The Legislative History of the Federal Antitrust Laws and Related Statutes

Other parts of this set (in preparation)

Part II
The Hart-Scott-Rodino Antitrust Improvements
Act of 1976

Part III
Antitrust Exemptions, Regulated Industries,
and FTC-Enforced Statutes

The Legislative History of the Federal Antitrust Laws and Related Statutes

Part I
The Antitrust Laws

Volume 1

Edited by Earl W. Kintner

Senior Partner
Arent, Fox, Kintner, Plotkin & Kahn
Washington, D.C.

Former Chairman and General Counsel
Federal Trade Commission

CHELSEA HOUSE PUBLISHERS
New York   London
1978

Chart: "Growth Of Drug Distribution In Leading Food Stores." From the February 1952 issue of *Progressive Grocer*. Reprinted by permission.

Table 1: June 5, 1951. ©1951 by The New York Times Company. Reprinted by permission.

"A Chance for Really Fair Trade." Reprinted from the March 1952 issue of *Fortune Magazine* by special permission; ©1952 Time Inc.

"The Schwegmann Case: An Economic Comment." From the November 1951 issue of the *University of Detroit Law Journal*. Reprinted by permission.

Project Editor	Jeanette Morrison
Associate Editor	Judy Susman
Editorial Staff	Karyn Browne, Don Coulter, Maxine Krasnow, Deborah Weiss
Design	Susan Lusk, Jeanette Morrison

©1978 by Earl W. Kintner
All rights reserved.
Printed and bound in the United States of America.

Published 1978 by Chelsea House Publishers

Library of Congress Cataloging in Publication Data

Kintner, Earl W
 The Federal antitrust laws.

 His Legislative history of the Federal antitrust laws and related statutes; pt. 1, v. 1—
 1. Antitrust law—United States. I. United States. Laws, statutes, etc. 1977. II. Title.
KF1635.8 1977. pt. 1. vol. 1 343'.73'072s
ISBN 0-87754-101-9 (v. 1) [343'.73'072] 77-21143

Kintner, Earl W.
 Legislative history of the Federal antitrust laws and related statutes.
 CONTENTS: pt. 1. The Federal antitrust laws. v.
 1. Antitrust law—United States. I. United States. Law, statutes, etc. 1977. II. Title.
KF1635.8 1977 343'.73'072 77-21144
ISBN 0-87754-100-0

CHELSEA HOUSE PUBLISHERS

Harold Steinberg, Chairman & Publisher   Andrew E. Norman, President
A Division of Chelsea House Educational Communications, Inc.
70 West 40th Street, New York, N.Y. 10018

*To Jerrold G. Van Cise—
peerless student, teacher and practitioner of antitrust law—
and to all other students of antitrust law.*

Guide to the use of this set

1. The materials are arranged statute by statute, each chapter bearing the name of the statute whose legislative history is covered therein. In a few cases, chapters include subsections setting forth the history of amendatory statutes (*e.g.*, Chapter 15, Expediting Act of 1903 and Amendments).

2. The following reference material appears at the beginning of each chapter:
    A detailed table of contents for each chapter.
    An *Introduction* covering the legislative, social, and economic context and history of the statute, its provisions, and its significance.
    A *Chronological Synopsis* of the significant events in the statute's history, with an emphasis on congressional consideration.
    A *Table of Reprinted Documents,* arranged by document type for ready reference.

For additional information see the *Introductory editorial note* on page xv.

Summary of the contents

Part I
The Antitrust Laws

A. THE SHERMAN ACT

Chapter 1 / Sherman Act of 1890

B. THE FAIR TRADE AMENDMENTS

Chapter 2 / Miller-Tydings Resale Price Maintenance Act of 1937
Chapter 3 / McGuire Resale Price Maintenance Act Amendment of 1952
Chapter 4 / Consumer Goods Pricing Act of 1975 (Fair Trade Repealer)

C. THE CLAYTON ACT AND AMENDMENTS

Chapter 5 / Clayton Act of 1914
Chapter 6 / Robinson-Patman Price Discrimination Act of 1936
Chapter 7 / Celler-Kefauver Act of 1950

D. THE FTC ACT AND AMENDMENTS

Chapter 8 / Federal Trade Commission Act of 1914
Chapter 9 / Wheeler-Lea Act of 1938
Chapter 10 / Antitrust Amendments of 1973
Chapter 11 / Federal Trade Commission Improvement Act of 1975

E. ACTS RELATING TO FOREIGN COMMERCE

Chapter 12 / Wilson Tariff Act of 1894 and Amendment
Chapter 13 / Section 11, Panama Canal Act of 1912
Chapter 14 / Section 337, Tariff Act of 1930 and Amendments

F. ACTS RELATING TO PROCEDURE AND ENFORCEMENT

Chapter 15 / Expediting Act of 1903 and Amendments
Chapter 16 / Antitrust Immunity Act of 1903 and Amendments
Chapter 17 / Publicity in Taking Evidence Act of 1913
Chapter 18 / Antitrust Civil Process Act of 1962
Chapter 19 / Antitrust Procedures and Penalties Act of 1974

Part II
The Hart-Scott-Rodino Antitrust Improvements Act of 1976

Part III
Antitrust Exemptions, Regulated Industries, and FTC-Enforced Statutes

Contents of Volume 1

Guide to the use of this set / **vi**
Summary of the contents / **vii**
Preface to Part I / **xi**
Acknowledgments / **xiii**
Introductory editorial note / **xv**

      A. THE SHERMAN ACT

Chapter 1 / Sherman Act of 1890 / **3**

      B. THE FAIR TRADE AMENDMENTS

Chapter 2 / Miller-Tydings Resale Price Maintenance Act of 1937 / **459**

Chapter 3 / McGuire Resale Price Maintenance Act Amendment of 1952 / **549**

Chapter 4 / Consumer Goods Pricing Act of 1975 (Fair Trade Repealer) / **937**

A detailed table of contents appears at the beginning of each chapter.

Preface to Part I

During my years first as General Counsel and later as Chairman of the Federal Trade Commission, I came to the conclusion that the antitrust and trade regulation laws are violated more often through ignorance than through intent. I learned that many businessmen and lawyers had a thirst for knowledge concerning those laws but were bewildered by their complexity and by the jargon all too often used in articles and books intended to explain the antitrust laws. Since then I have devoted a substantial amount of my time to explaining the antitrust and trade regulation laws by means of seven books, numerous legal articles, and over 400 speeches.

I was delighted when Chelsea House asked me to produce a legislative history of the federal antitrust laws. The absence of a comprehensive, authoritative compilation of the legislative histories of the federal antitrust statutes has long been a hindrance to an understanding of these laws by lawyers, courts, and businessmen. Although the labor involved in compiling such an exhaustive set of books is truly herculean, several colleagues in my law firm and I gladly undertook it as a service to our profession, to law libraries and law students, and to the innumerable businessmen whose plans and decisions are pervasively affected by the antitrust laws. Not the least of our compilation problems has been that of locating long out-of-print materials, sometimes available only in the dog-eared copy in an agency's library or archives.

The 19 statutes covered in the first part of this set are both substantive and procedural and range from the Sherman Act, which the Supreme Court has described as "a comprehensive charter of economic liberty aimed at preserving free and unfettered competition as the rule of trade,"* to the little-known and never-used antitrust provision of the Panama Canal Act. My intent in these first volumes has been to present a comprehensive history of the 19 federal statutes pertaining directly to the federal antitrust laws. Future volumes to be published by Chelsea House will cover the Hart-Scott-Rodino Antitrust Improvements Act of 1976 and the more than 40 statutes relating to antitrust exemptions, regulated industries, and FTC-enforced statutes.

For this set of books the primary source materials are the actual congressional bills, reports, and debates. In addition, materials such as presidential messages and addresses, annual and special agency reports, and letters and other documents from executive departments and congressional committees have been included to clarify statutory provisions and to document the concerns that motivated passage. The background and importance of each statute is explained in an introduction, which is extensively footnoted with references to pertinent materials. Major federal court decisions construing the legislative history or examining the nature of the statutes are also included, with explanatory commentaries where necessary.

The Introductions, Commentaries, and editorial selection of documents and cases are intended to give the reader an objective, well-informed view of the origins, congressional intent, and developments pertinent to each law. I have consciously avoided making any value judgments as to the efficacy or wisdom of the statutes. The documents are intended to speak for themselves. It is hoped that the product of our labors will serve as a useful tool, previously wholly lacking, to those interested in antitrust law and legislation in this country.

E.W.K.

---

* Northern Pac. Ry. v. United States, 356 U.S. 1, 4, 78 S. Ct. 514, 517, 2 L. Ed. 2d 545, 549 (1958).

Acknowledgments

As I noted in the Preface, the labor involved in researching, compiling, and editing the 19 legislative histories contained in the first part of this set was truly herculean. A number of colleagues in my law firm made significant contributions to these volumes and I gratefully acknowledge their assistance.

At the outset two of my colleagues deserve special thanks for their substantial contributions to this project. Joseph P. Griffin served as coordinator and managing editor for the project as a whole. Mark R. Joelson made substantial editorial and substantive contributions to each of the Introductions and Commentaries. I would also like to thank Jeanette Morrison, project editor at Chelsea House, for her substantial editorial assistance, and Judy Susman, her associate editor.

Grateful acknowledgment is also made to my colleagues below for their major contributions to individual chapters:

1 / Sherman Act   *John C. Filippini*
2 / Miller-Tydings Resale Price Maintenance Act   *Alan R. Malasky*
3 / McGuire Resale Price Maintenance Act Amendment   *Alan R. Malasky*
4 / Consumer Goods Pricing Act   *David B. Goldston*
5 / Clayton Act   *Robert W. Green*
6 / Robinson-Patman Price Discrimination Act   *Salvatore A. Romano*
7 / Celler-Kefauver Act   *Eugene J. Meigher, Robert B. Weintraub*
8 / Federal Trade Commission Act   *Stephen T. Phelps, Christopher Smith*
9 / Wheeler-Lea Act   *Christopher Smith*
10 / Antitrust Amendments of 1973   *Douglas G. Green*
11 / Federal Trade Commission Improvement Act   *Christopher Smith*
12 / Wilson Tariff Act and Amendment   *Marc L. Fleischaker*
13 / Section 11, Panama Canal Act   *Joseph P. Griffin*
14 / Section 337, Tariff Act of 1930   *Bruce E. Aitken, Joseph P. Griffin*
15 / Expediting Act and Amendments   *Marc L. Fleischaker*
16 / Antitrust Immunity Act and Amendments   *Paul F. Donahue, Joseph P. Griffin*
17 / Publicity in Taking Evidence Act   *Thomas J. Tourish, Jr.*
18 / Antitrust Civil Process Act   *David L. Cohen*
19 / Antitrust Procedures and Penalties Act   *Lee Calligaro*

Professor Bernie R. Burrus, Bruce V. Bordelon, David L. Carden, John Cushing, Paul F. Donahue, Debra Goldstein, Jeremy Mathis, Sherrill A. Sherman, Brison S. Shipley, and Daniel P. Sternberg, as well as several librarians at the Library of Congress and the Federal Trade Commission, provided valuable research assistance. Finally I would like to thank Inge Vogel for her skill and patience.

E.W.K.

Introductory editorial note

Part I of this set covers developments to January 1, 1977; significant later developments have been included where possible.

ORGANIZATION OF THE MATERIAL

This set is divided into three Parts:
  Part I / The Antitrust Laws
  Part II / The Hart-Scott-Rodino Antitrust Improvements Act of 1976
  Part III / Antitrust Exemptions, Regulated Industries, and FTC-Enforced Statutes

Where appropriate, parts are subdivided into sections reflecting traditional topical groupings. For example, Part I is divided as follows:
  A. The Sherman Act
  B. The Fair Trade Amendments
  C. The Clayton Act and Amendments
  D. The FTC Act and Amendments
  E. Statutes Relating to Foreign Commerce
  F. Statutes Relating to Procedure and Enforcement

EDITORIAL METHOD

In reprinting these documents, every effort has been made to preserve the integrity of the original texts.

Original pagination. An inverted T-bar system (employing the symbol ⊥) has been used to provide the original page numbers of all reprinted documents except the *United States Code* (always cited to section numbers).

Bill prints. All bill prints are reproduced line for line, together with the original line numbers.

Footnotes. Original document footnotes reprinted herein are separated from the text by a short, one-inch line that begins at the left margin. The original note numbers have been retained.

Footnotes added by the editor appear below any original footnotes and are separated from them or from the text by a line drawn across the entire page. Editor's footnotes are numbered consecutively throughout each chapter and each note number is preceded by the chapter number as a prefix. For example, the editor's footnotes in Chapter 1 are numbered 1.1, 1.2, 1.3, etc.

Case citations. Full citations to all significant cases named, partially cited, or otherwise referred to in the documents have been footnoted at the first appearance of each case in each chapter and as many times thereafter as would be helpful to the reader.

Deletions. The printed record of congressional hearings regarding the statutes covered in this series runs into the tens of thousands of pages, much of which is now only of historic interest. The editor has therefore limited such material to representative exhibits and to statements made by individuals who were directly responsible for the drafting of the legislation in question and/or its subsequent passage. The only other material excluded was that which was clearly irrelevant, procedural, or unnecessarily duplicative.

All deletions made by the editor have been indicated by ellipsis points. Since the original pagination has been provided, the omission of full paragraphs has been indicated by ellipsis points at the end of the paragraph preceding the omitted part, rather than by a full line of ellipsis points.

Congressional Record. In reprinting the congressional debate, the permanent, bound edition of the *Congressional Record* has been used except in the case of the most recent statutes, where only the daily edition of the *Record* was available at the time of compilation. Where the daily edition has been used, this is indicated in the title to the document.

The first name, state, and party affiliation of each Congressperson has been supplied in brackets at his or her first appearance in each chapter.

General style. Capitalization, abbreviation, and typographical style (insofar as possible) have all been retained.

Apparent errors in the original texts have been treated in several ways. In general, *sic* has been inserted in brackets to indicate "so in original" following obvious typographical errors, inadvertent grammatical slips that could mistakenly be attributed to typographical errors made in reprinting, incorrect spellings of proper names, and obvious factual discrepancies. *Sic* has not been used for every odd expression or spelling variation, or to indicate inconsistent capitalization, etc.

Missing punctuation has been added in brackets where needed for clarity.

A THE SHERMAN ACT

Chapter
1 Sherman Act of 1890

1 SHERMAN ACT OF 1890

7	Introduction
37	Chronological Synopsis
45	Table of Reprinted Documents

CURRENT VERSION

49   Sherman Antitrust Act as amended
     15 U.S.C. §§ 1-7

ORIGINAL VERSION

51   Sherman Antitrust Act, July 2, 1890

The Origins

53   House [Bacon] resolution authorizing the Committee on Manufactures to investigate trusts
     January 25, 1888

54   Antitrust plank of the Democratic Party platform
     June 5, 1888

54   Antitrust plank of the Republican Party platform
     June 19, 1888

54   Senate [Sherman] resolution directing the Committee on Finance to inquire into the control of trusts in connection with revenue bills
     July 10, 1888

55   Report of the House Committee on Manufactures
     H.R. Rep. No. 3112, 50th Cong., 1st Sess.
     [to accompany Misc. Doc. 124/Bacon resolution]
     July 30, 1888

57   Fourth annual message of President Grover Cleveland
     December 3, 1888

58   Report of the House Committee on Manufactures
     H.R. Rep. No. 4165, Pt. 1, 50th Cong., 2d Sess.
     [pursuant to Bacon resolution]
     March 2, 1889

59   Minority Views, H.R. Rep. No. 4165, Pt. 2
     March 2, 1889

60	First annual message of President Benjamin Harrison December 3, 1889

Senate Consideration (S. 3445)

61	Senate Debate, 50th Cong., 1st Sess. August 14, 1888
63	S. 3445, 50th Cong., 1st Sess. August 14, 1888
64	S. 3445 as reported by the Senate Committee on Finance 50th Cong., 1st Sess. September 11, 1888
	Senate Debate, 50th Cong., 2d Sess.
65	January 23, 1889
67	January 25, 1889
73	S. 3445 as amended by the Senate January 25, 1889
75	Senate Debate, 50th Cong., 2d Sess. February 4, 1889

Senate Consideration (S. 1)

89	S. 1, 51st Cong., 1st Sess. December 4, 1889
90	Resolution of Sen. David Turpie December 9, 1889
90	Remarks of Sen. David Turpie December 10, 1889
93	S. 1 as reported by the Senate Committee on Finance 51st Cong., 1st Sess. January 14, 1890
94	Senate Debate, 51st Cong., 1st Sess. February 27, 1890
112	Amendment to S. 1 reported by the Senate Committee on Finance 51st Cong., 1st Sess. March 18, 1890
	Senate Debate, 51st Cong., 1st Sess.
113	March 21, 1890
150	March 24, 1890
183	March 25, 1890
214	S. 1 as amended by the Senate March 25, 1890
219	Senate Debate, 51st Cong., 1st Sess. March 26, 1890
256	S. 1 as amended by the Senate March 26, 1890

262	Senate Debate, 51st Cong., 1st Sess. March 27, 1890
275	S. 1 as reported by the Senate Committee on the Judiciary 51st Cong., 1st Sess. April 2, 1890
	Senate Debate, 51st Cong., 1st Sess.
277	April 2, 1890
279	April 8, 1890

House Consideration (S. 1)

295	Report of the House Committee on the Judiciary H.R. Rep. No. 1707, 51st Cong., 1st Sess. [to accompany S. 1] April 25, 1890
296	S. 1 as reported by the House Committee on the Judiciary April 25, 1890
298	House Debate, 51st. Cong., 1st Sess. May 1, 1890

Senate Consideration (S. 1)

	Senate Debate, 51st Cong., 1st Sess.
325	May 2, 1890
326	May 12, 1890
329	May 13, 1890
329	May 16, 1890

Conference Consideration (S. 1)

	House Debate, 51st Cong., 1st Sess.
331	May 17, 1890
331	May 21, 1890
	First Conference Report and House Debate 51st Cong., 1st Sess.
331	June 11, 1890
353	June 12, 1890
355	June 14, 1890
355	Senate Debate, 51st Cong., 1st Sess. June 16, 1890
358	Second Conference Report and Senate Debate 51st Cong., 1st Sess. June 18, 1890
359	Second Conference Report and House Debate 51st Cong., 1st Sess. June 20, 1890

THE DECISIONS

365	Commentary

377 United States v. Joint Traffic Association, 171 U.S. 505 (1898)

382 Standard Oil Co. of New Jersey v. United States, 221 U.S. 1 (1911)

403 United States v. American Tobacco Co., 221 U.S. 106 (1911)

410 Board of Trade of the City of Chicago v. United States, 246 U.S. 231 (1918)

412 United States v. Trenton Potteries Co., 273 U.S. 392 (1927)

416 Apex Hosiery Co. v. Leader, 310 U.S. 469 (1940)

423 Parker v. Brown, 317 U.S. 341 (1943)

426 United States v. South-Eastern Underwriters Association, 322 U.S. 533 (1944)

437 United States v. E. I. du Pont de Nemours & Co., 351 U.S. 377 (1956)

446 United States v. Topco Associates, Inc., 405 U.S. 596 (1972)

Introduction

SHERMAN ACT OF 1890

The Sherman Act provides the basic pronouncement of American antitrust policy favoring a competitive, free enterprise economy unencumbered by unreasonable or monopolistic restrictions on free market forces. As the guiding principle for competitive economic behavior, its first two sections have retained, with certain limited exceptions, their original form for some 85 years.

One of the best ways to view the legislative history of the Sherman Act is to recognize that it represents an attempt to reconcile two major economic or business themes of long standing. These are the principles of combination and competition which, although they had existed in relative harmony for many decades, came into sharp conflict during the period of rapid economic change in the latter half of the 19th century. A host of economic, political, sociological, and legal factors and circumstances were undoubtedly responsible for the resolution of this conflict in the form of the Sherman Act. A general survey of some of the more significant of these factors will illuminate not only the reasons for the passage of the Act but also its essential purpose and its intended interpretation.

[1.1] Act of July 2, 1890, ch. 647, 26 Stat. 209, *as amended*, 15 U.S.C. §§ 1–7 (Supp. V, 1975). Through the years, there have been increases in the fines and criminal penalties authorized under the Act, as well as conforming amendments to changes in the federal judicial system. The only other substantive modification of the original Act was made by the Miller-Tydings Act of 1937, which provided an antitrust exemption for resale price maintenance agreements in jurisdictions where such arrangements were permitted under state fair-trade laws. Act of Aug. 17, 1937, ch. 690, tit. VIII, 50 Stat. 693. This exemption was subsequently repealed. Consumer Goods Pricing Act of 1975, Pub. L. No. 94–145, § 2, 89 Stat. 801. For the legislative histories of the Miller-Tydings Act, the Consumer Goods Pricing Act, and the 1974 Antitrust Procedures and Penalties Act, Pub. L. No. 93–528, 88 Stat. 1706, see *infra* at chapters 2, 4, and 19, respectively. As enacted, the Sherman Act comprised eight sections. In 1914, the original section 7 was reenacted with some modifications as section 4 of the Clayton Act. Act of Oct. 15, 1914, ch. 323, § 4, 38 Stat. 731, 15 U.S.C. § 15 (1970). The original section 7 was later repealed by the Act of July 7, 1955, ch. 283, § 3, 69 Stat. 283, and original section 8 accordingly became present section 7. For a complete account of all the amendments see *infra* at 51–52 & notes.

THE ORIGINS
Common Law Background

First English, and later American, common law had recognized that certain cooperative business agreements were both necessary and beneficial.[1.2] Thus, for example, agreements not to compete incident to the sale of a business, limited as to both duration and geographic area, were generally upheld as necessary to protect the goodwill and investment of the purchaser.[1.3] On the other hand, arrangements establishing prices at which items would be sold,[1.4] those which artificially restricted the supply of products,[1.5] and those which involved the use of economic force to prevent others from competing or which otherwise attempted to appropriate a monopoly were routinely condemned.[1.6] Indeed, the term "monopoly" itself had long been given a definite meaning related to the privilege given by the crown or government to one person to exercise exclusive control over a certain area of commerce.[1.7]

The common law doctrine which was eventually developed tested the legality of commercial agreements according to whether they were reasonable in the light of accepted business conduct and merely incidental to arrangements primarily designed to carry out such conduct, or whether they exceeded the acceptable limits so as to constitute unreasonable restraints upon commercial activity.[1.8] Accordingly, partial restraints that were only as broad as necessary to protect the legitimate business interests involved were held valid, while more encompassing restraints than were reasonably necessary were deemed to be void and contrary to public policy.[1.9] Likewise, arrangements that tended to promote a monopoly were also held to be unlawful and

---

[1.2] A good discussion of the English and American common law on restraints of trade may be found in United States v. Addyston Pipe & Steel Co., 85 F. 271 (6th Cir. 1898), aff'd, 175 U.S. 211 (1899). See generally 1 H. TOULMIN, A TREATISE ON THE ANTI-TRUST LAWS OF THE UNITED STATES 24–92 (1949); Letwin, *The English Common Law Concerning Monopolies*, 21 U. CHI. L. REV. 355 (1954); Eaton, *On Contracts in Restraint of Trade*, 4 HARV. L. REV. 128 (1890).

[1.3] An example of such a valid agreement is found in Oregon Steam Navigation Co. v. Winsor, 87 U.S. (20 Wall.) 64, 22 L. Ed. 315 (1874), which involved a 10-year covenant not to use a steamship on the Columbia River, where the seller remained in business, nor in California, where the prior owner—who had obtained a similar covenant from this seller—remained in business.

[1.4] For example, in Craft v. McConoughy, 79 Ill. 346 (1875), a price-fixing agreement among the grain dealers of Rochelle, Ill., was held to be an illegal restraint of trade. Similar agreements to fix prices, apportion markets, and compensate each other for any differences in prices received were held unlawful in Morris Run Coal Co. v. Barclay Coal Co., 68 Pa. 173 (1871).

[1.5] *See, e.g.,* Arnot v. Pittston & Elmira Coal Co., 68 N.Y. 558 (1877), in which contracts having the purpose of limiting the supply of coal coming into the Elmira, N.Y., market and maintaining unnaturally high prices were held void and unenforceable on public policy grounds; India Bagging Ass'n v. B. Kock & Co., 14 La. Ann. 164 (1859), in which eight firms unlawfully agreed not to sell any bagging for a three-month period without majority consent in order to raise prices.

[1.6] *See, e.g.,* Richardson v. Buhl, 77 Mich. 632, 43 N.W. 1102 (1889), the famous *Diamond Match* case, often referred to during the Sherman Act debates, in which contracts made in furtherance of the Diamond Match Co.'s goal of monopolizing the manufacture of friction matches were held void and unenforceable; People v. North River Sugar Ref. Co., 22 Abb. N. Cas. 164, 3 N.Y.S. 401 (Cir. Ct., N.Y. Co.), aff'd, 7 N.Y.S. 406 (Sup. Ct. 1st Dep't 1889), aff'd, 121 N.Y. 582, 24 N.E. 834 (1890), also referred to in the debates and congressional reports, involving an agreement to produce a monopoly by sugar refiners.

[1.7] In a classic statement of the term, Lord Coke defined monopoly as follows:
> ... A monopoly is an institution or allowance by the King by his grant, commission, or otherwise to any person or persons, bodies politic or corporate, of or for the sole buying, selling, making, working or using of anything whereby any person or persons, bodies politic or corporate, are sought to be restrained of any freedom or liberty that they had before, or hindered in their lawful trade.

E. COKE, THIRD PART OF THE INSTITUTES OF THE LAW OF ENGLAND 181 (1664).

[1.8] *See generally* 1 H. TOULMIN, *supra* note 1.2, at §§ 2.14–.17.

[1.9] Craft v. McConoughy, 79 Ill. 346, 349–50 (1875). *Compare* Oregon Steam Navigation Co. v. Winsor, 87 U.S. (20 Wall.) 64 (1874) (10-year covenant not to compete where seller remained in business held reasonable) *with* Herreshoff v. Boutineau, 17 R.I. 3, 19 A. 712 (1890) (covenant not to compete in the state of Rhode Island for one year held to be an unreasonable restraint because it covered a larger geographic area than was needed to protect the owner of a foreign language school from competition by a former employee).

unenforceable under common law.[1.10] These principles were well established in American common law by the third quarter of the 19th century,[1.11] and were repeatedly referred to during the congressional consideration of the Sherman Act.[1.12]

Economic, Social, and Political Forces Behind Passage of the Sherman Act

While these common law rules pertaining to business regulation were being developed, economic conditions underwent dramatic change during the latter half of the 19th century. The post-Civil War era saw rapid industrialization and economic expansion. Scientific and technological innovations stimulated development in the areas of manufacturing, agriculture, rail and water transportation, and communications, creating both new demands and new markets for goods and services. As a result, business firms found themselves competing in greatly widened areas of effective commerce. Industry and trade were further spurred by the growth of private banking, investment and speculation, and marketing of securities.[1.13]

The nation's economic expansion was fostered by the encouragement of individual entrepreneurial spirit and the rewards of economic and industrial success. Free enterprise was further nurtured by a governmental policy of laissez faire. Certain limitations existed in the form of laws protecting patent rights and tariff laws creating barriers to foreign trade,[1.14] but even these encouraged greater domestic production. Moreover, there were few legal restrictions on the use of the nation's work force, which grew during this period because of increasing urbanization and immigration.[1.15]

In this era, new forms of business organization were created to manage the enlarged scope of commercial activity. Although the corporate business form was not new, it became increasingly popular because corporations were easily created and

---

[1.10] See, e.g., Richardson v. Buhl, 77 Mich. 632, 43 N.W. 1102 (1889); People v. North River Sugar Ref. Co., 121 N.Y. 582, 24 N.E. 834 (1890). See also United States v. Addyston Pipe & Steel Co., 85 F. 271, 279-82 (6th Cir. 1898), aff'd, 175 U.S. 211 (1899).

[1.11] See Craft v. McConoughy, 79 Ill. 346, 349-50 (1875). See also 1 H. TOULMIN, supra note 1.2, at § 2.16. In addition to the case law developments, certain statutes were passed in England to prevent abuse of economic power by prohibiting practices such as "engrossing" (generally defined as buying up so much of a commodity as to obtain a monopoly and then selling it at a forced price) and "forestalling" (generally defined as buying or contracting for merchandise on its way to market with the intention of reselling at a higher price). These too are referred to in the congressional debates. Although many of these had been repealed in England, American common law continued to carry their effect. Moreover, several states had attempted to control anticompetitive behavior by enactment of statutes designed to prohibit certain practices. See H. SEAGER & C. GULICK, TRUST AND CORPORATION PROBLEMS 341-42 & n.1 (1929), identifying 14 states and territories with constitutional prohibitions, and 13 states and territories with statutory prohibitions, against anticompetitive combinations in 1890.

[1.12] For example, Senator Sherman's speech during Senate consideration of S. 1 reviewed several of the common law precedents. 21 CONG. REC. 2457-61 (1890), infra at 117-25.

[1.13] For discussions of the surging growth of American capitalism and industrialization during this era see generally C. & M. BEARD, THE BEARDS' NEW BASIC HISTORY OF THE UNITED STATES at ch. 18 (1968); Limbaugh, Historic Origins of Antitrust Legislation, 18 Mo. L. REV. 215, 230-42 (1953). Early in the debates, Senator Jones (D., Ark.) made specific reference to the rapid technological advances that had been made in transportation and to the expansion of commerce. 20 CONG. REC. 1457 (1889), infra at 75.

[1.14] The patent law in effect during this period was the Act of July 8, 1870, ch. 230, 16 Stat. 198. Tariff laws which had been enacted included the Act of March 2, 1861, ch. 68, 12 Stat. 178, and the Act of March 3, 1883, ch. 121, 22 Stat. 488. Within months after passage of the Sherman Act, Congress passed another tariff bill, the Act of Oct. 1, 1890, ch. 1244, 26 Stat. 567. The controversial protective tariff issue was frequently interjected into the Sherman Act debates, generally by anti-tariff proponents who saw the tariffs as protecting domestic industry from foreign competition thereby fostering the abuses of the large business organizations. This view was advanced in a New York Times article of April 7, 1890, at 4, col. 2, which criticized Senator Sherman's antitrust legislation as being inconsistent with his refusal to adopt an anti-tariff stand. The tariff supporters, however, pointed out that many of the industries dominated by trusts—such as beef, whisky, and oil—were not subject to protective tariffs. See, e.g., 21 CONG. REC. 2470-71 (1890), infra at 148. See also discussion infra at 19.

[1.15] 2 V. CLARK, HISTORY OF MANUFACTURES IN THE UNITED STATES 177-78 (1929).

offered continuity of control, accumulation of large amounts of investment capital, facilitated access to credit, and limited personal liability. Nevertheless, the corporation was chartered by the state, often by special acts of incorporation, and was therefore subject to some degree of control, including prohibition of, or restriction on, its activity in other states and possible revocation of its corporate charter.[1.16] During the latter half of the 19th century, however, general incorporation laws became more prevalent and encouraged greater and more expansive use of the corporate form.[1.17] Another form of business organization that came into prominence was known as the pool, whereby competitors would jointly agree to divide markets, share profits, discriminate jointly against less-favored entities, and otherwise wield their economic power.[1.18] This type of arrangement was used extensively by the railroads, which were among the largest and most powerful economic entities of the day.[1.19] Because of its dependence upon voluntary adherence and its lack of enforcement powers,[1.20] however, the pool was not a highly stable form of business organization.

The disadvantages of the pool and the corporation were largely absent in the trust, which soon became one of the most popular forms of business arrangement. A trust agreement, entered into by two or more corporations, not only could provide centralized control, greater stability, and greater aggregation of capital but also had a legally binding effect.[1.21] The shareholders of the member corporations would typically transfer their shares to a single trustee or board of trustees, who would be given full control over the management of the trust, the shareholders receiving trust certificates entitling them to share proportionally in the trust's profits. Moreover, because they were not themselves corporations, the trusts did not require state sanction in order to exist, nor were they subject to many of the controls or restrictions which the states were able to impose upon corporations.[1.22] Accordingly, huge trusts, such as the Standard Oil Co. and others in steel, whiskey, salt, and sugar, were able to control almost the entirety of a particular industry.[1.23] As popular hostility and legal barriers to trusts increased, however, a similar type of arrangement known as the holding company emerged, by which one corporation acquired ownership of shares or assets of another in expanded economic concentration.[1.24]

[1.16] *See* Limbaugh, *supra* note 1.13, at 219, 232; Jones, *Historical Development of the Law of Business Competition*, 36 YALE L. REV. 207 (1910).

[1.17] *See* H. SEAGER & C. GULICK, *supra* note 1.11, at ch. 4, for a discussion of the development of state general incorporation laws and the competition among many states to attract corporations, and thus revenue, from other states by passing permissive incorporation laws.

[1.18] The pooling agreement among five coal companies is set forth in Morris Run Coal Co. v. Barclay Coal Co., 68 Pa. 173, 175–78 (1871); a pooling agreement among the grain dealers of Rochelle, Ill., is found in Craft v. McConoughy, 79 Ill. 346, 347 (1875); and discussion of a pool arrangement among candle manufacturers appears in Emery v. Ohio Candle Co., 47 Ohio St. 320, 321 (1890). *See generally* H. THORELLI, THE FEDERAL ANTITRUST POLICY 75–76 (1955); H. SEAGER & C. GULICK, *supra* note 1.11, at ch. 7.

[1.19] A pooling arrangement involving railroads is described in United States v. Trans-Missouri Freight Ass'n, 166 U.S. 290, 292–97, 17 S. Ct. 540, 541–42, 41 L. Ed. 1007, 1011–13 (1897).

[1.20] H. THORELLI, *supra* note 1.18, at 76; Limbaugh, *supra* note 1.13, at 233.

[1.21] H. THORELLI, *supra* note 1.18, at 76–79; H. SEAGER & C. GULICK, *supra* note 1.11, at 49–54.

[1.22] *See* H. THORELLI, *supra* note 1.18, at 76.

[1.23] *See* Jones, *supra* note 1.16, at 217–18. The interesting nature and development of the Standard Oil trust, the first successful use of the trust form, is described in a report of the House Committee on Manufactures, H.R. REP. No. 3112, 50th Cong., 1st Sess. (1888), as well as in the Supreme Court's decision in Standard Oil Co. v. United States, 221 U.S. 1, 33–40, 31 S. Ct. 502, 505–07, 55 L. Ed. 619, 634–37 (1911), *infra* at 383–84. *See also* H. THORELLI, *supra* note 1.18, at 91–96. The entire Standard Oil trust agreement of 1882, which was held to be unlawful under Ohio law, can be found in State *ex rel.* v. Standard Oil Co., 49 Ohio St. 137, 142–52 (1892). The sugar trust agreement is set forth in People v. North River Sugar Ref. Co., 121 N.Y. 582, 585–95 (1890).

[1.24] Holding companies were made possible to a large degree by relaxation of state law prohibitions against ownership by one corporation of the stock or assets of another or doing business in states other than that of incorporation. Many states passed laws specifically allowing corporations to hold stock of other corporations. The first of these statutes was Laws of the State of New Jersey, ch. 265, § 4 (1889)—the relevant part of which is reprinted in H. THORELLI, *supra* note 1.18, at 84. The expanded use of holding companies played a greater role in the passage of the Clayton Act in 1914, when congressional concern was focused upon the problem of economic concentration and specific types

By the late 1880's, the accumulation and use of vast economic power by these various business organizations, coupled with a series of domestic ills, had caused great public hostility, evidenced by a popular, generalized hatred of trusts and commercial monopolies. In an effort to curb the abuses of these entities some states, notably Kansas and Missouri, enacted legislation aimed at regulating business activities within their borders.[1.25] Although state judicial actions against trusts had also been instituted with some success, such state activity was unable to achieve significant results because of the defects in much state legislation, the absence of a uniform common law, and the ability of the large economic entities to adapt their business forms to jurisdictional limitations or expand their activities beyond state borders in order to circumvent the reach of state jurisdiction.[1.26] The Sherman Act debates contain numerous references to this public resentment, which was one of the prime causal factors behind the legislation, although other socio-economic and political factors played significant roles as well.

Despite the general economic prosperity during this period of commercial expansion, many Americans resented the often ruthless manner in which many businesses were operated. Farmers as a group suffered from the discriminatory railroad rebate system. This group was also economically squeezed by the emergence of the industrialized state, receiving low prices for their produce while being forced to pay high prices for consumer goods.[1.27] Small independent businessmen were likewise often victims of the economic power wielded by their larger, more powerful competitors. Because a trust typically controlled the integrated levels of a particular industry, it could often control the means or sources of supply and dictate the prices or terms at which commodities would be bought, sold, or transported. Moreover, large concerns often agreed to divide markets and to fix prices, engaged in predatory pricing, and discriminated in favor of certain entities.[1.28]

Several social and political factors further spurred public discontent. In the minds of many persons, the large business organizations were supported by the protective tariff policy, which was viewed as sheltering them from foreign competition while increasing their stranglehold on domestic commerce.[1.29] The discriminatory rates and practices of the railroads were also very much political issues and were largely responsible for the enactment of the Interstate Commerce Act of 1887.[1.30] In addition, the public was outraged by instances of watered stock, fraudulent schemes, graft, and political corruption.[1.31] Moreover, most people—especially laborers, factory workers, and farmers—suffered during the two economic depressions of the 1870's and 1880's. Blaming big business in general and the trusts in particular for these economic and political ills, the public clamored for legislation which would eliminate either the power

---

of abuse of economic power. *See* E. KINTNER, AN ANTITRUST PRIMER 8-9 (2d ed. 1973). An example of the holding company arrangement was the Chicago Gas Trust Co., which purchased and held the majority of the capital stock of all four gas companies doing business in Chicago. *See* People ex rel. Peabody v. Chicago Gas Trust Co., 130 Ill. 268, 22 N.E. 798 (1889). The Supreme Court's decision in Northern Sec. Co. v. United States, 193 U.S. 197, 321-24, 24 S. Ct. 436, 450-51, 48 L. Ed. 679, 693-95 (1904), provides a good description of the Northern Securities Railroad holding company, and its decision in Standard Oil Co. v. United States, 221 U.S. 1, 41-42 (1911), *infra* at 384, discusses the Standard Oil Co. of New Jersey's holding company arrangement.

[1.25] *See* Limbaugh, *supra* note 1.13, at 244-47. By the time of passage of the Sherman Act in 1890, 14 states and territories prohibited monopolies by constitutional provision while 13 states had enacted antitrust statutes. *Id.* at 246; *see also* note 1.11 *supra*.

[1.26] *See* H. THORELLI, *supra* note 1.18, at 80-83; 1 J. VON KALINOWSKI, ANTITRUST LAWS AND TRADE REGULATION § 2.05[1] (1969). One notable exception, however, was People v. North River Sugar Ref. Co., 121 N.Y. 582, 24 N.E. 834 (1890), aff'g 7 N.Y.S. 406 (Sup. Ct. 1st Dep't), aff'g 22 Abb. N. Cas. 164, 3 N.Y.S. 401 (Cir. Ct., N.Y. Co. 1889), in which the New York Court of Appeals upheld a lower court's decision vacating the company's corporate charter.

[1.27] E. KINTNER, *supra* note 1.24, at 9. One expression of the hostility toward trusts appeared in a letter from a farmer to Representative Fithian (D., Ill.), which he had read into the *Record.* 21 CONG. REC. 4102-03 (1890).

[1.28] *See generally* E. KINTNER, *supra* note 1.24, at 5-9; 1 J. VON KALINOWSKI, *supra* note 1.26, at § 2.02[2]; Limbaugh, *supra* note 1.13, at 236-39.

[1.29] *See* W. LETWIN, LAW AND ECONOMIC POLICY IN AMERICA: THE EVOLUTION OF THE SHERMAN ANTITRUST ACT 58 (1965).

[1.30] Act of Feb. 4, 1887, ch. 104, 24 Stat. 379.

[1.31] *See* H. THORELLI, *supra* note 1.18, at 86-88; 1 J. VON KALINOWSKI, *supra* note 1.26, at § 2.03[3].

of such organizations or at least the perceived abuses of that power.[1.32] This sentiment was expressed in newspaper editorials, political cartoons, and magazine articles, which regularly portrayed the evils of the trusts and demanded corrective legislation.[1.33]

Political Concern over the Power of the Trusts and Similar Organizations

The post-Civil War period witnessed political developments which also helped to create the climate for enactment of antitrust legislation. Just as the agrarian movement aided in spurring passage of the Interstate Commerce Act of 1887,[1.34] opposition to the trusts on behalf of the agricultural sector was expressed by such political organizations as the Grangers and Greenbackers, and, later, the Populist Party.[1.35] The labor movement likewise provided an impetus for regulatory legislation because of its philosophical attitudes concerning big business and the plight of the worker,[1.36] while, as has been noted, the anti-tariff forces viewed the relationship between the protective tariffs and the growth of big business as a causal one. All in all, opposition to the trusts was extremely widespread and was evidenced in Congress not only by the nearly unanimous final votes in favor of the Sherman Act's passage but also by the almost uniform recognition of the need for some type of regulatory legislation voiced during the debates.[1.37]

Antitrust legislation found support in both major political parties. The Democrats, who generally favored fewer restrictions on foreign trade, were vocal in their objection to the trusts as well as to the protective tariff policy.[1.38] Thus, in his third annual message to the Congress on December 6, 1887, President Grover Cleveland, in referring to the high prices paid by consumers for many commodities due to protective tariffs, stated that domestic competition, which sometimes operated to keep prices down, was "too often strangled by combinations quite prevalent at this time, and frequently called trusts, which have for their object the regulation of the supply and price of commodities made and sold by members of the combination."[1.39] On the other hand, the Republican Party, referred to by some as the Party of Big Business, generally represented the manufacturing interests of the industrialized Northeast and supported the protective tariff policy.[1.40] Notwithstanding these philosophical leanings, by the late 1880's the Republicans could no longer afford to ignore the trust issue and may indeed

---

[1.32] 1 J. VON KALINOWSKI, *supra* note 1.26, at § 2.02[3]; W. LETWIN, *supra* note 1.29, at 70.

[1.33] Letwin states that in February 1888 the *New York Times* ran articles on trusts on all but one day and he also lists 23 articles on trusts published by the *Chicago Tribune* during the first week of February 1888. W. LETWIN, *supra* note 1.29, at 57 & n.9. *See also* H. THORELLI, *supra* note 1.18, at 132-43.

[1.34] *See* S. BUCK, THE GRANGER MOVEMENT 214-31 (Bison ed. 1913).

[1.35] 1 J. VON KALINOWSKI, *supra* note 1.26, at § 2.03[1]. *See also* J. HICKS, THE POPULIST REVOLT: A HISTORY OF THE FARMER'S ALLIANCE AND THE PEOPLE'S PARTY 78-80 (1931) for a discussion of agrarian opposition to trusts. The Union Labor Party, Antimonopoly Party, and Prohibition Party also adopted antimonopoly platforms. *See* H. THORELLI, *supra* note 1.18, at 148-52.

[1.36] H. THORELLI, *supra* note 1.18, at 147-49. The Sherman Act debates reflect congressional awareness of the opposition of both agriculture and labor to the trusts. An amendment exempting agricultural and labor organizations from the bill was adopted on March 25, 1890, during Senate consideration. 21 CONG. REC. 2611-12 (1890), *infra* at 205. This amendment was not, however, retained in the version of the bill reported out of the Senate Judiciary Committee. In addition, several of the trust bills proposed during the first session of the 51st Congress contained exemptions for labor and agricultural activities (S. 6, H.R. 91, H.R. 402, H.R. 509, H.R. 826, H.R. 846, H.R. 3819, H.R. 3844).

[1.37] The congressional debates demonstrate that the legislators were in essential agreement concerning the need to enact some type of regulatory legislation, the principal areas of disagreement being the form such legislation should take as well as the practical, legal, and constitutional implications of the various proposals. One of the few "pro-trust" speeches given was that of Senator Stewart (R., Neb.), 21 CONG. REC. 2564-66 (1890), *infra* at 167-70. *See also* discussion *infra* at 20.

[1.38] *See* W. LETWIN, *supra* note 1.29, at 85-86.

[1.39] 2 THE STATE OF THE UNION MESSAGES OF THE PRESIDENTS 1790-1966, at 1594 (F. Israel ed. 1966).

[1.40] *See* Letwin, *Congress and the Sherman Antitrust Law 1887-1890*, 23 U. CHI. L. REV. 221, 248 (1956).

have supported antitrust legislation partially as a defensive strategy against the overwhelming public outrage which had developed against the large commercial interests.[1.41] In any event, both the Republican and Democratic Party platforms for the national elections of 1888 contained planks opposing the trusts and other oppressive business combinations.[1.42]

In November 1888, the Republicans elected Benjamin Harrison to the Presidency and gained a decisive majority of the seats in the Congress.[1.43] In view of the public opposition to trusts and business combinations, and notwithstanding their pro-tariff stand, the Republicans were now seemingly in a position to enact the antitrust legislation which they were on record as favoring.[1.44] In his last annual message, delivered on the eve of the nation's centennial anniversary, outgoing President Grover Cleveland reviewed the changes which had occurred during the nation's first 100 years. While proud of the country's growth and prosperity, he criticized, perhaps for the benefit of the new Congress and administration, "the existence of trusts, combinations, and monopolies, while the citizen is struggling far in the rear or is trampled to death beneath an iron heel."[1.45]

CONGRESSIONAL ACTION

The Fiftieth Congress

During the 50th Congress, resolutions were introduced specifically authorizing congressional investigation and legislation with respect to the trusts.[1.46] A resolution introduced by Representative William E. Mason (R., Ill.) in the House of Representatives on January 4, 1888, called for the investigation of certain trusts in the coal and sugar industries by the House Judiciary Committee.[1.47] Later that month, the House Committee on Manufactures reported the resolution to the House[1.48] with an accompanying substitute resolution by Representative Henry Bacon (D., N.Y.) directing the Committee on Manufactures to inquire into the "names and number and extent" of trusts, pools, or other combinations, their methods of doing business, their effects on prices, and their other activities, and to report back to the House with recommendations for legislation if appropriate.[1.49] This resolution was amended during a brief debate on January 25, 1888, to reflect the concern that the investigation include all such combinations and their products within the scope of the congressional legislative power.[1.50]

[1.41] *Id.*

[1.42] These are reprinted in T. MCKEE, THE NATIONAL CONVENTIONS AND PLATFORMS OF ALL POLITICAL PARTIES 1789-1905, at 235, 241 (1906), and *infra* at 54. In his September 11, 1888, letter accepting the Republican nomination for the Presidency, Benjamin Harrison expressed his agreement with his party's opposition to the trusts' abuses and predicted that "the legislative authority should and will find a method of dealing fairly and effectively with those and other abuses connected with this subject." SPEECHES OF BENJAMIN HARRISON, TWENTY-THIRD PRESIDENT OF THE UNITED STATES 113 (C. Hedges ed. 1892). As has been noted above, popular third parties further reflected the growing public sentiment.

[1.43] The *Congressional Directory* for the 51st Congress, 1st session, shows a 47-36 Republican majority in the Senate and a 172-156 Republican majority in the House of Representatives.

[1.44] *See* Letwin, *supra* note 1.40, at 248, who suggests that the Republicans could not politically oppose antitrust legislation under the prevalent public climate for reform.

[1.45] Fourth Annual Message of Grover Cleveland, Dec. 3, 1888, in 2 THE STATE OF THE UNION MESSAGES OF THE PRESIDENTS 1790-1966, *supra* note 1.39, at 1599, *infra* at 58.

[1.46] In addition to those resolutions discussed herein, see H.R. MISC. DOC. NO. 584, 50th Cong., 1st Sess. (1888).

[1.47] H.R. MISC. DOC. NO. 69, 50th Cong., 1st Sess. (1888).

[1.48] H.R. REP. NO. 67, 50th Cong., 1st Sess. (1888).

[1.49] HOUSE RESOLUTION AUTHORIZING THE COMMITTEE ON MANUFACTURES TO INVESTIGATE TRUSTS, H.R. MISC. DOC. NO. 124, 50th Cong., 1st Sess. (1888).

[1.50] 19 CONG. REC. 719-23 (1888). The amended version of the resolution was apparently not printed as a House document but appears in other documents, such as H.R. REP. NO. 708, 50th Cong., 1st Sess. (1888), and is reprinted *infra* at 53.

Pursuant to the above resolution, the House Committee on Manufactures held hearings which focused upon the sugar trust and the Standard Oil trust.[1.51] An interim report was issued on July 30, 1888, which highlighted the scope of the inquiry thus far and described the nature of these two trust forms and their methods of operation.[1.52] The committee further reported that the number of combinations and trusts was "very large" and concluded that, with respect to the Standard Oil and sugar trusts at least, the trust form had been purposefully devised to avoid legal action under state conspiracy laws while permitting the respective organizations to control the prices and production of their commodities. The committee held further hearings with respect to the whiskey and cotton bagging trusts and issued a final report the following year in which it emphasized the large number of domestic trusts and combinations, their increasing rate of formation, and their influence upon a substantial portion of the important manufacturing and industrial interests in the country.[1.53] During this period, a number of bills designed to define, regulate, tax, or prohibit trusts were also introduced in the House,[1.54] although none of these were ever reported out of committee or independently considered.

The proceedings in the Senate, however, were of far greater significance in the enactment of the initial antitrust legislation. John Sherman, the eminent Ohio Republican in the 50th Congress, had had a long career in public service, including several terms as a member of the House of Representatives and of the Senate.[1.55] After losing a bid for his party's nomination for President at its national convention of 1888, he decided to make his last major legislative contribution in the regulation of domestic and foreign trade and commerce.[1.56] Senator Sherman was most widely recognized, however, as an expert in the field of public finance and taxation and was, during this time, the most influential member of the Senate Committee on Finance.[1.57] Despite the fact that he did not help draft the final version of the legislation that was to bear his name, there can be no real doubt concerning his sincere and substantial efforts in helping to secure the Act's passage.[1.58]

On July 10, 1888, Senator Sherman introduced in the Senate a resolution directing the Committee on Finance to inquire into and report, in connection with any revenue bills, such measures as the committee would recommend to prohibit anticompetitive arrangements, contracts, or combinations.[1.59] That resolution was accepted without debate by the Senate and referred to the Finance Committee.[1.60] On August 14, 1888, Senator Sherman introduced his first antitrust bill, S. 3445, which comprised a single section declaring all arrangements, contracts, agreements, trusts, or combinations to prevent full and free competition in the production, manufacture, or sale of goods, and all arrangements by which the price of goods was increased, to be against public policy,

---

[1.51] *Hearings Pursuant to H.R. Misc. Doc. No. 124 Before the House Comm. on Manufactures in Relation to Trusts*, 50th Cong., 1st Sess. (1888).

[1.52] H.R. REP. NO. 3112, 50th Cong., 1st Sess. (1888), *infra* at 55–57.

[1.53] H.R. REP. NO. 4165, 50th Cong., 2d Sess. (1889), *infra* at 58–59.

[1.54] These bills are collected in a document prepared by the United States Attorney General entitled BILLS AND DEBATES IN CONGRESS RELATING TO TRUSTS, S. DOC. NO. 147, 57th Cong., 2d Sess. 39–68 (1903) [hereinafter cited as BILLS & DEBATES].

[1.55] Senator Sherman served a total of 6 years in the House and 32 years in the Senate. He also served in the Cabinets of Presidents Hayes and McKinley, as Secretary of the Treasury and Secretary of State, respectively. John Sherman's autobiography was entitled *Recollections of Forty Years in the House, Senate and Cabinet—An Autobiography* (1895).

[1.56] *See also* Letwin, *supra* note 1.40, at 249; H. THORELLI, *supra* note 1.18, at 166–67.

[1.57] H. THORELLI, *supra* note 1.18, at 167.

[1.58] The Sherman Act was passed in the form in which it was reported out of the Senate Judiciary Committee, of which Sherman was not a member. That committee substantially revised the bill (S. 1, 51st Cong.) following its referral there on March 27, 1890. 21 CONG. REC. 2731 (1890), *infra* at 274. Although Sherman's two-volume autobiography, cited note 1.55 *supra*, devoted only six pages to the passage of the antitrust Act, Sherman there stated that he knew of no object of greater importance to the people than this legislation. *Id.* at 1076.

[1.59] 19 CONG. REC. 6041 (1888), *infra* at 54–55. It does not appear that Sherman's resolution was ever printed or numbered as part of the Senate's documents.

[1.60] *Id., infra* at 55.

unlawful, and void.[1.61] Sherman's bill was referred to his Committee on Finance without debate,[1.62] and an amended version was reported to the Senate on September 11, 1888.[1.63]

Senate Consideration of S. 3445

The Senate proceedings during the 50th Congress in relation to Senator Sherman's bill, in which it acted as a Committee of the Whole, were principally concerned with the source of Congress' power to regulate commerce in general, the constitutionality of the bill, and the nature and types of business arrangements intended to be covered. Significant portions of the debates touched upon the common law and statutory bases for the regulation of commerce and provided a review of existing law concerning the legality of business arrangements having restraining effects upon commerce. During these proceedings, the political forces and themes that were to play major roles in the bill's consideration began to emerge and take shape. Although the great majority of the Senate debates occurred before the final version of the bill was drafted by the Senate Judiciary Committee, these proceedings shed light on Congress' motivation and its assessment of the economic, political, and legal forces which were operating in the country. Accordingly, it may be helpful to highlight the course of the congressional proceedings and to make a few general observations where necessary to place them in the proper perspective.[1.64]

It is interesting to note, for example, that despite Senator Sherman's early statement, in relation to Senator John H. Reagan's (D., Tex.) bill,[1.65] to the effect that a trust bill could be predicated both upon Congress' authority to regulate commerce and upon its taxing authority,[1.66] neither the original nor the amended version of Sherman's bill specifically referred to the congressional power upon which it was to rest.[1.67] Because of the lack of legislative precedent in this area, the source and extent of appropriate congressional constitutional authority for the proposed legislation was debated at length. Another area of extensive debate was the scope of the bill's proposed coverage in relation to both commercial and noncommercial activity. For example, when Senator George F. Hoar (R., Mass.) complained early during the debate that the bill's general language appeared to apply not only to harmful but also to meritorious arrangements, Sherman answered, as he did several times during the course of the proceedings, that the bill merely set out the prevailing common law rule concerning unlawful contracts affecting interstate transportation of goods.[1.68]

A major speech in opposition to the trust bill was delivered on February 4, 1889, by Senator James Z. George (D., Miss.),[1.69] who was to play a significant role in shaping the legislation. He severely attacked the constitutionality of Sherman's bill and recited his basic objections to its substantive provisions. Senator George believed that

---

[1.61] S. 3445, 50th Cong., 1st Sess. (1888), *infra* at 63-64.

[1.62] 19 CONG. REC. 7513 (1888), *infra* at 63. Earlier that day, Senator John H. Reagan (D., Tex.) had introduced S. 3440, a bill which attempted to define trusts and their purposes and to make membership in them unlawful. Although Senator Reagan wished to have his bill referred to the Senate Judiciary Committee, Sherman convinced him that it should be sent to the Finance Committee. *Id.*, *infra* at 61-62.

[1.63] *See* pp. 64-65 *infra*. Other Senate antitrust bills introduced during the 50th Congress are reprinted in BILLS & DEBATES at 3-6, 33-37. None of these were ever reported out of committee.

[1.64] A good treatment of the passage of the Sherman Act may be found in H. THORELLI, *supra* note 1.18, at 166-210.

[1.65] S. 3440, 50th Cong., 1st Sess. (1888). *See* note 1.62 *supra*.

[1.66] 19 CONG. REC. 7513 (1888), *infra* at 62-63.

[1.67] During the Senate debates of January 23 and 25, 1889, Senator Sherman offered an amendment that included adding the words "in due course of trade" to the first section of his bill in an apparent attempt to rest the bill upon the interstate commerce power. 20 CONG. REC. 1121, 1167 (1889), *infra* at 66, 67.

[1.68] 20 CONG. REC. 1167 (1889), *infra* at 68-69. Sherman's remark clearly implied not only that the bill was based on the commerce power but also that it should be interpreted in the light of existing common law precedents and was intended to cover only those restraints found to be unlawful under such law.

[1.69] *Id.* at 1458-62, *infra* at 77-88.

his colleagues misunderstood the potential effects of the bill and that it would indiscriminately apply to arrangements which were "purely moral and defensive."[1.70] He doubted the bill would be effective because he believed that Congress could not constitutionally regulate the interstate sale of commodities because of the constitutional limitations then existing under the original package doctrine, which had been enunciated by the Supreme Court in several cases including *Brown v. Maryland*,[1.71] and which essentially provided that imported commodities passed out of interstate commerce and into local jurisdiction when their original packaging was opened and the goods sold. It was his further criticism that neither the anticompetitive acts themselves, as opposed to the mere trust agreements, nor the oppressive behavior of a single person was reached by the language of Sherman's bill.[1.72] In another interesting speech, Senator James K. Jones (D., Ark.) metaphorically characterized the antitrust attitude of the time.[1.73] In portraying the increasing size and power of these "commercial monsters," he used terminology pertaining to animals, declaring that these business organizations had "been allowed to grow and fatten upon the public," and had the "conscienceless rapacity of commercial sharks . . . in schools," and were "preying upon every industry, and by their unholy combinations robbing their victims, the general public, in defiance of every principle of law or morals."

Senate consideration of the bill during the 50th Congress essentially provided a vehicle for raising some of the basic objections to the bill held by several Senators while allowing them nevertheless to declare their opposition to the trusts and thus to respond in at least a preliminary manner to the popular demand for some form of antitrust legislation. No events of significance beyond the hearings previously mentioned occurred in the House of Representatives until it took up consideration, during the next Congress, of the trust bill following its passage by the Senate.[1.74]

The Fifty-first Congress

On December 3, 1889, in his first annual message to the Congress, President Harrison urged that body to give "earnest attention" to federal antitrust legislation.[1.75] The following day, Senator Sherman introduced the first Senate bill of the 51st Congress, S. 1, which was identical to the amended version of his bill reported by the Senate Finance Committee on September 11 of the previous year.[1.76] Sherman's bill was referred to the same committee and reported back with amendments on January 14, 1890.[1.77] On the same day that Sherman introduced S. 1, bills dealing with the trust problem were also introduced by Senators George[1.78] and Reagan.[1.79] Although neither was ever favorably reported back to the Senate, both were later considered as

---

[1.70] *Id.* at 1458, *infra* at 77-78.

[1.71] 25 U.S. (12 Wheat.) 419, 6 L. Ed. 419 (1827). Senator George was also concerned with such further constitutional limitations upon the scope of interstate commerce as had been expressed in Kidd v. Pearson, 128 U.S. 1, 9 S. Ct. 6, 32 L. Ed. 346 (1888), and in a speech on February 27, 1890, he referred to several Supreme Court decisions as bases for his constitutional objections to the bill. 21 CONG. REC. 1768-72 (1890), *infra* at 101-11.

[1.72] *Id.* at 1765, *infra* at 95. During his speech on February 27, 1890, Senator George also stated that Sherman's earlier view had premised the ability to regulate the trusts under the revenue system by its power to control taxation and tariff duties. *Id.* at 1768, *infra* at 100-01.

[1.73] 20 CONG. REC. 1457-58 (1889), *infra* at 75-77.

[1.74] As previously discussed, although several bills relating to trusts had been introduced in the House during the 50th Congress, none of these were ever reported out of committee. *See* note 1.54 *supra*.

[1.75] First Annual Message of Benjamin Harrison, Dec. 3, 1889, in 2 THE STATE OF THE UNION MESSAGES OF THE PRESIDENTS 1790-1966, *supra* note 1.39, at 1638, *infra* at 60.

[1.76] S. 1, 51st Cong., 1st Sess. (1889), *infra* at 89-90. *See also* 21 CONG. REC. 96 (1889). Thorelli suggests that Sherman chose to introduce this version, founded on the taxing power, rather than the amended January 25, 1890 version, because of the constitutional objections raised by Senator George. *See* H. THORELLI, *supra* note 1.18, at 177.

[1.77] 21 CONG. REC. 541 (1890). The bill as reported appears *infra* at 93-94.

[1.78] S. 6, 51st Cong., 1st Sess. (1889); *see* BILLS & DEBATES at 411-12. Senator George's bill was referred to the Senate Finance Committee. 21 CONG. REC. 96 (1889).

[1.79] S. 62, 51st Cong., 1st Sess. (1889); *see* BILLS & DEBATES at 413-14. Senator Reagan's bill was referred to the Senate Judiciary Committee, 21 CONG. REC. 97 (1889), and adversely reported back on June 30, 1890, after the Sherman bill had been passed by Congress. *Id.* at 6737.

amendments to S. 1.[1.80] These were the only bills relating to trusts introduced in the Senate during the 51st Congress, although Senator George, presumably because of his serious reservations concerning the adequacy of existing constitutional regulatory authority, on March 25, 1890, introduced a joint resolution proposing an amendment to the Constitution to grant Congress concurrent authority with the states to enact antitrust legislation.[1.81]

On March 2, 1889, the House Committee on Manufactures issued its final report, which illustrated the substantial power of the trusts.[1.82] Although these proceedings did not deal directly with Senator Sherman's trust bill, they reflect both Congress' concern with the trust problem and a desire on the part of the legislators to understand the nature and activities of some of the larger business organizations. No indication exists that any Senate hearings directly related to the specific trust legislation were held. Hearings were, however, conducted by a select Senate committee, pursuant to a resolution passed in May 1888 authorizing study of the production and transportation of meat in the United States.[1.83] On May 1, 1890, some six weeks before the Sherman Act's final passage, that committee issued its report,[1.84] in which it extensively outlined the centralized control of the beef industry and the corresponding dominant role played by a few railroad companies. The committee strongly recommended both federal legislation and supplemental state legislation and specifically recommended passage by the House of the Sherman bill, which had recently been passed by the Senate, observing that this measure encompassed the full extent of federal constitutional regulatory authority in relation to trusts and combinations affecting interstate and foreign commerce.[1.85]

Senate Consideration of S. 1

Once active consideration of the trust bill began in the 51st Congress, its passage was accomplished in relatively short time.[1.86] Most of the proceedings were held by the

---

[1.80] In addition, on December 9, 1889, a resolution was introduced by Senator Turpie (D., Ind.) providing that penal sanctions against trusts should include seizure, forfeiture, and sale of trust goods. 21 CONG. REC. 125 (1889), *infra* at 90. *See also infra* at 90-92. Although it does not appear that this resolution was considered during the Sherman Act debates, the Senate Judiciary Committee incorporated a seizure and forfeiture provision in section 6 of the final version of the bill. *See infra* at 277.

[1.81] S.J. Res. 67, 51st Cong., 1st Sess. (1890).

[1.82] REPORT OF THE HOUSE COMM. ON MANUFACTURES, H.R. REP. NO. 4165, 50th Cong., 2d Sess. (1889), *infra* at 58.

[1.83] *Hearings Pursuant to S.J. Res. 78 Before the Senate Select Comm. on the Transportation and Sale of Meat Products*, 51st Cong., 1st Sess. (1890).

[1.84] REPORT OF THE SENATE SELECT COMM. ON THE TRANSPORTATION AND SALE OF MEAT PRODUCTS, S. REP. NO. 829, 51st Cong., 1st Sess. (1890).

[1.85] The pertinent portion of the report containing this recommendation stated:
> So far as Congress can give relief against illegal trusts and conspiracies, its action must be confined under constitutional restrictions to commerce among the States and with foreign nations. It cannot legislate as to such trusts and combinations existing and limiting their operations within State lines. The State authorities alone can apply the proper remedy as to such illegal agreements and arrangements when operating exclusively within a State.
> The bill recently passed by the Senate on the subject of trusts, and now pending in the House of Representatives, was prepared with great care by the Senate Judiciary Committee and goes as far as the Federal Constitution permits. It will safely endure judicial criticism, and covers fully the whole subject of illegal trusts and combinations as affecting commerce among the States and with foreign countries.
> If any combine or trust, such as we believe is operating in the Chicago cattle market, engages in shipping its products from one State or Territory to another, or to a foreign country, it can be punished under the provisions of this bill, a copy of which is herewith filed.
> This, in our judgment, is all that can be done by Congress, without violating the Constitution, and it remains for the State legislatures to enact laws which will punish these combines operating within State lines.
> State legislation must supplement that by Congress, and active, intelligent, honest officials must be found to enforce the laws enacted.

Id. at 33.

[1.86] The bill was debated for seven days in the Senate, during the period of February 27 to April 8, 1890, at which time the bill was initially passed. The House debated and passed the bill with the addition of one amendment on May 1, 1890. An additional seven days' consideration was required, including two House-Senate conferences, in order to secure its final passage on June 20, 1890.

Senate acting as a Committee of the Whole until final consideration of the bill after it was reported by the Senate Judiciary Committee. On February 27, 1890, Senator George renewed his attack on Senator Sherman's bill in a lengthy speech in which he repeated some of his earlier objections and asserted that the bill was both "utterly unconstitutional" and "utterly worthless," and was not properly related to any specific congressional power.[1.87] Senator George ended by forcefully admonishing that passage of the bill would only aggravate the existing evils and add to the people's suffering. He proposed instead to offer, at the proper time, a substitute amendment which would utilize the power to reduce or abolish tariff duties on foreign competing articles as a means of combatting the trust problem.[1.88] At least two commentators have concluded that the impact of George's speech was not lost on the other Senators and apparently convinced many of them of the need for significant modification of the bill.[1.89]

On March 18, 1890, the Senate Finance Committee reported another amended version of Sherman's bill,[1.90] eliminating the criminal provisions contained in the earlier version and specifically applying it to "all arrangements, contracts, agreements, trusts, or combinations between two or more citizens or corporations, or both, of different States" with a view toward or tending to restrict competition. This language appears to have been drafted to meet one of Senator George's principal objections, namely, that the bill did not reach the unlawful activities of the trusts beyond the trust agreements themselves.

The bill was not further debated until March 21, 1890, at which time Senator Reagan offered his bill (S. 62) as an amendment to the bill under consideration.[1.91] In the course of that debate, Senator Sherman delivered his most important speech in support of his bill and attempted to answer Senator George's several specific objections.[1.92] He stated that the purpose of the bill was to enable the federal courts to apply the same remedies against combinations injuriously affecting the interests of the United States as the state courts had been applying to protect state interests under existing common or statutory law. In response to George's constitutional objections, he asserted that article III of the Constitution—the judicial article—was sufficient to vest the federal courts with jurisdiction to enforce the proposed statute and further declared that the bill could be supported by Congress' power to regulate interstate and foreign commerce and by its revenue power as well as by the federal judicial authority.[1.93]

Sherman reviewed the individual sections of the bill, distinguishing the first as remedial, which was intended to be liberally construed, from the third, criminal, section which had been deleted.[1.94] He clearly expressed the bill's intended limitations, remarking that it was aimed "only at unlawful combinations" and would not affect combinations operating where there was "free and fair competition."[1.95] He additionally discussed the power of the trusts and their anticompetitive effects and reviewed some of the existing common law precedents to illustrate the basis for holding

---

[1.87] 21 CONG. REC. 1765-72 (1890), *infra* at 94-111. Senator George prefaced his remarks by stating that he considered legislation on the subject matter covered by the bill "as possibly the most important matter to come before the present Congress." *Id.* at 1765, *infra* at 94.

[1.88] *Id.* at 1772, *infra* at 111. Although Senator George submitted an amendment, *id.* at 2474, *infra* at 150, he declined to offer it after a similar provision was tabled. *Id.* at 2616, *infra* at 213. Section 3 of George's bill (S. 6) contained a suspension-of-duties remedy. It was offered as a floor amendment to S. 1 by Senator Gray but rejected, 21-25. *Id.* at 2661, *infra* at 254-55.

[1.89] A. WALKER, HISTORY OF THE SHERMAN LAW OF THE UNITED STATES OF AMERICA 8 (1910); H. THORELLI, *supra* note 1.18, at 179.

[1.90] BILLS & DEBATES at 89, *infra* at 112.

[1.91] 21 CONG. REC. 2455 (1890), *infra* at 113.

[1.92] *Id.* at 2456-62, *infra* at 113-29.

[1.93] *Id.* at 2460-62, *infra* at 123-29.

[1.94] *Id.* at 2456, *infra* at 115. The second section of the bill provided for a private right of action with double the monetary recovery for injuries sustained by reason of violations of section 1. The third section had been deleted from the version reported by the Senate Finance Committee on March 18, 1889.

[1.95] *Id.* at 2457, *infra* at 116.

such practices unlawful.[1.96] In presenting his view of the function of the courts in determining the legality of any challenged conduct on a case-by-case basis according to the bill's guiding principle, Sherman candidly stated:

> I admit that it is difficult to define in legal language the precise line between lawful and unlawful combinations. This must be left for the courts to determine in each particular case. All that we, as lawmakers, can do is to declare general principles, and we can be assured that the courts will apply them so as to carry out the meaning of the law, as the courts of England and the United States have done for centuries. This bill is only an honest effort to declare a rule of action, and if it is imperfect it is for the wisdom of the Senate to perfect it. Although this body is always conservative, yet, whatever may be said of it, it has always been ready to preserve, not only popular rights in their broad sense, but the rights of individuals as against associated and corporate wealth and power.[1.97]

Sherman's speech was an eloquent and forceful presentation, in which he termed the proposed legislation "a bill of rights, a charter of liberty."[1.98]

Following introduction by Senator John J. Ingalls (R., Kan.) of his amendment concerning regulation of the options and futures markets,[1.99] Senator George G. Vest (D., Mo.)—another Senator who played a leading role in the proceedings—sided with George's constitutional objections and suggested the bill be referred to the Judiciary Committee in order to cure its constitutional infirmities.[1.100] His speech also emphasized a common theme of the debates—the tying of the antitrust legislation to the issue of reducing the protective tariff.[1.101] Next, Senator Reagan briefly discussed his substitute amendment, comparing it with Sherman's proposal.[1.102] His bill adopted a somewhat different approach from that taken by Sherman, in that it attempted to define a trust in terms of the specific purposes for which it was formed. Senator William B. Allison (R., Iowa), on the other hand, responded to Vest's position that reduction of the protective tariff was the means by which to resolve the trust problem by denying any causal relationship between the trust problem and the tariff policy. He ventured to say that the objectionable domestic combinations were practically independent of the tariff, arguing that such articles as woolen, cotton, leather, and silk goods were protected by tariffs yet not the subject of trusts, while, conversely, articles such as beef, oil, whiskey, and oatmeal were the subject of large trusts although not affected by protective tariffs.[1.103] While there existed a strong difference of opinion between the two political camps with respect to the relevance of the tariff issue, this difference was eventually overcome by their common desire to enact some form of remedial legislation regardless of the genesis of the target economic arrangements.[1.104]

During the Senate debate of March 24, 1890, Senator David Turpie (D., Ind.) rejected Sherman's use of the judicial power to support his bill and stated that the only foundation for such legislation existed under the commerce clause.[1.105] While generally

---

[1.96] *Id.* at 2457–60, *infra* at 117–23.

[1.97] *Id.* at 2460, *infra* at 122.

[1.98] *Id.* at 2461, *infra* at 126.

[1.99] *Id.* at 2462–63, *infra* at 129–30. This amendment was later debated at some length and adopted. *Id.* at 2613, *infra* at 209. It is of greater historical than practical importance, however, since it was not a part of the final version of the bill as reported by the Senate Judiciary Committee.

[1.100] *Id.* at 2463–67, *infra* at 131–40. Senator Vest urged that the bill be referred to the Senate Judiciary Committee because of its significance. *Id.* at 2467, *infra* at 140. This suggestion was eventually accepted despite repeated countereffoorts by Sherman. *Id.* at 2731, *infra* at 274. *See also* pp. 21–23 *infra*.

[1.101] *Id.* at 2466–67, *infra* at 138–40. Senator Vest directly related the protective tariff to the abuses of business organizations: "If the high protective tariff were removed the foreign competition would furnish, if not an absolute, certainly a most beneficial remedy to remove this evil." *Id.* at 2466, *infra* at 139.

[1.102] *Id.* at 2469–70, *infra* at 144–46. In Reagan's view, the commerce power was the appropriate basis for the proposed legislation.

[1.103] *Id.* at 2470–71, *infra* at 146–48.

[1.104] It should be noted that the 51st Congress was concurrently considering further tariff legislation, and the relationship between trusts and tariffs was therefore of immediate interest.

[1.105] 21 CONG. REC. 2556–57 (1890), *infra* at 150–53.

supporting the bill, Turpie believed it could have gone much further than it did, in contrast to previous criticisms that had emphasized the bill's overbroad reach into areas beyond congressional constitutional authority.[1.106] Turpie also expressed the difficulties many of the Senators were undoubtedly experiencing in attempting to formulate legislation in a new area but urged them to pass some form of legislation, even an imperfect measure, in order to give the executive branch, the courts, and the public a chance to voice their opinions about its construction and possible refinement.[1.107]

On March 24 also, Senator Reagan's bill was offered as an addition to the Sherman bill.[1.108] Because this bill itemized the practices that would be made unlawful, such as agreements to affect prices or to decrease production of commodities,[1.109] it evoked a fair amount of discussion as to its potential applicability to agricultural and labor organizations.[1.110] The consensus of these and subsequent statements addressed to this issue favored expressly excluding the activities of such organizations from the bill's coverage, and a specific amendment was later adopted by the Senate Committee of the Whole toward this end.[1.111] No such express exemptions were included in the bill's final version, however, and such statutory exemptions had to await passage of section 6 of the Clayton Act in 1914.[1.112] While it is not clear why this omission was made, there appears to be substantial evidence in the debates that Senators Sherman and Reagan believed that such groups would in any event be exempted from the coverage of their respective bills, and that such an express exemption would therefore be surplusage.[1.113] In any event, at this point in the debate Sherman objected that consideration of this issue and of the other bills that had been introduced were nothing more than attempts to defeat his bill.[1.114] While stating he would accept other amendments which would accomplish the basic purpose of his bill, he urged his fellow Senators, if they were so inclined, to "defeat it squarely by a fair vote" rather than "encumber it with propositions that lead to endless argument."[1.115]

Repeated reference was also made throughout the proceedings to the policy favoring "freedom and fairness" in commercial intercourse which was violated by the combinations at which the proposed bill was aimed.[1.116] One of the very few "protrust" speeches to challenge the underlying purpose of the Sherman bill was given by Senator William M. Stewart (R., Nev.); he asserted his basic agreement with the combinations themselves and stated that "[c]ombination, co-operation, is the foundation of all civilized society."[1.117] In his view, the solution to the trust problem was "counter combinations" among the people, and he urged the people to combine in order to combat the effects of the trusts.[1.118]

[1.106] *Id.* at 2557, *infra* at 152–53. Although he supported the bill, Turpie saw merit in both the Reagan and George amendments and urged their adoption as additions to, rather than substitutes for, the Sherman bill.

[1.107] *Id.* at 2557–58, *infra* at 153–54.

[1.108] *Id.* at 2560, *infra* at 158. Reagan had proposed it as a substitute three days earlier. See note 1.91 *supra*.

[1.109] See the second and fourth paragraphs of section 2, *infra* at 111.

[1.110] 21 CONG. REC. 2561–62 (1890), *infra* at 159–62.

[1.111] *See* text at note 1.130 *infra*. A related amendment was offered on March 26, 1890, by Senator Aldrich (R., R.I.) and adopted. *See* 21 CONG. REC. 2654–55, *infra* at 245.

[1.112] Act of Oct. 15, 1914, ch. 323, § 6, 38 Stat. 731, 15 U.S.C. § 17 (1970). This section expressly provides that human labor is not a commodity or article of commerce and that the antitrust laws should not be construed so as to prevent qualifying labor, agricultural, or horticultural organizations from engaging in their legitimate objectives nor to consider such persons or organizations as illegal combinations or conspiracies in restraint of trade within the meaning of the Sherman Act. The full treatment of the legislative history of the Clayton Act appears *infra* at chapter 5.

[1.113] *See* 21 CONG. REC. 2562 (1890) (remarks of Senator Sherman), *infra* at 162; *id.* at 2561–62 (remarks of Senator Reagan), *infra* at 161.

[1.114] *Id.* at 2562–63, *infra* at 162–64.

[1.115] *Id.* at 2563, *infra* at 163.

[1.116] *See, e.g., id.* at 2558–59 (remarks of Senator Pugh), *infra* at 154–57.

[1.117] *Id.* at 2564–66, *infra* at 167–70.

[1.118] *Id.* at 2565–66, *infra* at 167–69. Stewart's speech elicited no direct response.

Following a reiteration by Senator Hoar of his criticisms of the bill, Senator Sherman again defended it in a long speech largely repetitive of the one given on March 21, but which evidenced his strong commitment to the pending legislation.[1.119] His renewed argument that Congress was the only force which could effectively deal with the trust problem touched off some heated debates between Sherman and the more outspoken opponents of his bill.[1.120] During this exchange, earlier suggestions that the bill be referred to the Judiciary Committee were repeated.[1.121]

The Senate resumed consideration of S. 1 on March 25, 1890, with the reading of Senator Reagan's bill which was proposed to be added to S. 1.[1.122] Senator George then took the floor and gave a very good legislative history of the trust bill and the proposed amendments to that time.[1.123] In his speech, George referred to the serious problems in regard to each of the bills which had been introduced and moved that all bills be referred to the Committee on the Judiciary, of which he was a member. Senators Reagan,[1.124] James F. Wilson[1.125] (R., Iowa), and Sherman[1.126] opposed such reference of the bill, the latter quite naturally concerned about the fate of his bill before a committee of which two members, Senators George and Hoar, had previously questioned the existence of constitutional authority upon which it could rest. Substantial debate was directed to the proposition to refer the bill, with Senator James L. Pugh (D., Ala.), himself a member of the Judiciary Committee, opposing the motion upon the belief that such reference would destroy the bill.[1.127]

This motion to refer the bill was also defeated,[1.128] and the Senate quickly added to the bill in succession the Reagan amendment,[1.129] a proviso exempting labor and agricultural combinations offered by Senator Sherman and taken from Senator George's bill,[1.130] an amendment giving the state courts concurrent jurisdiction with the federal courts without respect to the amount in controversy,[1.131] an amendment offered by Senator Hoar striking reference to citizens and corporations of different states so that the bill would also apply to unlawful combinations existing in one state,[1.132] and the entirety of Senator Ingalls' amendment dealing with futures and options.[1.133] On the following day, the Senate added a series of additional amendments, including one placing "money trusts" within the scope of the bill,[1.134] and one offered by Senator John C. Spooner (R., Wis.) granting courts authority to issue nationwide injunctions and dealing with other aspects of judicial procedure.[1.135]

[1.119] *Id.* at 2568-69, *infra* at 175-78. Thorelli comments of this oration: "The entire speech displays the spirit of a crusader, a man impassioned with what he regards as a just cause." H. THORELLI, *supra* note 1.18, at 191.

[1.120] 21 CONG. REC. 2569-72 (1890), *infra* at 176-83.

[1.121] *Id.* at 2572, *infra* at 183. *See* note 1.100 *supra*.

[1.122] Senator Reagan's amendment as read incorporated a minor modification made the preceding day.

[1.123] *Id.* at 2597-600, *infra* at 184-88.

[1.124] *Id.* at 2601-02, *infra* at 189-92.

[1.125] *Id.* at 2602-03, *infra* at 193-94.

[1.126] *Id.* at 2604-05, *infra* at 196-98.

[1.127] *Id.* at 2606, *infra* at 200-01.

[1.128] The vote was 28 to 15 against referral to the Judiciary Committee. *Id.* at 2610-11, *infra* at 205.

[1.129] *Id.* at 2611, *infra* at 205.

[1.130] *Id.* at 2612, *infra* at 206.

[1.131] *Id.*, *infra* at 207-08.

[1.132] *Id.* at 2612-13, *infra* at 208.

[1.133] *Id.* at 2613, *infra* at 209. The Ingalls amendment included a minor amendment offered by Senator Hoar placing a $50 minimum jurisdictional requirement upon contracts. In addition, an amendment offered by Senator Coke was considered but tabled. *Id.* at 2613-16, *infra* at 209-13.

[1.134] *Id.* at 2640, *infra* at 219. This amendment had been offered by Senator Stewart on the previous day. *Id.* at 2616, *infra* at 213.

[1.135] *Id.* at 2652, *infra* at 241. Still another amendment was added, offered by Senator Aldrich (R., R.I.), which would have made the first section of the bill inapplicable to combinations that reduced the price of goods by means other than through a reduction of wages. *Id.* at 2654-55, *infra* at 245.

Senator Ingalls' amendment received a disproportionate amount of the Senate's attention during these debates. Moreover, additional amendments tacking on sundry commodities to the Ingalls amendment were offered amid some laughter. The introduction of these various "joker" amendments reflects the less-than-serious attitude of the Senate, caused, perhaps, by the length of the debate, the lateness of the hour, or the strain and uncertainty the Senators were experiencing in their task. In any event, these proceedings prompted objections by Senator Sherman, among others, to the effect that the Senate was bringing the bill into contempt in order to delay or prevent its passage.[1.136] Although several other amendments were also considered, there was a growing concern upon the part of an increasing number of Senators that the bill had been so hopelessly encumbered and confused that it should be recommitted to the Finance or Judiciary Committee for substantial revision, but Senator Sherman, with the assistance of some other Senators, was again successful in defeating all of these referral motions.[1.137] While agreeing that the bill should not be passed in its present form, Sherman expressed his confidence that it would eventually be sufficiently streamlined and the objectionable provisions deleted after it was reported to the Senate from the Committee of the Whole.[1.138] Following the addition of further minor amendments, the now lengthy bill was reported to the Senate from the Committee of the Whole.[1.139] Although the Senate's consideration of the bill had included adoption of several apparently frivolous amendments, it has been noted that such behavior was not unusual in the Committee of the Whole and should therefore not be taken as indicative of indifference or hostility to the bill on the part of the Senators.[1.140]

A more serious mood prevailed the following day, March 27, and more significant attention was given to the substantive provisions of the bill. Important contributions were made by Senator George F. Edmunds (R., Vt.), who was chairman of the Senate Judiciary Committee. He objected principally to the proposed labor exemption and to the constitutional aspects of the bill, which, he believed, involved an unlawful attempt by the Congress to legislate in an area reserved for state regulation.[1.141] In Edmunds' opinion, the bill could operate only as a regulation, under the commerce clause, of the movement of commodities in an interstate transaction.[1.142] Another important speech was that given by Senator Orville H. Platt (R., Conn.), in which he attacked the bill on several grounds, principally that it did not discriminate between legitimate and illegitimate business transactions, being, in his view, "a bill which is aimed at every business and every business transaction in the United States."[1.143] In commenting on the first section of Sherman's bill, he not only objected to its overbroad construction but also expressed his belief that it was based upon the false assumptions that all competition was beneficial and that all price increases were injurious.[1.144] He presented an interesting argument relating to the competing themes of combination and competition, which have been discussed above, and he attempted to demonstrate, through the use of examples, what he considered to be the destructive nature of unrestricted competition.[1.145] Platt believed that the bill had not been carefully drafted and that the Senate was merely attempting to pass some form of legislation to satisfy the public's demand. He concluded with a strong appeal against presenting the country

---

[1.136] *Id.* at 2655, *infra* at 246–47.

[1.137] *Id.* at 2657, *infra* at 248; *id.* at 2660, *infra* at 254.

[1.138] *Id.* at 2655 *infra* at 246–48.

[1.139] *Id.* at 2662, *infra* at 255.

[1.140] See H. THORELLI, *supra* note 1.18, at 196–97.

[1.141] 21 CONG. REC. 2726-28 (1890), *infra* at 264–69. Senator Edmunds' basic constitutional objection was that the bill transgressed the line between the Congress' commerce regulatory powers and the rights of the states themselves to exercise their own policies, especially as to aspects of Ingalls' amendment to tax and regulate certain commodities.

[1.142] *Id.* at 2727, *infra* at 267. In another significant speech, Senator Hoar defended the agricultural-labor exemption. *Id.* at 2728, *infra* at 269.

[1.143] *Id.* at 2729, *infra* at 271.

[1.144] *Id., infra* at 271–72.

[1.145] At one point in his presentation, Senator Platt stated: "Unrestricted competition is brutal warfare, and injurious to the whole country." *Id., infra* at 271.

with either meaningless legislation or legislation which would harm legitimate interests for a long time in the future.[1.146]

Following Senator Platt's performance, another motion was made to refer the bill and amendments to the Judiciary Committee with instructions to report back to the Senate within 20 days. This time, Senator Sherman did not object to the referral, asking only for a vote on the motion, which was adopted by a narrow margin.[1.147]

S. 1 as Reported by the Senate Committee on the Judiciary

On April 2, 1890, only six days after its referral, a substitute version of S. 1, in the form in which the bill was to be finally enacted, was reported to the Senate by the Committee on the Judiciary.[1.148] Although the first section of the substitute version of the bill generally resembled the first section of Senator Sherman's bill in that it declared unlawful and against public policy "every contract, combination in the form of trust or otherwise, or conspiracy, in restraint of commerce," the substitute bill constituted a major revision of the original Sherman proposal. A criminal provision similar to that which had appeared in a version of the bill reported by the Senate Finance Committee[1.149] was incorporated, and an entirely new section—numbered section 2—making unlawful the offenses of monopolization, attempted monopolization, and conspiracy to monopolize was added. In addition, the jurisdictional provision was expanded, a venue provision was added, and the remedial provision was modified to provide that anyone "injured in his business or property" by reason of a violation of the Act would be entitled to recover treble the damages suffered in addition to the costs of suit and a reasonable attorney's fee.[1.150]

When the bill was reported by Senator Edmunds, no reference was made to the authorship of its individual sections. Indeed, the debates indicated that, while committee members disagreed among themselves concerning particular sections, they were unanimous in their support of the bill.[1.151] Senator George, for example, stated: "I regard the bill, so far as it goes, as a very good one, the best I think that can be framed under that particular power of Congress, the power over commerce, which the committee have [sic] attempted to frame a bill under."[1.152]

Senator Sherman, although he was the prime mover of the bill, was not a member of the Judiciary Committee and, therefore, had no direct role in the drafting of the final version of the bill that was to bear his name. He had steadfastly resisted its referral to the Judiciary Committee and was dissatisfied with the revised version of the bill. Indeed, he was reported to have said that he considered the substitute version

---

[1.146] *Id.* at 2731, *infra* at 274.

[1.147] *Id., infra* at 274. The motion to commit the bill and amendments to the Judiciary Committee was passed by a 31-to-28 vote.

[1.148] S. 1 as reported by the Senate Committee on the Judiciary, 51st Cong., 1st Sess. (1890), *infra* at 275-77.

[1.149] Reprinted *infra* at 93-94.

[1.150] Other changes in the substitute bill included an expansion of the court subpoena power, a provision for forfeiture, seizure, and condemnation of property owned by a trust pursuant to any conspiracy mentioned under the first section of the bill, and a definitional section which made it clear the term "persons" was intended to apply to corporations. Finally, the measure's title was changed from "A bill to declare unlawful trusts and combinations in restraint of trade and production" to "A bill to protect trade and commerce against unlawful restraints and monopolies" in order to provide a positive emphasis. For a fuller discussion of the provisions of the Act see pp. 30-35 *infra*.

[1.151] 21 CONG. REC. 2901 (1890), *infra* at 277-78. That committee was chaired by Senator Edmunds (R., Vt.) and composed additionally of Senators Coke (D., Tex.), Everts (R., N.Y.), Hoar (R., Mass.), Ingalls (R., Kan.), Pugh (D., Ala.), Vest (D., Mo.), and Wilson (R., Iowa). H. THORELLI, *supra* note 1.18, at 199. The revised S. 1 was not accompanied by a report. The minutes of the Senate Committee on the Judiciary, which are preserved in the National Archives of the United States, provide evidence that Edmunds was primarily responsible for drafting the bill, having written the first (with the help of Everts), second, third, fifth, and sixth sections, while George was credited with having drafted the fourth, Hoar the seventh, and Ingalls the eighth, sections. *See generally* H. THORELLI, *supra* note 1.18, at 212-14; Letwin, *supra* note 1.40, at 254-55 & n.190.

[1.152] 21 CONG. REC. 2901 (1890), *infra* at 278. It was by now clear that the bill was premised upon the congressional power to regulate interstate commerce.

"worthless" and "totally ineffective" and that he was hopeful that amendments would be added to the bill in the House of Representatives which would "restore in substance the original design of the bill."[1.153] Nevertheless, Sherman supported the revised bill during its subsequent consideration.

It is interesting to note that, after relatively limited debate, the substantially revised bill passed the Senate on April 8, 1890, by a nearly unanimous vote. Despite the inclusion of several new substantive provisions in the bill, Senator Hoar, who was a member of the Judiciary Committee, opened that debate by stating he would not undertake to explain the bill, which was "well understood."[1.154] Likewise, Senator Sherman indicated that while he, too, did not propose to open debate on the bill, he intended to vote for it "not as being precisely what I want, but as the best under all the circumstances that the Senate is prepared to give in this direction."[1.155]

When the bill was reported out of the Committee of the Whole to the full Senate, Senator Reagan proposed an amendment giving state courts concurrent jurisdiction with federal courts.[1.156] Reagan doubted that private litigants would take advantage of the private damage remedy provision of the bill if they had to bring their actions in federal district courts but believed they might avail themselves of the civil remedy in a state court within their geographic location.[1.157] This amendment was defeated after argument that it would be beyond Congress' power to confer jurisdiction.[1.158] Senator George's amendment expressly permitting several persons having common claims against a defendant to join in a private action under the seventh section of the bill, which had been considered and rejected by the Judiciary Committee, was also rejected by the Senate,[1.159] as was Senator Reagan's further amendment making each day's violation of the Act a separate offense.[1.160]

There followed the only significant debate concerning the new second section of the bill, making unlawful monopolization, attempts to monopolize, and conspiracies to monopolize. A proposal by Senator George Gray (D., Del.) that would have limited the section merely to concerted combinations or conspiracies to monopolize—to parallel the concerted activity requirement of the first section of the bill, instead of proscribing monopolization or attempted monopolization by single persons—was rejected.[1.161] During this discussion, Senator Hoar gave a good definition of monopoly as a common law technical term, focusing upon intent and predatory conduct, and emphasized that the two main features of the bill were to provide a remedy for anticompetitive behavior and to extend the common law principles to the interstate and international commerce

---

[1.153] These terms were attributed to Senator Sherman by the *New York Times* in an article dated April 8, 1890, at 4, col. 4, entitled "Mr. Sherman Gives Up Hope," in which the *Times* reported some comments by Senator Sherman that had appeared in the *St. Louis Globe-Democrat*:
> Senator SHERMAN does not mince words in speaking of the fate of his Anti-trust bill. The bill which the Committee on the Judiciary has just reported as a substitute for the Sherman bill will, in the opinion of the Senator, "be totally ineffective in dealing with combinations and Trusts. All corporations can ride through it or over it without fear of punishment or detection. It is manifest," he says, "that if any relief is to be had it must be as a result of popular opinion or by the action of the House, where amendments may be provided which will restore in substance the original design of the bill." He gives up hope of seeing any legislation originate in the Senate of such a character as to cope with the Trust evil.

[1.154] 21 CONG. REC. 3145 (1890), *infra* at 279.

[1.155] *Id.*, *infra* at 279-80.

[1.156] *Id.* at 3146, *infra* at 280.

[1.157] *Id.*

[1.158] *Id.* at 3146-51, *infra* at 281-91. It is interesting to note that during this debate Edmunds declared that the bill did not exclude the jurisdiction of state courts to hear antitrust cases but merely permitted actions in the federal courts without regard to the requirement that the amount in controversy exceed the minimum jurisdictional amount then in effect. *Id.* at 3149, *infra* at 287.

[1.159] *Id.* at 3151, *infra* at 292. This proposal would have permitted a type of class action as is now possible under rule 23 of the Federal Rules of Civil Procedure.

[1.160] *Id.*

[1.161] *Id.* at 3152, *infra* at 294.

of the United States.[1.162] The bill passed the Senate without further debate, 52 Senators voting in favor of passage, 1 Senator voting against, and 29 not voting.[1.163]

House Consideration of S. 1

The House Committee on the Judiciary favorably reported the bill as passed by the Senate to the House on April 25, 1890, and recommended its passage.[1.164] That report defined the bill's objectives as twofold: (1) protection of trade and commerce among the several states or with foreign nations against unlawful restraints and monopolies, and (2) protection of trade and commerce in the territories and the District of Columbia against unlawful restraints. However, the report merely paraphrased the bill's substantive provisions, adding little information as to their intended purpose or effect. It concluded with the following observation:

It may be proper to state that while this measure is not precisely what any member of the committee would have proposed upon his own motion, there was a general acquiescence in the recommendation of its passage as perhaps the only legislation possible under existing circumstances by this Congress.[1.165]

On May 1, 1890, the House considered the trust bill as reported by the House Judiciary Committee.[1.166] Although of more limited scope and significance than the Senate consideration, the House debates are nevertheless important because, unlike most of the Senate debates, they were concerned with the bill in the form in which it was finally enacted.[1.167] Representative David B. Culberson (D., Tex.), who was the author of the House Judiciary Committee report and played a leading role in securing the bill's passage in the House, remarked that the trust bill would occupy far less time than other pending legislation and proposed a rather strict limitation on debate. Objection was immediately raised, however, by Congressman Richard P. Bland (D., Mo.), who warned against rushing the measure through without the proper opportunity for amendment and debate.[1.168]

During the House debate, Representative Culberson assumed initial responsibility

---

[1.162] *Id., infra* at 293.

[1.163] *Id.* at 3152-53, *infra* at 294. Upon its passage, the bill's title was amended as reported by the Judiciary Committee. *See* note 1.150 *supra*. Senator Blodgett (D., N.J.), who cast the sole negative vote, had taken no part in the debates on the bill. Among those Senators abstaining were Everts and George, both of whom were members of the Senate Judiciary Committee.

[1.164] HOUSE COMM. ON THE JUDICIARY, REPORT TO ACCOMPANY S. 1, H.R. REP. NO. 1707, 51st Cong., 1st Sess. (1890), *infra* at 295-96.

[1.165] *Id.* at 2, *infra* at 296. The report also attempted to assure the House members of the bill's constitutionality and of the care which had been taken not to exceed the legislative authority of the Congress or to trespass upon the legislative jurisdiction of the states. *Id.* at 1.

[1.166] 21 CONG. REC. 4088-104 (1890), *infra* at 298-324. Although there had been no separate proceedings in the House directly related to any specific legislative proposals concerning the trust problem, as has been discussed above, the House Committee on Manufactures had held significant hearings in this area which provided some impetus for and information concerning trust legislation. Reference has also been made to the fact that several antitrust bills had been introduced in the 50th Congress. Additional bills were also introduced in the House during the 51st Congress, but again, none of these were reported out of committee. These tended to follow generally the format of earlier versions of Senate or House bills and are reprinted in BILLS & DEBATES at 417-59.

[1.167] The Senate debate of April 8, 1890, had substantively considered the bill after its revision by the Senate Judiciary Committee, and the Senate also resumed consideration of the bill following adoption of one amendment by the House. The Senate debates prior to the Judiciary Committee substitute, however, are nevertheless important in evaluating legislative intent because they dealt with many of the general issues raised by the bill.

[1.168] 21 CONG. REC. 4088-89 (1890), *infra* at 299. Representative Bland believed that extreme haste in the bill's consideration would not serve the country. In his view, "[t]he bill is not worth a copper in its present shape without amendment, and we want an opportunity to make something out of it." *Id.* at 4089, *infra* at 299. As will be more fully discussed, he was the author of the only amendment to be added to the bill during the House consideration.

for explaining the bill, highlighting its various provisions, and giving examples of various business practices which he believed would fall within its scope.[1.169] He emphasized, however, that it could not be predicted with certainty which agreements would be embraced by the bill until the courts had construed and interpreted it. Although surprisingly little of the entire consideration of the bill dealt with how the legislators viewed its practical application to specific business practices, this exchange presents a significant amount of discussion along these lines. For example, during the course of Culberson's presentation, Congressman Benjamin Butterworth (R., Ohio) raised several questions concerning a company's resale price maintenance agreements with its dealers to which Culberson attempted to respond.[1.170] This exchange also demonstrated congressional awareness of practices in specific industries which had been the subjects of contemporaneous legislative study. In this regard, Butterworth raised the question of the bill's application to certain practices in the cattle industry, and Congressman David B. Henderson (R., Iowa) made reference to the Senate select committee investigating the cattle and transportation industries and its report, which had been issued that day, describing the activities of the beef trust and recommending passage of the Sherman bill.[1.171]

Representative William L. Wilson (D., W. Va.) was highly critical of both the substance of the bill and what he believed to be its abbreviated consideration by the House. He nevertheless assured that body that he would not oppose the bill, despite his objection that no one could tell him exactly what it meant, since he considered it essentially "experimental legislation." By his characterization, the bill was "a blind legislation, to answer a popular demand that something shall be done about trusts."[1.172] This was an unduly harsh criticism of the bill, and a more representative attitude of many of the legislators appears to be that of Congressman John H. Rogers (D., Ark.) who, later that day, expressed both his doubts concerning this new area of legislation as well as his desire to respond to the popular demand for legislation:

> . . . Mr. Speaker, while I am willing to give my sanction to this bill, I give it just as I gave it to the interstate-commerce bill, filled with doubts, yet compelled by a sense of the exigency and the emergency of the occasion to do whatever seems best that we have the power to do under the Constitution to afford a remedy for the evils under which the country is now suffering.[1.173]

Of major significance in the House proceedings was consideration of Representative Bland's amendment. Proposed as an addition to the end of section 8 of the bill, it sought to make unlawful agreements entered into for the purpose of preventing competition in the sale of commodities transported between states or territories, or for preventing competition in the transportation of persons or commodities between states.[1.174] Bland's remarks indicated that he was concerned with reaching companies such as Armour & Co. and preferred not to leave the construction of the bill entirely to the courts. Because of his uncertainty about the bill's scope, he expressed his desire to

---

[1.169] *Id.* at 4089–91, *infra* at 299–306. Mr. Culberson's discussion touched upon the bill's application to price-fixing arrangements, monopolization, and existing combinations such as the Standard Oil trust, in addition to the procedural, jurisdictional, and remedial portions of the bill. He also reiterated the recommendation appearing in the House Judiciary Committee report that the states enact supplemental legislation to control those business activities that were beyond the congressional jurisdiction over interstate commerce. *Id.* at 4091, *infra* at 305.

[1.170] *Id.* at 4089–90, *infra* at 300–03.

[1.171] *Id.* at 4090, 4091, *infra* at 302, 306. See also note 1.85 *supra* and accompanying text.

[1.172] 21 CONG. REC. 4095 (1890), *infra* at 312. This attitude was atypical. Indeed, two Congressmen, Ezra B. Taylor (R., Ohio), then chairman of the House Judiciary Committee, and Joseph Cannon (R., Ill.), gave rather forceful speeches in which they responded to some of Wilson's objections. *Id.* at 4098, *infra* at 314–15, and *id.* at 4099, *infra* at 315–16, respectively.

[1.173] *Id.* at 4101, *infra* at 321. See also H. THORELLI, *supra* note 1.18, at 205.

[1.174] 21 CONG. REC. 4099, *infra* at 316. Congressman Sayers (D., Tex.) had attempted to offer an amendment which would have added a ninth section to the bill, requiring the President to suspend the protective tariff on any commodity that was the subject of a trust. The amendment was, however, ruled out of order as constituting a revenue amendment. *Id.* at 4098, *infra* at 313. Senator Coke had introduced a similar amendment during the Senate consideration, which was tabled. *See id.* at 2613–16, *infra* at 209–13.

include specifically both the transportation and the cattle industries within its coverage, intending the bill to apply to every commodity on which a trust was formed once it was placed in interstate commerce. Representative Bland concluded his remarks by reiterating that the bill was "but the beginning, an experiment" and voiced his expectation that the interpretations given the Act by the courts would "point the way to a more perfect law."[1.175]

The Bland amendment itself received little substantive consideration. There followed, however, a display of partisan politics concerning the passage of antitrust legislation in general, as well as declarations as to the importance of the bill and the congressional unanimity in favor of its passage.[1.176] After some further parliamentary discussions, the Bland amendment was adopted, over the objection of Representative Culberson, and the amended bill was passed by the House.[1.177]

Senate Consideration of S. 1 as Amended by the House

The Senate received the bill with the added Bland amendment on May 2, 1890.[1.178] Senator Vest immediately moved to refer the bill with amendment to the Judiciary Committee, but Senator Sherman opposed such referral, believing that the amendment was merely one "in degree" which should be concurred in.[1.179] The bill with amendment was nevertheless referred to the Senate Judiciary Committee and reported back by Senator Hoar on May 12, 1890, with the recommendation that the Senate concur in the House amendment with the addition of a Senate amendment striking part of the House amendment and limiting it to unlawful contracts or agreements made to prevent competition in the transportation of persons or property in interstate commerce.[1.180] The Senate committee further requested that a conference between the two Houses be held concerning the amendment.

During the ensuing Senate debate, Senator Hoar explained that the Bland amendment had, in the view of the Judiciary Committee, contained two provisions. The first, which would have affected contracts entered into for the purpose of preventing competition in the sale of commodities purchased in interstate commerce, had been rejected by the Senate committee on constitutional grounds. The second part of the Bland amendment, which purported to cover agreements affecting interstate transportation, was agreeable to the committee although the majority believed such agreements were already prohibited by the bill.[1.181] The Senate soon thereafter adjourned, and on the following day the bill was recommitted to the Senate Judiciary Committee, largely because of Senator Hoar's concern that the language of the amendment was imprecise.[1.182]

On May 16, 1890, the Senate Judiciary Committee reported another version of the amendment, which would have made unlawful agreements entered into for the purpose of preventing competition in transportation "so that the rates of such transportation may be raised above what is just and reasonable."[1.183] The Senate agreed to this amendment of the House amendment and requested that a conference be held, Senators Edmunds, Hoar, and Vest being appointed Senate conferees.[1.184] The following day,

---

[1.175] *Id.* at 4099, *infra* at 317.

[1.176] *Id.* at 4100-04, *infra* at 317-24. Interestingly, additional reference was made to the report of the Senate select committee which specifically recommended passage of the bill. *See* note 1.85 *supra* and accompanying text.

[1.177] 21 CONG. REC. 4104 (1890), *infra* at 324. The *Congressional Record* does not reflect that a record vote was taken.

[1.178] *Id.* at 4123, *infra* at 325.

[1.179] *Id.*

[1.180] *Id.* at 4559, *infra* at 326.

[1.181] *Id.* at 4559-60, *infra* at 326-28. Senators Vest and Coke, who had dissented from the second Judiciary Committee report, expressed the reasons for their positions. *Id.* at 4560, *infra* at 327-28.

[1.182] *Id.* at 4598, *infra* at 329.

[1.183] *Id.* at 4753, *infra* at 329-30.

[1.184] *Id.*, *infra* at 330.

however, the House refused to concur in the Senate amendment and agreed to the requested conference, Congressmen Ezra B. Taylor (R., Ohio), John W. Stewart (R., Vt.), and Bland being later appointed as House conferees.[1.185]

Conference Consideration and Final Passage of S. 1

On June 11, 1890, the first conference committee report was submitted to the House. It recommended that the House agree to a further modification adding to the Senate version of the Bland amendment a clause to the effect that nothing contained in the bill would be deemed to impair the power of the states regarding any of the matters covered by the bill.[1.186] A statement accompanying the report explained that the House particularly desired application of the bill to the transportation industry, which was embodied in provisions making unlawful agreements that raised rates above what was justifiable and reasonable.[1.187] The statement also declared that state powers in these areas were not to be impaired by the federal legislation. The extended debate which followed was concerned with whether the "just and reasonable" clause would, in effect, operate to repeal the anti-pooling clause of the recent Interstate Commerce Act.[1.188] Stewart favored adoption of the conference committee report,[1.189] but Culberson opposed it and argued in favor of the original House amendment on the ground that inclusion of the "just and reasonable" clause would permit pooling and discourage competition in the establishment of transportation rates.[1.190] Congressman Bland also opposed inclusion of the "just and reasonable" clause. He emphasized that disagreement existed as to whether the bill as passed by the Senate applied to the interstate sale of commodities and interstate transportation, and stated that he wished to have a clear statement of affirmative congressional intent to this effect.[1.191]

During this consideration, an interesting speech was given by Representative Elijah A. Morse (R., Mass.). He said that, while he approved of the bill to the extent that it was directed against "trusts that oppress the people by cornering the necessities of life or . . . that put up the price of such necessities," he was opposed to denying sellers the right to control the prices at which their goods would be sold, the right to avoid entering into "ruinous competition," or the right to "exact a fair and living profit on the sale of their goods." In his view, such effects would violate "sound business principle[s]" and would be injurious to business interests in the country.[1.192] Congressman Stewart, who favored the conference committee report, continued this theme and emphasized the importance of balancing the two major economic forces in operation—competition and combination:

[1.185] *Id.* at 4837, 5113, *infra* at 331.

[1.186] *Id.* at 5950, *infra* at 331–32. Neither Senator Vest nor Congressman Bland joined in the first conference committee report.

[1.187] *Id.*, *infra* at 332.

[1.188] *Id.* at 5951–61, *infra* at 333–53. Section 5 of the ICC Act, ch. 104, pt. 1, § 5, 24 Stat. 380 (1887), *as amended*, 49 U.S.C. § 5 (1970), made it unlawful for common carriers to enter into pooling agreements.

[1.189] 21 Cong. Rec. 5950 *et seq.* (1890), *infra* at 331 *et seq.*

[1.190] *Id.* at 5951–52, *infra* at 334–36. It is interesting to note that during the exchange which followed, Culberson argued that a distinction existed between trade and transportation and that the bill as passed by the Senate did not cover anticompetitive practices in the field of transportation. *Id.* at 5952, *infra* at 335–36. In the early cases to arise under the Act involving the establishment of rates by freight associations, however, the Supreme Court nevertheless held the Act to be applicable to such arrangements. United States v. Trans-Missouri Freight Ass'n, 166 U.S. 290 (1897); United States v. Joint Traffic Ass'n, 171 U.S. 505, 19 S. Ct. 25, 43 L. Ed. 259 (1898), *infra* at 377. *See Commentary infra* at 367. Senator Hoar, however, asserted that transportation was already covered by the bill, being as much a part of commerce as was the sale of goods, but believed no harm would be done by adding this portion of the House amendment. 21 Cong. Rec. 4560 (1890), *infra* at 327.

[1.191] 21 Cong. Rec. 5952–53 (1890), *infra* at 336–39. Bland made apparent reference to Leisy & Co. v. Hardin, 135 U.S. 100, 10 S. Ct. 681, 34 L. Ed. 128 (1890), which had been very recently decided, and in which, he believed, the Supreme Court had expanded the scope of the commerce clause beyond the bounds recognized when original consideration had been given to the bill. 21 Cong. Rec. 5952 (1890), *infra* at 337.

[1.192] 21 Cong. Rec. 5953–54 (1890), *infra* at 339–40.

INTRODUCTION

Now, there are two great forces working in human society in this country to-day, and they have been contending for the mastery on one side or the other for the last two generations. Those two great forces are competition and combination. They are correctives of each other, and both ought to exist. Both ought to be under restraint. Either of them, if allowed to be unrestrained, is destructive of the material interests of this country. It is just as necessary to restrict competition as it is to restrict combination, and any student of the times who has failed to see this has missed the lesson of the hour.[1.193]

Following additional debate upon the merits of the Senate amendment and its perceived effects upon competition in the railroad industry,[1.194] Congressman Mason suggested that the Bland amendment had been interjected in an effort to defeat the bill, a statement which resulted in some political name-calling between Mason and Bland.[1.195] Mason then stated his preference for the bill as originally passed by the Senate and requested another conference in which the amendment in its entirety would be deleted and a vote would be taken on the bill without amendment.[1.196] The House overwhelmingly rejected the first conference report the following day[1.197] and subsequently requested a further conference, instructing its conferees to recede from its amendment.[1.198]

On June 16, 1890, the Senate agreed to another conference, and two days later the second conference report, approved by five of the six conferees, was reported to the Senate, recommending that both Houses recede from their respective amendments.[1.199] The Senate concurred in the report without debate and, apparently, without opposition.[1.200] On June 20, 1890, the same report was presented to the House[1.201] where it was briefly considered. While each party attempted to claim political credit for the bill, there was no attempt made to reinstate some form of the Bland amendment.[1.202] In his closing remarks, Congressman Stewart summarized his view of the bill:

... The provisions of this trust bill are just as broad, sweeping, and explicit as the English language can make them to express the power of Congress over this subject under the Constitution of the United States. If the bill does not go far enough, then the proposition of my friend from Tennessee [Mr. ENLOE],[1.203] made some time ago, will be in order. When it is

---

[1.193] *Id.* at 5956, *infra* at 341.

[1.194] *Id.* at 5956-60, *infra* at 341-51. It is interesting to note that Congressman Stewart originally questioned why agreements between railroads to establish rates would be objectionable if the rates were in fact reasonable, to which Congressman Anderson (R., Kan.) replied that such concerted activity was the essential evil that the bill attempted to prevent, regardless of the reasonableness of the rates themselves. *Id.* at 5958-59, *infra* at 346-48. The Supreme Court adopted this latter view in the railroad association cases, *supra* note 1.190, which were among the first to reach it under the Act.

[1.195] 21 CONG. REC. 5960 (1890), *infra* at 351.

[1.196] *Id.* at 5960-61, *infra* at 351-52. Congressman Stewart acknowledged that the railroads could not exempt themselves from operation of the Interstate Commerce Act and, reversing his field, agreed that the amendment under debate was not germane to the trust bill. He joined in the request that the House pass the bill as originally enacted by the Senate. *Id.* at 5961, *infra* at 353.

[1.197] *Id.* at 5981, *infra* at 353.

[1.198] *Id.* at 5983, *infra* at 355. Congressman Bland, stating he "took no further interest in the conference," requested that another conferee be appointed in his place since his amendment was no longer supported by the House, and Culberson was appointed. *Id.* at 6099, *infra* at 355.

[1.199] *Id.* at 6208, *infra* at 358. Senator Vest abstained from arguing the report. During the brief Senate debate which preceded the second conference, Senator Edmunds moved that the Senate insist upon its amendment to the House amendment, asserting that the first conference amendment would not have had the effect of repealing the anti-pooling provision of the ICC Act. Since he considered the Bland amendment "wholly unnecessary," however, he stated no objection to a second conference in order to recommend approval of the bill in its original form. *Id.* at 6116, *infra* at 355-56.

[1.200] *Id.* at 6208, *infra* at 358. *See* H. THORELLI, *supra* note 1.18, at 210.

[1.201] 21 CONG. REC. 6312 (1890), *infra* at 359.

[1.202] *Id.* at 6313-14, *infra* at 359-62. Congressman Bland now expressed his support for the bill, although stating he would have preferred his amendment to have been appended. *Id.* at 6313, *infra* at 360.

[1.203] Congressman Enloe (D., Tenn.) had earlier proposed a constitutional amendment granting express power to the Congress to legislate on the subject of trusts. H. Res. 30, 51st Cong., 1st Sess. (1889), BILLS & DEBATES at 459.

found that the power of Congress as it now exists has been exhausted in this legislation, then it will be time to look for some amendment to the Constitution.[1.204]

The House immediately adopted the second conference report by a vote of 242 to 0, with 85 Congressmen not voting.[1.205] On July 2, 1890, the Sherman Act was signed into law by President Benjamin Harrison, apparently without comment.

SECTIONAL ANALYSIS OF THE SHERMAN ACT

According to the House Judiciary Committee report, the trust bill was intended to serve a dual function. The first stated purpose was to protect interstate and foreign trade and commerce against unlawful restraints and monopolies; the second, more limited articulated purpose was to protect trade and commerce in or between the federal territories and in the District of Columbia against unlawful restraints. Although these two purposes largely overlap, as will be further discussed, the first was primarily concerned with transactions involving interstate and foreign commerce, while the second focused upon the District of Columbia and the territories, and transactions involving them or states or foreign countries. Sections 1 and 2 applied to interstate and foreign commerce, while section 3 applied only to commerce involving territories, the District, and foreign commerce.[1.206] The bill was intended to apply existing common law principles to the trusts and other business organizations of the day and, from the beginning, took a broad and sweeping approach, leaving to the courts the determination as to where the line between lawful and unlawful behavior should be drawn in any particular instance.[1.207]

Despite the numerous criticisms directed at the bill during its consideration for its failure to discriminate between harmful and meritorious business agreements, it survived the legislative process with its first, and principal, **substantive provision drafted** in general terms. Moreover, with the exception of the Senate consideration of the Reagan amendment, which attempted to define a trust in terms of the purposes for which it was created, no other serious attempts were made to spell out what objectionable acts and practices would be contemplated by the first section of the bill.[1.208] The House Judiciary Committee report merely paraphrased the bill's provisions without further elaboration as to the meaning which was intended to be given to the terms employed therein. In addition, the **statute contained no substantive definitions to govern its application; the single definitional** section merely stated its affirmative intention to include artificial as well as natural persons within the Act's coverage.[1.209] Some legislators accordingly criticized the bill and the congressional proceedings as being spurred primarily by the desire to present some form of regulatory legislation to satisfy the public demand. Nevertheless, it is largely because of its general terms evoking Congress' plenary commerce power that the Sherman Act has served essentially without alteration as the cornerstone of American antitrust law.

While based upon the common law pertaining to restraints of trade, the Act nevertheless went beyond existing common law in several important respects. First, although unreasonable restraints at common law were deemed to be void, unenforce-

---

[1.204] 21 CONG. REC. 6314 (1890), *infra* at 362. Stewart was by this time apparently convinced that the provisions of the bill were "very general and sweeping, and perhaps cover the whole ground." *Id.* at 6313, *infra* at 359.

[1.205] *Id.* at 6314, *infra* at 362–63.

[1.206] HOUSE COMM. ON THE JUDICIARY, REPORT TO ACCOMPANY S. 1, H.R. REP. NO. 1707, 51st Cong., 1st Sess. (1890), *infra* at 295–96. *See* discussion *supra* at 25.

[1.207] *See, e.g.*, 21 CONG. REC. 2460 (1890) (remarks of Senator Sherman), *infra* at 122–23; *id.* at 3146 (remarks of Senator Hoar), *infra* at 281–82.

[1.208] Senator Reagan's Bill (S. 62) was added to the Sherman bill during the debate of March 25, 1890, following considerable discussion. *Id.* at 2611, *infra* at 205. It should also be noted, however, that the Senate Judiciary Committee, on May 16, 1890, recommended amending the Bland amendment previously adopted by the House to prohibit anticompetitive agreements raising the rates for interstate transportation of persons or property above what was deemed "just and reasonable." 21 CONG. REC. 4753 (1890), *infra* at 330. Neither provision was retained in the final bill.

[1.209] Section 8 of the Act defined the term "person" to include associations and corporations and is further discussed *infra* at 35.

able, and without effect,[1.210] the statute provided that persons engaging in such restraints would face possible criminal prosecution and sanction. Second, as will be further discussed, the Act for the first time provided for civil actions by the federal government and private parties by which to seek equitable injunctive relief, as well as recovery of monetary damages by private parties. Third, while the common law had evolved according to precedents established in individual jurisdictions, which often produced inconsistent results, the new statute served to create a comprehensive federal law by which to evaluate transactions.[1.211]

Substantive Provisions

The substantive provisions of the Sherman Act are contained in its first three sections, the first two being of primary significance. Section 1 of the Act broadly announces that "[e]very contract, combination in the form of trust or otherwise, or conspiracy, in restraint of trade or commerce among the several States, or with foreign nations, is hereby declared to be illegal." Section 1 as originally enacted also provided that every person who criminally violated the Act would be guilty of a misdemeanor and subject to a potential fine of $5,000 and/or one year's imprisonment.[1.212] Section 1 applies only to concerted activity between two or more persons and the terms "contract," "combination," and "conspiracy" have generally been applied interchangeably by the courts.[1.213]

As we have seen, by the latter half of the 19th century the term "unreasonable restraint of trade" had a well-recognized meaning, *i.e.*, agreements to establish prices, to control production, and to divide markets and similar restrictive practices.[1.214] Despite the Act's exact wording in proscribing "every agreement in restraint of trade," the courts soon held that this language was meant only to be given its common law meaning, which recognized the need to balance the interests of both competition and combination and which accordingly prohibited only those arrangements that unreasonably restrained trade. Hence, a judicial standard was developed utilizing a Rule of Reason by which to evaluate particular arrangements according to current business standards.[1.215]

Under judicial interpretation of the Act, the phrase "restraint of trade or commerce" has been applied to varied types of concerted activity to limit competition, which necessarily require some form of agreement between two or more persons. These include agreements to establish prices, to affect levels of production, to divide markets (both horizontally and vertically), and to engage in concerted boycotts of, or refusals to deal with, third parties. Other practices which may also be encompassed within this section in particular circumstances are discriminatory or predatory pricing or other such conduct; limitations upon a customer's resale markets; reciprocal dealing, exclusive dealing, and tying arrangements; restrictive or exclusionary practices in association membership; restrictive patent licensing or trademark franchising arrangements; and mergers, joint ventures, and other cooperative endeavors resulting in a substantial

---

[1.210] *See* discussion and cases cited at notes 1.2–.11 *supra*.

[1.211] Although the early cases decided under the Act substantially relied upon the common law precedents, *see, e.g.*, United States v. Addyston Pipe & Steel Co., 85 F. 271 (6th Cir. 1898), *aff'd*, 175 U.S. 211 (1899), such reference to common law precedents is now rare because of the existence of a substantial body of federal antitrust case law.

[1.212] As stated by Senator Hoar, while the bill "affirmed the old doctrine of the common law," it also provided the courts of the states with injunctive power to prohibit unlawful restraints, and it also contained a "grave penalty." 21 Cong. Rec. 3146, *infra* at 282. Criminal violation of the Act is now a felony and is subject to a potential fine of $100,000 or, in the case of a corporation, $1 million. Antitrust Procedures and Penalties Act of 1974, Pub. L. No. 93-528, § 3, 88 Stat. 1708. The legislative history of the Act appears *infra* at chapter 19.

[1.213] *See* Perma Life Mufflers, Inc. v. International Parts Corp., 392 U.S. 134, 141-42, 88 S. Ct. 1981, 1986, 20 L. Ed. 2d 982, 991-92 (1968).

[1.214] *See* discussion and cases cited at notes 1.2–.11 *supra*.

[1.215] The Rule of Reason was first formally enunciated by the Supreme Court in Standard Oil Co. v. United States, 221 U.S. 1 (1911), *infra* at 382, and is discussed more fully in the *Commentary infra* at 372–73.

lessening of competition.[1.216] In short, the term "restraint of trade" is intended to encompass essentially any concerted effort to unreasonably restrain competition in interstate or foreign commerce. As will be further discussed in connection with some of the significant cases decided under the Sherman Act, the courts have evolved a rule of *per se* illegality because judicial experience with certain types of restraints may allow them to be conclusively presumed unreasonable without further analysis of their particular anticompetitive market effects.[1.217]

There was a considerable amount of disagreement during the consideration of the bill concerning its constitutional foundation and the scope of congressional authority over interstate commerce. As a study of the debates makes clear, and subsequent Supreme Court decisions have recognized, Congress chose, in enacting the Sherman Act, to exercise the full extent of its constitutional power to regulate interstate commerce. Accordingly, the "in trade or commerce" requirement has eventually been extended so as to bring within the scope of the Act all activity having a substantial effect upon interstate or foreign commerce.[1.218]

Section 2 of the Act provides criminal penalties, which parallel those of section 1, for the three distinct offenses of monopolization, attempted monopolization, and combination or conspiracy to monopolize any part of the interstate or foreign commerce of the United States. Unlike the first section, which pertains solely to concerted activity, the second section of the Act applies both to concerted and individual activity. This section received very little consideration during the congressional debates beyond the basic recognition that the attainment or use of monopolistic control over any identifiable portion of commerce should also be proscribed.[1.219] Accordingly, this section is principally concerned with situations in which a single entity achieves or seeks to achieve, either alone or in combination with others, a position of such size and power that it is itself capable of restraining trade.

Although, as we have seen, the term "monopolization" had a rather precise meaning at common law, related to the privilege given by the government to one person to exercise exclusive control over a certain portion of commerce,[1.220] the three offenses delineated in section 2 are concerned with conduct which gives or threatens to give an unwarranted control over a particular market, even though such control may not be exclusive. Monopolization as proscribed by the Sherman Act has perhaps best been defined as the ability of a firm to control prices or exclude competitors from the market.[1.221] In *United States v. Grinnell Corp.*,[1.222] the Supreme Court held that the offense of monopolization contained two essential elements: (1) the possession of monopoly power in the relevant market, and (2) the willful acquisition or maintenance of that power as distinguished from growth or development as a consequence of a superior product, business acumen, or historic accident. The means by which market

---

[1.216] It should be noted that some of these acts or practices may also be violative of other antitrust or trade regulation statutes, most notably the Clayton Act, 15 U.S.C. § 12 *et seq., as amended,* and the Federal Trade Commission Act, 15 U.S.C. § 41 *et seq., as amended.* A full substantive discussion of each of these types of business activities and conduct that may be found violative of section 1 of the Sherman Act is beyond the scope of this treatment. For textual treatments of these matters, the reader is referred to ABA ANTITRUST LAW DEVELOPMENTS 2–46 (1975); E. KINTNER, *supra* note 1.24, at chs. 3–8; REPORT OF THE ATTORNEY GENERAL'S NATIONAL COMMITTEE TO STUDY THE ANTITRUST LAWS 12–42 (1955); 1 H. TOULMIN, *supra* note 1.2, at ch. 13; 1 J. VON KALINOWSKI, *supra* note 1.26, at chs. 4–6.

[1.217] See discussion in *Commentary infra* at 374–76.

[1.218] See *id.* at 367–70.

[1.219] On April 8, 1890, during the Senate consideration of S. 1 as reported by the Senate Judiciary Committee, an amendment proposed by Senator Gray (D., Del.) that would have limited section 2 only to combinations or conspiracies to monopolize—to parallel the concerted activity required under section 1—was rejected. See discussion *supra* at 24. In addition, the passage cited in United States v. E.I. du Pont de Nemours & Co., 351 U.S. 377, 389–90 n.15, 76 S. Ct. 994, 1004–05, 100 L. Ed. 1264, 1277–78 (1956), *infra* at 440–41, evidences that that section also was to be given its common law meaning and would not apply where monopolization does not result from an anticompetitive purpose or intent.

[1.220] See discussion *supra* at 8.

[1.221] United States v. E.I. du Pont de Nemours & Co., 351 U.S. 377, 391 (1956), *infra* at 441.

[1.222] 384 U.S. 563, 86 S. Ct. 1698, 16 L. Ed. 2d 778 (1966).

power is unlawfully achieved or maintained may often involve conduct which is also proscribed by section 1 of the Act, which is unlawful under other antitrust or trade regulation statutes, or which somehow evidences the affirmative desire to gain or hold a monopoly position. Not all instances of monopoly are proscribed, however, and mere size, power, and virtual absence of competition are not necessarily unlawful. Rather, it is the attainment or use of such power in the marketplace by unlawful or unfair means for the purpose of excluding competition which is proscribed. Thus, for example, a firm may lawfully have a monopoly on a particular product or process because the nature of the market dictates such result, as with the so-called natural monopolies involving a distinct brand or trademark for certain products.[1.223] Similarly, practical considerations may provide a monopoly, as with a market that will support the existence of only a single enterprise.[1.224] Moreover, in other cases, the monopoly may simply be "thrust" upon the firm because it was the first to enter a particular market or the only one to grow and survive in such market.[1.225] In short, it is the conduct, not the mere status, of a firm which is dealt with in this section.

The offense of attempted monopolization, on the other hand, generally involves four distinct but necessary elements of proof: (1) a specific or relevant geographic market of trade or commerce in which the attempt to monopolize is to take place; (2) a specific or relevant product market embracing the defendant's products and other reasonably competing products; (3) a specific intent to monopolize that market, evidenced by or inferred from predatory acts taken in furtherance of the attempt; and (4) a dangerous probability that the attempt will be successful.[1.226] In evaluating alleged combinations or conspiracies to monopolize, however, the courts utilize essentially the same tests as those applied to single-entity monopolization resulting from internal growth, although a lesser degree of market control may be required.[1.227] The existence of any of the three separate offenses cognizable under section 2 of the Sherman Act is therefore predicated upon the existence of sufficient market power, which is usually measured in terms of the share of a particular product and geographic market held, plus some additional factor evidencing an intent to use or acquire such power in an unfair or anticompetitive manner. Under traditional concepts, the offense of monopolization requires a greater market share than is required for either attempted monopolization or conspiracy or combination to monopolize,[1.228] the logical consideration being that specifically attempted or concerted activity towards market domination is to be more feared than individual growth.

Section 3 of the Sherman Act essentially applies the proscriptions of section 1 of that Act to commerce in any United States territory or the District of Columbia or between any two territories, or between any territory and any state or the District of Columbia, or with foreign countries, or between the District of Columbia and any state or foreign country. It also provides criminal sanctions equal to those contained in section 1. This section has not been of major significance. It is interesting to note, however, that although section 3 incorporates within its terms the prohibitions of

---

[1.223] *See, e.g.,* United States v. E.I. du Pont de Nemours & Co., 351 U.S. 377, 390-91 (1956), *infra* at 441.

[1.224] *See* Union Leader Corp. v. Newspapers of New England, Inc., 284 F.2d 582, 584 (1st Cir. 1960), *cert. denied,* 365 U.S. 833 (1961); *see also* United States v. Aluminum Co. of America, 148 F.2d 416, 429-30 (2d Cir. 1945).

[1.225] *See* American Tobacco Co. v. United States, 328 U.S. 781, 786, 66 S. Ct. 1125, 1128, 90 L. Ed. 1575, 1582 (1946); United States v. Aluminum Co. of America, 148 F.2d 416, 429 (2d Cir. 1945). *See generally* ABA ANTITRUST LAW DEVELOPMENTS, *supra* note 1.216, at 56-59 and cases discussed therein.

[1.226] *See, e.g.,* United States v. Aluminum Co. of America, 148 F.2d 416, 431-32 (2d Cir. 1945). *See also* United States v. E.I. du Pont de Nemours & Co., 351 U.S. 377, 395 n.23 (1956). For a comprehensive review of the cases involving attempted monopolization *see* Cooper, *Attempts and Monopolization: A Mildly Expansionary Answer to the Prophylactic Riddle of Section Two,* 72 MICH. L. REV. 373 (1974).

[1.227] *See* ABA ANTITRUST LAW DEVELOPMENTS, *supra* note 1.216, at 59-60; 2 J. VON KALINOWSKI, *supra* note 1.26, at § 9.02.

[1.228] American Football League v. National Football League, 205 F. Supp. 60, 64 (D. Md. 1962), *aff'd,* 323 F.2d 124 (4th Cir. 1963).

section 1, it does not likewise include those of section 2, perhaps because Congress did not believe that particular or isolated monopolies in the District of Columbia or the United States territories would constitute a significant regulatory problem.[1.229]

Procedural Sections

Original sections 4 through 8 of the Sherman Act were essentially procedural sections and constituted other significant ways in which it went beyond existing common law. Section 4 invests jurisdiction in the federal courts for both criminal prosecutions and civil injunctive actions brought under the Act; provides that prosecutions in the name of the United States be instituted by the United States attorneys (district attorneys in the original version)[1.230] under the direction of the Attorney General; and provides the basis for temporary and permanent injunctions to prevent and restrain violations of the Act. These injunctive provisions represent another significant departure from the common law in that while unlawful restraints and combinations were there declared to be void and against public policy, and accordingly unenforceable, the statute for the first time provided a specific authorization by which to affirmatively enjoin such practices. It should be borne in mind that, under section 4, the government may institute either a criminal or a civil antitrust action. While the substantive elements of the alleged violation are essentially the same, the standard of proof in criminal actions is higher.[1.231] It is a common practice for the government to file a parallel civil action requesting future injunctive relief once an indictment has been obtained.

Section 5 of the Act provides that a court before which an action has been instituted by the government may subpoena any additional party as may be required by the interests of justice, regardless of the residence of such party, and, accordingly, provides for service of subpoenas nationwide. Section 6 provides that any property that is owned under, or subject to, any contract, combination, or conspiracy which is engaged in interstate or foreign commerce and is found to be unlawful under section 1 of the Act, shall be forfeited to the United States and subject to seizure and condemnation as provided by law.

The original section 7 of the Act (now found in section 4 of the Clayton Act, as modified) was of primary importance in that it created a private right of action not present under common law whereby any person "injured in his business or property" by reason of any violation of the Act is entitled to sue for treble the damages sustained including the costs of suit and a reasonable attorney's fee. The rationale behind providing a private litigant with the potential for such multiple-damage recovery was not only to provide an economic incentive for private enforcement but also to help deter violations of the Act.[1.232] Private litigation has, in fact, aided in establishing a significant body of antitrust case law. The original section of the Act also provided that venue in a private action would lie in the district in which the defendant resided or was found.[1.233] Furthermore, the section allowed access to the federal courts without

---

[1.229] See H. THORELLI, supra note 1.18, at 224.

[1.230] In 1948, the title "United States district attorney" was changed to "United States attorney." Act of June 25, 1948, ch. 646, § 1, 62 Stat. 909.

[1.231] In a civil action, the allegations must be established by a preponderance of the evidence; in a criminal action, a conviction must be obtained by showing guilt beyond a reasonable doubt, as in the case of any other prosecution under the penal laws.

[1.232] The remedial section of the bill was modified during the consideration of the various versions of the Sherman bill, and the concept of multiple recovery was utilized in order to provide both relief for injured parties and an incentive for private parties to bring actions for enforcement of the Act. See 21 CONG. REC. 2569 (1890) (remarks of Senator Sherman), infra at 177-78, and id. at 3147 (remarks of Senator Reagan), infra at 283. The Senate Judiciary Committee increased the recoverable damages from double to treble. Compare S. 1, § 2, as printed March 26, 1890, infra at 257-58, with S. 1, § 7, as reported April 2, 1890, infra at 277.

[1.233] Original section 7 of the Sherman Act was later reenacted, with expanded venue provisions, as section 4 of the Clayton Act of 1914, ch. 323, § 4, 38 Stat. 731, 15 U.S.C. § 15 (1970), the legislative history of which appears infra at chapter 5. Under section 4 of the Clayton Act, venue in antitrust actions will lie either where the defendant resides, where it is found, or where it has an agent. The Act of July 7, 1955, ch. 283, § 3, 69 Stat. 283, subsequently repealed original section 7. As has been noted above (see discussion supra at 24), an amendment was rejected which would have

regard to the amount in controversy.[1.234] A significant body of case law has been developed with regard to issues arising under this section, including what persons have standing to bring actions, what causal relationship is required between an antitrust violation and an individual injury suffered, and how the jurisdictional and venue provisions will be applied to individuals, corporations, or other business entities.[1.235]

Present section 7 (original section 8) is the Act's only definitional section and provides that the words "person" or "persons" shall be deemed to include corporations and associations, both domestic and foreign. Given Congress' recognition of the corporations, trusts, and other forms of business organization which were prevalent during the period in which the Act was passed, it is not surprising that it specifically wished to include artificial as well as natural persons within coverage of the Act.[1.236] This definition applies to the term "person" whenever used in the Act, and thus embraces not only those entities that may have been found to have violated the Act but also those entitled to institute private actions thereunder.[1.237]

---

explicitly stated that the state courts had concurrent jurisdiction to enforce the Act. The Supreme Court subsequently stated that the federal courts have exclusive jurisdiction over suits brought under the Sherman Act. Blumenstock Bros. Advertising Agency v. Curtis Publishing Co., 252 U.S. 436, 440, 40 S. Ct. 385, 386, 64 L. Ed. 649, 652 (1920). Section 16 of the Clayton Act, 15 U.S.C. § 26 (1970), provides the present basis for injunctive actions on behalf of persons, firms, corporations, or associations.

[1.234] The Judiciary Act of 1789, ch. 20, 1 Stat. 73, which established the federal court system, also required that a minimum amount be in controversy before a private litigant could invoke the general jurisdiction of the federal courts.

[1.235] One area of significant development has been the increasing utilization of rule 23 of the Federal Rules of Civil Procedure to institute antitrust class actions. A considerable body of case law also exists in relation to issues therein encountered.

[1.236] Nevertheless, even before 1890 the Supreme Court had considered corporations to be "persons" in other contexts, and even this lone definition may well have been superfluous to the legislation. *See* H. THORELLI, *supra* note 1.18, at 225.

[1.237] *See* 1 J. VON KALINOWSKI, *supra* note 1.26, at § 3.03[7]. Besides corporations and associations, it has also been held that partnerships as well as other entities are "persons" for purposes of the Sherman Act. *See* United States v. Brookman Co., 229 F. Supp. 862 (N.D. Cal. 1964). Other significant issues arise, however, in connection with concerted activity, for the "intra-enterprise conspiracy" doctrine provides that a corporation cannot combine or conspire with its officers or agents, Nelson Radio & Supply Co. v. Motorola, Inc., 200 F.2d 911 (5th Cir. 1952), *cert. denied*, 345 U.S. 925 (1953), or with its unincorporated divisions, Joseph E. Seagram & Sons, Inc. v. Hawaiian Oke & Liquors, Ltd., 416 F.2d 71 (9th Cir. 1969), *cert. denied*, 396 U.S. 1062 (1970).

Chronological Synopsis

SHERMAN ACT OF 1890

50th Congress, 1st Session

January 4, 1888

Rep. Mason introduced a resolution (H.R. Misc. Doc. No. 69) directing the House Judiciary Committee to investigate charges that trusts taking advantage of the tariff laws were setting unreasonably high prices for certain "necessities of life."

January 21, 1888

Mason resolution was reported to the House (H.R. Rep. No. 67) with a recommended substitute resolution (H.R. Misc. Doc. No. 124) by Rep. Bacon directing the House Committee on Manufactures to investigate trusts and recommend appropriate legislation.

January 25, 1888

Bacon resolution (H.R. Misc. Doc. No. 124) was debated, amended, and passed by the House [19 Cong. Rec. 719-23; text of amended resolution at 719] 53

February 6, 1888

Rep. Milliken introduced a resolution directing the Secretary of the Treasury to investigate the New York sugar trust, which was referred to the House Committee on Manufactures [19 Cong. Rec. 983].

February 24, 1888

House Committee on Manufactures recommended tabling the Milliken resolution, since the investigation pursuant to the Bacon resolution was proceeding.

May 16, 1888

Senate adopted a resolution (S. Res. 78), introduced by Sen. Vest, creating a select committee to investigate the meat industry, particularly regarding alleged combinations among the meat-packing and -dressing companies.

June 5, 1888

Democratic Party adopted an antitrust platform plank 54

June 19, 1888

Republican Party adopted an antitrust platform plank 54

July 10, 1888

Sen. Sherman submitted a resolution directing the Senate Finance Committee to inquire into and report, in connection with revenue bills referred to it, measures to control anticompetitive agreements and combinations, which was agreed to without debate and referred to the Senate Finance Committee [19 Cong. Rec. 6041] 54

July 30, 1888

House Committee on Manufactures issued an interim report on its investigation pursuant to the Bacon resolution (H.R. Misc. Doc. No. 124).
[House Report No. 3112] 55

August 14, 1888

S. 3440 was introduced by Sen. Reagan and, after a brief debate, referred to the Senate Finance Committee [19 Cong. Rec. 7512-13; text of bill printed] 61

S. 3445 was introduced by Sen. Sherman and referred to the Senate Finance Committee [19 Cong. Rec. 7513] .. 63
[Bill print] 63

September 11, 1888

Benjamin Harrison endorsed the Republican antitrust platform plank in his letter accepting the party's presidential nomination.

S. 3445 (Sherman bill) was reported, with an amendment in the nature of a substitute, by the Senate Finance Committee.
[Bill print] 64

December 3, 1888

President Cleveland expressed concern about the abuse of corporate powers by expanding business combinations in his fourth annual message to Congress. 57

50th Congress, 2d Session

January 23, 1889

Senate, as in Committee of the Whole, began debate on S. 3445 (as reported by Senate Finance Committee Sept. 11, 1888) [20 Cong. Rec. 1120] 65

Sen. Sherman proposed an amendment to § 1, substituting the words "in due course of trade" for the words "competes with any similar article upon which a duty is levied by the United States," thus apparently shifting the basis of the bill from the taxing power to the commerce power [20 Cong. Rec. 1121] 66

January 25, 1889

Senate, as in Committee of the Whole, resumed debate on S. 3445 (as reported by the Senate Finance Committee Sept. 11, 1888) [20 Cong. Rec. 1167] 67

Pending Sherman amendment to § 1 (proposed Jan. 23) was adopted [20 Cong. Rec. 1167] 67

Hoar amendment to § 1, adding articles transported to or from the District of Columbia to the bill's jurisdictional scope, was proposed and adopted [20 Cong. Rec. 1167] 67

Hoar amendment to add a new § 3, establishing a private right of action for persons compelled to become parties to unlawful arrangements or to sell or give up any lawful business, was proposed and adopted [20 Cong. Rec. 1167-68] 67

Eustis amendment adding a new section (§ 5), to clarify the Act's applicability to existing trusts, was proposed, modified, agreed to, and further modified at the suggestion of Sen. Platt [20 Cong. Rec. 1168-69] 70

S. 3445 as amended by the Senate, as in Committee of the Whole, through Jan. 25 was ordered printed.
[Bill print] 73

February 4, 1889

Senate, as in Committee of the Whole, resumed debate on S. 3445 (as amended and printed Jan. 25, 1889) [20 Cong. Rec. 1457] 75

Speech by Sen. George attacking the efficacy and constitutionality of the bill [20 Cong. Rec. 1458-62] ... 77

March 2, 1889

House Committee on Manufactures issued final reports (majority and minority) on its investigation pursuant to

the Bacon resolution (H.R. Misc. Doc. No. 124).
  [House Report No. 4165, part 1] 58
  [House Report No. 4165, part 2] 59

51st Congress, 1st Session

December 3, 1889

President Harrison urged Congress to enact antitrust legislation in his first annual message 60

December 4, 1889

S. 1 (identical with S. 3445, 50th Cong., as reported Sept. 11, 1888) was introduced by Sen. Sherman and referred to the Senate Finance Committee [21 Cong. Rec. 96].
  [Bill print] 89

S. 6 (an antitrust bill) was introduced by Sen. George and referred to the Senate Finance Committee [21 Cong. Rec. 96].

S. 62 (an antitrust bill) was introduced by Sen. Reagan and referred to the Senate Judiciary Committee [21 Cong. Rec. 97].

December 9, 1889

Sen. Turpie introduced a resolution providing that penal sanctions against trusts should include the seizure, confiscation, and sale of trust property [21 Cong. Rec. 125] 90

December 10, 1889

Remarks of Sen. Turpie on his resolution (introduced Dec. 9) [21 Cong. Rec. 137-40] 90

December 18, 1889

Twelve antitrust bills were introduced in the House.

Rep. Enloe introduced a resolution (H.R. Res. 30) proposing a constitutional amendment granting express power to the Congress to legislate on the subject of trusts.

January 14, 1890

S. 1 (Sherman Bill) was reported, with minor amendments, by the Senate Finance Committee [21 Cong. Rec. 541].
  [Bill print] 93

February 27, 1890

Senate, as in Committee of the Whole, began debate on S. 1 (as reported by the Senate Finance Committee Jan. 14) [21 Cong. Rec. 1765] 94

  Additional Senate Finance Committee amendment, to strike § 3 (penal clause), was reported by Sen. Sherman [21 Cong. Rec. 1765] 94

  Speech by Sen. George criticizing the efficacy and constitutionality of the bill [21 Cong. Rec. 1765-72] .. 94

  Notice of an intended amendment in the nature of a substitute, to strike the text of S. 1 and insert in lieu thereof the provisions of S. 62, was given by Sen. Reagan [21 Cong. Rec. 1772; text of proposed substitute, printed] 111

March 18, 1890

Amendment in the nature of a substitute for S. 1 was reported by the Senate Finance Committee.
  [Bill print] 112

March 21, 1890

Senate, as in Committee of the Whole, resumed debate on S. 1 (Senate Finance Committee substitute) [21 Cong. Rec. 2455] 113

March 21, 1890 — *Cont.*

Substitute bill (printed March 18) was reported from the Senate Finance Committee by Sen. Sherman [21 Cong. Rec. 2455] 113

Reagan amendment (introduced Feb. 27) in the nature of a substitute for S. 1 was offered [21 Cong. Rec. 2455-56] 113

Speech by Sen. Sherman in defense of his bill [21 Cong. Rec. 2456-62] 113

Notice of an intended amendment in the nature of a substitute, to strike the text of S. 1 and insert in lieu thereof a bill concerning the regulation of options and futures contracts and taxing dealings in options and futures, was given by Sen. Ingalls [21 Cong. Rec. 2462-63; text of proposed substitute printed] 129

March 24, 1890

Senate, as in Committee of the Whole, resumed debate on S. 1 (Senate Finance Committee substitute printed March 18) [21 Cong. Rec. 2556] 150

Sen. Reagan requested that his amendment be changed from a substitute for, to an addition to, S. 1 after the Chair reported that the Ingalls amendment was now proposed as an amendment in the nature of an addition to S. 1; Reagan amendment to add new §§ 3-5 (formerly §§ 1-3 of S. 62) was read [21 Cong. Rec. 2560] 158

Debate on applicability of provisions to labor and agricultural organizations [21 Cong. Rec. 2560-64] ... 158

Modifications of proposed § 3 suggested by Sen. Platt, accepted by Sen. Reagan, and agreed to without objection [21 Cong. Rec. 2564] 166

March 25, 1890

Sen. George introduced a joint resolution (S.J. Res. 67) proposing a constitutional amendment to grant Congress concurrent authority with the states to enact antitrust legislation.

Senate, as in Committee of the Whole, resumed debate on S. 1 (Senate Finance Committee substitute printed March 18) [21 Cong. Rec. 2597] 183

Pending Reagan amendment adding new §§ 3-5 was read, incorporating minor amendments that had been made the previous day [21 Cong. Rec. 2597; text of amendment printed] 183

After debate on George referral motion, the Reagan amendment was adopted by a rollcall vote [21 Cong. Rec. 2611] 205

Motion made by Sen. George to refer S. 1 and pending amendments to the Senate Judiciary Committee was debated [21 Cong. Rec. 2597-611] 184

Speech by Sen. George reviewing legislative history and analyzing constitutional and legal questions raised by the Sherman bills [21 Cong. Rec. 2598-600] 184

Motion to refer defeated by rollcall vote, yeas 15, nays 28 [21 Cong. Rec. 2610-11] 205

Sherman amendment to § 1, to add a proviso exempting labor and agricultural organizations from the operation of the Act, was proposed, modified, and agreed to [21 Cong. Rec. 2611-12] 205

Reagan amendment to § 2, giving state courts concurrent jurisdiction with federal courts to hear civil actions brought under the Act, was agreed to, after a second part of the amendment, striking the words "without respect to the amount in controversy" (which would have made the minimum jurisdictional amounts of the various courts applicable to such actions), was withdrawn [21 Cong. Rec. 2612] 208

Hoar amendment to § 1, making the Act applicable to members of illegal combinations whether in the same or different states, was proposed and accepted [21 Cong. Rec. 2612-13] 208

Ingalls amendment (introduced March 21) was offered as an amendment in the nature of an addition to S. 1, with a minor modification [21 Cong. Rec. 2613] 208

Hoar amendment to § 2 of Ingalls amendment (§ 7 of bill), to add a proviso that the Act would not apply to contracts for the delivery at any one time of articles less than $50 in value, was adopted without objection [21 Cong. Rec. 2613] 209

Ingalls amendment as amended was agreed to (later numbered new §§ 6-16 of S. 1) [21 Cong. Rec. 2613] 209

Coke amendment was offered as an amendment in the nature of an addition to S. 1 but striking out all of the bill except the Ingalls amendment and the labor–agricultural exemption. (This amendment, which had been drafted as a substitute for S. 1, defined trusts, declared their formation in the territories or the District of

Columbia illegal, imposed criminal sanctions upon persons connected with a trust, prohibited and imposed criminal sanctions on the interstate transportation of trust products, declared contracts entered into by trusts illegal, and directed the President to suspend import duties on like items to those subject to a trust.) After being read, debated, and explained, the amendment was tabled on a motion by Sen. Sherman, agreed to by a vote of yeas 26, nays 16 [21 Cong. Rec. 2613-16] 209

Stewart amendment to § 1, placing "money trusts" within the scope of the bill by declaring unlawful combinations that controlled the "value of money" and artificially advanced costs to the consumer, was proposed [21 Cong. Rec. 2616] 213

    Hoar amendment to the amendment, to insert, after "value of money," the words "or of gold or silver," was offered [21 Cong. Rec. 2616] 213

S. 1 as amended by the Senate, as in Committee of the Whole, through March 25 was ordered printed. [Bill print] 214

March 26, 1890

Senate, as in Committee of the Whole, resumed debate on S. 1 (as amended and printed March 25) [21 Cong. Rec. 2639] 219

    Several technical amendments were proposed and agreed to without debate [21 Cong. Rec. 2639-40] ... 219

    Pending Stewart amendment to § 1 (proposed March 25) was agreed to, after Sen. Hoar withdrew his amendment to the amendment [21 Cong. Rec. 2640] 219

    Spooner amendment to § 1, relating to several aspects of judicial authority and procedures (granting courts power to issue nationwide injunctions and to impose fines of $1,000 a day in addition to other penalties for contempt), and to venue of the courts in actions brought by the government, was proposed [21 Cong. Rec. 2639, 2640] and adopted [21 Cong. Rec. 2652], as modified by Sen. Hoar's perfecting amendment [21 Cong. Rec. 2642-43] 219

    Ingalls amendment (adopted March 25) was further debated [21 Cong. Rec. 2644-52] and amended as follows:

        Sec. 7 [21 Cong. Rec. 2650, 2653-55] 239

        Sec. 8 [21 Cong. Rec. 2655] 245

        Sec. 9 [21 Cong. Rec. 2661] 255

        Sec. 10, amendment proposed but ruled out of order [21 Cong. Rec. 2662] 255

    Aldrich amendment to § 1, to add a further proviso exempting from the Act's coverage combinations and associations made with a view to reduce the cost of any necessity of life by means other than a reduction of wages, and combinations and associations made with a view to increase the earnings of persons engaged in useful employment, was proposed and adopted [21 Cong. Rec. 2654-55] 245

    Motion made by Sen. Gorman to refer S. 1 to the Senate Judiciary Committee with instructions to report back within 20 days was debated and withdrawn [21 Cong. Rec. 2655-57] 246

    Gray amendment, to substitute the text of S. 6 (the bill originally drafted and introduced by Sen. George) for the text of S. 1, was proposed and read [21 Cong. Rec. 2657], and rejected by a vote of yeas 18, nays 26 [21 Cong. Rec. 2660-61] 249

    Wilson amendment to § 1, exempting temperance societies from the Act's coverage by making it inapplicable to associations for the enforcement of the laws of any state enacted in pursuance of its police powers, was proposed and agreed to, after a clarifying amendment proposed by Sen. Hoar was withdrawn [21 Cong. Rec. 2658-60] 250

    Motion made by Sen. Cullom to recommit S. 1 with proposed and adopted amendments to the Senate Finance Committee was defeated, 17 to 31 [21 Cong. Rec. 2659-60] 252

    Motion made by Sen. Hawley to refer S. 1 and all amendments to the Senate Judiciary Committee was defeated, 24 to 29 [21 Cong. Rec. 2660] 254

    Gray amendment, to add a new section (taken from George bill § 3) requiring the President to suspend all import duties on foreign goods when the prices of similar domestic goods had been enhanced as the result of the formation of a trust, was proposed and rejected by a rollcall vote, yeas 21, nays 25 [21 Cong. Rec. 2661] 254

S. 1 was reported from the Committee of the Whole to the Senate, as amended [21 Cong. Rec. 2662] 255

S. 1 as amended by the Senate, as in Committee of the Whole, through March 26 was ordered printed. [Bill print] 256

March 27, 1890

Senate resumed debate on S. 1 (as amended in Committee of the Whole and printed March 26) [21 Cong. Rec. 2723] 262

    Senate concurred in several amendments to § 1 adopted in the Committee of the Whole and adopted several technical amendments to § 1 [21 Cong. Rec. 2724-25] 262

    Spooner amendment to § 1 (adopted March 26) was passed over after Sen. Edmunds raised the objection that it would allow a court to obtain jurisdiction over persons having property in the district without personal service of process [21 Cong. Rec. 2725-26] 263

    Motion made by Sen. Walthall to refer the bill and the amendments to the Senate Judiciary Committee with instructions to report back within 20 days was accepted by a rollcall vote, 31-28 [21 Cong. Rec. 2731] 274

March 31; April 1-2, 1890

S. 1 was considered, amended, and redrafted by the Senate Judiciary Committee.

April 2, 1890

S. 1 was reported, with an amendment in the nature of a substitute, by the Senate Judiciary Committee [21 Cong. Rec. 2901] 277
    [Bill print] 275

April 8, 1890

Senate, as in Committee of the Whole, agreed to the amendment in the nature of a substitute reported April 2 by the Senate Judiciary Committee [21 Cong. Rec. 3145] 280

S. 1 was reported from the Committee of the Whole to the Senate, as amended [21 Cong. Rec. 3146] 280

    Reagan amendment to § 7, to give state courts concurrent jurisdiction with federal courts to hear private treble-damage actions brought under the Act, was proposed, modified, debated, and rejected, by a vote of yeas 13, nays 36 [21 Cong. Rec. 3146, 3151] 280

    George amendment to § 7, to allow joinder of private actions brought under the Act, was proposed and rejected [21 Cong. Rec. 3148-51] 285

    Gray amendment, to strike monopolization and attempts to monopolize from the Act's prohibitions (thereby limiting § 2 to concerted activity, to parallel § 1), was offered, debated, and rejected [21 Cong. Rec. 3151] 292

    Reagan amendment to § 3, making each day's violation a separate offense, was offered and rejected [21 Cong. Rec. 3152] 292

S. 1 as amended was passed by the Senate by a rollcall vote of yeas 52, nay 1 [21 Cong. Rec. 3152-53] 294

Title of S. 1 was amended to read "A bill to protect trade and commerce against unlawful restraints and monopolies" [21 Cong. Rec. 3153] 294

April 25, 1890

S. 1 was reported favorably, without amendment, by the House Judiciary Committee.
    [House Report No. 1707] 295
    [Bill print] 296

May 1, 1890

Senate Select Committee on Transportation and Sale of Meat Products issued its final report (S. Rep. No. 829), recommending passage by the House of the Sherman bill.

House debated, amended, and passed S. 1 [21 Cong. Rec. 4088-104] 298

    Rep. Culberson, the bill's floor manager, explained the major provisions [21 Cong. Rec. 4089-91]...... 299

    Remarks by Rep. Wilson criticizing the bill on the ground that the most effective remedy for the evils of trusts was not in Congress but in the states and that the proper federal remedy was the elimination of the protective tariff, which promoted the formation of trusts [21 Cong. Rec. 4092-96] 306

    Sayers amendment, to add a section directing the President to suspend import duties on like articles to those covered by a trust, was proposed and ruled out of order [21 Cong. Rec. 4098] 313

Bland amendment, to extend the scope of the bill to all agreements entered into for the purpose of preventing competition either in the purchase or sale of commodities, or in the transportation of persons or property within the jurisdiction of Congress, was proposed as new § 8 [21 Cong. Rec. 4099] 316

    This section was made an independent section (later § 2), was modified expressly to cover interstate sales of commodities and interstate transportation of persons or property, and containing a final proviso, and was agreed to [21 Cong. Rec. 4104] 324

    S. 1, as amended by the Bland amendment, was passed by the House [21 Cong. Rec. 4104] 324

May 2, 1890

S. 1, as amended and passed by the House, was received by the Senate. Motion made by Sen. Vest to refer the bill with the House amendments to the Senate Judiciary Committee was agreed to, despite Sen. Sherman's suggestion that the Senate concur in the Bland amendment [21 Cong. Rec. 4123-24] 325

May 12, 1890

S. 1 was reported by the Senate Judiciary Committee, with a further amendment to the House amendment, striking out the provision pertaining to interstate sale of commodities and striking the final proviso [21 Cong. Rec. 4559] 326

    Senate report debated and ordered to lie over until the next day; subsequently withdrawn [21 Cong. Rec. 4559-60] 326

May 13, 1890

Senate Judiciary Committee amendment to the House amendment, reported the previous day by Sen. Hoar, was again reported to the Senate floor. Motion made by Sen. Hoar to recommit the bill and amendments was agreed to [21 Cong. Rec. 4598-99] 329

May 16, 1890

S. 1 was reported by the Senate Judiciary Committee, with amendments to the House amendment striking out the provision relating to interstate sale of commodities and the final proviso of the Bland amendment, and inserting language making unlawful only contracts and agreements that raised the rate of transportation above what was deemed "just and reasonable." Motion that the Senate agree to the House amendments as thus amended and request a conference was made and agreed to, and conferees were appointed [21 Cong. Rec. 4753] 329

May 17, 1890

House disagreed to the Senate amendments to the Bland amendment and agreed to a conference [21 Cong. Rec. 4837] 331

May 21, 1890

House conferees were appointed [21 Cong. Rec. 5113] 331

June 11, 1890

House began consideration of the first conference report on S. 1, recommending that the House recede from its disagreement to the Senate amendments and agree to the same as modified by an additional proviso that nothing contained in the Act should be deemed to impair the power of the states regarding matters covered by the Act; Bland amendment and conference report debated [21 Cong. Rec. 5950-61; text of conference report and accompanying statement at 5950] 331

June 12, 1890

House rejected the first conference report by a vote of ayes 12, noes 115. Motion made by Rep. Stewart to request another conference and to instruct the House conferees to recede from the Bland amendment was agreed to by a vote of yeas 106, nays 98 [21 Cong. Rec. 5981-83] 353

June 14, 1890

House conferees were appointed [21 Cong. Rec. 6099] 355

June 16, 1890

Senate agreed to a second conference committee and appointed conferees [21 Cong. Rec. 6116-17] 355

June 18, 1890

Second conference report, recommending that both Houses recede from their respective amendments, leaving the bill as originally passed by the Senate, was submitted in the Senate and concurred in without debate [21 Cong. Rec. 6208; text of conference report printed] 358

June 20, 1890

Second conference report was submitted in the House, debated, and adopted by a vote of yeas 242, nay 0, not voting 85 [21 Cong. Rec. 6312-14; text of conference report and accompanying statement of House conferees at 6312] 359

July 2, 1890

S. 1 was signed into law by President Harrison.
  [*Statutes at Large* print] 51

Table of Reprinted Documents

SHERMAN ACT OF 1890

Statutory Materials

Sherman Act, ch. 647, 26 Stat. 209 (July 2, 1890) 51
Sherman Act as amended, 15 U.S.C. §§ 1-7 (Supp. V, 1975) 49

Legislative Materials

Bills

S. 3440, 50th Cong., 1st Sess., 19 Cong. Rec. 7512-13 (Aug. 14, 1888) 61
S. 3445, 50th Cong., 1st Sess. (Aug. 14, 1888) 63
S. 3445 as reported by Senate Finance Committee, 50th Cong., 1st Sess. (Sept. 11, 1888) 64
S. 3445 as amended by Senate, 50th Cong., 2d Sess. (Jan. 25, 1889) 73
S. 1, 51st Cong., 1st Sess. (Dec. 4, 1889) 89
S. 1 as reported by Senate Finance Committee, 51st Cong., 1st Sess. (Jan. 14, 1890) 93
Amendment in the nature of a substitute for S. 1 reported by Senate Finance Committee (March 18, 1890) 112
S. 1 as amended by the Senate, 51st Cong., 1st Sess. (March 25, 1890) 214
S. 1 as amended by the Senate, 51st Cong., 1st Sess. (March 26, 1890) 256
S. 1 as reported by Senate Judiciary Committee, 51st Cong., 1st Sess. (April 2, 1890) 275
S. 1 as reported by House Judiciary Committee, 51st Cong., 1st Sess. (April 25, 1890) 296

Reports

H.R. Rep. No. 3112, 50th Cong., 1st Sess. (July 30, 1888) 55
H.R. Rep. No. 4165, Pt. 1, 50th Cong., 2d Sess. (March 2, 1889) 58
H.R. Rep. No. 4165, Pt. 2, 50th Cong., 2d Sess. (March 2, 1890) 59
H.R. Rep. No. 1707, 51st Cong., 1st Sess. (April 25, 1890) 295
First conference report on S. 1, 21 Cong. Rec. 5950 (June 11, 1890) 332
Second conference report on S. 1, 21 Cong. Rec. 6208 (June 18, 1890) 358
   21 Cong. Rec. 6312 (June 20, 1890) 359

Congressional Record

Volume 19 – 50th Congress, 1st Session

Date	Pages	
Jan. 25, 1888	719	53
July 10, 1888	6041	54
Aug. 14, 1888	7512-13	61

Volume 20 – 50th Congress, 2d Session

Date	Pages	
Jan. 23, 1889	1120-21	65
Jan. 25, 1889	1167-69	67
Feb. 4, 1889	1457-62	75

Volume 21 – 51st Congress, 1st Session

Date	Pages	
Dec. 9, 1889	125	90
Dec. 10, 1889	137, 139, 140	90
Feb. 27, 1890	1765-72	94
March 21, 1890	2455-74	113
March 24, 1890	2556-72	150
March 25, 1890	2597-616	183
March 26, 1890	2639-60	219
March 27, 1890	2723-31	262
April 2, 1890	2901	277
April 8, 1890	3145-53	279
May 1, 1890	4088-96, 4098-104	298
May 2, 1890	4123-24	325
May 12, 1890	4559-60	326
May 13, 1890	4598-99	329
May 16, 1890	4753	329
May 17, 1890	4837	331
May 21, 1890	5113	331
June 11, 1890	5950-61	331
June 12, 1890	5981-83	353
June 14, 1890	6099	355
June 16, 1890	6116-17	355
June 18, 1890	6208	358
June 20, 1890	6312-14	359

Presidential Documents

Fourth annual message of President Grover Cleveland (Dec. 3, 1888) 57

First annual message of President Benjamin Harrison (Dec. 3, 1889) 60

Case Reports

Apex Hosiery Co. v. Leader, 310 U.S. 469, 60 S. Ct. 982, 84 L. Ed. 1311 (1940) 416

Board of Trade of the City of Chicago v. United States, 246 U.S. 231, 38 S. Ct. 242,
62 L. Ed. 683 (1918) 410

Parker v. Brown, 317 U.S. 341, 63 S. Ct. 307, 87 L. Ed. 315 (1943) 423

Standard Oil Co. of New Jersey v. United States, 221 U.S. 1, 31 S. Ct. 502,
55 L. Ed. 619 (1911) 382

United States v. American Tobacco Co., 221 U.S. 106, 31 S. Ct. 632, 55 L. Ed. 663 (1911) 403

United States v. E. I. du Pont de Nemours & Co., 351 U.S. 377, 76 S. Ct. 994,
100 L. Ed. 1264 (1956) 437

United States v. Joint Traffic Association, 171 U.S. 505, 19 S. Ct. 25, 43 L. Ed. 259 (1898) 377

United States v. South-Eastern Underwriters Association, 322 U.S. 533, 64 S. Ct. 1162,
88 L. Ed. 1440 (1944) 426

United States v. Topco Associates, Inc., 405 U.S. 596, 92 S. Ct. 1126, 31 L. Ed. 2d
515 (1972) 446

United States v. Trenton Potteries Co., 273 U.S. 392, 47 S. Ct. 377, 71 L. Ed. 700 (1927) 412

Miscellaneous

Democratic party platform, antitrust plank (June 5, 1888) 54

Republican party platform, antitrust plank (June 19, 1888) 54

Current Version

SHERMAN ANTITRUST ACT AS AMENDED

15 U.S.C. §§ 1-7 (Supp. V, 1975)

[ED. NOTE: The Hart-Scott-Rodino Antitrust Improvements Act of 1976, Pub. L. No. 94-435 § 305(a), 90 Stat. 1397, amended the Sherman Act by inserting immediately after the enacting clause the language "That this Act may be cited as the 'Sherman Act.'" This amendment is codified in a note to the *United States Code*.]

§ 1. Trusts, etc., in restraint of trade illegal; penalty.

Every contract, combination in the form of trust or otherwise, or conspiracy, in restraint of trade or commerce among the several States, or with foreign nations, is declared to be illegal. Every person who shall make any contract or engage in any combination or conspiracy declared by sections 1 to 7 of this title to be illegal shall be deemed guilty of a felony, and, on conviction thereof, shall be punished by fine not exceeding one million dollars if a corporation, or, if any other person, one hundred thousand dollars or by imprisonment not exceeding three years, or by both said punishments, in the discretion of the court. (July 2, 1890, ch. 647, § 1, 26 Stat. 209; Aug. 17, 1937, ch. 690, title VIII, 50 Stat. 693; July 7, 1955, ch. 281, 69 Stat. 282; Dec. 21, 1974, Pub. L. 93-528, § 3, 88 Stat. 1708; Dec. 12, 1975, Pub. L. 94-145, § 2, 89 Stat. 801.)

§ 2. Monopolizing trade a felony; penalty.

Every person who shall monopolize, or attempt to monopolize, or combine or conspire with any other person or persons, to monopolize any part of the trade or commerce among the several States, or with foreign nations, shall be deemed guilty of a felony, and, on conviction thereof, shall be punished by fine not exceeding one million dollars if a corporation, or, if any other person, one hundred thousand dollars or by imprisonment not exceeding three years, or by both said punishments, in the discretion of the court. (July 2, 1890, ch. 647, § 2, 26 Stat. 209; July 7, 1955, ch. 281, 69 Stat. 282; Dec. 21, 1974, Pub. L. 93-528, § 3, 88 Stat. 1708.)

§ 3. Trusts in Territories or District of Columbia illegal; combination a felony.

Every contract, combination in form of trust or otherwise, or conspiracy, in restraint of trade or commerce in any Territory of the United States or of the District of Columbia, or in restraint of trade or commerce between any such Territory and another, or between any such Territory or Territories and any State or States or the District of Columbia, or with foreign nations, is declared illegal. Every person who shall make any such contract or engage in any such combination or conspiracy, shall be deemed guilty of a felony, and, on conviction thereof, shall be punished by fine not exceeding one million dollars if a corporation, or, if any other person, one hundred thousand dollars or by imprisonment not exceeding three years, or by both said punishments, in the discretion of the court. (July 2, 1890, ch. 647, § 3, 26 Stat. 209; July 7, 1955, ch. 281, 69 Stat. 282; Dec. 21, 1974, Pub. L. 93-528, § 3, 88 Stat. 1708.)

§ 4. Jurisdiction of courts; duty of United States attorneys; procedure.

The several district courts of the United States are invested with jurisdiction to prevent and restrain violations of sections 1 to 7 of this title; and it shall be the duty of the several United States attorneys, in their respective districts, under the direction of the Attorney General, to institute proceedings in equity to prevent and restrain such violations. Such proceedings may be by way of petition setting forth the case and praying that such violation shall be enjoined or otherwise prohibited. When the parties complained of shall have been duly notified of such petition the court shall proceed, as soon as may be, to the hearing and determination of the case; and pending such petition and before final decree, the court may at any time make such temporary restraining order or prohibition as shall be deemed just in the premises. (July 2, 1890, ch. 647, § 4, 26 Stat. 209; Mar. 3, 1911, ch. 231, § 291, 36 Stat. 1167; June 25, 1948, ch. 646, § 1, 62 Stat. 909.)

§ 5. Bringing in additional parties.

Whenever it shall appear to the court before which any proceeding under section 4 of this title may be pending, that the ends of justice require that other parties should be brought before the court, the court may cause them to be summoned, whether they reside in the district in which the court is held or not; and subpoenas to that end may be served in any district by the marshal thereof. (July 2, 1890, ch. 647, § 5, 26 Stat. 210.)

§ 6. Forfeiture of property in transit.

Any property owned under any contract or by any combination, or pursuant to any conspiracy (and being the subject thereof) mentioned in section 1 of this title, and being in the course of transportation from one State to another, or to a foreign country, shall be forfeited to the United States, and may be seized and condemned by like proceedings as those provided by law for the forfeiture, seizure, and condemnation of property imported into the United States contrary to law. (July 2, 1890, ch. 647, § 6, 26 Stat. 210.)

§ 7. "Person" defined.

The word "person", or "persons", wherever used in sections 1 to 7 of this title shall be deemed to include corporations and associations existing under or authorized by the laws of either the United States, the laws of any of the Territories, the laws of any State, or the laws of any foreign country. (July 2, 1890, ch. 647, § 8, 26 Stat. 210.)

Original Version

SHERMAN ANTITRUST ACT
July 2, 1890

Ch. 647, 26 Stat. 209

An Act To protect trade and commerce against unlawful restraints and monopolies.

Be it enacted by the Senate and House of Representatives of the United States of America in Congress assembled,[1.237a]

SEC. 1. Every contract, combination in the form of trust of otherwise, or conspiracy, in restraint of trade or commerce among the several States, or with foreign nations, is hereby declared to be illegal.[1.238] Every person who shall make any such contract or engage in any such combination or conspiracy, shall be deemed guilty of a misdemeanor, and, on conviction thereof, shall be punished by fine not exceeding five thousand dollars, or by imprisonment not exceeding one year, or by both said punishments, in the discretion of the court.[1.239]

SEC. 2. Every person who shall monopolize, or attempt to monopolize, or combine or conspire with any other person or persons, to monopolize any part of the trade or commerce among the several States, or with foreign nations, shall be deemed guilty of a misdemeanor, and, on conviction thereof, shall be punished by fine not exceeding five thousand dollars, or by imprisonment not exceeding one year, or by both said punishments, in the discretion of the court.

SEC. 3. Every contract, combination in form of trust or otherwise, or conspiracy, in restraint of trade or commerce in any Territory of the United States or of the District of Columbia, or in restraint of trade or commerce between any such Territory and another, or between any such Territory or Territories and any State or States or the District of Columbia, or with foreign nations, or between the District of Columbia and any State or States or foreign nations, is hereby declared illegal. Every person who shall make any such contract or engage in any such combination or conspiracy, shall be deemed guilty of a misdemeanor, and, on conviction thereof, shall be punished by fine

---

[1.237a] The language "That this Act may be cited as the 'Sherman Act' " was added by the Hart-Scott-Rodino Antitrust Improvements Act of 1976, Pub. L. No. 94-435, § 305(a), 90 Stat. 1397, the legislative history of which will be covered in subsequent volumes.

[1.238] Section 1 of the Sherman Act was amended by the Miller-Tydings Act of 1937, ch. 690, tit. VIII, 50 Stat. 693, which inserted two provisos between the two original sentences of the Sherman Act, permitting resale price maintenance by owners of trademarked goods where state fair-trade laws authorized such contracts. For the legislative history of the Miller-Tydings Act see chapter 2 *infra*. This statute was subsequently repealed by the Consumer Goods Pricing Act of 1975, Pub. L. No. 94-145, 89 Stat. 801, the legislative history of which appears *infra* at chapter 4.

[1.239] Sections 1, 2, and 3 of the Sherman Act were first amended to increase the criminal penalties from $5,000 to $50,000 by the Act of July 7, 1955, ch. 281, 69 Stat. 282. These sections have recently been further amended by section 3 of the Antitrust Procedures and Penalties Act of 1974, Pub. L. No. 93-528, § 3, 88 Stat. 1708, which increased the offenses from misdemeanors to felonies, increased the maximum fine to $1 million for corporations and $100,000 for any other person, and increased the maximum term of imprisonment to three years. For the legislative history of the Antitrust Procedures and Penalties Act see chapter 19 *infra*.

not exceeding five thousand dollars, or by imprisonment not exceeding one year, or by both said punishments, in the discretion of the court.

SEC. 4. The several circuit courts[1.240] of the United States are hereby invested with jurisdiction to prevent and restrain violations of this act; and it shall be the duty of the several district attorneys of the United States,[1.241] in their respective districts, under the direction of the Attorney-General, to institute proceedings in equity to prevent and restrain such violations. Such proceedings may be by way of petition setting forth the case and praying that such violation shall be enjoined or otherwise prohibited. When the parties complained of shall have been duly notified of such petition the court shall proceed, as soon as may be, to the hearing and determination of the case; and pending such petition and before final decree, the court may at any time make such temporary restraining order or prohibition as shall be deemed just in the premises.

SEC. 5. Whenever it shall appear to the court before which any proceeding under section four of this act may be pending, that the ends of justice require that other parties should be brought before the court, the court may cause them to be summoned, whether they reside in the district in which the court is held or not; and subpoenas to that end may be served in any district by the marshal thereof.

SEC. 6. Any property owned under any contract or by any combination, or pursuant to any conspiracy (and being the subject thereof) mentioned in section one of this act, and being in the course of transportation from one State to another, or to a foreign country, shall be forfeited to the United States, and may be seized and condemned by like proceedings as those provided by law for the forfeiture, seizure, and condemnation of property imported into the United States contrary to law.

SEC. 7. Any person who shall be injured in his business or property by any other person or corporation by reason of anything forbidden or declared to be unlawful by this act, may sue therefor in any circuit court of the United States in the district in which the defendant resides or is found, without respect to the amount in controversy, and shall recover three fold the damages by him sustained, and the costs of suit, including a reasonable attorney's fee.[1.242]

SEC. 8.[1.243] That the word "person," or "persons," wherever used in this act shall be deemed to include corporations and associations existing under or authorized by the laws of either the United States, the laws of any of the Territories, the laws of any State, or the laws of any foreign country.

[1.240] By the Act of March 3, 1911, ch. 231, § 291, 36 Stat. 1167, jurisdiction in cases arising under the Sherman Act was vested in the district courts, instead of the circuit courts, of the United States.

[1.241] By the Act of June 25, 1948, ch. 646, § 1, 62 Stat. 909, effective September 1, 1948, the title "United States attorneys" was substituted for "district attorneys of the United States."

[1.242] Repealed by the Act of July 7, 1955, ch. 283, § 3, 69 Stat. 283. Original section 7 had been reenacted with some modifications as section 4 of the Clayton Act of 1914, ch. 323, § 4, 38 Stat. 731, 15 U.S.C. § 15 (1970). For the legislative history of the Clayton Act see chapter 5 *infra*.

[1.243] Present section 7.

THE ORIGINS

HOUSE RESOLUTION AUTHORIZING THE COMMITTEE ON MANUFACTURES TO INVESTIGATE TRUSTS[1.244]
50th Cong., 1st Sess.
January 25, 1888

19 CONG. REC. 719

"In the House of Representatives, January 25, 1888.

"Mr. BACON, from the Committee on Manufactures, submitted the following; which was agreed to:

"Whereas it is alleged that certain individuals and corporations in the United States engaged in manufacturing, producing, mining, or dealing in some of the necessaries of life and other productions, have combined for the purpose of controlling or curtailing the production or supply of the same, and thereby increasing their price to the people of the country, which combinations are known as associations, trusts, pools, and like names; and

"Whereas such combinations not only injuriously affect commerce between the States, but impair the revenues of the United States as derived from its duties on imports: Therefore,

"*Resolved,* That the Committee on Manufactures be, and the same is hereby, directed to inquire into the names and number and extent of such alleged combinations, under whatever name known, their methods of combination or doing business, their effect upon the prices of any of the necessaries of life and of all productions to the people of the country, upon its internal or foreign commerce, and its revenues from import duties, together with any and all other matters relating to the same which may call for or suggest legislation by Congress, and report the same to the House with such recommendations as the said committee may agree upon. And for these purposes the Commitee on Manufactures is authorized to sit during the sessions of the House, to employ a stenographer, to administer oaths, examine witnesses, compel the attendance of persons, and the production of papers. And the expense of such investigation shall be paid out of the contingent fund of the House.

"Attest:

"JOHN B. CLARK, Clerk."

[1.244] The original version of this resolution was reported to the House on January 21, 1888, by Representative Bacon from the Committee on Manufactures and printed as H.R. MISC. DOC. NO. 124, 50th Cong., 1st Sess. (1888), not reprinted herein. On January 25, 1888, the resolution was debated, amended, and passed by the House, 19 CONG. REC. 719-23 (1888). The amended version, reprinted here, was also printed at H.R. REP. NO. 708, 50th Cong., 1st Sess. 3-4 (1888). See notes 1.48-.50 *supra* and accompanying text.

ANTITRUST PLANK OF THE DEMOCRATIC PARTY PLATFORM[1.245]
June 5, 1888

. . . Judged by Democratic principles, the interests of the people are betrayed when, by unnecessary taxation, trusts and combinations are permitted to exist, which, while unduly enriching the few that combine, rob the body of our citizens, by depriving them of the benefits of natural competition.

ANTITRUST PLANK OF THE REPUBLICAN PARTY PLATFORM[1.246]
June 19, 1888

COMBINATIONS OF CAPITAL.

We declare our opposition to all combinations of capital, organized in trusts or otherwise, to control arbitrarily the condition of trade among our citizens; and we recommend to Congress and the state legislatures, in their respective jurisdictions, such legislation as will prevent the execution of all schemes to oppress the people by undue charges on their supplies, or by unjust rates for the transportation of their products to market.

SENATE RESOLUTION DIRECTING THE COMMITTEE ON FINANCE TO INQUIRE INTO CONTROL OF TRUSTS IN CONNECTION WITH REVENUE BILLS
50th Cong., 1st Sess.
July 10, 1888

19 CONG. REC. 6041

Mr. [JOHN] SHERMAN [R., Ohio]. I submit a resolution for which I ask present consideration.

The PRESIDENT *pro tempore*. The resolution will be read.

The Chief Clerk read as follows:

Resolved, That the Committee on Finance be directed to inquire into and report, in connection with any bill raising or reducing revenue that may be referred to it, such measures as it may deem expedient to set aside, control, restrain, or prohibit all arrangements, contracts, agreements, trusts, or combinations between persons or corporations, made with a view, or which tend to prevent free and full competition in the production, manufacture, or sale of

---

[1.245] The entire platform is reprinted in T. MCKEE, THE NATIONAL CONVENTIONS AND PLATFORMS OF ALL POLITICAL PARTIES 1789-1905, at 235 (1906).

[1.246] The entire platform is reprinted in T. MCKEE, *supra* note 1.245, at 241.

articles of domestic growth or production, or of the sale of articles imported into the United States, or which, against public policy, are designed or tend to foster monopoly or to artificially advance the cost to the consumer of necessary articles of human life, with such penalties and provisions, and as to corporations, with such forfeitures, as will tend to preserve freedom of trade and production, the natural competition of increasing production, the lowering of prices by such competition, and the full benefit designed by and hitherto conferred by the policy of the Government to protect and encourage American industries by levying duties on imported goods.

The PRESIDENT *pro tempore*. Is there objection to the present consideration of this resolution?
Mr. [FRANCIS] COCKRELL [D., Mo.]. I did not hear the first part of it.
The PRESIDENT *pro tempore*. It will be again reported.
The Chief Clerk read the first clause of the resolution.
The resolution was considered by unanimous consent, and agreed to.

REPORT OF THE HOUSE COMMITTEE ON MANUFACTURES
H.R. Rep. No. 3112
50th Cong., 1st Sess.
July 30, 1888

Mr. BACON, from the Committee on Manufactures, submitted the following

REPORT:

[To accompany Mis. Doc. 124.]

The Committee of [*sic*] Manufactures respectfully report that, acting under the authority and direction of a resolution of this House passed on the 25th day of January, 1888, they have proceeded to investigate and inquire into the matters and things referred to in said resolution, and having examined witnesses and papers in relation thereto they have been unable to complete such inquiry and investigation, and respectfully report the following resolution, with the recommendation that it do pass.

Your committee further report that the names of various combinations and trusts have been from time to time furnished to your committee; that the number of such combinations is very large; and that your committee, in calling witnesses and taking testimony, proceeded upon the following plan of investigation, *i.e.*, to inquire—

(1) With relation to trusts or combinations in lines of business which are connected with or use articles in which there exists a competition in our markets between the domestic product and the foreign product imported and dutiable under our tariff laws.

(2) With relation to such combinations dealing in articles which are not imported into this country or are not subject to import duties.

(3) With relation to such combinations dealing in articles which are subject to taxation under the internal-revenue laws of the United States.

Your committee has particularly directed its inquiry into the methods of and the extent of the business done or controlled by, the sugar trust and the Standard Oil trust, and respectfully submit herewith the testimony taken before it in relation to these two trusts.*

In submitting this testimony your committee desire to call the attention of the House to the form of organization of these two trusts. Both of them are organized upon substantially the same plan. From the testimony it appears that there exists a certain

---

* Not reprinted herein.

number of corporations organized under the laws of the different States and subject to their control; that these corporations have issued their stock to various individuals and that these individual stockholders have surrendered their stock to the trustees named in the agreement creating these trusts and accepted in lieu thereof certificates issued by the trustees named therein. The agreements provide that the various corporations whose stock is surrendered to the trustees shall preserve their identity ⊥ and carry on their business. In the Sugar Trust agreement the provision is that the several corporations shall maintain their separate organizations and each shall carry on and conduct its own business.

In the Standard Oil Trust agreement it is provided that all property, real and personal, assets, and business shall be transferred to and vested in the said several companies. The duties of the trustees are restricted to the receipt of the dividends declared by the various corporations and the distribution of the aggregate of them to the holders of the trust's certificates, pro rata, and to holding and voting upon the stock of the corporations. The trustees in both cases, upon the stand as witnesses, specifically denied that the trustees, as such, ever do any other business than to receive and distribute these dividends and exercise the only other function given to them by the trust agreements, that is, to hold the stock of the various corporations and exercise the right of stockholders in such corporation.

The care with which the trustees avoid making any agreement relating to commodities appears from the testimony as to the arrangement made with the Oil Producers' Association in the fall of 1887. The officers of the Producers' Association testified that an arrangement was then made with the Standard Oil Trust by which 5,000,000 barrels of oil belonging to the Standard Oil Trust were set apart for the benefit of the association, upon its agreeing to curtail the production of crude oil at least 17,500 barrels per diem. These witnesses undoubtedly understand that their arrangement was with the trustees of the Standard Oil Trust. But the written agreement produced, and now in evidence, shows that it was made with and is signed by the Standard Oil Company of New York, one of the companies whose stock is held by the trustees, and that the Standard Oil Trust or the trustees thereof, as such, are not parties to it, nor is either of them responsible for the carrying out of that agreement.

This form of combination was obviously devised for the purpose of relieving the trusts and trustees from the charge of any breach of the conspiracy laws of the various States, or of being a combination to regulate or control the price or production of any commodity; hence they assert that the corporations themselves, which control and regulate the price of commodities and the extent of production and have tangible property, remain with their organization intact and distinct, and not in combination with each other; that the stockholders, who owned only the stock, and by well-settled legal rules had no legal title in the property of the corporations, entered into the agreements and sold their stock in the corporations and accepted in payment trust certificates, and that the trustees receive and hold only the stock of corporations, and have no legal title to any of the property of the corporations, and neither buy nor sell anything nor combine with any one to fix prices or regulate production of any commodity.

Your committee have deemed it proper to call attention to this feature of these combinations because it is believed that it will be found that all trade combinations having similar aims either have adopted this method or speedily will do so; and also, because the legislation which has been proposed to this House and referred to your committee has been directed against combinations to fix the price or regulate the production of articles of merchandise or commerce. It is plain that the two combinations, the testimony concerning which is herewith submitted, have been intentionally formed so as to avoid, if possible, the charge that the trust, as such, or the trustees, in that capacity, either fixed the ⊥ price or regulated the production of any article of merchandise or commerce.

Complaint having been made to him by citizens of the State of New York against the sugar trust and one of the corporations whose stock it holds, the attorney-general of that State has, after hearing, directed prosecutions to be commenced against that trust and the corporation complained of, upon grounds which are set forth in an elaborate opinion, which is submitted as part of the evidence in relation to that trust, and as containing a careful statement of the law of that State so far as it affords any remedy against such trusts.

FOURTH ANNUAL MESSAGE OF PRESIDENT GROVER CLEVELAND
December 3, 1888

2 THE STATE OF THE UNION MESSAGES OF THE PRESIDENTS 1790-1966, at 1598 (F. Israel ed. 1966)

Washington, December 3, 1888.

To the Congress of the United States:

As you assemble for the discharge of the duties you have assumed as the representatives of a free and generous people, your meeting is marked by an interesting and impressive incident. With the expiration of the present session of the Congress the first century of our constitutional existence as a nation will be completed.

Our survival for one hundred years is not sufficient to assure us that we no longer have dangers to fear in the maintenance, with all its promised blessings, of a government founded upon the freedom of the people. The time rather admonishes us to soberly inquire whether in the past we have always closely kept in the course of safety, and whether we have before us a way plain and clear which leads to happiness and perpetuity.

When the experiment of our Government was undertaken, the chart adopted for our guidance was the Constitution. Departure from the lines there laid down is failure. It is only by a strict adherence to the direction they indicate and by restraint within the limitations they fix that we can furnish proof to the world of the fitness of the American people for self-government.

The equal and exact justice of which we boast as the underlying principle of our institutions should not be confined to the relations of our citizens to each other. The Government itself is under bond to the American people that in the exercise of its functions and powers it will deal with the body of our citizens in a manner scrupulously honest and fair and absolutely just. It has agreed that American citizenship shall be the only credential necessary to justify the claim of equality before the law, and that no condition in life shall give rise to discrimination in the treatment of the people by their Government.

The citizen of our Republic in its early days rigidly insisted upon full compliance with the letter of this bond, and saw stretching out before him a clear field for individual endeavor. His tribute to the support of his Government was measured by the cost of its economical maintenance, and he was secure in the enjoyment of the remaining recompense of his steady and contented toil. In those days the frugality of the people was stamped upon their Government, and was enforced by the free, thoughtful, and intelligent suffrage of the citizen. Combinations, monopolies, and aggregations of capital were either avoided or sternly regulated and restrained. The pomp and glitter of governments less free offered no temptation and presented no delusion to the plain people who, side by side, in friendly competition, wrought for the ennoblement and dignity of man, for the solution of the problem of free government, and for the achievement of the grand destiny awaiting the land which God had given them.

A century has passed. Our cities are the abiding places of wealth and luxury; our manufactories yield fortunes never dreamed of by the fathers of the Republic; our business men are madly striving in the race for riches, and immense aggregations of capital outrun the imagination in the magnitude of their undertakings.

We view with pride and satisfaction this bright picture of our country's growth and prosperity, while only a closer scrutiny develops a somber shading. Upon more careful inspection we find the wealth and luxury of our cities mingled with poverty and wretchedness and unremunerative toil. A crowded and constantly increasing urban population suggests the impoverishment of rural sections and discontent with agricultural pursuits. The farmer's son, not satisfied with his father's simple and laborious life, joins the eager chase for easily acquired wealth.

We discover that the fortunes realized by our manufacturers are no longer solely the reward of sturdy industry and enlightened foresight, but that they result from the discriminating favor of the Government and are largely built upon undue exactions from the masses of our people. The gulf between employers and the employed is constantly widening, and classes are rapidly forming, one comprising the very rich and powerful, while in another are found the toiling poor.

As we view the achievements of aggregated capital, we discover the existence of trusts, combinations, and monopolies, while the citizen is struggling far in the rear or is trampled to death beneath an iron heel. Corporations, which should be the carefully restrained creatures of the law and the servants of the people, are fast becoming the people's masters.

Still congratulating ourselves upon the wealth and prosperity of our country and complacently contemplating every incident of change inseparable from these conditions, it is our duty as patriotic citizens to inquire at the present stage of our progress how the bond of the Government made with the people has been kept and performed. . . .

. . . Others of our citizens, whose comforts and expenditures are measured by moderate salaries and fixed incomes, will insist upon the fairness and justice of cheapening the cost of necessaries for themselves and their families.

When to the selfishness of the beneficiaries of unjust discrimination under our laws there shall be added the discontent of those who suffer from such discrimination, we will realize the fact that the beneficent purposes of our Government, dependent upon the patriotism and contentment of our people, are endangered.

REPORT OF THE HOUSE COMMITTEE ON MANUFACTURES
H.R. Rep. No. 4165, Pt. 1
50th Cong., 2d Sess.
March 2, 1889

Mr. BACON, from the Committee on Manufactures, submitted the following

REPORT:

Your committee respectfully submit herewith the testimony taken before them in relation to the whisky trust and the combination affecting the article of cotton bagging. Your committee believe that the testimony heretofore submitted to the House and that which accompanies this report* discloses the nature, form, and causes of trusts and combinations, and that all others in existence are formed in substantially the same way as those referred to in such testimony.

They respectfully report that the number of combinations and trusts formed and

---

* Not reprinted herein.

forming in this country is, as your committee has ascertained, very large, and affects a large portion of the important manufacturing and industrial interests of the country. They do not report any list of these combinations, for the reason that new ones are constantly forming and that old ones are constantly extending their relations so as to cover new branches of business and invade new territories.

Your committee further report that, owing to present differences of opinion between the members of the committee, they limit this report to submitting to the careful consideration of subsequent Congresses the facts shown by the testimony taken before the committee.

REPORT OF THE HOUSE COMMITTEE ON MANUFACTURES (MINORITY VIEWS)
H.R. Rep. No. 4165, Pt. 2
50th Cong., 2d Sess.
March 2, 1889

Mr. BUCHANAN, from the Committee on Manufactures, submitted the following as

VIEWS OF THE MINORITY:

The undersigned deems the record in this case incomplete without the documents hereto annexed as appendices.* "A" is a very able review of the authorities bearing upon the legality of trusts. "B" is the opinion of Judge Barrett, of the supreme court of New York, in the sugar-refining case,[1.247] discussing the same question. "C" is the offer by the solicitor of the Standard Oil Trust to disprove certain matters in testimony relating to such trust. As these matters appear of record, uncontradicted, it would seem but fair to put upon record the offer to disprove. "D" and "E" are submitted as fair specimens of the crudeness and limited operation of remedies proposed in the measures submitted to the committee.

James Buchanan.

---

* Not reprinted herein.

[1.247] New York v. North River Sugar Ref. Co., 22 Abb. N. Cas. 164, 3 N.Y.S. 401 (1889).

FIRST ANNUAL MESSAGE OF PRESIDENT BENJAMIN HARRISON
December 3, 1889

2 THE STATE OF THE UNION MESSAGES OF THE PRESIDENTS
1790-1966, at 1628 (F. Israel ed. 1966)

Executive Mansion,
Washington, December 3, 1889.

To the Senate and House of Representatives: . . .

⊥ Earnest attention should be given by Congress to a consideration of the question how far the restraint of those combinations of capital commonly ⊥ called "trusts" is matter of Federal jurisdiction. When organized, as they often are, to crush out all healthy competition and to monopolize the production or sale of an article of commerce and general necessity, they are dangerous conspiracies against the public good, and should be made the subject of prohibitory and even penal legislation.

SENATE CONSIDERATION (S. 3445)

SENATE DEBATE
50th Cong., 1st Sess.
August 14, 1888

19 CONG. REC. 7512

Mr. [JOHN H.] REAGAN [D., Tex.] introduced a bill (S. 3440) to define trusts and to provide for the punishment of persons connected with them or carrying them on; which was read the first time by its title.

Mr. [JAMES B.] BECK [D., Ky.]. Let that bill be read in full.

The PRESIDENT *pro tempore* [JOHN J. INGALLS, R., Kan.]. The bill will be read the second time at length, if there be no objection.

The bill was read the second time at length, as follows:

Be it enacted, etc., That a trust is the combination of capital or skill by two or more persons for the following purposes:

First. To create or carry out restrictions on trade.

Second. To limit, to reduce, or to increase the production or prices of merchandise or commodities.

Third. To prevent competition in the manufacture, making, sale, or purchase of merchandise or commodities.

Fourth. To create a monopoly.

SEC. 2. That any person who may be or may become a member of any such trust, or who may be or may become engaged in the business of any such trust in any trade or business carried on with foreign countries, or between the States, or between any State or Territory and the District of Columbia, or between the ⊥ District of Columbia and any Territory, or between the United States and the waters adjacent to any foreign country, shall be guilty of a high misdemeanor, and on conviction thereof in any district or circuit court of the United States after indictment shall be fined a sum of not more than $10,000 nor less than $1,000, and may be imprisoned in the penitentiary for a period of not more than five years and not less than one year. ⊥7513

SEC. 3. That the purchase by any trust, or by the agent of any trust, of merchandise or commodities in a foreign country for sale in this country; or the manufacture, making, or purchase of any merchandise or commodity in this country for sale in a foreign country; or the manufacture, making, or purchase of any merchandise or commodity in one State for sale in another; or in any State or Territory for sale in the District of Columbia; or in the District of Columbia for sale in any State or Territory; or in any Territory for sale in any other Territory or in any State or in the District of Columbia, shall constitute a violation of this act, and shall subject the offender to the aforesaid penalties.

Mr. SHERMAN. To what committee is it proposed to refer the bill?

The PRESIDENT *pro tempore*. To the Committee on the Judiciary.

Mr. BECK. It should go to the Committee on Commerce.

Mr. SHERMAN. Upon the question of reference I desire to say something.

Mr. REAGAN. I had marked it to go to the Committee on the Judiciary, but it is immaterial to me whether it goes to that committee or the Committee on Commerce.

Mr. SHERMAN. The Committee on Finance is already in charge of that subject. It has been instructed by the Senate to inquire into and report whether there is any remedy for trusts, combinations, etc.

Mr. REAGAN. Very well; I have no objection then. If the Committee on Finance has the subject before it the bill may go to that committee.

Mr. BECK. I desire to say that the Committee on Finance has got its hands very full just now, and is likely to have until the end of the session. I do not believe the Committee on Finance can look into this question any further, and the bill ought to go either to the Committee on Commerce or the Committee on the Judiciary on that account.

Mr. REAGAN. I indicated the reference to the Committee on the Judiciary because the bill involves an exceedingly interesting and important question of law, and I supposed that that committee perhaps had better have the consideration of it. But if the Senator from Ohio prefers that it should go to the Committee on Finance, or prefers it should go to any other committee, it will be agreeable to me.

Mr. SHERMAN. I wish to say that the Committee on Finance has already been charged with the consideration of this subject. I have myself given some attention to it, to see how far it is within the constitutional power of Congress to prohibit trusts and combinations in restraint of trade. It is very clear there is no such power unless it is derived from the power of levying taxes; that it is a power which must be exercised by each State for itself. Similar laws have been passed in England and in other countries. Indeed, in Blackstone's Commentaries there are declarations and denunciations of trusts, monopolies, etc., as strong as can be written in the English language. Whether such legislation can be ingrafted in our peculiar system of government by the national authority, there is some doubt. If it can be done at all, it must be done upon a tariff bill or upon a revenue bill. I do not see in what other way it can be done.

My impression is that in any bill reported to the Senate in respect to the collection of the revenue there will be provisions offered seeking, if possible, to prevent the evils which unquestionably grow out of these combinations and trusts, especially by corporations. The difficulty, however, is that many of these combinations and trusts, some of the most dangerous of them, like the Standard Oil Company, grow out of matters as to which there is no tax, and where they do not grow out of the revenue laws. Whether in such cases we can reach the combinations and trusts, which affect every citizen of the United States, I do not know; but it is certain that where these combinations grow out of revenue laws, as the sugar trust, which is one of the most dangeroas [sic] and wrongful trusts ever organized in this country, the trust can certainly be reached by the operation of our revenue laws.

Perhaps it is the best way to let this matter go where the Senate have already sent it—to the Committee on Finance—and if the provisions reported by that committee should not be deemed wise, or if it is thought better to take the opinion of the Judiciary Committee upon their constitutionality or efficiency, then I should have no objection to having the subject go there. But, as a matter of course, legislation upon the subject of trusts and combinations in trade will naturally grow out of our revenue laws, and if it does not grow out of our revenue laws, it is not within the power of Congress to deal with it.

Mr. REAGAN. This bill was framed with a view—whether it has been successful in accomplishing that purpose or not—of avoiding the constitutional difficulty of assuming to legislate upon matters within State jurisdiction; and that question arises, as well as the difficulty of defining what a trust is, and providing proper penalties. I have indicated the reason why I had mentioned its reference to the Committee on the Judiciary, but I am willing to leave it to the Senate to make whatever reference it chooses.

The PRESIDENT *pro tempore*. The Chair recognizes the right of a Senator introducing a bill to move its reference to any committee he may prefer, but if no motion is made the Chair will then exercise his own judgment in referring the bill.

Mr. SHERMAN. I move that the bill be referred to the Committee on Finance. . . .

The Chief Clerk again read the bill.

The PRESIDENT *pro tempore*. Does the Chair understand the Senator from Texas to withdraw his motion to refer the bill to the Committee on the Judiciary?

Mr. REAGAN. The Senator from Ohio, I believe, has moved to refer it to the Committee on Finance.

The PRESIDENT *pro tempore.* The question is on agreeing to the motion of the Senator from Ohio to refer the bill to the Committee on Finance.

Mr. [MATT W.] RANSOM [D., N.C.]. I have no objection whatever to the bill being referred to the Committee on Finance, but I will venture to make a suggestion to the Senator from Ohio, if he will permit me.

That Senator intimates that if this power is to be derived at all, it is to be derived from the authority of Congress to lay and collect taxes.

Mr. SHERMAN. And to regulate commerce.

Mr. RANSOM. It strikes me, with great deference to the Senator from Ohio, that the best source of this power, if found at all, and I think it can be found, is in the power of Congress to regulate commerce.

Mr. SHERMAN. I always take the revenue laws as commercial laws. They always go together, interchangeably. But this very subject was embraced by a resolution offered by me, which was referred to the Committee on Finance, under which that committee was instructed to inquire into the subject and consider it.

Mr. RANSOM. As that committee has it in charge I agree with the Senator from Ohio in thinking that it had best continue to consider it, although it properly belongs to the Committee on Commerce.

The PRESIDENT *pro tempore.* The bill will be referred to the Committee on Finance, if there be no objection. . . .

Mr. SHERMAN introduced a bill (S. 3445) to declare unlawful trusts and combinations in restraint of trade and production; which was read twice by its title and referred to the Committee on Finance.

S. 3445
50th Cong., 1st Sess.
August 14, 1888

Mr. SHERMAN introduced the following bill; which was read twice and referred to the Committee on Finance.

A BILL

To declare unlawful trusts and combinations in restraint of trade and production.

```
 1    Be it enacted by the Senate and House of Representa-
 2    tives of the United States of America in Congress assembled,
 3    That all arrangements, contracts, agreements, trusts, or com-
 4    binations between persons or corporations made with a view,
 5    or which tend, to prevent full and free competition in the
 6    production, manufacture, or sale of articles of domestic growth
 7    or production, or of the sale of articles imported into the
 8    United States, and all arrangements, contracts, agreements,
 9    trusts, or combinations between persons or corporations de-
10    signed, or which tend, to advance the cost to the consumer of
11    any of such articles, are hereby declared to be against public
12    policy, unlawful, and void; and any person or corporation in-
13    jured or damnified by such arrangement, contract, agreement,
14    trust, or corporation [sic] may sue for and recover in any court of
15    the United States of competent jurisdiction double the amount
16    of damages suffered by such person or corporation. And any
```

17 corporation doing business within the United States that acts
18 or takes part in any such arrangement, contract, agreement,
19 trust, or corporation [*sic*] shall forfeit its corporate franchise; and
20 it shall be the duty of the district attorney of the United
21 States of the district in which such corporation exists or does
22 business to institute the proper proceedings to enforce such
23 forfeiture.

S. 3445 AS REPORTED BY THE SENATE COMMITTEE ON FINANCE
50th Cong., 1st Sess.
September 11, 1888

[ED. NOTE: This revised version of S. 3445 was not accompanied by a report.]

⊥ Reported by Mr. SHERMAN with an amendment, viz: Strike out all after the enacting clause and insert the part printed in *italics*.

A BILL

To declare unlawful trusts and combinations in restraint of trade and production.

1 *Be it enacted by the Senate and House of Representa-*
2 *tives of the United States of America in Congress assembled,*
3 ~~That all arrangements, contracts, agreements, trusts, or com-~~
4 ~~binations between persons or corporations made with a view~~
5 ~~or which tend to prevent full and free competition in the~~
6 ~~production, manufacture, or sale of articles of domestic growth~~
7 ~~or production, or of the sales of articles imported into the~~
8 ~~United States, and all arrangements, contracts, agreements,~~
9 ~~trusts, or combinations between persons or corporations de-~~
10 ~~signed, or which tend, to advance the cost to the consumer of~~
11 ~~any of such articles, are hereby declared to be against public~~
12 ~~policy, unlawful, and void; and any person or corporation in-~~
13 ~~jured or damnified by such arrangement, contract, agreement,~~
14 ~~trust, or corporation [sic] may sue for and recover in any court of~~
15 ~~the United States of competent jurisdiction double the amount~~
16 ~~of damages suffered by such person or corporation. And any~~
17 ~~corporation doing business within the United States that acts~~
18 ~~or takes part in any such arrangement, contract, agreement,~~
19 ~~trust, or corporation [sic] shall forfeit its corporate franchise; and~~
20 ~~it shall be the duty of the district attorney of the United~~
21 ~~States of the district in which such corporation exists or does~~
22 ~~business to institute the proper proceedings to enforce such~~
23 ~~forfeiture.~~
3 *That all arrangements, contracts, agreements, trusts, or com-*
4 *binations between persons or corporations made with a view,*
5 *or which tend, to prevent full and free competition in the im-*

    6 *portation, transportation, or sale of articles imported into the*
    7 *United States or in the production, manufacture, or sale of*
    8 *articles of domestic growth or production, or domestic raw*
    9 *material that competes with any similar article upon which a*
  10 *duty is levied by the United States, or which shall be trans-*
  11 *ported from one State or Territory to another, and all ar-*
  12 *rangements, contracts, agreements, trusts, or combinations*
  13 *between persons or corporations designed, or which tend, to*
  14 *advance the cost to the consumer of any such articles, are*
  15 *hereby declared to be against public policy, unlawful, and*
  16 *void.*
    1   SEC. 2. *That any person or corporation injured or dam-*
    2 *nified by such arrangement, contract, agreement, trust, or com-*
    3 *bination may sue for and recover in any court of the United*
    4 *States of competent jurisdiction of any person or corporation*
    5 *a party to a combination described in the first section of this*
    6 *act, the full consideration or sum paid by him for any goods,*
    7 *wares, and merchandise included in or advanced in price by*
    8 *said combination.*
    1   SEC. 3. *That all persons entering into any such ar-*
    2 *rangement, contract, agreement, trust, or combination de-*
    3 *scribed in section one of this act, either on his own account or*
    4 *as agent or attorney for another, or as an officer, agent, or*
    5 *stockholder of any corporation, or as a trustee, committee, or*
    6 *in any capacity whatever, shall be guilty of a high misde-*
    7 *meanor, and on conviction thereof in any district or circuit*
    8 *court of the United States shall be subject to a fine of not*
    9 *more than ten thousand dollars, or to imprisonment in the*
  10 *penitentiary for a term of not more than five years, or to*
  11 *both such fine and imprisonment, in the discretion of the*
  12 *court. And it shall be the duty of the district attorney of*
  13 *the United States of the district in which such persons reside*
  14 *to institute the proper proceedings to enforce the provisions*
  15 *of this act.*

SENATE DEBATE
50th Cong., 2d Sess.
January 23, 1889

20 CONG. REC. 1120

    Mr. SHERMAN. I now move that the Senate proceed to the consideration of what is known as the trust bill, stating that at the request of the Senator from Massachusetts [Mr. HOAR] I will not ask for a final vote until to-morrow, as he desires to offer one or two amendments; but I should like to have it read now.
    The PRESIDING OFFICER [Mr. COCKRELL in the chair]. The Senator from Ohio moves that the Senate proceed to the consideration of the bill (S. 3445) to declare unlawful trusts and combinations in restraint of trade and production.
    The motion was agreed to; and the Senate, as in Committee of the Whole, proceeded to consider the bill.

The bill was reported from the Committee on Finance with an amendment, to strike out all after the enacting clause and insert: . . .[1.248]

⊥1121 ⊥ Mr. SHERMAN. I move to strike out, in lines 9 and 10 of section 1, the words "competes with any similar article upon which a duty is levied by the United States, or which," and to insert in lieu thereof, after the word "that," in line 9, the words "in due course of trade;" so as to read:

> Or in the production, manufacture, or sale of articles of domestic growth or production, or domestic raw material that in due course of trade shall be transported from one State or Territory to another, etc.

I ask for the adoption of the amendment.

The PRESIDING OFFICER. The Senator from Ohio proposes an amendment to the amendment reported by the Finance Committee, which will be read.

The CHIEF CLERK. In lines 9 and 10 of the amendment reported by the committee, it is proposed to strike out the words "competes with any similar articles upon which a duty is levied by the United States, or which," and insert in lieu thereof the words "in due course of trade;" so as to read:

> That all arrangements, contracts, agreements, trusts, or combinations between persons or corporations made with a view or which tend to prevent full and free competition in the importation, transportation, or sale of articles imported into the United States or in the production, manufacture, or sale of articles of domestic growth or production, or domestic raw material that in due course of trade shall be transported from one State or Territory to another.

Mr. SHERMAN. I promised the Senator from Massachusetts to let the bill lie over until to-morrow, as he has some amendments that he desires to propose. I wish to call the attention of the Senate to the importance of the bill. I do not wish to say a word about it, but to-morrow I will call it up for final action. . . .

Mr. [SHELBY M.] CULLOM [R., Ill.]. I was going to inquire of the Senator from Ohio whether he had made any amendment to the bill reported by his committee?

Mr. SHERMAN. The amendment is a substitute for the original bill, and contains three sections, one of which I believe was mainly taken from a bill introduced by the Senator—the punitive clause.

Mr. CULLOM. The bill reported from the committee. I was out and did not know whether the Senator made any suggestion to further amend the bill.

Mr. SHERMAN. I submitted one amendment from the Committee on Finance; and the bill will come up for further amendment to-morrow.

Mr. [ORVILLE H.] PLATT [R., Conn.]. Has the bill been read as amended?

The PRESIDING OFFICER. The amendment proposed by the committee, reported as a substitute, has been read and an amendment offered to it and agreed to.

Mr. PLATT. Let us have an order that the bill as now amended shall be printed in the RECORD, so that we may all see it.

The PRESIDING OFFICER. The amendment reported by the committee has not been agreed to. The Senate has not acted on that. The committee reported an amendment which was practically a substitute, and the Senator from Ohio offered an amendment to that amendment, which was agreed to. Now the question is on the amendment of the committee as amended.

Mr. SHERMAN. What the Senator desires will be done anyway, because the Secretary has read the bill, and the bill as it now stands will be printed in the RECORD to-morrow.

Mr. PLATT. That is all I desire.

The PRESIDING OFFICER. The bill will be postponed until to-morrow, if there be no objection.

[1.248] The amended version of S. 3445 as reported by the Committee on Finance on September 11, 1888, 50th Cong., 1st Sess., *supra* at 64–65, was read.

SENATE DEBATE
50th Cong., 2d Sess.
January 25, 1889

20 CONG. REC. 1167

Mr. SHERMAN. I renew my motion.

The PRESIDING OFFICER. The Senator from Ohio moves that the Senate proceed to the consideration of Senate bill 3445.

The motion was agreed to; and the Senate, as in Committee of the Whole, resumed the consideration of the bill (S. 3445) to declare unlawful trusts and combinations in restraint of trade and production, the pending question being on the amendment proposed by Mr. SHERMAN, in lines 9 and 10 of the amendment reported by the Committee on Finance, to strike out the words "competes with any similar articles upon which a duty is levied by the United States, or which," and to insert in lieu thereof the words "in due course of trade;" so as to read:

> That all arrangements, contracts, agreements, trusts, or combinations between persons or corporations made with a view or which tend to prevent full and free competition in the importation, transportation, or sale of articles imported into the United States or in the production, manufacture, or sale of articles of domestic growth or production, or domestic raw material that in due course of trade shall be transported from one State or Territory to another.

The amendment to the amendment was agreed to.

Mr. [GEORGE F.] HOAR [R., Mass.]. I move to amend, in line 11 of the substitute, by inserting after the word "another," the words "or to the District of Columbia, or from the District of Columbia to any State or Territory." The District is omitted in the enumeration of the political bodies to or from which the transportation is to be made.

Mr. SHERMAN. I have no objection to that amendment.

The PRESIDING OFFICER. The amendment to the amendment will be stated from the desk.

The CHIEF CLERK. In line 11, section 1, after the word "another," it is proposed to insert:

> Or to the District of Columbia, or from the District of Columbia to any State or Territory.

So as to read:

> Or which shall be transported from one State or Territory to another or to the District of Columbia, or from the District of Columbia to any State or Territory, etc.

The amendment to the amendment was agreed to.

Mr. HOAR. I now move an amendment, to come in as a second section, not as a substitute for the present second section, but preceding that, making that present second section the third section.

The PRESIDING OFFICER. The amendment will be read.

The Chief Clerk read as follows:

> SEC. 2. If one of the purposes of any such arrangement, contract, agreement, trust, or combination shall be to compel any person, partnership, or corporation to become a party thereto, or to cease from doing any lawful business, or to sell and dispose of any lawful business, or if acts shall be done under any such arrangement, contract, agreement, trust, or combination which have for their purpose or which shall tend to compel the giving up or sale of any lawful business, the person, partnership, or corporation injured thereby may sue for and recover in any court of the United States of competent jurisdiction the damages sustained thereby of any person or corporation a party to any such arrangement, contract, agreement, trust, or combination, or of all or any number less than all of such parties, and if any purchaser of articles specified in the preceding section shall be put to additional cost by the advancing of the price of such articles by means or because of any such arrangement, contract,

agreement, trust, or combination, he may in like manner sue for and recover the damages sustained, which shall in such case be estimated at the full consideration or sum paid by him for the articles so advanced in price as aforesaid.

Mr. HOAR. I think, on reflection, that the suggestion made by the Senator from Ohio is a wise one, that this proposed section had better come in after the second section as section 3.

The PRESIDING OFFICER. It will be considered as a proposed amendment to come in after section 2, and to be, if adopted, section 3.

Mr. PLATT. Let it be read once more.

Mr. SHERMAN. Before it is read I wish to say that I have read the section very carefully, and although I am not authorized, as a matter of course, in reporting this bill from the Committee on Finance to accept it, yet I believe it does amplify and make clearer and stronger the provisions of the second section. As far as I am concerned, I shall vote for it with pleasure. It has evidently been very carefully drawn by persons who understand the matter.

Mr. [M. C.] BUTLER [D., S.C.] May I inquire if this bill has been reported by a committee?

Mr. SHERMAN. It has been reported twice by the Committee on Finance with a substitute for the original bill.

Mr. BUTLER. This amendment, it seems to me from a casual reading of it, is a very important one. . . .

Mr. SHERMAN. The bill was introduced at the last session, and it has been printed two or three times. It has been up before, and, after being carefully considered, went over at the request of Senators. There is not a single thing, I am satisfied, but what the Senator will heartily approve. There are three sections of the measure as reported. The first declares the principle of the common law against combinations, trusts, etc., to affect the value of articles necessary to human life. The second section authorizes any person injured by such a combination to sue for the recovery of damages, etc. The section now offered simply emphasizes that by providing for cases where the combination extends to preventing a man from carrying on his business. The third section as reported, but which will be the fourth section now, is simply a penal clause declaring that any one who violates the preceding sections shall be guilty of a misdemeanor.

Mr. [ELI] SAULSBURY [D., Del.]. If I understood the reading of the section proposed by the Senator from Massachusetts aright, one of its provisions was that any persons compelling another to give up his business and join with them should be liable to the provisions of the act. I inquire whether that is sufficient, whether you ought not to go so far as to say "or shall induce by offers of stock?" The object, I suppose, is to break up these combinations, and if you limit the prohibition simply to cases of compelling persons to give up their business you do not cover proceedings by which persons are brought into combinations by being induced to give up their business. Why not after the word "compel" insert "or who shall induce?"

Mr. HOAR. It seems to me that language would apply not only to a harmful but to a meritorious arrangement. That was the difficulty with the bill of the Senator from Texas [Mr. REAGAN], which would prevent lawful partnerships from uniting for a proper purpose. If there be a railroad from Wilmington toward Dover and a separate railroad leading from Dover southward, it could transact business for the public in Delaware more cheaply by having one president and one treasurer, one salaried officer instead of two. It would be for the public convenience that such companies should unite. So a mere agreement to induce them to unite, putting no constraint or compulsion on them, should not be prohibited.

Mr. SAULSBURY. This applies to trusts, so that parties engaged in the same business shall not absorb the whole business by some means. Now, I understand that sometimes by use of force men are compelled by threats to give up their own business and become parts of the combination.

Mr. HOAR. That may be. The Senator, as I understand, asks why in my amendment—I do not undertake to speak for the Senator from Ohio in regard to the general bill—I did not put in the word "induce?" It was because I supposed the mere inducing such things as I suggested is strictly lawful and may be proper and meritorious.

Mr. SAULSBURY. But if they come to offer a share—

Mr. SHERMAN. If the Senator will read the first section he will find that it provides—

That all arrangements, contracts, agreements, trusts, or combinations between persons or corporations made with a view, or which tend, to prevent full and free competition in the importation, transportation, or sale of articles imported into the United States or in the production, manufacture, or sale of articles of domestic growth or production, or domestic raw material that competes with any similar article upon which a duty is levied by the United States, or which shall be transported from one State or Territory to another, and all arrangements, contracts, agreements, trusts, or combinations between persons or corporations designed, or which tend, to advance the cost to the consumer of any of such articles, are hereby declared to be against public policy, unlawful, and void.

In other words, it sets out in the most specific language the rule of the common law which prevails in England and this country, especially declared by the supreme court of the State of New York in a very clear and able opinion, which I have here on my desk. That section makes such agreements and combinations unlawful, and it goes as far as the Constitution permits Congress to go, because it only deals with two classes of matters: contracts which affect the importation of goods into the United States, which is foreign commerce, and contracts which affect the transportation and passage of goods from one State to another. The Congress of the United States can go no farther than that. It is not claimed by anybody it can. So that covers the whole thing.

The second section provides that any person or corporation injured or damnified by such arrangement, contract, agreement, trust, or combination may bring an action for damages. If any combination should be made to strike down any particular person or corporation, if that ⊥ person or corporation should be injured by the combination, he or it can sue in the courts and recover according to the language of the bill.

Then the section now offered simply provides for cases where a corporation seeks to compel other corporations or persons to enter into combinations, etc. If they enter into them willingly by persuasion or inducement, as the Senator from Delaware suggests, the case is covered fully by the first section, and the section now offered simply aims to protect a weak person from being compelled by surrounding circumstances, by force or violence, or by threats or intimidation against being forced into a combination of this kind. . . .

The PRESIDING OFFICER. The amendment reported by the Committee on Finance is now pending, being a substitute for the original bill, and this is an amendment to that amendment. . . .

Mr. [ISHAM G.] HARRIS [D., Tenn.]. I should like the attention of the Senator from Massachusetts. I suppose the power that Congress has over the subject-matter of this bill is derived chiefly, if not entirely, from the power to regulate foreign and interstate commerce. On listening to the amendment as read, I do not see any provision in it that applies it especially to such commerce as either foreign or interstate.

Mr. HOAR. It does. It is there.

Mr. HARRIS. I have only heard it read, and it may be that my ear did not catch the description; but if it is not there, it seems to me it ought to be there.

Mr. SHERMAN. It refers to the arrangements, contracts, agreements, etc., described in the first section of the bill.

Mr. HARRIS. That may correct the defect which had occurred to me.

Mr. HOAR. "If one of the purposes of such arrangement"—the arrangement being an arrangement previously described in the foregoing section of the bill—

Mr. HARRIS. And that previous description applies to foreign and interstate commerce?

Mr. HOAR. Yes.

The PRESIDING OFFICER. The question is on the amendment of the Senator from Massachusetts to the amendment of the Committee on Finance.

The amendment to the amendment was agreed to.

The PRESIDING OFFICER. If there be no objection, section 3 will be changed to section 4.

Mr. [JAMES B.] EUSTIS [D., La.]. I would ask the Senator from Ohio whether this proposed law is to apply, as I understand it, only to future trusts, or whether he desires that it shall be applied to existing trusts? The reason I ask the question is this: A great many of these trusts are already in existence. That is the evil which, as I understand, is to be reached by this new legislation. I do not think the provisions of the bill as it stands apply to existing trusts. They are combinations or agreements, it is true, but the first section says "made," of course meaning "made after the passage" of the act. I call the Senator's attention to the fact that the first section contains no sanction—that is, there is no penalty attached. It simply is a declaration that these trusts are void. In the other section, where a penalty is provided, that applies only to future trusts. Therefore in order that this proposed law shall cover existing trusts as well as future trusts, I shall offer the following amendment:

> That any person who thirty days after the passage of this law shall act as a manager, officer, trustee, or agent of any trust or combination as described in the first section, shall be liable to the penalties prescribed in the fourth section.

That is, the fourth section as it now stands. . . .

Mr. SHERMAN. As far as I can perceive, I think that the continuing agreement, arrangement, combination, etc., such as described in the first section will become illegal on the passage of this act and not before. Our laws can not be made retroactive. But I do not see myself any objection to making the continuance of a combination like this after proper days' notice an offense. I think, however, thirty days' notice is too short because a law of this kind ought to have a broad circulation before it becomes operative.

Mr. EUSTIS. I will accept any reasonable change in regard to the number of days.

Mr. SHERMAN. I am not at liberty to accept any amendment on behalf of the committee, but I should be inclined to vote for it if the Senator should say six months or a year.

Mr. EUSTIS. Say "ninety days."

Mr. SHERMAN. I would say six months or a year, because I do not think anybody ought to be charged with an offense of this kind with such severe consequences until he has had ample notice. A year would answer just as well.

Mr. HARRIS. Ninety days is certainly sufficient for every man to be informed as to the state of the law.

Mr. SHERMAN. Very well.

Mr. HARRIS. And the shorter the time that immunity is given to offenders such as these, the better.

The PRESIDING OFFICER. The question is on the amendment of the Senator from Louisiana [Mr. EUSTIS] as modified.

The amendment to the amendment was agreed to.

The PRESIDING OFFICER. This amendment will be section 5, if there be no objection.

Mr. PLATT. Let the amendment which has just been agreed to be read again.

The Secretary read as follows:

> SEC. 5. That any person who ninety days after the passage of this law shall act as manager, officer, trustee, or agent of any trust or combination as described in the first section, shall be liable to the penalties of the fourth section.

Mr. PLATT. I ask whether there is any distinction between these several words "arrangement," "contract," "agreement," "trust, or combination," and if there is, to suggest that section 2 only applies to what may be done under a combination and not to what may be done under an arrangement, agreement, or trust; and the amendment which has just been adopted only applies to what may be done under a combination or a trust, and has no reference to the other words which are used in section 1, "arrangement," "contract," "agreement."

I do not know that there is anything in the suggestion, but if not, why are all those words used in the first section? The second section is this:

SEC. 2. That any person or corporation injured or damnified by such arrangement, contract, agreement, trust, or combination may sue for and recover in any court of the United States of competent jurisdiction of any person or corporation a party to a combination described in the first section of this act, the full consideration or price paid by him for any goods, wares, and merchandise included in or advanced in price by said combination.

Mr. EUSTIS. That is not part of the section I offered.

Mr. PLATT. I know, but that uses only the word "combination." The Senator's amendment uses one other word, "combination or trust."

Mr. EUSTIS. "As described in the first section," where there is a full description.

Mr. PLATT. The second section does not even refer to the first section.

Mr. EUSTIS. I have not referred to the second section at all.

Mr. PLATT. I merely make this suggestion: If there is any difference between the legal definition of those words as used in the first section, they ought all to be employed in the second section and also in the Senator's amendment.

Mr. EUSTIS. My amendment does not refer to the second section at all. It refers to the first section. . . .

. . . I have no objection to the insertion of the words, but the first section defines specifically what this act prohibits. It was not necessary to insert the other words in my amendment. I am perfectly willing to have them inserted.

The PRESIDING OFFICER. The amendment last adopted will be read.

The Secretary read the amendment of Mr. EUSTIS.

Mr. PLATT. Now let me say—

Mr. EUSTIS. I will amend the amendment, with the Senator's permission, by including the other words, "arrangement, contract, agreement, trust, or combination," as described.

Mr. PLATT. If there is any legal difference, the subsequent sections ought to include all the words in the first.

The PRESIDING OFFICER. Is there any objection to the modification suggested by the Senator from Louisiana? The amendment already voted on will be considered not agreed to, and the Senator from Louisiana modifies it as indicated, by the insertion of the words reported. His amendment will now be read as amended.

Mr. EUSTIS. Put in the words "arrangement, contract, agreement, trust, or combination." . . .

Mr. PLATT. While the change is being made, I want to make my point clear, if I can, to the Senator from Ohio, because it seems to me that the act ought to be perfected, and my suggestion applies as well to the second section as to the amendment offered by the Senator from Louisiana.

The first section describes several different things, I suppose—if it does not, then the superfluous words ought to be stricken out—"arrangement, contract, agreement, trust, or combination." If it means trust and combination simply, and is not intended to go any further, then the words "arrangement, contract, agreement" ought to be stricken out; but if it is intended to go further than reaching what are technically known as trusts and combinations, then those words, as it seems to me, ought to be inserted in line 5 and line 8 of section 2, which reads:

SEC. 2. That any person or corporation injured or damnified by such arrangement, contract, agreement, trust, or combination may sue for and recover, in any court of the United States of competent jurisdiction, of any person or corporation a party to a combination described in the first section of this act, the full consideration or sum paid by him for any goods, wares, and merchandise included in or advanced in price by said combination.

If there is any technical distinction between these words, the second section does not permit a party injured to recover damages from anybody except a party to a combination. If he is a party to an agreement, an arrangement, a contract, or a trust which does not amount in legal definition as it shall be determined by the court to be a combination, then there is no liability.

The PRESIDING OFFICER. The amendment of the Senator from Louisiana will now be read as modified.

The Secretary read as follows:

> SEC. —. That any person who, ninety days after the passage of this law, shall act as a manager, officer, trustee, or agent of any arrangement, contract, agreement, trust, or combination as described in the first section, shall be liable to the penalties prescribed in the fourth section.

The amendment was agreed to. . . .

Mr. REAGAN. I think it is to be regretted that a measure of this great importance should come up as an amendment to an appropriation bill. It is unquestionably a subject-matter that deserves the earliest and most careful consideration.

The PRESIDING OFFICER. Does the Chair understand the Senator to say it comes up on an appropriation bill?

Mr. REAGAN. I understand so.

The PRESIDING OFFICER. The Senator is mistaken. This is an independent bill reported by the Committee on Finance. It is the bill (S. 3445) to declare unlawful trusts and combinations in restraint of trade and production.

Mr. REAGAN. Very well. I misunderstood it, then. . . .

Mr. SHERMAN. This bill has been here now for almost a year.

Mr. REAGAN. I understand. I desire to call attention to the language contained in the first section because it is a matter of very great moment. There are some things which we have the power to do and some things, I take it, that we have not the power to do. The first section provides—

> That all arrangements, contracts, agreements, trusts, or combinations between persons or corporations made with a view, or which tend, to prevent full and free competition in the importation, transportation, or sale of articles imported into the United States—

That is all right; then it proceeds—

> or in the production, manufacture, or sale of articles of domestic growth or production, or domestic raw material that competes with any similar article upon which a duty is levied by the United States,

That language evidently rests upon the idea that we obtain jurisdiction over this question by virtue of the revenue policy of the United States, which it seems to me is a great mistake. If we have the power to deal with this subject, it seems to me it must be under the clause of the Constitution authorizing Congress to regulate commerce among the States and with foreign countries. If I am right as to that, then the language which I last read and which I will reread seems to me to be unwarranted and I fear it would be inoperative; that is:

> Or in the production, manufacture, or sale of articles of domestic growth or production, or domestic raw material that competes with any similar article upon which a duty is levied by the United States.

That would extend the jurisdiction of Congress, if it could be made effective, to all such combinations, arrangements, agreements, or trusts made wholly within a State and made with reference to commerce wholly within a State. I do not think the courts would give effect to such a provision, nor do I think it would be safe for the Senate to attempt to do what it appears to me is clearly not within the power of Congress. If the language were changed so as to read (I do not know that this precise language is the proper phraseology, but I suggest it as an improvement):

> That all arrangements, contracts, agreements, trusts, or combinations between persons or corporations, made with a view or which tend to prevent full and free competition in the importation, transportation, or sale of articles imported into the United States—

Then these new words I would suggest—

> Or for transportation from State to State, or to or from a foreign country, or within the District of Columbia, or any of the Territories of the United States.

And then I would proceed with the language of the bill:

> And all arrangements, contracts, agreements, trusts, or combinations.

SENATE CONSIDERATION (S. 3445)

The PRESIDING OFFICER. If the Senator from Texas will permit, the Chair will suggest that amendments have already been adopted probably covering the same ground about which he is speaking. The Chair will have the amendments read for his information. . . .

The Secretary will read the amendments agreed to.

The SECRETARY. In section 1, line 9, after the word "that," the words "competes with any similar article upon which a duty is levied by the United States, or which" have been stricken out, and the words "in due course of trade" inserted; and after the word "another," in line 11, the words "or to the District of Columbia, or from the District of Columbia to any State or Territory" have been inserted; so as to make the section read:

That all arrangements, contracts, agreements, trusts, or combinations between persons or corporations made with a view or which tend to prevent full and free competition in the importation, transportation, or sale of articles imported into the United States, or in the production, manufacture, or sale of articles of domestic growth or production, or domestic raw material that in due course of trade shall be transported from one State or Territory to another, or to the District of Columbia, or from the District of Columbia to any State or Territory, and all arrangements, contracts, agreements, trusts, or combinations between persons or corporations designed or which tend to advance the cost to the consumer of any of such articles, are hereby declared to be against public policy, unlawful, and void.

Mr. REAGAN. I think it likely that that covers the idea I had in view, but I am not entirely certain of it. Not having been present when that action was taken is my apology for presenting the amendment which I intended to suggest to cover the difficulty. If the Senator from Mississippi [Mr. GEORGE] thinks that covers the difficulty, I am satisfied.

Mr. [JAMES Z.] GEORGE [D., Miss.]. The Senator is mistaken about my supposing that the amendment covers the difficulty. I called his attention to the amendment so that he might discuss the bill as it stood. I do not think it removes the difficulty by any means.

Mr. REAGAN. I misunderstood the Senator, then. That would leave in the bill the words "or in the production, manufacture, or sale of articles of domestic growth or production, or domestic raw material" that are transported. I do not feel able to determine at this time whether the language there covers the idea that I have presented or not. I have not had an opportunity to consider the subject, was not present when it was up before, and did not know it would be up this morning, or I should have been prepared for it.

S. 3445 AS AMENDED BY THE SENATE
50th Cong., 2d Sess.
January 25, 1889

⊥ Ordered to be reprinted as amended.   ⊥⊥

A BILL

To declare unlawful trusts and combinations in restraint of trade and production.

1 *Be it enacted by the Senate and House of Representa-*
2 *tives of the United States of America in Congress assembled,*
3 That all arrangements, contracts, agreements, trusts, or com-
4 binations between persons or corporations made with a view,
5 or which tend, to prevent full and free competition in the im-

portation, transportation, or sale of articles imported into the United States or in the production, manufacture, or sale of articles of domestic growth or production, or domestic raw material that in due course of trade shall be transported from one State or Territory to another, or to the District of Columbia, or from the District of Columbia to any State or Territory, and all arrangements, contracts, agreements, trusts, or combinations between persons or corporations designed, or which tend, to advance the cost to the consumer of any of such articles, are hereby declared to be against public policy, unlawful, and void.

SEC. 2. That any person or corporation injured or damnified by such arrangement, contract, agreement, trust, or combination may sue for and recover in any court of the United States of competent jurisdiction of any person or corporation a party to a combination described in the first section of this act the full consideration or sum paid by him for any goods, wares, and merchandise included in or advanced in price by said combination.

SEC. 3. That if one of the purposes of any such arrangement, contract, agreement, trust, or combination shall be to compel any person, partnership, or corporation to become a party thereto, or to cease from doing any lawful business, or to sell and dispose of any lawful business, or if acts shall be done under any such arrangement, contract, agreement, trust, or combination, which have for their purpose, or which shall tend to compel the giving up or sale of any lawful business, the person, partnership, or corporation injured thereby may sue for and recover in any court of the United States of competent jurisdiction the damages sustained thereby of any person or corporation a party to any such arrangement, contract, agreement, trust, or combination, or of all or any number less than all of such parties. And if any purchaser of articles specified in the preceding section shall be put to additional cost by the advancing of the price of such articles by means or because of any such arrangement, contract, agreement, trust, or combination, he may, in like manner, sue for and recover the damages sustained, which shall in such case be estimated at the full consideration or sum paid by him for the article so advanced in price as aforesaid.

SEC. 4. That all persons entering into any such arrangement, contract, agreement, trust, or combination described in section one of this act, either on his own account or as agent or attorney for another, or as an officer, agent, or stockholder of any corporation, or as a trustee, committee, or in any capacity whatever, shall be guilty of a high misdemeanor, and, on conviction thereof in any district or circuit court of the United States, shall be subject to a fine of not more than ten thousand dollars, or to imprisonment in the penitentiary for a term of not more than five years, or to both such fine and imprisonment, in the discretion of the court. And it shall be the duty of the district attorney of the United States of the district in which such persons reside

⊥14 to institute the proper proceedings to enforce the provisions
15 of this act.
1 SEC. 5. That any person, who, ninety days after the pas-
2 sage of this law, shall act as a manager, officer, trustee, or
3 agent of any arrangement, contract, agreement, trust, or com-
4 bination as described in the first section, shall be liable to the
5 penalties prescribed in the fourth section.

⊥4

SENATE DEBATE
50th Cong., 2d Sess.
February 4, 1889

20 CONG. REC. 1457

The Senate, as in Committee of the Whole, resumed the consideration of the bill (S. 3445) to declare unlawful trusts and combinations in restraint of trade and production.

Mr. [JAMES K.] JONES [D., Ark.]. Mr. President, when the framers of the Constitution of the United States conferred upon Congress the power "to regulate commerce among the several States" they had no conception of what those words would import within a century. "Commerce among the several States" then meant an interchange by slow and laborious methods of a few scattered products, insignificant in quantity and value. Steam was then practically unknown; ships, such as were then in existence, were sailing vessels, while the boats upon the few known navigable rivers were propelled either by the current or by human labor.

Overland transportation of commodities was confined to a few miles from the point of production. Judging at that time by the history of the human race for six thousand years it looked as if there was never to be any "commerce among the States" except this primitive, inconsequential, and slow method of exchanging commodities. "Commerce among the States" as we know it, it had not "entered into the heart of man to conceive."

Man had not learned to harness "that wayward daughter of fire and water, steam." The marvel of vessels driven by this power with the speed of the wind against the current and against the wind was yet to be unfolded to the human mind, while carriages carrying tons of freight overland with the rapidity, smoothness, and ease of our time, and at a cost of less than 1 cent per ton per mile, had never been thought of.

These things have now, however, come to be so common that it seems strange, incredible almost, that the time ever was when they were not. The products of the most remote sections of our Union find their way so easily and so inexpensively into the homes of all classes that the fruits and fish of the Pacific have become to be necessaries of life to even such citizens of the Atlantic seaboard as make no pretensions to wealth. The tropical fruits of the far South are at home in the streets of the cities of the North, while the products of the North are laid at the doors of our Southern homes almost as cheaply as to the neighbors of the producers.

Steam and electricity have well-nigh abolished time and distance, until every citizen of the great Republic is, if not actually present, at least at home in every part of our great country.

Every village in the broad land is the recipient of the blessings that a beneficent Providence has showered upon the varied and diverse soils, climate, characteristics, in endless variety in our wonderful country.

Whether, if this vast and intricate system of "commerce among the States" had been comprehended in all its immensity by the framers of the Constitution, this power of control, unlimited save by the discretion of Congress, would have been conferred upon us we may well doubt; and, doubting this, we should proceed with caution in the exercise of this great power.

For myself, I confess frankly that I have always regarded the exercise of the powers conveyed by this section of the Constitution as full of danger; for if we exercise all the power that we may under this clause, we practically assume control of everything. The details of "commerce among the States" have become so vast and complicated that there is not a home, a business, or a human being who is not more or less affected by it; and the exercise of all the power conferred by this section upon Congress might be made to absorb almost everything else.

No one can deny that there is great danger in centralization, and it becomes every patriotic citizen to watch with jealous care the encroachments of Federal power and to check and restrain them by every legitimate means. Powers once assumed and exercised are rarely, if ever, relinquished, and we should be sure that we never enter upon the exercise of a new power or an old power in a new way except upon the clearest evidence that such exercise is absolutely demanded by the best interests of the nation.

I hesitated long before fully making up my mind that a law regulating interstate commerce should pass, but mature reflection convinced me of the utter inability of the States to deal with the class of evils that it was intended to remedy, and after judicial decisions had settled this as true, there was absolutely nothing left except the exercise of power by the Federal Government. I believe the exercise of that power has already brought great good to the general public, and I hope that the intelligence and patriotism of the people will prevent the evils that might quite naturally grow up out of it.

The enactment of the bill under consideration into a law will be another and a most important exercise of authority conferred by this clause of the Constitution; and for myself, while I am keenly alive to the dangers to flow from it, the demand for some such action is so great that I am most heartily in favor of some such bill. The details of the bill and its construction I leave to the committee having the matter in charge. I simply mean to declare myself in favor of legislation to suppress a gross wrong. The dangers to come from this exercise of power are in the future and may never come, while the wrongs which it is intended to remedy are here present and pressing upon us and demanding attention.

The growth of these commercial monsters called trusts in the last few years has become appalling. For a long while they were limited in numbers and applied to but a few articles, and while even then they excited the detestation of good men, they did not exist in such numbers and power as to cause apprehensions for the public safety.

Now, however, having been allowed to grow and fatten upon the public, their success is an example of evil that has excited the greed and conscienceless rapacity of commercial sharks until in schools they are to be found now in every branch of trade, preying upon every industry, and by their unholy combinations robbing their victims, the general public, in defiance of every principle of law or morals.

The iron hand of the law must be laid heavily upon this system, or the boasted liberty of the citizen is a myth. If the proceeds of the labor of our men and women are not to be their own we have no liberty and our Government is a farce and a fraud.

The interstate-commerce law was aimed at a tendency to combination in railroading. This was wise; but it will be utterly useless if combinations in restraint of competition in all other branches of trade should be allowed. We are advised by the newpapers that a monster salt trust intended to control the salt market of the world, and which is to pay an annual dividend of 25 per cent, is now in process of organization.

The steel trust has with a mailed hand laid the entire country under tribute for years; its profits, if the "swag" it has pocketed may be called by so respectable a name, has [sic] reached fabulous sums; and now we are regaled by assurances that a pig-iron trust is to come in and control the trade and the price in that article.

The iniquities of the Standard Oil Company have been enumerated and recounted until some of them are familiar to every one, and the colossal fortunes which have grown from it, which in all their vastness do not represent one dollar of honest toil or one trace of benefit to mankind, nor any addition to the products of human labor, are known everywhere.

The sugar trust has its "long, felonious fingers" at this moment in every man's pocket in the United States, deftly extracting with the same audacity the pennies from the pockets of the poor and dollars from the pockets of the rich. But why name them? There is scarcely an article of commerce which is not now or soon to be controlled by some combination of plunderers.

When Robin Hood undertook to rob his fellow-citizens he took his life in his hand and with at least some sort of courage took the consequences of his crimes, but these modern foot-pads have not the grace of his courage, but commit their robberies by stealth. I am in favor of so changing the laws that their robberies can not be committed in safety any longer, and so that even planning them will make the offenders amenable to punishment.

This bill is a step in the right direction, and if it shall prove the beginning of the end of this system of conspiracies and combinations it will be hailed as the dawn of genuine freedom, and if it is not so constructed as to accomplish this purpose, I hope the Senate will so amend it as to make it effective. I hope it may serve to set people to thinking of the wrong of either permitting people or authorizing people to combine to plunder the public. If it does this there will not be a repetition in this Chamber of what has recently passed here. Proposed financial legislation, which has received the sanction of the majority here, will, if it ever becomes law, promote and build up just such conspiracies, combinations, trusts, "sympathetic movements," as we propose in this bill to condemn. We have been actually paving the way for such things for weeks—making the way for them easy—practically making the Government of the United States *particeps criminis* in those that are to grow up hereafter.

If, however, this bill shall become a law, and I hope it will, it may prove a great educator, and people may come to believe after a while that no class of persons in this country has any right to be enriched by indirect means at the expense of the many, and if this shall come to be fully accepted as correct and just by the whole people, your system of protection—that system of "concealed bounties," to use the expressive words of the honorable Senator from Iowa—will, like many another pirate that has gone before, have to "walk the plank."

Mr. GEORGE. Mr. President, this is a very important subject. The bill undertakes to deal with very great evils which in the last few years have done great injury to the people of the United States. I am in favor of legislation to prevent trusts and combinations, but I want effective legislation—legislation that will crush out these combinations and trusts. The trouble is in finding the constitutional power to do exactly what ought to be done, and if we exceed our constitutional power, our action, however well meant, will be of no value; it will be utterly void. The bill before us seeks to get under the commercial clause of the Constitution jurisdiction to pass a criminal law in relation to trusts, agreements, and combinations as described in the bill. This power is simply the power to regulate interstate and foreign commerce.

I have given some thought and some reflection to this matter, and I am extremely anxious that some bill shall receive the assent of this Congress which will put an end forever to the practice, now becoming too common, of large corporations, and of single persons, too, of large wealth, so arranging that they dictate to the people of this country what they shall pay when they purchase, and what they shall receive when they sell.

I have considered with some care the provisions of this bill. I do not believe that the effect of its provisions is accurately understood by members of this body. I propose, therefore, to make an analysis of its provisions to see, if we can, what it means, what evils it undertakes to remedy, and what remedy it provides, and how efficacious this remedy may prove to be.

In the beginning, I desire to call the attention of the Senate to the fact that the provisions of this bill are not confined to trusts, to combinations, to arrangements and agreements made between parties who are engaged in business; or, in other words, taking the language of the bill in its plain meaning, it refers to and brings within the punitory provisions of the fourth section not only arrangements and agreements between manufacturers, between sellers, between transporters, but it brings within its grasp arrangements made by any persons, though merely for moral and for defensive purposes. The bill provides—

> That all arrangements, contracts, agreements, trusts, or combinations between persons or corporations made with a view, or which tend, to prevent full and free competition in the importation, transportation, or sale of articles imported into the United States shall be unlawful.

That would apply to an arrangement, to an agreement, to a combination, not of a business character, but, as I before remarked, to such as is purely moral and defensive. It does not say that all arrangements, contracts, etc., made between persons and corporations engaged in selling, transporting, importing, manufacturing, or producing the articles described in the bill shall be unlawful; but it applies to all persons whether so engaged or not. So if this bill passes as it now stands, the farmers and laborers of this country who are sending up their voices to the Congress of the United States, asking, pleading, imploring us to take action to put down trusts, these farmers and these laborers will find that they themselves in their most innocent and necessary arrangements, made solely for defensive purposes against the operations of these trusts, will be brought within the punitory provisions of this bill.

It will strike the Senate probably with some astonishment if it be ascertained that under this bill the arrangements made by the Southern farmers during the last season to prevent the consummation of the robbery of them by the jute-bagging trust are made highly criminal. Under it the farmers of the South who combine to prevent and defeat that most iniquitous and unjust combination will find that they themselves rather than the jute-bagging trust will be the subjects of severe punishment.

The bill declares that any arrangement, any agreement, any combination made by any person, whether engaged in trade or not, which tends to prevent full and free competition in the importation, transportation, or sale of the articles described in the bill, shall be subject to indictment, and, on conviction, to punishment by fine of $5,000 or imprisonment in the penitentiary not exceeding five years, or to both such fine and imprisonment.

Upon the formation of this bagging trust the cotton farmers of the South, many of them in their granges and in their alliances, agreed that they would not purchase jute bagging, and by that agreement to a very large extent the rich rewards anticipated by the men who formed that trust were defeated. These combinations tended to prevent full and free competition in the sale of this article. But if that is not very clear, if Senators think these arrangements of the farmers did not have the effect of preventing this full and free competition, I call their attention to another provision contained in the third section of the bill, which reads in this way:

> If acts shall be done under any such arrangement, contract, agreement, trust, or combination, which have for their purpose, or which shall tend to compel the giving up or sale of any lawful business, the person, partnership, or corporation injured thereby may sue for and recover in any court of the United States of competent jurisdiction the damages sustained thereby.

The very object of this combination of Southern farmers was to break down the trust in jute bagging, to compel the men who had seized and got control of the bagging manufacture of this country to give up their business—to loose their grip upon the business of the farmers. It also very clearly violated the other provision of the bill to which I have just called attention. The fact that the bill does not restrict these combinations, these agreements, to persons engaged in trade, engaged in transportation, engaged in importation, engaged in selling—the fact that it applies to all arrangements, all agreements, all combinations, by whomsoever made, would bring within its reach all defensive agreements made by farmers for the purpose of enhancing the price of their products. This bill, instead of preventing trusts, would have the effect of crushing out all efforts of the people to rid themselves of their injurious effects. . . .

Mr. SHERMAN. Do I understand my friend from Mississippi to claim that under this bill an agreement made by farmers not to buy cotton-bagging or not to buy anything else is a combination within the meaning of the act?

Mr. GEORGE. Yes, sir; directly within the meaning of the act.

Mr. SHERMAN. That is a very extraordinary proposition. There is nothing in the bill to prevent a refusal by anybody to buy anything. All that it says is that the people producing or selling a particular article shall not make combinations to advance the price of the necessaries of life. However, I simply wished to get the answer of the Senator.

Mr. GEORGE. That is the true construction of this bill which I put on it.

Mr. SHERMAN. I desire to say distinctly that that is not my idea or the idea of any one of the committee.

Mr. GEORGE. I presume it is not.

Mr. SHERMAN. Nor do I believe it is a fair construction of the bill.

Mr. GEORGE. But yet that is the legal meaning and force of the bill; and I will state to the Senate and to the Senator from Ohio that it is directly within the terms of this bill to forbid any number of persons belonging to or joining a temperance society whose object is to compel retailers of intoxicating liquors to give up their business.

Mr. SHERMAN. Where men agree that they will not drink at all, does the Senator think that is a combination in restraint of the trade of liquor-sellers?

Mr. GEORGE. What is it?

Mr. SHERMAN. The Senator, as I understand, now claims that an agreement among several people not to drink whisky or brandy is in restraint of the trade of selling whisky or brandy and is therefore a combination within the meaning of this bill?

Mr. GEORGE. I insist that a society, making an agreement or a combination between citizens of a town anywhere in the Union not to drink, not to use in any way vinous or spirituous liquors, and to persuade others to a similar abstention, does, in the language of this bill, tend to compel persons engaged in retailing liquor in that community to give up their business, and the doing of that is expressly condemned by the third section of this bill. . . .

Mr. [WILLIAM M.] STEWART [R., Nev.]. If an organization for the purpose of having laws passed creating high license is formed, would not that enhance the value of the things prohibited in this bill?

Mr. GEORGE. I have considered that question. I have thought possibly that the courts might say that the right of political organization to bring about political results by legislation was not embraced within the provisions of the bill.

But this bill not only prevents combinations between farmers to raise the price of their products, but it would (though not so intended by the framers) embrace combinations among workingmen to increase the amount of their wages. For an increase in their wages would tend to increase the price of the product to the consumer, and thus the combination would come within the express terms of the bill.

But the bill is futile; it amounts to nothing. In the first place there are two subjects, as named in the first section, concerning which these arrangements or agreements are to be made. The first subject is imports. Now, if there is anything settled in the constitutional law of this country, commencing with the decision of Chief-Justice Marshall in the case of Brown *vs.* Maryland, in 12 Wheaton's Reports,[1.249] and coming down to the present time, it is that the jurisdiction of the Government of the United States under the commercial clause of the Constitution over imports ceases at the moment the import passes out of the hands of the importer, or, remaining in his hands, the package in which it was imported is broken up.

So, then, the first clause of the first section can have no effect beyond an agreement with reference to imports whilst they are still in the hands of the importer and before the package is broken up. Will any Senator say that there has ever been a trust, a combination, or an agreement within the United States between importers before the package had been broken up and before sale in reference to the sale of the imported goods? In all the long list of trusts, of combinations, of arrangements, and of agreements which have been made within the United States for the purpose of fleecing the people I have not as yet heard of a single combination between importers made

---

[1.249] 25 U.S. (12 Wheat.) 419, 6 L. Ed. 419 (1827).

with reference to the sale of the goods imported by them in the original package. So, then, the first clause of this bill is aimed at a phantom, is aimed at an evil which does not exist and which can not exist.

As soon as the article passes out of the hands of the importer, or, remaining in his hands, as soon as the package in which it was imported is broken, it passes beyond the jurisdiction of the United States and is subject to State authority alone, and therefore combinations with reference to these imports in that condition are not reached by this bill, because they are without the jurisdiction of Congress.

We will next go to the other provision in the first section and see how that is. It is as follows:

That all arrangements, contracts, agreements, trusts, or combinations between persons or corporations made with a view, or which tend, to prevent full and free competition * * * in the production, manufacture, or sale of articles of domestic growth or production, or domestic raw material that in due course of trade shall be transported from one State or Territory to another—

Shall be unlawful.

By this provision is drawn within the punitive provisions of this bill every agreement made by farmers not to sell any particular article of their production unless they receive a certain price for it, for that would be an agreement which, under the clause of the first section, which is under consideration, would tend to advance the cost to the consumer of any such articles, and is therefore condemned by the bill. This is another phantom at which this bill is aimed. There is no complaint, there have been no complaints that the farmers of this country have combined for the purpose of raising the price of agricultural products. There have been combinations of that sort, lawful in their character, meritorious in their aims, which have tended to prevent the farmers of this country from being fleeced by these great trusts; and yet under this bill they are condemned and punished. Under its plain provisions, if any grange in the United States, if any agricultural club, if any society called a farmers' alliance, if any number of farmers not embraced in these organizations should agree that they would withhold their products from sale until they could receive a certain price for them, every one of them would be liable to be fined $5,000 and put in the penitentiary for five years. The same is true, as I have shown, of combinations and arrangements made by laborers to increase their wages.

I am not prepared to sustain a bill of that sort merely because it is entitled "A bill to declare trusts and combinations unlawful." It seems that the bill, however honestly intended for good, has its effectual aim at phantoms, and not at the real grievances of the people, nor at the real culprits who have combined to plunder the great mass of the people.

I have shown how little can be done under the import clause to relieve the people of trusts; now let us see how much can be done under the interstate-transportation clause. Let me read that so that we may understand it:

That all arrangements, contracts, etc., made with a view—

I am reading from the first section—

or which tend, to prevent full and free competition * * * in the production, manufacture, or sale of articles of domestic growth or production, or domestic raw material that in due course of trade shall be transported from one State or Territory to another—

Are prohibited.

How much can be done under that? And here note that in the first section of the bill there is not a single provision against the unlawful acts themselves done under these agreements. The first section of the bill is aimed at the agreement alone. If the agreement be made, whether or not it does in fact increase the price or does in fact prevent full and free competition, if it be made with that purpose or with that view, or if it have that tendency, whether these evil results follow or not, then it is liable to the condemnation of the bill. No act however injurious done in pursuance of it is made criminal. The country may be robbed to the amount of millions, and, so far as these acts of pillage and plunder are concerned, they are not condemned by the bill. It is only agreements that are condemned. Here we find another trouble upon that subject. If the agreement be not made within the jurisdiction of the United States, as if it be made in Canada, it is not within the terms of the bill. So that under this bill an agreement may be made at Montreal or on the other side of Niagara Falls or at any other place outside of the jurisdiction of the United States, and then the wrongful acts may be done within the United States and there is no punishment, no redress. You can not punish the agreement, because it was made outside of the jurisdiction of the United States; you can not punish the acts done under the agreement, because there is no provision in the bill which makes these acts subject to its punitory provisions. Scrutinize the bill, read it, study it, and you will find that is its legal effect.

But here is another anomaly about this second clause of the first section. Suppose the agreement be made within the United States. Then whether it shall be held lawful or unlawful, whether it shall come within the provisions of this bill or not, depends upon an act to take place after the agreement is made. So far as this bill is concerned, the agreement may be perfectly lawful at the time it is made and it will become unlawful by a matter which may take place months afterwards, and by an act—and I desire to call the especial attention of the Senator from Ohio to that—and by an act to which the parties to the agreement were in no way privy, and for which they are in no way responsible. For instance, A and B combine to raise the price of domestic products. If the thing stops there they can not be punished under this bill, although that agreement be made within the city of New York; but if C, months afterwards, having acquired some of the goods, some of the articles of merchandise with reference to which this original agreement was made, transports them from one State to another, then the crime is consummated.

What a remarkable anomaly is that in legislation! The agreement when made is lawful, it only becomes unlawful by the subsequent act of men, not parties to it, not privies to it, and, what is more remarkable, it becomes unlawful by the lawful act of these subsequent parties, for it must be noted there is nothing in this bill which makes it unlawful to transport from one State to another goods, merchandise, or articles which are the subject-matter of the prohibited agreement. The original agreement is and so remains lawful because the fact has not transpired and may never transpire, or if it transpires at all it may not transpire for months after the agreement is made, and when that fact does transpire it is a thing which is perfectly lawful in itself. It is not only lawful, but it is meritorious, and yet this subsequent innocent, lawful, and meritorious act relates back to the agreement, and makes it criminal without bringing on itself any criminality whatever. So, then, we have this remarkable anomaly, that two acts both of which are perfectly lawful, done by separate and distinct persons without any privity or connection between the two, just simply by the mere sequence in time of one to the other are compounded into a high crime, and punished by a heavy fine and imprisonment in the penitentiary.

Mr. President, I make that statement deliberately. Senators who have not studied this bill will be astonished to find it so, but it is so nevertheless. The original agreement is not made unlawful until the subsequent transportation takes place. The transportation is not unlawful, nor is it made so by this bill, but it is a meritorious act, being commerce between the States; and yet these two acts done by two separate and distinct persons without the slightest privity, without the slightest concert between them, both being innocent and lawful when they are performed, are by this bill compounded into a high misdemeanor punished by a fine of $5,000 and imprisonment in the penitentiary for five years.

Mr. President, a bill of that sort will not do. You can not make a crime out of a lawful act by matter *ex post facto* done by a person without connection with the original actor. It is lawful to make a gun, but it is unlawful to kill a person with it. In that case when one of the acts was manifestly unlawful, the mind and the conscience would be shocked if by the subsequent unlawful act of the man who committed murder with the gun you should provide that the maker of the gun should be guilty of a crime. In that case one of the acts would be unlawful, but in the case made by this bill both are lawful, and yet a crime results; results, too, from the performance of the subsequent act, which under no circumstances does the bill condemn, but seeks to promote and encourage.

I am asked by a Senator who sits near me to give a specific illustration of the argument which I am making. I will do so. There is a combination made in relation to jute bagging, for instance, produced in this country, not imported. That combination, under the terms of this bill, is not unlawful until there shall be a transportation of the article from one State to another. I will again read the clause under consideration:

> That all arrangements, contracts, * * * to prevent full and free competition in the production, manufacture, or sale of articles of domestic growth or production, or domestic raw material that in due course of trade shall be transported from one State or Territory to another, etc., shall be unlawful.

So that the Senator will clearly see that it is not the agreement or combination *per se* that is made unlawful, nor is the subsequent transportation unlawful; but if the lawful agreement be followed, however distant in time, by the subsequent transportation, then by this sequence alone a crime is made of the agreement.

This provision about transportation is inserted to draw this subject within the commercial power of Congress. Without the subject of transportation or without some provision with reference to transportation from one State to another, the bill would be manifestly unconstitutional, and therefore its framers were compelled to put in a subsequent act of transportation from one State to another, so that up to the time that transportation takes place the agreement, the trust, the combination is perfectly lawful, not only by the terms of the bill, but for want of constitutional power in us to make it anything else. . . .

Mr. EUSTIS. If I understand the difficulty which is presented by the argument of the Senator from Mississippi, it is that the jurisdiction, the power of Congress is derived from the fact of transportation from one State to another, in order to exercise that power under the commercial clause. I would ask the Senator whether the power of Congress would exist if the language were "shall or may be transported," etc.? In other words, I ask whether the power of Congress is conferred by the Constitution, dependent on the act of actual transportation and is confined to that, or whether the power of Congress may be applied to the transportable merchandise; so that if this bill were to read "shall or may be transported," would that correct the defect which has been pointed out by the Senator from Mississippi?

Mr. GEORGE. Upon that point in the latter part of my remarks I expect to be full and explicit. At this stage I will merely state to the Senator in answer to his question that "shall or may be" would make no difference; that the power of Congress exists only over the subject so far as it comes from transportation, while the transportation is being carried on; that the power of Congress does not begin as to the subject until transportation begins, and it ends when transportation is completed. Upon that point I expect to make some remarks before I get through.

The trouble about this bill is that it is an attempt to do the impossible. It is an attempt to draw within the commercial power of Congress jurisdiction over this subject by the provision about transportation. That is the trouble.

There is another serious defect in the bill. It relates only to agreements, combinations, arrangements between two or more. It leaves wholly out of view acts of oppression and plunder when done by a single individual. If he be a great capitalist, so that by his own unaided means he can so provide to increase prices to the consumer or reduce prices to the producer, he is not touched by this bill. For, as I have shown, it is the agreements, combinations, between two or more, and the like which are punished, and not the wrongful acts which these agreements and combinations were designed to promote.

Mr. President, I believe that I have said about all I desire to say in the way of analysis and comment upon the bill, and I will go now to the point to which my attention was directed by the question of the Senator from Louisiana.

It is not denied anywhere by the friends and supporters of this bill that the power to pass it is claimed under the commerce clause of the Constitution. Certainly under no other clause can there be the slightest pretense for the claim of this power.

Now, let us see what is the extent of that power under the commercial clause of the Constitution. It is a power to "regulate commerce," foreign and interstate, not a police power to regulate the general business of the people. That power is reserved to the States. The Supreme Court said in Railroad Company *vs.* Husen, 95 United States Reports, page 465, that this police power of the States extends—

to the protection of all property within the State. * * * By it persons and property are subject to all kinds of restraint and burdens in order to secure the general comfort, health, and prosperity of the State.[1.250]

And Judge McLean, in the License Cases, 5 Howard, page 588, said:

The States, resting upon their original basis of sovereignty, * * * exercise their powers over everything connected with their social and internal condition. A State regulates domestic commerce, contracts, the transmission of estates, real and personal, and acts upon all internal matters which relate to its moral and political welfare. Over these subjects the Federal Government has no power.[1.251]

These combinations and trusts, therefore, are clearly within the police power of the States. I ask the Senator from Louisiana, would it be lawful or constitutional for the State of Louisiana, or any other State, to pass a law punishing persons entering into these combinations and trusts within their respective limits, whether or not the subjects about which the trusts were made should afterwards become subjects of foreign or of interstate commerce?

Mr. EUSTIS. I think the States have the power.

Mr. GEORGE. You think they have, and I agree with you. If they have Congress has not, because there is a dividing line plainly marked by the decisions of the Supreme Court of the United States, upon one side of which rests the police power of the State, and on the other the commercial power of Congress. That power is granted in these words: "Congress shall have power to regulate commerce with foreign nations and among the several States." It is a power of regulation, and a regulation only of commerce, not a regulation of something which may in the near or remote future become a subject of foreign or interstate commerce. The regulation must be of the act or the transaction of commerce itself. . . .

Mr. EUSTIS. In a case where the State of Kansas or the State of Iowa prohibits the sale of intoxicating liquors, I should like to ask the Senator whether, in his opinion, Congress has the constitutional power to prohibit the transportation of liquors into those States?

Mr. GEORGE. The States have no such power. That has been settled.

Mr. EUSTIS. I ask if Congress has.

Mr. GEORGE. Congress would have the power to prevent anything from being transported into the States.

Mr. EUSTIS. Very well. Now the argument of the Senator from Mississippi has been that the actual fact of transportation is what gives Congress power and jurisdiction under the commercial clause. Now he admits that in the absence of any act of transportation Congress can exercise that power.

Mr. GEORGE. Why, Mr. President, the regulation of commerce—

Mr. EUSTIS. It is no transportation.

Mr. GEORGE. It is a prohibition of transportation. It regulates the transportation. This is done in a prohibition of transportation, and this is a regulation of commerce as was decided with reference to the embargo enacted under the administration of Jefferson.

Mr. EUSTIS. Therefore I do not understand how the Senator reconciles the argument he has made with the position he now takes, that the fact of actual transportation is what confers the jurisdiction upon Congress, and yet he admits that Congress has the power to prohibit the transportation of goods and exercises that power in a case where there is no actual transportation.

Mr. GEORGE. The answer to that is this: Congress has the power to regulate interstate transportation; it may either prohibit it altogether, or when it takes place may regulate the means and methods of carrying it on. But because Congress may prohibit

---

[1.250] 95 U.S. 465, 471, 24 L. Ed. 527, 530 (1878).

[1.251] Thurlow v. Massachusetts, 46 U.S. (5 How.) 504, 588, 12 L. Ed. 256, 294 (1847).

the transportation of an article in interstate or in foreign commerce, it does not follow, as would seem to be the view of the Senator from Louisiana, that Congress may assume jurisdiction over matters entirely within the jurisdiction of the States merely because they may become the subject of interstate commerce, transportation being one of the means of interstate commerce.

Mr. EUSTIS. That is exactly the case that I stated, where Congress prohibits the transportation of liquors, for instance, to the State of Kansas. The power conferred upon Congress is not to prohibit, it is to regulate, and that power of regulation is exercised in the absence of any actual transportation; and the Senator from Mississippi informs us that in his opinion that power is rightfully exercised. Therefore I ask him if that be so how can it be necessary that the actual transportation should be the jurisdictional fact with reference to this bill?

Mr. GEORGE. Whenever Congress undertakes to regulate interstate transportation, as it does in this bill, then there must be transportation to regulate; but where Congress in the exercise of its power, as it has the undoubted power, in regulating interstate commerce, to prohibit the transportation of certain articles, they may do that. The power of Congress, says Chief-Justice Marshall, is to regulate commerce, which includes intercourse.

It is regulated by prescribing rules for carrying on that intercourse.

Not prescribing rules for subjects, as I will show hereafter by the decisions of the Supreme Court, which are within the jurisdiction of the States, merely because those subjects may afterwards become the subjects of interstate commerce. Chief-Justice Marshall's language is, "to make rules for carrying on that intercourse." It is not "carrying on that intercourse" until there is actual commerce or the beginning of commerce between two or more States.

I am now trying to ascertain the limits of the power of Congress on the subject. I now quote from Chief-Justice Taney in the License Cases, in 5 Howard's Reports:[1.252]

That imports ceased to be such when sold by the importer, or the original package was broken. This—

Chief-Justice Taney understands—

to be substantially the line between foreign commerce, which is subject to the regulation of Congress, and internal and domestic commerce, which belongs to the States, and over which Congress can exercise no control.[1.253]

McLean, justice, in the same case, after adopting the rule as to imports ceasing to be such when this happens, says of the imported article:

The imported article becomes mingled with the other property of the State and is subject to its laws.[1.254]

This power is claimed here, as I understand it, not because there is any actual commerce between States or citizens of States, but because the subjects to which this bill relates may afterwards become the subjects of interstate commerce. Now, let us see how that stands in constitutional law. . . .

I have shown as to imports that the power of Congress ceased when they passed out of the hands of the importer or when the original package was broken up. That is the end of the power of Congress. Now, I desire to call the attention of the Senate to some decisions of the Supreme Court of the United States which fix the time when the power begins, and especially I desire to call the attention of the Senator from Louisiana to that subject. This bill is framed on the idea that Congress may take jurisdiction of the subject, because at some time hereafter this subject may become a matter of interstate commerce; and on that point the decisions of the Supreme Court of the United States are uniform without one single break. I propose now to read some extracts from the decisions of the Supreme Court on that point.

[1.252] 46 U.S. (5 How.) at 574-75.
[1.253] *Id.*
[1.254] *Id.* at 589 (concurring opinion).

In the case of Veazie vs. Moore [sic], 14 Howard, 568, the court say [sic]:

Commerce with foreign nations must signify commerce which is necessarily connected with these nations, transactions which either immediately or at some stage of their progress must be extraterritorial.[1.255]

Not "may be," but "must be extraterritorial." This bill is framed on the idea that "may be" will do. This is expressly overruled in the language I have read.

The phrase can never be applied to transactions wholly internal between citizens of the same community, or to a polity and laws whose end and purposes and operations are restricted to the territory and soil and jurisdiction of such community.

Nor can it be properly concluded that because the products of domestic enterprise in agriculture, or manufactures, or in the arts, may ultimately become subjects of foreign commerce, that the control of the means or the encouragements by which enterprise is fostered is legitimately within the import of the phrase "foreign commerce," or fairly implied in any investiture of the power to regulate such commerce.[1.256]

That decision overthrows the theory of this bill that these products of agriculture, of manufactures, and of the mines may ultimately become the subjects of foreign or interstate commerce, and therefore before they do actually become such the United States Congress will interpose and regulate them. The court go [sic] on to say:

A pretension as far-reaching as this would extend to contracts between citizen and citizen of the same State, and would control the pursuits of the planter, the grazier, the mechanic, the immense operations of the collieries and mines and furnaces of the country, for there is not one of these avocations the results of which may not become the subjects of foreign commerce.[1.257]

And afterwards this same language is applied to interstate commerce. This case is exactly in point, and establishes the unconstitutionality of this bill. Though an old case it never has been overruled nor its doctrines departed from. In a very recent case, to wit, Lord *vs.* Steam-ship Company, 102 United States Reports,[1.258] it was cited and confirmed. But there is another case, and a very recent one, which defines this matter with some care and precision. I read now from the case of Coe *vs.* Errol, volume 116 United States Reports, page 525:

There must be a point of time when they—

That is, articles of merchandise—

cease to be governed exclusively by the domestic law and begin to be governed and protected by the national law of commercial regulation, and that moment seems to us to be a legitimate one for this purpose, in which they commence their final movement for transportation from the State of their origin to that of their destination. When the products of the farm or the forest are collected and brought in from the surrounding country to a town or station serving as an entrepôt for that particular region, whether on a river or a line of railroad, such products are not yet exports, nor are they in process of exportation, nor is exportation begun until they are committed to the common carrier for transportation out of the State to the State of their destination, or have started on their ultimate passage to that State. Until then it is reasonable to regard them as not only within the State of their origin, but as a part of the general mass of property of that State, subject to its jurisdiction.[1.259]

Here is another sentence a little more explicit answering the argument that they were intended for exportation, and when they were thus intended they become the subjects of the power of Congress. The court say [sic] on that subject:

Though intended for exportation, they may never be exported; the owner has a perfect right to change his mind; and until actually put in motion, for some place out of the State, or committed to the custody of a carrier for transportation to such place, why may they not be regarded as still remaining a part of the general mass of property in the State?[1.260]

[1.255] Veazie v. Moor, 55 U.S. (14 How.) 568, 573, 14 L. Ed. 545, 547 (1852).
[1.256] 55 U.S. (14 How.) at 574.
[1.257] *Id.*
[1.258] Lord v. Goodall, Nelson & Perkins S.S. Co., 102 U.S. 541, 26 L. Ed. 224 (1881).
[1.259] Coe v. Town of Errol, 116 U.S. 517, 525, 6 S. Ct. 475, 477, 29 L. Ed. 715, 718 (1886).
[1.260] 116 U.S. at 526.

The court proceeds on page 528 thus:

Some of the Western States produce very little except wheat and corn, most of which is intended for export; and so of cotton in the Southern States. Certainly as long as these articles are on the land which produced them they are a part of the general property of the State, and so we think they continue to be until they have entered upon their final journey for leaving the State and going into another state. * * * This movement does not begin until the articles have been shipped or started for transportation from one State to another.

* * * * * * *

Until actually launched on its way to another State or committed to a common carrier for transportation to such State, its destination is not fixed and certain. It may be sold or otherwise disposed of within the State, and never put in course of transportation out of the State. * * * Until shipped or started on its final journey out of the State, its exportation is matter *in fieri*, and not at all a fixed and certain thing.

So that if anything is settled in the constitutional law of this country it is that an article of commerce, an article of merchandise, does not become the subject of Congressional jurisdiction under the commercial clause of the Constitution until it has actually become the subject of interstate or foreign commerce, and that this does not begin, though it may be intended for that purpose, until transportation has actually commenced. That was the decision in Veazie *vs.* Moore [*sic*], made many years ago, and also in the case to which I have just called the attention of the Senate.

My attention is called by my colleague [Mr. WALTHALL] to a still more recent case decided at the October term, 1888, the case of Kidd *vs.* Pearson, in which the court say [*sic*]:

This court has already decided that the fact that an article was manufactured for export to another State does not of itself make it an article of interstate commerce within the meaning of section 8, Article I, of the Constitution, and that the intent of the manufacturer—

The intent of the manufacturer—

does not determine the time when the article or product passes from the control of the State and belongs to commerce.[1.261]

Then the court refer [*sic*] to the case which I have just read and approve [*sic*] it. That was the view of the Senator from Ohio himself in the beginning of this controversy, as shown by the RECORD. I do not state this for the purpose of convicting the Senator from Ohio of any inconsistency, but as a support and a strong support of the views which I entertain. On August 14, 1888, the Senator from Texas [Mr. REAGAN] introduced a bill on the subject of trusts, which will be found printed on page 7512 of volume 19, part 8, of the CONGRESSIONAL RECORD, and is as follows:

Mr. REAGAN, introduced a bill (S. 3440) to define trusts and to provide for the punishment of persons connected with them or carrying them on; . . .

"*Be it enacted, etc.*, That a trust is the combination of capital or skill by two or more persons for the following purposes:

"First. To create or carry out restrictions on trade.

"Second. To limit, to reduce, or to increase the production or prices of merchandise or commodities.

"Third. To prevant [*sic*] competition in the manufacture, making, sale, or purchase of merchandise or commodities.

"Fourth. To create a monopoly.

"SEC. 2. That any person who may be or may become a member of any such trust, or who may be or may become engaged in the business of any such trust in any trade or business carried on with foreign countries, or between the States or between any State or Territory and the District of Columbia, or between the District of Columbia and any Territory, or between the United States and the waters adjacent to any foreign country, shall be guilty of a high misdemeanor, and on conviction thereof in any district or circuit court of the United States, after indictment shall be fined in a sum of not more than $10,000 nor less than $1,000, and may be imprisoned in the penitentiary for a period of not more than five years and not less than one year.

[1.261] 128 U.S. 1, 24, 9 S. Ct. 6, 11, 32 L. Ed. 346, 351 (1888).

"SEC. 3. That the purchase by any trust, or by the agent of any trust, of merchandise or commodities in a foreign country for sale in this country; or the manufacture, making, or purchase of any merchandise or commodity in this country for sale in a foreign country; or the manufacture, making, or purchase of any merchandise or commodity in one State for sale in another; or in any State or Territory for sale in the District of Columbia; or in the District of Columbia for sale in any State or Territory; or in any Territory for sale in any other Territory or in any State or in the District of Columbia, shall constitute a violation of this act, and shall subject the offender to the aforesaid penalties."

On the motion to refer that bill to the Committee on the Judiciary the Senator from Ohio said this:

Mr. SHERMAN. I wish to say that the Committee on Finance has already been charged with the consideration of this subject. I have myself given some ⊥ attention to it, to see how far it is within the constitutional power of Congress to prohibit trusts and combinations in restraint of trade. It is very clear there is no such power unless it is derived from the power of levying taxes—

⊥1462

Not from the power to regulate commerce, but from the power of levying taxes—

that it is a power which must be exercised by each State for itself. Similar laws have been passed in England and in other countries. Indeed, in Blackstone's Commentaries there are declarations and denunciations of trusts, monopolies, etc., as strong as can be written in the English language. Whether such legislation can be ingrafted in our peculiar system of government by the national authority there is some doubt. If it can be done at all, it must be done upon a tariff bill or upon a revenue bill. I do not see in what other way it can be done.

So at that time the Senator who is the author of this bill concurred in the views which I have expressed upon that subject; and on July 10 of the same year—I read from the CONGRESSIONAL RECORD, volume 19, part 7—the Senator introduced the following resolution:

Resolved, That the Committee on Finance be directed to inquire into and report, in connection with any bill raising or reducing revenue that may be referred to it, such measures as it may deem expedient to set aside, control, restrain, or prohibit all arrangements, contracts, agreements, trusts, or combinations between persons or corporations, made with a view, or which tend to prevent free and full competition in the production, manufacture, or sale of articles of domestic growth or production, or of the sale of articles imported into the United States, or which, against public policy, are designed or tend to foster monopoly or to artificially advance the cost to the consumer of necessary articles of human life, with such penalties and provisions, and as to corporations, with such forfeitures, as will tend to preserve freedom of trade and production, the natural competition of increasing production, the lowering of prices by such competition, and the full benefit designed by and hitherto conferred by the policy of the Government to protect and encourage American industries by levying duties on imported goods.[1.262]

The referring of the matter to the Committee on Finance would have been inappropriate, unless it was designed that legislation on this subject should be a part of the revenue system of this country.

So that the Senator who is the author of this bill, with his great learning and his great experience and his well-trained mind, in the beginning of our consideration of this subject took the same view of it that I do. To show what he meant by taking jurisdiction of it in connection with the tariff and the power to levy taxes, I will read from a speech made by that Senator on January 4, 1888, in which he commented upon the President's message,[1.263] from the President as follows:

But it is notorious that this competition is too often strangled by combinations quite prevalent at this time, and frequently called trusts, which have for their object the regulation of the supply and price of commodities made and sold by members of the combination.

That was a quotation from the President. Now here is the reply of the Senator from Ohio:

[1.262] 19 CONG. REC. 6041 (1888), *supra* at 54-55.

[1.263] President Grover Cleveland's third annual message, Dec. 6, 1887.

When such combinations to prevent a reduction of price by fair competition exist, I agree that they may and ought to be met by a reduction of duty.

That is what was meant by the Senator from Ohio in restricting the power of Congress over the subject of trusts to legislation in connection with the revenue laws of the country.

Mr. President, I have said about all I desire to say on this subject at present. I shall offer some amendments to the bill at a later stage of these proceedings, based upon the ideas announced by the Senator from Ohio, amendments which look to a suspension or a reduction of the duties on imports where combinations and trusts have been formed in this country with reference to similar and competing articles.

I will also offer amendments which look to outlawing these trusts by preventing their admission into the courts of the United States to collect any debt due them or to redress any wrong done them; and also declaring the products and manufactures of all such trusts shall not be lawful subjects of interstate commerce.

For the present I desire simply to say in addition to what I have already said that the bill as now framed is ineffectual to carry out the objects and purposes for which it was introduced, and for which it was designed by its framer; that it is without constitutional authority, as settled by the Supreme Court of the United States in a long line of decisions coming down even to the present term of the court, and that in response to the demand of the people of this country, coming from every part of it, if we now pass this bill and nothing more we shall do nothing effectual in respect to the suppression of trusts. If the bill be constitutional it does not contain the provisions which are necessary to make it effective, and it does contain provisions which bring within the force and operation of the law numerous arrangements and agreements made by the producers of raw material in this country which have hitherto been regarded as a perfectly innocent exercise of the power of combination, and which have never been brought into operation to the extent of injuring a single human being, and which have been used solely for the purpose of defensive measures against the trusts which this bill vainly attempts to put down.

[ED. NOTE: There was no further debate on S. 3445.]

SENATE CONSIDERATION (S. 1)

S. 1[1.264]
51st Cong., 1st Sess.
December 4, 1889

Mr. SHERMAN introduced the following bill; which was read twice and referred to the Committee on Finance.

A BILL

To declare unlawful trusts and combinations in restraint of trade and production.

1   *Be it enacted by the Senate and House of Representa-*
2   *tives of the United States of America in Congress assembled,*
3   That all arrangements, contracts, agreements, trusts, or com-
4   binations between persons or corporations made with a view,
5   or which tend, to prevent full and free competition in the im-
6   portation, transportation, or sale of articles imported into the
7   United States, or in the production, manufacture, or sale of
8   articles of domestic growth or production, or domestic raw
9   material that competes with any similar article upon which a
10 duty is levied by the United States, or which shall be trans-
11 ported from one State or Territory to another, and all ar-
12 rangements, contracts, agreements, trusts, or combinations
13 between persons or corporations designed, or which tend, to
14 advance the cost to the consumer of any such articles, are
15 hereby declared to be against public policy, unlawful, and
16 void.
1   SEC. 2. That any person or corporation injured or damni-
2   fied by such arrangement, contract, agreement, trust, or com-
3   bination may sue for and recover, in any court of the United
4   States of competent jurisdiction of any person or corporation
5   a party to a combination described in the first section of this
6   act, the full consideration or sum paid by him for any goods,
7   wares, and merchandise included in or advanced in price by
8   said combination.
1   SEC. 3. That all persons entering into any such ar-
2   rangement, contract, agreement, trust, or combination de-

---

[1.264] S. 1 was identical to S. 3445, 50th Cong., 2d Sess., as reported with an amendment by Senator Sherman from the Committee on Finance on September 11, 1888. *See supra* at 64–65.

3   scribed in section one of this act, either on his own account or
4   as agent or attorney for another, or as an officer, agent, or
5   stockholder of any corporation, or as a trustee, committee, or
6   in any capacity whatever, shall be guilty of a high misde-
7   meanor, and on conviction thereof in any district or circuit
8   court of the United States shall be subject to a fine of not
9   more than ten thousand dollars, or to imprisonment in the
10 penitentiary for a term of not more than five years, or to
11 both such fine and imprisonment, in the discretion of the
12 court. And it shall be the duty of the district attorney of
13 the United States of the district in which such persons reside
14 to institute the proper proceedings to enforce the provisions
15 of this act.

RESOLUTION OF SEN. DAVID TURPIE
51st Cong., 1st Sess.
December 9, 1889

21 CONG. REC. 125

Mr. TURPIE [D., Ind.]. I offer a resolution, which I ask to have read.
The PRESIDENT *pro tempore*. The resolution will be read.
The Chief Clerk read as follows:

Resolved, That the proposed penal enactments against trusts affecting commerce among the several States should provide for the seizure of trust goods, as such, upon lawful warrant and information, and for the forfeiture, confiscation, and sale of the same, upon due process of trial and hearing, if they be adjudged and found to be such, the proceeds to be paid into the Treasury of the United States, less the costs of prosecution.

Mr. TURPIE. Mr. President, I ask that the resolution for the present be laid upon the table and printed, and I give notice that tomorrow, immediately after the conclusion of the morning hour, I shall move to take it from the table for consideration, with a view of making some remarks.
The PRESIDENT *pro tempore*. The resolution will be laid on the table and printed.

REMARKS OF SEN. DAVID TURPIE
51st Cong., 1st Sess.
December 10, 1889

21 CONG. REC. 137

[ED. NOTE: While Senator Turpie's remarks were not made when the Senate was considering S. 1, the concepts of forfeiture, seizure, and condemnation of trust property were embodied in the final version of the bill reported by the Senate Judiciary Committee. *See infra* at **277**. Provisions for seizure, forfeiture, and condemnation were also contained in a bill offered by Senator Cullom, S. 3510, 50th Cong., 1st Sess. (1888), which was referred to the Finance Committee but never reported out of committee. See BILLS & DEBATES at 35-37.]

The PRESIDENT *pro tempore*. The question is on agreeing to the resolution, upon which the Senator from Indiana is entitled to the floor.

Mr. TURPIE. Mr. President, a trust, in the most recent acceptation of the term, is a union or combination, rarely of individuals, usually of corporations, dealing in or producing a certain commodity, of the total amount of which belonging to them a common stock is made with the intention of holding and selling the same at an enhanced price, by suppressing or limiting the supply and by other devices, so that the price of such trust commodity shall depend merely upon the agreement made about it by those in the combination, without reference to the cost of its production, the quantity of the article held for consumption, or the demand therefor among buyers.

The act of fixing the price of the commodity, the ultimate result of this confederated association, and sometimes the handling of its goods and funds, are intrusted to one or more persons, called the syndicate, or executive committee, from which intrusting the scheme takes its name. The ultimate fixing of a price upon the common stock is done without the least consideration of any legitimate element either of a sale or purchase in the open market, and depends for its efficiency not upon any law or known rule of trade or commerce, but only upon the binding force, tenor, and tension of the trust agreement. . . .

⊥ The bill of the Senator from Ohio [Mr. SHERMAN] and that of the Senator from Mississippi [Mr. GEORGE] providing for the suppression of trusts ought to meet with general favor. It is proposed to make the organization of these combinations a penal offense, and to punish those engaged therein. Such a law ought to include all those who in any manner aid or abet such organizations, whether they be accessories before or after the fact. While I would not hold as amenable to such penalties a shipper or forwarder who, without knowledge, received and carried trust commodities, yet one of this class who knowingly did so, thus intentionally lending aid to the consummation of the criminal purpose, ought to be charged, tried, convicted, and punished as a confederate. . . . ⊥ 139

. . . [T]his great commonwealth of traffic, briefly described in modern phrase as interstate commerce, is the peculiar sphere and field, a republic within a republic, segregated, set apart, held in suspension as it were, as subject to the special supervisory regulation of Congress. It embraces in its jurisdiction all the persons, all the things, all the means and instrumentalities engaged or employed in commerce among the several States in the same manner and to the same extent as those used or concerned in commerce with foreign nations or with the Indian tribes. This is a high national police power, and Congress within the scope of it has the same right to deal with the actors in and subjects of interstate commerce, in the interest of honest trade and public policy, as a State may have over traffic within its own limits. . . .

⊥ There is no doubt that the methods of regulation adopted by us in the three provinces of Indian, foreign, and interstate commerce are mutually interchangeable by legislative enactment, in our discretion. The power is neither more nor less in one of these provinces than another. . . . ⊥ 140

Congress has made the importation of dutiable goods, without the payment of duty, a penal offense. The regulation for the punishment of those guilty thereof is as old as the Government. But legislation has not stopped here. The goods themselves, made use of to defraud the revenue, are, by the same regulation, liable to seizure, forfeiture, and sale. The sale of certain commodities to the Indian tribes is interdicted, and those engaged in such sales are denounced and punished; but it is a part of the same regulation that the goods used or designed for use in such illegal traffic shall be liable to seizure and the like condemnation.

The goods and wares of a trust placed in transit or in store, designed to carry out the objects and purposes of such conspiracy, are contraband of good faith, of common honesty, of all honorable and fair dealing, and should also be subject in like manner to seizure, forfeiture, and sale. They are no more entitled to protection, exemption, or favor than the goods of the smuggler or the Indian contrabandist.

In making a regulation of commerce among the several States which shall denounce the trust as a penal offense, we ought to add to it a provision that on information filed by the proper district attorney, upon affidavit of any collector of internal revenue or of the customs, or any private citizen, the goods, wares, and merchandise of any trust combination shall be seized, and ascertained, upon due process and trial, to be such, shall be forfeited, confiscated, and sold, the proceeds to go to the public treasury, except what may be necessary to pay the costs of the prosecution and a substantial reward to the informer.

It may be said such a policy will fill the country with spies and informers—it will empty it of trusts. The remedy may be considered harsh—the wrong is not a mild one. It is the gigantic commercial sin of this age and generation. I do not wish to palliate the offense of smuggling, of false invoicing, of fraudulent undervaluation, or of illicit trade with Indians; but what are these compared to the iniquity of a system which honeycombs the whole world of domestic commerce with fraud, with falsehood, with suspicion, distrust, and impurity?

There is nothing in the proposed legislation against trusts which encroaches upon or infringes the just rights of persons or property. The trust is a nuisance, open and notorious, but can not itself be taken, destroyed, or abated as other unlawful injuries to the public. It is an enormous obstruction to interstate trade and commerce, more dangerous than any of those whose removal has ever been contemplated by the acts for the improvement of rivers, harbors, or highways; but it can not be reached, apprehended, or dealt with like these.

The essence of the trust is the guilty intention of the conspirators. This intention is invisible, intangible, not the subject of physical prehension or discernment. Wherefore, in this class of cases the most ancient usage of the law-maker is to attach and seize upon the things made use of in the perpetration of the crime. The guilt in such cases, without quitting the offender, is transferred, extended to the means and implements he uses. These are deemed by their use to be forfeit, as lawful deodands, to the Government whose law has been violated. Also, it sometimes occurs that the owner of smuggled goods or merchandise otherwise contraband of law can not be known, or if known can not be apprehended, yet the things themselves can be known, designated, identified as designed for an illicit purpose, wherefore the rights of proprietorship of the owner, known or unknown, are justly deemed to be lost and abandoned.

It is not probable that these seizures of trust goods would be frequent or that the number of informers would be very great. A few convictions and sales under such an act would suffice to break the spine of this monopoly. The risk and hazard of the adventure would be such as to soon banish these combinations from our trade and to work their perpetual final dissolution.

The conspirators of the trust, these scoffing assassins of our commercial liberties, are now in the full and undisturbed enjoyment of successful operation. They are hunting the prey, dividing the spoil in every market. They are making use of the courts and the laws of the country to enforce their contracts, to uphold their credit, and to clothe and cloak their designs with efficiency and validity.

Is the law, then, to be used as a shield to shelter and defend these baneful forces, and is there no weapon in the arsenal of legislative stores to grapple with and throttle these depredators upon our commerce and spoliators of public faith and credit? It is not to be conceived but that the framers and founders of our form of government did foresee the vast and profluent current of trade among the several States; did clearly perceive the evils which might threaten it—the evils which itself might induce upon the body-politic. They have not left us without a way of escape or without the means of remedy.

The trusts are strong, based upon the principle of voluntary association for an unlawful purpose, backed by millions of treasure, directed by sagacity and ability of the highest character; but there is an organization yet stronger. It is the nation, the people of the United States; their representative is the Government, their authority is that of law, and armed with this we may assail and overthrow these enemies. If injustice and the most flagrant wrong have shaped, formed, and organized themselves to pirate upon the earnings of the people, justice may bare and use, not in vain, its sword, to strike down the offense and the offenders.

S. 1 AS REPORTED BY THE SENATE COMMITTEE ON FINANCE
51st Cong., 1st Sess.
January 14, 1890

[ED. NOTE: This revised version of S. 1 was not accompanied by a report.]

Reported by Mr. SHERMAN with amendments, viz: Omit the parts struck through and insert the parts printed in *italics*.

A BILL

To declare unlawful trusts and combinations in restraint of trade and production.

1 *Be it enacted by the Senate and House of Representa-*
2 *tives of the United States of America in Congress assembled,*
3 That all arrangements, contracts, agreements, trusts or com-
4 binations between persons or corporations made with ~~a view,~~
5 ~~or which tend~~ *the intention* to prevent full and free competi-
6 tion in the importation, transportation, or sale of articles im-
7 ported into the United States, or in the production, manu-
8 facture, or sale of articles of domestic growth or production,
9 or domestic raw material, that competes with any similar
10 article upon which a duty is levied by the United States, or
11 *intended for and* which shall be transported from one State or
12 Territory to another *for sale,* and all *such* arrangements, con-
13 tracts, agreements, trusts, or combinations between persons
14 or corporations ~~designed, or which tend,~~ *intended* to ad-
15 vance the cost to the consumer of any such articles, a [*sic*]
16 hereby declared to be against public policy, unlawful, and
17 void.

1 SEC. 2. That any person or corporation injured or damni-
2 fied by such arrangement, contract, agreement, trust, or com-
3 bination may sue for and recover, in any court of the United
4 States of competent jurisdiction, of any person or corporation
5 a party to a combination described in the first section of this
6 act, ~~the full consideration or sum paid by him for any goods,~~
7 ~~wares, and merchandise included in or advanced in price by~~
8 ~~said combination~~ *twice the amount of the damages sustained,*
9 *and the costs of suit.*

1 SEC. 3. That all persons entering into any such ar-
2 rangement, contract, agreement, trust, or combination de-
3 scribed in section one of this act, either on his own account or
4 as agent or attorney for another, or as an officer, agent, or
5 stockholder of any corporation, or as a trustee, committee, or
6 in any capacity whatever, shall be guilty of a high misde-
7 meanor, and on conviction thereof in any district or circuit
8 court of the United States shall be subject to a fine of not

9 more than ten thousand dollars, or to imprisonment in the
10 penitentiary for a term of not more than five years, or to
11 both such fine and imprisonment, in the discretion of the
12 court. And it shall be the duty of the district attorney of
13 the United States of the district in which such persons reside
14 to institute the proper proceedings to enforce the provisions
15 of this act.

SENATE DEBATE
51st Cong., 1st Sess.
February 27, 1890

21 CONG. REC. 1765

The Senate, as in Committee of the Whole, proceeded to the consideration of the bill (S. 1) to declare unlawful trusts and combinations in restraint of trade and production. . . .

Mr. SHERMAN. I do not intend to say anything with respect to the bill at this time; perhaps not at all, unless it becomes necessary. I wish to give notice, however, that I am directed by the Committee on Finance to move to strike out the third section of the bill, so that Senators may understand that that amendment is proposed by the Committee on Finance, and probably some modification will be made of the amendments that have already been reported. With this remark I leave the matter to the Senator from Mississippi.

Mr. GEORGE. Mr. President, I regard this legislation, or rather legislation on the subject-matter of this bill, as possibly the most important matter to come before the present Congress, and for that reason I have prepared with some care the remarks which I propose to submit to the Senate in opposition to the bill as it now stands, both as to its efficiency, if it be constitutional, and also upon the question of the constitutional power of Congress to enact it.

A careful analysis of the terms of the bill is essential. We must know what it means, what its legal effect is, if we give force to it as it is written. It is somewhat obscure; in some parts ambiguous. It is a criminal and penal statute. Its second section provides for the recovery of a penalty. Its third and last section provides for an indictment and punishment of offenders for crimes defined in the first.

In considering such a bill Congress must necessarily determine with care what will be its meaning and effect in the courts. This is essential to prevent a result which would be both absurd and highly prejudicial, to wit, that Congress means one thing in passing the bill and the courts in enforcing it shall give it another and different meaning.

We must adopt, therefore, the known methods of the courts in determining what the bill means. Before passage this is a high duty, to prevent misconception and, from that, injustice. After its enactment we have no power of construction. It is then the sole duty of the courts to construe it to find out our meaning and intention in making the law. In the sense in which they interpret it, it becomes the law of the land, however contrary that intent may be to the individual opinion of Senators who vote for it.

Being a penal statute, and nothing else, it will be construed strictly in favor of alleged violators. Nothing will be brought within it which is outside of its plain words. Enlargement by construction will not be allowed. The party charged with violating it can stand, and will stand, on the strict letter of the statute. The courts will not go an inch beyond this in trying and punishing alleged offenders.

I proceed now to the analysis of the bill, to see what it provides for, what it prohibits, what it punishes, and what it permits as lawful.

In the first place, it must be noted that the bill deals only with agreements, arrangements, and combinations. It denounces and punishes these when made with a certain intent, but it neither punishes nor affects in the least any act done in pursuance of these combinations. It punishes a conspiracy with intent to do certain things, but treats these things when done as perfectly lawful, as harmless, even meritorious.

The making of the combination with the prohibited intent is the *corpus delicti*, the criminal act denounced by the statute. That and nothing more is the crime. The crime, in the main, is complete and perfect when this agreement is made. It makes no difference, so far as the bill goes, except in one case, whether acts are afterwards done in pursuance of the agreement or not. If no such act be done, still the making or entering into the agreement is criminal and punishable. If such act be done, it is neither punishable in itself, nor does it aggravate ⊥ in any way the criminality of the combination, or agreement, or whatever else the thing may be called. It is not a case (and this must be borne in mind) where the original agreement is one of a series of acts, all of which are necessary to be done in order to constitute the crime. But the entering into the agreement or combination (for these words cover the whole of the words descriptive of the crime as used in the bill) is *per se* the crime and the whole of it.

The first thing which attracts our attention, therefore, is that if the agreement or combination, which is the crime, be made outside of the jurisdiction of the United States it is also without the terms of the law and can not be punished in the United States. Mark that. Then if these conspirators are foreigners and remain at home, or, being citizens, shall cross our borders and enter into any foreign territory and there make the combination or agreement they escape the criminal part of this law; and proceedings carrying out the combination may be carried on with impunity in the United States. The raising of prices and the prevention of free and full competition may all take place in the United States, and yet no crime has been committed.

That this is a serious and not a mere fanciful and hypothetical objection is manifest. For it is certain, if the bill become a law, all combinations and agreements involving large amounts and therefore seriously affecting the welfare of the people of the United States will be made outside of the jurisdiction of the United States. Canada and Mexico are near neighbors, and the former will certainly become the locality in which these agreements will be made, as it has become the refuge of embezzlers at this day. The law will therefore operate only on little sinners, little men, combining with reference to interests so small as not to justify the expense and trouble of a visit to Canada or Mexico in order to make the agreement or combination. So that the bill is a sham so far as the real criminals are concerned, the men whose wealth enables them to fleece and rob the people.

But suppose, what I think, however, is highly improbable, some of these great combinations should be made in the United States. Will the case be any better for the people in whose interests we profess to legislate? The combination, agreement, or trusts, etc., must, under the bill, be made "with the intention to prevent full and free competition in the importation, transportation, or sale of articles imported into the United States."

Here we have serious ambiguity and doubt, and it is impossible to say with certainty what the bill means. The word "imported," which describes the article about which the agreement is to be made, is in the past tense, and means, grammatically, articles already imported, and shows that the agreement must be in reference to articles which have then at the time of making the agreement been imported; yet in the same sentence we have denounced an agreement to prevent full and free competition in the importation of the articles described, and this necessarily means that the agreement shall precede the final act of importation. For it is certain that an agreement made after the act of importation is complete can not have any effect on that past and completed transaction. It is not in the power of man to change or affect the past. What has transpired is not a matter in action; it is only a matter of history.

So that we have this contradictory enactment contained in the same sentence, that the agreement denounced by the bill shall precede importation, and that it shall also come after importation. There is no way to reconcile this except to strike out the word "importation" in the sentence "prevent full and free competition in the importation, transportation, or sale of articles imported" or to insert "which shall be" before "imported." It certainly is not allowable to strike out a word in a criminal statute, nor can we insert words which change its meaning. If we insert "which shall be," then we make the "transportation and sale" prohibited precede the final act of importation. They will thus not only precede importation, but there is nothing in the bill to limit the time, so it be preceding time, in which such sale and transportation shall take place. It therefore covers any time in which, and any place, though in a foreign country, at which, such transportation and sale might take place. A provision so broad would make the statute unconstitutional, as embracing matters within a foreign jurisdiction and subject to regulation only by a foreign power.

There is only one other conceivable meaning, and that is, the phrase "agreements, etc., made with intention to prevent full and free competition in the importation, transportation, or sale of articles imported into the United States," means, with reference to importation, that the agreement must precede the act of importation; and with reference to "transportation and sale," this agreement refers to those acts done after importation. With this meaning, if we are allowed to conjecture it in a criminal statute, the bill would be plainly unconstitutional. It would then include transportation and sale generally, there being no words to limit them. Transportation and sale generally are not within the jurisdiction of Congress, but only transportation and sale in interstate and foreign commerce. It will be hereafter shown to be an undeniable rule of constitutional law that where the language of a statute embraces matters within and without the constitutional power of Congress the whole of it is unconstitutional.

But if we were allowed to do this in this case, the result would be to demonstrate in the clearest manner the utter worthlessness of the bill as a remedy for the evils which afflict our country. For in this view we would have the prohibited agreement so far as importation is concerned preceding that event. As importation is the result of a transportation of goods from a foreign country, the agreement in relation to it would generally be made there, and would always be made there if such agreements were prohibited and punishable by law here. And as to the transportation and sales here, they would take place or could be made to take place after the article [sic] imported ceased to be imports in the constitutional sense of the term or after the original package in which they were imported had been broken. An agreement made with reference to them in that connection would be beyond the jurisdiction of Congress. This will be proven before I conclude.

There is another trouble—a very serious obstacle—in enforcing the bill as a law. The agreement or combination must be made with a certain specified intent. A combination or arrangement between two or more in relation to the business mentioned in the bill is altogether an innocent and lawful transaction, unless it be made with the intent named in the bill. The unlawful intent therefore is the gist of the offense. Without this intent the act is lawful, even meritorious. With it the act is unlawful and criminal.

In such cases it is settled law that the specific intent which constitutes the crime must be proven on the trial to exist as is stated in the statute. A lawful act made unlawful when done with a specific intent mentioned in the statute remains still lawful, so far as that statute is concerned, if not done with that specific intent, though it may have been done with some other intent, which may be recognized in morals and even in law as equally objectionable as the specific intent named in the statute.

In all such cases the specific intent named in the statute must not only exist, but must on the trial be proven to exist beyond a reasonable doubt, or the party indicted must be acquitted: the proof of a different intent, though it be also unlawful, will not do. So that under the first branch of the statute relating to imported goods, it must be proven that the intention was to prevent competition in the transportation, when it is not purely internal and domestic, or in the sale of the article whilst it was still an import in the constitutional sense; that is, before it has been sold by the importer or before the original package in which it is imported has been broken. If the combination relates to sales to be made by others than the importers or even by the importers themselves after the original package is broken, then it is with different intention than the one included in the statute, and with an intention that can not be constitutionally included in it, and therefore there can be no conviction under the statute.

So that all the benefits of this bill, so far as preventing increased price coming from combinations to prevent free competition in the sale of imported goods, come to naught if the parties making the combinations will only make them with the intent to operate on sales taking place after they have ceased to be imports by either having been sold by the importer, or he, still being owner, has broken the package in which they were imported. Of course if the bill becomes a law, the combinations and arrangements will be made outside of it when that can be so easily done.

I pass now to the second branch of the bill: Combinations and arrangements "with intention to prevent full and free competition in the production, manufacture, or sale of articles of domestic growth or production or domestic raw material" that competes with any similar article upon which a duty is levied by the United States, intended for and which shall be transported in interstate commerce for sale.

This is a most remarkable provision, possibly unparalleled in penal legislation.

To constitute the crime under this part of the bill there must be combined three intents, entirely distinct, two of them not unlawful, and one act which may be done by a third party in no wise connected with the party who is made criminal. This act of such third party is not only not criminal, but is even meritorious and the subject of encouragement by law. That is, a crime is by statute compounded of three intents, two of them lawful, and of the separate and independent and subsequent lawful act of another, all of these concurring to constitute the crime.

To convict a party indicted under this clause of the bill, it must be proved beyond a reasonable doubt—

First. That he entered into the combination or arrangement named with another, or others, with the specific intent to prevent the full and free competition in the production, manufacture, or sale of domestic articles which compete with dutiable foreign goods;

Second. That these domestic articles must be intended for transportation in interstate commerce for sale; and

Third. That these goods have been so transported for sale.

Suppose the United States succeeds in proving the unlawful combinations or arrangement to permit full and free competition. This alone will not do, as under the first branch of the bill something further must be proven. It must be further shown that the articles in relation to which the combination was made do actually compete with the dutiable foreign article. The language is that the domestic article "competes" with the foreign article, not that it may compete or has the tendency to compete. There must be actual competition. If we may, as this bill does, apply the action indicated by the verb "to compete" to inanimate and insensible subjects, as articles of merchandise, we can do it only in the sense that the separate owners of these articles are maintaining a contest, seeking and striving for the same thing; that is, each is striving to sell his own article, as against the other, in the same market and to the same set of customers or buyers.

This actual competition in the sense above named must be proven as stated. The statute is a penal one and must not only be construed strictly in favor of the alleged violator, but the acts constituting the crime must be proven beyond reasonable doubt. It must be shown, then, that the domestic article, in the language of the bill, "competes" with the foreign article; that this competition must be actual, a real, substantive fact actually transpiring and capable of observation, not a mere potentiality or possibility, or even probability, of competition. This it will be impossible to prove unless both articles should be actually in a particular market, as New York, and their owners are seeking and striving against each other to sell them. If the foreign article be absent and not offered in the market, there is no competition. If the domestic article be absent there is no competition, for in neither case can it be said the domestic article, in the language of the statute, "competes" with the other. And it makes no difference what may cause the absence of the foreign article, except that such absence shall not be caused by the combination. For if the foreign owner will not on any account bring or send his goods to our markets, there can be nothing here which competes with them. And so if the foreign goods be excluded by a law of the United States denouncing them as unlawful objects of commerce, for then they can not be brought here at all.

Is not the same thing true if their entrance into our ports be excluded by the imposition of a duty so high that it is prohibitory? In either case it is prohibition of competition, complete and effectual. In the one case the prohibition is absolute and *eo nomine;* in the other it is equally effectual, though prohibition is not expressly and by that name enacted. In both cases there is no actual competition, nor does the *casus* named in the bill, that the domestic articles "compete" with the foreign article, arise.

So it appears that in a large majority of instances under our protective tariff, enacted expressly, as the friends of it claim, to prevent full and free competition between foreign and domestic goods, this bill, if enacted, will furnish no remedy. It will be a sham and nothing more.

But suppose the difficulty is surmounted and the actual competition is proven beyond a reasonable doubt, then it must also be proven that the domestic goods or raw materials were intended by the parties to the combination for transportation from one State or Territory to another for sale.

The intention to transport for sale must be the intention of the parties to the combination and the party on trial. However we may make one man responsible for the open and overt acts of another, I believe it has never been contended that we could make one man liable for the secret and uncommunicated intention and thoughts of another. So it must be proven that the combination was made not only with the intent to prevent full and free competition between the goods produced under it and the foreign article, but that the intent was that the goods produced should be transported from State to State for sale. These intents must coexist at the making of the arrangement in the minds of the parties to it. If either is wanting there can be no crime under this bill.

Parties, therefore, entering into these combinations after this bill becomes a law will of course make them according to law. It is their duty to make their action conform to the law. It will be presumed that they did so conform to law unless the contrary is proven. Seeing, then, when the bill passes, that it is not unlawful to make combinations and arrangements in the production, manufacture, and sale of goods with intent to prevent the competition denounced by the bill, unless is shown the further intent that these goods shall be transported for sale from one State to another, they will limit the intention to selling them or exchanging them in the State in which they are produced. They will refuse to sell except at their doors. They will agree to make and produce goods to sell to whosoever will there at that very place and in that State buy them. Calling to mind the rule of law before alluded to, that when the specific intent is the gist of the crime, it must exist and be proven to exist, specifically as stated in the statute, we see that no crime is established.

That a part of the goods produced may and actually does go into interstate commerce will not do to prove the specific intent mentioned in the bill; for that would only prove that the intent of the combination was to produce goods which parties to whom they were sold and over whom the combination had no control might or might not put into interstate commerce as circumstances of trade might afterward indicate as most profitable. This is a very different intent from the specific intent named in the statute, the intent solely to transport in interstate commerce.

To show how impossible it is to produce a conviction upon a statute where the gist of the offense is the intent to transport in the manufacture of goods, I read from a decision of the Supreme Court at the October term, 1888, Kidd *vs.* Pearson:

> Even in the exercise of the power contended for Congress would be confined to the regulation, not of certain branches of industry, however numerous, but to those instances in each and every branch where the producer contemplated an interstate market. These instances would be almost infinite, as we have seen, but still there would always remain the possibility, and often it would be the case, that the producer contemplated a domestic market. In that case the supervisory power must be executed by the State, and the interminable trouble would be presented that whether the one power or the other should exercise the authority in question would be determined, not by any general or intelligible rule, but by the secret and changeable intention of the producer in each and every act of production. A situation more paralyzing to

the State governments and more provocative of conflicts between the General Government and the States, and less likely to have been what the framers of the Constitution intended, it would be difficult to imagine.[1.265]

But, Mr. President, if this trouble should be removed there remains another. It must also be shown that the goods produced were actually so transported, and that, too, with another specific intent, namely, for sale.

It is not stated in the statute who shall entertain this last intent. We are left to conjecture as to whether the purpose of sale shall be the purpose of the persons making the combination, or of any person to whom they may have sold the goods, or of a subpurchaser from them, being the consignor in the transportation, or of the consignee in the State in which the transportation ends. But though doubtful we must assume that the intent or purpose of sale was the intent and purpose of the party on trial, of the parties to the combination, for, as stated before, one man can not be punished for the secret and uncommunicated intent of another.

But if this obstacle, insurmountable as it appears to be, should be found in fact removable, then we will find that the statute will nevertheless be a worthless remedy against the evils arising from these combinations. For, as the transportation must be for sale, and not for anything else, it must be negatived in the proof that it was for exchange or for consumption.

But up to this point, if all the proof be made as required, there must be proven a superadded or fourth intention; that is, it shall be the intent of the parties to the combination to advance the cost of the articles described to the consumer. The intent to advance the price to the wholesale or retail dealer alone will not do; it must be to advance it to the consumer. This leaves unpunished and perfectly lawful all those combinations which have proven so disastrous, that have for their object a decrease in the price to be given to the producer, and also those speculative movements now so common by which there shall be a temporary advance in the market, to last till a day not far off, when there shall be a settlement.

These arrangements, combinations, or corners, or whatever else they may be called, are made wholly for speculative purposes—intended alone to squeeze those who are "short," as the saying is. It is true they do, as an incident, sometimes affect, while they last, the price paid by the consumer; but that is not the intent, the specific intent with which they are formed, and they are, therefore, not embraced in the statute. Nor are such combinations made in reference to articles intended for interstate transportation and sale, for such speculations are made wholly without expectation of a delivery of the articles, and settlements are made by merely paying the price on the day agreed upon.

Mr. President, up to this point I have been considering the bill in its aspect as a punisher of crime. But there is a section which gives the injured party a civil action to recover a penalty; that is, double damages. If we suppose that such a suit would ever be brought, an event almost certain not to transpire, the plaintiff would encounter all the difficulties of a criminal prosecution, as I have pointed them out, with one single exception and only one. That exception is that he would not be compelled to make out his case beyond a reasonable doubt. He would, however, be compelled to prove every fact shown to be necessary in the criminal proceeding by clear evidence to the satisfaction of the court and jury. He would not be allowed to rely on mere conjecture or supposition, but he must establish his case affirmatively so as to satisfy the court and jury that all the facts and all the intents existed which I have shown to be necessary in the criminal prosecution. That this would be impossible is seen from what I have stated, and is also shown more clearly even by what follows.

The right of action against the persons in the combination is given to the party damnified. Who is this party injured, when, as prescribed in the bill, there has been an advance in the price by the combination? The answer is found in the bill itself in the words, "intended to advance the cost to the consumer of any such articles." The consumer is the party "damnified or injured."

This is the express provision of the bill, as I think is clear from the last clause of the first section. But even if it were not the express language of the bill, it so results as

---

[1.265] 128 U.S. 1, 22 (1888).

a logical necessity. An advance in price to the middlemen is not mentioned in the bill, for the obvious reason that no such advance would damnify them; it would rather be a benefit, as it would increase the value of the goods he has on hand. He buys to sell again. He buys only for profit on a subsequent sale. So whatever he pays he receives when he sells, together with a profit on his investment; and so of all of them, including the last, who sells directly to the consumer. The consumer, therefore, paying all the increased price advanced by the middlemen and profits on the same, is the party necessarily damnified or injured.

Who are the consumers? The people of the United States as individuals; whatever each individual consumes, or his family, marks the amount of his interest in the price advanced by the combination. It is manifest that in nearly every instance the damage by the advanced price of each article affected by these combinations would be—though in the aggregate large, indeed—so small as not to justify the expense and trouble of a suit in a distant court. The consumer claims a loss of, say, $25, on a particular article, as sugar, affected by the combination. If he succeeds he gets double damages; that is $50. He may live in Missouri, or Texas, or Kansas; he must go to New York, or Boston, or Chicago, or some distant city to bring his suit. He is poor, a farmer, or mechanic, or laborer. He undertakes to get damages from a powerful and rich corporation, or combination of corporations and persons. He must employ lawyers; he must hunt up and interview witnesses, many of them unwilling to communicate what they know and some interested in misleading him. He must summon them; pay their expenses. He must attend the court. If he is ready for trial the cause will be probably continued. The result will be in nearly every case that, crushed by the expense, wearied by the delays, he will abandon the suit in despair.

I do not hesitate to say that few, if any, of such suits will ever be instituted, and not one will ever be successful.

Mr. President, I have proven this bill to be worthless even if it be constitutional. These trusts and combinations are great wrongs to the people. They have invaded many of the most important branches of business. They operate with a double-edged sword. They increase beyond reason the cost of the necessaries of life and business and they decrease the cost of the raw material, the farm products of the country. They regulate prices at their will, depress the price of what they buy and increase the price of what they sell. They aggregate to themselves great, enormous wealth by extortion which make [sic] the people poor. Then making this extorted wealth the means of further extortion from their unfortunate victims, the people of the United States, they pursue unmolested, unrestrained by law, their ceaseless round of peculation under the law, till they are fast producing that condition in our people in which the great mass of them are the servitors of those who have this aggregated wealth at their command.

The people see this and they are restless and discontented. The farmers especially have been the victims of this and other policies which have brought them to the verge of ruin. Debts and mortgages accumulate. The home, the farm, the workshop, are becoming the properties by encumbrances of lordly creditors, who, by methods encouraged and fostered by law in some instances and permitted by law in others, have extorted their ill-gotten gains from the poor and then used the money thus obtained to complete the ruin of the people. The people ask us for redress. They plead for security against these wrongs. What is offered them is this bill, which, even if it be constitutional, is, as I have shown it to be, utterly worthless. It will aggravate rather than diminish the evils.

Mr. President, I do not charge the committee with bad faith in the presentation of this bill. I have faith in the fairness and justice of their intentions. The truth is, sir, the committee, by its methods, undertook to accomplish the impossible. They have undertaken to compound from reserved and granted powers a valid bill, and the result is the incongruities I have pointed out, that curious commingling of inconsistent and inefficient provisions which has produced this abortion. There is one power in the Constitution which would have been efficient if it had been resorted to. It is the power to levy taxes, duties, imposts, etc. The author of this bill at one time concurred in the opinion that this was the only power in Congress on the subject which would be efficient. Speaking of legislation to suppress trusts, on August 14, 1888, Mr. SHERMAN said:

Whether such legislation can be ingrafted in our peculiar system by the national authority there is some doubt. If it can be done at all it must be done upon a tariff bill or revenue bill. I do not see in what other way it can be done.

That, sir, is exactly my position. There is no other way under the Constitution.

And to show what he meant by legislation on a tariff bill the same great Senator on January 2, 1888, commenting on a passage in President Cleveland's message recommending lower duties to prevent trusts, said:

Where such combinations to prevent a reduction of price by fair competition exist I agree that they may and ought to be met by a reduction of duty.

But that distinguished Senator and the great Committee on Finance who have produced this bill believe in high duties, in protective duties, in even prohibitive duties. They are wedded to the conviction that the home market is the best market, and that the American manufacturer is entitled to this American market as against the world. They are unwilling to give up this theory. Notwithstanding they see "that combinations to prevent a reduction of price by fair competition do exist" and that a fair and effectual "way to meet them is by a reduction of duty," they can not make up their minds to do this. So, contrary to the views expressed, as above quoted, by Mr. SHERMAN, they have sought another power in the Constitution to suppress trusts. But they have sought in vain, as Mr. SHERMAN said they would. They seek to make two inconsistent, even repellant, things coexist and harmonize, to wit: a high protective tariff, which shuts out foreign competition, and the vain prohibition that the protected parties shall not avail themselves of the advantage thus given them. They throw the coveted sop to the hungry and greedy Cerberus and then say to the dog, "You shall not eat it."

The attempt to do this must fail. Success is impossible. You can no more make moral contradictory laws coalesce and work in harmony than you can construct a system dependent on contradictory physical and mathematical laws. The power of Congress is impotent to reconcile and harmonize truth and error. It is powerless also to make truth error or to make error truth. We can not enact that the three angles of a triangle shall be more or less than two right angles. We can not repeal the law of gravity. We can not enact that vice shall be virtue, that falsehood shall be truth. We can not change human nature. We can not by our tariff laws administer to and stimulate the greed of men, and then, without removing the stimulant, enact successfully, as is attempted by this bill, that this greed shall be generosity and self-abnegation. By our tariff laws we hold out to the owners of the protected industries the offer of 47 per cent advance in price. We tell them they are entitled to it; that it is right and just. By this bill we say to them, "You must not take the offer."

Of course, Mr. President, a bill framed with these utterly contradictory and irreconcilable ends will be inefficient, the miserable sham I have shown this to be.

THE BILL UNCONSTITUTIONAL.

Mr. President, I now proceed to show that the bill is utterly unconstitutional.

This task is an easy one, since the principles applicable to this examination have again and again been settled by the Supreme Court. I warn Senators now that no attempt will be made to show the bill unconstitutional upon that narrow and strict theory of State rights which they may suppose is entertained by the Southern people and by them only. In all I shall say on this subject I shall plant my argument on an exposition of the Constitution made by the tribunal which the Constitution itself appoints to perform that duty.

The power to enact the bill is claimed in the bill itself under the commercial clause of the Constitution—the power "to regulate commerce with foreign nations and among the States."

A statute enacted under this grant must be the exercise of a power of regulation, a regulation of commerce, either foreign or interstate. It must be this and nothing else.

A regulation of commerce is prescribing rules for carrying on that commerce; that is, regulating the doing of the things which of themselves constitute that commerce; the very transactions between men which are commerce, interstate or foreign, are the things to be regulated.

The transactions which take place before this interstate or foreign commerce begins and the transactions occurring after it ends, though they be strictly commercial, do not constitute interstate or foreign commerce nor any part of it. They are only domestic commerce in the State in which they take place, and are beyond the power of Congress to regulate. They belong exclusively to the State in which they originate and are consummated. The power of Congress commences with the initiation of interstate or foreign commerce and ceases with its termination. The regulation, therefore, must be of things done, transactions taking place, after this initial point and before the point of termination. The power of Congress extends to nothing before the beginning and to nothing occuring after the end of this commerce.

So far as this bill is concerned, it is needful only to specify the acts, without reference to the citizenship of the actors, which constitute interstate or foreign commerce. They embrace purchase, sale, exchange, barter, transportation, and intercourse for the purpose of trade in all its forms. (See Welborn [sic] vs. Missouri, 91 U. S. R.[1.266] and Mobile vs. Kimball, 102 U. S. R., 702.[1.267]) Of these acts this bill specifies and claims jurisdiction over importation (purchase and transportation combined), transportation, and sale of imported articles. This relates to foreign commerce. So far as interstate commerce is concerned, it specifies transportation for sale only. The extent of these under the power of Congress will be discussed further on.

But, Mr. President, among these commercial acts are not manufactures or any other kind of production, nor sales, nor transportation purely within a State or wholly outside the territorial jurisdiction of the United States. The bill proceeds on the idea that as to interstate commerce the jurisdiction of Congress extends to the regulation of the production and manufacture of articles taking place in a State, if only it be intended that, after such manufacture or production shall be complete, all or a portion of the articles shall become subjects of interstate commerce, and shall in fact be transported as such.

This basis of the bill is expressly confuted by the decisions I shall quote.

The Supreme Court in Veazie vs. Moor, 14 How. R., on page 574, speaking of the commercial clause of the Constitution, says it can not "be properly concluded that because the products of domestic enterprise in agriculture or manufactures or in the arts may ultimately become the subjects of foreign" (or interstate) "commerce, the control of the means or the encouragements by which enterprise is fostered and protected is legitimately within the import of the phrase 'foreign commerce,' or fairly implied in any investiture of the power to regulate such commerce. A pretension so far-reaching as this would extend to contracts between citizen and citizen of the same State; would control ⊥ the pursuits of the planter, the grazier, the manufacturer, the mechanic, the immense operations of the collieries and mines and furnaces of the country; for there is not one of these vocations the results of which may not become the subject of foreign" (interstate) "commerce."[1.268]

The court further condemns the position that Congress has jurisdiction over a commerce "which * * * is unquestionably internal, although intermediately or ultimately it might become foreign."

This case, though decided in 1852, was very recently (in 1880) confirmed by the Supreme Court in Lord vs. Steam-Ship Company, 102 U. S.[1.269]

This case expressly condemns that provision in the bill which seeks for jurisdiction in Congress over production and sales in a State merely upon the ground that the articles so produced or so sold might be afterwards transported in interstate commerce. There are other cases to the same effect.

But the bill, though originally written by its author to stand on this basis only, of a subsequent interstate transportation in interstate commerce, seems now, as amended by the committee, to abandon that position and to place the power of Congress on such subsequent transportation, combined with an intention existing in the mind of the

---

[1.266] Welton v. Missouri, 91 U.S. 275, 23 L. Ed. 347 (1876).

[1.267] 102 U.S. 691. 26 L. Ed. 238 (1881).

[1.268] See note 1.255 supra.

[1.269] See note 1.258 supra.

parties to these arrangements or trusts, at the time of production and manufacture, that the articles should be so transported.

That the conjoining of this intent in the production, with the subsequent transportation, does not help the case for the validity of the bill, I now proceed to show.

Production of all kinds, manufactures of all kinds, as we have seen, are subject to the jurisdiction and power of the State in which they are carried on. Whatever regulations, therefore, may be made for carrying on these must be made by State authority. The methods of these operations of industry and art are exclusively for the States to regulate.

What is lawful by the State regulation can not be made unlawful by the United States. The bill concedes this, for it professes not to undertake to condemn these operations as carried on under State authority. So far as this bill goes, these manufactures and productions are perfectly lawful, even when made with the intent of subsequent interstate transportation. Nor is interstate commerce in them interdicted or even regulated in any manner or to the smallest extent.

Whether Congress can interdict commerce between two States in articles lawfully produced in either, and which one State wishes to sell and another wishes to buy, merely upon the ground that Congress dissapproves the methods of production or dislikes the motive on which production took place, these methods and motives being perfectly lawful in these States, I shall not discuss now. That question does not arise on the bill as it now stands.

The question is, Can Congress, in the exercise of the power to regulate commerce among the States, make a law—prescribe a regulation—which punishes the intent with which an article is produced in a State and then permit it to be a lawful subject of interstate commerce, with no regulation whatever of that commerce in that article? That is exactly what this bill undertakes to do; neither more nor less. The result is that there is no regulation of interstate commerce, but there is a regulation of something else. That something is the domestic and internal production and business of a State. The power to do this will not be contended for.

Mr. President, if it be conceded that the punishment of an intent with which goods are produced, and which, when produced, are lawful subjects of interstate commerce, exactly as all other goods are, is a regulation of commerce, and not of production merely, still the bill is unconstitutional. This results from the fact that the acts and the intent with which they are associated, and which are punished by the bill, are not the carrying on of interstate commerce, but precede the commencement of that commerce, and therefore are not subject to the jurisdiction of Congress.

I now, therefore, proceed to inquire when goods intended for interstate commerce become subject to the jurisdiction of Congress. The answer to that is furnished by well-considered decisions of the Supreme Court.

In Coe *vs.* Errol (116 United States,—)[1.270] the articles of commerce were logs cut in the State of New Hampshire for transportation by floating on the Androscoggin River to Lewiston, in the State of Maine. So in that case the production of the article, the cutting of the logs, was with the intent to transport them to another State. But the logs were not only cut with this intent, but they were actually transported to the river with the intent to transport them as soon as the water should rise. They had gone through the initial domestic transportation necessary to enable them to be started on the final journey from New Hampshire to Maine. In that condition they were taxed by New Hampshire. If they were the subjects of interstate commerce, if the jurisdiction of New Hampshire had ceased and the power of the United States had commenced, the tax was unconstitutional.

On this case the Supreme Court say [*sic*]:

There must be a point of time when they [the logs] cease to be governed exclusively—

Yes, exclusively—

by the domestic law, and begin—

[1.270] *See* note 1.259 *supra*.

Note the point of time when they begin—

begin to be governed and protected by the law of commercial regulation; and that moment seems to us to be a legitimate one for this purpose—in which they commence their final movement for transportation from the State of their origin to the State of their destination. (Coe vs. Errol, 116 U. S. R., 525.)

The court then quotes from its own decision in the case of the Daniel Ball (10 Wallace R., 565) as follows:

Whenever a commodity has begun to move as an article of trade from one State to another, commerce in that commodity has commenced.[1.271]

The decision is that when the article of commerce has begun to move—not begun to be produced with an intent to move—from one State to another, then at that time interstate commerce in that commodity has commenced. Not before that time, but then, at the commencement of the interstate movement.

And in Coe vs. Errol, the court, speaking of an article intended for transportation to another State and moved by internal transportation to a depot from which the final transportation was intended to be commenced, proceeds to say:

Until actually launched on its way to another State or committed to a common carrier for transportation to such State, its destination is not fixed and certain. It may be sold or otherwise disposed of within the State and never be put in course of transportation out of the State. Carrying it from the farm or the forest to the depot is only an interior movement of the property, entirely within the State, for the purpose it is true, but only for the purpose—

What is the purpose but the intent?—

of putting it into a course of exportation. It is no part of the exportation itself.

And therefore no part of interstate transportation and of interstate commerce.

Until shipped or started on its final journey out of the State its exportation is altogether a matter *in fiere*, and not at all a fixed and certain thing. (*Ibid.*, page 528.)

That case, Mr. President, would seem to settle this question forever. There seems to be no escape from the conclusion that it fixes the unconstitutionality of this bill. Here was the intent to transport to another State, not only in the production of the logs, the cutting of them from the forest with intent to send them to another State, but there was transportation to a depot in the same State from which it was intended to ship them to another State. We have the goods produced with the intent to put them in interstate commerce. We have all the preparation necessary, with the same intent. But because the final act of transportation had not commenced the goods were not subject to the jurisdiction of Congress. They were not interstate commerce.

The case of Coe vs. Errol, just commented on, was confirmed in the late case of Kidd vs. Pearson (128 U. S. R., page 1), decided in 1888.

In that case the attempt was made to bring the production of goods in a State within the jurisdiction of the commercial clause of the Constitution, because they were manufactured with the intent to export them in interstate commerce. The court, after alluding to the right of the State to regulate the manufacture of an article of commerce as being settled beyond dispute, say [*sic*]:

Is this right overthrown by the fact that the manufacturer intends to export the liquors when made? Does the statute, in omitting to except from its operations the manufacture of intoxicating liquor within the limits of the State for export, constitute an unauthorized interference with the power given to Congress to regulate commerce?

These questions are well answered in the language of this court in the License Tax cases (5 Wallace, 462, 470). Over this commerce and trade (the internal commerce and domestic trade of the States) Congress has no power of regulation or control. This power belongs exclusively to the State. No interference by Congress with the business of citizens transacted within a State is warranted by the Constitution except such as is strictly incidental to the exercise of powers

---

[1.271] The Steamer Daniel Ball v. United States, 77 U.S. (10 Wall.) 557, 565, 19 L. Ed. 999, 1002 (1871).

clearly granted to the legislature. The power to authorize a business within a State is plainly repugnant to the exclusive power of the State over the same subject.

The manufacture of intoxicating liquors in a State is none the less a business within that State because the manufacturer intends, at his convenience, to export such liquors to foreign countries or to other States.

This court has already decided that the fact that an article was manufactured for export to another State does not of itself make it an article of interstate commerce within the meaning of section 8, Article I, of the Constitution, and that the intent of the manufacturer does not determine the time when the article or product passes from the control of the State and belongs to commerce.[1.272]

The court then referred to Coe vs. Errol, above cited, for this position, and then quote largely from it to show that was its true meaning.

There is but one remaining point in this part of the bill—referring to domestic production with the intent named—which may be considered as pointing to a fact giving Congress jurisdiction. The point is embraced in the language which describes the goods as competing with dutiable goods imported into the United States.

The question on this point is, has Congress jurisdiction, under the power to regulate commerce, to regulate the manufacture, production, and sale in purely internal State commerce of goods because they compete with dutiable goods imported into the United States? An answer is found in the proposition that if the power exists as to production, to regulate by prescribing the rule laid down in this bill as to full and free competition, it may prescribe any other regulation. There is nothing in the prevention of full and free competition in the manufacture and production of goods which of itself would give Congress jurisdiction as to goods competing with dutiable goods which would not authorize Congress to make any other regulation they might deem wise in such production of such goods.

If competition with dutiable goods gives jurisdiction for one regulation, it gives it for all regulations deemed wise by Congress. It results, therefore, that if such competition be a ground of Federal jurisdiction, then Congress can assume or acquire the jurisdiction over the manufacture and production of all goods whatever manufactured and produced in any State by simply levying a duty on the competing foreign articles, and in this way would the whole internal business of the State be brought within the jurisdiction of Congress to regulate and control as Congress might deem proper. The two facts, dutiable foreign goods and competing domestic goods, co-existing, would, in this view, give Congress full jurisdiction as to the manufacture and sale of the latter. As the power of Congress is unlimited as to the selection of articles on which duties are to be levied, so by the exercise of this power its jurisdiction over domestic production and manufactures would be unlimited, and nothing would remain to the States of their ancient and undoubted jurisdiction over their internal business.

This *reductio ad absurdum* is a sufficient answer. But there is another answer as full and complete by direct argument. It is that the power of Congress is simply a power to regulate interstate and foreign commerce; that is, a power to prescribe rules for carrying on this commerce where it exists and as it is being actually carried on as between States and between the United States and foreign countries. This statute prescribes no rule for carrying on this commerce. On the contrary it prescribes a rule for carrying on something else; that is, for carrying on the business of manufacturing and producing domestic articles within the limits of a State and the sale of them even in the State of their origin.

I come now, Mr. President, to consider the power of Congress as proposed to be exerted in this bill in its first clause in relation to imports.

This clause makes it criminal to enter into a combination or arrangement "with intent to prevent full and free competition in the importation, transportation, or sale of articles imported into the United States."

This is, to say the least of it, a singular provision. It is difficult to extract the meaning of the draughtsman.

Evidently as to "importation" preventing full and free competition in the

---

[1.272] *See* note 1.261 *supra.*

importing of goods, the combination must precede the act of importation; otherwise it could not affect the importation. A combination to affect importation could not by any human power change or alter that which has already transpired, an act of importation already complete. So if the bill be not absurd and impracticable on its face we must make the unlawful agreement precede the act of importation. What, then, are we to do with the other words of the sentence, "transportation or sale of articles imported into the United States?" "Imported" means an act of importation already transpired. Note that the phrases "articles imported" means articles already imported. If it does not mean this, but is to be construed as if written "articles which shall be imported," then the agreement condemned must not only precede importation, but must precede the transportation and sale, which must also precede importation.

Then we have a provision which makes criminal an agreement to prevent competition in the transportation or sale of an article produced in a foreign country by whomsoever made and wheresoever made, and as to the time of the making indefinite and unlimited, except only that it shall precede the transportation and sale affected by it, which transportation and sale may have taken place anywhere on the face of the globe and at any time within the lives of the parties to the agreement. Of course a statute of that sort, embracing within its provisions transactions wholly without the territorial jurisdiction of Congress can not stand. It will not help it that it may also embrace transactions within the jurisdiction of Congress, for in such a case, as I will show hereafter, the courts can not restrict the plain meaning of the words used, by running a line which Congress itself would not run, excluding the unconstitutional part and giving the statute operation and effect on those transactions which might fall within Congressional power.

There is only one other conjectural meaning of this language, and that is, that as to transportation and sale of the imported articles the meaning is: that the transportation and sale of the articles shall be after they are imported. This would confine the acts of transportation and sale to the United States—a place at least in which Congress has some jurisdiction. But here again we encounter the difficulty above alluded to, that the language embraces too much, embraces transactions within the power of Congress and transactions beyond or outside of this power. It embraces both interstate and domestic transportation; that is, transportation generally. Besides, the words "articles imported" are not the same as, nor equivalent in meaning to, the word "imports" in its constitutional sense. Articles once imported from a foreign country, always, as long as they remain in the United States, wherever situated and in whosesoever hands they may be and in whatsoever condition, as to being in the original package or not, continue to be "imported articles." That is, they are articles not of domestic production, but foreign articles which have been imported into the United States.

But "imports" in a constitutional sense are imported articles in the hands of the importer and in the original package. When they are sold to another or the package is broken, though there be no sale, then they cease to be "imports" in the constitutional sense; they cease to be within the jurisdiction of Congress to regulate and control, and become subject to State jurisdiction exclusively. They might be regulated as to interstate transportation, but, as we have seen, this is not provided for, but only transportation generally.

This rule is well settled and well known; but, since this distinction is not recognized in this bill and since the power of Congress is asserted in it to regulate "imported articles" generally in their transportation and sale, without reference to their condition as imports, as I have defined them, I will now read some authorities on that point.

The first case in which it was settled when imported articles ceased to be imports under the jurisdiction of Congress and become a part of the great mass of the property of the State in which they were located was Brown *vs.* Maryland, reported in 12 Wheat. R., 419.[1.273] I take the exposition of that case as made by Chief Justice Taney and Justice McLean in the License Cases, in 5 Howard Reports,[1.274] because it is not

---

[1.273] *See* note 1.249 *supra.*

[1.274] *See* note 1.251 *supra.*

only correct, but because it illustrates the last-named cases, which I also wish to bring to the consideration of the Senate.

In that case (Brown *vs.* Maryland)—

Says Chief Justice Taney—

the court held that an import continued to be a part of the foreign commerce of the country while it remained in the hands of the importer for sale in the original bale, package, or vessel in which it was imported, * * * but that when the original package was broken up for use or retail by the importer, and also when the commodity had passed from the hands of the importer into the hands of a purchaser, it ceased to be an import or a part of the foreign commerce and became subject to the laws of the State and might be taxed for State purposes and the sale regulated by the State like any other property.

This I understand to be substantially the decision in Brown *vs.* Maryland, drawing the line between foreign commerce, which is subject to the regulation of Congress, and internal or domestic commerce, which belongs to the States, and over which Congress can exercise no control. (See License Cases, 5 Howard R., on page 575.)[1.275]

Mr. Justice McLean, in the same case, after adopting the same rule above defined by Judge Taney, as to when imports ceased to be such and got beyond the control of Congress, says:

When this happens the imported article becomes mingled with the other property of the State and is subject to its laws.[1.276]

And in the same case, referring to the police powers of the States and the "powers of Congress," Judge McLean says they—

must stand together. Neither of them can be so exercised as materially to affect the other. The source and object of these powers are exclusive, distinct, and independent. The one operates on foreign—

Or interstate—

commerce, the other upon the internal commerce of the States. The former—

Power of Congress—

ceases when the product becomes commingled with the other property in the State. At this point the local law attaches and regulates it as it does other property. (5 Howard R., page 592.)

A rule even more liberal than this, it may as well be stated here, is allowed in favor of the power of a State over goods brought into it from another State. In that case the goods are not imports at all, and as soon as they arrive at their destination, in whosesoever hands they may be, they are subject to the jurisdiction of the State, just as other goods therein are. (Woodruff *vs.* Parham, 8 Wall.;[1.277] Hinson *vs.* Lott, ib.[1.278])

Mr. President, tested by these principles all that part of the bill that relates to these combinations in reference to the importation, transportation, and sale of goods imported into the United States must be unconstitutional, unless we restrict the plain meaning of the general language employed in the bill and confine it to transportation and sale of goods imported whilst they still remain imports; that is, to sale or transportation of the goods whilst they remain in the hands of the importer and also in the original bale or package in which they were imported. If we so restrict the meaning of the bill, it is utterly worthless, for the agreement may be made to relate only to the transportation of the goods after they have been sold by the importer, or being still owned by him after he has put them in a different bale or package from the one in which they were imported.

How worthless such a provision would be to suppress trusts is so evident as to need no comment. So of the sales of such articles. The combination need only relate to

---

[1.275] 46 U.S. (5 How.) at 574–75.
[1.276] *Id.* at 589
[1.277] 75 U.S. (8 Wall.) 123, 19 L. Ed. 382 (1869).
[1.278] 75 U.S. (8 Wall.) 148, 19 L. Ed. 387 (1869).

such sales by a purchaser from the importer, or even by the importer himself if he will only take the trouble to sell them in bales and packages made and put up after importation, to be wholly without the restraint of this bill. How near these transactions when they are beyond the jurisdiction of Congress may come to the act of importation is shown by the decision of the Supreme Court in Waring *vs.* Mayor (8 Wall. R., 110).[1.279] In that case it was held that a purchaser of goods in transit from a foreign country to the United States and whilst at sea was not an importer if the agreement was that they should be at the risk of the seller till delivery. This purchaser not being an importer, the goods even in his hands and in the original packages after delivery remained no longer a part of the foreign commerce and subject to the jurisdiction of the United States. So it is seen again how utterly worthless this bill is if we restrict its meaning so as to make it constitutional.

But, Mr. President, we are not allowed to so restrict the language of the bill in this provision nor in the others which I have pointed out.

In United States *vs.* Reese, 92 U. S. R., 214,[1.280] this matter was up for decision. The court stated the question in these words:

> We are, therefore, directly called upon to decide whether a penal statute enacted by Congress with its limited power, which is in general language broad enough to cover wrongful acts without as well as within the constitutional jurisdiction, can be limited by judicial construction so as to make it operate only on that which Congress may rightfully prohibit and punish.[1.281]

In answering this question the court says:

> It would certainly be dangerous if the legislature should set a net large enough to catch all possible offenders, and leave it to the court to step inside and say who might rightfully be detained and who should be set at large. That would, to some extent, substitute the judicial for the legislative department of the Government.
>
> To limit this statute in the manner now asked for would be to make a new law, not to enforce an old one.[1.282]

In Trade-Mark cases, 100 U. S. R., page 82,[1.283] the same question arose. In that case, as in this bill, the language of the statute was general, embracing interstate and foreign commerce as well as domestic commerce. The acts condemned embraced equally acts done in domestic commerce and in interstate and foreign commerce, and Congress had power over the latter only. The court was asked to restrict the language so as to apply it only to foreign and interstate commerce, and therefore make the statute constitutional. This the court refused to do, saying:

> While it may be true that, where one part of a statute is valid and constitutional and another part unconstitutional and void, the court may enforce the valid part where they are distinctly separated so that each can stand alone, it it not within the judicial province to give to the words used by Congress a narrower meaning than they are manifestly intended to bear in order that crimes may be punished which are not described in language that brings them within the constitutional power of that body. (100 U. S. R., page 100 [*sic*].)[1.284]

This settles the unconstitutionality of the whole bill. That there are some things included in the general words of the bill which, if separately stated and disconnected from the great mass of the provisions of the bill, Congress can constitutionally enact, is admitted. But they are not so separated, and if they were they are utterly without efficacy in remedying the great evil of these trusts and combinations, as has been shown.

But, Mr. President, there is another ground upon which the bill is clearly

---

[1.279] Waring v. Aldermen & Common Council, 75 U.S. (8 Wall.) 110, 19 L. Ed. 342 (1869).

[1.280] 92 U.S. 214, 23 L. Ed. 563 (1876).

[1.281] 92 U.S. at 221.

[1.282] *Id*.

[1.283] United States v. Steffens, 100 U.S. 82, 25 L. Ed. 550 (1879).

[1.284] The correct citation is 100 U.S. at 98.

unconstitutional. I mention these various grounds with that prolixity of detail which I know is calculated to weary the attention of the Senate. My excuse is that the objects sought to be attained by the bill are of the greatest importance to the people of the United States. The wrongs perpetrated by these combinations inflict a deep wound upon the prosperity and welfare of the people. They demand redress. It is our duty to furnish the remedy. It is our duty, therefore, to scrutinize this bill in all its parts, to examine its force and effect, so that, if indeed it be, as I have shown it to be, wholly inadequate, a mere delusion, and not a real and efficient measure, its true character may be known, and that we may seek another remedy, if one can be found; and there is no doubt that it can be found.

The objection I now insist on is fundamental. It destroys the whole framework of the bill. If it be good, no part of the bill can stand, even it we separate from it those parts which on other grounds might be unconstitutional.

The bill is a proposition for the enactment of a penal or criminal statute. It does nothing but inflict penalties, either by civil or criminal procedure.

There are but few express powers granted by the Constitution for the enactment of criminal laws. They relate to punishing the counterfeiting of the coin and the securities of the United States, and piracies and felonies on the high seas, and offenses against the law of nations. These are all the express powers for enacting criminal and penal legislation by Congress found in the Constitution.

Every other exercise of the power must be as an incident to some express power. In the language of the Constitution, it must "be necessary and proper for carrying into execution" an expressly granted power. Congress must first determine to execute an express power before it can consider the propriety and necessity of assuming the incidental power. If the express power is found, that does not authorize Congress to exercise a power which might of itself be necessary and proper to the execution of that express power, if in fact there be no attempt to exercise the express power. The express power in this case is the power to regulate commerce among the States and with foreign nations.

Is there such a regulation in the bill? This question is easily answered. Recurring to what has been said—that regulation is the prescribing a rule for the actual carrying on of this commerce; that is, prescribing a rule for doing the acts which constitute this commerce—we look in vain to the provisions of this bill to find such a regulation or rule.

Bearing in mind, Mr. President, that interstate commerce begins—so far as Federal jurisdiction over it comes from property, and not from the citizenship of the parties—with the beginning of transportation and ends with its completion, and that foreign commerce ends with the breaking of the original package or with a sale by the importer; that neither embraces production, manufacturing, or fitting articles for this commerce, with intent that they should be so afterwards employed, but that both relate only to articles already made and already actually embarked in interstate or foreign commerce, we see that there is not the slightest attempt in this bill to prescribe a rule by which such commerce shall be carried on.

Acts done with reference to the production of articles which are intended for such commerce—acts done with reference to articles which have been the subjects of such commerce—are by this bill made criminal, whilst that very commerce in these very articles which were so produced, brought into existence, or imported in violation of the provisions of the bill is wholly untouched. If the bill becomes a law, that commerce in these very articles will go on, or, as Chief Justice Marshall expresses it, will be carried on exactly in the same way in all respects whatsoever as if this bill had never been passed, and without the slightest variation or change, as in all other articles. Can that be a regulation of interstate or foreign commerce which regulates nothing done in that commerce, but something else? The something else is production and selling in a State, which all agree can not be regulated by Congress. Being such a regulation and being as such undoubtedly beyond the power of Congress, the bill can not be made constitutional as an incident to a regulation of interstate or foreign commerce, which is not only not regulated at all, but is left wholly untouched.

The Constitution is a reasonable instrument, designed to specify powers delegated to a general government. So far as these powers are granted expressly or by necessary implication for the execution of express powers, they are full and complete, as well as supreme; but the Constitution neither authorizes nor tolerates the absurdity of the exercise of a power as a necessary incident to and in aid of the execution of an express power when no attempt is made to execute the express power. We can not, therefore, assume a power which would be proper in the execution of an express power, and then pervert it, so that it will not be an execution of the express power, but will be, as exercised, a regulation of something else not within the jurisdiction of the Federal Government. For no incidental power is given as a separate and substantive power, independent of the execution of an express power to be exercised by Congress whenever and wherever it may seem desirable.

Such a power is always subordinate and conditioned for its existence on the necessity for its exercise for the proper execution of an express power; that is, for making effectual the actual exercise by Congress of the express power. All incidental powers are dormant, even nonexistent, except in the promise of possible life to begin when their exercise is necessary to do their proper work in the actual execution of an express power. If the express power is not executed or not executed on the point to which an assumed incidental power is directed, then the alleged incidental power can not be evoked, for it can be constitutionally evoked only for execution, and only when its exercise is necessary and proper for executing the express power, and not for something else.

This bill regulates, not interstate or foreign commerce, but regulates, by penalties, contracts and agreements, etc., that are conspiracies of a certain character with the intent to do something else. That something else, or the end sought by the conspiracy is not regulated at all. It remains perfectly lawful; lawful not only as a principal end, but lawful in the methods by which it is sought to be attained; lawful notwithstanding the criminal conspiracy. There is, be it remembered, no prohibition of the importation or transportation or sale of the articles imported, produced, manufactured, or sold by the conspiracy. Interstate and foreign traffic transportation and full and free commerce in them are wholly unregulated, but remain perfectly lawful and unrestrained. They remain not only unprohibited, but even meritorious—things fostered and promoted by our laws.

A criminal conspiracy is a combination or agreement of two or more to do an unlawful act or to do a lawful act in an unlawful manner. But here in this bill we have a criminal conspiracy made out of an agreement to do a thing, with the intent that it shall result in another thing, which is not only not unlawful but meritorious, not only as to the act to be done, but as to the methods named in the bill as the gist of the crime. In other words, Congress usurps, as an incident to the power to regulate interstate and foreign commerce, the power to punish a thing, a conspiracy, over which it has *per se* no jurisdiction, and, at the same time and by the same law, the results of this conspiracy, when they become a part of that commerce and thereby become for the first time subject to the jurisdiction of Congress, are not only not criminal, but are encouraged and protected by our laws. Can such a usurpation stand?

The States may punish the conspiracy denounced in the bill without going further and declaring that commerce in the articles so produced shall be unlawful, because the States have full jurisdiction over the main or principle thing, the production, without reference to any subsequent commerce in them.

Mr. President, what I have just said in relation to the powers of Congress is fully sustained by the Supreme Court in United States *vs.* Fox, 95 United States Reports, 692,[1.285] wherein the court declares unconstitutional an act of Congress passed under the power to enact a bankrupt law, which act made criminal the doing of an act which Congress might have embraced, but did not, in the purview of the act. On this point the court say [*sic*]:

Any act committed with a view of evading the legislation of Congress, passed in the execution of any of its powers, or of fraudulently securing the benefit of such legislation may properly be made an offense against the United States. But—

[1.285] 95 U.S. 670, 24 L. Ed. 538 (1878).

Continues the court—

an act committed within a State—

As the act condemned in this bill is—

whether with an honest or criminal intent, can not be made an offense against ⊥ the United ⊥1772
States, unless it has some relation to the execution of a power of Congress or to some matter
within the jurisdiction of the United States.[1-286]

 Mr. President, I have shown that this bill is utterly unconstitutional, and, even if
constitutional, utterly worthless. If we pass it we do not only a vain and useless thing;
we do a wicked thing. We give to a suffering people, as a remedy for a great wrong,
that which will not only prove utterly inefficient, but will prove an aggravation of the
evils. There is, however, a power we can exercise, the power to reduce or abolish duties
on the foreign competing articles. At the proper time I shall offer as a substitute for
this bill an amendment looking to the exercise of that power.

 Mr. REAGAN. Mr. President, I wish to give notice of an amendment which I
shall offer when this bill comes up for final action. I shall move to strike out all after
the enacting clause of the bill reported by the Committee on Finance and to insert in
place of the matter stricken out the following:

That all persons engaged in the creation of any trust, or as owner or part owner, agent, or
manager of any trust, employed in any business carried on with any foreign country, or
between the States, or between any State and the District of Columbia, or between any State
and any Territory of the United States, or any owner or part owner, agent, or manager of any
corporation using its powers for either of the purposes specified in the second section of this
act, shall be deemed guilty of a high misdemeanor, and, on conviction thereof, shall be fined in
a sum not exceeding $10,000, or imprisonment at hard labor in the penitentiary not exceeding
five years, or by both of said penalties, in the discretion of the court trying the same.

SEC. 2. That a trust is a combination of capital, skill, or acts by two or more persons, firms,
corporations, or associations of persons, or of any two or more of them for either, any, or all of
the following purposes:

First. To create or carry out any restrictions in trade

Second. To limit or reduce the production or to increase or reduce the price of merchandise
or commodities.

Third. To prevent competition in the manufacture, making, purchase, sale, or transportation
of merchandise, produce, or commodities.

Fourth. To fix a standard or figure whereby the price to the public shall be in any manner
controlled or established of any article, commodity, merchandise, produce, or commerce intended
for sale, use, or consumption.

Fifth. To create a monopoly in the making, manufacture, purchase, sale, or transportation of
any merchandise, article, produce, or commodity.

Sixth. To make, or enter into, or execute, or carry out any contract, obligation, or
agreement, of any kind or description, by which they shall bind or shall have bound themselves
not to manufacture, sell, dispose of, or transport any article or commodity, or article of trade,
use, merchandise, or consumption below a common standard figure, or by which they shall
agree in any manner to keep the price of such article, commodity, or transportation at a fixed
or graduated figure; or by which they shall in any manner establish or settle the price of any
article, commodity, or transportation between themselves or between themselves and others so as
to preclude free and unrestricted competition among themselves and others in the sale and
transportation of any such article or commodity; or by which they shall agree to pool, combine,
or unite in any interest they may have in connection with the sale or transportation of any such
article or commodity that its price may in any manner be so affected.

SEC. 3. That each day any of the persons, associations, or corporations aforesaid shall be
engaged in violating the provisions of this act shall be held to be a separate offense.

 I shall desire to offer that amendment when the bill comes up for consideration
again, and I shall hope to have the opportunity of expressing some views upon the
subject.

 Mr. SHERMAN. The Senator's amendment is printed, is it not?

 Mr. REAGAN. I will mention that what I propose to offer as an amendment is in

---

[1-286] 95 U.S. at 672.

the terms of the bill introduced by me on this subject on the 4th of December last, and which has been printed.[1.287]

Mr. SHERMAN. All right. I move that the Senate proceed to the consideration of executive business.

The motion was agreed to.

AMENDMENT TO S. 1 REPORTED BY THE SENATE COMMITTEE ON FINANCE
51st Cong., 1st Sess.
March 18, 1890

⊥ Ordered to be printed.

AMENDMENT,

Reported by Mr. SHERMAN, from the Committee on Finance, and intended to be proposed to the bill (S. 1) to declare unlawful trusts and combinations in restraint of trade and production, viz: Strike out all after the enacting clause and insert the following:

```
 3    That all arrangements, contracts, agreements, trusts, or com-
 4    binations between two or more citizens or corporations, or
 5    both, of different States, or between two or more citizens or
 6    corporations, or both, of the United States and foreign states,
 7    or citizens or corporations thereof, made with a view or which
 8    tend to prevent full and free competition in the importation,
 9    transportation, or sale of articles imported into the United
10    States; or with a view or which tend to prevent full and
11    free competition in articles of growth, production, or manu-
12    facture of any State or Territory of the United States, with
13    similar articles of the growth, production, or manufacture of
14    any other State or Territory, or in the transportation or sale
15    of like articles, the production of any State or Territory of
16    the United States into or within any other State or Territory
17    of the United States; and all arrangements, trusts, or combina-
18    tions between such citizens or corporations, made with
19    a view or which tend to advance the cost to the consumer
20    of any such articles, are hereby declared to be against public
21    policy, unlawful, and void. And the circuit court of the
22    United States shall have original jurisdiction of all suits of a
23    civil nature at common law or in equity arising under this
24    section, and to issue all remedial process, orders, or writs
25    proper and necessary to enforce its provisions. And the
26    Attorney-General and the several district attorneys are hereby
27    directed, in the name of the United States, to commence
```

[1.287] Senator Reagan's bill (S. 62), which had been introduced the same day as the Sherman and George bills and referred to the Senate Judiciary Committee, 21 CONG. REC. 97 (1889), was adversely reported out on June 30, 1890, after passage of S. 1. *Id.* at 6737. Senator Reagan offered it as an amendment in the nature of a substitute for S. 1 on March 21; it was subsequently proposed as an addition to the Sherman bill and adopted in that form. *See infra* at 113, 158, 205.

```
28        and prosecute all such cases to final judgment and execution, [sic]
 1           SEC. 2. That any person or corporation injured or
 2        damnified by such arrangement, contract, agreement, trust,
 3        or combination defined in the first section of this act may
 4        sue for and recover, in any court of the United States of
 5        competent jurisdiction, without respect to the amount involved
 6        of any person or corporation a party to a combination de-
 7        scribed in the first section of this act, twice the amount of
 8        damages sustained and the costs of the suit, together with a
 9        reasonable attorney's fee.
```

SENATE DEBATE
51st Cong., 1st Sess.
March 21, 1890

21 CONG. REC. 2455

Mr. SHERMAN. If there is no further morning business, I move that the Senate proceed to the consideration of the bill (S. 1) to declare unlawful trusts and combinations in restraint of trade and production. It is really the unfinished business.

The motion was agreed to; and the Senate, as in Committee of the Whole, proceeded to consider the bill.

Mr. SHERMAN. I ask that the bill be read.

The VICE-PRESIDENT. The bill will be read at length.

The Chief Clerk read the bill.

Mr. SHERMAN. I will state that upon further consideration the Committee on Finance have reported a substitute for the bill, which I ask to have read.

The VICE-PRESIDENT. The substitute proposed by the Committee on Finance will be read.

The CHIEF CLERK. The Committee on Finance report to strike out all after the enacting clause of the bill and to insert: . . .[1.288]

Mr. REAGAN. If the Senator from Ohio will permit me and if it is the proper time now, I wish to present for consideration the amendment that I submitted on a former day.

Mr. SHERMAN. It would not now be in order. An amendment is pending.

Mr. REAGAN. It is an amendment in the second degree, and I believe that is allowable under the rules.

Mr. SHERMAN. If the Senator prefers to offer it now, very well. . . .

Mr. REAGAN. I offer it now, not to interfere with the Senator from Ohio at all. . . .

The VICE-PRESIDENT. The amendment proposed by the Senator from Texas [Mr. REAGAN] will be read.

The CHIEF CLERK. It is proposed to substitute for the amendment reported by the Committee on Finance the following: . . .[1.289]

The VICE-PRESIDENT. The question is on agreeing to the amendment submitted by the Senator from Texas to the amendment reported from the Committee on Finance.

Mr. SHERMAN. Mr. President, I did not originally intend to make any extended argument on this trust bill, because I supposed that the public facts upon which it is

---

[1.288] The amended version of S. 1 reported by the Senate Finance Committee on March 18, 1890, was read; it appears immediately *supra*.

[1.289] The text of Senator Reagan's bill (S. 62), which appears *supra* at 111, was read.

founded and the general necessity of some legislation were so manifest that no debate was necessary to bring those facts to the attention of the Senate.

But the different views taken by Senators in regard to the legal questions involved in the bill and the very able speech made by the Senator from Mississippi [Mr. GEORGE] relative to the details of the bill led me to the conclusion that it was my duty, having reported the bill from the Committee on Finance, to present in as clear and logical a way as I can the legal and practical questions involved in the bill.

Mr. President, the object of this bill, as shown by the title, is "to declare unlawful trusts and combinations in restraint of trade and production." It declares that certain contracts are against public policy, null and void. It does not announce a new principle of law, but applies old and well recognized principles of the common law to the complicated jurisdiction of our State and Federal Government. Similar contracts in any State in the Union are now, by common or statute law, null and void. Each State can and does prevent and control combinations within the limit of the State. This we do not propose to interfere with. The power of the State courts has been repeatedly exercised to set aside such combinations as I shall hereafter show, but these courts are limited in their jurisdiction to the State, and, in our complex system of government, are admitted to be unable to deal with the great evil that now threatens us.

Unlawful combinations, unlawful at common law, now extend to all the States and interfere with our foreign and domestic commerce and with the importation and sale of goods subject to duty under the laws of the United States, against which only the General Government can secure relief. They not only affect our commerce with foreign nations, but trade and transportation among the several States. The purpose of this bill is to enable the courts of the United States to apply the same remedies against combinations which injuriously affect the interests of the United States that have been applied in the several States to protect local interests.

The first section declares: . . .[1.290]

This section will enable the courts of the United States to restrain, limit, and control such combinations as interfere injuriously with our foreign and interstate commerce, to the same extent that the State courts habitually control such combinations as interfere with the commerce of a State.

The question has arisen whether express jurisdiction should be conferred on the circuit courts of the United States to enforce this section, with authority to issue the ordinary remedial process of courts of law and equity, or whether such power is already sufficiently contained in the several acts organizing the courts of the United States. The third article of the Constitution vests the judicial power of the United States in one Supreme Court and in such inferior courts as Congress may ordain and establish.

The judiciary act of 1789 defines the jurisdiction of the several courts, and, by separate acts, this jurisdiction has been, from time to time, extended to new subjects of legislation. The committee therefore deemed it proper by express legislation to confer on the circuit courts of the United States original jurisdiction of all suits of a civil nature at common law or in equity arising under this section, with authority to issue all remedial process or writs proper and necessary to enforce its provisions, and to require the Attorney-General and the several district attorneys, in the name of the United States, to commence and prosecute all such suits to final judgment and execution.

The second section of the bill provides that any person or corporation injured or damnified by such a combination may sue for and recover in any court of the United States of competent jurisdiction, of any person or corporation a party to such a combination, all damages sustained by him. The measure of damages, whether merely compensatory, putative, or vindictive, is a matter of detail depending upon the judgment of Congress. My own opinion is that the damages should be commensurate with the difficulty of maintaining a private suit against a combination such as is described.

[1.290] At this point Senator Sherman read section 1 of his bill as amended by the Committee on Finance; it appears *supra* at 112-13.

These two sections are distinct and different in their scope and object. The first invokes the power of the National Government, in proper cases, to restrain such a combination, by mandatory proceedings, from interfering with the trade and commerce of the country, and the second section is to give to private parties a remedy for personal injury caused by such a combination.

A third section was added when the bill was first reported by the Committee on Finance which declares that all persons entering into such a combination, either on his own account or as an attorney for another or as an officer, attorney, or as a trustee or in any capacity whatever, shall be guilty of a misdemeanor, and on conviction shall be punished by fine or imprisonment, in the discretion of the court.

The amendments, then, proposed by the Committee on Finance to the first section would be proper amendments to the third section, but not to the first, where they have no proper place. The first section, being a remedial statute, would be construed liberally, with a view to promote its object. It defines a civil remedy, and the courts will construe it liberally; they will prescribe the precise limits of the constitutional power of the Government; they will distinguish between lawful combinations in aid of production and unlawful combinations to prevent competition and in restraint of trade; they can operate on corporations by restraining orders and rules; they can declare the particular combination null and void and deal with it according to the nature and extent of the injuries.

In providing a remedy the intention of the combination is immaterial. The intention of a corporation can not be proven. If the natural effects of its acts are injurious, if they tend to produce evil results, if their policy is denounced by the law as against the common good, it may be restrained, be punished with a penalty or with damages, and in a proper case it may be deprived of its corporate powers and franchises. It is the tendency of a corporation, and not its intention, that the courts can deal with. Therefore the amendments first reported to the first section are not in the substitute.

The third section is a criminal statute, which would be construed strictly and is difficult to be enforced. In the present state of the law it is impossible to describe, in precise language, the nature and limits of the offense in terms specific enough for an indictment. This section is applicable only to individuals.

A corporation can not be indicted or punished except through civil process. The criminal law can only reach officers or agents employed by the corporation. Whether this law should extend to mere clerks, as was proposed in the third section, is a matter of grave doubt. The business conducted by them may be innocent and lawful, and they should not be punished or threatened for the offenses of others. I am, therefore, clearly of the opinion that at present at least it is not wise to include this section in this bill. Such penalties may come later when the limits of the power of Congress over the subject-matter shall be defined by the courts.

It is sometimes said that without this section the law would be nugatory. I do not think so. The powers granted by the first section are ample to check and prevent the great body of illegal combinations that ⊥ may be made; but, if not, it is easy enough hereafter to provide a suitable punishment for a violation of this statute. But if the criminal section is retained the amendments first proposed by the Committee on Finance should apply only to that section, and not to the civil section. Every corporation engaged in business must be responsible for the tendency of its business, whether lawful or unlawful, but individuals can only be punished for criminal intentions. To require the intentions of a corporation to be proven is to impose an impossible condition and would defeat the object of the law. To restrain and prevent the illegal tendency of a corporation is the proper duty of a court of equity. To punish the criminal intention of an officer is a much more difficult process and might be well left to the future.

⊥2457

This bill, as I would have it, has for its single object to invoke the aid of the courts of the United States to deal with the combinations described in the first section when they affect injuriously our foreign and interstate commerce and our revenue laws, and in this way to supplement the enforcement of the established rules of the common and statute law by the courts of the several States in dealing with combinations that affect injuriously the industrial liberty of the citizens of these States. It is to arm the Federal courts within the limits of their constitutional power that they may co-operate with the State courts in checking, curbing, and controlling the most dangerous combinations that now threaten the business, property, and trade of the people of the United States. And for one I do not intend to be turned from this course by fine-spun constitutional quibbles or by the plausible pretexts of associated or corporate wealth and power.

It is said that this bill will interfere with lawful trade, with the customary business of life. I deny it. It aims only at unlawful combinations. It does not in the least affect combinations in aid of production where there is free and fair competition. It is the right of every man to work, labor, and produce in any lawful vocation and to transport his production on equal terms and conditions and under like circumstances. This is industrial liberty and lies at the foundation of the equality of all rights and privileges.

The right to combine the capital and labor of two or more persons in a given pursuit with a community of profit and loss under the name of a partnership is open to all and is not an infringement of industrial liberty, but is an aid to production. The law of partnership clearly defines what is a lawful and what is an unlawful partnership. The same business is open to every other partnership, and, while it is a combination, it does not in the slightest degree prevent competition.

The combination of labor and capital in the form of a corporation to carry on any lawful business is a proper and useful expedient, especially for great enterprises of a quasi public character, and ought to be encouraged and protected as tending to cheapen the cost of production, but these corporate rights should be open to all upon the same terms and conditions. Such corporations, being mere creatures of law, can only exercise the powers specially granted and defined. Experience has shown that they are the most useful agencies of modern civilization. They have enabled individuals to unite to undertake great enterprises only attempted in former times by powerful governments. The good results of corporate power are shown in the vast development of our railroads and the enormous increase of business and production of all kinds.

When corporations unite merely to extend their business, as connecting lines of railway without interfering with competing lines, they are proper and lawful. Corporations tend to cheapen transportation, lessen the cost of production, and bring within the reach of millions comforts and luxuries formerly enjoyed by thousands. Formerly corporations were special grants to favored companies, but now the principle is generally adopted that no private corporation shall be created with exclusive rights or privileges. The corporate rights granted to one are open to all. In this way more than three thousand national banks have been formed with the same rights and privileges, and the business is open to all competitors. In most of the States general railroad laws provide the terms on which all railroads may be built, with like rights and privileges. Corporate rights open to all are not in any sense a monopoly, but tend to promote free competition of all on the same conditions. They are mere creatures of the law, to exercise only well defined powers, and are not in any way interfered with by this bill.

This bill does not seek to cripple combinations of capital and labor, the formation of partnerships or of corporations, but only to prevent and control combinations made with a view to prevent competition, or for the restraint of trade, or to increase the profits of the producer at the cost of the consumer. It is the unlawful combination, tested by the rules of common law and human experience, that is aimed at by this bill, and not the lawful and useful combination. Unlawful combinations made by individuals are declared by the several States to be against public policy and void, and in proper cases they may be punished as criminals. If their business is lawful they can combine in any way and enjoy the advantage of their united skill and capital, provided they do not combine to prevent competition. A limited monopoly secured by a patent right is an admitted exception, for this is the only way by which an inventor can be paid for his invention.

Any other attempt by individuals to secure a monopoly should be subject to the same law of restraint applied to partnerships and corporations. A partnership is unlawful when its business tends to restrain trade, to deal in forbidden productions, or to encourage immoral and injurious pursuits, such as lotteries and the like; but if its business is lawful and open to competition with others with like skill and capital, it can not be dangerous. A corporation may be, and usually is, a more powerful and useful combination than a partnership. It is an artificial person without fear of death, without a soul to save or body to punish; but if other corporations can be formed on equal terms a monopoly is impossible. If it becomes powerful enough to exercise an undue influence in one State it is met by free competition with producers in all the other States in the Union and by importation from all the world, subject only to such duties as the public necessities demand.

Mr. President, I have thus far confined my argument to the statement of what this bill does not do; that is, it does not interfere with any lawful business in the United States, whether conducted by a corporation, or a partnership, or an individual. It deals only with unlawful combinations, unlawful by the code of any law of any civilized nation of ancient or modern times.

But associated enterprise and capital are not satisfied with partnerships and corporations competing with each other, and have invented a new form of combination commonly called trusts, that seeks to avoid competition by combining the controlling corporations, partnerships, and individuals engaged in the same business, and placing the power and property of the combination under the government of a few individuals, and often under the control of a single man called a trustee, a chairman, or a president.

The sole object of such a combination is to make competition impossible. It can control the market, raise or lower prices, as will best promote its selfish interests, reduce prices in a particular locality and break down competition and advance prices at will where competition does not exist. Its governing motive is to increase the profits of the parties composing it. The law of selfishness, uncontrolled by competition, compels it to disregard the interest of the consumer. It dictates terms to transportation companies, it commands the price of labor without fear of strikes, for in its field it allows no competitors. Such a combination is far more dangerous than any heretofore invented, and, when it embraces the great body of all the corporations engaged in a particular industry in all of the States of the Union, it tends to advance the price to the consumer of any article produced, it is a substantial monopoly injurious to the public, and, by the rule of both the common and the civil law, is null and void and the just subject of restraint by the courts, of forfeiture of corporate rights and privileges, and in some cases should be denounced as a crime, and the individuals engaged in it should be punished as criminals. It is this kind of a combination we have to deal with now.

If the concentered powers of this combination are intrusted to a single man, it is a kingly prerogative, inconsistent with our form of government, and should be subject to the strong resistance of the State and national authorities. If anything is wrong this is wrong. If we will not endure a king as a political power we should not endure a king over the production, transportation, and sale of any of the necessaries of life. If we would not submit to an emperor we should not submit to an autocrat of trade, with power to prevent competition and to fix the price of any commodity. If the combination is confined to a State the State should apply the remedy; if it is interstate and controls any production in many States, Congress must apply the remedy. If the combination is aided by our tariff laws they should be promptly changed, and, if necessary, equal competition with all the world should be invited in the monopolized article. If the combination affects interstate transportation or is aided in any way by a transportation company, it falls clearly within the power of Congress, and the remedy should be aimed at the corporations embraced in it, and should be swift and sure.

Do I exaggerate the evil we have to deal with? I do not think so. I do not wish to single out any particular trust or combination. It is not a particular trust, but the system I am [sic] at. I will only cite a very few instances of combinations that have been the subject of judicial or legislative inquiry, to show what has been and what can be done by them.

I quote from the opinion of Judge Baxter, in the case of Handy *et al.*, trustees, *vs.* Cleveland and Marietta Railroad Company, Federal Reporter, volume 31, pages 689 to 693, inclusive, where it appears, to quote the exact language of the learned judge:

That the Standard Oil Company and George Rice were competitors in the business of refining oil; that each obtained supplies in the neighborhood of Macksburgh, a station of said railroad, from whence the same was carried to Marietta or Cleveland, and that for this service both were equally dependent upon the railroad, then in the hands of the receiver.

It further appears that the Standard Oil Company desired to "crush" Rice and his business, and that under a threat of building a pipe for the conveyance of its oil and withdrawing its patronage from the receiver, O'Day, one of its agents, "compelled" Terry, who was acting for and on behalf of the receiver, to carry its oil at 10 cents per barrel and charge Rice 35 cents per barrel for a like service, and pay the Standard Oil Company 25 cents out of the 35 cents thus exacted from Rice, "making," in the judgment of the receiver, "$25 per day clear money" for it (the Standard Oil Company) "on Rice's oil alone."[1.291]

It also appears in an equity suit in which the Commonwealth of Pennsylvania was complainant and the Pennsylvania Railroad Company was ⊥ defendant, filed in the supreme court of Pennsylvania for the western district, in the year 1879, and where A. J. Cassatt, then third vice-president in charge of the transportation department of the Pennsylvania Railroad Company, testified that the Standard Oil Company were [sic] receiving over and above current drawbacks the following rebates and allowances, namely:

Forty-nine cents per barrel on crude oil from the Bradford oil region to tide water; 51 1/2 cents per barrel crude oil from the lower oil region to tide water; and 61 1/2 cents on refined oil from Cleveland to tide water.

In the year 1878 the railroad shipments of oil had reached 13,700,000 barrels. Assuming 80 per cent. of this to be the traffic of the Standard Oil Company and that but 50 cents per barrel rebate was paid by the railroad companies, the annual illegal receipts by the Standard Oil Company would have been $5,480,000, not including the receipts of the American Transfer Company from such traffic as was not embraced within the 80 per cent. of the Standard Oil Company.

Another case of unlawful combination was the case of David M. Richardson vs. Russell A. Alger et al.,[1.292] recently decided in the supreme court of the State of Michigan. I have the opinion by the chief-justice which sufficiently states the nature of the combination and the view taken of it by that court. This is quite a leading case. In order that I may not do injustice to any one I will lay before the Senate the judgment of the court in full, as expressed by the judges of the supreme court of Michigan: . . .[1.293]

Mr. PLATT. What was the conclusion of the court?

Mr. SHERMAN. They declared the combination null and void, against public policy, and refused to entertain jurisdiction to settle the accounts between the parties, because this case arose on a dispute between two of the parties, Mr. Richardson and General Alger. They declared it unlawful and void and set aside the contract.

Mr. PLATT. If the Senator will permit me, the object of my inquiry was to make it appear clearly that the court as at present constituted has so decided.

Mr. SHERMAN. That was a State matter between parties living within the State, and therefore did not involve any of the questions which are requisite to impart jurisdiction to United States courts under this bill.

Mr. CULLOM. Where was this?

Mr. SHERMAN. It was in Michigan. The supreme court of Michigan made the decision. I have here the case of Craft et al. vs. McConoughy, in the supreme court of Illinois, reported in the seventy-ninth volume of Illinois Reports.[1.294] I am showing that the State courts in different States have declared this thing, when it exists in a State, to be unlawful and void.

Mr. CULLOM. Everywhere.

Mr. SHERMAN. In every case, everywhere, and all I wish is to have the courts of

---

[1.291] 31 F. 689, 692 (C.C.S.D. Ohio 1887).

[1.292] Richardson v. Buhl, 77 Mich. 632, 43 N.W. 1102 (1889).

[1.293] Senator Sherman read the opinion of the court in which it was held that the Diamond Match Co.'s practices in excluding competition were unlawful, and its contracts were void as against public policy.

[1.294] 79 Ill. 346 (1875).

the United States do by these greater combinations what has been done already by the courts of the States.

In the case of Richard C. Craft *et al. vs*. James O. McConoughy, in the supreme court of Illinois, reported in the seventy-ninth volume of Illinois Reports, it was decided that—

> A contract entered into by the grain dealers of a town which, on its face, indicates that they have formed a partnership for the purpose of dealing in grain, but the true object of which is to form a secret combination which would stifle all competition and enable the parties, by secret and fraudulent means, to control the price of grain, costs of storage, and expense of shipment at such town, is in restraint of trade, and consequently void on the ground of public policy.[1.295]

I will insert in my remarks the decision of Mr. Justice Craig without reading it at this time.

Mr. GEORGE. Will the Senator state what was the decision of the court in that case?

Mr. SHERMAN. They set aside the contract.

Mr GEORGE. The suit was to annul the contract?

Mr. SHERMAN. To annul the contract, and they said they would treat it as illegal. This is the decision:

> While these parties were in business, in competition, they had the undoubted right to establish their own rates for grain stored and commissions for shipment and sale. They would pay as high or low a price for grain as they saw proper and as they could make contracts with the producer. So long as competition was free the interest of the public was safe. The laws of trade, in connection with the rigor of competition, was all the guaranty the public required, but the secret combination created by the contract destroyed all competition and created a monopoly, against which the public interest had no protection.[1.296]

I find another case, that of the Chicago Gas-Light and Coke Company *vs*. The People's Gas-Light and Coke Company, on page 531, 121 Illinois Reports,[1.297] in which it appears that the Chicago Gas-Light and Coke Company was incorporated in 1849 with the exclusive privilege of supplying Chicago and its inhabitants with gas for a period of ten years. Subsequently another company, under the name of the People's Gas-Light and Coke Company, was chartered, with power to manufacture and sell gas in the city of Chicago and to erect the necessary apparatus for that purpose, with the usual provisions as to laying their pipes in the streets of the city. Subsequently the two companies divided the city between them, allowing each the exclusive right of supplying gas therein for one hundred years and stipulating that neither would interfere with the business of the other in its own territory.

Here is the judgment of the court setting aside that contract as preventing competition, as null and void by the rules of the common law. I have only now been able to get this, but I will see that it is correctly quoted from the regular report, and will read the brief statement I have:

> The defendant company, claiming as the assignee of the exclusive privilege in the territory set off to it, filed a bill against the other for a specific performance of the contract of assignment. The court refused the relief sought, holding "that by the grant of the second charter the Legislature intended to do away with the monopoly" granted under the first; "that, although the contract involved a partial restraint of trade, and therefore might not, by the general rule of law, be invalid, yet that the general rule does not apply to corporations engaged in a public business in which the public have an interest," and that the contract was void.[1.298]

In a recent case, that of the People of Illinois *vs*. The Chicago Gas Trust Company,[1.299] which I find reported in a late paper—

[1.295] *Id*. The quoted material is a headnote.
[1.296] *Id*. at 350.
[1.297] The correct citation is 121 Ill. 530, 13 N.E. 169 (1889).
[1.298] *Id*. at 544-45, 13 N.E. at 174-75.
[1.299] 130 Ill. 268, 22 N.E. 798 (1889).

the trust combination consisted of a new corporation holding a separate charter under the general incorporation law of Illinois. In applying for its charter the Gas Trust Company stated the objects of its incorporation to be "the erection and operation of works in Chicago and other places in Illinois for the manufacture, sale, and distribution of gas and electricity, and to purchase and hold or sell the capital stock of any gas or electric company or companies in Chicago or elsewhere in Illinois." Having received its charter the company purchased a majority of the capital stock of each of the gas companies doing business in Chicago, four in number.

The information charges that, by so purchasing and holding a majority of the shares of the capital stock of each of the four companies, the appellee usurps and exercises "powers, liberties, privileges, and franchises not conferred by law."

* * * * * * *

"That by purchasing and holding such stock it secured the control of each of the companies; that such control 'by the appellee, an outside and independent corporation, suppresses outside competition between them and destroys their diversity of interest and all motive for competition. There is thus built up a virtual monopoly in the manufacture and sale of gas.' It also held that 'a corporation thus formed for the purpose of manufacturing and selling gas * * * has no power to purchase and hold or sell shares of stock in other gas companies as an incident to the purpose of its formation, even though such power is specified in its articles of incorporation.' "[1.300]

Mr. CULLOM. That is a recent decision.

Mr. SHERMAN. Yes, a very recent decision, and it has not yet gone into the reports. There is a still more recent case, and I am reminded of it by the remark of the Senator from Connecticut [Mr. PLATT], that of The People of New York *vs.* The North River Sugar-Refining Company, a trust which was investigated by a committee of the House of Representatives, of which Mr. Bacon was chairman, and which came before the supreme court of New York at circuit in January, 1889, was carried to the general term in November last, and is reported in volume 2 [*sic*], Abbott's New Cases, page 164,[1.301] both decisions being against the defendant, a member of the so-called trust company. This is a statement of the case together with the decision of Mr. Justice Daniels in rendering judgment:

The case was that seventeen corporations, in at least six different States, all engaged in the sugar-refining business, arranged to transfer their stock to a board of eleven members and were to receive in return from the association shares of stock to be issued by it and to be distributed among the several corporations in proportion to the amounts of stock held by them. The profits of the business were to be divided among the holders of certificates for shares issued by the board. No limit for the duration of the association was fixed, and its capital stock was fixed at $50,000,000. A suit was brought by the attorney-general in the name of the people of New York against one of the associate corporations to vacate and annul its charter for "abuse of its powers" and for exercising "privileges or franchises not conferred upon it by law" by participating "in a combination with certain sugar refineries." Upon both grounds the court found against the defendant.

Daniels, Justice, in rendering his judgment, said:

"The defendant had disabled itself from exercising its functions and employing its franchises, as it was intended it should by the act under which it was incorporated, and had by the action which was taken placed itself in complete subordination to another and different organization, to be used for an unlawful purpose detrimental and injurious to the public. * * * This was a subversion of the object for which the company was created, and it authorized the attorney-general to maintain and prosecute this action to vacate and annul its charter."[1.302]

This case may be said to be a leading case and was throughly discussed and considered. The opinion of the court at the general term pronounced by Mr. Justice Barrett covers the whole ground upon which the great body of the trusts in the United States rests. The suit presented the distinct question raised by many of the contracts which are the bases of these combinations. To use the language of that judge:

Any combination the tendency of which is to prevent competition in its broad and general sense, and to control, and thus at will enhance, prices to the detriment of the public, is a legal monopoly. And this rule is applicable to every monopoly whether the supply be restricted by

---

[1.300] The quoted material does not appear in the court's opinion.

[1.301] 22 Abb. N. Cas. 164, 3 N.Y.S. 401 (1889).

[1.302] 7 N.Y.S. 406, 415 (Sup. Ct., Gen. Term, 1st Dep't 1889).

nature or susceptible of indefinite production. The difficulty of effecting the unlawful purpose may be greater in the one case than in the other, but it is never impossible. Nor need it be permanent or complete. It is enough that it may be even temporarily and partially successful. The question in the end is, does it inevitably tend to public injury?[1.303]

Then follows a long and elaborate decision, and I think it is the unanimous judgment of the court—at least I see no dissent marked, and I presume it is the unanimous judgment of that high court of the State of New York—in a case which occurred only last year when it had before it this sugar company. That being a corporation of New York, it could deal with that corporation alone, but the combination was between that company and sixteen others, if I remember aright—perhaps the number was greater. In the courts of the United States all of them might have been parties, but as a matter of course the supreme court of New York could not extend its jurisdiction beyond the limits of its own territory.

I might add to the cases cited innumerable cases in nearly all the States and in England, and in all of them it will appear that while the law in respect to contracts in restraint of trade and combinations to prevent competition and to advance the price of necessaries of life has varied somewhat, but in all of them, whether the combinations are by individuals, partnerships, or corporations, when the purpose of the combination or its plain tendency is to prevent competition, the courts have enforced the rule of the common law and have vigorously used the judicial power in subverting them.

And now it is for Congress to say, when the devices of able lawyers and the cupidity of powerful corporations have united to spread these combinations over all the States of the Union, embracing in their folds nearly every necessary of life, whether it is not time to invoke the judicial power conferred upon the courts of the United States to deal with these combinations; when lawful to support them and when unlawful to suppress them.

I might state the case of all the combinations which now control the transportation and sale of nearly all the leading productions of the country that have recently been made familiar by the public press, such as the cotton trust, the whisky trust, the sugar-refiners' trust, the cotton-bagging trust, the copper trust, the salt trust, and many others, some of which have been the subjects of legislative inquiry and others of judicial process; but it is scarcely necessary to do so, as they are all modeled upon the same plan and involve the same principles. They are all combinations of corporations and individuals of many States forming a league and covenant, under the control of trustees with power to suspend the production of some and enlarge the production of others, and absolutely control the supply of the article which they produce, and with a uniform design to prevent competition, to break it down wherever it appears to threaten their interest.

I have seen within a few days in the public prints a notice of a combination intended to affect the price of silver bullion, as follows:

WITH A CAPITAL OF TWENTY-FIVE MILLION DOLLARS.

Chicago, March 2.

The Herald to-day says that, with the exception of five companies, all the refining and smelting companies of the United States have formed a trust, with a capital of $25,000,000, of which $15,000,000 is to be common stock and the remaining preferred.

If such a combination is formed it will enable a few corporations in different States to corner the Government of the United States in its proposed effort, by a bill pending in the Senate, to purchase silver bullion as the basis and security for paper money. Can any one doubt that such a combination is unlawful, against public policy, with power enough to control the operation of your laws, and destructive to all competition which you invite? It is scarcely necessary on this point to quote further from the law books. Every decision or treatise on the law of contracts agrees in denouncing such a combination.

Judge Gibson, in the case of the Commonwealth of Pennsylvania *vs.* Carlisle,[1.304] states the general principle in terse and vigorous language:

[1.303] The correct citation is 22 Abb N. Cas. at 207, 3 N.Y.S. at 413.

[1.304] Commonwealth *ex rel.* Chew v. Carlisle, Brightly's N.P. 36 (Ct. of Nisi Prius 1821).

A combination is criminal whenever the act to be done has a necessary tendency to prejudice the public or to oppress individuals by unjustly subjecting them to the power of the confederates, and giving effect to the purpose of the latter, whether of extortion or of mischief.[1.305]

The solicitor of the Standard Oil Trust, Mr. Dodd, in an argument which I have before me, admits that certain combinations are null and void. He says:

When I speak of unrestricted combinations I do not mean that combinations should be allowed under all circumstances and for all purposes. While combination is not, *per se,* evil, its purposes may be. The law is possibly our best guide on this subject. It has progressed as experience and the necessities of business required it to progress, from the idea that all combinations were wrong to the idea that all persons should be left free to combine for all legitimate purposes. To this day, however, the law is properly very jealous of certain classes of combinations, such as—

First. Where the parties combining exercise a public employment or possess exclusive privileges, and are to that extent monopolies.

Second. Where the purpose and effect of the combination is to "corner" any article necessary to the public.

Third. Where the purpose and effect of the combination is to limit production, and thereby to unduly enhance prices.

* * * * * * *

These things are just as unlawful without combination as with it. In other words, the evil is not in the combination, but in its purposes and results.

* * * * * * *

The law condemns any arrangement the purpose or necessary tendency of which is to destroy all competition and thus to prejudice the public.

⊥2460 ⊥ I accept the law as stated by Mr. Dodd, that all combinations are not void, a proposition which no one doubts, but I assert that the tendency of all combinations of corporations, such as those commonly called trusts, and the inevitable effect of them, is to prevent competition and to restrain trade. This must be manifest to every intelligent mind. Still this can not be assumed as against any combination unless upon a fair hearing it should appear to a court of competent jurisdiction that the agreement composing such combination is necessarily injurious to the public and destructive to fair trade. These modern combinations are uniformly composed of citizens and corporations of many States, and therefore they can only be dealt with by a jurisdiction as broad as their combination. The State courts have held in many cases that they can not interfere in controlling the action of corporations of other States. If corporations from other States do business within a State, the courts may control their action within the limits of the State, but when a trust is created by a combination of many corporations from many States, there are no courts with jurisdiction broad enough to deal with them except the courts of the United States.

I admit that it is difficult to define in legal language the precise line between lawful and unlawful combinations. This must be left for the courts to determine in each particular case. All that we, as lawmakers, can do is to declare general principles, and we can be assured that the courts will apply them so as to carry out the meaning of the law, as the courts of England and the United States have done for centuries. This bill is only an honest effort to declare a rule of action, and if it is imperfect it is for the wisdom of the Senate to perfect it. Although this body is always conservative, yet, whatever may be said of it, it has always been ready to preserve, not only popular rights in their broad sense, but the rights of individuals as against associated and corporate wealth and power.

It is sometimes said of these combinations that they reduce prices to the consumer by better methods of production, but all experience shows that this saving of cost goes to the pockets of the producer. The price to the consumer depends upon the supply, which can be reduced at pleasure by the combination. It will vary in time and place by the extent of competition, and when that ceases it will depend upon the urgency of the demand for the article. The aim is always for the highest price that will not check the demand, and, for the most of the necessaries of life, that is perennial and perpetual.

[1.305] *Id.* at 40.

But, they say, competition is open to all; if you do not like our prices, establish another combination or trust. As was said by the supreme court of New York, when the combination already includes all or nearly all the producers, what room is there for another? And if another is formed and is legal, what is to prevent another combination? Sir, now the people of the United States as well as of other countries are feeling the power and grasp of these combinations, and are demanding of every Legislature and of Congress a remedy for this evil, only grown into huge proportions in recent times. They had monopolies and mortmains of old, but never before such giants as in our day. You must heed their appeal or be ready for the socialist, the communist, and the nihilist. Society is now disturbed by forces never felt before.

The popular mind is agitated with problems that may disturb social order, and among them all none is more threatening than the inequality of condition, of wealth, and opportunity that has grown within a single generation out of the concentration of capital into vast combinations to control production and trade and to break down competition. These combinations already defy or control powerful transportation corporations and reach State authorities. They reach out their Briarean arms to every part of our country. They are imported from abroad. Congress alone can deal with them, and if we are unwilling or unable there will soon be a trust for every production and a master to fix the price for every necessity of life.

But it is said by the Senator from Mississippi [Mr. GEORGE], who honors me with his attention, that this bill is unconstitutional, that Congress can not confer jurisdiction on the courts of the United States in this class of cases. I respectfully submit that, in his subtle argument, he has entirely overlooked the broad jurisdiction conferred by the Constitution upon courts of the United States in ordinary cases of law and equity between certain parties, as well as cases arising under the Constitution, laws, and treaties of the United States. Much the greater proportion of the cases decided in these courts have no relation to the Constitution, laws, or treaties. They embrace admiralty and maritime law, all controversies in which the United States are a party, controversies between two or more States, between a State and citizens of another State, between citizens of different States, between citizens of the same State claiming lands under grants of different States, and between a State, or the citizens thereof, and foreign states, citizens, or subjects.

This jurisdiction embraces the whole field of the common law and of commercial law, especially of the law of contracts, in all cases where the United States is a party and in all cases between citizens of different States. The jurisdiction is as broad as the earth, except only it does not extend to controversies within a State between citizens of a State. All the combinations at which this bill aims are combinations embracing persons and corporations of several States. Each State can deal with a combination within the State, but only the General Government can deal with combinations reaching not only the several States, but the commercial world. This bill does not include combinations within a State, but if the Senator from Mississippi can make this clearer any proposition he will make to that effect will certainly be accepted and I will cheerfully vote for his proposition. Can any one doubt the jurisdiction of the courts of the United States in all cases in which the United States is a party and in all cases between citizens, including corporations, of different States? I will read a note from Story on the Constitution:

> It has been very correctly remarked by Mr. Justice Iredell that "the judicial power of the United States is of a peculiar kind. It is, indeed, commensurate with the ordinary legislative and executive government and the powers which concern treaties.["] But it also goes further. When certain parties are concerned, although the subject in controversy does not relate to any special objects of authority of the General Government, wherein the separate sovereignties of the separate States are blended in one common mass of supremacy, yet the General Government has a judicial authority in regard to such subjects of controversy; and the Legislature of the United States may pass all laws necessary to give such judicial authority its proper effect.[1.306]

The judicial power of the United States extends to all questions of law and equity which arise between citizens of different States or between the other classes named. The jurisdiction of the courts of the United States may depend either upon the nature of the

---

[1.306] 3 J. STORY, COMMENTARIES ON THE CONSTITUTION OF THE UNITED STATES 499 (1833).

cause arising under the Constitution, laws, or treaties of the United States, or upon the parties to the case.

Chief-Justice Marshall, in the case of Cohens *vs.* Virginia, 6 Wheaton, page 378, says:

> The second section of the third article of the Constitution defines the extent of the judicial power of the United States. Jurisdiction is given to the courts of the Union in two classes of cases. In the first, their jurisdiction depends on the character of the cause, whoever may be the parties. This class comprehends "all cases, in law and equity, arising under this Constitution, the laws of the United States, and treaties made, or which shall be made, under their authority." This clause extends the jurisdiction of the court to all the cases described, without making in its terms any exceptions whatever, and without any regard to the condition of the party. If there be any exception, it is to be implied against the express words of the article.
>
> In the second class the jurisdiction depends entirely on the character of the parties. In this are comprehended "controversies between two or more States, between a State and citizens of another State, and between a State and foreign states, citizens, or subjects." If these be the parties, it is entirely unimportant what may be the subject of controversy. Be it what it may, these parties have a constitutional right to come into the courts of the Union.[1.307]

The same question was involved in the celebrated case of Osborn *vs.* Bank of the United States (9 Wheaton, page 738),[1.308] in which it was contended that the courts of the United States could not exercise jurisdiction because several questions might arise in such suits, which might depend upon the general principles of law, and not upon any act of Congress. It was held that Congress did constitutionally possess the power and had rightfully conferred it in that charter. Chief-Justice Marshall said there, in one of the most famous of his opinions involving grave constitutional questions:

> A cause may depend upon several questions of fact and law. Some of these may depend on the construction of a law of the United States; others, on principles unconnected with that law.[1.309]

It was held in that case that the Bank of the United States being created by Congress the right might be conferred upon it by Congress to sue in the courts of the United States without respect to the nature or character of the controversy.

> The clause giving the bank a right to sue in the circuit courts of the United States stands on the same principle with the acts authorizing officers of the United States who sue in their own names to sue in the courts of the United States.
>
> * * * * * * *
>
> If it be said that a suit brought by the bank may depend in fact altogether on questions unconnected with any law of the United States, it is equally true with respect to suits brought by the Postmaster-General.
>
> * * * * * * *
>
> Cases may also arise under laws of the United States by implication as well as by express enactment, so that due redress may be administered by the judicial power of the United States.[1.310]

This goes to show that, the jurisdiction once acquired by having the parties before the court, it extends to any kind of remedial jurisdiction, any kind of a case.

It has also been asked, and may again be asked—

Chief-Justice Marshall says—

> why the words "cases in equity" are found in this clause. What equitable causes can grow out of the Constitution, laws, and treaties of the United States? To this the general answer of the Federalist seems at once clear and satisfactory. There is hardly a subject of litigation between individuals which may not involve those ingredients of fraud, accident, trust, or hardship which would render the matter an object of equitable rather than of legal jurisdiction, as the distinction is known and established in several of the States. It is the peculiar province, for

---

[1.307] 19 U.S. (6 Wheat.) 264, 378, 5 L. Ed. 257, 284–85 (1821).
[1.308] 22 U.S. (9 Wheat.) 738, 6 L. Ed. 204 (1824).
[1.309] 22 U.S. (9 Wheat.) at 821–22.
[1.310] *Id.* at 825.

instance, of a court of equity to relieve against what are called hard bargains. These are contracts in which, though there may have been no direct fraud or deceit sufficient to invalidate them in a court of law, yet there may have been some undue and unconscionable advantage taken of the necessities or misfortunes of one of the parties which a court of equity would not tolerate.[1.311]

By the Constitution of the United States this jurisdiction of the courts of the United States extends to all cases in law and equity between certain parties. What is meant by the words of "cases in law and equity?" Does this include only cases growing out of the Constitution, statutes, and treaties of the United States? It has been held over and over again that, by these words, the Constitution has adopted ⊥ as a rule of remedial justice the common law of England as administered by courts of law and equity.

⊥2461

Judge Story, in his work on the Constitution, volume 2, page 485,[1.312] says:

What is to be understood by "cases in law and equity" in this clause? Plainly, cases at the common law, as contradistinguished from cases in equity, according to the known distinctions in the jurisprudence of England, which our ancestors brought with them upon their emigration, and with which all the American States were familiarly acquainted. Here, then, at least, the Constitution of the United States appeals to and adopts the common law to the extent of making it a rule in the pursuit of remedial justice in the courts of the Union. If the remedy must be in law or in equity, according to the course of proceedings at the common law, in cases arising under the Constitution, laws, and treaties of the United States, it would seem irresistibly to follow that the principles of decision by which these remedies must be administered must be derived from the same source. Hitherto such has been the uniform interpretation and mode of administering justice in all civil cases in the courts of the United States in this class of cases.

But I need not pursue the matter further. The question of the character and nature of the controversy when the proper legal parties are before the court is never entered into. In some cases, where the rules of law and equity have been modified by legislation, the courts of the United States have followed the local law as construed and administered by the courts of the State where the controversy arose, but it is clearly within the power of Congress to prescribe the rule as well as to define the methods of procedure in the courts of law and equity of the United States; so I submit that this bill as it stands, without any reference to the specific powers granted to Congress by the Constitution, is clearly authorized under the judicial article of the Constitution. This bill declares a rule of public policy in accordance with the rule of the common law. It limits its operation to certain important functions of the Government, among which are the importation, transportation, and sale of articles imported into the United States, the production, manufacture, or sale of articles of domestic growth or production, and domestic raw materials competing with a similar article upon which a duty is levied by the United States.

If this bill were broader than it is and declared unlawful all trusts and combinations in restraint of trade and production null and void, there could be no question that in suits brought by the United States to enforce it, or suits between individuals or corporations of different States for injuries done in violation of it, it would be clearly within the power of Congress and the jurisdiction of the court. The mere limitation of this jurisdiction to certain classes of combinations does not affect in the slightest degree the power of Congress to pass a much broader and more comprehensive bill.

Nor is it necessary to limit the jurisdiction of the courts of the United States to suits between citizens of different States. It extends also to suits by the United States when authorized by law. It is eminently proper that when a combination of persons or corporations of different States tends to affect injuriously the interests or powers of the United States, as well as of citizens of the United States, the proceeding should be in the courts of the United States and in the name of the United States. The legal process of quo warranto or mandamus ought, in such cases, to be issued at the suit of the

---

[1.311] This quote does not appear in either *Cohens* or *Osborn*.

[1.312] The correct citation is 3 J. STORY, COMMENTARIES ON THE CONSTITUTION OF THE UNITED STATES 506 (1833).

United States. A citizen would appear in such a suit at every disadvantage, and even the United States is scarcely the equal of a powerful corporation in a suit where a single officer with insufficient pay is required to compete with the ablest lawyers encouraged with compensation far beyond the limits allowed to the highest government officer. It is in such proceedings that the battle with these great combinations is to be fought.

But, aside from the power drawn from the third article of the Constitution, I believe this bill is clearly within the power conferred expressly upon Congress to regulate commerce with foreign nations and among the several States and its power to levy and collects [sic] taxes, duties, imposts, and excises.

And here, Mr. President, I wish to again call attention to the argument of the Senator from Mississippi [Mr. GEORGE]. He treats this bill as a criminal statute from beginning to end, and not as a remedial statute with civil remedies. He says:

> The first thing which attracts our attention, therefore, is that if the agreement or combination, which is the crime, be made outside of the jurisdiction of the United States it is also without the terms of the law and can not be punished in the United States.

It is true that if a crime is committed outside of the United States it can not be punished in the United States. But if an unlawful combination is made outside of the United States and in pursuance of it property is brought within the United States such property is subject to our laws. It may be seized. A civil remedy by attachment could be had. Any person interested in the United States could be made a party.

Either a foreigner or a native may escape "the criminal part of the law," as he says, by staying out of our jurisdiction, as very many do, but if they have property here it is subject to civil process. I do not see what harm a foreigner can do us if neither his person nor his property is here. He may combine or conspire to his heart's content if none of his co-conspirators are here or his property is not here.

Again he says:

> But suppose, what I think, however, is highly improbable, some of these great combinations should be made in the United States. Will the case be any better for the people in whose interest we profess to legislate? The combination, agreement, or trusts, etc., must, under the bill, be made "with the intention to prevent full and free competition in the importation, transportation, or sale of articles imported into the United States."

The word "intention" is not in the bill. It was proposed as an amendment.

Mr. GEORGE. It was in the bill as reported.

Mr. SHERMAN. Ah, it was proposed as an amendment.

Mr. GEORGE. By the Committee on Finance?

Mr. SHERMAN. Yes, but the Senator treated it as being a part of the bill. It was a proposed amendment to the bill and was never adopted.

Mr. GEORGE. The original bill was proposed by the Senator from Ohio.

Mr. SHERMAN. That had no such word in it.

Mr. GEORGE. That had no such word in it, but when the bill came back from the committee it did have the word in it.

Mr. SHERMAN. But the bill as it comes from the committee now has certainly no such word in it. It was proposed as an amendment, but has no place in the first section. The language is: "made with a view or which tend." The "*intention*" can not be proved, though "*tendency*" can. The tendency is the test of legality. The intention is the test of a crime.

And so all through his speech he quotes the phrases of a "certain specified intent," "specific intent," "penal legislation," "reasonable doubt," "indicted must be acquitted." He treats this bill very much as he does the Constitution of the United States, something to be evaded, to be strictly construed, instead of being what it is, a remedial statute, a bill of rights, a charter of liberty. He no doubt is partly justified in this by the amendments proposed but not adopted, and by the third section, which would be subject to his criticism, and which I will join him in striking out.

Mr. GEORGE. It was an amendment proposed by the committee?

Mr. SHERMAN. Yes. Now, Mr. President, what is this bill? A remedial statute to enforce by civil process in the courts of the United States the common law against monopolies. How is such a law to be construed? Liberally with a view to promote its objects. What are the evils complained of? They are well depicted by the Senator from Mississippi in this language, and I will read it as my own with quotation marks.

Mr. GEORGE. I am very much obliged for the compliment.

Mr. SHERMAN. "These trusts and combinations are great wrongs to the people. They have invaded many of the most important branches of business. They operate with a double-edged sword. They increase beyond reason the cost of the necessaries of life and business, and they decrease the cost of the raw material, the farm products of the country. They regulate prices at their will, depress the price of what they buy and increase the price of what they sell. They aggregate to themselves great, enormous wealth by extortion which makes the people poor. Then, making this extorted wealth the means of further extortion from their unfortunate victims, the people of the United States, they pursue unmolested, unrestrained by law, their ceaseless round of peculation under the law, till they are fast producing that condition in our people in which the great mass of them are the servitors of those who have this aggregated wealth at their command."

One would think that with this conception of the evil to be dealt with he would for once turn his telescope upon the Constitution to find out power to deal with so great a wrong, and not, as usual, to reverse it, to turn the little end of the telescope to the Constitution, and then, with subtle reasoning, to dissipate the powers of the Government into thin air. He overlooks the judicial power of the courts of the United States extending to all cases where the United States is a party, or where a State may sue in the courts of the United States, or where citizens of different States are contesting parties with full power to apply a remedy by quo warranto, mandamus, judgment, and execution. He treats the question as depending alone upon the power to regulate foreign and domestic commerce and of taxation. I submit that, without reference to the judicial power, they are amply sufficient to justify this bill. What are they?

Congress shall have power to regulate commerce with foreign nations and among the several States and with the Indian tribes.

The want of this power was one of the leading defects of the Confederation, and probably as much as any one cause conduced to the establishment of a Constitution. It is a power vital to the prosperity of the Union; and without it the Government could scarcely deserve the name of a National Government and would soon sink into discredit and imbecility. It would stand as a mere shadow of sovereignty to mock our hopes and involve us in a common ruin. (Story on the Constitution, volume 2, page 2.)

What is the extent of this power? What is the meaning of the word "commerce?" It means the exchange of all commodities between different places or communities. It includes all trade and traffic, all modes of transportation by land or by sea, all kinds of navigation, every species of ship or sail, every mode of transit, from the dog-cart to the Pullman car, every kind of motive power, from the mule or horse to the most recent application of steam or electricity applied on every road, from the trail over the mountain or the plain to the perfected railway or the steel bridges over great rivers or arms of the sea. The power of Congress extends to all this commerce, except only that limited within the bounds of a State.

Under this power no bridge can be built over a navigable stream except by the consent of Congress. All the network of railroads crossing from State to State, from ocean to ocean, from east to west, and from north to south are now curbed, regulated, and controlled by the power of Congress over commerce. Most of the combinations aimed at by this bill are directly engaged in this commerce. They command and control in many cases and even own some of the agencies of this commerce. They have invented or own new modes of transportation, such as pipelines for petroleum or gas, reaching from State to State, crossing farms and highways and public property.

Can it be that with this vast power Congress can not protect the people from combinations in restraint of trade that are unlawful by every code of civil law adopted by civilized nations? It may "regulate commerce;" can it not protect commerce, nullify contracts that restrain commerce, turn it from its natural courses, increase the price of articles, and therefore diminish the amount of commerce?

It is said that commerce does not commence until production ends and the voyage commences. This may be true as far as the actual ownership or sale of articles within a State is subject to State authorities. I do not question the decision of the Supreme Court in the case of Coe vs. Errol,[1.313] quoted by the Senator from Mississippi, that property within a State is subject to taxation though intended to be transported into another State. This bill does not propose to deal with property within a State or with combinations within the State, but only when the combination extends to two or more States or engages in either State or foreign commerce. It is said that these combinations can and will evade this bill. I have no doubt they will do so in many cases, but they can do so only by ceasing to interfere with foreign and interstate commerce.

Their power for mischief will be greatly crippled by this bill. Their present plan of organization was adopted only to evade the jurisdiction of State courts. They still maintain their workshops, their mode of production, by means of partnerships or corporations in a State. If their productions competed with those of similar partnerships or corporations in other States it would be all right. But to prevent such competition they unite the interests of all these partnerships and corporations into a combination, sometimes called a trust, sometimes a new corporation located in a city remote from the places of production, and then regulate and control the sale and transportation of all the products of many States, discontinuing one at their will, some running at half time, others pressed at their full capacity, fixing the price at pleasure in every mart of the United States, dictating terms to transportation companies, controlling your commerce; and yet it is said that Congress, armed with full power to regulate commerce, is helpless and unable to deal with this monster.

Sir, the object aimed at by this bill is to secure competition of the productions of different States which necessarily enter into interstate and foreign commerce. These combinations strike directly at the commerce over which Congress alone has jurisdiction. "Congress may regulate interstate and foreign commerce," and it is absurd to contend that Congress may not prohibit contracts and arrangements that are hostile to such commerce.

Congress also has power "to lay and collect taxes, duties, imposts, and excises." It may exercise its own discretion in acting upon this power, and is only responsible to the people for the abuse of the power. All parties, from the foundation of the Government, have held that Congress may discriminate in selecting the objects and rates of taxation. Some of these taxes are levied for the direct and some for the incidental encouragement and increase of home industries. The people pay high taxes on the foreign article to induce competition at home, in the hope that the price may be reduced by competition, and with the benefit of diversifying our industries and increasing the common wealth.

Suppose one of these combinations should unite all, or nearly all, the domestic producers of an article of prime necessity with a view to prevent competition and to keep the price up to the foreign cost and duty added, would not this be in restraint of trade and commerce and affect injuriously the operation of our revenue laws? Can Congress prescribe no remedy except to repeal its taxes? Surely it may authorize the executive authorities to appeal to the courts of the United States for such a remedy, as courts habitually apply in the States for the forfeiture of charters thus abused and the punishment of officers who practice such wrongs to the public. It may also give to our citizens the right to sue for such damages as they have suffered.

In no respect does the work of our fathers in framing the Constitution of the United States appear more like the work of the Almighty Ruler of the Universe rather than the conception of human minds than by the gradual development and application of the powers conferred by it upon different branches of the Federal Government. Many of these powers have remained dormant, unused, but plainly there, awaiting the growth and progress of our country, and when the time comes and the occasion demands we find in that instrument, provided for thirteen States, a thread along the Atlantic and containing four millions of people, without manufactures, without commerce, bankrupt with debt, without credit or wealth, all the powers necessary to govern a continental empire of forty-two States, with sixty-five millions of people, the

---

[1.313] See note 1.259 *supra*.

largest in manufactures, the second in wealth, and the happiest in its institutions of all the nations of the world.

While we should not stretch the powers granted to Congress by strained construction, we can not surrender any of them; they are not ours to surrender, but whenever occasion calls we should exercise them for the benefit and protection of the people of the United States. And, sir, while I have no doubt that every word of this bill is within the powers granted to Congress, I feel that its defects are in its moderation, and that its best effect will be a warning that all trade and commerce, all agreements and arrangements, all struggles for money or property, must be governed by the universal law that the public good must be the test of all.

Mr. INGALLS and Mr. VEST addressed the Chair.

The PRESIDING OFFICER (Mr. MANDERSON in the chair). Does the Senator from Kansas rise to speak to this bill?

Mr. INGALLS. I rose to inquire if an amendment in the second degree is now pending.

Mr. REAGAN. There is.

The PRESIDING OFFICER. The amendment of the Senator from Texas to the amendment reported from the Committee on Finance is pending.

Mr. INGALLS. I give notice, then, of my intention, when it shall be in order, to offer the amendment which I send to the desk, and which I ask may be now read, and ordered to be printed.

The PRESIDING OFFICER. The amendment will be read for the information of the Senate, and ordered to be printed.

The CHIEF CLERK. It is proposed to substitute the following:

That for the purposes of this act the words "options" shall be understood to mean any contract or agreement whereby a party thereto, or any person, corporation, partnership, or association for whom or in whose behalf such contract or agreement is made acquires the right or privilege, but is not thereby obligated, to deliver to another at a future time or period any of the articles mentioned in section 3 of this act.

SEC. 2. That for the purposes of this act the word "futures" shall be understood to mean any contract or agreement whereby a party agrees to sell and deliver at a future time to another any of the articles mentioned in section 3 of this act, when at the time of making such contract or agreement the party so agreeing to make such delivery, or the party for whom he acts as agent, broker, or employé in making such contract or agreement, is not at the time of making the same the owner of the article so contracted and agreed to be delivered.

SEC. 3. That the articles of which the foregoing sections relate are wheat, corn, oats, rye, barley, cotton, and all other farm products; also, beef, pork, lard, and all other hog and cattle products.

SEC. 4. That special taxes are imposed as follows: Dealers in "options" or "futures" shall pay annually the sum of $1,000, and shall also pay the further sum of 5 cents per pound for each and every pound of cotton, or of beef, pork, lard, or other hog and cattle products, and the sum of 20 cents per bushel for each and every bushel of any of the other articles mentioned in section 3 of this act, the right or privilege of delivering which may be acquired under any "options" contract or agreement, as defined by section 1 of this act, or which may be sold to be delivered at a future time or period under any "futures" contract or agreement as defined in section 2 of this act, which said amounts shall be paid to the collector of internal revenue, as hereinafter provided, and by him accounted for, as required in respect to other special taxes collected by him. Every person, association, copartnership, or corporation who shall, in their own behalf, or as broker, agent, or employé of another, deal in "options," or make any "options" contract or agreement, as hereinbefore defined, shall be deemed a dealer in "options," and every person, association, copartnership, or corporation who shall, in their own behalf or as broker, agent, or employé of another, deal in "futures," or make any "futures" contract or agreement, as hereinbefore defined, shall be deemed a dealer in "futures."

SEC. 5. That every person, association, copartnership, or corporation engaged in or proposing to engage in the business of dealer in "options" or of dealer in "futures" as hereinbefore defined shall, before commencing such business or making any such "options" or "futures" contract or agreement, make application in writing to the collector of internal revenue for the district in which he proposes to engage in such business or make such contract or agreement, setting forth the name of the person, association, partnership, or corporation, place of residence of the applicant, the business engaged in, and where such business is to be carried on, and in case of partnership, association, or corporation the names and places of residence of the several persons constituting the same, and shall thereupon pay to such collector the sum aforesaid of $1,000, and shall also execute and deliver to such collector a bond in the penal sum of $50,000, with two or more sureties satisfactory to the collector, conditioned upon the full and faithful compliance by the obligor therein with all the requirements of this act; and thereupon the collector shall issue to such applicant a certificate in such form as the Commissioner of Internal Revenue shall prescribe that such applicant is authorized for the period of one year from the date of such certificate to be a dealer in "options" or "futures" and to make "options" or "futures" contracts or agreements as hereinbefore defined, and for the period specified in such certificate the party to whom it is issued may conduct the business of dealer as aforesaid. Such certificate may be renewed annually upon the compliance with the provisions of this act, and any "options" or "futures" contract or agreement as defined by this act shall be absolutely void as between the parties thereto and their respective assigns unless the party making such contract or agreement shall have at the time of making the same a certificate as aforesaid authorizing the making thereof.

SEC. 6. That it shall be the duty of the collector to keep in his office a register containing a copy of each and every application made to him under the foregoing section and a statement in connection therewith as to whether a certificate had been issued thereon and for what period, which book or register shall be a public record and be subject to inspection of any and all persons desiring to examine the same.

SEC. 7. That every "option" [sic] or "futures" contract or agreement as hereinbefore defined shall be in writing and signed in duplicate by the parties making the same; and any such contract or agreement not so made and signed shall, as between the parties thereto and their assigns, be absolutely void.

SEC. 8. That it shall be the duty of every person, copartnership, association, or corporation, on the first day of the week next succeeding the date of the certificate issued to them, and on the first day of each and every week thereafter, to make to the collector of the district in which any "options" or "futures" contract or agreement has been made full and complete return and report, under oath, of any and all such contracts and agreements made or entered into by such person, copartnership, association or corporation during the previous week, together with a statement of the article or articles embraced in or covered by such contracts or agreements, and the amounts, respectively, of each, and the name of the party or parties with whom such contracts or agreements have been made, and at the same time to pay to such collector the amount of the tax hereinbefore required of 5 cents per pound on each and every pound of cotton, and of pork, lard, or other hog products, and of 20 cents per bushel on each and every bushel of any of the other articles mentioned in section 3 of this act, which are the subject of or covered by such contracts or agreements, or any of them, for which sums such collector shall give his receipt to the party so paying, and the sums so collected shall be accounted for by the collector as provided by law in respect to other taxes collected by him.

SEC. 9. That every person who shall, in his own behalf or in behalf of any other person, association, partnership, or corporation, enter into any "options" or "futures" contract or agreement, as defined by this act, without having a certificate of authority from the collector, as hereinbefore provided, and covering the time at which such contract or agreement shall be made, shall, besides being liable for the amounts prescribed in section 4 of this act, be fined not less than $5,000 and not more than $10,000 for each and every such offense. And every person who shall make to the collector a false or fraudulent return or report required by section 8 of this act shall be subject to a fine of not less than $5,000 nor more than $10,000, or to imprisonment for not less than six months or more than two years, or to both such fine and imprisonment.

SEC. 10. That neither the payment of the taxes required nor the certificate issued by the collector under this act shall be held to legalize dealing in options and futures, nor to exempt any person, association, copartnership, or corporation from any penalty or punishment, now or hereafter provided by the laws of any State for making contracts or agreements such as are hereinbefore defined as "options" or "futures" contracts or agreements, or in any manner to authorize the making of such contracts or agreements within any State or locality contrary to the laws of such State or locality; nor shall the payment of the taxes imposed by this act be held to prohibit any State or municipality from placing a tax or duty on the same trade, transaction, or business for State, municipal, or other purposes.

SEC. 11. That section 3209 of the Revised Statutes of the United States is, so far as applicable, made to extend and apply to the taxes imposed by this act and to the persons upon whom they are imposed.

Amend the title so as to read: "A bill to suppress and punish unlawful trusts and combinations, to prevent dealing in options and futures, and for other purposes." . . .

The PRESIDING OFFICER. The Chair will state the parliamentary condition of the bill. The substitute reported by the committee upon the 18th day of March is considered as the original bill for the consideration of the Senate. The amendment proposed by the Senator from Texas [Mr. REAGAN] is an amendment in the first degree, and that proposed by the Senator from Kansas [Mr. INGALLS] an amendment in the second degree. The question now is on the amendment proposed as a substitute by the Senator from Kansas, on which the Senator from Missouri is entitled to the floor.

Mr. [GEORGE GRAHAM] VEST [D., Mo.]. Mr. President, no one can exaggerate the importance of the question pending before the Senate or the intensity of feeling which exists, especially in the agricultural portions of the country in regard to it. I take it that there will be no controversy with the Senator from Ohio as to the enormity of the abuses that have grown up under the system of trusts and combinations which now prevail in every portion of the Union. What we desire is one thing; what we can accomplish under the autonomy of our Government is another.

We live, very fortunately, in my judgment, under a written Constitution, and we are governed by the decisions of the Supreme Court in regard to the legislative powers vested in us. Acts of Congress and treaties are the supreme law of the land, if in accordance with the Constitution. I deprecate as much as the Senator from Ohio can possibly do that spirit of hypercriticism which would consider the Constitution of the United States as a bill of indictment. I believe that it is a great bill of human rights, conservative, liberty-preserving, liberty-administering; and it is conservative, it preserves and administers liberty because it is a written Constitution and not because it is given to Congress to legislate as it sees proper, under the general and nebulous presumption of the general welfare, without regard to the grants that are made by the people to them as their legislative servants.

The grants of power to the courts of the United States are limited also by this written Constitution, and the grants of power in the judicial clause of the Constitution consist of two sorts: first, the jurisdiction which comes from the character of the litigants and, secondly, the jurisdiction that comes from the subject-matter involved. This is elementary law, and I simply announce it as one of the necessary premises in any discussion such as that in which we are now engaged.

As I understand the provisions of the original bill reported by the Senator from Ohio and the amendment which he offers now as a substitute, the attempt is made under one or the other of these two classes of jurisdiction, and then, permit me to say respectfully, by an uncertain and nebulous commingling of the two to give the power to Congress to pass this proposed act.

I know how ungrateful and dangerous it is now for a public man to object to this kind of legislation against this terrible evil, this enormous abuse of trusts and combines which the whole country is properly denouncing. I appreciate fully the significance of the remark of the Senator from Ohio when he says that unless relief is given, to use the language of Mr. Jefferson, "worse will ensue."

But, sir, even in the face of the popular indignation which may be visited upon any one who criticises any measure that looks to the destruction of this evil, I can not violate my oath to support the Constitution and all the habitudes of thought which have come to me as a lawyer educated and trained in my profession.

As I said, what we want is one thing, what we can do is another; and for Congress to pass a law which will be thrown out of the Supreme Court under the terrible criticism that any such law must invoke is simply to subject ourselves to ridicule and to say to our constituents that we are powerless to enact laws which will give them relief.

This bill, if it becomes a law, must go through the crucible of a legal criticism which will avail itself of the highest legal talent throughout the entire Union. It will go through a furnace not seven times but seventy-seven times heated, because the ablest lawyers in this country, it goes without saying, are on the side of the corporations and of aggregated wealth.

Without invoking this spirit of hypercriticism, which the Senator from Ohio deprecates, let us look at the provisions of the original bill and then of the amendment which he proposes shall take its place. In the original bill the Senator from Ohio undertakes to derive jurisdiction in Congress, not from the character of the litigants, but from the subject-matter in litigation, and this is evident from a cursory reading even of the first section of the original bill.

That all arrangements, contracts, agreements, trusts, or combinations between persons or corporations—

Not between corporations or persons residing in different States, not between corporations whose stockholders are citizens of different States, but between "persons or corporations"—

made with a view or which tend to prevent full and free competition in the importation, transportation, or sale of articles imported into the United States, or in the production, manufacture, or sale of articles of domestic growth or production, or domestic raw material that competes with any similar article upon which a duty is levied by the United States, or which shall be transported from one State or Territory to another, etc.

Here the Senator from Ohio puts the legislative jurisdiction of Congress, which he invokes, not upon the fact that persons living in different States compose these corporations, but the subject-matter is invoked. It must be as to productions going from one State to another or coming from a foreign country into the area of territory composing the United States.

For the able argument of the Senator from Mississippi [Mr. GEORGE], I have no words to express my admiration as a lawyer. I was exceedingly glad that it was made, because it is just through that species of argumentation that this legislation must pass.

It must be subjected to the crucible which was brought here by the Senator from Mississippi in that admirable dissertation upon constitutional power. After that argument was made the Senator from Ohio found it necessary to amend this original bill, and he did so by putting into it another element of jurisdiction; and that was the character of the litigants, in addition to the jurisdiction he had already invoked as to the subject-matter. This is evident from the first clause of the substitute.

That all arrangements, contracts, agreements, trusts, or combinations between two or more citizens or corporations—

Now, there is the original bill, and if it had stopped there the substitute would have agreed with it, but mark the addition—

or both, of different States, or between two or more citizens or corporations, or both, of the United States and foreign states, or citizens or corporations thereof, made with a view, etc.

It is plain that the Senator from Ohio, recognizing the weakness of the original bill, then determined or attempted to invoke that idea which is found in the Constitution of the United States and the judiciary act of 1789, that citizenship in different States conferred Federal jurisdiction.

Now, let us see if the Senator by any such process as that can evade the argument made by the Senator from Mississippi. Sir, I shall not attempt to make any elaborate argument, but will simply read the Constitution and then inquire under what clause the legislative jurisdiction to enact this bill can be found. The Constitution of the United States provides as to the judicial power as follows:

The judicial power shall extend to all cases, in law and equity.

⊥2464 ⊥ If it had stopped there much of the argument of the Senator from Ohio would have been pertinent; but it goes further:

All cases, in law and equity, arising under this Constitution.

That is to say, you must find the jurisdiction within the limits of this instrument.

Mr. SHERMAN. I do not want to interrupt the Senator, but he reads the clause relating to cases in law and equity when there is an independent clause relating to controversies between citizens of different States.

Mr. VEST. I will come to that.

Mr. SHERMAN. The decisions of Chief-Justice Marshall set forth the power distinctly.

Mr. VEST. I do not think there will be any disagreement among lawyers as to the meaning of this clause. I am simply analyzing the grants of the Constitution.

Mr. SHERMAN. I think Chief-Justice Marshall was a pretty good lawyer.

Mr. VEST. I am taking the clauses as they come. The first is:

All cases in law and equity arising under this Constitution—

Under this particular instrument, coming from the Constitution itself—

the laws of the United States—

There is another grant—

and treaties made, or which shall be made, under their authority.

Now, there are three distinct clauses of jurisdiction: first, under the Constitution; next, under the laws made in pursuance thereof; next, under the treaties made with foreign countries. It proceeds:

To all cases affecting ambassadors, other public ministers and consuls; to all cases of admiralty and maritime jurisdiction; to controversies to which the United States shall be a party; to controversies between two or more States; between a State and citizens of another State; between citizens of different States,—between citizens of the same State claiming lands under grants of different States, and between a State, or the citizens thereof, and foreign States, citizens or subjects.

Mr. President, let us take these clauses separately and see whether the power to pass this bill can be found under all or any of them. I shall reserve until the last my comments upon the first clause, which is, "To all cases, in law and equity, arising under this Constitution, the laws of the United States, and treaties made, or which shall be made, under their authority," because I think it can be established beyond any doubt that the jurisdiction is not found in the other clauses that follow. If this bill can be sustained at all, it is because there is a clause in the Constitution which authorizes it outside of the other clauses, which I shall proceed to enumerate. For instance, the next clause is:

To all cases affecting ambassadors, other public ministers and consuls.

Unquestionably the power is not there. No minister, no consul is involved in this legislation.

To all cases of admiralty and maritime jurisdiction.

Unquestionably it is not found there, because the bill proposes only to affect contracts made upon land, not upon the ocean, and there is no admiralty or maritime question involved. Next:

To controversies in which the United States shall be a party.

Unquestionably it does not affect that unless it be in that uncertain and unsatisfactory statement of the Senator from Ohio that he means in one clause of his amendment to give to the United States the power to proceed by *quo warranto,* injunction, or otherwise. In his original bill he had a direct criminal proceeding on the part of the Government of the United States against these trusts and he struck it out in the substitute. He has eliminated from this discussion the direct criminal proceeding in the name of the United States against the parties composing this trust and against the trust itself. There is no machinery provided for any proceeding by the United States in his amendment; but only the uncertain statement that the United States may proceed by remedial process. There is nothing else to lead us to believe that he intends that the United States shall do anything else except proceed in some fashion by information against the persons composing these trusts or the trusts themselves.

To controversies between two or more States.

Unquestionably the bill is not under that clause.

Between a State and citizens of another State.

There is nothing in this amendment which gives jurisdiction under that clause.

Between citizens of different States, between citizens of the same State claiming lands under grants of different States, and between a State, or the citizens thereof, and foreign states, citizens, or subjects.

Of course there will be no contention that the jurisdiction is found under that clause. It must be then found under the clause—

Mr. SHERMAN. I have stated that the jurisdiction is sufficiently conferred in the ordinary language of the judiciary act of 1789, in all controversies in which the United States is a party and in controversies between citizens of different States.

Mr. VEST. Unquestionably.

Mr. SHERMAN. Those are the two clauses to which I referred. I did not claim any other power.

Mr. VEST. Unquestionably where there is any litigation between citizens of different States the Federal courts have jurisdiction, no matter what is the subject-matter. That is elementary law known to every student. But here is a bill which is put upon no such ground. The bill says:

All arrangements, contracts, agreements, trusts, or combinations between two or more citizens or corporations, or both, of different States, or between two or more citizens or corporations, or both, of the United States and foreign states.

Not where there are litigants, not where one is plaintiff and the other is defendant. There is where the Constitution gives Federal jurisdiction. If the corporation itself is composed of citizens of different States then this jurisdiction attaches. Any citizen can sue although he lives in the same State with the corporation. There is the distinction.

Let me say that it excludes all the remedy that can be given to any citizen of the United States against the enormous evils depicted by the Senator from Ohio, because if this bill be passed and the Supreme Court of the United States decides it constitutional, you will never hear of the corporation which proposes to create or manipulate a trust that does not have the *personnel* of its stockholders all in the same State. That goes without saying, and it is to impute idiocy to the men whose schemes and machinations we are now attacking to suppose that they would do anything else. The idea that they, with the best counsel in the United States and even in the world, with the highest legal talent upon their side, will not immediately construct their corporations so as to nullify such a law is to impute to them a degree of mental imbecility that is simply ludicrous.

The Senator makes no distinction between the parties to the suit and the composition of the corporation which is itself a plaintiff or a defendant, He puts this jurisdiction upon something unknown to the Constitution, and the result would be (and it can be read between the lines) that if we enacted this into law the Supreme Court of the United States would immediately confront us with that clause of the Constitution and the judiciary act of 1789 and throw the case out of court.

It is very obvious that this attempt to invoke the web and woof of the judiciary act of 1789, which was made in pursuance of the clause of the Constitution that I have read, is an uncertain commingling of two elements utterly incongruous and utterly inconsistent.

Mr. SHERMAN. Does the Senator from Missouri say that there is anything in the bill that confers jurisdiction when they are citizens or members of a corporation of different States? There is nothing of that. The language of the bill is plain. I have read it. I do not see what the Senator is driving at.

Between two or more citizens or corporations—

The corporation is considered as a unit and the citizen as a unit—

or both, of different States.

This must be some persons and some corporations, distinct and separate personalities, not citizens who are members of the corporation. There is no such provision— . . .

Mr. VEST. Here is what I mean, and I think the Senator must agree with me: The Constitution of the United States makes one basis of jurisdiction to be the diverse citizenship of the litigants.

Mr. SHERMAN. Very well.

Mr. VEST. Nothing can be plainer than that.

Mr. SHERMAN. This points that out. They must be citizens of different States or corporations of different States, or both.

Mr. VEST. Of course. Although it is so simple a matter that it hardly needs elucidation, I may put it thus: If Mr. Brown lives in the State of Missouri and Mr. Smith lives in Ohio they can sue each other without regard to the subject-matter, provided it comes within the limits which was [sic] fixed in the judiciary act as to the jurisdiction of a Federal tribunal. The Senator does not put his bill upon that ground at all. He undertakes to put it upon the composition of one of the litigants alone. He does not say, if one of these citizens lives in one State and one in another, which we would all admit to confer Federal jurisdiction, but he gives Federal jurisdiction because the corporation which makes the trust is composed of citizens of different States. If it does not mean that, then the English language has lost all its flavor and I have lost my power to understand it.

Here is what he says; I will read it again *ad nauseam*:

> All arrangements, contracts, agreements, trusts, or combinations between two or more citizens or corporations, or both, of different States.

And that gives jurisdiction, provided they go on and undertake to do the other things enumerated in the other part of the section as to goods brought from foreign countries or goods carried from one State to another.

The Senator does not follow the Constitution, which says that when a suit shall be brought by a citizen of one State against a citizen of another State for doing the thing which he enumerates afterwards, which is another matter of argument, but he says if the corporation offending is composed of people living in different States, then the Federal courts have jurisdiction, which I submit is an unheard-of proposition and no lawyer ever advanced it before. As I undertook to show, how easy is it for these corporations to evade any such provision by simply having their stockholders all living in the limits of any particular State? It affords no remedy, even if the argument of the Senator from Ohio could stand for a moment, which it can not.

⊥2465

But, Mr. President, I proceed now, for it is not my disposition to make any elaborate argument, to the latter clause of the amendment, disregarding entirely the original bill, which for the purposes of discussion has been removed. If a corporation is composed of two or more persons living in different States or if it is composed of citizens or corporations, or both, in the United States and a foreign country, and they make a combination to prevent full and free competition in the importation, transportation, or sale of articles imported into the United States, then this proposed law takes effect, and they become subject to the jurisdiction we invoke legislatively.

I do not propose to make any hypercritical argument, but I do insist that unless we adhere to the opinions of the Supreme Court, especially in the great case of Brown *vs.* The State of Maryland,[1.314] we are at sea without rudder or compass in this whole discussion.

The Senator invokes the commerce clause of the Constitution, that clause which gives to Congress the power to regulate commerce with foreign countries, among the States, and with the Indian tribes. The first question that meets us *in limine*, which any lawyer would be ashamed to confess that he did not invoke at the very beginning of his argument on this commerce clause, is the material question, what is commerce? What is commerce with a foreign country? There is the point in this whole legislation, the point that has given me the most trouble after long and exhaustive thought to the extent of my ability.

I will confess now, parenthetically but honestly, that in all my experience as a lawyer I have never encountered a subject so full of difficulty as that now before the Senate. I can very well understand how it is full of difficulty. Notwithstanding the

---

[1.314] See note 1.249 *supra*.

eulogium in which I cordially unite with the Senator from Ohio upon the framers of the Constitution, it is simply impossible, unless we attribute to the framers of this instrument the intellect of gods, that they in the thirteen original colonies, poor, struggling for existence, limited in their territorial area to the Atlantic sea-board, should ever have contemplated the immense country for which we are now legislating, and the enormous aggregation of wealth which startles and amazes the world. They undertook in the Constitution to meet contingencies, but here is one which beggars Aladdin's lamp in the reality that is before us and with us to-day. It is no reflection, then, upon their intellect or their patriotism to say that they could not have contemplated an emergency such as that which now rests upon the people of the United States.

Mr. President, I come back to the question. What is commerce? We have the power to regulate it, but we must first find what commerce is in order to exercise our legislative power. I shall not undertake to read the decisions of the Supreme Court of the United States, which are elementary law upon this subject. In the great case of Brown against The State of Maryland, which leads upon this subject, and to which every lawyer goes first, decided by the most eminent men who ever sat upon the bench in this country, and the equals of any in the world, the regulation of foreign commerce was declared to be the regulation of the importation and sale of articles brought from a foreign country before they had left the hands of the importer and been broken as to the original package. I state crudely, but I think accurately.

The Supreme Court in that case settled the question of foreign commerce by declaring, as to the power of a State to tax foreign importations, that so long as the original package remained in the hands of the importer unbroken it was the subject of foreign commerce. When it left his hands and the package was broken, and the goods went into the common mass of the property of the people of the State, then the commercial clause of the Constitution as to foreign commerce ceased to operate.

Mr. President, apply that decision to the provisions of this bill. Here is one clause of the amendment which provides that if a corporation composed of citizens of different States does any act "with a view or which tends to prevent full and free competition in the importation, transportation, or sale of articles imported into the United States," this proposed law shall take effect.

Does the Senator from Ohio pretend that, after the importer has brought in the goods and the package has been broken and the merchandise has been mingled or commingled with the other goods of the people of the State into which the importation is made, under this clause of the Constitution we can enact such a law as is proposed? I take it that the statement of the case is sufficient to answer the proposition. But it is undertaken to get this jurisdiction under another clause of the Constitution. The bill proceeds:

> Or with a view or which tends to prevent full and free competition in articles of growth, production, or manufacture of any State or Territory of the United States with similar articles of the growth, production, or manufacture of any other State or Territory, or in the transportation or sale of like articles, the production of any State or Territory of the United States into or within any other State or Territory of the United States.

I shall not repeat the argument made by the Senator from Mississippi as lucidly and conclusively as any argument could have been made, that we have no power under any clause of the Federal Constitution to legislate as to any article simply because it is manufactured in any State of the Union and may be at some time carried to another State. That clause in the Constitution of the United States which affects interstate commerce, or, to speak more accurately, commerce among the States, has been defined by the Supreme Court in three leading cases to mean the power to regulate commerce in articles, whether manufactured in the State or not, after they have gone into commerce and are *in transitu* from one State to another.

The Supreme Court of the United States has decided that it is not for the manufacturer or the owner to say, "I intend these goods to go into another State." They must actually be *in transitu;* they must be in the hands of the common carrier, or in his depot or warehouse, with the impression distinctively made upon them that, to use the expression of one judge, they are dedicated to commerce among the States.

The Senator from Ohio makes the fatal mistake as a lawyer that, because goods manufactured in one State may be at some time or other taken into another, which as a matter of course is possible in every contingency, therefore he can invoke the general interstate commerce clause of the Constitution. He can not do it. If we pass this bill upon any such assumption and it goes to the Supreme Court of the United States, we shall simply be told that all we have done here is *vox et praeterea nihil,* sound and fury, signifying nothing.

Mr. President, one year ago the Senator from Ohio struck the keynote as to all these trusts and combinations in the United States. It was in the expression made in this Chamber that whenever he was satisfied that any trust or combination was protected by a high tariff duty he would be in favor of reducing that duty. This is the remedy; and any other remedy, without an amendment of the Constitution of the United States, any remedy such as is proposed in this bill, will be absolutely nugatory and ineffectual.

The Senator from Ohio has drawn an eloquent picture of the operations of trusts in the United States. Sir, these trusts—and every intelligent man knows it, whether a legislator or a citizen—are protected by your high tariff, and are enabled to work their iniquitous purposes under that buttress which the tariff law erects around them. . . .

Mr. [WILLIAM B.] ALLISON [R., Iowa]. Am I to understand the Senator as saying that the only remedy as respects trusts is that which enables us to reduce tariff duties upon particular articles, and therefore if a trust or combination is made which is not in any way influenced by duties there is no remedy without an amendment to the Constitution?

Mr. VEST. Mr. President, if I stated it that strongly perhaps I went beyond my exact meaning. I believe there is a remedy if you take the jurisdiction of the State and also the jurisdiction of Congress and put them together, but I do not believe there is any complete remedy in the action of either separately and of itself. What I meant to say was that as to nearly all the trusts which have been denounced here to-day the most apparent remedy is to take away the protection which these trusts have from the high tariff that is now upon our statute-books and in operation. . . .

Mr. PLATT. What is the difficulty of the States dealing with this matter? What prevents any State from dealing with the matter of trusts?

Mr. VEST. I do not think there is any difficulty whatever as to that class of cases in which the products, or the transactions, to speak more accurately, take place entirely within the limits of a State; but we know that these trusts evade the State statutes even when they are made, and if we desire to apply a remedy we must remove the cause or else we are legislative empirics. If it is true that the tariff permits these trusts and protects them and we do not seek to remove the cause, all the remedies we attempt to apply are simply surface and skin, expedients that amount to nothing, and the real cause of the difficulty still remains.

Mr. INGALLS. Will the Senator inform me upon what ground the Missouri antitrust bill was declared unconstitutional in his own State?

Mr. VEST. The circuit court at St. Louis, Mo., decided the act of the Legislature to be unconstitutional upon the ground that the forfeiture of the charter of a corporation was a judicial act, and could not be done by the act of the secretary of state. It was decided in the court at St. Louis by Judge Dillon, but it has not yet been decided in the supreme court, that the forfeiture of the charter of a corporation was a judicial act, and that the act of the Legislature which gave to the secretary of state the power of himself to declare the forfeiture of the charter was therefore unconstitutional. That was the ground.

But, Mr. President, whether it was on one ground or another, these corporations, with the amount of legal talent they are enabled to employ and invoke, will be able in almost every instance to avoid these statutes, and I solemnly assert here that in my judgment the only real remedy is to be found in taking away the protection and origin of these trusts, which is in the high tariff taxes which stand like a wall and enable these trusts to exist.

The Senator from Ohio has spoken of these trusts. Now, Mr. President, I happen to have here a list of them, and these are only a few. The first is the steel-rail trust, buttressed by a tariff tax of $17 per ton.

Mr. GEORGE. What per cent. is that?

Mr. VEST. I do not recollect the per cent. We discussed it in the last Congress. Seventeen dollars is the taxation per ton; steel rails are protected that much. As my friend from Iowa very well knows, I tried to reduce it, and he resisted the attempt. . . .

Mr. ALLISON. I ask the Senator if it is not true that at this moment the price of steel rails in England is practically the same as it is in the United States, or within a dollar or two? If that be so, how is it that the $17 duty upon steel rails at this moment is injuring the great body of the rail purchasers in this country?

Mr. VEST. Why, Mr. President, if we were told anything in the discussion in which my friend and myself participated rather largely in the last Congress—and I know it was urged by the Senator from New York [Mr. HISCOCK] now in my sight—it was that whenever you reduce the price in any one country you reduce it all over the world, and necessarily in every other country. We know very well that competition always reduces prices. It is no argument to say that steel rails are as cheap, even if it were true, in England to-day as they are in the United States; that will not do. I say if you let these two manufacturing interests compete together and create competition, you then secure lower prices to the consumer. That is the law of trade and that is the law of manufactures the world over. . . .

Mr. [HENRY M.] TELLER [R., Colo.]. Is not the Senator from Missouri aware that there is a steel trust in Great Britain that includes every steel establishment in Great Britain except one, and includes the German and Belgian establishments also?

Mr. VEST. I know that statement was made, but I never took the trouble to investigate it. Now, I make this statement to supplement it, and it is as absolutely true as that I am standing in this Senate Chamber. I know that there are trusts in Great Britain, and I have no doubt there will be trusts in any country under the present conditions of manufactures and of commerce; but here is the difference between trusts in Great Britain and the United States:

When you make a trust or attempt to make a trust in Great Britain, you must corner the products of all the world and you must have enough capital to do this, because you compete with every part of the civilized globe and you have no tariff to protect you and prevent competition, and therefore the capital necessary to effect the purposes of the combine must be at hand; but when you come to the United States the combine is helped by the tariff because the tariff tax shuts out the foreign producer and foreign importer, and limits necessarily the amount of capital necessary to achieve the purpose.

Mr. [WILLIAM P.] FRYE [R., Me.]. If that is true, will the Senator from Missouri please account for the fact that 25,000 tons of steel rails manufactured in the United States were last week sold in Mexico, where all the nations of the earth have free competition one with the other?

Mr. VEST. Mr. President, I am obliged to my friend from Maine. That shows the blessings and the equities of the high protective tariff! These very people making steel rails in the United States, who must be protected in order to live by a subsidy of $17 per ton, are able to go into Mexico and in a free-trade market to undersell the English, the Belgians, or anybody else!

Mr. FRYE. But the Senator does not reply to the question which I asked him.

Mr. VEST. I was attempting to do so.

Mr. FRYE. The Senator was asserting that a protective tariff prevented competition and created the trusts. I say there is no protective tariff which prevents competition in Mexico, because there is the same tariff against the products of England as against the products of the United States, and yet the United States sells 25,000 tons of steel rails to Mexico.

Mr. VEST. As a matter of course, Mr. Disston, of Philadelphia, who is protected on his saws, it was testified before the committees of the Senate and the House of Representatives, can sell his saws in England and undersell the English manufacturers, and yet Mr. Disston gets his protection in the United States. How will the Senator answer my proposition when he says that we sell 25,000 tons of steel rails in Mexico?

I have a letter in my possession from a gentleman who lives at Piedras Negras on the Rio Grande, which I believe is translated Black Rock, upon the Mexican side, and opposite to it is a small American village, and there are two stores belonging to the same party, one on American soil and one in Mexico, and in Mexico the same goods are sold one-third cheaper than in the United States, because on the Mexican side this man is bound to compete with the whole world, whilst on the American side he is protected by the tariff and competition does not exist.

Is it any argument to tell me that we sell our saws, our watches, our machinery, our cutlery, all over the world, and do it successfully? I say it is an argument against the high protective tariff because it shows that the subsidy we are paying inside of the United States to enrich these manufacturers is a sham and fraud. They do not need it.

That is what is the matter with the people of the West to-day; that is why the complaint is made of combines and trusts; that is why the farmers are combining or attempting to do so in order to protect themselves against the aggregation of capital, which by this legislation is enabled to compete outside of the United States successfully, and yet to shut out the competition after they reach our own shores. Let me give the facts:

THE TARIFFS AND THE TRUSTS.
[From Justice, Philadelphia.]

1. The Steel Rail Trust, buttressed by a tariff tax of $17 per ton.
2. The Nail Trust, by a tariff tax of $1.25 per 100 pounds.
3. The Iron Nut and Washer Trust, by a tax of $2 per 100 pounds.
4. The Barbed Fence-Wire Trust, by a tax of 60 cents per 100 pounds.
5. The Copper Trust, by a tax of $2.50 per 100 pounds.
6. The Lead Trust, by a tax of $1.50 per 100 pounds.
7. The Slate-Pencil Trust, by a tax of 30 per cent.

I should like to hear my friend from North Carolina [Mr. VANCE] on that

8. The Nickel Trust, by a tax of $15 per one hundred pounds.
9. The Zinc Trust, by a tax of $2.50 per one hundred pounds.
10. The Sugar Trust, by a tax of $2 per one hundred pounds.
11. The Oilcloth Trust, by a tax of 40 per cent.
12. The Jute Bag Trust, by a tax of 40 per cent.
13. The Cordage Trust, by a tax of 30 per cent.
14. The Paper Envelope Trust, by a tax of 25 per cent.
15. The Gutta Percha Trust, by a tax of 35 per cent.
16. The Castor Oil Trust, by a tax of 80 cents per gallon.
17. The Linseed Oil Trust, by a tax of 25 cents per gallon.
18. The Cottonseed Oil Trust, by a tax of 25 cents per gallon.
19. The Borax Trust, by a tax of $5 per one hundred pounds.
20. The Ultramarine Trust, by a tax of $5 per one hundred pounds.

And so on, and they are adding to them day by day. Now, Mr. President, the favorite argument of our friends who sustain the high protective tariff is that high duties lower the cost of products to the consumer by reason of the competition between the manufacturers inside of the United States. If that be so, why are these trusts created? They are created because when foreign competition has been shut out and competition becomes acute and severe between American manufacturers they come together and create these combines at the expense of the consumer in order to enhance their own profits. If the high protective tariff were removed the foreign competition would furnish, if not an absolute, certainly a most beneficial remedy to remove this evil.

We have been told in some directions that the trusts and combines have nothing to do with the tariff. Mr. President, that reminds me of a very suspicious old gentleman who when the Siamese twins were in this country thought he would invest twenty-five cents in looking at this great natural curiosity. He paid the tax, went into the exhibition room, and there found two grown young men posing before the audience in the most approved style. He was very suspicious and he examined them critically, and finally examined the ligament that bound them together in that world-renowned connection which scientists, even, were not able to explain, and he found in this ligament the pulsation which indicated animal life to the fullest extent. He stepped back, still suspicious, and said to them, "Now, boys, tell me the truth; are you brothers?" [Laughter.] So with the connection between the trusts and the tariff. . . .

Mr. [HENRY L.] DAWES [R., Mass.]. I appreciate the difficulties of this subject as well as the Senator does. I understand him to say that the remedy, the method of putting down the trusts in this country is to open these trusts to the competition of the foreign trusts. Now, the query I want to put to him is this: What is to hinder taking one more into a trust and taking the foreign trust into the American trust or the American trust into the foreign trust and then having it beyond all control?

Mr. VEST. Mr. President, I am against all trusts, and the Senator—

Mr. DAWES. The Senator does not get my point. I asked him what remedy he would get by erecting free trade so as to cause active competition between the two trusts. Would there not be just the same motive and just the same opportunity and just the same facility to put these two trusts together when they were competing as there would be to have two competing with each other here at home?

Mr. VEST. Mr. President, any sort of assumption could be made as to what parties would come in as competitors from a foreign country. With that I have nothing to do so far as the purposes of my arguments are concerned. I take it that in the natural course of trade the foreign importer would come in and compete with the American manufacturer. I know absolutely that the purpose of the friends of a high protective tariff is to shut out foreign competition. If I had any doubts about that, they were removed in the last Congress when my friend from Iowa [Mr. ALLISON] and my friend from Rhode Island [Mr. ALDRICH] and my friend from New York [Mr. HISCOCK] applied in every case as to every item in the tariff bill that they reported, not the test whether protection was needed for the manufacturer in this country or for the consumer, but how much of the competing article was brought in during the last year. . . .

. . . [W]ithout wanting to go into that argument and thrash over old straw I say now that the Senator and his colleagues took pains to increase the duties on all the necessaries of life that were imported in competition with American manufactures.

Mr. DAWES. To wit, duties on what?

Mr. VEST. On hardware, on woolen goods, on a dozen other articles that are absolutely necessaries of life, and refused to take them off lumber and salt and other things that enter into the daily consumption of the American people. That is the fact, and the Senators know it.

As a matter of course they reduced the duties upon coarse cotton cloths, because they are made in the South, but they took care to put the duties up on fine cotton cloths, that are made in New England; and now the Senator from Iowa says they reduced the duties on sugar. That was because sugar was raised in Louisiana. It was for a climatic reason, and that only. If the sugar had been raised in the North, all of them, I think, would have "taken sugar in theirs," and if the Senate wanted to reduce the duties upon necessaries why was it not done? It was not done because the Republican party could not afford to do it and did not do it.

Sir, I have spoken longer than I intended. I hope that some member of the majority, because it will be useless for me to do so, will move to refer this question to the Judiciary Committee. The amendment of the Senator from Texas is now pending before a subcommittee of that committee, together with other proposed legislation on this subject, which has been introduced into the Senate. This is a subject so elaborate, so important, so overwhelming, that it should be approached with the greatest caution and treated with the greatest care.

I sympathize with the objects of the Senator from Ohio. I am willing to vote for any bill which I think as a law will stand judicial criticism and construction, but in my judgment to pass a law which the Supreme Court would declare to be unconstitutional is simply to invite additional disaster.

Mr. [FRANK] HISCOCK [R., N.Y.]. Mr. President, I sympathize with a great deal that has been said by the Senator from Ohio [Mr. SHERMAN] and agree to all that he has said against trusts and combinations, and I am willing to join hands with him in every effort that promises success to defeat them. I do not, however, sympathize with the expression which has been made here that a public legislator can not afford to resist efforts in the direction of unwise, illegal, and unconstitutional legislation because his action may be misconstrued. One is always safe in predicating his action upon the intelligence of the people, and they will understand that the bill or the amendment to the bill now offered by the Senator from Ohio is absolutely ineffectual to remedy the evils which he has so elaborately and ably commented upon.

In reference to interstate and foreign commerce, I understand that he states the proposition to be that the initial point with us in respect of foreign and interstate commerce is when the merchandise is launched on its way to its destination, or at least is in the hands or possession of the common carrier who transports it there. There is no doubt that is the law of the land. Bearing that in mind, let us briefly take this amendment and see precisely what it means and what it proposes, what merchandise it covers and what transactions it declares void. It provides—

> that all arrangements, contracts, agreements, trusts, or combinations between two or more citizens or corporations, or both, of different States, or between two or more citizens or corporations, or both, of the United States and foreign states, or citizens or corporations thereof, made with a view or which tend to prevent full and free competition in the importation—

It prohibits a contract and arrangement preceding the very act which gives Congress jurisdiction over it—

> importation, transportation, or sale of articles imported into the United States.

The provision on the face of it applies to contracts which are made before importation has commenced, before the article is within the purview of the Constitution, and they are declared to be void. It is in the purchase of the goods, Mr. President, within the language of the provision, that the combination may not be made to prevent importation into this country and "with a view or which tend to prevent full and free competition," is the preceding language. Goods may be purchased and diverted from the United States, and that may be the object of the combination, to send them elsewhere, divert them from coming here and flooding our markets, and the amendment proposed takes jurisdiction of that.

I hope that the Senator from Ohio will point out the clause of the Constitution that gives us the power and the right to take jurisdiction of goods which may never be imported here; never come within the jurisdiction of the Federal Constitution or of the laws which have been passed under it. But an article reaches here, and, as has been well said, it has passed beyond the hands of the importer.

It is then subject to State law, State taxation; and yet this amendment follows it, and under this provision if it becomes a law penalties are imposed. At both ends it legislates with reference to commerce before the merchandise has been dispatched on its way to this country, and after it has reached here and after it has been taken out of the volume of commerce. Let us take the next clause of this amendment:

> Or with a view or which tend to prevent full and free competition in articles of growth, production, or manufacture of any other State or Territory of the United States, with similar articles of the growth, production, or manufacture of any other State or Territory, or in the transportation or sale of like articles, the production of any State or Territory of the United States into or within any other State or Territory of the United States.

That clause provides that if the trust may prevent competition of property which is grown in one State or Territory and merchandise which is manufactured in one State or Territory with that produced in another, then it is illegal and void; it need not be transported. I call the Senator's attention to the effect. There may never have been an intention of transporting it into another State, and yet the provision of this section of the bill applies to it.

It takes control of the manufacturing, of the mining, and of the agricultural industries of the whole country wherever there may be competition as between the people of one State and the people of another. The language is explicit. As I remarked, the article may never have been produced for the purpose of transportation or delivery from one State into another, still this amendment reaches out and takes jurisdiction of it.

The damages which may have resulted from the trust may have been incurred by the individual before it has entered upon transit from one State to another, and yet, under the provisions of this bill a plaintiff can recover. What follows?

> And all arrangements, trusts, or combinations between such citizens or corporations, made with a view or which tend to advance the cost to the consumer of any such articles, are hereby declared to be against public policy, unlawful, and void.

There is no limitation upon the language. It does not pretend to regulate interstate commerce. Let us go back again to the first lines of the bill, "made with a view or which tend" to do this; and these arrangements are void, under the provisions of the bill, as against public policy. It takes the control of every manufacturing industry; it takes the control of every mine; it takes the control of all the merchants, because, as I have said, it does not limit its operations and effects to goods in interstate commerce.

And the circuit court of the United States shall have original jurisdiction of all suits of a civil nature at common law or in equity arising under this section, and to issue all remedial process, orders, or writs proper and necessary to enforce its provisions. And the Attorney-General and the several district attorneys are hereby directed, in the name of the United States, to commence and prosecute all such cases to final judgment and execution.

Inquisitorial power is given to the officers of the General Government to reach into the management of every industry in the United States, and I repeat it does not depend upon the fact that the merchandise is to be involved in interstate commerce. Not at all. If by its production a certain effect may be had, if it may compete in any way, the penalties follow. Now, with the interchange of commodities we have in this country, it is fair to say that wheat raised in Dakota competes with wheat raised in New York if not a bushel of that wheat is transported to the State of New York. Competition is now in the markets of the world, and it is not confined to States or the markets of States between themselves.

If this bill shall be carried into effect I shall expect the Senator from Ohio to present here next year an amendment to it that manufacturers are to be licensed and their business carried on under the restrictions of that license and under the inquisitorial power of the Attorney-General, the district attorneys, or some other officials.

It seems to me, Mr. President, that I have commented enough on the enormities, the far-reaching effect of this bill if it shall become a law and be declared by the courts to be constitutional. The logic of the decision will be for Congress to take control of every producing interest in the respective States of the Union.

⊥2468 The Senator from Ohio has read several decisions here upon the subject of the power of the courts over this question and the illegality of ⊥ these trusts. In each case that he cited the court established its jurisdiction and its power to afford a remedy, and the Senate would have been under great obligation to the Senator from Ohio if he had pointed to a single case as to which there is not a complete remedy or may not be a complete remedy under State laws. I should be obliged to him if, in the progress of this discussion, before its close, he would point out and describe the cases in which there is not ample jurisdiction in the Legislatures and courts of the States, respectively, in respect to all these trusts and combines.

As I have already said, interstate commerce commences when the goods are entered for transportation from one State to another. Up to that point of time every contract made in reference to them, the control of the goods themselves, is within the jurisdiction of the State courts and of the Legislatures of the States, respectively.

I think something has been said here that the framers of the Constitution neglected to put something in the Constitution that might properly have been placed there giving Congress the proper authority in respect to this subject.

Why did they need to put it there? I ask, Mr. President, bearing in mind what I have stated, that up to the point when an article of production is delivered to the common carrier every contract in reference to it and the custody of the goods is within the jurisdiction of the Legislature of the State in which it starts, and when it reaches another State it is subject to the jurisdiction of the courts and of the laws of that State.

It is with reference to interstate commerce that Congress has the right to take jurisdiction; that is the act of exchange from one State to another; and we all know why that provision was placed in the Constitution. One of the chief reasons was that the General Government might prevent States from practically prohibiting commerce between each other, for the purpose of regulating taxation upon property which was to go from one State to another. The purpose was obvious; but it was not the intention of the framers of the Constitution to take the jurisdiction of the property until it had passed beyond the point when it was subject to State taxation and State control.

The Senator from Ohio has seemed to think, and has argued here, that we might take control of this subject on account of that provision of the Constitution which gives jurisdiction to the courts of persons, forms of action, and all that. I hope in the progress of this discussion the Senator will tell us if he believes that our courts can create a cause of action. That is the question involved here as he presents it. They may have jurisdiction of the litigants and of the cause of action in actions of law and in equity, but it should be borne in mind they have no power to create a cause of action. They have ample and full jurisdiction over the remedies, but the creation of the cause of action rests with the law-making power, and not with the court, and Congress, the law-making power, looks to the Constitution for its authority to create a cause of action, and nowhere else.

Mr. President, criticisms have been made upon this bill that in my judgment may be obviated by amendments to it. I have devoted no time to defects of that kind. The objections that I make to the bill are fundamental; they can not be obviated by any amendments that possibly can be proposed.

What I maintain is that whenever property, either in process of manufacture or completely manufactured, has not already been put on its course of transit either into this country or from one State to another, whatever the intention may have been in its production, up to the point of time when it is started to its destination, absolute and complete control of that property is within the legislative power, the law-making power, and the jurisdiction of the courts, of the States and countries respectively in which it is situated.

If the Senator from Ohio will point to a single case in which the Legislature and the courts have not the one the power to give the other jurisdiction, and the latter to administer it, I will join hands with him in an effort to perfect a bill by Congress that shall give to the Federal courts jurisdiction with reference to that subject. But it must be borne in mind that this is not a jurisdiction that can be abdicated by the States. It is not a jurisdiction that can be possessed by a State and the General Government at the same time. There is no partnership in respect to it, and there can be none. If the States have jurisdiction the National Government can not have it, and if the National Government has jurisdiction, or can take it, it can not be possessed by the States.

As I said some time since, my objections to the bill are fundamental; they can not be reached by Congressional legislation. According to the cases that have been read here, there is full and ample power on the part of each State Legislature in respect to this very subject. Why not then leave it there as a matter of right and wrong between the States? Local and State sentiment will take care of these questions. It does not depend upon one State alone. The State from which the goods are started has jurisdiction and the States to which they are consigned has it also.

Mr. President, I have not gone through with this bill to elaborate the different subjects, all the matters of which it proposes to take jurisdiction. The language is remarkable in it:

Made with a view or which tend to prevent full and free competition.

I can summon here to answer those who would be injured by the bill whose voice would be as potential to put up or down the supporter of it as all those who can be invoked by popular clamor against trusts; and I hope we shall be told in the progress of this discussion if there is a labor organization in the United State that is not affected by it. Every organization which attempts to take the control of the labor that it puts into the market to advance its price is interdicted by this bill.

Sir, I am one of those who believe in labor organizations. I believe the only safety to labor rests in the power to combine as against capital and assert its rights and defend itself.

The criminal section of this proposed law has been eliminated from it. Perhaps it was wise to do that, because under that section these organizations and their promoters might have been reached. Possibly under the damage provisions in the bill they never would be pursued; but it strikes at them as viciously as it is possible to conceive of. Will it be said that their combinations are not made with a view of advancing costs and regulating the sale of property? Will it be argued that they do not directly do it? If we have entered upon a race to outstrip each other in the denunciation of capital, the manufacturing industries, the combinations of capital, and it is to be on the line of the support of this bill, I announce that there are two sides to it. If Senators are to be deterred from their opposition to it by this clamor, I call their attention to the fact that the bill takes within its embrace those affected by its provisions and injured by its provisions who are very potential in asserting their rights and respect for their wishes.

In my judgment, Mr. President, neither this bill nor any like it should be enacted into law unless it is within the warrant of our charter, unless we are satisfied that it is legal and constitutional. No attempt should be made to reach into the States and take from the jurisdiction of the State Legislatures the subjects of which they have full and ample control. . . .

⊥ Mr. REAGAN. Mr. President, with some of the criticisms made upon the bill reported by the Senator from Ohio I agree. I think the country is debtor to that distinguished Senator for his efforts to furnish a remedy for a great and dangerous evil. I know the difficulty of preparing a bill to be enacted by Congress to meet this evil. I have presented an amendment by way of substitute for the bill reported by the Senator from Ohio. I do not know but that when it becomes subject to criticism it may fare as badly as his bill has done, and yet I have tried to formulate a measure which would obviate the objections that have been urged to his. Whatever authority we have here over this subject is derived from the provision in the Constitution which confers upon Congress the power to regulate commerce with foreign nations and between the States. Keeping that in view, I will read the first section of the amendment which I have offered:

That all persons engaged in the creation of any trust, or as owner or part owner, agent, or manager of any trust, employed in any business carried on with any foreign country, or between the States, or between any State and the District of Columbia, or between any State and any Territory of the United States, or any owner or part owner, agent, or manager of any corporation using its powers for either of the purposes specified in the second section of this act, shall be deemed guilty of a high misdemeanor, and, on conviction thereof, shall be fined in a sum not exceeding $10,000, or imprisonment at hard labor in the penitentiary not exceeding five years, or by both of said penalties, in the discretion of the court trying the same.

I concede that the penalty provided here is a very strong one, but it is designed to meet a very great evil perpetrated by powerful and wealthy parties. It is designed to arrest and prevent an evil which can only be met, in my judgment, by strong, coercive measures. Now, I desire to call attention to the second section of my amendment, which is simply intended as a definition of the things prohibited in the first section. The second section is:

That a trust is a combination of capital, skill, or acts by two or more persons, firms, corporations, or associations of persons, or of any two or more of them for either, any, or all of the following purposes:

It will be understood that it is for these purposes when performed under the influence of the first section of this proposed act, that is, by persons engaged in commerce with foreign countries or between the States:

First. To create or carry out any restrictions in trade.
Second. To limit or reduce the production or to increase or reduce the price of merchandise or commodities.
Third. To prevent competition in the manufacture, making, purchase, sale, or transportation of merchandise, produce, or commodities.
Fourth. To fix a standard or figure whereby the price to the public shall be in any manner controlled or established of any article, commodity, merchandise, produce, or commerce intended for sale, use, or consumption.
Fifth. To create a monopoly in the making, manufacture, purchase, sale, or transportation of any merchandise, article, produce, or commodity.
Sixth. To make, or enter into, or execute, or carry out any contract, obligation, or agreement of any kind or description by which they shall bind or shall have bound themselves not to manufacture[,] sell, dispose of, or transport any article or commodity, or article of trade, use, merchandise, or consumption below a common standard figure, or by which they shall agree, in any manner, to keep the price of such article, commodity, or transportation at a fixed or graduated figure or by which they shall, in any manner, establish or settle the price of any article, commodity, or transportation between themselves, or between themselves and others, so

as to preclude free and unrestricted competition among themselves and others in the sale and transportation of any such article or commodity, or by which they shall agree to pool, combine, or unite in any interest they may have in connection with the sale or transportation of any such article or commodity that its price may, in any manner, be so affected.

SEC. 3. That each day any of the persons, associations, or corporations aforesaid shall be engaged in violating the provisions of this act shall be held to be a separate offense.

I am advised that some criticisms have been made upon the second section; that it relates to things which it is said Congress has no jurisdiction of. I apprehend that those who make that criticism read the second section of the bill without considering that everything in the second section is controlled by the provision of the first section, which makes the things referred to in the second section those which are involved in commerce with foreign nations or among the several States.

As to the authority of Congress to act upon the subject, that is all I now care to say upon that point. I deem it proper to say that, though I was present when the Senator from Ohio gave notice yesterday evening that he would call the subject up today, other duties prevented any consideration of it which might prepare me to discuss it now as its importance and merits deserve.

It will be seen that, as between the bill reported by the Senator from Ohio and my amendment, his provides for civil suits only for damages by persons who conceive themselves to be injured, damaged by these unlawful combinations, while the amendment which I have presented does not make provision for civil suits, but provides for a criminal prosecution and severe penalties against those who may be engaged in these unlawful occupations. After what has been said by other Senators this morning on the subject, if we were better prepared to discuss these points it is not necessary that I should go over the evils which it is intended to prevent by this character of legislation. I am inclined, however, to think that if the amendment which I present should be adopted as a substitute for the bill of the Senator from Ohio, it would be well to incorporate in it after its adoption, or at some time, a provision of that measure authorizing civil suits. I am inclined to think that it would be well that whatever law should be adopted on this subject should embrace both jurisdiction of civil and criminal proceedings to prevent and punish these evils.

In speaking of this subject and in looking at its difficulties, I feel sure, notwithstanding the great demand for action by Congress, that the people interested, the people oppressed and distressed by operation of these trusts, look too much to the Congress of the United States for the desired relief. Congress can go no further, as I understand its authority under the Constitution, than to provide a remedy with reference to those things which come into the category of commerce with foreign nations and commerce between the States. That is as far as it may rightfully go; and it seems to me that it is one of the highest and most important duties under the circumstances that it should go that far. But if the people of this country expect salutary relief on this subject they must look to their State governments, for they have jurisdiction over the great mass of transactions out of which these troubles grow. If the Federal Government will act upon those things which relate to international and interstate commerce, and the States, responding to the necessity of the country and the complaints of the people, will act upon the branch of subjects of which the States have jurisdiction, we may, it seems to me, arrest the evil of trusts and combinations to augment prices or to depress prices in the interest of monopoly and for the oppression and wrong of the people.

I am inclined to say right here, Mr. President, that it seems to me unfortunate that of late years the people of this country, whenever a grievance arises, feel that they must appeal to Congress for the redress of that grievance without considering whether it is one that Congress can redress or not. The idea seems to have become prevalent all over the country that anything which is wrong, anything which oppresses or depresses the people, must be remedied by Congress. I think it most ⊥ unfortunate that the people forget that their own local governments at home, controlled by their immediate representatives, are able to furnish the remedies for most of the grievances of which they complain, and for many of which they complain over which Congress has no power whatever. On this subject, however, Congress does have a limited power; but the exercise of its power under the Constitution and the doing of what it may do rightfully under the Constitution will not give relief to the people of the country unless the Legislatures of the several States take hold of the subject and make provisions there which will cover the larger number and the greater amount of the wrongs complained of by the people.

I had intended to make a criticism upon the bill of the Senator from Ohio which has in part been made by the Senator from Missouri [Mr. VEST] and in part by the Senator from New York [Mr. HISCOCK]; and inasmuch as those criticisms have been made I do not feel disposed to occupy the attention of the Senate by going over them again. I simply say in conclusion that I think the bill presented by the committee is objectionable on account of its not being within the provisions of the Constitution for the most part of it. The first clause of the first section is within the provisions of the Constitution, that which relates to commerce with foreign nations. A good deal of it, I think, is not within the provisions of the Constitution; and if the Senate should agree with me upon that point and should then agree with me that the provisions of the amendment which I have presented are within the purview of the Constitution, I shall hope they will adopt the amendment which I have presented.

Mr. ALLISON. Mr. President, I do not desire at this hour of the day, or at any time indeed, to discuss the merits of the bill presented by the Committee of Finance. I only rise now to occupy a few moments somewhat in response to the suggestions made by the Senator from Missouri [Mr. VEST], who has discussed the question so fully.

I must say that his argument as a lawyer discourages me somewhat as respects a remedy for these so-called trusts or combinations. If I understood the Senator correctly, he says that without an amendment of the Constitution the only practical remedy there is at this time is either an abolition or a great reduction of tariff duties or concurrent legislation of the States and of the United States, I suppose as respects interstate commerce; that beyond this narrow limit we have no power here to legislate upon this subject.

To fortify his argument as respects the tariff, he stated, as I understood him, that the tariff is the fruitful source of these combinations. If that be true, it is a curious thing to me that all these great combinations in our country are practically outside of and independent of the tariff.

The Senator read a number of trusts from a statement which he held in his hand, showing that the articles in the combinations alluded to by him were also articles that were included in the tariff schedules. But the complaint of the people, as I understand it, is not in respect mainly to the articles embraced within the tariff. I know it is true as respects the great article of sugar. Those whom I represent upon this floor in part, living in the State of Iowa, and those represented I have no doubt in part by the Senator from Missouri, are in favor practically of no tariff duty upon sugar. They believe that sugar is a necessary of life, and they believe that because of the fact that our entire production of sugar in this country amounts to but one-tenth of the consumption, the duty upon sugar is a tax upon that consumption, and therefore they are for its abolition or practical abolition if we can spare the revenue from that source.

With the exception of sugar and with the exception perhaps of steel rails, I know of no product in this country to-day (and in this I shall be glad to be corrected if I am mistaken) of any great magnitude that is affected by the tariff.

Nor will I admit that the tariff duty in and of itself produces even the sugar trust. I am not sure but that if sugar was to-day free, as it is in Great Britain, there would still be a combination among the sugar-refiners of our country to hold the market of our country. Whilst I have no doubt the present high rate of duty upon sugar has to some extent the effect to enable refiners and others more thoroughly to complete this combination, as fewer men can engage in sugar refining because of the high duty, yet I believe that if there was no duty upon sugar it would still be possible for a combination to exist here as respects the refining of sugar.

So it is practically with steel rails. The price of steel rails in England is substantially the price of steel rails in the United States to-day. Therefore the combination, if there be a combination, has not at this time any effect upon the price of steel rails in the United States. I will join the Senator from Missouri in making a proper and fair reduction of the duty on steel rails when we reach the question of the tariff, but the tariff on steel rails to-day has practically no effect upon the price, because, as I have stated, the price abroad is nearly equal to the price at home.

The Senator from Missouri illustrated his argument by reference to the copper trust. It is well known to every man who has studied the copper question that we can put copper upon the free-list any moment we choose to do so. We reduced the duty one-half upon copper in the proposed act of 1888, and it might just as well have been put upon the free-list. There has been a trust in copper. I do not know whether it exists now, but I presume it does. But that trust has not even an existence in the United States. It is a combination in a foreign jurisdiction which comes here and buys all the copper we produce and all the copper produced in the world. We are the largest producers of copper in the world. We are large exporters of copper to foreign countries. Therefore the duty upon copper has no more effect as respects trusts than if copper was upon the free-list.

The Senator from Missouri read one or two little instances or illustrations of trusts as respects our tariff, but I waited for him to show illustrations from the great tariff schedules as respects trusts and combinations resulting from the tariff. What are the great schedules that we deem important to protect American manufactures against similar manufactures and products of foreign countries? They are the great staples of woolen and cotton and leather and iron and steel.

The Senator from Missouri, with a production of steel of perhaps one thousand five hundred million dollars per annum, only illustrated by his statement as respects steel rails and nails. Those two items as compared with the great production of steel and iron in our country are infinitesimal and mere "leather and prunella." The manufactures of iron extend throughout the length and breadth of our country. Although there may be a few instances where iron production or steel production is under these trust combinations, I maintain that they are not there, because there is a tariff duty upon the articles.

Who has ever heard of a trust in woolen goods and woolen manufactures? The Senator from Missouri said the Committee on Finance of last year failed to reduce the duties upon woolen goods, and upon wool, and thereby oppressed the consumers of the country. Those consumers, whatever may be their conditions and relations to the tariff duties, which I will not discuss now, are not oppressed by reason of trust combinations. I state without fear of successful contradiction that in the two or three hundred millions of woolen goods manufactured in the United States there is no trust combination as respects those manufactures, and if I am mistaken in this I should be glad to be corrected now by any Senator.

Take the great manufacture of cotton, which the Senator from Missouri says in our tariff bill last year we reduced as respects the lower grades of cotton, and not upon the higher, and he undertook to criticise the committee by saying that that was done because the coarser cottons were manufactured in the Southern States and the finer products in the North. Mr. President, for myself, and for myself alone, I want to say to the Senator from Missouri that in dealing with the tariff I know no section of the Union, whether it be North or South. The reason why the duties upon cotton fabrics of a coarser character were proposed to be reduced was because those who produced those fabrics said they could produce them in competition with the world upon the rate we fixed. Yet with all these millions of cotton manufactures in the United States there is not a trust in any one of them of which I have ever heard.

Take another great article which is protected by the tariff, the article of leather and its productions. Boots and shoes and all the products of leather are produced in the United States, and are produced relatively at as cheap a rate as they are produced abroad, notwithstanding our tariff duties. They amount to hundreds of millions of dollars per annum. There is not within the range of all the States of this Union a trust or combination in the manufacture of boots and shoes.

So we are developing in this country a great silk industry. I have not heard, I do not know, how many millions of production we have, certainly up to the fifties, being nearly one-half of the silk consumed in the United States, and protected by a heavy duty upon silk manufactures. If there is now or ever has been a trust or combination as respects the silk manufactures of the United States, I have not heard of it.

So, Mr. President, agreeing to what the Senator says as respects trusts and combinations, I differ with him absolutely in the statement that they originate wholly in our tariff legislation. If we shall put wool and woolens upon the free-list, if we shall put cotton and manufactures of cotton upon the free-list, if we shall put leather and all its products upon the free-list, there will be no more and no less combinations in this country. If we should put practically all the iron upon the free-list, it would not change the trust relations and combinations except as to a few articles which were named by the Senator from Missouri.

These combinations exist, I admit, under the tariff in some of its relations, but the mass of these great combinations exist outside of it and beyond it. The Senator from Missouri himself is chairman of an important committee looking into a very important industry in our Western States, as respects the slaughtering of beef. He has been engaged in taking testimony upon that question. It is the common and the current belief among the farmers of the State in which I reside and of all the West that there is a combination in the city of Chicago which not only keeps down the price of cattle upon the hoof, but also has such relations and situations as respects the internal commerce of this country that its members are enabled to make the consumers of beef pay a high price for that article. Does anybody for a moment say that this great combination, involving the price of cattle perhaps in all the ⊥ Northwestern States and Territories, has in the slightest degree its origin in the tariff? Certainly not.

So I might illustrate by going into other great trusts in our country, like the whisky trust. Is that controlled in any way by the tariff? Yet it is perfectly well known that the production of distilled spirits is and has been under a close trust for a good many years.

Take the Standard Oil Trust, another great and ramifying corporation, not only in this country, but throughout the world. That combination, whatever it is, not only controls practically the price of the raw material in our country, but it controls the price of the refined oil throughout the civilized world. Year by year as we go on we not only produce more of this raw material in our own country, but we add year by year to the exports of refined oil in competition with the rest of the globe, and without any relation or without any respect whatever to the tariff.

Mr. President, there has been in our Western country for four years a combination as respects the production of oatmeal. Is that affected in any way by the tariff? Yet the producers of oatmeal have had a legal combination whereby they have been enabled to keep up the price of oatmeal, not only to the cost of production, but to a point of reasonable profit, and sometimes beyond it, as I have heard.

So, when I heard the declamation of the Senator from Indiana [Mr. VOORHEES] the other day, and again repeated in substance by the Senator from Missouri [Mr. VEST] to-day, that our tariff system is the fruitful source of all our woes, I can not forbear for a single moment to show, not by going into debate, but by mere illustration, that although I agreed with those gentlemen who are in favor of remodeling and revising the tariff, if we are to correct the great evils which arise from combinations and trusts in this country, we shall fall far short of our duty and far short of accomplishing what we propose if we undertake to do it simply by a change and modification of tariff rates.

Therefore, Mr. President, I welcome this discussion as respects the measure of our duty here and as respects the means whereby we can accomplish the desired result. I undertake to say that it is our duty to the extent of our power, whatever that power may be, to put upon our statute-books such national legislation as we can put there inhibiting these combinations and trusts, and I merely call attention to the fact that that is our duty in connection with the fact, that we can not do it by merely modifying or changing existing tariff rates.

Mr. TELLER. Mr. President, the Senator from Kansas [Mr. INGALLS] has offered a very important amendment. . . .

I rose to call the attention of the Senate a little more in detail to a question I asked the Senator from Missouri [Mr. VEST], who on several occasions I have heard express the opinion that these trusts, which have become very prevalent in this country, were the result of the tariff, and that, too, in the face of what the Senator from Iowa [Mr. ALLISON] has so well just said, that the principal trusts in this country and against which there is the greatest complaint, and under which the people are suffering the most, have no relation whatever to the tariff. There is not a civilized country anywhere in the world now that is not more or less cursed with trusts. A trust may not be always an evil. A trust for certain purposes, which may mean simply a combination of capital, may be a valuable thing to the community and the country. There have been trusts in this country that have not been injurious. But the general complaint against trusts is that they prevent competition.

I have before me, and I propose to read, testimony taken in 1886 before the British Commission to inquire into the cause of the depression of trade. If I had known that this discussion was coming up to-day (and it is only by accident that I have this book with me) I could have read other testimony showing that there are other trusts besides the one I am going to mention. . . .[1.315]

⊥ The Senator from Missouri has on several occasions complained of the tariff, especially with reference to steel rails, as I understood he did today, and as to steel generally, notwithstanding, as stated by the Senator from Iowa, practically steel rails and steel have been at the same price in Great Britain and in this country for a number of years. In December, 1885, steel rails were sold in Great Britain, according to the testimony to be found in this book, for more money than they were selling for in New York, and I want to call the attention of the Senator from Missouri and the Senate to a statement made here as to the manufacture of steel generally.

This is the testimony of Mr. Vickers, who is a steel manufacturer. . . .

Mr. VEST. I should like to ask the Senator from Colorado a question, which it seems to me concerns the people of this country a great deal more than the evidence taken before that commission. Does he not know that it is a fact that the steel-makers, including the steel-rail men, in this country entered into a trust a few years ago; that they made a trust here in the United States in order to put up the price and keep up the price of steel rails and other steel products?

Mr. TELLER. I understand they did, but they made it just exactly as it was made in Great Britain, and they will make it without any tariff; and if we had been exporters of rails, which we are now to some extent, but not largely, our American rail manufacturers would have entered into that trust with the British. I have no doubt about it at all. I am not saying that the men who manage these great industries will not get all they can out of the people. I am not defending trusts. I intend to vote for any measure that is constitutional and legal to break up these trusts, and I propose to say something about the bill which I do not care to say to-night, because I want to examine more carefully the amendment offered by the Senator from Kansas. I wish, however, to read from this volume about the price of steel.

Mr. Vickers went on then to tell about a pool, which is another name for a trust, that existed among the manufacturers of other steel besides steel rails. . . .

That is proof positive, if he would have the favor of the buyer, that there is an opinion among the buyers in that country that these pools do put up unduly the price of the product. . . .

⊥ There is not a Senator on the other side of the Chamber who has ever made a speech on free trade or the tariff who has not over and over again reiterated that we paid the duty, not only on steel rails, but on everything else.

Mr. VEST. I suggest to the Senator from Colorado that I wish the Senator from Rhode Island [Mr. ALDRICH] was in the Chamber, who stated in the last Congress that the tariff was put on in order to put up the price. That was said in debate.

Mr. TELLER. The tariff is put on to protect our people from just what these trusts did with reference to France and Austria, so that when we want to export or when we want to trade with our own people these trusts shall not come in and break down our enterprises. That is what he said.

Mr. VEST. No, sir.

Mr. TELLER. And it compels them to do just what he said it was for their interest to do, to sell at a loss rather than to shut up their establishments. . . .

Mr. President, I suggest that the Senators who are so certain that the tariff always

---

[1.315] The testimony read by Senator Teller, omitted here, concerned the operation of a trust composed of steel manufacturers.

raises the prices of all articles and that the consumer pays the tariff duty under all circumstances should get a copy of this work and give some attention to this testimony. . . .

. . . I can demonstrate, and I intend to do so some day on this floor, that the trouble with Great Britain, as with us, is not because of the tariff duties, but it is owing to a lack of money, and that is what the whole world is suffering from to-day.

Mr. COKE. I should like . . . to submit an amendment, which I intend to propose as a substitute for the trust bill at the proper time. I ask that it be printed and lie on the table. . . .

Mr. GEORGE. I offer an amendment which I intend to propose to the pending bill, and I ask that it be printed.[1.316]

SENATE DEBATE
51st Cong., 1st Sess.
March 24, 1890

21 CONG. REC. 2556

Mr. SHERMAN. I insist now on my motion to proceed to the consideration of the unfinished business of Friday, being the bill (S. 1) to declare unlawful trusts and combinations in restraint of trade and production.

The Senate, as in Committee of the Whole, resumed the consideration of the bill (S. 1) to declare unlawful trusts and combinations in restraint of trade and production.

Mr. TURPIE. Mr. President, I do not believe that the clause of the Constitution concerning controversies in which the United States shall be a party, controversies between two or more States, between a State and citizens of another State, between citizens of different States, has any relation except to the named controversies and to suits in equity and at law known and recognized to be such at the time of the adoption of the Constitution and now known and recognized to be such. I do not think such personal or mutual relations as are named in this clause have any connection with that large domain, the jurisdiction conferred in the beginning of the section arising "under the Constitution and laws of the United States." On the contrary, while the laws of the United States have granted special rights, remedies, or recoveries, those rights, remedies, and recoveries are to be entertained by the Federal courts without reference to the personal condition of the parties who may be interested in them. Such, I think, has been the invariable interpretation and practice under the first grant of power in this section, as far as we have gone into the domain characterized as "arising under the Constitution and laws of the United States."

I apprehend there are very few of us of this generation who have the slightest conception what this domain, very extensive in its character, shall yet include or embrace. Congress has seen fit heretofore to enter this domain very partially, only upon one or two or at the most three lines, and then to go no very great distance. The progress made in it has been always and must be dual. The jurisdiction conferred on the United States courts, arising under the Constitution and laws of the United States, is not self-operative. It always requires the act of Congress in the first place and the judgment of the court in the second place to make any progress at all in that domain. Congress must take the initiative. We must take action upon the subject-matter, and if our own jurisdiction in respect to such subject-matter is sustained by the courts the

---

[1.316] The Coke amendment was subsequently proposed on March 25 but tabled. *See infra* at 209-13. *See also infra* at 180-81, 192-95 (remarks of Senators Vest, Reagan, and Wilson on proposed amendment).

Senator George had introduced a bill (S. 6) on December 4, 1889, the same day as the Sherman and Reagan bills, which was referred to the Senate Finance Committee, 21 CONG. REC. 96 (1889), but never reported out. It was offered as an amendment to S. 1 by Senator Gray on March 26. *See*

judicial jurisdiction in the courts is then sustained in respect to such subject-matter and the methods by which it is to be adjudicated.

The Senator from Missouri [Mr. VEST] spoke the other day about the difficulty of defining the word "commerce," especially as contained in the phrase "interstate commerce." I recollect one judicial decision upon this subject very definitely. The Supreme Court has decided that insurance is not commerce, and I suppose by following the circle of negations long enough and excluding all the things not commerce we should come at last to the residuum, which must be commerce or interstate commerce, because it can be nothing else. *A fortiori,* judging from this principle, I should myself have decided that transportation is not commerce nor interstate commerce either. It can not be. It is only a means of conducting commerce, notwithstanding the courts and Congress have decided and have judicially determined that transportation is a matter so nearly related to interstate commerce that both Congress and the Federal courts have jurisdiction in relation to it under the clause giving us the power to regulate interstate commerce.

Now, sir, we have created a special tribunal to try cases under the interstate-commerce act. We have legislated very fully and very elaborately upon the incident to interstate commerce called transportation by railway. We need not have created a special tribunal. We could have referred the whole matter to the Federal courts in the first instance. But whether this matter of interstate transportation by railway be dealt with by Congress or the courts, by special tribunals or by the regular tribunals, the law with regard to it provides for a special class of cases arising under the law of Congress, affording special remedies and relief, affording special rights for recovery, and it is not therefore necessary that litigants in this subject-matter should occupy to each other the personal relations mentioned in the latter clause of the section, and no inquiry has been made by the commission upon interstate commerce, upon transportation, or by a court trying a cause in relation to such measure, as to whether litigants were residents of different States or whether the suit was between a citizen of one State and a citizen of another State, or what might be their personal or official relations. It is only required to give jurisdiction in such matter that the party shall be interested in the subject-matter which Congress has taken under its jurisdiction; that is, railway transportation in interstate commerce.

Take another instance. I should myself have determined, reasoning in the same manner as before stated, that if there were any subject necessarily committed solely and exclusively to State action, it would be the relation between debtor and creditor. Had it not been for a long precedent history of determination upon the subject, I should say that it was clear Congress had no power to deal with such relations; yet the history of the general bankruptcy law in this country has been so long settled, so well known, that our authority to deal herein is no longer questioned, it is *res adjudicata* [*sic*], and the only inquiry now made with respect to the passage of a general bankrupt law, with all its special rights and remedies and its utter indifference to parties, would be ⊥ whether it is expedient to do so. Congress having taken jurisdiction of the subject and having created special writs, processes, rights, remedies, recoveries, and defenses in this matter, it is never inquired in any case in a Federal court as to whether the parties in such cases were citizens of different States, were litigating with their own State or another, or whether they were representing any of the peculiar relations named and alluded to in the closing clause of the jurisdictional section which I first read.

I have known, and so has every attorney here known, litigants in the Federal courts under this special act of Congress, under both the acts of Congress in relation to bankruptcy, to be residents of the same State, of the same town in the same State, next-door neighbors, so absolute is the usage upon that subject-matter and so absolutely does the special provision of rights and remedies under an act of Congress confer unquestioned jurisdiction without any inquiry in respect to peculiar personal relations or official relations between the litigants.

I feel inclined to make the prediction, as one of the things to come in this vast

⊥2557

---

infra at 249. Specific provisions of the George bill were also proposed as amendments to S. 1. See *infra* at 205–06, 254.

Senator George declined to offer his proposed amendment after a similar proposition in the Coke amendment was voted down. See *infra* at 213.

domain, scarcely touched, of cases arising under the Constitution and laws of Congress, that the whole mass of merchantable paper known as negotiable by the law merchant, made at one place, negotiable at another, payable at another, transcending in its negotiation State lines, will be remitted to Congressional action, and with respect to its creation, its formation, its negotiation, with respect to all the rights and liabilities which may arise under it, the people, stunned with the eternal dissonance of conflicting decisions and judgments of forty-eight or fifty tribunals of last resort in the States upon the subject of interstate negotiable paper, will require Congress to act therein, and that, unconstitutional as I now deem it or think it, it will as a matter of necessity be done, and in any such legislation with respect to that paper, the whole bulk of it, the personal and peculiar conditions of litigants will not be inquired about, but simply whether the one party or the other is entitled to relief or liable to recovery against him by reason of being a party to interstate commercial paper, negotiable and payable and suable under the action of Congress which may finally take place upon that subject.

I go now, though, to another department of the domain which has been partially entered. I think we have only three times entered it since the existence of the Government. . . .

Mr. [JOHN H.] MITCHELL [R., Ore.]. In discussing this negotiable paper business—

Mr. TURPIE. That was a mere suggestion.

Mr. MITCHELL. I understand the law is now that where the parties to negotiable paper are citizens of different States the Federal courts have jurisdiction.

Mr. TURPIE. Certainly.

Mr. MITCHELL. Does the Senator hold that Congress could go further and give parties a remedy in the Federal courts irrespective of the question as to whether the real parties to the paper were citizens of different States at the time?

Mr. TURPIE. I have stated what I have to say on that subject. The RECORD will show it, and I do not wish to be asked except as to what I have said.

Congress passed a law concerning the creation and existence of national banks, one entering upon this same domain of formerly disputed, and in fact now disputed, questions. One of the sections of that bill provided that the national banks should have the right to sue in the Federal courts and conferred jurisdiction upon the Federal courts, and suits were brought under that section in the Federal courts. No question was ever made as to what the relation of the parties was to each other in respect to residence—none whatever. It was simply necessary, Congress having conferred jurisdiction, that one of the parties should be a national bank to avail itself of this special remedy, and that the other should be liable or claimed to be liable as a debtor in some way to such national bank.

The legislation respecting transportation, the legislation respecting bankruptcy, and the other partial legislation respecting national banks are perhaps the only three instances in which we have entered upon this great domain of cases arising under the laws of Congress.

From the interpretation and practice under all three of these instances, I should think that when we assume special legislative jurisdiction and create causes of action by special enactment and confer the judicial jurisdiction upon Federal courts, it is not necessary to define further any relations, personal or official, as between the litigants in these courts. No inquiry will ever be made, should Congress assume this jurisdiction, create the rights and remedies, and give to the courts the power to pass upon them, where the parties live, whether they are private citizens or otherwise, what the corporations may be, except that they shall be both related as plaintiff and defendant, adversely or favorably, to some question connected with this subject-matter, the prevention of trusts in interstate commerce.

I do not feel like entering into any strictures upon the phraseology of the bill of the honorable Senator from Ohio. I am too favorably inclined to the main purpose of this measure to indulge in any criticism of any effort made in good faith to prevent or avert these evils. There are some of them with which I think it is necessary to deal; but there is nothing in the bill which is not amendable. I am very far from saying with the Senator from New York [Mr. HISCOCK] that the objections to the bill of the Senator from Ohio are fundamental and that the scope of the measure lies beyond our power.

On the contrary, I believe that Congress has the same power to regulate interstate commerce that the States have to regulate commerce within their own lines, and that, as a matter of public policy, we have the same right to make this regulation affording civil remedies for those injured by the trusts, denouncing the trusts penally and all the others which are contemplated, as a State has under similar circumstances. Nor do I think with the Senator from New York that we are discharged from duty or released from our obligation to legislate upon the subject of trusts because the States have a right to do so.

They unquestionably have a right to do so, but there comes a time when the States have not that right. There comes a time, sometimes it may be a few hours, sometimes a few days, it is always a brief time, but it is a time of transit, in which the goods are moving from one State to another. It is a creating, formative, procreative, profit-bearing time. If at that time, by reason of the condition imposed by it, we may at that very moment strike a blow at these mischiefs, it will be more effective and more remedial in its character than any amount of State legislation upon the subject; and although with reference to a single transaction it is admitted it may be very brief, yet with reference to the whole of the transactions of trusts in interstate commerce there is not an hour of the day or night whose moments are not filled by violations of the law here proposed, whose moments are not filled with the perpetration of that crime against the people which this bill denounces and which these measures aim to punish.

The purpose of the bill of the Senator from Ohio is to nullify civilly the agreements and obligations of the trusts of these fraudulent combinations; I favor it. There is another purpose: to give to parties injured a civil remedy in damages for injury inflicted; I am in favor of that.

Those are the two principal measures embraced in that bill. I am willing to go much further, and I think the Senators generally will also. There is a bill introduced by the Senator from Texas [Mr. REAGAN]. It is a most carefully and elaborately prepared bill as far as the penal section is concerned. It has been introduced into the Senate, but I am sorry that the Senator himself speaks of it as a substitute for the bill of the Senator from Ohio. It is in no sense a substitute. Allow me to suggest that it be made an additional section in the one bill which is to receive our sanction.

There can be no objection to the proposition to nullify civilly trust-contracts, the contracts of fraudulent trusts described here. There can be no objection to giving a civil remedy for those injured thereby. And there ought to be still less objection to punishing penally those who are guilty of these fraudulent combinations. This much will be accomplished by a bill embracing such sections as those proposed by the Senator from Ohio and the Senator from Texas, not using either as a substitute, but all as additional, incidental, and closely connected with the main object and purposes of the whole body of legislation upon the matter about which and over which we are about to assume jurisdiction.

There is another bill here having very great merit. I allude now to the bill of the Senator from Mississippi, [Mr. GEORGE] upon the same subject. I have not heard that Senator say that it was offered as a substitute, but I suggest that it ought to go into the same bill as auxiliary thereto. I am perfectly willing to authorize the President to suspend the collection of duty with respect to commodities which have become the subject of fraudulent trusts, so that we shall have the action of Congress, the action of the courts, and the action of the Executive all directed to the same purpose.

Sir, a good deal has been said about the difficulties which are involved in this kind of legislation and the difficulties of administering a law or passing a law of this nature. We should have all these sections put into the same bill, making an act of only six or seven sections, upon the subject of trusts, and I think that would be a very brief enactment upon that subject. I do not think it would be a perfect enactment. No first legislation is ever perfect. I would rather favor imperfect legislation upon this subject than to be silent. It is only by commencing and prosecuting these different projects to the form of law, entering this domain, and asking the opinions of the Federal tribunals as to our own jurisdictional power, first, that we shall ever be able to lay hands upon these conspiracies which have done so much to injure the commercial credit and prosperity of interstate trade. It is our duty to do that first.

After all, these difficulties may be greatly overrated. It is a very difficult thing to convict a man under the numerous penal statutes in all the States of fraudulent conveyance. I have known a great many prosecutions of that kind in my life and not a single conviction; yet I would not vote for the repeal of such a statute. It is a valuable law and has prevented much fraud. It is *in terrorem* over offenders, and whether prosecutions have been sustained or not it has exercised a valuable moral influence in the business of the country.

In the same respect we have it as part of the statute of frauds that ⊥ such conveyances shall be void; also a very useful enactment. Now, I would add as a part of the Congressional statute of frauds exactly the provision in the bill of the Senator from Ohio that all agreements, notes, bonds, securities, and contracts of any nature made by a trust for trust purposes, or made by one of these fraudulent combinations, shall be null and void. The civil nullification of all the paper creatures of these combinations is a thing we have certainly in our power.

Again, sir, there may be some difficulty in defining this offense. To describe it is impossible. It is like the penal offense of fraud. The courts have never attempted to define it. In the statute the definition of it is very brief, "a conveyance with intent to hinder or delay creditors." Notwithstanding, the definition has been made practical, it has been made useful, and it has become a measure of the first importance in the conduct of the business of the country; and notwithstanding this definition may be imperfect and there may be no description and can be none altogether applicable to fraudulent commercial trusts, they vary so much and are so multiform in their character, yet the definition here attempted will, if it do nothing else, lead us to a better form and a more explicit definition or description of the offense here meant to be denounced.

Notwithstanding the difficulty which courts and juries have had in punishing men, or in investigating cases brought upon complaints of fraudulent conveyance or of procuring goods upon false pretenses, yet this jurisdiction has been of extreme worth and is still of great utility. We know that in the revenue acts there are very great difficulties accompanying sometimes the conviction of a smuggler, at other times of parties who are charged with making false invoices and false inventories, and there are many of the definitions or attempted descriptions of offenses in the customs acts which are even now, after years of adjudication, more vague and more indefinite than anything contained in the bill of the Senator from Mississippi, and the Senator from Ohio, or the Senator from Texas upon this subject; and yet they have not practically failed to prevent those frauds and to punish offenders.

We need not conceive, and I do not think any of us have, that Congress takes upon itself the entire charge of the administration of justice in the country. We have only one branch of it. We make the laws which are to be civilly and penally administered. The moment we denounce these trusts penally, the moment we declare these fraudulent trust combinations to be conspiracies, to be felonies or misdemeanors, that moment, under their own maxim, the courts are bound to carry out the intention and purpose of the legislation, and even to favor that purpose and intention, that the will of the people may prevail and not perish. This is one of the fundamental maxims. I have no doubt that when this law goes into practical operation it will receive a construction and a definition very useful to us; it will be aided by courts and juries; it will be aided by advocates upon both sides in stating different views of construction, and above all it will be supported and upheld by a public opinion expressed in a denunciation of those evils which this kind of legislation would avert and avoid.

Mr. [JAMES L.] PUGH [D., Ala.]. Mr. President, it will take me but a short time to give my views to the Senate upon the important bill now before us. I have listened with interest and instruction to the speech of the Senator from Indiana [Mr. TURPIE], and in the main I fully indorse it.

Mr. President, the existence of trusts and combinations to limit the production of articles of consumption entering into interstate and foreign commerce for the purpose of destroying competition in production and thereby increasing prices to consumers has become a matter of public history, and the magnitude and oppressive and merciless character of the evils resulting directly to consumers and to our interstate and foreign commerce from such organizations are known and admitted everywhere, and the universal inquiry is, What shall be done that can be done by Congress to prevent or mitigate these evils and intolerable exactions?

Congress may declare these trusts and combinations to be unlawful, if they are against the public policy of the United States, and without any act of Congress prohibiting their creation or existence they could not now be enforced in any court, because they are manifestly contrary to the public policy of the United States. Such trusts and combinations could not be enforced even as against the parties to them, for the reason that the wrongdoing of any party to them can not be visited upon him by the courts on account of his conduct when to do so would be detrimental to the public policy of the United States, and in such cases the courts relieve the wrongdoer to protect the public policy, which is paramount.

Why are such trusts and combinations contrary to the public policy of the United States? For the plain reason that they hinder, interrupt, and impair the freedom and fairness of commerce with foreign nations and among the States.

To use the language of the bill before the Senate, are "arrangements, contracts, agreements, trusts, or combinations between two or more citizens or corporations, or both, of different States, or between two or more citizens or corporations, or both, of the United States and foreign states, or citizens or corporations thereof, made with a view or which tend to prevent full and free competition in the importation, transportation, or sale of articles imported into the United States; or with a view or which tend to prevent full and free competition in articles of growth, production, or manufacture of any State or Territory of the United States, with similar articles of the growth, production, or manufacture of any other State or Territory, or in the transportation or sale of like articles the production of any other State or Territory of the United States; and all arrangements, trusts, or combinations between such citizens or corporations made with a view or which tend to advance the cost to the consumer of any such articles," against the public policy of the United States?

Can any Senator doubt that the recitals of the first section of the bill are true, and that they amount to a violation of the public policy of the United States, and, if so, that Congress can declare such transactions to be unlawful and void for that reason? What public policy of the United States is violated by the acts recited in the bill? Manifestly the public policy founded on and to be encouraged and promoted by the freedom and fairness of our commerce with foreign nations and among the States and the unrestricted interchange of their productions. Has Congress no power to protect the public policy? If no such power exists in Congress, then our public policy is at the mercy of conspirators against it, and, although clothed with an express grant of power to regulate commerce, no power exists by implication which Congress decides to be "necessary and proper" to execute the express grant.

But it may be conceded that Congress has the power under the commerce clause of the Constitution to define what acts are detrimental to our commercial policy and to prohibit them. What is the value of such a power if it is limited to mere declaration and prohibition? If the acts denounced in the bill are unlawful or become so by declaration and prohibition by Congress because they have the effect or tend to violate our commercial policy, why should Congress be powerless to enact penalties and provide remedies? I have heard no answer to this inquiry except that the Federal courts have no jurisdiction and Congress can confer upon them no jurisdiction to enforce any remedies for the evils recited in the bill.

Let us see if this opinion is well founded. In Cohens *vs.* Virginia, 6 Wheaton, page 378, many times cited, Chief-Justice Marshall delivered the opinion of the court in these words:

> The second section of the third article of the Constitution defines the extent of the judicial power of the United States. Jurisdiction is given to the courts of the Union in two classes of cases. In the first their jurisdiction depends on the character of the cause, whoever may be the parties. This class comprehends "all cases in law and equity arising under the Constitution, the laws of the United States, and treaties," etc. This clause extends the jurisdiction of the court to all the cases described, without making in its terms any exceptions whatever and without any

regard to the condition of the party. If there be any exception it is to be implied against the express words of the article.[1.317]

It is solely from the subject-matter, "the character of the cause," that I desire the power of Congress to pass the bill under consideration and to confer jurisdiction to the Federal courts to execute the law. The subject-matter is commerce with foreign nations and among the States, and the public policy founded on its encouragement and promotion. In my humble judgment it was unnecessary for the bill to make the parties to the trust and combination citizens or corporations of different States, and it should be amended so as to include citizens of the same State or Territory. It matters not where the parties reside if their acts or combinations hinder, delay, interrupt, or prejudice the freedom and fairness of our commerce or violate our commercial policy in the manner specified in the bill. I have no doubt Congress has the power to make such trusts and combinations criminal and punishable by fine and imprisonment.

Whenever the bill before the Senate becomes a law of the United States, the Constitution declares, in the language of Chief-Justice Marshall, that "the judicial power of the United States extends the jurisdiction of the court to all cases in law and equity arising under the laws of the United States, without any exceptions whatever and without any regard to the condition of the party." Make the bill before the Senate a law of the United States. I know of no law Congress has the constitutional power to enact that Congress can not authorize and require the courts of its own creation to execute.

Where did Congress get the power to enact into a law the fifth section of the act "to regulate commerce," known as the interstate-commerce law, which declares—

That it shall be unlawful for any common carrier subject to the provisions of this act to enter into any contract, agreement, or combination with any other common carrier or carriers for the pooling of freights of different and competing railroads, or to divide between them the aggregate or net proceeds of the earnings of such railroads or any portion thereof; and in any case of an agreement for the pooling of freights as aforesaid, each day of its continuance shall be deemed a separate offense?

I know it will be at once claimed that these common carriers are engaged in interstate transportation on public highways, and that it is their pursuit there that subjects them to the jurisdiction of Congress and the Federal courts. This is true; but what I wish to show is that the crucial test urged by Senators opposed to the proposed legislation for want of constitutional power in Congress is the judicial definition of commerce with foreign nations and between the States.

It is claimed that the Supreme Court in the leading case of Brown *vs.* The State of Maryland[1.318] crystalized the law as to the meaning of foreign commerce by saying that it was "imports in the original package remaining in the hands of the importer unbroken; and when and so long as the original package was in that condition it was the subject of foreign commerce. When it left his hands and the package was broken, and the goods went into the common mass of the property of the people of the State, then the commercial clause of the Constitution as to foreign commerce ceased to operate."

Again, it is correctly stated that the Supreme Court in three leading cases has also defined the constitutional meaning of "commerce among the States" to be in "articles, commodities, productions that become the subject of sale or barter and are in the custody of the carrier and *in transitu,* actually moving from one State to another to purchasers and consumers." When these articles, commodities, or productions of one State are in the condition of being moved and are labeled for carriage and for sale or other disposition in another State, then they become subject to the operation of the commerce clause of the Constitution as to "commerce among the States."

It is important that Senators should understand that the definitions of commerce with foreign nations and among the States relate exclusively to the *corpus* of foreign and interstate commerce. The physical body, the articles, the productions, the goods, wares, and merchandise, the freight—when these become the subject of "regulations" by

---

[1.317] 19 U.S. (6 Wheat.) 264, 378 (1821).
[1.318] *See* note 1.249 *supra.*

Congress they can be reached only when in the original unbroken package in the hands of the importer and when *in transitu* from one State to another. But there is a wide difference, in my humble judgement, between the power regulating the *corpus* of foreign and interstate commerce in its transition state between the producer and the consumer, and the power of reaching and regulating individuals, companies, and corporations who enter into agreements, trusts, and combines to hinder, delay, interrupt, or in any way to prevent the full, free, and fair transit and interchange of the *corpus* of commerce with foreign nations and among the States.

The one jurisdiction is over the physical body, the other jurisdiction is over persons and corporations who conspire against the freedom, the health, and well-being of the physical body. It is the latter power that Congress exercised in the passage of the fifth section of the interstate-commerce act. There the power is exercised to reach and punish by fine and imprisonment individual carriers who "enter into any contract, agreement, or combination with any other carrier for the pooling of freights of different and competing railroads, or to divide between them the aggregate or net proceeds of the earnings of such railroads or any portion thereof." The law of the fifth section of the act "to regulate commerce" is aimed at the persons and their trusts and combines that interfere with the freedom and fairness of commerce among the States. It embraces carriers who never handle the freight and railroads that have never had or carried a pound of the freight while *in transitu* or otherwise, the earnings for carrying which by other and different railroads are to be equally divided. . . .[1.319]

Thus we discover that power was found in the commerce clause of the Constitution to protect commerce with foreign nations and among the States against diseased cattle, but it is denied by the same Senators who voted for the cattle bill that any power exists to protect our commerce against the greater evil of trusts and combines.

The commerce clause of the Constitution has also furnished power to Congress to prevent the spread of cholera and yellow fever and small-pox by prohibiting and punishing the transportation of goods infected or that have been exposed to the infection of these epidemic diseases. There is no epidemic disease that is as destructive to human health and life as trusts and combines are destructive to the health and happiness and well-being of industrial pursuits, and the freedom, growth, and prosperity of our foreign and domestic commerce.

Mr. President, I am thankful that I have no capacity to indulge in hair splitting so I can see how many hairs I can make out of one, neither have I any ambition to excel in ciphering to show into how many decimal fractions I can reduce the constitutional grants of power to Congress. The framers of the Constitution were practical men with a large stock of common sense and not enough uncommon sense to interfere with the wisdom, safety, and perfection of their great work. The grants of power to Congress are defined in plain language, and, although specific, the grants are comprehensive in their scope, to be exercised by Congress within the common-sense limitations of the Constitution. . . .

The PRESIDING OFFICER. There being a quorum present, forty-seven Senators having answered to their names, the Senate will proceed with the consideration of the unfinished business. The pending question is on the amendment of the Senator from Kansas [Mr. INGALLS]. Is the Senate ready for the question?

Mr. SHERMAN. I have no objection to so much of this amendment as seeks to make illegal the class of contracts described in the first and second sections of the bill, but the amendment also creates a tax and is therefore not within the originating power of the Senate. I think we ought not to violate the Constitution by voting for an amendment which we have no right to pass as a bill. I shall, therefore, content myself by simply voting against the amendment. I do not know that any question of order can be raised, but it is a question of constitutional law. We have no power in the Senate to originate tax bills, ⊥ and I hope, therefore, the amendment will be voted down on this ⊥2560 ground, although I am in favor of the general proposition of making these contracts null and void.

[1.319] Senator Pugh also referred to section 6 of the Act establishing a Bureau of Animal Industry (Act of May 24, 1884, ch. 60, § 6, 23 Stat. 32), which prohibited the exportation of diseased cattle, as another example of the use of the commerce clause of the Constitution to regulate interstate commerce.

Mr. REAGAN. Mr. President, I wish to suggest also in that connection—I do not see the Senator from Kansas present—that the amendment proposed by the Senator from Kansas is not germane to the subject-matter of the original bill. It is on an entirely different subject and has no reference to the bill. It proposes to deal with the question of futures and subjects of that kind, not the subject of trusts.

The PRESIDING OFFICER. The question is upon the amendment proposed by the Senator from Kansas. Does the Chair understand the Senator from Texas as presenting a question of order?

Mr. REAGAN. Yes, sir.

The PRESIDING OFFICER. There is no rule in the Senate of relevancy or requiring that an amendment shall be germane. The Chair overrules the point of order.

Mr. REAGAN. All right.

The PRESIDING OFFICER. The question is upon the amendment of the Senator from Kansas. . . .

The amendment of the Senator from Kansas is in the nature of perfecting the original bill, as it is offered as an addition to the original bill, and not as a substitute. . . .[1.320]

Then the Senator's [Mr. Reagan's] amendment is first in order, having been first introduced; and the question is upon the amendment of the Senator from Texas [Mr. REAGAN]. Is the Senate ready for the question? . . .[1.321]

Mr. GEORGE. Mr. President, I regard that amendment as I do the bill, as utterly without warrant in the Constitution, by which Congress is bound, but I regard it as more efficient, if an unconstitutional bill can be efficient, than the original bill, and at this stage of the proceedings, as we are perfecting the bill, and if the bill is passed at all in my opinion the Constitution will be violated, I think it is well, if we are to have a violation of the Constitution, that we shall have a bill that will do the people some good, if it is to operate at all, and for that reason I shall at this stage of the proceedings vote for the proposition of the Senator from Texas as an amendment to the bill of the Senator from Ohio.

Mr. TELLER. Mr. President, I am in full sympathy with the efforts on the part of the Senator who introduced this bill and the several amendments to it to control the trusts, of which we hear so much complaint. The only question seems to be just how the trusts can be controlled. My own judgment on that point is that the States are the most competent to control trusts and to control them efficiently. It is suggested by a Senator near by, "Suppose the trusts control the State." I do not know that they are any more likely to control a State than they are to control this body or any other legislative body. These combinations have, of course, become very powerful; they have vast sums of money at command and generally a vast army of people engaged in connection with them whose interests are with them, and of course they have become powerful, but still not so powerful, I think, but that the States can and ought to control them.

So far as the General Government can control them, I am in favor of the General Government undertaking to control them. I am inclined to vote for this bill because it seems to me that it is possible to do something in that direction. I want to say, however, that I am not so sanguine of its accomplishing the purpose for which the bill is intended as some who have spoken upon the subject. I doubt whether very much benefit will be derived from this bill, and unless the States take hold of the question and devise appropriate legislation for suppressing these trusts or limiting the amount of capital that can be aggregated in one corporation this trouble will continue, in my judgment.

I understand that some of these trusts have been disturbed by the recent decisions of the courts of the country, which, as the Senator from Ohio [Mr. SHERMAN] showed the other day, have been all in one line, and I suppose no lawyer needs to have any argument made to him that these combinations and trusts are illegal without statute.

[1.320] At this point Senator Reagan changed his amendment from a substitute for, to an addition to, the Sherman bill and requested that it be voted upon before the Ingalls amendment.

[1.321] Senator Reagan's bill, which appears *supra* at 111, was read as an addition to the Sherman bill, the paragraphs being renumbered 3 through 5.

But frightened somewhat by the decisions of the courts they have gone to work and have united what were many corporations into one with all the characteristics of a corporation and none of a trust as we now speak of and treat trusts. When that is done, it is beyond the power of this body to deal with them unless they impede or impair or hinder or delay interstate commerce. When they do that, of course they bring themselves within the jurisdiction of the General Government. But the ⊥ great evil against which the people are complaining, these corporations perpetrate at home in the respective States, untouched by any legislation of ours.

⊥2561

I do not know whether this bill will be used for the benefit of the people or whether it will be used against them, especially the amendment which is now proposed to be voted on. I realize that the Senator from Texas [Mr. REAGAN] is an honest enemy to these combinations, and that he intends as far as possible to control them by the legislation proposed. But take the fourth paragraph of section 2 of the Senator's amendment. Among the things that are spoken of and made illegal is this:

Fourth. To fix a standard or figure whereby the price to the public shall be in any manner controlled or established of any article, commodity, merchandise, produce, or commerce intended for sale, use, or consumption.

The second is:

Second. To limit or reduce the production or to increase or reduce the price of merchandise or commodities.

There are legitimate and proper efforts that can be made for the advancement of prices. This refers to reduction in price as well as to advance in price. If there is a combination to put down the price of an article or to put it up, it is equally punishable under this provision by a criminal prosecution. There may be a condition of things where it is perfectly proper to put down the price of an article and on the other hand there may be a condition of affairs where it would be perfectly proper and legitimate to put up the price of an article.

I know it will be said in answer that these things should be left to the natural course of affairs, of commerce, and trade. But there has been recently organized all over this country what is called the Farmers' Alliance. What is the object and what is the purpose of it? The very purpose of it is to increase the price of farm products, and that I regard as a thing most desirable to be done, and I regard it as absolutely essential to the prosperity of this country. There has recently been organized, in the Northern States more particularly, and I suppose it will spread all over the country, what is called a National League amongst the farmers for the same identical purpose that the Farmers' Alliance has been organized for. Shall it be said that these organizations are forbidden by law? Is it possible that we are putting it in the power of some men to coerce and force the farmers to abandon these organizations? Does anybody believe that these organizations are inimical and hostile to the public welfare? On the contrary, does not everybody know that unless we can by some method increase the price of farm products in this country a great many farmers in the United States will be in bankruptcy and turned out of their homes? . . .

Mr. GEORGE. I think that is a very good point that the Senator has made against the amendment offered by the Senator from Texas, but can not the same point be made against the original bill as introduced by the Senator from Ohio and amended by the Committee on Finance?

Mr. TELLER. The same point can be made with this difference, that one is a civil proceeding and the other is criminal. That is all the difference. I was going to say the same of the original bill.

Mr. GEORGE. But still, if I understand the Senator, he admits that under the bill as last reported by the Committee on Finance the Farmers' Alliance, being composed of citizens of different States, is an organization which is condemned by the bill.

Mr. TELLER. I think so, by the bill itself. I think it is objectionable to that criticism, although, of course, it is not so objectionable, because the one is a civil and the other is a criminal proceeding. . . .

Mr. GEORGE. Under the original bill as reported by the Committee on Finance, every farmer belonging to one of these alliances would be liable to a civil action and to the recovery of double damages against him for being a member of that organization, the tendency of which is to increase the price of his farm products.

Mr. TELLER. That is what I was saying. It seems to me that is the fact. While I am extremely anxious to take hold of and control these great trusts, these combinations of capital which are disturbing the commerce of the country and are disturbing legitimate trade, I do not want to go to the extent of interfering with organizations which I think are absolutely justifiable by the remarkable condition of things now existing in this country.

I believe this bill will go further than that. I believe it will interfere with the Knights of Labor as an organization. While I have never been very much in love with the Knights of Labor, because of some of their methods, yet their right to combine for their mutual protection and for their advancement can not be denied. While in many instances I think they have gone beyond what they should have done, beyond what was legitimate and proper, yet on the whole we can not deny to the laborers of the country the opportunity to combine either for the purpose of putting up the price of their labor or securing to themselves a better position in the world, provided always, of course, that they use lawful means. I do not believe the mere fact of combining to secure to themselves a half-dollar a day more wages or greater influence and power in the country can be said to be an unlawful combination. . . .

Mr. GEORGE. The Knights of Labor, as I understand, are [sic] an organization composed of citizens of the different States of the Union, probably of every State of the Union. The object of that organization, as I understand furthermore, is to increase the price of their wages. Now, increasing the price of wages has a tendency, in the language of this bill, to increase the price of the product of their labor. Are they not also included, then, in the bill of the Senator from Ohio?

Mr. TELLER. When I said that the Knights of Labor were included I meant that they were included both in the civil provisions and in the criminal provisions. In my judgment they are in both. I do not believe that anybody in the Senate proposes to go to that extent. It is suggested to me by a Senator near me that the Typographical Union would come in in the same way.

Mr. HISCOCK. And it would practically include all the trades unions.

Mr. TELLER. It would practically include perhaps all the trades unions in this country. Many of these organizations are corporations. If they are not, at least they will be termed "combinations" under this bill.

Mr. President I admit as a general rule the principle should be to let trade and commerce go on in the natural way, and yet we can not object to men putting up the price of certain things or under some circumstances putting down the price of certain things when the great mass of the people are benefited by that movement. I have not learned the doctrine that cheapness is the only thing in the world that we are to go for. I do not believe that the great object of life is to make everything cheap. I have before me now, in the morning papers, a statement of the condition of tailors in London. It is headed:

PATHETIC PLEA FOR AID—EAST END TAILORS OF LONDON PETITION THE QUEEN FOR HELP—A HOPELESS SET OF WORKMEN.

It is dated yesterday, London, March 23: . . .[1.322]

If a condition of that kind existed in this country and a class of laborers should combine to raise the price of their labor, and thus have a tendency to increase the price of the product, whether it was in a mill or in a shop or on a farm, would it not fall within the inhibition of this bill, both the original bill and the amendment of the Senator from Texas? . . .

Mr. REAGAN. . . .

In reference to the point made by the Senator from Colorado [Mr. TELLER], I wish to remark that he is doubtless misled as to the effect of the fourth clause of the second section of my amendment, to which he has referred, by considering it isolated from the provisions of the first section. He will see that the first section, as introduced by me,

---

[1.322] The newspaper article describing the "wretched condition" of the tailors was read.

limits its operation to matters involved in commerce with foreign nations and between the States, in this language:

> That all persons engaged in the creation of any trust, or as owner or part owner, agent, or manager of any trust, employed in any business carried on with any foreign country, or between the States, or between any State and the District of Columbia, or between any State and any Territory of the United States, or any owner or part owner, agent, or manager of any corporation using its powers for either of the purposes specified in the second section of this act—

The second section of the bill as I introduced it, but the fourth section of this amendment—

shall be deemed guilty of a high misdemeanor, etc.

⊥ The second section in each of these clauses relates back as to the question of authority to the first section, so that whatever view may be taken as to the constitutional question presented by the Senator from Indiana [Mr. TURPIE] and the Senator from Alabama [Mr. PUGH], that point can not arise on this, which relates to the criminal part of the proceeding because it is limited to business in international or interstate commerce, and I suggest that the Farmers' Alliance and the Knights of Labor would not come under that clause; but, if they did, the way to prevent all such organizations is to strike down first the organizations which give rise and necessity to this local labor association. ⊥2562

Mr. PLATT. If the Senator from Colorado will permit me, and if the Senator from Texas will give me his attention, I desire to say a word.

I had supposed it to be true that the first part of the section, that is, down to line 6, referred to trusts employed in any business carried on with any foreign country or between the States, or between the States and the District of Columbia, or between the States and Territories, but from line 6 down I supposed, as the language reads "or any owner or part owner, agent, or manager of any corporation using its powers for either of the purposes specified in the second section of this act," had no reference whatever to a business carried on which might be called foreign commerce or interstate commerce, but was intended to punish a stockholder in any corporation who should do any of the things included in the several heads of the second section. That is the way I have understood it.

Mr. REAGAN. The object was as I have stated.

Mr. TELLER. The Senator from Connecticut has explained that provision exactly as I understood it. Of course I may be all wrong about it and it may be entirely different. It may not be objectionable but it would be well to put this in form so that there can be no question about it.

Mr. President, I had not quite concluded reading the newspaper extract which I wanted to read. . . .

I know that nobody here proposes to interfere with the class of men I have mentioned. Nobody here intends that by any of these provisions, either in the original bill or in any amendment; and I have only called attention to it to see if the efforts of those who have undertaken to manage this subject can not in some way confine the bill to dealing with trusts which we all admit are offensive to good morals.

I do not myself desire to interfere with the management of this bill which has been reported from the Committee on Finance and is in the hands of such able gentlemen as those who proposed it originally, or those who have attempted to interfere with it and to aid in its perfection.

Mr. President, I was greatly struck with the amendment offered by the Senator from Kansas [Mr. INGALLS], and I believe if that can be enacted into law it will greatly relieve the agricultural interests of this country. I was, however, somewhat disturbed in my idea of supporting that proposition by the suggestion made by the Senator from Ohio that it was beyond the jurisdiction of this body to pass it. That is the only objection I can see to it. It seems to me that the measure is well intended and very desirable; and it strikes me that if it could be carried out it would go far to relieve the people of this country. I do not know what the Senator who introduced it would say upon the constitutional question, but I shall listen when he takes the floor on that point.

I want to repeat that I am exceedingly anxious myself to join in anything that shall break up and destroy these unholy combinations, but I want to be careful that in doing that we do not do more damage than we do good. I know how these great trusts, these great corporations, these large moneyed institutions can escape the provisions of a penal statute, and I know how much more likely they are to escape than the men who have less influence and less money. Therefore, I suggest that the Senators who have this subject in charge give it special attention, and by a little modification it may be possible to relieve the bill of any doubt on that point.

Mr. SHERMAN. Mr. President, all I desire is that this bill, the object of which I believe is approved of by more than three-fourths of the Senate, should be treated like all other bills that have been carefully considered by a committee of this body and reported to the Senate. To attempt to defeat this bill by offering various other bills from other committees or from the other House on different branches of the same subject or on entirely different subjects, is not the proper way to deal with the work of a committee.

Now, let us look at it. The bill as reported contains three or four simple propositions which relate only to contracts, combinations, agreements made with a view and designed to carry out a certain purpose, which the laws of all the States and of every civilized community declare to be unlawful. It does not interfere in the slightest degree with voluntary associations made to affect public opinion to advance the interests of a particular trade or occupation. It does not interfere with the Farmers' Alliance at all, because that is an association of farmers to advance their interests and to improve the growth and manner of production of their crops and to secure intelligent growth and to introduce new methods. No organizations in this country can be more beneficial in their character than Farmers' Alliances and farmers' associations. They are not business combinations. They do not deal with contracts, agreements, etc. They have no connection with them. And so the combinations of workingmen to promote their interests, promote their welfare, and increase their pay if you please, to get their fair share in the division of production, are not affected in the slightest degree, nor can they be included in the words or intent of the bill as now reported.

On the other hand, the Senator from Kansas [Mr. INGALLS] offers a bill which was framed by one of my colleagues in the House of Representatives, and the fact that it is pending there is a matter known and shown by the record, and it is still being considered by a committee of that body. It proposes to deal with a class of contracts that do not have to do with production, that are based upon the idea that there is no production at all. They are options on property that does not exist. They are what are called mere contracts without regard to production, based upon nothing, upon empty air. They are gambling contracts. If the Senator from Kansas wishes to introduce a proposition to prevent gambling in property which does not exist, to prevent agreements to deliver property without any intention to deliver it, that is one question and an entirely different matter from the one covered by the bill. That is a question to be considered by itself, and it ought not to be attached or annexed to this bill.

But there is another fatal objection to that measure, it seems to me. We can not vote for it without violating our obligations under the Constitution of the United States. The Senate has no power to originate any form of taxation, and yet here is a proposition to tax in various ways these illegal contracts, with a view to deter them from being made, just as we imposed the tax upon the issue of State bank paper, in order to drive it out of existence, but still we levied it in the form of a tax; it was part of a tax bill, and the proper place for this proposition, so far as it attempts to levy a tax, is upon a tax bill. It would be proper upon the tariff bill when it comes to us, but it has no relation to the subject-matter of the pending bill.

The original bill deals with a combination, agreement, or contract to advance the price of productions on hand; it relates to actual commerce in things tangible passing from State to State; while the proposition of the Senator from Kansas is to deal with things intangible, with contracts in the nature of gambling, and it has no relation to this matter, and to put it on as an amendment to this bill, it seems to me, is not treating the subject fairly unless the Senate wants to defeat the original proposition. It seems to me it is a great deal better for us to have a fair vote on the original proposition, disconnected with any other measure pending at this time.

Take the proposition of the Senator from Texas. It does contain some matter germane to or connected with the original proposition, but it introduces into this debate a criminal law, and that was one of the objections made to the original bill as first reported by the Committee on Finance. When we undertook to amend it and put on a criminal clause, and after full reconsideration of the subject, it was thought best to omit the criminal clause and to leave that for future consideration, because we were dealing with a new subject-matter and it was deemed a great deal better to declare the general principle of law, without any criminal section, leaving Congress to provide hereafter criminal penalties, as I have no doubt it will do if they shall be found to be necessary.

The objection I have to the proposition of the Senator from Texas is, first, that it is a proposition pending in another committee of this body, and there it is being considered. The Senator from Vermont says it has been referred to a subcommittee and they have not reported upon it. Now, is it wise to ingraft here that proposition which has not yet been considered by the committee in charge of it, relating to a different subject-matter? I think it is not fair; it is not right. In this way, by antagonizing friendly propositions, you may defeat any bill.

Suppose, for instance, the amendment of the Senator from Kansas should be ingrafted on the bill; a Senator might say, "I can not vote for that because it undertakes to do what the Constitution plainly declares the Senate can not do," and that would result in defeating the original proposition. So with the proposition of the Senator form [sic] Texas. He offers here a criminal statute defining various kinds and various forms of combinations; it has not yet been subject to scrutiny, and it is now pending before a committee of this body which has not yet considered it. Suppose that is ingrafted on this bill. Some member of the Senate might with great propriety say, "Why, this is a new proposition; it has never been fully considered; it does not come to us perfected by the judgment of a committee; it is drawn out, wrested, taken from the jurisdiction of the Judiciary Committee, and put upon a bill which has already been considered and fully considered by another committee."

⊥ I am actuated by no desire to have this bill and nothing else, because I would ⊥2563 accept any amendment that met my judgment, and I will vote for any proposition that will make it clear and confine it to its proper objects; but I do think the Senate of the United States in dealing with a question which at this time commands the attention the people of the United States as much as any other should deal with it in a fair way. In other words, there should be fair play on all these various propositions, and we should not combine incongruous elements in order to defeat the original proposition. If you do not like the bill, vote it down. If you can propose any amendments to carry out the object of the bill, to limit its operation, or in any way to improve it, they are proper and ought to be offered; but do not put on different propositions. I might with the same propriety take the pension bill which is now pending here, giving a pension to dependent relatives of soldiers, and a thousand other bills on the Calendar and offer them as amendments. That is sometimes a way of trying to defeat an original bill. I think, however, it is better for Senators of the United States to defeat it squarely by a fair vote, and say that the original bill ought not to pass rather than to encumber it with propositions that lead to endless argument.

I shall vote against all these amendments which do not seem to carry out the object defined in the original bill, not because I disapprove of them, for I approve of all attempts to destroy and to declare illegal, null, and void all those gambling contracts which now pester the business of the country. I shall at the proper time be perfectly willing to denounce criminal penalties upon any man who violates the principles of this bill; but I do not think at this time it is wise for us to introduce criminal legislation upon a remedial bill of this character. As I said in my argument—and I do not want to repeat it over again—this bill is simply an attempt to extend the jurisdiction of the courts of the United States, to declare unlawful contracts which have been held unlawful in every State of the Union where the subject has been brought before the courts; nothing more, nothing less.

The only ground of objection to this is that we can not extend the jurisdiction of the courts of the United States thus far. That argument has been fully answered by Senators on the other side. I attempted to answer it myself by showing a great number of authorities. The honorable Senator from Alabama [Mr. PUGH] and the honorable Senator from Indiana [Mr. TURPIE] have shown that this bill as it now stands is not only constitutional, but that it is the duty and right of the United States to aid the States in declaring null and void these combinations and agreements in restraint of trade. I hope, therefore, we shall have a fair vote on these different measures as they come up and as they are reported by committees, and that when the bill of the Senator from Texas is reported from the Judiciary Committee we shall have the judgment of that committee upon that bill. When the proposition which is now made by the Senator from Kansas comes up to us it is to go first to the Committee on Finance, because it is a part of a scheme for raising revenue and can only be treated as a revenue measure. The other provisions of that bill are simply incidental to the main point.

I say it is better and fairer in dealing with this great subject to take the bill which has been reported by the Committee on Finance, reject it if you will, improve it if you can, and confine the attention and intelligence of the Senate to the provisions and objects of this bill, and go no further until the other bills are reported and have gone through the same scrutiny, and then we shall have time enough to do it. So far as I can see, there are no provisions in the bill offered by the Senator from Kansas but what meet my judgment in a general way. I have only had time to read it this morning. The first two sections I am entirely agreed to, but they have never been matured, never have been reported by any committee, never have been considered by a committee. When they are so considered, we shall have time enough to act upon them. . . .

Mr. HOAR. I wish to ask the Senator from Ohio one or two practical questions about the details of the bill, which will take but a moment. The bill provides that—

The circuit court of the United States shall have original jurisdiction of all suits of a civil nature at common law or in equity.

I suppose it is the purpose of the Senator from Ohio to give private citizens who are injured by these combinations or monopolies for the advancement of cost or preventing men from freely competing, a civil remedy in the courts, is it not?

Mr. SHERMAN. Certainly.

Mr. HOAR. I suppose that is the object, and I suppose any citizen of the United States might bring a suit in the courts if he had been wronged or claimed that he had been wronged in this way. Now the bill goes on and says:

And the Attorney-General and the several district attorneys are hereby directed, in the name of the United States, to commence and prosecute all such cases to final judgment and execution.

Mr. SHERMAN. That is confined to the first section of the bill.

Mr. HOAR. I understand that, and my question is confined to the first section of the bill.

Mr. SHERMAN. The first section of the bill does not give a civil remedy at all; it is the second section that gives a civil remedy.

Mr. HOAR. The first section says that—

The circuit court of the United States shall have original jurisdiction of all suits of a civil nature at common law or in equity arising under this section.

Now the Senator says the first section does not give the civil suit at all.

Mr. SHERMAN. It does give a suit in the name of the United States:

And the Attorney-General and the several district attorneys are hereby directed, in the name of the United States, to commence and prosecute all such cases to final judgment and execution.

Mr. HOAR. Then the Senator avoids my first question and does not mean to answer it.

Mr. SHERMAN. I do.

Mr. HOAR. Let me put the question again. The first section of the bill declares:

The circuit court of the United States shall have original jurisdiction of all suits of a civil nature at common law or in equity arising under this section, and to issue all remedial process, orders, or writs proper and necessary to enforce its provisions.

Now, this section has declared that all these arrangements are wrongful and unlawful, and that is the only declaration which gives any private citizen any right to sue under them. That is the declaration of the first section. It seems to me that as the Senator has got this bill so drawn that any citizen of the United States can invoke the civil remedy and the civil jurisdiction provided in the first section under the bill—it seems to me there is no doubt of it whatever—and when he has done it the bill makes it the duty of a United States officer, the Attorney-General or the district attorney, not merely to commence and prosecute the suit, but to prosecute it without compromise or abandonment, because he is expressly commanded to prosecute it "to final judgment and execution."

Mr. SHERMAN. Well, Mr. President, the Senator has confounded the two sections together. They are absolutely distinct and independent, each conveying the proper authority and jurisdiction to the courts of the United States. The first deals only with combinations made in restraint of trade or to prevent free competition in the importation, transportation, etc., of articles. They are in the nature of public offenses against public policy. In regard to those in the first section it is declared that—

The Attorney-General and the several district attorneys are hereby directed in the name of the United States to commence and prosecute all such cases to final judgment and execution.

And before that it is provided—

The circuit court of the United States shall have original jurisdiction of all suits of a civil nature.

Mr. HOAR. Are they of a civil nature? The Senator has just said that these are public offenses and the statute says that they are suits of a civil nature.

Mr. SHERMAN. Can not the United States commence a suit of a civil nature?

Mr. HOAR. For a crime?

Mr. SHERMAN. Not for a crime, but for a remedial proceeding. It is a proceeding such as is known in every State of the Union, as in the Commonwealth of Massachusetts and in other States. There are suits by the people of New York against these combinations. We have a suit of the people of Ohio and the people of Missouri; I quoted here a decision in a suit of the people of Illinois—just such things as are contemplated by this bill. If the Senator from Massachusetts will read the second section of the bill he will find that that alone deals with private suits.

SEC. 2. That any person or corporation injured or damnified by such arrangement, contract, agreement, trust, or combination defined in the first section of this act may sue for and recover, in any court of the United States of competent jurisdiction, without respect to the amount involved, of any person or corporation a party to a combination described in the first section of this act, twice the amount of damages sustained and the costs of the suit, together with a reasonable attorney's fee.

It is the second section that gives the civil suit, and that is not to be prosecuted at all by the United States or by the officers of the United States. The first section deals with the public injury to the people of the United States and there the suit is brought in the name of the United States to restrain, limit, and control such arrangements so far as they are illegal. The second section gives a private remedy to every person injured. It seems to me the two sections are as distinct from each other as possible.

Mr. HOAR. The Senator from Ohio states, in my very humble judgment, two entirely different and conflicting and inconsistent propositions. I agree and thoroughly understand that the second section of the bill gives individuals the right to private suits. I leave that out as settled. I am looking at the first section alone. The Senator says that the first section provides nothing but suits for public offenses, which are criminal suits and to be tried in the name of the United States, as for an offense against the United States. The language of the section is:

And the circuit court of the United States shall have original jurisdiction of all suits of a civil nature at common law or in equity arising under this section.

⊥ I should like to ask the Senator again, does he understand that the United ⊥2564 States is to enforce this proposed statute by a civil suit, and not by a criminal proceeding?

Mr. SHERMAN. I say that in a civil suit brought in the name of the United States the United States may sue on a contract; they may sue for a neglect; they may sue for a great many things. Those are civil suits. The distinction between a civil suit and a criminal suit, I need not tell the Senator from Massachusetts.

Mr. HOAR. I understand that. What will be the judgment?

Mr. SHERMAN. It may be a judgment of ouster of the corporation; it may be a judgment for damages. Civil suits and criminal suits are easily distinguished.

Mr. HOAR. There is no difficulty in that.

Mr. SHERMAN. Very well. This is a civil proceeding commenced by the people of the United States against these corporations, and a judgment may be, as in ordinary cases, an ouster of the power of a corporation; it may be for damages; there may be an injunction; there may be proceedings in *quo warranto*, and so of the other ordinary civil proceedings which are fixed by the judiciary act of the United States.

But the second section provides purely a personal remedy, a civil suit also by citizens of the United States. The Senator from Texas wishes to add to it a criminal remedy. In that I differ from him. I think it is better not to put a criminal section in this bill. Still, if it is adopted by the Senate, that would not deter me from voting for the measure, because that at least is in harmony with the bill and seeks to carry out the same object. However, in my judgment, his measure ought to undergo the same scrutiny that this bill has undergone. Let it be reported from the Judiciary Committee, and then we can consider it and probably vote for it, if so reported after full scrutiny.

Mr. REAGAN. I ask unanimous consent, if it is necessary, to modify my amendment by inserting after the word "corporation," in line 9 of section 3 (in the first section of the amendment), the words "company or person employed in any such business." I make this modification because I think there was force in the objection made by the Senator from Connecticut [Mr. PLATT], and I think these words cure that difficulty. That puts it all under the interstate and international commerce clause.

The VICE-PRESIDENT. Without objection that modification will be considered as agreed to. The Chair hears no objection, and the amendment of the Senator from Texas is so modified.

Mr. REAGAN. Mr. President, I confess to a little surprise at the suggestions of the Senator from Ohio that the amendment which I have submitted is different in character from the measure which he has reported, and that they ought to be separately acted upon by the Senate. What is the object of the bill reported by the Senator from Ohio? It is to prevent and to punish persons engaged in trusts and combinations for unlawful purposes. What is his remedy? It is a civil suit, and a civil suit to be brought in the circuit court of the United States. Who can avail themselves of that remedy? Rich corporations and rich men may, but the great mass of the people are not able to employ counsel and go with witnesses to the circuit court for the vindication of their rights.

So the remedy as presented (and I intend at the proper time to offer an amendment to meet that) is inadequate; it is insufficient. I propose to aid the Senator in the prevention and punishment of trusts and combinations for unlawful purposes by providing that their formation, and the action under them when in connection with the international and interstate trade, shall be unlawful and shall be punished as provided in my bill. That certainly gives an efficient remedy, and a much more efficient remedy than that proposed by him for the very evil which he seeks to prevent.

The Senator suggests that my amendment ought to undergo the revision of a committee. I may say to the Senator that much of it is copied out of a law, not a law of Congress but of one of the States, which underwent very thorough and searching discussion. So all I had to do in this case (and that is the purpose I had) was to make the provisions of the State law applicable to international and interstate commerce. That is as far as it has seemed to me our powers go.

When first discussing this bill I suggested that I thought it proper that a clause giving a civil remedy should be inserted, but that the most efficient means of preventing the very evil which the Senator from Ohio is driving at is to make these offenses penal and provide for their prosecution in the courts of the country. I suggest that if the purpose is to prevent these things it is much more efficient than the remedy proposed by the Senator and exactly in the same line and for the same purpose.

I call again the attention of the Senator to the fact that his bill gives this jurisdiction to the circuit court of the United States, and that only the corporations and the rich men will be able to go into that court to assert the remedy which he proposes; and that the great mass of the people who are the sufferers from these combinations and trusts will not have the means to employ counsel and to take witnesses to the Federal courts, often at a great distance from them, to vindicate and enforce their rights.

We need a law upon this subject that will punish every man engaged in this business and that will give an adequate remedy in a convenient jurisdiction to every person who is damaged by these associations. I trust that the Senate will sustain the amendment which I have offered to the bill for the purpose of giving it efficiency, for the purpose of affording to the people that protection which he desires to secure.

Mr. STEWART. Mr. President, this whole subject is surrounded by difficulties of the gravest character. Men must unite their efforts to have any civilization at all. An individual by himself can be but a savage. Combination, co-operation, is the foundation of all civilized society. When you permit that at all, the question is where you are to stop and say there shall be no more combinations.

These combinations seem almost like a necessary evil resulting from civilization. Our ancestors have tried to check them in England for hundreds of years. They had their common-law rules, they had their statutory regulations, and finally they came to the conclusion in that country that legislation would not reach the subject, but that it simply retards trade and embarrasses those whom they do not desire to embarrass. If we attempt it in this country, we shall have a similar history. Besides, the Congress of the United States is laboring under special difficulties on account of its limited jurisdiction.

To show the experience in England in dealing with this particular question, I have here a statute passed in 1844 which wiped out all that had preceded it, and left trade and commerce free, and I think it is so instructive a lesson that it ought to be incorporated in the RECORD. I send it to the desk and ask that the statute be read. The statute itself is its own commentary.

The VICE-PRESIDENT. The Chief Clerk will read, as requested.

The Chief Clerk read as follows:

> An act for abolishing the offenses of forestalling, regrating, and engrossing, and for repealing certain statutes passed in restraint of trade. . . .[1.323]

Mr. STEWART. The difficulty in dealing with this question is well illustrated by hundreds of years of experience in Great Britain, where Parliament was supreme, where they could pass and enforce any law they pleased on this subject. They found after all this experience that such laws were simply hurtful, and so they passed an act repealing the law, changing the common law with regard to it, and leaving trade and commerce free.

The difficulty in the whole subject is in reaching any precise evil or defining the offense. If you say there shall be no combination the tendency of which shall put up prices, how far would that reach? It would reach to nearly every transaction in life and would be particularly oppressive upon the struggling masses who are making combinations to resist accumulated wealth. Accumulated wealth has the power to prosecute, and if the laborers combine in any form to protect themselves there will be means found of prosecuting them.

If small traders combine together to meet some great trust so as to enable them to carry on their business, the power will be in the hands of the great trust and the opposition will be trusts. This scheme seems to me to put in the hands of accumulated capital the power to have all associations that can possibly be rivals prosecuted, because the associations that seek to resist trusts are not organized so artfully. Their purpose has to be avowed; they must state what their purpose is in order to get the inexperienced masses to go with them. It must be for the purpose of protecting themselves, whereas the experienced few who handle accumulated capital can do this in such a manner as to preclude all the possibility of proof.

[1.323] 7 & 8 Vict., c. 24 (1844).

So I believe the practical working of this bill, if it were constitutional and we had a right to pass it, would be to crush out competition where the people are trying to protect themselves against oppressive monopolies. I think that it is the way it would work practically.

Besides, I do not find any warrant in the Constitution for this particular class of legislation. It is stated in the first section of the bill that when combinations between citizens of different States and citizens of the United States combine with aliens to do certain things they shall be amenable to the law and shall be prosecuted in certain ways. I suppose that is the jurisdictional provision.

Mr. GEORGE. That is the jurisdictional provision.

Mr. STEWART. Now, that jurisdictional provision is referred to citizenship, and the provision in the Constitution gives the United States courts jurisdiction when and of what? First, it gives them jurisdiction in cases of equity and actions at law, and nothing else. This is given in certain cases on account of citizenship. Where citizens reside in different States they can have their controversies settled in the United States courts. But this is not a controversy. On the contrary, it is a combination; it is an agreement.

There is no dispute between these citizens resident in different States, but it is a partnership formed of citizens of different States that confers no jurisdiction upon the Federal courts. There is a difference between a partnership where all the parties agree and a litigation where the two parties disagree. The fact that they reside in different States and agree to do something does not add to the jurisdiction one particle. That part of it may be eliminated from the bill as having nothing to do with it.

Then the bill provides in a separate clause by itself:

And all arrangements, trusts, or combinations between such citizens or corporations—

Meaning combinations between citizens of different States or between citizens of the United States and aliens—

made with a view or which tends to advance the cost to the consumer of any such articles, are hereby declared to be against public policy, unlawful, and void.

It might just as well read, and it would be just as constitutional if it had said, that "all combinations having that tendency should be unconstitutional and void."

Now, it is the struggle of every community, it is the struggle of all the people who are attempting to better themselves, to get a good price for their commodities. Why might not the citizens of Iowa and Kansas unite and say, "We will hold back our corn; we will not sell it at these ruinous prices; we will combine and hold it until prices are better; we will put up the prices; they are robbing us. There is an organization in Chicago that is bearing this article, that is selling it short, that is putting it down; they are robbing us and we will not sell; we will combine?"

Suppose all the people of the different States should combine together and say, "We will stand against this Chicago combine that is attempting to get our produce for nothing," why would not they be liable to prosecution, the whole of them, if it were a constitutional law? But have they not a natural right to hold their products back until they can get a better price?

This is only one of a thousand instances in which this measure would be abused if it were passed. It is not the intention of anybody here to make that construction of it; we are trying to remedy the evil; but it is very probable that if this bill were passed the very first prosecution would be against combinations of producers and laborers whose combinations tend to put up the cost of commodities to consumers. It would be a weapon in the hands of the rich against the poor, and if you will trace the history of such legislation you will find that the experience of Great Britain was that such laws have always been turned against the people. After several hundred years of experience Parliament wiped them all out.

I believe that the true remedy against such trusts is that of counter combinations among the people. I believe in co-operation. Take, for instance, the most notorious trust in the West that there has been so much said about—the beef trust in Chicago. You can not reach that by such legislation as this. But suppose that you had a general law on your statute-books passed by the United States, that has the power to regulate interstate commerce, or suppose there was such a law in Illinois allowing the consumers to combine and have a co-operative organization, and suppose five thousand consumers in Chicago would form an association and supply themselves?

The trouble is, these combinations monopolize the market. Suppose those who are oppressed should do that? They might unite and get beef in for enough people, so that under this law they, too, would unite ⊥ together. They could so co-operate that they can supply themselves with beef. It is because they do not take that means that the beef-combine has control. This law would prevent them from combining against the other combine. If they did co-operate, however, they would be certain to get enough inhabitants who consume beef to meet together and say "We will buy of nobody else." That would break up your trust. If you pass this proposed law, however, and such a combination were attempted in Chicago, it would be prosecuted the next day.

These evils of combination, of course, are great, but the question is, do they not grow out of civilization itself, the foundation of which is organization, and without organization men would be savages? Should we not rather encourage organizations among the people to meet the grasping disposition of the favored few? The great trouble from the beginning of civilization has been that the few have combined against the many, being more competent, and that the few in various ways secure to themselves special privileges against the masses. I say let the masses combine.

One of the worst combines that have ever been inaugurated on earth from the beginning has been the combine on money, which has been an organization sanctioned by law to put up prices and put them down at the option of the speculator; to make it scarce or dear whenever they desired. That is the great trust that is pressing upon the country today. The labor organizations in this land are beginning to wake up to what is hurting them, and they are demanding legislation whereby the amount of money in the country shall be kept stationary in proportion and business, so that they shall not be robbed by low wages or half pay. They are getting waked up to that.

Let the people organize, I say, to get proper legislation for the whole country, but do not strike at civilization and say that you will abandon the idea of co-operation, which is absolutely necessary, without which we could not exist as a nation or remain in any civilized state.

I think that this bill is on the wrong basis and it will cut in the wrong direction if it passes, inasmuch as I find no warrant in the Constitution for Congress to pass this kind of a law and no warrant in the exigencies of our condition.

The amendment of the Senator from Kansas [Mr. INGALLS] has a good feature in it. It aims at a particular thing. It strikes at these options, where men are selling something they do not have, where they are selling other people's property short. That is one of the few things in the list that might be selected, and dealing in options, selling other people's property short might be remedied or stopped.

There is some difficulty about that, because there must be limited agreements to deliver property in the future which has not yet been produced; but the mere dealing in other people's property without any intention of furnishing the property, simply to destroy its market value, is a dangerous thing. If that could be properly guarded there might be something gained. It is dangerous also to attempt that. It has been attempted and has thus far failed. I would not advise any legislator to vote to sanction any dealing of that kind, but when you say that all combinations of the people to protect themselves against monopoly shall be criminally prosecuted in the United States courts, you go too far; you attack the wrong people.

Then, the bill provides for another thing which will be very vexatious. It makes it the duty of the district attorney and of the Attorney-General, all the law portion of the Government, to prosecute these actions, and you will have the whole country converted into a most vexatious lawsuit. It will be against people who are illy prepared to defend themselves. Those who are cunning will work by their secret organizations. The power of those who understand this will not be touched; but if it is carried out you will fill the whole country with litigation and retard business and development. You will do the very thing which you would regret the most of all.

If this question is to be dealt with, I say it is within the jurisdiction of the States. What jurisdiction has the United States to go into the States? These combinations and organizations are in the States. Bring suits in the States to abolish them or to punish them for having formed trusts and partnerships in the States! What authority have you? The attempt in the first section to acquire jurisdiction by citizenship in different States will not reach the point. What is the difference? A partnership is not a case presented at all. United States courts have jurisdiction of controversies, not partnerships. Stripped of that, it authorizes the law officers of the United States to sue persons for making business combinations in the States, making it their duty, of course, to bring suits. The law would either be a dead letter or it would be a weapon of injury to the people who want redress in some substantial way.

I think the best way to legislate is to legislate upon those subjects which Congress has the confessed jurisdiction of, and to relieve the present depression in business as rapidly as possible.

The VICE-PRESIDENT. The question is on the amendment of the Senator from Texas [Mr. REAGAN], as modified, to the bill reported by the Committee on Finance.

Mr. [HENRY W.] BLAIR [R., N.H.]. Mr. President, I am a little troubled by the amendment of the Senator from Kansas [Mr. INGALLS], which, to be sure, seems to aim at the destruction of the business of gambling, dealing in futures and options, by imposing so heavy a tax upon the articles to be dealt in as to amount to a prohibition. Nevertheless, the amendment does legalize such transactions. It expressly legalizes gambling in options and in futures. It licenses the practice, fixes the conditions and terms under which this gambling, universally denounced to be a crime, is to be conducted, under and by authority of the laws of the United States. It is not business, like the dealing in oleomargarine, which is understood to be useful food, but there being abuses connected with it likely to become serious it was thought worth while, by a very slight tax, so that there could be a regulation of the subject, to guard the public against evils resulting from unrestrained traffic.

Mr. INGALLS. Did the Senator do me the honor to examine section 10 of my proposed amendment before making that remark?

Mr. BLAIR. Section 10 of the Senator's amendment provides—

That neither the payment of the taxes required nor the certificates issued by the collector under this act shall be held to legalize dealing in options and futures, nor to exempt any person, association, copartnership, or corporation, etc.

Certainly I had read that; but the Senator, I suppose, understands very well (at least I understand) that, although there might be a provision of that kind, nevertheless the enactment of conditions under which the business may be conducted is a license; and that the acceptance of a tax on the part of the United States from the party who exercises that business is a practical exemption of the party from all penalties and is a legalization of the practice itself. It is not sufficient to insert these nugatory words in the proposed statute and yet say to the party, "You can do this business if you pay us so much." It is not in the power of the lawgiver to authorize a thing to be done upon condition that a certain amount of money be paid, and then by words which are practically nugatory prohibit the exercise of the privilege a license to do which is given.

The Senator from Nevada [Mr. STEWART] said that dealing in options and futures, or at least in futures, under certain circumstances, is sometimes necessary. Very likely that may be true in some conceivable cases. I do not find fault with the Senator's statement, but the point I wish to make is this: If that be true, a measure like this, which does not except those cases wherein the practice is a right one, a measure like this, which in general terms by this tremendous imposition of taxes upon the exercise of the right renders the exercise of that legitimate and proper right impossible, certainly should not be adopted by the Senate. The amendment contains no exceptions reaching a case such as may have been referred to by the Senator from Nevada. It is an intended prohibition of just those cases, as well as of the abuse of actual gambling, which constitutes the great abuse under which the country suffers.

It is no reply to say that this is an important thing and will prohibit generally the hurtful practices which are ruining the farmers of Kansas and Nebraska, as they understand, and throughout the West generally. It is no remedy for the difficulty under which they are laboring to enact the proposed amendment presented into law. First, it legalizes the practice, and, in the second place, it proposes to put upon the statute book a law which, in the next session—it may be at this very session—may be so amended and modified by the reduction of the taxes as to become practically inoperative as a prohibition of the practice itself. It seems to me that the amendment, if it is to accomplish anything as a remedy to the farmers in the West or elsewhere, should be pretty thoroughly examined.

I think if the sharp and critical Senator from Kansas looks his amendment over he will find that he can correct it grammatically in quite a number of important particulars. . . . But that is not of so much importance. I call his attention to the possible evil operation of the amendment in the regards I have pointed out of a more substantial character.

I suggest to the Senator from Ohio, in order to meet the difficulties he seems to be laboring under, and which are inevitably to destroy his bill if one may judge from the criticisms of the Senate, that in the fifth line of the first section he strike out the words, "to prevent full and free competition" and insert instead the words, "to permit a monopoly." Everybody knows what a monopoly is, and nobody will object to prohibiting a monopoly. In the seventh line I suggest to insert after the word "or" the words "a monopoly;" and again in the eleventh line, where the words "intended for and which" occur, it would be necessary, in order to have good grammar, to insert the word "transportation" after the word "for." Likewise, if he will look a little farther along, in the fourteenth and fifteenth lines I suggest that it would at least make the bill better in the direction which he evidently intends the bill to operate, to strike out the words "intended to advance" before "the cost" and to insert the words "primarily intended to enchance [sic]," so as to read: "primarily intended to enchance [sic] the cost to the consumer of any such articles;" and after the word "articles" to insert "and for the promotion of a monopoly." I give notice that I shall move these amendments. Let them be taken down, with the idea that they may be moved when the proper time comes.

The VICE-PRESIDENT. The Chair desires to call the attention of the Senator from New Hampshire to the fact that the original bill is not now before the Senate for amendment. . . .

Mr. BLAIR. . . . The other phraseology which I thought might be worthy of consideration comes in the fourteenth and fifteenth lines in section 1, striking out, as I indicated, and inserting the words "primarily intended to enhance;" so as to read: "primarily intended to enhance the cost to the consumer of any such articles;" and then to insert after the word "articles" the words "and for the promotion of a monopoly." I shall have these amendments ready to go in a different arrangement, applying the same phraseology to different lines.

Mr. HOAR. Mr. President, I do not understand why the Senator from Ohio has inserted in the bill the language of the first few lines, confining his penalty to citizens or corporations of different States or citizens or corporations of the United States and foreign States. I suppose it was prepared with some idea on the part of the draughtsman of the bill that contracts between citizens of foreign States and our citizens or between citizens of different States were necessarily commerce between those States, and that that was essential to bring the proposed statute within the constitutional power of Congress to regulate commerce between the different States or with foreign States. But that, as it seems to me, is very clearly a mistake. It is not commerce between the States for a citizen of Massachusetts to go into Ohio and buy a farm there, or buy a barrel of flour there, or even make an unlawful contract there.

This bill must stand, if at all, upon the fact that it is a bill to protect what is described alone, and that is the importation, transportation, or sale of articles imported into the United States or transported from one State to another or from a State to a Territory or the District of Columbia.

The Senator, it seems to me, would make his bill much more comprehensive if he struck out, after the word "combinations" in the fourth line, down to the word "thereof" in the seventh line, and it would stand within the Constitution as a measure for the protection of foreign or interstate commerce. I suppose we could punish a single person who did not combine with anybody else in another State who committed an act which was clearly to the injury of foreign commerce or commerce between the States, as, for instance, if he should adulterate some article which was to be exported or taken from one State to another, and perhaps we could punish him even for putting obstructions on the track of a railroad engaged in interstate commerce itself. There are a great many illustrations that could be put.

So it seems to me that the Senator has aimed his shot at a very small portion of the offenders when he has a perfect right to include them all. That is the first criticism of the bill that I have to make.

Mr. SHERMAN. In the bill as originally draughted by myself I did not insert the words "between two or more citizens or corporations."

Mr. HOAR. I do not lose the floor by yielding to the Senator. The Chair will understand that he is merely making an explanation.

Mr. SHERMAN. I have the original bill before me, and it reads precisely as the Senator proposes:

> That all arrangements, contracts, agreements, trusts, or combinations between persons or corporations made with the intention to prevent full and free competition, etc.

But these very words were inserted with a view to confine the operation of the bill to contracts made between citizens or corporations of different States, so as not to invade, by possibility, the jurisdiction of the courts of the States. I prefer a great deal the original draught, but to avoid somewhat the criticism of the Senator from Mississippi [Mr. GEORGE] I put in those words so as to describe contracts made between citizens and corporations of different States dealing in interstate commerce. As a matter of course I have no objection if the Senator should propose to strike out the words "two or more citizens or corporations, or both, of different States," but then it would only lead again to the objection. I do not want to fight both Senators, however.

Mr. HOAR. Of course, if the Senator does not want to interfere with the State jurisdiction and the State does what he would consider its duty in the premises, the State can equally punish as far as the bill is concerned any act which it has the power to make unlawful, whether it is done by two citizens of its own State or a citizen of its own and a citizen of another State, an act done within its borders, if the act be unlawful. The only jurisdiction over this subject is the jurisdiction to protect foreign and interstate commerce. That we have; that we can regulate; that the States can not regulate under the recent railroad decisions of the Supreme Court overruling a case from Illinois and that class of decisions where it was held that the jurisdiction was concurrent.

I suppose that, so far as this is a regulation of the commerce between this country and a foreign country or between two different States of this country, the jurisdiction of Congress is conclusive over it; the States can not touch it. A State can no more touch it when two of its own citizens do the act than it can when two citizens, one of its own State and another of another State, do the act, because it is a regulation of foreign or interstate commerce with which a State does not undertake to deal. If that be true, it seems to me, with great respect to the learned and able Senator, that he was right in his original judgment, and that the error of the amendment is in yielding to an untenable attack which was made on the bill as he originally drew it. I should hope that before the bill is voted upon that amendment will be made, because otherwise it will be easy to avoid its operation altogether by the offenders taking up their residence or citizenship in the same State, and this bill does not touch them.

Mr. HISCOCK. Do I understand that the Senator from Massachusetts is arguing the jurisdiction in reference to this subject on account of residence?

Mr. HOAR. That is the very thing I am attacking.

Mr. HISCOCK. That is, the Senator thinks that no jurisdiction is given on account of residence?

Mr. HOAR. Certainly; that is the proposition I am endeavoring to maintain, and I hope I have the concurrence of my honorable friend from New York.

Mr. HISCOCK. You have.

Mr. HOAR. In the next place, I want to come to the subject which was the matter of a colloquy between the honorable Senator from Ohio and myself when he was addressing the Senate in his own right, in his own time, and that is, that this bill fails to afford any considerable remedy to anybody, either to the public or to any private citizen, except so far as it may give a power to private citizens to bring their suits. It provides, in the first place, only for jurisdiction in the courts of the United States in suits of a civil nature to enforce the provisions of the bill. There is no remedy by penal suit; there is no remedy by indictment or by any other criminal process, if there be any other criminal process known.

The Senator says the suit of a civil nature gives, as against these corporations or partnerships, all the remedy which could exist for individuals when brought on the part of the United States. But what will it amount to? You can not prove in any court that the United States will suffer damages, though you can say why, in a civil suit brought by the Attorney-General or district attorney, the United States shall recover $100,000, or $200,000, or $500,000. It is an injury to the public, but there is no injury to the United States as a Government in respect of any of its property, or ownership, or function.

But the honorable Senator says they can get judgment against the corporation by ouster or *quo warranto*. I respectfully submit to the Senate and to the careful reflection of my honorable friend from Ohio that that is not a sound legal proposition.

A *quo warranto*, as I understand it, is a process by which a corporation is deprived of its corporate power by a judgment in a proceeding instituted in behalf of the authority which created it, because it has exceeded its functions or disobeyed the law in a matter which, by the law of its being, makes that disobedience a forfeiture of its franchise.

Mr. SPOONER. Or by non-user.

Mr. HOAR. Or by non-user, which is another basis of proceeding by *quo warranto*, as the Senator from Wisconsin suggests. But it is perfectly clear to my humble judgment as a legal proposition that an offense by a corporation created by the State of Ohio or the State of Massachusetts against a law of the United States can not, even if it were expressly declared by the law of the United States to accomplish that result (which this proposed law does not at all declare), constitutionally operate as a deprivation of a State corporation of its State charter and function.

Mr. HISCOCK. If the Senator from Massachusetts will allow me to interrupt him again, I will make this suggestion: The purpose of that provision, if it has any purpose, is, first, to make these contracts void. No one, then, has suffered any damages. If the first section has any purpose it is to reach out and commence actions to set aside contracts of that kind that have been made, to institute, so far as you can by suit, investigations into all of the business affairs of the people who may be engaged in interstate commerce possibly. Before there has been any sale of the property, if you please, the contract has been made; before any manufacturing has been done you commence then and there to start a sort of bureau of protection against this sort of thing.

Mr. HOAR. I will answer that presently. I am at present dealing with the suggestion of my honorable friend from Ohio. I submit to the lawyers of the Senate, including my honorable friend from Ohio, who is one of the ablest members of this body, as we all know, that it ⊥ is an utterly untenable proposition to claim that the ⊥2568 United States can have a forfeiture of the charter of a State corporation for an offense against the United States law. The Senator sees that it is not because of an offense against the law of its being. Then the sole jurisdiction over the right of the corporation to live and go on, to proceed in order, as the Chair says when anybody is out of order, is in the State courts.

The honorable Senator made one suggestion in which I agree with him, that in a proper case there might be an injunction in equity which would prohibit the future exercise of these unlawful powers by these corporations. It seems to me from all the reflection I can give to this section that is all there is left of it, a possibility in proper cases of an injunction in equity where some future offense against this proposed law is threatened; but as a remedy by way of a punishment, as a penal enactment for the past, which of course will be the great terror of these offenders, the injunction will not hurt them much, because they will merely have tried to do the thing and failed, and in nine cases out of ten they will have had their purpose accomplished before the injunction is issued. To that extent I agree that the section has virility.

The honorable Senator from New York inquires whether the object of this section will not be accomplished by treating it as a section which provides for an investigation to inquire into the jurisdiction.

Mr. HISCOCK. I refer to suits brought with reference to declaring these arrangements void, and, if you please, coupled with a prayer for an injunction against the continuance of them, and I ask whether practically the Government is not to follow them up in that way? Wherever they have been effecting a combination of that kind, suit is to be commenced by the district attorney in the locality, and he is to appear against them and have them indicted. As I suggested the other day, I expected, if that is held to be valid, it will be followed by some sort of provision in the future that every concern or every manufacturing industry shall be compelled to take out a license.

Mr. HOAR. When we have the provision in the future presented here, that will be one thing; but who ever heard, either as a matter of sound public policy or as a matter of constitutional authority, a provision for a mere inquiry into the business and affairs of citizens, whether corporations or individuals, which was conducted by a civil suit brought against them on the part of the Government?

Mr. HISCOCK. I agree with the Senator on that question.

Mr. HOAR. That would be one of the unreasonable processes against which all of our constitutional theories militate.

Mr. HISCOCK. I should like to ask the Senator if he can conceive of a possible cause of action on the part of either the Government or a private individual up to the time when the goods have been transported or entered for transportation from one State to another that could be maintained?

Mr. HOAR. I conceive that my honorable friend from Ohio proposes in this section of the bill that if the Attorney-General or district attorney in a proper case is informed that a contract has been made, whether between citizens of different States or of the same State, which is an offense against the provisions of this bill, he can get in with his preliminary injunction. I say again, if he can get in with his injunction between the illegal contract and its execution, I do not see at present why the bill does not answer that purpose and accomplish so much good; and that, it seems to me, respectfully, is all there is in it, so far as that first section goes.

Mr. PLATT. May I ask the Senator from Massachusetts a question? Suppose that there was a combination existing in Chicago to put up the price of wheat? Wheat is a commodity which may be transported between the different States or it may not. Does he think that that combination could be reached under the power of Congress to deal with commerce between the States?

Mr. HOAR. That is a totally different question from the point I was discussing at the moment. It does not relate to it at all. But I will say that unless it can be shown that that combination is to put up the price of wheat elsewhere than in Chicago, that it is to affect the price which is to be paid by the person who is to acquire that wheat of the man in Chicago to be delivered to him in another State or abroad, you can not constitutionally accomplish that.

If I understand the question of my honorable friend from Connecticut, I suppose he means to imply (and certainly I should agree with him if he does), for instance, that an elevator full of wheat or any other quantity of wheat which is bought by one man of another in Chicago to be delivered in Chicago, so that the only transaction between them is the exchange of property in a State, although that property may be intended to be resold in the South, may be intended to be resold in the East, may be intended to be resold in Liverpool, would not be within the constitutional power of Congress, that the States have to deal with that themselves if they can.

Mr. PLATT. So, it seems to me, if the Senator will permit me, that the particular contract, or agreement, or combination which might be reached under the power to regulate commerce between the States must be exceedingly limited. Indeed, since he has been making his argument here I have been sitting listening to the argument and trying to think what particular things could be reached under it, and it is very difficult to see that anything could be reached.

Mr. HOAR. Mr. President, I want merely to add one observation, and I think it is an observation which is worth thinking of by the Senate, especially at the present time. We have great currents of public sentiment in this country, breezes of popular opinion and indignation. Something goes wrong, or the people fancy something is going wrong, or an influential portion of them think that something is going wrong, and they come in here setting forth their grievance or their opinion that they are aggrieved, and there is very great danger that in the haste for the sake of satisfying the present feeling of discontent we shall get up some crude, hasty legislation which does not cure the evil, which keeps the word of promise to the ear and breaks it to the hope, and the people will be contented for a week or two, and then the evil continues, and the discontent grows stronger, and it is aggravated by the popular feeling that they have been played with and juggled with, and that we have given them pretenses of remedies and cures which, if we were fit for our place here, we ought to know are no remedies and no cures.

The history of this country for the last thirty years in finance, in protection, in our land policies, in our homestead policies, in our dealing with the great question which separates the sections, has shown that those statesmen and those parties who deal with the people on the theory that they have some sense themselves and see the difference between sham and reality are those who permanently retain their confidence and maintain their own strength. Every time the price of wheat goes down, or that there is a bad year in agriculture, or that the manufacturers are pinched, or that the mines are unprofitable, or that there is such a good year for agriculture abroad that our people do not get the prices which they have had the year before, I do not believe that it is good policy for me, or for the men who associate with me, or the party to which I belong, or the body of which that party is but a component part, to hold out to the people false remedies or pretended cures.

Mr. FRYE. I should like to ask the Senator from Massachusetts if the pending bill and amendments suggest that last remark.

Mr. SHERMAN. Mr. President, the Senator from Massachusetts looks upon this matter a little differently from what he would if the duty on cotton cloth or woolen cloth was a little too low to protect the people of Massachusetts. Then not one month or one day would pass before there would be a speedy demand for a remedy.

Mr. HOAR. And I would have one that would accomplish the object, and not one that would not.

Mr. SHERMAN. By raising the duty. Now, here is a remedy for a greater wrong than can be imposed by a tariff law. We know that within twenty years, for the first time in the history of our country, combinations have been made involving from eighty to one hundred million dollars, combinations so strong that it was impossible for any other combinations to compete with them, combinations so powerful and extensive as to reach every branch of trade and business in the United States. This has been going on during that time. The State courts have attempted to wrestle with this difficulty. I produced decisions of the supreme courts of several of the States.

Take the State of New York, where the sugar trust was composed of seventeen corporations. What remedy had the people of New York in the suit that they had against that combination? None whatever, except as against one corporation out of the seventeen. No proceeding could be instituted in the State of New York by which all those corporations could be brought in one suit under the common jurisdiction of the United States. No remedy could be extended by the courts, although they were eager and earnest in search of a remedy. All that they could do was to declare a forfeiture of the corporate power of one single corporation, while all the associated companies still held together in their combination, and not only did they hold together, but they went on making huge and enormous profits. You may almost say that while we have been sitting here debating this bill, since this bill has been pending, they have made a large dividend to all the associated corporations, and all have shared in it on the amount of watered stock and all other kinds of stock. They could not pay to the defunct corporation, which was suspended and inert for the time, until a final decision could be made by the court of appeals of New York, and so they put the dividend of that corporation in trust, but the other corporations went on; the combination continued and it continues today. So it is on many other articles. I do not care to single out all the corporations and point to the history of their transactions as I know it.

Is there no remedy for this? Is this no evil that we ought to remedy? If this remedy proposed is a sham and a quack, where is your genuine remedy? It will never come from the men or the class of men who are engaged in these monopolies. That there is an evil which must be dealt with, which the people of the United States demand shall be dealt with, no man can deny. Where is your remedy? If this is a quack medicine, produce something better. But it will never come from that source, never.

Mr. President, this thing must not be dealt with too lightly. No man can question my object in this matter. I have no interest to subserve and no interest to injure, and care nothing for the consequence; but I say I have seen the gradual growth of these combinations. I have been familiar with them, so far as I could gather from the public prints and public investigations. I know that the evil the bill is aimed at is growing greater and greater, and stronger and stronger. If you are impotent and unable to deal with the question and can not prescribe any remedy but quack medicine, then you are utterly unfit to perform your duties as the representatives of the people of the United States.

There are classes of contracts springing up here and being enforced day by day which have tended more than all else combined to bring these complaints upon us, complaints from the workingmen all over our land, from the farmers in their alliances and in their other organizations. They can not see the cause or source of this evil, but they demand a remedy and that demand will be heard. Nor will it be turned aside by any combination here or anywhere else. It must be met openly, and if you are unable to do anything with it let it be so and announce your inability.

Look at our dealing with interstate commerce. Some years ago it came up here on the bill of my honorable friend from Illinois [Mr. CULLOM], and it was hooted and jeered at; and when the Senator from Texas [Mr. REAGAN] started out on that road in the other House he was met with constitutional objections without number. The railroads were then too powerful to be dealt with. They combined together. There was one striking case which I introduced in my argument the other day where they gave a single other corporation in the combine the advantage of $5,400,000 a year in one transportation contract. But fortunately my honorable friend from Illinois here and the Senator from Texas and others elsewhere took hold of the matter and they prescribed a remedy, and now do you say that is a quack remedy, that it is an ineffective remedy? Yet their proposition was met by the same class of arguments that this bill is met with.

No, sir; the power of Congress is the only power that can deal with these corporations. The power of Congress is the only one that can regulate the internal commerce of this country. The power of Congress is the only one that can bring all the parties to combinations before a tribunal, and have that tribunal pronounce judgment, not in a criminal suit, but in a civil suit.

These corporations do not care about your criminal statutes aimed at their servants. They could give up at once one or two or three of their servants to bear this penalty for them. But when you strike at their powers, at their franchises, at their corporate existence, when you deal with them directly, then they begin to feel the power of the Government. So in regard to interstate commerce by rail. All those corporations and organizations opposed that law, but when it went into force it produced enormously good effects, and everybody appreciates it, and nobody proposes to dispense with the Interstate Commerce Commission, which was organized to enforce the interstate-commerce law.

Sir, I have that confidence in the courts of the United States that I believe if you even give them a single grip, if you give them jurisdiction of this class of cases by law—because this jurisdiction can only be conferred by the law—they will administer the law. The Senator from Massachusetts says we are providing here only for cases of a civil nature. Strike it out, if you please. I would say "all cases at law or in equity arising under this statute;" or, better yet, I would use the broader terms, "all controversies between citizens of different States," the language used by the Constitution. Strike out the words "of a civil nature." Those words are properly in the bill, because the remedies pointed out in this measure are of a civil nature, and therefore they are properly defined as cases at law or in equity of a civil nature. Strike out the words and then the jurisdiction will be broader. That would be an amendment I should favor.

But the Senator says that I have crippled this measure by inserting words of limitation, so that these combinations must be between citizens and corporations of different states. Only the other day I met with a different kind of objection. It was said here that we were reaching out so as to bring citizens of the same State into court as defendants; that I was reaching out after a jurisdiction that ought to be limited to the State itself; and to avoid that objection I propose to provide that the combinations must extend beyond the State.

I think that is a wise provision. I think it is well to do it. Why? Because these combinations are always in many States and, as the Senator from Missouri says, it will be very easy for them to make a corporation within a State. So they can; but that is only one corporation of the combination. The combination is always of two or more, and in one case of forty-odd corporations, all bound together by a link which holds them under the name of trustees, who are themselves incorporated under the laws of one of the States. You can not make a combination such as is described by this bill unless it embraces the members of many corporations of many States.

Gentlemen say you must show when the commerce commenced and when it ended; you must distinguish between production and commerce. The agreements point out and mean transportation from place to place. What do these great combinations—take for instance the Standard Oil Company—do when they transport oil to Ohio, or Chicago, or Indiana, east and west? They transfer oil from Pennsylvania to every part of the country. It is necessarily a part of their business to do so, it is an incident of their business. If you could confine their business to a single State or if their contracts could only reach commerce within a State, their profits would dwindle into the air; but they are able to make these combinations embracing corporations without number, extending their operations not only through every State of the Union, as the Standard Oil Company does, but throughout the civilized world, competing as they do—and I am glad they do compete—with all foreign nations and all foreign productions. If they conducted their business lawfully, without any attempt by these combinations to raise the price of an article consumed by the people of the United States, I would say let them pursue that business.

I am not opposed to combinations in and of themselves; I do not care how much men combine for proper objects; but when they combine with a purpose to prevent competition, so that if a humble man starts a business in opposition to them, solitary and alone, in Ohio or anywhere else, they will crowd him down and they will sell their product at a loss or give it away in order to prevent competition, and when that is established by evidence that can not be questioned, then it is the duty of the courts to intervene and prevent it by injunction and by the ordinary remedial rights afforded by the courts.

Not only that, but this provision allowing any party to sue is of vital importance. Why, sir, I know of one case where a man in good circumstances, a thrifty, strong, healthy American, was engaged in this kind of competition. He was met in just the way I have mentioned. If he had had the right to sue this company in the courts of the United States under this section he would have been able to indemnify himself for the losses that he suffered. I have known of other cases of the kind. Sometimes the damages would be too slight to give the courts of the United States jurisdiction. In the case of a single individual whose bread has been advanced in price or whose small expenditures have been somewhat increased, there is no remedy for him. The remedy is only for those who are largely enough interested to sue in the courts of the United States.

This bill does only two things. It authorizes the Government officers in a proper case where these combinations are plainly made with a view that is declared by the law of every civilized country to be unlawful and void and destructive to trade—when such a combination does exist the United States may come in and as a suitor in the name of the people of the United States may sue for and prevent and, if possible, enjoin, restrain, or tie up these combinations. That is authorized to be done by the first section.

The first section only provides for that wrong a general remedy, and if any injustice be done a suit is brought in the name of the people of the United States by the Attorney-General, and the courts of the United States must decide. Will they be governed by wild and arrogant feelings, like the Communists or Nihilists? No; the United States, the power of the country, sues these corporations, calls upon them for information, proves, if possible, the extent of the evil, and then administers the remedy.

It is said that damages are not given. Well, sir, it is not so much the object of the first section to give damages as it is to provide restraint, limitation, regulation, and the exertion of the power of the Government over these corporations.

In the other section there is a civil remedy provided. When a man is injured by an unlawful combination why should he not have the power to sue in the courts of the United States? It would not answer to send him to a State court. It would not answer at all to send him to a court of limited jurisdiction. Then, besides, it is a court of the United States that alone has jurisdiction over all parts of the United States. The United States can send its writs into every part of a State and make parties in different States submit to its process. The States can not do that.

Now, sir, under these circumstances it is important to citizens that they should have some remedy in a court of general jurisdiction in the United States to sue for and recover the damages they have suffered. I think myself the rule of damages is too small. It provides double the damages and reasonable attorneys' fees. Very few actions will probably be brought, but the cases that will be brought will be by men of spirit, who will contest against these combinations. . . .

Mr. HOAR. Is the Senator quite right in saying that without making some change in the law the United States court would have the right to send out its writs at large into the States?

Mr. SHERMAN. To what extent I do not know, but I think so. I suppose myself the writs of the United States courts would go to the several States. How far they may go is regulated by the law, and can be ascertained by an examination of the statutes.

Mr. [JOHN C.] SPOONER [R., Wis.]. If the Senator will permit me, I think the statutory rule is that no man can be sued except in the jurisdiction where he resides, with one exception. There is a general exception, as I recollect the statute, and that is where the suit is to enforce a lien upon real estate or remove a cloud from title to real estate, in which case leave can be obtained from the court to serve process in another district and by publication.

Mr. SHERMAN. Then, clearly, here is a matter in which the honorable gentlemen of the Judiciary Committee can give us some relief. Let them frame a provision that will allow the process of the United States courts to go all over the United States. Why not, if that is necessary? I supposed that was provided for in existing law. It is in some cases. . . .

Mr. GEORGE. The Senator has alluded to the Standard Oil Company as one of the evils which are to be suppressed by this bill. I should like to ask him whether the Standard Oil Company is not a corporation created by the laws of the State of Ohio, and is that not all there is in it? As a combination, who else is to combine with it except its own stockholders in the corporation?

Mr. SHERMAN. The Senator is greatly mistaken. I can show him by the papers—the Standard Oil Company was no doubt the original company—that it was organized in the modest sum, I think, of $200,000 capital, and it is running now an ordinary refining business, but other corporations all over this country—

Mr. GEORGE. What other corporation now besides the Standard Oil Company, located at Cleveland, Ohio, is in that Standard Oil combination?

Mr. SHERMAN. I am not prepared to say, but an examination was made into this matter by a committee of the other House, of which Mr. Bacon was chairman, and, I think, in the report which was made he gave a list of the corporations, and, if I am not mistaken, there are forty or fifty, all interlaced with each other, having different interests nominally, different incorporators, different charters. I think there are forty or fifty great combinations. I do not know the exact number, but perhaps some gentleman who has gone into the reading of that report may be able to answer.

So with the other combinations. I do not wish to single out the Standard Oil Company, which is a great and powerful corporation, composed in great part of citizens of my own State, and some of the very best men I know of. Still, they are controlling and can control the market as absolutely as they choose to do it; it is a question of their will. The point for us to consider is whether, on the whole, it is safe in this country to leave the production of property, the transportation of our whole country, to depend upon the will of a few men sitting at their council board in the city of New York, for there the whole machine is operated? I do not say anything against these men. Many of them are my personal friends and acquaintances. I only refer to them because they are the oldest of these combinations founded upon contracts which have been copied by the other combinations.

That is all I wish to say. If Senators find any difficulty in this bill, if they want to strengthen it in any way, in the name of Heaven let them offer their amendments. If they think it goes too far in any particular, let them strike out the objectionable clauses. If it does not go far enough, do not call it a quack medicine, because it is honestly gotten up, even if it is nothing but paregoric. If it is not strong enough, put some stronger element into it. That is the business of the Senate. What I have done is to aid it step by step. I was in favor of the broad declaration that certain contracts should be null and void, and invoking the jurisdiction of the courts of the United States, but I have modified it to meet the fears and the timidity of others who were afraid we were going too far, and now, as I said the other day, the objection to the bill is its weakness, but it is weakness drawn into the bill because of the objections made in the Senate.

Mr. HOAR. I called the attention of the Senator from Ohio to certain propositions in his bill showing, in the first place, that it did not include a tenth part, and perhaps not a hundredth part, of the cases that would arise in the country; second, that it did not contain all the remedies which he supposed it did, and that it was defective in sundry other particulars; and if I have not misunderstood my honorable friend he has agreed with every one of these criticisms. He says in regard to the first one that he had the bill as I think it ought to have been, but changed that to please some one. Then he says in regard to the next one he thought there ought to have been a provision declaring unlawful contracts criminal and so punishable, but that he did not put it in because of somebody else. Then, he meets all the objections by conceding them, and he says in another place he thinks the bill is very admirable because the process will run all over the United States, and on asking him if he is sure of that he replies that on the whole he is not—

Mr. SHERMAN. I will take your word for it.

Mr. HOAR. And that he thinks some committee will propose a law which he does not provide himself. Then he answers, having agreed to all the objections, which, so far as I now remember, establish the fact that the bill ought to be strengthened, by an impassioned statement of the great evil which he wants to reach. We all agree with that, and we have trusted to him to give us a vigorous remedy. That is what we expect of him. Now, if a member of my family is suffering with an incipient cancer and a doctor comes in who proposes a piece of court-plaster as a remedy, and I ask him if he thinks court-plaster will cure that cancer and save that valuable life, and he says, "No, it will not," and then turns around on me with an impassioned and an eloquent statement of the horrors of the disease called cancer and how much it is going to ruin the lives of my family threatened with it, I am obliged to say—I do not know whether the phrase "quack medicine" would be a proper phrase to use—but I would rather call in another doctor, and if he were a doctor that I had thorough confidence in, like my friend from Ohio, I should ask him to substitute some other prescription for his court-plaster. . . .

Mr. VEST. Mr. President, I deny the right of the Senator from Ohio to assume that there is no other way to reach this great evil of combines and trusts in this country except through his intellectual effort and through the bill that he has reported to this body. Illustrious as has been the career of that Senator, there is nothing in it which gives him the right to assume that he has discovered the only remedy and the only road to success in a contest against these combinations.

I object to his bill because, in my judgment, it will effect nothing; because, as a lawyer, I believe that the courts will not entertain it for one moment when it is brought before them. I object to it because it destroys all my ideas of the limitations of the Constitution. I object to it because it is against the spirit and letter of the judiciary act of 1789. I object to it because it is "sound and fury, signifying nothing." If I believed that the bill of the Senator from Ohio, coming from him or any other Senator here, would effect what he claims for it, I should vote and speak for it until my strength was exhausted in this Chamber. I am not here to claim that I have any pre-eminence as an enemy of combines and trusts, but I think, although my career has not been as long or as illustrious as that of the Senator from Ohio, but limited and slight as it has been, I have shown in my legislative labors that I am as much opposed to these combines as he can possibly be.

Sir, I object to the bill because I am certain, as a lawyer, that the Supreme Court of the United States will never declare it to be constitutional, and for the Senator to assume that he, and he alone, has found the remedy in this case, is, to say the least, transcending the limits of parliamentary modesty.

Now, Mr. President, I will ask the Secretary to read a bill that I think, although I am not the author of it (and I have been for over six months attempting to find some legislation that would meet this evil)—I freely accord to another gentleman the merit of having framed a bill that, in my judgment, comes nearer to furnishing a remedy than that presented by any other person, and I ask the Secretary to read the fifth, sixth, and seventh sections of the amendment proposed by the Senator from Texas [Mr. COKE]. That is a bill that has been offered in the House of Representatives, and was offered here as an amendment by the Senator, and I ask the attention of the Senate to it.

The Secretary read as follows:

SEC. 5. That when any State shall declare, or heretofore has declared by law, trusts as defined by the true intent and meaning of this act to be unlawful and against public policy, it shall not be lawful thereafter for any person, firm, or corporation to cause to be transported any product or article covered or embraced by such trust from such State to or into any other State or Territory or the District of Columbia.

SEC. 6. That any common carrier or agent of any common carrier who shall knowingly receive such product or commodity for transportation from such State into another State or Territory or the District of Columbia shall be deemed guilty of a misdemeanor, and upon conviction thereof shall be fined not less than five hundred nor more than ten thousand dollars or shall be imprisoned for any period of time not less than one year and not more than five years, or by both such fine and imprisonment in the discretion of the court. And any person who shall knowingly deliver to any common carrier or agent thereof, any such product or commodity to be transported into another State or Territory or the District of Columbia shall be deemed guilty of a misdemeanor, and upon conviction thereof shall be fined in any sum not less than five hundred nor more than ten thousand dollars or by imprisonment for any period of time not less than one year nor more than five years, or by both such fine and imprisonment, in the discretion of the court.

SEC. 7. That whenever the President of the United States shall be advised that a trust has been or is about to be organized for either of the purposes named in the first section of this act, and that a like product or commodity covered or proposed to be covered or handled by such trust, when produced out of the United States, is liable to an import duty when imported into the United States, he shall be, and is hereby, authorized and directed to suspend the operation of so much of the laws as impose a duty upon such product, commodity, or merchandise for such time as he may deem proper.[1.324]

Mr. VEST. Now, Mr. President, there is a measure much more radical than that of the Senator from Ohio, far more effective, and not subject to any constitutional objection. Not even the most hair-splitting constitutional casuist, such as to-day has been denounced by the Senator from Alabama [Mr. PUGH], can find any objection to that measure; and if my friends on the opposite side of the Chamber object to the seventh section because it deals with the question of import duties, if they do not want to give the President of the United States discretion to take off import duties when they protect a trust, let them strike it out.

If my friend from Illinois [Mr. CULLOM] or my friend from Texas [Mr. REAGAN] objects to the sixth section because it interferes in any way indirectly with the interstate-commerce law, let him strike it out; but in the fifth section is the gist of all legislation upon the subject in the line indicated by the Senator from Ohio. We must rely, as I said on Friday last, in two jurisdictions: in the States and in the Federal Government; and, sir, when the States declare any article to be the product of a trust, when they declare any trust itself to be unlawful, or any combination or corporation or individuals to be unlawful, then let the Congress of the United States supplement that with the declaration, under the interstate-commerce clause of the Constitution, that the products of that trust, so put under the ban of State legislation, shall not be carried from one State or Territory to another.

That bill, more than any other bill introduced into Congress or ever invented,

---

[1.324] Senator Coke offered his comprehensive amendment on March 25. *See infra* at 209–10 & note 1.341. *See also infra* at 192–95 (remarks of Senators Reagan, Vest, and Wilson on proposed amendment).

obviates constitutional objections and scruples and at the same time reaches, in my judgment, this great evil, if it ever can be reached by one act upon the part of Congress.

Mr. HISCOCK. Mr. President, I do not believe that by impassioned eloquence the defects of this bill are to be obscured. We have been told that if this bill should be passed into law the Federal courts might take jurisdiction of all the parties to one of these combinations and that the defect in the State law was that the State courts could only take jurisdiction of the subjects of the State, or whoever might be domiciled in the State; and before we get through with the discussion we are told that the process which is to be issued in a suit of that kind can not go out of the district in which the party is found. Where, then, is the difference between the jurisdiction and power of the State courts and of the Federal courts? The State courts take jurisdiction in the State.

In the State of New York we have three Federal judicial districts. Suppose the process can reach a party in the entire circuit; grant that it does extend to him; go as far as that; and are we to be asked on this bill inconsiderately to put in it a provision that process may reach the offending parties in the United States wherever they are, and disregard the settled practice in the United States since the foundation of the Government? An amendment of that kind would be too far-reaching to be adopted in this bill with the consideration that it would receive in this debate. So, then, under the bill we can go no further and we have no more power, it seems to be conceded, than the State courts have.

Now, then, let us look at the only remedy that the bill affords to an oppressed people.

SEC. 2. That any person or corporation injured or damnified by such arrangement, contract, agreement, trust, or combination defined in the first section of this act may sue for and recover, in any court of the United States of competent jurisdiction, without respect to the amount involved, of any person or corporation a party to a combination described in the first section of this act, twice the amount of damages sustained, and the costs of the suit, together with a reasonable attorney's fee.

A person sues the corporation or the combination or party to the combination. The combination is in twine, we will say, but the man who is injured is in Minnesota, and he is invited by this bill to travel to New York, where the combination, we will say, was created, or to St. Louis, where I think the last one was created, and commence his action in the circuit court of the United States and recover twice the damages that he has sustained. The middlemen will never commence these actions. I mean the parties who in the first instance purchase of the combination. That will be guarded against, and the people who are to suffer the damages are those who are distributed all over this broad land, the consumers of the article, the consumers of the merchandise, buying perhaps a hundred dollars' worth and damaged possibly $10, and they have the right to follow this combination or a party to it wherever he is domiciled and recover twice the amount of damages they have sustained!

Seriously, Mr. President, it is a fearful attack upon trusts! I am not going over the argument that I have made heretofore against the constitutionality of the bill. I am one of those who believe that because we have parties named in this bill that reside in the different States that gives us jurisdiction. It is only when the property is in commerce and in the course of commerce that we can take jurisdiction, and I say for myself, if I had made up my mind to vote for an unconstitutional measure and one which I believed to be unconstitutional, I should vote for the amendment of the Senator from Texas [Mr. REAGAN], because, unconstitutional as it is, in my judgment it would upon its face afford some remedy.

This bill, however, does not promise any relief, even if it is valid. But I shall not follow the example of the Senator who said that possibly he might vote for the Reagan amendment in some stage of our deliberations, although he believed it was unconstitutional, because I most heartily indorse the sentiment of the Senator from Massachusetts that it is always safe to predicate your action, here or elsewhere, upon the intelligence of your people, and not upon their ignorance.

Mr. TELLER. Mr. President, I do not propose to allow the Senator from Ohio to presume that everybody who does not agree with him on this bill and what it will do is against the relief that he seeks. My real objection to this bill is that it is delusive. I do not know but that it may be of some benefit; possibly it may. As I said before, I do not know but that I may vote for it; but I want it distinctly understood, as far as I am concerned, that I am not very much moved by it.

Now, how does the bill reach the great evil against which it is aimed? The Standard Oil Trust has been spoken of. What is the Standard Oil Trust? A corporation in Ohio, a corporation in Pennsylvania, a corporation in Colorado, and so on through all the States. Each corporation is a creature by itself. Ohio can deal with the corporation in Ohio.

Mr. SHERMAN. But they have combinations in other States.

Mr. TELLER. And the Ohio Legislature can say that any corporation created by that State, which combines with any corporation in another State for this purpose, shall be dissolved. What can we do about it? If Ohio declines to do that, some other State may do that. But what can we do about it? We do not dissolve the corporation. What do we do? Anybody who is damaged can sue them. When they interfere with somebody who has sunk a well in Ohio and they run down the price of oil until they shut him up, he may have his remedy against them. But that is not what we are complaining of. We are complaining that that Standard Oil Company has a tendency to reduce and destroy competition, and thereby, by destroying competition, to put up improperly the price of oil. Who suffers by that? The sixty-five millions of people in the United States who use oil; and how do they suffer? How much damage have they sustained? It is inconsequential individually, but great to the whole mass of the people.

What remedy does this bill give the people for any such misconduct on the part of that corporation? None whatever, because it does not destroy the corporation, it does not attempt to destroy the corporation, and could not if it did. It will not dissolve it. It will remain, although a judgment may be rendered against it. On the contrary, in my judgment, it is a bill that may be seized upon to prevent just what everybody admits ought to be done in this country. It may seize, as I said before, the organizations of labor, the organizations of farmers; it may take hold of them, and while it will not dissolve them they are not the class of men that can afford to be brought into court once or twice even, while these great corporations do not care how frequently they are brought into court where the damages that the parties get are just simply twice what the individual who makes the complaint has sustained. . . .

I do not know—I am not absolutely certain—that under this bill the Knights of Labor, the Alliance, the Wheel, the National League, could be attacked, but it strikes me there is a great deal more probability of their being attacked than there is of these great, strong corporations being. They are the men who, if they keep on, will destroy these combinations in Chicago, these dealers in futures; they are the people who will take hold eventually of the interstate-commerce question in such a way as to make the railroads feel their power, because, after all, the farmers are the moving and the influential body of this country whenever they unite; they have the intelligence and the virtue and the control when they say so.

Mr. President, all other industries are nothing compared with the agricultural interests in numbers and in influence when they take hold, and if you give those who are opposed to their combination the slightest opportunity to interfere with them they will do it. I have not much faith in any national control over these associations. I do not believe it is possible, because, as I have said, we can not dissolve the corporation; we can not reach it; but the States can. Every corporation that is created is created at the will of a State, and the State can put upon it just such conditions as it sees fit. The State can say, "If you combine with anybody in this State, or out of this State, and do certain acts which we declare improper and unlawful, then your charter shall be taken away by a proper proceeding in court." We can not do that; and therefore it is not possible that we should meet the difficulty by any bill that may pass this body.

It is not to be said to me, because I do not agree with the Senator from Ohio that here is the remedy and here only, that I am not in favor of taking hold of this evil with a strong hand where it can be done. The Senator says if we can not do this then there is no remedy at all. Not so; even if we had the power, the bill, in my judgment, is not well drawn, though I might vote for it as the best thing that could be had. I was glad to hear from a Senator on this floor that the Judiciary Committee was dealing with this subject, and I think it would be well now to refer this bill to the Judiciary Committee and wait until we can hear what they propose, something that would be within the constitutional limits of Congress and at the same time would be vigorous and effective; that would take hold with a strong hand and do what I have no doubt the Senator from Ohio wants to do, but which he does not want to do any more than a majority of this Senate on both sides of this Chamber want to do.

SENATE DEBATE
51st Cong., 1st Sess.
March 25, 1890

21 CONG. REC. 2597

. . . [T]he Senate, as in Committee of the Whole, resumed the consideration of the bill (S. 1) to declare unlawful trusts and combinations in restraint of trade and production.

The VICE-PRESIDENT. The pending question is on the amendment submitted by the Senator from Texas [Mr. REAGAN].

Mr. STEWART. Let the amendment be read.

The CHIEF CLERK. It is proposed to add as additional sections the following:

SEC. 3. That all persons engaged in the creation of any trust, or as owner or part owner, agent, or manager of any trust, employed in any business carried on with any foreign country, or between the States, or between any State and the District of Columbia, or between any State and any Territory of the United States, or any owner or part owner, agent, or manager of any corporation, company, or person employed in any such business, using its powers for either of the purposes specified in the second section of this act, shall be deemed guilty of a high misdemeanor, and, on conviction thereof, shall be fined in a sum not exceeding $10,000 or imprisonment at hard labor in the penitentiary not exceeding five years or by both of said penalties, in the discretion of the court trying the same.[1.325]

SEC. 4. That a trust is a combination of capital, skill, or acts by two or more persons, firms, or associations of persons, or of any two or more of them, for either, any, or all of the following purposes:

First. To create or carry out any restrictions in trade.

Second. To limit or reduce the production or to increase or reduce the price of merchandise or commodities.

Third. To prevent competition in the manufacture, making, purchase, sale, or transportation of merchandise, produce, or commodities.

Fourth. To fix a standard or figure whereby the price to the public shall be in any manner controlled or established of any article, commodity, merchandise, produce, or commerce intended for sale, use, or consumption.

Fifth. To create a monopoly in the making, manufacture, purchase, sale, or transportation of any merchandise, article, produce, or commodity.

Sixth. To make, or enter into, or execute, or carry out any contract, obligation, or agreement of any kind or description by which they shall bind, or shall have bound themselves not to manufacture, sell, dispose of, or transport any article or commodity or article of trade, use, merchandise, or consumption below a common standard figure, or by which they shall agree in any manner to keep the price of such article, commodity, or transportation at a fixed or graduated figure, or by which they shall in any manner establish or settle the price of any article, commodity, or transportation between themselves, or between themselves and others so as to preclude free and unrestricted competition among themselves and others in the sale and transportation of any such article or commodity, or by which they shall agree to pool, combine, or unite in any interest they may have in connection with the sale or transportation of any such article or commodity that its price may in any manner be so affected.

[1.325] Section 3 incorporated the minor modification agreed to during the previous day's debate.

SEC. 5. That each day any of the persons, associations, or corporations aforesaid shall be engaged in violating the provisions of this act shall be held to be a separate offense.

Mr. GEORGE. Mr. President, the wish has been expressed in my hearing by several Senators that this bill and the various amendments which have been offered to it and which are proposed to be offered shall be referred to the Committee on the Judiciary. I concur in the propriety of that course. I shall make that motion and do now make it, and on that I ask the indulgence of the Senate to state some reasons why that course should be pursued.

⊥2598   ⊥ Certainly there is no subject likely to engage the attention of the present Congress in which the people of this country are more deeply interested than in the subject of trusts and combinations. These evils have grown within the last few years to an enormous magnitude; enormous also in their numbers. They cover nearly all the great branches of trade and of production in which our country is interested. They grow out of the present tendency of economic affairs throughout the world. It is a sad thought to the philanthropist that the present system of production and of exchange is having that tendency which is sure at some not very distant day to crush out all small men, all small capitalists, all small enterprises. This is being done now. We find everywhere over our land the wrecks of small, independent enterprises thrown in our pathway. So now the American Congress and the American people are brought face to face with this sad, this great problem: Is production, is trade, to be taken away from the great mass of the people and concentrated in the hands of a few men who, I am obliged to add, by the policies pursued by our Government, have been enabled to aggregate to themselves large, enormous fortunes?

This is the evil before us. Any time within the last nine years since I have had the honor to be a member of this body I would have introduced a bill to prevent these evils, to suppress these combinations and these trusts if I could have found the constitutional power to enact the bill. I find myself to-day, with every wish to exercise every power conferred by the Constitution upon Congress to suppress these trusts, unable to find in that instrument a power under which the Senate can originate a measure that in my opinion will be efficient.

The people complain; the people suffer; the people in many parts of our country, especially the agricultural people, are in greater distress than they have ever been before. They look with longing eyes, they turn their faces to us with pleading hands asking us to do something to relieve them from their trouble. I believe the sentiment that something ought to be done pervades this body almost universally. The question for us and the problem for us is how, consistently with the limited powers which the Constitution has conferred upon us, we can deal with these great evils.

There is a power, a power which the learned and distinguished Senator from Ohio [Mr. SHERMAN] on the 14th day of September, 1888, declared in this body was the only power which could be efficiently used. That is the taxing power. But by the forms of our Constitution no tax law, no bill to raise revenue can originate in this body. But for that the amendment offered to this bill by the Senator from Kansas [Mr. INGALLS] would receive and ought to receive the vote of every member of this body. We can go further. In that amendment the taxing power is applied to options and to futures. There is no reason why this same power could not be applied as it was applied for the purpose of supressing the circulation of State bank notes, to the suppression of these trusts, the suppression of these combinations which are eating up the substance of our people. But, sir, we can not originate that in this body; a revenue bill must be first sent to us from the other House before we can enter into that business. The Senate, however, seems determined, leaving out the taxing power, to pass some measure on this very intricate and very difficult subject.

I say it is difficult and intricate, and if the Senate will bear with me while I call attention to the several bills which have been introduced by the Senator from Ohio partly on his own account and partly as the organ of the Committee on Finance, the Senate will see what difficulties that Senator and the great committee of which he is the organ have encountered in the pursuit of this subject.

On the 14th day of August, 1888, the Senator from Ohio introduced a bill. I desire all these bills to be printed as a part of my remarks. I do not wish to read them all, and I shall ask that the Reporter will note at this point the bill to be inserted.

The bill referred to is as follows: . . .[1.326]

This was the first bill that was introduced in the Senate on this subject. In that the Senator from Ohio assumed, as the Senator from Alabama [Mr. PUGH] did yesterday, that Congress had full, complete jurisdiction over the subject of trusts and combinations, whether they affect interstate or foreign commerce or not. It will be seen by reading the bill that it denounced all arrangements, contracts, agreements, and trusts made by anybody about anything which is an article of commerce, whether in domestic, interstate, or foreign commerce.

Mr. REAGAN. Is the Senator from Mississippi sure that is the first bill introduced on that subject?

Mr. GEORGE. That is the first one introduced here that I know of.

Mr. REAGAN. I introduced one the same day, or previously to that time, on the same subject.

Mr. GEORGE. I stand corrected upon that. I have been pursuing in most of my investigations the action of the Senator from Ohio and the committee of which he is the organ.

That bill had no reference to transactions in interstate or foreign commerce, but assuming that the Congress of the United States had throughout the Union, as a separate State has within its own borders, full and complete jurisdiction over the subject of trusts it legislated in that way. It applied to contracts made by anybody; it applied to all subjects of commerce, interstate, foreign, and domestic; and it contained the remarkable provision that Congress could enact a law declearing [sic] the ground of forfeiture for a State corporation of its charter and directing proceedings in a Federal court by a Federal officer against a State corporation for the purpose of declaring the forfeiture of its charter. That was the first bill introduced by the Senator. That was introduced August 14, 1888.

The Committee on Finance kept the bill under consideration until September 11, nearly one month, and then we have bill No. 2, which the Reporter will note.

The bill reported September 11, 1888, is as follows: . . .[1.327]

By that bill all of the first bill was stricken out and the committee sought to get jurisdiction upon a ground which I will now proceed to state. The committee began to discover that this subject of trusts and combinations in restraint of trade was not a matter of Federal jurisdiction in its full extent. They began to discover that they must look to some particular power granted by the Constitution to Congress under which they could pass this bill. So they undertook and so they provided that these arrangements and contracts should be in reference to preventing "full and free competition in the importation, transportation, or sale of articles imported into the United States, or in the production, manufacture, or sale of articles of domestic growth or production, or domestic raw material that competes with any similar article" introduced into the United States "or which shall be transported from one State or Territory to another."

The committee sought jurisdiction upon the ground that these trusts were interfering with full and free competition with articles imported which were dutiable articles. The idea of the committee seemed to be this: If Congress can impose a duty upon a foreign article, Congress may prevent an arrangement or a trust which interferes with the sale of that imported article. That was the first ground. The second ground was that if these arrangements were made about articles which were afterwards transported in interstate commerce that would bring them within Federal jurisdiction.

At this stage there was some discussion in this body, in which cases were cited and principles of constitutional law well known were introduced and brought to the attention of the Senate, which showed the utter fallacy of the grounds upon which the committee had placed the jurisdiction of Congress to enact the bill. Some discussion followed and some amendments were made, so that on the 25th of January, 1889, there was another bill reported from the committee. That is bill No. 3.

[1.326] S. 3445 as originally introduced by Senator Sherman on August 14, 1888, during the first session of the 50th Congress, appears *supra* at 63-64.

[1.327] S. 3445 as reported by the Committee on Finance on September 11, 1888, appears *supra* at 64-65.

⊥2599

The bill referred to is as follows: . . . [1.328]

⊥ In that bill, either by the acceptance of the Senator from Ohio or by the vote of the Senate—and I do not remember which—section 3 and section 5 were introduced for the first time in this legislation.

Mr. SHERMAN. What bill is that?

Mr. GEORGE. This is Senate bill 3445, ordered to be printed January 25, 1889. I will read section 3 so that the Senator can catch my idea more perfectly. I believe this section was offered by the Senator from Massachusetts [Mr. HOAR]. At all events it appears to be ordered reprinted as amended. In section 3 of this bill it was proposed—

> That if one of the purposes of any such arrangement, contract, agreement, trust, or combination shall be to compel any person, partnership, or corporation to become a party thereto, or to cease from doing any lawful business, or to sell and dispose of any lawful business, or if acts shall be done under any such arrangement, contract, agreement, trust, or combination, which have for their purpose or which shall tend to compel the giving up or sale of any lawful business, the person, partnership, or corporation injured thereby may sue for and recover in any court of the United States of competent jurisdiction the damages sustained thereby of any person or corporation a party to any such arrangement, contract, agreement, trust, or combination, or of all or any number less than all of such parties.

And then there was a provision in that same section for recovering further damages. The fifth section was intended to have operation upon trusts and combinations already formed, and is in the following words:

> That any person who, ninety days after the passage of this law, shall act as manager, officer, trustee, or agent of any arrangement, contract, agreement, trust, or combination as described in the first section, shall be liable to the penalties prescribed in the fourth section.

In that connection there was also some discussion. It was shown in that debate very fully that under the power to regulate foreign and interstate commerce the provisions of the bill could not stand. It was also shown that the bill covered very innocent combinations and transactions, such as the alliances among farmers and grangers and combinations among laborers to advance their wages, etc. That bill submitted on the 25th day of January, 1889, after that debate was closed, was never called up for action during the last Congress.

That disposes, Mr. President, of the history of this legislation or attempted legislation in the Fiftieth Congress. But the Senator from Ohio was not disposed, as he understood his duty, to let the matter rest there; so that on the first day or the next day after we met at this session, at least on December 4—I believe we met on the 2d—the Senator from Ohio introduced this bill: . . . [1.329]

In this the effort was made to evade—I suppose I ought not to use the word "evade," as that is sometimes used in a sinister sense, and I do not use it in that sense—but an effort was made to get rid of the constitutional objections which had been urged in the last Congress; so that we have here some provisions which had been left out of No. 3. The committee seem to have been uncertain about the ground upon which they had placed it. In No. 2, the second bill introduced, one of the grounds of jurisdiction was stated in these words: The article must "compete with any similar article upon which a duty is levied by the United States." That was left out of the next bill. The committee thought they could get along with the jurisdiction without this competing clause, and so with that omission the Senator from Ohio, in the original bill introduced at this session, presented the bill in other respects substantially like the last bill that had been reported in the last Congress, except that section 3 and section 5 which I have read were omitted.

That went to the committee, and on the 14th of January, 1890, it was reported back to the Senate with some changes with the view of getting at jurisdiction. It had been shown in the debate, and conclusively shown by citations from the decisions of

---

[1.328] S. 3445 as reprinted on January 25, 1889, appears *supra* at 73–75.

[1.329] S. 1 51st Cong., 1st Sess., as introduced by Senator Sherman on December 4, 1889, appears *supra* at 89–90. It was identical to S. 3445, 50th Cong., 2d Sess., as reported by the Senate Finance Committee on September 11, 1888, *supra* at 64–65.

the Supreme Court of the United States, that articles which might become subjects of interstate commerce did not so become until they were actually delivered at the depot of the common carrier for transportation. Several cases were cited which settled that doctrine beyond dispute. So when the Committee on Finance, able and learned as it [sic], came to consider the bill introduced by the Senator from Ohio on the second day of the session, they discovered that the bill would not stand the constitutional test, and so they changed the bill in the particulars to which I will now call the attention of the Senate.

The bill reported January 14, 1890, is as follows: . . .[1.330]

As the bill originally read it stood as follows:

> That all arrangements, contracts, agreements, trusts, or combinations between persons or corporations made with a view or which tend to prevent full and free competition.

The committee struck out the words "a view or which tend" and inserted the words "the intention;" so that the bill read in this way:

> That all such arrangements, etc., made with the intention to prevent full and free competition.

And then in order to meet the objection which has been made, based upon the decision in Coe vs. Errol, in 116 United States Reports,[1.331] the committee inserted in that part of the bill which referred to the transportation of these goods the words "intended for;" so that that part of the bill read in this way: That these arrangements and contracts made "to prevent full and free competition in the" goods above described, which goods are "intended for and which shall be transported from one State or Territory to another for sale," and then in the general clause which condemns all sorts of arrangements and trusts between persons or corporations to advance the cost to the consumer, the committee again struck out the words "designed, or which tend" and inserted the word "intended." So the effort of the committee in this bill was to get jurisdiction under the commercial clause upon the ground that the articles about which the arrangement was made, about which the trust was formed, were intended for and afterwards transported in interstate commerce.

In that condition the bill stood on the 17th day of last month when it was called up for discussion in this Chamber, and was discussed by myself. I claim that the debate showed, not by force of the argument of the speaker, but by the citation of cases decided by the Supreme Court, that the words "intended for transportation in interstate com⊥merce" gave no additional power to Congress. That argument has never been answered. I believe I might say it has never been attempted to be answered. I feel authorized to say that it can not be answered because every position taken was based upon a decision of the Supreme Court of the United States.

With that array of authority it was supposed by some that this controversy was at an end, and yet in that we were mistaken, for on the 18th day of March, 1890, we had the bill in its present shape, as thus reported by the Senator from Ohio: . . .[1.332]

In the first bill the jurisdiction was claimed to be absolute, plenary, and original, not dependent upon the commerce clause of the Constitution. In the four subsequent ones the committee undertook to get jurisdiction from the commerce clause of the Constitution. In all these efforts the committee have been defeated, and now we have this bill based upon the extraordinary proposition, the unparalleled proposition that, because the Constitution has granted to the courts of the United States jurisdiction in controversies between citizens of different States and between citizens of the United States and of foreign countries, therefore the Constitution has granted to Congress legislative power to regulate the transactions between citizens of different States and between citizens of the United States and foreign countries.

A judicial power, it is unnecessary for me to state, I hope, in this body, is a power *jus dicere*, a power to say what the law is. A legislative power is a power *jus dare*, a

---

[1.330] S. 1 as reported by the Committee on Finance on January 14, 1890, appears *supra* at 93-94.

[1.331] 116 U.S. 517, 6 S. Ct. 475, 129 L. Ed. 715 (1886).

[1.332] S. 1 as reported by Senator Sherman on March 18, 1890, appears *supra* at 112-13.

power to say what the law shall be. The judicial power ascertains the existing law and applies it to transactions occurring, the legislative power makes new rules, new regulations for transactions thereafter to occur. Yet strange as it may seem, because the Constitution gave a judicial power to settle controversies between citizens of different States and between citizens of the United States and of foreign countries, the bill is formulated to legislate to make rules and regulations concerning these transactions.

I am not going into that argument any further at present. I shall do it, though, unless my motion prevails. I have only gone thus far to show to the Senate the difficulty which the Committee on Finance have encountered in framing this bill. I have pointed out the differences between the various bills to show that all along for now more than a year the committee have not been able to find a single solid stone in the Constitution upon which it could place this bill, but as often as it has been discussed, as often as the fallacies upon which one of these bills rests have been exposed, the committee, uncertain, doubtful, have sought refuge in another pretense. That is the meaning of the history which I have given this morning. The committee in no part of all these six bills which they have presented for the consideration of the Senate have ever been able to place the jurisdiction of Congress to enact them twice upon the same proposition. When beaten from one rampart behind which they have fortified themselves, they have fallen back and made another. Beaten out of that they have retreated to a third; beaten out of that they have retreated to a fourth, and so again to a fifth, and so again to this last ditch in which they place the jurisdiction of Congress on the extraordinary proposition to which I have called the attention of the Senate.

Mr. President, under these circumstances of doubt and difficulty, this changing attitude of the Committee on Finance, the immense importance of this question to the people of the United States, our grave and solemn duty which we owe to the people of the United States to do something, and something effectual, it becomes us to stop, to think, to deliberate. Are Senators willing, in face of this great demand of the people of the United States for redress against these enormous evils, to give to these crying and supplicating sufferers a mere sham? The people call to us for redress. They ask us for security against wrong and evil. Shall we, upon any idea that we will do something, that we will throw some sop to the dog Cerberus, pass a bill which will accomplish nothing, unless it be to demonstrate the inability or the unwillingness of the American Congress to pass an efficient measure?

In view of these things, Mr. President, I think I do a duty, I think I discharge a proper duty to the people of the United States when I ask the Senate to refer all these various propositions to that committee which by the rules of the Senate has charge of these great questions. . . .

Mr. [JOHN T.] MORGAN [D., Ala.]. In view of the pressure of business here, I will move an amendment to that effect, that the committee be required to report a bill within twenty days.

Mr. GEORGE. Very well; I do not object to that. . . .

The PRESIDING OFFICER (Mr. MOODY in the chair). The question is on the motion of the Senator from Mississippi to refer the bill and amendments to the Committee on the Judiciary.

Mr. INGALLS. What was the motion of the Senator from Alabama? To amend?

The PRESIDING OFFICER. The Chair understands the amendment to the motion has been accepted by the Senator from Mississippi.

Mr. GEORGE. No; the Senator from Alabama moves the amendment himself. I do not accept it, because I doubt the propriety of it.

Mr. INGALLS. What is the amendment to the motion?

The PRESIDING OFFICER. The Senator from Mississippi moves that the bill and pending amendments be referred to the Committee on the Judiciary. The Senator from Alabama moves to amend by instructing the committee to report within twenty days. The question is upon the amendment of the Senator from Alabama to limit the time within which the committee shall report. The Senator from Texas [Mr. REAGAN] has the floor.

Mr. REAGAN. Mr. President, the honorable Senator who makes the motion to refer these bills to the Judiciary Committee is a member of that committee. He told us in his opening remarks this morning that for several years he had been endeavoring to formulate in his mind some bill that would give relief against the great evil to which he has referred growing out of unlawful trusts and combinations. He favored us a few weeks ago with a very learned and able argument to demonstrate that the bill reported by the Committee on Finance was not warranted by the Constitution. He is a member of a committee which has had a bill[1.333] before it from the first day of this session of the Senate until now and has never acted upon it. I confess that it seems to me not very encouraging to refer bills of this description to that committee.

Mr. GEORGE. If the Senator will allow me, I will state (I am not sure I am right about it, but I think I am) that one reason of the delay in the action of the Judiciary Committee upon the matter was that the subject was before the Committee on Finance.

Mr. REAGAN. But the honorable Senator has just told us that the Judiciary Committee is the right committee for this subject to be before, and it had a bill referred to it. I think that is an answer to his suggestion.

Mr. VEST. Will the Senator allow me? I do not know that it is a matter which is very material, but the reason why the Judiciary Committee did not act upon this matter was on account of the sickness of the chairman of that committee. I am not a very experienced parliamentarian and never took much interest in that sort of business, but if it is within the rules for me to state what happened in committee, I wish to say that more than six weeks ago, two months ago, I moved myself, as a member of the Judiciary Committee, for the appointment of a subcommittee to take under consideration the subject of trusts, there being then pending before us the bill of the Senator from Texas and one other measure. I collated all the bills that had been offered in Congress, together with a large number that had been before the State Legislatures; but the sickness of the chairman of the committee delayed the matter until a few days ago. That subcommittee has now been appointed, and about the time that we commenced the consideration of this matter the bill coming from the Committee on Finance of which the Senator from Ohio has charge was called up in the Senate. Those are the facts, and it is but justice to the Judiciary Committee to state them.

Mr. HOAR. Will the Senator from Texas allow me to make a little additional statement? I suppose it is not a breach of any rule of this body to say that a very large number of nominations for important offices have been before that committee during the few months of the present session. . . . ⊥ [T]he command of that committee has ⊥2601 been very much occupied and engrossed by that class of its duties.

Mr. REAGAN. I have no doubt that the Judiciary Committee has had a great deal of such labor before it, as is suggested by the Senator from Massachusetts. In connection with these explanations, I desire to read what the Senator from Vermont [Mr. EDMUNDS], the chairman of the Judiciary Committee, said on that very point yesterday:

> The amendment proposed by the Senator from Texas [Mr. REAGAN] is the substance and for aught I know now literally the body of the bill that he introduced, I see by the top of it, on the 4th day of December last, I think about the first day of the session, and which was referred to the Committee on the Judiciary. I think it due to the Senator and to the Senate to state that according to our course the chairman very soon, almost immediately, referred that bill to a subcommittee of three among the most eminent and earnest of the members of that committee, but the committee has not yet been able to act upon it, owing, I have no doubt, to other important business in the committee, our time having been almost exclusively and necessarily devoted to the consideration of executive business. I think it is due to the Senator from Texas and to the Senate, he having introduced the bill so early, to say that.

I can understand very well, with the multiplied duties of the Judiciary Committee and with the difficulties which attend the formulation of a bill on this subject, that there may have been delay; and I do not complain of the delay, because the members of that committee were the better judges of what they were able to do than I can be, who was less informed as to what was before them. The point I made was this: The motion to refer comes from a member of the committee who confesses his inability to formulate a bill upon the subject and who combats, as far as I know, all the bills presented.

I can not state in as strong terms as the Senator from Mississippi has done the

---

[1.333] S. 62, Senator Reagan's bill.

great need for legislation upon this subject, the demand of the public for legislation upon this subject, the importance and necessity of legislation upon this subject; and is it possible that the Senate of the United States, having this subject before it in the last Congress and the present, has not been able to reach a conclusion that it could act or that it could not act, and to state the reasons why it could act or why it could not act? I think the country has a right to expect the Senate of the United States, if it can, to say that it has the power to act and the extent and character of that power, or to say that it has not power to act and that the people must rely exclusively upon the action of the State governments.

Mr. President, I have stated from the beginning that the power of Congress over this subject comes from the commerce clause of the Constitution. If there is any other power for legislation by us upon this subject I do not know where it comes from. . . .

I have examined with a good deal of care, and certainly with no disposition to be hypercritical, the bill reported by the Finance Committee, to which I shall refer for one moment. I think, as I stated on a former occasion, that the country owes to the distinguished Senator from Ohio a debt of gratitude for his efforts to bring this subject before the Senate and to secure action, whether he has been successful in bringing it before the Senate in a proper form or not. The bill, as I understand it, which is reported by the committee, is not wholly unconstitutional. The first clause of the first section, it seems to me, is clearly within the Constitution.

That all arrangements, contracts, agreements, trusts, or combinations between two or more citizens or corporations, or both, of different States, or between two or more citizens or corporations, or both, of the United States and foreign states, or citizens or corporations thereof, made with a view or which tend to prevent full and free competition in the importation, transportation, or sale of articles imported into the United States.

What is here described is made unlawful. The words "or sale of articles" ought to have added to them, "while the original packages remain unbroken," to have brought it within the constitutional clause. Then, it does not seem to me to have been necessary to say that these individuals or corporations should be citizens of different States, when it refers to the importation of articles under the Constitution. That brings it under the commerce clause. The other part of the paragraph was unnecessary to give Congress jurisdiction, in my judgment. So, while I would not employ the words used in this bill, because it assigns for jurisdiction some things not necessary to give jurisdiction, it is, within the purview of the Constitution, a regulation of foreign commerce.

Then the second provision pointing out the ground of jurisdiction, which I shall not go over, beginning on line 10, and the third provision giving jurisdiction, which I shall not read, beginning on line 3, on the second page, and ending at line 21, while well intended, it seems to me can not be sustained by the courts of the country, for they do not lay any known predicate for jurisdiction; that is, any predicate that I have learned from the Constitution or from the reading of the commentaries upon it.

The Senator from Mississippi spoke of the various bills introduced by the Senator from Ohio and reported from the Finance Committee in his argument in favor of a reference of all these bills to the Judiciary Committee. I listened to see whether he would not take up the bill now under consideration as an amendment, and give his reasons why that ought to be referred to the Judiciary Committee. I allude to the bill which I have offered as an amendment to the Finance Committee's bill. My amendment has been read two or three times, but I will venture to tax the Senate to read it again, prefacing what I have to say by the statement that it is based alone upon the commerce clause of the Constitution of the United States, and that in my judgment, though we may seek as many sources of power as we choose, we shall find none outside of that and outside of the taxing power, which can not be applied to bills originating in the Senate.

Besides what Congress can do under the commerce clause of the Constitution, the rest, as I took occasion to say a few days ago, must be done by the State Legislatures. One of the great mistakes that seem to me to be made by the people of the country—and it appears to some extent to permeate the Halls of Congress—is that all grievances must be dealt with by Congress, without reference to the question of the source of power enabling us to deal with the subject. When we have exhausted our power under the commerce clause of the Constitution, which must be a confessed power for this purpose, then the people must rely upon the Legislatures of the several States for the rest of the legislation on the subject. I do not mean by this to be understood that no legislation ought to be adopted by Congress. I believe that it is the duty of Congress to pass such legislation as is within its constitutional power in order that it may be supplemented by appropriate legislation of a much larger scope in the several States.

With these preliminary remarks I desire again to call attention (and I am sorry the Senator from Mississippi is not in his seat) to the provisions of the amendment pending before the Senate: . . .[1.334]

It has been suggested to me that the penalty is pretty high. It will be observed that simply the maximum penalties are given,[1.335] and they are given the same as in the committee's bill. The courts have all the way from nothing up to the maximum given here in their discretion in trying these cases, so that the judgment of the court will determine how much of this penalty shall be applied in each case, according to the special circumstances of the case. I would have no objection if it was thought necessary to reduce the maximum; but when we remember that these penalties have relation to great and powerful corporations as well as to less important combinations, it will be seen that strong measures will be necessary to control and repress the mischievous action.

The second section of my amendment, which would be the fourth section of the bill, if adopted, is:

That a trust is a combination of capital, skill, or acts by two or more persons, firms, corporations, or associations of persons, or of any two or more of them, for either, any, or all of the following purposes—

These are trusts under the power of the first section, resting upon the commerce clause of the Constitution—

First. To create or carry out any restrictions in trade.
Second. To limit or reduce the production or to increase or reduce the price of merchandise or commodities.

That is for the purpose and under the authority mentioned in the first section. . . .[1.336]

The third section, which will be the fifth of the bill if it shall be adopted, provides that each day's violation of the law shall be a separate offense.

I apprehend that those who have looked at my amendment and taken up the clauses in the second section have considered them as independent, and assumed that they were questions to be dealt with by the ⊥ State authority, and so they would be if the first section was out of the amendment, but that limits them, as I will read again for emphasis:

That all persons engaged in the creation of any trust, or as owner or part owner, agent, or manager of any trust, employed in any business carried on with any foreign country, or between the States, or between any State and the District of Columbia, or between any State and any Territory of the United States, or any owner or part owner, agent, or manager of any corporation, company, or person employed in any such business, using its powers for either of the purposes specified in the second section of this act—

That is, all those things that I have just enumerated—

shall be deemed guilty of a high misdemeanor.

So I beg of those who come to criticise this amendment that they will look to see that it is all brought distinctly and clearly under the commerce clause of the Constitution, and I should like to see some of the constitutional lawyers who are

---

[1.334] Senator Reagan read the first section of his amendment, the proposed section 3 of the Sherman bill; it appears *supra* at 183. This section was originally introduced as section 1 of Reagan's bill (S. 62); *see* pp. 111 and 112 *supra*.

[1.335] $10,000 fine and/or five years' imprisonment.

[1.336] Senator Reagan read the remainder of proposed new section 4, which appears *supra* at 183.

discussing this subject place themselves in opposition to that—if they choose to risk their reputations there as lawyers, I mean.

It was said yesterday by the distinguished Senator from Missouri [Mr. VEST] that a clause of a bill which he read, which made the power to act rest upon the idea that the subject was declared to be contrary to the policy of a State, was the foundation for Federal jurisdiction to enact a law. For safety I will read the clause:

> That when any State shall declare, or heretofore has declared by law, trusts as defined by the true intent and meaning of this act to be unlawful and against public policy, it shall not be lawful thereafter for any person, firm, or corporation to cause to be transported any product or article covered or embraced by such trust from such State to or into any State or Territory or the District of Columbia.

That section is the one the Senator from Missouri alluded to as the only oasis in this great desert of unconstitutionality, and he made it to rest upon the fact that the State has passed a law declaring certain things to be against public policy. I am inclined to think my friend, the Senator from Iowa [Mr. WILSON] who sits farthest from me, would accept that for a very different reason from the one which the Senator from Missouri asserts it for. The State of Iowa thinks that the manufacture or sale of intoxicating liquors and wines and beer is against public policy. The State of Missouri and the Senator from Missouri do not so think, but his constitutional argument would enable Congress to determine, not as a constitutional question, but as a question of expediency and morality and policy, that if that State chooses to forbid those things the United States may forbid them also. If the United States can forbid a thing, it must be upon another authority, and not because the State of Iowa has adopted such a provision of law. At least I suggest that; and I suggest further that, if this be a source of constitutional power, it is a new source of power just discovered, not heretofore invoked.

Mr. President, I am inclined to think, in view of the fact that but one member of the Committee on the Judiciary has given any expression that indicates a purpose to mature a law to repress the evil effects of trusts and to punish those engaged in them, that it is not best to refer these measures to that committee. I would rather trust them to the action of the Senate, unless we can have some assurance that that committee will take the subject up and act upon it. If we can have the judgment of that committee, with its reputation for legal and constitutional ability, put to the test, I should be willing to accept it. I do feel that in the multiplied number of bills before us there is danger that we may get provisions adopted which will not be constitutional.

I confess that in offering the measure which I offered as an amendment to the bill reported by the Senator from Ohio, I presented it with the full belief that two of the sources of power invoked by the bill reported by that Senator are not within the Constitution, but I believed if this one is it covers the whole case so far as the criminal part of the law is concerned, and if the other part of it failed the country would not be much at a loss. So I was willing to accept, because I did not well see how to avoid it, that which I did not think strictly conformable to the Constitution, in order to get enough in the law to give it vigor and efficiency, and to protect the people of this country against longer being plundered by the corporations and trusts that are driving the people of the country to despair while other bills are now being acted upon here; and what is the use of sending them to a wet nurse that does not seem to favor them much? . . .

Mr. PLATT. . . . I wish to know from the Senator from Texas how far these words in his amendment reach in his construction: "Any business carried on * * * between the States." Let me direct the Senator's attention to what is in my mind—

Mr. REAGAN. In what line are those words found?

Mr. PLATT. In the third and fourth lines of the first section of the Senator's amendment. . . .

Mr. REAGAN. In the first place it would punish persons engaged in the transportation of things by virtue of trusts, and it is possible that it would go beyond that to some extent, but I am not prepared to say exactly the extent to which it would go.

Mr. PLATT. Then the particular purpose in the use of those words, which are the important words, is to reach the transportation which is carried on between the States?

Mr. REAGAN. That is one of the reasons. I need not repeat to the Senator, as I have stated over and over, that I have given the formulation of what seems to me to meet the question under the commerce clause of the Constitution, and I trust that to the Senate and to the country.

Mr. [JAMES F.] WILSON [R., Iowa]. . . .

Mr. President, I am glad that as time goes on opinions change. It took ten years of agitation to bring about the enactment of the law for the regulation of interstate commerce, but it came at last. Through the processes inducing its final enactment changes of opinion were frequent, and I am glad to see in the RECORD of this morning, as I heard yesterday when the Senator from Missouri[1.337] was speaking, that a change has come over the spirit of his dream since . . . the last Congress. . . .

⊥ But the broad ground is assumed and occupied by the Senator that the ⊥2603 provisions embraced in the three sections of the bill offered as an amendment by the Senator from Texas [Mr. COKE] are wholly beyond constitutional objection. If that be so, I should like to know why that bill of the Fiftieth Congress relating to the importation of foreign intoxicating liquors was obnoxious to constitutional objection. And is it possible that we are to be driven to the extreme of saying that the State is entitled to that remedy provided first (leaving its police power wholly out of the case) it shall declare that a trust exists within its borders in respect of the manufacture and sale of intoxicating liquors; and yet if that should be done what protection would that give to the State of Iowa, or any other State which in the exercise of its police powers should enact legislation similar to that now in force in Iowa?

This only provides that in case the States declare a trust in accordance with the provisions of the first section of the bill, then it shall be operative. But suppose there were no trust for the manufacture and sale of liquor in the State of Iowa, still this flood can be poured on; and yet if in the State of Illinois or the State of Missouri, or any other of the surrounding States, there should be a statutory declaration against a trust or alleging the existence of a trust for the manufacture of these liquors within that State, then the provision of this bill would be effective and remedy might be had under its provisions.

Mr. President, you may debate the question as to where the line of constitutional power to enact legislation of this kind will go, and support it, because it is seemingly a new field where by your Congressional legislation you first ask the State to define the object upon which your national legislation may act, overlooking that more substantial field which has been recognized from the foundation of the Government down to the present time, in which it is affirmed that the police powers of the States were retained by them at the formation of the Government, and not surrendered to the United States, but that in regard to those things not surrendered no Congrssional action can be had to aid the States in the enforcement of their laws or in protecting them against the infractions which are practiced under color of the United States laws.

What then? States that do not care to exercise their police powers for the protection of the health and morals of their people may be protected by Congressional legislation against a combination to reduce the price of anything as well as to raise it, and yet I think that Senators who engage in this discussion would find it difficult to induce all the people who have been asking for legislation of this character to approve of a measure which should put up a stone wall against the reduction of price. People are generally willing to accept the advantages of reduction, while they may be crying out against the disadvantages of a sudden rise.

So, Mr. President, it is well enough, in the discussion of these great public questions, to be certain, at least reasonably so, that in our endeavor to answer a widespread public demand such as has induced the introduction of these trust bills, we do not overlook and trample into the dust the recognized powers of the States in other fields. . . .

Now, Mr. President, I am in favor of legislation upon this subject. I desire to

---

[1.337] Senator Vest.

reach it at the earliest practicable moment. I remember well, and I have already stated, that through the long lines of ten years the agitation moved before it brought the result of the enactment of the law for the regulation of interstate commerce. I do not want this agitation to run through ten years of time, and yet I do not expect a perfect remedy from any act which this Congress may pass. These things are of gradual growth, and it is well for us and all the people who are looking for a remedy to keep in mind one prominent fact, and that is that no act of Congress, no act of any legislative body will enforce itself, so that not only officers of the United States intrusted with the administration of the law and the officers of the States intrusted with the administration of the laws must take care to see that it is enforced, but the citizen who may be injured by infractions also must give his attention and aid in order to make the remedy effective and perfect.

Now, in order that we may reach action as early as practicable, I am inclined to, and at present believe I shall, vote against the reference of this bill to the Committee on the Judiciary; not that I fear that it would not have conservative and forceful consideration and reasonably early action there, but for the very different reason that I want some bill passed by this body that may go to the other House for action, and where doubtless there may be disagreement; and if that disagreement should bring us to the position of a conference between the two bodies, from it may be evolved a start at least towards legislation in this very important field. For that reason I shall so vote as to bring us to as early a resolution in the Senate as possible, so that we may put ourselves in the same attitude we were in in connection with the bill for the regulation of interstate commerce, a conference between the two Houses, and the result, at least to a considerable degree, effective legislation looking to the accomplishment of the ends so generally desired.

Mr. VEST. Mr. President, I do not know that, if it were, the fact that I occupied a position inconsistent with that which I occupy in regard to the bills now before the Senate during the last Congress, as to the bill referred to by the Senator from Iowa, would practically affect the question now pending at all. I am unable, however, to see that there is anything inconsistent in the position or the vote which I gave in the Judiciary Committee in regard to the bill to which the Senator has referred with that occupied by me to-day. But whether the inconsistency exists or not is really an immaterial question. . . .

Now, Mr. President, it is absolutely within the power of the Congress of the United States, under the interstate-commerce clause of the Constitution, in its power to regulate commerce, to prohibit the carrying of any article from one State to another. That is absolutely and exclusively within the power of the General Government and of Congressional action. The police power of the State is an entirely different jurisdiction, as distinct and separate from the interstate-commerce clause in the Federal Constitution as any two subjects can possibly be. What analogy can be drawn between the traffic in ardent spirits and the subject of trusts in regard to which we are legislating now? Is there any State in this Union that can ever be expected to legislate in favor of these unlawful combines and trusts as defined in the first amendment submitted by the Senator from Texas [Mr. COKE]? That section reads as follows:

> That a trust is a combination of capital or skill by two or more persons, firms, or corporations for the purpose of creating or employing restrictions on trade, or limiting the production, increasing or reducing the price of merchandise or commodities, or preventing competition in the making, manufacture, sale, or purchase of merchandise or commodities, or creating a monopoly in the manufacture, making, sale, or purchase of any merchandise or commodity with intent to forestall the market value of any merchandise or commodity.

There is a trust unlawful under the common law. There is no common law of the United States, but the common law prevails in all the States of the Union. They have in the State of Louisiana a mixed jurisdiction or a mixed system of laws composed of the common law of ⊥ England and the Code Napoléon, or the civil law of France, but in all the other States the common law prevails, and that law without statutory enactment makes all such combinations as are prescribed or defined in the States of the Union and this amendment to be unlawful. The section which I condemned reads as follows:

SEC. 5. That when any State shall declare, or heretofore has declared by law, trusts as defined by the true intent and meaning of this act to be unlawful and against public policy.

That is surplusage, because by the common law, which obtains in all the States, the combination, as defined in the first section, which I have read, is unlawful and void; and is it pretended that there is anything in the Constitution of the United States that militates against the idea that under the interstate-commerce clause of the Federal Constitution Congress can treat as unlawful and void and prohibit the transportation of the products of any such combinations as are here defined from one State to another?

The Senator from Iowa speaks of a policy law which is enacted against a commodity that is unlawful under the common law, an article of merchandise. Alcoholic stimulants are as much an article of merchandise under the common law and under the laws of a majority of the States of this Union as corn or wheat or pork; and because the Senator from Iowa or the Senator from Texas believes that traffic to be unlawful, the law is not changed as it is in the common law or as it is upon the statute-books of the respective States. What analogy is there between the two? In the one case there is an unlawful combination by the laws of all the States, and if there were a common law of the United States it would be unlawful under that. In the other case there is simply a police regulation as to an article of drink which many intelligent and worthy men believe to be absolutely necessary to human life and human comfort.

I must confess, sir, that I am unable to see even in the exigencies of debate a justification for the assumption made by the Senator from Iowa that the two cases are parallel, and that my [sic] inconsistency is therefore apparent.

Mr. WILSON, of Iowa. Mr. President, I do not see the inconsistency on this side of the line that the Senator from Missouri has referred to. Now, the remedy that he proposes by giving his indorsement and support to the amendment presented by the Senator from Texas [Mr. COKE] amounts to this, so far as the question that he addressed his attention to is concerned, that if the State of Iowa or the State of Missouri should find within its borders a combination to put down or put up the price of intoxicating liquors it might pass an act declaring that to be an unlawful combination, and then if this amendment should become a law the State would get the help of the United States and its power to prevent the exportation from that State of the products of that trust, but it would not get the aid of the United States to protect the State that had thus declared a trust existing within its borders from the intrusion of the same article from other States where that trust had not been declared. So then, instead of aiding the States in the enforcement of their police powers, it would simply be an additional means for overriding those powers, notwithstanding the desire of the State. . . .

Mr. VEST. He makes his argument from one standpoint and I make mine from another. He is now going upon the assumption that the General Government exercises this power under the interstate-commerce clause of the Constitution to aid the police powers of the State. That is not my idea. I hold and claim that the General Government, under the interstate-commerce clause, has a right to prohibit an article from going from one State into another, without regard to any police regulation by any State in the Union. It is a very broad, comprehensive, general power that is vested in Congress alone.

Mr. WILSON, of Iowa. That is to say, Congress may enact a law which shall declare that certain articles recognized as belonging to the field of interstate commerce may be taken into Missouri from Iowa and taken into Illinois from Minnesota, but they shall not be returned from those States into the States from which they were shipped, nor shall they go there from any other State. That is, there shall be a kind of checkerboard enacted by Congress, so that the States may jump from one to another and pick up one another as you do in playing a game of checkers. That is not constitutional law, Mr. President. You must recognize a principle which will apply to all alike, and when you have applied it to one it will allow the application to others. So that, as has always been recognized in regard to the police powers of the State, belonging as they do wholly to the State, recognized as they were in all the early decisions of the Supreme Court as belonging there, you have got to give your aid so that the States will possess them all, and not obtrude obstacles in the way of their enforcement.

Mr. President, as I said when I was on the floor first to-day, the conditions existing in the country seem to change the opinions of men with regard to the same character of question, and I have no doubt that there are supporters of this amendment of the Senator from Texas and other amendments which have been offered here, that if they had been prepared with equal vigor in some other line of action as clearly constitutional as this would have expressed quite a different judgment in respect to them, just as we see in the case of the bill of the last Congress to which I have referred and the bill we are now discussing. But there must be that consistency which will give each State the same rights in the enforcement of its powers and the enjoyment of its privileges under the Constitution and which shall impose the same kind of conditions upon others. The State which I in part represent asks no departure from that line. Her Senators and Representatives are ready to aid in the enactment of proper legislation for the protection and for the indorsement of the rights of the other States as well as hers, and in regard to the illustration which I used in connection with the bill of the last Congress, all that we ask is that there shall be that proper recognition of the doctrine of State rights that will protect the State of Iowa or any other State and recognize her police powers within her own borders without asking any other State to follow her example except by her own voluntary election.

Mr. SHERMAN. I ask the Chair to state the pending question.

The VICE-PRESIDENT. The pending question is the amendment moved by the Senator from Alabama [Mr. MORGAN] to the motion made by the Senator from Mississippi [Mr. GEORGE] to commit the bill to the Committee on the Judiciary.

Mr. SHERMAN. What was the amendment of the Senator from Alabama?

The VICE-PRESIDENT. To commit with instructions that the Committee on the Judiciary should report within twenty days.

Mr. SHERMAN. Mr. President, it is a very unusual proceeding in the Senate of the United States, very rarely resorted to, to refer the action of one committee to another. It is not a wise proceeding to take at any time. Although there have been cases of the kind, they are very rare. Such a course would create controversies and contention and rivalry between committees, each of which is supposed to understand the duty that is enjoined upon it. As a general rule, such a proposition ought not to be made; but in this particular case I appeal to every Senator to say whether it would be wise to do it. One of these propositions is now pending before the Judiciary Committee, and it has been there for two, three, or four months—I do not know how long. When did the Senator from Texas introduce his proposition?

Mr. REAGAN. I introduced it on the first day of the session, I think, as a bill.

Mr. SHERMAN. On the first day of the session. It has been in that committee almost four months, and nothing has been done. Now, the Committee on Finance was charged with somewhat the same subject-matter. It has been deliberated upon carefully; the committee revised its decision once or twice. Perhaps the criticism of the Senator from Mississippi [Mr. GEORGE] in that respect is correct. It made changes and withdrew from them. But we have considered the subject and very carefully considered it, and opinions have been expressed to the Senate and they are here. Now to send that work to a committee which has already had charge of the subject-matter for four months and has not acted upon it, is rather a damaging proposition. If it is proposed to kill this measure, let it be done in a fair and legitimate way. . . .

As to the pending amendment, I have no sensibility about it. I am perfectly willing to accept any amendment that may be adopted by the Senate. If the Senate by a vote should adopt the amendment proposed by the Senator from Texas, well and good. As I stated, I do not believe in it; that is, I think it is better not now to put upon this proposed law a criminal proceeding, although I originally voted for such a proposition. Still, if the Senate chooses to put it on, well and good. It will probably, in the opinion of some, strengthen the bill, and in the opinion of others it will probably weaken it. Let the judgment of the Senate be carried out when expressed.

Then as to the proposition made by the Senator from Wisconsin [Mr. SPOONER] that some distinct proposition of law should be inserted in this bill giving the court in proper cases the power to send its process, its summons, or notice to parties in other States, there is no objection to such a provision. Indeed, as I lost the suit of my first client some thirty-five years ago, when I entered public life, I am not very familiar with the practice of the courts; but I find, on examination, that the law already provides, in certain cases, that just that thing may be done. Such a statute has existed for many years, and here is a decision of the Supreme Court of the United States upon the subject regulating and pointing out the necessity of having parties from other States and from all over the jurisdiction of the United States in certain cases. The case decided was a case where the suit was to quiet title to land, a suit in equity, and notice was sent under the law of 1875, I think it was, to different parties in different States. So there is no trouble in meeting ⊥ that difficulty. The court may, in the exercise of its discretion, serve notice of the pendency of this proceeding upon all the parties wherever they may live, and it goes broadcast wherever they may live, and even from foreign countries it may summon them to take their part in the trial of the case. The Senator from Wisconsin, who is a practicing lawyer and engaged now in cases in the United States courts, is thoroughly familiar with that matter, and he has prepared a section that will cover it entirely. I have not only no objection to it, but I shall be very glad indeed to have it provided for.

⊥2605

The language which was inserted by the Committee on Finance required these combinations to be made between persons or corporations in different States in order to come within the jurisdiction thereby created. That language was inserted by the Committee on Finance. I did not think it was necessary on the first draughting of the bill, but that was deemed necessary, and now the Senator from Massachusetts [Mr. HOAR] thinks those words ought to be stricken out. I do not care whether they are in or out. It does not make any difference in my judgment as to the effect of this bill. I shall be glad to have it either way in order to satisfy Senators, but I can not satisfy them all.

The Senator from Massachusetts objects to the words "in a civil suit." I have no objection to their being stricken out. I would say, using the language of the Constitution of the United States, "all cases in law or equity," or, which is better, "all controversies between persons living in different States."

Mr. HOAR. The Senator will pardon me.

Mr. SHERMAN. I would have it either way. The second section refers to controversies between parties.

Mr. HOAR. The Senator will allow me to call his attention to one thing. That first section being criticised yesterday, he stated that it was intended to apply to suits brought by the United States. Now, as I understand him, he is willing to substitute the phrase in the first section, "controversies between citizens of different States." That clearly would exclude the United States altogether.

Mr. SHERMAN. The Senator does not correctly state my case.

Mr. HOAR. If the Senator would make that amendment he would have a section which provided that controversies between citizens of different States should be taken possession of by the district attorney or the Attorney-General and conducted to final judgment and execution.

Mr. SHERMAN. I will explain to the Senator from Massachusetts in regard to the bill. It is strange he can not distinguish between the first and second sections. He dislikes the bill so much that he can not state the case fairly. I refer to all actions at law or in equity in the first section of the bill. I use the language of the Constitution of the United States in defining the cases that arise under the Constitution and laws of the United States, and so "all cases at law or in equity of a civil nature." These words he objects to, and I am willing to strike them out. These words are there because they are used in the Constitution of the United States.

When I come to describe these things in the second section, there the words "controversies between citizens of different States" are used, so that there can be no misunderstanding.

The first section deals with suits brought by the United States in the name of the United States to check, and control, and enjoin, and regulate these corporations. The second section provides for suits between parties, and there, I think, they ought to be classed as controversies between parties of different States; and that is the distinction laid down.

Now, Mr. President, all I desire is that this bill shall be voted upon. I believe that in a half-hour we can take the vote on the proposition of the Senator from Texas [Mr.

REAGAN]. If that is adopted, well and good. We can vote then upon the proposition of the Senator from Kansas [Mr. INGALLS] and then adopt the amendments that are suggested on either side. Correct this bill as you will, and we can have a bill which, while it may not be perfect, while it may not go far enough to suit me or may in some respects go further than I think is wise, yet we shall have a tangible proposition that we can send to the House of Representatives for their consideration, and in that way we can dismiss from the Senate of the United States, for this session at least, this question and controversy about trusts and combinations. If we send this bill to the Judiciary Committee and await their report to come back to us, we shall have to go over all this ground again and we shall be simply wasting time that is valuable to the people of the United States. . . .

Mr. HOAR. . . . I think if the Senator from Ohio will look at the Reporter's notes of his speech he will find that he said just now that he had put into this bill the words "all suits of a civil nature at common law or in equity," and that he put them in because they were the words of the Constitution.

Mr. SHERMAN. Substantially.

Mr. HOAR. But he said he thought he would like to substitute for them, as on the whole better, "controversies between citizens of different States." That is exactly what he said. I think that will be found in the Senator's remarks, and I think it will be found in the memory of every Senator who listened to him. Then I called his attention to the fact that he said yesterday the first section was intended to provide for suits by the United States, and that the substitution of the words "between citizens of different States" cut off suits by the United States altogether. He says in reply to that that I misunderstood him, and that he was talking about the second section; but if he will look at the second section he will find that there is no place in that section where those words belong; that there is nothing appropriate to them; that there is nothing to be stricken out for which they are to be substituted. The second section provides—

That any person or corporation injured or damnified by such arrangement, contract, agreement, trust, or combination * * * may sue for and recover, in any court of the United States, * * * twice the amount of damages sustained.

Does the Senator mean to limit the second section to cases of controversies between citizens of different States? Of course not. If the combination against which the bill is leveled has injured me through foreign or interstate commerce, does he mean to say that his purpose in the bill is to provide that I can only have a remedy when I am damaged by citizens of different States from my own? The second section has nothing at all to do with residence in different States.

My honorable friend says that I dislike his bill. I do not. I like his bill very much; and I like it as he had it; but he has proposed this amendment. He has answered to every single criticism I have made upon it, if I recollect aright—there may be possibly one exception—that he was of that way of thinking himself in the first place, but that he yielded his judgment to the opinion of others in order to make the bill go through. What I want is to have the great authority of the Senator in his original judgment, not in his yielding to other people, in favor of a bill which I should like to vote for.

That is the difference between the Senator and me. I want him to strike out these words which made the bill apply to only one-one-hundredth part of the cases that it ought to apply to, and to have it as the Senator first reported it. Then I want a penal provision put in and have it as the Senator originally designed it, and with one or two other little amendments in which I shall have the Senator's entire concurrence, if I understand him, I propose heartily to support his bill.

My honorable friend seems to me, owing to my great dullness of expression and failure of clearness, to have understood a concurrence with his opinion somehow or other as a criticism upon his bill. I say again that in making those amendments I do not see where he can put in the words "controversies between citizens of different States" in the second section. There is nothing to be stricken out for which they can be properly a substitute. The second section is not drawn on the theory that makes it proper, and if he does he will do in the second section what, contrary to his judgment, if put in the first, will make the bill apply to but a very small proportion or fraction of the cases it ought to reach.

Mr. SHERMAN. The whole idea is that the Senator differs as to my statement of the case; but when he comes to offer the amendments he will find them not very important and probably those I shall cheerfully accede to. I hope we shall have a vote on the question of reference. . . .

Mr. STEWART. Mr. President, while this debate has been proceeding I have been thinking about the practical operation of the bill reported from the Committee on Finance if it should be passed and could be enforced as a constitutional law. I call particular attention to the clause commencing in the seventeenth line:

> And all arrangements, trusts, or combinations between such citizens or corporations, made with a view or which tend to advance the cost to the consumer of any such articles, are hereby declared to be against public policy, unlawful, and void.

Now, it is a well known fact that since the money power abandoned ⊥ the old ⊥2606 automatic system of allowing the quantity of money to be governed by the product of the mines or by the quantity of gold and silver obtainable, and provided that only one metal should be manufactured and both should enter into production, there has been a decline in prices and that it has now reached a point where there is great distress in the country. There is now great distress on account of falling prices, which necessarily follow contraction. There are many manufacturing establishments that find they can not make any money; they are losing money and see that they will have to go into bankruptcy if something is not done. Men agree, for instance, that they will manufacture only a certain amount, no more than the market will take, in order to keep up the prices, so as to avoid bankruptcy. Those arrangements are common; they are of every-day occurrence. But under this bill would they not be subject to the pains and penalties prescribed? If producers did not have the power to make such an agreement in times like these, when prices are declining, when they are putting their money in one year and can not get it out the next year because prices have declined—if they could not make an agreement to check production and wait for better times to bridge over the trouble, they would be ruined; and this bill would probably, if carried out literally, in times of depression, break up half the manufacturing establishments in the country. That is one of the ordinary effects, one of the ordinary arrangements which are necessary in times like these, that would be in violation of the bill.

Then again we will take, for example, the beef trust in Chicago. There is a trust which has put up the price of beef, a trust that we have been investigating and want to remedy. There is a plain remedy for that trust, not in legislation perhaps, but in the action of the parties interested. Farmers who are producing beef have to sell it at an enormous sacrifice, at starvation prices. Cattle are cheap all through the country. Still beef is high in Chicago. Suppose the farmers in the West should unite and say, "We will not sell our beef except at a certain price." Suppose they should unite to beat this combination; they would all be criminals under this bill; they could not combine to beat it at all.

Suppose, again, a combination is formed in Chicago by citizens of Chicago, not citizens of different States, but all citizens of Chicago, to bear the prices. The farmers of different States would have no right to combine and say, "We will not sell any wheat; we will help each other; we will advance money to each other; we will not sell any wheat until this combination is broken up; we will not allow them to sell our wheat short, to sell something they have not got and bear the market, and we will not take our wheat to market to be robbed." That they could not do under this proposed law. They would be liable to all the pains and penalties of the law if they did.

Again, suppose that the employers, railroad companies, and manufacturing establishments should say that labor shall be put down to two bits a day. Suppose that capital should combine against labor, as it is very much inclined to do, and there should be a combination among the laborers which would increase the cost of production and increase the cost of all articles consumed. Suppose there should be a combination among the laborers to protect themselves from grasping monopolies; they would all be criminals for doing it.

This measure strikes at the very root of competition. It strikes at the very root of self-preservation. It strikes at the very root of organization. It strikes at the very root of co-operation. . . .

Co-operation is necessary; but co-operation has its evils. When capital is combined and strong, it will for a time produce evils, but if you take away the right of co-operation you take away the power to redress those evils; it gives rise to monopolies that are protected by law, against which the people can not combine. They can not have other monopolies equal to them. It is that which depresses the people.

For instance, the patent laws of the United States create monopolies, and there is more money made by speculators under the patent laws, because they have monopolies. There is no way for the people to combine and form co-operation against the patent laws. While in England every privilege was parceled out to corporations and to private individuals, favorites of the Crown, there was no way for the people to compete with them; but now, in the march of progress, we find everything has been changed and there is freedom of action, freedom of combination, and when one combination is formed, if it is not beneficent, if it puts up the price, others will be formed that will put the price down, and there will be competition. But if you deny the right to combine in order to compete with the capitalists, in order to compete with strong establishments, you go back hundreds of years.

This bill is a step in the wrong direction. It is a step back towards the dark ages. It is a declaration against the freedom of man, against freedom of action. If one corporation is making too much money there will be other corporations, and that is the remedy which modern civilization has invented. That is the remedy which has brought about the present development of the civilized world. All the States, instead of having corporations dealt out to private individuals by private statutes, have passed general incorporation laws, and there is as much freedom of competition between corporations now as there is between individuals.

The great harmfulness of corporations was that they were monopolies; that others could not form them. It required special acts or special favors to create them; the people could not form them. If you take away the right to form combinations to meet combination, you will have monopoly in this country to your heart's content. It would be the accumulated capital that would prosecute the new concerns that are starting. This bill would be an engine of oppression to break down all competition, because as soon as one was forming those in existence would bring suit immediately. They would have the power and the money, and the poor people struggling to meet the combinations in existence would not have the power to resist them. What could a labor organization do when its individual members were sued by the Government for belonging to a labor organization, a combination which has a tendency to put up the price of labor or its products? It would be helpless against the power of these great corporations, which have abundance of money to prosecute these suits.

Why take away the right of the laborers of America to compete in production with these great corporations? Why take away from the people the power to resist corporations, the power to organize for the purpose of bettering themselves? Organization is everything; individuals literally nothing. No great enterprises are conducted now without organization. As I said yesterday, the individual man by himself can be but little above a savage. He can not supply himself with the wants, let alone the luxuries of life. He must be as a savage if he is alone. He must avail himself of the labor of others. Inter-association (and in my judgment this bill strikes at the principle of association) is necessary to afford competition; it is necessary to provide means for the development of the country; it is necessary for the laboring men and the producers of the country. If they will develop its resources they will benefit themselves, and if they will resist oppression they must have this right. The bill takes away the sacred right of co-operation, and it ought not to be passed into a law.

Mr. PUGH. Mr. President, as a member of the Committee on the Judiciary I simply desire to say that in my opinion a reference of this bill to that committee will be the last of it for this session. I think I have knowledge enough to enable me to say that the enemies of the bill can not adopt more efficient action to destroy it than to send it to that committee.

I am a friend of this bill and of many of the amendments that have been offered to it. The Senate is in just as good condition, is just as well informed and prepared to pass upon the amendments now as it will be hereafter, or as the Judiciary Committee are. I have no idea that the Judiciary Committee can formulate a bill, that will meet with the concurrence of a majority of that committee, that has any life in it, and I insist that we should dispose of the bill and the amendments, and vote down the proposition to refer to the Judiciary Committee.

Mr. HISCOCK. I should like to make an inquiry of the Senator before he takes his seat. Do I understand from him that he thinks a majority of the very able lawyers constituting the Judiciary Committee would come to the conclusion that the bill is unconstitutional and void?

Mr. PUGH. On that subject I am not prepared to speak; I am not sufficiently familiar with the constitutional opinions of the members of that committee, except as to those who have expressed them in this debate.

Mr. HISCOCK. I suppose if the bill and the amendments should be referred to the Judiciary Committee, it would be for the purpose of having the opinion of that committee upon the constitutional objections that have been urged against the bill, and my inquiry pointed to the fact whether the Senator knows that a majority of the eminent gentlemen who constitute that committee believe that this scheme of legislation would be unconstitutional and void.

Mr. PUGH. We have had the opinion of two very able members of that committee, learned and able lawyers, that there is no power under the Constitution to pass the bill or any amendment now pending or proposed except the one offered by the Senator from Texas [Mr. COKE]. While I am ready to vote for that amendment, I have no idea that a majority of the Judiciary Committee will favor it. The difficulty in that committee is with the variety of opinion that it has both as to constitutional power and as to the provisions of a bill to reach this evil. My opinion is that the variety of that opinion will prevent any concurrence in favor of a bill that has any vitality in it, and we are more apt to give it by voting in the Senate on the amendments as they are presented and will be in order than by letting that committee deal with this question and make a report to the Senate. I have no idea but what any report that it may make of any bill would be subjected to the same number of amendments, if not more, than the bill now pending before the Senate.

Mr. HISCOCK. I will say to the Senator upon the same question and upon the same line that if the bill with the amendments is to be referred to the Committee on the Judiciary I would like the motion to ⊥ be modified so as to call for a report from ⊥2607 that committee upon the constitutional and legal questions involved, not upon the framework of a bill especially, for that we could take care of here. I could have my opinion as to what the provisions ought to be, as well as any one else. I hope that the Senator who made the motion to refer the bill to the Committee on the Judiciary will amend his motion in that they shall be called upon to express themselves as to the constitutional power of enacting this legislation. . . .

Mr. GEORGE. The remark made by the Senator from Alabama calls for some response from me. The Senator said if the bill should be referred to the Judiciary Committee, he had no idea it would be heard from during the remainder of this session. The Senator from Alabama has no warrant for making any such statements, I think.

Mr. PUGH. It is merely my opinion, of course.

Mr. GEORGE. The Judiciary Committee, I believe, have been as diligent in performing the duties which the Senate have imposed upon them as any other committee of this body. There is the motion now pending, made by the Senator's colleague [Mr. MORGAN], requiring that committee to report within twenty days, and then there is the parliamentary power in this body, which the Senator seems to have overlooked, that when a matter is referred to a committee and that committee fails and neglects for an unreasonable time to report, to discharge the committee and bring the matter before the Senate directly.

Taking these things into consideration, I think the Senator's remark is wholly unwarranted. It is not the intention of the Senator, that is, myself, who made the motion to refer, to dispose of the bill in that way. My object in making the motion is to give us a bill, if one be possible—and I believe one is possible—which will be a real remedy for the ills and the evils which afflict the people of the United States, instead of the sham which the pending bill will turn out to be.

Mr. PLATT. Mr. President, I shall, notwithstanding the embarrassment which a motion of this sort creates, vote to refer the bill and the various amendments to the Judiciary Committee, and I do it not as an enemy of some bill which may be properly framed to meet the evil complained of, but I do it because I believe there is in the bill nothing at all which will meet the evil complained of. The people who are suffering from the unlawful acts of associated corporations are asking relief, and when they ask for bread the Senator from Ohio proposes to give them a stone; when they ask for fish he proposes to give them a serpent. As the author of this bill he has been, first and last, something over a year in bringing forward his experiments to meet the evil, and constantly revising his own impressions as to the method in which it could be done, until I venture to say the last proposition is the least effective of any one that he has made.

I allude to this, as I do to the fact that five amendments have been presented, and I believe presented in good faith, to this bill, to show the very great difficulty which surrounds the subject. There is not a single member of the Senate who has thought upon this subject who does not recognize that it is one full of difficulty, of legal difficulty, of constitutional difficulty. The very fact that these amendments have been offered proves the difficulty of the situation, and proves, not that Senators are opposed to granting relief from the ills which are complained of, but that they desire to grant efficient relief if they attempt to grant relief at all.

It is no answer to the criticisms which are made on this bill to declaim against the enormities of trusts and combinations. It is no answer to the objection which is made to this bill, that it will not touch any single trust or combination in this country, to denounce the operations of trusts. It will not do to say that a person who is not ready to vote for this bill wants to perpetuate the illegal and injurious acts of combinations and associations and trusts. We are very often as legislators placed in this dilemma: An evil exists, an evil which ought to be remedied, which ought to be remedied in an efficient, legal, and constitutional way, and some measure is proposed which either does not remedy it at all or runs against every constitutional method of reaching it; and then the persons who are not ready to take that measure are held up as being opposed to rendering any relief whatever.

My objection to this bill, which I have already stated, is that it will not touch or reach the unlawful or injurious acts of any trust, association, or combination, whether of individuals or corporations, in this country. The fact that it is confined to arrangements between persons or corporations residing in different States of the Union or residing in this country and in foreign countries, is an admission on the face of it that the author of the bill or the amendment admits his inability to do anything else in this direction. It is an admission on the part of the author of the bill that all trusts, all combinations, all agreements, all associations existing between people of the same State, between corporations of the same State, for the unlawful purposes which we all understand, are beyond the reach of Congressional action.

That is the admission in this bill. It is an admission which I do not make, but it is an admission of this bill, because it is confined simply to those arrangements, associations, combinations, and trusts existing between persons of different States or corporations of different States or persons of this country and another country or corporations of this country and another country. So having eliminated from the effect of the bill all the great combinations which have been formed and may be formed within States it proposes to deal with them where the parties composing them reside in different States; that, and that only.

If we could do that we should simply transfer the parties who compose these corporations from different States to a single State. The great sugar trust, if it is now a combination existing between corporations in different States, would organize as a single corporation of a single State, and then would be beyond the reach of this bill.

But that is not the real difficulty. The real difficulty is that under the Constitution of the United States you can not reach an agreement made between parties residing in different States, no matter for what purpose. It is the controversies arising between persons residing in different States, between corporations residing in different States, which can be reached in the courts of the United States.

The Senator from Ohio seems entirely unable to comprehend this distinction—but it is a distinction which, as it seems to me, every lawyer ought to comprehend—that he is not providing for controversies between persons residing in different States and corporations of different States, but he is trying to stop agreements between persons of different States and corporations of different States, under that clause of the Constitution which gives the courts of the United States jurisdiction of controversies arising between persons so residing. I believe that I can understand the difference between a controversy and an agreement. It is not claimed (at least I have not heard it claimed by the honorable and able Senator from Ohio) that he reaches these combinations under any provision of the Constitution except that which confers jurisdiction upon the United States courts in controversies arising between citizens of different States. If that be true, then every particle of meat, every particle of efficiency, every particle of force in this bill disappears.

I am not to be told that because I am not willing to stand here and vote for a bill which is a snare and a delusion I am not therefore willing to do all in my power to put down these unlawful acts which are ruining the business and injuring the people of the country.

I think it highly appropriate that the bill should be referred to the Judiciary Committee, and it is no answer to that proposition to suggest, as the Senator from Alabama has done, that it is to be referred to a committee several of whose members are enemies of the bill. Any lawyer ought to be, not an enemy of the bill, but opposed to the bill, if he desires to do anything to remedy the evils which have been complained of.

How far the bill may represent the matured judgment of the Finance Committee we are not informed. Certainly one Senator upon the Finance Committee, and an able lawyer, has expressed his dissent from the bill. The other members of the Finance Committee, with the exception of the Senator from Ohio, have not spoken; but I apprehend that when they come to speak by their vote on the bill it will be seen that the bill represents, not a majority, but a decided minority of the Finance Committee.

I do not vote to refer the bill in any spirit of criticism of the Finance Committee, but I vote to refer it by reason of the difficulty of the subject, by reason of the honest doubts of Senators as to the method of relief proposed in the bill and the power of Congress to exercise such relief, because of the earnest desire on the part of members of the Senate to enact some legislation which shall be effectual. I think it ought to be referred to that committee which by common consent embraces the largest amount of judicial ability in the Senate; and to say that it is to be smothered there is to attack and impugn the motives of the honorable gentlemen who compose that committee. I have every confidence that that committee will deal with the subject; that if there is a constitutional way of reaching this difficulty, of remedying these evils, of punishing the men and the corporations who are engaged in these unlawful conspiracies and acts, it will be found out by that committee, and a bill framed along that line; and if there is none that they will say in their opinion there is none; and if that be true we had better face that proposition now than to deal in what in my judgment will be found, if this bill shall pass, to be nothing more nor less than a humbugging of the people of the United States.

I do not use that language imputing to the author of the bill or to anyone who may vote for it a desire to humbug the people of the United States, but in my judgment, after having given this matter careful attention and careful thought for two or three years' time, if we pass this bill we shall show the people of the United States who desire to have these evils remedied that we have passed a bill which is utterly powerless and inefficient to reach the evils, and then they will say that they have been humbugged, and they will say more than that, which will not be true, however, that they have been intentionally humbugged by the Congress of the United States. . . .

⊥ Mr. [WILLIAM D.] WASHBURN [R., Minn.]. I should like to ask the Senator ⊥2608 also if any special harm would come to the country or anybody else by the passage of the bill if it should be afterwards held to be unconstitutional by the Supreme Court of the United States. Would any damage be done to anybody?

Mr. PLATT. I pointed out one damage. Whenever Congress passes a bill which the concurrent sentiment of Congress believes to be unconstitutional it does a greater damage to the people of this country that is well to be calculated.

Mr. WASHBURN. I do not see how we are ever going to know whether this bill is constitutional or not until it has been referred to the Supreme Court. The most eminent lawyers in this Chamber differ in opinion, and it seems to me that we shall never reach any definite result until some law goes to the Supreme Court.

So far as I am concerned I know the sentiment of the country with regard to the question of monopolies and trusts, and I believe the people expect the Congress of the United States to make an attempt to secure some valid and satisfactory legislation. While the bill of the Senator from Ohio may not be perfect, while it may not reach every point, and may finally be declared unconstitutional, yet it is a move in the right direction, and for one I should dislike very much to have it sent to the Committee on the Judiciary, which would be sending it to "the tomb of the Capulets," I believe. I believe it would be sent there for that purpose, and I believe, furthermore, that when all other means fail to defeat a bill the constitutionality of it is usually invoked for that purpose. I hope that will not be done in this case. . . .

⊥2609   ⊥ Mr. MORGAN. . . .

I think there has been as much ingenious argumentation upon this question as I have ever heard in the same length of time in the Senate of the United States, and it has taxed the abilities of almost every gentleman on this floor to find out exactly what is the extent and boundary of our power and what are the lawful methods by which we can put it into exercise in the Federal courts. It is a very intricate subject, and, in my judgment, we are going entirely too fast if we do not get the opinion of our Judiciary Committee upon it.

There is a feature in this case that nobody has ever suggested, so far as I have heard, that has always struck me with a good deal of force. I think a proceeding *in rem* can be had under a libel for condemnation of goods, wares, and merchandise carried between the States, to seize, condemn, and confiscate goods that may have been manufactured under a conspiracy or bought and collected together under a conspiracy to control the markets. That subject seems not to have had any attention from Senators here. I never have proposed to myself to interfere in any way to try to make the legislation one thing or the other except so far as my mere vote would go, but it seems to me there is a field here for the enterprise of Senators.

Here is a sugar trust in New York. They say it consists of a number of corporations that are banded together, who have their local habitation in various different States; but they refine sugar under a combination that puts the price up to a certain figure and does not allow it to go any lower than that. Now, when their sugar is in transit from New York to Chicago, what is the reason why some person may not sieze [*sic*] it under a proceeding *in rem*, and in that way touch the very chord that would run to the heart of the whole establishment? Why could not that be done? It seems to me that is as easy a way to get at it as any you could mention, certainly far better than the declaration of nullity of the contract or referring some poor fellow who bought ten pounds to a Federal court somewhere to recover double damages according to the percentage of loss he sustained in the amount taxed upon him through the conspiracy. . . .[1.338]

⊥2610   ⊥ . . . There will not be a suit brought in twenty-five years to come under the bill of the Senator from Ohio, if it becomes a law. What does a man get? Double damages. For what? The enhanced price that he has to pay for a commodity in the market. You would never trace it back to them in the world. You have got to identify the sugar, or the molasses, or whatever it is, and run it back to the manufacturer or to the refiner and prove the conspiracy. There would not be a recovery in twenty-five years, and it is not expected that there would be. This bill does not contemplate such a thing. This bill is a good preface to an argument upon the protective tariff when that comes up: "We have sunk the trust question out of sight by a bill that has smothered it for the present."

Mr. SHERMAN. Why could not the Senator's friend in Alabama sue the combination in the courts of the United States and make them pay for all the damages he suffered?

Mr. MORGAN. In the courts of the United States?

[1.338] Senator Morgan proceeded to describe a case in Alabama involving an alleged predatory incident by the cottonseed oil trust.

Mr. SHERMAN. Certainly, why not? Why could not your citizens, whom you describe so pathetically, sue in the Federal court under this bill?

Mr. MORGAN. He would find, as everybody else would find under the bill of the Senator, that it is cheaper not to sue. It is not a pleasant thing to have a lawsuit. . . .

Mr. [ZEBULEN B.] VANCE [D., N.C.]. Mr. President, I never have a bill in which I feel any interest referred to this grand mausoleum of Senatorial literature, the Judiciary Committee, without feeling that I have attended a funeral. This occasion is no exception to that feeling. The grand air of magisterial dominion which surrounds those gentlemen who constitute that committee, the awful profundity and gravity with which they are enveloped, naturally tend to produce a funereal impression upon a serious mind, and the whole atmosphere seems to be resonant with the strains of that familiar old hymn:

> Hark! from the tombs a doleful sound;
> Mine ears attend the cry.
> Come, living men, and view the ground
> Where your bills must shortly lie.

[Laughter.] . . .

I am satisfied, sir, that when this bill does come back it will be so mutilated, that it will have everything that can possibly be of any benefit to the people of this country so entirely eliminated and eradicated, that it will for practical purposes not be worth the paper that it is written upon, and the country will so accept it. The country knows the receptacles where we deposit our dead by this time. We can no longer hope to conceal them. . . .

The VICE-PRESIDENT. Is the Senate ready for the question? The question is on the amendment offered by the Senator from Alabama [Mr. MORGAN] to the motion made by the Senator from Mississippi [Mr. GEORGE] to commit the bill to the Judiciary Committee.

Mr. GEORGE. I will accept the amendment if I have a right to do so.

The VICE-PRESIDENT. Is the Senate ready for the question?

Mr. SHERMAN. I ask for the yeas and nays.

The yeas and nays were ordered. . . .

Mr. INGALLS. Let the pending question be now stated.

The VICE-PRESIDENT. The Chair omitted to state that the amendment was instructing the committee to report within twenty days. The roll will be called.

The Secretary proceeded to call the roll. . . .

⊥ The result was announced—yeas 15, nays 28; as follows: . . . ⊥2611

So the motion to refer was not agreed to.

Mr. HOAR. What is now the pending question?

The VICE-PRESIDENT. The question now is on agreeing to the amendment submitted by the Senator from Texas [Mr. REAGAN].

Mr. HOAR. I inquire if that be an amendment to the entire bill, a substitute.

The VICE-PRESIDENT. It is not. . . .

The Chair will again state his understanding of the question before the Senate. It is on the amendment offered by the Senator from Texas, [Mr. REAGAN] to the substitute agreed upon for the original bill, adding new sections to the substitute accepted for the original bill.

It is not in any sense a substitute for the original bill, but an amendment to the substitute which was accepted in place of the original bill.

The Secretary proceeded to call the roll. . . .

The result was announced—yeas 34, nays 12, as follows: . . .

So the amendment was agreed to.

Mr. SHERMAN. Mr. President, I offer a proviso at the end of the first section of the bill reported by the Committee on Finance. I take this proviso from the amendment proposed by the Senator from Mississippi [Mr. GEORGE]. I do not think it necessary, but, at the same time to avoid any confusion, I submit it to come in at the end of the first section.

The CHIEF CLERK. It is proposed to add the following proviso to section 1:

Provided, That this act shall not be construed to apply to any arrangements, agreements, or combinations between laborers made with the view of lessening the number of hours of labor or of increasing their wages; nor to any arrangements, agreements, or combinations among persons engaged in horticulture or agriculture made with the view of enhancing the price of agricultural or horticultural products.

Mr. [PRESTON B.] PLUMB [R., Kan.]. Let me suggest to the Senator from Ohio that the word "their" should come in there, so that the limitation should be upon the exercise of the combination concerning their own products and nobody else's. The point is, if that is carried out, the provisions of the bill would not apply to a person who happened to own a ten-acre tract of land who is engaged in horticulture or agriculture. . . .

Mr. SHERMAN. The word "their" ought to be inserted before "labor" and also before "agricultural."

Mr. TELLER. I should like to suggest to the Senator from Ohio that he add there something about associations as well as combinations.

Mr. SHERMAN. I do not think those words describe the arrangement.

Mr. TURPIE. I think the amendment would be still clearer by inserting the word "own" after "their:" so as to read "their own."

Mr. SHERMAN. Yes, and inserting "associations," because that is what they are. . . .

⊥2612 ⊥ The VICE-PRESIDENT. The question is on the amendment offered by the Senator from Ohio [Mr. SHERMAN], which will be read again as modified:

The Chief Clerk read as follows:

Provided, That this act shall not be construed to apply to any arrangements, agreements, or combinations between laborers, made with the view of lessening the number of hours of their labor or of increasing their wages; nor to any arrangements, agreements, associations, or combinations among persons engaged in horticulture or agriculture, made with a view of enhancing the price of their own agricultural or horticultural products.

Mr. PLATT. I should like to inquire of the Senator from Ohio whether he understands by this language agricultural products would include wool. They have, I believe, a wool-growing association—

Mr. BLAIR. There are not many sheep in Connecticut.

Mr. SHERMAN. I think it would include their own wool. [Laughter.] . . .

The amendment was agreed to.

Mr. REAGAN. I desire to offer an amendment in line 4 of section 2 of the committee's bill. After "United States" I wish to add the words "or any State," and then in the next line to strike out the words "without respect to the amount involved;" so as to make the section read:

SEC. 2. That any person or corporation injured or damnified by such arrangement, contract, agreement, trust, or combination defined in the first section of this act may sue for and recover, in any court of the United States or any State of competent jurisdiction, of any person or corporation a party to a combination described in the first section of this act, twice the amount of damages sustained and the costs of the suit, together with a reasonable attorney's fee.

The object is, in the first place, to give concurrent jurisdiction to the State courts in civil suits; of course in criminal prosecutions that could not be done; and to that end it would be proper to strike out the words "without respect to the amount involved," because the law of the United States and of the States would fix the jurisdictional amount, and those words would not be necessary. . . .

Mr. SHERMAN. Those words were inserted with a view to giving a remedy to persons who had suffered in a minor degree. The jurisdictional amount in the courts of the United States is a pretty large sum; I understand $2,000 is the minimum, and it seemed to the Committee on Finance when this was inserted that to limit the jurisdiction to cases of $2,000 or over that amount would be to close the courts to most suitors. However, it is for the Senate to decide. . . .

Mr. TELLER. It strikes me that the words proposed to be stricken out are most desirable to be retained. We want to give the United States courts jurisdiction without reference to the amount involved. It is the subject-matter simply that we want the court to have jurisdiction of, and not the amount, and if we limit the amount there is not one man out of a hundred who are damaged who will ever have an opportunity of getting redress. It may be that there will not be a case prosecuted where there is a large amount of damage. It is to be presumed that there may be cases gotten up for the purpose of trying to abate what appears to be a sort of public nuisance. I think we had better let the parties go into court on any amount. If they are damaged by these proceedings which we are about to declare illegal, they ought to be allowed to sue, no matter what the amount of damage may be. I am opposed to the amendment.

Mr. PLATT. Mr. President, this is the old question which has been so frequently before Congress and before the Senate, where it is attempted to give State courts of all descriptions concurrent jurisidiction with the United States courts over remedies provided by United States statutes. It has, I think, never been done in Congress, though it has been often attempted. The result of it is to give every court in the United States, certainly every court that is a court of record, and justices of the peace, if they are courts of record, jurisdiction over remedies prescribed by United States statutes. I am opposed to it, as I have been in every case in which it has been attempted before Congress.

Mr. [CUSHMAN K.] DAVIS [R., Minn.]. I suppose the amendment would amount to this: That the statute creates a cause of action under certain circumstances, and, that being the case, it gives the right to assert that cause of action in any court of competent jurisdiction. It is not a question of whether the amount involved or the person suing is the jurisdictional test, but the creation by statute of the universal right of action under certain circumstances, which can be enforced in any court of competent jurisdiction, State or national, especially if the jurisdiction of the national court is not made exclusive by the terms of the bill.

Mr. REAGAN. There are a number of statutes which I can not refer to now, but I have referred to them heretofore, saying, in effect, that there are a number of subjects in which civil suits under United States authority may be maintained in the State courts.

Mr. HOAR. Cases of suits against national banks, for example.

Mr. REAGAN. Yes, sir, and a number of other subjects; so that I do not think there is any question about that. My reason for presenting this amendment is that under the original bill persons of moderate means would not be able to go into the Federal courts and employ lawyers and take witnesses there and prosecute suits, so that, while the bill would nominally afford a remedy for the evils, it would really be no remedy at all for the great class of persons who might be injured by the sort of things we are legislating against.

If the law is to be efficient to give a remedy, it seems to me it ought to be put in courts that will be accessible to litigants and as cheaply accessible to the litigants as we can make them. If, as suggested by the Senator from Colorado [Mr. TELLER], there is objection to striking out the words in the fifth line, I have no particular choice about that. I thought, perhaps, it would be safest to let the laws of the United States and of the States fix the jurisdictional amount, but if it is thought better that that part should stand as it is in the committee's bill, I have no objection. If any one objects, I will limit the amendment to the first part which I have proposed.

Mr. SPOONER. Let the amendment be again reported.

The VICE-PRESIDENT. The amendment will be again read.

The CHIEF CLERK. In line 4 of section 2, after "United States," it is proposed to insert "or any State;" so as to make the section read:

SEC. 2. That any person or corporation injured or damnified by such arrangement, contract, agreement, trust, or combination defined in the first section of this act may sue for and recover in any court of the United States or any State of competent jurisdiction without respect to the amount involved.

Mr. TELLER. I have no objection to the attempt to confer upon the State courts authority to hear these cases. Of course, that will depend upon what the State says about it. What I objected to was the provision striking out the words "without respect to the amount involved," in line 5.

Mr. SHERMAN. That part of the amendment is withdrawn.

Mr. TELLER. I was under the impression that the present statutes which require that there shall be a certain amount involved to give jurisdiction might be invoked against these claimants, and I think it would; but, if that is withdrawn, I have no objection to the rest of the amendment.

The VICE-PRESIDENT. The question is on agreeing to the amendment offered by the Senator from Texas [Mr. REAGAN] as modified.

The amendment was agreed to.

Mr. HOAR. I move now to strike out, beginning in line 4 of section 1 of the committee's substitute, from the word "corporations," at the end of that line, down to the word "thereof," in line 7, so that the bill will then punish these illegal combinations whether they are in the same State or in different States.

The VICE-PRESIDENT. The amendment will be reported.

The CHIEF CLERK. In line 4 of section 1, after the word "corporations," it is proposed to strike out all down to and including the word "thereof," in line 7, as follows:

Or both, of different States, or between two or more citizens or corporations, or both, of the United States and foreign states, or citizens or corporations thereof.

So as to read—

Mr. HOAR. Before the Secretary proceeds to read, I wish to say that the words "or both" should not be included in the language to be stricken out. The amendment should begin with the words "of different States," in the fifth line.

The CHIEF CLERK. So as to read:

That all arrangements, contracts, agreements, trusts, or combinations between two or more citizens or corporations, or both, made with a view or which tend to prevent full and free competition in the importation, transportation, or sale of articles imported into the United States, etc.

The amendment was agreed to.

Mr. INGALLS. What became of the amendment I offered some time since?

The VICE-PRESIDENT. The amendment next in order is the amendment of the Senator from Kansas [Mr. INGALLS], which will be read.

The CHIEF CLERK. It is proposed to add to the bill as new sections the following: . . .[1.339]

Mr. INGALLS. In section 4, after the first word "That," I ask leave to modify the amendment by inserting the following words:

For the purpose of preventing and suppressing, as far as may be, the dealing in options and futures as herein defined.

The PRESIDING OFFICER (Mr. CULLOM in the chair). The section will be read as modified by the Senator from Kansas.

The Chief Clerk read section 4 as modified, as follows:

SEC. —. That, for the purpose of preventing and suppressing, as far as may be, the dealing in options and futures as herein defined, special taxes are imposed as follows: Dealers in "options" or "futures" shall pay annually the sum of $1,000, and shall also pay the further sum of 5 cents per pound for each and every pound of cotton, or of beef, pork, lard, or other hog and cattle products, and the sum of 20 cents per bushel for each and every bushel of any of the articles mentioned in section 3 of this act, the right or privilege of delivering which may be acquired under any "options" contract or agreement, as defined by section 1 of this act, or which may be sold to be delivered at a future time or period under any "futures" contract or agreement as defined in section 2 of this act, which said amounts shall be paid to the collector of internal revenue, as hereinafter provided, and by him accounted for, as required in respect to other special taxes collected by him. Every person, association, copartnership, or corporation who shall, in their own behalf or as broker, agent, or employe of another, deal in "options," or make any "options" contract or agreement, as hereinbefore defined, shall be deemed a dealer in "options," and every person, association, copartnership, or corporation who shall, in their own behalf or as broker, agent, or employe of another, deal in "futures" or make any "futures" contract or agreement, as hereinbefore defined, shall be deemed a dealer in "futures." . . .

[1.339] The first three sections of Senator Ingalls' amendment, which appear *supra* at 129, were read at this point.

The PRESIDING OFFICER. If no further reading of the amendment be called for it will be dispensed with.

The remaining sections of the amendment are as follows: . . .[1.340]

Mr. HOAR. I should like to ask the Senator from Kansas whether it would not be best to insert in the second section:

Provided, That this [act] shall not apply to contracts or agreements for articles less than $50 in value to be delivered at one time.

Literally construed, this section would prohibit a man's grocer from engaging to deliver any farm product or articles in common family use. It seems to me there should be some limit in amount. I will suggest an amendment in these words:

Provided, That this act shall not apply to contracts for the delivery at any one time of articles less than $50 in value.

The PRESIDING OFFICER. The amendment to the amendment will be stated.

The CHIEF CLERK. It is proposed to add to section 2 the following proviso:

Provided, That this act shall not apply to contracts for the delivery at any one time of articles less than $50 in value.

The PRESIDING OFFICER. This amendment to the amendment will be considered adopted unless objection is made. The Chair hears no objection. The question now is on the adoption of the amendment offered by the Senator from Kansas as amended.

The amendment as amended was agreed to. . . .

Mr. [RICHARD] COKE [D., Tex.]. I desire, if I can get it in the proper shape, to offer what I send to the desk as additional sections to the bill.

The PRESIDING OFFICER. The amendment of the Senator from Texas [Mr. COKE] will be read.

The CHIEF CLERK. It is proposed to add to the bill the following:

That a trust is a combination of capital or skill by two or more persons, firms, or corporations for the purpose of creating or employing restrictions on trades or limiting the production, increasing or reducing the price of merchandise or commodities, or preventing competition in the making, manufacture, sale, or purchase of merchandise or commodities, or creating a monopoly in the manufacture, making, sale, or purchase of any merchandise or commodity with intent to forestall the market value of any merchandise or commodity.

SEC. —. That the formation or organization of a trust within the Territories of the United States or the District of Columbia is hereby declared to be against public policy and unlawful.

SEC. —. That any person acting in his own behalf or as the agent, attorney, or representative of any firm, copartnership, corporation, or any association whatsoever, who shall in any Territory or the District of Columbia aid in the organization of a trust, or who shall be a party thereto or in any manner interested therein, or who shall, after the passage of this act, knowingly aid in the business of a trust heretofore organized, or be in any way interested therein, shall be deemed guilty of a misdemeanor, and upon conviction thereof shall be fined not less than five hundred nor more than ten thousand dollars.

SEC. —. That all contracts made in either of the Territories of the United States or District of Columbia by a trust, or by any person, firm, or corporation acting for a trust in furtherance of the object of such trust, or in respect of the price or sum to be paid for any commodity or merchandise controlled or handled by such trust, are hereby declared to be illegal and against public policy.

SEC. —. That when any State shall declare, or heretofore has declared by law, trusts as defined by the true intent and meaning of this act to be unlawful and against public policy, it shall not be lawful thereafter for any person, firm, or corporation to cause to be transported any product or article covered or embraced by such trust from such State to or into any other State or Territory or the District of Columbia.

SEC. —. That any common carrier or agent of any common carrier who shall knowingly receive such product or commodity for transportation from such State into another State or Territory or the District of Columbia shall be deemed guilty of a misdemeanor, and upon

---

[1.340] Sections 5 through 11 of Senator Ingalls' amendment, which appear *supra* at 129–30, were printed at this point.

conviction thereof shall be fined not less than five hundred nor more then ten thousand dollars or shall be imprisoned for any period of time not less than one year or not more than five years, or by both such fine and imprisonment, in the discretion of the court. And any person who shall knowingly deliver to any common carrier, or agent thereof, any such product or commodity to be transported into another State or Territory or the District of Columbia shall be deemed guilty of a misdemeanor, and upon conviction thereof shall be fined in any sum not less than five hundred nor more than ten thousand dollars or by imprisonment for any period of time not less than one year nor more than five years, or by both such fine and imprisonment, in the discretion of the court.

SEC. —. That whenever the President of the United States shall be advised that a trust has been or is about to be organized for either of the purposes named in the first section of this act, and that a like product or commodity covered or proposed to be covered or handled by such trust, when produced out of the United States, is liable to an import duty when imported into the United States, he shall be, and is hereby, authorized and directed to suspend the operation of so much of the laws as impose a duty upon such product, commodity, or merchandise for such time as he may deem proper.

SEC. —. That all laws and parts of laws inconsistent with the provisions of this act be, and the same are hereby, repealed.[1.341] . . .

Mr. COKE. My proposed substitute was printed several days ago and laid upon the table. I desire to say a word or two in explanation of my reasons for offering it. It was my purpose to introduce it, if I could have done so, prior to the introduction of the amendment of the Senator from Kansas [Mr. INGALLS], because I did not wish to antagonize that amendment. This was intended as a substitute for the original bill and for any amendment which might be made to it, and I propose, if I can do so in accordance with parliamentary law, to so shape my action with reference to it as to seek to have this amendment, which I now propose, put in the place of the original bill and its amendments, except the amendment of the Senator from Kansas. As I said, I favor the amendment of the Senator from Kansas. I desire to put this measure in the place of the original bill as amended by the amendment of my colleague from Texas.[1.342] How I shall do that, I am not now fully advised, but I will attempt to do it in proper parliamentary form.

This amendment contains in its first clause a definition of trusts and combinations. It contains in its second clause a declaration that such trusts and combinations are contrary to public policy and unlawful. The third clause denounces the action of persons acting in their own behalf or as agents, attorneys, or representatives of any firm, copartnership, corporation, or any association whatsoever, who shall in any Territory or the District of Columbia aid in the organization of a trust, etc., and declares that such persons shall be guilty of a misdemeanor, and upon conviction thereof shall be fined not less than $500 nor more than $10,000.

In theory the amendment is operative only in the Territories and the District of Columbia until it gets to the fifth section, and that section declares:

SEC. 5. That when any State shall declare, or heretofore has declared by law, trusts as defined by the true intent and meaning of this act to be unlawful and against public policy, it shall not be lawful thereafter for any person, firm, or corporation to cause to be transported any product or article covered or embraced by such trust from such State to or into any other State or Territory or the District of Columbia.

Section 6 provides penalties for the breach of the other sections, making it a misdemeanor punishable by fine and by imprisonment in the penitentiary.

Section 7 is the section which requires the President of the United States, when advised that a trust has been or is about to be organized for either of the purposes named in the first section, to suspend the collection of import duties on articles the subject-matter of such trust.

There is no bill, there has been none before the Senate—and the bill which has already been adopted in the amended form now before the Senate is like all the

---

[1.341] The Coke amendment was never introduced as a Senate bill. It appears to have been heavily drawn from two House bills, H.R. 3925 (Representative Abbott) and H.R. 8980 (Representative Culberson), 51st Cong., 1st Sess. *See also supra* at 180–81, 192–95 (remarks of Senators Vest, Reagan, and Wilson).

[1.342] Mr. Reagan.

others—that is not seriously doubted as to its constitutionality by the legal talent of this body.

It is demonstrable that the bill of my colleague, as well as that of the Senator from Ohio, being the original bill amended by that of my colleague, is as liable to all of the objections made by the Senator from Mississippi [Mr. GEORGE] in his argument on this subject a few days ago as was the bill then before the Senate. A brief reference to the bill of my colleague will show this. Bearing in mind that interstate commerce commences only when the product gets into the hands of the common carrier for transportation to another State and ends as soon as it reaches its destination there, I call attention to some of the provisions of the amendment submitted by my colleague. The first thing denounced is:

First. To create or carry out any restrictions in trade.

Restrictions in trade is a very general proposition. There may possibly be found some restrictions in commerce after the product has gotten into the interstate channel, but it will be extremely rare that such will be the case. Restrictions, if any, will occur almost universally before the product goes into commerce at all and when under State jurisdiction, out of the reach of Congressional legislation.

Second. To limit or reduce the production or to increase or reduce the price of merchandise or commodities.

These things must result from the production of the commodities or the suppression of their production in the States. They must occur before interstate commerce commences in the commodities, and therefore outside of and beyond the jurisdiction of Congress, and wholly under State jurisdiction.

Third. To prevent competition in the manufacture, making, purchase, sale, or transportation of merchandise, produce, or commodities.

How is competition to be prevented? Every combination must have a local habitation and a name. It must be in a State, and of course under the local jurisdiction. All the conditions denounced in that clause are things that must necessarily occur before the product gets into the channel of interstate commerce where the jurisdiction of Congress can take hold of it.

Fourth. To fix a standard or figure whereby the price to the public shall be in any manner controlled or established of any article, commodity, merchandise, produce, or commerce intended for sale, use, or consumption.

All the things forbidden in this bill are acts. They are acts which are done in a State, under State, not Congressional, jurisdiction, and are acts which are done before the products get into interstate commerce, and therefore before they come under the jurisdiction of Congress. The intention to do these things contravenes no law. The intention amounts to nothing. Although there may be goods manufactured on one bank of the Mississippi River, in St. Louis, intended to be transported for consumption across into Illinois, that intention cuts no figure whatever in the consideration of the transaction until the goods are actually put into the hands of the common carrier to be taken over the Mississippi River, and as soon as they land in the State of Illinois are again outside of Congressional jurisdiction, and under the State jurisdiction of Illinois.

You may take the bill of my colleague, you may take the bill of the Senator from Ohio, examine them and test them under the rulings of the Supreme Court which we have heard cited here, and they are clearly and, as it seems to me, grossly unconstitutional. I want a bill that will stand. I want a bill that shall not be a promise to be broken, that shall not be a delusion and a sham.

Mr. President, the bill of my colleague is infinitely better and stronger than that of the Senator from Ohio. There is greatly more force and vitality in it, and yet I challenge any man to answer the arguments which can be made against its constitutionality. If you read the different propositions contained in the first, second, third, fourth, and fifth clauses they are plausible, but will not bear analysis or close inspection.

We are all working for the same end. We are all desiring the same purpose. We all want a bill that will accomplish some good, that will relieve the people of the robbery being perpetrated on them, one that the Supreme Court will sustain; and hence we have been offering amendments and suggestions with reference to the subject.

The measure which I have offered I believe to be clear of any constitutional objection. I believe it would be sustained by the Supreme Court. It co-operates with the States, it invokes the power and authority of the States in their own behalf, and does not act upon a State except in aid of her own action.

If there is a State that has not acted, the people of that State will see that they should act in order to get the benefit of the protection of this law if it shall be passed by Congress. If they want the protection they will enact statutes on this subject.

We have all seen that Congress has not the power to deal fully with this subject. My amendment exhausts the power of Congress, and then uses all the aid the States can give in order to carry out its purpose. . . .

⊥2615 ⊥ Mr. BLAIR. . . . I should like to know whether in striking out it strikes out all but the amendment of the Senator from Kansas. If so, what, then, will become of the proviso of the Senator from Ohio, exempting the farmers from prosecution for combinations and trusts and the like?

Mr. COKE. We will not strike that out. I did not propose to strike that out.

Mr. BLAIR. I thought the line was very strictly drawn.

Mr. COKE. I say my colleague's bill is stronger than that of the Senator from Ohio. I regard the bill of the Senator from Ohio as being almost without a clause for its enforcement.

The last section of his bill reads thus:

> SEC. 2. That any person or corporation injured or damnified by such arrangement, contract, agreement, trust, or combination defined in the first section of this act may sue for and recover, in any court of the United States of competent jurisdiction, without respect to the amount involved, of any person or corporation, a party to a combination described in the first section of this act, twice the amount of damages sustained and the costs of the suit, together with a reasonable attorney's fee.

How would a citizen who has been plundered in his family consumption of sugar by the sugar trust, or in his consumption of cotton-bagging under the trust covering that indispensable article, or in his consumption of iron or steel by the iron and steel trust recover his damages under that clause? It is simply an impossible remedy offered him. The bill is as vague as the world.

Mr. BLAIR. Without form and void?

Mr. COKE. I do not believe that a recovery can be had under it. It is a wasp without a sting; it is a law without a clause for its enforcement. If the party damnified, as has been said heretofore in this debate, were a great corporation, a wealthy association, it could employ lawyers and perhaps be able to show some direct damage, but how could the consumers of the articles produced by these trusts, the great mass of our people—the individuals—go about showing the damages they had suffered?

How would they establish the damage which they had sustained so as to get a judgment under this bill? I do not believe they could do it. I do not believe it is possible to do it. I think the constituents of all of us, the consumers of products which are raised and manufactured in this country, would be absolutely without a remedy under the bill of the Senator from Ohio. The bill of my colleague is more specific and contains clauses under which it can be strictly and fully enforced if the courts should hold it constitutional. But, as I remarked before, I do not think that either of these bills is constitutional and I have offered this amendment hoping that it may be adopted. . . .

The PRESIDING OFFICER. The question is on the amendment of the Senator from Texas [Mr. COKE] to strike out all of the original bill after the enacting clause and the amendments heretofore adopted, except that offered by the Senator from Kansas [Mr. INGALLS], and insert the amendment last read in lieu thereof.

Mr. COKE. I do not mean to strike out the proviso adopted on the motion of the Senator from Ohio [Mr. SHERMAN].

Mr. SHERMAN. I move that the amendment lie on the table. . . .

The PRESIDING OFFICER. . . . The motion is to lay the amendment on the table. The Secretary will call the roll on that motion.

The Secretary proceeded to call the roll. . . .

The result was announced—yeas 26, nays 16; as follows: . . .

⊥ So the motion to lay on the table was agreed to. ⊥2616

The PRESIDING OFFICER. Are there further amendments in Committee of the Whole?

Mr. GEORGE. Mr. President, I gave notice of an amendment and had it printed, which I intended to offer, but substantially the proposition of that amendment is contained in the amendment of the Senator from Texas [Mr. COKE], and as that had been voted down I do not wish to detain the Senate by offering the amendment of which I gave notice.

Mr. STEWART. I offer an amendment to come in in section 1, line 20, after the word "articles," by inserting "or of the value of money by which such cost may be advanced or reduced." . . .

Mr. HOAR. I move to amend, and give notice of a motion to amend, after the word "money," by inserting "or of gold or silver." . . .

Mr. STEWART. I wish to make a remark in regard to my amendment. It is offered in as good faith as anything in this bill. Every time there is a scheme to affect the price of products, the first thing that is done is for the operators to form a combination to borrow the money from the banks, lock it up, and so make money tight, and they make it a regular business in every gambling center in the United States by forming combinations of that character. . . .

The PRESIDING OFFICER. The amendment as proposed to be amended will be read.

The CHIEF CLERK. In the proposed amendment, after the word "money," it is proposed to insert the words "or of gold or silver;" so that the amendment as amended will read:

Or of the value of money or of gold or silver by which such cost may be advanced or reduced. . . .

Mr. STEWART. I think that confuses it. My amendment is simply directed against combinations in money for the purpose of affecting prices as part of a gambling scheme.

Mr. HOAR. Will the Senator from Nevada inform the Senate why an unlawful combination of this kind to raise the price of gold or silver is not as reprehensible as anything in this bill?

Mr. PLATT. That is already in the bill.

Mr. STEWART. But it appears that the Government by law is engaged in raising the price of gold and depressing the price of silver. You will have to make it unlawful for the United States to do that. . . .

Mr. TELLER. Mr. President, it is quite evident that we can not finish this bill tonight, and I move that the Senate do now adjourn.

Mr. SPOONER. I ask the Senator to yield to me to have an order made that this bill and the amendments may be printed. . . .

The PRESIDING OFFICER. The Senator from Wisconsin [Mr. SPOONER] has asked that the bill may be printed with the amendments. That order will be made, if there be no objection.

Mr. SHERMAN. I have no objection to having the bill and amendments printed, but I hope the Senate will be ready to say that at a certain hour to-morrow the debate shall close and the vote be taken.

S. 1 AS AMENDED BY THE SENATE
51st Cong., 1st Sess.
March 25, 1890

⊥ Ordered to be reprinted as amended.

A BILL

To declare unlawful trusts and combinations in restraint of trade and production.

Be it enacted by the Senate and House of Representatives of the United States of America in Congress assembled, That all arrangements, contracts, agreements, trusts, or combinations between two or more citizens or corporations, or both, made with a view or which tend to prevent full and free competition in the importation, transportation, or sale of articles imported into the United States; or with a view or which tend to prevent full and free competition in articles of growth, production, or manufacture of any State or Territory of the United States with similar articles of the growth, production, or manufacture of any other State or Territory, or in the transportation or sale of like articles, the production of any State or Territory of the United States, into or within any other State or Territory of the United States; and all arrangements, trusts, or combinations between such citizens or corporations made with a view or which tend to advance the cost to the consumer of any such articles are hereby declared to be against public policy, unlawful, and void. And the circuit court of the United States shall have original jurisdiction of all suits of a civil nature at common law or in equity arising under this section and to issue all remedial process, orders, or writs proper and necessary to enforce its provisions. And the Attorney-General and the several district attorneys are hereby directed, in the name of the United States, to commence and prosecute all such cases to final judgment and execution: *Provided,* That this act shall not be construed to apply to any arrangements, agreements, or combinations between laborers made with the view of lessening the number of hours of their labor or of increasing their wages; nor to any arrangements, agreements, associations, or combinations among persons engaged in horticulture or agriculture made with the view of enhancing the price of their own agricultural or horticultural products.

SEC. 2. That any person or corporation injured or damnified by such arrangement, contract, agreement, trust, or combination defined in the first section of this act may sue for and recover, in any court of the United States or any State of competent jurisdiction, without respect to the amount involved, of any person or corporation a party to a combination described in the first section of this act twice the amount of damages sustained and the costs of the suit, together with a reasonable attorney's fee.

SEC. 3. That all persons engaged in the creation of any trust, or as owner or part owner, agent, or manager of any trust, employed in any business carried on with any foreign country, or between the States, or between any State and the District of Columbia, or between any State and any Territory of the United States, or any owner or part owner, agent, or manager of any corporation, company, or person employed in any such business using its powers for either of the purposes specified in the fourth section of this act, shall be deemed guilty of a high misdemeanor, and, on conviction thereof, shall be fined in a sum not exceeding ten thousand dollars, or imprisonment at hard labor in the penitentiary not exceeding five years, or by both of said penalties, in the discretion of the court trying the same.

SEC. 4. That a trust is a combination of capital, skill, or acts by two or more persons, firms, corporations, or associations of persons, or of any two or more of them for either, any, or all of the following purposes:

First. To create or carry out any restrictions in trade.

Second. To limit or reduce the production or to increase or reduce the price of merchandise or commodities.

Third. To prevent competition in the manufacture, making, purchase, sale, or transportation of merchandise, produce, or commodities.

Fourth. To fix a standard or figure whereby the price to the public shall be in any manner controlled or established of any article, commodity, merchandise, produce, or commerce intended for sale, use, or consumption.

Fifth. To create a monopoly in the making, manufacture, purchase, sale, or transportation of any merchandise, article, produce, or commodity.

Sixth. To make, or enter into, or execute, or carry out any contract, obligation, or agreement of any kind or description by which they shall bind, or shall have bound themselves, not to manufacture, sell, dispose of, or transport any article or commodity, or article of trade, use, merchandise, or consumption below a common standard figure, or by which they shall agree, in any manner, to keep the price of such article, commodity, or transportation at a fixed or graduated figure, or by which they shall in any manner establish or settle the price of any article, commodity, or transportation between themselves, or between themselves and others, so as to preclude free and unrestricted competition among themselves and others in the sale and transportation of any such article or commodity, or by which they shall agree to pool, combine, or unite in any interest they may have in connection with the sale or transportation of any such article or commodity that its price may in any manner be so affected.

SEC. 5. That each day any of the persons, associations, or corporations aforesaid shall be engaged in violating the provisions of this act shall be held to be a separate offense.

SEC. 6. That for the purposes of this act the word "options" shall be understood to mean any contract or agreement whereby a party thereto, or any person, corporation, partnership, or association, for whom or in whose behalf such contract or agreement is made, acquires the right or privilege, but is not thereby obligated, to deliver to another at a future time or period any of the articles mentioned in section three of this act.

SEC. 7. That for the purposes of this act the word "futures" shall be understood to mean any contract or agreement whereby a party agrees to sell and deliver at a future time to another any of the articles mentioned in section three of this act when at the time of making such contract or agreement the party so agreeing to make such delivery, or the party for whom he acts as agent, broker, or employee in making such contract or agreement, is not at the time of making the same the owner of the article so contracted and agreed to be delivered: *Provided,* That this act shall not apply to contracts for the delivery at any one time of articles of not more than fifty dollars in value.

SEC. 8. That the articles to which the foregoing sections relate are wheat, corn, oats, rye, barley, cotton, and all other farm products; also beef, pork, lard, and all other hog and cattle products.

SEC. 9. That for the purpose of preventing and suppressing, as far as may be, the dealing in options and futures as herein defined, special taxes are imposed as follows: Dealers in "options" or "futures" shall pay annually the sum of one thousand dollars, and shall also pay the further sum of five cents per pound for each and every pound of cotton or of beef, pork, lard, or other hog and cattle products, and the sum of twenty cents per bushel for each and every bushel of any of the articles mentioned in section three of this act, the right or privilege of delivering which may be acquired under any "options" contract or agreement, as defined by section one of this act, or which may be sold to be delivered at a future time or period under any "futures" contract or agreement as defined in section two of this act, which said amounts shall be paid to the collector of internal revenue, as hereinafter provided, and by him accounted for, as required in respect to other special taxes collected by him. Every person, association, copartnership, or corporation who shall, in their own behalf, or as broker, agent, or employee of another, deal in "options," or make any "options" contract or agreement, as hereinbefore defined, shall be deemed a dealer in "options," and every person, association, copartnership, or corporation who shall, in their own behalf, or as broker, agent, or employee of another, deal in "futures," or make any "futures" contract or agreement, as hereinbefore defined, shall be deemed a dealer in "futures."

SEC. 10. That every person, association, copartnership, or corporation engaged in, or proposing to engage in, the business of dealer in "options" or of dealer in "futures," as hereinbefore defined, shall, before commencing such business or making any such "options" or "futures" contract or agreement, make application in writing to the collector of internal revenue for the district in which he proposes to engage in such business or make such contract or agreement, setting forth the name of the person, association, partnership, or corporation, place of residence of the applicant, the business engaged in, and where such business is to be carried on, and in case of partnership, association, or corporation, the names and places of residence of the several persons constituting the same, and shall thereupon pay to such collector the sum aforesaid of one thousand dollars, and shall also execute and deliver to such collector a bond in the penal sum of fifty thousand dollars with two or more sureties satisfactory to the collector, conditioned upon the full and faithful compliance by the obligor therein with all the requirements of this act. And thereupon the collector shall issue to such applicant a certificate in such form as the Commissioner of Internal Revenue shall prescribe, that such applicant is authorized for the period of one year from the date of such certificate to be a dealer in "options" or "futures" and to make "options" or "futures" contracts or agreements, as hereinbefore defined; and for the period specified in such certificate the party to whom it is issued may conduct the business of dealer as aforesaid. Such certificate may be renewed annually upon the compliance with the provisions of this act, and any "options" or "futures" contract or agreement as defined by this act shall be absolutely void between the parties thereto and their respective assigns, unless the party making such contract or agreement shall have at the time of making the same a certificate as aforesaid authorizing the making thereof.

SEC. 11. That it shall be the duty of the collector to keep in his office a register containing a copy of each and every application made to him under the foregoing section and a statement in connection therewith as to whether a certificate had been issued thereon and for what period, which book or register shall be a public record and be subject to inspection of any and all persons desiring to examine the same.

SEC. 12. That every "options" or "futures" contract or agreement as hereinbefore defined shall be in writing and signed in duplicate by the parties making the same; and any such contract or agreement not so made and signed shall, as between the parties thereto and their assigns, be absolutely void.

SEC. 13. That it shall be the duty of every person, copartnership, association, or corporation, on the first day of the week next succeeding the date of the certificate issued to them, and on the first day of each and every week thereafter, to make to the collector of the district in which any "options" or "futures" contract or agreement has been made full and complete return and report under oath of any and all such contracts or agreements made or entered into by such person, copartnership, association, or corporation during the previous week, together with a statement of the article or articles embraced in or covered by such contracts or agreements, and the amounts, respectively, of each, and the name of the party or parties with whom such contracts or agreements have been made, and at the same time to pay to such collector the amount of the tax hereinbefore required of five cents per pound on each and every pound of cotton, and of beef, pork, lard, or any other hog and cattle products, and of twenty cents per bushel on each and every bushel of any of the other articles mentioned in section three of this act, which are the subject of or covered by such contracts or agreements, or any of them, for which sums such collector shall give his receipt to the party so paying, and the sums so collected shall be accounted for by the collector as provided by law in respect to other taxes collected by him.

SEC. 14. That every person who shall in his own behalf, or in behalf of any other person, association, partnership, or corporation, enter into any "options" or "futures" contract or agreement as defined by this act, without having a certificate of authority from the collector as hereinbefore provided, and covering the time at which such contract or agreement shall be made, shall, besides being liable for the amounts prescribed in section four of this act, be fined not less than five thousand dollars and not more than ten thousand dollars for each and every such offense. And every person who shall make to the collector a false or fraudulent return or report required by section eight of this act shall be subject to a fine of not less than five thousand dollars nor more than ten thousand dollars, or to imprisonment for not less than six months or more than two years, or to both such fine and imprisonment.

SEC. 15. That neither the payment of the taxes required or the certificate issued by the collector under this act shall be held to legalize dealing in "options" and "futures," nor to exempt any person, association, copartnership, or corporation from any penalty or punishment now or hereafter provided by the laws of any State for making contracts or agreements such as are hereinbefore defined as "options" o [sic] "futures" contracts or agreements, or in any manner to authorize the making of such contracts or agreements within any State or locality contrary to the laws of such State or locality; nor shall the payment of the taxes imposed by this act be held to prohibit any State or municipality from placing a tax or duty on the same trade, transaction, or business for State, municipal, or other purposes.

SEC. 16. That section thirty-two hundred and nine of the Revised Statutes of the United States is, so far as applicable, made to extend and apply to the taxes imposed by this act and to the persons upon whom they are imposed.

SENATE DEBATE
51st Cong., 1st Sess.
March 26, 1890

21 CONG. REC. 2639

The Senate, as in Committee of the Whole, resumed the consideration of the bill (S. 1) to declare unlawful trusts and combinations in restraint of trade and production.

Mr. SHERMAN. There are one or two verbal amendments that I should like to have made. They are made necessary by the amendments agreed to yesterday. In line 4 of the first section of the reprinted bill I move to strike out the word "citizens" and insert the word "persons."

The amendment was agreed to.

Mr. SHERMAN. In line 15 of the first section I move to strike out the word "citizens" and insert the word "persons."

The amendment was agreed to.

Mr. SHERMAN. There is an amendment prepared by the Senator from Wisconsin [Mr. SPOONER] to come in on line 26. If he is ready to offer it now, I should be very glad to have it presented.

Mr. SPOONER. I offer the amendment which I send to the desk to come in after the word "execution" in line 26 of section 1.

Mr. INGALLS. Is that an amendment of substance?

Mr. SPOONER. I think it is.

Mr. INGALLS. If the Senator will allow me a few moments, I wish to offer certain amendments which are rendered necessary by the change in the enumeration of the sections. . . .[1.343]

⊥ Mr. VEST. Does that conclude the amendments?   ⊥2640

Mr. SHERMAN. No; there is another amendment to be offered by the Senator from Wisconsin [Mr. SPOONER].

The VICE-PRESIDENT. There is an amendment, and there is also an amendment to an amendment pending now. Yesterday the Senator from Nevada [Mr. STEWART] offered an amendment, to which the Senator from Massachusetts [Mr. HOAR] proposed an amendment. The amendment and the amendment to the amendment will be read.

Mr. HOAR. I will withdraw the amendment to the amendment.

The VICE-PRESIDENT. The amendment proposed by the Senator from Massachusetts to the amendment offered by the Senator from Nevada is withdrawn. . . .

The pending amendment, offered by the Senator from Nevada, will be read.

The CHIEF CLERK. On page 2, section 1, line 17, of the reprinted bill, after the word "articles," insert the words "or of the value of money by which such cost may be advanced or reduced;" so as to read:

And all arrangements, trusts, or combinations between such persons or corporations made with a view or which tend to advance the cost to the consumer of any such articles, or of the value of money by which such cost may be advanced or reduced, are hereby declared to be against public policy, unlawful, and void.

The VICE-PRESIDENT. The question is on agreeing to the amendment offered by the Senator from Nevada [Mr. STEWART].

The amendment was agreed to. . . .

Mr. SPOONER. I offer now the amendment which I send to the desk, to come in after the word "execution," in the twenty-sixth line of section one of the reprint.

[1.343] Several technical and renumbering amendments were agreed to at this point.

The VICE-PRESIDENT. The amendment will be read.

The CHIEF CLERK. In section one, line 26, of the reprinted bill, after the word "execution," insert:

> And whenever in any action commenced under the provisions of this act in the name of the United States any arrangement, trust, or combination herein declared void is found by any such court to exist, the court may, in addition to other remedies, issue its writ of injunction, temporary or final, running and to be served anywhere within the jurisdiction of the United States, prohibiting and restraining the defendants or any thereof, or their or any of their servants, agents, or attorneys, from proceeding further in the business of said arrangement, trust, or combination, except to wind up its affairs; and in case of any disobedience of any such writ of injunction or other proper process, mandatory or otherwise, issued in any such cause, it shall be lawful for said court to issue writs of attachment, running and to be served anywhere within the United States, against the defendants or any thereof, and against their or any of their agents, attorneys, or servants, of whatever name or office, disobeying said injunction or other process; and the court may, if it shall think fit, in addition to fine or imprisonment for contempt, make an order directing any such defendants disobeying such writ of injunction or other process to pay such sum of money, not exceeding $1,000, for every day after a date to be named in such order that such defendant or defendants or their or any of their agents, attorneys, or servants as aforesaid shall refuse or neglect to obey such injunction or other process; and such money shall be paid into court, and may be paid in whole or in part to the party or parties upon whose complaint said action was instituted, or into the Treasury of the United States, as the court shall direct. And in any action brought by the United States under the provisions of this act the Attorney-General may bring the action in any district in which anyone of the parties defendant resides or transacts business, and any other parties, corporate or otherwise, may, regardless of residence or location of business, be brought into court in said action in the manner provided by section 738 of the Revised Statutes, and the court shall thereupon have jurisdiction of the defendant or defendants so brought in, as fully to all intents and purposes as if they had appeared in said action.

Mr. SPOONER. Mr. President, I offer this amendment to cure what seems to me to be a very great defect in the bill. Most if not all of the combinations, however they may be called, aimed at by the bill, are detrimental to the public interest. I think of them all it will be agreed that two of them, whose ramifications extend throughout the whole country and who directly affect the people generally in the country, the sugar trust and what is called the beef combine, are infamous in their oppression, the sugar trust dealing with an article which goes into the daily consumption of the people, which goes into every house, to every family. I believe 52 pounds per year per capita are used by the people of the United States. The object of this trust is to keep up to consumers the price of sugar. The beef combine, with which the Senator from Missouri [Mr. VEST] has been endeavoring to deal, has been so successful as to maintain at the war rate the price of beef to consumers throughout the United States, and to depress it among those, the farmers and others, who raise cattle, so as to render that industry no longer a profitable one.

The sugar trust is made up, as I understand it, of seventeen different corporations, some of them citizens of different States. Manifestly to deal efficiently with a trust or combination of that character it must be possible to bring into one action, into one court, the essential parties defendant. One of the arguments made by the Senator from Ohio in favor of this bill was that there might be under its provisions such a concentration of defendants; but as the law stands to-day there could be none, and I desire to call the attention of the Senate for a moment to the sections of the Revised Statutes bearing upon the subject. Section 737 provides:

> SEC. 737. When there are several defendants in any suit at law or in equity, and one or more of them are neither inhabitants of nor found within the district in which the suit is brought, and do not voluntarily appear, the court may entertain jurisdiction, and proceed to the trial and adjudication of the suit between the parties who are properly before it; but the judgment or decree rendered therein shall not conclude or prejudice other parties not regularly served with process nor voluntarily appearing to answer; and non-joinder of parties who are not inhabitants of nor found within the district, as aforesaid, shall not constitute matter of abatement or objection to the suit.[1.344]

[1.344] Act of Feb. 28, 1839, ch. 36, § 1, 5 Stat. 321.

Whoever may be parties defendant in the action, under that section the court might proceed as to those within the jurisdiction; but its judgment could have no effect whatever upon those not served or not voluntarily appearing.

Section 738 provides: [1.345]

SEC. 738. When any defendant in a suit in equity to enforce any legal or equitable lien or claim against real or personal property within the district where the suit is brought—

And it was amended[1.346] so as to include suits brought to remove a cloud upon title to land in a district—

is not an inhabitant of nor found within the said district, and does not voluntarily appear thereto, it shall be lawful for the court to make an order directing such absent defendant to appear, plead, answer, or demur to the complainant's bill at a certain day, therein to be designated.

Then follows a provision for obtaining jurisdiction in a mode to be pointed out by the order of publication or otherwise:

But the said adjudication shall, as regards such absent defendant without appearance, affect his property within such district only.

Then comes this section, to which I call the attention of the Senator from Ohio:

SEC. 739. Except in the cases provided in the next three sections, no person shall be arrested in one district for trial in another, in any civil action before a circuit or district court; and except in the said cases and the cases provided by the preceding section, no civil suit shall be brought before either of said courts against an inhabitant of the United States, by any original process, in any other district than that of which he is an inhabitant or in which he is found at the time of serving the writ.

One object of the amendment is to provide that the court may bring in these parties wherever they reside or wherever they are doing business and have as full and complete jurisdiction over them upon publication as if they voluntarily appeared in the action. This provision I regard as absolutely essential to the efficiency of the bill.

Another matter which is covered by the amendment is this. For myself, I think the efficacious remedy will be found to be, not the criminal prosecution provided for by the Senator from Texas [Mr. REAGAN], but the vigorous and drastic use of the writ of injunction. Under the law as it stands to-day that writ can only be served and punishment for its disobedience enforced within the district over which the court has jurisdiction. By the amendment which I have sent to the desk, this writ of injunction may be served anywhere within the United States and if it is disobeyed the attachment for contempt may be served anywhere within the United States. I think the amendment ought to be adopted. . . .

Mr. [GEORGE] GRAY [D., Del.]. Mr. President, I did not have the pleasure of hearing the remarks of the Senator from Wisconsin, explanatory, I suppose, of this amendment, owing to the confusion in the Chamber; but so far as I can understand the amendment proposed by him as just read at the desk, it is that when jurisdiction once is obtained by a court there shall be attached also these additional remedies, a general power to issue remedial process by injunction and otherwise, which are recited in the amendment of the Senator, process and remedies which I agree with him in thinking would be exceedingly important to effect any proper object under this bill. But I should like to ask the Senator from Wisconsin, who has no doubt studied carefully the provisions to which he has offered the amendment, as to the clause he seeks to amend, commencing at line 18 of the first section of the bill and reading as follows:

And the circuit court of the United States shall have original jurisdiction of all suits of a civil nature at common law or in equity arising under this section, and to issue all remedial process, orders, or writs proper and necessary to enforce its provisions. And the Attorney-General and the several district attorneys are hereby directed, in the name of the United States, to commence and prosecute all such cases to final judgment and execution.

[1.345] Act of June 1, 1872, ch. 255, § 1, 17 Stat. 198.

[1.346] Act of March 3, 1875, ch. 137, § 8, 18 Stat. 472.

I should like to ask him how under that language, taken in connection with what precedes it in the prior part of the first section, the court is in the first place to obtain any jurisdiction of any matter or thing or parties with reference to the subject of this first section. The Senator will remember the previous part of the first section declares:

> That all arrangements, contracts, agreements, trusts, or combinations between two or more citizens or corporations, or both, made with a view or which tend to prevent full and free competition in the importation, transportation, or sale of articles imported into the United States.

And so on; I do not read further. These arrangements, etc., are declared to be against public policy, unlawful, and void; and then the section goes on to declare in the language that I have just read that the circuit courts of the United States shall have original jurisdiction of all suits of a civil nature at common law and in equity. I ask the Senator how that jurisdiction is to be invoked? What is to be the *lis mota* in any circuit court of the United States whereby the provisions of this first section shall be brought into activity? I grant you that when jurisdiction has attached the amendment offered by the Senator from Wisconsin would be exceedingly important in rendering thorough and effectual that jurisdiction; but I do not understand how or under what circumstances the circuit court of the United States is to obtain the jurisdiction spoken of in the language which the Senator seeks to amend.

Mr. SPOONER. Mr. President, the observations submitted by the Senator from Delaware are aimed really not at the amendment which I have offered, as it seems to me—

Mr. GRAY. Not at all. I was asking for information.

Mr. SPOONER. But at the bill. I have some doubts about the efficacy of the section. I should have been glad, for I want the best bill that can be drawn, if this bill had been in the first instance—and I say that with all due respect to the Senator from Ohio and the Committee on Finance—referred to the Committee on the Judiciary, in order that it might receive from that committee careful examination and study. I think it will be agreed that no subject has been brought before the Senate involving questions of law of a more complicated character and more difficult of solution than the propositions involved in this bill.

The Senate saw fit yesterday to reject the proposition to refer the bill to the Committee on the Judiciary, and in view of the protest made by the Senator from Ohio on behalf of the Committee on Finance I voted against the reference. I am assuming that the bill will be a constitutional enactment and that it will give to the circuit courts of the United States jurisdiction at the suit of the United States to dissolve, suppress, and enjoin these combinations which are declared by this bill to be void, as against public policy. . . .

Mr. PUGH. Would not the court under the general jurisdiction already conferred by the bill have the power to issue any remedial process?

Mr. SPOONER. Of course, in any case in which the court would have jurisdiction, the suit being in equity, the court would have the power to issue remedial writs within its territorial jurisdiction.

Mr. PUGH. Then what is the necessity for the amendment of the Senator from Wisconsin?

Mr. SPOONER. I will explain again to the Senator from Alabama. How far this bill will give jurisdiction in any case in which the United States courts are not now possessed of it, I do not undertake now to say.

The bill declares certain trusts, combinations, and agreements void. It gives the circuit courts of the United States original jurisdiction of all suits of a civil nature at common law or in equity arising under this section. That would include, of course, controversies between citizens of different States.

Mr. GRAY. That is just the point if the Senator will allow me: How shall a suit at common law or in equity, arising under this section be brought?

Mr. SPOONER. It is not my province to attempt now to satisfy the Senator on that question, for I am only discussing my amendment. I am only, on the assumption that there is something of substance in this bill, endeavoring to incorporate in it a provision without which, to my mind, it will be in any event utterly without strength or efficiency. . . .

Mr. HOAR. I rise to ask the Senator from Wisconsin a question in reference to his amendment. I understand that the amendment assumes that somehow or other the court has obtained jurisdiction, and that it has found that somewhere in the United States this offense or injury has been committed. Then it issues an injunction. The court may be held in Maine and the party against whom the injunction is to issue, or the transaction which it strikes at, the business which it strikes at, may have been carried on or performed in California in whole or in part. Now, the amendment of the Senator, as I heard it read and as I read it, provides that the court shall have jurisdiction and shall have power to punish by fine and imprisonment for contempt for the disobedience of its orders. For the purposes of my question we may concede legality, constitutionality, and the wisdom of the section up to that point, without going into any such question. Now, the Senator, in addition to that, if I understand his amendment, says that the court shall have power to order a penalty for the carrying on of the business of $1,000 a day.

Now, that is a clear penalty and nothing but a penalty for an offense. It is a part of the civil remedy of the individual who suffers; it is not the sum which is to be recovered by the United States if it has suffered in any of its properties or functions which would make it a suitor for it to assert its own rights, but it is a clear, sheer penalty. The contempt of court has been satisfied previously by the assumption of the amendment. The injury to the United States or to anybody else in the way of property or business or any other material necessity is satisfied in another way. Then is this anything more than asserting the principle that you may enforce the penal or criminal laws of the United States by getting an injunction against a man in advance against offending against those criminal or penal laws and having judgment without a jury and punish him by a fine of $1,000 for every day? You are not trying that offense; or rather I put that question to the Senate at this point. You are not trying that offense in the vicinity where it happened, in the district where it was committed previously ascertained by law. You are not trying it by a jury; you are not trying it in the presence of the party accused, where he has met the witnesses against him face to face. Now, is it the constitutional right of the law-making power to say that, in addition to all civil remedies, including the remedy for contempt of court, you may suppress offenses against public order by getting an injunction in advance against permitting the act, and then having so acted the judge in his discretion may fine the party?

Mr. SPOONER. Mr President, the bill as it now stands, if I may continue what I was saying, declares that certain trusts, combinations, and agreements are void. I repeat it gives to the circuit courts—

> jurisdiction of all suits of a civil nature at common law or in equity arising under this section, and to issue all remedial process, orders, or writs proper and necessary to enforce its provisions. And the Attorney-General and the several district attorneys are hereby directed, in the name of the United States, to commence and prosecute all such cases to final judgment and execution.

The amendment which I have sent to the desk does not apply to any suit which is a controversy between citizens of different States to recover damages because of such unlawful arrangement. It is limited in its operation to suits commenced by the Attorney-General and the several district attorneys in the name of the United States, and to be prosecuted to final judgment, to suppress, dissolve, and destroy the combinations found to exist detrimental to the public interests and declared void by this act.

As I said in explaining this amendment at the outset, all of these trusts, or nearly all of them, are made up of different firms, of corporations, and of citizens of different States. The Senator from Ohio argued that in the suits brought by the United States under the provisions of this act all of the parties to the trust might be made defendants, and the court having acquired jurisdiction of the subject-matter and of the defendants could deal with them. I brought to the attention of the Senate the fact that that assumption by the Senator from Ohio is a mistaken one as the law now stands, and that the statutory rule is that no man shall, with a single exception or so, be sued in the United States courts except in the district where he happens to reside or where he happens to be found. So, then, in prosecuting the sugar trust under the provisions of this act, made up of seventeen distinct corporations, as I understand it, only one of which, if you please, is a citizen of the State of New York, there would be no power to obtain jurisdiction in a single suit except over one. Seventeen different suits would be necessary, possibly. That, it seemed to me, was a weakness in this bill which ought to be remedied.

It seems to me that in dealing with it we ought to deal with it, although a civil suit brought in the name of the United States, just as we would deal with it if it were a criminal case involving as defendants half a dozen citizens of different States, because the combination aimed at is criminal, is a crime against the people, and it requires strong measures to afford any remedy for it.

To remedy this defect I provide in the pending amendment that the action may be brought in any district where any one of the defendants resides or is doing business, and that if there be other defendants, other members of the combine or trust, located in other districts in the same State or in other States, they may be brought into court and made defendants in that action, in order that the parties to the trust may be consolidated and dealt with at the suit of the United States by one of its courts in one case, under the provisions of section 738 of the Revised Statutes, with which I suppose every Senator is familiar. That is a section which provides— . . .[1.347]

Now, the object of one branch of the amendment is to enable the United States court, when the suit is brought in the name of the United States to suppress one of these combinations or trusts made up of citizens or corporations of different States, to bring them all into that suit, wherever they may happen to reside. I have no doubt it is within the constitutional power of Congress to do this, because I think the entire power to regulate the procedure is under the Constitution in Congress.

So much for that. I stated, although I did not get the attention of some, that I thought the only efficient remedy in this bill, if it shall become a law, is not in the penal clause introduced by the amendment of the Senator from Texas, but is in the merit of injunction.

As the law stands to-day that writ can not be made effective except where it is served within the jurisdiction of the court; it can have no effect whatever beyond the jurisdiction of the court; and so I have provided (which I think is also clearly within the constitutional power of Congress) that in addition to other remedial process the court shall have the power to issue its writ of injunction running anywhere and to be served anywhere within the United States. I would not agree to that in any ordinary case; I would not agree to it in controversies between citizens of different States; but it has seemed to me, as it was necessary to make this an efficient bill in view of the fact that we were dealing with a set of combinations of great power whose oppressions are criminal, that we ought to make these writs of injunction run throughout the country and to be served anywhere.

Now, Mr. President, I come to the suggestion made by the Senator from Massachusetts [Mr. HOAR]. The amendment provides—and of course the proposition to make the writ of injunction servable anywhere must carry with it, to make it forceful, the proposition to make the writ of attachment run anywhere—that the writ of attachment also for disobedience to the writ of injunction, it having been so served, may go anywhere within the United States. And it provides—I am not particular about this provision—that the court may, in addition to the imprisonment for contempt, direct the payment of a thousand dollars a day for every day after a date to be fixed in the order that the defendants or any one of the defendants shall neglect or refuse to obey the injunction.

I took that from the interstate-commerce law. . . .

Mr. HOAR. The Senator will pardon me. My attention was not called to that when that law passed as a particular item of the bill; but without going into any discussion as to whether that is valid or not, my question to the Senator was whether it would be valid, in his judgment, having fully exhausted the punishment by fine for contempt, then to make an additional penalty which should be in the nature of the case

---

[1.347] Senator Spooner read sections 738 and 739 of the Revised Statutes, which appear *supra* at 221.

only something in the nature of a penalty, not for contempt, but for the offense against public order. If that be true, if that be the difference between that and the Senator's amendment, is it within the constitutional power of Congress, in authorizing the courts to punish for contempt, to provide that any offense against the law shall be reached by a judge imposing a fine, by way of penalty, trying him in a different district from the one in which he lives? In other words, what is the thousand dollars' fine for which the Senator provides? It is not a fine for contempt. You have got that in addition. Is it anything else than a penal punishment?

Mr. SPOONER. I think it can not fairly be regarded otherwise than an additional penalty. I am not strenuous about that feature of the amendment at all. It might be so amended as to make it in the disjunctive, so that the court might punish by fine or imprisonment, or by requiring payment of a sum of money for each day's disobedience. . . .

Mr. HOAR. I suggest that the Senator say "in addition to fine or imprisonment for contempt make an order punishing for contempt."

Mr. SPOONER. I am quite willing to accept that amendment. It seemed to me that there ought to be something more than an ordinary fine for contempt. These corporations and trusts, which make tremendous profits, can very well afford to pay such a fine; but I think that in such cases, just as in the operation of the interstate-commerce law, it would have an excellent deterrent effect if every day's indulgence in the luxury of disobeying the injunction of the court is made to be a costly one. I am quite willing to accept the amendment proposed by the Senator from Massachusetts.

Mr. GRAY. I should like to ask the Senator what is the amendment he accepts?

Mr. HOAR. I suggest to the Senator from Wisconsin where he says "in addition to the fine or imprisonment for contempt" to say "in addition to other lawful punishment for contempt make an order" directing so and so.

Mr. SPOONER. I accept the amendment. . . .

The SECRETARY. In line 8 of the amendment of the Senator from Wisconsin [Mr. SPOONER], on the second page, after the word "to," it is proposed to strike out the words "fine or imprisonment" and insert the words "lawful punishment;" so as to read:

And the court may, if it shall think fit, in addition to other lawful punishment for contempt, make an order directing any such defendant disobeying such order of injunction, etc.

The VICE-PRESIDENT. The question is on the amendment of the Senator from Massachusetts to the amendment of the Senator from Wisconsin.

⊥ The amendment to the amendment was agreed to.

The VICE-PRESIDENT. The question is on the amendment of the Senator from Wisconsin as amended.

Mr. GRAY. Before the amendment is adopted, I want to ask the Senator from Wisconsin another question, because, if there is to be a jurisdiction provided for in the courts that is to be effectual, it might as well be in the line indicated by the Senator.

The jurisdiction given in the first section, in the clause which the Senator from Wisconsin seeks to amend, is in "all suits of a civil nature at common law or in equity." That embraces the whole judicial power of the United States. Now, in all suits at common law, Article VII of the amendments to the Constitution of the United States provides:

In suits at common law, where the value in controversy shall exceed $20, the right of trial by jury shall be preserved, and no fact tried by a jury shall be otherwise re-examined in any court of the United States than according to the rules of the common law.

I ask the Senator from Wisconsin if his amendment goes to the extent of providing by way of execution of a judgment at common law that the court may issue this writ of injunction for which he provides.

Mr. SPOONER. My intention was that in any action in which it would be appropriate to issue the writ of injunction it might be issued.

Mr. GRAY. If the Senator will allow me, I will make my question a little broader. He knows very well that the Supreme Court of the United States has decided that in the conferring of jurisdiction by the Constitution of suits at common law and in equity where equity jurisdiction is obtained it must be according to the interpretation of that word in the law of England at the time of the adoption of the Constitution; that is, it must be the general equitable or chancery jurisdiction as known then by lawyers to exist in English jurisprudence, and in suits in equity in which juries are not required the process by injunction is appropriate and ancillary to the main process, and I know no reason why it should not be to the minor process; that is, the amendment would be appropriate. But does the Senator from Wisconsin undertake by his amendment to make the remedy by injunction as by way of execution appropriate to a common-law suit?

Mr. SPOONER. I did not intend to change the cases in which the writ of injunction is within the jurisdiction of the Federal court as a proper writ. I think the Federal courts sometimes in actions at law issue a writ of injunction. It is in those cases where the proceedings in the cause conform to the laws of the State in actions at law, and in many of the States it is provided as one of the remedies that the writ of injunction may issue. In an action of ejectment sometimes a writ of injunction is issued pending the determination of the cause. I did not intend by the amendment to work any revolution in the law on that subject as it now stands. . . .

It was intended to have reference to what preceded:

And the circuit court of the United States shall have original jurisdiction of all suits of a civil nature at common law or in equity arising under this section, and to issue all remedial process, orders, or writs proper and necessary to enforce its provisions.

I thought that left it where it is now, and my amendment was intended to have reference to that general language which preceded it; and I think, taking the section together, there can be no doubt as to that construction. In other words, I have not intended by the amendment, nor will it have that effect, to impart to or to ingraft upon an ordinary action at law commenced in a Federal court the remedy by injunction where, under the general jurisdiction of the country, it does not now exist.

Mr. GRAY. Inasmuch as the remedy by injunction and the power to issue injunction is a peculiar feature and power of an equitable court exercising equitable jurisdiction, I suggest to the Senator from Wisconsin that it might be well to confine the scope of his amendment to a suit so arising.

Mr. SPOONER. I have no objection to that, although I think it quite plain, taking the section as it will read, that the writ of injunction would under this amendment be only authorized to issue where under the law now it would be authorized to issue. This bill does confer upon the court the right in any action to issue a writ which it would not be at liberty in an action of the same nature to issue now, as I understand it, and the amendment, I think, would have no larger scope or effect.

Mr. STEWART. Mr. President, the original bill has been very much improved, and one of the great objections has been removed from it by the amendment offered by the Senator from Ohio [Mr. SHERMAN], which relieves the class of persons who would have been the first prosecuted under the original bill without the amendment. I am very much gratified that the Senator offered the amendment and that the Senate adopted it, which reads as follows: . . .[1.348]

Those were the points to which I called the attention of the Senate yesterday. I am glad that much is granted, and I am glad of other additions which have been made. The bill ought now in some respects to be satisfactory to every person who is opposed to the oppression of labor and desires to see it properly rewarded.

I beg leave of the Senate, however, to call attention to the way, if this should become a law, in which everybody might be put in the penitentiary who attempted to carry on any kind of business, provided the bill becomes a law and can be enforced. The third section of the bill as amended provides that certain things which are enumerated in that section shall be high crimes and misdemeanors and punished by a fine—

not exceeding $10,000 or imprisonment at hard labor in the penitentiary not exceeding five years, or by both of said penalties, in the discretion of the court trying the same.

[1.348] Senator Sherman's amendment appears *supra* at 205–06.

It then, in order to warn people so that they may not fall into the penitentiary inadvertently, defines what a trust is. The fourth section commences with the definition of a trust, as follows:

That a trust is a combination of capital, skill, or acts by two or more persons, firms, corporations, or associations of persons, or of any two or more of them, for either, any, or all of the following purposes:
First. To create or carry out any restrictions in trade.

Well, just what would be a restriction in trade it would be difficult to define, but we will not comment upon that particular provision now. It is vague, and a man might be liable under it without knowing exactly what he had done. The second provision reads:

Second. To limit or reduce the production or to increase or reduce the price of merchandise or commodities.

That would make pretty nearly everybody criminal. It says "to limit or reduce the production." That would apply to a case where, if in one line of industry there was overproduction and the volume of money was being rapidly contracted and those engaged in that industry were on the eve of bankruptcy and they should attempt to make an agreement to limit their production until they could bridge over the particular difficulties, they would all have to go to the penitentiary. The alternative would be the penitentiary or bankruptcy.

Then, "to increase or reduce the price of merchandise or commodities." If a person should make an invention which would have a tendency to reduce the price of any article he would, if he formed a combination to carry that invention into execution—if two or more persons united to push that invention (and that is the usual means by which inventions have been brought into use), all who united themselves together would certainly be engaged in an effort to reduce the price of a commodity or of the merchandise which the improved method would produce. So the inventors would all pretty much have to go to the penitentiary, because all useful inventions have a tendency to reduce the price of articles to the consumer; and if two or more of them unite together they are criminals. That, I think, would put a very great damper upon all enterprise if it were carried out according to the terms of this bill.

The third clause of the same section reads:

Third. To prevent competition in the manufacture, making, purchase, sale, or transportation of merchandise, produce, or commodities.

I suppose that trade-marks are a legitimate thing, and we have many laws on our statute-book protecting trade-marks so that one man shall not have the advantage of another in the use of his credit or standing as a business man or as an inventor. I thought a trade-mark was a right which parties could be protected in, so that they might have their goods distinguished from other people's goods. I know most of the States have criminal laws to protect trade-marks, so that each individual may have the benefit of his own enterprise and industry in the conduct of his business.

Mr. REAGAN. Will the Senator from Nevada allow me to make an explanation? I think his reasoning upon the subject is utterly wrong. The Senator will see that what gives the court jurisdiction is the third section. That fixes what is the offense. The fourth section simply enumerates certain things which being done are made, in pursuance of the first section, unlawful. If the Senator supposes that the paragraphs to which he refers are meant to give power to Congress to regulate and do these things independent of the first section, he will see that is not my purpose, for it would be confessedly what Congress can not do. But I will put it so that he will understand it by a transposition of the sentence:

"That all persons engaged in the creation of any trust, or as owner or part owner, agent, or manager of any trust engaged in any business carried on, first, with a foreign country; second, between the States; third or between any State and the District of Columbia; fourth, or between any State or any Territory of the United States."

That is, as between foreign countries and States and Territories, using its powers for either of the purposes specified in the fourth section of this act. That is what the provision is. Now, look at the first paragraph: "Using its powers to create or carry out any restrictions in trade." That is, in dealing with the commerce between this country and others, or between the States and Territories, or the States and the District of Columbia; those who create restrictions in trade become subject to the penal clause. Then that clause operates. You have to read each one of these separate paragraphs, not that Congress may undertake to do these things independently of the first section, but it is one ⊥ of the definitions of the class of things that would come within the province and purview of the first section.

Mr. STEWART. I think I comprehend it. The business made unlawful, as I understand it, is business that is carried on with any foreign country, or between any of the States, or between a State and a Territory, or between a State and the District of Columbia. Any business of that kind that extends throughout the States is the business referred to. The trust defined in the fourth section is to be composed of "two or more persons, firms, corporations, or associations of persons." Any two or more persons engaged in the business of manufacturing any article vended in different States or in any foreign country who attempt to have an exclusive trade-mark would have to go to the penitentiary, as I understand the bill.

We ought to know who is to go to the penitentiary, and whether a man would be liable to go to the penitentiary if he confines the products of his manufactures to his own State. I admit this bill would not apply if he did not send his goods out of the State; and some of the Eastern States are so small that they would have a very small custom if they were compelled to keep their goods within their own State. When the goods are sent into other States, of course they are liable to go to the penitentiary under this bill.

The next clause is:

Fourth. To fix a standard or figure whereby the price to the public shall be in any manner controlled or established of any article, commodity, merchandise, produce, or commerce intended for sale, use, or consumption.

If two or more persons fix the price at which they will sell any article they have got to go to the penitentiary. Well, I think they ought to. [Laughter.]

The next clause is:

Fifth. To create a monopoly in the making, manufacture, purchase, sale, or transportation of any merchandise, article, produce, or commodity.

If two or more persons combine to create a monopoly they are to go to the penitentiary. "Monopoly" is a very difficult word to define. It has several significations. Its legal signification is something created by law which gives a special privilege. Of course it can not apply when all the world can go into the manufacture. It is not then, legally speaking, a monopoly. Popularly speaking, where a man has accumulated a large amount of money and carries on a large business, he is called a monopolist. Whether this to abolish all the laws of all the States which have organized corporations, and the patent laws of the United States, which create the greatest monopolies of the country, will be left for the courts to construe, and they will have some difficulty, I think, in doing it. Next:

Sixth. To make, or enter into, or execute, or carry out any contract, obligation, or agreement of any kind or description by which they shall bind or shall have bound themselves not to manufacture, sell, dispose of, or transport any article or commodity, or article of trade, use, merchandise, or consumption below a common standard figure, or by which they shall agree, in any manner, to keep the price of such article, commodity, or transportation at a fixed or graduated figure or by which they shall in any manner establish or settle the price of any article, commodity, or transportation between themselves, or between themselves and others, so as to preclude free and unrestricted competition among themselves and others in the sale and transportation of any such article or commodity, or by which they shall agree to pool, combine, or unite in any interest they may have in connection with the sale or transportation of any such article or commodity that its price may in any manner be so affected.

That would absolutely preclude the possibility of those engaged in any kind of business fixing any price upon their goods which they are going to sell in other States. If two or more persons or firms should agree not to dispose of their goods unless a certain price should be obtained, which goods were to be transported to another State, that would be criminal under this clause; and the multiplicity of crimes that business men would be likely to commit every day would be beyond conception if that were the law.

I think that as the bill now stands it will answer every purpose that anybody may desire in the embarrassment of trade and business.

The PRESIDING OFFICER (Mr. HARRIS in the chair). The question is on the amendment proposed by the Senator from Wisconsin [Mr. SPOONER]. The Chair would suggest that the Senator from Wisconsin desires to modify his amendment. The modification will be stated.

The SECRETARY. In line 12 of the amendment after the word "within," strike out the words "the jurisdiction of," so as to read:

Running and to be served anywhere within the United States.

The PRESIDING OFFICER. The question is on the amendment as modified.

Mr. VEST. Mr. President, it is not my purpose to offer the slightest obstacle to the passage of this measure. I have expressed my doubts in regard to this bill, and have said all I propose to say as to its provisions, but I find in the RECORD of this morning a statement by the Senator from Texas [Mr. REAGAN] that I feel called upon to notice. I find this statement made by him which I did not hear, or I should have answered it at the time:

Mr. President, I am inclined to think, in view of the fact that but one member of the Committee on the Judiciary has given any expression that indicates a purpose to mature a law to repress the evil effects of trusts and to punish those engaged in them, that it is not best to refer these measures to that committee.

Now, there are but three members of the Judiciary Committee who have spoken at all upon this question—the Senator from Mississippi [Mr. GEORGE], the Senator from Alabama [Mr. PUGH]—and he is entirely in accord with every portion of the bill—and myself; but, as only two of us criticised the bill, it is fair to assume, and I take it for granted, that the remarks of the Senator from Texas were intended for the Senator from Mississippi and myself.

Mr. President, the statement is unjust and it is not based upon the facts. . . .

But what have we here to-day? Here is a bill that upon its very face says, as it stands now before the Senate, that it proposed to use the revenue power for the undisguised purpose of effecting police purposes, in language so distinct and plain that a wayfaring man, although he could not read, would be able to understand it.

That for the purpose of preventing as far as may be the dealing in options and futures as herein defined special taxes are imposed.

No pretense that it is to collect revenue, no pretense that it is anything else but the bald, naked use of the revenue power of the Government for police regulation; and yet, sir, it will be supported with a unanimity utterly unparalleled in this Chamber.

For myself I shall say nothing more about the Constitution. I am prepared to join the procession. I heard once of a hunting party who went into camp and made an agreement that the first man who complained of any dish set before him at the camp table should cook for a week. One happened to kill an old and very tough crow, and, as he was acting as cook for the mess, he prepared it for the table, and every man swore it was the most delicious morsel that ever went into his mouth. The Farmers' Alliance are cooking now, and there is no dish that can be put on this Senatorial table which will not go down with a gusto that will astonish any gourmand from the restaurants of Paris.

Mr. President, I simply rise, not to make an argument, but to suggest that I should like before the debate closes to hear from the Senator from Ohio whether he believes the clauses now incorporated in this bill which propose to originate in the Senate of the United States a revenue measure are constitutional or not. This bill does not come from the House of Representatives. It has not even the poor excuse that it was originated in the House, and that we have struck out the whole and put in a substitute by way of amendment. This is an original bill to raise revenue, providing revenue, putting on a tax, and it performs the most remarkable act of legislative legerdemain ever known since the foundation of the world. It licenses an illegal combination which it denounces as opposed to the laws of the United States and all the States. In other words, we say to the option dealers, "You are a lot of criminals, thieves, and robbers, but if you will give us a thousand dollars we will let you go on robbing." I shall be obliged to the Senator from Ohio if he will explain what is his opinion of those clauses of ⊥ this bill, to say nothing about the feature which we have discussed before, that propose to levy taxes under the revenue power of the Government exercised by the Senate of the United States without any originating act upon the part of the House of Representatives.

Mr. REAGAN. Mr. President, it was certainly the furthest from my desire to do any wrong to any Senator by any statement I may have made. . . .

The idea which I intended to convey—perhaps I may not have been happy in the choice of the words I employed—was that but one member of the Judiciary Committee had expressed himself favorable to legislation on this subject, and that in the discussion the Senator from Missouri and the Senator from Mississippi[1.349] had furnished us with many criticisms upon the propositions before the Senate. No doubt there was ground for a good deal of the criticism which they made; but it occurred to me that the criticisms were so general, so sweeping, as to cover everything which had been presented or could be presented to the Senate on this subject.

I called attention to the fact that the Senator from Mississippi said that he had been five years trying to formulate something on this subject and the Senator from Missouri has just told us that he has been five months trying to formulate something on this subject.

Now, Mr. President, is it true that the Constitution of the United States gives Congress no power over this subject? Will either of the distinguished Senators affirm that that is true? Are they not compelled to concede that we have certainly some power over the subject. If we have some power over the subject, has it taken that long for these Senators to discover that they can not find where that power exists nor how it is to be exercised?

Mr. President, I have made my share of criticism on the provisions of the bill, and I have had an ample amount of criticism on the portion which I have participated in making. However, I have not been hunting for criticisms and speculations that would defeat this bill or any bill with this object in view; but I have been trying to see if it were not possible for this Senate to mature a measure which would arrest and punish combinations and trusts that are robbing and plundering the people of this country. That is what I am hunting for.

I stated, when giving my consent to place my bill as an amendment to the bill of the Senator from Ohio, that while I doubted whether the provisions of that bill were sufficient, except so far as the general purpose of the first part of the first section was declared, I believed that the part which I added to it had actual virtue in it and would do good, and I felt under the circumstances that it was better to put it there, if possible, and get all we could of good in order to meet the great evils which the Senator from Missouri concedes, and which all other Senators here concede, and which are notorious to the country.

The Senator has alluded to the great cattle trust which he has been combating; he has seen and known of evils growing out of that; and the great sugar trust has been referred to, which the whole country feels the effects of; and so of the cotton-seed-oil trust, by which a combination has crushed the cotton-seed-oil manufacturers throughout the South and stopped the mills wherever it was to their interest to do so by paying interest upon the investment rather than let the establishments run in competition, and thus they fix the price of oil and cotton-seed as they please and by their monopoly they put down the price of cotton seed about one-third and put up the price of oil to whatever they please by a monopoly.

The people that I in part represent feel the effects of these trusts both in cattle and cotton-seed oil. They feel their effects in many other things. So I have felt and so I

[1.349] Senators Vest and George, respectively.

have tried, during this and the last Congress, by the best efforts I was able to make, to see if we could not devise a law that would arrest and prevent these trusts as far as the jurisdiction of Congress would go. I have said from the beginning, and I repeat again, that the power which we have over this question comes from the commerce clause of the Constitution. If it comes from any other source, I do not know where to trace it. I have limited the bill which I presented to an execution of the commerce power of the Constitution and to preventing the evils complained of as far as it seemed to me they might be prevented by Congress. It would be assuming a great deal for me to say that I know I have succeeded in doing it, but I say I believe I have presented a proposition to the Senate under which the owners and managers of trusts and persons connected with them may be indicted and convicted. . . .

Mr. VEST. . . .

The Senator speaks of the interstate-commerce clause of the Constitution. I agree with him as to that, but I confess at the beginning under the decisions of the Supreme Court of the United States the remedy that was in us to exercise under that clause of the Constitution was not at all commensurate with the enormous evils which we propose to remedy. That is the trouble. Because I am not able to say honestly that I believe these bills presented here are full and complete and in accordance with the Constitution, I am to be told that I am trying to do nothing, and we have here *par excellence* the friends of the people, who are struggling and worrying to preserve them, while some of us are sitting here spectators and worse than spectators, attempting to throw obstacles in the way of this gigantic reform!

Now, sir, I only claim that I am endeavoring to do my duty as I see it, and I do not interfere with anybody else's conscientious convictions upon that subject. If I am not able to see that these bills are in accordance with the Constitution, if I am not able to see that they will not stand the crucible of the criticism through which they must go in the Supreme Court of the United States, I do not propose to have it said to me that I am in the way of the judicial or legal ability of my colleagues. That is all, sir.

Mr. EUSTIS. Mr. President, I was not present yesterday when the amendments to this bill were adopted. In looking over the RECORD of the last sitting, and considering the amendments which have been adopted, I ask myself whether the Senate of the United States is seriously engaged in the attempt to impair or destroy what are known as trusts, or whether it is simply engaged in a sham battle, playing the role of Don Quixotes [*sic*].

When this bill came up at the last session, I rose and asked the Senator from Ohio whether it was his intention by this bill to deal with existing trusts or future trusts; that is to say, we know that all the great trusts have been already formed, they could be easily enumerated, and their enumeration would include all the great products and industries known to our country. Strange to say, the Senator could not then state distinctly whether the bill referred to actually existing trusts—that is, trusts *in esse*, such as the sugar trust, the lead trust, and other trusts—or whether it applied to the shadowy and non-existent trusts to be formed in the future. Under the law which was then proposed and under this bill—for, of course, when the Congress of the United States enacts a penal statute it can only operate in the future—I take it that there will be very few trusts created in defiance of the law. Therefore, if the bill did not apply to the existing trusts, you would have a statute which did not reach any existing evil, and you would have a statute which would operate in the future, which would be entirely inoperative and nugatory.

I have the colloquy which took place between the Senator from Ohio and myself at that time, and I will read it:

> Mr. EUSTIS. I would ask the Senator from Ohio whether this proposed law is to apply, as I understand it, only to future trusts, or whether he desires that it shall be applied to existing trusts? The reason I ask the question is this: A great many of these trusts are already in existence. That is the evil which, as I understand, is to be reached by this new legislation.

The Senator from Ohio replied to my question as follows:

> Mr. SHERMAN. As far as I can perceive I think that the continuing agreement, arrangement, combination, etc., such as described in the first section will become illegal on the passage of this act, and not before. Our laws can not be made retroactive.

Then I offered the following amendment in order to reach existing trusts:

SEC. —. That any person who, ninety days after the passage of this law, shall act as a manager, officer, trustee, or agent of any arrangement, contract, agreement, trust, or combination as described in the first section, shall be liable to the penalties prescribed in the fourth section.

⊥ The language of the bill which we are discussing is the same as the language which is used in the bill that I criticise; that is to say:

That all arrangements and contracts made with a view or which tend to prevent full and free competition, etc.

So that if the Senate of the United States had adopted my amendment, which provided a penalty and which struck at existing trusts, the effect of the legislation under my amendment would have been to destroy the existing trusts. Yet, in the face of that, we have a bill reported by the Senator from Ohio, which, under his own interpretation at the last session, does not in the remotest degree affect any existing trust. . . .

Mr. GRAY. I should like to ask the Senator from Louisiana on this point what construction he puts upon section 3 of the bill in regard to its efficiency.

Mr. SHERMAN. Will the Senator from Louisiana be kind enough to read again the words he quotes as to my declaration? I do not remember to have made a declaration as broad as that. If I did it could not have any weight.

Mr. EUSTIS. The Senator from Ohio, in answer to the question which I propounded whether this proposed law was to apply to future trusts or whether he desires that it should be applied to existing trusts, said:

Mr. SHERMAN. As far as I can perceive, I think that the continuing agreement, arrangement, combination, etc., such as described in the first section will become illegal on the passage of this act, and not before. Our laws can not be made retroactive. But I do not see myself any objection to making the continuance of a combination like this after proper days' notice an offense. I think, however, thirty days' notice is too short, because a law of this kind ought to have a broad circulation before it becomes operative.

Mr. SHERMAN. I think it does apply to existing trusts where they continue to do the acts complained of after the passage of the law.

Mr. EUSTIS. They are simply declared null and void. Now, the proposition of the Senator from Texas [Mr. REAGAN] is that all persons engaged in the creation of any trust commit a misdemeanor. Of course, that only applies to the future.

Mr. REAGAN. I hope the Senator will not stop reading there.

Mr. EUSTIS. I will read the whole of it:

That all persons engaged in the creation of any trust—

Mr. REAGAN. It goes on:

or as owner or part owner, agent, or manager of any trust.

Mr. EUSTIS. Yes, "employed." Does not that refer to the creation, I ask the Senator from Texas?

That all persons engaged in the creation of any trust, or as owner or part owner, agent, or manager of any trust employed in any business carried on with any foreign country.

Does the Senator construe that to apply immediately after the passage of this act?
Mr. REAGAN. That is the way I understand it.
Mr. EUSTIS. Immediately after the passage of this act?
Mr. REAGAN. It commences to take trusts as they are and make them unlawful.
Mr. EUSTIS. But immediately after the passage of this act?
Mr. REAGAN. It can not operate until after its passage.
Mr. EUSTIS. Of course; I understand that.
Mr. REAGAN. And at common law they are unlawful already.
Mr. EUSTIS. Then do I understand the Senator's amendment to mean that the manager or agent of any trust company existing at the time of the passage of this act commits a misdemeanor the day after its passage?

Mr. REAGAN. Yes, sir.

Mr. EUSTIS. I ask the Senator whether he does not think that is too harsh, and whether it would not be better to provide that the act shall not take effect for ninety days?

Mr. REAGAN. I have no objection, if it is thought best, to give them reasonable notice. I would accept an amendment, if it is thought advisable to do so, which would give notice and give time for people to abandon these combinations, though they are not entitled to much mercy. . . .

These combinations have robbed the people without mercy themselves, and they are doing about what is unlawful at common law. I do not know; I think probably I shall not accept the amendment suggested. . . .

Mr. EUSTIS. If the provisions of the bill, beginning at the first section, apply to existing trusts, and if the penal provision applies to the managers or agents of an existing trust immediately after the passage of the law—

Mr. HOAR. It also, I will suggest to the Senator from Louisiana, includes the owner of stock in a corporation so employed.

Mr. EUSTIS. It is to cover the case of existing trusts; and I am perfectly willing to strain a point to vote for such a bill as that. I have had some very serious difficulty in reaching that conclusion, but very able lawyers think that it is constitutional, and I am willing to acquiesce in their judgment so far; but I can not vote for this measure for the reason that upon many propositions I have no sort of doubt whatever as to its unconstitutionality. I refer to contracts in what are known as "futures." I should like to know what the Congress of the United States has to do with the Cotton Exchange, for instance, in New Orleans dealing in futures. I notice that nearly all the articles which are referred to with regard to future contracts are things that people consume: wheat, corn, oats, rye, barley; but the authors of the measure have included cotton. If we are going to include cotton why do we not include steel rails? People are as liable to eat steel rails as they are to eat cotton.

Why do we not include lead or salt? Why do we not include everything? Why do we not include manufactured cotton goods, a subject with reference to which there are very large operations in futures in Boston and in New York, Philadelphia, and elsewhere? If the broad proposition be that Congress should declare its policy upon the question of gambling, of which I confess I know very little; if the States have become so debilitated and emasculated and if the people of the States have become so demoralized that we are to surrender the whole question of police, of policy, and of public morality to the Congress of the United States, for one it will not be done by my vote.

Where are we going to stop? If the State of Louisiana, for its own interest and from its own motives, owing no apology to any other State or to the Government of the United States, chooses to legalize contracts in futures with reference to cotton, by which a large and most respectable portion of our population make a living, which many and many a time have enabled the planter to get a much higher price for his product than he would get in the absence of a cotton exchange, when the planter many and many a time has been able to protect himself against flood and unfavorable seasons by making a future contract in cotton—if the State of Louisiana chooses to consider that a perfectly proper and legitimate business, a business that should exist and should be sustained by the State, from which the State derives a revenue, and legalizes that business, where is the authority of Congress to step in and tell the State of Louisiana or any other State that those contracts are illegal and immoral and shall be suppressed by the power of Congressional legislation?

Mr. President, I am not surprised that a Republican Senator should have introduced such an amendment as this. I am not surprised that it should receive votes from Republican Senators, who believe that what they call nationality has been substituted for the Constitution of the United States, who believe that we have nothing in fact but a parliamentary government whose powers are supreme and indisputable, a government of the majority which can control the minority, that there are no balances, no adjustments, no limitations in our system of government; but it would be amazing to me to find that a Democratic Senator should vote for it, who believes that the police powers, ever since the foundation of this Government, belong exclusively to the State;

that each State government is reponsible [sic] to the people inhabiting that State for the exercise of that police power; and that whenever the Congress of the United States undertakes to regulate that State power, that police power, in defiance of the sovereign will of the State, then you attempt the grossest usurpation that has ever been attempted in the history of our Government. Then it will be that the people will be ready to lay down their liberties and their rights on the footstool that you create by your legislation, and surrender every principle of local and self government. It will then be that our Federal Government will become not only central, but overshadowing. It will be the only voice that can speak to the people of the United States. To this source alone will they look for their rights and for their liberties, if any they have left. Strike down once the police power of the State, which is the supremest attribute of its sovereignty, invade that sacred domain by this bill, declare what is immoral, what is illegal, what is proper, what is reprehensible with reference to a purely domestic, local, and State question, and then you will have statehood stand as nothing but a mockery and a sham, an emblem of what was great in the past, but has disappeared for the future.

Mr. VANCE. . . .

⊥2647　⊥ We are all the friends of the people. We are all enemies to these illegal combinations of capital which devour the substance of the people and grind the faces of the poor. But when it comes to putting that friendship to the test we find that every proposition which human Senatorial ingenuity can suggest bristles with legal and constitutional objections. "We are your friend, farmer; we are your friend, little fish who are being swallowed up by the big ones; would to God we could help you, but we can not."

Now, Mr. President, my profession of regard for the people and their interests, as contradistinguished from those of the combinations of capital in this country, is a sincere one, and those expressions have characterized me ever since I was in political life. So far as my recollection extends, there is not a single vote that I have ever given in this or other legislative bodies which was not as I believed in the interests of the people.

It may be, sir, that these constitutional objections are valid, but at all events there is certainly ingenuity and legal learning enough in this body to devise some measure to correct these evils of which every one complains, these trusts that have even extended to the bagging that envelops the cotton of the planter in the South, to the plow with which the Western and Southern farmers stir the soil. There is scarcely any article of prime necessity in this country as to which the people do not complain that its price has been enhanced by these combinations.

Now, we ought either to do something or we ought to say to the people "It is not worth while to talk about the subject; the Constitution of the United States gives no power whatsoever to Congress to redress these evils, and you must look to the States alone." As honest men we must tell them that if it be the truth, and let them endeavor to find redress in their State Legislatures.

For one, sir, I am willing to make an effort to do something. So far as the amendment which was proposed by the Senator from Kansas [Mr. INGALLS], which has been adopted and has now become a part of the bill, is concerned, I did not vote for it. I was not in the Chamber when it was adopted. It was agreed to without a yea-and-nay vote, in the confusion which was in the Senate yesterday in regard to the various amendments and propositions submitted upon the bill. I acknowledge that is an unconstitutional amendment. I believe it to be so, so far as a layman has any right to express a constitutional view.

Mr. GEORGE. Which amendment is that?

Mr. VANCE. The amendment of the Senator from Kansas [Mr. INGALLS], which is undoubtedly a revenue bill, and such a bill can not under the Constitution originate in this body. I admit that. I expect to vote to strike it out of the bill, but should it be adopted I believe that I shall still continue in support of the bill, believing that the courts can decide that portion of the law as it will then be, unconstitutional, without interfering with or disturbing the remainder, for it is not at all dependent upon the remainder of the bill, nor is the remainder of the bill dependent upon it.

I am determined, so far as it is in my power, to do something to repress the operation of these trusts and combinations, and having done my endeavor so far as I am able to do it, then the results rest not with me. I make no imputations upon other Senators. If I ever have done it, I have not been correct in doing so, because it is not the thing to do here. We are all responsible to our own consciences for our actions and for our views of the Constitution. But I say that it is our duty either to do something to repress these trusts and combinations or stop talking to the people about them. So far as the imputation is made that my action or that of any other Senator is influenced by the Farmers' Alliance, I say that the demagogy of the whole proposition consists in continuing to talk to the people as though we could do something when we know that we can not do anything. . . .

Mr. GEORGE. Does the Senator know any gentleman on this side of the Chamber who denies that Congress has the constitutional power to do something?

Mr. VANCE. Yes.

Mr. GEORGE. Who is it?

Mr. VANCE. I am one of the Senators myself who believe that Congress can do something to remedy these evils.

Mr. GEORGE. Who denies that Congress can do something, I ask?

Mr. VANCE. Oh, I did not understand the question. I do not deny it, but it so happens that every proposition ever made so far meets with a constitutional objection. . . .

Mr. GEORGE. Does he not believe that the great mother of these trusts lies in a protective tariff?

Mr. VANCE. I do.

Mr. GEORGE. Then if the duty were taken off the articles which are manufactured by the trusts, would not that be a constitutional remedy?

Mr. VANCE. It would, so far as those performances are concerned which are enacted behind the wall of the protective tariff; but there are others which are not behind that wall, and I want to strike at them all, every one of them. As a matter of course, the great bulk of the articles the purchase price of which is enhanced by combinations are protected by the tariff law which excludes the competition of foreign articles, and it would break down their combination if those articles were admitted freely into this country or upon the payment of a reasonable duty. There is no doubt about that; but there are many other articles which would be unaffected by any action we might take in regard to the tariff, and for that reason I am in favor of doing what is before us to be done, rather than waiting for the trusts to be broken down by a reduction of tariff duties.

The Senator from Mississippi knows as well as I do and as well as any other Senator that there is no earthly prospect of reducing tariff duties for the purpose of suppressing trusts. Yesterday, upon the vote on the amendment of the Senator from Texas [Mr. COKE], which authorized the President of the United States to suspend the tariff duties whenever he may be satisfied that trusts are formed under their protection, the Senator saw at once how promptly every Senator on the other side rallied to the rescue of the tariff. . . .

Mr. GEORGE. The Senator from North Carolina, in alluding to the vote yesterday upon the amendment offered by the Senator from Texas [Mr. COKE], which struck down tariff duties when they were fostering these trusts, said that every Senator on the other side of the Chamber very promptly voted against it. I called his attention to the fact—(I thought it was a fact, and, if it is not, the Senator from Texas [Mr. REAGAN] can correct me)—that the Senator from Texas [Mr. REAGAN] voted with the other side on that proposition.

Mr. REAGAN. I voted against the adoption of my colleague's amendment as a substitute for the entire bill. I understand that the provision which the Senator from Mississippi and the Senator from North Carolina refer to is in that substitute, but it had not been mentioned in the debate, and I doubt if many members knew it was there. I did not vote against it on that ground, but for the reason that I had a better provision to substitute for it, in my judgment, than that was, because I relied on the commerce clause of the Constitution for my authority and because that relied for its constitutional authority upon an act of a State Legislature to create Federal jurisdiction, and I did not choose to vote for a substitute which I did not believe derived its power from the right source to supplant another which I did believe was derived from the right source. I hope the Senator from Mississippi will not set me down as a high-tariff man because of that vote. . . .

The VICE-PRESIDENT. The question is on agreeing to the amendment submitted by the Senator from Wisconsin [Mr. SPOONER], which has been read.

Mr. PUGH. Mr. President, I desire to say that there seems to be a very great misconception of the character of the amendment of the Senator from Kansas [Mr. INGALLS]. I think myself that that amendment is not germane to the subject of the bill introduced by the Senator from Ohio [Mr. SHERMAN], and I believe it is totally out of place and ought never to have been connected at all with the bill for the suppression of trusts and combinations. The amendment of the Senator from Kansas, it seems to be understood by my friend from Louisiana [Mr. EUSTIS], operates against dealing in futures by cotton exchanges in the South. There is nothing whatever in the bill that prevents a cotton exchange, or any farmer, any cotton-owner, in the South or anywhere else, from selling his cotton to be delivered at any time in the future. It only aims at dealing in these commodities when they are not owned, and when it is a part of the contract of sale that they are not to be delivered. I understand that to be the express provision of the bill. . . .

Mr. EUSTIS. Does not the amendment aim to prevent what is known as dealing in futures?

Mr. PUGH. In the way specified in the bill—that is, by making contracts to deliver commodities not owned by the parties to the contract at the time and never intended to be delivered.

I will state further that, as a lawyer engaged in the trial of a case involving the character of this business, I examined the best-informed men in the city of New York upon that subject, and every one of the witnesses testified that in that system established in New York by which they dealt in futures there was not a single transaction in which any party to it would say it was no part of the agreement that there was not to be an actual delivery of the commodity. Every one of them will testify to-day, I have no doubt, as they have done in the past within my knowledge, every member of these cotton exchanges, every man who is engaged in this business of selling for future delivery, will swear that it is no part of the contract between the parties that there is not to be a delivery of the article sold for future delivery.

I say that under this bill there will be no license issued to any man who wants to engage in the business as it is going on to-day in the country, and I look upon the amendment as being utterly useless and harmless in its operation. I state these facts from personal knowledge and from the express provisions of the bill.

Mr. EUSTIS. Mr. President, I desire to correct my friend from Alabama. What is known as a contract in futures is this: A person buys or sells a thousand bales of cotton deliverable at a fixed date. There is nothing whatsoever in the contract to show whether he intends to deliver the thousand bales or not. When the contract matures he can do one of two things, at his option: He can either deliver actually the thousand bales of cotton according to the grade called for by the contract, and the seller is bound to receive the thousand bales of cotton, or he can pay the difference in the market between the time that the contract was made and the time of the delivery. That is the way the business is conducted in New Orleans; that is the way the business is conducted in Liverpool. Not quite a year ago there was a man by the name of Steiner, who made a corner in cotton at Liverpool, and every ship that he could get all over the world was loaded with cotton by those people who had made contracts in order to tender him the actual cotton, which they did, and that prevented him from reaping the enormous profit which he otherwise would have secured.

There is no question whatever that in New Orleans and in Liverpool, and I take it in New York and Mobile, and Memphis, and every other city they have only one system of business, and that regulated by what is known as the National Exchange, composed of all these cotton exchanges in the various cities, and that is one of their rules. I know that is the way they conduct their business; there is nothing in the contract to show what the intention of the parties is except that it is understood generally that they will settle the difference when the contract matures; but if a man chooses to go and sell one hundred thousand bales of cotton and tender them to the purchaser he has the right to do that, and the purchaser is obliged to take them under what is known as a future contract. That is the business that is conducted in New Orleans.

Mr. PUGH. Mr. President, I understood the Senator to state that this bill prevented cotton-growers in the South from selling their cotton for future delivery. I deny that that can be the effect of the bill. In the next place, I would ask that Senator what there is in the bill which would prevent the Cotton Exchange in New Orleans from selling to a manufacturer at Lowell a thousand bales of cotton for delivery, selling them in the spring or summer for delivery to a manufacturer in Lowell? What is there in the bill to prevent that transaction?

Then again, if it is no part of the contract, as he admits, that this commodity, whatever it may be, provisions, food, or cotton, is not to be delivered at the time when the contract is to be performed by delivery, what is there in the bill to prevent the parties from arranging to settle upon the actual value of the cotton in the market at the time of the delivery and accepting the money in the place of cotton? What is there in the bill to prevent a man from selling 10,000 bushels of wheat for future delivery, and at the time when the contract requires the actual delivery, can not the parties under that contract agree upon the value of the wheat and settle the difference? I do not see anything whatever in the bill to prevent that transaction, to prevent dealings of that character.

Mr. BUTLER. Mr. President, I have no desire whatever to enter into this debate at this stage of it, but I think my friend from Alabama has clearly overlooked the whole object and purport of the bill. If I understand the text, the first thing that a man must do before he can carry out the agreement to which the Senator refers, he must pay a tax under the internal-revenue system.

Mr. PUGH. There is no tax necessary to enable parties, any number of them, members of the Cotton Exchange or producers, to deal in these commodities when they are to be actually delivered. There is the bill to speak for itself.

Mr. BUTLER. Then I have misunderstood the entire purport of it; that is very certain.

Mr. PUGH. I call on the author of the bill, the Senator from Kansas [Mr. INGALLS], to know if I am not correct in my construction.

Mr. INGALLS. Mr President, the statement of the Senator from Alabama who sits farthest from me [Mr. PUGH] correctly indicates the purpose of the amendment which I had the honor to submit and which has been adopted by a practically unanimous vote of the Senate. It is not intended in any manner whatever to interfere with the bargain, purchase, sale, or exchange of any product of which the parties may be possessed, or of which they may be the producers, or which they intend actually to deliver, provided they are the owners of it. It is directed against that gigantic modern invention known as dealing in futures, conspiracies artificially to raise the prices of products, to change the value of products, to create artificial scarcity of products, to juggle with values irrespective of ownership by processes that are just as nefarious and just as reprehensible as those of the poker-table or the faro-bank, in which there is no pretense of ownership, in which there is often an agreement to sell ten or fifty times more than the annual product of what is offered in the market, the sole purpose being to enable those "who neither toil nor spin," but who are clad in purple and fare sumptuously every day, to settle up on the 1st day of October, or the 1st day of November, if it may be, the difference between the price that they had bet a certain product would bear on that date and the price at which the producer is compelled to sell it on that day. . . .

⊥ Mr. President, the people of the United States have a reasonable degree of respect for the Constitution, but they are not afraid of it. A constitution is a growth, and not a manufacture, and the Constitution of 1890, by reason of the operation of the will of the people who made it, is a vastly different instrument from the Constitution of 1789. Its authors would not know it. They made it for specific purposes, not for the object of enabling country lawyers to devise definitions, not for the purpose of interposing obstacles and barriers to the will of the people.

Let us refresh our recollection for an instant to see what the Constitution was made for—not by the States, either.

⊥2649

We the people of the United States—

And for what?—

in order to form a more perfect union, establish justice, insure domestic tranquillity, provide for the common defense, promote the general welfare, and secure the blessings of liberty to ourselves and our posterity, do ordain and establish this Constitution for the United States of America.

Therefore, Mr. President, we are instructed what the purpose and object of "the people of the United States" was in the formation of the Constitution under which we live and which is perpetually invoked by the narrow and rigid and illiberal constructionists to interpose an insuperable barrier against every effort to better the condition of the people. Sir, the people of the United States do not regard the Constitution with superstition or awe. They know that there are some things more venerable than charters, more sacred than constitutions, and those are the rights and the privileges which charters and constitutions were ordained to establish and to maintain. At every stage of national growth and progress we have been met by the interposition of these minute and insectivorous propositions that the Constitution was a barrier against the determined and resolute will of the people, and we are taunted with bad faith, with false chivalry, with fighting sham battles when we attempt here to carry into effect a provision which I shall show before I get through with my statement is entirely within the limits and purview of the Constitution itself. . . .

I commend, Mr. President, to these construers of the Constitution the contemplation of the results of their criticisms for the last thirty years, and suggest whether it is not barely possible that they may be mistaken in invoking against this effort to relieve the people, for whom the Constitution was made, of one of the great, monstrous, crying evils of any century.

The Senator from North Carolina, prematurely, I think, the Senator from Alabama, improvidently, I think, said that the amendment proposed by me was outside the limits and purview of the Constitution in this, that it was a violation of the privilege and prerogative of the House of Representatives. To the two operating clauses of the Constitution I will call the attention of the Senate. Article I, section 7, says:

All bills for raising revenue shall originate in the House of Representatives.

That is plain; that is explicit; that is unmistakable. If this is a bill for raising revenue, I admit that it is improperly introduced into this body.

Section 8 says:

The Congress shall have power to lay and collect taxes, duties, imposts, and excises—

For what?

to pay the debts and provide for the common defense and general welfare of the United States.

I go further and I admit that if this measure which proposes to lay a tax is a bill for raising revenue then it is not properly in this body. I accept logically all the consequences of those declarations. There is the major premise; there is the minor premise; there is the conclusion. It is a syllogism. Bills for raising revenue must originate in the House of Representatives; this is a bill for raising revenue; therefore it can not properly originate in the Senate. But are the power to tax and the raising of revenue the same thing? Are they identical under the Constitution? Under section 8 is the exercise of the power to tax for the purpose of paying debts, providing for the common defense and general welfare of the United States, a bill for raising revenue? I deny it. I affirm that this is in no sense whatever a bill for raising revenue. It is not intended as a bill for raising revenue any more than the bill for the taxation of oleomargarine was intended for raising revenue. Everybody who voted for that bill or against it knew that it was not a bill for raising revenue. It was a bill that was introduced and passed for the purpose of suppressing the production of an article that was believed to be injurious to the general welfare of the United States, whether that belief was right or wrong. I did not believe in it myself. . . .

⊥ . . . I read from Story on the Constitution, volume 1, page 687 of the edition ⊥2650 that I hold in my hand, section 965: . . .[1.350]

If the authority of this great writer on constitutional law is worth anything, the power to raise revenue and the power to levy a tax are absolutely different. They are capable of being exercised by entirely different functions. We may tax irrespective of the question of revenue, and that is what is intended to be done in the amendment I proposed to the bill reported by the Senator from Ohio. That is the reason why the language in the ninth section, in the first and second lines, upon which the Senator from Louisiana animadverted, was inserted, not with any idea of leaving it doubtful whether this was a tax bill for the purpose of revenue or a bill for the suppression of a nefarious and reprehensible practice. I do not desire to be misunderstood, or mistaken, or misapprehended. Those words were inserted for a purpose, for the purpose of asserting affirmatively that under the Constitution, the power to tax being admitted to exist in order to suppress a traffic believed to be injurious, this was the intention and the design of the amendment. . . .

I think, unless some decisions or some argument or some evidence or the authority of some great writer can be adduced to the contrary, that those who have pronounced against the validity, the legality, the constitutionality of this amendment will see fit to revise their opinion. Unless this amendment which proposes to tax is intended to raise revenue it need not originate in the House of Representatives, because only those measures which are for raising revenue must originate in that place. I have shown by authority, by the express declaration of purpose, that this is not intended for the purpose of raising revenue, but for another purpose, in itself constitutional and expressed in the body of the bill itself; and therefore I contend that it is not obnoxious to the objections which have been urged.

Mr. HOAR. I desire to ask the attention of the Senator from Kansas to a little matter of detail, which I may forget if I do not call his attention to it now. I wish to propose an amendment which I believe he will accede to. At the bottom of the fifth page, after the proviso at the end of section 7, I wish to add the words:

Or of articles to be consumed by the person to whom they are delivered or in his establishment.

The Senator will observe that the bill as it is now drawn, especially section 8, will be open to the criticism that it prohibits contracts for the delivery to large establishments like hotels of beef, or lard, or milk for the daily use of their customers, and that class of contracts which have no sort of connection with those aimed at; but it is better, I suppose, to have the phraseology of the bill clearly exclude that intention, and I ask him, therefore, if he sees any objection to the amendment which I propose.

Mr. INGALLS. I see none. I ask that it be adopted. . . .

The CHIEF CLERK. It is proposed to add at the end of the proviso in section 7 "or of articles to be consumed by the person to whom they are delivered or in his establishment;" so as to make the proviso read:

Provided, That this act shall not apply to contracts for the delivery at any one time of articles of not more than $50 in value or of articles to be consumed by the person to whom they are delivered or in his establishment.

The VICE-PRESIDENT. If there be no objection, the amendment proposed by the Senator from Massachusetts will be agreed to. The Chair hears none, and it is agreed to. The question recurs on agreeing to the amendment proposed by the Senator from Wisconsin [Mr. SPOONER]. . . .

⊥ Mr. VEST. . . . He [Senator Ingalls] tells us that this portion of the bill which I ⊥2651 have before me is not intended for revenue purposes, but is intended to legislate out of existence these unlawful combinations and trusts. If that is so, why is a license issued to them? Why are they given the right under the authority of the United States to continue their unlawful and wicked machinations and evils?

[1.350] Senator Ingalls quoted from 1 J. STORY, *supra* note 1.306, at 677–81, regarding the use of taxation for purposes of regulating commerce in addition to raising revenue.

Mr. INGALLS. They will not continue, if this proposed law goes into effect.

Mr. VEST. I shall propose an amendment to this portion of the bill. I shall propose to strike out the words "one thousand dollars" wherever they occur and to insert "ten thousand dollars." If the object of the bill is to make these combinations impossible, if it is to use the taxing power to tax them out of existence, why put upon those immense and wealthy combinations the paltry tax of $1,000 in order to allow them to continue their nefarious business?

Mr. President, my only object in rising was to move that in section 10 where ever [sic] the words "one thousand dollars" occur they be stricken out and there be inserted the words "ten thousand dollars."

Mr. EUSTIS. Mr. President, the Senator from Kansas would have us understand that we know nothing about the Constitution of the United States.

Mr. INGALLS. I beg pardon, Mr. President.

Mr. EUSTIS. I say the Senator from Kansas would intimate that we are not able to understand the Constitution of the United States.

Mr. INGALLS. Oh, no; not exactly. You have been on both sides of it; you ought to understand it.

Mr. EUSTIS. Therefore I will limit my endeavor to the understanding of this bill. I ask the Senator from Kansas, suppose I agree to sell a thousand bales of cotton to A, deliverable on the 1st of May. I make that contract to-day. Suppose that on the morning of the 1st of May the purchaser A actually gets the thousand bales of cotton, that I actually deliver the thousand bales of cotton, is that a future contract under this proposed law which is to be suppressed?

Mr. INGALLS. Not if I correctly understand the statement of the Senator from Louisiana. . . .

And I will go further and say that if a contract based upon the actual delivery of property that is in the possession of the person agreeing to sell is covered by this bill, it ought not to be. I am entirely candid about it. . . .

Mr. EUSTIS. Suppose that to-day I make a contract selling a thousand bales of cotton to A, deliverable on the 1st of May.

Mr. INGALLS. Which cotton you do not now possess?

Mr. EUSTIS. Yes. On the 1st of May I get that cotton and deliver it. I ask whether in the contemplation of this proposed law that is a future contract to be suppressed.

Mr. INGALLS. If on the 1st of May the contracting party has the cotton actually in his possession and delivers it, the transaction ought not to be obnoxious to the provisions of the bill.

Mr. EUSTIS. Then I understand that if I do not own it at the date of the contract, but I do at the date of the execution of the contract, it is not amenable to this bill?

Mr. INGALLS. It ought not to be.

Mr. EUSTIS. It ought not to be! I assume that the Senator knows what amendment he has offered to the bill.

Mr. INGALLS. It is not intended to be.

Mr. EUSTIS. Section 7 covers exactly the case which I stated, because it requires that the person shall own the property at the date of the contract. It provides:

> That for the purposes of this act the word "futures" shall be understood to mean any contract or agreement whereby a party agrees to sell and deliver at a future time to another any of the articles mentioned in section 8 of this act when at the time of making such contract or agreement the party so agreeing to make such delivery, or the party for whom he acts as agent, broker, or employe in making such contract or agreement is not at the time of making the same the owner of the article so contracted and agreed to be delivered.

So this amendment does prohibit and suppress the making of a contract for future delivery unless the party making the contract is the actual owner of the thing sold and to be delivered. . . .

Yet, Mr. President, when I come to the practical question of asking him what does he mean by his bill, I absolutely demonstrate that he does not know what it means, and that he thought it meant directly contrary to what it does mean. I say that the bill does provide that, if any man in Kansas, in Massachusetts, or in Louisiana makes a contract with another man for the delivery of cotton, or wheat, or cotton print goods (that will come afterwards, not in this bill), at the time he makes that contract he must be the owner of the property which he sells and which he proposes to deliver. The Senator from Kansas did not know that that was in the amendment. He thought it was just the opposite. I wish to inform him that whenever the Congress of the United States undertakes to legislate in that direction, whether it be unconstitutional or constitutional, it will be a sorry day for the citizens of Kansas as well as the citizens of Louisiana. The people of the States have not been accustomed to come to Washington to ask the privilege of anybody of a license from Congress as to what contracts they shall and what contracts they shall not make. . . .

Mr. BLAIR. I should like to ask a question of the Senator from Kansas purely for information, for I had not supposed the bill went quite to the extent now alleged. The cotton manufactured in New England is nearly all of it purchased from brokers or farmers and institutions at the South, prior to its growth oftentimes, and nearly always before it is in the possession of the parties with whom the corporations, the mill-owners at the North, make their contracts for future delivery. So, then, the manufacture of cotton in New England is based upon contracts for the future delivery of cotton which is not in the possession of the other contracting party at the time the contract is made. I should like to know if the Senator means or understands this amendment of his to render illegal that practice, the regular business practice between New England and the South, between the manufacturers at the North and the cotton producers and middle-men at the South?

Mr. INGALLS. It is not aimed at any legitimate business. It is aimed at gambling in agricultural products, dealings between men who own none of the products they purport to sell and buy, and only intend to settle up the margin between the price at the time when they are to adjust their differences and the market price. . . .

The VICE-PRESIDENT. The question is on the amendment proposed by the Senator from Wisconsin [Mr. SPOONER].

The amendment was agreed to. . . .

Mr. SHERMAN. Mr. President, the plain purpose and meaning of the Senator from Kansas and the meaning of section 7 is to prevent gambling contracts, to prohibit what is done in all the boards, especially where wheat and corn not in existence are sold in immense quantities, to prevent such contracts and I think the sentiment of every member of the Senate would be against such contracts. They are very injurious. They enable persons without any property whatever, and sometimes without any money, to combine and put up the price of corn, wheat, etc. I am more familiar with the combinations in regard to corn and wheat than to cotton, but I can see that the same rule applies to that great staple. The language I think is too strong in the seventh section, and I would suggest to the Senator from Kansas to add to it in describing the contracts words which will indicate that there was no intention on the part of either party to deliver the actual article.

I can imagine many cases where men could go into the market and buy wheat, expecting the wheat to be delivered and to be sold again to the miller or somebody else. There are transactions of that kind occurring constantly, and it certainly is not the desire or intention of the Senator from Kansas to interfere with that kind of a contract. . . .

I think the words in the preceding section if carried into section 7 will cover the whole thing, that is to say, "the seller is not hereby obligated to deliver to another (that is the purchaser) at a future time or period any of the articles mentioned in the contract."

Mr. MITCHELL. A man may have a thousand acres of land sown in wheat; it may be growing, and if at any time before that wheat ripens or is harvested he makes a contract, based on the expectation that he is going to have a crop, to deliver a thousand bushels of wheat on the 1st day of October to A, that is declared an unlawful contract by this section plainly. Now, I want that amended.

Mr. SHERMAN. I do not care what words are used, but it is one of those cases certainly where words ought to be found to define exactly the difference between a gambling contract and a contract made by a broker. . . .

Mr. ALLISON. I had made a note of an amendment to the section covering the suggestions made by the Senator from Oregon [Mr. MITCHELL], and that is, to add after the word "owner," in line 9, the words "or producer."

Mr. [ARTHUR P.] GORMAN [D., Md.]. Where is that?

Mr. ALLISON. On page 5, section 7, line 9; so as to read:

Is not at the time of making the same the owner or producer of the article so contracted and agreed to be delivered.

There is a very common practice in every agricultural State of the Union to contract for farm products in advance of their actual existence. That is the case referred to by the Senator from Oregon [Mr. MITCHELL] and as indicated by the Senator from Louisiana [Mr. EUSTIS], I take it, in respect to cotton. A cotton producer in one of the States makes some arrangements with what is called a factor in New Orleans to secure advances on his crop and agrees to sell him that crop, I suppose, at the market price at the time of the delivery. Certainly, there should be no law to prevent a transaction of that character.

Mr. BLAIR. That factor is the same that the New England corporation or manufacturer contracts with and they make their contracts as early as, or earlier than, the factor contracts with the producer. Now, unless this language enables the manufacturers of New England to contract seasonably with this factor, not the producer, but the factor, the man who gathers in from the producer and who relies upon his contract with the producer as the basis for his contract with the manufacturer, unless the language reaches the New Englander, you see my difficulty. [Laughter.]

Mr. ALLISON. I see the difficulty under which the Senator from New Hampshire labors, and I think that if under the conditions I named a New England manufacturer, under the provisions of this bill with the words which I suggest added, were to contract with a factor or agent in New Orleans, if that agent at the time was an agent of the producer, and not otherwise, for the future delivery of cotton, it would be entirely proper.

Mr. BLAIR. But the factor is not necessarily the agent of the producer, and he often is not so. He makes his contract with the New Englander a long time before he has begun to gather in from the producer. . . .

Mr. MITCHELL. The word "producer" would cover the case I stated.

Mr. ALLISON. That is exactly what I want to do. In line 9 of section 7, on page 5, after the word "owner," I move to insert the words "or producer." . . .

. . . The cotton producer—and he is the producer in the language of this section as I propose to amend it—agrees to sell to the agent or factor or purchaser the product of his crop at the end of the season, or at a time which may be agreed upon, or which may be indefinite.

So I think the language I have employed here will cover that situation. It will not cover, however, the situation where a broker in New Orleans steps out upon 'change and sells 10,000 bales of cotton, to be delivered at a future time, without having a bale of cotton or the expectation or hope of having a bale, but is selling that cotton with a view of purchasing it, if necessary, to make the delivery on the 1st of May, or whatever the time may be, as the Senator from Louisiana said. This bill, I agree, does not cover that situation. Not only does it not cover it, but I think the language employed here is intended to prohibit it, and it does seem to me that it will be difficult to frame language here that will cover the entire situation and will break up this gambling in futures without breaking up the power of any man to sell that which he does not have or to buy that which he does not expect to receive. . . .

Mr. HOAR. Why would it not do to insert after the word "deliver," in line 10, the words "or does not at the time of such contract intend in good faith to deliver?"

Mr. MITCHELL. That is substantially what I suggested a few moments ago.

Mr. HOAR. It is a little different in phraseology, but it is in substance the Senator's idea. That, of course, puts upon the Government, if you are undertaking to indict, the *onus* of proving the intent; but that runs through all the great class of crimes. You know you have to prove the illegal intent and the surroundings and circumstances in general.

Mr. ALLISON. Mr. President, I do not object to the language suggested by the Senator from Massachusetts, but I submit that after this measure becomes a law with that language inserted every man who makes a contract to deliver an article in the future will have it inserted in the contract that the sale is made for the purpose of delivery, because these provisions require that these contracts shall be in writing.

Now, then, the intent is an intent at the time that the contract is made. The man who makes that sale will have in the intent to make the delivery at the time the sale is made, but it may happen that at the time of the delivery, which is a future time, it will not be possible for him to deliver the actual thing which he intended to deliver under that condition of selling, because occasions have arisen in Chicago and New York when it was physically impossible to deliver upon a given day the amount sold to be delivered on the day. So the man's intent will be, as the Senator from Massachusetts suggests it will be, an intent to deliver, but when the time comes it is impracticable to deliver, and then the two parties who make the contract will be compelled to make a new one or adjust their differences as they do now.

Mr. President, I want to say, as respects the modifications of this seventh section, that the complaint in the region of country in which I live is that this gambling in futures, this selling what people do not have to sell in quantities fifty times that which is in existence at the time, has a tendency to greatly depress the price of agricultural products. What our people want to do is to break up that habit, and that is the reason why they are in favor of some legislation such as is proposed by the Senator from Kansas; and I submit to the Senator from Louisiana that any serious modification of this provision which will enable the cotton brokers in New Orleans or in Chicago to do what he suggests they ought to be permitted to do, will have the effect of absolutely rendering nugatory the provisions of this bill as proposed by its author. Therefore it is that, if we are undertaking to deal with this question in the sense that the people who are opposed to these trusts want us to deal with it, we must, in essence at least, prohibit what the Senator from Louisiana says we ought not to prohibit.

I am not at this moment arguing whether or not the seventh section will do what the people who are opposed to these transactions think ought to be done; but I am very clear that the suggestions made by the Senator from Louisiana, if they are carried out, will make this seventh section absolutely a nugatory section.

Mr. BUTLER. . . . The question I want to get at is, and it is a practical one, whether or not that factor or broker or merchant, or whatever you may please to call him, would not be compelled under this bill in making a contract of that kind to take out a license and pay the tax imposed.

⊥ Mr. ALLISON. Under this bill as I propose to amend it I do not undertand ⊥2654 that such a broker would be obliged to take out a license. . . .

Mr. [JUSTIN S.] MORILL [R., Vt.]. I desire to suggest an amendment to the Senator from Iowa. A person making a sale of iron, of cotton, of cotton goods, or of woolen goods may not own a single dollar's worth, and may not be a producer thereof, and I suggest to the Senator to add, after the word "producer," the words "or the agent of such owner or producer."

The VICE-PRESIDENT. The Chair desires to call the attention of the Senator from Iowa to the fact that the amendment which he proposes is an amendment to the amendment offered by the Senator from Kansas [Mr. INGALLS], which was agreed to in Committee of the Whole, and an amendment to that amendment is therefore not now in order except by unanimous consent. The amendment will be in order when the bill is reported to the Senate.

Mr. BUTLER. . . .

I submit that under a fair construction of that language the merchant in New York, or in Baltimore, or in any of the commercial centers of Iowa, or in Illinois, or the South will be compelled, before he can enter into a contract with a farmer, to take out this license and pay that $1,000 and so much per pound for every pound of cotton, pork, lard, etc., that he deals in. Well, what will be the practical effect of it?

It will be that that merchant will charge the license tax to the farmer. The merchant is not going to pay it. . . .

Mr. HISCOCK. I desire to have the attention of the Senator from Kansas a moment. All over the State of New York there are located depots for the collection of milk, extending 300 miles from the city of New York, in regard to which the collector from the farmer or the middleman makes his contract with the dealer in New York

City to furnish him with so much milk per day, amounting, say, to not more than $50 a year in value. He makes the contract with the farmers in the neighborhood where his depot is located for them to furnish him with milk from day to day. Now, is there any doubt that such a middle-man would be compelled to take out a license?

Mr. INGALLS. Mr. President, I will answer the suggestion of the Senator from New York by reading the amendment that I shall propose to this section, in order to exclude any such possible definition. I propose, in line 9 of section 7, after the word "owner," to insert "or producer, or the lawful agent of such owner or producer." At the end of the proviso, after the word "value," I propose to strike out the period and insert a comma, and add, "nor to bona fide contracts for the actual delivery of the property contracted for." . . .

The VICE-PRESIDENT. The amendment will be read.

The CHIEF CLERK. Section 7, line 9, after the word "owner," it is proposed to insert the words "or producer or the lawful agent of such owner or producer," and after the amendment already agreed to at the end of the proviso, it is proposed to add the words "nor to bona fide contracts for the actual delivery of the property contracted for;" so as to read:

SEC. 7. That for the purposes of this act the word "futures" shall be understood to mean any contract or agreement whereby a party agrees to sell and deliver at a future time to another any of the articles mentioned in section 3 of this act when at the time of making such contract or agreement the party so agreeing to make such delivery, or the party for whom he acts as agent, broker, or employe in making such contract or agreement, is not at the time of making the same the owner or producer or the lawful agent of such owner or producer of the article so contracted and agreed to be delivered: *Provided*, that this act shall not apply to contracts for the delivery at any one time of not more than $50 in value, or of articles to be consumed by the person to whom they are to be delivered or in his establishment, nor to bona fide contracts for the actual delivery of the property contracted for.

Mr. [JOSEPH N.] DOLPH [R., Ore.]. It appears to me that there might be an easier way of getting rid of the section than by the amendment proposed to the proviso by the Senator from Kansas.

The sixth section provides—

That for the purposes of this act the word "options" shall be understood to mean any contract or agreement whereby a party thereto, or any person, corporation, partnership, or association for whom or in whose behalf such contract or agreement is made acquires the right or privilege, but is not thereby obligated, to deliver to another at a future time or period any of the articles mentioned in section 3 of this act.

A man who makes a contract with regard to personal property is obligated to deliver the property. If he fails to deliver it he pays damages. There is no law to enforce the specific performance of a contract to deliver farm produce, so that there is no real practical difference between options and futures. The provision of this bill which is to be effective is contained in the seventh section, which prevents dealing in futures. Now, to say that it shall not apply to any one who makes a bona fide contract for the delivery of these articles, in the first place complicates the matter by bringing in the question of bona fides. The contract may be bona fide; it may be the intention of the party to make the delivery; he may expect to do it, and he may prove that he did make such a contract; but if he does not make the delivery all that can be done is to get damages against him and make him pay the difference between the price at the time of delivery, if it is greater than at the time of sale. That is all there is of it. Therefore, these words will make both sections entirely inoperative.

I suppose that the real intention of the amendment of the Senator from Kansas was to prevent dealing in options. That is what we are striking at. How are you going to distinguish between a gambling contract and a contract made in good faith? There is the same facility in gambling, in speculating in futures, in a contract which is made in good faith, as in a contract made without any intention of actual delivery of the article.

Now, in regard to the purchase of articles from the producer, if there is no prohibition against this, there is nothing to prevent forestalling the market by securing control of the farm products of the West. A purchaser may buy the entire wheat crop, and so determine and fix the price for the consumer; and I say that nothing would be gained by providing that a farmer may sell, if everybody has the right to buy, and to forestall the market.

Then, again, if you prevent the purchaser of the crop, at least where it is intended for exportation, from making a contract for the sale of the article before he has purchased it, unless he buys it for speculation in advance of the time of delivery, he will not buy it at all.

It appears to me that the bill, while it deals with the producer and with articles that are imported, omits to deal with articles which are purchased and combinations formed to advance the price of articles which are purchased for export.

The VICE-PRESIDENT. The amendment now proposed being an amendment to the part of the bill inserted in Committee of the Whole, it may be received and reported by unanimous consent. The Chair hears no objection.

The CHIEF CLERK. In section 7, line 9, after the word "owner," it is proposed to insert:

Or producer or the lawful agent of such owner or producer.

And after the proviso in section 7 it is proposed to add:

Nor to bona fide contracts for the actual delivery of the property contracted for.

The amendment was agreed to. . . .

Mr. [N. W.] ALDRICH [R., R.I.]. I offer an amendment, which I think there will be no objection to, in section 1, after line 23.

The VICE-PRESIDENT. The amendment will be stated.

The CHIEF CLERK. It is proposed to add to section 1 an additional proviso, as follows:

Provided further, That this act shall not be construed to apply to or to declare unlawful combinations or associations made with a view or which tend, by means other than by a reduction of the wages of labor, to lessen the cost of production or reduce the price of any of the necessaries of life, nor to the combinations or associations made with a view or which tend to increase the earnings of persons engaged in any useful employment.

The amendment was agreed to.

Mr. BUTLER. I move to add, after the word "products," in line 4, at the end of section 8, the words "and also stocks and bonds."

The VICE-PRESIDENT. If there be no objection to receiving the amendment offered by the Senator from South Carolina, it will be stated.

The CHIEF CLERK. At the end of section 8 it is proposed to add "and also stocks and bonds;" so as to read:

SEC. 8. That the articles to which the foregoing sections relate are wheat, corn, oats, rye, barley, cotton, and all other farm products; also beef, pork, lard, and all other hog and cattle products; and also stocks and bonds.

Mr. REAGAN. Why, Mr. President, more harm is done by dealing in stocks and bonds than in nearly all other things put together. If we are going to adopt that amendment, we had better say the bill shall not apply to anything.

Mr. BUTLER. I was in hopes my friend would favor my amendment. If harm results from gambling in stocks and bonds, it is exactly what I want to get at. I want to suppress that evil as well as others. It is perfectly germane to the bill, and I think there is more gambling in stocks and bonds than in oats, rye, barley, cotton, and other things. . . .

The VICE-PRESIDENT. The question is on agreeing to the amendment offered by the Senator from South Carolina [Mr. BUTLER].

The amendment was agreed to.

Mr. EUSTIS. I move to add "cotton prints, steel rails, salt, boots and shoes, lumber, and lead," and anything else I can think of. [Laughter.]

The VICE-PRESIDENT. The amendment offered by the Senator from Louisiana will be read.

The CHIEF CLERK. At the end of section 8 it is proposed to add:

Also cotton prints, steel rails, salt, boots and shoes, lumber, and lead.

Mr. FRYE. I hope the Senator will not put in "lumber." I understood him to say "rubber." I would rather it would go in "rubber."

Mr. BLAIR. You did not hear right.

Mr. INGALLS. I forgot to ask the Senator from South Carolina when his amendment was pending whether stocks and bonds were to be taxed by the pound or by the bushel. [Laughter].

Mr. BUTLER. I think by the bushel, Mr. President, or the ton, if the Senator would prefer it. [Laughter.]

The VICE-PRESIDENT. The question is on agreeing to the amendment offered by the Senator from Louisiana [Mr. EUSTIS].

The amendment was agreed to.

Mr. BLAIR. I move to add "whisky and all manner of intoxicating drinks."

Mr. SHERMAN. This would be very funny if the hour was not so late, but I hope we may be able to pass this bill in half an hour or so; and as all these amendments have to be reported to the Senate, I ask Senators to let the bill be reported with the pending amendments, and then, of course, we can have a vote on these various propositions. . . .

Mr. BLAIR. I wish the amendment to read in this way:

Woolen goods, also whisky and all kinds of intoxicating liquors.

I mention whisky because I know that some of the Senators would understand what the rest of the amendment meant. [Laughter.]

The VICE-PRESIDENT. The amendment will be stated.

The CHIEF CLERK. It is proposed to add to section 8:

Also woolen goods, whisky, and all manner of intoxicating drinks.

The VICE-PRESIDENT. The question is on the amendment offered by the Senator from New Hampshire [Mr. BLAIR].

The amendment was agreed to.

Mr. GORMAN. Mr. President, I have not taken any part in the consideration of this measure except to give my votes very cheerfully in favor of the bill, which I think the entire country has been looking forward to the passage of in some shape that would correct the great evil which as been complained of, and properly complained of.

When the motion was made yesterday to refer this bill to the Committee on the Judiciary I voted against that proposition, hoping and believing that the bill would be so phrased and shaped that some practical good would come of the effort of the Senator from Ohio and those in charge of the bill. It is very evident, however, from what occurred late yesterday and from what has occurred to-day that we have so amended the present proposition as to make it inoperative and ineffectual. It will be worse than a sham and a delusion.

Being heartily in favor of the general proposition and with a desire to accomplish something for the people of this country, who have complained long of the evil which we are seeking to deal with, I now move that this measure be committed to the Committee on the Judiciary, with the suggestion of the Senator from Alabama [Mr. MORGAN] that that committee be requested to report the measure within twenty days; and on that motion I ask for the yeas and nays.

Mr. SHERMAN. About that I have something to say. I give notice to the Senate that there are features of this bill that I do not intend shall be defeated by indirection and by the mode which has been adopted here within the last hour. I give fair notice, so far as I am concerned, that this bill shall have fair play, I do not care who opposes it.

Mr. President, the amendments which have been put upon this bill in the last few minutes are such as simply bring it into contempt, and the manner in which this has been done tends to bring the whole bill into contempt. But the bill is worth preserving. There are three propositions in the bill, one the original bill amended, and I think very much strengthened and a better bill than it was at first, because it is a better bill than probably the committee would report. The first two or three or four sections of the bill there can be now no reasonable objection to. Most of the difficulties have been overcome. The proposition made by the Senator from Texas [Mr. REAGAN] is also in the right direction, and, after careful consideration of that proposition, there can be no objection to it so far as any one who is in favor of the principle of the bill is concerned. It adds a criminal clause and defines somewhat the meaning of words in the original bill. So far so good.

The attempt now to belittle the proposition of the Senator from Kansas seems to me an attempt to destroy and defeat this bill. I am to [sic] old a stager here not to understand the meaning of these various amendments. I know it perfectly well. But I say now that, for one, I do not care how long it takes, I do not propose that this bill shall be defeated in that way without at least a pretty fair chance to vote upon it.

There is some question as to the amendment proposed by the Senator from Kansas. Although it is wise in its purpose and in the main its provisions are wise, yet, as it has not been considered by a committee, it may very well possibly be postponed and be treated of in another and separate measure.

The fact that gambling contracts, made under the names given by brokers as "options" and "futures," are illegal contracts which tend to depreciate the value of agricultural products and tend to do a great deal of injury to the country is admitted on all hands. The men engaged in them know that they are unlawful. They are conducted in immense amounts.

I do not think that the sixth and seventh sections of the bill are framed with sufficient caution to prevent interference with ordinary legal and proper contracts between parties. It seems to me it would be very wise to mark out the line between a regular business transaction and a gambling contract where neither party contemplates the delivery of the article, where it is a mere bet on the value of the article. These bets tend to depreciate the value of agricultural products of the country at the time when they are offered for sale and tend to advance the price of articles at the time when men want to realize on their bets, their puts, and futures, and options.

I hope the Senator from Kansas will allow us to take a vote. This bill must be reported to the Senate. There are two propositions in it of great importance. The amendment of the Senator from Texas [Mr. REAGAN], which is now a distinct and separate amendment, and the vote upon that amendment will carry with it the amendments which have been made, and so with the proposition offered by the Senator from Kansas. As a matter of course, if that amendment is agreed to, it should be stripped of the various amendments which have been proposed here in humor and joke, or if it should be disagreed to—because it is not now in a fit condition to be made a part of this bill—it might be disagreed to by a single vote.

But I appeal to the Senate, now that we have this question of trusts and combinations before us, now that we have got a reasonable definition of trusts so as to meet the opinion of all Senators, when we have the machinery of law to carry the bill into effect and we have the additional sanction of a criminal provision to it, that we ought not to allow this bill to be defeated under these circumstances. If we do, the people of the United States will feel that the Senate of the United States is playing with a question which affects nearly and dearly the vital interests of our country.

That is all I have to say. I intend, so far as I can to try to strip this bill of anything that is objectionable to a majority of the Senate and then to pass what there is of virtual good in it.

Mr. INGALLS. Mr. President, so far as the suggestion of the Senator from Ohio about the abandonment of my amendment is concerned, I beg leave to say to him, with great deference and profound respect, that my amendment is the best thing there is about his bill. It is the only substantial proposition that offers definite, palpable, and tangible relief against what is acknowledged to be one of the gigantic evils of this century. This criticism and censure is idle and frivolous. There is not a man in this country who will read these proceedings tomorrow morning, if this provision is defeated, who will not know what it means. There is no farmer so remote or so obscure that he will not understand what these various amendments that have been offered mean. Nobody will be deluded by them. This is not the first time, Mr. President, that Nero has fiddled while Rome has burned. . . .

I ask that the bill may be reported to the Senate, and I shall demand a yea-and-nay vote in the Senate upon agreeing to these amendments that have been humorously inserted while the bill has been in Committee of the Whole. I know that sometimes the Senate has to unbend itself; the bow can not be always stretched. These amendments, I am confident, have been put on in a spirit of jocularity and recreation and refreshment. There has been a little time of recreation from labor. I feel confident that when the bill is reported to the Senate and such amendments are reserved they will, upon a yea-and-nay vote, be voted down. . . .

Mr. BUTLER. Mr. President, I do not think it is altogether fair to those of us who have not been within the charmed circle of the Judiciary Committee or the Committee on Finance to be told, as we have been by one Senator on one hand and another on another, that this bill must go through *nolens volens*, and that there will be no trifling with it, when they themselves admit, the Senator from Ohio himself admits, that there is some doubt about the constitutionality or form of the amendment of the Senator from Kansas, and therefore there ought to be some modifications in that; whereupon the Senator from Kansas rises with great indignation and assures the Senator from Ohio that his amendment is all there is in the bill that is worth anything.

Now, I want to say for one that my sympathies are with this bill. I should be very glad indeed to vote for it. But I have a little more respect for the Constitution than the Senator from Kansas appears to have, and I must be allowed to consult my own conscience and my own judgment as to what I think is constitutional and what is unconstitutional. If this bill can be put in such shape as to relieve it from the difficulties which have been suggested, I shall be most happy to vote for it. The Senator from Ohio says that he scarcely recognizes his own bill as it came from the Committee on Finance.

Mr. President, I think that this question will stand a little further ⊥ delay. It is a very important one, involving very complicated questions, so admitted by all parties, by the most distinguished lawyers of this body and by the laymen of the body. It has been discussed for four days, and the more we discuss it the more those complications and difficulties appear to increase. I want to vote for the bill. I want to vote for the amendment of the Senator from Kansas if I can. The amendments I offered were not offered for the purpose of depreciating the measure or in any spirit of humor or jocularity, as he says: but I was in earnest, and it so happened that the last amendment I suggested was adopted by his motion. . . .

Mr. GORMAN. Mr. President, from the discussion which has occurred since my motion to commit the bill to the Committee on the Judiciary was made, and the motion was only made for the purpose of perfecting the bill, as the Senator from Ohio who has charge of it insists upon going on with it in its present shape and letting it be reported to the Senate, I withdraw the motion.

Mr. SHERMAN, Mr. INGALLS, and others. Let the bill be reported to the Senate.

The VICE-PRESIDENT. Are there further amendments to the bill as in Committee of the Whole? If not, the bill will be reported to the Senate.

Mr. GRAY. Mr. President, I can not vote for the bill in its present shape. Notwithstanding the lecture which the Senator from Kansas gave us upon our duty in regard to questions of constitutional law, I still conceive it to have been the intention of those who sent us here that we should exercise the powers conferred by the Constitution on the legislative department of the Government, and not attempt to exercise those which were not conferred. . . .

We are not altogether without remedy. The States have the power to deal with many phases of this subject, in fact with all phases of it.

The only way in which they can fall short of a complete remedy is the territorial limit of their powers, but so far as they go the States which compose this Union can in a large measure apply a remedy that will meet the evil complained of. . . .

I should be quite willing just so far as I can find constitutional warrant for such legislation, to aid the States in suppressing these combinations and trusts which have undoubtedly produced many of the evils complained of. I would so reform the tariff as to take out of these combines the most important factor in them, eliminate from them the most important member, and that is the Government of the United States. By the provisions of our monstrous war tariff the Government of the United States has become a partner in these combines. It stands guard while the individual members of the partnership work their designs and carry out their purposes in regard to the objects of these combinations. I should be glad to unite in legislation that would reform this altogether.

But, sir, I have been very much struck in the course of this argument at the present session and also at the last Congress more than a year ago, by the amendment introduced by the Senator from Mississippi [Mr. GEORGE] to the bill of the Senator from Ohio when it was first presented to this body and referred to a committee, and which seemed to me to present for our consideration a proposition for Congressional action entirely within the powers conferred by the Constitution upon Congress, and which would go a long way, much further in my opinion even than the bill now before the Senate, towards correcting these evils. That was the amendment which the Senator from Mississippi has declined to offer to the bill at the present time, and which I have his permission to make my own. I therefore offer as an amendment to the bill the amendment which I send to the desk, and ask that it may be considered as in the nature of a substitute for the bill now before the Senate.

The PRESIDING OFFICER (Mr. HARRIS in the chair). The Chief Clerk will read the amendment proposed by the Senator from Delaware.

The CHIEF CLERK. It is proposed to strike out all after the enacting clause of the bill and to insert:

That all contacts, arrangements, agreements, trusts, or combinations between two or more persons or corporations, or between a corporation and a natural person engaged in selling, importing, manufacturing, or transporting articles of merchandise, made with a view of preventing or which tend to prevent, and all acts done by any person with a view of preventing or which tend to prevent, full and free competition in the importation, transportation, manufacturing, or sale of any article of merchandise, or which shall have the effect of advancing the cost of any such article to the consumer, are hereby declared to be unlawful to the extent herein provided, and subject to the provisions of the following section of this act: *Provided,* That this act shall not be construed to apply to any arrangements, agreements, or combinations between laborers made with the view of lessening the number of hours of labor or of increasing their wages; nor to any arrangements, agreements, or combinations among persons engaged in horticulture or agriculture made with the view of enhancing the price of agricultural or horticultural products.

SEC. 2. That when any action or suit in law or equity shall be commenced or shall be pending in any court of the United States, it shall be lawful for any defendant therein to except to the jurisdiction of such court upon the ground that the cause of action or suit is for the enforcement of a right of a person or corporation violating any of the provisions of the first section of this act based on a contract for the sale, exchange, or transportation, or based on any damage arising from any wrong committed in respect to any article of merchandise manufactured, transported, imported, bought, or sold in violation of the provisions of said first section; and if such ground of exception shall be proven to the satisfaction of the court, judgment of dismissal shall be entered, with double costs to the defendant and with such reasonable sum for the attorney's fees for the defense thereof as may be allowed by the court.

SEC. 3. That when the President of the United States shall be satisfied that any arrangement, trust, contract, agreement, or combination, as described in the first section of this act, has been formed, and that in consequence thereof there has been an enhancement of the price of any article of merchandise, he shall have power, and it is hereby made his duty, to issue his proclamation suspending the collection of all customs duties or import taxes on similar articles when imported into the United States from any foreign country. Such suspension shall continue for ninety days after the President, upon being satisfied that such enhancement in price no longer exists, shall issue his proclamation withdrawing his former proclamation of suspension. And the President of the United States may, from time to time, as may in his judgment be proper, reissue, modify, or withdraw any proclamation he may have issued.[1.351] . . .

Mr. GRAY. Mr. President, I desire to say only a few words in regard to this amendment which I have offered. It seems to me to have very carefully considered the question of what legislative power conferred by the Constitution upon Congress is appropriately applicable to this subject. It attempts in its second section, by invoking

---

[1.351] The amendment was identical with the George bill (S. 6) as introduced on December 4, 1889. The proviso in section 1 had been offered as an amendment to S. 1 and adopted, as modified, on March 25. *See supra* at 205–06.

the judicial power of the Government, to provide, as it may do, that whenever the judicial power of the United States is appealed to by a citizen of any State, if it shall appear that the subject-matter of the suit between the parties is a contract which is based upon an arrangement, combination, or trust that is declared unlawful by the bill which is now before the Senate, or when either of the parties to the suit or proposed suit shall have violated any of the provisions in regard to unlawful combinations, trusts, and arrangements, then that fact may be pleaded by the party sought to be affected by the suit, and the United States court in which the suit is brought shall dismiss for want of jurisdiction any such cause of action before it, thus withholding from all ⊥ who attempt to use the courts of the United States as a means of enforcing any matter or right claimed or growing out of such unlawful combinations, refusing the aid of the court to enforce such right or allowing that department of the Federal Government to be in any way ancillary to the cause of such arrangement or combination.

That goes a great way. The courts of the United States are the favorite resort for litigation between parties who are residents of different States, and where these large interests are concerned, stretching over the whole country, the parties generally being powerful corporations, the United States courts in ninety-nine cases out of a hundred would be the resort of litigants in matters growing out of such combinations or trusts. Then by this proposed legislation we absolutely forbid this class of suits being entertained, and thus disarm in a most important matter the power for evil of these combinations and illegal trusts.

That is one point of this proposed amendment. Another is that we shall attempt to do what I alluded to awhile ago, and that is measurably to dissever this great Government of the United States from its unworthy association with these combines and trusts which are now formed under the operation of our high protective tariff, and to allow the President of the United States whenever he is satisfied that the price of any article is raised to the consumer by means of these combinations or trusts, and such articles are imported into the United States under the provisions of the protective tariff, to suspend the operation of that law imposing customs duties for a period not exceeding ninety days, and to exercise that power in such a manner and with such discretion as will enable him to accomplish the result sought.

Here is a practicable, constitutional, and effective remedy that, if applied, will be sustained by the courts; will strike a deadly blow at the existence of this complaint of combinations, associations, and trusts; will not be mere *brutum fulmen*, if passed; will not be an act merely of show. We shall not be merely prancing like a hobby-horse and making no advancement on the enemy, but we shall have directly, constitutionally, and effectually disabled and disarmed these impolitic organizations of the power for evil that they now possess.

Mr. President, if we are in earnest, as I profess to be about this matter, let us adopt a measure of legislation which is within the admitted powers of Congress, and not merely content ourselves by declarations as to the immorality and impolicy of these trusts, declaring, as this bill does in its first section, that these impolitic and illegal combinations may be attacked in some unprovided-for way by the Attorney-General of the United States; not contenting ourselves merely with providing that the circuit court of the United States shall have original jurisdiction of all suits of a civil nature at law or in equity arising under this section, and to issue by remedial process the orders or writs proper and necessary to enforce its provisions, when there is not from beginning to end of that section any provision or any clause that makes it possible for a circuit court of the United States to obtain jurisdiction over any of the matters arising out of these trusts or combinations. It is all well enough to provide that the Attorney-General shall appear for the United States, but no process, no form of suit, no means by which a *lis mota* can be created on behalf of the United States is found from beginning to end in that section. . . .

Mr. WILSON, of Iowa. I desire to offer an amendment to come in at the end of section 1 of the bill, and as an addition to the proviso contained in that section.

The PRESIDING OFFICER. The Secretary will state the amendment proposed by the Senator from Iowa.

The CHIEF CLERK. It is proposed to add at the end of the second proviso to section 1:

Nor to any arrangements, agreements, associations, or combinations among persons for the enforcement and execution of the laws of any State enacted in pursuance of its police powers; nor shall this act be held to control or abridge such powers of the States.

The PRESIDING OFFICER. The question is on agreeing to the amendment proposed by the Senator from Iowa. . . .

Mr. EUSTIS. Where does the Senator propose his amendment to come in?

Mr. WILSON, of Iowa. I propose it as an addition to the proviso of section 1, and it is simply for the purpose of avoiding an effect which is likely to flow from the earlier provisions of that section. That section provides as follows:

That all arrangements, contracts, agreements, trusts, or combinations between two or more persons or corporations, or both, made with a view or which tend to prevent full and free competition in the importation, transportation, or sale of articles imported into the United States, or with a view or which tend to prevent full and free competition in articles of growth, production, or manufacture of any State or Territory of the United States with similar articles of the growth, production, or manufacture of any other State or Territory, or in the transportation or sale of like articles, the production of any State or Territory of the United States, into or within any other State or Territory of the United States: and all arrangements, trusts, or combinations between such persons or corporations made with a view or which tend to advance the cost to the consumer of any such articles are hereby declared to be against public policy, unlawful, and void.

I will state frankly my purpose in offering the amendment. Under the provisions of this section, should it become a law, every organization in such a State as Iowa, for instance, of the character of the Woman's Christian Temperance Union, the Temperance Alliance, and other organizations intended to promote the execution of the laws of that State in respect of the manufacture and sale of intoxicating liquors would become illegal bodies and their movements subject to the terms and provisions of this bill. I know that was not intended, and yet the language, without being stripped of its power by the amendment I propose, would include all organizations of that kind. All I ask is that the subjects within the police power of the States as embraced within that legislation, of Iowa and any other State which may desire similar legislation, shall not be embraced within this provision, but that the States shall be left free in the execution of their police powers. . . .

I will just add to what I have said that the proviso to which I offered this as an amendment excepts from the operations of this section of the bill arrangements, agreements, or combinations between laborers, made with a view of lessening the number of hours of their labor or of increasing their wages, and it also excepts arrangements, agreements, associations, or combinations among persons engaged in horticulture or agriculture, made with a view of enhancing the price of their own agricultural or horticultural products. I think that the exception which I ask to have made by this amendment is quite as worthy of the support of the Senate as either of these.

Mr. HOAR. Allow me to ask the Senator if his amendment accomplishes his object. I understand his object is to protect combinations of persons intended to discourage the use and manufacture of intoxicating liquors.

Mr. WILSON, of Iowa. My object is to exclude them from the operation of the bill.

Mr. HOAR. I understand, to protect them from being affected by it. But the only description in his amendment is of such associations as are in aid of the execution of the laws of a State in pursuance of its police power. Now, if this bill without his amendment would render the class of persons he has described subject to the penal provision, all temperance societies whose object is to persuade mankind not to use intoxicating liquors would still remain in spite of his amendment within the purview of the bill. It seems to me he should extend his amendment a little further, because, as far as my State goes, this class of associations which he has described do not confine their efforts to the execution of the law, but their efforts are a great deal more extensive and extend to discouraging the use or manufacture of intoxicating liquors altogether. This is what he means, and we would all vote for it.

Mr. WILSON, of Iowa. I am satisfied that my amendment will cover the purpose I have in view concerning my State. If other Senators desire something further in regard to their States, they can move it.

Mr. HOAR. I move to amend the Senator's amendment by adding to it:

Or to discourage the use or manufacture of intoxicating liquors.

And we will take a vote on that. . . .

The PRESIDING OFFICER. The question is on agreeing to the amendment to the amendment.

Mr. SHERMAN. The Senator from Iowa showed me his amendment. As these organizations in Iowa are associated and organized something in the nature of a corporation, there might be some reason for believing that they possibly might fall within the meaning of the clauses of the bill. Therefore, I have no objection to his amendment, but I do not see any reason for putting in temperance societies any more than churches or school-houses or any other kind of moral or educational associations that may be organized. Such an association is not in any sense a combination or arrangement made to interfere with interstate commerce; but under the peculiar circumstances, upon the facts stated by the Senator from Iowa, I think it is very proper to make an exception of those organizations in Iowa which are really in aid of the execution of State law. I would apply it to all organizations which are using either moral or any other kind of means for the enforcement of local laws; but I do not think it is worth while to adopt the amendment of the Senator from Massachusetts, because that would include temperance societies. You might as well include churches and Sunday schools.

Mr. CULLOM. . . .

While I am very anxious to pass a proper bill that will prohibit trusts and break them up and protect the people of this country I should much prefer having a bill carefully considered by a committee in order that we may intelligently vote upon it.

While I do not know whether the honorable Senator from Ohio will consent to it or not, yet I very much hope he will consent to a recommittal of the bill, with all the amendments, to the Committee on Finance.

Mr. SHERMAN. It would take two weeks longer.

Mr. CULLOM. I do not care if it does. I want to get something out of this measure that will do some good and not do any harm. In my judgment we are liable to pass something here that will destroy business instead of protecting the legitimate business of the country. Everybody who knows me, in the Senate and elsewhere, I think, knows me well enough to be assured that I am for the interest of the people, if I can find out what that is and if we can do it constitutionally and legitimately. But I am not willing to vote for a bill about which there is very serious doubt as to whether we will not injure the interests of the people, instead of protecting and benefiting them. . . .

Sir, I do not want to delay this subject, neither do I desire that the business of the Senate shall be interfered with, but this is as important a question as can come before us, and it is important that we should get the bill in proper shape before we pass it. I know that the Senator from Ohio is anxious to pass a proper bill on this subject, and I trust he will consent that the Senate shall recommit the bill to the Committee on Finance in order that they may report it to the Senate again after they have maturely considered the different amendments before them.

I hope the Senate will vote upon a motion and vote in favor of a motion, whether the Senator from Ohio desires the bill to go back to that committee or not, to send it back to the Finance Committee, with all of the amendments that have been offered, the most of which have been adopted, and let them consider the various propositions in their committee room carefully, and then bring in here a measure which they think ought to be passed, and I have no doubt the Senate will pass it. I make that motion, Mr. President.

The PRESIDING OFFICER. The Senator from Illinois moves that the bill be recommitted to the Committee on Finance. Is the Senate ready for the question?

Mr. SHERMAN. After four days' debate, all that is required is for us to have a vote upon these amendments. The Senate have now got all the information that can be communicated by the committee. There is no use in a reference of the bill; and if we go on in that way transacting the business of the country we shall never close this session. . . .

I know that every sentence and every line of the bill has been read to the Senate over and over again. It has been printed three times and the only point of difference now (and but for that point I believe the bill would have passed before this time) is whether the seventh section sufficiently defines what are called "futures." That doubt has arrested the passage of the bill, and but for that it would have passed before this time. Now that doubt has practically been removed by the amendment proposed by the Senator from Kansas. . . .

Mr. INGALLS. If the Committee on Finance should see fit to report the bill without the amendment that has been offered by me, I pledge myself distinctly to offer it again when the bill comes to the Senate.

Mr. DOLPH. I wish to say that I believe the amendment of the Senator from Kansas to be the important part of this bill. If any portion of the bill will accomplish the purpose designed this will, and if any part of the bill, in my judgment, is within the constitutional power of Congress the amendment offered by the Senator from Kansas is. But I think the Senator from Kansas has inadvertently, not having given the matter his usual careful consideration, taken the life out of his entire amendment. He has destroyed by the amendment to the proviso sections 6 and 7, and if those sections are destroyed there is nothing left of his proposition, because it now provides that the whole act shall not apply to bona fide contracts for the actual delivery of the property contracted for.

If there is such a contract it is not necessary for the party to deliver the article. If the contract is made in good faith and the seller does not choose to deliver the article he simply pays the damages, he pays the difference in the price; but if you were to go further and had the power, which you have not, to provide that it shall be delivered, it would not stop gambling in futures at all, because if there were half a million bushels of corn in the elevators in Chicago the warehouse receipts of that grain would be floating around the city; they would pass from hand to hand like checks upon money deposited in a bank, and you could every day in the year deliver, because the delivery of the receipt for the corn in the warehouse would be a delivery of the corn, and you could actually deliver and contract every day in the year for ten or twenty million bushels of corn.

Mr. [JOSEPH R.] HAWLEY [R. Conn.]. Mr. President, every Senator who speaks discloses to me the hopelessness of this situation. It is quite impossible to specify what propositions will receive the approval of a majority of the Senate, and yet the combinations of all the propositions may be such that nobody will vote for the bill, and that is just about where we stand now. I think the bill as it stands now literally has not a friend in the Senate. The Senator from Ohio indicates practically that it is an impossibility for anybody to vote for it as it stands.

Mr. SHERMAN. Oh, no.

Mr. HAWLEY. I understood the Senator to say that the bill as it is just now ought not to pass.

Mr. SHERMAN. Oh, no.

Mr. HAWLEY. Very well; I think that nine-tenths of the Senate would say so. That is my opinion of it.

Mr. INGALLS. A majority of the amendments have been offered subsequently to the last amendment adopted to section 7.

Mr. HAWLEY. Yet that was adopted by the Senate. There are half a dozen amendments there bunched together that received the approval of the Senate apparently.

Mr. President, I have a few words more to say. Nobody from the Committee on Finance has advocated this bill except its distinguished reporter and perhaps author. I do not remember that any one else has spoken for it from that committee. But we have a committee in the Senate chosen for the express purpose of considering great general laws, statutes that are intended to remain and do great work. . . .

⊥ I can not vote for the bill as it stands now. You may shear off any one of half a dozen things that remain and yet I could not vote for it. But there is a broad, general purpose of the bill as originally reported that I approve.

⊥2660

Now, I move sincerely, and with a desire to get at the truth, to amend the motion of the Senator from Illinois by inserting the Judiciary Committee, so as to refer the bill to the Judiciary Committee.

Mr. SHERMAN. The vote must be taken separately on that question. . . .

The PRESIDING OFFICER. The question is on the motion of the Senator from Illinois to recommit the bill to the Committee on Finance.

The motion was not agreed to, there being on a division—ayes 17, noes 31.

The PRESIDING OFFICER. The question recurs on the amendment of the Senator from Massachusetts [Mr. HOAR] to the amendment of the Senator from Iowa [Mr. WILSON].

Mr. HAWLEY. I move to refer the bill and all amendments to the Committee on the Judiciary, and if it be proper I would add, with instructions to report within a fortnight.

The PRESIDING OFFICER. The Chair holds that that motion is in order. The Senator from Connecticut moves that the bill and amendments be referred to the Committee on the Judiciary, with instructions that that committee shall report back to the Senate within two weeks. The question is on agreeing to the motion of the Senator from Connecticut.

The motion was not agreed to, there being on a division—ayes 24, noes 29.

The PRESIDING OFFICER. The question recurs on the amendment of the Senator from Massachusetts to the amendment of the Senator from Iowa.

Mr. VANCE (at 6 o'clock and 15 minutes p.m.). I move that the Senate do now adjourn.

Mr. SHERMAN and others. Oh, no. . . .

The PRESIDING OFFICER. The question is on the motion of the Senator from North Carolina that the Senate do now adjourn.

The motion was not agreed to.

The PRESIDING OFFICER. The question recurs on the amendment of the Senator from Massachusetts to the amendment of the Senator from Iowa.

Mr. HOAR. I will withdraw my amendment, solely in the interest of saving time.

The PRESIDING OFFICER. The question then recurs on the amendment of the Senator from Iowa [Mr. WILSON].

The amendment was agreed to.

The PRESIDING OFFICER. The question is on the amendment in the nature of a substitute proposed by the Senator from Delaware [Mr. GRAY]. Is the Senate ready for the question?

Mr. BUTLER. Let us have the yeas and nays.

The yeas and nays were ordered; and the Secretary proceeded to call the roll. . . .

⊥ The result was announced—yeas 18, nays 26; as follows: . . .

So the amendment was rejected.

Mr. GRAY. I offer the amendment which I send to the desk, to the bill, and ask that it be read. Is the bill in the Senate or in Committee of the Whole?

The PRESIDING OFFICER. The bill is in Committee of the Whole and open to amendment.

Mr. GRAY. I move to add after section 5 the section which I have sent to the desk.

The PRESIDING OFFICER. The Secretary will report the amendment proposed.

The CHIEF CLERK. After section 5 it is proposed to insert the following new section:

SEC. —. That when the President of the United States shall be satisfied that any arrangement, trust, contract, agreement or combination, as described in the first section of this act, has been formed, and that in consequence thereof there has been an enhancement of the price of any article of merchandise, he shall have power, and it is hereby made his duty to issue his proclamation suspending the collection of all customs duties or import taxes on similar articles when imported into the United States from any foreign country. Such suspension shall continue for ninety days after the President, upon being satisfied that such enhancement in price no longer exists, shall issue his proclamation withdrawing his former proclamation of suspension. And the President of the United States may, from time to time, as may in his judgment be proper, reissue, modify, or withdraw any proclamation he may have issued.

The PRESIDING OFFICER. The question is, Will the Senate agree to the amendment?

Mr. VEST. I call for the yeas and nays on that amendment.

The yeas and nays were ordered, and the Secretary proceeded to call the roll. . . .

The result was announced—yeas 21, nays 25; as follows: . . .

So the amendment was rejected.

Mr. VEST. I move to amend the bill, in section 9, line 5, by striking out the word "one," before the word "thousand," and inserting "ten."

The PRESIDING OFFICER. The amendment will be stated.

The CHIEF CLERK. In section 9, line 5, before the word "thousand," it is proposed to strike out "one" and insert "ten," so as to read:

Dealers in "options" or "futures" shall pay annually the sum of $10,000.

The amendment was agreed to—ayes 28, noes not counted. . . .

Mr. VEST. In line 15 of section 10, before the word "thousand," I move to strike out "one" and insert "ten;" so as to conform to the former amendment made on my motion.

The PRESIDING OFFICER. The amendment will be stated.

The CHIEF CLERK. In section 10, line 15, before the word "thousand," it it [sic] proposed to strike out "one" and insert "ten," so as to read:

And shall thereupon pay to such collector the sum aforesaid of $10,000.

Mr. SHERMAN. I raise the point of order on the amendment.

The PRESIDING OFFICER. The Senator will state his point of order.

Mr. SHERMAN. These amounts have been inserted by an amendment made as in Committee of the Whole, and consequently they are not now amendable. Most of these amendments have been out of order. I feel bound to raise the point.

The PRESIDING OFFICER. The amendment, being an amendment already agreed to as in Committee of the Whole, is not now amendable by the change proposed by the Senator from Missouri, and his amendment is not in order.

Mr. VEST. I suppose I can offer the amendment in the Senate.

The PRESIDING OFFICER. It will be in order in the Senate. The bill is still in Committee of the Whole and open to amendment. If there are no further amendments, the bill will be reported to the Senate.

The bill was reported to the Senate as amended.

The PRESIDING OFFICER. The Senate has made sundry amendments to the bill.

Mr. VEST. Now I submit my amendment.

Mr. INGALLS. The first question is on the amendments made as in Committee of the Whole.

The PRESIDING OFFICER. The question is on concurring in the amendments made as in Committee of the Whole; and then the Chair asks whether the question shall be put in gross or whether certain amendments shall be reserved.

Mr. INGALLS. I wish to reserve all the amendments made to section 7, I think it is, beginning with that offered by the Senator from South Carolina [Mr. BUTLER].

Mr. EDMUNDS. Reserve all the amendments; take them all one by one.

The PRESIDING OFFICER. All the amendments are reserved. The question will be put on each amendment separately, and the Secretary will report for information the first amendment made as in Committee of the Whole. . . .

Mr. SHERMAN. I ask for an order to reprint the bill with the amendments which have been made to it.

The PRESIDING OFFICER. That order will be made, in the absence of objection.

S. 1 AS AMENDED BY THE SENATE
51st Cong., 1st Sess.
March 26, 1890

⊥ Ordered to be reprinted as amended in Committee of the Whole, viz: Omit the parts struck through and insert the parts printed in *italics*.

A BILL

To declare unlawful trusts and combinations in restraint of trade and production.

1 *Be it enacted by the Senate and House of Representa-*
2 *tives of the United States of America in Congress assembled,*
3 That all arrangements, contracts, agreements, trusts, or com-
4 binations between two or more ~~citizens~~ *persons* or corporations,
5 or both, made with a view or which tend to prevent full and
6 free competition in the importation, transportation, or sale of
7 articles imported into the United States; or with a view or
8 which tend to prevent full and free competition in articles of
9 growth, production, or manufacture of any State or Territory
10 of the United States with similar articles of the growth, pro-
11 duction, or manufacture of any other State or Territory, or in
12 the transportation or sale of like articles, the production of
13 any State or Territory of the United States, into or within any
14 other State or Territory of the United States; and all arrange-
15 ments, trusts, or combinations between such ~~citizens~~ *persons*
16 or corporations made with a view or which tend to advance
17 the cost to the consumer of any such articles *or of the value*
18 *of money by which such cost may be advanced or reduced* are
19 hereby declared to be against public policy, unlawful, and void.
20 And the circuit court of the United States shall have original
21 jurisdiction of all suits of a civil nature at common law or in
22 equity arising under this section, and to issue all remedial
23 process, orders, or writs proper and necessary to enforce its
24 provisions. And the Attorney-General and the several dis-
25 trict attorneys are hereby directed, in the name of the United
26 States, to commence and prosecute all such cases to final judg-
27 ment and execution. *And whenever in any action commenced*
28 *under the provisions of this act in the name of the United*
29 *States any arrangement, trust, or combination herein declared*
30 *void is found by any such court to exist, the court may, in*
31 *addition to other remedies, issue its writ of injunction, tem-*
32 *porary or final, running and to be served anywhere within*
33 *the United States, prohibiting and restraining the defendants,*
34 *or any thereof, or their or any of their servants, agents, or*
35 *attorneys, from proceeding further in the business of said*
36 *arrangement, trust, or combination, except to wind up its*
37 *affairs; and in case of any disobedience of any such writ of*
38 *injunction, or other proper process, mandatory or otherwise,*

39 issued in any such cause, it shall be lawful for said court to
40 issue writs of attachment, running and to be served any-
41 where within the United States, against the defendants, or
42 any thereof, and against their or any of their agents, attor-
43 neys, or servants, of whatever name or office, disobeying said
44 injunction or other process; and the court may, if
45 it shall think fit, in addition to other lawful punishment for
46 contempt, make an order directing any such defendants dis-
47 obeying such writ of injunction, or other process, to
48 pay such sum of money, not exceeding one thousand dollars,
49 for every day after a date to be named in such order that
50 such defendant or defendants, or their or any of their agents,
51 attorneys, or servants, as aforesaid, shall refuse or neglect to
52 obey such injunction or other process; and such money shall
53 be paid into court, and may be paid in whole or in part to
54 the party or parties upon whose complaint said action was
55 instituted, or into the Treasury of the United States, as the
56 court shall direct, and in any action brought by the United
57 States under the provisions of this act the Attorney-General
58 may bring the action in any district in which any one of the
59 parties defendant resides or transacts business, and any other
60 parties, corporate or otherwise, may, regardless of residence
61 or location of business, be brought into court in said action
62 in the manner provided by section seven hundred and
63 thirty-eight of the Revised Statutes, and the court shall there-
64 upon have jurisdiction of the defendant or defendants so
65 brought in, as fully to all intents and purposes as if they had
66 appeared in said action. Provided, That this act shall not be
67 construed to apply to any arrangements, agreements, or com-
68 binations between laborers made with a view of lessening
69 the number of hours of their labor or of increasing their
70 wages; nor to any arrangements, agreements, associations
71 or combinations among persons engaged in horticulture or
72 agriculture made with the view of enhancing the price of their
73 own agricultural or horticultural products: *Provided further,*
74 *That this act shall not be construed to apply to or to declare*
75 *unlawful combinations or associations made with a view or*
76 *which tend, by means other than by a reduction of the wages*
77 *of labor, to lessen the cost of production or reduce the price*
78 *of any of the necessities of life; nor to combinations or as-*
79 *sociations made with a view or which tend to increase the*
80 *earnings of persons engaged in any useful employment; nor*
81 *to any arrangements, agreements, associations, or combina-*
82 *tions among persons for the enforcement and execution of*
83 *the laws of any State enacted in pursuance of its police*
84 *powers; nor shall this act be held to control or abridge such*
85 *powers of the States.*
1   SEC. 2. That any person or corporation injured or dam-
2   nified by such arrangement, contract, agreement, trust, or
3   combination defined in the first section of this act may sue
4   for and recover, in any court of the United States or any State
5   of competent jurisdiction, without respect to the amount in-
6   volved, of any person or corporation a party to a combination

described in the first section of this act, twice the amount of damages sustained and the costs of the suit, together with a reasonable attorney's fee.

SEC. 3. That all persons engaged in the creation of any trust, or as owner or part owner, agent, or manager of any trust, ~~employed~~ engaged in any business carried on with any foreign country, or between the States, or between any State and the District of Columbia, or between any State and any Territory of the United States, or any owner or part owner, agent or manager of any corporation, company or person ~~employed~~ engaged in any such business using its powers for either of the purposes specified in the fourth section of this act, shall be deemed guilty of a high misdemeanor, and, on conviction thereof, shall be fined in a sum not exceeding ten thousand dollars, or imprisonment at hard labor in the penitentiary not exceeding five years, or by both of said penalties, in the discretion of the court trying the same.

SEC. 4. That a trust is a combination of capital, skill, or acts by two or more persons, firms, or corporations, or associations of persons, or of any two or more of them for either, any, or all of the following purposes:

First. To create or carry out any restrictions in trade.

Second. To limit or reduce the production or to increase or reduce the price of merchandise or commodities.

Third. To prevent competition in the manufacture, making, purchase, sale, or transportation of merchandise, produce, or commodities.

Fourth. To fix a standard or figure whereby the price to the public shall be in any manner controlled or established of an article, commodity, merchandise, produce, or commerce intended for sale, use, or consumption.

Fifth. To create a monopoly in the making, manufacture, purchase, sale, or transportation of any merchandise, article, produce, or commodity.

Sixth. To make, or enter into, or execute, or carry out any contract, obligation, or agreement of any kind or description by which they shall bind, or shall have bound themselves, not to manufacture, sell, dispose of, or transport any article or commodity, or article of trade, use, merchandise, or consumption below a common standard figure, or by which they shall agree, in any manner, to keep the price of such article, commodity, or transportation at a fixed or graduated figure or by which they shall in any manner establish or settle the price of any article, commodity, or transportation between themselves, or between themselves and others, so as to preclude free and unrestricted competition among themselves and others in the sale and transportation of any such article or commodity, or by which they shall agree to pool, combine, or unite in any interest they may have in connection with the sale or transportation of any such article or commodity that its price may in any manner be so affected.

SEC. 5. That each day any of the persons, associations, or corporations aforesaid shall be engaged in violating the provisions of this act shall be held to be a separate offense.

SEC. 6. That for the purposes of this act the word "options" shall be understood to mean any contract or agreement whereby a party thereto, or any person, corporation, or partnership, or association, for whom or in whose behalf such contract or agreement is made, acquires the right or privilege, but is not thereby obligated, to deliver to another at a future time or period any of the articles mentioned in section ~~three~~ *eight* of this act.

SEC. 7. That for the purposes of this act the word "futures" shall be understood to mean any contract or agreement whereby a party agrees to sell and deliver at a future time to another any of the articles mentioned in section ~~three~~ *eight* of this act when at the time of making such contract or agreement the party so agreeing to make such delivery, or the party for whom he acts as agent, broker, or employee in making such contract or agreement, is not at the time of making the same the owner, *or producer, or the lawful agent of such owner or producer* of the article so contracted and agreed to be delivered: *Provided,* That this act shall not apply to contracts for the delivery at any one time of articles of not more than fifty dollars in value, *or of articles to be consumed by the person to whom they are delivered, or in his establishment.*

Nor to bona fide contracts for the actual delivery of the property contracted for.

SEC. 8. That the articles to which the foregoing sections relate are wheat, corn, oats, rye, barley, cotton, and all other farm products; also beef, pork, lard, and all other hog and cattle products, *and also stocks and bonds;*

Also cotton prints, steel rails, lead, salt, boots and shoes, and lumber;

Also woolen goods, whiskey, and all manner of intoxicating drinks.

SEC. 9. That for the purpose of preventing and suppressing, as far as may be, the dealing in options and futures as herein defined, special taxes are imposed as follows: Dealers in "options" or "futures" shall pay annually the sum of ~~one~~ *ten* thousand dollars, and shall also pay the further sum of five cents per pound for each and every pound of cotton or of beef, pork, lard, or other hog and cattle products, and the sum of twenty cents per bushel for each and every bushel of any of the articles mentioned in section ~~three~~ *eight* of this act, the right or privilege of delivering which may be acquired under any "options" contract or agreement, as defined by section ~~one~~ *six* of this act, or which may be sold to be delivered at a future time or period under any "futures" contract or agreement as defined in section ~~two~~ *seven* of this act, which said amounts shall be paid to the collector of internal revenue as hereinafter provided, and by him accounted for, as required in respect to other special taxes collected by him. Every person, association, copartnership, or corporation who shall, in their own behalf, or as broker, agent, or employee of another, deal in "options," or make any "options" contract or agreement, as hereinbefore defined, shall be deemed a dealer in "options," and every person, association, copartnership, or corporation who shall, in their own behalf, or as broker, agent, or employee of another, deal in "futures," or make any "futures" contract or agreement as hereinbefore defined, shall be deemed a dealer in "futures."

SEC. 10. That every person, association, copartnership, or corporation engaged in, or proposing to engage in, the business of dealer in "options" or of dealer in "futures," as hereinbefore defined, shall, before commencing such business or making any such "options" or "futures" contract or agreement, make application in writing to the collector of internal revenue for the district in which he proposes to engage in such business or make such contract or agreement, setting forth the name of the person, association, partnership, or corporation, place of residence of the applicant, the business engaged in, and where such business is to be carried on, and in case of partnership, association, or corporation, the names and places of residence of the several persons constituting the same, and shall thereupon pay to such collector the sum aforesaid of one thousand dollars, and shall also execute and deliver to such collector a bond in the penal sum of fifty thousand dollars with two or more sureties satisfactory to the collector, conditioned upon the full and faithful compliance by the obligor therein with all the requirements of this act. And thereupon the collector shall issue to such applicant a certificate, in such form as the Commissioner of Internal Revenue shall prescribe, that such applicant is authorized for the period of one year from the date of such certificate to be a dealer in "options" or "futures" and to make "options" or "futures" contracts or agreements as hereinbefore defined; and for the period specified in such certificate the party to whom it is issued may conduct the business of dealer as aforesaid. Such certificate may be renewed annually upon the compliance with the provisions of this act and any "options" or "futures" contract or agreement as defined by this act shall be absolutely void between the parties thereto and their respective assigns, unless the party making such contract or agreement shall have at the time of making the same a certificate as aforesaid authorizing the making thereof.

SEC. 11. That it shall be the duty of the collector to keep in his office a register containing a copy of each and every application made to him under the foregoing section and a statement in connection therewith as to whether a certificate had been issued thereon and for what period, which book or register shall be a public record and be subject to inspection of any and all persons desiring to examine the same.

SEC. 12. That every "options" or "futures" contract or agreement as hereinbefore defined shall be in writing and signed in duplicate by the parties making the same; and any such contract or agreement not so made and signed shall, as between the parties thereto and their assigns, be absolutely void.

SEC. 13. That it shall be the duty of every person, copartnership, association, or corporation, on the first day of the week next succeeding the date of the certificate issued to them, and on the first day of each and every week thereafter, to make to the collector of the district in which any "options" or "futures" contract or agreement has been made full and complete return and report under oath of any and all such contracts or agreements made or entered into by such person, copartnership, association, or corporation during the previous week, together with a statement of the article or articles embraced in or covered by such contracts or agreements, and the amounts, respectively, of each, and the name of the party or parties with whom such contracts or agreements have been made, and at the same time to pay to such collector the amount of the tax hereinbefore required of five cents per pound on each and every pound of cotton, and of beef, pork, lard, or any other hog and cattle products, and of twenty cents per bushel on each and every bushel of any of the other articles mentioned in section ~~three~~ *eight* of this act, which are the subject of or covered by such contracts or agreements, or any of them, for which sums such collector shall give his receipt to the party so paying, and the sums so collected shall be accounted for by the collector as provided by law in respect to other taxes collected by him.

SEC. 14. That every person who shall in his own behalf, or in behalf of any other person, association, partnership, or corporation, enter into any "options" or "futures" contract or agreement as defined by this act, without having a certificate of authority from the collector as hereinbefore provided, and covering the time at which such contract or agreement shall be made, shall, besides being liable for the amounts prescribed in section ~~four~~ *nine* of this act, be fined not less than five thousand dollars and not more than ten thousand dollars for each and every such offense. And every person who shall make to the collector a false or fraudulent return or report required by section ~~eight~~ *thirteen* of this act shall be subject to a fine of not less than five thousand dollars nor more than ten thousand dollars, or to imprisonment for not less than six months or more than two years, or to both such fine and imprisonment.

SEC. 15. That neither the payment of the taxes required or the certificate issued by the collector under this act shall be held to legalize dealing in "options" and "futures," nor to exempt any person, association, copartnership, or corporation from any penalty or punishment now or hereafter provided by the laws of any State for making contracts or agreements such as are hereinbefore defined as "options" or "futures" contracts or agreements, or in any manner to authorize the making of such contracts or agreements within any State or locality contrary to the laws of such State or locality; nor shall the payment of the taxes imposed by this act be held to prohibit any State or municipality from placing a tax or duty on the same trade, transaction, or business for State, municipal, or other purposes.

SEC. 16. That section thirty-two hundred and nine of the Revised Statutes of the United States is, so far as applicable, made to extend and apply to the taxes imposed by this act and to the persons upon whom they are imposed.

SENATE DEBATE
51st Cong., 1st Sess.
March 27, 1890

21 CONG. REC. 2723

Mr. SHERMAN. I now move that the Senate proceed to the consideration of the unfinished business of yesterday, Senate bill No. 1.

The motion was agreed to; and the Senate resumed the consideration of the bill (S. 1) to declare unlawful trusts and combinations in restraint of trade and production.

The VICE-PRESIDENT. The question is on concurring in the amendments made as in Committee of the Whole.

Mr. SHERMAN. I ask that the vote on the amendments be taken separately. They can be disposed of rapidly in that way.

The VICE-PRESIDENT. The first amendment will be read. . . .

The amendments will be stated in their order.

The CHIEF CLERK. The first reserved amendment is, in line 4 of section 1, to strike out "citizens" and insert "persons;" so as to read:

Two or more persons or corporations. . . .

⊥ Mr. SHERMAN. The only mistake the clerks made—and it was a very small mistake—was this: There was one amendment made which does not appear in this print, and the only one that I know of. If the Senator from Connecticut can find any other he may point it out. The Senator from Massachusetts [Mr. HOAR] moved to strike out three lines of the bill specifying combinations made by citizens of different States. That language was put in by the Committee on Finance, and was not in the original bill. He moved to strike it out and it was stricken out. That amendment does not appear on the face of the printed bill, but it will be reported, as a matter of course, by the Chief Clerk in reading the amendments in their order as they are noted in the copy of the bill before him.

Mr. ALLISON. What I fear is that proceeding to treat these amendments in the manner and order indicated here by taking, for example, the first amendment stated, which is, striking out "citizens" and inserting "persons," we shall get into confusion. That is not the first amendment.

Mr. SHERMAN. It is the first amendment in the bill.

Mr. PLATT. No.

Mr. SHERMAN. We do not take them in point of time as they were offered, but as they occur in the bill. In the order of place the word "persons" occurs before the line that was stricken out. . . .

⊥ The VICE-PRESIDENT. The question is on the first amendment made in Committee of the Whole.

Mr. [GEORGE F.] EDMUNDS [R., Vt.]. Let it be again read.

The CHIEF CLERK. In line 4 of the reprinted bill, after the word "more," strike out "citizens" and insert "persons;" so as to read:

That all arrangements, contracts, agreements, trusts, or combinations between two or more persons and corporations.

The amendment was concurred in.

The next amendment made as in Committee of the Whole was, in section 1, line 5, after the word "both," to strike out "of different States or between two or more corporations, or both, of the United States and foreign states, or citizens or corporations thereof." . . .

The amendment was concurred in.

The next amendment made as in Committee of the Whole was, in section 1, line 15, page 2, after the word "such," to strike out "citizens" and insert "persons."

The amendment was concurred in.

The next amendment was, in section 1, line 17, page 2, after the word "articles," to insert "or of the value of money by which such cost may be advanced or reduced."

The amendment was concurred in.

The next amendment was, in section 1, line 27, page 2, after the word "execution," to insert: . . .[1.352]

Mr. EDMUNDS. Mr. President, I wish to call the attention of the honorable member of the Committee on Finance in charge of this bill to the clause on page 3, lines 61, 62, 63, and so on, which provides that the Attorney-General may bring the action before mentioned—

> In any district in which any one of the parties defendant resides or transacts business, and any other parties, corporate or otherwise, may, regardless of residence or location of business, be brought into court in said action in the manner provided by section 738 of the Revised Statutes, and the court shall thereupon have jurisdiction of the defendant or defendants so brought in as fully, to all intents and purposes, as if they had appeared in said action.

Section 738 of the Revised Statutes is a section that has existed for nearly twenty years respecting suits concerning real estate. The real estate being located in a particular district and therefore there being the *res*, as the lawyers call it, the thing in controversy, within the jurisdiction of the court, the court is authorized, if direct service in that district by the marshal can not be obtained, to give notice by publication or otherwise, what is called a substituted service, to that party to appear and take care of his interests in regard to the property that the court has in hand. All that is right and safe and constitutional.

Now, this provision, as I understand it—perhaps I am wrong—is for a suit concerning a wrong done, and not concerning the right, title, or possession of property that is in the jurisdiction or possession of the court. I respectfully submit to the Committee on Finance that it is impossible under the Constitution of the United States, which provides for the preservation of private rights, for Congress to enact that a court in a particular district of the United States in a personal action between parties, and not in an action that relates to property which the court has in its jurisdiction or possession, can proceed by a publication or in any other such way—publication is enough for the illustration—to bind the defendant to the extent that a judgment against him would induce.

You can provide in this bill with entire safety that the process of the court shall run into any district of the United States, so that if a suit be commenced at Philadelphia and one of the defendants is in San Francisco, a part of a sugar trust, if you please, the court may direct a subpoena to the marshal at San Francisco, or the Philadelphia marshal, if it wishes him to travel so far, to serve that subpoena upon that defendant there and require him to appear at Philadelphia. It not being a criminal action, all this is easy enough; but to undertake to say under the Constitution, which was meant for the preservation of private rights in the United States and in all the States, that a person can be brought within the jurisdiction in this way is to me utterly unreasonable. The law seems, I think, to be perfectly well settled in that respect for a hundred years. It is impossible to give a court jurisdiction of a person unless you give that person personal notice that the matter which is to be tried about him is in hand in the court. If you are dealing with his property and the court has the property, then

---

[1.352] The amendment offered by Senator Spooner on March 26, 1890, concerning the issuance of writs of injunction, which appears *supra* at 220, was read. Several technical amendments were offered and agreed to, by which the language of this amendment was made to conform to the first part of this section (which contained the terms "arrangement," "contract," and "agreements").

you may provide—because he is supposed to look out for his property and see what is being done about it—that publication will do; but if I sue my friend from Delaware [Mr. GRAY], who is doing me the honor to attend to what I am saying, in the district court of the State of Vermont on a promissory note, he having no property there to garnishee, as the old phrase was, or to attach, as we call it in Vermont, I deny that Congress has the power to say that the circuit court for the district of Vermont may publish a notice in the Burlington Free Press or any other newspaper to the Senator from Delaware to appear and answer to that action, and that if judgment goes against him it binds him. It is totally out of the question.

Mr. GRAY. Let me ask the Senator from Vermont before he takes his seat whether I properly understand him. Section 738 of the Revised Statutes . . . refers entirely to this substituted service, and not at all to any provision enlarging the power of the United States courts to extend their process over an enlarged territory.

Mr. EDMUNDS. Not at all. It only provides that the court in its discretion may publish or do what it likes—and that is perfectly right—in respect of what the lawyers call the *res*, in respect of property that ⊥ the court is dealing with in the hands of the court, which is not the case that this bill provides for at all.

Mr. SHERMAN. This amendment was prepared by the Senator from Wisconsin. I am not able to say whether the suggestion of the Senator from Vermont is right or not. I would suggest, however, that the matter be passed over until the Senator from Wisconsin and the Senator from Vermont can consult about the phraseology.

The VICE-PRESIDENT. The amendment will be passed over temporarily, if there be no objection. . . .[1.353]

The next amendment made in Committee of the Whole was, in section 1, page 4, line 66, after the word "products," to insert the following:

Provided, That this act shall not be construed to apply to any arrangements, agreements, or combinations between laborers made with a view of lessening the number of hours of their labor or of increasing their wages; nor to any arrangements, agreements, associations, or combinations among persons engaged in horticulture or agriculture made with the view of enhancing the price of their own agricultural or horticultural products.

Mr. SHERMAN. That is an amendment offered by the Senator from Rhode Island [Mr. ALDRICH], and I call the attention of the Senate to it. In my judgment this amendment practically fritters away the substantial elements of this bill.

Mr. VANCE. What amendment is being considered?

Mr. SHERMAN. The amendment offered by the Senator from Rhode Island.

Mr. BLAIR. That is not the amendment offered by the Senator from Rhode Island. That is the one offered by the Senator from Ohio himself. . . .

Mr. SHERMAN. It is the amendment below that in italics that I object to.[1.354]

Mr. HARRIS. Still, that language is an amendment to the amendment made as in Committee of the Whole.

Mr. SHERMAN. Oh, yes.

Mr. HARRIS. Then it must be acted upon. . . .

Mr. EDMUNDS. I think I may just as well say the little I have to say about the general feature of this bill on this pending amendment as on any other, and perhaps better, because this pending amendment illustrates what I think are some of the intrinsic difficulties in the scheme.

I am in favor of the scheme in its fundamental desire and motive—most heartily in favor of it—directed to the breaking up of great monopolies which get hold of the whole of a particular business or production in the country and are enabled, therefore, to command everybody, laborer, consumer, producer, and everybody else, as the sugar trust and the oil trust, and whatever. Although for the time being the sugar trust has perhaps reduced the price of sugar, and the oil trust certainly has reduced the price of oil immensely, that does not alter the wrong of the principle of any trust; and that, in

---

[1.353] At this point, following a further technical amendment, Senator Wilson's amendment was agreed to.

[1.354] After some confusion, Senator Sherman made it clear that it was not his own exemption, which had just been read, to which he objected; rather, he objected to Senator Aldrich's exemption, which was offered as a further exemption to Sherman's and which appears *supra* at 245.

the brief definition of my friend from Texas [Mr. REAGAN], is a phrase which covers every combination to get control of the life and the industry and the producing and the consuming classes of the country. I am in favor, most earnestly in favor, of doing everything that the Constitution of the United States has given Congress power to do, to repress and break up and destroy forever the monopolies of that character, because in the long run, however seductive they may appear in lowering prices to the consumer for the time being, all human experience and all human philosophy have proved that they are destructive of the public welfare and come to be tyrannies, grinding tyrannies, that have sometimes in other countries produced riots, just riots in the moral sense, and so on.

We can not shut up our eyes, Mr. President, to the fact that if capital combines, if great industrial establishments combine, like mining industries, iron industries, coal industries, gold industries, pork-packing industries, if any kind of the great operations of society combine, if the people who own the capital and the plant combine to regulate the price of the wages of laborers, just like the great armaments of Europe, labor is compelled to combine to defend itself; and so the country has been turned and other countries have been turned in the last forty years into great social camps of enemies when they ought to be one great camp of co-operative friends. The laborers, therefore, were quite right in combining to resist and defend themselves against the combinations of capital and property and plants, as they may be called. And it runs everywhere. It has run through every class of society, and it is one of the great evils in the social progress of this country, and every other which exists, that there is hardly a trade and there is scarcely an industry except the farmers that, in one way or another, has not combined to defend itself, and make aggressive warfare upon those with whom it is brought in contact by employment upon the one side or the other, or by purchase or sale. In this very Capital of the country, where we have exclusive power of legislation, supreme and unlimited within the boundaries of natural right, that everybody recognizes, every trade nearly, speaking broadly I can say every trade, masons, carpenters, plumbers, bakers, tailors, merchants, printers, have their combinations that are armed camps in the moral sense, making, when they think they can gain anything by it, aggressive warfare against that part of the rest of mankind that they are brought in relation and contact with one day, and defending themselves the next, it may be, against the aggressive warfare of another competition.

Mr. MORGAN. I would like to ask the Senator from Vermont if he has not knowledge of combinations in this city or elsewhere between bar associations and doctors for raising their price or fees also?

Mr. EDMUNDS. I do not. I do not belong to the bar association of this city, if there is one, and I do not know but that they may have a combination; but, as I have not the honor to be a member of that association, or any other that I know of in this world, except the humble church to which I belong, I can not say.

Mr. MORGAN. Does this bill reach any case of that kind?

Mr. EDMUNDS. I do not know whether it does or not. I am speaking of the general subject.

Mr. HOAR. Will the Senator from Vermont allow me to make a statement as to these bar associations, that are very common and almost universal? In the early days in Massachusetts, I have seen the records of one to which some very eminent lawyers belonged, including a gentleman afterwards the Attorney-General of the United States in Mr. Jefferson's time, where they agreed never to charge less to a client for advice than $1. [Laughter.] I do not know whether the Senator from Vermont ever belonged to that association or not.

Mr. EDMUNDS. I never did. I never got up to a dollar. I gave most of my advice free gratis, as the saying is. [Laughter.] . . .

Well, here we are. I do not blame the farmers of the United States at all. On the contrary, I support them, when everybody has turned into an armament against their interests, in organizing themselves to defend them. They must do it so long as the thing goes on in this way, and therefore, so far as it is possible for the legislative power to exert itself to break up this international and interstate and intersocial warfare that is going on between classes—not classes of citizens as such, not classes of races as such, but classes of employment and interest, each one of which is right in itself and ought to be promoted to the best of the extent of the endeavors of all persons that are engaged in it—it should interpose against this warfare which is destructive of the welfare of them all.

But, if capital and plants and manufacturing industries organize to regulate and so to repress and diminish, if you please, below what it ought to be, the price of all the labor everywhere that is engaged in that kind of business, labor must organize to defend itself on the other side. If transportation companies and middlemen and exporters and dealers organize and arrange that they will give only so much for wheat, or corn, or pork, or whatever, the people who produce the wheat, the corn, the pork, or whatever, are driven to organize to defend themselves so far as they can against that species of tyranny. However, the whole thing is wrong, as it appears to me; and so I think the amendment is wrong, in the same way, which says that while the capital and the plant in any enterprise shall not combine to defend and protect itself, to increase the price of the product of that capital and plant, the labor which is essential to the production of that plant may combine to increase the price of the work that is to be done to make the production of that enterprise.

What is the consequence, Mr. President? The laborers of the United States, I will say for illustration—and one illustration is as good as the hundreds that might be brought forward—the laborers of the United States engaged in the manufacture of iron (which is, perhaps, the most largely valuable, take it altogether, of all the manufactured products of the United States) combine, as this bill authorizes them to do, to put up the price of their wages; they put them up 50 per cent., for illustration. The manufacturer of iron, the men who and whose fathers by their labor have found the iron mine and have built the iron-mill and the rolling mill, and the steel-process-mill, and all that sort of thing, are prohibited under penalties, as they ought to be under penalties, if they are prohibited at all, from combining to raise the price of the iron that the workmen have made cost 50 per cent. more and to sell at the advanced price if they can.

The consequence would be that, if the labor of the United States thus organized chose through its head men to put up the price of the manufactured iron, that iron could not be produced unless the price at which it was to be sold should be enhanced accordingly. The result is that every iron-mill in the United States must break, or live, not according to the demand for iron, not according to its production, but according to the will of the men employed to make it. Now, put it the other way— . . .

Mr. GEORGE. Can not the manufacturers of iron practically put up the price, each for himself, according to the cost that it may be to him to manufacture, without combinations?

Mr. EDMUNDS. So he can undoubtedly, and so can the laborer put up the price in any particular mill of his labor in making that iron. They stand on a perfect equality before the law and in morals. There is no sin, I take it, in owning an iron mine or an iron-mill; it is morally right. There is no sin in being a puddler in a furnace, I take it; it is moral and right, and the income of the work of that puddler, his labor and his muscle and his intellect, are the capital that he puts into it. The product is the iron. . . .

Mr. GEORGE. If the capitalists, the manufacturers, are allowed to combine, they having large capital, they having the means to live and support their families during a shut out or a shut-down of the work, what good will a combination of the laborers do when they would starve for want of their daily wages to feed themselves and their wives and children?

Mr. EDMUNDS. It will not do any good at all; and if on the other hand the laborers combine and say, "We will not do this thing anywhere in the United States of America unless you give us all there is in it, and you shall not arrange among yourselves not to destroy each other and sell your things by common consent at a higher price than you did before, unless you go to the penitentiary" (for that is prohibited), what good will that do except to break down the whole interests of society and destroy everybody?

The fact is that this matter of capital, as it is called, of business, and of labor is an equation, and you can not disturb one side of the equation without disturbing the other. If it costs for labor 50 per cent. more to produce a ton of iron, that 50 per cent.

more goes into what that iron must sell for, or some part of it. I take it everybody will agree to that.

Very well. Now, if you say to one side of that equation, "You may make the value or the price of this iron by your combination for wages in the whole Republic or on the continent, but the man for whom you have made the iron shall not arrange with his neighbors as to the price they will all sell it for, so as not to destroy each other," the whole business will certainly break, because the connection between the plant, as I will call it for short, and the labor that works that plant is one that no legislation and no force in the world—and there is only one outside of the world that can do it—can possibly separate. They can not be divorced. Neither speeches nor laws nor judgments of courts nor anything else can change it; and therefore I say that to provide on one side of that equation that there may be combination and on the other side that there shall not, is contrary to the very inherent principle upon which such business must depend. If we are to have equality, as we ought to have, if the combination on the one side is to be prohibited, the combination on the other side must be prohibited or there will be certain destruction in the end.

Mr. President, as I said before—and I am not going to take up the time of the Senate—I shall be glad within the constitutional limits, which are narrow but clear, in the regulation of commerce to go just as far as Congress has the power to go in breaking up these great monopolies that exist to the detriment and the injury of mankind in this country and in every other. They are in every other country as well as in this. They exist in free-trade countries and in tariff countries and under all social conditions, and have come up mainly within the last twenty or thirty years. But I can not go any further. I do not wish to hold out a false hope to the people of the United States, be they farmers or mere workingmen, as they are sometimes called, although everybody in the United States who is fit to be a citizen and is well ought to be and generally is a workingman in the best sense of the term; whether he drives a cart or whether he devotes himself to the business of the country in the Senate of the United States, he is equally, in my judgment, a workingman. . . .

The constitutional question, Mr. President, has been discussed so fully that I could add very little, if anything, to the argument; and on that point I will only state, now at any rate, very briefly indeed what I think about it.

The Constitution of the United States intended to leave and did leave, as I think—and I think so because the Constitution says so—to the States of the Union the right of local self-government in every respect except those named that were granted to the National Government. It did not give to the Congress of the United States, and it did not mean to give, and it ought not to have given to it, and ought not to give to it now, I think, the power to enter into the police regulations of the people of the United States to endeavor to conduct or to manage or to regulate their affairs as the States, in every State of the Union, have been authorized—not authorized, but left by the Constitution in their original right to do.

I believe, Mr. President, that the safety of the Republic as a nation, one people, one hope, one destiny, depends more largely upon the preservation of what are called the rights of the States covering a continent than upon any other one thing. I therefore should be slow to step over that line by voting for any act of Congress that I thought went beyond it, over the boundary that the Constitution has prescribed to the authority of the United States in Congress assembled in dealing with the business of the people of the several States, no matter how evil that business may be, no matter how injurious to the public welfare apparently or really at the moment it may be. I think it is better to endure a present evil of even the most grinding and most stupendous of monopolies than to step by one inch or attempt to step by one inch over the clear boundary line that has been established and continued between the Congress of the United States and the legislative and judicial powers of the States in respect of such subjects.

The Constitution has given to Congress the power to impose taxes. It has given to Congress the power to regulate commerce among the several States and with foreign nations. Just as far as we can go in regulating the transition of property from State to State, as we have done in the interstate-commerce law for the benefit of the whole people whose interests are common, as I said before, it is our right to go; and when a clear evil appears, as undoubtedly now exists, just as far as we can go in exerting the power that is given to us, I am willing to go; but I am not willing to go any further.

I am not willing to hold out to the people of the United States, the citizens of each State, any or all of them, an illusory and deceptive attempt at the redress of grievances, which will turn out in the end to be purely deceptive and illusory, mere dust and ashes, when it comes to the test of the resistance of anybody who is undertaken to be dealt with under our law. I have more confidence, Mr. President, in the people of the United States. . . .

I do not think, therefore, Mr. President, that we need concern ourselves about any popular impulse at this present moment of time, about any outcry in the newspapers, or at meetings, or at alliances, or whatever methods the people have of getting together to express their views concerning what we ought to do or ought not to do beyond what we clearly have a right to do. I do not believe that the people of the United States wish to have the Senate make haste in running to please them with a delusion and a snare which they will find out next year has been perfectly ineffective and perfectly incapable of execution, because Congress had gone beyond the power that it ought to have known it possessed.

That is my faith, Mr. President, in the people of the United States. Having that faith, I do not feel impelled by any sentiment or desire of popularity to-day to go beyond the lines that the Constitution has clearly marked out to us.

If we can exert the taxing power to repress and discourage "futures" and "options," as they are called, I shall be glad to exert it, as we exerted the taxing power in order to diminish the evil of the fraudulent butter or oleomargarine business; but in order to exert the taxing power I had supposed that it was indispensable that what are called the more immediate representatives of the people at the other end of the Capitol should be first appealed to and that they should first act. If, however, you put it, as this bill does, upon the ground of a license, I am unable to see, a license being a police measure, where the Congress of the United States gets the power to license anything whatever, except in the District of Columbia and the Territories, over which the Constitution says Congress shall have control. This bill on the face of it says that this tax is imposed as a police measure in order to repress and suppress the real evil, as it is, of this gambling, for that is what it is, in what are called "futures" and "options" and so on.

It is true that for the purpose of taxation and on the face of the statutes for the purpose of taxation, Congress, in order to raise a tax out of whisky, for instance, provides that every person producing whisky shall be identified. Call it a license if you please; I do not know that it is, but we will call it that if you please; still, it is a tax and a tax as a tax, and by whatever name the phrase of the statute may call it, it is a measure of revenue on its face, whatever may be the motive; and I suppose the motive in the case of whisky is the motive of revenue alone, and in the case of oleomargarine I suppose the motive was the general welfare of the people, to prevent frauds.

But when a statute of the United States is presented to the Supreme Court saying that this license tax which we impose is a police tax, as the bill now says, I am very much afraid, speaking with the greatest possible deference, that the court would say, "We can not inquire into the motives of the legislative body in passing a particular act, but when they put into the statute the ground upon which it rests and the purpose for which it is enacted we are compelled to take it as Congress has stated, and that this is an undertaking to regulate the good order of society" by regulating a business in each State for the purpose of regulating it, just as the State of Vermont and the State of Alabama and every other State provide for the licensing of inn-keepers, if you please, in order to the protection of travelers, and so on, the licensing of doctors in order to protect human life and health against quacks and humbugs and nostrums and all that sort of thing, and so on through; but within our power of levying a tax as a tax upon any kind of business, putting it as a tax and beginning as it ought to do upon any object which is injurious to the general welfare, of course that is the kind of occupation that ought to be taxed.

Every State, when it makes any discrimination at all, taxes those employments and occupations that are least useful to the community and gets the most money it can out of those things that if taken out of it prove the least burden upon the best and the well ordered people of the community. That is all right. That is motive, but it is a tax.

So, Mr. President, so far as we can provide in the regulation of commerce for impeding and harassing and cutting up the commercial transactions between the States of these great monopolies, I am most earnestly for it. So far as we can not do it, I am opposed to it, because I believe that the ultimate and the immediate welfare of the people of the United States is much more largely concerned in not overstepping the Constitution by what will turn out to be illusory and ineffectual and void operations merely for the reason that there is a present trouble.

If this bill can be brought within the provisions of impeding just as far as we may as a regulation of commerce the movement of the commodities of these great concerns and the arrangement of their transactions between the different States, as the Senator from Texas had the broad idea in his bill, I should certainly be most glad to do it, but as the thing now stands it is quite impossible for me—very likely I am entirely wrong—but it is quite impossible for me to support it.

I am sorry, Mr. President, to have taken the time which I have.

The PRESIDING OFFICER. The question is upon the amendment last reported.

Mr. EDMUNDS. Let it be read again.

The CHIEF CLERK. On page 4, line 66, section 1, after the word "action," the Senate, as in Committee of the Whole, inserted the following clause:

Provided, That this act shall not be construed to apply to any arrangements, agreements, or combinations between laborers made with a view of lessening the number of hours of their labor or of increasing their wages; nor to any arrangements, agreements, associations, or combinations among persons engaged in horticulture or agriculture made with the view of enhancing the price of their own agricultural or horticultural products.

Mr. HOAR. Mr. President, I wish to state in one single sentence my opinion in regard to this particular provision. If I correctly understood the Senator from Vermont . . . he thought that the applying to laborers in this respect a principle which was not applied to persons engaged in the large commercial transactions which are chiefly aimed at by this bill was indefensible in principle. Now, it seems to me there is a very broad distinction which, if borne in mind, will warrant not only this exception to the general provision of the bill, but a great deal of other legislation which we enact, or attempt to enact, relating to the matter of labor.

When you are speaking of providing to regulate the transactions of men who are making corners in wheat, or in iron, or in woolen or in cotton goods, speculating in them or lawfully dealing in them without speculation, you are aiming at a mere commercial transaction, the beginning and end of which is the making of money for the parties, and nothing else. That is the only relation that transaction has to the State. It is the creation or diffusion or change of ownership of the wealth of the community. But when a laborer is trying to raise his wages or is endeavoring to shorten the hours of his labor, he is dealing with something that touches closely, more closely than anything else, the Government and the character of the state itself.

The maintenance of a certain standard of profit in dealing in large transactions in wheat, or cotton, or wool is a question whether a particular merchant or a particular class of merchants shall make money or not, or shall deal lawfully or not, shall affect the state injuriously or not; but the question whether the standard of the laborer's wages shall be maintained or advanced, or whether the leisure for instruction, for improvement, shall be shortened or lengthened, is a question which touches the very existence and character of government of the state itself. The laborer who is engaged lawfully and usefully and accomplishing his purpose in whole or in part in endeavoring to raise the standard of wages is engaged in an occupation the success of which makes republican government itself possible and without which the Republic can not in substance, however it may nominally do in form, continue to exist.

I hold, therefore, that as legislators we may constitutionally, properly, and wisely allow laborers to make associations, combinations, contracts, agreements for the sake of maintaining and advancing their wages, in regard to which, as a rule, their contracts are to be made with large corporations who are themselves but an association or combination or aggregation of capital on the other side. When we are permitting and even encouraging that, we are permitting and encouraging what is not only lawful, wise, and profitable, but absolutely essential to the existence of the commonwealth itself.

When, on the other hand, we are dealing with one of the other classes, the combinations aimed at chiefly by this bill, we are dealing with a transaction the only purpose of which is to extort from the community, monopolize, segregate, and apply to individual use, for the purposes of individual greed, wealth which ought properly and lawfully and for the public interest to be generally diffused over the whole community.

Without entering upon a general discussion of the merits of this bill, it seemed to me proper to make this observation in regard to what, if I understand him correctly, had fallen from my honorable and distinguished friend from Vermont.

Mr. EDMUNDS. Mr. President, the Senator from Massachusetts, for whose opinions I have the greatest possible respect, understood me quite correctly, as he has stated, and he has stated a great deal better and more strongly than I could the value of improving the condition of the laboring people of the United States, in the sense in which he uses that term, as people who earn their daily bread by the work of their hands, not having accumulated sufficient capital or not having had sufficient opportunity to go into business for themselves. I agree to all that entirely. But when the laborer, unless he labors for himself in his own plant—and then he is not laboring for wages—when the wage-earner is to earn wages he must earn them from somebody that employs him. That is absolutely indispensable, and it only needs stating; it is the merest commonplace. There must be somebody on the other side of what I called a little while ago the equation. They are inseparable. . . .

On the one side you say that is a crime and on the other side you say it is a valuable and proper undertaking. That will not do, Mr. President. You can not get on in that way. It is impossible to separate them; and the principle of it, therefore, is that if one side, no matter which it is, is authorized to combine the other side must be authorized to combine, or the thing will break and there will be universal bankruptcy. That is what it will come to, and then the laborer, whose interest and welfare we are all so really desirous to promote, will turn around and justly say to the Senate of the United States, "Why did you go to such legislation as that? Why did you attempt to stimulate and almost require us to combine against our employers, and thus break down the whole industry of the country and leave us all beggars? When you allowed us to combine and to regulate our wages, why did you not allow the products that our hands produced to be raised in price by an arrangement, so that everybody that bought them might pay the increased price, and everybody that was making them all around for whom we were working could live also?" I do not think, as a practical thing, Mr. President, that anybody will thank us for making a distinction of that kind.

Mr. PLATT. Mr. President, a word or two which fell from the lips of the Senator from Massachusetts [Mr. HOAR] induces me to think that he does not comprehend the scope of this bill. In pointing out the difference between allowing associations and combinations of laborers to unite in order to increase their wages and the combinations forbidden by the bill, he spoke of the object of this bill being to reach the great monopolistic and capitalistic corporations and associations which are oppressing the people.

Mr. HOAR. The Senator will pardon me. I did not. If he will allow me I certainly made no such suggestion consciously.

Mr. PLATT. What did the Senator think was the object of the bill?

Mr. HOAR. I said the object of this bill was to prevent the speculation in and engrossing of wheat and similar commodities. I did not speak in that connection of corporations. I said, in speaking generally of the lawfulness and propriety of laborers combining in regard to the matter of their wages, that the persons with whom they were to contract were very largely the corporations which were themselves nothing but a combination or aggregation of capital for that purpose. I made no such suggestion as that corporations were the persons aimed at by this bill. That was in a different connection.

Mr. PLATT. Taking the explanation of the Senator from Massachusetts as he now makes it, that the object of the bill is chiefly to reach the transactions of associated capital engaged in putting up the price of wheat and the necessaries of life or putting them down, gambling in them or dealing in them, I want to say that the scope of this bill is very much wider and broader than that, and for that reason I can not vote for it.

If this bill were aimed only at people who are doing wrong, if it were aimed only at illegitimate business transactions, if it were aimed only at those men and that kind of business which ought to be repressed in this country, it would not have a stronger defender or a more enthusiastic supporter than myself. But it is because it is utterly without discrimination in its provisions that I oppose it. While its supporters say that it is a bill aimed at wrongful transactions, at wrongful combinations of capital, it is in its very terms a bill which is aimed at every business and every business transaction in the United States, and if it should reach, repress, restrain, and prevent the wrongful acts of wrongful associations and combinations, the benefit that would be thereby accomplished would be a hundred, a thousand times outweighed by the disastrous effects which it would have upon the legitimate business interests of this country.

That is the fault with this bill. It attempts, because it sees some guilty persons, to punish all persons, guilty and innocent alike; because certain persons in business are doing things which are deemed to be reprehensible, it would strike an unjust and cruel blow at all business transactions in the country; and it seems strange, Mr. President, that the authors of the bill can not see this.

Now, take the portion of the bill as it stands to-day which was in the original bill reported by the Senator from Ohio [Mr. SHERMAN].

Mr. HOAR. Before my honorable friend proceeds, I should like to ask him to do perhaps what he is about to proceed to do, but I wish to remark that what I said in response to the Senator from Vermont [Mr. EDMUNDS] was not intended either as a defense of the bill or an attack upon it, but to point out what I thought the Senator from Vermont failed to appreciate thoroughly, the distinction between the associations of laborers and this class of cases at which this bill aims.

Now, I should like to ask the Senator from Connecticut to point out to the Senate and to me what he thinks is prohibited in this bill which is not prohibited by the general common law, as he and I learned it in our studies, in regard to such things as are covered by the English common law.

I wish to say in all sincerity that my mind is yet in a state of doubt whether I can or not vote for this bill as it is finally left. I think it has been improved very much since it was reported, and, on the other hand, I have grave doubt whether it is not liable to the objection which the Senator has just stated to us, that it attacks what is innocent and lawful and necessary.

Mr. PLATT. Mr. President, the first section of this bill, which I am now commenting on, is complicated and involved, and I desire to read, leaving out some things from this section, but leaving out nothing which in any way changes the effect or the real intent and meaning of the bill as applied to the persons of whom I am now speaking, and I beg Senators to listen.

The bill provides that—

All arrangements, contracts, agreements between two or more persons, which tend to prevent full and free competition in articles of growth, production, or manufacture of any State or Territory of the United States with similar articles of the growth, production, or manufacture by any other State or Territory, and all arrangements between such persons which tend to advance the cost to the consumer of any such article are hereby declared to be against public policy, unlawful, and void.

That is the real meaning of this bill. That is, all arrangements whatever looking to the objects which are pointed out in the bill, between any two or more persons, are unlawful. In other words, this bill proceeds upon the false assumption that all competition is beneficent to the country, and that every advance of price is an injury to the country. That is the assumption upon which this bill proceeds. There never was a greater fallacy in the world. Competition, which this bill provides for as between any two persons, must be full and free. Unrestricted competition is brutal warfare, and injurious to the whole country. The great corporations of this country, the great monopolies of this country are every one of them built upon the graves of weaker competitors that have been forced to their death by remorseless competition. I am entirely sick of this idea that the lower the prices are the better for the country, and that any effort to advance prices, no matter how low they may be, and that any arrangement between persons engaged in business to advance prices, no matter how low they may be, is a wrong and ought to be repressed and punished.

The true theory of this matter is that prices should be just and reasonable and fair, that prices, no matter who is the producer or what the article, should be such as will render a fair return to all persons engaged in its production, a fair profit on capital, on labor, and on everything else that enters into its production. When the price of any commodity, I do not care whether it is wheat or iron, I do not care whether it is corn or silverware—whenever the price of any commodity is forced below that standard, the whole country suffers. We have been running to bankruptcy and ruin and distress. But the theory of this bill is that, no matter how much the price may have been depressed, no matter how losing the business may be, the parties engaged in it must have no understanding between themselves by which they will come together and say that they will obtain a fair and a fairly remunerative price for the article which they produce. That is wicked, the bill says.

We have five thousand manufacturing establishments in the State of Connecticut, or had by the last census, and I think that gentlemen will ⊥ hunt up and down that State and its borders without finding many of the trusts at which it is said this bill is aimed. . . .

What I mean to say is that the great bulk of manufacturing in Connecticut, both as to the establishments and the amount of production, is carried on by men and associations of comparatively small capital, most of whom have sprung up from the ranks of labor themselves, and who have largely associated with laborers in engaging in their business. I do not deny that there may be some trusts there; but the bill which is aimed at those trusts reaches every arrangement, all arrangements, innocent or guilty, which those persons may make under any circumstances to preserve themselves from ruin and bankruptcy. It reaches more than that: every merchant in the State of Connecticut; all business in which persons who are engaged in this deadly, brutal warfare which is called competition think it for their advantage to come together and obtain fair prices for the articles in which they are dealing.

Mr. HAWLEY. Will my colleague allow me to ask him a question? He says the bill reaches all those corporations and individuals. I want to know how it can reach every citizen in Connecticut whose bargain shall begin and be carried on and finally consummated in the midst of that State? . . .

Mr. PLATT. I am not by any means a very strict constructionist of the Constitution; I think in a great many matters I am deemed to be extremely liberal in my views of the powers which Congress may exercise under the Constitution of the United States; but at the risk of unpopularity and of being declared to be unfashionable and of being criticised, I will say that in this whole bill, so far as I read it, there is but one constitutional provision, and that is that provision of the Senator from Texas [Mr. REAGAN] in his amendment which confines the bills to persons engaged in transportation—for that is the effect of his amendment—that uproots the interstate-commerce law, drives that by the board, repeals the law. If it be thought by the Senate that that is good policy, I do not object to that on the ground of unconstitutionality.

I am being diverted for the moment from the answer to the question asked by my colleague, but while I am diverted I desire to say this: It is not two years since this Senate was exercised over the idea that there must be something done to prevent the ruinous rate wars between railroads or that impending disaster was to be precipitated upon the country. And so we provided, in the interstate-commerce act, provisions which we thought would prevent these ruinous rate wars. We agreed then that ruinous competition among railroads was not for the interest of any portion of the people of this country. We provided that if they advanced rates in their joint tariffs they should give ten days' notice; that if they reduced rates by their joint tariffs they should give three days' notice. But here comes this amendment of the Senator from Texas, who has been godfather at least to the interstate-commerce act, and sweeps that all away and says that if those engaged in making joint tariffs shall ever advance a rate they shall go to State prison and pay $10,000 fine. That is the effect of the amendment of the Senator from Texas.

Now let me return to the question asked me by my colleague. He asked me how it could be done. I do not think it can, but I propose to deal with this bill as it reads. It seizes, lays hold of all articles of growth, production, or manufacture of any State which compete with similar articles of growth, production, or manufacture of any other State. That is what it attempts to lay its hand upon, and that is all-inclusive. It takes all articles. You can scarcely find an article of commerce, an article of merchandise in any State which does not compete with similar articles which are the growth, production, or manufacture of another State. So then, this bill sweeps in all business. It sweeps in the dealing in every article; it sweeps in the transactions of every merchant; it sweeps in the transactions of every manufacturer and of every producer. What does it say shall happen, what does it say is wrong with regard to such articles? for it includes all articles of trade. That all arrangements and agreements between two or more persons which tend to advance the cost to the consumer of any such article is "hereby declared to be against public policy, unlawful, and void."

Now, I want to illustrate a little. . . .[1.355]

. . . They are running their business at a loss; they are making articles to which this bill refers; and this bill says that if those eight men should combine to get a fair, living profit upon their manufacture, that contract, that agreement is against public policy, unlawful and void. That is but an illustration. It runs all through the business of my State and of the United States.

I do not like to vote against this bill. I believe that there are combinations in this country which are criminal, but I believe that every man in business—I do not care whether he is a farmer, a laborer, a miner, a sailor, a manufacturer, a merchant—has a right, a legal and a moral right, to obtain a fair profit upon his business and his work; and if he is driven by fierce competition to a spot where his business is unremunerative, I believe it is his right to combine for the purpose of raising prices until they shall be fair and remunerative. This bill makes no distinction. It says that every combination which has the effect in any way to advance prices is illegal and void. The Senator from Ohio in the first speech which he made here admitted that there were combinations in which there was no wrong, and yet he leveled his bill at them equally with the combinations which are doing wrong.

I do not believe there is in this country among any class of people a real desire that anybody shall do business without receiving a fair profit, without receiving a fair remuneration for the capital, skill, and work employed in carrying on the business, and I do not believe that there is any class of people in this country who, when they face this false assumption that cheap prices are the great, beneficent thing for the country and think of it, will agree to that proposition. Whenever the price of anything is below what it costs to produce it, it ought to be raised, and any combination for the purpose of raising it to a point where the price is fair and reasonable ought not to be condemned; it ought to be encouraged. It will not do, because a few concerns in this country are attempting to put prices where they are unreasonable, to enrich themselves beyond a fair compensation or equivalent for their capital, their skill, and their enterprise—it will not do to cast out your drag-net and bring within the condemnation of your law all the legitimate business enterprises of the country that are struggling along and trying to obtain only fair and reasonable prices for their goods, and who are giving life to labor, and peace and plenty to the whole land.

As I said, there is no greater fallacy than that the cheaper prices are the better it is for the community. It is not true. The farmer understands it when his wheat or his corn does not bring the cost of production, and this Senate is quick to see it and provide in this bill that there may be combinations in such cases. The farmer is not outside of the general economic principle. We do not raise wheat in the East; we consume it. Why should the Eastern man not be permitted to say, then, being a

---

[1.355] Senator Platt stated that eight "representative" woolen manufacturers had reported a net loss in 1887.

consumer of wheat, according to the theory of this bill, that as the price is down you must not raise it; you must not enhance the cost of flour to the consumer. We make no such contention as that. But there can not be two principles upon which a law shall stand. It must stand upon one principle. The theory of this bill is that prices must never be advanced by any two or more purposes [sic], no matter how ruinously low they may be. That theory I denounce as utterly untenable, as immoral.

So, Mr. President, I can not vote for this bill in the shape in which ⊥ I think it will come to a vote or in any shape in which I think it will be perfected. I am ready to go to the people of the State of Connecticut; I have faith and confidence in them; and when I tell them that here is a bill which, under the guise of dealing with trusts, would strike a cruel blow at their entire industries, I know that they will see it and understand it; and if there be a people anywhere in this country who can not understand it it is better for a Senator to answer to his judgment and his conscience than it is to answer to their misapprehension.

I am sorry, Mr. President, that we have not had a bill which had been carefully prepared, which had been thoughtfully prepared, which had been honestly prepared, to meet the object which we all desire to meet. The conduct of this Senate for the past three days—and I make no personal allusions—has not been in the line of the honest preparation of a bill to prohibit and punish trusts. It has been in the line of getting some bill with that title that we might go to the country with. The questions of whether a bill would be operative, of how it would operate, or whether it was within the power of Congress to enact it, have been whistled down the wind in this Senate as idle talk, and the whole effort has been to get some bill headed "A bill to punish trusts" with which to go to the country.

The distinguished author of the bill, the Senator in charge of it on this floor, when the Senator from Texas proposed his amendment, opposed it, and when the Senator from Kansas proposed his amendment opposed it and said that it ought to be voted down; and yet the moment they were put on the bill he seemed to be as thoroughly anxious for the passage of the bill with those amendments upon it as he had been of his own. We should legislate better than that. Every effort to refer this bill to any committee that would give it careful and honest consideration has been voted down in this Senate, and it is better to vote the bill down than it is to go to the people with a measure which shall resemble the apples which grow in the region of that fated plain on which once stood the city of Sodom. We may make this bill look like a beautiful remedy; we may call it a bill to punish trusts, but when you attempt to put it in operation it will be,

> Like that Dead Sea fruit,
> All ashes to the taste;

or it will be found to be a blow struck at the legitimate industries of the country such as they will not recover from in years and years.

Mr. [C.] WALTHALL [D., Miss.]. Mr. President, if it be in order at this time, I will move to refer this bill and the amendments to the Committee on the Judiciary with instructions to report within twenty days.

The VICE-PRESIDENT. Is the Senate ready for the question?

Mr. SHERMAN. I call for the yeas and nays.

The VICE-PRESIDENT. The question is on the motion of the Senator from Mississippi [Mr. WALTHALL] to refer the bill to the Committee on the Judiciary with instructions to report within twenty days. On that motion the yeas and nays and [sic] demanded.

The yeas and nays were ordered, and the Secretary proceeded to call the roll. . . .

The result was announced—yeas 31, nays 28; as follows: . . .

So the motion to refer the bill to the Committee on the Judiciary with instructions was agreed to.

Mr. SPOONER. The vote included the pending amendments?

Mr. EDMUNDS. They go with the bill as a matter of parliamentary law.

S. 1 AS REPORTED BY THE SENATE COMMITTEE ON THE JUDICIARY
51st Cong., 1st Sess.
April 2, 1890

[ED. NOTE: This redrafted version of S. 1 was not accompanied by a report.]

⊥ Reported by Mr. EDMUNDS with an amendment, viz: Strike out all after the enacting clause and insert the part printed in *italics*.

A BILL

To declare unlawful trusts and combinations in restraint of trade and production.

1 *Be it enacted by the Senate and House of Representa-*
2 *tives of the United States of America in Congress assembled,*
3 That all arrangements, contracts, agreements, trusts, or com-
4 binations between two or more citizens or corporations, or
5 both, of different States, or between two or more citizens or
6 corporations, or both, of the United States and foreign states,
7 or citizens or corporations thereof made with a view or which
8 tend to prevent full and [free] competition in the importation,
9 transportation, or sale of articles imported into the United
10 States, or with a view or which tend to prevent full and
11 free competition in articles of growth, production, or manu-
12 facture of any State or Territory of the United States with
13 similar articles of the growth, production, or manufacture of
14 any other state or territory, or in the transportation or sale
15 of like articles, the production of any State or Territory of
16 the United States into or within any other State or Territory
17 of the United States; and all arrangements, trusts, or combi-
18 nations between such citizens or corporations, made with
19 a view or which tend to advance the cost to the consumer
20 of any such articles, are hereby declared to be against public
21 policy, unlawful, and void. And the circuit court of the
22 United States shall have original jurisdiction of all suits of a
23 civil nature at common law or in equity arising under this
24 section, and to issue all remedial process, orders, or writs
25 proper and necessary to enforce its provisions. And the
26 Attorney-General and the several district attorneys are hereby
27 directed, in the name of the United States, to commence
28 and prosecute all such cases to final judgment and execution.
1 SEC. 2. That any person or corporation injured or
2 damnified by such arrangement, contract, agreement, trust,
3 or combination defined in the first section of this act may
4 sue for and recover, in any court of the United States of
5 competent jurisdiction, without respect to the amount involved,
6 of any person or corporation a party to a combination de-

~~scribed in the first section of this act, twice the amount of damages sustained and the cost of the suit, together with a reasonable attorney's fee.~~

SEC. 1. Every contract, combination in the form of trust or otherwise, or conspiracy, in restraint of trade or commerce among the several States, or with foreign nations, is hereby declared to be illegal. Every person who shall make any such contract or engage in any such combination or conspiracy, shall be deemed guilty of a misdemeanor, and, on conviction thereof, shall be punished by [a] fine not exceeding five thousand dollars, or by imprisonment not exceeding one year, or by both said punishments, in the discretion of the court.

SEC. 2. Every person who shall monopolize, or attempt to monopolize, or combine or conspire with any other person or persons, to monopolize, any part of the trade or commerce among the several States, or with foreign nations, shall be deemed guilty of a misdemeanor, and, on conviction thereof, shall be punished by fine not exceeding five thousand dollars or by imprisonment not exceeding one year, or by both said punishments, in the discretion of the court.

SEC. 3. Every contract, combination in form of trust or otherwise, or conspiracy, in restraint of trade or commerce in any Territory of the United States or of the District of Columbia, or in restraint of trade or commerce between any such Territory and another, or between any such Territory or Territories and any State or States or the District of Columbia, or with foreign nations, or between the District of Columbia and any State or States or foreign nations, is hereby declared illegal. Every person who shall make any such contract or engage in any such combination or conspiracy shall be deemed guilty of a misdemeanor, and on conviction thereof, shall be punished by fine not exceeding five thousand dollars, or by imprisonment not exceeding one year, or by both said punishments, in the discretion of the court.

SEC. 4. The several circuit courts of the United States are hereby invested with jurisdiction to prevent and restrain violations of this act; and it shall be the duty of the several district attorneys of the United States, in their respective districts, under the direction of the Attorney-General, to institute proceedings in equity to prevent and restrain such violations. Such proceedings may be by way of petition setting forth the case and praying that such violation shall be enjoined or otherwise prohibited. When the parties complained of shall have been duly notified of such petition the court shall proceed, as soon as may be, to the hearing and determination of the case; and pending such petition and before final decree, the court may at any time make such temporary restraining order or prohibition as shall be deemed just in the premises.

SEC. 5. Whenever it shall appear to the court before which any proceeding under section four of this act may be pending that the ends of justice require that other parties should be brought before the court, the court may cause them

5   to be summoned, whether they reside in the district in which
6   the court is held or not; and subpoenas to that end may be
7   served in any district by the marshal thereof.
1   SEC. 6. Any property owned under any contract or by
2   any combination, or pursuant to any conspiracy (and being
3   the subject thereof) mentioned in section one of this act, and
4   being in the course of transportation from one State to another,
5   or to a foreign country, shall be forfeited to the United States,
6   and may be seized and condemned by like proceedings as
7   those provided by law for the forfeiture, seizure, and con-
8   demnation of property imported into the United States con-
9   trary to law.
1   SEC. 7. Any person who shall be injured in his business
2   or property by any other person or corporation by reason of
3   anything forbidden or declared to be unlawful by this act,
4   may sue therefor in any circuit court of the United States in
5   the district in which the defendant resides or is found, with-
6   out respect to the amount in controversy, and shall recover
7   three fold the damages by him sustained, and the costs of suit,
8   including a reasonable attorney's fee.
1   SEC. 8. That the word "person" or "persons" wher-
2   ever used in this act shall be deemed to include corporations
3   and associations existing under or authorized by the laws of
4   either the United States, the laws of any of the Territories,
5   the laws of any State, or the laws of any foreign country.

Amend the title so as to read: "A bill to protect trade and commerce against unlawful restraints and monopolies."

SENATE DEBATE
51st Cong., 1st Sess.
April 2, 1890

21 CONG. REC. 2901

Mr. EDMUNDS. I am instructed by the Committee on the Judiciary, in obedience to the order of the Senate sending to that committee the bill (S. 1) to declare unlawful trusts and combinations in restraint of trade and production, to report back the bill within the time mentioned by the Senate in its order with an amendment—one amendment—striking out all after the enacting clause and inserting the measure that the committee reports.

I will state that there is one section in the amendment which I think goes further than it ought to do, but for the sake of unity all around I shall be entirely willing to support the measure as it is reported. I ought to say, as I stated to the committee, that owing to a little necessity of health I shall probably not be in town at the time the matter may be properly and fairly taken up, and so some other gentleman of the committee will move it whenever it is convenient to the Senate to consider it.

Mr. MORGAN. I should like to hear the bill, as reported, read.

Mr. VEST. I want to state in connection with the report made by the chairman of the Committee on the Judiciary that I agreed to that report, but with the understanding that there was one section of the bill as now reported which I desired amended. In my judgment, it does not go far enough. I wish to state that in justice to myself.

Mr. CULLOM. I will inquire if it is the same section the Senator from Vermont says goes too far in some provisions of it, which the Senator from Missouri thinks does not go far enough?

Mr. EDMUNDS. It is the same provision.

Mr. CULLOM. It is the same section?

Mr. VEST. It is the same section. I think it is numbered 7 in the substitute reported by the committee.

Mr. GEORGE. Some Senators on the committee have deemed it necessary to state their exact position with reference to the bill and I will state mine.

I regard the bill, so far as it goes, as a very good one, the best I think that can be framed under that particular power of Congress, the power over commerce, which the committee have attempted to frame a bill under. There are one or two powers of Congress which may be exercised, in my judgment, very effectually in the direction of the suppression of these trusts and combinations, which the committee did not see proper to exercise.

I shall support the bill as it has been reported, and if, on consultation with friends who agree with me, it should be deemed the best course, I may then ask the Senate to look to other and additional powers in the way of suppressing these trusts; and I may offer amendments which will look to additions to the bill, not to striking out or amending anything that is in the substitute reported by the committee. . . .

Mr. COKE. I desire to state that I concur with the bill as reported, with the exception that I would prefer one of the sections, the one referred to by the Senator from Missouri, to be in a little different form, and if an amendment placing it in a different shape shall be offered I shall support it.

The VICE-PRESIDENT. The substitute reported by the Committee on the Judiciary will be read.

The CHIEF CLERK. The committee report to strike out all after the enacting clause of the bill and to insert:

SECTION 1. Every contract, combination in the form of trust or otherwise, or conspiracy in restraint of trade or commerce among the several States or with foreign nations is hereby declared to be illegal. Every person who shall make any such contract or engage in any such combination or conspiracy shall be deemed guilty of a misdemeanor, and, on conviction thereof, shall be punished by fine not exceeding $5,000 or by imprisonment not exceeding one year, or by both said punishments, in the discretion of the court.

SEC. 2. Every person who shall monopolize, or attempt to monopolize, or combine or conspire with any other person or persons to monopolize any part of the trade or commerce among the several States or with foreign nations, shall be deemed guilty of a misdemeanor, and, on conviction thereof, shall be punished by fine not exceeding $5,000 or by imprisonment not exceeding one year, or by both said punishments, in the discretion of the court.

SEC. 3. Every contract, combination in form of trust or otherwise, or conspiracy in restraint of trade or commerce in any Territory of the United States or of the District of Columbia, or in restraint of trade or commerce between any such Territory and another, or between any such Territory or Territories and any State or States or the District of Columbia, or with foreign nations, or between the District of Columbia and any State or States or foreign nations is hereby declared illegal. Every person who shall make any such contract or engage in any such combination or conspiracy shall be deemed guilty of a misdemeanor, and, on conviction thereof, shall be punished by fine not exceeding $5,000 or by imprisonment not exceeding one year, or by both said punishments, in the discretion of the court.

SEC. 4. The several circuit courts of the United States are hereby invested with jurisdiction to prevent and restrain violations of this act; and it shall be the duty of the several district attorneys of the United States in their respective districts, under the direction of the Attorney-General, to institute proceedings in equity to prevent and restrain such violations. Such proceedings may be by way of petition setting forth the case and praying that such violation shall be enjoined or otherwise prohibited. When the parties complained of shall have been duly notified of such petition the court shall proceed, as soon as may be, to the hearing and determination of the case; and, pending such petition and before final decree, the court may at any time make such temporary restraining order or prohibition as shall be deemed just in the premises.

SEC. 5. Whenever it shall appear to the court before which any proceeding under section 4 of this act may be pending that the ends of justice require that other parties should be brought before the court, the court may cause them to be summoned, whether they reside in the district in which the court is held or not; and subpoenas to that end may be served in any district by the marshal thereof.

SEC. 6. Any property owned under any contract or by any combination or pursuant to any conspiracy (and being the subject thereof) mentioned in section 1 of this act, and being in the course of transportation from one State to another, or to a foreign country, shall be forfeited to the United States, and may be seized and condemned by like proceedings as those provided by law for the forfeiture, seizure, and condemnation of property imported into the United States contrary to law.

SEC. 7. Any person who shall be injured in his business or property by any other person or corporation by reason of anything forbidden or declared to be unlawful by this act may sue therefor in any circuit court of the United States in the district in which the defendant resides or is found, without respect to the amount in controversy, and shall recover threefold the damages by him sustained and the costs of suit, including a reasonable attorney's fee.

SEC. 8. That the word "person" or "persons" wherever used in this act shall be deemed to include corporations and associations existing under or authorized by the laws of either the United States, the laws of any of the Territories, the laws of any State, or the laws of any foreign country.

Amend the title so as to read: "A bill to protect trade and commerce against unlawful restraints and monopolies."

Mr. EDMUNDS. I ought to say that as this bill was under discussion and had the lead on the Calendar when it was referred to the Committee on the Judiciary I shall hope it will be the pleasure of the Senate to take it up very soon, indeed perhaps as soon as the pending matter of privilege is out of the way.

SENATE DEBATE
51st Cong., 1st Sess.
April 8, 1890

21 CONG. REC. 3145

Mr. HOAR. I ask unanimous consent that the trust bill be taken up.

The PRESIDENT *pro tempore*. The Senator from Massachusetts asks unanimous consent that the pending business be informally laid aside, and that the Senate proceed to the consideration of the bill (S. 1) to declare unlawful trusts and combinations in restraint of trade and production. Is there objection? The Chair hears none. The Senator from Alabama [Mr. PUGH] will be recognized as entitled to the floor when the Montana case is next considered.

The Senate, as in Committee of the Whole, resumed the consideration of the bill (S. 1) to declare unlawful trusts and combinations in restraint of trade and production, which had been reported from the Committee on the Judiciary with an amendment to strike out all after the enacting clause and insert a substitute.

The PRESIDENT *pro tempore*. The question is on agreeing to the amendment proposed by the Committee on the Judiciary, which will be read.

The SECRETARY. The committee report to strike out all after the enacting clause of the bill and to insert: . . .[1.356]

The PRESIDENT *pro tempore*. The question is on agreeing to the amendment proposed by the Committee on the Judiciary.

Mr. HOAR. I desire to say that I hope we may have a vote. I shall not undertake to explain the bill, which is well understood. . . .

Mr. SHERMAN. I do not intend to open any debate on the subject, but I wish to state that, after having fairly and fully considered the amendment proposed by the Committee on the Judiciary, I shall vote for it, not as being precisely what I want, but as the best under all the circumstances that the Senate is prepared to give in this

---

[1.356] The bill as reported by the Committee on the Judiciary was read; it appears *supra* at 275–77.

direction. Therefore, without enlarging or entering into debate, I shall vote for the proposition of the Judiciary Committee as it stands.

Mr. VEST. I stated the other day when the bill was reported from the committee that there was one section that I thought ought to be extended further than its present provisions go, but on reflection I am satisfied that the public interest demands the passage of this bill as it came from the committee, and I am prepared to sacrifice my private judgment to a certain extent in order to facilitate its immediate passage. I sincerely hope that it may go through without any delay and without amendment. . . .

The PRESIDENT *pro tempore*. The question now is upon the amendment proposed by the committee.

The amendment was agreed to.

⊥ The PRESIDENT *pro tempore*. Are there further amendments to the bill as in Committee of the Whole?

Mr. REAGAN. I will ask the Secretary to take down an amendment in section 7, lines 4 and 5. I move that the words "circuit court of the United States in the district in which the defendant resides or is found" may be stricken out and the following words inserted in lieu of those—

The PRESIDENT *pro tempore*. That amendment can not now be entertained. The amendment having been agreed to as in Committee of the Whole, it is not subject to amendment until the bill is reported to the Senate.

Mr. REAGAN. Very well.

The PRESIDENT *pro tempore*. Are there further amendments to the bill as in Committee of the Whole? If there are none, the bill will be reported to the Senate.

The bill was reported to the Senate as amended.

The PRESIDENT *pro tempore*. The Senate have made one amendment to the bill as in Committee of the Whole. The question is, Shall the amendment made as in Committee of the Whole be concurred in in the Senate?

Mr. REAGAN. In lines 4 and 5, in section 7, I move to strike out the words "circuit court of the United States in the district in which the defendant resides or is found" and to insert in lieu thereof the words "court of the United States or of any State of competent jurisdiction."

The PRESIDENT *pro tempore*. The amendment proposed by the Senator from Texas will be read.

The SECRETARY. In section 7, line 4, after the word "any," it is proposed to strike out the words "circuit court of the United States in the district in which the defendant resides or is found" and to insert "court of the United States or of any State of competent jurisdiction;" so as to read:

Any person who shall be injured in his business or property by any other person or corporation by reason of anything forbidden or declared to be unlawful by this act may sue therefor in any court of the United States or of any State of competent jurisdiction, without respect to the amount in controversy, and shall recover threefold the damages by him sustained and the costs of suit, including a reasonable attorney's fee.

Mr. REAGAN. Mr. President, I offer this amendment for the reason that this is the section which gives a remedy for damages in a civil suit, and while it purports to give a remedy, as it is in the original section, it really in most cases amounts to no remedy at all, because no one except a corporation or a rich man would attempt to institute a proceeding under this section. Men of ordinary means (and that is the class of men who are usually subjected to wrongs of this kind) would not be able to employ lawyers and to take witnesses to the circuit court of the United States, and perhaps travel a great distance to reach there, in order to prosecute a suit for a few hundred dollars.

If we intend to give a civil remedy we ought to give it in a jurisdiction within reach of the people of the United States so as to make the remedy available to the people. If we do not mean to give them a remedy we had better strike this section out, because this would be only a remedy for corporations or wealthy men, and would not be a remedy for the great mass of the people.

I trust that the Senate will adopt the amendment so as to give a remedy to all the people.

Mr. HOAR. I ask the Senator before he sits down to say whether he means by the term "competent jurisdiction" and by striking out the words "in the district in which the defendant resides or is found" to give to individuals a right to sue in any United States court anywhere in the country a defendant who may reside anywhere else in the country.

Mr. REAGAN. I believe that the general law fixes the question of the territorial jurisdiction of the various courts; and if I am right as to that, it is not necessary to repeat it in this act.

Mr. HOAR. Then the Senator, I understand, does not intend to accomplish that result?

Mr. REAGAN. It is not my purpose to change the law of territorial jurisdiction so far as the United States courts are concerned.

Mr. HOAR. Then why does not the Senator make it safe and clear by leaving in the phrase "in the district in which the defendant resides or is found?"

Mr. VEST. If my friend from Texas will permit me, I do not want to take any advantage of the phraseology, though I am not prepared to support his amendment, and I suggest that he put his amendment in after the word "found" in line 5, adding the words "or in any State court of competent jurisdiction." Of course he does not wish that a suit should be instituted in a circuit court of the United States against a defendant in a district where he neither resides nor is found. I take it for granted that is not his object; and if he would insert after the word "found," in line 5, the words "or in any State court of competent jurisdiction" it would leave the Federal jurisdiction as it is in the bill and would add to it the State jurisdiction, which I take it is the salient point at which my friend aims.

Mr. REAGAN. I will adopt the suggestion of the Senator from Missouri and insert after the word "found," in line 5, the words "or in any State court of competent jurisdiction."

The PRESIDENT *pro tempore*. The Senator from Texas withdraws his amendment and proposes to amend as will be stated.

The SECRETARY. In section 7, line 5, after the word "found," insert the words "or in any State court of competent jurisdiction;" so as to read:

Any person who shall be injured in his business or property by any other person or corporation by reason of anything forbidden or declared to be unlawful by this act, may sue therefor in any circuit court of the United States in the district in which the defendant resides or is found, or in any State court of competent jurisdiction, without respect to the amount in controversy, etc.

Mr. VEST. I sympathize with the object of the Senator from Texas, but unless we change the entire practice in the Federal courts as it now exists upon the general statute-book of the United States, his amendment is simply in the right direction without reaching the real difficulty. As the law now stands, if a suit under the proposed act should be instituted in a State court, taking it for granted that the Senator's amendment is adopted, the corporation attacked would only be compelled under existing law to appear and make affidavit through its agents or officers that the suit involved a statute of the United States, which it unquestionably would do, and that would take the case into the Federal tribunal.

It is absolutely necessary, then, in order to reach the object of my friend from Texas, with which I entirely sympathize, to change the existing general statute, and he is simply going one step, and a very short step, towards the object which he seeks to attain. I do not know that without an entire revolution in the present Federal judiciary system of the United States we can ever do anything toward equalizing the difference in wealth and in the ability to sue and defend between persons; and therefore this by no means attains the full object of the Senator from Texas. I believe it would be infinitely better to take the bill as it comes from the committee.

Mr. HOAR. I hope the Senator from Texas and those who like him in the Senate on both sides of the Chamber would desire a more sweeping and vigorous remedy will consent so far as this bill is concerned, whatever separate measures may be proposed hereafter, to take it as it has come from the Committee on the Judiciary. Senators will remember that this is entering upon a new and untrodden field of legislation. It is undertaking to curb by national authority an evil which, under the opinions which have prevailed of old under all our legislative precedents and policies, has been left to be dealt with either by the ordinary laws of trade or to be dealt with by the States.

The complaint which has come from all parts and all classes of the country of these great monopolies, which are becoming not only in some cases an actual injury to the comfort of ordinary life, but are a menace to republican institutions themselves, has induced Congress to take the matter up. I suppose no member of this body who remembers the history of the processes by which this bill reached the shape in which it went to the Judiciary Committee will doubt that the opinions of Senators themselves, of able and learned and experienced lawyers, were exceedingly crude in this matter. One Senator who had taken charge of a bill and had drawn one supposed that the processes of the United States courts ran into every district in the United States, and framed his bill on that theory. Another bill was framed on the theory that a bargain between two citizens of different States for an unlawful purpose constituted a controversy between these two citizens within the meaning of the Constitution and gave jurisdiction.

Now, the Judiciary Committee has carefully and as thoroughly as it could agreed upon what we believe will be a very efficient measure, under which one long forward step will be taken in suppressing this evil. We have affirmed the old doctrine of the common law in regard to all interstate and international commercial transactions, and have clothed the United States courts with authority to enforce that doctrine by injunction. We have put in also a grave penalty.

But look at this amendment. I am sorry that I have not the attention of the Senator from Missouri [Mr. VEST], who is on the committee and who expressed himself generally as in favor of the amendment. Oh, there he is. It seems to me, and I wish to suggest to my honorable friend from Missouri, that this amendment of the Senator from Texas is clearly unconstitutional, and that it injures the bill by inserting an unconstitutional proposition, when the whole bill itself is constitutional.

Mr. VEST. I am opposed to the amendment.

Mr. HOAR. I know, but I thought the Senator said he thought he would agree with its purpose.

Mr. VEST. I said I sympathize with the object the Senator from Texas has in view.

Mr. HOAR. What I wish to point out to the Senate and to the Senator from Texas is this: This section which is proposed to be amended is a section establishing a penalty, threefold damages. Now, you can not clothe a State court with the authority to enforce a penalty.

If we create a legal right like a debt by a United States statute, then undoubtedly a State court of general jurisdiction, which has authority to enforce and aid in the collection of debts, without any express enactment by the Congress of the United States, would sustain an action to recover that debt. If there is a debt due from one citizen to another the State court of competent jurisdiction enforces it, no matter what is the nature of the law under which the debt was created; it may ⊥ have been created in a foreign country, it may have been created in another State.

But when you come to penalties, no court enforces penalties except those created by the authority which creates the court, and no statute of any foreign or other authority but that can clothe the court with that power. Take, for instance, the familiar case of usury. If the State of Mississippi enacts that a payment of usurious interest shall not vest the title to that sum in the person to whom it is paid, it may be recovered in an action for money had and received. To that extent that could be enforced in any State in the country or in any foreign country, because the person who receives the usurious interest instantly owes as a debt the money had and received under the law where that transaction took place. But it is very well settled that a statute of a State creating a penalty for usury by enabling the party to recover threefold the usurious interest, or twice the usurious interest, or any other sum, as a penalty, can be enforced only within the jurisdictional limits of the State where the transaction took place and under whose law the transaction is made penal.

We might perhaps say that a person who owed to another a sum of money under an obligation solely the creature of a statute of the United States might recover in any State court; and if the obligation were created he could recover it equally, whether we said so or not; but we can not say that a State court shall be clothed with jurisdiction to enforce a claim for threefold the damages suffered, which is purely penal and punitive.

Mr. MORGAN. And the attorney's fee.

Mr. HOAR. Yes; and the attorney's fee. So I submit to my honorable friend from Texas that his amendment, though intended in the same direction as the bill is intended, will not bear examination.

Mr. REAGAN. In response to the suggestion made by my friend from Missouri that the general law would authorize the transfer of a suit brought in a State court to the Federal court, I have this to say, that without this proposed statute in the form that it would be if my amendment were adopted, his proposition would be true; but if we have the constitutional power to enact the language as it would be if amended, that would be a law fixing the restriction, and would certainly form an exception to the provision of the general law, because this would give an alternative jurisdiction, and being subsequent to the general law the Senator speaks of, it would, it seems to me, carry the State jurisdiction.

As to the question presented by the Senator from Massachusetts that the provision would not be warranted by the Constitution, I understand of course that the State courts will not, as a rule, enforce penal statutes; but it will be remembered, if I am not mistaken, that in the laws in relation to post-offices, perhaps in the laws in relation to national banks, and on quite a number of subjects that I once collected the laws about, the United States gave jurisdiction to the State courts, and that jurisdiction is being asserted upon various subjects and not specially with reference to the collection of debts.

This measure is giving a civil remedy. It is not in the nature of prosecution for crime. It is a civil remedy for damage done. It is true that it fixes a part of the measure of the damages in a civil suit providing that the defendant may be required to pay triple damages and costs, and attorney's fees; but that is a part of the measure of damages in a civil suit and is not in the nature of a prosecution for a crime. . . .

So I do not feel prepared to accept the suggestions of either of the Senators and will ask for a vote of the Senate upon my amendment.

Mr. GEORGE. Mr. President, I am afraid we have got into this condition about the pending bill, that we have a disposition to do something, and that very speedily, whether that something amounts to much or not. I am afraid that there will be great disappointment among the people of this country about the effects of this bill when it shall become a law. It covers professedly a very narrow territory, leaving a very large number of these institutions, these trusts, or whatever we may call them, entirely without the purview of the bill.

That is not the fault of the committee, Mr. President. The bill has been very ingeniously and properly drawn to cover every case which comes within what is called the commercial power of Congress. There is a great deal of this matter outside of that. The bill being of that character, it necessarily will be a disappointing measure to the people of this country.

I sympathize with the amendment offered by the Senator from Texas. If the parties who are injured by these trusts are compelled in all cases to resort to the Federal courts, in many States held at a very long distance from the residence of the parties, it will amount, in effect, to a denial of justice to the small men, the people of small means, the people who have suffered small injuries individually, though very large ones in the aggregate. It will in a measure deprive them of any remedy against the wrongs perpetrated by the combinations and conspiracies against which the bill is directed.

It is not competent for Congress to confer a jurisdiction upon a State court any more than it is for a State to confer jurisdiction upon a United States court. But there is a rule of law of this sort which we can obviate, and which will be obviated by the amendment of the Senator from Texas. As to actions or suits arising under the laws of Congress, Congress can make the jurisdiction of the Federal courts exclusive, so that if a State, or any number of States, or all of the States were willing to allow their courts to try cases arising under such a law, they could not authorize their courts to try them.

The object and purpose and the legal effect of the amendment offered by the Senator from Texas are not to confer *in invitum* on the State courts a jurisdiction which the States do not desire the courts to possess, but it simply means that, if the States are willing or if any State is willing that its courts may entertain jurisdiction and try cases arising under this law, the consent of Congress is given for that to be done.

Mr. President, I think we ought, in view of what is said by the Senator from Texas and in view of what we all know about these matters, to give that consent; in other words, we ought to leave it to the option of each State to give its courts concurrent jurisdiction with the United States courts in cases arising under this act if it should become a law. I hope, therefore, that the amendment of the Senator from Texas, as it does not change in the least the general structure of the bill, but merely furnishes an additional facility to the people of the United States to get redress for their wrongs in a cheap and easy and convenient mode, will be adopted by the Senate.

As to the suggestion made by the Senator from Missouri that it would be unavailing because as soon as a suit was brought in the State courts it could be immediately removed into the Federal courts, if that be true (and I am not sure whether it is so with reference to the amount involved) that trouble can be very easily remedied by adding this provision:

And suits commencing in the State courts under this act shall not be removed into any Federal court. . . .

Mr. BUTLER. How will the Senator reconcile the amendment of the Senator from Texas with section 5 of this bill, which says:

SEC. 5. Whenever it shall appear to the court before which any proceeding under section 4 of this act may be pending that the ends of justice require that other parties should be brought before the court, the court may cause them to be summoned, whether they reside in the district in which the court is held or not; and subpoenas to that end may be served in any district by the marshal thereof.

Mr. GEORGE. That only applies to the remedial process of injunction and things of that kind.

Mr. BUTLER. Precisely, but if the suit is begun in a State court, how is the process of the State court to go outside of the limits of the State?

Mr. GEORGE. If the Senator will look at the amendment he will find that it applies to section 7, which has reference only to actions brought by persons injured to recover damages for the injury, and does not affect that remedial process in courts of equity mentioned in the section to which he has called my attention.

I hope that the amendment will be adopted; and I propose—though I am urged by Senators in whose judgment and in whose disposition to do right about this matter on both sides of the Chamber I have confidence not to offer any further amendments—to take the sense of the Senate upon an amendment which I have drawn up, which will still further facilitate the small men, the men of small capital in getting redress for the great wrongs that are perpetrated against them by these trusts.

Whilst I am up, as it is objected to by Senators, I will explain the object and purpose of the amendment which I shall offer.

It is well known that the great evil of these combinations, these conspiracies, as they are called, these monopolies, as they are denominated by the bill, consists in the fact that by combination, by association, there have been gathered together the money and the means of large numbers of persons, and under these combinations, or conspiracies, or trusts, this great aggregated capital is wielded by a single hand and guided by a single brain, or at least by hands and brains acting in complete harmony and co-operation, and that in this way, by this association, by this direction of this immense amount of capital, by one organized will, to a very large extent, these wrongs have been perpetrated upon the American people.

They come about by the association of men of large capital living in various States of the Union. They come about by corporations organized in various States of the Union acting in concert. They come about, too, by single individuals organizing as a single corporation in one State in the Union. By the use of this organized force of wealth and money the small men engaged in competition with them are crushed out, and that is the great evil at which all this legislation ought to be directed.

The amendment which I intend to offer gives the right of combination in suits under the seventh section of this bill to the wretched victims of these great combinations and trusts. For instance, these combinations and trusts raise the price of articles of consumption; take for instance that article which has been made the subject of a trust and has been so injurious to the section of country from which I come, the cotton-bagging trust. They double the price of cotton-bagging. Cotton-bagging is bought in the South, and the men who are injured by the trust are those small farmers, white and colored, who raise a few bales of cotton. They will probably, on each bale of cotton, lose by the combination, by the increased price, from one to two dollars. The small farmer will make from three to twenty bales of cotton. So he will be injured by this cotton-bagging trust from ten to fifty or sixty dollars. How can a single man thus injured—I put it to Senators to think about this thing candidly—how can the small farmer thus injured from $10 to $50, with his witnesses, go to a distant town or city, employ a lawyer, and sue one of these great trusts in a United States court?

Sir, it is like a single man, a citizen untrained in military affairs, taking his musket or his shotgun and attacking a drilled army. So of every other trust.

The object of my amendment is to allow combination against combination, to allow these small farmers, these mechanics who have been injured in small sums by the advanced price which they have been compelled to pay for articles they must use to unite in the same suit against one of these combinations, and to require the court when proof of this union has been made to try the case and to ascertain the damages done to each one and to render judgment in favor of each one for the damages sustained by him. I think without a provision of that sort you might as well write on the face of your bill, "This is not intended for small men, for small people; this is intended only for those who have money enough to fight these great corporations, these great trusts, these great combinations."

Now, a word or two more and I shall have done, because when I have said what I think is proper to say in this matter I shall conclude. The country calls on us loudly for relief; the Senate is being pressed now, urged now to go on with this bill, because we ought to take some step, make a beginning to show that we are opposed to trusts. That is a proper sentiment when not carried too far; but it ought not, I submit to this honorable body, to be allowed to have sufficient strength and vigor to deprive us of the power of reasoning upon the bill we are about to pass and give it such amendments and such perfection as will prevent its turning out Dead Sea fruit.

I hope that the amendment of the Senator from Texas, as the first step in the line of giving the real sufferers of this country a chance to get something back from these combinations and conspiracies, will be adopted. . . .

Mr. EDMUNDS. I hope we shall finish the bill to-night; but let the Senator send his amendment up to be read. It was considered in the committee[1.357] and I should like other Senators to know what it is, I should like the whole body of the Senate to know what it is. The Committee on the Judiciary knew what it was when it was submitted there. . . .

Mr. GEORGE. I will read it here in the aisle. I propose to add at the end of section 7:

And in all such actions in any court of the United States it shall be lawful for any number of persons complaining of such injuries committed by the same defendant against each of them separately, to join as plaintiffs, and the court or jury trying the issues of fact in any such cause shall find the amount of the separate damages sustained by each plaintiff and may also find in favor of a part of said plaintiffs and against the others, as the proof shall warrant, and the court shall render judgment accordingly. And in the proceedings in such cause the court may, if justice so requires, proceed with the trial thereof as to a part of said plaintiffs and continue the cause to a future day as to the remainder, and this may be done as often as justice may require. And whenever there shall be a motion for a new trial in any such cause, the court may sustain the same as to a part of said plaintiffs and overrule it as to others, accordingly as the right and justice of the case may require. Execution shall issue on any judgment rendered in such cause in favor of each plaintiff for the amount recovered by him and for his reasonable attorney's fees, and also for such share of the costs as the court shall determine to be fair and reasonable.

Mr. EDMUNDS. This amendment in substance, and perhaps in very form, was

---

[1.357] Senator Edmund's reference is to the Senate Committee on the Judiciary.

submitted by my friend from Mississippi and carefully considered by the Committee on the Judiciary, and I am under the impression that we all agreed excepting himself that it was entirely inadmissible for the purposes of the safety of the very people who are concerned in it. So much for that. . . .

The trouble about this business is as I have seen a good many times before when we were trying to strike at great evils in a broad way and leave the details and difficulties that might afterwards arise to be repaired by legislation, as we do about all such things, that Congress has failed to make a law because the very persons against whom it was intended to operate in their mischievous performances got up, as they say on the prairies, a counter-fire and added to the fuel and stimulated men to carry the law so far that it could not be executed at all.

That was the aspect of this thing when this subject was sent to the Committee on the Judiciary. We all felt it, and the committee, I think unanimously, including my friend from Mississippi, thought that if we were really in earnest in wishing to strike at these evils broadly, in the first instance, as a new line of legislation, we would frame a bill that should be clearly within our constitutional power, that we should make its definition out of terms that were well known to the law already, and would leave it to the courts in the first instance to say how far they could carry it or its definitions as applicable to each particular case as it might arise.

Therefore I say as to the suggested amendment of my friend from Mississippi—and I repeat it in all earnestness—that if I were a lobbyist and wanted to entangle this business, I should provide that everybody might sue everybody else in one common suit and have a regular *pot-pourri* of the affair, as his amendment proposes, and leave it to the lawyers of the trust to have an interminable litigation in respect of the proper parties, whether their interests were common or diverse or how they were affected, and take twenty years in order to get a result as to a single one of them. The Judiciary Committee did not think it wise to do that sort of thing, because we were in earnest about the business, as I know my friend is.

Now I come to the amendment of my friend from Texas [Mr. REAGAN], to section 7, I believe it is, that a person aggrieved may sue in the State courts. I wish to call the attention of my friend from Texas—and I know he is perfectly earnest about this business and I think he introduced the best and the first bill upon the subject—I wish to call his attention to this seventh section as framed in the very line of what he is speaking of.

The law of the United States as it is now prevents anybody from going into the circuit court of the United States unless he has a two-thousand-dollar controversy.

This section provides that any person who shall be injured, etc., by anything declared unlawful in this act may sue therefor in the circuit court of the United States in the district where the defendant resides or is found, without regard to the amount in controversy. That is all. The whole object of the seventh section is to relieve the circuit court of the United States from the question of the *quantum* in dispute. It leaves everybody, as everybody now has the power under any law of the United States, to sue anybody who wrongs him, whether against the law of the State or of the United States, in a State court if he chooses to do so. So I appeal to my friend from Texas and make the suggestion to him that his amendment is quite useless and unnecessary, because this section merely gives in the circuit court of the United States the right of anybody to sue who chooses to sue, without regard to the amount in controversy, leaving anybody to sue in the State courts against anybody who wrongs him under the common practices of the law that apply in all the States.

So I should hope, if the Senator is really in earnest, he will be satisfied to leave the section as it is. Of course the man who writes for a newspaper in the fifth story of a large building in some city, that is properly furnished and carpeted and lighted by electricity, etc., is "public opinion." Whatever we might think about his opinion if he came here and told it to us without regard to what he may say in a newspaper, I should hope that the Senate of the United States, being in earnest about this business, would allow us to pass a bill that is clear in its terms, is definite in its definitions, and is broad in its comprehension, without winding it up into infinite details which those whom we are trying to repress would be most glad to have us do.

Mr. REAGAN. Mr. President, I certainly for one feel gratified at the result of the action of the Judiciary Committee in getting before the Senate a bill which is probably not obnoxious to constitutional objections and one that may afford some relief against the evils towards which it is directed. But it seems to me that we need not be afraid to do that which would bring the beneficial operations of the law within the reach of the people intended to be protected by it.

On the bills that were before the Senate and that were referred to the Judiciary Committee we encountered the trouble of coming in contact with the Constitution, and certainly there were many suggestions made in them which were liable to objections of that kind. The objection which we now meet is the danger of the lobby. Well, the lobby is composed of a troublesome set sometimes; but the lobby can not change the meaning of words, nor can it change legal principles.

The Senator from Vermont suggests that the bill is in the line which I have in view, of extending the law so as to put it within the reach of everybody by waiving the $2,000 limit, which fixes the jurisdiction of the circuit courts. The Senator certainly is right in that, and I feel gratified that the Committee on the Judiciary have put the clause into the section providing that these suits may be there prosecuted without respect to the amount in controversy.

That, however—and I call the attention of the Senator from Vermont to it—is not the point that I presented as a reason for the amendment which I offered. The difficulty is in getting into the circuit court of the United States. Take any one of the great States of this country, especially those most sparsely settled; the litigants may in many cases be very far removed from the place of holding the circuit court and may be unable and would, if only a few hundred dollars were involved, be unable to employ counsel and go to the place where the court sits and bring suit and take witnesses and prosecute the claim. So, then, even with the provision as submitted by the Judiciary Committee and the words "without reference to the amount involved" inserted, still, the distance from the court and the expense of employing attorneys in that court would be involved, and justice would be denied to the great mass of the people under the bill as it is presented.

Mr. EDMUNDS. But my point about that is that this seventh section only is intended to and only does give a right to sue in the courts of the United States, which becomes a right common to sue in the courts of all the States and in the courts of the United States without regard to the $2,000 limitation which prevails by general law. It has been suggested to me by my friend from Massachusetts who sits behind me [Mr. HOAR], and there may be force in it, but I am not sure about it (certainly there must be force in it or he would not have suggested it), that possibly if suit were brought in the State court, as triple damages are fixed by the act of Congress, the plaintiff in the State court could not recover the triple damages. But I wish to repeat that in respect of this seventh section, waiving the point of triple damages, it has been suggested that any person who has a right of action for a wrong done to him in violation of this statute may sue in any court of any State where he may find the defendant or any of his property, according to the laws of the jurisdiction, and apart from the question my friend from Massachusetts suggested about whether the triple damages, being allowed by act of Congress, and not by the laws of the State, could be recoverd in a State court.

I repeat that this section was intended by the Committee on the Judiciary to allow anybody who wished, to sue in a court of the United States without regard to the $2,000 limitation, leaving to any man the original right to sue anybody that offended him in the courts of his own State and in the courts of his own county.

Mr. REAGAN. I understand the Senator, and I always have great respect for him, especially on legal questions; but under this section I submit to him and to the Senate, as it limits the right to sue to the circuit court of the United States, I do not exactly see how men could sue in the State courts.

Mr. EDMUNDS. I was about to address my friend as "my good friend," but I address the Chair. I submit to him that he will see that the language is an authority that the man "may sue in the circuit court of the United States" without regard to the amount in controversy. It is not intended and designed by a long-settled line of decisions to exclude the jurisdiction of the courts of the States.

Mr. REAGAN. I should be afraid that "may" would be held by the courts in that case to mean "shall," and certainly, if it be subject to that interpretation, then the only suggestion I have to make further in response to what the Senator from Vermont has said is the same I have made in response to what the Senator from Massachusetts said, that this is not a section which provides for punishing a crime; if it were, of course it would have to be enforced by the Federal courts; but it is a section that governs a civil suit and fixes the measure of damages in that civil suit. It provides for triple damages, and for costs as a matter of course. If I am right about that, my amendment would simply place it in the power of the people to institute suits in a jurisdiction which would be accessible to them and where they could enforce their rights; and I do not care to go further into the discussion of that subject at this time.

Mr. MORGAN. Mr. President, suppose we should undertake to give to the States criminal jurisdiction under this statute. I presume there is not a lawyer in this body or anywhere else who would not deny that we had any authority of that kind; and yet we have just the same power to confer criminal jurisdiction upon the State courts as we have to confer upon the State courts the power to recover a penalty, something that must be enforced in a *qui tam* action or something like that.

Now, whoever recovers upon this statute, in whatever court he may go to, will recover upon the statute. It is very true that we use common-law terms here and common-law definitions in order to define an offense which is in itself comparatively new, but it is not a common-law jurisdiction that we are conferring upon the circuit courts of the United States. It is a Federal jurisdiction, arising under the Constitution of the United States. If it did not arise there we could not confer it.

In the great criminal feature of the bill and in the feature which declares a forfeiture for the offense of the transportation of goods contrary to this statute, it provides for a recovery and punishment upon the same footing that such proceedings are put by our laws in relation to the importation of goods into the United States contrary to the statutes provided in such cases.

Now, if the amendment of the Senator from Texas should prevail, the first question that would arise in any case in a State court would be, Where did this State court get its jurisdiction? It has not got it now. That is very clear. Where would it get it? Would it get it from the act of Congress?

The Senator from Vermont did not say, as I understood him, that the common-law remedy, which he considers exists in all common-law countries and in all the State courts, still exists in the common-law courts, but you can not get your triple damages and attorney's fees there. You would have to get your damages as they are measured by the common law in the State courts, because the jurisdiction comes from that source.

I think, Mr. President, it is time the Congress of the United States had reconciled as many of the difficulties about this matter as it can and we had gotten some strong, general, useful legislation upon this question. Now, the Committee on the Judiciary have been, I think, remarkably successful in the suggestion of their remedies. They certainly have been very cautious, indeed, in their definitions, so far as giving power to the courts and limiting the authority of the courts, and prescribing some enlargement, perhaps, in cases of injunction and in the service of process upon parties interested or concerned who may be beyond the borders of the particular jurisdiction. It seems to me that this is the best bill on that subject that I have ever seen in this body, and I shall expect real, wholesome, good fruit from it.

The Senator from Texas [Mr. REAGAN] has been for many years trying to reform the transportation of this country, trying to reform its interstate commerce, and he is very eager and very anxious to give every remedy that ingenuity could possibly suggest, but I submit to the Senator that there is no occasion for going so far as to bring up a great constitutional difficulty over which war will be had. This bill ought not to be a breeder of lawsuits. If there is any one duty we have got higher than another in respect of the general judiciary of the United States, it is to suppress litigation and have justice done without litigation as far as we can.

Mr. REAGAN. If the Senator will allow me I will suggest that the very object of this is to make litigation, or there would be no use for it.

Mr. MORGAN. No; it is not. Every man can not go to the circuit court of the United States and bring his suit. My view of the bill was that there was a little too much temptation of that kind presented in it, for when a plaintiff is allowed reasonable attorney's fees, if he has but 75 cents interest, he will always be very likely to find an attorney who will prosecute his case.

Mr. HOAR. And civil damages also.

Mr. EDMUNDS. If my friend from Alabama will allow me, I wish to add that the framework of this bill provides, first, for a declaration of the illegality of these things; it provides, second, for the criminal punishment of the parties engaged in that illegal combination; it provides, third, for an institution of a suit on the part of the United States to repress it as you suppress a nuisance, although it is liable to indictment; it provides, fourth, that, on the part of the United States defending all small people, any part of the property which is the subject of this combination that is moved from State to State (that is as far as we can go, as everybody knows) shall be an illegal movement and subject to confiscation. Then we say that anybody, without respect to the amount in controversy, may bring suit in the circuit court.

Mr. MORGAN. I should have been perfectly satisfied with this bill, or the first three propositions of it, as a bill that would cover the evil, but we have gone further and given a personal remedy, to whoever may be injured in his business or property by the unlawful act defined and denounced in the statute. We can not go to every length. We can not bring in a bill in the nature of a creditor's bill for the purpose of enabling a man to sue in favor of himself and of other persons who may find themselves injured and therefore is given a creditor's bill to recover debts. That is something that does not belong to our statutory jurisdiction. It would be very hard to give it. It is admitted here there would have to be a jury trial in each case, and they might rise to fifty, and we should have perhaps fifty jury trials, and the probability of new trials; and when would that case ever end and when would you get an appeal?

There is as much harm in trying to do too much as there is in not trying to do anything, and I think we have stopped at about the proper line in this bill, and I shall support it just as it is. . . .

⊥ Mr. GEORGE. I understand they[1.358] infest the Capitol and are passing around ⊥3150 here, and so I suppose I must have seen at some time or other an individual who occupies that position in reference to Congress. But this amendment is not to be put down in that way. It was the duty of the Senator to show, first, that this amendment of mine was an obstacle to the successful operation of this bill if it should become a law, and not, as I believe it to be, a necessary thing to have it operate at all.

It is very well to talk about the symmetry of the work of the Judiciary Committee, but when you pass a bill by which you throw the poor unlettered and unskilled American farmer and American mechanic and American laborer, who are the great sufferers by these trusts and combinations, unaided, single-handed, against these large corporations, you just simply pass a bill that will amount to nothing, and I predict—and I put it on the record now as my deliberate judgment—that not one suit will ever be brought under this seventh section by any person who is simply damaged in his character as consumer. I repeat it. I do not propose silently to sit here and be a silent partner, an assenting partner, to the enactment of what I know to be, so far as a remedy to the real parties injured by these trusts is concerned, a sham, a snare, and a delusion.

I do not mean by that to say that there are not other classes of the community that will be benefited by this bill. I do not mean by that to say that this bill ought not to pass. I believe it ought to pass. I believe it ought to pass whether amended as proposed by the Senator from Texas and myself or not. There is enough of good in it to justify the American Senate and the American Congress in putting it in the shape of a law; but when we are performing this operation, when we are legislating for the benefit of the people of this country, I do not think that, out of any mere sentiment or out of any mere objection to taking a little pains and care in perfecting this bill, we ought to leave out the essential matters contained in the amendment of the Senator from Texas and in the amendment offered by myself. I should like some Senator to get up and show by a specific statement, not by general allegations, in what respect the amendment offered by me would interfere with the beneficial operation of this bill.

[1.358] Senator George's reference is to lobbyists.

Suppose twenty consumers combine in a suit. They have bought cotton-bagging; they have been robbed of the amount of five, twenty, fifty, or one hundred dollars each, according to the amount of cotton-bagging they have bought. They have all been injured by the same combination, by the same conspiracy. This combination—this conspiracy—controls millions of dollars. The parties injured separately are poor men. Why not allow them to combine in a suit to enforce from this great combination proper redress for the wrongs they have suffered? Suppose they bring the suit. Suppose at the trial term half of them are not ready for trial and half of them are.

The court, according to the provisions of this bill, continues the case as to half, proceeds with the trial as to half, settles their rights, gives judgment in their favor, gives them full redress, and continues the case as to the others until the next term of the court. At the next term they try the rest. How does that injure anybody? Some Senator suggested that if a hundred persons were injured you would have a hundred jury trials in one case. No, sir; the whole matter can be tried by the same jury. Will gentlemen tell me that in a case which I have suggested, where all have been injured by the same act, and you prove that act, you prove the combination, you prove the rise in the price of bagging, a jury is not competent to say that when the proof is that the plaintiff A was damaged to the amount of $10 they can not find that, that where plaintiff B was damaged to the amount of $20 they can not find that, and so on to the end of the list? Certainly that is not an extraordinary feat for a jury to perform.

So, then, the objection made by the Senator from Vermont, and I think, though I could not hear him distinctly, as his back was to me, participated in by the Senator from Alabama [Mr. MORGAN], amounts simply to nothing. What is the effect if you do not pass the amendment? Will any single one of those men who have been thus wronged to the amount of ten, fifteen, twenty, or fifty dollars bring a separate suit? How can he maintain it? He is to employ a lawyer; he has to go to a distance of from 100 to 500 miles, perhaps to a distant State, to maintain his suit. Who will do it? I ask Senators to stop and reflect who will do it? Not one of them. If some great manufacturer has been injured by an advance in the price of his raw material he can sue, but the poor man, the consumer, the laborer, the farmer, the mechanic, the country merchant, all that large class of American citizens who constitute 90 per cent. of our population and who are the real sufferers will have no opportunity of redress, and the bill, so far as they are concerned, will be a snare and a mere delusion.

A word now about whether or not the triple damages could be recovered in a State court. There is no doubt that they can not be recovered unless we give permission to the State courts to entertain the suit, because, being a penalty, the courts will construe the statute which is passed here as giving exclusive jurisdiction to the United States courts. . . .

Mr. EDMUNDS. . . . How can Congress impute to a State court of sovereign jurisdiction the right to enforce its own penalties?

Mr. GEORGE. If the Senator had honored me with his attention when I first addressed the Senate upon this subject he would not have asked that question. I stated distinctly that it was no more competent for Congress to give or confer a jurisdiction upon a State court than it was competent for a State to confer a jurisdiction upon a United States court. That is not the point. We, in passing laws of this sort, may give concurrent jurisdiction to the States or we may take exclusive jurisdiction for the United States courts. When we manifest a disposition to allow the jurisdiction to be concurrent that does not give the State courts jurisdiction. It allows the States themselves to give that jurisdiction to their courts. That is all there is of it.

We remove the bar created by the presumption or the enactment that we intended the jurisdiction to be exclusive, and we allow each State to give or withhold the jurisdiction to its own courts as it sees proper. Then when a State comes to do that, suppose we give them the permission, the State courts will enforce the exact jurisdiction which the States allow their court to assume. The State of Mississippi, for instance, says, and the State of Vermont says, and some other State says, "We confer upon our common-law courts jurisdiction under this bill, and they shall take and assume the jurisdiction which Congress allows them to take and assume under this bill." Suppose that is done. The suit is brought in a State court. What prevents the State court from rendering just such judgment as the law we pass allows the United States court to render? It is the State having the permission of Congress that can regulate this matter. . . .

Mr. HOAR. I should like to understand the Senator's view of this point: What is it that the State renders judgment upon?

Mr. GEORGE. The Senator made his question too laconic. I do not understand it.

Mr. HOAR. Is it a contract, and what is the cause of action?

Mr. GEORGE. The cause of action under this seventh section would be a wrong.

Mr. HOAR. A penalty.

Mr. GEORGE. A wrong or a penalty.

Mr. HOAR. How can a State render judgment for a penalty or wrong committed by a man in another State?

Mr. GEORGE. That depends entirely upon what jurisdiction the State gives its own courts. If it be a foreign country, for instance, if it be a penalty under the law of England, the State may or it may not, as it sees proper, invest its courts with the jurisdiction to enforce it. The States ordinarily do not give that jurisdiction, but there is nothing to prevent it being given in the case of a Federal law. If it be a Federal law, a national law, there is something else besides the mere will of the State to be considered: the Federal relation to the State. If the United States allow, the State can give that jurisdiction to its courts, and if the Federal Government will not allow it, the State can not. If the Senator disputes that proposition, he must show me some principle of constitutional law restricting the powers of the States which prevents them from investing their courts with jurisdiction to enforce penalties incurred under a foreign jurisdiction or under the United States laws, if the United States shall consent that the State courts may do it.

Mr. REAGAN. If the Senator will allow me, I wish to state in that connection that there are numbers of cases in which State jurisdiction is given under Federal laws.

The PRESIDENT *pro tempore*. Is the Senate ready for the question upon the amendment offered by the Senator from Texas [Mr. REAGAN]? . . .

The question is upon agreeing to the amendment proposed by the Senator from Texas. It will be again read.

The CHIEF CLERK. In section 7, line 5, after the word "found," it is proposed to insert the words "or in any State court of competent jurisdiction;" so as to read:

SEC. 7. Any person who shall be injured in his business or property by any ⊥ other person ⊥3151 or corporation by reason of anything forbidden or declared to be unlawful by this act, may sue therefor in any circuit court of the United States in the district in which the defendant resides or is found, or in any State court of competent jurisdiction without respect to the amount in controversy, and shall recover threefold the damages by him sustained and the costs of suit, including a reasonable attorney's fee.

Mr. BUTLER. I am not going to inflict a speech on the Senate at this late hour, but I want to explain my vote.

I shall vote against this amendment and I shall vote against all amendments to this bill, and if the difficulties which have been pointed out by the Senator from Texas and the Senator from Mississippi exist, there is nothing easier than for Congress to amend this law in the future.

It seems to me that this is a very good bill as it stands, and I shall therefore vote for it as it stands, and shall vote against all amendments, because I desire to get some legislation upon this subject; and if, as I said awhile ago, in the future it shall turn out that these additional provisions shall be found necessary it will be a very easy thing for Congress to add them.

The yeas and nays were ordered; and the Secretary proceeded to call the roll. . . .

The result was announced—yeas 13, nays 36; as follows: . . .

So the amendment of Mr. REAGAN was rejected.

Mr. GEORGE. Mr. President, I now offer the amendment I send to the desk. . . .

The PRESIDENT *pro tempore*. The amendment proposed by the Senator from Mississippi will be read.

The CHIEF CLERK. It is proposed to add to section 7 the following: . . . [1.359]

The PRESIDENT *pro tempore*. The question is on agreeing to the amendment of the Senator from Mississippi [Mr. GEORGE].

The amendment was rejected.

The PRESIDENT *pro tempore*. Are there further amendments to the bill in the Senate?

Mr. REAGAN. I offer the following to come in as a proviso at the end of the third section:

Provided, That each day's violation of any of the provisions of this act shall be held to be a separate offense.

The PRESIDENT *pro tempore*. The question is on agreeing to the amendment proposed by the Senator from Texas [Mr. REAGAN].

The amendment was rejected.

Mr. [JOHN E.] KENNA [D., W. Va.]. Mr. President, I have no disposition to delay a vote on the bill, but I would like to ask, with his permission, the Senator from Vermont a question touching the second section:

Every person who shall monopolize, or attempt to monopolize, or combine or conspire with any other person or persons, to monopolize any part of the trade, etc.

Is it intended by the committee, as the section seems to indicate, that if an individual engaged in trade between States or between States and Territories, or between States or Territories and the District of Columbia, or between a State and a foreign country, by his own skill and energy, by the propriety of his conduct generally, shall pursue his calling in such a way as to monopolize a trade, his action shall be a crime under this proposed act? To make myself understood, if I am not clear—

Mr. EDMUNDS. I think I understand the Senator.

Mr. KENNA. Suppose a citizen of Kentucky is dealing in shorthorn cattle and by virtue of his superior skill in that particular product it turns out that he is the only one in the United States to whom an order comes from Mexico for cattle of that stock for a considerable period, so that he is conceded to have a monopoly of that trade with Mexico; is it intended by the committee that the bill shall make that man a culprit?

Mr. EDMUNDS. It is not intended by it and the bill does not do it. Anybody who knows the meaning of the word "monopoly," as the courts apply it, would not apply it to such a person at all; and I am sure my friend must understand that.

Mr. KENNA. I think I understand what the word "monopoly" means, and my ignorance may have caused me to propound the inquiry; but it does not make any difference how the courts have explained or interpreted the word "monopoly." I do not know that the courts have done it, but no matter how they have explained it, here is a provision in the bill which, if plain English means anything in the courts or elsewhere, provides a penalty for such conduct on the part of any citizen of this country engaged in the commonest and most legitimate callings of the country, who happens by his skill and energy to command an innocent and legitimate monopoly of a business.

Mr. EDMUNDS. It does not do anything of the kind, because in the case stated the gentleman has not any monopoly at all. He has ⊥ not bought off his adversaries. He has not got the possession of all the horned cattle in the United States. He has not done anything but compete with his adversaries in trade, if he had any, to furnish the commodity for the lowest price. So I assure my friend he need not be disturbed upon that subject.

Mr. GRAY. Before the Senator from West Virginia arose I had the bill before me and was about to offer an amendment which was directed precisely to the point he has raised, and I shall offer that amendment now. It is to strike out of section 2, in lines 1 and 2, the words "monopolize, or attempt to monopolize, or;" so that the section shall read:

Every person who shall combine or conspire with any other person or persons to monopolize any part of the trade or commerce among the several States, etc.

[1.359] Senator George's amendment appears *supra* at 285.

We will avoid by that amendment the objection which I think the Senator from West Virginia has very pertinently raised. I do not know what definition the courts of the United States have ever given to the word "monopoly" or "monopolize." It is true that, because I do not know it, it does not follow that they may not have defined those terms; but we avoid the danger by this amendment of incorporating in the bill words that are not susceptible of exact legal interpretation, and we confine the provisions of this bill to an inhibition of the combination or conspiracy to monopolize, which we all agree should be the object of its denunciation.

Mr. HOAR. I put in the committee, if I may be permitted to say so (I suppose there is no impropriety in it), the precise question which has been put by the Senator from West Virginia, and I had that precise difficulty in the first place with this bill, but I was answered, and I think all the other members of the committee agreed in the answer, that "monopoly" is a technical term known to the common law, and that it signifies—I do not mean to say that they stated what the signification was, but I became satisfied that they were right and that the word "monopoly" is a merely technical term which has a clear and legal signification, and it is this: It is the sole engrossing to a man's self by means which prevent other men from engaging in fair competition with him.

Of course a monopoly granted by the King was a direct inhibition of all other persons to engage in that business or calling or to acquire that particular article, except the man who had a monopoly granted him by the sovereign power. I suppose, therefore, that the courts of the United States would say in the case put by the Senator from West Virginia that a man who merely by superior skill and intelligence, a breeder of horses or raiser of cattle, or manufacturer or artisan of any kind, got the whole business because nobody could do it as well as he could was not a monopolist, but that it involved something like the use of means which made it impossible for other persons to engage in fair competition, like the engrossing, the buying up of all other persons engaged in the same business.

Mr. KENNA. If the Senator will permit me, I should like to ask him whether a monopoly such as he defines is prohibited at common law. I ask the Senator from Massachusetts whether a monopoly coming within the definition which he gives is prohibited at common law.

Mr. HOAR. I so understand it.

Mr. KENNA. Then why should this bill proceed to denounce that very monopoly?

Mr. HOAR. Because there is not any common law of the United States.

Mr. KENNA. There is common law in nearly every State in the Union.

Mr. HOAR. I know. The common law in the States of the Union of course extends over citizens and subjects over which the State itself has jurisdiction. Now we are dealing with an offense against interstate or international commerce, which the State can not regulate by penal enactment, and we find the United States without any common law. The great thing that this bill does, except affording a remedy, is to extend the common-law principles, which protected fair competition in trade in old times in England, to international and interstate commerce in the United States.

Mr. EDMUNDS. I have only to say, in regard to the amendment suggested by my friend from Delaware and the suggestions of the Senator from West Virginia, that this subject was not lightly considered in the committee, and that we studied it with whatever little ability we had, and the best answer I can make to both my friends is to read from Webster's Dictionary the definition of the verb "to monopolize:"

1. To purchase or obtain possession of the whole of, as a commodity or goods in market, with the view to appropriate or control the exclusive sale of; as, to monopolize sugar or tea.

Like the sugar trust. One man, if he had capital enough, could do it just as well as two.

2. To engross or obtain by any means the exclusive right of, especially the right of trading to any place, or with any country or district; as, to monopolize the India or Levant trade.

The old definition. So I assure my friends that although we may be mistaken (we do not pretend to know all the law) we were not blind to the very suggestions which have been made, and we thought we had done the right thing in providing, in the very phrase we did, that if one person instead of two, by a combination, if one person alone, as we have heard about the wheat market in Chicago, for instance, did it, it was just as offensive and injurious to the public interest as if two had combined to do it.

The PRESIDENT *pro tempore*. The question is on the amendment proposed by the Senator from Delaware [Mr. GRAY].

Mr. HOAR. Let it be read.

The PRESIDENT *pro tempore*. The amendment will be stated.

The CHIEF CLERK. In lines 1 and 2 of section 2 it is proposed to strike out the words "monopolize, or attempt to monopolize, or," so as to read:

Every person who shall combine or conspire with any other person or persons to monopolize any part of the trade, etc.

The amendment was rejected.

The PRESIDENT *pro tempore*. Are there further amendments? If there are none, the question recurs on concurring in the amendment made as in Committee of the Whole.

The amendment was concurred in.

The bill was ordered to be engrossed for a third reading, and was read the third time.

The PRESIDENT *pro tempore*. Having been read three times, shall the bill pass?

Mr. EDMUNDS. I wish to have the yeas and nays on that, Mr. President.

The yeas and nays were ordered; and the Secretary proceeded to call the roll. . . .

⊥ The result was announced—yeas 52, nay 1; as follows:

YEAS—52.

Allison,	Davis,	Ingalls,	Ransom,
Bate,	Dawes,	Jones of Nevada,	Reagan,
Berry,	Dixon,	Kenna,	Sawyer,
Blackburn,	Dolph,	McMillan,	Sherman,
Butler,	Edmunds,	McPherson,	Spooner,
Call,	Faulkner,	Manderson,	Stewart,
Casey,	Frye,	Mitchell,	Stockbridge,
Chandler,	Gibson,	Morgan,	Teller,
Cockrell,	Gorman,	Paddock,	Turpie,
Coke,	Gray,	Pierce,	Vest,
Colquitt,	Harris,	Platt,	Walthall,
Cullom,	Higgins,	Plumb,	Wilson of Iowa,
Daniel,	Hoar,	Pugh,	Wilson of Md.

NAY—1.
Blodgett.

ABSENT—29.

Aldrich,	Evarts,	Jones of Arkansas,	Stanford,
Allen,	Farwell,	Moody,	Vance,
Barbour,	George,	Morrill,	Voorhees,
Beck,	Hale,	Pasco,	Washburn,
Blair,	Hampton,	Payne,	Wolcott.
Brown,	Hawley,	Pettigrew,	
Cameron,	Hearst,	Quay,	
Eustis,	Hiscock,	Squire,	

So the bill was passed.

The title was amended so as to read: "A bill to protect trade and commerce against unlawful restraints and monopolies."

[ED. NOTE: S. 1 as passed by the Senate was identical with the bill as redrafted by the Senate Judiciary Committee (reported out on April 2, 1890, and reprinted *supra*).]

HOUSE CONSIDERATION (S. 1)

REPORT OF THE HOUSE COMMITTEE ON THE JUDICIARY
H.R. Rep. No. 1707
51st Cong., 1st Sess.
April 25, 1890

Mr. CULBERSON, from the Committee on the Judiciary, submitted the following

REPORT:

[To accompany S. 1.]

The Committee on the Judiciary have had under consideration Senate bill No. 1, "to protect trade and commerce against unlawful restraints and monopolies," and recommend its passage.

The object of the bill is twofold:

(1) To protect trade and commerce among the several States or with foreign nations against unlawful restraints and monopoly; and

(2) To protect trade and commerce in the Territories of the United States or of the District of Columbia, or between any such Territory and another, or between any such Territory or Territories, or any State or States, or the District of Columbia, or with foreign nations, or between the District of Columbia and any State or States or foreign nations against unlawful restraints.

It will be observed that the provisions of the bill are carefully confined to such subjects of legislation as are clearly within the legislative authority of Congress.

No attempt is made to invade the legislative authority of the several States or even to occupy doubtful grounds. No system of laws can be devised by Congress alone which would effectually protect the people of the United States against the evils and oppression of trusts and monopolies. Congress has no authority to deal, generally, with the subject within the States, and the States have no authority to legislate in respect of commerce between the several States or with foreign nations.

It follows, therefore, that the legislative authority of Congress and that of the several States must be exerted to secure the suppression of restraints upon trade and monopolies. Whatever legislation Congress may enact on this subject, within the limits of its authority, will prove of little value unless the States shall supplement it by such auxiliary and proper legislation as may be within their legislative authority.

It is proposed to accomplish the first object of the bill by declaring every contract, combination in the form of trust or otherwise, or conspiracy in restraint of trade or commerce among the several States or with foreign nations illegal, and by declaring every person who shall monopolize or attempt to monopolize, or who combines or conspires with any other person or persons to monopolize, any part of the trade or commerce among the several States or with foreign nations guilty of a misdemeanor.

The penalty proposed to each of these offenses is fixed at a fine not to exceed $5,000 or imprisonment not to exceed one year, or both said punishments in discretion of the court.

In order to accomplish the second object of the bill any contract, combination in form of trust or otherwise, or conspiracy in restraint of trade or commerce in a Territory of the United States or of the District of Columbia, or in restraint of trade or commerce between any such Territory and another, or between any such Territory or Territories, or any State or States, or the District of Columbia, or with foreign nations, or between the District of Columbia and any State or States, or foreign nations, is declared illegal. Any person offending against this provision shall be deemed guilty of a misdemeanor, and is made liable to the same penalty.

In addition to the penal provisions of the bill, the circuit courts of the United States are invested with jurisdiction to prevent and restrain violations of the act, and it is made the duty of the several district attorneys of the United States, under the direction of the Attorney-General, to institute proceedings in equity to prevent and restrain such violations.

It is also provided that property owned under any contract, or by any combination, or pursuant to any conspiracy (and being the subject thereof), denounced as illegal and being in the course of transportation from one State to another or to a foreign country, shall be forfeited to the United States and may be seized and condemned by like proceedings as those provided by law for the seizure, forfeiture, and condemnation of, [sic] imported into the United States according to law.

Any person injured or damaged in his business or property by any other person or corporation by reason of anything forbidden or declared to be unlawful by the act may sue in the circuit courts of the United States in the district in which the defendant resides or is found, without regard to the amount in controversy, and shall recover threefold the damages sustained by him and the costs of suit, including attorney fees.

It may be proper to state that while this measure is not precisely what any member of the committee would have proposed upon his own motion, there was a general acquiescence in the recommendation of its passage as perhaps the only legislation possible under existing circumstances by this Congress.

S. 1 AS REPORTED BY THE HOUSE COMMITTEE ON THE JUDICIARY
51st Cong., 1st Sess.
April 25, 1890

⊥ Referred to the House Calendar and ordered to be printed.

AN ACT

To protect trade and commerce against unlawful restraints and monopolies.

```
 1      Be it enacted by the Senate and House of Representa-
 2    tives of the United States of America in Congress assembled,
 3         SEC. 1. Every contract, combination in the form of trust
 4    or otherwise, or conspiracy, in restraint of trade or commerce
 5    among the several States, or with foreign nations, is hereby
 6    declared to be illegal. Every person who shall make any
 7    such contract or engage in any such combination or con-
 8    spiracy, shall be deemed guilty of a misdemeanor, and, on
 9    conviction thereof, shall be punished by fine not exceeding five
10    thousand dollars, or by imprisonment not exceeding one year,
11    or by both said punishments, in the discretion of the court.
 1         SEC. 2. Every person who shall monopolize, or at-
 2    tempt to monopolize, or combine or conspire with any other
```

person or persons, to monopolize any part of the trade or commerce among the several States, or with foreign nations, shall be deemed guilty of a misdemeanor, and, on conviction thereof, shall be punished by fine not exceeding five thousand dollars, or by imprisonment not exceeding one year, or by both said punishments, in the discretion of the court.

SEC. 3. Every contract, combination in form of trust or otherwise, or conspiracy, in restraint of trade or commerce in any Territory of the United States or of the District of Columbia, or in restraint of trade or commerce between any such Territory and another, or between any such Territory or Territories and any State or States or the District of Columbia, or with foreign nations, or between the District of Columbia and any State or States or foreign nations, is hereby declared illegal. Every person who shall make any such contract or engage in any such combination or conspiracy, shall be deemed guilty of a misdemeanor, and, on conviction thereof, shall be punished by fine not exceeding five thousand dollars, or by imprisonment not exceeding one year, or by both said punishments, in the discretion of the court.

SEC. 4. The several circuit courts of the United States are hereby invested with jurisdiction to prevent and restrain violations of this act; and it shall be the duty of the several district attorneys of the United States, in their respective districts, under the direction of the Attorney-General, to institute proceedings in equity to prevent and restrain such violations. Such proceedings may be by way of petition setting forth the case and praying that such violation shall be enjoined or otherwise prohibited. When the parties complained of shall have been duly notified of such petition the court shall proceed, as soon as may be, to the hearing and determination of the case; and pending such petition and before final decree, the court may at any time make such temporary restraining order or prohibition as shall be deemed just in the premises.

SEC. 5. Whenever it shall appear to the court before which any proceeding under section four of this act may be pending, that the ends of justice require that other parties should be brought before the court, the court may cause them to be summoned, whether they reside in the district in which the court is held or not; and subpoenas to that end may be served in any district by the marshal thereof.

SEC. 6. Any property owned under any contract or by any combination, or pursuant to any conspiracy (and being the subject thereof) mentioned in section one of this act, and being in the course of transportation from one State to another, or to a foreign country, shall be forfeited to the United States, and may be seized and condemned by like proceedings as those provided by law for the forfeiture, seizure, and condemnation of property imported into the United States contrary to law.

SEC. 7. Any person who shall be injured in his business or property by any other person or corporation by reason of

3   anything forbidden or declared to be unlawful by this act,
4   may sue therefor in any circuit court of the United States in
5   the district in which the defendant resides or is found, with-
6   out respect to the amount in controversy, and shall recover
7   three fold the damages by him sustained, and the costs of
8   suit, including a reasonable attorney's fee.
1   SEC. 8. That the word "person," or "persons," wher-
2   ever used in this act shall be deemed to include corporations
3   and associations existing under or authorized by the laws of
4   either the United States, the laws of any of the Territories,
5   the laws of any State, or the laws of any foreign country.

Passed the Senate April 8, 1890.
Attest: ANSON G. MCCOOK, *Secretary.*

HOUSE DEBATE
51st Cong., 1st Sess.
May 1, 1890

21 CONG. REC. 4088

The SPEAKER *pro tempore* [LEWIS E. PAYSON, R., Ill.]. The Chair recognizes the chairman of the Judiciary Committee, the gentleman from Ohio [Mr. EZRA B. TAYLOR].

Mr. EZRA B. TAYLOR [R., Ohio]. I yield to my colleague on the committee, the gentleman from Texas [Mr. CULBERSON].

Mr. [D. B.] CULBERSON [D., Tex.]. In accordance with the order of the House, I call up for consideration the bill (S. 1) to protect trade and commerce against unlawful restraints and monopolies. . . .

The SPEAKER *pro tempore.* The Clerk is proceeding to read the bill for the information of the House.

The bill was read, as follows:

Be it enacted, etc., Every contract, combination in the form of trust or otherwise, or conspiracy in restraint of trade or commerce among the several States or with foreign nations is hereby declared to be illegal. Every person who shall make any such contract or engage in any such combination or conspiracy shall be deemed guilty of a misdemeanor, and, on conviction thereof, shall be punished by a fine not exceeding $5,000 or by imprisonment not exceeding one year, or by both said punishments, in the discretion of the court.

SEC. 2. Every person who shall monopolize, or attempt to monopolize, or combine or conspire with any other person or persons to monopolize, any part of the trade or commerce among the several States, or with foreign nations, shall be deemed guilty of a misdemeanor, and, on conviction thereof, shall be punished by fine not exceeding $5,000 or by imprisonment not exceeding one year, or by both said punishments, in the discretion of the court.

SEC. 3. Every contract, combination in form of trust or otherwise, or conspiracy in restraint of trade or commerce in any Territory of the United States or of the District of Columbia, or in restraint of trade or commerce between any such Territory and another, or between any such Territory or Territories and any State or States or the District of Columbia, or with foreign nations, or between the District of Columbia and any State or States or foreign nations, is hereby declared illegal. Every person who shall make any such contract or engage in any such combination or conspiracy shall be deemed guilty of a misdemeanor, and, on conviction thereof, shall be punished by fine not exceeding $5,000 or by imprisonment not exceeding one year, or by both said punishments, in the discretion of the court.

SEC. 4. The several circuit courts of the United States are hereby invested with jurisdiction to prevent and restrain violations of this act; and it shall be the duty of the several district attorneys of the United States, in their respective districts, under the direction of the Attorney-General, to institute proceedings in equity to prevent and restrain such violations. Such proceedings may be by way of petition setting forth the case and praying that such violation shall be enjoined or otherwise prohibited. When the parties complained of shall have been duly notified of such petition the court shall proceed, as soon as may be, to the hearing and determination of the case; and pending such petition and before final decree the court may at any time make such temporary restraining order or prohibition as shall be deemed just in the premises.

SEC. 5. Whenever it shall appear to the court before which any proceeding under section 4 of this act may be pending that the ends of justice require that other parties should be brought before the court, the court may cause them to be summoned, whether they reside in the district in which the court is held or not; and subpoenas to that end may be served in any district by the marshal thereof.

SEC. 6. Any property owned under any contract or by any combination or pursuant to any conspiracy (and being the subject thereof) mentioned in section 1 of this act, and being in the course of transportation from one State to another, or to a foreign country, shall be forfeited to the United States, and may be seized and condemned by like proceedings as those provided by law for the forfeiture, seizure, and condemnation of property imported in the United States contrary to law.

SEC. 7. Any person who shall be injured in his business or property by any other person or corporation by reason of anything forbidden or declared to be unlawful by this act may sue therefor in any circuit court of the United States in the district in which the defendant resides or is found, without respect to the amount in controversy, and shall recover threefold the damages by him sustained, and the costs of suit, including a reasonable attorney's fee.

SEC. 8. That the word "person" or "persons" wherever used in this act shall be deemed to include corporations and associations existing under or authorized by the laws of either the United States, the laws of any of the Territories, the laws of any State, or the laws of any foreign country. . . .

The SPEAKER *pro tempore*. The bill is now before the House for consideration under the rules, and amendments will be in order from any gentleman whenever he has the floor.

Mr. CULBERSON, of Texas. Mr. Speaker, in view of the pressure upon the Judiciary Committee for time in respect to the three bills named in the order, I would like to have some intimation from the House as to about how much time may be necessary upon the bill now called up. It is supposed that it should consume far less time than either of the other bills named in the order. I do not expect to occupy more than a very little time myself. I am willing to hold the floor for an hour, dealing out time for five-minute speeches, with leave to extend the remarks of those who speak, and with leave on the part of those who may not speak to print in the RECORD whatever they may see proper; and then the previous question might be called at the end of an hour.

Several MEMBERS. Oh, no.

Mr. [J. D.] SAYERS [D., Tex.]. Is there to be no opportunity for amendments?

Mr. [RICHARD P.] BLAND [D., Mo.]. I hope we shall not pursue the course suggested by the gentleman from Texas [Mr. CULBERSON]. This is a very important bill, and certainly the country would not regard it as fair to rush through a measure like this without opportunity for amendment and without proper debate. The bill is one in which the whole country is interested, and we ought to have the opportunity to debate and amend it. I do not believe that rushing a bill of this importance through in the way indicated will meet the approbation of the country. The bill is not worth a copper in its present shape without amendment, and we want an opportunity to make something out of it. . . .

Mr. CULBERSON, of Texas. I observe, Mr. Speaker, that there is no opportunity now to fix a limit upon this debate; and therefore I shall proceed to give some explanation of the bill before the House.

This is a Senate measure which has been reported from the Judiciary Committee of the House without any amendment. Its passage has been recommended by that committee without opposition, as perhaps the only legislation on this subject that we can secure under the circumstances at this session of Congress. This legislation occupies a new field, and as the Constitution has wisely left with the several States of this Union the right to local self-government, the legislative field of Congress with reference to questions of this character, except in a few instances where power has been granted to the Federal or General Government, is extremely limited.

There is no attempt to exercise any doubtful authority on this subject, but the bill is confined strictly and alone to subjects over which, confessedly, there is no question about the legislative power of Congress, and as my time will not permit a discussion of the general subject of trusts I will confine what I have to say to the measure before the House.

I call attention to the first section of the bill. It provides that "every contract, combination in the form of trust or otherwise, or conspiracy in restraint of trade or commerce among the several States, or with foreign nations, is hereby declared to be illegal."

Now, it will be observed, Mr. Speaker, that this is a very important principle embodied in the very outset of the bill, and may be stated in this way: Every contract made in restraint of trade between the States, or among the States, or with foreign nations, and every combination in the form of a trust or otherwise, or every conspiracy in restraint of trade or commerce among the several States or with foreign nations, is denounced as illegal.

Now, just what contracts, what combinations in the form of trusts, or what conspiracies will be in restraint of trade or commerce mentioned in the bill will not be known until the courts have construed and interpreted this provision. . . .

Mr. [LEOPOLD] MORSE [D., Mass.]. I would like to ask the gentleman from Texas, who I suppose understands the bill—

Mr. CULBERSON, of Texas. I have some opinion of the scope of the bill.

Mr. MORSE. And for the information of the House and the country, to explain what will be the bearing of the bill upon the manufacturers of proprietary articles, who fix a price upon their own goods.

Mr. CULBERSON, of Texas. I will try to do so.

I wish to be understood, Mr. Speaker, as having stated in the outset that I do not know, nor can any man know, just what contracts will be embraced by this section of the bill until the courts determine. But the gentleman from Massachusetts asks a question which I will endeavor to answer. . . .

. . . I will suppose, Mr. Speaker, that there is a corporation in Massachusetts manufacturing a polish called the "Rising Glory," for instance. They sell to their patrons in Texas this product at what they call a bottom price, provided the dealer with the firm in question will sign a written agreement that he will not sell the product below a given price. If he signs such contract they allow him 5 per cent. profit on the sales, and besides the 5 per cent. profit they allow him a drawback in the shape of a percentage, the amount of which I do not need to specify. That may vary.

Now, I take it, with all due deference to what the Supreme Court may ultimately decide, that that is a contract in restraint of trade within the meaning of the bill. In other words, this firm sells this product to a purchaser, who refuses to give this written obligation, not at the bottom, but at a far different and higher price, reserving the lower rate for the person who may agree to the private terms they impose.

The object of this peculiar contract is to force every dealer in the country who deals in that particular product to purchase from them, and if he does not, or if he does not conform to the price they choose to fix upon the commodity, they will make him pay more than if he was a regular customer, and more than another man who enters into the contract or private agreement with the manufacturers. That is in restraint of free and liberal trade, as I take it, and tends to destroy competition. The customers of the manufacturer are not allowed to sell at a lower rate than that fixed by the manufacturer—I do not, of course, allude to the occupation of the gentleman, for I do not know whether I strike it or not in the illustration—but goods shipped from one State to another under such contracts would be liable to forfeiture under the provisions of this bill.

Mr. [BENJAMIN] BUTTERWORTH [R., Ohio]. Will the gentleman permit me to interrupt him for a moment? I understand, if the honorable gentleman from Massachusetts—carrying out the illustration of the gentleman from Texas—should fix the price at which his customers should sell the article he produces, not a natural product, but his article, and sell it as his agents, agreeing to pay forfeit if they sell for less than the price fixed—do I understand my friend from Texas to say that that is a contract in the terms of this bill and in his opinion in restraint of trade?

Mr. CULBERSON, of Texas. Taking it in connection with the other conditions, if he sells to parties at a different price—

Mr. BUTTERWORTH. No; let me make the point clear. I understood the gentleman to put the case of his selling his manufactured product, whatever it is, to Brown, Smith & Co., of Galveston, Tex., and has a written contract with them that they shall not sell below the schedule price, which he fixes—

Mr. [JOHN A.] ANDERSON [R., Kan.]. But they are not his agents.

Mr. BUTTERWORTH. But I am putting the case of his agents, contracting not to sell below the schedule price, and if they do they are to forfeit something, $10 or $25, whatever you please. Would that be a contract in restraint of trade under the provisions of this bill?

Mr. CULBERSON, of Texas. Perhaps not. . . .

Mr. [JULIUS C.] BURROWS [R., Mich.]. If the gentleman from Texas has a case in mind that would be covered by the first section of the bill I would be glad to know it.

Mr. CULBERSON. Yes; there are cases.

Mr. BURROWS. I would like to have the gentleman cite one of them as an illustration.

Mr. CULBERSON, of Texas. Well, I will take the Standard Oil Company, for instance.

Mr. [CHARLES J.] BOATNER [D., La.]. Just there let me ask, does this bill propose to affect existing combinations?

Mr. CULBERSON, of Texas. Yes, sir.

Now, I take it the Standard Oil Company manufactures its product in Ohio and sells it in another State.

Mr. BURROWS. Let us have an illustration.

Mr. CULBERSON, of Texas. I was about to say that the Standard Oil Company, as I understand the operations of that concern, sell their oil in different States under special contract. They make a contract with the merchant to whom they sell their goods obligating the merchant not to sell at below a certain price, and they give full power and authority to the merchant if any competing oil is offered for sale in the neighborhood to drive it out of the trade by underselling it.

Now, I understand such contracts to be directly in restraint of trade and commerce. This corporation exercises its power and its wealth with a view of driving out of competition every other oil [sic] in that locality in which they sell their own products. Such contracts not only tend to restrain trade, but by destroying competition they secure for the corporation a monopoly, in part, of interstate trade, which is made an offense under this bill. . . .

Mr. Speaker, the remarks which I have made in respect to the Standard Oil Company apply to the celebrated dressed-beef combine. These are some of the cases, Mr. Speaker, which I think fall within the operation of the bill. If I am not mistaken in this and this measure should become the law, the people will be protected from the merciless extortion made possible by such contracts.

It is certainly within the power of Congress to regulate trade between the States, and it is certainly the duty of Congress to protect this trade from such restraints as tend to foster monopoly and promote extortion.

The third section of the bill provides "that all such contracts, such ⊥ combinations, such conspiracies in restraint of trade or commerce within the Territories, or within the District of Columbia, or between a Territory and another Territory, or between a State and a Territory, or between a State and the District of Columbia, or between the District of Columbia and a foreign nation, or between the Territories and and [sic] foreign nations" shall be unlawful, and severe penalties are provided for all violations of the provisions of the act.

It will be observed that this is a sphere in which Congress has absolute dominion and control. It has full and unlimited authority to legislate in respect of trade within a Territory or within the District of Columbia, and between a Territory and a State, or a State and a Territory, or a Territory and the District of Columbia, and also between them and foreign nations.

It is provided by the bill that any person who shall monopolize or attempt to monopolize or combine or conspire with any other person or persons to monopolize any part of the trade or commerce among the several States or with foreign nations shall be deemed guilty of a misdemeanor. This is a very important and far-reaching provision. I will read to the House what appears to be Webster's definition of a monopoly:

> To engross, to obtain by any means exclusive right of trade to any place or within any country or district, as to monopolize the trade.

That is the definition of monopoly as given by Webster. Every person, therefore, who shall attempt to monopolize, to engross, or to obtain by any means exclusive control of interstate trade to any place or within any country or district will be guilty of a misdemeanor under the provisions of the bill. I need only say that there are many cases within our observation in which combinations have succeeded in monopolizing, in part at least, trade between localities in different States. It is to be hoped that if this measure becomes a law an end may be put to such practices and the people relieved of extortion which the destruction of competition always produces.

Mr. BUTTERWORTH. Now, before the gentleman leaves that point, if my friend will indulge me, I want to ask him a question or two which are pertinent, because they are presenting themselves to the minds of men engaged in considering the question. Now, the case of the Standard Oil Company put by my friend: He says that if that company shall consign oil, for instance, from Ohio to a consignee in Texas, and fix the price at which that consignee or purchaser may sell, and authorizes him also in case of competition to drive out that competition by underselling his competitor, would that come under the terms of this bill?

Mr. CULBERSON, of Texas. I believe it would.

Mr. BUTTERWORTH. Yes. Now, suppose, however, they stop there in that, and simply fix the price at which every consignee may sell. For instance, they say, "We will sell you this oil, but we want it understood or agreed that it shall not be sold at less than 10 cents a gallon." Now, suppose we take a step further and say that they shall sell or deal only in the output of this company consigned to this dealer. Would that be in restraint of the trade to sell this particular oil.

Mr. CULBERSON, of Texas. Do I understand your question covers a case of this sort, that while they make this consignment or sale and I am dealing with them as sales?

Mr. BUTTERWORTH. I mean sales, for that is what we are driving at.

Mr. CULBERSON, of Texas. I do not distinctly hear your question.

Mr. BUTTERWORTH. Well, I will take this case alone. The Standard Oil Company consigns its goods to Smith, Brown & Co., of Galveston, Tex., agreeing to sell only to those parties in that place, and fixing a schedule of prices, and stopping there. They simply say: "We want to contract with you, gentlemen, not to sell the goods you purchase of us at less than a certain rate," which rate is agreed upon. Now, would that case come within the terms of this bill?

Mr. CULBERSON, of Texas. That would be in violation of the Texas law against trusts and corporations; and—

Mr. BUTTERWORTH. But I speak of this bill. Of course I know that it is not easy to draw the line, but what is the opinion of my friend from Texas?

Mr. CULBERSON, of Texas. I am inclined to think that the Standard Oil Company can sell its product at just such prices as it pleases, but when it enters into a combination to drive out competition, by giving a sliding scale of prices, or anything of that sort, then the transaction falls within the terms of this bill.

Mr. BUTTERWORTH. But in my question I leave out the element of a sliding scale. The company fixes the selling price, but does not authorize its representatives to attempt to drive out competitors by putting prices down. It simply fixes a schedule and stops there.

Mr. CULBERSON, of Texas. I think the company might fix one price and sell to everybody in that way.

Mr. BUTTERWORTH. One question more. Suppose a "combine"—if I may use a term that is offensive to some people, and the thing is certainly offensive for what it does in this country—suppose a "combine" at Chicago should purchase beef consigned from Indiana, Kansas, and so on, and should, by the manipulation of the market there, keep the price below a certain figure, by arrangements with agents throughout the States, paying them a commission upon all sales from that quarter whether sold to them or not, would that transaction come within this bill?

Mr. CULBERSON, of Texas. I should think it would be within the scope of this bill.

Mr. ANDERSON, of Kansas. It ought to be.

Mr. CULBERSON, of Texas. If I understand the gentleman's question I should think it would be, because I believe it would be in the nature of a restraint of commerce. . . .

Mr. BUTTERWORTH. One other question, if the gentleman will permit. Suppose a Chicago firm should consign its beef to a butcher in my town, and should afterwards, upon his insisting upon selling the meat at a lower price than they directed, establish another butcher by his side, refusing to sell any more to the first and authorizing the second to sell at a lower price until the first was driven out of the business; would that be reached by this bill?

Mr. CULBERSON, of Texas. I think so.

Mr. Speaker, I wish to call attention to the fourth section of this bill, which provides that the circuit courts of the United States are invested with jurisdiction to restrain and prevent violations of this act. I regard that as a very important provision of the bill, in this respect: Whenever it shall come to the knowledge of a district attorney that such contracts are being made or that such combinations are being formed, it shall be his duty to commence proceedings in equity in the circuit courts of the United States to restrain such violations of this act.

Under the law as it now stands a defendant is required to be sued in the district in which he lives or in which he may be found, and it was therefore objected that these combinations could never be, in all cases, reached, inasmuch as all of them might never be found in the same district. Hence the law is enlarged by this bill, so that whenever it becomes necessary in the progress of a suit to bring before the court any person, firm, or corporation engaged in such transactions with the party who is before the court, the court shall have the power to bring them in, by process issued to another State if necessary, and require them to answer the petition filed by the district attorney. . . .

Mr. [DAVID B.] HENDERSON [R., Iowa]. Will not the district attorneys have to first apply to the Attorney-General for authority before they can take any such proceedings?

Mr. CULBERSON, of Texas. I believe they will.

Mr. HENDERSON, of Iowa. Ought not that to be corrected?

Mr. CULBERSON, of Texas. They will have to proceed under the direction of the Attorney-General.

Mr. HENDERSON, of Iowa. But is not that too cumbersome? Ought not they to have authority to proceed without waiting for instructions from the Attorney-General?

Mr. CULBERSON, of Texas. This is a very grave proceeding. It will probably involve immense litigation in the courts. The legislation contemplated is so far-reaching, affecting such large and important interests, that I do not think a district attorney in a rural district or elsewhere outside of the great commercial centers should be empowered to bring a suit to restrain these combinations unless under the direction of the Attorney-General. Gentlemen will understand that these suits must proceed in the name of the United States. It is not the custom to give district attorneys authority to bring suits in the name of the United States all over the country. It is necessary to have some head to direct this great body of litigation. Otherwise you would involve the United States in interminable costs and litigation.

Mr. [JOHN T.] HEARD [D., Mo.]. Would not the language of the bill authorize the formulation of general directions so that it would not be necessary to apply to the Attorney-General for instructions in each individual case?

Mr. CULBERSON, of Texas. I do not think that would fall within the meaning of the language employed.

Mr. HENDERSON, of Iowa. I call the gentleman's attention to that point for this reason: Cases might arise where an injunction or a restraining order ought to be obtained promptly from the court, and it might involve too much delay if, for instance, a district attorney in Texas had to write to the Attorney-General in Washington to get authority to act.

Mr. CULBERSON, of Texas. Well, in such matters we rely now upon the telegraph. I do not think the bill can be improved in that respect. It would be very unwise, in my judgment, to invest the district attorneys throughout the United States with such authority. . . .

Now, Mr. Speaker, I will call the attention of the House to section 6 of the bill. I find that I am occupying so much time that I must omit mere details.

> Any property owned under any contract or by any combination or pursuant to any conspiracy (and being the subject thereof) mentioned in section 1 of this ⊥ act, and being in the course of transportation from one State to another or to a foreign country, shall be forfeited to the United States, and may be seized and condemned by like proceedings as those provided by law for the forfeiture, seizure, and condemnation of property imported into the United States contrary to law.

Whenever, therefore, any property owned under any contract or by any combination, or pursuant to any conspiracy in restraint of trade, is found in course of transportation—and it will be recollected the Supreme Court of the United States has decided that interstate commerce commences when the article to be shipped is delivered to the common carrier—the moment it is delivered to the common carrier for shipment it becomes the subject of interstate commerce; whenever, therefore, any property the subject of a contract, combination, or conspiracy in restraint of trade is found in a warehouse to be shipped from one State to another, or is found *in transitu*, it is liable to be forfeited to the Government of the United States as in cases of goods wrongfully imported into the country. And the manner of doing this is for the district attorney of the United States to direct the seizure of the property; it is libeled in the United States district court and sold to the highest bidder for cash.

I desire to call attention to the seventh section:

> Any person who shall be injured in his business or property by any other person or corporation by reason of anything forbidden or declared to be unlawful by this act may sue therefor in any circuit court of the United States in the district in which the defendant resides or is found, without respect to the amount in controversy, and shall recover threefold the damages by him sustained, and the costs of suit, including a reasonable attorney's fee.

I beg to call the attention of the House for a moment or two to this provision, because it is objected by some that in the construction of this bill entire and sole jurisdiction to enforce a claim for damages on the part of a person injured by any other person or corporation by reason of anything forbidden by this act is limited to the circuit courts of the United States. That is a misconstruction. Let me state my understanding of the existing law on this subject. Under the law as it now exists no suit can be brought, ordinarily, in the circuit court of the United States, unless the *quantum* of value involved exceeds the sum of $2,000.

Therefore, it will be seen that, unless Congress provides that these claims shall be heard in the circuit court without regard to the amount involved, any person desiring to sue in that court would be excluded if his claim was less than $2,000.

One further matter I wish to call attention to in this relation. It is suggested, "Why may not this jurisdiction be given to the State courts? Why restrain or attempt to restrain the jurisdiction to the circuit courts of the United States only?" I submit that this bill does no such thing and does not attempt to do any such thing. Congress has no more power to invest a State court with jurisdiction than a State has to invest a United States court with jurisdiction. I am aware that in some bills passed by Congress there is permissive language declaring that suits may be brought in the State courts; but that is all surplusage and unnecessary.

I look at the matter in this way: A has a cause of action against a corporation for an act forbidden by this bill. He may sue in a State court if he wishes to do so, provided he is willing to waive the penalty named in this statute and sue for actual damages, or he may, if he chooses, go into the circuit court of the United States and sue for the actual damages sustained as well as the penalty.

If Congress had declared that the circuit court should have exclusive jurisdiction over these subjects, then as a matter of course the State courts would be deprived of any right or power under the laws of the several States to entertain jurisdiction of any case of this character. But it is simply provided that the circuit court shall have jurisdiction without regard to the amount, leaving the State courts open to every person who may desire to go into them to recover actual damages.

You will understand, Mr. Speaker, that this bill allows a punitory verdict to be rendered; that is to say, the person who sues is not restricted in the amount which may be recovered to the damages actually sustained, but may recover in addition thereto a reasonable attorney's fee (a very wise forethought on the part of the Senate) and may also recover treble damages. Now, those who insist that the State courts should take charge of this matter overlook the fact that no court can enforce a penalty except those enacted by the authority which created the court. Therefore any person having a claim under this statute, if he should go into a State court to enforce it, would be obliged to waive the tort and claim actual damages only.

Mr. [NATHAN] FRANK [R., Mo.]. I would like to ask the gentleman a question. Does not this section confer on the Federal court jurisdiction of a suit in which the plaintiff and the defendant may both be citizens of the same State? In other words, does it not confer jurisdiction irrespective of citizenship? May not both parties be residents of the same State and the Federal court have jurisdiction irrespective of that fact?

Mr. CULBERSON, of Texas. If the gentleman will reflect a moment he will see that every cause arising under a law of Congress is cognizable in a United States court without regard to the citizenship of the parties when the amount in controversy is $2,000; therefore citizenship cuts no figure in this case at all. The law would give a right of removal in certain cases perhaps from a State court to the Federal court.

Now, Mr. Speaker, I want to say that it is impossible, I believe, for Congress to enact any law or devise any system of laws that will crush out absolutely trusts and combinations.

Mr. MORSE. Then why do you not let the business alone?

Mr. CULBERSON, of Texas. What I mean is this, I will state to the gentleman: If Congress will legislate within its sphere and to the limit to which it may go, and if the Legislatures of the several States will do their duty and supplement that legislation, the trusts and combinations which are devouring the substance of the people of the country may be effectually suppressed. The States are powerless unless Congress will take charge of the trade between the States and make unlawful traffic that operates in restraint of trade and which promotes and encourages monopoly. Persons, corporations, or associations should be prevented from carrying into the several States products covered by trusts. If the States will do their duty and supplement this act, the people can be relieved of the outrages inflicted upon them.

Now, it is suggested that Congress ought to go further. It is very difficult to say how it could do so. It occupies now in this bill, or attempts to occupy, the sphere allotted to it in the regulation of commerce between the States. It attempts to control and regulate the trade within the Territories and District of Columbia and between the District of Columbia and the Territories of the United States and between them and the States.

What else, then, could Congress do? There is one thing it might do. The taxing power is given to Congress for the purpose of collecting revenue with which to pay ordinary expenses of the Government only, as I understand it. Now, if Congress saw proper to omit to exercise the taxing power in the levying of import duties in respect to products manufactured abroad, the counterpart of which in the United States was the subject of these trusts—if the Congress did that, then Congress might crush out and uproot this whole business.

But no one possibly can advocate that scheme to-day for the reason that there are so many products covered and handled by these combinations and trusts in the United States that if we were to omit to exercise the power of Congress and levy an import duty upon similar products from abroad we would strip the Government of revenue and deprive it of the means of defraying the expenses except by the imposition of a direct tax.

Mr. BLAND. Have we not the power to levy an income tax or to derive additional taxes, for instance, from whisky and tobacco?

Mr. CULBERSON, of Texas. Undoubtedly we might. But we could hardly expect to raise the amount that would be necessary to carry on the Government from such sources, or even to supply the deficiency in revenues which would result from placing on the free-list all products manufactured abroad the counterparts of which produced in the United States are the subjects of trusts.

I am in favor of a law which would impose a reasonable income tax. I think it was unwise and absolutely unjust to the people of the United States to relieve the wealth of the country from its just share of the burden of taxation. The income-tax law ought not to have been repealed. I would gladly aid my friend from Missouri [Mr. BLAND] in restoring it. . . .

Mr. HENDERSON, of Iowa. This is a matter in which I feel deeply interested, and I would like to be informed upon this point. I think it has been well settled by the investigation of a Congressional committee within the last year[1.360] that a trust or combination of a few men in Chicago, Ill., has been able to reduce the price of Western cattle from one-third to one-half, controlling, as they do, the stock-yards, the cattle-yards, and the transportation in Chicago, and it seems at the same time they have been enabled to keep up the price of every beef-steak that is used in this country—

Mr. [JOHN H.] ROGERS [D., Ark.]. To raise the price.

Mr. HENDERSON, of Iowa. Yes; to raise the price of every beef-steak that is used in the country. Now, I want to ask the gentleman from Texas, who has carefully considered this matter in his committee whether this bill, in his judgment, reaches that difficulty or not.

Mr. CULBERSON, of Texas. I believe it will, if it is construed as we think it ought to be construed by the courts.

Mr. HENDERSON, of Iowa. Does the bill go as far as Congress has the power to go to strike at that damnable system?

Mr. CULBERSON, of Texas. That is the opinion of the committee.

Mr. HENDERSON, of Iowa. Then, I am very glad of it. . . .

⊥4092 ⊥ Mr. [WILLIAM L.] WILSON [D., W. Va.]. Mr. Speaker, I do not believe there could be a more striking illustration or a swifter condemnation of the system of rules under which this House is now operating than the consideration of the bill just brought before us. The theory of our Government is that it is a Government by public discussion, and that at least in the law-making branch of it the representatives of the people shall have ample opportunity for mature, intelligent, and full discussion of all important matters come before them for action.

We know that at best this is a vanishing theory so far as this House is concerned, and that its members have such a burden of labor put upon them that does not properly belong to the representative office that they have little time for the study and investigation of measures of the highest moment to the welfare of the country. . . .

Now, sir, here again is a bill dealing with a novel and most important question, a bill that is a new departure in Federal legislation, bristling with pains and penalties, denouncing a new class of crimes, and imposing prohibitions and penalties on many acts not now illegal and some perhaps not properly punishable. Here is a bill that may derange the course of trade among the States, that will bring doubt and uncertainty in many lines of business, both of production and distribution in the country.

It was reported by the Judiciary Committee but five days ago, and the report printed since that time has been exhausted, so that when the bill is suddenly and prematurely called up this morning members can procure copies of neither bill nor report, and we are now called upon to pass it, blindly and promptly, without deliberate discussion or any general and intelligent understanding of its provisions, simply because something must be done to meet the demand of the people for some legislation against trusts and like combinations.

Sir, its first section proposes to punish with heavy fines and imprisonment the making of certain contracts, combinations, and conspiracies, and the gentleman from

---

[1.360] *See Introduction supra* at 17 & notes 1.83–.85, 26, 27 & note 1.176.

Texas in charge of the bill, as able and clear-headed a lawyer as we have upon this floor, frankly informs the House that just what these "contracts, combinations, and conspiracies" will be can not be known until the courts have construed and interpreted this section.

Yet we are to consider and pass this bill after an hour or two of discussion only; a bill seriously affecting the business and prosperity of the country, and, what is more, the rights and liberties of the people. Was ever criminal law made in this fashion before? And who are to be the first victims that must be fined and sent to the penitentiary, in order that the courts may interpret and declare what are the crimes which we punish, but do not define?

I, for one, Mr. Speaker, do not believe that this bill will accomplish the purposes for which it purports to be enacted.

It was prepared, as we have already been informed, by the Judiciary Committee of the Senate, in response to a popular demand for some Congressional legislation against trusts. I think that is a just demand, and one that required at the hands of Congress careful and well considered legislation, as to the meaning and effect of which, at least, there should be no uncertainty. And, Mr. Speaker, believing this, I had intended and desired to submit some deliberate and orderly remarks upon this matter of trusts whenever such a bill was brought before the House for action.

As I had no warning that the bill would be brought up to-day, I find myself unprepared to take up its discussion as I proposed. I desire, however, even in this irregular way, to make a few observations on the subject of dealing with trusts. I was a member in the last House, as the gentleman from Kentucky [Mr. BRECKINRIDGE] requests me to state, of the Committee on Manufactures, which investigated the organization of three or four of the great trusts of the country. Now, Mr. Speaker, in order to legislate effectively against trusts, this House ought to know exactly what a trust is, its structure and mode of operation and the conditions that produce or make possible a successful trust.

In general terms, we all know that a trust is the latest and most perfect form of combination among competing producers to control the supply of their product, in order that they may dictate the terms on which they shall sell in the market and may secure release from stress of competition among themselves. From the very beginning of trade perhaps, certainly in all its known history, there have been various forms of combination, and we have long been familiar with them in this country under the name of pools, corners, combines, and the like. These have awakened the distrust and anger of the people, but never the same uneasiness and resentment as have been kindled by these so-called trusts.

If I may use an illustration that seems to me an apt and expressive one, I would say that the trust bears the same relation to all previous modes of combination in trade that the Government of the United States under the Constitution bears to the Government of the United States under the Articles of Confederation. A combination or pool is a voluntary association depending upon the good faith of the parties associating and carrying with it those elements of weakness and disintegration that necessarily belong to a voluntary association. A trust is a legal consolidation of properties, a legal concentration of control.

Historically, it grew out of the greatness and the necessities of the Standard Oil combination. When that combination in its triumphal progress found itself practically the sole producer of refined oil in this country, it had its properties in many States, vested in and controlled, as the case might be, by corporations, partnerships, and individually, and including many separate lines of business. It had its refineries, its pipe lines, its terminal facilities, its manufactures of barrels, and cans, and lamp-wicks, and other articles.

It became necessary that all these scattered properties and all these different kinds of business should be brought under some simple and effectual central control.

Accordingly the able solicitor of the Standard alliance worked out for that alliance the trust scheme of combination, which has subsequently swept over the field of American industry and has been adopted, with greater or less success, by so many other would-be monopolies.

⊥ That scheme, as first outlined, provided for the formation in each State of a single corporation to be known as the Standard Oil Company of New York, Kentucky, Ohio, or Pennsylvania, as the case might be, in which were to be vested all the property, business, and interests of the combination in that particular State. The shares of stock in these various State corporations were then to be transferred by the holders of the stock to the legal ownership of nine trustees, who in return, therefor, gave to the owners of stock in the several companies certificates of stock in the Standard Oil trust.

In this way the legal ownership and the efficient and permanent control of all the corporations were vested in the nine trustees, who held all the stock and managed them as a central directory in the interest of the entire combination. They could throw the full power of the entire combination as the interests and supremacy of the monopoly might require, whether to overawe railroad companies and secure preferential rates, to oppress producers of crude oil, or crush out a troublesome competition in any line of business. Just as we can add new States to the Union, they could add new corporations to their trust, either to extend into new fields its legitimate business to receive under a new name and in a hidden disguise the tributes or rebates of common carriers, or to strike a deadly blow at a rival, which blow might be direct or indirect, by immediate and destructive competition or by remote and unsuspected attack.

Now, sir, I have said enough, I hope, in a general way, to indicate the distinctive features of the trust as differentiating it from other and previous forms of monopolies. It was soon discovered, Mr. Speaker, that the trust scheme devised for the purposes of an existing combination offered a new and admirable scheme for forming monopolies out of existing competitors, and it spread with rapidity as soon as its form became divulged.

Now, Mr. Speaker, I shall not go into an examination or discussion of individual trusts. I have said this much only to show that the common basis of trusts is the corporation. The deed under which the sugar trust was organized required that all the refineries should first become corporations and that all subsequent applicants for admission should qualify themselves in like manner. Indeed, it may be affirmed that no permanent trust can be built on a less solid basis. Combinations very effective for some temporary purpose or within a limited area may be formed by individuals or partnership, but they will be subject to all the contingencies of death, bankruptcy, bad faith, and voluntary withdrawal.

Those which are to become a menace to the public can not be built upon a foundation so shifting. Moreover, Mr. Speaker, we all know that the individual has disappeared in the corporation, which alone offers the aggregation of means, the exemption from physical death, and the unity of control that are indispensable for the gigantic enterprises of modern production and trade.

If, therefore, the organization of a trust must have the corporation as a basis, it is clear, Mr. Speaker, that the first and most effective blow at that organization must be struck, not by Congress, but by the States.

The States, not Congress, grant the charters for these corporations. It is at once their duty, as it is easily and clearly within the sphere of their lawful power, to supervise the creatures which they bring into being, so as to prevent the franchises granted by the people being used for the oppression and detriment of the people. The courts of New York have already shown how this may be done. In the proceeding against one of the companies that went into the sugar trust, Judge Barrett held that a corporation has no authority to enter into a partnership or combination of that kind and by the mere act of doing so forfeited its charter.[1.361]

I believe, Mr. Speaker, that both his decision and the reasoning by which he sustained it are sound law and that the courts of other States will adopt them. But even if Judge Barrett's decision be not adopted by the courts in other States, it may readily be made the statutory law of them all. And it deals with trusts by a remedy that calls for no doubtful exercise of power, but is in itself just and salutary.

And now, sir, what can the Federal Government do for suppressing or at least rendering harmless these new and dangerous monopolies? When it has recourse to

---

[1.361] New York v. North River Sugar Ref. Co., 22 Abb. N. Cas. 164, 3 N.Y.S. 401 (1889).

criminal law and seeks to destroy them by pains and penalties its lawful authority is limited to interstate trade, except when legislating for the District of Columbia and the Territories. If any one supposes that such a bill as this, no matter how severe the punishment it threatens or how sweeping may be its prohibitions, will prevent such combinations as it seeks to destroy, he does not, I fear, fully understand the structure and operation of trusts. How would such a law as this reach the Standard Oil trust or materially interfere with its operations? Had not the members of that great alliance the legal right to vest the various properties and businesses they already had in the nine trustees?

The trustees of the sugar trust when put upon the witness stand denied that they exercised any functions except receiving profits and distributing dividends. They denied all privacy [sic] with contracts, combinations, or conspiracies, and how can you prove guilt upon them under the rules of evidence required in criminal proceedings?

Now, Mr. Speaker, you are not going to have a trust formed unless that trust can control and practically monopolize the production or sale of some article in this country—some article, I might add, of universal or common consumption. A trust is not merely such a combination as I have described. It is a combination for the very purpose of forming a monopoly, and to form a monopoly it must be possible to do away as nearly as may be with competition.

You can not, therefore, form a trust in articles of which the producers are scattered all over the country; but any article like sugar, the refining or manufacturing of which can be concentrated in a few or in a moderate number of establishments, can be consolidated into a trust that will have a monopoly of the home market unless there be sources of supply outside the trust. Now, sir, it is just here that the Federal Government, by its system of import duties, already prohibitory as to many articles of common consumption and soon to be made so as to others, presents the most favorable and tempting field in the world for the successful formation and growth of trusts.

Where the Government by high or prohibitory duties shuts out foreign supplies from our markets, it makes it practicable and easy for home producers to unite in the trust organization and maintain a monopoly in those markets. And this is the present working of protective tariffs in other countries as well as in our own. Mr. David A. Wells tells us that Germany leads all other countries in the number, variety, and power of its trusts, and that it is admitted that they sprang up immediately after the high tariff law of 1879 in that empire.

I venture to say that there are few, if any, trusts in the correct sense of that word in England to-day. I know we were told in the campaign of 1888 that "free-trade England" was "plastered with trusts," but I went personally last summer to the professor of political economy at the University of Oxford, himself for some years a member of Parliament and a distinguished Liberal—I refer to Professor Thorold Rogers—and asked him if there were such things as trusts in England, and he told me he had never heard of any and indeed could not well see how they could thrive there. An attempt was made some months ago to form some sort of a combination among the paper mills there, but the consumers of paper promptly informed the combination that if it attempted to run up prices on them they would buy their paper abroad.

But, Mr. Speaker, if our tariff encourages the formation of trusts by shutting out foreign supplies and outside competition from our markets, it is in another sense scarcely less responsible for them. If there is a remunerative demand for products there is little temptation and no necessity for forming trusts. It is only when the power of production has outstripped the power of consumption that this temptation and almost necessity exist.

Now, I need not say that such is the condition of production in the United States to-day. As the foremost of all peoples in mechanical invention, as the quickest and readiest at all times to adopt every improved appliance and every scientific discovery, we have in many important manufactures already far outrun remunerative demand in this country. We have done likewise in our staple farm products.

A Kansas farmer, in a recent number of The Forum, presenting figures which I am sure are not understatements, says that our present supply of beef is sufficient for

71,000,000 people, of swine for 76,000,000, of wheat for 79,000,000, of corn for 70,500,000, and of oats for more than 100,000,000. Our population is something less than 65,000,000.

Now, I say that for a congested market, for overproduction, there are but two remedies possible. The one remedy is commerce and the other is trusts. You must throw open your ports and let out your surplus agricultural products or your surplus manufactured products to outside buyers and to a larger market, or you must put your hand upon the throttle and bring down supply to the measure of consumption in this country.

Mr. [E. H.] FUNSTON [R., Kan.]. Will the gentleman kindly point out the tariff laws, the duties on imports or exports, that prevent us from shipping farm products from this country now? . . . .[1.362]

Mr. WILSON, of West Virginia. Again, Mr. Speaker, take wool as an illustration. We have been keeping out foreign wool under our tariff, which, as I said the other day, was absolutely merciless, because in this great and rich country, with all of its various sources of taxation, with its great corporations, its wealth and property of all kinds, the Government gathers more than one-tenth part of all of the revenue from the people who use woolen goods. This illustrates just what the men of Massachusetts said would be the working of a tax of 8 cents per gallon on molasses.

It is a merciless tax upon the consumer; it cripples the woolen industry by taxing its raw material and it increases the agricultural surplus by depriving the producers of this country of a foreign market. Why, do you not know that the people of the Argentine Confederation, who are anxious to sell us wool, and whose wool we will not take, and by refusing to take it have so depressed its price in foreign markets that it is not profitable, as a consequence are now plowing up their sheep pastures and are going into the production of wheat, thus coming into competition in another branch of industry with the already distressed wheat-growers of America? [Applause on the Democratic side.] . . .

. . . Leave, as far as possible, the internal-revenue system alone and cut down the taxes that cripple commerce and destroy navigation. And let me read you an extract from Mr. Hamilton's writings in the Federalist bearing upon that very point. We are told in the majority report of the Committee on Ways and Means that they have not cared so much about the consumer—Lord bless you no; what do they care about the consumer?—but that the bill is framed upon the idea of checking importations.

In other words, it is the continuation of the war that has been going on in this country for a quarter of a century against commerce. You talk about these taxes being war taxes. In a sense—in a historic sense—they are, because we continue to-day the same rates that we enacted when war was flagrant in the land, and even higher rates. But in a more pregnant sense and in a more disastrous sense they are war taxes, because they represent twenty-five years' unrelenting war against American commerce.

Now, Mr. Hamilton wrote:

A prosperous commerce is now believed and acknowledged by all enlightened statesmen to be the most useful as well as the most productive source of national wealth, and has accordingly become the prime object of their political care.

A prosperous commerce, say the majority of the Ways and Means Committee, is a menace to American industry. [Applause on the Democratic side.]

Such is the contrast between the legislation proposed to-day and the views of that great statesman, one of the fathers of the protective system:

By multiplying the means of gratification, by promoting the introduction and circulation of the precious metals, those darling objects of human avarice and enterprise, it serves to vivify and invigorate all the channels of industry and to make them flow with greater activity and copiousness.

That is what the prosperous commerce would do for this country. It invigorates and vivifies every channel of industry, making them flow with greater copiousness; but by refusing commerce and warring against it you compel men to resort to such

---

[1.362] At this point an exchange took place regarding the duties on molasses and tin plate.

machinery as trusts to reduce production to the demands of the home market, and where this can not be done, as with the farmer, to throw their productions at ruinous prices upon these markets. . . .

Mr. [GEORGE E.] ADAMS [R., Ill.]. I desire to know if it is the gentleman's argument that the tariff stimulates production so that it gets to be overproduction? Is it his argument that trusts arise from overproduction; that is, from an excess of production, and the competition engendered between producers, so that they must necessarily form a combination, or else the competition would bring the prices down below the cost of production?

Mr. WILSON, of West Virginia. But, Mr. Chairman, the gentleman himself goes round the whole circle. I am not arguing just now that the tariff stimulates home production, because that is not the line that I am discussing, and I had not intended to refer to it particularly. But the argument is a sound one, that by offering profits greater than those which can be made in a normal condition of trade it does tempt men to go into the protected industries, and that having thus stimulated production it is responsible in that way also for the formation of trusts. . . .

Mr. ADAMS. Simply supposing, as the gentleman has stated in general terms, as I understand, that these trusts are the result of tariff legislation, I have the impression that a trust did not exist specifically on those articles which may be presumed to have felt the effect of tariff as much as others. Now, I ask simply for information what articles affected by the tariff have developed into a trust in a large degree and what articles imported from abroad have developed into trusts upon any special articles. I ask these questions because the gentleman has given much attention to the subject.

Mr. WILSON, of West Virginia. I will give by way of illustration the sugar trust, the lead trust, and I could roll off a number of them. . . .

Mr. [LOUIS E.] McCOMAS [R., Md.]. Does my friend from West Virginia not remember that the English papers and French and German papers condemned the conduct of some trusts, as the copper trust and the salt trust, in France and England?

Mr. WILSON, of West Virginia. The copper trust—which, however, was not a trust, but a corner—is but an illustration of what I have said or what I should say; that you can not form an international trust. ⊥ The whole world is too big a thing, and it fails. The copper trust, as you know, fell to pieces and wrecked the second biggest bank of France.

The salt trust is such a combination as I have spoken of. It is a voluntary combination, because, as the gentleman from Ohio says, there is a natural limitation to the supply. Now, England could not have a salt trust if Germany had salt; and England could not have a sugar trust, because if it had, Germany, Holland, and France could pour their sugar into England.

Mr. McCOMAS. Did not my friend find in those papers that there were half a dozen different trusts?

Mr. WILSON, of West Virginia. I did not.

Mr. McCOMAS. I could give a dozen different trusts.

Mr. WILSON, of West Virginia. In answer to that, I would say that when the gentleman from Maryland and myself were over the sea I went to the gentleman I have already referred to, who was recommended to me as being the best informed man as to British industries and trade, and he told me that he had never heard of such a thing in England and that he did not know how there could be one.

Mr. McCOMAS. But you and I had read of them in the papers—

Mr. WILSON, of West Virginia. I admit, of course, that there could be a trust in England where there is a natural limitation of supply, but I was arguing against the Government coming in and making an artificial limitation of supply. [Loud applause on the Democratic side.]

Mr. ADAMS. Will the gentleman allow me—

Mr. WILSON, of West Virginia. I was defining a trust and speaking against such action as the gentleman from Ohio [Mr. McKINLEY] is attempting. [Applause.]

Now, one sentence more, Mr. Speaker. Mr. Alexander Hamilton said—and I know it will commend itself to gentlemen who are talking so much about the agricultural distress in this country, for a great truth was never stated more clearly—

It has been found in various countries that in proportion as commerce has flourished land has risen in value.

And how could it have been otherwise?

Now, my friends, when you come in here with your bill to cripple commerce, to destroy or minimize it, what are you going to say to the farmer who understands that great truth "that in proportion as commerce has flourished the land has everywhere risen in value?" . . .

Now, Mr. Speaker, I shall not oppose this bill, although even so great a lawyer as the gentleman from Texas [Mr. CULBERSON] is not able to tell us what it means. I do not believe that anybody can tell us what it means. This is merely experimental legislation. It is a blind legislation, to answer a popular demand that something shall be done about trusts.

You bring in with one hand a bill to make trusts more permanent in this country; you bring in with one hand a bill that offers such temptations to the formation of trusts that no laws which you may pass merely imposing penalties will prevent people from availing themselves of the opportunities presented, and with the other hand you bring in a bill of which nobody can tell the meaning, but which may introduce chaos into the business of this country, for the professed purpose of suppressing trusts.

Mr. [CHARLES AUGUSTUS] HILL [R., Ill.]. As a lawyer, does not the gentleman think that this bill is within the scope and limits of the Constitution and fully up to the jurisdiction of Congress under the Constitution?

Mr. WILSON, of West Virginia. I would not vote for it blindly even if it were constitutional. I believe that it is within the jurisdiction of the Federal Government to legislate concerning interstate and foreign commerce.

Mr. HILL. But the point of my inquiry was whether this does not furnish all the relief that Congress under the Constitution can furnish?

Mr. WILSON, of West Virginia. You hold out to a man great prizes, you dangle before his eyes the opportunity of making great wealth, and then you say, "If you seize upon these prizes we are going to punish you." Now, human ingenuity is going to be sharp enough to evade the threat of punishment and to get the prizes.

I remember an old rhyme that runs something like this:

> I hear a lion in the lobby roar.
> Say, Mr. Speaker, shall we shut the door
> And keep him there, or shall we let him in
> To try if we can turn him out again?

[Laughter.]

⊥ This is your position in regard to trusts. Instead of keeping out the lion Brother MCKINLEY comes opening the door and says "Let him in, and then we are going to chase him around and try to get him out again." [Laughter.] . . .

Mr. HEARD. Does not the gentleman think he is unfair to those on this side who urge the passage of this bill to repress "trusts" when he couples them with those who favor the McKinley bill? Does he not know that the two sides of this House stand upon different footing and support the measure from different points of view?

Mr. WILSON, of West Virginia. Oh, we are all going to support the bill; we are all solid against trusts.

Mr. HEARD. But we on this side are not in the same boat with the men on the other side.

Mr. WILSON, of West Virginia. What I am saying is that the party in control of this House comes in here, carrying in one hand a bill to encourage trusts in this country, to consolidate and perpetuate their dominion, to offer them even higher prizes than were heretofore possible, by shutting out the only thing that really can destroy them, and that is the stream of competition; and then they attempt with the other hand to pass some sort of a measure that will chase the lion out after they have let him in.

Moreover, this bill does not interfere with trusts formed in a single State. You might concentrate all the sugar production of this country in the State of New York, consolidate it into a trust with $100,000,000 capital, a trust that could destroy competition wherever it dared to raise its head in the country. Why, sir, it is one of the subtleties of the trust system that it can always have on hand a supply of corporations to be used as light cavalry to chase down the first competitor that dares to appear to contest the dominion of the trust over the home market. The trust may form its corporations *ad libitum*. Nobody can say whether they belong to the trust or not; you can not find it out.

But I am contending, not that you should not attempt to punish trusts—I am in favor of that—but that you should bring about such a healthful condition of trade in this country that trusts can not possibly exist; and that is only possible when your tariff law is so arranged that when men get beyond a reasonable profit the stream of healthful competition from abroad shall be let in to prevent combinations to oppress the people. That was the measure of protection that the elder statesmen of the Republican party contended for. Mr. Garfield wished nothing more.

As late as 1883 Senator SHERMAN, in discussing the tariff bill of that year, said the just measure of protection was only to the extent of creating competition, not home monopoly. There is nothing more true.

And coming again to the point raised by the gentleman from Kansas, I will say in conclusion that whenever you shut out the things which people are ready to exchange for our products you are shutting in these products upon the home market.

And just as the men of Massachusetts exclaimed against the high tariff on molasses, "Without the molasses trade is continued the fisheries can not be carried on; the weapon which wounds the one will stab the other," so we may say to-day every blow at commerce is a blow at some home industry. The weapon which wounds the trade in wool, or hides, or tin-plate will stab the home production of wheat and corn and manufactured products.

Mr. Speaker, as the unexpected calling up of this bill has prevented my discussing it with the preparation I had desired, I will append to my remarks when printed some extracts from published articles in which I have stated my views with more care and fullness on the points I have just touched. I now yield for a moment to the gentleman from Texas [Mr. SAYERS]. . . .[1.363]

⊥ The SPEAKER. The gentleman from Texas [Mr. SAYERS] has two minutes. ⊥4098

Mr. SAYERS. I send up an amendment which I desire to offer.

The Clerk read as follows:

Amend by adding the following as section 9:

"SEC. 9. That whenever the President of the United States shall be advised that a trust has been or is about to be organized for either of the purposes named in the first section of this act, and that a like product or commodity covered or proposed to be covered or handled by such trust, when produced out of the United States, is liable to an import duty when imported into the United States, he shall be, and is hereby, authorized and directed to suspend the operation of so much of the laws as impose a duty upon such product, commodity, or merchandise for such time as he may deem proper."

Mr. EZRA B. TAYLOR. Mr. Speaker, I raise the question of order against that amendment. I will reserve it if the gentleman desires to be heard.

Mr. SAYERS. I offer that in response to the remarks of the gentleman from West Virginia, to meet the point he makes.

Mr. McCOMAS. Will my friend accept an amendment providing for keeping out those imports on which there are trusts in other countries?

Mr. SAYERS. No, sir; that does not meet the point. . . .

The gentleman has not stated the point of order.

Mr. EZRA B. TAYLOR. The point of order is that this is a revenue amendment not germane to this bill; that it is not upon the subject of the bill.

Mr. SAYERS. Mr. Speaker, this is a question dealing entirely with trusts, and the purposes of the bill are, first, to suppress trusts, and, to aid in the accomplishment of that which the bill seeks to accomplish and which its friends think it will not accomplish, the amendment is offered.

[1.363] The appended articles on trusts, not reprinted here, were written for the *Baltimore Sun*.

The SPEAKER. The Chair sustains the point of order.

Mr. EZRA B. TAYLOR. Mr. Speaker, the gentleman from West Virginia [Mr. WILSON] complained that the time allowed for debate on this bill was insufficient and that no opportunity had been given for due consideration of its scope and purpose.

The bill bears the earliest number of the Senate bills, has been before the country for months, and has been duly considered by the Committee on the Judiciary of the House, of which committee the gentleman is a member. Whoever may plead ignorance of the provisions of the bill, surely my friend ought not to be included in the number.

If there is piteous need of discussion and instruction, as the gentleman asserts there is, it is to be regretted that he occupied one full hour of the time so much needed in debating the tariff question, with only an occasional allusion to trusts as connected with the tariff. . . .

I regret that my friend did not withhold his tariff speech till next week, when that subject will be under discussion. It would then be in better time and the delay would have enabled him to avoid serious errors and mistakes. He seemed desirous of conveying the impression that in free-trade England trusts were unknown, and he informed us that a certain "professor," name reserved, informed him while in England last year that he had never heard the name of "trust." I do hope the gentleman will not long allow the name of this dear, unsophisticated old gentleman to remain unknown and unsung. He should at once take his place with the spectacled crew of revenue reformers in this country, who can follow a theory beyond the stars, but do not recognize a fact when they meet it, and are wholly unacquainted with the common and practical affairs of every-day life and experience.

My friend also has a theory to the effect that tariffs create and foster trusts, and would like to believe that trusts exist only where protection prevails; but he does not, can not, so believe; whatever the "professor" may have informed him to the contrary, he knows that England is the great home of combinations of capital to control business, call them by whatever name you choose—syndicates, companies limited, or trusts—and yet he insists that to abandon protection would ruin trusts in this country. He was asked, during the delivery of his speech, to name a single trust, just one, which had been created or fostered by the tariff, and he did not succeed in naming one. The great trusts to which all thoughts are turned when the word is spoken are the whisky, the oil, and the beef trusts, not one of which is protected.

If tariff promotes trusts we would reasonably expect to find the products and commodities most largely protected involved in trusts, but such is not the case. Iron, steel, woolen, cotton, glass, and pottery industries are not, nor are they suspected of being, involved in trusts. I invite attention to these facts, not in the hope of stopping the eternal iteration and reiteration alluded to, but trusting that the candid will follow the thoughts the facts suggest.

Of course no tariff-reform speech has the true ring of free-trade orthodoxy unless it contains an attack on the wool-growers' interests and asserts the necessity of free wool, and my friend is not guilty of the heresy of such omission. Such attack and assertion have become a habit of speech, unfortunately, not a subject of thought. If our wool-growing industry is crippled or destroyed, what then? Will wool, and clothing made of wool, be cheaper or dearer?

I answer unhesitatingly, dearer. You answer not at all or with a double tongue, as you sometimes do, that untaxed wool makes cheap clothing and that wool is higher in price when not taxed. At such times and in such arguments you do not explain how the tariff cheapens wool or how dear wool makes cheap clothing, but both those propositions may be found in more than one speech delivered on this floor by leading revenue reformers.

But why dearer? Because no competition would then exist in the wool trade. The high-priced wool would be foreign wool, not American wool. The wool of the world, except ours, is now and in the future will continue to be under the control and finally owned by the great London syndicate or trust, and it would fix the price to suit its own selfish ends.

If under the high prices so fixed the flocks reappear on the hills and plains of America the price would again be cut so low as to cause their disappearance, and only so long. Believe it or not, regard it as a fact or put it aside as a fancy, it is as true as prophesy that the only safety of the American wool-producer and the American wool-consumer lies in a fair and full protective tariff, and I plead for both classes at once.

The proposed increased duty on tin-plate also received the criticism of the gentleman from West Virginia. It is assumed that tin will be dearer in that case, but the assumption is unwarranted and false. The tin-plate business is now in the hands of a close corporation, so to speak, a syndicate, a trust. Prices do not respond to cost of production, but no competition can be organized against it in the absence of protection; without it any attempt at competition would be crushed.

This is not only theory, but experience. We can make tin-plate cheaper than it is now sold, but not so cheap as the powerful and wealthy monopoly which now controls it would sell it to remove opposition. Men competent to judge and abundantly able financially to back their pledges are ready to give bond that under the proposed advance tin-plate will not become dearer for a moment, but will become permanently cheaper; and such would be the result. A foreign trust would no longer control this immense industry and grow rich by oppressing us.

I am opposed to trusts, foreign or domestic; they toil not, neither do they spin, and yet they accumulate their numberless millions from the toil of others. They lay burdens, but bear none. The beef trust fixes arbitrarily the daily price of cattle, from which there is no appeal, for there is no other market. The farmers get from one-third to half of the former value of their cattle and yet beef is as costly as ever. Even if the conscience of the retailer is touched and he reduces his price the trust steps on him and refuses to sell to him or undersells him till he is ruined.

This monster robs the farmer on the one hand and the consumer on the other. This bill proposes to destroy such monopolies, such destructive tyrants, and goes as far in that direction as Congress has the power to go under the Constitution. Our action must be supplemented by action of the States, for we can only deal with interstate transactions.

It describes and condemns the wrong, fixes the penalty, both civil and criminal, gives the United States courts new jurisdiction, and allows a concurrent jurisdiction in the State courts so far as recovery for civil damages are concerned, as well as to restraining orders. It is clearly drawn, is practical, and will prove efficacious and valuable. . . .

Mr. [JOSEPH G.] CANNON [R., Ill.]. . . .

⊥ Now, then, I want to say I believe this bill to be a good one; and I will be honest enough to say that I have not been able to give its provisions much consideration. I have not been a legislative drone this session of Congress; but after reading it and listening to the explanation of its provisions, it seems to me that it is a measure of great value, conservatively drawn, and discussed at the other end of the Capitol, and comes into this House with the unanimous report of the able committee presided over by the able gentleman from Ohio [Mr. EZRA B. TAYLOR]. What does it do? It defines combinations and conspiracies in restraint of trade among the several States and with foreign countries and declares them illegal. Then it furnishes a remedy: ⊥4099

First. It makes such combination or conspiracy a misdemeanor punishable by fine or imprisonment.

Second. It gives to any person injured by such combination an action for damages, and he can recover three times the damages sustained with costs, including a reasonable attorney's fee.

Third. It invokes the equity side—the great restraining power of the court—and makes it the duty of the United States district attorneys under the direction of the Attorney-General to go upon the equity side of the court and invoke the strong hand of the chancellor, backed by the whole power of the United States, and cause the same to be laid upon any person or corporation in the United States that is violating, or about to violate, the provisions of this act, and compel him to halt, to refrain from or to cease violating the same.

Fourth. It forfeits to the United States any property owned under any contract or by any combination which is used in violation of the provisions of the act.

Gentlemen say that they do not know how the courts will construe the act. It is for us to enact the law and for courts to construe and enforce it. If we do our duty it is reasonable to believe that the coordinate branch of the Government will do its duty. I believe that this is a valuable bill, and I shall vote for it with pleasure. . . .

Mr. BLAND. Mr. Speaker, I desire to offer the following amendment, to come in at the end of section 8, the last section of the bill.

The SPEAKER. Does the gentleman from Ohio yield to the gentleman from Missouri?

Mr. EZRA B. TAYLOR. I do.

Mr. BLAND. Then I desire to offer the following amendment.

The Clerk read as follows:

Every contract or agreement entered into for the purpose of preventing competition in the sale or purchase of any commodity transported from one State or Territory to be sold in another, or so contracted to be sold, or for the transportation of persons or property from one State or Territory into another, shall be deemed unlawful within the meaning of this act: *Provided*, That the contracts here enumerated shall not be construed to exclude any other contract or agreement declared unlawful in this act.

Mr. CULBERSON, of Texas. I reserve the point of order, Mr. Speaker.

Mr. BLAND. Oh, there is no point of order on this. I was somewhat struck, Mr. Speaker, with the frankness of my friend from Texas [Mr. CULBERSON] in his explanation of this bill. If the House or the country is advised up to this very time as to any particular kind of contract or agreement that is covered by the bill, the gentlemen who have reported it and who have advocated it upon this floor have not designated that particular contract. It is true that my friend from Iowa [Mr. HENDERSON] mentioned the beef trust of the Big Four, so called, and my friend from Texas thought that possibly the bill would cover such a trust. Now, I hope my friend from Iowa will join me—for Iowa and Missouri are particularly interested in suppressing this trust—and I think this amendment of mine will reach it beyond any question or doubt, and not leave it to the construction of the Supreme Court.

This amendment declares unlawful a contract for the sale or purchase of any commodity on which a trust is formed the moment it becomes a commodity of interstate commerce. The moment it is put upon the car to be transported into another State and sold, or the moment it arrives in another State before, as a matter of course, it is delivered to the purchaser, it is still the subject of interstate commerce, and will come within the provisions of this amendment, and that will cover this beef trust. We know that the contract with the Big Four, so called, covers every State in this Union. They compel butchers in every town of any population, East or West, to purchase of them or else they establish by the side of those butchers other shops for the sale of beef and, by underselling for a short time, they compel the home seller to submit to their dictation.

Now, this amendment covers that situation. It provides that where the Big Four or any other corporation or company are proven to be in a trust as to any commodity, the moment that commodity leaves the State or is to be sold in another State and is *in transitu* it becomes subject to this law. This provision does reach Armour & Co. without leaving the matter to the construction of the Supreme Court. It does it in direct terms in the law, and I want my friends to join with me to make that definite and certain, for there is no trust in this country that to-day is robbing the farmers of the great West and Northwest of more millions of their hard-earned money than this so-called Big Four beef trust of Chicago. This amendment, however, goes a little further than that, and provides that where there is a combination or an agreement to combine between railroad companies or transportation companies for the transportation of persons or property from one State into another, a "pool," so to speak, it is declared to be subject to this bill. I want at least two things to be known to be covered by this bill, and these two are the most important: the transportation monopoly and the monopoly of the great cattle industry of this country. This amendment will cover these two things, but God knows, for no man in this House knows, what else the bill will cover.

To be more explicit, Mr. Speaker, the amendment declares it to be unlawful to combine or make any agreement to prevent competition in the purchase or sale of anything transported from a State or Territory for sale in another State or Territory. Thus cattle shipped from any other State for sale in Chicago, Ill., will come within the express provisions of the amendment, and any trust or combine to prevent competition in the sale or purchase of this commodity is denounced by the amendment as unlawful and subject to the penalties imposed by the bill. So, also, where the Big Four, so called, agree not to compete with each other in the sale of dressed beef shipped from Chicago, Ill., to any other State or Territory for sale will come within the provisions of the bill and subject the combine to its penalties.

That part of the amendment which makes it unlawful for transportation companies to pool or agree not to compete in the matter of transporting persons or property from one State or Territory into another State or Territory will greatly aid the enforcement of the principles of the interstate-commerce law.

These remedies being cumulative may be applied where the interstate-commerce act does not afford adequate relief. Of course the amendment, like the bill, is confined to interstate commerce, since Congress has no jurisdiction over State commerce. State laws must supplement Congressional enactment if we are to reach the whole disease.

This act is but the beginning, an experiment. The decisions of the courts under it, it is to be hoped, will point the way to a more perfect law.

I trust the House will adopt the amendment. The bill may reach the case without the amendment, but I fear it will not, and from abundant caution I have offered it. . . .

Mr. [BENTON] McMILLIN [D., Tenn.]. Mr. Speaker, I favor and shall vote for the bill now under consideration, and think that it is not only expedient, but that it is the duty of this Congress to exercise every legitimate power for the prevention of these combinations called trusts—

The SPEAKER. The gentleman will suspend for a moment. The Chair supposes it is understood that the question of order is still pending.

Mr. CULBERSON, of Texas. Yes, sir.

The SPEAKER. The gentleman from Tennessee [Mr. MCMILLIN] will continue. The Chair did not wish that there should be any misunderstanding.

Mr. McMILLIN. I was saying, Mr. Speaker, that I think it is the duty of Congress to exert every legitimate power for the prevention of the organization of these trusts which are so detrimental to trade and so destructive to the best interests of the citizen. Whether this bill accomplishes all that could be wished or not may be doubted. I recognize that the question is a very difficult one with which to deal, but this bill is certainly a step in the right direction. It is a condemnation of that which is vicious and which can result only in evil. Amendments proposed have been ruled out on a point of order, and it is possible the House may be restrained thereby from applying more stringent remedies. . . .

⊥ Mr. [WILLIAM E.] MASON [R., Ill.]. Mr. Speaker, I had the pleasure of ⊥4100 introducing in a Democratic Congress the first resolution introduced on this subject,[1.364] and for six months, before a committee controlled by what is now the minority, the majority then, evidence was taken upon the subject of "trusts." The Republicans stood here ready to vote upon that question; but after you had spent thousands of dollars of the people's money in taking evidence no bill was ever presented in that Democratic House to give the people's representatives a chance to vote on the question.

The real cry that comes up from the other side of the House to-day is, "Feed the 'trusts.'" You had told us for years that the tariff protected the "trusts." As a friend of the tariff, as a friend of protection, representing the working people of my district, I asked an investigation by this House to ascertain the effect, if any, that the tariff had upon "trusts;" but you gave us no chance to vote upon the question. You use the "trust" as a bugaboo to frighten the people away from the Republican party into your

---

[1.364] Mr. Mason's resolution, H.R. MISC. DOC. NO. 69, 50th Cong., 1st Sess. (1888), which was introduced on January 4, 1889, called for the investigation of trusts in the coal and sugar industries. It was later replaced by a substitute resolution introduced by Representative Bacon and printed as H.R. MISC. DOC. NO. 124, 50th Cong., 1st Sess. (1888), which led to hearings on the trust issue by the House Committee on Manufactures. *See Introduction supra* at 13–14.

ranks. That is the reason you do not want the Republican party to strike a blow at trusts to-day. The moment we strike down trusts in this country that moment there is taken away one of the principal elements of your political talk in seeking to drive the farmers away from the Republican party into the Democratic party. [Applause.] This is why gentlemen on the other side seem fearful that we may strike a blow at the trusts. You have complained against them for years. Ever since I have heard you talk you have talked about "monopolies and trusts;" you have said, "The tariff produces the trusts; the trusts are robbing the people." And now we propose that one of the first acts of this Republican Congress shall be to strike down this giant which every man knows has destroyed legitimate competition.

Some say that the trusts have made products cheaper, have reduced prices; but if the price of oil, for instance, were reduced to 1 cent a barrel it would not right the wrong done to the people of this country by the "trusts" which have destroyed legitimate competition and driven honest men from legitimate business enterprises. We propose now to strike down these "trusts;" and you stand there and say, "The trusts are protected by the tariff." My friend from West Virginia [Mr. WILSON] says: "Do not destroy these giants; let them grow; let them stalk through this country; we will use them as an argument to drive the people away from the Republican party and into our ranks." Consistency is a jewel!

One word more and I am done. The gentleman says, "We do not know what the Supreme Court will decide on this question." You never passed a law aimed at a giant of this kind that you did not have to take it to the Supreme Court to settle it. They will take us there, of course. If you are honest in the position you take on this question—if you believe, as you say, that the "trust" is a bad thing for the people—help us to strike one blow at this great evil, or refuse, and then go home to your constituents and explain your position on this matter. . . .

But in regard to the particular question now before us we say to you, help us to help the people of the country; do not stand back.

My friend from West Virginia says: "You invite trusts, and then when you have brought them in you want to kill them." If the protection of American industry is an invitation to trusts, if there are combinations in this country that want to take advantage of just laws designed for the protection of the American workingmen, then I say let us give just protection to the laboring classes and as a part of the same protection let us strike at those combinations the blow which we are seeking to strike in this bill.

This question of protection will not "down" in this country. You can not in striking at "trusts" "down" the protective system. It has come to stay. The young men of this country have settled it, the old men are agreed, that there shall be and there can be no further competition with American labor except upon American soil. [Applause on the Republican side.] . . .

Mr. EZRA B. TAYLOR. I now yield the remainder of my time to the gentleman from Texas, and hope that he will have occasion to use but little of it.

Mr. CULBERSON, of Texas. How much time have I remaining?

The SPEAKER. Thirty minutes.

Mr. CULBERSON, of Texas. I desire to give notice that I would like to call the previous question on this bill as soon as possible within thirty minutes. I will be compelled to yield time to some of the requests of gentlemen on this side of the House. I now yield to the gentleman from Missouri [Mr. HEARD].

Mr. HEARD. Mr. Speaker, considering the importance of the bill under discussion and that it has been projected upon the consideration of the House without an hour's notice, I think that the feeling of surprise expressed by the gentleman from Ohio [Mr. BUTTERWORTH] at the course which was pursued by the Committee on Rules in thus precipitately bringing the question forward for immediate disposition is a very natural one. . . .

Under such conditions, Mr. Speaker, I shall not hesitate to accept the bill as it came from the Senate, and hope that the House may be willing to thus accept it, rather than to amend it inconsiderately, or in such way as to detract from its symmetry, or to imperil, in the slightest degree, the chances for agreement between the two branches of

Congress on a measure which will at least serve as a foundation for proper legislation on this vitally important subject.

The bill as it is now presented to us has the sanction of an almost unanimous vote in the Senate and the unanimous approval of the Judiciary Committee of this House. I confess, Mr. Speaker, that this status justly commands our respect, for in neither of those bodies was this question a new one. In the last House no less than twelve different bills upon this subject were referred to the Judiciary Committee and were there considered, and a majority of those members constituting the Judiciary Committee in the present House had the benefit of that investigation.

In the Senate, also, bills aimed to accomplish the object for which this is designed were considered and discussed in the Fiftieth Congress, and at the beginning of the present one the bill for which the one now before us is a substitute had the distinction of being the first introduced in that body. After having been considered by the Finance Committee and favorably reported therefrom, it was most ably discussed, and its defects as they then appeared were pointed out, whereupon it was referred to the Judiciary Committee, composed of some of the ablest lawyers in the country, who, happily being led by the light of extended investigation and full discussion, reached by unanimous agreement the result presented in this bill.

I insist, therefore, Mr. Speaker, that in the presence of the great demand for legislation upon this subject, and the high commendation with which this measure comes to us, there is nothing left to us under existing circumstances but to accept it, hoping that it may justify the expectations of its framers and reach effectively the giant evils at which it is aimed. It may not be perfect; indeed, sir, it would be strange if the initial act upon this subject should not call for amendment and development; but, as has been well said by the distinguished gentleman from Texas [Mr. CULBERSON] who reported this bill to the House, "It is at least a step in the right direction."

Experience teaches us that original legislation upon important subjects should always be conservative, for the reason that when you shall have applied to a law the test of its operation, under the influence of judicial interpretation, upon the persons and things which it was designed to affect, you are not only prepared to judge it correctly but also qualified to propose those amendments necessary to remove friction in action, and to give vitality to weak provisions, as well as to relax those clauses which are too harsh for enforcement. We must remember, Mr. Speaker, the magnitude of the interests to be affected by this legislation, as well as the imperative demand of an outraged people for its enactment; and in the contemplation of this prudence will dictate our course.

It will be remembered that the present interstate-commerce laws of this country[1.365] are not the work of a day, nor of one Congress; but that it was ten years from the date of the first determined effort, led by such men as REAGAN, Clardy, HOLMAN, and others in the House of Representatives, till the first law upon that subject went on our statute-book, and that after four years of experience under it, administered as it is by a commission of the highest character for ability, energy, and integrity, aided by the courts of the country, Congress learns, year by year, changes that are necessary to make effective the wise and patriotic purposes of that law.

So, Mr. Speaker, we will hereafter find it necessary, no doubt, to add to and perhaps take from some of the provisions of the bill before us; but having once started on the right course, animated by a desire to secure for our people relief from the most odious despotism of monopoly that ever cursed any country, who can doubt the ultimate result? Some gentlemen express the opinion that this bill does not go far enough. It should be sufficient answer to such criticism, Mr. Speaker, to state that such lawyers as EDMUNDS, VEST, and COKE, of the Senate, and such as CULBERSON, EZRA B. TAYLOR, ROGERS, and STEWART, in the House, declare that in this bill we go as far as in their judgment is permitted under a safe construction of constitutional limitations.

It has been well said by the gentleman from West Virginia [Mr. WILSON] that the place to go for authority to strike the root of these evils growing out of trusts is to the Legislatures of the different States from which the charters of incorporation issue. That

---

[1.365] Act of Feb. 4, 1887, ch. 104, 24 Stat. 379.

is unquestionably true so far as concerns the trusts and combines composed of different corporations united, but not in the case of combination among individuals, whose power to oppress comes not from authority of any kind, granted from any source, but from the absence of legislation of a national character which might restrain their nefarious operations carried on in any State or States, under conditions which subject them to Federal control.

The States may forfeit the charters granted by them respectively to corporations which abuse their grants, and thus reach, with some measure of punishment, the citizen—natural or artificial—operating illegally within their borders; but proper investigation of this subject teaches that when the States shall have respectively done all that lies within their power there still is left to Congress a part to perform in this work, which in order to be effective must extend over all the States and Territories of this country.

Some of the States have begun their work, and begun it courageously and with the determination to properly co-operate with other States and the National Government in doing whatever may be necessary, within the limitations of their constitutions and of the restrictions contained in the Constitution of the United States, to crush out those unholy and defiant combinations which for the enrichment of a few persons have made paupers of millions of honest and helpless people. I am proud to say that my own State has taken advanced ground in the fight so well begun, and in her support and on behalf of her citizens I now call upon the Representatives here of all the States to do their duty and to strike hard the blow aimed at the existence of these arrogant oppressors of all our people.

A single combination, or trust, known as the "dressed-beef combine" of Chicago and New York, aided and abetted by certain railroad lines, has within a few years last past absolutely prostrated the live-stock interest of the West and impoverished whole States and Territories by their infamous operations; and unless Congress, in aid of the States and Territories affected, puts forth its hand to stay this wholesale destruction of that great agricultural section, universal ruin will be the portion of its people.

As the result of an honest, able, and fearless investigation made by a committee specially raised in the Senate for the purpose of exposing the practices of said combination and of pointing out to Congress and to the country the course necessary to be pursued in legislation for the correction of its evils,[1.366] we have all the evidence necessary to prove its existence, power, and audacity, and the provisions of this bill are believed by its authors to be broad enough to enable the people to crush out the existence of this great curse. If this belief be well founded, the good that will be accomplished by the operation of the act upon the one combination referred to will be sufficient to establish its value as one of the wisest and best laws ever passed by an American Congress with reference to the commerce of the country.

But, Mr. Speaker, this giant robber combination, while perhaps the most damaging of all of its class to the interests of our people, is only one of many which by their methods extort millions from the citizens of this Republic without adding one cent of value to our productions or one iota of increase to our prosperity. In fact, the very object of these giant schemes of combined capital is not to increase the volume of supply, and thus lesson [sic] the cost of any useful commodity, but rather to repress, reduce, and control the volume of every article that they touch, so that the cost to consumers is increased while the expenditure for production is lessened, and thereby their profit secured.

We know that by such means the trusts which control the markets on sugar, nails, oils, lead, and almost every other article of use in the commerce of this country have advanced the cost of such articles to every consumer, and that without rendering the slightest equivalent therefor these illegal conspiracies against honest trade have stolen untold millions from the people.

Then, with a knowledge of all these facts and acknowledging our duty to the people who are being robbed, and who must rely upon us for protection against the robbers, we must this day decide whether we will make an effort to destroy these

---

[1.366] See REPORT OF THE SENATE SELECT COMM. ON THE TRANSPORTATION AND SALE OF MEAT PRODUCTS, S. REP. NO. 829, 51st Cong., 1st Sess. (1890). See also Introduction supra at 17 & notes 1.83–.85, 26, 27 & note 1.176.

combinations or by acquiescence in the continuation of the wrongs become parties to the wrongdoing. I believe we have the power to uproot and utterly destroy these evils and I know that it is our duty to try it and try it now; and I sincerely hope that this House may entitle itself to the respect and confidence of the people of the country by this day giving to this our best effort the indorsement of a unanimous support. . . .

Mr. ROGERS. Mr. Speaker, the origin of this measure entitles it to the most friendly consideration. So high a body as the Committee on Finance of the Senate of the United States, headed by Senator SHERMAN, whose large and long experience as well as great ability is known to all, formulated and presented to that body a measure which, when brought under the scrutiny of the law, was completely eviscerated and destroyed. After nearly ten days of consecutive debate in the Senate, participated in by some of the ablest lawyers in this country, that bill was recommitted to the Judiciary Committee of the Senate, and in that committee this bill originated.

I mention these facts to show how unwise it would be for us to adopt any amendment framed upon the desk of a member, without the most earnest and careful consideration in the light of cases adjudicated by the Supreme Court of the United States. I undertake to say now that if the amendment offered by the gentleman from Missouri [Mr. BLAND], earnest and conscientious as he always is upon public questions, were brought to the test of adjudicated cases, it would not hold water for a minute.

One word now about this bill. I have read, I believe, almost every measure presented in either body during the present and the last Congress upon the subject of trusts. I have never yet seen one except this, based upon the judicial power of the Constitution, that could receive my sanction in this great body under the obligation of my oath. Various bills upon this subject have been introduced. Some have been sent to the Judiciary Committee of the House, framed upon the taxing power of the Constitution, that I would be very glad to have an opportunity to support.

Yet, Mr. Speaker, while I am willing to give my sanction to this bill, I give it just as I gave it to the interstate-commerce bill, filled with doubts, yet compelled by a sense of the exigency and the emergency of the occasion to do whatever seems best that we have the power to do under the Constitution to afford a remedy for the evils under which the country is now suffering. And so, Mr. Speaker, not satisfied even that there is not great harm in this conservative measure—which I believe to be within the scope of the Constitution, for otherwise it could not receive the sanction of my vote or my voice—I yet fear that we will not achieve by it, when it is brought into practical application, that which we so much hope for and which is so much to be desired.

When the interstate-commerce law passed I felt precisely that way, and I am not yet prepared to say that we have seen enough of the operation of that law to justify the belief that the people of this country have derived any substantial benefit from it. But, Mr. Speaker, that law is here to stay, it is here to be improved, it is here to be amplified, ⊥ it is here to be enforced, as this law is here to stay, to be amplified in the light of experience, and to be enforced for the correction of the great evils which it is intended to remedy. ⊥4102

I hope from it the very best results, in this, that it gives a precedent for State legislation, and the courts will soon demonstrate to the country that Congress can not, unaided, afford the relief desired, but that all the States must act in the premises if they would be freed from the oppressions of trusts. However far the bill may fall short of the ends we desire, nevertheless I believe its author is entitled to the thanks of the country. . . .

Mr. [GEORGE W.] FITHIAN [D., Ill.]. Mr. Speaker, the bill under consideration receives my most hearty approval, and I shall take great pleasure in giving it my support. I regret that in dealing with a measure so important to the country sufficient time has not been allowed to give it that full consideration to which it is entitled. I have been listening, not without hope, for some measure or measures to be taken up during this session looking to the relief of the farming constituents that I have the honor to represent. . . .

. . . The creation of a trust is dishonest in its inception, it is hurtful to the whole people, and it renders to no one "his just due." Trusts and unlawful combinations to interfere with commerce were denounced by the common law of England, and if the people of the United States have not the power to prohibit and punish such pernicious evils the Government may as well be pronounced a failure. While the legislation in this bill may not be all that is needed for the suppression of the evil of trusts it is a forcible recognition of the contrary doctrine to that announced in the last campaign by an eminent gentleman and a member of the present Cabinet, that "trusts are private affairs, about which the people and the Government have no concern."

At the beginning of this session of Congress I introduced a bill in this House which, if enacted into law, with a few needed amendments which I now see necessary, would effectually eradicate the evil of trusts or transfer the scenes of operation of the gentlemen engaged in these unlawful, swindling combinations behind the bars. The bill under consideration may not be all that the friends of the masses would desire, but, as the best measure that can be passed at this session of Congress for the suppression of the evil of trusts I shall give it my support.

As a measure in the right direction I hope to see the bill become a law, leaving it to the future to remedy any defects or imperfections that it may possibly contain. It has passed the examination of the Judiciary Committees of the Senate and House, and received the careful consideration of the gentleman from Texas, [Mr. CULBERSON], who is recognized by every one as a constitutional lawyer of great ability, and I believe that it will stand the test in the courts.

I shall not bandy words with gentlemen who may want to differ with me as to the primary cause of trusts. It is sufficient for me to know that they exist; that they are an evil; that they are destroying the legitimate commerce of the country; that they enhance the price of commodities to the people beyond an honest profit, and that they are a crime against the Government and against the people. These causes are sufficient to call for the intervention of the power of the Government for their suppression. They are destructive to commerce by interfering with competition. Skill is created and is stimulated by competition. A recent writer on political economy says:

> Wherever monopoly is dominant, the incentive for improvement and skill is deadened. It is only when competitors contend with each other for the favor of the consumer that they are stimulated to attract that consumer by presenting him with wares both skillfully and cheaply made.

Competition when left free, and when combinations are not formed to prevent the operation of natural laws, will regulate the price of every commodity and will bring the price down to the level of an honest profit. No one, however, who studies the question with a view of obtaining the truth will assert that a protective tariff does not have more or less influence in creating and fostering trust combinations.

Wherever there is free, healthy competition there can be no combination to create fictitious prices of commodities, except where the supply of the article is limited by natural causes. The tariff has its influence in fostering trusts by shutting out foreign importations and thereby preventing competition with the domestic article. This kind of legislation is necessary to reach trusts which control the prices upon articles where the supply is limited by natural laws, but the most effective way to deal with trusts where they operate to increase the prices on articles upon which a tariff duty prevents the competition of the foreign article with the domestic article is to repeal the tariff duty and place the foreign article on the free-list.

With that idea in view I have introduced bills to place sugar, salt, hemp, manila, jute, twine, lumber, and all kinds of agricultural implements on the free-list, which I afterwards followed up with a resolution asking the Ways and Means Committee to make separate and independent reports upon each bill, so that the question of placing on the free-list these articles, the prices of all of which are more or less affected by trust combinations, might be considered independent and separate from the consideration of other questions in a general tariff bill. My bills to place these articles on the free-list and my resolution, like my anti-trust bill, sleep, in the committees to which they were respectively referred, that sleep that knows no wakening.

I believe that the Government in the exercise of its sovereign power has the right and that it is its duty to enact such legislation as will both prohibit and punish crime.

Legislation in the interest of the people should not stop with this bill. Many other measures are needed in the interest of the farmers of this country whose business has almost been destroyed by unjust legislation. They see the product of their toil annually taken from them and bestowed upon the favored classes. They begin to think that the Government is no longer a Government of the masses, but is a Government of the classes, and is administered upon—

> The good old rule,
> * * * * * the simple plan,
> That they should take who have the power,
> And they should keep who can.

• • • •

Born and raised on a farm, I was taught in my early youth to know its daily hardships and labors, its needs and its wants, and having continued to be more or less identified with the interests of the farm, I have learned by practical experience that farming has become unprofitable. I feel that it is my duty, not only as a representative of a farming constituency, but as one who knows from observation of the great depression in this most honorable pursuit, to call the attention of the House and the country to some of the wants of our agricultural people, although no member of this House can excuse himself on the plea of ignorance of the dire distress that confronts the farmer in his effort to support his family and save his home.

I desire to have read as a part of my remarks extracts from a very lengthy personal letter from one of my constituents, a plain honest farmer, a man of good judgment and ordinarily of conservative views.

The Clerk read as follows: . . .[1.367]

⊥ Mr. FITHIAN. This letter shows how seriously the situation is regarded by the farmers and shows the excited state of the public mind among the agricultural people and their dissatisfaction and unrest.

The condition of affairs that exists to-day among the farmers is not without cause. No class of laborers in this broad land put in more faithful hours of honest toil than the farmers. Other laborers are demanding eight hours for a day's labor. The farmer's labor does not end with eight or ten hours, but begins with the peep of day and ends only when the darkness of night obscures the heavens and spreads its mantle over the face of the earth. The demands of the farmers for remedial legislation are both reasonable and just. I ask the members of this House what has been done in recognition of the rights of these hard-working people. . . .

The question is, What is to become of the agricultural interests of this country if something is not done, and that speedily, too, for its relief? The time has come when class legislation must cease. Those who are familiar with the depressed condition of agriculture will not deny that the farmers have just, righteous cause for complaint. This Government is ceasing to be the Government of the people, for the people, and by the people, but is becoming a Government of the classes, for the classes, and by the classes. . . .

⊥ Class legislation can not be justified upon any theory consistent with honest government. Let us go back to first principles and have no privileged classes. Let every person sell the product of his toil in fair and legitimate competition in the market that will afford him the best prices and buy his necessaries in the market where he can buy the cheapest. . . .

Reduce the revenues to the legitimate needs of the Government, stop the looters of the national Treasury, suppress trusts, and give the plain, common, honest people of this country a chance; give the masses of the people a chance for once, and stop the unceasing and never-ending grabbing of the avaricious few. Do this, and let the farmer buy his necessaries in the same market where he is compelled to sell his surplus; stop class legislation, give the people free and unlimited coinage of silver, make the circulating medium sufficient to meet the demands of trade, put the money in circulation and stop giving it to national banks, and hard times will disappear to return no more. The farmer will lift the mortgage from his farm, will be able to supply his family with all the comforts of life, and will have money to loan, instead of being compelled to borrow.

[1.367] The letter pertained to farm-mortgage indebtedness and expressed the hostility of farmers toward the trusts.

Mr. CULBERSON, of Texas. I yield three minutes to the gentleman from Mississippi [Mr. STOCKDALE], and I desire to state now that after three minutes more, which I shall yield to the gentleman from Tennessee [Mr. ENLOE], I will call the previous question.[1.368] . . .

I now call the previous question on the passage of the bill.

The SPEAKER. The Chair desires to state that there is a point of order pending.

Mr. CULBERSON, of Texas. I reserved a point of order on the amendment of the gentleman from Missouri [Mr. BLAND].

The SPEAKER. Does the gentleman desire to be heard on the question of order?

Mr. CULBERSON, of Texas. I do not.

The SPEAKER. The Chair does not think the amendment in order in the place where the gentleman from Missouri proposes to add it; that is, to the eighth section. It might more properly come in as section 2.

Mr. BLAND. Very well; I will offer it as an independent section, in accordance with the suggestion of the Chair.

Mr. CULBERSON, of Texas. I do not know whether the gentleman has the floor to offer it. I make the point that he has not the floor. I hope he will let this bill pass without the amendment.

Mr. BLAND. The bill may pass without it, and be utterly worthless; with it, it may be worth something.

Mr. CULBERSON, of Texas. That may be a question of opinion.

Mr. BLAND. I do not understand that because a bill is reported by a committee it must be perfect and nobody can amend it. The amendment I desire to offer may give the bill some little vitality. I submit that the amendment is pending, no matter where it comes in.

The SPEAKER. A point of order was reserved upon the amendment; but from anything that has been said the Chair does not know what the point of order is. If it is founded upon the idea that the gentleman had not the floor except for debate, that is one thing; if founded upon the question whether the amendment is germane or not, that would be another thing.

Mr. BLAND. I told the gentleman from Ohio I wanted to offer that amendment.

Mr. EZRA B. TAYLOR. The point that the gentleman had not the floor for the purpose of offering the amendment ought not to be made, because I said to him that he might offer it.

The SPEAKER. Then the Chair will have to overrule the point of order.

Mr. CULBERSON, of Texas. I demand the previous question on the bill and amendment.

The previous question was ordered.

The SPEAKER. The Clerk will report the amendment, as modified, of the gentleman from Missouri, on which the first question will be taken.

The Clerk read as follows:

Every contract or agreement entered into for the purpose of preventing competition in the sale or purchase of a commodity transported from one State or Territory to be sold in another, or so contracted to be sold, or to prevent competition in transportation of persons or property from one State or Territory into another, shall be deemed unlawful within the meaning of this act: *Provided*, That the contracts here enumerated shall not be construed to exclude any other contract or agreement declared unlawful in this act.

The amendment was adopted.

The bill as amended was ordered to a third reading; and being read the third time, was passed.

[1.368] Representatives Stockdale and Enloe withheld their remarks for revision. Congressman Stockdale's remarks were inserted at 21 CONG. REC. A321–23 (1890). However, the *Congressional Record* index does not reveal any remarks inserted by Representative Enloe.

SENATE CONSIDERATION (S. 1)

SENATE DEBATE
51st Cong., 1st Sess.
May 2, 1890

21 Cong. Rec. 4123

Mr. VEST. I move that the trust bill, with the amendments of the House of Representatives, be referred to the Judiciary Committee.

Mr. SHERMAN. I should like to have the amendments read.

The VICE-PRESIDENT. The Chair will lay the bill before the Senate.

The SECRETARY. A bill (S. 1) to protect trade and commerce against unlawful restraints and monopolies.

Mr. SHERMAN. Let the amendments be read.

The SECRETARY. Page 1, after line 10, insert as section 2:

SEC. 2. Every contract or agreement entered into for the purpose of preventing competition in the sale or purchase of a commodity transported from one State or Territory to be sold in another, or so contracted to be sold, or to prevent competition in transportation of persons or property from one State or Territory into another, shall be deemed unlawful within the meaning of this act: *Provided,* That the contracts here enumerated shall not be construed to exclude any other contract or agreement declared unlawful in this act.

Page 1, line 11, change section 2 to section 3, change section 3 to section 4, change section 4 to section 5, change section 5 to section 6, change section 6 to section 7, change section 7 to section 8, and change section 8 to section 9.

The VICE-PRESIDENT. The amendments will be referred with the bill to the Committee on the Judiciary.

Mr. SHERMAN. I suppose that the amendment proposing a substitute for section 2 could be concurred in, so far as I know, without a reference. That is merely an amendment in degree. I will move that it be concurred in.

Mr. VEST. I prefer that the amendment should go to the Committee on the Judiciary.

Mr. SHERMAN. I will submit my motion.

Mr. VEST. I looked at it in the RECORD this morning, and it seemed to me an amendment which was entirely unnecessary.

Mr. SHERMAN. I will submit the motion to concur in the amendment, and then if the Senator desires it can go to the Committee on the Judiciary. I do not see anything in the amendment out of the way.

The VICE-PRESIDENT. The question is on the motion of the Senator from Ohio to concur in the amendments of the House of Representatives.

Mr. SHERMAN. I only move to concur and then it is quite proper for the Senator from Missouri to move to refer that motion. . . .

The VICE-PRESIDENT. The question is on the motion made by the Senator from Missouri to refer the bill with the amendments of the House of Representatives to the Judiciary Committee.

The motion was agreed to.

SENATE DEBATE
51st Cong., 1st Sess.
May 12, 1890

21 Cong. Rec. 4559

Mr. HOAR. I am directed by the Committee on the Judiciary, to whom was referred the bill (S. 1) to protect trade and commerce against unlawful restraints and monopolies, which had passed the other House with a certain amendment, to report that the Senate concur with the House amendment with an amendment; and that a conference be asked. The amendment of the committee consists in striking out from the House amendment the words which are inclosed in red brackets. I ask for the present consideration of the report.

The VICE-PRESIDENT. The amendment of the House of Representatives will be read.

The CHIEF CLERK. The bill passed the House of Representatives with an amendment, to add as section 2 the following:

SEC. 2. Every contract or agreement entered into for the purpose of preventing competition in the sale or purchase of any commodity transported from one State or Territory to be sold in another, or so contracted to be sold, or to prevent competition in the transportation of persons or property from one State or Territory into another, shall be deemed unlawful within the meaning of this act: *Provided,* That the contracts here enumerated shall not be construed to exclude any other contract or agreement declared unlawful in this act.

Also, on page 1, line 11, change "section 2" to "section 3," and change the numbering of the remaining sections.

Mr. HOAR. We propose to concur in the House amendment with an amendment striking out certain language.

The VICE-PRESIDENT. The amendment of the committee to the amendment of the House will be read.

The CHIEF CLERK. In line 1, after the word "preventing," strike out all down to and including the word "prevent," as follows:

Competition in the sale or purchase of any commodity transported from one State or Territory to be sold in another, or so contracted to be sold, or to prevent.

In line 6, after the work "act," strike out the proviso, as follows:

Provided, That the contracts here enumerated shall not be construed to exclude any other contract or agreement declared unlawful in this act.

So that section 2 as thus amended would read:

SEC. 2. Every contract or agreement entered into for the purpose of preventing competition in the transportation of persons or property from one State or Territory into another shall be deemed unlawful within the meaning of this act.

The VICE-PRESIDENT. The question is on concurring in the amendment of the House of Representatives with an amendment.

Mr. HOAR. And that a conference be requested.

Mr. VEST. I simply wish to state that as I understand the Senator from Massachusetts he reports this bill, leaving the impression that it is the unanimous report of the committee.

Mr. HOAR. I did not make any such statement as that.

Mr. VEST. I say it leaves that impression. I simply want to state that I did not concur in that report; that is all. I have no objection to a committee of conference, but I do not agree to the section as reported.

Mr. COKE. Mr. President, I desire to say also as a member of the committee that I do not concur in the report.

Mr. STEWART. I think it would be better to have the amendment printed.

Mr. HOAR. It is very simple, and I think it would be better to hasten the passage of the bill. I will state for the information of the Senate that the House concurred in the Senate bill with an amendment inserting this as the second section:

> Every contract or agreement entered into for the purpose of preventing competition in the sale or purchase of any commodity transported from one State or Territory to be sold in another, or so contracted to be sold, or to prevent competition in the transportation of persons or property from one State or Territory into another, shall be deemed unlawful within the meaning of this act: *Provided,* That the contracts here enumerated shall not be construed to exclude any other contract or agreement declared unlawful in this act.

The addition proposed by the other House contains two things. First, it provides that any contract or agreement entered into for the purpose of preventing competition in the sale or purchase of a commodity transported from one State or Territory to another shall be prohibited, and then that contracts to prevent competition in the transportation of persons or property from one State to another shall be prohibited.

The first proposition goes on what I think the whole Senate, at any rate with very slight exceptions, agreed was a mistaken conception of the constitutional power of Congress. The mere fact that an article has once been the subject of transportation from one State to another ⊥ does not authorize the Congress to treat forever after the dealing in that article as interstate commerce. If I have contracted for a hundred thousand barrels of flour in Chicago to be delivered to me in Boston and that delivery has been completed and that flour has entered into the general mass of merchandise in Massachusetts, Congress can not pursue it and prohibit dealing in that article ever after. We carefully eliminated from the Senate bill all such propositions. So the proposition of the committee is to strike out that clause of the House amendment.

⊥4560

The other clause of the House amendment is that contracts or agreements entered into for the purpose of preventing competition in the transportation of persons or property from one State or Territory into another shall be deemed unlawful. That the committee recommend shall be concurred in. We suppose that it is already covered by the bill as it stands; that is, that transportation is as much trade or commerce among the several States as the sale of goods in one State to be delivered in another, and therefore that it is covered already by the bill as it stands. But there is no harm in concurring in an amendment which expressly describes it, and an objection to the amendment might be construed as if the Senate did not mean to include it. So we let that stand.

Then the proviso which we propose to strike out is ungrammatical and unmeaning, and we suppose the bill has exactly the same meaning without it that it would have if it were inserted. The proviso is:

> That the contracts here enumerated shall not be construed to exclude any other contract or agreement declared unlawful in this act.

How a contract could be construed to exclude another contract, in the first place, we do not see; and, in the next place, no contract has been enumerated whatever in the bill.

Mr. VEST. The Senator from Massachusetts states correctly; I suppose there is not a Senator here who claims that the power of Congress applies to every article of merchandise indefinitely which has been transported from one State or Territory into another. That goes without saying.

But the difference between the majority and the minority of the committee as to their action is simply this, that the whole of the House amendment which applies to interstate commerce and to the article of merchandise itself, to all articles carried from one State or Territory to another, is stricken out, and the only portion of the House amendment that is left is that in regard to transportation.

Mr. HOAR. And also a majority of the committee understand that, so far as the Senate thinks the bill should and could constitutionally prohibit this, it is already covered by the rest of the bill.

Mr. VEST. I am perfectly willing myself to remove the argument as to the first portion of the amendment by inserting after the word "commodity" and before the word "transported" the word "being," so that it would apply to all articles being transported from one State or Territory to another. That would limit the operation of the bill to the articles which are the immediate subject of interstate transportation, and would do away with the objection made to applying the power of Congress to an article which has been transported from one State or Territory to another without limitation as to time.

It seems to me that the action of the committee goes too far. The first portion of the amendment could be made a valuable one. It certainly could be so framed that it would not antagonize the provisions of the bill as it passed the Senate. As to the latter portion of it, in regard to transportation, I understand ffrm [sic] the Senator from Massachusetts there is no controversy about that at all.

Mr. COKE. Mr. President, this amendment has been very little discussed in the committee, and the Senate know very little about it. It is too important, in my judgment, to be passed upon without further understanding it. I ask that the amendment go over and be printed, so that we can understand exactly what the report is.

Mr. SHERMAN. As the motion is that this matter go to a committee of conference I do not see what is the object of this debate. It would be better to let it go to a committee of conference and let them report it back.

Mr. COKE. I should like to see the report printed. If my motion is in order I ask that the matter go over and be printed.

The VICE-PRESIDENT. Objection being made, the report will lie over and be printed.

Mr. HOAR. I hope the Senator will allow it to go into conference, because the whole matter will be before the Senate when the representatives of the two branches have agreed and this postponement delays the passage of the bill. It is a very unimportant point that is raised now. There is not a thing which the Senator from Texas desires to accomplish by this bill, in my judgment, so far as this matter is concerned, that is not in the bill already.

Mr. COKE. I desire to know, and the Senate wishes to know, what is being voted on, and we can not know without further explanation than has appeared in the remarks of the Senator from Massachusetts, nor can we know as we ought to know until the report is printed.

Mr. HOAR. Very well; let it go over. I suppose it is a privileged matter, and I shall call it up after it is printed to-morrow.

The VICE-PRESIDENT. Objection being made, the report will lie over.

Mr. COKE. I am perfectly willing to have it called up, and will expedite it as much as possible whenever it is printed.

Mr. HOAR subsequently said: I ask unanimous consent to withdraw the report which was just made upon the trust bill and to have the bill printed as proposed to be amended by the report. I shall report it again to-morrow morning. I make the request in order that it shall not go upon the Calendar.

The VICE-PRESIDENT. It will be so ordered, in the absence of objection.

SENATE DEBATE
51st Cong., 1st Sess.
May 13, 1890

21 Cong. Rec. 4598

Mr. HOAR. I am directed by the Committee on the Judiciary to report in regard to the bill (S. 1) to protect trade and commerce against unlawful restraints and monopolies, recommending concurrence in the House amendment with an amendment. I shall not call up the matter this morning, as I understand there are some Senators who would like to examine it further. Let it go to the Calendar.

The VICE-PRESIDENT. The bill and amendments will be placed on the Calendar. . . .

⊥ Mr. HOAR subsequently said: I reported from the Judiciary Committee an ⊥4599 amendment to the trust bill yesterday, and again to-day, which came from the other House with an amendment. I find that some Senators on both sides of the Chamber think that the language of that amendment is not as precise and well guarded as it should be. I desire, therefore, to move to recommit the matter to the committee. I will say that the committee undoubtedly will be able to report it before the time that the Senate would have taken it up if it were not recommitted.

The PRESIDING OFFICER (CHARLES JAS. FAULKNER [D., W. Va.] in the chair). The Senator from Massachusetts moves to recommit the bill (S. 1) to protect trade and commerce against unlawful restraints and monopolies, with the amendment of the House of Representatives and the committee amendment thereto, to the Committee on the Judiciary.

The motion was agreed to.

SENATE DEBATE
51st Cong., 1st Sess.
May 16, 1890

21 Cong. Rec. 4753

Mr. EDMUNDS. I am instructed by the Committee on the Judiciary, to which was referred a House amendment to the bill (S. 1) to protect trade and commerce against unlawful restraints and monopolies, to report the same back with a recommendation of amendment which I send to the desk and ask may be read, and after it is read I shall ask the Senate to consider it at this time in order that we may have a conference, if the Senate agrees to our view.

The CHIEF CLERK. The Committee on the Judiciary recommend that the Senate agree to the amendment of the House of Representatives, amended as follows:

Strike out the words, in lines 2, 3, and 4 of the House amendment from the word "competition," in line 2, to the word "prevent," in line 4, inclusive.

Strike out of the House amendment the whole of the proviso, and insert after the word "another," in line 5 of the House amendment, the words "so that the rates of such transportation may be raised above what is just and reasonable;" so as to make the amendment of the House of Representatives read:

SEC. 2. That every contract or agreement entered into for the purpose of preventing competition in transportation of persons or property from one State or Territory into another, so that the rates of such transportation may be raised above what is just and reasonable, shall be deemed unlawful within the meaning of this act.

Mr. EDMUNDS. I move that the Senate agree to the House amendment thus amended and insist upon its amendment to the House amendment and ask a conference.

The VICE-PRESIDENT. The Senator from Vermont moves that the Senate agree to the House amendment as amended and request a committee of conference on the disagreeing votes of the two Houses.

The motion was agreed to.

By unanimous consent, the Vice-President was authorized to appoint the conferees on the part of the; [sic] Senate and Mr. EDMUNDS, Mr. HOAR, and Mr. VEST were appointed.

CONFERENCE CONSIDERATION (S. 1)

HOUSE DEBATE
51st Cong., 1st Sess.
May 17, 1890

21 Cong. Rec. 4837

The bill (S. 1) to protect trade and commerce against unlawful restraints and monopolies was laid before the House with the notification that the Senate had concurred in the amendment of the House with amendments, and requested a conference with the House on the bill and amendments.

Mr. EZRA B. TAYLOR. I move that the House non-concur in the amendments of the Senate and agree to the conference asked.

The motion was agreed to.

HOUSE DEBATE
51st Cong., 1st Sess.
May 21, 1890

21 Cong. Rec. 5113

The SPEAKER. The Chair will appoint as conferees on the disagreeing votes of the two Houses on the bill (S. 1) to protect trade and commerce against unlawful restraints and monopolies, or what is known as the trust bill, Mr. EZRA B. TAYLOR, Mr. STEWART of Vermont, and Mr. BLAND.

FIRST CONFERENCE REPORT AND HOUSE DEBATE
51st Cong., 1st Sess.
June 11, 1890

21 Cong. Rec. 5950

Mr. [JOHN W.] STEWART [R., Vt.]. Mr. Speaker, I desire to present a report from a committee of conference.[1.369]

The report was read, as follows:

[1.369] The report of the conference committee was apparently not printed as a separate document.

The committee of conference on the disagreeing votes of the two Houses on the amendment of the House of Representatives to the bill of the Senate S. 1, entitled "An act to protect trade and commerce against unlawful restraints and monopolies," having met, after full and free conference have agreed to recommend and do recommend to their respective Houses as follows:

That the House of Representatives recede from its disagreement to the amendments of the Senate and agree to the same modified to read as follows, in lieu of the whole House amendment:

"SEC. 2. Every contract or agreement entered into for the purpose of preventing competition in the transportation of persons or property from one State or Territory into another so that the rates of such transportation may be raised above what is just and reasonable, shall be deemed unlawful within the meaning of this act, and nothing in this act shall be deemed or held to impair the powers of the several States in respect of any of the matters in this act mentioned."

And the Senate agree to the same.

E. B. TAYLOR,
J. W. STEWART,
Managers on the part of the House.
GEORGE F. EDMUNDS,
GEORGE F. HOAR,
Managers on the part of the Senate.

Mr. BLAND. Mr. Speaker, I desire to submit a minority report, and ask for a further conference.

The SPEAKER. The Chair does not know any way in which a minority report can be submitted.

Mr. BLAND. Then I give notice that I will ask for a new conference with instructions. . . .

Mr. STEWART, of Vermont. Mr. Speaker, I send to the Clerk's desk the statement of the House conferees.

The statement was read, as follows:

Statement accompanying report of conferees on the disagreeing votes
of the two Houses on S. 1.

A majority of the committee of conference on the part of the House on the disagreeing votes of the two Houses on Senate bill 1 submit the following statement:

In the original bill two things were declared illegal, namely: Contracts in restraint of interstate trade or commerce, and the monopolization of such trade.

Its only object was the control of trusts, so called, so far as such combinations in their relation to interstate trade are within reach of Federal legislation.

The House amendment extends the scope of the act to all agreements entered into for the purpose of preventing competition either in the purchase or sale of commodities, or in the transportation of persons or property within the jurisdiction of Congress.

It declares illegal any agreement for relief from the effects of competition in the two industries of transportation and merchandising, however excessive or destructive such competition may be.

The amendment reported by the conferees is the Senate amendment with the added proviso that the power of the States over the subjects embraced in the act shall not be impaired thereby.

It strikes from the House amendment the clause relating to contracts for the purchase of merchandise, and modifies the transportation clause by making unlawful agreements which raise rates above what is just and reasonable.

J. W. STEWART,
For Conferees.

Mr. CULBERSON, of Texas. Mr. Speaker, this is a very important amendment which is suggested by the conference. I was not a member of that committee, but I think the action of that committee raises a very important question, and I ask the gentleman [Mr. STEWART, of Vermont] now to yield to me to ask unanimous consent that we have debate upon this proposition for one hour on each side, as quite a number of gentlemen desire to be heard.

Mr. STEWART, of Vermont. Mr. Speaker, there has been a good deal of interest expressed in the questions which are raised by this report, which are more important, more intricate, and less understood, in my judgment, than any questions which have been recently submitted to this House; so I am not disposed to avail myself of any power which I may have to cut off reasonable debate. I think, however, that my friend from Texas might agree to an hour and a half, forty-five minutes on each side. . . .

The SPEAKER. The question is on the request of the gentleman from Texas for unanimous consent for two hours' debate. Is there objection?

Mr. ANDERSON, of Kansas. Yes. I suggest to the gentleman from Vermont that, as I understand it, this conference report substantially repeals the anti-pooling clause of the interstate-commerce law.

Mr. STEWART, of Vermont. My friend is mistaken. I think I can satisfy him on that point. . . .

⊥ The SPEAKER. The gentleman from Vermont [Mr. STEWART] asks unanimous ⊥5951 consent that debate on this question be continued for two hours and a half. Is there objection? The Chair hears none.

Mr. STEWART, of Vermont. Mr. Speaker, I have no desire at this stage of the debate to make any general statement other than what I have submitted, which has been read at the Clerk's desk. The effect of the conference report as will be understood by those who have listened to the reading of the statement is to eliminate from the amendment adopted by the House those provisions which are evidently intended to prevent any contract affecting competition either in transportation or in the purchase and sale of commodities. The Senate amendment which is incorporated in the conference report eliminates those provisions, and only permits the transportation companies to contract at such rates as shall be just and reasonable. That provision has no relation whatever to the clause in the interstate-commerce law which forbids "pooling."

And let me state right here that the traffic associations, under whose management the transportation of this country has been conducted ever since and before the passage of the interstate-commerce law, have been constantly doing with the approbation of the Interstate Commerce Commission precisely what my friend from Kansas thinks would be contrary to the pooling clause of the interstate-commerce law; that is to say, they have been obliged to agree upon rates, which this amendment of the gentleman from Missouri would forbid. But agreeing upon rates between the different trunk lines from one terminal point to another is quite a different thing from "pooling," as I think I can satisfy my friend later on. . . .

Mr. CULBERSON, of Texas. Mr. Speaker, I think that the state of the case, as presented by the House amendment and the action of the Senate upon the House amendment and the action of the conference committee, may be briefly stated as follows: The House amendment to this bill contains two distinct propositions. By the first, every contract or agreement entered into for the purpose of preventing competition in the sale or purchase of any commodity transported from one State or Territory to be sold in another, or so contracted to be sold, is made unlawful.

The second proposition contained in the House amendment, submitted by my friend from Missouri [Mr. BLAND], is that every contract or agreement to prevent competition in the transportation of persons or property from one State or Territory into another shall be deemed unlawful. There follows a proviso to this amendment which it is unnecessary to read, inasmuch as it is wholly superfluous.

I think that the first proposition, that every contract or agreement which seeks to prevent competition in the sale or purchase of an article, commodity, or product to be transported from one State to another shall be unlawful, is entirely covered by the original bill; and therefore the Senate and the conference committee did right in rejecting that part of this amendment. The reason I make this statement is that the original bill contains the following proposition:

> Every contract, combination in the form of a trust, or otherwise, or conspiracy, in restraint of trade or commerce among the several States or with foreign nations, is hereby declared to be illegal.

It would seem that the thing denounced by the first clause of the amendment of the House is a contract or agreement to prevent competition in the sale or purchase of a commodity to be transported. The original bill makes every contract in restraint of trade unlawful; and therefore the proposition of the amendment is covered by the original bill, clearly and distinctly—there is no doubt about it.

The conference report eliminates that proposition from the House amendment altogether; and I think the House loses nothing by it, because the proposition, as I stated before, is covered by the original bill.

Now, the second proposition, I think, is a very material one. It relates to transportation from one State into another. The exact terms of the amendment in relation to this are that any contract or agreement to prevent competition in the transportation of a product from one State to another is declared to be illegal. I think the House, if it can do so, ought to retain that amendment in the bill. The conference committee substitutes an entirely different proposition for this clause of the House amendment. They entirely ignore it; or, in other words, they reverse the proposition contained in that clause of the House amendment. Now, what is it?

The conference committee recommends that the House shall recede from its disagreement to the Senate amendment, and that both Houses agree to the amendment with an amendment to read as follows:

> Every contract or agreement entered into for the purpose of preventing competition in the transportation of persons or property from one State or Territory into another, so that the rates of such transportation may be raised above what is just and reasonable, shall be declared unlawful. . . .

Now, the House proposition makes every contract and agreement to prevent competition in transportation unlawful. That is the substance of the House proposition. The proposition of the conference committee, on the other hand, provides that every contract or agreement made to prevent competition in the transportation of any product from one State into another whereby the rate of freight is raised above what is deemed reasonable and just is declared to be unlawful. That is to say, if the contract contemplates a rate of freight which is reasonable and just, this report legalizes the contract or agreement; whereas the House proposition is to make all contracts of that character, whether the rates are reasonable or unreasonable, unlawful.

I think that the House ought to maintain its own proposition at least on transportation, for the reasons briefly stated, which I will illustrate as follows: Two trunk lines of railroad running from the city of St. Louis to Chicago can make a contract in respect to transportation and fix the rates, by which contract both roads are to be bound. If these rates, so fixed by that contract, are reasonable, this legislation proposed in the conference report legalizes it. But if the rate so fixed by the two competing lines are unreasonable, the contract is declared to be unlawful.

In the interstate-commerce act there is a provision making pooling unlawful. The very object of that was to encourage competition between railroads. That was the purpose of inserting the provision. It was contemplated, of course, that the contract upon which the pool was or might be based should be reasonable and just. But yet Congress said, "You shall not pool at all." Why? For the reason that if you are permitted to pool your freight rates, then you will discourage competition and thereby impose unnecessary burdens on the people.

Now, the proposition of the conference committee virtually repeals that law in this respect: A half dozen trunk lines running out of any city in the Union may agree upon a rate of freight which the Interstate Commerce Commission, if you please, might hold to be reasonable. After they may have fixed the rate by such a contract there is absolutely no more competition between these trunk-competing roads, none whatever; because this contract is binding upon all of them, and they know that each and every one of them must stand by the contract, and each and every one of them will get the exact amount provided in the contract so fixed.

Mr. STEWART, of Vermont. What is the objection, if the rate is just and reasonable?

Mr. CULBERSON, of Texas. Why, the very reason why we insist, and that is about one of the very best provisions in the interstate-commerce law—the very reason why we insisted that there should be no more pooling between railroads in the United States was to encourage, incite, and, if you please, excite competition among competing lines of railway.

Mr. [WILLIAM C.] OATES [D., Ala.]. Has not the effect of that attempt been a union of all of the smaller roads under the control of the larger ones, and has it not resulted in accomplishing just the contrary to what was expected?

Mr. CULBERSON, of Texas. I would rather not go into what is an unknown field, the actual results of the operation of the interstate-commerce act. I am inclined to think, however, that in some respects the operation of that act has not met the expectations of the public.

I understand that the very same question now before Congress is before the Interstate Commerce Commission in this way: The commission is discussing the proposition whether or not competing lines, going to or from the same point, may not agree upon a specified rate of freight.

If you adopt this conference report in this shape, there will be no necessity for the commission to decide it; because we will legalize the very proposition which is now a matter of dispute before the commission, and if this provision should become the law, all the evils now restrained by the law which forbids pooling will return to oppress the people. . . .

Mr. HILL. Who is to decide under this section (section 2) reported by the conference committee as to whether the contracts are just and reasonable or not—the courts or the commission?

Mr. CULBERSON, of Texas. The courts.

Mr. STEWART, of Vermont. The Interstate Commerce Commission has authority as to freights.

Mr. BLAND. The Interstate Commerce Commission, if this becomes a law, has no power over it at all. It throws it all into the power of the railroads and transportation companies. That is the serious objection to this provision.

Mr. STEWART, of Vermont. The question of rates would come before the commission. . . .

Mr. CULBERSON, of Texas. Now, I understand, Mr. Speaker, that one of the main objects of this report is to prevent railroad wars on freight rates. That I understand to be the object. Whether it would have that effect or not I do not know, but I suppose it would. Is it important for the people of this country to promote competition among competing lines of railways? I think so; and the only way to encourage competition is to forbid pooling, as Congress has done, and reject all propositions which propose to authorize railroad companies to enter into contracts for the purpose of preventing competition. . . .

Mr. STEWART, of Vermont. I want to call your attention to the jurisdiction. What jurisdiction has Congress over this subject of interstate transportation except under that clause of the Constitution? Now, does not the phrase in the section you have read in the original bill cover this question just as much as the other?

Mr. CULBERSON, of Texas. I do not think it does.

Mr. STEWART, of Vermont. Why not?

Mr. CULBERSON, of Texas. I would have to go back and state the matter over again in order to answer that.

Mr. STEWART, of Vermont. If that is the source of our jurisdiction, that declares all contracts in restraint of trade by anybody—and of course that means interstate trade, because we have no jurisdiction over anything else—to be illegal. Now, does not that cover this proposition?

Mr. CULBERSON, of Texas. I understand you, and I have already stated that the first proposition contained in this amendment was covered by the original bill, but the second proposition is not contained in the original bill.

Mr. [N. P.] HAUGEN [R., Wis.]. You make a distinction between trade and transportation?

Mr. CULBERSON, of Texas. Yes, sir.

Mr. STEWART, of Vermont. The only jurisdiction we have over this subject is in relation to interstate trade, under that clause of the Constitution.

Mr. CULBERSON, of Texas. I understand that.

Mr. STEWART, of Vermont. The original bill provided that any contract in restraint of trade—and that means interstate trade—is illegal.

Mr. CULBERSON, of Texas. I understand that.

Mr. STEWART, of Vermont. I say that phrase is broad enough to cover this, too.

Mr. CULBERSON, of Texas. If you think so, then you ought not to have reported this amendment; but the fact is that the conference committee proceeded upon the idea that there was a distinction between the first proposition contained in the amendment and the second, and there is no doubt but that is so, because the first proposition—

Mr. STEWART, of Vermont. Not any distinction in law.

Mr. CULBERSON, of Texas. Oh, yes. The first proposition refers simply to contracts made in restraint of trade.

Mr. STEWART, of Vermont. Yes, but interstate trade.

Mr. CULBERSON, of Texas. Of course; the sale or purchase of commodities to be transported from one State into another.

Now, the second proposition deals with contracts which have for their object the destruction of competition in rates of transportation from one State to another.

Mr. HILL. Will the gentleman permit me? Is not the direct effect of this second section to legalize, or at least to authorize *prima facie,* all contracts between railroads relating to transportation, until the matter is finally submitted to the courts, and if the courts finally decided that a certain schedule, or rather contract or agreement, is illegal, they can immediately make another a little lower or a little different, so that the practical effect will be to continue these contracts or agreements in force?

Mr. STEWART, of Vermont. That is exactly what the law is now.

Mr. CULBERSON, of Texas. As a matter of course the law is now that the railroad company can not charge an unreasonable rate. That is the law now, and there was no necessity of putting that in this conference report.

Mr. STEWART, of Vermont. Not at all; it does not change the law in that.

Mr. CULBERSON, of Texas. That, if I remember, provided that an unreasonable rate should be unlawful. That is the law; but you understand, gentlemen, the object of this—I will not say the object, because I do not know what the object was—but the effect of this proposition submitted by the conference committee is to legalize every contract made between competing roads when that contract fixes a reasonable rate. That is what it does, and it in effect destroys the law against pooling.

Mr. [ISAAC S.] STRUBLE [R., Iowa]. And against competition?

Mr. CULBERSON, of Texas. Yes, it destroys competition. . . .

Mr. STRUBLE. I would like to have the gentleman read the first section as proposed by the Senate, if he can. . . .

Will you read that section?

Mr. BLAND. Yes. In order to ascertain whether the gentleman from Vermont [Mr. STEWART] is correct with regard to the question asked the gentleman from Texas [Mr. CULBERSON], as to whether the bill as it now stands will not cover this proposition, one of these gentlemen thought it did cover the proposition and the other that it did not.

Now, here are two lawyers of the Judiciary Committee who differ about this subject-matter.

Mr. STEWART, of Vermont. Lawyers do disagree, you know.

Mr. PEEL. Sometimes.

Mr. BLAND. The gentleman from Vermont [Mr. STEWART] claims in his report that the House amendment does extend the scope of the bill, for he states:

> In the original bill two things are declared illegal, to wit, contracts in restraint of interstate trade or commerce and the monopolization of such trade. Its only object was the control of trusts, so called, so far as such combinations in their relation to interstate trade are within reach of Federal legislation.
>
> The House amendment extends the scope of the act to all agreements entered into for the purpose of preventing competition either in the sale of commodities or in the transportation of persons or property within the jurisdiction of Congress.

Now, there is a direct admission on the part of the majority of the conferees that the House amendment does extend the scope of the bill. And it is very singular, Mr. Speaker, that this bill went through the Senate without any practical opposition, that it came to the House and was about to pass the House without any dissent or practical opposition, but the moment two amendments are put in the bill we ascertain there is some fighting ground in the measure for the first time. Now, what is that fighting ground? I must dissent from my friend from Texas and my friends on the conference committee both. Every lawyer here who has read what is called the liquor cases, the unbroken-package cases,[1.370] which it is unnecessary for me to read—I have the decision here—will find that in that decision the Supreme Court has gone beyond what probably most lawyers in this country expected it would go, in holding what is an article of interstate commerce and the power of Congress over it.

When the bill passed the Senate and passed the House that decision had not been rendered.[1.371] Now, the amendment that is stricken out by the Senate that my friend from Texas claims was covered by the original bill provides substantially that where an article of interstate commerce is transported from one State or Territory into another, there to be sold, that any contract or agreement to prevent competition of the first sale of that article is unlawful. The Supreme Court holds that it is an article of interstate commerce until the first sale is had and until that sale—that is the language—by that sale it becomes mingled with the property of the State and passes out of the jurisdiction of the courts.

Now, we had some controversy here the other day when this bill was up as to the power of Congress over what is called the "Big Four" of Chicago, in relation to the purchase of beef, cattle, and hogs that are shipped from the Northwest and Western States to Chicago. It is said that there are four companies there that by agreement among themselves do not compete in the purchase of this class of property. One firm will purchase to-day, another firm will purchase next day, another the next day, and another the next. They have their particular days to purchase so as not to compete with each other, and in that way they have contracts that interfere with a fair sale of property imported, so to speak, from other States.

Now, if the language of the bill as put in by the House, that any property transported from one State or Territory to be sold in another, be retained there is no question whatever, under the decision of the Supreme Court, that combinations such as we have, and such as we of the West and Northwest complain of, are covered by the bill in express terms and express language. Nothing is left for construction in that regard. My friend from Texas [Mr. CULBERSON] thinks it is covered by the original bill, and my friend from Vermont thinks that ⊥ railroad transportation is covered in the original bill. Here are lawyers differing. We do not know what the court will hold in regard to contracts to prevent fair competition in interstate commerce or in restraint of trade.

⊥5953

That is a question yet to be decided by the courts of the country if the original bill pass in its present shape. That is a question that Congress remits to the courts to determine as a judicial question; but with the House amendment in, it is no longer a judicial question at all. It is simply a question of fact. Congress would then make a legislative declaration that it is illegal, and puts the condemnation of a law upon it without asking the court whether or not interstate trade is interfered with by such transactions. Wherever commodities are shipped from one State to another it covers them all. It covers them by a legislative declaration that can not be mistaken, and I think that amendment is more important than the other and ought to have remained in the bill, but it was stricken out by the Senate.

Now, as to railroad transportation or any other transportation. The original bill, although it denounces combinations and trusts in restraint of trade, my friend from Vermont thinks will cover railroad transportation, but he does not say so in his report, for his report specifically says that this amendment goes beyond the scope of the bill, and that it makes unlawful all contracts or agreements by which competition is to be protected in transportation or in the sale of the property. That he acknowledges in his report, and if it is all covered by the bill, why all this difficulty about it?

Now, the interstate-commerce law in the fifth section prevents pooling, and that is as far as it goes. That is, that railroads shall not enter into combinations and agreements by which they will divide up the profits, etc. There is no law authorizing

---

[1.370] Representative Bland was apparently referring to Leisy v. Hardin, 135 U.S. 100, 10 S. Ct. 681, 34 L. Ed. 128 (1890).

[1.371] Actually, *Leisy* was decided on April 28, 1890—three days before the House passed S. 1.

them to make contracts between companies to establish rates among themselves. They want that, and there is a bill pending in the Senate for that purpose; and this amendment is intended to give them that. The Interstate Commerce Commission have no power over that subject except in regard to pooling.

Mr. STEWART, of Vermont. What bill does my friend refer to as pending in the Senate?

Mr. BLAND. I understand that a bill has been introduced by Senator DAWES in the Senate that practically covers this proposition. I have not seen the bill, and merely state that on information without knowing that I am correct about it.

Now, as I said before, here is a proposition not to place the roads under the jurisdiction of the Interstate Commerce Commission at all. This is an effort to get them from under the control of the Interstate Commerce Commission, as I understand the act. It does not say that any contract or agreement where it raises the freights may be reasonable. It provides that the Interstate Commerce Commission shall say that this contract is reasonable, or that the freights are reasonable, and fix the manner in which they are to divide the charge. The Interstate Commerce Commission wants no jurisdiction over such a subject, and ought not to have it. There ought to be no tribunal in this country to determine between the different transportation companies what is reasonable and what is not, except the courts of the country.

As stated by my friend from Texas [Mr. CULBERSON], two trunk lines may agree between themselves to establish rates to prevent competition, and the Interstate Commerce Commission would have no power over it at all. It is left simply for the shipper and those who do business on the road to contest that thing in the courts. Whatever rates they may establish themselves are *prima facie* lawful, proper, legal, just, equitable, and reasonable. Now, do we propose to betray the people of this country in a contest of that sort with the great trunk lines of this country? Why, certainly we ought not to do so.

We know the difficulties they have to contend with in such contests. We know the great power of these corporations by way of changes of venue; changes from one court to another, and from one district to another. We know, also, the power they have in procuring the testimony of experts who claim to know all about transportation and about the "reasonableness" of freight charges. They are always able, in some way or other, to get "expert" witnesses who will overwhelm the suitor and drive him out of court every time. That is the real situation, and that is where this conference report proposes to relegate the people of this country in their contests with the railroads. I do not believe this House will do that. But I think now is the time and here is the place to insist not only on that amendment, but also on the other amendment which is equally important so far as my people and the people of the great Northwest are concerned, the amendment to declare any contract or agreement illegal within the meaning of this act which prevents competition in the purchase or sale of property transported from one State or Territory to another.

That makes it definite and certain, beyond dispute and beyond conjecture, as to what the Supreme Court may hold with regard to what is or is not an interference with interstate freight or a restriction of interstate freight. The court may hold an agreement of that sort to be a restriction of interstate freight or they may not. They may hold it to be a monopoly denounced by the original bill or by the bill as it came from the House, or they may not. We do not know what the court may hold. It is the duty of the legislator to make a clear legislative declaration as to what is intended to be denounced as "unlawful," and that this amendment does beyond all question. Now, if we want to legislate upon this subject in a way to leave no doubt as to what we mean, then it is highly important that that amendment shall remain in the bill. As I stated before, when this bill passed the House and the Senate these questions had not been settled as they have been since.

The Supreme Court have gone probably further than the Judiciary Committee of either the House or the Senate expected they would go with respect to interstate commerce. We are now legislating in the light of that opinion of the court, which throws new light upon this subject and extends the jurisdiction of the courts over interstate commerce beyond what was contemplated before that opinion was delivered.

Hence I say those who framed this bill did not frame it in view of the powers now possessed under the decision of the Supreme Court, but this amendment does come within the scope of that opinion. It is clearly and legally within that opinion, and since the court has settled that question, and we are thus called upon to legislate with regard to it, I say this Congress would be negligent of the interests of the people of this country if they did not both maintain these amendments with regard to contracts for the sale of property transported from one State to another and also strike out that provision which permits the railroads to combine and make contracts provided somebody can show that they are not "unreasonable." . . .

Mr. MORSE. Mr. Speaker, this legislation is based upon that provision of the Constitution, as I understand it, that gives Congress a right to regulate commerce between the States. It is plain that Congress has no right to regulate trusts within a State, but the bill proposes to regulate transactions in restraint of trade between citizens of different States.

The recent decisions of the Supreme Court on the original-package case as well as the interstate-commerce law are based on this provision of the Constitution. I have not the slightest idea that the framers of the Constitution ever intended by this provision a regulation of commerce and trade by land. Commerce was understood by them as a division of traffic or trade carried on in ships and by water, as nearly all the commerce was in that time between the different colonies, and this provision was to prevent any form of taxation or regulation upon such commerce by the different States and without the consent of Congress.

No such condition as exists to-day was contemplated or dreamed of in which the country is interlaced by railroads and State lines are obliterated, and instead of distant and distinct colonies we have in many sections run together and become one people. And for purposes of trade State lines are ignored and obliterated. But a different and vastly wider construction has been given this provision of the Constitution, and under it it is claimed that Congress has a right to regulate all transactions between citizens of different States by land or water, though such a construction is denied by good lawyers and has never been passed upon by the Supreme Court.

Under this provision of the Constitution the pending bill is now before us and under consideration. Mr. Speaker, no one will go further than I in legislation to suppress trusts that oppress the people by cornering the necessities of life or by injurious combinations that put up the price of such necessities; but, Mr. Speaker, let us be sure that the bill now under consideration means that. The gentleman from Texas told us in a former debate upon this bill that no one knew how wide a swath the bill would cut, and that the application of the bill to different transactions carried on in this country among business men would have to be determined by the courts.

Mr. Speaker, here is a bill that proposes fine and imprisonment as a penalty, and the chairman of the committee, in answer to my question, says that he can not tell or explain its scope, and that the courts will have to define and expound this law. In other words, we must try and punish by fine and imprisonment, if convicted, some of our citizens to get a definition of the scope of the law. I submit that we had better go slow. If the chairman of the committee does not understand this law, who does? It seems very much to me like taking a leap in the dark, and to my mind is not wise legislation. . . .

. . . Mr. Speaker, the interstate-commerce law was supposed to be in the interest of the consumer and the people; it has proved to be the opposite. In its practical workings it has strengthened chains that it was intended to loosen.

The gentleman from Kansas [Mr. PERKINS] stood up here the other day, when the tariff bill was under consideration, and stated a fact which is borne out by testimony from every section of the country, that three years ago a depression in the farming interests of the country began—a depreciation began three years ago, he said, in farm lands and farm products, expecially in the extreme Western States.

⊥ I called the attention of the gentleman from Kansas to the fact that the interstate-commerce law was enacted when this depression began, and the remedy for that depression was the repeal of that law. He said that the farmers of his State were burning their corn for fuel; the cause is the "long and short haul clause" of the

⊥5954

interstate-commerce law that prevents the farmer in his State from exchanging his corn with the miner of Pennsylvania for coal at nominal freight on long hauls, to the mutual advantage of the Kansas farmer and the Pennsylvania miner.

Now, I want to be sure that this bill means what it says, and that it is not a bill to injure the people. I desire here to call attention to an important business method adopted by many large manufacturers and merchants in this country an interference with which would work injury to large business interests and the people. There is a practice among manufacturers of proprietary articles known as the "contract system" of selling goods, the intention of which is to fix a fair and living profit to the merchant handling their goods and to prevent cut-throat competition; and so far it may be said to be in restraint of trade. Such restraint, I claim, is in the interests of the consumer. It means 16 ounces in a pound of soap; it means 24 sheets in a quire; it means a high grade and uniform quality of goods, so that a purchaser can know what he is buying and what to depend upon. Very many large manufactories in this country have adopted this method of controlling the price at which their goods shall be sold.

Deny manufacturers this right to control the selling price of their goods and compel them to enter into ruinous competition and the effect is a constantly deteriorating quality of goods to meet such ruinous competition; deny manufacturers this right, it means adulterated food, adulterated spice, it means short weight and short count to meet the constant demand for cheaper goods that will still afford a profit; deny the stove manufacturers the right to regulate the selling price of their goods, as is the custom of many stove manufacturers now, and it means thinner castings and poorer quality of iron to meet the demand for a cheaper stove that will still afford a profit, and no one will suffer so much as the people who buy the goods. So far as I know, the manufacturers of this country who have adopted this system of selling their goods have fixed a fair living profit only on their products, and require the merchant, in order to secure the bottom price, to sign an agreement that he will sell at such living profit; and this arrangement, I claim for the reasons I have stated, is for the interest of the manufacturer, the merchant, and the consumer.

So far as this bill does what its friends claim for it, namely, so far as it suppresses unlawful combinations cornering the necessities of life, so far as it will suppress great combinations that oppress the people, like the Standard Oil Company, like the beef trust in Chicago, like the sugar trust in New York, I believe in so much of this bill, but if it proposes to deny to manufacturers and merchants the right to control the price at which their goods shall be sold, the right to say they shall not enter into ruinous competition, the right to exact a fair and living profit on the sale of their goods by the merchant who handles them, it will be unwise legislation and injurious to the manufacturer, to the merchant, to the consumer, and the whole people, and strike a blow at the business interests of the country, because it will violate a sound business principle, "to live and let live."

I submit that if such a construction could be given this bill the question of its constitutionality might be raised; and in this connection I desire to incorporate in my remarks the following opinion of the Supreme Court of the United States, which is self-explanatory, and I commend it to the careful consideration of the House and the committee in charge of this bill: . . .[1.372]

⊥ Mr. STEWART, of Vermont. Mr. Speaker, the jurisdiction of Congress over this subject is conferred by that clause of the Constitution which gives us the power to control commerce among the States; it is derived only from that clause. The statement which I submitted referred more particularly to what the gentleman from Missouri [Mr. BLAND] intended rather than what he effected. As I understand the scope of the original bill, I insist that neither his amendment nor the Senate amendment extends at all the effect of the Senate bill. I think the amendment reported by the conference committee leaves the law exactly where it is.

[1.372] Representative Morse entered into the *Record* the Court's opinion in Fowle v. Park, 131 U.S. 88, 9 S. Ct. 658, 33 L. Ed. 67 (1889), which held that contract provisions restricting the geographic area of sale and establishing a minimum resale price for a secret patent medicine were not unreasonable nor invalid as in restraint of trade.

Now, this is a conference report. It has been a matter of agreement. There it stands. It is a sort of a "tub to the whale." I do not think it amounts to anything. It does not do any harm, because the interstate-commerce law as it stands to-day leaves the law precisely where this does. A contract to prevent competition is an illegal contract to-day. It is not necessary that Congress should enact the proposition into law; it is the law now. A contract in restraint of interstate trade, whether its object is to prevent competition, or whatever else may be its object, may be made an illegal contract under an act of Congress; and it is only because it is in restraint of interstate trade that it becomes a proper subject of legislation by Congress.

⊥ Now, there are two great forces working in human society in this country to-day, and they have been contending for the mastery on one side or the other for the last two generations. Those two great forces are competition and combination. They are correctives of each other, and both ought to exist. Both ought to be under restraint. Either of them, if allowed to be unrestrained, is destructive of the material interests of this country. It is just as necessary to restrict competition as it is to restrict combination, and any student of the times who has failed to see this has missed the lesson of the hour. ⊥5956

Why, Mr. Speaker, when this trust bill came up for consideration before the Committee on the Judiciary I could not but smile at the proposition. Here is a furious assault upon combinations; and my friends from Kansas and Missouri, who have protested so much here in the interest of the laborer and the farmer, make haste to fight combinations, while they seem to forget that they are representing a constituency to-day that are in combinations. There is hardly a class in this country to-day that I know anything about that is not in some form of combination. This system of combination pervades human society from the highest classes to the lowest.

Now let us look for one moment at the cause of this. All these great social and sociological changes are produced by causes which are constantly working in human society. Why do the laborers organize and combine to put up the price of labor, and so enhance the cost of everything to the consumer? Because of excessive competition. Yet my friend from Missouri does not propose to apply any remedy in that direction. Nothing more largely affects the cost of articles to every consumer—and I will not except the tariff if my friend Mr. MILLS will allow me to make that allusion in this connection—nothing enhances the cost of commodities to the consumer to-day in this country more than the combinations of labor. Who complains of it? I do not. I think the laborer is justified, where competition is excessive and is becoming destructive to the interests of his class, I think the laborer is justified in entering into combinations for self-protection.

The other day we began to hear whispers of a "Farmers' Alliance"—

Mr. STRUBLE. "Whispers," did you say?

Mr. STEWART, of Vermont. Well, thunders—thunders of a Farmers' Alliance. So far as the Farmers' Alliance is a combination of the farmers for the protection of their material interests I bid them God speed. So far as it is an organization of one class for the purpose of getting political power and legislating against other classes I protest against it. There are probably ten million farmers among the sixty-five million people of this country, a country where every laborer in every department stands equal to everybody else, where we have diversities of industry, and where no one class has a right to assume any dominant influence either in the Government or in the protection which the Government affords. And yet I understand that the Farmers' Alliance—and I think they were right, they were wise in it—entered into a sort of combination to withhold their products from the markets and enhance their prices.

So, when I buy corn and fodder in Vermont I make a contribution, because the fodder comes from the West, to the farmers of Kansas, and I am perfectly willing that it shall be so. I have no objection to doing it. But what leads the farmers of Kansas and everywhere else to make a combination? What has driven them to do it? They were driven to it by competition. And yet my friend from Missouri seeks to apply to that one class a rigid legal statute against combination, which will affect property valued at over $8,000,000,000 of investments and covering over 160,000 miles of railroads in the United States, in which the agricultural interests of the country, and especially the farmers of the West, are more interested than in anything else, especially in their productive management.

Mr. BLAND. I understood the original bill covered every point of the amendment and I can not understand the contention between my friend and myself.

Mr. STEWART, of Vermont. I am endeavoring to answer some of the objections contained in remarks submitted by gentlemen on the other side, who seem to think that competition ought to be unrestrained, especially as applicable to two classes in the country, and leave all the rest to cut loose and prey upon the community at their own sweet will. . . .

Why, my friend from Texas says that this is a repeal of the clause of the interstate-commerce law forbidding pools; but permit me to say here, and I venture the prediction, that in five years from now not a man in this House will be opposed to pooling in some form or other and will favor the repeal of that clause—

Mr. ANDERSON, of Kansas. That is just it; now you have said it.

Mr. STEWART, of Vermont. Yes, and I can justify it.

Mr. ANDERSON, of Kansas. Yes; that is just what this means.

Mr. MORSE. And every man in the House will favor the repeal of the long and short haul clause.

Mr. STEWART, of Vermont. Let me say to the gentleman from Kansas that that is not what it means. He entirely misapprehends the matter. I undertake to say if the Bland amendment becomes a law and is enforced that the railroad industries of this country will be paralyzed within three months.

Mr. SPRINGER. Paralyzed! Why?

Mr. STEWART, of Vermont. I will tell you. Look at the traffic associations which have been in existence ever since the passage of the interstate-commerce law, and which, as I said before, have the approval of the Interstate Commerce Commission, and without which it can not do its work. They do what? Why, they fix through rates for the traffic from the territory of my friend from Missouri. They fix equable and uniform rates of traffic. The gentleman from Texas says if the trunk-lines from St. Louis agree upon rates which are "just and reasonable" it is not competition.

Mr. CULBERSON, of Texas. On that particular contract.

Mr. STEWART, of Vermont. But the competitive agency enters into the competition at the very start. The gentleman apparently forgets that before the contract is made the traffic agency does the work; and what my friend from Missouri does, if he succeeds in getting his amendment adopted, is to accomplish the destruction of these agencies. What would be the effect of such a provision as that the gentleman proposes to incorporate in the bill? Why, simply to drive out the weak lines or to drive them to the wall. It is the survival of the fittest, and the cat with the longest tail survives.

Why, take the illustration submitted by my friend from Texas [Mr. CULBERSON]. You have the trunk-lines from St. Louis running to some terminal point on the Atlantic, two or three of them, we will suppose, which enter into a combination.

Now, do you say that these three lines shall not make any traffic agreement for the transportation of the products of the State of Missouri from that distributive point? What is the result if you do? You give each one of the roads a right to establish its own rate. I may make an agreement with one to ship my freight at a certain rate, and my friend from Wisconsin may go to another line and pay a somewhat higher rate, and when we go to the market it is just a difference between profit and loss. I gain; he loses. It is the very spirit of discrimination which the interstate-commerce law is designed to meet. It was not so much the destruction of competition, for I know something of the law, because I happened to be a member of the Committee on Commerce which framed it. It was not so much aimed at that or the destruction of it, but was more an effort to secure uniformity of rates, and nothing more. It was to prevent unjust discriminations. Now, what is the effect here?

Mr. BLAND. The sixth section itself prohibited pooling.

Mr. STEWART, of Vermont. I agree with the gentleman that pooling was prohibited; that is a part of the law, and I respect the law while it stands.

Mr. OATES. I would like to ask the gentleman if, in his opinion, the results of the interstate-commerce law have not been somewhat disappointing.

Mr. STEWART, of Vermont. I suppose they have. The trouble with such legislation is that the measure involves so much complicated machinery that it is utterly impossible for any gentlemen to understand it unless they make it a special study. There is nothing in our legislation which equals the complexity of the railroad problem or the railroad system in this country.

That system, Mr. Speaker, is of wonderful development, and on the whole the railroad service in this country has been better performed than in any other country in the world. In the last fifteen years these roads have reduced freight on an average from about 4 cents per ton per mile to less than 1 cent per ton per mile.

Mr. [JOHN M.] FARQUHAR [R., N.Y.]. Is it not true, as a matter of fact, that freight rates and passenger rates in the United States are from 25 to 30 per cent. less than in any other country in the world to-day?

Mr. STEWART, of Vermont. In reply to the question of my friend from New York [Mr. FARQUHAR] I understand, although I have not the precise figures, that there is not any doubt about the fact that the railway service in this country is very much cheaper than any other other [sic]. Now, to go back to my illustration–

Mr. [JOHN] LIND [R., Minn.]. In that connection will the gentleman permit a question which is very simple? Is it not a fact that our trunk lines carry more than three times the volume of trade that any line carries, which you can call a trunk line, on the the continent of Europe?

Mr. STEWART, of Vermont. I suppose that is true. I do not know.

Mr. ANDERSON, of Kansas. And they make more profits.

Mr. LIND. And as a result of their carrying so much more, should not the charge be less?

Mr. STEWART, of Vermont. That result has been brought about by combination in spite of the interstate law; that is, by consolidation. Instead of having a lot of distinct lines, lines have been consolidated. What was the effect? Why, it was to cheapen transportation by lessen⊥ing the expense of administration, and everybody has had the benefit of it. Now, my friend from Missouri [Mr. BLAND] seems to omit the idea, or to forget, that discrimination on two parallel lines in his State, which may be 10 miles apart, in favor of the farmers on one line as against the farmers on another, is just as injurious as discrimination on one line would be if they were all on the same line; and that is precisely what happens unless you permit the railroads to make some adjustment for uniformity of rates.

It is just as clear as the sun in heaven, and no Western man can do a greater injury to the interests he represents than to stand here and advocate a measure by which the hands of railroad men are to be tied so that they can not agree upon uniform rates from the same region. As I said before, the great object of the interstate-commerce law was to prevent unjust discriminations, not only between individuals, but between localities, and the short and long haul clause was put in for the same purpose. When they came along to the end of it they put into the bill the clause against pooling, because it was supposed that that would excite competition and that competition would be greatly beneficial to the country.

Now, let me say right there—and I think I am justified in the statement, and I think every man who has observed the course of events with reference to railroad transportation in this country will bear me out—that a rate war between railroads is absolutely injurious to the community. Why, it can not be otherwise. In the first place the doctrine of fair play requires, and everybody concedes, that the railroads should have a just compensation for their services. We ought not to ask them to do anything for less than will pay the interest on the investment and the running expenses. That is only reasonable and fair, and that is all that this amendment provides for. And yet you propose to throttle these companies so that when a rate war comes, as it will from time to time, it must go on forever.

Rate wars will come. The roads are managed by men subject to like passions as we are, and they have their tantrums and their quarrels and their disagreements. Competition is sharp and strife is tremendous, and they get after one another, and presently there is a rate war, and they do what they did the other day, when they carried people from Chicago to Kansas City for a dollar. Why was that? Simply because the association which had control of the subject of agreeing upon rates among competing lines got into a war, and they were running business at a great loss to themselves and which was of no benefit to anybody.

Mr. BLAND. Is it not possible that they made more money? It has been stated that they carried more people back and forth than they ever had carried at any other time.

Mr. FARQUHAR. That is nonsensical.

Mr. STEWART, of Vermont. I trust to the candor of my friend from Missouri. I think we will admit that a rate war must necessarily be destructive. In the first place, in such a war, the railroads do not make any money. In the next place, it begets the very spirit of discrimination which the law was intended to prevent, because the moment you have a rate war you have the very worst form of discrimination. I get a rate on a thousand barrels of beef from Chicago to New York, and my friend from Missouri gets another rate, and he gets the advantage of me. That is the discrimination which we want to avoid; and of course it begets a spirit of speculation. It demoralizes all business.

If you look at the reports of the Interstate Commerce Commission you will find that nothing is more deprecated than these rate wars. Now, does my friend from Kansas, through whose State there are half a dozen railroads running, say that he is going to permit one road to discriminate against the people on another road, and if they get into a rate war does he say they must stay there eternally? Because that is the effect of this proposed bill, for if they undertake to make a contract to get out of their war that is an illegal contract, because it is a contract which prevents any competition and there will be no end to the war until somebody is absolutely destroyed. Then the fact is that the railroad will recoup its loss some time, so that ultimately the people will have to pay for it. They make the thing even in the long run.

Mr. ANDERSON, of Kansas. Does my friend want an answer to his question?

Mr. STEWART, of Vermont. Yes, if you can answer it.

Mr. ANDERSON, of Kansas. I hold that it is public policy and for the public good that common carriers shall compete with each other, just as merchants do; that if there be a dozen roads in my district, it is for the good of the people in that district that those roads shall not enter into combinations which may prevent competition, and by preventing competition increase the rates; and that is your purpose, to make it protect a monopoly.

Mr. STEWART, of Vermont. I agree to my friend's proposition except the last clause. The only trouble with his proposition is that it has no application to the question before the House. The amendment which my friend from Missouri seeks to thrust into this bill goes too far.

We all agree that we want competition. We all agree that these competitive agencies must exist, but we ought not to agree that it becomes necessary, in order to get justice for a community and preserve the interests that these corporations have in their hands, where an unjust, discriminating, and injurious rate war is going on, that we should tie their hands so that they can not get an adjustment; and that is what you are proposing to do.

Mr. CULBERSON, of Texas. Do I understand the gentleman to hold that the railroad companies of this country now demand a change in the existing law or are not content with the law as it is?

Mr. STEWART, of Vermont. I understand the railroad companies of this country are demanding a relaxation of the law so that they can permit some of your Western roads to exist that some of these gentlemen here represent; and that is not the pooling provision. I think my friend from Missouri [Mr. BLAND] is mistaken as to the character of the bill. If I understand it, it is this: They propose—and they have the approbation of the Interstate Commission—a relaxation of the law so that the strong railroads may give to the weaker competitive roads, and roads that perhaps have a little longer line and fewer facilities for doing business, but which still ought to exist and have business enough to exist, a fair division; that they may make an arrangement for a division of the business, and that they shall receive pay for the proportion of the business they do.

Mr. BLAND. The gentleman is mistaken as to the Interstate Commission acceding to that. On the contrary, they hold that if they make this agreement it is in violation of law, and also without the knowledge or consent of the commission. That is the contest now going on between the railroads and the commission.

Mr. STEWART, of Vermont. I do not understand, if my friend will allow me, that there is a collision with the Interstate Commission and the theory which I am advocating, to wit, that traffic associations may exist for the purpose of making adjustment for through rates.

Now, let me say to my friend—

Mr. LIND. Is not that usually called a traffic arrangement?

Mr. STEWART, of Vermont. That is what it is sometimes called.

Mr. ANDERSON, of Kansas. Is it not in violation of the law?

Mr. STEWART, of Vermont. Oh, no.

Mr. ANDERSON, of Kansas. It is most the subtle and damnable of all forms of pooling.

Mr. STEWART, of Vermont. Now, Mr. Speaker, what was understood as a pool was an arrangement for a division of the earnings upon a certain percentage. That was a pool. It is not a pool in any proper sense of the term which permits trunk lines that are competitors—for instance the four or eight lines from Chicago to New York—to make an arrangement as to the rates instead of having a great confusion and diversity of the rates. Let me say right here, Mr. Speaker, that if the amendment of the gentleman from Missouri [Mr. BLAND] becomes a law it prevents classification. The question of classification enters into the question of competition. He can see, and everybody can see, that if you say that a railroad shall not classify their freight (they agree to that now), why then you introduce an element of confusion which would absolutely paralyze business.

Mr. BLAND. There is nothing about classification in the amendment.

Mr. STEWART, of Vermont. The question of classification of freight has a very practical bearing upon competition in rates; and the whole scale of rates depends on the different classifications. You put an article which would be carried under class 4 at one rate into class 2 at another rate, and then you have competition on that article classified in a different way on another road. So in through traffic. You can not make a through-traffic arrangement but what it would be hit by this amendment of the gentleman from Missouri [Mr. BLAND]. This brings confusion into the transportation between one terminal point and another. You are constantly striking competitive lines; and the shippers want to know exactly what rate they are going to get; and if there is no understanding or agreement about what rates they are going to charge, you are at sea and can not transact your business.

Mr. Speaker, gentlemen are not aware of what would be the effect of hastily determining this subject, which is so complicated a machine, nor can it be determined with as little debate as we have had to-day, when we have comparatively little understanding of the subject. I say this with great respect for my friend from Missouri [Mr. BLAND], who thinks he knows as much about it as I do, and I presume a good deal more.

I think it is a dangerous thing for us to thrust in such a proposition as this, which is entirely new, and which I affirm is against the whole trend of public sentiment in this country.

When everybody is in combination and everybody is doing something to defeat competition, it seems to me a dangerous thing to undertake to set up a new crime here and make it an offense for people to seek to protect these great interests which are so intimately connected with all the commercial, agricultural, and manufacturing interests of the country. I think it is a very dangerous experiment, and I trust the House will not go as far as my friend from Missouri thinks it ought to go.

Mr. HILL. Let me ask the gentleman whether or not the effect of this bill, if it is passed, will not be to take this matter of contracts or agreements between the railroad companies as to rates out of the hands and out of the jurisdiction of the Interstate Commerce Commission?

Mr. STEWART, of Vermont. I think not.

Mr. HILL. Let me call the gentleman's attention to section 7, ⊥ which provides that any person who shall be injured in his business and so on may sue therefor in any circuit court.

⊥5958

Mr. STEWART, of Vermont. There is the same provision in the interstate-commerce law. It is only concurrent jurisdiction.

Mr. HILL. But there is not anything said here to the effect that it is concurrent, and this act is subsequent to the other.

Mr. STEWART, of Vermont. There is nothing there to take away the jusisdiction [sic] of the Interstate Commerce Commission. Everybody who is aggrieved by the rates of freight has a right to go before the Interstate Commerce Commission; there is no doubt anywhere about that.

Mr. HILL. Then why not say so in this bill, as well as say that they may sue in any circuit court?

Mr. STEWART, of Vermont. Well, I was not here when the bill passed. I would have no objection myself to saying it.

Mr. BLAND. I think there is a reservation in the conference report that nothing contained in the act shall be construed to take away any jurisdiction of any State over the same subject-matter.

Mr. STEWART, of Vermont. Yes. Here is what the Interstate Commerce Commission report, written by Judge Cooley, says upon this subject. . . .

The pooling of freights and of railroad earnings, so far as the commission has knowledge or information on the subject, came to an end when the act took effect.

The pooling of earnings—I call the attention of my friend from Kansas [Mr. ANDERSON] to that expression.

But as pooling was only one of several purposes had in view in forming railroad associations, the leading associations have not been dissolved, but have been continued in existence for other objects. Among these objects are the making of regulations for uninterrupted and harmonious railroad communication and exchange of traffic within the territory embraced by their workings. Some regulations in addition to those made by the law are almost, if not absolutely, necessary.[1.373]

There is a recognition of the very form of railway association which this amendment strikes at, because if the amendment means anything it means that the railroads shall be powerless to make any arrangement by which they can avoid the effects of rate wars, the cutting of rates, and unjust discriminations.

Now, I ask, in the interest of my farmer friends in Kansas [laughter]—I have not protested very much about my devotion to the farmers and I have sometimes thought that some of my friends here did protest a little too much on that subject—I have not protested very much, but I say here now, in all sincerity, that it is my most earnest and solemn conviction that no greater injury can be inflicted on the farmers of the West than the passage of an act intended to work the effect which my friend from Missouri [Mr. BLAND] has in view.

I am sorry to differ with him, and I say this with great respect for his intelligence, but it is my sincere conviction. I would rather myself that the whole amendment was stricken out, but I trust that the conference report may receive the sanction of the House. . . .

Mr. ANDERSON, of Kansas. . . .

Now, I hope the House will come back to the proposition before it, which is the question whether the section of the interstate-commerce act relating to pooling shall virtually have its whole pith and force taken out by this Senate amendment or whether the amendment shall be beaten. That is all of it. In the former event it is for the interest of the East and the owners of railroads; in the latter event it is for the interest of cotton-planters, wheat-growers, and men who raise and ship agricultural products. There is the precise issue.

Everybody knows that the interstate-commerce act—the culmination of a ten-year struggle—was passed upon the idea and with the purpose of securing competition between carriers, and of thus providing safeguards against extortionate charges upon the shipper. The whole law was based upon the long-established principle that

---

[1.373] 1 I.C.C. 311 (1887).

competition prevented extortion. The pooling clause especially was based on that principle. Let me read the language of that clause:

> That it shall be unlawful for any common carrier subject to the provisions of this act to enter into any contract, agreement, or combination with any other common carrier or carriers for the pooling of freight of different and competing railroads—

At that time everybody in the country understood the "pooling" of freight to be a generic term. The Interstate Commerce Commission has interpreted it as a specific term. They have applied it to the division of the aggregate earnings of several roads; this they construe to be pooling. But the House in passing that bill certainly understood and believed that it was striking at any and every combination between the carriers of freight for the prevention of competition as to rates. That was what we understood pooling to be and what the country understood it to be; in fact what it was. That this is the correct construction is shown by the clause which succeeds what I have just read—

> or to divide between them the aggregate or net proceeds of the earnings of such railroads or any portion thereof.

The commission interprets this latter clause to be pooling; but if Congress meant the latter clause as a definition of pooling, why in the world did they insert the former clause?

After the passage of the act the railroads ostensibly stopped pooling in one sense, yet they kept up their same "associations," and to-day they have the most effective pool that was ever formed on the continent, namely, that of their freight agents or traffic managers. There is before the Interstate Commerce Commission to-day a case in which it appears that the roads through their freight associations have agreed to charge 16 cents for transporting from Philadelphia to Chicago 100 pounds of tin-plate imported from Liverpool, while the rate on domestic tin from Philadelphia to Chicago is 28 cents. And the same thing applies to other items of transportation. . . .

Mark you that these are the rates charged by each and all of the trunk lines. There is neither difference nor competition between them, the reason being that by some "agreement or combination" through their traffic associations they as completely eliminate competition as if all the roads were owned by one man. It is the perfection of pooling, and every member of the Commerce Commission knows it. Each man of them knows down in his very soul that all the roads are violating the law.

The Senate amendment—and I want the House to understand precisely what it is—justifies, legalizes, and makes permanent this most subtle, infamous, and damnable form of pooling. It says to the presidents of the trunk-line associations, "Hereafter, just as long as you do not charge what you deem an unreasonable rate, you may enter into any combination you please," and by so saying it takes the whole question of regulating rates away from the Interstate Commerce Commission; that commission will then have nothing more to do with rates. Thus the pith is taken out of the anti-pooling clause, and by so doing we ruin the West and the South for the benefit of railway officers, owners, and investors. And gentlemen here will find that the Farmers' Alliance, the Knights of Labor, the great masses of the people who pay these freights, will, as they should, hold responsible any ⊥ man or any party that thus cuts the throat of that interstate-commerce clause with respect to pooling.

The House amendment made unlawful—

> Every contract or agreement entered into for the purpose of preventing competition in the transportation of persons or property from one State or Territory into another—

This the Senate exactly reverses by adding—

> so that the rates of such transportation may be raised above what is just and reasonable.

The gentleman from Vermont lays great stress upon the point that so long as the rates are not raised above what is just and reasonable it is all right. Who is to determine that? The court. What has the commission to do with it? Nothing. But, gentlemen, that is not the only crime daily committed by the roads; the crime is not simply in charging over and above what is just and reasonable, as every one of them does; the crime is that of a conspiracy between competing lines to bleed and fleece the people. That is the great crime.

Mr. STEWART, of Vermont. Do they "bleed the people" if they do not charge more than is just and reasonable?

Mr. ANDERSON, of Kansas. Yes, if they combine to do it. There are two crimes to which this legislation refers. One is robbery, where the roads charge more than is just and reasonable; the other is conspiracy, where they agree together to rob the people. And I would like to see the president and officers of any railroad that does so put in the penitentiary for life. [Laughter.]

I hope the House will not be misled by all the talk of my friend from Vermont on different topics from understanding exactly what is before it. I tell you, gentlemen—and I would like to ring it out with a clarion voice to all the people of the nation if I could—in my belief the welfare and prosperity of this country are more at stake on the defeat of this amendment than on the tariff bill, the silver bill, or any other legislation which has come or will come before this Congress. I never yet knew the time when the Senate did not get in a little railroad "deal" somewhere in a conference report; that is what they are for. [Laughter.] And they have got their work in here magnificently. They, by this flank legislation, repeal the interstate-commerce law in effect; and I am sorry that my friend from Vermont should have given his consent to any such proposition.

Mr. Speaker, this is a question that directly affects three-fourths of the people of the United States, and indirectly it affects the other fourth. The question is whether the people shall be protected by the safeguard of competition between carriers, as they are by competition between merchants, or whether we shall legalize combinations so that the railroads may hereafter charge whatever they see fit in defiance of common law and justice.

The gentleman from Vermont talks about "indiscriminate competition" between railroads. What about "indiscriminate competition" between merchants, or between lawyers, or between doctors, or between mechanics?

Does anybody say you should pass a law preventing "indiscriminate competition" between merchants? Not at all. But when these high and holy railroad millionaires come here—these men who allege themselves to have put money into a road when they really put in only "water," this greatest and most fateful of all trusts before whom New England and the East bow down and worship as a slave a master—when they come up here urging their interests, then for some mysterious reason we are called upon to legalize their pools, to "regulate" competition between them lest they hurt each other, to abolish the little law we have against them and which the commission does not enforce or execute.

The gentleman from Vermont has said outright that pooling must and will be legalized. If so, then the law which does it will deliver over to the roads all shippers, bound hand and foot. It will never be enacted; or, if it is, the men who enact it never will and never ought to be re-elected. The trouble to-day is not in the law, but in the fact that the commission which was created to enforce the law does not enforce it. Until the last Congress they said they lacked the legal power so to do. By an amendment of mine that power was given them, and the Attorney-General was required to prosecute any case they reported to him. The commission has power on its own motion to proceed against any offending road. Every man on it knows that every road in the United States is daily violating the law, and yet if any legal proceedings have been instituted I never heard of them. There is the trouble. The commission was intended to be an executive rather than a judicial agent, and it is paid by the people of the United States to do its sworn duty. That it is not doing it nobody knows half so well as do the railroad companies. . . .

Mr. HILL. Mr. Speaker, in the short time allowed me to talk upon this bill and the amendments I shall hardly have time to touch upon more than one or two of them. There are two points to which I wish to call the attention of the committee directly and sharply, and first as to the meaning and effect of this new section that has been reported from the conference committee, section 2. I have a copy of that section in my hand. It provides that every contract or agreement entered into for the purpose of preventing competition in the transportation of persons or property from one State or Territory into another, so that the rates of such transportation may be raised above what is just and reasonable, shall be deemed unlawful.

Now, the practical effect of this proposition if enacted into a law is to legalize in the first instance and *prima facie* all contracts or agreements between railroad companies relating to rates of transportation. In the first instance they are made *prima facie* lawful, and the party contesting them—of course the railroads themselves who enter into these contracts will not contest—the private individual contesting them must go into the courts, and there at his own expense, after years of litigation running through all the courts, from the circuit to the Supreme Court of the United States, find out as best he can from judicial authority whether or not those rates are reasonable and just.

Mr. [JOHN A.] PICKLER [R., S.D.]. He had better be dead than have to do that.

Mr. HILL. You can readily see what a burden that would impose upon an individual, what a risk he would take upon himself, and how reluctant he would be to enter upon an investigation of that kind at his own expense. The practical result would be that, except in very exceptional cases, where great interests were at stake and where those interests could be combined to foot the bill, no such contest would be made, and these contracts and combinations thus legalized and entered into between the railroad companies would be the law of the land. And if, perchance, such a case should pass from the circuit to the Supreme Court and finally be adjudged against the railroad companies, all the railroad companies would have to do would be to enter into a new combination, a new arrangement, or a new contract, and then run that contract or that combination for a series of years until some other poor man could test it through all the courts to a decision in the Supreme Court of the United States. The practical effect of this is to place this matter of railroad rates almost exclusively in the hands of the railroad companies.

Mr. STEWART, of Vermont. It is there now.

Mr. HILL. The gentleman says it is there now.

Mr. STEWART, of Vermont. And always will be.

Mr. HILL. The gentleman is mistaken.

Mr. STEWART, of Vermont. Do they not fix the rates?

Mr. HILL. So far as the individual railroad is concerned, that is true, and it is also true that the Supreme Court of the United States has decided that there is no right to fix a rate that is unjust or unreasonable; so that each individual railroad company can fix its rates, but they can not do it by combining or by contract or agreement between themselves. There is no law now under which they can enter into such a contract. They are the creatures of the statute. They can do nothing except what the statute will authorize them to do, and they can not enter into any such contract or agreement between themselves either for the purpose of putting up or putting down, or controlling railroad rates unless the law expressly authorizes them to do that.

Now, another point. I call the gentleman's attention to section 7 of this act, which provides in substance that any person feeling himself aggrieved by violations of this statute, or assumed violations of this statute, on the part of any other person or corporation, may go into the circuit court and there test the matter, and if he recovers, he is entitled to recover threefold the damages sustained and an attorney's fee. Now, I submit this subsequent act having provided that the person aggrieved may go into the circuit court and there test his rights, whether the legal effect of that is not to take away the jurisdiction of the Interstate Commerce Commission over these railroads as affecting the question of rights. . . .

. . . At any rate, that is a matter that ought to be explained. If, as suggested by the chairman of this committee, it means that it is not to take away the jurisdiction of the Interstate Commerce Commission, an amendment should be ingrafted upon this act to that effect, to make plain what at least in the opinion of every lawyer upon this floor must be regarded uncertain. In my judgment this remedy provided here would be regarded as exclusive in the eye of the law, as an implied repeal or revocation of the right of the individual to go before the Interstate Commerce Commission and there have a rate revised and passed upon by the commission.

I believe, Mr. Chairman, that is all that I wish to say upon this question in the limited time at my command. . . .

Mr. BLAND. Mr. Speaker, I will state in closing this debate that it was rather a strange spectacle that the bill should pass the Senate without any opposition whatever. It did not seem to tread on any one's toes. Nobody seemed to resist it; no interest seemed to be affected; no one seemed to think it was going to touch him at all. It came to the House. It was about to pass the House. Everybody was ready to vote for it; no one seemed to be opposed to it; and by general consent the House was about to pass the bill that was to denounce, check, and punish all the combines and trusts in the country, railroads or otherwise, and there was not a railroad or a trust that ever resisted its passage or had made any contest against it.

But the moment two simple amendments got into this bill; the very moment that a legislative declaration was put in the bill, so that no one could misunderstand its purpose, providing that where property was transported from one State to be sold in another State it was an article of interstate commerce and the courts were to protect it from combines and monopolies, then there seemed to be an interest taken in it. That was the first amendment I offered, and it was put into the bill.

The next amendment offered was that any transportation company or companies that entered into an agreement to prevent competition in the transportation of persons or property from one State or Territory into another should be considered as having made an unlawful agreement under this bill. We were doing that by legislative enactment and not referring it to the courts for judicial interpretation. The very moment these expressions came into this bill, covering the whole subject of trusts, and pointing out what was desired to be declared illegal, then we have a contest, of course.

The amendments go to the Senate, and what do they do? They strike out entirely the first proposition—that where property is transported from one State to be sold in another State it shall be protected from these trusts and combines till its first sale. That went out entirely, and they left all these trusts and combines intact. Gentlemen, that is the true situation. What did they do with the other proposition? They simply convert it from a declaration on the part of Congress that transportation companies should compete with each other into a declaration that they may agree not to compete, and there is the contention.

We provide that where any transportation companies enter into contracts or agreement to prevent competition, such contracts shall be illegal; that they shall be declared illegal and unlawful by law. Why, I had supposed in my simplicity that the idea of building railroads throughout the country was that we might have competition. The common people of this country have so regarded it. They have regarded every new railroad as a blessing, because it tended to compete with other roads, and thereby to cheapen transportation, but this amendment has been converted by the Senate into a legalization of agreements made on the part of transportation companies of this country to prevent competition among themselves. The whole tenor of it has been changed. Now, Mr. Speaker, I hope the House will insist upon its amendment and not recede from it. If we are to have a trust bill let us have one, and not a sham, for, as I stated before, here are two propositions that are contested and that reach the whole matter, and if this House will stand upon this proposition we can enact it into law. . . .

Mr. MASON. Mr. Speaker, all legislation is the outgrowth of the wish of the people. There came a time in the history of this country when the interstate-commerce law had to be enacted. It was passed by both Houses of Congress, approved by the President, and it touched upon all of the questions in which the shippers were interested. The gentleman from Missouri [Mr. BLAND] congratulates himself that he was enabled to put an amendment to this Senate bill which has placed us in the position in which we are now. I think the gentleman is not to be congratulated upon that point. The Senator from Ohio [Mr. SHERMAN], in response to the unanimous wish of the people of this country, desired to introduce and pass some legislation which would strike a blow at the trusts and monopolies which "corner" the necessaries of life, and which have constantly, as our Democratic brethren tell us, taken advantage of the tariff laws for their own advantage, and he drew a bill which, in my judgment, is as perfect as any that could have been drawn in the present state of affairs.

That bill, as the gentleman from Missouri [Mr. BLAND] has said, passed the Senate; and, while I do not question the motives of the gentleman from Missouri, there are gentlemen upon the other side of the House, judging from the speeches made here, who desire to defeat this anti-trust bill, so called; and certainly there is no more need of including a clause here in regard to the interstate-commerce law than there is of inserting a clause in regard to the Ten Commandments. Interstate commerce is controlled by the interstate-commerce statute, and if the gentleman is acting in good faith and wants to amend that law, why not introduce his bill for that purpose, refer it to the proper committee, and let it come here through the proper channels? But when the Republican party are in possession of both the House and the Senate, and after they take care of the pooling interests, so called, of the railroad companies, by previous legislation prohibiting pooling, the moment they present a bill which strikes a substantial blow at the trusts of the country, which are not covered by the interstate-commerce law, the gentleman from Missouri [Mr. BLAND] injects into that bill, which is intended for the benefit of the whole people, something not analagous to the bill, something not germane to the bill, something which Congress has already attempted to deal with by other legislation, and so by his amendment has put us in a position where, by conference and reconference, consideration and reconsideration, the people may be deprived of legitimate legislation upon this subject. . . .

Mr. BLAND. The gentleman protested in the beginning that he did not doubt my motives and then proceeded to question them.

Mr. MASON. I say now I do not doubt them; but I say the effect of your action is to create antagonism against a bill which the people of this country have called for and which the Democratic party for years refused to introduce and pass.

In your Democratic House you had a resolution[1.374] before your committee in regard to these trusts; for six months you took evidence; you paid $10,000 attorneys' fees in that case; but you never gave us a bill or resolution. The moment that Republican Representatives in a Republican Congress, taking care of the commerce and the commercial laws of the country, introduce resolutions or bills to relieve the people from the oppression of combinations and trusts you proceed to inject amendments which in effect may defeat the legislation.

Mr. BLAND. The gentleman represents Chicago, where the "Big Four" reside.

Mr. MASON. I presume there is no one here who does not know that I live in Chicago. If the gentleman wants to get that fact in the RECORD he is welcome to do so. I am proud of Chicago, as I wish the gentleman were of the great State of Missouri.

Mr. BLAND. My State is so far ahead that you ought to be proud of her.

Mr. MASON. I hope this does not come out of my time.

Mr. Speaker I want to be understood. I am willing to vote for this conference report, if I have to vote for it. It is not my preference. I prefer the bill as it came from the Senate in its simple form. Let us have a bill declaring in effect that all combinations against the peace, good-will, and prosperity of the country are illegal. If the gentleman from Missouri tries to insert in a conference report upon such a bill an amendment in regard to silver or in regard to the pooling by railroads or any other matter already covered by legislation, I think this House ought to refuse to concur in any such report and send it back with instructions to bring in a bill in simple form embracing one single branch of legislation.

Gentlemen here can understand what may be the effect of introducing into this legislation these subjects which do not properly belong here. Judging from the remarks of my friend from Minnesota [Mr. LIND], I infer that he and I represent a large number of members on ⊥ this floor who do not care, in connection with this bill, to ⊥5961 vote on the interstate-commerce law directly or indirectly. We are willing to leave it as it is. We are willing to have the Interstate Commerce Commissioners or the Committees on Commerce of the two Houses pass in the ordinary way upon any proposed amendment to that law. But the gentleman from Kansas [Mr. ANDERSON] and

---

[1.374] House Resolution Authorizing the Committee on Manufactures to Investigate Trusts, 50th Cong., 1st Sess., 19 CONG. REC. 719 (1888), reprinted *supra* at 53.

the gentleman from Missouri [Mr. BLAND], if we were considering the adoption of the Ten Commandments as a moral code or if we were attending the wedding ceremony of a friend, would be ready to stop to attend to the hanging of a railroad official.

It is all very well that the railroad law should be amended at the proper time, and perhaps it ought to be amended; I will help you to adopt any necessary amendment. But why inject such legislation into a bill of this kind which the people of the country have demanded ever since these trusts and combinations took possession of us? We have an anti-pooling clause in the interstate-commerce law—

Mr. ANDERSON, of Kansas. Is the gentleman addressing me?

Mr. MASON. I am addressing the whole House. The gentleman may take my remarks to himself if they fit.

Mr. ANDERSON, of Kansas. The gentleman looked at me.

Mr. MASON. The gentleman is so handsome I can not look at anybody else when he is here. [Laughter.]

Mr. ANDERSON, of Kansas. I will answer you if you want an answer.

Mr. MASON. I will telegraph you if I want you.

Mr. ANDERSON, of Kansas. Do not fail to prepay the message.

Mr. MASON. Mr. Speaker, let me occupy one moment further in restating my position. Let us have a vote upon the original bill, which declares that "every combination, in the form of trust or otherwise, or conspiracy, in restraint of trade or commerce among the several States, or with foreign nations, is hereby declared to be illegal." Let us send this matter back to the conference committee, and let them take out everything affecting subjects which we have undertaken to cover by other laws passed by previous Congresses. Let us vote upon the simple proposition of the Senator from Ohio, passed by the Senate, and substantially agreed to by every Republican in this House. . . .

Mr. [JOHN F.] LACEY [R., Iowa]. Mr. Speaker, there is one feature of this conference report to which the attention of the House has not been called. There is danger of Congress legislating upon the question of trusts without making any reservation to the States of their right to legislate upon these trusts when they are local in their character. This was not provided for in the original bill. I suggested to the conference committee the introduction of an amendment reserving to the States the power to enforce such laws on this subject, local in their character, as they might deem proper. That amendment is embraced in the bill as now reported. It has not been referred to in this discussion, because I believe the gentleman in charge of the conference report thinks it is not really necessary.

It seems to me, sir, that this reservation ought to be distinctly made. In giving to the country Congressional legislation on the subject of trusts, we ought not to endanger the local legislation such as Missouri and Iowa have adopted. We ought not to place the courts in the position of being able to say, in construing our local laws, "Congress has acted on this subject; the jurisdiction of Congress is exclusive; it has passed a trust bill; whether adequate or not, it is not for us to say, but it is at any rate exclusive; and the statutes of the States with refenceg [sic] to trusts are thereby entirely superseded." I think, whatevererisla-eltion [sic] we may adopt on this subject, this reservation of the authority of the States ought to be preserved. I desired simply to call attention to this matter, as it seems to have been overlooked. . . .

Mr. [HENRY C.] McCORMICK [R., Pa.]. The gentleman will concede the power of Congress extends only to interstate commerce?

Mr. LACEY. Certainly.

Mr. McCORMICK. Then, if that be so, how can this legislation affect local trusts?

Mr. LACEY. In this way: It is grounded on the interstate-commerce law. When the articles which are the subject of commerce reach a State and come within the regulations of the State, the trust in them is controlled by the State; but this bill, attempting through commerce to follow them into the State, would control the trust, and may have force enough to control the local or State laws on that subject. At all events it is wise to put in a reservation to place that beyond question.

Mr. STEWART, of Vermont. I do not desire to add to anything that has been said except simply to call the attention of some gentlemen to the provisions of the interstate-commerce act. I understood the gentleman from Illinois [Mr. HILL], my friend from

Kansas [Mr. ANDERSON] also, and other gentlemen to express some doubts as to the jurisdiction of the Interstate Commerce Commission. It is perfectly clear from an examination of that act that no railroad can put itself outside the operation of the provisions of that act. The language of the first section is that all common carriers engaged in such business are subject to the provisions of the act. Every member knows that all contracts between corporations shall be subject to these provisions, and no railroad shall lay any unjust rates; and the same act gives jurisdiction to the circuit courts, as in this case. So there is no question of the jurisdiction.

Now, Mr. Speaker, I desire to add one word.

Personally, I should prefer that the House recede from its amendment and that the Senate also recede from its amendment, and let us pass the trust bill, because, as has been said by the gentleman from Illinois, this provision is not at all germane to the original bill. It deals with an entirely different subject. It confuses the interstate-commerce matter, which is a separate and distinct subject in our statutes, with the matter of trusts; and it would be better, if any legislation was had or is necessary, that it should be entirely independent. Personally, therefore, I do not desire that the report of the conference committee should be sustained, provided the House entertains the same idea I do in regard to the general question. . . .

. . . I ask unanimous consent that the vote be taken immediately after the reading of the Journal to-morrow; and I now move the previous question upon the report.

The SPEAKER *pro tempore* (Mr. PAYSON). The debate is exhausted under the order of the House, and so the Chair thinks that motion would be unnecessary. But the Chair thinks the request for unanimous consent would be proper.

The gentleman from Vermont asks unanimous consent that the vote be postponed to-night and made the first thing in order after the reading of the Journal in the morning. Is there objection?

There was no objection, and it was so ordered.

HOUSE DEBATE
51st Cong., 1st Sess.
June 12, 1890

21 CONG. REC. 5981

The SPEAKER. The first matter before the House is the conference report which was under consideration yesterday evening. The Clerk will read the title of the bill.

The Clerk read as follows:

A bill (S. 1) to protect trade and commerce against unlawful restraints and monopolies. . . .

The SPEAKER. The question recurs upon the adoption of the conference report.
The question was taken; and on a division there were—ayes 12, noes 115.
So the conference report was rejected.
Mr. STEWART, of Vermont. I rise to a parliamentary inquiry.
The SPEAKER. The gentleman will state it.
Mr. STEWART, of Vermont. Would it not be in order at this stage of the proceedings to move that the House recede from its original amendments?
The SPEAKER. The Chair thinks it would be in order.
Mr. STEWART, of Vermont. Then I make the motion that the House recede from its original amendments. . . .
Mr. [EDWARD P.] ALLEN [R., Mich.]. A parliamentary inquiry, Mr. Speaker. If the motion of the gentleman from Vermont is carried, does it leave the bill as it came from the Senate?
The SPEAKER. In the opinion of the Chair it leaves the bill as it came from the Senate.

Mr. SPRINGER. Mr. Speaker—

The SPEAKER. One moment. The Chair desires to examine the matter. [After a pause.] The Chair desires to call the attention of the gentleman from Vermont to the exact situation. The House passed an amendment to the Senate bill; thereupon the bill was returned to the Senate, and the Senate passed an amendment to the House amendment and asked for a conference. The Senate having amended the House amendment, it would not be competent for the House to withdraw its original amendment by recession.

Mr. STEWART, of Vermont. Then, Mr. Speaker, I desire to make another parliamentary inquiry. Would it be in order to move for a further conference with instruction to the conferees on the part of the House to withdraw the House amendment?

The SPEAKER. It would be in order.

Mr. STEWART, of Vermont. I make that motion. . . .

⊥5982 ⊥ The SPEAKER. The gentleman from Vermont moves that the House insist on its disagreement to the Senate amendment to the House amendment and ask for a committee of conference, and that the conferees on the part of the House be instructed to withdraw the House amendment or to propose a recession from the House amendment.

Mr. [JAMES B.] McCREARY [D., Ky.]. And on that the gentleman from Vermont moves the previous question.

The SPEAKER. On that the gentleman moves the previous question. If the previous question should be ordered the vote will then come directly upon the proposition of the gentleman from Vermont. If it be not ordered, then his proposition will be open to amendment.

Mr. BLAND. Let us have the amendments read before we vote.

The SPEAKER. The Chair thinks that the amendments should be reported so that the House may understand what it is voting upon. The Clerk will read first the original House amendment, then the Senate amendment thereto.

The Clerk read as follows:

After line 10 insert as section 2 the following:

"Every contract or agreement entered into for the purpose of preventing competition in the sale or purchase of any commodity transported from one State or Territory to be sold in another, or so contracted to be sold, or to prevent competition in the transportation of persons or property from one State or Territory into another, shall be deemed unlawful within the meaning of this act: *Provided,* That the contracts herein enumerated shall not be construed to exclude any other contract or agreement declared unlawful in this act."

The Senate proposed to amend the House amendment as follows:

Strike out in lines 2, 3, and 4 of said amendment the words "competition in the sale or purchase of any commodity transported from one State or Territory to be sold in another or so contracted to be sold, or to prevent."

After the word "another," in line 5 of said amendment, insert "so that the rates of such transportation may be raised above what is just and reasonable."

Strike out all after "act," in line 6 of said amendment, down to and including "act" in line 8; so that the amendment of the House as amended will read:

"Every contract or agreement entered into for the purpose of preventing competition in the transportation of persons or property from one State or Territory into another, so that the rates of such transportation may be raised above what is just and reasonable, shall be deemed unlawful within the meaning of this act."

The SPEAKER. The gentleman from Vermont demands the previous question on his motion.

The question being taken on ordering the previous question, there were—ayes 82, nays 95.

Mr. STEWART, of Vermont. I call for the yeas and nays.

The yeas and nays were ordered, 53 voting in favor thereof.

The question was taken; and it was decided in the affirmative—yeas 110, nays 97, not voting 120; as follows: . . .

So the previous question was ordered. . . .

⊥5983 ⊥ The SPEAKER. The question recurs on the motion of the gentleman from

Vermont that the House ask a further conference, and instruct its conferees to recede from the House amendment. . . .

The yeas and nays were ordered.

The question was taken; and there were—yeas 106, nays 98, not voting 123; as follows: . . .

So the motion of Mr. STEWART, of Vermont, was agreed to.

HOUSE DEBATE
51st Cong., 1st Sess.
June 14, 1890

21 CONG. REC. 6099

The SPEAKER announced the appointment of Mr. EZRA B. TAYLOR, Mr. STEWART of Vermont, and Mr. BLAND as the House conferees on the disagreeing votes of the two Houses on the bill (S. 1) to declare unlawful trusts and combinations in restraint of trade and production.

Mr. BLAND. Mr. Speaker, inasmuch as the House has instructed the conferees to recede from the House amendment, I take no further interest in the conference and would prefer that the Chair should appoint some one else.

The SPEAKER. The gentleman from Missouri [Mr. BLAND] asks to be excused from serving as one of the House conferees on Senate bill 1, the trust bill. Is there objection?

There was no objection.

The SPEAKER appointed Mr. CULBERSON of Texas instead of Mr. BLAND.

SENATE DEBATE
51st Cong., 1st Sess.
June 16, 1890

21 CONG. REC. 6116

The PRESIDENT *pro tempore* laid before the Senate the action of the House of Representatives on the bill (S. 1) to protect trade and commerce against unlawful restraints and monopolies; which was read, as follows:

Resolved, That the House disagree to the report of the committee of conference on the disagreeing votes of the two Houses on the amendment of the House to the bill (S. 1) to protect trade and commerce against unlawful restraints and monopolies.

Resolved, That the House further insist on its disagreement to the amendment of the Senate to the amendment of the House to the bill (S. 1) to protect trade and commerce against unlawful restraints and monopolies, and ask for a further conference, with instructions that the House conferees recede from the original amendment of the House.

Ordered, That Mr. E. B. TAYLOR, Mr. STEWART of Vermont, and Mr. CULBERSON of Texas be the managers at the further conference on the part of the House.

Mr. EDMUNDS. I move that the Senate further insist upon its amendment to the House amendment and agree to the conference asked by the other House.

In making that motion I wish to say a word. It has been stated, and appears to have been believed in some quarters, that the Senate amendment to the House amendment had the effect to repeal or modify the provision of the interstate-commerce law prohibiting pooling. I wish to say (I think I may safely say it for all the members of the Committee on the Judiciary, certainly for myself) that the amendment as reported from the Committee on the Judiciary had no such effect whatever, and that it is impossible for anybody who looks at the whole section as it would read amended to imagine any such thing. I think it is due to the House of Representatives and the Senate to say that.

I have seen it stated, Mr. President, in a newspaper (and that is the only way I can allude to it, and that is all that I have a right to know about it) that the Senate amendment was got through the Senate by the influence of railways and corporations, and that the Senate was given to that sort of influence, and not much else could be expected from it in that behalf. I wish to recall to the attention of the Senate that every piece of important legislation in the last ten years or more that has affected great corporations and important interests has been the work, so far as I remember, in the outset, of the Senate of the United States. The bill which brought the Pacific railroads into some sort of obedience to the laws of the United States, and some sort of sense of their obligations in respect of what was due the United States, was the work of the Senate. The interstate-commerce bill was a Senate bill, although I believe the House had a bill of the same character as well. It is, therefore, entirely unjust for anybody to say anywhere (and perhaps I dignify it a little too much by alluding to it at all) that any act of the Senate or any act of any Senator can be referred to at any time which would justify what I have seen in the newspapers.

It may be further said, Mr. President, in respect of this very amendment of the Senate, which the House of Representatives has now disagreed to and proposes to recede entirely from its own amendment and leave the bill as it passed the Senate originally, that the very force, and the only force that I have known to be exerted—and I have known of it—has been a somewhat organized and persistent and powerful effort on the part of railroad and other corporations through well-known agents and influences (well known to me) to induce simple-minded persons somewhere—I am unable to say where, of course—to defeat the Senate amendment and to mislead those persons into opposition to it by betraying them into the false position that they were defending the people in defeating an amendment which the railroads did not want; and the railroads and other corporations appear to have accomplished their purpose.

Now, if the newspapers think they are doing any public good under such a state of things, which everybody outside of the newspapers knows perfectly well, by imputing to the Senate a subserviency to railroad or corporate influence in respect to this amendment, or indeed any other, speaking particularly now of this which is up, and are not wise enough and bright enough to see that the scheme of these great corporations is brought to bear upon people who do not know any better, to fire them up with the idea that the railroads do want it and get them to vote against it, when, as I say, to my personal knowledge the exertion of very potent but ineffectual railway influence with me and with others that I know of has been tried, but it was to accomplish exactly the thing that the House of Representatives, not subservient I suppose to railroads, but hungry for the public good, has done.

I think myself that this amendment of the House was wholly unnecessary, but the original bill as it passed the Senate was adequate to cover every case over which Congress had power, and broad enough to include every case of wrongdoing of any kind of that nature. So if the House of Representatives, led or misled by railway influence, wishes to retreat from its position altogether, I do not know that I shall have any objection; but I thought it due to the Senate and to the committee to say thus much.

Mr. [ALGERNON S.] PADDOCK [R., Neb.]. I should like to ask the Senator from Vermont what section of the interstate-commerce act it is proposed by this bill to amend?

Mr. EDMUNDS. Not any section.

Mr. PADDOCK. Ah!

Mr. EDMUNDS. It was an effect, it was said.

Mr. VEST. Mr. President, when the trust bill, as it is called, was pending before the Judiciary Committee prior to its being reported to the Senate, I was under the impression that the bill could have been made much more effective and valuable in the direction which all of us were pursuing if an additional section had been put to it specifically attacking the practice of destroying competition in the rates of transportation as to interstate commerce. A majority of my colleagues upon that committee were under the impression that the bill without that provision was sufficiently stringent, and I yielded my opinion to theirs upon that subject. The courts must at last construe this bill, because we are entering upon a new and untried field of legislation, and I was under the impression that the courts would construe the original bill as being sufficiently effective in prohibiting those pooling arrangements by which the prices of transportation to the people at large were kept up to ruinous and dangerous rates.

When the bill went to the House of Representatives a provision was put upon it, crudely drawn, imperfect in its language, but the object of which was to strike specifically at the evil; and when it came back to the Senate I was under the impression that with a modification of that provision as to its language and structure the amendment ought to be adopted. It could not possibly, in my judgment, have done any harm, and it might have done a vast amount of good. The Committee on the Judiciary came to the conclusion that the amendment of the House was unnecessary. I was appointed one of the conferees, but was unable to agree with the other two conferees on the part of the Senate in the conclusions which were reached. I am under the impression that the following provision, which I intended, if opportunity had come, to have offered in the Senate, would strengthen the bill:

> Every contract, combination in the form of trust or otherwise, or conspiracy entered into for the purpose of preventing competition in the sale or purchase of any commodity while the subject of interstate commerce, or to prevent competition in the transportation of persons or property from any State or Territory to another, or from any State or Territory to the District of Columbia, or from the District of Columbia to any State or Territory, except such contracts or agreements in regard to transportation as may be approved by the Interstate Commerce Commission, shall be deemed unlawful within the meaning of this act. Nothing herein shall be deemed or held to impair the powers of the several States in respect of any of the matters in this act mentioned.

If that amendment had been placed upon the bill, in my opinion it would have put the meaning of this legislation beyond any question. It would have made a salient issue between a great evil which now exists in this country and the Congress of the United States representing the people. It goes without saying, with our knowledge of the present transportation system of the United States, that railroad companies do by combination, unlawfully, in my opinion, fix the price of rates to suit themselves, without regard to the public at large or to the consumers of the country. If our bill with all its provisions be worth anything, it is to strike down that sort of unlawful conspiracy against the people of the United States. As I said before, sir, I hope that the courts will construe the original bill as sufficient to do away with this monstrous evil, but it is certainly to be desired that Congress should be so explicit on the subject as to their intent in this legislation that there can be no question in regard to their intent.

Now, Mr. President, in regard to what has been said in another part of this Capitol as to the influence of railroads upon our legislation, to which the Senator from Vermont, the chairman of our committee, has alluded, I have this to say: As a matter of course it would be undignified and unparliamentary to indulge in recrimination in reply to such statements as these, but I can not resist the temptation of saying that within my personal knowledge one bill has passed the Senate repeatedly, a bill which simply provided for the government of a public park belonging to the people of the United States, and when that bill has gone to the House of Representatives it has been repeatedly defeated because the Senate would not agree that a railroad corporation should be permitted to construct its railroad through that park. If railroad influences be potent in this Capitol, there is a glaring and conspicuous example of the iron hand of corporations grasping the legislation of this country for their own private purposes.

I was never approached about this subject except, after the amendment of the House had been adopted, by a friend connected with a large railroad system in the

United States, who objected to that amendment because he said it would prevent railroads from making legitimate rates by agreement as between themselves. My reply to him then was, and my reply now is, that there never has been known a case in which railroads ever combined except for their own benefit. It is safe to assume, without making any attack upon them, that there are no interests in this country so well provided for by the exertions of their attorneys and the influence of their wealth, by their appeals to sectional and other interests, as the railroad companies in this country. It will always be so, and it is, in my judgement, impossible that the Congress of the United States inside of the Constitution can go far enough to make any of their legislation immoderate or unjust when we are attempting to protect the interests of the people. . . .

The PRESIDENT *pro tempore*. The question is on the motion of the Senator from Vermont that the Senate still further insist upon its amendment to the amendment of the House and agree to the request for a further conference thereon. It is a privileged question. The Senator from Texas has the floor.

Mr. REAGAN. I merely wanted to inquire if it would not be better to have the report printed. Then we can be able to see it. It is a very important matter, and I think we ought to be able to know what we are voting on, as certainly we do not now.

Mr. EDMUNDS. All we are voting on now is simply to agree to the request of the House of Representatives to have further conference on the subject.

Mr. REAGAN. Very well.

The PRESIDENT *pro tempore*. The question is on the motion of the Senator from Vermont.

The motion was agreed to.

By unanimous consent, the President *pro tempore* was authorized to appoint the managers of the further conference on the part of the Senate, and Mr. EDMUNDS, Mr. HOAR, and Mr. VEST were appointed.

SECOND CONFERENCE REPORT AND SENATE DEBATE
51st Cong., 1st Sess.
June 18, 1890

21 CONG. REC. 6208

TRUSTS AND COMBINATIONS.

Mr. EDMUNDS submitted the following report:

The committee of conference on the disagreeing votes of the two Houses on the amendment of the Senate to the amendment of the House of Representatives to the bill (S. 1) to protect trade and commerce against unlawful restraints and monopolies, having met, after full and free conference have agreed to recommend and do recommend to their respective Houses as follows:

That both Houses recede from their respective amendments.

GEORGE F. EDMUNDS,
GEORGE F. HOAR,
Managers on the part of the Senate.
E. B. TAYLOR,
J. W. STEWART,
D. B. CULBERSON,
Managers on the part of the House.

The report was concurred in.

SECOND CONFERENCE REPORT AND HOUSE DEBATE
51st Cong., 1st Sess.
June 20, 1890

21 CONG. REC. 6312

Mr. STEWART, of Vermont. Mr. Speaker, I desire to submit the following conference report. . . .

The SPEAKER. The Clerk will read the conference report.

The Clerk read as follows:

The committee of conference on the disagreeing votes of the two Houses on the amendment of the House of Representatives to the bill (S. 1) to protect trade and commerce against unlawful restraints and monopolies, having met, after full and free conference have agreed to recommend and do recommend to their respective Houses as follows:

That both Houses recede from their respective amendments.

E. B. TAYLOR,
J. W. STEWART,
D. B. CULBERSON,
Managers on the part of the House of Representatives.
GEO. F. EDMUNDS,
GEO. F. HOAR,
Managers on the part of the Senate.

The statement submitted by the House conferees was read, as follows:

STATEMENT.

The committee of conference on the part of the House on the disagreeing votes of the two Houses on the amendment of the House of Representatives to the bill (S. 1) to protect trade and commerce against unlawful restraints and monopolies submit the following statement:

The report recommends recession by the House from the House amendment and by the Senate from the Senate amendment to the House amendment.

The adoption of the report therefore leaves the bill as it passed the Senate.

J. W. STEWART, *For House Conferees.*

Mr. BLAND. Now, Mr. Speaker, I raise the question of consideration, in order to go to the Speaker's table and take up the silver bill.

Mr. STEWART, of Vermont. On that question I demand the yeas and nays.

The SPEAKER. The question is: Will the House now consider the conference report; and on that the gentleman from Vermont demands the yeas and nays.

The yeas and nays were ordered.

The question was taken; and it was decided in the affirmative—yeas 144, nays 103, not voting 80; as follows: . . .

So the House determined to consider the conference report. . . .

Mr. STEWART, of Vermont. Mr. Speaker, the statement submitted with the conference report is perhaps all that is necessary in order to give the information desired by the House, and as the conference report submits the question to the House it stands upon the Senate bill as it came originally to the House, which gentlemen perhaps will remember as a bill against trusts and combinations. Its provisions are very general and sweeping, and perhaps cover the whole ground. Inasmuch as the amendments made by the House to the Senate bill and the Senate amendment to that amendment are all withdrawn by the conference and inasmuch as these amendments were discussed at considerable length the other day, unless some gentleman desires further debate, I shall ask for a vote on the adoption of the report. . . .

Mr. CULBERSON, of Texas. Mr. Speaker, I desire to state to the House that I rise simply to state that we agree to this report because it is in compliance with the instructions of the House. Individually I thought the amendment originally made by the House was desirable, but, the House having instructed otherwise, I agree to this report in accordance with that instruction. . . .

Mr. BLAND. I regret that the amendments that the House put upon the bill were stricken out; and while I fear the bill in its present shape is not what its friends expect of it I shall cheerfully vote for it. I raised the question of consideration simply for the purpose of going to the Speaker's table and taking up the silver bill. I am not opposed to the bill itself. [Cries of "Vote!" "Vote!"]

Mr. STEWART, of Vermont. As there seems to be no disposition, or at least I am not advised of any disposition, to discuss the bill, I will ask for a vote.

Mr. [DANIEL] KERR [R., Iowa]. Mr. Speaker, this bill, as it came from the Senate, as was stated by the gentleman from Texas [Mr. CULBERSON]—

Mr. STEWART, of Vermont. Do I understand the gentleman from Iowa [Mr. KERR] desires to discuss this question?

Mr. KERR, of Iowa. I do.

The SPEAKER. The Chair so understood.

Mr. STEWART, of Vermont. Then I yield the floor to the gentleman if he desires to discuss the measure.

Mr. KERR, of Iowa. When this bill was before the House recently the gentleman from Texas [Mr. CULBERSON], in discussing its provisions, made the statement that the power given in this bill was an exercise of the entire power of the General Government over the subject of trusts, and that its provisions presented the matter in a shape to obtain the decisions of the courts, out of which we might gather the full extent of the power of the Government on that subject. Now, as a great deal has been said in this Congress about trusts, it seems to me but justice to this side of the Chamber that a statement of the facts should be made to the House and the country in regard to the situation before this question is put to the House.

For four years during the last Administration we heard a great deal on the other side of this Chamber about trusts, and all over the country a great clamor has been raised about trusts. It was stated in this Chamber and to the people that the trusts were crushing the life-blood out of the people, and that everything that we bought was being enhanced in value by the trusts in various parts of the country, and so increasing the prices. While, perhaps, there was a great deal of misstatement about this proposition, there was, perhaps, also a great deal of truth in it; and we know that the sugar trust came before the last Congress and exacted from the Democratic side of the House, as was generally believed, some concession making it possible for that great monopoly to exact from the people of the United States a vast sum of money out of the products of their enriched business, and we know that many millions of dollars were obtained by them through the trust.

The stock of the sugar trust became a very profitable investment, and vast sums of money were made out of it. Now, this was true; but it is also true that, while so much was being said on the subject, not one single syllable of legislation came from that side of the House during the four years of the last Administration on the subject of trusts. The leading gentlemen on that side of the Chamber went so far as to say that the only method by which we could control the trusts of this country was by a change of the Constitution, granting additional power to the General Government over the subject of trusts, and the fact that no legislation was proposed by this House seemed to imply that that view was a generally accepted theory of the Democratic party, and that Congress could only control trusts after a change of the Constitution.

Mr. HEARD. Who said that?

Mr. KERR, of Iowa. And the gentleman from Tennessee [Mr. ENLOE], in order to further that view of the case, took occasion to introduce a proposition for an amendment to the Constitution of the United States, making a grant of power to the General Government over the subject.[1.375]

Mr. [BENJAMIN A.] ENLOE [D., Tenn.]. I would like to ask the gentleman from

---

[1.375] H.R.J. Res. 30, 51st Cong., 1st Sess. (1889), BILLS AND DEBATES IN CONGRESS RELATING TO TRUSTS, S. DOC. NO. 147, 57th Cong., 2d Sess. 459 (1903).

Iowa [Mr. KERR] if he believes that when this bill is passed into a law it will be worth even the blank paper it is written on.

Mr. KERR, of Iowa. We have a statement from the gentleman from Texas [Mr. CULBERSON] and other members of the committee who framed this bill—

Mr. ENLOE. I am asking your opinion.

Mr. KERR, of Iowa. My opinion is that it will be the exercise of the entire power of the Government over the subject, except in so far as it applies to the Territories and the District of Columbia.

Mr. ENLOE. But will it accomplish anything?

Mr. KERR, of Iowa. I think it will accomplish a great deal. The gentleman from Texas [Mr. CULBERSON] very truly said that this was an unexplored field, that this was new legislation, that it was a case which demanded that the Government should declare the law, and that out of that declaration of the law would be evolved the decisions of the court, which would settle the question and determine the extent of our control over the subject. When the gentleman from Texas made that statement he had the approval, I believe, of every gentleman on this side of the House, and also of a number of gentlemen on the other side.

Mr. ENLOE. The gentleman from Iowa [Mr. KERR] says that the gentleman from Texas [Mr. CULBERSON] stated that this bill was the complete exercise of the powers of the Federal Government, under the Constitution, to control trusts. If I remember the statement of the gentleman from Texas correctly it was that this bill was the exercise of all the constitutional power that Congress had except the power to repeal the duties which protect these trusts, and I would like to ask the gentleman from Iowa a question on that point.

Mr. KERR, of Iowa. So far as the question of duties is concerned, that entire question has been gone over fully in this House, and we know that some of the most injurious trusts, those from which the people of this country have suffered most, have been beyond our control, trusts existing in other countries. We know, further, that the only way in which we can control those foreign trusts and prevent their exactions upon our people is to establish or maintain industries in this country which will compete against the exactions of the trusts existing on the other side of the ocean, and the policy which is favored by some gentlemen, including the gentleman from Tennessee, would leave us entirely at the mercy of those monopolies on the other side of the ocean.

Mr. ENLOE. I would like the gentleman to name some of the trusts that exist on the other side of the ocean that interfere with business here.

Mr. KERR, of Iowa. Well, since we have had our tariff laws in operation they have not been so extensive in their effects, but we know that until our tariff laws were passed, protecting our American industries, the combinations among the foreign producers of articles that had no competition in this country compelled our people to pay very high prices. Steel rails, for example, cost three or four times what our people have to pay for them to-day.

Mr. ENLOE. That was twenty-five years ago.

Mr. KERR, of Iowa. But when we got our American competition established against these foreign trusts, which were exacting such high prices from our people, prices began to fall, and the cost to the consumer has been steadily reduced.

Mr. ENLOE. I venture to say that the gentleman never heard of a "trust" twenty-five years ago.

Mr. KERR, of Iowa. But everybody knows that they were in existence. As to hearing of them, we have only heard much about trusts since the Democratic party began to think that they could make political capital out of that question. [Applause on the Republican side.]

Mr. ENLOE. You heard of them when Mr. Cleveland said that they were all over this country and when Mr. Blaine responded that they were private affairs, with which the Government had nothing to do.

Mr. BUCHANAN, of New Jersey. And that England was "plastered with them." . . .

⊥ Mr. KERR, of Iowa. But, Mr. Speaker, I suppose I shall have to draw my ⊥6314
remarks to a close, as the gentleman in charge of this bill seems to be in a hurry to

have it disposed of. I only wanted to call attention to the fact that this is the first bill that has ever passed the American Congress undertaking or pretending to regulate trusts in this country, and also to the fact that this is a bill passed by a Republican Congress. For fourteen years the Democratic party had control of the legislation of this country, and until now no legislation has ever been carried through for the purpose of regulating trusts.

Mr. ENLOE. Where was your Republican Senate, that it did not pass such a bill?

Mr. STEWART, of Vermont. I had no idea that I was going to open such a Pandora's box. The tariff, Mr. Speaker, is a very amusing subject, and I think I have heard something about it during this session. [Laughter.] It is, however, so far as this question is concerned, a mere "local issue," as our Democratic friends used to say. At all events, it does not seem to me that it has any particular relation to the bill under consideration. The provisions of this trust bill are just as broad, sweeping, and explicit as the English language can make them to express the power of Congress over this subject under the Constitution of the United States. If the bill does not go far enough, then the proposition of my friend from Tennessee [Mr. ENLOE], made some time ago, will be in order. When it is found that the power of Congress as it now exists has been exhausted in this legislation, then it will be time to look for some amendment to the Constitution. Mr. Speaker, I demand the previous question on the adoption of the conference report.

The previous question was ordered.

Mr. HEARD. On that I demand the yeas and nays.

The yeas and nays were ordered.

The question was taken; and there were—yeas 242, nay 0, not voting 85; as follows:

YEAS—242.

Abbott,	Burrows,	Evans,	Kerr, Iowa
Adams,	Burton,	Ewart,	Ketcham,
Alderson,	Butterworth,	Farquhar,	Kilgore,
Allen, Mich.	Bynum,	Finley,	Kinsey,
Anderson, Kans.	Caldwell,	Fithian,	Knapp,
Anderson, Miss.	Campbell,	Flick,	Lacey,
Arnold,	Candler, Mass.	Flood,	La Follette,
Atkinson, W. Va.	Cannon,	Forman,	Laidlaw,
Baker,	Carlton,	Forney,	Lane,
Bankhead,	Carter,	Fowler,	Lanham,
Banks,	Caruth,	Frank,	Laws,
Barnes,	Caswell,	Funston,	Lee,
Bartine,	Cheadle,	Gear,	Lehlbach,
Beckwith,	Chipman,	Geissenhainer,	Lester, Ga.
Belden,	Clements,	Gest,	Lester, Va.
Belknap,	Clunie,	Gibson,	Lewis,
Bergen,	Cobb,	Gifford,	Lind,
Bingham,	Cogswell,	Goodnight,	Lodge,
Blanchard,	Comstock,	Greenhalge,	Magner,
Bland,	Conger,	Grimes,	Maish,
Bliss,	Cooper, Ind.	Grosvenor,	Mansur,
Boatner,	Cothran,	Hall,	Martin, Ind.
Boothman,	Cowles,	Hansbrough,	McAdoo,
Boutelle,	Crain,	Hare,	McClammy,
Bowden,	Crisp,	Haugen,	McClellan,
Breckinridge, Ark.,	Culberson, Tex.	Hayes,	McComas,
Breckinridge, Ky.	Culbertson, Pa.	Haynes,	McCormick,
Brewer,	Cummings,	Heard,	McCreary,
Brickner,	Cutcheon,	Hemphill,	McKenna,
Brookshire,	Dalzell,	Henderson, Ill.	McKinley,
Brosius,	Davidson,	Henderson, Iowa	McMillin,
Brown, J. B.	De Lano,	Henderson, N.C.	McRae,
Browne, Va.	Dockery,	Herbert,	Miles,
Brunner,	Dolliver,	Hermann,	Mills,
Buchanan, N. J.	Dunnell,	Hill,	Moffitt,
Buchanan, Va.	Dunphy,	Hitt,	Montgomery,
Buckalew,	Elliott,	Holman,	Moore, N. H.
Bullock,	Ellis,	Kelley,	Moore, Tex.
Bunn,	Enloe,	Kennedy,	Morey,

CONFERENCE CONSIDERATION (S. 1)

Morrill,
Morrow,
Morse,
Mudd,
Niedringhaus,
Norton,
Oates,
O'Neall, Ind.
O'Neil, Mass.
O'Neill, Pa.
Osborne,
Owen, Ind.
Owens, Ohio
Parrett,
Paynter,
Payson,
Peel,
Penington,
Perkins,
Perry,
Pickler,
Post,
Pugsley,
Quinn,
Raines,
Reed, Iowa
Reilly,
Richardson,
Rife,
Robertson,
Rockwell,
Rowell,
Rowland,
Rusk,
Russell,
Sanford,
Sayers,
Scull,
Sherman,
Shively,
Simonds,
Smith, Ill.
Smith, W. Va.
Smyser,
Snider,
Spinola,
Spooner,
Springer,
Stephenson,
Stewart, Ga.
Stewart, Tex.
Stewart, Vt.
Stivers,
Stockdale,
Stone, Ky.
Stone, Mo.
Struble,
Stump,
Swency,
Tarsney,
Taylor, J.D.
Thomas,
Tillman,
Townsend, Colo.
Tracey,
Tucker,
Turner, Ga.
Turner, Kans.
Vandever,
Vaux,
Venable,
Walker, Mass.
Wallace, N.Y.
Wheeler, Ala.
Whiting,
Whitthorne,
Wickham,
Wike,
Wilkinson,
Willcox,
Williams, Ill.
Williams, Ohio
Wilson, Ky.
Wilson, Mo.
Wilson, W. Va.
Wright

NAY—0.

NOT VOTING—85.

Allen, Miss.
Andrew,
Atkinson, Pa.
Barwig,
Bayne,
Biggs,
Blount,
Brower,
Browne, T. M.
Candler, Ga.
Catchings,
Cheatham,
Clancy,
Clark, Wis.
Clarke, Ala.
Coleman,
Connell,
Cooper, Ohio
Covert,
Craig,
Dargan,
Darlington,
De Haven,
Dibble,
Dingley,
Dorsey,
Edmunds,
Featherston,
Fitch,
Flower,
Grout,
Harmer,
Hatch,
Hooker,
Hopkins,
Houk,
Kerr, Pa.
Lansing,
Lawler,
Martin, Tex.
Mason,
McCarthy,
McCord,
McDuffie,
Milliken,
Morgan,
Mutchler,
Nute,
O'Donnell,
O'Ferrall,
Oathwaite,
Payne,
Peters,
Phelan,
Pierce,
Price,
Quackenbush,
Randall,
Ray,
Reyburn,
Rogers,
Sawyer,
Scranton,
Seney,
Skinner,
Stahlnecker,
Stockbridge,
Taylor, E. B.
Taylor, Ill.
Taylor, Tenn.
Thompson,
Townsend, Pa.
Turner, N. Y.
Van Schaick,
Waddill,
Wade,
Walker, Mo.
Wallace, Mass.
Washington,
Watson,
Wheeler, Mich.
Wiley,
Wilson, Wash.
Yardley,
Yoder.

So the conference report was adopted.

The Decisions

Commentary

In passing the Sherman Antitrust Act, Congress declared the general principle that competition should be free and unrestricted by abuses of the vast economic power concentrated in the prevalent business organizations of the day. It was accordingly left to the courts to flesh out the form of this skeletal principle through a case-by-case analysis of particular business arrangements encountered in their specific factual contexts. While the congressional debates and the legislative materials evidence a unity of purpose in prohibiting the abuse of economic power,[1.376] Congress was nonetheless cognizant of the desirability of various types of business arrangements that were deemed valid under existing law. Despite having enacted the Interstate Commerce Act[1.377] three years earlier in an attempt to regulate the nation's railroads and to curb specific abuses in that industry, the Congress of 1890 was engaged in a considerably broader task in attempting to define acceptable standards of competitive conduct for business behavior as a whole. It is not surprising that in enacting the Sherman Act during an era of changing economic conditions Congress chose the course of enunciating guiding principles rather than defining specific types of prohibited conduct.[1.378]

This intentionally flexible legislative approach has become well recognized by the courts in their interpretation of the Act and was reflected in the "Rule of Reason," first formally enunciated in 1911 in *Standard Oil Co. v. United States*.[1.379] The development of this judicial standard not only is of prime significance for an understanding of the Act's current application but also illustrates the Supreme Court's interpretation of legislative history, congressional debates, and the forces operative at the time the statute was enacted. In the cases here presented, the Court has made reference to and use of these considerations in its decisions involving both section 1 and section 2 of the Act. These cases should not, however, be viewed as surveying the various types of business arrangements or conduct that have been found to fall within the Sherman Act's proscription, but rather as illustrating the development of the judicial standards applied to evaluate such activity.[1.380] The basic issues of the Act's constitutionality, the definition of interstate commerce, the business arrangements affected, and the evolution of the doctrine of *per se* illegality are closely related to the development of the Rule of Reason. These topics are also treated in the decisions that

---

[1.376] This conclusion follows from a reading of the debates themselves, as well as from the almost unanimous final vote in favor of passage of the bill.

[1.377] Act of Feb. 4, 1887, ch. 104, 24 Stat. 379.

[1.378] One able student of the background and history of the Sherman Act has termed Congress' choice of this flexible approach "elegant." H. THORELLI, THE FEDERAL ANTITRUST POLICY 229 (1955).

[1.379] 221 U.S. 1, 31 S. Ct. 502, 55 L. Ed. 619 (1911), *infra* at 382.

[1.380] For a brief general discussion of the types of business activities and conduct which may be found violative of section 1 of the Sherman Act see *Introduction supra* at 31–32. For more detailed discussions of these matters the reader is referred to those authorities listed at note 1.216 *supra*. Section 2 of the Act is also discussed in the *Introduction supra* at 32–33, and similar textual authorities dealing with that section are provided. Discussion of the procedural and remedial provisions of the Act is likewise beyond the scope of this treatment, but these provisions are generally discussed in connection with the sectional analysis of the Act; see *Introduction supra* at 34–35.

follow. Although reference to the Act's legislative history is considerably less in cases involving section 2 of the Act, brief treatment of this section is also included.

Early Enforcement

The Sherman Act was passed during the Republican administration of Benjamin Harrison. Although President Harrison sought the Presidency on a platform that urged legislation to curb the power of monopolies and trusts[1.381] and endorsed this principle in both his letter accepting the nomination[1.382] and his first annual message to the Congress in 1889,[1.383] there is no evidence he paid any further attention to the statute.[1.384] Indeed, it does not appear that President Harrison made any formal statement upon signing the Act into law on July 2, 1890. Enforcement of the new statute during the remaining 32 months of his administration was certainly not vigorous but, in fairness, some of this inactivity was undoubtedly due to unfamiliarity on the part of United States attorneys with the new, broad law as well as to the paucity of early government victories and other political and economic considerations.[1.385] However, the Trans-Missouri Association[1.386] and sugar trust[1.387] prosecutions, both of which eventually reached the Supreme Court, were instituted during this period.

No significant change in enforcement attitude occurred during the administrations of Grover Cleveland and William McKinley,[1.388] although governmental antitrust attacks were mounted against the Joint Traffic Association[1.389] and six members of the cast iron pipe trust, including the Addyston Pipe & Steel Co.[1.390] in addition to several cases instituted against organized labor activities.[1.391] Thus, despite increasing economic concentration and the prevalence of large business associations in the form of trusts and, later, holding companies, the Act was not effectively utilized during its first 11 years to suppress the combinations upon which the attention of its enacting Congress

---

[1.381] The relevant portion of the Republican Party platform of 1888 appears *supra* at 54 and is reprinted in its entirety in T. MCKEE, THE NATIONAL CONVENTIONS AND PLATFORMS OF ALL POLITICAL PARTIES 1789-1905, at 241 (1906).

[1.382] SPEECHES OF BENJAMIN HARRISON, TWENTY-THIRD PRESIDENT OF THE UNITED STATES 113 (C. Hedges ed. 1892).

[1.383] The relevant portion of President Harrison's first annual message appears *supra* at 60 and is reprinted in its entirety in 2 THE STATE OF THE UNION MESSAGES OF THE PRESIDENTS 1790-1966, at 1628-53 (F. Israel ed. 1966).

[1.384] *See* H. THORELLI, *supra* note 1.378, at 371.

[1.385] According to the compilation of cases prepared by the Antitrust Division of the Department of Justice, only six antitrust actions were instituted by the government during the administration of President Harrison. CCH, THE FEDERAL ANTITRUST LAWS, WITH SUMMARY OF CASES INSTITUTED BY THE UNITED STATES 1890-1951, at 67-69 (1952) [hereinafter cited as FEDERAL ANTITRUST LAWS]. For good discussions of early antitrust enforcement and interpretation of the Sherman Act, including reviews of the actions initiated both by the government and by private parties, see H. THORELLI, *supra* note 1.378, at 369-431, 477-99; A. WALKER, HISTORY OF THE SHERMAN LAW OF THE UNITED STATES OF AMERICA 62-269 (1910); W. LETWIN, LAW AND ECONOMIC POLICY IN AMERICA: THE EVOLUTION OF THE SHERMAN ANTITRUST ACT 145-237 (1965).

[1.386] FEDERAL ANTITRUST LAWS at 67. *See also* United States v. Trans-Missouri Freight Ass'n, 166 U.S. 290, 17 S. Ct. 540, 41 L. Ed. 1007 (1897).

[1.387] FEDERAL ANTITRUST LAWS at 68. *See also* United States v. E.C. Knight Co., 156 U.S. 1, 15 S. Ct. 249, 39 L. Ed. 325 (1895).

[1.388] During the period March 4, 1893, to September 14, 1901, a total of 12 government antitrust actions were instituted, 9 of which were filed during the second administration of President Cleveland and 3 of which were filed during the administration of President McKinley. FEDERAL ANTITRUST LAWS at 69-72. (Related actions filed in the same case are considered as a single case for purposes of this compilation.)

[1.389] *Id.* at 70-71. *See also* United States v. Joint Traffic Ass'n, 171 U.S. 505, 19 S. Ct. 25, 43 L. Ed. 259 (1898), *infra* at 377.

[1.390] FEDERAL ANTITRUST LAWS at 71. *See also* United States v. Addyston Pipe & Steel Co., 175 U.S. 211, 20 S. Ct. 96, 44 L. Ed. 136 (1899).

[1.391] The celebrated Pullman strike occurred in 1894 during the second Cleveland administration. The antitrust Act was used as an antistrike weapon in an effort to prevent concerted labor activity in the famous *Debs* and related cases; *see generally* FEDERAL ANTITRUST LAWS at 69-70; H. THORELLI, *supra* note 1.378, at 389-94.

had been generally focused and at which the Act had been primarily aimed.[1.392] This period did, however, witness significant final victories for the government in the *Trans-Missouri, Joint Traffic,* and *Addyston Pipe* cases.[1.393] During the administration of President Theodore Roosevelt, antitrust enforcement gained new momentum,[1.394] and major actions destined to reach the Supreme Court were instituted against, among others, the Northern Securities (railroad),[1.395] Swift (beef),[1.396] Standard Oil,[1.397] and American Tobacco[1.398] companies.

Constitutionality of the Sherman Act

The first direct challenge to the constitutionality of the Sherman Act was not directly presented to the Supreme Court until 1898 in *United States v. Joint Traffic Association*.[1.399] In that case, the defendants had contended that the statute violated the due process clause of the fifth amendment to the Constitution and that it constituted an improper limitation on their ability to enter into contracts. Despite the significant attention devoted during the congressional debates to the constitutionality of the bill and the appropriate congressional power upon which it should be rested, the Justices concisely affirmed Congress' power to regulate interstate commerce without reference to the debates. In upholding the constitutionality of the Act, the Court concluded:

> . . . The question comes back whether the statute under review is a legitimate exercise of the power of Congress over interstate commerce and a valid regulation thereof. The question is, for us, one of power only, and not of policy. We think the power exists in Congress, and that the statute is therefore valid.[1.400]

Scope of Interstate Commerce

Considerably greater difficulty existed for the Court in defining the scope of interstate commerce and extending the Act to its intended limits. The Court recognized in two early cases[1.401] that interstate commerce was affected by railroad association agreements establishing rates for interstate traffic. Nevertheless, in the first case to reach the High Court under the new statute, *United States v. E. C. Knight Co.*,[1.402] it was held that purchase of the stock of several Philadelphia, Pennsylvania, sugar refineries, which gave the defendant members of the sugar trust nearly monopolistic control of the manufacture of refined sugar within the United States, was not within the sphere of interstate commerce. While the Court did not broadly exempt manufacturers from application of the Act, it did distinguish between manufacturing activity itself and the

---

[1.392] *See* A. WALKER, *supra* note 1.385, at 167. Principal among those combinations to which repeated references were made during the congressional debates were the Standard Oil, tobacco, salt, whiskey, and beef trusts.

[1.393] *See* discussion *infra* at 370–72.

[1.394] During Theodore Roosevelt's administration, 44 governmental antitrust cases were filed. FEDERAL ANTITRUST LAWS at 72–82. Under President Taft, antitrust enforcement experienced an even greater increase as 77 cases were filed during the four-year period March 4, 1909, to March 3, 1913. *Id.* at 82–102.

[1.395] *Id.* at 72. *See also* Northern Sec. Co. v. United States, 193 U.S. 197, 24 S. Ct. 436, 48 L. Ed. 679 (1904). By the early 1900's, many of the trusts had been reorganized into holding companies which permitted aggregate centralized control in much the same way as provided under trust arrangements. *See* note 1.24 *supra*.

[1.396] FEDERAL ANTITRUST LAWS at 72–73. *See also* Swift & Co. v. United States, 196 U.S. 375, 25 S. Ct. 276, 49 L. Ed. 518 (1905).

[1.397] FEDERAL ANTITRUST LAWS at 77. *See also* Standard Oil Co. v. United States, 221 U.S. 1 (1911), *infra* at 382.

[1.398] FEDERAL ANTITRUST LAWS at 79. *See also* United States v. American Tobacco Co., 221 U.S. 106, 31 S. Ct. 632, 55 L. Ed. 663 (1911), *infra* at 403.

[1.399] 171 U.S. 505 (1898), *infra* at 377.

[1.400] *Id.* at 573, *infra* at 382.

[1.401] United States v. Trans-Missouri Freight Ass'n, 166 U.S. 290 (1897); United States v. Joint Traffic Ass'n, 171 U.S. 505 (1898), *infra* at 377.

[1.402] 156 U.S. 1 (1895).

subsequent shipment or sale of manufactured goods across state lines. Only this latter activity, which had not been emphasized in the government's action, was found to be within the reach of the statute.[1.403]

This restricted view of interstate commerce was soon expanded, however. In *United States v. Addyston Pipe & Steel Co.*[1.404] the Sixth Circuit Court of Appeals, in a significant opinion written by Judge William Howard Taft, the future President of the United States and Chief Justice of the Supreme Court, expanded upon the approach previously taken in the *E. C. Knight* case. Judge Taft distinguished negotiations and contracts for the sale of goods across state lines from manufacture of the merchandise itself, holding that the former constituted interstate commerce even before the actual interstate transportation of the goods had commenced.[1.405] Judge Taft's decision was affirmed by the Supreme Court in 1899,[1.406] in which opinion Mr. Justice Peckham stated that the Sherman Act applied to any "agreement or combination [which] directly restrains not alone the manufacture, but the purchase, sale, or exchange of the manufactured commodity among the several states."[1.407]

The genesis of the current expansive, but not unlimited, view of the Sherman Act's jurisdictional requirement can be traced to *Swift & Co. v. United States*,[1.408] in which the Supreme Court utilized a "flow of commerce" test, emphasizing that the direct effect upon interstate commerce was sufficient to bring the challenged combination within the perimeter of the statute.[1.409] *United States v. South-Eastern Underwriters Association* further illustrates the expanded notion of interstate commerce, the Supreme Court observing that the statute "[o]n its face . . . shows a carefully studied attempt to bring within the Act every person engaged in business whose activities might restrain or monopolize commercial intercourse among the states."[1.410] In that opinion, the Court made extensive reference to the congressional debates and other legislative materials in support of its position.[1.411] Stated another way, "If it is interstate commerce that feels the pinch, it does not matter how local the operation which applies the squeeze."[1.412] In *Gulf Oil Corp. v. Copp Paving Co.*, the Supreme Court declared that the Sherman Act's jurisdictional reach "is keyed directly to effects on interstate markets and the interstate flow of goods."[1.413] It emphasized that Congress' intent in enacting the Sherman Act was to exercise the full degree of congressional regulatory power over interstate commerce and that "however local its immediate object, a 'contract, combination . . . or conspiracy' nonetheless may constitute a restraint within the meaning of [section 1 of the Sherman Act] if it substantially and adversely affects interstate commerce."[1.414] In its 1975 pronouncement on the subject, *Goldfarb v. Virginia State Bar*, the Court found real property title examinations to be integral parts of and inseparable from the interstate aspects of real estate transactions, so that a

---

[1.403] *Id.* at 13, 17.

[1.404] 85 F. 271 (6th Cir. 1898), *aff'd,* 175 U.S. 211 (1899).

[1.405] *Id.* at 298.

[1.406] Addyston Pipe & Steel Co. v. United States, 175 U.S. 211 (1899).

[1.407] *Id.* at 241.

[1.408] 196 U.S. 375 (1905).

[1.409] *Id.* at 396-97. Mr. Justice Holmes distinguished *E. C. Knight* on the ground that that case had involved restraints which were directly aimed at monopolizing manufacture within a single state. *Id.* at 397.

[1.410] 322 U.S. 533, 553, 64 S. Ct. 1162, 1174, 88 L. Ed. 1440, 1457-58 (1944), *infra* at 430.

[1.411] 322 U.S. at 556-59 & nn.40-42, 45-47, *infra* at 430-31. In his dissenting opinion, Mr. Chief Justice Stone argued that the Court's holding that the insurance industry was part of interstate commerce was erroneous. He, too, made extensive reference to the congressional debates and what he perceived to be the state of the law at the time the Sherman Act was enacted in support of his view. *Id.* at 573-75 & nn.3-5 (dissenting opinion), *infra* at 434-35.

[1.412] United States v. Women's Sportswear Mfrs. Ass'n, 336 U.S. 460, 464, 69 S. Ct. 714, 716, 93 L. Ed. 805, 811 (1949).

[1.413] 419 U.S. 186, 194, 95 S. Ct. 392, 398, 42 L. Ed. 2d 378, 386 (1974).

[1.414] 419 U.S. at 195.

restraint upon these legal services sufficiently affected interstate commerce for purposes of the Sherman Act.[1.415]

That the Sherman Act was intended to apply only to business arrangements or conduct is illustrated by *Apex Hosiery Co. v. Leader*[1.416] and by *Parker v. Brown*.[1.417] In these cases, the Supreme Court placed reliance upon the congressional debates and expressed its view that Congress was concerned about "restraints to free competition in business and commercial transactions,"[1.418] and about "business combinations,"[1.419] respectively, to illustrate the appropriateness of this limitation of the Act's coverage. Accordingly, in the light of its legislative history, the Act was held inapplicable to the concerted activities of labor organizations and to the activities of governmental entities in these respective cases.[1.420] Although the definition of commercial conduct has been a matter of substantial contemporary dispute, as evidenced by the series of cases grappling with whether there existed an exemption from the Sherman Act for the so-

---

[1.415] 421 U.S. 773, 95 S. Ct. 2004, 44 L. Ed. 2d 572 (1975). The Court did not, however, state or imply that all legal services would be within the jurisdictional reach of the Act, for it recognized that some legal services may involve interstate commerce in other fashions, just as other legal services might have no nexus with interstate commerce and thus be beyond the reach of the Sherman Act.

Despite the broad language of *Copp Paving* and *Goldfarb*, however, there is still some uncertainty as to whether the jurisdictional requirements of interstate commerce and restraint under the Act may be satisfied separately or whether jurisdiction requires that the restraint be found to be upon interstate commerce. Thus, a question remains whether the Act is applicable when a business engaged in interstate commerce participates in anticompetitive activity having only, or substantially only, a local effect, or whether the restraint itself must also operate upon interstate commerce. The Supreme Court has never decided this precise question. A recent decision by the United States Court of Appeals for the Seventh Circuit, United States v. Finis P. Ernest, Inc., 509 F.2d 1256 (7th Cir.), *cert. denied*, 423 U.S. 893 (1975), while not deciding the issue, reviewed the precedents and found support for both positions. That court suggested, however, that language used by the Supreme Court in deciding related issues might favor the latter jurisdictional requirement. *Id.* at 1260-61.

However, in Hospital Building Co. v. Trustees of Rex Hospital, 425 U.S. 738 (1976), the Supreme Court, observing that "Sherman Act coverage requires only that the conduct complained of have a substantial effect on interstate commerce," held that alleged efforts to block a private hospital's efforts to expand its hospital services within a single city sufficiently stated a cause of action under the Act. In reversing the Court of Appeals' finding that the Act was inapplicable, 511 F.2d 678, 684 (4th Cir. 1975), the Supreme Court observed that conduct that was not "purposely directed" toward interstate commerce did not necessarily fall outside the Act merely because its effect on interstate commerce was termed "indirect." 425 U.S. at 744.

[1.416] 310 U.S. 469, 60 S. Ct. 982, 84 L. Ed. 1311 (1940), *infra* at 416.

[1.417] 317 U.S. 341, 63 S. Ct. 307, 87 L. Ed. 315 (1943), *infra* at 423.

[1.418] 310 U.S. at 493 & n.15, *infra* at 419.

[1.419] 317 U.S. at 351, *infra* at 425.

[1.420] These cases are intended to illustrate only the legislative purpose behind enactment of the Sherman Act, not necessarily the current status of the labor and agricultural exemptions to concerted activity. Although an amendment specifically exempting labor and agricultural organizations from the antitrust bill's coverage was attached during its consideration by the Senate Committee of the Whole, the bill's final version contained no such provision. Section 6 of the Clayton Act of 1914, however, provided for a limited exemption for the activities of both these groups. *See Introduction supra* at 20.

There has also been considerable uncertainty as to the scope of the state action exemption under *Parker v. Brown*, even within the factual context of minimum attorney fee schedules established by county and state bar associations. In *Goldfarb*, 421 U.S. 773 (1975), the Supreme Court held that such activities were not exempt as state action "compelled by direction of the State acting as a sovereign." In reversing the appellate court's ruling, 497 F.2d 1 (4th Cir. 1974), the Supreme Court aligned itself with the previous federal district court decision in United States v. Oregon State Bar, 385 F. Supp. 507 (D. Ore. 1974), which had held that state bar's minimum fee schedule not exempt from the Sherman Act under the state action doctrine.

Similarly, in Cantor v. Detroit Edison Co., 428 U.S. 579 (1976), the Supreme Court held that approval by a state public service commission of a private utility's tariff schedule did not immunize that portion of the tariff relating to a challenged light-bulb exchange program, where the state approval and required continuance of the privately initiated action did not implement any statewide policy in conflict with federal antitrust policy, and where the legality of any acts of the state or its officials was not in question. In his dissenting opinion, Mr. Justice Stewart quoted freely from the Sherman Act's legislative history, contending that its draftsmen, who narrowly viewed the scope of interstate commerce, had not intended to intrude upon state regulatory authority. *Id.* at 632-35.

called learned professions,[1.421] in 1975 the Supreme Court ruled in *Goldfarb v. Virginia State Bar* that the legal profession enjoys no such exemption for otherwise anticompetitive conduct.[1.422] The Court found no explicit exemption or legislative history to support the proposition that Congress intended to provide any such sweeping exclusion under the Sherman Act. Rather, it emphasized that Congress endeavored to strike as broadly as it could in enacting section 1 of the Sherman Act and that to read into that section such a wide exemption would be inconsistent with that purpose.[1.423]

Development of the Rule of Reason

The cases utilizing the Rule of Reason approach in interpreting the Sherman Act are numerous, and space considerations permit selection of only a few in order to give the reader an understanding of how the rule has evolved over the Act's 85-year history. As these decisions illustrate, during the Act's first two decades the courts came to grips with its intended purpose; later decisions refined the rule in the light of experience gained in earlier cases involving a diversity of business arrangements and conduct.

In the early cases to come before the Supreme Court involving the rate-fixing arrangements of railroad associations, the Court applied a literal interpretation of the Act's first section. In *United States v. Trans-Missouri Freight Association*,[1.424] the Supreme Court in 1897 rejected the argument that the statute was intended to apply only to those restraints that were held to be invalid under common law. Instead, it emphasized the language of the statute itself, declaring that the Act was intended to prohibit *every* contract, combination, or conspiracy that restrained trade without regard to whether such restraint had previously been held reasonable under common law:

It is now ... urged that the statute ... does not mean what the language used therein plainly imports, but that it only means to declare illegal any such contract which is in *unreasonable* restraint of trade, while leaving all others unaffected by the provisions of the act; that the common-law meaning of the term "contract in restraint of trade" includes only such contracts as are in *unreasonable* restraint of trade, and when that term is used in the Federal statute it is not intended to include all contracts in restraint of trade, but only those which are in unreasonable restraint thereof.

The term is not of such limited signification. Contracts in restraint of trade have been known and spoken of for hundreds of years both in England and in this country, and the term includes all kinds of those contracts which in fact restrain or may restrain trade. Some of such contracts have been held void and unenforceable in the courts by reason of their restraint being unreasonable, while others have been held valid because they were not of that nature. A contract may be in restraint of trade and still be valid at common law. Although valid, it is nevertheless a contract in restraint of trade, and would be so described either at common law

---

[1.421] *Compare* Goldfarb v. Virginia State Bar, 497 F.2d 1 (4th Cir. 1974), *rev'd*, 421 U.S. 773 (1975) (practice of law exempt from Sherman Act as a learned profession) *and* Bank Bldg. & Equip. Corp. of America v. National Council of Architectural Registration Bds., 1975 Trade Cas. ¶ 60,108 (D.D.C. 1975) (architecture a learned profession) *with* United States v. Oregon State Bar, 385 F. Supp. 507 (D. Ore. 1974) (practice of law not exempt from Sherman Act as a learned profession) *and* United States v. National Soc'y of Professional Eng'rs, 389 F. Supp. 1193 (D.D.C. 1974) (professional engineering not a learned profession), *vacated and remanded for further consideration in light of Goldfarb v. Virginia State Bar*, 422 U.S. 1031 (1975), *reaffirmed*, 404 F. Supp. 457 (D.D.C. 1975). For the genesis of the theory that the so-called learned professions enjoyed such an exemption see the Supreme Court's decision in *Goldfarb*, 421 U.S. at 786 n.15 and cases cited therein.

[1.422] 421 U.S. 773 (1975).

[1.423] *Id.* at 785-88. It is interesting to note in this regard that the issue whether the antitrust bill would apply to professional fee schedules established by bar associations was raised briefly, but inconclusively, during the Senate debate in connection with the antitrust bill, 21 CONG. REC. 2726 (1890), *supra* at 265. Although the court in *Goldfarb* expressly limited its holding to the factual situation with which it was presented in that case, 421 U.S. at 787-88 n.17, it may be expected that its finding that section 1 of the Sherman Act contained no exemption for the so-called learned professions, as well as other aspects of its opinion, would likewise preclude the existence of such exemption for other professions. By the same token, however, it was expressly recognized that the fact that a restraint operated upon a profession, as distinguished from a business, would be relevant in determining whether the particular restraint violated the Act, thus permitting possible differences in application of the Act to the professions as compared to business enterprises. *See id.*

[1.424] 166 U.S. 290 (1897).

or elsewhere. By the simple use of the term "contract in restraint of trade," all contracts of that nature, whether valid or otherwise, would be included, and not alone that kind of contract which was invalid and unenforceable as being in unreasonable restraint of trade. When, therefore, the body of an act pronounces as illegal every contract or combination in restraint of trade or commerce among the several states, etc., the plain and ordinary meaning of such language is not limited to that kind of contract alone which is in unreasonable restraint of trade, but all contracts are included in such language, and no exception or limitation can be added without placing in the act that which has been omitted by Congress.[1.425]

To hold otherwise, according to Mr. Justice Peckham, would be tantamount to the Court's engaging in judicial legislation by engrafting upon the plain wording of the statute a limitation that was not intended.[1.426]

Mr. Justice White dissented from the majority opinion, and his view was later to prevail in his opinions for the majority of the Court in the *Standard Oil*[1.427] and *American Tobacco*[1.428] cases after he became Chief Justice. However, his dissent in *Trans-Missouri* did not refer to those portions of the congressional debates which strongly supported his view that the statute was intended to be interpreted according to the common law principles that were commonly recognized at the time the statute was enacted.[1.429]

The following year, in *Hopkins v. United States*,[1.430] the Supreme Court held the Act to apply only to those contracts having "a direct and immediate effect" upon interstate commerce, as opposed to those which were indirect or incidental to a legitimate business purpose.[1.431] The same day, when faced with an arrangement for the establishment of railroad rates in *United States v. Joint Traffic Association*[1.432] similar to that which had been presented in the *Trans-Missouri* case, the Court, after holding the Act constitutional as discussed above, declined to alter or reconsider its position expressed in that earlier case. In rejecting the constitutional challenge to the Act in *Joint Traffic*, however, the Court did repeat an obiter dictum from *Hopkins* that "the act of Congress must have a reasonable construction, or else there would scarcely be an agreement or contract among business men that could not be said to have, indirectly or remotely, some bearing upon interstate commerce, and possibly to restrain it."[1.433] Thus, while refusing to alter its basic ideological approach, the Court began to loosen somewhat its insistence upon a strictly literal interpretation of the statute.

Meanwhile, in an important decision foreshadowing the trend toward a more flexible interpretation of the Sherman Act, Judge William Howard Taft, writing for the United States Court of Appeals for the Sixth Circuit in *United States v. Addyston Pipe & Steel Co.*,[1.434] utilized a different jurisprudential approach. In response to the

---

[1.425] *Id.* at 327-28.

[1.426] *Id.* at 340.

[1.427] Standard Oil Co. v. United States, 221 U.S. 1 (1911), *infra* at 382.

[1.428] United States v. American Tobacco Co., 221 U.S. 106 (1911), *infra* at 403.

[1.429] For example, in his first major speech in support of his bill, Senator Sherman announced that it was not intended to void all commonly accepted business arrangements, nor to announce a new principle of law, but was to apply "old and well recognized principles of the common law to the complicated jurisdiction of our State and Federal Government." 21 CONG. REC. 2456 (1890), *supra* at 114. Later in the same speech, Senator Sherman stated: "All that we, as lawmakers, can do is to declare general principles, and we can be assured that the courts will apply them so as to carry out the meaning of the law, as the courts of England and the United States have done for centuries." 21 CONG. REC. 2460 (1890), *supra* at 122. Likewise, Senator Hoar declared: "We have affirmed the old doctrine of the common law in regard to all interstate and international commercial transactions, and have clothed the United States courts with authority to enforce that doctrine by injunction. We have put in also a grave penalty." 21 CONG. REC. 3146 (1890), *supra* at 282.

Mr. Justice White in *Trans-Missouri*, however, did make reference to the Sherman Act's legislative history, as well as to reports of the Interstate Commerce Commission, to urge that the statute was not intended to interfere with the ICC's authority to regulate railroads. 166 U.S. at 358-73.

[1.430] 171 U.S. 578, 19 S. Ct. 40, 43 L. Ed. 290 (1898).

[1.431] 171 U.S. at 592.

[1.432] 171 U.S. 505 (1898), *infra* at 377.

[1.433] *Id.* at 568, *infra* at 379-80.

[1.434] 85 F. 271 (6th Cir. 1898), *aff'd,* 175 U.S. 211 (1899).

contention that the defendants and their association, in allocating territories and establishing prices for their products, had merely engaged in conduct valid at common law, Judge Taft intimated that the Supreme Court's rejection of this view in *Trans-Missouri* "might be a sufficient answer."[1.435] Rather than decide whether that case was controlling precedent for one involving private manufacturers rather than "quasi-public" railroads, however, Judge Taft analyzed the common law precedents and determined that the arrangement would nonetheless have been invalid at common law.[1.436] His opinion was affirmed by the Supreme Court the following year.[1.437] Speaking for a unanimous Court, Mr. Justice Peckham observed that even assuming a defense could be predicated upon a showing that the restraints were reasonable, the Court agreed with Judge Taft's analysis that the restraints in fact were not so.[1.438] While Judge Taft's approach to the common law precedents was undoubtedly of great significance in signaling a different interpretation of the Act, it received no express recognition by Chief Justice White in his subsequent *Standard Oil* or *American Tobacco* opinions. On the other hand, Mr. Justice Peckham's tacit approval of the Taft[1.439] approach has been recognized by one commentator as evidencing a retreat from the Supreme Court's earlier, inflexible approach.[1.440]

Mr. Chief Justice White's landmark opinion in *Standard Oil Co. v. United States*[1.441] represents the clean break with the earlier approach and the formal statement of the Rule of Reason. After making brief reference to English and American common law history applicable to business restraints, he directed that the words employed in the Sherman Act be interpreted according to the common law meaning they had at the time the statute was enacted. In Chief Justice White's view, the statute was intended to protect interstate and foreign commerce from "an undue restraint" and was not intended to restrain the right to make and enforce a contract that did not constitute such "an undue restraint."[1.442] Thus, in interpreting section 1 of the Act, he determined that a court must, in each case, exercise its judgment to measure the

---

[1.435] *Id.* at 278.

[1.436] *Id.* at 278-91.

[1.437] Addyston Pipe & Steel Co. v. United States, 175 U.S. 211 (1899).

[1.438] *Id.* at 235.

[1.439] It is interesting to note that another future eminent member of the Supreme Court, John M. Harlan of Kentucky, was a member of the Sixth Circuit Court of Appeals in 1898 and had joined in Judge Taft's *Addyston Pipe* opinion. When sitting upon the Supreme Court, however, Mr. Justice Harlan vigorously dissented from that part of the Supreme Court's decision in *Standard Oil* which established the Rule of Reason, principally on the ground that the statute should continue to be given the literal interpretation it had received in the earlier *Trans-Missouri* and *Joint Traffic* decisions. 221 U.S. at 82-106, *infra* at 396-403. It appears, therefore, that all members of the Sixth Circuit *Addyston Pipe* panel may not have had in mind the same logical extension of the Rule of Reason as was eventually developed after Judge Taft's opinion.

[1.440] H. THORELLI, *supra* note 1.378, at 470. Still another signal of retreat from the earlier, inflexible approach was Northern Sec. Co. v. United States, 193 U.S. 197 (1904), in which five Justices avoided a literal interpretation of the Sherman Act and leaned towards applying a standard of common law reasonableness. Mr. Justice Harlan's majority opinion, joined in by Justices Brown, Day, and McKenna, followed the *Trans-Missouri* and *Joint Traffic* approach, holding that the Sherman Act applied to "*all direct restraints* imposed by combination, conspiracy or monopoly upon . . . trade or commerce." *Id.* at 331. However, Mr. Justice Brewer, who concurred in the majority opinion, and the dissenters—Chief Justice Fuller and Justices Holmes, Peckham, and White—interpreted the Sherman Act to apply only to restraints of trade that were unreasonable at common law. *Id.* at 361, 403-05. As with the Sixth Circuit's decision in *Addyston Pipe*, though, this opinion did not constitute part of Chief Justice White's authority in *Standard Oil* for the formal launching of the Rule of Reason.

[1.441] 221 U.S. 1 (1911), *infra* at 382.

[1.442] *Id.* at 59-60, *infra* at 389. Mr. Chief Justice White's resort to the congressional debates was limited to "ascertaining the environment at the time of the enactment of a particular law." *Id.* at 50, *infra* at 386. Recognition of the value of legislative history in general, and congressional debates specifically, has been considerably broadened since that time, as evidenced by increased judicial reliance upon such materials to evaluate legislative intent. *See, e.g.*, Supreme Court's decisions in, among others, Apex Hosiery Co. v. Leader, 310 U.S. 469 (1940), *infra* at 416; Parker v. Brown, 317 U.S. 341 (1943), *infra* at 423; United States v. South-Eastern Underwriters Ass'n, 322 U.S. 533 (1944), *infra* at 426; United States v. Topco Associates, Inc., 405 U.S. 596, 92 S. Ct. 1126, 31 L. Ed. 2d 515 (1972) (Burger, C.J., dissenting), *infra* at 446; and Gulf Oil Corp. v. Copp Paving Co., 419 U.S. 186 (1974).

particular arrangement against the "standard of reason" which had been applied to such arrangements at common law.[1.443] In like manner, the Act's complementary second section was to be harmonized with the first, and the challenged conduct tested by the criterion of "the rule of reason guided by the established law and by the plain duty to enforce the prohibitions of the act and thus the public policy which its restrictions were obviously enacted to subserve."[1.444]

Although the Court in *Standard Oil* did not make specific reference to the congressional debates, there is ample legislative evidence to support the Court's essential conclusion that the statute was to be applied by utilization of a flexible, practical approach to the challenged conduct in the light of experience as to its effect on competition.[1.445] It should be noted, however, that despite the departure of *Standard Oil* from an inflexible analytical approach to the statute's construction, Chief Justice White nevertheless maintained that its announced rationale was consistent with the Court's earlier decisions. He accordingly stated that the *Trans-Missouri* and *Joint Traffic* decisions were not overruled by the *Standard Oil* formulation because, in each of those cases, the restraints had in fact been found unlawful "by the light of reason," that is, by resort to the standard that the Court was that day expressly formulating.[1.446] Chief Justice White, again speaking for the Court a mere two weeks later in *United States v. American Tobacco Co.*,[1.447] reaffirmed the broad, flexible approach to the Act's construction taken in *Standard Oil*. In this opinion, the previously stated need to give the Act a "reasonable construction" was reemphasized, and the Rule of Reason standard further elaborated.[1.448]

The remaining decisions selected present further elaborations and refinements of the rule. The often-quoted, classic statement describing the "true test of legality" by which to distinguish the competitive impact of a particular restraint appears in the Supreme Court's succinct opinion in *[Chicago] Board of Trade v. United States*.[1.449] In addition, *United States v. Trenton Potteries Co.*[1.450] emphasized that the standard of "reasonableness" was a changing one and that any particular conduct must be controlled by the Act's underlying purpose in protecting and maintaining free competition.[1.451]

The Court's decision in *United States v. E. I. du Pont de Nemours & Co.*[1.452] is one of the few cases arising exclusively under section 2 of the Act in which reference is made to its legislative proceedings. That case illustrates the Act's flexible application to

---

[1.443] 221 U.S. at 60, *infra* at 389.

[1.444] *Id.* at 61–62, *infra* at 390.

[1.445] See note 1.429 *supra*.

[1.446] 221 U.S. at 64–65, *infra* at 391. Chief Justice White declared that while those earlier cases had made use of certain "general language . . . which, when separated from its context, would justify the conclusion that it was decided that reason could not be resorted to for the purpose of determining whether the acts complained of were within the statute," those opinions had fully referred to the nature of the respective arrangements and demonstrated their unreasonableness. *Id.* at 64, *infra* at 391. In his partially dissenting opinion, Mr. Justice Harlan took his brother Justices to task for allegedly engaging in exactly the same type of "judicial legislation" which the Court had previously stated in those cases it was to avoid. *Id.* at 98–100, *infra* at 400–01.

[1.447] 221 U.S. 106 (1911), *infra* at 403.

[1.448] *Id.* at 178–80, *infra* at 406–07.

[1.449] 246 U.S. 231, 38 S. Ct. 242, 62 L. Ed. 683 (1918), *infra* at 410. In connection with the factors which the Court in that case said must be considered, it should be noted that in Goldfarb v. Virginia State Bar, 421 U.S. 773, 787–88 n.17 (1975), the Supreme Court intimated that section 1 of the Sherman Act may be susceptible to different application to some activities of the professions than would be the case if the activity under inquiry were to be engaged in by a business enterprise, presumably under a Rule of Reason analysis. *See* note 1.423 *supra*.

[1.450] 273 U.S. 392, 47 S. Ct. 377, 71 L. Ed. 700 (1927), *infra* at 412.

[1.451] 273 U.S. at 397, *infra* at 414. A comprehensive article dealing with the evolution of the Rule of Reason, which emphasizes the early Sherman Act cases and gives greater credit to Justice Peckham for the rule's development than has generally been accorded him, is Bork, *The Rule of Reason and the Per Se Concept: Price Fixing and Market Division* (pts. 1–2), 74, 75 YALE L.J. 775, 377 (1965–1966); another good treatment of the subject is found in M. HANDLER, *The Judicial Architects of the Rule of Reason*, in 1 TWENTY-FIVE YEARS OF ANTITRUST 1 (1973).

[1.452] 351 U.S. 377 (1956), *infra* at 437.

technological developments in determining the market definition for the products there being considered. It also demonstrates that the offense of monopolization involves some conduct beyond "superior skill and intelligence" by which a person gains an unlawful competitive advantage. In *United States v. Aluminum Co. of America*,[1.453] Judge Learned Hand, dealing with the offense of monopolization, had engaged in an economic analysis similar to that used in *du Pont* in formulating the appropriate market definition. In discussing the economic reasons which forbid monopoly, Judge Hand made passing reference to one of Senator Sherman's speeches to demonstrate that "among the purposes of Congress in 1890 was a desire to put an end to great aggregations of capital because of the helplessness of the individual before them." Moreover, he quoted the following passage from Sherman's remarks:

> If the concerted powers of this combination are intrusted to a single man, it is a kingly prerogative, inconsistent with our form of government, and should be subject to the strong resistance of the State and national authorities. . . . 21 Cong. Record, 2457.
>
> The popular mind is agitated with problems that may disturb social order, and among them all none is more threatening than the inequality of condition, of wealth, and opportunity that has grown within a single generation out of the concentration of capital into vast combinations to control production and trade and to break down competition. These combinations already defy or control powerful transportation corporations and reach State authorities. They reach out their Briarean arms to every part of our country. They are imported from abroad. Congress alone can deal with them, and if we are unwilling or unable there will soon be a trust for every production and a master to fix the price for every necessity of life. . . . 21 Cong. Record, 2460. See also 21 Cong. Record, 2598.[1.454]

That case is also significant for its discussion of the elements involved in the offense of monopolization and the nature of the conduct which is proscribed under section 2 of the Act.[1.455]

Evolution of the Rule of Per Se Illegality

In refusing to consider the reasonableness of the prices actually established, the Court in *Trenton Potteries* held that price-fixing agreements, because they involved the power to control the market and to fix arbitrary and unreasonable prices, were unlawful in and of themselves and did not require an inquiry in each case as to the reasonableness of the prices established.[1.456] Although drawing somewhat upon precedent, this was an early formulation of the doctrine of *per se* illegality, which permits courts, having experience with certain forms of business conduct shown to have

---

[1.453] 148 F.2d 416 (2d Cir. 1945).

[1.454] *Id.* at 428–29 n.1.

[1.455] As discussed in the *Introduction*, section 2 of the Sherman Act was added to the bill during its substantial revision by the Senate Judiciary Committee and was the subject of sparse debate, limited generally to the proposition that a single firm's or person's conduct could also be subject to the Act. *See* pp. 23, 24–25 *supra*. Development of judicial standards for this major operative section of the Act has not, accordingly, proceeded by judicial resort to the congressional debates or legislative history in as extensive a manner as the first section.

It should be noted that both the *Standard Oil* and *American Tobacco* opinions also analyzed and construed section 2 of the Act. In each of these cases, it was found that the challenged conduct constituted monopolization and attempted monopolization as well as unlawful restraints of trade. In addition to the *du Pont (Cellophane)* opinion, which is included in this compilation, *infra* at 437, some of the other leading section 2 cases, including Judge Learned Hand's opinion in United States v. Aluminum Co. of America, 148 F.2d 416 (2d Cir. 1945), and the Supreme Court's decision in United States v. Grinnell Corp., 384 U.S. 563 (1966), are briefly discussed in the *Introduction supra* at 32–33. For additional textual discussions of the substantive elements of section 2 offenses, the reader is referred to ABA Antitrust Law Developments 47–63 (1975); E. Kintner, An Antitrust Primer, at ch. 12 (2d ed. 1973); Report of the Attorney General's National Committee to Study the Antitrust Laws 43–62 (1955); 1 H. Toulmin, A Treatise on the Anti-Trust Laws of the United States, at chs. 14–15 (1949); 1 J. von Kalinowski, Antitrust Laws and Trade Regulation, at chs. 7–8 (1969); and 2 *id.* at ch. 9.

[1.456] 273 U.S. at 397–98, *infra* at 414. The Court in *Trenton Potteries* also cited with approval from the *Trans-Missouri*, *Standard Oil*, and *American Tobacco* decisions concerning the refusal of those Courts to consider the reasonableness of the prices involved in those cases. *Id.* at 398–400, *infra* at 414–15. *See also* United States v. Addyston Pipe & Steel Co., 85 F. 271, 293 (6th Cir. 1898), *aff'd*, 175 U.S. 211 (1899).

been restrictive, to find such conduct presumptively unlawful without inquiring into the precise impact upon competition. As later succinctly explained by the Supreme Court in *Northern Pacific Railway Co. v. United States*,[1.457] the principle of *per se* illegality is not inconsistent with the flexible Rule of Reason approach, because judicial experience with certain restraints may allow them to be conclusively presumed illegal without further analysis of their particular market effect:

> The Sherman Act was designed to be a comprehensive charter of economic liberty aimed at preserving free and unfettered competition as the rule of trade. It rests on the premise that the unrestrained interaction of competitive forces will yield the best allocation of our economic resources, the lowest prices, the highest quality and the greatest material progress, while at the same time providing an environment conducive to the preservation of our democratic political and social institutions. But even were that premise open to question, the policy unequivocally laid down by the Act is competition. And to this end it prohibits "Every contract, combination . . . or conspiracy, in restraint of trade or commerce among the several States." Although this prohibition is literally all-encompassing, the courts have construed it as precluding only those contracts or combinations which "unreasonably" restrain competition. *Standard Oil Co. of New Jersey v. United States*, 221 U.S. 1; *Chicago Board of Trade v. United States*, 246 U.S. 231.
>
> However, there are certain agreements or practices which because of their pernicious effect on competition and lack of any redeeming virtue are conclusively presumed to be unreasonable and therefore illegal without elaborate inquiry as to the precise harm they have caused or the business excuse for their use. This principle of *per se* unreasonableness not only makes the type of restraints which are proscribed by the Sherman Act more certain to the benefit of everyone concerned, but it also avoids the necessity for an incredibly complicated and prolonged economic investigation into the entire history of the industry involved, as well as related industries, in an effort to determine at large whether a particular restraint has been unreasonable—an inquiry too often wholly fruitless when undertaken. Among the practices which the courts have heretofore deemed to be unlawful in and of themselves are price fixing, *United States v. Socony-Vacuum Oil Co.*, 310 U.S. 150, 210; [horizontal] division of markets, *United States v. Addyston Pipe & Steel Co.*, 85 F. 271, aff'd, 175 U.S. 211; group boycotts, *Fashion Originators' Guild v. Federal Trade Comm'n*, 312 U.S. 457; and tying arrangements, *International Salt Co. v. United States*, 332 U.S. 392.[1.458]

Nonetheless, the Supreme Court's 1972 decision in *United States v. Topco Associates, Inc.*,[1.459] illustrates that some jurisprudential difficulties may be encountered in utilizing both a Rule of Reason and a *per se* approach in that the latter may prevent the courts from analyzing the reasonableness of restraints in unique or troublesome situations. In holding the horizontal territorial allocation by the cooperative association unlawful, despite the trial court's finding that such arrangement enabled its smaller member grocery chains to compete more effectively with the larger integrated chains,

---

[1.457] 356 U.S. 1, 78 S. Ct. 514, 2 L. Ed. 2d 545 (1958).

[1.458] 356 U.S. at 4–5. Two other types of arrangements which in the past appeared to have been given *per se* status are vertical allocation of markets where the seller has parted with title, dominion, and risk of loss over the product, *see* United States v. Arnold, Schwinn & Co., 388 U.S. 365, 379, 87 S. Ct. 1856, 1865, 18 L. Ed. 2d 1249, 1260 (1967), *overruled by* Continental T.V., Inc. v. GTE Sylvania, Inc., 97 S. Ct. 2549 (1977), and reciprocal dealing where there has been foreclosure of a not insubstantial amount of commerce, *see* United States v. General Dynamics Corp., 258 F. Supp. 36, 66 (S.D.N.Y. 1966).

For a good example of an opinion in which the Court assessed the considerations involved in applying a test of *per se* illegality to arrangements that established vertical customer and territorial restraints—in which the Court declined to apply such a *per se* rule because it did not "know enough of the economic and business stuff out of which these arrangements emerge[d]"—see White Motor Co. v. United States, 372 U.S. 253, 83 S. Ct. 696, 9 L. Ed. 2d 738 (1963). Some four years later, however, in *Schwinn*, the Court appeared to hold that such arrangements were *per se* illegal where the manufacturer had parted with title, dominion, or risk of loss with respect to the products involved, but the *per se* approach was subsequently rejected in *GTE Sylvania*.

It should be noted, however, that to the extent that traditional antitrust concepts are applied to the professions rather than to business enterprises, the Supreme Court in Goldfarb v. Virginia State Bar, 421 U.S. 773, 787–88 n. 17 (1975), intimated that a different application of the Act may be appropriate with regard to activities engaged in by the former, presumably requiring a Rule of Reason analysis in such situations, even where a *per se* approach may be applied to such conduct involving business enterprises. *See* notes 1.423 & 1.499 *supra*.

[1.459] 405 U.S. 596 (1972), *infra* at 446.

Mr. Justice Marshall declared the lower court's reasoning to have been fallacious in that the Sherman Act does not authorize businessmen to make judgments as to the respective value of competition in various sectors of the economy.[1.460] On the other hand, Chief Justice Burger presented a thorough and analytical dissent, in which he appealed to the legislative intent that the statute be applied on a case-by-case basis in order to effectuate the legislative policy of protecting competition.[1.461] In a separate, short opinion, Mr. Justice Blackmun referred to what he termed the "anomalous aspects" of the Court's decision.[1.462] While acknowledging the established nature of the *per se* rule, he predicted that one effect of the decision would be to inhibit the ability of smaller firms to compete effectively with large chains. Although there may be no logical inconsistency in utilizing both the Rule of Reason and *per se* concepts, the practical difficulties inherent in such an approach are highlighted in cases such as *Topco*. The majority of the Court recognized that, in applying a statute such as the Sherman Act which enunciates only general principles of protecting free competition, specific judgments as to the comparative value of different kinds of competition can only be left for further legislative resolution.[1.463]

[1.460] *Id.* at 611, *infra* at 450–51.

[1.461] *Id.* at 620–21 (dissenting opinion), *infra* at 454.

[1.462] *Id.* at 612 (concurring opinion), *infra* at 451.

[1.463] *Id.* at 611–12, *infra* at 451.

UNITED STATES v. JOINT TRAFFIC ASSOCIATION

171 U.S. 505, 19 S. Ct. 25, 43 L. Ed. 259 (1898)

The bill was filed in this case in the Circuit Court of the United States for the Southern District of New York for the purpose of obtaining an adjudication that an agreement ⊥ entered into between some thirty-one different railroad companies was ⊥506 illegal, and enjoining its further execution.

These railroad companies formed most (but not all) of the lines engaged in the business of railroad transportation between Chicago and the Atlantic coast, and the object of the agreement, as expressed in its preamble, was to form an association of railroad companies "to aid in fulfilling the purpose of the Interstate Commerce act, to coöperate with each other and adjacent transportation associations to establish and maintain reasonable and just rates, fares, rules and regulations on state and interstate traffic, to prevent unjust discrimination and to secure the reduction and concentration of agencies and the introduction of economies in the conduct of the freight and passenger service." To accomplish these purposes the railroad companies adopted articles of association, by which they agreed that the affairs of the association should be administered by several different boards, and that it should have jurisdiction over all competitive traffic (with certain exceptions therein noted) which passed through the western termini of the trunk lines (naming them), and such other points as might be thereafter designated by the managers. The duly published schedules of rates, fares and charges, and the rules applicable thereto, which were in force at the time of the execution of the agreement and authorized by the different companies and filed with the Interstate Commerce Commission, were reaffirmed by the companies composing the association. From time to time the managers were to recommend such changes in the rates, fares, charges and rules as might be reasonable and just and necessary for governing the traffic covered by the agreement and for protecting the interests of the parties to the agreement, and a failure to observe such recommendations by any of the parties to the agreement was to be deemed a violation of the agreement. No company which was a party to it was permitted in any way to deviate from or to change the rates, fares, charges or rules set forth in the agreement or recommended by the managers, except by a resolution of the board of directors of the company, and its action was not to affect the rates, etc., disapproved, except to the ex⊥tent of its interest ⊥507 therein over its own road. . . . It was further stated in the agreement that "the powers conferred upon the managers shall be so construed and exercised as not to permit violation of the Interstate Commerce act, or any other law applicable to the premises or any provision of the charters or the laws applicable to any of the companies parties hereto, and the managers shall coöperate with the Interstate Commerce Commission to secure stability and uniformity in the rates, fares, charges and rules established hereunder." . . .

⊥ . . . Any violation of the agreement was to be followed by a forfeiture of the ⊥508 offending company in a sum to be determined by the managers, which should not exceed five thousand dollars, or if the gross receipts of the transaction which violated the agreement should exceed five thousand dollars, the offending party should, in the discretion of the managers, forfeit a sum not exceeding such gross receipts. The sums thus collected were to go to the payment of the expenses of the association, except that the offending company should not participate in the application of its own forfeiture. . . .

The bill filed by the Government . . . ⊥ charged that the agreement was an ⊥509 unlawful one, and a combination and conspiracy, and that it was entered into in order to terminate all competition among the parties to it for freight and passenger traffic, and that the agreement unlawfully restrained trade and commerce among the several States and Territories of the United States, and unlawfully attempted to monopolize a part of such interstate trade and commerce. . . . [T]he relief sought was a judgment declaring the agreement void and enjoining the parties from operating their roads under the same. . . .

The case came on for hearing on bill and answer, and the Circuit Court, after a hearing, dismissed the bill, and upon appeal its decree was affirmed by the Circuit Court of Appeals for the Second Circuit, and the Government has appealed here. . . .

⊥558 ⊥ MR. JUSTICE PECKHAM, after stating the case, delivered the opinion of the court.

. . . The suit is brought to obtain a decree declaring null and void the agreement mentioned in the bill. Upon comparing that agreement with the one set forth in the case of *United States* v. *Trans-Missouri Freight Association,* 166 U. S. 290, the great similarity between them suggests that a similar result should be reached in the two cases. The respondents, however, object to this, and give several reasons why this case should not be controlled by the other. . . .

⊥559 ⊥ It is also objected that the statute, if construed as it has been construed in the *Trans-Missouri case,* is unconstitutional, in that it unduly interferes with the liberty of the individual and takes away from him the right to make contracts regarding his own affairs, which is guaranteed to him by the Fifth Amendment to the Constitution, which provides that "no person shall be . . . deprived of life, liberty or property without due process of law; nor shall private property be taken for public use without just compensation." This objection was not advanced in the arguments in the other case. . . .

⊥562 ⊥ So far as the establishment of rates and fares is concerned, we do not see any substantial difference between this agreement and the one set forth in the *Trans-Missouri case.* . . .

⊥565 ⊥ It is also said that the agreement in the first case conferred upon the association an unlimited power to fix rates in the first instance, and that the authority was not confined to reasonable rates, while in the case now before us the agreement starts out with rates fixed by each company for itself and filed with the Interstate Commerce Commission, and which rates are alleged to be reasonable. The distinction is unimportant. It was considered in the other case that the rates actually fixed upon were reasonable, while the rates fixed upon in this case are also admitted to be reasonable. By this agreement the board of managers is in substance and as a result thereof placed in control of the business and rates of transportation, and its duty is to see to it that each company charges the rates agreed upon and receives its equitable proportion of the traffic.

The natural and direct effect of the two agreements is the same, viz., to maintain rates at a higher level than would otherwise prevail, and the differences between them are not sufficiently important or material to call for different judgments in the two cases on any such ground. Indeed, counsel for one of the railroad companies on this argument, in speaking of the agreement in the *Trans-Missouri case,* says of it that its terms, while substantially similar to those of the agreement here, were less explicit in making it just and reasonable.

Regarding the two agreements as alike in their main and material features, we are brought to an examination of the question of the constitutionality of the act, construed ⊥566 as it has ⊥ been in the *Trans-Missouri case.* It is worthy of remark that this question was never raised or hinted at upon the argument of that case, although, if the respondents' present contention be sound, it would have furnished a conclusive objection to the enforcement of the act as construed. The fact that not one of the many astute and able counsel for the transportation companies in that case raised an objection of so conclusive a character, if well founded, is strong evidence that the reasons showing the invalidity of the act as construed do not lie on the surface and were not then apparent to those counsel.

The point not being raised and the decision of that case having proceeded upon an assumption of the validity of the act under either construction, it can, of course, constitute no authority upon this question. Upon the constitutionality of the act it is now earnestly contended that contracts in restraint of trade are not necessarily prejudicial to the security or welfare of society, and that Congress is without power to prohibit generally all contracts in restraint of trade, and the effort to do this invalidates the act in question. It is urged that it is for the court to decide whether the mere fact that a contract or arrangement, whatever its purpose or character, may restrain trade in some degree, renders it injurious or prejudicial to the welfare or security of society, and if the court be of opinion that such welfare or security is not prejudiced by a contract of that kind, then Congress has no power to prohibit it, and the act must be declared unconstitutional. It is claimed that the act can be supported only as an exercise of the police power, and that the constitutional guarantees furnished by the Fifth Amendment secure to all persons freedom in the pursuit of their vocations and the use of their property, and in making such contracts or arrangements as may be necessary therefor. In dwelling upon the far-reaching nature of the language used in the act as construed in the case mentioned, counsel contend that the extent to which it limits the freedom and destroys the property of the individual can scarcely be exaggerated, and that ordinary contracts and combinations, which are at the same time most indispensable, have the effect of somewhat ⊥ restraining trade and commerce, although to a very slight extent, but yet, under the construction adopted, they are illegal.

As examples of the kinds of contracts which are rendered illegal by this construction of the act, the learned counsel suggest all organizations of mechanics engaged in the same business for the purpose of limiting the number of persons employed in the business, or of maintaining wages; the formation of a corporation to carry on any particular line of business by those already engaged therein; a contract of partnership or of employment between two persons previously engaged in the same line of business; the appointment by two producers of the same person to sell their goods on commission; the purchase by one wholesale merchant of the product of two producers; the lease or purchase by a farmer, manufacturer or merchant of an additional farm, manufactory or shop; the withdrawal from business of any farmer, merchant or manufacturer; a sale of the good will of a business with an agreement not to destroy its value by engaging in similar business; and a covenant in a deed restricting the use of real estate. It is added that the effect of most business contracts or combinations is to restrain trade in some degree.

This makes quite a formidable list. It will be observed, however, that no contract of the nature above described is now before the court, and there is some embarrassment in assuming to decide herein just how far the act goes in the direction claimed. Nevertheless, we might say that the formation of corporations for business or manufacturing purposes has never, to our knowledge, been regarded in the nature of a contract in restraint of trade or commerce. The same may be said of the contract of partnership. It might also be difficult to show that the appointment by two or more producers of the same person to sell their goods on commission was a matter in any degree in restraint of trade.

We are not aware that it has ever been claimed that a lease or purchase by a farmer, manufacturer or merchant of an additional farm, manufactory or shop, or the withdrawal from business of any farmer, merchant or manufacturer, restrained commerce or trade within any legal definition of that term; ⊥ and the sale of a good will of a business with an accompanying agreement not to engage in a similar business was instanced in the *Trans-Missouri case* as a contract not within the meaning of the act; and it was said that such a contract was collateral to the main contract of sale and was entered into for the purpose of enhancing the price at which the vendor sells his business. The instances cited by counsel have in our judgment little or no bearing upon the question under consideration. In *Hopkins* v. *United States,* decided at this term, *post,* 578, we say that the statute applies only to those contracts whose direct and immediate effect is a restraint upon interstate commerce, and that to treat the act as condemning all agreements under which, as a result, the cost of conducting an interstate commercial business may be increased, would enlarge the application of the act far beyond the fair meaning of the language used. The effect upon interstate commerce must not be indirect or incidental only. An agreement entered into for the purpose of promoting the legitimate business of an individual or corporation, with no purpose to thereby affect or restrain interstate commerce, and which does not directly restrain such commerce, is not, as we think, covered by the act, although the agreement may indirectly and remotely affect that commerce. We also repeat what is said in the case above cited, that "the act of Congress must have a reasonable construction, or else there would scarcely be an agreement or contract among business men that could not be said to have, indirectly or remotely, some bearing upon interstate commerce, and possibly to restrain it." To suppose, as is assumed by counsel, that the effect of the decision in the *Trans-Missouri case* is to render illegal most business contracts or combinations, however indispensable and necessary they may be, because, as they assert, they all restrain trade in some remote and indirect degree, is to make a most violent assumption and one not called for or justified by the decision mentioned, or by any other decision of this court.

The question really before us is whether Congress, in the exercise of its right to regulate commerce among the several States, or otherwise, has the power to prohibit, as in restraint of interstate commerce, a contract or combination between competing railroad corporations entered into and formed for the purpose of establishing and maintaining interstate rates and fares for the transportation of freight and passengers on any of the railroads parties to the contract or combination, even though the rates and fares thus established are reasonable. Such an agreement directly affects and of course is intended to affect the cost of transportation of commodities, and commerce consists, among other things, of the transportation of commodities, and if such transportation be between States it is interstate commerce. The agreement affects interstate commerce by destroying competition and by maintaining rates above what competition might produce.

If it did not do that, its existence would be useless, and it would soon be rescinded or abandoned. Its acknowledged purpose is to maintain rates, and if executed, it does so. It must be remembered, however, that the act does not prohibit any railroad company from charging reasonable rates. If in the absence of any contract or combination among the railroad companies the rates and fares would be less than they are under such contract or combination, that is not by reason of any provision of the act which itself lowers rates, but only because the railroad companies would, as it is urged, voluntarily and at once inaugurate a war of competition among themselves, and thereby themselves reduce their rates and fares.

Has not Congress with regard to interstate commerce and in the course of regulating it, in the case of railroad corporations, the power to say that no contract or combination shall be legal which shall restrain trade and commerce by shutting out the operation of the general law of competition? We think it has.

As counsel for the Traffic Association has truly said, the ordinary highways on land have generally been established and maintained by the public. When the matter of the building of railroads as highways arose, a question was presented whether the State should itself build them or permit others to do it. The State did not build them, and as their building required, among other things, the appropriation of land, private individuals could not enforce such appropriation without a grant from the State.

The building and operation of a railroad thus required a public franchise. The State would have had no power to grant the right of appropriation unless the use to which the land was to be put was a public one. Taking land for railroad purposes is a taking for a public purpose, and the fact that it is taken for a public purpose is the sole justification for taking it at all. The business of a railroad carrier is of a public nature, and in performing it the carrier is also performing to a certain extent a function of government which, as counsel observed, requires them to perform the service upon equal terms to all. This public service, that of transportation of passengers and freight, is a part of trade and commerce, and when transported between States such commerce becomes what is described as interstate, and comes, to a certain extent, under the jurisdiction of Congress by virtue of its power to regulate commerce among the several States.

Where the grantees of this public franchise are competing railroad companies for interstate commerce, we think Congress is competent to forbid any agreement or combination among them by means of which competition is to be smothered.

Although the franchise when granted by the State becomes by the grant the property of the grantee, yet there are some regulations respecting the exercise of such grants which Congress may make under its power to regulate commerce among the several States. This will be conceded by all, the only question being as to the extent of the power.

We think it extends at least to the prohibition of contracts relating to interstate commerce, which would extinguish all competition between otherwise competing railroad corporations, and which would in that way restrain interstate trade or commerce. We do not think, when the grantees of this public franchise are competing railroads seeking the business of transportation of men and goods from one State to another, that ordinary freedom of contract in the use and management of their property requires the right to combine ⊥ as one consolidated and powerful association for the purpose of stifling competition among themselves, and of thus keeping their rates and charges higher than they might otherwise be under the laws of competition. And this is so, even though the rates provided for in the agreement may for the time be not more than are reasonable. They may easily and at any time be increased. It is the combination of these large and powerful corporations, covering vast sections of territory and influencing trade throughout the whole extent thereof, and acting as one body in all the matters over which the combination extends, that constitutes the alleged evil, and in regard to which, so far as the combination operates upon and restrains interstate commerce, Congress has power to legislate and to prohibit.

The prohibition of such contracts may in the judgment of Congress be one of the reasonable necessities for the proper regulation of commerce, and Congress is the judge of such necessity and propriety, unless, in case of a possible gross perversion of the principle, the courts might be applied to for relief.

The cases cited by the respondents' counsel in regard to the general constitutional right of the citizen to make contracts relating to his lawful business are not inconsistent with the existence of the power of Congress to prohibit contracts of the nature involved in this case. The power to regulate commerce has no limitation other than those prescribed in the Constitution. The power, however, does not carry with it the right to destroy or impair those limitations and guarantees which are also placed in the Constitution or in any of the amendments to that instrument. *Monongahela Navigation Co.* v. *United States,* 148 U. S. 312-336; *Interstate Commerce Commission* v. *Brimson,* 154 U. S. 447-479.

Among these limitations and guarantees counsel refer to those which provide that no person shall be deprived of life, liberty or property without due process of law, and that private property shall not be taken for public use without just compensation. The latter limitation is, we think, plainly irrelevant.

⊥ As to the former, it is claimed that the citizen is deprived of his liberty without due process of law when, by a general statute, he is arbitrarily deprived of the right to make a contract of the nature herein involved.

The case of *Allgeyer* v. *Louisiana,* 165 U. S. 578, is cited as authority for the statement concerning the right to contract. In speaking of the meaning of the word "liberty," as used in the Fourteenth Amendment to the Constitution, it was said in that case to include, among other things, the liberty of the citizen to pursue any livelihood or vocation, and for that purpose to enter into all contracts which might be proper, necessary and essential to his carrying out those objects to a successful conclusion.

We do not impugn the correctness of that statement. The citizen may have the right to make a proper (that is, a lawful) contract, one which is also essential and necessary for carrying out his lawful purposes. The question which arises here is, whether the contract is a proper or lawful one, and we have not advanced a step towards its solution by saying that the citizen is protected by the Fifth, or any other amendment, in his right to make proper contracts to enable him to carry out his lawful purposes. We presume it will not be contended that the court meant, in stating the right of the citizen "to pursue any livelihood or vocation," to include every means of obtaining a livelihood, whether it was lawful or otherwise. Precisely how far a legislature can go in declaring a certain means of obtaining a livelihood unlawful, it is unnecessary here to speak of. It will be conceded it has power to make some kinds of vocations and some methods of obtaining a livelihood unlawful, and in regard to those the citizen would have no right to contract to carry them on.

Congress may restrain individuals from making contracts under certain circumstances and upon certain subjects. *Frisbie* v. *United States,* 157 U. S. 160.

Notwithstanding the general liberty of contract which is possessed by the citizen under the Constitution, we find that there are many kinds of contracts which, while not in themselves immoral or *mala in se,* may yet be prohibited by the ⊥ legislation of the

States or, in certain cases, by Congress. The question comes back whether the statute under review is a legitimate exercise of the power of Congress over interstate commerce and a valid regulation thereof. The question is, for us, one of power only, and not of policy. We think the power exists in Congress, and that the statute is therefore valid. . . .

⊥ *The judgments of the Circuit Court of the United States for the Southern District of New York and of the Circuit Court of Appeals for the Second Circuit are reversed, and the case remanded to the Circuit Court with directions to take such further proceedings therein as may be in conformity with this opinion.*

MR. JUSTICE GRAY, MR. JUSTICE SHIRAS and MR. JUSTICE WHITE dissented.

MR. JUSTICE MCKENNA took no part in the decision of the case.

STANDARD OIL CO. OF NEW JERSEY v. UNITED STATES

221 U.S. 1, 31 S. Ct. 502, 55 L. Ed. 619 (1911)

[ED. NOTE: All original Court footnotes have been omitted.]

⊥ MR. CHIEF JUSTICE WHITE delivered the opinion of the court.

The Standard Oil Company of New Jersey and 33 other corporations, John D. Rockefeller, William Rockefeller and five other individual defendants prosecute this appeal to reverse a decree of the court below. Such decree was entered upon a bill filed by the United States under authority of § 4, of the act of July 2, 1890, c. 647, p. 209, known as the Anti-trust Act, and had for its object the enforcement of the provisions of that act. . . .

⊥ The bill and exhibits, covering one hundred and seventy pages of the printed record, was [sic] filed on November 15, 1906. Corporations known as Standard Oil Company of New Jersey, Standard Oil Company of California, Standard Oil Company of Indiana, Standard Oil Company of Iowa, Standard Oil Company of Kansas, Standard Oil Company of Kentucky, Standard Oil Company of Nebraska, Standard Oil Company of New York, Standard Oil Company of Ohio and sixty-two other corporations and partnerships, as also seven individuals were named as defendants. The bill was divided into thirty numbered sections, and sought relief upon the theory that the various defendants were engaged in conspiring "to restrain the trade and commerce in petroleum, commonly called 'crude oil,' in refined oil, and in the other products of petroleum, among the several States and Territories of the United States and the District of Columbia and with foreign nations, and to monopolize the said commerce." The conspiracy was alleged to have been formed in or about the year 1870 by three of the individual defendants, viz: John D. Rockefeller, William Rockefeller and Henry M. Flagler. The detailed averments concerning the alleged conspiracy were arranged with reference to three periods, the first from 1870 to 1882, the second from 1882 to 1899, and the third from 1899 to the time of the filing of the bill.

The general charge concerning the period from 1870 to 1882 was as follows:

⊥ "That during said first period the said individual defendants, in connection with the Standard Oil Company of Ohio, purchased and obtained interests through stock ownership and otherwise in, and entered into agreements with, various persons, firms, corporations, and limited partnerships engaged in purchasing, shipping, refining, and selling petroleum and its products among the various States for the purpose of fixing the price of crude and refined oil and the products thereof, limiting the production thereof, and controlling the transportation therein, and thereby restraining trade and commerce among the several States, and monopolizing the said commerce."

To establish this charge it was averred that John D. and William Rockefeller and several other named individuals, who, prior to 1870, composed three separate partnerships engaged in the business of refining crude oil and shipping its products in interstate commerce, organized in the year 1870, a corporation known as the Standard Oil Company of Ohio and transferred to that company the business of the said partnerships, the members thereof becoming, in proportion to their prior ownership, stockholders in the corporation. It was averred that the other individual defendants soon afterwards became participants in the illegal combination and either transferred property to the corporation or to individuals to be held for the benefit of all parties in interest in proportion to their respective interests in the combination; that is, in proportion to their stock ownership in the Standard Oil Company of Ohio. By the means thus stated, it was charged that by the year 1872, the combination had acquired substantially all but three or four of the thirty-five or forty oil refineries located in Cleveland, Ohio. By reason of the power thus obtained and in further execution of the intent and purpose to restrain trade and to monopolize the commerce, interstate as well as intrastate, in petroleum and its products, the bill alleged that the combination and its members obtained large preferential rates and rebates in many and devious ways over their competitors from various railroad companies, and that by means of the advantage thus obtained many, if not virtually all, competitors were forced either to become members of the combination or were driven out of business; and thus, it was alleged, during the period in question the following results were brought about: *a.* That the combination, in addition to the refineries in Cleveland which it had acquired as previously stated, and which it had either dismantled to limit production or continued to operate, also from time to time acquired a large number of refineries of crude petroleum, situated in New York, Pennsylvania, Ohio and elsewhere. . . . *b.* That the combination had obtained control of the pipe lines available for transporting oil from the oil fields to the refineries in Cleveland, Pittsburg [*sic*], Titusville, Philadelphia, New York and New Jersey. *c.* That the combination during the period named had obtained a complete mastery over the oil industry, controlling 90 per cent of the business of producing, shipping, refining and selling petroleum and its products, and thus was able to fix the price of crude and refined petroleum and to restrain and monopolize all interstate commerce in those products.

The averments bearing upon the second period (1882 to 1899) had relation to the claim:

"That during the said second period of conspiracy the defendants entered into a contract and trust agreement, by which various independent firms, corporations, limited partnerships and individuals engaged in purchasing, transporting, refining, shipping and selling oil and the products thereof among the various States turned over the management of their said business, corporations and limited partnerships to nine trustees, composed chiefly of certain individuals defendant herein, which said trust agreement was in restraint of trade and commerce and in violation of law, as hereinafter more particularly alleged."

The trust agreement . . . was made in January, 1882. By its terms the stock of forty corporations, including the Standard Oil Company of Ohio, and a large quantity of various properties which had been previously acquired by the alleged combination and which was held in diverse forms, as we have previously indicated, for the benefit of the members of the combination, was vested in the trustees and their successors, "to be held for all parties in interest jointly." . . .

The agreement made provision for the method of controlling and managing the property by the trustees, for the formation of additional manufacturing, etc., corporations in various States, and the trust, unless terminated by a mode specified, was to continue "during the lives of the survivors and survivor of the trustees named in the agreement and for twenty-one years thereafter." The agreement provided for the issue of Standard Oil Trust certificates to represent the interest arising under the trust in the properties affected by the trust, which of course in view of the provisions of the agreement and the subject to which it related caused the interest in the certificates to be coincident with and the exact representative of the interest in the combination, that is, in the Standard Oil Company of Ohio. . . .

The bill charged that during the second period quo warranto proceedings were commenced against the Standard Oil Company of Ohio, which resulted in the entry by the Supreme Court of Ohio, on March 2, 1892, of a decree ⊥ adjudging the trust agreement to be void, not only because the Standard Oil Company of Ohio was a party to the same, but also because the agreement in and of itself ⊥ was in restraint of trade and amounted to the creation of an unlawful monopoly. It was alleged that shortly after this decision, seemingly for the purpose of complying therewith, voluntary proceedings were had apparently to dissolve the trust, but that these proceedings were a subterfuge and a sham because they simply amounted to a transfer of the stock held by the trust in 64 of the companies which it controlled to some of the remaining 20 companies, it having controlled before the decree 84 in all, thereby, while seemingly in part giving up its dominion, yet in reality preserving the same by means of the control of the companies as to which it had retained complete authority. It was charged that especially was this the case, as the stock in the companies selected for transfer was virtually owned by the nine trustees or the members of their immediate families or associates. The bill further alleged that in 1897 the Attorney-General of Ohio instituted contempt proceedings in the quo warranto case based upon the claim that the trust had not been dissolved as required by the decree in that case. . . .

⊥ The result of these proceedings, the bill charged, caused a resort to the alleged wrongful acts asserted to have been committed during the third period, as follows:

"That during the third period of said conspiracy and in pursuance thereof the said individual defendants operated through the Standard Oil Company of New Jersey, as a holding corporation, which corporation obtained and acquired the majority of the stocks of the various corporations engaged in purchasing, transporting, refining, shipping, and selling oil into and among the various States and Territories of the United States and the District of Columbia and with foreign nations, and thereby managed and controlled the same, in violation of the laws of the United States, as hereinafter more particularly alleged." . . .

⊥ Reiterating in substance the averments that both the Standard Oil Trust from 1882 to 1899 and the Standard Oil Company of New Jersey since 1899 had monopolized and restrained interstate commerce in petroleum and its products, the bill at great length additionally set forth various means by which during the second and third periods, in addition to the effect occasioned by the combination of alleged previously independent concerns, the monopoly and restraint complained of was continued. . . . [I]t suffices to say that such averments may properly be grouped under the following heads: Rebates, preferences and other discriminatory practises in favor of the combination by railroad companies; restraint and monopolization by control of pipe lines, and unfair practises against com⊥peting pipe lines; contracts with competitors in restraint of trade; unfair methods of competition, such as local price cutting at the points where necessary to suppress competition; espionage of the business of competitors, the operation of bogus independent companies, and payment of rebates on oil, with the like intent; the division of the United States into districts and the limiting of the operations of the various subsidiary corporations as to such districts so that competition in the sale of petroleum products between such corporations had been entirely eliminated and destroyed; and finally reference was made to what was alleged to be the "enormous and unreasonable profits" earned by the Standard Oil Trust and the Standard Oil Company as a result of the alleged monopoly; which presumably was averred as a means of reflexly inferring the scope and power acquired by the alleged combination.

Coming to the prayer of the bill, it suffices to say that in general terms the substantial relief asked was, first, that the combination in restraint of interstate trade and commerce and which had monopolized the same, as alleged in the bill, be found to have existence and that the parties thereto be perpetually enjoined from doing any further act to give effect to it; second, that the transfer of the stocks of the various corporations to the Standard Oil Company of New Jersey, as alleged in the bill, be held to be in violation of the first and second sections of the Anti-trust Act, and that the Standard Oil Company of New Jersey be enjoined and restrained from in any manner continuing to exert control over the subsidiary corporations by means of ownership of said stock or otherwise; third, that specific relief by injunction be awarded against further violation of the statute by any of the acts specifically complained of in the bill. There was also a prayer for general relief. . . .

On June 24, 1907, the cause being at issue, a special examiner was appointed to take the evidence, and his report was filed March 22, 1909. It was heard on April 5 to 10, 1909, under the expediting act of February 11, 1903, before a Circuit Court consisting of four judges.

The court decided in favor of the United States. In the opinion delivered, all the multitude of acts of wrong-doing charged in the bill were put aside, in so far as they were alleged to have been committed prior to the passage of the Anti-trust Act, "except as evidence of their (the defendants') purpose, of their continuing conduct and of its effect." (173 Fed. Rep. 177.)

By the decree which was entered it was adjudged that the combining of the stocks of various companies in the hands of the Standard Oil Company of New Jersey in 1899 constituted a combination in restraint of trade and also an attempt to monopolize and a monopolization under § 2 of the Anti-trust Act. The decree was against seven individual defendants, the Standard Oil Company of New Jersey, thirty-six domestic companies and one foreign company which the Standard Oil Company of New Jersey controls by stock ownership; these 38 corporate defendants being held to be parties to the combination found to exist. . . .

The Standard Oil Company of New Jersey was enjoined from voting the stocks or exerting any control over the said 37 subsidiary companies, and the subsidiary companies were enjoined from paying any dividends as to the Standard Oil Company or permitting it to exercise any control over them by virtue of the stock ownership or power acquired by means of the combination. The individuals and corporations were also enjoined from entering into or carrying into effect any like combination which would evade the decree. Further, the individual defendants, the Standard Oil Company, and the 37 subsidiary corporations were enjoined from engaging or continuing in interstate commerce in petroleum or its products during the continuance of the illegal combination. . . .

. . . [W]e shall make our investigation under four separate headings: First. The text of the first and second sections of the act originally considered and its meaning in the light of the common law and the law of this country at the time of its adoption. Second. The contentions of the parties concerning the act, and the scope and effect of the decisions of this court upon which they rely. Third. The application of the statute to facts, and, Fourth. The remedy, if any, to be afforded as the result of such application.

First. The text of the act and its meaning.

We quote the text of the first and second sections of the act, as follows:

"SECTION 1. Every contract, combination in the form of trust or otherwise, or conspiracy, in restraint of trade or commerce, among the several States, or with foreign nations, is hereby declared to be illegal. Every person who shall make any such contract, or engage in any such combination or conspiracy, shall be deemed guilty of a misdemeanor, and, on conviction thereof, shall be punished by fine not exceeding five thousand dollars, or by imprisonment not exceeding one year, or by both said punishments, in the discretion of the court.

"SEC. 2. Every person who shall monopolize, or attempt to monopolize, or combine or conspire with any other person or persons, to monopolize any part of the trade or commerce among the several States, or with foreign nations, shall be deemed guilty of a misdemeanor, and, on conviction thereof, shall be punished by fine not exceeding five thousand dollars, or by imprisonment not exceeding one year, or by both said punishments, in the discretion of the court."

The debates show that doubt as to whether there was a common law of the United States which governed the subject in the absence of legislation was among the influences leading to the passage of the act. They conclusively show, however, that the main cause which led to the legislation was the thought that it was required by the economic condition of the times, that is, the vast accumulation of wealth in the hands of corporations and individuals, the enormous development of corporate organization, the facility for combination which such organizations afforded, the fact that the facility was being used, and that combinations known as trusts were being multiplied, and the widespread impression that their power had been and would be exerted to oppress individuals and injure the public generally. Although debates may not be used as a means for interpreting a statute (*United States* v. *Trans-Missouri Freight Association,* 166 U. S. 318, and cases cited) that rule in the nature of things is not violated by resorting to debates as a means of ascertaining the environment at the time of the enactment of a particular law, that is, the history of the period when it was adopted.

There can be no doubt that the sole subject with which the first section deals is restraint of trade as therein contemplated, and that the attempt to monopolize and monopolization is the subject with which the second section is concerned. It is certain that those terms, at least in their rudimentary meaning, took their origin in the common law, and were also familiar in the law of this country prior to and at the time of the adoption of the act in question.

We shall endeavor then, first to seek their meaning, not by indulging in an elaborate and learned analysis of the English law and of the law of this country, but by making a very brief reference to the elementary and indisputable conceptions of both the English and American law on the subject prior to the passage of the Anti-trust Act.

a. It is certain that at a very remote period the words "contract in restraint of trade" in England came to refer to some voluntary restraint put by contract by an individual on his right to carry on his trade or calling. Originally all such contracts were considered to be illegal, because it was deemed they were injurious to the public as well as to the individuals who made them. In the interest of the freedom of individuals to contract this doctrine was modified so that it was only when a restraint by contract was so general as to be coterminous with the kingdom that it was treated as void. That is to say, if the restraint was partial in its operation and was otherwise reasonable the contract was held to be valid:

b. Monopolies were defined by Lord Coke as follows:

" 'A monopoly is an institution, or allowance by the king by his grant, commission, or otherwise to any person or persons, bodies politic or corporate, of or for the sole buying, selling, making, working, or using of anything, whereby any person or persons, bodies politic or corporate, are sought to be restrained of any freedom or liberty that they had before, or hindered in their lawful trade.' (3 Just. 181, c. 85.)"

Hawkins thus defined them:

" 'A monopoly is an allowance by the king to a particular person or persons of the sole buying, selling, making, working, or using of anything whereby the subject in general is restrained from the freedom of manufacturing or trading which he had before.' (Hawk. P. C. bk. 1, c. 29.)"

The frequent granting of monopolies and the struggle which led to a denial of the power to create them, that is to say, to the establishment that they were incompatible with the English constitution is known to all and need not be reviewed. The evils which led to the public outcry against monopolies and to the final denial of the power to make them may be thus summarily stated: 1. The power which the monopoly gave to the one who enjoyed it to fix the price and thereby injure the public; 2. The power which it engendered of enabling a limitation on production; and, 3. The danger of deterioration in quality of the monopolized article which it was deemed was the inevitable resultant of the monopolistic control over its production and sale. As monopoly as thus conceived embraced only a consequence arising from an exertion of sovereign power, no express restrictions or prohibitions obtained against the creation by an individual of a monopoly as such. But as it was considered, at least so far as the necessaries of life were concerned, that individuals by the abuse of their right to contract might be able to usurp the power arbitrarily to enhance prices, one of the wrongs arising from monopoly, it came to be that laws were passed relating to offenses such as forestalling, regrating and engrossing by which prohibitions were placed upon the power of individuals to deal under such circumstances and conditions as, according to the conception of the times, created a presumption that the dealings were not simply the honest exertion of one's right to contract for his own benefit unaccompanied by a wrongful motive to injure others, but were the consequence of a contract or course of dealing of such a character as to give rise to the presumption of an intent to injure others through the means, for instance, of a monopolistic increase of prices. . . .

⊥ As by the statutes providing against engrossing the quantity engrossed was not required to be the whole or a proximate part of the whole of an article, it is clear that there was a wide difference between monopoly and engrossing, etc. But as the principal wrong which it was deemed would result from monopoly, that is, an enhancement of the price, was the same wrong to which it was thought the prohibited engrossment would give rise, it came to pass that monopoly and engrossing were regarded as virtually one and the same thing. In other words, the prohibited act of engrossing because of its inevitable accomplishment of one of the evils deemed to be engendered by monopoly, came to be referred to as being a monopoly or constituting an attempt to monopolize. . . .

⊥ And by operation of the mental process which led to considering as a monopoly acts which although they did not constitute a monopoly were thought to produce some of its baneful effects, so also because of the impediment or burden to the due course of trade which they produced, such acts came to be referred to as in restraint of trade. This is shown by my Lord Coke's definition of monopoly as being "an institution or allowance . . . whereby any person or persons, bodies politic or corporate, are sought to be restrained of any freedom or liberty that they had before or hindered in their lawful trade." It is illustrated also by the definition which Hawkins gives of monopoly wherein it is said that the effect of monopoly is to restrain the citizen "from the freedom of manufacturing or trading which he had before." And see especially the opinion of Parker, C. J., in *Mitchel* v. *Reynolds* (1711), 1. P. Williams, 181, where a classification is made of monopoly which brings it generically within the description of restraint of trade.

Generalizing these considerations, the situation is this: 1. That by the common law monopolies were unlawful because of their restriction upon individual freedom of contract and their injury to the public. 2. That as to necessaries of life the freedom of the individual to deal was restricted where the nature and character of the dealing was such as to engender the presumption of intent to bring about at least one of the injuries which it was deemed would result from monopoly, that is an undue enhancement of price. 3. That to protect the freedom of contract of the individual not only in his own interest, but principally in the interest of the common weal, a contract of an individual by which he put an unreasonable restraint upon himself as to carrying on his trade or busi⊥ness was void. And that at common law the evils consequent upon engrossing, etc., caused those things to be treated as coming within monopoly and sometimes to be called monopoly and the same considerations caused monopoly because of its operation and effect, to be brought within and spoken of generally as impeding the due course of or being in restraint of trade.

From the development of more accurate economic conceptions and the changes in conditions of society it came to be recognized that the acts prohibited by the engrossing, forestalling, etc., statutes did not have the harmful tendency which they were presumed to have when the legislation concerning them was enacted, and therefore did not justify the presumption which had previously been deduced from them, but, on the contrary, such acts tended to fructify and develop trade. See the statutes of 12th George III, ch. 71, enacted in 1772, and statute of 7 and 8 Victoria, ch. 24, enacted in 1844, repealing the prohibitions against engrossing, forestalling, etc., upon the express ground that the prohibited acts had come to be considered as favorable to the development of and not in restraint of trade. It is remarkable that nowhere at common law can there be found a prohibition against the creation of monopoly by an individual. This would seem to manifest, either consciously or intuitively, a profound conception as to the inevitable operation of economic forces and the equipoise or balance in favor of the protection of the rights of individuals which resulted. That is to say, as it was deemed that monopoly in the concrete could only arise from an act of sovereign power, and, such sovereign power being restrained, prohibitions as to individuals were directed, not against the creation of monopoly, but were only applied to such acts in relation to particular subjects as to which it was deemed, if not restrained, some of the consequences of monopoly might result. After all, this was but an instinctive recognition ⊥ of the truisms that the course of trade could not be made free by obstructing it, and that an individual's right to trade could not be protected by destroying such right.

From the review just made it clearly results that outside of the restrictions resulting from the want of power in an individual to voluntarily and unreasonably restrain his right to carry on his trade or business and outside of the want of right to restrain the free course of trade by contracts or acts which implied a wrongful purpose, freedom to contract and to abstain from contracting and to exercise every reasonable right incident thereto became the rule in the English law. The scope and effect of this freedom to trade and contract is clearly shown by the decision in *Mogul Steamship Co. v. McGregor* (1892), A. C. 25. While it is true that the decision of the House of Lords in the case in question was announced shortly after the passage of the Anti-trust Act, it serves reflexly to show the exact state of the law in England at the time the Anti-trust statute was enacted.

In this country also the acts from which it was deemed there resulted a part if not all of the injurious consequences ascribed to monopoly, came to be referred to as a monopoly itself. In other words, here as had been the case in England, practical common sense caused attention to be concentrated not upon the theoretically correct name to be given to the condition or acts which gave rise to a harmful result, but to the result itself and to the remedying of the evils which it produced. The statement just made is illustrated by an early statute of the Province of Massachusetts, that is, chap. 31 of the laws of 1778-1779, by which monopoly and forestalling were expressly treated as one and the same thing.

It is also true that while the principles concerning contracts in restraint of trade, that is, voluntary restraint put by a person on his right to pursue his calling, hence only operating subjectively, came generally to be recognized ⊥ in accordance with the English rule, it came moreover to pass that contracts or acts which it was considered had a monopolistic tendency especially those which were thought to unduly diminish competition and hence to enhance prices—in other words, to monopolize—came also in a generic sense to be spoken of and treated as they had been in England, as restricting the due course of trade, and therefore as being in restraint of trade. The dread of monopoly as an emanation of governmental power, while it passed at an early date out of mind in this country, as a result of the structure of our Government, did not serve to assuage the fear as to the evil consequences which might arise from the acts of individuals producing or tending to produce the consequences of monopoly. It resulted that treating such acts as we have said as amounting to monopoly, sometimes constitutional restrictions, again legislative enactments or judicial decisions, served to enforce and illustrate the purpose to prevent the occurence of the evils recognized in the mother country as consequent upon monopoly, by providing against contracts or acts of individuals or combinations of individuals or corporations deemed to be conducive to such results. . . .

It will be found that as modern conditions arose the trend of legislation and judicial decision came more and more to adapt the recognized restrictions to new manifestations of conduct or of dealing which it was thought ⊥ justified the inference of intent to do the wrongs which it had been the purpose to prevent from the beginning. The evolution is clearly pointed out in *National Cotton Oil Co. v. Texas,* 197 U. S. 115, and *Shawnee Compress Co. v. Anderson,* 209 U. S. 423; and, indeed will be found to be illustrated in various aspects by the decisions of this court which have been concerned with the enforcement of the act we are now considering.

Without going into detail and but very briefly surveying the whole field, it may be with accuracy said that the dread of enhancement of prices and of other wrongs which it was thought would flow from the undue limitation on competitive conditions caused by contracts or other acts of individuals or corporations, led, as a matter of public policy, to the prohibition or treating as illegal all contracts or acts which were unreasonably restrictive of competitive conditions, either from the nature or character of the contract or act or where the surrounding circumstances were such as to justify the conclusion that they had not been entered into or performed with the legitimate purpose of reasonably forwarding personal interest and developing trade, but on the contrary were of such a character as to give rise to the inference or presumption that they had been entered into or done with the intent to do wrong to the general public and to limit the right of individuals, thus restraining the free flow of commerce and tending to bring about the evils, such as enhancement of prices, which were considered to be against public policy. It is equally true to say that the survey of the legislation in this country on this subject from the beginning will show, depending as it did upon the economic conceptions which obtained at the time when the legislation was adopted or judicial decision was rendered, that contracts or acts were at one time deemed to be of such a character as to justify the inference of wrongful intent which were at another period thought not to be ⊥ of that character. But this again, as we have seen, simply ⊥59 followed the line of development of the law of England.

Let us consider the language of the first and second sections, guided by the principle that where words are employed in a statute which had at the time a well-known meaning at common law or in the law of this country they are presumed to have been used in that sense unless the context compels to the contrary.

As to the first section, the words to be interpreted are: "Every contract, combination in the form of trust or otherwise, or conspiracy in restraint of trade or commerce . . . is hereby declared to be illegal." As there is no room for dispute that the statute was intended to formulate a rule for the regulation of interstate and foreign commerce, the question is what was the rule which it adopted?

In view of the common law and the law in this country as to restraint of trade, which we have reviewed, and the illuminating effect which that history must have under the rule to which we have referred, we think it results:

a. That the context manifests that the statute was drawn in the light of the existing practical conception of the law of restraint of trade, because it groups as within that class, not only contracts which were in restraint of trade in the subjective sense, but all contracts or acts which theoretically were attempts to monopolize, yet which in practice had come to be considered as in restraint of trade in a broad sense.

b. That in view of the many new forms of contracts and combinations which were being evolved from existing economic conditions, it was deemed essential by an all-embracing enumeration to make sure that no form of contract or combination by which an undue restraint of ⊥ interstate or foreign commerce was brought about could save ⊥60 such restraint from condemnation. The statute under this view evidenced the intent not to restrain the right to make and enforce contracts, whether resulting from combination or otherwise, which did not unduly restrain interstate or foreign commerce, but to protect that commerce from being restrained by methods, whether old or new, which would constitute an interference that is an undue restraint.

c. And as the contracts or acts embraced in the provision were not expressly defined, since the enumeration addressed itself simply to classes of acts, those classes being broad enough to embrace every conceivable contract or combination which could be made concerning trade or commerce or the subjects of such commerce, and thus caused any act done by any of the enumerated methods anywhere in the whole field of human activity to be illegal if in restraint of trade, it inevitably follows that the provision necessarily called for the exercise of judgment which required that some standard should be resorted to for the purpose of determining whether the prohibitions contained in the statute had or had not in any given case been violated. Thus not specifying but indubitably contemplating and requiring a standard, it follows that it was intended that the standard of reason which had been applied at the common law and in this country in dealing with subjects of the character embraced by the statute, was intended to be the measure used for the purpose of determining whether in a given case a particular act had or had not brought about the wrong against which the statute provided.

And a consideration of the text of the second section serves to establish that it was intended to supplement the first and to make sure that by no possible guise could the public policy embodied in the first section be frustrated or evaded. The prohibitions of the second embrace ⊥ "Every person who shall monopolize, or attempt to monopolize, ⊥61 or combine or conspire with any other person or persons, to monopolize any part of the trade or commerce among the several states, or with foreign nations, . . ." By reference to the terms of § 8 it is certain that the word person clearly implies a corporation as well as an individual.

The commerce referred to by the words "any part" construed in the light of the manifest purpose of the statute has both a geographical and a distributive significance, that is it includes any portion of the United States and any one of the classes of things forming a part of interstate or foreign commerce.

Undoubtedly, the words "to monopolize" and "monopolize" as used in the section reach every act bringing about the prohibited results. The ambiguity, if any, is involved in determining what is intended by monopolize. But this ambiguity is readily dispelled in the light of the previous history of the law of restraint of trade to which we have referred and the indication which it gives of the practical evolution by which monopoly and the acts which produce the same result as monopoly, that is, an undue restraint of the course of trade, all came to be spoken of as, and to be indeed synonymous with, restraint of trade. In other words, having by the first section forbidden all means of monopolizing trade, that is, unduly restraining it by means of every contract, combination, etc., the second section seeks, if possible, to make the prohibitions of the act all the more complete and perfect by embracing all attempts to reach the end prohibited by the first section, that is, restraints of trade, by any attempt to monopolize, or monopolization thereof, even although the acts by which such results are attempted to be brought about or are brought about be not embraced within the general enumeration of the first section. And, of course, when the second section is thus harmonized with and made as it ⊥ was intended to be the complement of the first, it becomes obvious that the criteria to be resorted to in any given case for the purpose of ascertaining whether violations of the section have been committed, is the rule of reason guided by the established law and by the plain duty to enforce the prohibitions of the act and thus the public policy which its restrictions were obviously enacted to subserve. And it is worthy of observation, as we have previously remarked concerning the common law, that although the statute by the comprehensiveness of the enumerations embodied in both the first and second sections makes it certain that its purpose was to prevent undue restraints of every kind or nature, nevertheless by the omission of any direct prohibition against monopoly in the concrete it indicates a consciousness that the freedom of the individual right to contract when not unduly or improperly exercised was the most efficient means for the prevention of monopoly, since the operation of the centrifugal and centripetal forces resulting from the right to freely contract was the means by which monopoly would be inevitably prevented if no extraneous or sovereign power imposed it and no right to make unlawful contracts having a monopolistic tendency were permitted. In other words that freedom to contract was the essence of freedom from undue restraint on the right to contract.

Clear as it seems to us is the meaning of the provisions of the statute in the light of the review which we have made, nevertheless before definitively applying that meaning it behooves us to consider the contentions urged on one side or the other concerning the meaning of the statute, which, if maintained, would give to it, in some aspects a much wider and in every view at least a somewhat different significance. And to do this brings us to the second question which, at the outset, we have stated it was our purpose to consider and dispose of.

⊥ *Second. The contentions of the parties as to the meaning of the statute and the decisions of this court relied upon concerning those contentions.*

In substance, the propositions urged by the Government are reducible to this: That the language of the statute embraces every contract, combination, etc., in restraint of trade, and hence its text leaves no room for the exercise of judgment, but simply imposes the plain duty of applying its prohibitions to every case within its literal language. The error involved lies in assuming the matter to be decided. This is true because as the acts which may come under the classes stated in the first section and the restraint of trade to which that section applies are not specifically enumerated or defined, it is obvious that judgment must in every case be called into play in order to determine whether a particular act is embraced within the statutory classes, and whether if the act is within such classes its nature or effect causes it to be a restraint of trade within the intendment of the act. To hold to the contrary would require the conclusion either that every contract, act or combination of any kind or nature, whether it operated a restraint on trade or not, was within the statute, and thus the statute would be destructive of all right to contract or agree or combine in any respect whatever as to subjects embraced in interstate trade or commerce, or if this conclusion were not reached, then the contention would require it to be held that as the statute did not define the things to which it related and excluded resort to the only means by which the acts to which it relates could be ascertained—the light of reason—the enforcement of the statute was impossible because of its uncertainty. The merely generic enumeration which the statute makes of the acts to which it refers and the absence of any definition of restraint of trade as used in the statute leaves room for but one conclusion, which is, that it was expressly designed not to unduly limit the application of the act by precise definition, but while clearly fixing a standard, that is, by defining the ulterior boundaries which could not be transgressed with impunity, to leave it to be determined by the light of reason, guided by the principles of law and the duty to apply and enforce the public policy embodied in the statute, in every given case whether any particular act or contract was within the contemplation of the statute.

But, it is said, persuasive as these views may be, they may not be here applied, because the previous decisions of this court have given to the statute a meaning which expressly excludes the construction which must result from the reasoning stated. The cases are *United States* v. *Freight Association,* 166 U. S. 290, and *United States* v. *Joint Traffic Association,* 171 U. S. 505. Both the cases involved the legality of combinations or associations of railroads engaged in interstate commerce for the purpose of controlling the conduct of the parties to the association or combination in many particulars. The association or combination was assailed in each case as being in violation of the statute. It was held that they were. It is undoubted that in the opinion in each case general language was made use of, which, when separated from its context, would justify the conclusion that it was decided that reason could not be resorted to for the purpose of determining whether the acts complained of were within the statute. It is, however, also true that the nature and character of the contract or agreement in each case was fully referred to and suggestions as to their unreasonableness pointed out in order to indicate that they were within the prohibitions of the statute. As the cases cannot by any possible conception be treated as authoritative without the certitude that reason was resorted to for the purpose of deciding them, it follows as a matter of course that it must have been held by the light of reason, since the conclusion could not have been otherwise reached, that the assailed contracts or agreements were within the general enumeration of the statute, and that their operation and effect brought about the restraint of trade which the statute prohibited. This being inevitable, the deduction can in reason only be this: That in the cases relied upon it having been found that the acts complained of were within the statute and operated to produce the injuries which the statute forbade, that resort to reason was not permissible in order to allow that to be done which the statute prohibited. This being true, the rulings in the cases relied upon when rightly appreciated were therefore this and nothing more: That as considering the contracts or agreements, their necessary effect and the character of the parties by whom they were made, they were clearly restraints of trade within the purview of the statute, they could not be taken out of that category by indulging in general reasoning as to the expediency or non-expediency of having made the contracts or the wisdom or want of wisdom of the statute which prohibited their being made. That is to say, the cases but decided that the nature and character of the contracts, creating as they did a conclusive presumption which brought them within the statute, such result was not to be disregarded by the substitution of a judicial appreciation of what the law ought to be for the plain judicial duty of enforcing the law as it was made.

But aside from reasoning it is true to say that the cases relied upon do not when rightly construed sustain the doctrine contended for is established by all of the numerous decisions of this court which have applied and enforced the Anti-trust Act, since they all in the very nature of things rest upon the premise that reason was the guide by which the provisions of the act were in every case interpreted. Indeed intermediate the decision of the two cases, that is, after the decision in the *Freight Association Case* and before the decision in the *Joint Traffic Case,* the case of *Hopkins* v. *United States,* 171 U. S. 578, was decided, the opinion being delivered by Mr. Justice Peckham, who wrote both the opinions in the *Freight Association* and the *Joint Traffic cases.* And, referring in the *Hopkins Case* to the broad claim made as to the rule of interpretation announced in the *Freight Association Case,* it was said (p. 592):

"To treat as condemned by the act all agreements under which, as a result, the cost of conducting an interstate commercial business may be increased would enlarge the application of the act far beyond the fair meaning of the language used. There must be some direct and immediate effect upon interstate commerce in order to come within the act." And in the *Joint Traffic Case* this statement was expressly reiterated and approved and illustrated by example; like limitation on the general language used in *Freight Association* and *Joint Traffic Cases* is also the clear result of *Bement* v. *National Harrow Co.,* 186 U. S. 70, 92, and especially of *Cincinnati Packet Co.* v. *Bay,* 200 U. S. 179.

If the criterion by which it is to be determined in all cases whether every contract, combination, etc., is a restraint of trade within the intendment of the law, is the direct or indirect effect of the acts involved, then of course the rule of reason becomes the guide, and the construction which we have given the statute, instead of being refuted by the cases relied upon, is by those cases demonstrated to be correct. This is true, because as the construction which we have deduced from the history of the act and the analysis of its text is simply that in every case where it is claimed that an act or acts are in violation of the statute the rule of reason, in the light of the principles of law and the public policy which the act embodies, must be applied. From this it follows, since that rule and the result of the test as to direct or indirect, in their ultimate aspect, come to one and the same thing, that the difference between the two is therefore only that which obtains between things which do not differ at all.

⊥67 ⊥ If it be true that there is this identity of result between the rule intended to be applied in the *Freight Association Case,* that is, the rule of direct and indirect, and the rule of reason which under the statute as we construe it should be here applied, it may be asked how was it that in the opinion in the *Freight Association Case* much consideration was given to the subject of whether the agreement or combination which was involved in that case could be taken out of the prohibitions of the statute upon the theory of its reasonableness. The question is pertinent and must be fully and frankly met, for if it be now deemed that the *Freight Association Case* was mistakenly decided or too broadly stated, the doctrine which it announced should be either expressly overruled or limited.

The confusion which gives rise to the question results from failing to distinguish between the want of power to take a case which by its terms or the circumstances which surrounded it, considering among such circumstances the character of the parties, is plainly within the statute, out of the operation of the statute by resort to reason in effect to establish that the contract ought not to be treated as within the statute, and the duty in every case where it becomes necessary from the nature and character of the parties to decide whether it was within the statute to pass upon that question by the light of reason. This distinction, we think, serves to point out what in its ultimate conception was the thought underlying the reference to the rule of reason made in the *Freight Association Case,* especially when such reference is interpreted by the context of the opinion and in the light of the subsequent opinion in the *Hopkins Case* and in *Cincinnati Packet Company* v. *Bay,* 200 U. S. 179.

And in order not in the slightest degree to be wanting in frankness, we say that in so far, however, as by separating the general language used in the opinions in the
⊥68 *Freight Assocation* and *Joint Traffic cases* from the con⊥text and the subject and parties with which the cases were concerned, it may be conceived that the language referred to conflicts with the construction which we give the statute, they are necessarily now limited and qualified. We see no possible escape from this conclusion if we are to adhere to the many cases decided in this court in which the Anti-trust Law has been applied and enforced and if the duty to apply and enforce that law in the future is to continue to exist. The first is true, because the construction which we now give the statute does not in the slightest degree conflict with a single previous case decided concerning the Anti-trust Law aside from the contention as to the *Freight Association* and *Joint Traffic cases,* and because every one of those cases applied the rule of reason for the purpose of determining whether the subject before the court was within the statute. The second is also true, since, as we have already pointed out, unaided by the light of reason it is impossible to understand how the statute may in the future be enforced and the public policy which it establishes be made efficacious.

So far as the objections of the defendants are concerned they are all embraced under two headings:—

a. That the act, even if the averments of the bill be true, cannot be constitutionally applied, because to do so would extend the power of Congress to subjects *dehors* the reach of its authority to regulate commerce, by enabling that body to deal with mere questions of production of commodities within the States. But all the structure upon which this argument proceeds is based upon the decision in *United States* v. *E. C. Knight Co.,* 156 U. S. 1. The view, however, which the argument takes of that case and the arguments based upon that view have been so repeatedly pressed upon this court in connection with the interpretation and enforcement of the Anti-trust Act, and have been so necessarily and expressly decided to be unsound as to cause the contentions to be plainly foreclosed and to require no ex⊥press notice. *United States* v. *Northern Securities Co.,* 193 U. S. 197, 334; *Loewe* v. *Lawlor,* 208 U. S. 274; *Swift & Co.* v. *United States,* 196 U. S. 375; *Montague* v. *Lowry,* 193 U. S. 38; *Shawnee Compress Co.* v. *Anderson,* 209 U. S. 423.

b. Many arguments are pressed in various forms of statement which in substance amount to contending that the statute cannot be applied under the facts of this case without impairing rights of property and destroying the freedom of contract or trade, which is essentially necessary to the well-being of society and which it is insisted is protected by the constitutional guaranty of due process of law. But the ultimate foundation of all these arguments is the assumption that reason may not be resorted to in interpreting and applying the statute, and therefore that the statute unreasonably restricts the right to contract and unreasonably operates upon the right to acquire and hold property. As the premise is demonstrated to be unsound by the construction we have given the statute, of course the propositions which rest upon that premise need not be further noticed.

So far as the arguments proceed upon the conception that in view of the generality of the statute it is not susceptible of being enforced by the courts because it cannot be carried out without a judicial exertion of legislative power, they are clearly unsound. The statute certainly generically enumerates the character of acts which it prohibits and the wrong which it was intended to prevent. The propositions therefore but insist that, consistently with the fundamental principles of due process of law, it never can be left to the judiciary to decide whether in a given case particular acts come within a generic statutory provision. But to reduce the propositions, however, to this their final meaning makes it clear that in substance they deny the existence of essential legislative authority and challenge the right of the judiciary to perform duties which that department of the government has exerted from ⊥ the beginning. This is so clear as to require no elaboration. . . .

Third. The facts and the application of the statute to them.

Beyond dispute the proofs establish substantially as alleged in the bill the following facts:

1. The creation of the Standard Oil Company of Ohio;
2. The organization of the Standard Oil Trust of 1882, and also a previous one of 1879, not referred to in the bill, and the proceedings in the Supreme Court of Ohio, culminating in a decree based upon the finding that the company was unlawfully a party to that trust; the transfer by the trustees of stocks in certain of the companies; the contempt proceedings; and, finally, the increase of the capital of the Standard Oil Company of New Jersey and the acquisition by that company of the shares of the stock of the other corporations in exchange for its certificates.

The vast amount of property and the possibilities of far-reaching control which resulted from the facts last stated are shown by the statement which we have previously annexed concerning the parties to the trust agreement of 1882, and the corporations whose stock was held by the trustees under the trust and which came therefore to be held by the New Jersey corporation. But these statements do not with accuracy convey an appreciation of the ⊥ situation as it existed at the time of the entry of the decree below, since during the more than ten years which elapsed between the acquiring by the New Jersey corporation of the stock and other property which was formerly held by the trustees under the trust agreement, the situation of course had somewhat changed, a change which when analyzed in the light of the proof, we think, establishes that the result of enlarging the capital stock of the New Jersey company and giving it the vast power to which we have referred produced its normal consequence, that is, it gave to the corporation, despite enormous dividends and despite the dropping out of certain corporations enumerated in the decree of the court below, an enlarged and more perfect sway and control over the trade and commerce in petroleum and its products. The ultimate situation referred to will be made manifest by an examination of §§ 2 and 4 of the decree below. . . .

⊥ Giving to the facts just stated, the weight which it was deemed they were entitled to, in the light afforded by the ⊥ proof of other cognate facts and circumstances, the court below held that the acts and dealings established by the ⊥ proof operated to destroy the "potentiality of competition" which otherwise would have existed to such an extent as to cause the transfers of stock which were made to the New Jersey corporation and the control which resulted over the many and various subsidiary corporations to be a combination or conspiracy in restraint of trade in violation of the first section of the act, but also to be an attempt to monopolize and a monopolization bringing about a perennial violation of the second section.

We see no cause to doubt the correctness of these conclusions, considering the subject from every aspect, that is, both in view of the facts established by the record and the necessary operation and effect of the law as we have ⊥ construed it upon the inferences deducible from the facts, for the following reasons:

a. Because the unification of power and control over petroleum and its products which was the inevitable result of the combining in the New Jersey corporation by the increase of its stock and the transfer to it of the stocks of so many other corporations, aggregating so vast a capital, gives rise, in and of itself, in the absence of countervailing circumstances, to say the least, to the *prima facie* presumption of intent and purpose to maintain the dominancy over the oil industry, not as a result of normal methods of industrial development, but by new means of combination which were resorted to in order that greater power might be added than would otherwise have arisen had normal methods been followed, the whole with the purpose of excluding others from the trade and thus centralizing in the combination a perpetual control of the movements of petroleum and its products in the channels of interstate commerce.

b. Because the *prima facie* presumption of intent to restrain trade, to monopolize and to bring about monopolization resulting from the act of expanding the stock of the New Jersey corporation and vesting it with such vast control of the oil industry, is made conclusive by considering, *1*, the conduct of the persons or corporations who were mainly instrumental in bringing about the extension of power in the New Jersey corporation before the consummation of that result and prior to the formation of the trust agreements of 1879 and 1882; *2*, by considering the proof as to what was done under those agreements and the acts which immediately preceded the vesting of power in the New Jersey corporation as well as by weighing the modes in which the power vested in that corporation has been exerted and the results which have arisen from it.

Recurring to the acts done by the individuals or corporations who were mainly instrumental in bringing about the ⊥ expansion of the New Jersey corporation during the period prior to the formation of the trust agreements of 1879 and 1882, including those agreements, not for the purpose of weighing the substantial merit of the numerous charges of wrongdoing made during such period, but solely as an aid for discovering intent and purpose, we think no disinterested mind can survey the period in question without being irresistibly driven to the conclusion that the very genius for commercial development and organization which it would seem was manifested from the beginning soon begot an intent and purpose to exclude others which was frequently manifested by acts and dealings wholly inconsistent with the theory that they were made with the single conception of advancing the development of business power by usual methods, but which on the contrary necessarily involved the intent to drive others from the field and to exclude them from their right to trade and thus accomplish the mastery which was the end in view. And, considering the period from the date of the trust agreements of 1879 and 1882, up to the time of the expansion of the New Jersey corporation, the gradual extension of the power over the commerce in oil which ensued, the decision of the Supreme Court of Ohio, the tardiness or reluctance in conforming to the commands of that decision, the method first adopted and that which finally culminated in the plan of the New Jersey corporation, all additionally serve to make manifest the continued existence of the intent which we have previously indicated and which among other things impelled the expansion of the New Jersey corporation. The exercise of the power which resulted from that organization fortifies the foregoing conclusions, since the development which came, the acquisition here and there which ensued of every efficient means by which competition could have been asserted, the slow but resistless methods which followed by which means of transportation were absorbed and brought under control, the system of marketing which was adopted by which the country was divided into districts and the trade in each district in oil was turned over to a designated corporation within the combination and all others were excluded, all lead the mind up to a conviction of a purpose and intent which we think is so certain as practically to cause the subject not to be within the domain of reasonable contention.

The inference that no attempt to monopolize could have been intended, and that no monopolization resulted from the acts complained of, since it is established that a very small percentage of the crude oil produced was controlled by the combination, is unwarranted. As substantial power over the crude product was the inevitable result of the absolute control which existed over the refined product, the monopolization of the one carried with it the power to control the other, and if the inferences which this situation suggests were developed, which we deem it unnecessary to do, they might well serve to add additional cogency to the presumption of intent to monopolize which we have found arises from the unquestioned proof on other subjects.

We are thus brought to the last subject which we are called upon to consider, viz:

Fourth. The remedy to be administered.

It may be conceded that ordinarily where it was found that acts had been done in violation of the statute, adequate measure of relief would result from restraining the doing of such acts in the future. *Swift* v. *United States,* 196 U. S. 375. But in a case like this, where the condition which has been brought about in violation of the statute, in and of itself, is not only a continued attempt to monopolize, but also a monopolization, the duty to enforce the statute requires the application of broader and more controlling remedies. As penalties which are not authorized by law may not be inflicted by judicial authority, it follows that to meet the situation with which we are confronted the application of remedies two-fold in character becomes essential: 1st. To forbid the doing in the future of acts like those which we have found to have been done in the past which would be violative of the statute. 2d. The exertion of such measure of relief as will effectually dissolve the combination found to exist in violation of the statute, and thus neutralize the extension and continually operating force which the possession of the power unlawfully obtained has brought and will continue to bring about.

In applying remedies for this purpose, however, the fact must not be overlooked that injury to the public by the prevention of an undue restraint on, or the monopolization of trade or commerce is the foundation upon which the prohibitions of the statute rest, and moreover that one of the fundamental purposes of the statute is to protect, not to destroy, rights of property.

Let us then, as a means of accurately determining what relief we are to afford, first come to consider what relief was afforded by the court below, in order to fix how far it is necessary to take from or add to that relief, to the end that the prohibitions of the statute may have complete and operative force.

The court below by virtue of §§ 1, 2, and 4 of its decree, which we have in part previously excerpted in the margin, adjudged that the New Jersey corporation in so far as it held the stock of the various corporations, recited in §§ 2 and 4 of the decree, or controlled the same was a combination in violation of the first section of the act, and an attempt to monopolize or a monopolization contrary to the second section of the act. It commanded the dissolution of the combination, and therefore in effect, directed the transfer by the New Jersey corporation back to the stockholders of the various subsidiary corporations entitled to the same of the stock which had been turned over to the New Jersey company in exchange for its stock. To make this command effective § 5 of the decree forbade the New Jersey corporation from in any form or manner exercising any ownership or exerting any power directly or indirectly in virtue of its apparent title to the stocks of the subsidiary corporations, and prohibited those subsidiary corporations from paying any dividends to the New Jersey corporation or doing any act which would recognize further power in that company, except to the extent that it was necessary to enable that company to transfer the stock. So far as the owners of the stock of the subsidiary corporations and the corporations themselves were concerned after the stock had been transferred, § 6 of the decree enjoined them from in any way conspiring or combining to violate the act or to monopolize or attempt to monopolize in virtue of their ownership of the stock transferred to them, and prohibited all agreements between the subsidiary corporations or other stockholders in the future, tending to produce or bring about further violations of the act. . . .

So far as the decree held that the ownership of the stock of the New Jersey corporation constituted a combination in violation of the first section and an attempt to create a monopoly or to monopolize under the second section and commanded the dissolution of the combination, the decree was clearly appropriate. And this also is true of § 5 of the decree which restrained both the New Jersey corporation and the subsidiary corporations from doing anything which would recognize or give effect to further ownership ⊥ in the New Jersey corporation of the stocks which were ordered to be retransferred.

But the contention is that, in so far as the relief by way of injunction which was awarded by § 6 against the stockholders of the subsidiary corporations or the subsidiary corporations themselves after the transfer of stock by the New Jersey corporation was completed in conformity to the decree, the relief awarded was too broad: *a.* Because it was not sufficiently specific and tended to cause those who were within the embrace of the order to cease to be under the protection of the law of the land and required them to thereafter conduct their business under the jeopardy of punishments for contempt for violating a general injunction. *New Haven R. R. v. Interstate Commerce Commission,* 200 U. S. 404. Besides it is said that the restraint imposed by § 6—even putting out of view the consideration just stated—was moreover calculated to do injury to the public and it may be in and of itself to produce the very restraint on the due course of trade which it was intended to prevent. We say this since it does not necessarily follow because an illegal restraint of trade or an attempt to monopolize or a monopolization resulted from the combination and the transfer of the stocks of the subsidiary corporations to the New Jersey corporation that a like restraint or attempt to monopolize or monopolization would necessarily arise from agreements between one or more of the subsidiary corporations after the transfer of the stock by the New Jersey corporation. . . . ⊥ [W]e construe the sixth paragraph of the decree, not as depriving the stockholders or the corporations, after the dissolution of the combination, of the power to make normal and lawful contracts or agreements, but as restraining them from, by any device whatever, recreating directly or indirectly the illegal combination which the decree dissolved. In other words we construe the sixth paragraph of the decree, not as depriving the stockholders or corporations of the right to live under the law of the land, but as compelling obedience to that law. As therefore the sixth paragraph as thus construed is not amenable to the criticism directed against it and cannot produce the harmful results which the arguments suggest it was obviously right. . . .

Our conclusion is that the decree below was right and ⊥ should be affirmed, except as to the minor matters concerning which we have indicated the decree should be modified. Our order will therefore be one of affirmance with directions, however, to modify the decree in accordance with this opinion. The court below to retain jurisdiction to the extent necessary to compel compliance in every respect with its decree.

And it is so ordered.

MR. JUSTICE HARLAN concurring in part, and dissenting in part.

A sense of duty constrains me to express the objections which I have to certain declarations in the opinion just delivered on behalf of the court.

I concur in holding that the Standard Oil Company of New Jersey and its subsidiary companies constitute a combination in restraint of interstate commerce, and that they have attempted to monopolize and have monopolized parts of such commerce—all in violation of what is known as the Anti-trust Act of 1890. 26 Stat. 209, c. 647. The evidence in this case overwhelmingly sustained that view and led the Circuit Court, by its final decree, to order the dissolution of the New Jersey corporation and the discontinuance of the illegal combination between that corporation and its subsidiary companies.

In my judgment, the decree below should have been affirmed without qualification. But the court, while affirming the decree, directs some modifications in respect of what it characterizes as "minor matters." It is to be apprehended that those modifications may prove to be mischievous. In saying this, I have particularly in view the statement in the opinion that "it does not necessarily follow that because an illegal restraint of trade or an attempt to monopolize or a monopolization resulted from the combination and the transfer of the stocks of the subsidiary corporations to the New Jersey corporation, that a like restraint of trade or attempt to monopolize or monopolization would necessarily arise from agreements between one or more of the subsidiary corporations after the transfer of the stock by the New Jersey corporation." Taking this language, in connection with other parts of the opinion, the subsidiary companies are thus, in effect, informed—unwisely, I think—that although the New Jersey corporation, being an illegal combination, must go out of existence, *they* may join in an agreement to *restrain commerce* among the States if such restraint be not "undue."

In order that my objections to certain parts of the court's opinion may distinctly appear, I must state the circumstances under which Congress passed the Anti-trust Act, and trace the course of judicial decisions as to its meaning and scope. This is the more necessary because the court by its decision, when interpreted by the language of its opinion, has not only upset the long-settled interpretation of the act, but has usurped the constitutional functions of the legislative branch of the Government. With all due respect for the opinions of others, I feel bound to say that what the court has said may well cause some alarm for the integrity of our institutions. Let us see how the matter stands.

All who recall the condition of the country in 1890 will remember that there was everywhere, among the people generally, a deep feeling of unrest. The Nation had been rid of human slavery—fortunately, as all now feel—but the conviction was universal that the country was in real danger from another kind of slavery sought to be fastened on the American people, namely, the slavery that would result from aggregations of capital in the hands of a few individuals and corporations controlling, for their own profit and advantage exclusively, the entire business of the country, including the production and sale of the necessaries of life. Such a danger was thought to be then imminent, and all felt that it must be met firmly and by such statutory regulations as would adequately protect the people against oppression and wrong. Congress therefore took up the matter and gave the whole subject the fullest consideration. All agreed that the National Government could not, by legislation, regulate the domestic trade carried on wholly within the several States; for, power to regulate such trade remained with, because never surrendered by, the States. But, under authority expressly granted to it by the Constitution, Congress could regulate commerce among the several States and with foreign states. Its authority to regulate such commerce was and is paramount, due force being given to other provisions of the fundamental law devised by the fathers for the safety of the Government and for the protection and security of the essential rights inhering in life, liberty and property.

Guided by these considerations, and to the end that the people, *so far as interstate commerce* was concerned, might not be dominated by vast combinations and monopolies, having power to advance their own selfish ends, regardless of the general interests and welfare, Congress passed the Anti-trust Act of 1890 in these words (the italics here and elsewhere in this opinion are mine):

"SEC. 1. *Every* contract, combination in the form of trust or otherwise, or conspiracy, in restraint of trade or commerce among the several States, or with foreign nations, is hereby declared to be illegal. Every person who shall make *any such contract or engage in any such combination or conspiracy,* shall be deemed guilty of a misdemeanor, and, on conviction thereof, shall be punished by fine not exceeding five thousand dollars, or by imprisonment not exceeding one year, or by both said punishments, in the discretion of the court. § 2. Every person who shall monopolize, or attempt to monopolize, or combine or conspire with any other person or persons, to monopolize *any part* of the trade or commerce among the several States, or with foreign nations, shall be deemed guilty of a misdemeanor, and, on conviction thereof, shall be punished by fine not exceeding five thousand dollars, or by imprisonment not exceeding one year, or by both said punishments, in the discretion of the court. § 3. *Every* contract, combination in form of trust *or otherwise,* or conspiracy, in restraint of trade or commerce in any Territory of the United States or in the District of Columbia, or in restraint of trade or commerce between any such Territory and another, or between any such Territory or Territories and any State or States or the District of Columbia, or with foreign nations, or between the District of Columbia and any State or States or foreign nations, is hereby declared illegal. Every person who shall make any *such* contract or engage in any *such* combination or conspiracy, shall be deemed guilty of a misdemeanor, and, on conviction thereof, shall be punished by fine not exceeding five thousand dollars, or by imprisonment not exceeding one year, or by both said punishments, in the discretion of the court." 26 Stat. 209, c. 647.

The important inquiry in the present case is as to the meaning and scope of that act in its application to interstate commerce.

In 1896 this court had occasion to determine the meaning and scope of the act in an important case known as the *Trans-Missouri Freight Case.* 166 U. S. 290. The question there was as to the validity under the Anti-trust Act of a certain agreement between numerous railroad companies, whereby they formed an association for the purpose of establishing and maintaining rates, rules and regulations in respect of freight traffic over specified routes. Two questions were involved: first, whether the act applied to railroad carriers; second, whether the agreement the annulment of which as illegal was the basis of the suit which the United States brought. The court held that railroad carriers were embraced by the act. In determining that question, the court, among other things, said:

"The language of the act includes *every* contract, combination in the form of trust or otherwise, or conspiracy, in restraint of trade or commerce among the several States or with foreign nations. So far as the very terms of the statute go, they apply to *any* contract of the nature described. A contract therefore that is in restraint of trade or commerce is, by the strict language of the act prohibited, even though such contract is entered into between competing common carriers by railroad, and only for the purposes of thereby affecting traffic rates for the transportation of persons and property. If such an agreement restrains trade or commerce, it is prohibited by the statute, unless it can be said that an agreement, no matter what its terms, relating only to transportation cannot restrain trade or commerce. We see no escape from the conclusion that if an agreement of such a nature does restrain it, the agreement is condemned by this act. . . ." 166 U. S. 290, 312, 324, 326. . . .

I have made these extended extracts from the opinion of the court in the *Trans-Missouri Freight Case* in order to show beyond question, that the point was there urged by counsel that the Anti-trust Act condemned *only* contracts, combinations, trusts and conspiracies that were in *unreasonable* restraint of interstate commerce, and that the court in clear and decisive language met that point. It adjudged that Congress had in unequivocal words declared that "*every* contract, combination, in the form of trust or otherwise, or conspiracy, in restraint of commerce among the several States" shall be illegal, and that no distinction, *so far as interstate commerce was concerned,* was to be tolerated between restraints of such commerce as were undue or unreasonable, and restraints that were due or reasonable. With full knowledge of the then condition of the country and of its business, Congress determined to meet, and did meet, the situation by an absolute, statutory prohibition of "*every* contract, combination in the form of trust or otherwise, in restraint of trade or commerce." Still more; in response to the suggestion by able counsel that Congress intended only to strike down such contracts, combinations and monopolies as unreasonably restrained interstate commerce, this court, in words too clear to be misunderstood, said that to so hold was "to read into the act by way of *judicial legislation,* an exception not placed there by the law-making branch of the Government." "This," the court said, as we have seen, "*we cannot* and *ought not* to do."

It thus appears that fifteen years ago, when the purpose of Congress in passing the Anti-trust Act was fresh in the minds of courts, lawyers, statesmen and the general public, this court expressly declined to indulge in judicial legislation, by inserting in the act the word "unreasonable" or any other word of like import. It may be stated here that the country at large accepted this view of the act, and the Federal courts throughout the entire country enforced its provisions according to the interpretation given in the *Freight Association Case.* What, then, was to be done by those who questioned the soundness of the interpretation placed on the act by this court in that case? As the court had decided that to insert the word "unreasonable" in the act would be "judicial legislation" on its part, the only alternative left to those who opposed the decision in that case was to induce Congress to so *amend* the act as to recognize the right to restrain interstate commerce to a *reasonable* extent. The public press, magazines and law journals, the debates in Congress, speeches and addresses by public men and jurists, all contain abundant evidence of the general understanding that the meaning, extent and scope of the Anti-trust Act had been judicially determined by this court, and that the only question remaining open for discussion was the ⊥ wisdom of the policy declared by the act—a matter that was exclusively within the cognizance of Congress. But at every session of Congress since the decision of 1896, the lawmaking branch of the Government, with full knowledge of that decision, has refused to change the policy it had declared or to so amend the act of 1890 as to except from its operation contracts, combinations and trusts that *reasonably* restrain interstate commerce.

⊥91

But those who were in combinations that were illegal did not despair. They at once set up the baseless claim that the decision of 1896 disturbed the "business interests of the country," and let it be known that they would never be content until the rule was established that would permit interstate commerce to be subjected to *reasonable* restraints. Finally, an opportunity came again to raise the same question which this court had, upon full consideration, determined in 1896. I now allude to the case of *United States* v. *Joint Traffic Association,* 171 U. S. 505, decided in 1898. . . .

It is important to state the points urged in that case by the defendant companies charged with violating the Anti-trust Act, and to show that the court promptly met them. To that end I make a copious extract from the opinion in the *Joint Traffic Case.* Among other things, the court said: "Upon comparing that agreement [the one in the *Joint Traffic Case,* then under consideration, 171 U. S. 505] with the one set forth in the case of *United States* v. *Trans-Missouri Freight Association,* 166 U. S. 290, the great similarity between them suggests that a similar result should be reached in the two cases" (p. 558). ⊥ Learned counsel in the *Joint Traffic Case* urged a reconsideration of the question decided in the *Trans-Missouri Case* contending that "the decision in that case [the *Trans-Missouri Freight Case*] is quite plainly erroneous, and the consequences of such error are far reaching and disastrous, and clearly at war with justice and sound policy, and the construction placed upon the Anti-trust statute has been received by the public with surprise and alarm." . . .

⊥92

The question whether the court should again consider the point decided in the *Trans-Missouri Case,* 171 U. S. 573, was disposed of in the most decisive language. . . .

⊥ These utterances [from the Supreme Court's opinion in *United States* v. *Joint Traffic Association,* 171 U. S. 505 (1898)], taken in connection with what was previously said in the *Trans-Missouri Freight Case,* show so clearly and affirmatively as to admit of no doubt that this court, many years ago, upon the fullest consideration, interpreted the Anti-trust Act as prohibiting and making illegal not only *every* contract or combination, in whatever form, which was in restraint of interstate commerce, without regard to its reasonableness or unreasonableness, but all monopolies or attempts to monopolize "any part" of such trade or commerce. . . .

⊥94

⊥ In the opinion delivered on behalf of the minority in the *Northern Securities Case,* 193 U. S. 197, our present Chief Justice referred to the contentions made by the defendants in the *Freight Association Case,* one of which was that the agreement there

⊥96

involved did not unreasonably restrain interstate commerce, and said: "Both these contentions were decided against the association, the court holding that the Anti-trust Act did embrace interstate carriage by railroad corporations, and as that act prohibited *any* contract in restraint of interstate commerce, *it hence embraced all contracts of that character, whether they were reasonable or unreasonable.*" One of the Justices who dissented in the *Northern Securities Case* in a separate opinion, concurred in by the minority, thus referred to the *Freight* and *Joint Traffic cases*: "For it cannot be too carefully remembered that that clause applies to 'every' contract of the forbidden kind— a consideration which was the turning point of the *Trans-Missouri Freight Association* case. . . . Size has nothing to do with the matter. A monopoly of 'any part' of commerce among the States is unlawful."

In this connection it may be well to refer to the adverse report made in 1909, by Senator Nelson, on behalf of the Senate Judiciary Committee, in reference to a certain bill ⊥ offered in the Senate and which proposed to amend the Anti-trust Act in various particulars. That report contains a full, careful and able analysis of judicial decisions relating to combinations and monopolies in restraint of trade and commerce. Among other things said in it which bear on the questions involved in the present case are these: "The Anti-trust Act makes it a criminal offense to violate the law, and provides a punishment both by fine and imprisonment. To inject into the act the question of whether an agreement or combination is *reasonable* or *unreasonable* would render the act as a criminal or penal statute indefinite and uncertain, and hence, to that extent, utterly nugatory and void, and would practically amount to a repeal of that part of the act. . . . And while the same technical objection does not apply to civil prosecutions, *the injection of the rule of reasonableness or unreasonableness would lead to the greatest variableness and uncertainty in the enforcement of the law. The defense of reasonable restraint would be made in every case and there would be as many different rules of reasonableness as cases, courts and juries.* What one court or jury might deem unreasonable another court or jury might deem reasonable. A court or jury in Ohio might find a given agreement or combination reasonable, while a court and jury in Wisconsin might find the same agreement and combination unreasonable. In the case of *People* v. *Sheldon,* 139 N. Y. 264, Chief Justice Andrews remarks: 'If agreements and combinations to prevent competition in prices are or may be hurtful to trade, *the only sure remedy is to prohibit all agreements of that character.* If the validity of such an agreement was made to depend upon actual proof of public prejudice or injury, it would be very difficult in any case to establish the invalidity, although the moral evidence might be very convincing.' . . . To amend the Anti-trust Act, as suggested by this bill, would be to entirely emasculate it, and for all practical purposes render it nugatory as a remedial statute. Criminal prosecutions would not lie and civil remedies would labor under the greatest doubt and uncertainty. The act as it exists is clear, comprehensive, certain and highly remedial. It practically covers the field of Federal jurisdiction, and is in every respect a model law. To destroy or undermine it at the present juncture, when combinations are on the increase, and appear to be as oblivious as ever of the rights of the public, would be a calamity." The result was the indefinite postponement by the Senate of any further consideration of the proposed amendments of the Anti-trust Act.

After what has been adjudged, upon full consideration, as to the meaning and scope of the Anti-trust Act, and in view of the usages of this court when attorneys for litigants have attempted to reopen questions that have been deliberately decided, I confess to no little surprise as to what has occurred in the present case. The court says that the previous cases, above cited, "cannot by any possible conception be treated as authoritative without the certitude that *reason* was resorted to for the purpose of deciding them." And its opinion is full of intimations that this court proceeded in those cases, so far as the present question is concerned, without being guided by the "rule of reason," or "the light of reason." It is more than once intimated, if not suggested, that if the Anti-trust Act is to be construed as prohibiting *every* contract or combination, of whatever nature, which is in fact in restraint of commerce, regardless of the reasonableness or unreasonableness of such restraint, that fact would show that the court had not proceeded, in its decision, according to "the light of reason," but had disregarded the "rule of reason." If the court, in those cases, was wrong in its construction of the act, it is certain that it fully apprehended the views advanced by learned counsel in previous cases and pronounced them to be untenable. The published reports place this beyond all question. . . . ⊥ Is it to be supposed that any point escaped notice in those cases when we think of the sagacity of the Justice who expressed the views of the court, or of the ability of the profound, astute lawyers, who sought such an interpretation of the act as would compel the court to insert words in the statute which Congress had not put there, and the insertion of which words, would amount to "judicial legislation"? Now this court is asked to do that which it has distinctly declared it could not and would not do, and has now done what it then said it could not constitutionally do. It has, by mere interpretation, modified the act of Congress, and deprived it of practical value as a defensive measure against the evils to be remedied. On reading the opinion just delivered, the first inquiry will be, that as the court is unanimous in holding that the particular things done by the Standard Oil Company and its subsidiary companies, in this case, were illegal under the Anti-trust Act, whether those things were in reasonable or unreasonable restraint of interstate commerce, why was it necessary to make an elaborate argument, as is done in the opinion, to show that according to the "rule of reason" the act as passed by Congress should be interpreted as if it contained the word "unreasonable" or the word "undue"? The only answer which, in frankness, can be given to this question is, that the court intends to decide that its deliberate judgment, fifteen years ago, to the effect that the act permitted no restraint whatever of interstate commerce, whether reasonable or unreasonable, was not in accordance with ⊥ the "rule of reason." In effect the court says, that it will now, for the first time, bring the discussion under the "light of reason" and apply the "rule of reason" to the questions to be decided. I have the authority of this court for saying that such a course of proceeding on its part would be "judicial legislation."

Still more, what is now done involves a serious departure from the settled usages of this court. Counsel have not ordinarily been allowed to discuss questions already settled by previous decisions. . . . ⊥ When counsel in the present case insisted upon a reversal of the former rulings of this court, and asked such an interpretation of the Anti-trust Act as would allow reasonable restraints of interstate commerce, this ⊥ court, in deference to established practice, should, I submit, have said to them: "That question, according to our practice, is not open for further discussion here. This court long ago deliberately held (1) that the act, interpreting its words in their ordinary acceptation, prohibits *all* restraints of interstate commerce by combinations in whatever form, and whether reasonable or unreasonable; (2) the question relates to matters of public policy in reference to commerce among the States and with foreign nations, and Congress alone can deal with the subject; (3) this court would encroach upon the authority of Congress if, under the guise of construction, it should assume to determine a matter of public policy; (4) the parties must go to Congress and obtain an amendment of the Anti-trust Act if they think this court was wrong in its former decisions; and (5) this court cannot and will not *judicially legislate,* since its function is to declare the law, while it belongs to the legislative department to make the law. Such a course, I am sure, would not have offended the "rule of reason."

But my brethren, in their wisdom, have deemed it best to pursue a different course. They have now said to those who condemn our former decisions and who object to all legislative prohibitions of contracts, combinations and trusts in restraint of interstate commerce, "You may *now* restrain such commerce, provided you are reasonable about it; only take care that the restraint in not undue." The disposition of the case under consideration, according to the views of the defendants, will, it is claimed, quiet and give rest to "the business of the country." On the contrary, I have a strong conviction that it will throw the business of the country into confusion and invite widely-extended and harassing litigation, the injurious effects of which will be felt for many years to come. When Congress prohibited *every* contract, combination or monopoly, in restraint of commerce, it prescribed a simple, definite rule that all could understand, and which could be easily ap⊥plied by everyone wishing to obey the law, and not to conduct their business in violation of law. But now, it is to be feared, we are to have, in cases without number, the constantly recurring inquiry—difficult to solve by proof—whether the particular contract, combination, or trust involved in each case is or is not an "unreasonable" or "undue" restraint of trade. Congress, in effect, said that there should be *no* restraint of trade, *in any form,* and this court solemnly adjudged many years ago that Congress meant what it thus said in clear and explicit words, and that it *could not* add to the words of the act. But those who condemn the action of Congress are now, in effect, informed that the courts will allow such restraints of interstate commerce as are shown not to be unreasonable or undue.

It remains for me to refer, more fully than I have heretofore done, to another, and, in my judgment—if we look to the future—the most important aspect of this case. That aspect concerns the usurpation by the judicial branch of the Government of the functions of the legislative department. The illustrious men who laid the foundations of our institutions, deemed no part of the National Constitution of more consequence or more essential to the permanancy of our form of government than the provisions under which were distributed the powers of Government among three separate, equal and coördinate departments—legislative, executive, and judicial. This was at that time a new feature of governmental regulation among the nations of the earth, and it is deemed by the people of every section of our own country as most vital in the workings of a representative republic whose Constitution was ordained and established in order to accomplish the objects stated in its Preamble by the means, *but only by the means,* provided either expressly or by necessary implication, by the instrument itself. No department of that government can constitutionally exercise the ⊥ powers committed strictly to another and separate department.

I said at the outset that the action of the court in this case might well alarm thoughtful men who revered the Constitution. I meant by this that many things are intimated and said in the court's opinion which will not be regarded otherwise than as sanctioning an invasion by the judiciary of the constitutional domain of Congress—an attempt by interpretation to soften or modify what some regard as a harsh public policy. This court, let me repeat, solemnly adjudged many years ago that it could not, except by *"judicial legislation,"* read words into the Anti-trust Act not put there by Congress, and which, being inserted, give it a meaning which the words of the Act, as passed, if properly interpreted, would not justify. The court has decided that it could not thus change a public policy formulated and declared by Congress; that Congress has paramount authority to regulate interstate commerce, and that it alone can change a policy once inaugurated by legislation. The courts have nothing to do with the wisdom or policy of an act of Congress. Their duty is to ascertain the will of Congress, and if the statute embodying the expression of that will is constitutional, the courts must respect it. They have no function to declare a public policy, nor to *amend* legislative enactments. "What is termed the policy of the Government with reference to any particular legislation," as this court has said, "is generally a very uncertain thing, upon which all sorts of opinions, each variant from the other, may be formed by different persons. It is a ground much too unstable upon which to rest the judgment of the court in the interpretation of statutes." *Hadden* v. *Collector,* 5 Wall. 107. Nevertheless, if I do not misapprehend its opinion, the court has now read into the act of Congress words which are not to be found there, and has thereby done that which it adjudged in 1896 and 1898 could not be done without violating ⊥ the Constitution, namely, by interpretation of a statute, changed a public policy declared by the legislative department.

After many years of public service at the National Capital, and after a somewhat close observation of the conduct of public affairs, I am impelled to say that there is abroad, in our land, a most harmful tendency to bring about the amending of constitutions and legislative enactments by means alone of judicial construction. As a public policy has been declared by the legislative department in respect of interstate commerce, over which Congress has entire control, under the Constitution, all concerned must patiently submit to what has been lawfully done, until the People of the United States—the source of all National power—shall, in their own time, upon reflection and through the legislative department of the Government, require a change of that policy. There are some who say that it is a part of one's liberty to conduct commerce among the States without being subject to governmental authority. But that would not be liberty, regulated by law, and liberty, which cannot be regulated by law, is not to be desired. The Supreme Law of the Land—which is binding alike upon all—

upon Presidents, Congresses, the Courts and the People—gives to Congress, and to Congress alone, authority to regulate interstate commerce, and when Congress forbids *any* restraint of such commerce, in any form, all must obey its mandate. To overreach the action of Congress merely by judicial construction, that is, by indirection, is a blow at the integrity of our governmental system, and in the end will prove most dangerous to all. Mr. Justice Bradley wisely said, when on this Bench, that illegitimate and unconstitutional practices get their first footing by silent approaches and slight deviations from legal modes of legal procedure. *Boyd* v. *United States,* 116 U. S. 616, 635. We shall do well to heed the warnings of that great jurist.

I do not stop to discuss the merits of the policy embodied in the Anti-trust Act of 1890; for, as has been often adjudged, the courts, under our constitutional system, have no rightful concern with the wisdom or policy of legislation enacted by that branch of the Government which alone can make laws.

For the reasons stated, while concurring in the general affirmance of the decree of the Circuit Court, I dissent from that part of the judgment of this court which directs the modification of the decree of the Circuit Court, as well as from those parts of the opinion which, in effect, assert authority, in this court, to insert words in the Anti-trust Act which Congress did not put there, and which, being inserted, Congress is made to declare, as part of the public policy of the country, what it has not chosen to declare.

UNITED STATES v. AMERICAN TOBACCO CO.

221 U.S. 106, 31 S. Ct. 632, 55 L. Ed. 663 (1911)

MR. CHIEF JUSTICE WHITE delivered the opinion of the court.

This suit was commenced on July 19, 1907, by the United States, to prevent the continuance of alleged violations of the first and second sections of the Anti-trust Act of July 2, 1890. The defendants were twenty-nine individuals, . . . sixty-five American corporations, most of them created in the State of New Jersey, and two English corporations. . . .

The ground of complaint against the American Tobacco Company rested not alone upon the nature and character of that corporation and the power which it exerted directly over the five accessory corporations and some of the subsidiary corporations by stock ownership in such corporations, but also upon the control which it exercised over the subsidiary companies by virtue of stock held in said companies by the accessory companies by stock ownership in which the American Tobacco Company exerted its power of control. . . .

. . . [T]he bill averred the origin and nature of the American Tobacco Company and the origin and nature of all the other defendant corporations, whether accessory or subsidiary, and the connection of the individual defendants with such corporations. In effect the bill charged that the individual defendants and the defendant corporations were engaged in a conspiracy in restraint of interstate and foreign trade in tobacco and the products of tobacco and constituted a combination in restraint of such trade in violation of the first section of the act, and also were attempting to monopolize and were actually a monopolization of such trade in violation of the second section. In support of these charges general averments were made in the bill as to the wrongful purpose and intent with which acts were committed which it was alleged brought about the alleged wrongful result.

The prayer of the bill was as follows:

"Wherefore petitioner prays:

"1. That the contracts, combinations, and conspiracies in restraint of trade and commerce among the States and with foreign nations, together with the attempts to monopolize and the monopolies of the same hereinbefore described be declared illegal and in violation of the act of Congress passed July 2, 1890, and subsequent acts, and that they be prevented and restrained by proper orders of the court.

"2. That the agreements, contracts, combinations, and conspiracies entered into by the defendants on or about September 27, 1902, and thereafter, and evidenced among other things by the two written agreements of that date, Exhibits 1 and 2 hereto, be declared illegal, and that injunctions issue restraining and prohibiting defendants from doing anything in pursuance of or in furtherance of the same within the jurisdiction of the United States. . . ."

. . . .

After the taking of much testimony before a special examiner, the case was heard before a court consisting of four judges, constituted under the expediting act of February 11, 1903. In deciding the case in favor of the Government each of the four judges delivered an opinion (164 Fed. Rep. 700). A final decree was entered on December 15, 1908. The petition was dismissed as to the English corporations, three of the subsidiary corporations, the United Cigar Stores Company and all the individual defendants. It was decreed that the defendants other than those against whom the petition was dismissed, had theretofore entered into and were parties to combinations in restraint of trade, etc., in violation of the Anti-trust Act and said defendants and each of them, their officers, agents, etc., were restrained and enjoined "from directly or indirectly doing any act or thing whatsoever in furtherance of the objects and purposes of said combinations and from continuing as parties thereto." It specifically found that each of the defendants . . . "constitutes and is itself a combination in violation of the said Act of Congress." The corporations thus named, their officers, etc., were next restrained and enjoined "from further directly or indirectly engaging in interstate or foreign trade and commerce in leaf tobacco or the products manufactured therefrom or articles necessary or useful in connection therewith. But if any of said last-named defendants can hereafter affirmatively show the restoration of reasonably competitive conditions, such defendant may apply to this court for a modification, suspension or dissolution of the injunction herein granted against it." . . .

The United States appealed, as did also the various defendants against whom the decree was entered. . . .

The elaborate arguments made by both sides at bar present in many forms of statement the conflicting contentions resulting from the nature and character of the suit and the defense thereto, the decree of the lower court and the propositions assigned as error to which we have just referred. In so far as all or any of these contentions, as many of them in fact do, involve a conflict as to the application and effect of §§ 1 and 2 of the Anti-trust Act, their consideration has been greatly simplified by the analysis and review of that act and the construction affixed to the sections in question in the case of *Standard Oil Company* v. *United States*, quite recently decided, *ante*, p. 1. In so far as the contentions relate to the disputed propositions of fact, we think from the view which we take of the case they need not be referred to, since in our opinion the case can be disposed of by considering only those facts which are indisputable and by applying to the inferences properly deducible from such facts the meaning and effect of the law as expounded in accordance with the previous decisions of this court. . . .

. . . [I]t is well briefly to point out the increase in the power and control of the American Tobacco Company and the extension of its activities to all forms of tobacco products which had been accomplished just prior to the organization of the Continental Tobacco Company. Nothing could show it more clearly than the following: At the end of the time the company was manufacturing eighty-six per cent or thereabouts of all the cigarettes produced in the United States, above twenty-six per cent of all the smoking tobacco, more than twenty-two per cent of all plug tobacco, fifty-one per cent of all little cigars, six per cent each of all snuff and fine cut tobacco, and over two per cent of all cigars and cheroots.

A brief reference to the occurrences of the second period, that is, from and after the organization of the Continental Tobacco Company up to the time of the bringing of this suit, will serve to make evident that the transactions in their essence had all the characteristics of the occurrences of the first period. . . .

By proceedings in New Jersey, October, 1904, the (old) American Tobacco Company, Continental Tobacco Company and Consolidated Tobacco Company were merged into one corporation, under the name of The American Tobacco Company, the principal defendant here. The merged company, with perpetual existence, was capitalized at $180,000,000 ($80,000,000 preferred, ordinarily without power to vote). . . .

The record indisputably discloses that after this merger the same methods which were used from the beginning continued to be employed. Thus, it is beyond dispute: First, that since the organization of the new American Tobacco Company that company has acquired four large tobacco concerns, that restrictive covenants against engaging in the tobacco business were taken from the sellers, and that the plants were not continued in operation but were at once abandoned. Second, that the new company has besides acquired control of eight additional concerns, the business of such concerns being now carried on by four separate corporations, all absolutely controlled by the American Tobacco Company, although the connection as to two of these companies with that corporation was long and persistently denied.

Thus reaching the end of the second period and coming to the time of the bringing of the suit, brevity prevents us from stopping to portray the difference between the condition in 1890 when the (old) American Tobacco Company was organized by the consolidation of five competing cigarette concerns and that which existed at the commencement of the suit. That situation and the vast power which the principal and accessory corporate defendants and the small number of individuals who own a majority of the common stock of the new American Tobacco Company exert over the marketing of tobacco as a raw product, its manufacture, its marketing when manufactured, and its consequent movement in the channels of interstate commerce indeed relatively over foreign commerce, and the commerce of the whole world, in the raw and manufactured products stand out in such bold relief from the undisputed facts which have been stated as to lead us to pass at once to the second fundamental proposition which we are required to consider. That is, the construction of the Anti-trust Act and the application of the act as rightly construed to the situation as proven in consequence of having determined the ultimate and final inferences properly deducible from the undisputed facts which we have stated.

The construction and application of the Anti-trust Act.

If the Anti-trust Act is applicable to the entire situation here presented and is adequate to afford complete relief for the evils which the United States insists that situation presents it can only be because that law will be given a more comprehensive application than has been affixed to it in any previous decision. This will be the case because the undisputed facts as we have stated them involve questions as to the operation of the Anti-trust Act not hitherto presented in any case. Thus, even if the ownership of stock by the American Tobacco Company in the accessory and subsidiary companies and the ownership of stock in any of those companies among themselves were held, as was decided in *United States* v. *Standard Oil Co.*, to be a violation of the act and all relations resulting from such stock ownership were therefore set aside, the question would yet remain whether the principal defendant, the American Tobacco Company, and the five accessory defendants, even when divested of their stock ownership in other corporations, by virtue of the power which they would continue to possess, even although thus stripped, would amount to a violation of both the first and second sections of the act. Again, if it were held that the corporations, the existence whereof was due to a combination between such companies and other companies was a violation of the act, the question would remain whether such of the companies as did not owe their existence and power to combinations but whose power alone arose from the exercise of the right to acquire and own property would be amenable to the prohibitions of the act. Yet further: Even if this proposition was held in the affirmative the question would remain whether the principal defendant, the American Tobacco Company, when stripped of its stock ownership, would be in and of itself within the prohibitions of the act although that company was organized and took being before the Anti-trust Act was passed. Still further, the question would yet remain whether particular corporations which, when bereft of the power which they possessed as resulting from stock ownership, although they were not inherently possessed of a sufficient residuum of power to cause them to be in and of themselves either a restraint of trade or a monopolization or an attempt to monopolize, should nevertheless be restrained because of their intimate connection and association with other corporations found to be within the prohibitions of the act. The necessity of relief as to all these aspects, we think, seemed to the Government so essential, and the difficulty of giving to the act such a comprehensive and coherent construction as would be adequate to enable it to meet the entire situation, led to what appears to us to be in their essence a resort to methods of construction not compatible one with the other. And the same apparent conflict is presented by the views of the act taken by the defendants when their contentions are accurately tested. Thus the Government, for the purpose of fixing the illegal character of the original combination which organized the old American Tobacco Company, asserts that the illegal character of the combination is plainly shown because the combination was brought about to stay the progress of a flagrant and ruinous trade war. In other words, the contention is that as the act forbids every contract, and combination, it hence prohibits a reasonable and just agreement made for the purpose of ending a trade war. But as thus construing the act by the rule of the letter which kills, would necessarily operate to take out of the reach of the act some one of the accessory and many subsidiary corporations, the existence of which depend not at all upon combination or agreement or contract, but upon mere purchases of property, it is insisted in many forms of argument that the rule of construction to be applied must be the spirit and intent of the act and therefore its prohibitions must be held to extend to acts even if not within the literal terms of the statute if they are within its spirit because done with an intent to bring about the harmful results which it was the purpose of the statute to prohibit. So as to the defendants. While it is argued on the one hand that the forms by which various properties ⊥ were acquired in view of the letter of the act exclude many of the assailed transactions from condemnation, it is yet urged that giving to the act the broad construction which it should rightfully receive, whatever may be the form, no condemnation should follow, because, looking at the case as a whole, every act assailed is shown to have been but a legitimate and lawful result of the exertion of honest business methods brought into play for the purpose of advancing trade instead of with the object of obstructing and restraining the same. But the difficulties which arise, from the complexity of the particular dealings which are here involved and the situation which they produce, we think grows out of a plain misconception of both the letter and spirit of the Anti-trust Act. We say of the letter, because while seeking by a narrow rule of the letter to include things which it is deemed would otherwise be excluded, the contention really destroys the great purpose of the act, since it renders it impossible to apply the law to a multitude of wrongful acts, which would come within the scope of its remedial purposes by resort to a reasonable construction, although they would not be within its reach by a too narrow and unreasonable adherence to the strict letter. This must be the case unless it be possible in reason to say that for the purpose of including one class of acts which would not otherwise be embraced a literal construction although in conflict with reason must be applied and for the purpose of including other acts which would not otherwise be embraced a reasonable construction must be resorted to. That is to say two conflicting rules of construction must at one and the same time be applied and adhered to.

The obscurity and resulting uncertainty however, is now but an abstraction because it has been removed by the consideration which we have given quite recently to the construction of the Anti-trust Act in the *Standard Oil Case*. In that case it was held, without departing from ⊥ any previous decision of the court that as the statute had not defined the words restraint of trade, it became necessary to construe those words, a duty which could only be discharged by a resort to reason. We say the doctrine thus stated was in accord with all the previous decisions of this court, despite the fact that the contrary view was sometimes erroneously attributed to some of the expressions used in two prior decisions (the *Trans-Missouri Freight Association* and *Joint Traffic cases*, 166 U. S. 290, and 171 U. S. 505). That such view was a mistaken one was fully pointed out in the *Standard Oil Case* and is additionally shown by a passage in the opinion in the *Joint Traffic Case* as follows (171 U. S. 568): "The act of Congress must have a reasonable construction, or else there would scarcely be an agreement or contract among business men that could not be said to have, indirectly or remotely, some bearing on interstate commerce, and possibly to restrain it." Applying the rule of reason to the construction of the statute, it was held in the *Standard Oil Case* that as the words "restraint of trade" at common law and in the law of this country at the time of the adoption of the Anti-trust Act only embraced acts or contracts or agreements or combinations which operated to the prejudice of the public interests by unduly restricting competition or unduly obstructing the due course of trade or which, either because of their inherent nature or effect or because of the evident purpose of the acts, etc., injuriously restrained trade, that the words as used in the statute were designed to have and did have but a like significance. It was therefore pointed out that the statute did not forbid or restrain the power to make normal and usual contracts to further trade by resorting to all normal methods, whether by agreement or otherwise, to accomplish such purpose. In other words, it was held, not that acts which the statute prohibited could be removed from the control of its prohibitions by a finding that they were reasonable, but that the duty to interpret which inevitably arose from the general character of the term restraint of trade required that the words restraint of trade should be given a meaning which would not destroy the individual right to contract and render difficult if not impossible any movement of trade in the channels of interstate commerce—the free movement of which it was the purpose of the statute to protect. The soundness of the rule that the statute should receive a reasonable construction, after further mature deliberation, we see no reason to doubt. Indeed, the necessity for not departing in this case from the standard of the rule of reason which is universal in its application is so plainly required in order to give effect to the remedial purposes which the act under consideration contemplates, and to prevent that act from destroying all liberty of contract and all substantial right to trade, and thus causing the act to be at war with itself by annihilating the fundamental right of freedom to trade which, on the very face of the act, it was enacted to preserve, is illustrated by the record before us. In truth, the plain demonstration which this record gives of the injury which would arise from and the promotion of the wrongs which the statute was intended to guard against which would result from giving to the statute a narrow, unreasoning and unheard of construction, as illustrated by the record before us, if possible serves to strengthen our conviction as to the correctness of the rule of construction, the rule of reason, which was applied in the *Standard Oil Case,* the application of which rule to the statute we now, in the most unequivocal terms, reexpress and re-affirm.

Coming then to apply to the case before us the act as interpreted in the Standard Oil and previous cases, all the difficulties suggested by the mere form in which the assailed transactions are clothed become of no moment. This follows because although it was held in the *Standard Oil Case* that, giving to the statute a reasonable construction, the words "restraint of trade" did not embrace all those normal and usual contracts essential to individual freedom and the right to make which were necessary in order that the course of trade might be free, yet, as a result of the reasonable construction which was affixed to the statute, it was pointed out that the generic designation of the first and second sections of the law, when taken together, embraced every conceivable act which could possibly come within the spirit or purpose of the prohibitions of the law, without regard to the garb in which such acts were clothed. That is to say, it was held that in view of the general language of the statute and the public policy which it manifested, there was no possibility of frustrating that policy by resorting to any disguise or subterfuge of form, since resort to reason rendered it impossible to escape by any indirection the prohibitions of the statute.

Considering then the undisputed facts which we have previously stated, it remains only to determine whether they establish that the acts, contracts, agreements, combinations, etc., which were assailed were of such an unusual and wrongful character as to bring them within the prohibitions of the law. That they were, in our opinion, so overwhelmingly results from the undisputed facts that it seems only necessary to refer to the facts as we have stated them to demonstrate the correctness of this conclusion. Indeed, the history of the combination is so replete with the doing of acts which it was the obvious purpose of the statute to forbid, so demonstrative of the existence from the beginning of a purpose to acquire dominion and control of the tobacco trade, not by the mere exertion of the ordinary right to contract and to trade, but by methods devised in order to monopolize the trade by driving competitors out of business, which were ruthlessly carried out upon the assumption that to work upon the fears or play upon the cupidity of competitors would make success possible. We say these conclusions are inevitable, not because of the vast amount of property aggregated by the combination, not because alone of the many corporations which the proof shows were united by resort to one device or another. Again, not alone because of the dominion and control over the tobacco trade which actually exists, but because we think the conclusion of wrongful purpose and illegal combination is overwhelmingly established by the following considerations: *a.* By the fact that the very first organization or combination was impelled by a previously existing fierce trade war, evidently inspired by one or more of the minds which brought about and became parties to that combination. *b.* Because, immediately after that combination and the increase of capital which followed, the acts which ensued justify the inference that the intention existed to use the power of the combination as a vantage ground to further monopolize the trade in tobacco by means of trade conflicts designed to injure others, either by driving competitors out of the business or compelling them to become parties to a combination—a purpose whose execution was illustrated by the plug war which ensued and its results, by the snuff war which followed and its results, and by the conflict which immediately followed the entry of the combination in England and the division of the world's business by the two foreign contracts which ensued. *c.* By the ever-present manifestation which is exhibited of a conscious wrongdoing by the form in which the various transactions were embodied from the beginning, ever changing but ever in substance the same. Now the organization of a new company, now the control exerted by the taking of stock in one or another or in several, so as to obscure the result actually attained, nevertheless uniform, in their manifestations of the purpose to restrain others and to monopolize and retain power in the hands of the ⊥ few who, it would seem, from the beginning contemplated the mastery of the trade which practically followed. *d.* By the gradual absorption of control over all the elements essential to the successful manufacture of tobacco products, and placing such control in the hands of seemingly independent corporations serving as perpetual barriers to the entry of others into the tobacco trade. *e.* By persistent expenditure of millions upon millions of dollars in buying out plants, not for the purpose of utilizing them, but in order to close them up and render them useless for the purposes of trade. *f.* By the constantly recurring stipulations, whose legality, isolatedly viewed, we are not considering, by which numbers of persons, whether manufacturers, stockholders or employés, were required to bind themselves, generally for long periods, not to compete in the future. Indeed, when the results of the undisputed proof which we have stated are fully apprehended, and the wrongful acts which they exhibit are considered, there comes inevitably to the mind the conviction that it was the danger which it was deemed would arise to individual liberty and the public well-being from acts like those which this record exhibits, which led the legislative mind to conceive and to enact the Anti-trust Act, considerations which also serve to clearly demonstrate that the combination here assailed is within the law as to leave no doubt that it is our plain duty to apply its prohibitions. . . .

⊥ Leading as this does to the conclusion that the assailed combination in all its aspects—that is to say, whether it be looked at from the point of view of stock ownership or from the standpoint of the principal corporation and the accessory or subsidiary corporations viewed independently, including the foreign corporations in so far as by the contracts made by them they became cooperators in the combination—comes within the prohibitions of the first and second sections of the Anti-trust Act, it remains only finally to consider the remedy which it is our duty to apply to the situation thus found to exist.

The remedy.

Our conclusion being that the combination as a whole, involving all its cooperating or associated parts, in whatever form clothed, constitutes a restraint of trade within the first section, and an attempt to monopolize or a monopolization within the second section of the Anti-trust Act, it follows that the relief which we are to afford must be wider than that awarded by the lower court, since that court merely decided that certain of the corporate defendants constituted combinations in violation of the first section of the act, because of the fact that they were formed by the union of previously competing concerns and that the other defendants not dismissed from the action were parties to such combinations or promoted their purposes. . . . ⊥ [W]e think that the court below clearly erred in dismissing the individual defendants, the United Cigar Stores Company, and the foreign corporations and their subsidiary corporations.

Looking at the situation as we have hitherto pointed it out, it involves difficulties in the application of remedies greater than have been presented by any case involving the Anti-trust Act which has been hitherto considered by this court: First. Because in this case it is obvious that a mere decree forbidding stock ownership by one part of the combination in another part or entity thereof, would afford no adequate measure of relief, since different ⊥ ingredients of the combination would remain unaffected, and by the very nature and character of their organization would be able to continue the wrongful situation which it is our duty to destroy. Second. Because the methods of apparent ownership by which the wrongful intent was, in part, carried out and the subtle devices which, as we have seen, were resorted to for the purpose of accomplishing the wrong contemplated, by way of ownership or otherwise, are of such a character that it is difficult if not impossible to formulate a remedy which could restore in their entirety the prior lawful conditions. Third. Because the methods devised by which the various essential elements to the successful operation of the tobacco business from any particular aspect have been so separated under various subordinate combinations, yet so unified by way of the control worked out by the scheme here condemned, are so involved that any specific form of relief which we might now order in substance and effect might operate really to injure the public and, it may be, to perpetuate the wrong. . . . ⊥ Under these circumstances, taking into mind the complexity of the situation in all of its aspects and giving weight to the many-sided considerations which must control our judgment, we think, so far as the permanent relief to be awarded is concerned, we should decree as follows: 1st. That the combination in and of itself, as well as each and all of the elements composing it, whether corporate or individual, whether considered collectively or separately, be decreed to be in restraint of trade and an attempt to monopolize and a monopolization within the first and second sections of the Anti-trust Act. 2d. That the court below, in order to give effective force to our decree in this regard, be directed to hear the parties, by evidence or otherwise, as it may be deemed proper, for the purpose of ascertaining and determining upon some plan or method of dissolving the combination and of recreating, out of the elements now composing it, a new condition which shall be honestly in harmony with and not repugnant to the law. . . .

⊥ Pending the bringing about of the result just stated, each and all of the defendants, individuals as well as corporations, should be restrained from doing any act which might further extend or enlarge the power of the combination, by any means or device whatsoever. In view of the considerations we have stated we leave the matter to the court below to work out a compliance with the law without unnecessary injury to the public or the rights of private property.

While in many substantial respects our conclusion is in accord with that reached by the court below, and while also the relief which we think should be awarded in some respects is coincident with that which the court granted, in order to prevent any complication and to clearly define the situation we think instead of affirming and modifying, our decree, in view of the broad nature of our conclusions, should be one of reversal and remanding with directions to the court below to enter a decree in conformity with this opinion and to take such further steps as may be necessary to fully carry out the directions which we have given.

And it is so ordered.

[ED. NOTE: Mr. Justice Harlan concurred in part and dissented in part. His opinion, in which he essentially restated his views as expressed in his opinion in *Standard Oil,* has been omitted.]

BOARD OF TRADE OF THE CITY OF CHICAGO
v.
UNITED STATES

246 U.S. 231, 38 S. Ct. 242, 62 L. Ed. 683 (1918)

[ED. NOTE: All original Court footnotes have been omitted.]

MR. JUSTICE BRANDEIS delivered the opinion of the court.

Chicago is the leading grain market in the world. Its Board of Trade is the commercial center through which most of the trading in grain is done. The character of the organization is described in *Board of Trade* v. *Christie Grain & Stock Co.*, 198 U. S. 236. Its 1600 members include brokers, commission merchants, dealers, millers, maltsters, manufacturers of corn products and proprietors of elevators. Grains there dealt in are graded according to kind and quality and are sold usually "Chicago weight, inspection and delivery." The standard forms of trading are: (*a*) Spot sales; that is, sales of grain already in Chicago in railroad cars or elevators for immediate delivery by order on carrier or transfer of warehouse receipt. (*b*) Future sales; that is, agreements for delivery later in the current or in some future month. (*c*) Sales "to arrive"; that is, agreements to deliver on arrival grain which is already in transit to Chicago or is to be shipped there within a time specified. On every business day sessions of the Board are held at which all bids and sales are publicly made. Spot sales and future sales are made at the regular sessions of the Board from 9.30 A. M. to 1.15 P. M., except on Saturdays, when the session closes at 12 M. Special sessions, termed the "Call," are held immediately after the close of the regular session, at which sales "to arrive" are made. These sessions are not limited as to duration, but last usually about half an hour. At all these sessions transactions are between members only; but they may trade either for themselves or on behalf of others. Members may also trade privately with one another at any place, either during the sessions or after, and they may trade with non-members at any time except on the premises occupied by the Board.

Purchases of grain "to arrive" are made largely from country dealers and farmers throughout the whole territory tributary to Chicago, which includes besides Illinois and Iowa, Indiana, Ohio, Wisconsin, Minnesota, Missouri, Kansas, Nebraska, and even South and North Dakota. The purchases are sometimes the result of bids to individual country dealers made by telegraph or telephone either during the sessions or after; but most purchases are made by the sending out from Chicago by the afternoon mails to hundreds of country dealers offers to buy, at the prices named, any number of carloads, subject to acceptance before 9.30 A. M. on the next business day.

In 1906 the Board adopted what is known as the "Call" rule. By it members were prohibited from purchasing or offering to purchase, during the period between the close of the Call and the opening of the session on the next business day, any wheat, corn, oats or rye "to arrive" at a price other than the closing bid at the Call. The Call was over, with rare exceptions, by two o'clock. The change effected was this: Before the adoption of the rule, members fixed their bids throughout the day at such prices as they respectively saw fit; after the adoption of the rule, the bids had to be fixed at the day's closing bid on the Call until the opening of the next session.

In 1913 the United States filed in the District Court for the Northern District of Illinois this suit against the Board and its executive officers and directors, to enjoin the enforcement of the Call rule, alleging it to be in violation of the Anti-Trust Law (July 2, 1890, c. 647, 26 Stat. 209). The defendants admitted the adoption and enforcement of the Call rule, and averred that its purpose was not to prevent competition or to control prices, but to promote the convenience of members by restricting their hours of business and to break up a monopoly in that branch of the grain trade acquired by four or five warehousemen in Chicago. On motion of the Government the allegations concerning the purpose of establishing the regulation were stricken from the record. The case was then heard upon evidence; and a decree was entered which declared that defendants became parties to a combination or conspiracy to restrain interstate and foreign trade and commerce "by adopting, acting upon and enforcing" the "Call" rule; and enjoined them from acting upon the same or from adopting or acting upon any similar rule.

No opinion was delivered by the District Judge. The Government proved the existence of the rule and described its application and the change in business practice involved. It made no attempt to show that the rule was designed to or that it had the effect of limiting the amount of grain shipped to Chicago; or of retarding or accelerating shipment; or of raising or depressing prices; or of discriminating against any part of the public; or that it resulted in hardship to anyone. The case was rested upon the bald proposition, that a rule or agreement by which men occupying positions of strength in any branch of trade, fixed prices at which they would buy or sell during an important part of the business day, is an illegal restraint of trade under the Anti-Trust Law. But the legality of an agreement or regulation cannot be determined by so simple a test, as whether it restrains competition. Every agreement concerning trade, every regulation of trade, restrains. To bind, to restrain, is of their very essence. The true test of legality is whether the restraint imposed is such as merely regulates and perhaps thereby promotes competition or whether it is such as may suppress or even destroy competition. To determine that question the court must ordinarily consider the facts peculiar to the business to which the restraint is applied; its condition before and after the restraint was imposed; the nature of the restraint and its effect, actual or probable. The history of the restraint, the evil believed to exist, the reason for adopting the particular remedy, the purpose or end sought to be attained, are all relevant facts. This is not because a good intention will save an otherwise objectionable regulation or the reverse; but because knowledge of intent may help the court to interpret facts and to predict consequences. The District Court erred, therefore, in striking from the answer allegations concerning the history and purpose of the Call rule and in later excluding evidence on that subject. But the evidence admitted makes it clear that the rule was a reasonable regulation of business consistent with the provisions of the Anti-Trust Law.

First: The nature of the rule: The restriction was upon the period of price-making. It required members to desist from further price-making after the close of the Call until 9.30 A. M. the next business day: but there was no restriction upon the sending out of bids after close of the Call. Thus it required members who desired to buy grain "to arrive" to make up their minds before the close of the Call how much they were willing to pay during the interval before the next session of the Board. The rule made it to their interest to attend the Call; and if they did not fill their wants by purchases there, to make the final bid high enough to enable them to purchase from country dealers.

Second: The scope of the rule: It is restricted in operation to grain "to arrive." It applies only to a small part of the grain shipped from day to day to Chicago, and to an even smaller part of the day's sales: members were left free to purchase grain already in Chicago from anyone at any price throughout the day. It applies only during a small part of the business day; members were left free to purchase during the sessions of the Board grain "to arrive," at any price, from members anywhere and from non-members anywhere except on the premises of the Board. It applied only to grain shipped to Chicago: members were left free to purchase at any price throughout the day from either members or non-members, grain "to arrive" at any other market. Country dealers and farmers had available in practically every part of the territory called tributary to Chicago some other market for grain "to arrive." . . .

Third: The effects of the rule: As it applies to only a small part of the grain shipped to Chicago and to that only during a part of the business day and does not apply at all to grain shipped to other markets, the rule had no appreciable effect on general market prices; nor did it materially affect the total volume of grain coming to Chicago. But within the narrow limits of its operation the rule helped to improve market conditions thus:

(a) It created a public market for grain "to arrive." Before its adoption, bids were made privately. Men had to buy and sell without adequate knowledge of actual market conditions. This was disadvantageous to all concerned, but particularly so to country dealers and farmers.

(b) It brought into the regular market hours of the Board sessions more of the trading in grain "to arrive."

(c) It brought buyers and sellers into more direct relations; because on the Call they gathered together for a free and open interchange of bids and offers.

(d) It distributed the business in grain "to arrive" among a far larger number of Chicago receivers and commission merchants than had been the case there before.

(e) It increased the number of country dealers engaging in this branch of the business; supplied them more regularly with bids from Chicago; and also increased the number of bids received by them from competing markets.

(f) It eliminated risks necessarily incident to a private market, and thus enabled country dealers to do business on a smaller margin. In that way the rule made it possible for them to pay more to farmers without raising the price to consumers.

(g) It enabled country dealers to sell some grain to arrive which they would otherwise have been obliged either to ship to Chicago commission merchants or to sell for "future delivery."

(h) It enabled those grain merchants of Chicago who sell to millers and exporters to trade on a smaller margin and, by paying more for grain or selling it for less, to make the Chicago market more attractive for both shippers and buyers of grain.

(i) Incidentally it facilitated trading "to arrive" by enabling those engaged in these transactions to fulfil their contracts by tendering grain arriving at Chicago on any railroad, whereas formerly shipments had to be made over the particular railroad designated by the buyer.

The restraint imposed by the rule is less severe than that sustained in *Anderson* v. *United States*, 171 U. S. 604. Every board of trade and nearly every trade organization imposes some restraint upon the conduct of business by its members. Those relating to the hours in which business may be done are common; and they make a special appeal where, as here, they tend to shorten the working day or, at least, limit the period of most exacting activity. The decree of the District Court is reversed with directions to dismiss the bill.

Reversed.

MR. JUSTICE MCREYNOLDS took no part in the consideration or decision of this case.

UNITED STATES v. TRENTON POTTERIES CO.

273 U.S. 392, 47 S. Ct. 377, 71 L. Ed. 700 (1927)

[ED. NOTE: All original Court footnotes have been omitted.]

MR. JUSTICE STONE delivered the opinion of the Court.

Respondents, twenty individuals and twenty-three corporations, were convicted in the district court for southern New York of violating the Sherman Anti-Trust Law, Act of July 2, 1890, c. 647, 26 Stat. 209. The indictment was in two counts. The first charged a combination to fix and maintain uniform prices for the sale of sanitary pottery, in restraint of interstate commerce; the second, a combination to restrain interstate commerce by limiting sales of pottery to a special group known to respondents as "legitimate jobbers." On appeal, the court of appeals for the second circuit reversed the judgment of conviction on both counts on the ground that there were errors in the conduct of the trial. 300 Fed. 550. This Court granted certiorari. 266 U. S. 597. Jud. Code, § 240.

Respondents, engaged in the manufacture or distribution of 82 per cent. of the vitreous pottery fixtures produced in the United States for use in bathrooms and lavatories, were members of a trade organization known as the Sanitary Potters' Association. . . .

There is no contention here that the verdict was not supported by sufficient evidence that respondents, controlling some 82 per cent. of the business of manufacturing and distributing in the United States vitreous pottery of the type described, combined to fix prices and to limit sales in interstate commerce to jobbers.

The issues raised here by the government's specification of errors relate only to the decision of the court of appeals upon its review of certain rulings of the district court made in the course of the trial. It is urged that the court below erred in holding in effect (1) that the trial court should have submitted to the jury the question whether the price agreement complained of constituted an unreasonable restraint of trade. . . .

REASONABLENESS OF RESTRAINT.

The trial court charged, in submitting the case to the jury, that if it found the agreements or combination complained of, it might return a verdict of guilty without regard to the reasonableness of the prices fixed, or the good intentions of the combining units, whether prices were actually lowered or raised or whether sales were restricted to the special jobbers, since both agreements of themselves were unreasonable restraints. These instructions repeated in various forms applied to both counts of the indictment. The trial court refused various requests to charge that both the agreement to fix prices and the agreement to limit sales to a particular group, if found, did not in themselves constitute violations of law unless it was also found that they unreasonably restrained interstate commerce. In particular the court refused the request to charge the following:

"The essence of the law is injury to the public. It is not every restraint of competition and not every restraint of trade that works an injury to the public; it is only an undue and unreasonable restraint of trade that has such an effect and is deemed to be unlawful."

Other requests of similar purport were refused including a quotation from the opinion of this Court in *Chicago Board of Trade* v. *United States*, 246 U. S. 231, 238.

The court below held specifically that the trial court erred in refusing to charge as requested and held in effect that the charge as given on this branch of the case was erroneous. This determination was based upon the assumption that the charge and refusals could be attributed only to a mistaken view of the trial judge, expressed in denying a motion at the close of the case to quash and dismiss the indictment, that the "rule of reason" announced in *Standard Oil Co.* v. *United States*, 221 U. S. 1, and in *American Tobacco Co.* v. *United States*, 221 U. S. 106, which were suits for injunctions, had no application in a criminal prosecution. Compare *Nash* v. *United States*, 229 U. S. 373.

This disposition of the matter ignored the fact that the trial judge plainly and variously charged the jury that the combinations alleged in the indictment, if found, were violations of the statute as a matter of law, saying:

". . . the law is clear that an agreement on the part of the members of a combination controlling a substantial part of an industry, upon the prices which the members are to charge for their commodity, is in itself an undue and unreasonable restraint of trade and commerce; . . ."

If the charge itself was correctly given and adequately covered the various aspects of the case, the refusal to charge in another correct form or to quote to the jury extracts from opinions of this Court was not error, nor should the court below have been concerned with the wrong reasons that may have inspired the charge, if correctly given. The question therefore to be considered here is whether the trial judge correctly withdrew from the jury the consideration of the reasonableness of the particular restraints charged.

That only those restraints upon interstate commerce which are unreasonable are prohibited by the Sherman Law was the rule laid down by the opinions of this Court in the *Standard Oil* and *Tobacco* cases. But it does not follow that agreements to fix or maintain prices are reasonable restraints and therefore permitted by the statute, merely because the prices themselves are reasonable. Reasonableness is not a concept of definite and unchanging content. Its meaning necessarily varies in the different fields of the law, because it is used as a convenient summary of the dominant considerations which control in the application of legal doctrines. Our view of what is a reasonable restraint of commerce is controlled by the recognized purpose of the Sherman Law itself. Whether this type of restraint is reasonable or not must be judged in part at least in the light of its effect on competition, for whatever difference of opinion there may be among economists as to the social and economic desirability of an unrestrained competitive system, it cannot be doubted that the Sherman Law and the judicial decisions interpreting it are based upon the assumption that the public interest is best protected from the evils of monopoly and price control by the maintenance of competition. See *United States* v. *Trans-Missouri Freight Association*, 166 U. S. 290; *Standard Oil Co.* v. *United States, supra; American Column Co.* v. *United States*, 257 U. S. 377, 400; *United States* v. *Linseed Oil Co.*, 262 U. S. 371, 388; *Eastern States Lumber Association* v. *United States*, 234 U. S. 600, 614.

The aim and result of every price-fixing agreement, if effective, is the elimination of one form of competition. The power to fix prices, whether reasonably exercised or not, involves power to control the market and to fix arbitrary and unreasonable prices. The reasonable price fixed today may through economic and business changes become the unreasonable price of tomorrow. Once established, it may be maintained unchanged because of the absence of competition secured by the agreement for a price reasonable when fixed. Agreements which create such potential power may well be held to be in themselves unreasonable or unlawful restraints, without the necessity of minute inquiry whether a particular price is reasonable or unreasonable as fixed and without placing on the government in enforcing the Sherman Law the burden of ascertaining from day to day whether it has become unreasonable through the mere variation of economic conditions. Moreover, in the absence of express legislation requiring it, we should hesitate to adopt a construction making the difference between legal and illegal conduct in the field of business relations depend upon so uncertain a test as whether prices are reasonable—a determination which can be satisfactorily made only after a complete survey of our economic organization and a choice between rival philosophies. Compare *United States* v. *Cohen Grocery Co.*, 255 U. S. 81; *International Harvester Co.* v. *Kentucky*, 234 U. S. 216; *Nash* v. *United States, supra*. Thus viewed, the Sherman law is not only a prohibition against the infliction of a particular type of public injury. It "is a limitation of rights, . . . which may be pushed to evil consequences and therefore restrained." *Standard Sanitary Mfg. Co.* v. *United States*, 226 U. S. 20, 49.

That such was the view of this Court in deciding the *Standard Oil* and *Tobacco* cases, and that such is the effect of its decisions both before and after those cases, does not seem fairly open to question. Beginning with *United States* v. *Trans-Missouri Freight Association, supra; United States* v. *Joint Traffic Association*, 171 U. S. 505, where agreements for establishing reasonable and uniform freight rates by competing lines of railroad were held unlawful, it has since often been decided and always assumed that uniform price-fixing by those controlling in any substantial manner a trade or business in interstate commerce is prohibited by the Sherman Law, despite the reasonableness of the particular prices agreed upon. . . .

That the opinions in the *Standard Oil* and *Tobacco* cases were not intended to affect this view of the illegality of price-fixing agreements affirmatively appears from the opinion in the *Standard Oil* case where, in considering the *Freight Association* case, the court said (p. 65):

"That as considering the contracts or agreements, their necessary effect and the character of the parties by whom they were made, they were clearly restraints of trade within the purview of the statute, they could not be taken out of that category by indulging in general reasoning as to the expediency or non-expediency of having made the contracts or the wisdom or want of wisdom of the statute which prohibited their being made. That is to say, the cases but decided that the nature and character of the contracts, creating as they did a conclusive presumption which brought them within the statute, such result was not to be disregarded by the substitution of a judicial appreciation of what the law ought to be for the plain judicial duty of enforcing the law as it was made."

And in *Thompson* v. *Cayser*, 234 U. S. 66, 84, it was specifically pointed out that the *Standard Oil* and *Tobacco* cases did not overrule the earlier cases. The decisions in *Maple Flooring Association* v. *United States,* 268 U. S. 563, and in *Cement Manufacturer's Protective Association* v. *United States*, 268 U. S. 588, were made on the assumption that any agreement for price-fixing, if found, would have been illegal as a matter of law. In *Federal Trade Commission* v. *Pacific States Paper Trade Association, ante,* p. 52, we upheld orders of the Commission forbidding price-fixing and prohibiting the use of agreed price lists by wholesale dealers in interstate commerce, without regard to the reasonableness of the prices.

Cases in both the federal and state courts have generally proceeded on a like assumption, and in the second circuit the view maintained below that the reasonableness or unreasonableness of the prices fixed must be submitted ⊥ to the jury has apparently been abandoned. See *Poultry Dealers' Association* v. *United States*, 4 Fed. (2d) 840. While not necessarily controlling, the decisions of this Court denying the validity of resale price agreements, regardless of the reasonableness of the price, are persuasive. See *Dr. Miles Medical Co.* v. *Park & Sons Co.*, [220 U. S. 373]; *Boston Store of Chicago* v. *American Graphophone Co.,* 246 U. S. 8; *United States* v. *Schrader's Sons*, 252 U. S. 85; *Federal Trade Commission* v. *Beechnut Packing Co.*, 257 U. S. 441.

Respondents rely upon *Chicago Board of Trade* v. *United States, supra*, in which an agreement by members of the Chicago Board of Trade controlling prices during certain hours of the day in a special class of grain contracts and affecting only a small proportion of the commerce in question was upheld. The purpose and effect of the agreement there was to maintain for a part of each business day the price which had been that day determined by open competition on the floor of the Exchange. That decision, dealing as it did with a regulation of a board of trade, does not sanction a price agreement among competitors in an open market such as is presented here.

The charge of the trial court, viewed as a whole, fairly submitted to the jury the question whether a price-fixing agreement as described in the first count was entered into by the respondents. Whether the prices actually agreed upon were reasonable or unreasonable was immaterial in the circumstances charged in the indictment and necessarily found by the verdict. The requested charge which we have quoted, and others of similar tenor, while true as abstract propositions, were inapplicable to the case in hand and rightly refused. . . .

⊥ It follows that the judgment of the circuit court of appeals must be reversed and the judgment of the district court reinstated.

Reversed.

MR. JUSTICE VAN DEVANTER, MR. JUSTICE SUTHERLAND and MR. JUSTICE BUTLER dissent.

MR. JUSTICE BRANDEIS took no part in the consideration or decision of this case.

APEX HOSIERY CO. v. LEADER

310 U.S. 469, 60 S. Ct. 982, 84 L. Ed. 1311 (1940)

[ED. NOTE: Selected original Court footnotes have been omitted.]

MR. JUSTICE STONE delivered the opinion of the Court.

Petitioner, a Pennsylvania corporation, is engaged in the manufacture, at its factory in Philadelphia, of hosiery, a substantial part of which is shipped in interstate commerce. It brought the present suit in the federal district court for Eastern Pennsylvania against respondent Federation, a labor organization, and its officers, to recover treble the amount of damage inflicted on it by respondents in conducting a strike at petitioner's factory alleged to be a conspiracy in violation of the Sherman Anti-Trust Act. 26 Stat. 209, 15 U. S. C. § 1. The trial to a jury resulted in a verdict for petitioner . . . [and the trial judge] gave judgment accordingly. The Court of Appeals for the Third Circuit reversed, 108 F. 2d 71, on the ground that the interstate commerce restrained or affected by respondents' acts was unsubstantial, the total shipment of merchandise from petitioner's factory being less than three per cent. of the total value of the output in the entire industry of the country, and on the further ground that the evidence failed to show an intent on the part of respondents to restrain interstate commerce. We granted certiorari, 309 U. S. 644, the questions presented being of importance in the administration of the Sherman Act.

The facts are undisputed. There was evidence from which the jury could have found as follows. Petitioner employs at its Philadelphia factory about twenty-five hundred persons in the manufacture of hosiery, and manufactures annually merchandise of the value of about $5,000,000. Its principal raw materials are silk and cotton, which are shipped to it from points outside the state. It ships interstate more than 80 per cent. of its finished product, and in the last eight months of 1937 it shipped in all 274,791 dozen pairs of stockings. In April, 1937, petitioner was operating a non-union shop. A demand of the respondent Federation at that time for a closed shop agreement came to nothing. On May 4, 1937, when only eight of petitioner's employees were members of the Federation, it ordered a strike. Shortly after midday on May 6, 1937, when petitioner's factory was shut down, members of the union, employed by other factories in Philadelphia who had stopped work, gathered at petitioner's plant. Respondent Leader, president of the Federation, then made a further demand for a closed shop agreement. When this was refused Leader declared a "sit down strike." Immediately, acts of violence against petitioner's plant and the employees in charge of it were committed by the assembled mob. It forcibly seized the plant, whereupon, under union leadership, its members were organized to maintain themselves as sit-down strikers in possession of the plant, and it remained in possession until June 23, 1937, when the strikers were forcibly ejected pursuant to an injunction. . . .

. . . While occupying the factory, the strikers wilfully wrecked machinery of great value, and did extensive damage to other property and equipment of the company. All manufacturing operations by petitioner ceased on May 6th. As the result of the destruction of the company's machinery and plant, it did not resume even partial manufacturing operations until August 19, 1937. The record discloses a lawless invasion of petitioner's plant and destruction of its property by force and violence of the most brutal and wanton character, under leadership and direction of respondents, and without interference by the local authorities.

For more than three months, by reason of respondents' acts, manufacture was suspended at petitioner's plant and the flow of petitioner's product into interstate commerce was stopped. . . . Shipment was prevented by the occupation of the factory by the strikers. Three times in the course of the strike respondents refused requests made by petitioner to be allowed to remove the merchandise for the purpose of shipment in filling the orders.

Section 1 of the Sherman Act provides: "Every contract, combination in the form of trust or otherwise, or conspiracy, in restraint of trade or commerce among the several States, or with foreign nations, is hereby declared to be illegal." Only a single question is presented by the record for our decision, whether the evidence which we have detailed, whose verity must be taken to be established by the jury's verdict, establishes a restraint of trade or commerce which the Sherman Act condemns.

It is not denied, and we assume for present purposes, that respondents by substituting the primitive method of trial by combat, for the ordinary processes of justice and more civilized means of deciding an industrial dispute, violated the civil and penal laws of Pennsylvania which authorize the recovery of full compensation and impose criminal penalties for the wrongs done. But in this suit, in which no diversity of citizenship of the parties is alleged or shown, the federal courts are without authority to enforce state laws. Their only jurisdiction is to vindicate such federal right as Congress has conferred on petitioner by the Sherman Act and violence, ⊥ as will appear hereafter, however reprehensible, does not give the federal courts jurisdiction.

At the outset . . . [w]e find abundant support for petitioner's contention that the effect of the sit-down strike was to restrict substantially the interstate transportation of its manufactured product, so as to bring the acts of respondents by which the restriction was effected within the reach of the commerce power if Congress has seen fit to exercise it. Cessation of petitioner's manufacturing operations, which respondents compelled, indubitably meant the cessation of shipment interstate. The effect upon the commerce resulted naturally and inevitably from the cause. . . .

⊥ [T]he Sherman Act admittedly does not condemn all combinations and conspiracies which interrupt interstate transportation. *United Mine Workers* v. *Coronado Coal Co.*, 259 U. S. 344 (*First Coronado* case); *United Leather Workers* v. *Herkert Co.* 265 U. S. 457 (*Leather Workers* case). In *In re Debs*, 158 U. S. 564, 600, this Court declined to consider whether the stoppage of trains on an interstate railroad resulting from a strike, was a violation of the Sherman Act—a question which it has not since been called on to decide. It is not seriously ⊥ contended here that a conspiracy to derail and rob an interstate train, even though it were laden with 100,000 dozen pairs of stockings, necessarily would involve a violation of the Sherman Act. This Court has never applied the Act to laborers or to others as a means of policing interstate transportation, and so the question to which we must address ourselves is whether a conspiracy of strikers in a labor dispute to stop the operation of the employer's factory in order to enforce their demands against the employer is the kind of restraint of trade or commerce at which the Act is aimed, even though a natural and probable consequence of their acts and the only effect on trade or commerce was to prevent substantial shipments interstate by the employer.

A point strongly urged in behalf of respondents in brief and argument before us is that Congress intended to exclude labor organizations and their activities wholly from the operation of the Sherman Act. To this the short answer must be made that for the thirty-two years which have elapsed since the decision of *Loewe* v. *Lawlor*, 208 U. S. 274, this Court, in its efforts to determine the true meaning and application of the Sherman Act has repeatedly held that the words of the act, "Every contract, combination . . . or conspiracy in restraint of trade or commerce" do embrace to some extent and in some circumstances labor unions and their activities; and that during that period Congress, although often asked to do so, has passed no act purporting to exclude labor unions ⊥ wholly from the operation of the Act. On the contrary Congress has repeatedly enacted laws restricting or purporting to curtail the application of the Act to labor organizations and their activities, thus recognizing that to some extent not defined they remain subject to it.

Whether labor organizations and their activities are wholly excluded from the Sherman Act is a question of statutory construction, not constitutional power. The long time failure of Congress to alter the Act after it had been judicially construed, and the enactment by Congress of legislation which implicitly recognizes the judicial construction as effective, is persuasive of legislative recognition that the judicial construction is the correct one. This is the more so where, as here, the application of the statute ⊥ to labor unions has brought forth sharply conflicting views both on the Court and in Congress, and where after the matter has been fully brought to the attention of the public and the Congress, the latter has not seen fit to change the statute.

While we must regard the question whether labor unions are to some extent and in some circumstances subject to the Act as settled in the affirmative, it is equally plain that this Court has never thought the Act to apply to all labor union activities affecting interstate commerce. The prohibitions of the Sherman Act were not stated in terms of precision or of crystal clarity and the Act itself did not define them. In consequence of the vagueness of its language, perhaps not uncalculated,[10] the courts have been left to give content to the statute, and in the performance of that function it is appropriate that courts should interpret its word in the light of its legislative history and of the particular evils at which the legislation was aimed. Cf. *Standard Oil Co.* v. *United States*, 221 U. S. 1; *Nash* v. *United States*, 229 U. S. 373; *Appalachian Coals* v. *United States*, 288 U. S. 344, 359, 360.

⊥ The critical words which circumscribe the judicial performance of this function so far as the present case is concerned are "Every . . . combination . . . or conspiracy in restraint of trade or commerce." Since in the present case, as we have seen, the natural and predictable consequence of the strike was the restraint of interstate transportation the precise question which we are called upon to decide is whether that restraint resulting from the strike maintained to enforce union demands by compelling a shutdown of petitioner's factory is the kind of "restraint of trade or commerce" which the Act condemns.

In considering whether union activities like the present may fairly be deemed to be embraced within this phrase, three circumstances relating to the history and application of the Act which are of striking significance must first be taken into account. The legislative history of the Sherman Act as well as the decisions of this Court interpreting it, show that it was not aimed at policing interstate transportation or movement of goods and property. The legislative history and the voluminous literature which was generated in the course of the enactment and during fifty years of litigation of the Sherman Act give no hint that such was its purpose.[11] They do not suggest ⊥ that, in general, state laws or law enforcement machinery were inadequate to prevent local obstructions or interferences with interstate transportation, or presented any problem requiring the interposition of federal authority. In 1890 when the Sherman Act was adopted there were only a few federal statutes imposing penalties for obstructing or misusing interstate transporation. With an expanding commerce, many others have since been enacted safeguarding transportation in interstate commerce as the need was seen, including statutes declaring conspiracies to interfere or actual interference with

---

[10] See Debates, 21 Cong. Rec. 2460, 3148; 2 Hoar, Autobiography of Seventy Years 364; Senator Edmunds, *The Interstate Trust and Commerce Act of 1890*, 194 No. Am. Rev. 801, 813, "after most careful and earnest consideration by the Judiciary Committee of the Senate it was agreed by every member that it was quite impracticable to include by specific description all the acts which should come within the meaning and purpose of the words 'trade' and 'commerce' or 'trust,' or the words 'restraint' or 'monopolize,' by precise and all-inclusive definitions; and that these were truly matters for judicial consideration."

See also Senator Hoar who with Senator Edmunds probably drafted the bill (see A. H. Walker, History of the Sherman Law (1910), p. 27-28) in 36 Cong. Rec. 522, Jan. 6, 1903: "We undertook by law to clothe the courts with the power and impose on them and the Department of Justice the duty of preventing all combinations in restraint of trade. It was believed that the phrase, 'in restraint of trade,' had a technical and well-understood meaning in the law."

[11] See the Bibliography on Trusts (1913) prepared by the Library of Congress. Cf. Homan, "Industrial Combination as Surveyed in Recent Literature," 44 Quart. J. Econ., 345 (1930). With few exceptions the articles, scientific and popular, reflected the popular idea that the Act was aimed at the prevention of monopolistic practices and restraints upon trade injurious to purchasers and consumers of goods and services by preservation of business competition. See e. g. Seager and Gulick, Trusts and Corporation Problems (1929), 367 *et seq.*, 42 Ann. Am. Acad., Industrial Competition and Combination (July, 1912); P. L. Anderson, Combination *v.* Competition, 4 Edit. Rev. 500 (1911); Gilbert Holland Montague, Trust Regulation Today, 105 Atl. Monthly, 1 (1910); Federal Regulation of Industry, 32 Ann. Am. Acad. of Pol. Sci., No. 108 (1908) *passim;* Clark, Federal Trust Policy (1931), Ch. II, V; Homan, Trusts, 15 Ency. Soc. Sciences 111, 113, "clearly the law was inspired by the predatory competitive tactics of the great trusts and its primary purpose was ⊥ the maintenance of the competitive system in industry." See also, Shulman, Labor and the Anti-Trust Laws, 34 Ill. L. Rev. 769; Boudin, The Sherman Law and Labor Disputes, 39 Col. L. Rev. 1283; 40 Col. L. Rev. 14.

interstate commerce by violence or threats of violence to be felonies. It was another and quite a different evil at ⊥ which the Sherman Act was aimed. It was enacted in the era of "trusts" and of "combinations" of businesses ⊥ and of capital organized and directed to control of the market by suppression of competition in the marketing of goods and services, the monopolistic tendency of which had become a matter of public concern. The end sought was the prevention of restraints to free competition in business and commercial transactions which tended to restrict production, raise prices or otherwise control the market to the detriment of purchasers or consumers of goods and services, all of which had come to be regarded as a special form of public injury.[15]

⊥ For that reason the phrase "restraint of trade" which, as will presently appear, had a well-understood meaning at ⊥ common law, was made the means of defining the activities prohibited. The addition of the words "or commerce among the several states" was not an additional kind of restraint to be prohibited by the Sherman Act but was the means used to relate the prohibited restraint of trade to interstate commerce for constitutional purposes, *Atlantic Cleaners & Dyers* v. *United States*, 286 U. S. 427, 434, so that Congress, through its commerce power, might suppress and penalize restraints on the competitive system which involved or affected interstate commerce. Because many forms of restraint upon commercial competition extended across state lines so as to make regulation by state action difficult or impossible, Congress enacted the Sherman Act, 21 Cong. Rec. 2456. It was in this sense of preventing restraints on commercial competition that Congress exercised "all the power it possessed." *Atlantic Cleaners & Dyers* v. *United States, supra*, 435.

---

[15] The history of the Sherman Act as contained in the legislative proceedings is emphatic in its support for the conclusion that "business competition" was the problem considered and that the act was designed to prevent restraints of trade which had a significant effect on such competition.

On July 10, 1888, the Senate adopted without discussion a resolution offered by Senator Sherman which directed the Committee on Finance to inquire into and report in connection with revenue bills, "such measures as it may deem expedient to set aside, control, restrain, or prohibit all arrangements, contracts, agreements, trusts, or combinations between persons or corporations, made with a view, or ⊥ which tend to prevent *free and full competition* . . . with such penalties and provisions . . . as will tend to preserve freedom of trade and production, the natural competition of increasing production, the lowering of prices by such competition . . . ." (19 Cong. Rec. 6041.)

This resolution explicitly presented the economic theory of the proponents of such legislation. The various bills introduced between 1888 and 1890 follow the theory of this resolution. Many bills sought to make void all arrangements "made with a view, or which tend, to prevent full and free competition in the production, manufacture, or sale of articles of domestic growth or production," S. 3445; S. 3510; H. R. 11339, all of the 50th Cong., 1st Sess. (1888) were bills of this type. In the 51st Cong. (1889) the bills were in a similar vein. See S. 1, § 1 (this bill as redrafted by the Judiciary Committee ultimately became the Sherman Law); H. R. 202, § 3; H. R. 270; H. R. 286; H. R. 402; H. R. 509; H. R. 826; H. R. 3819. See Bills and Debates in Congress relating to Trusts (1909), Vol. 1, pp. 1025-1031.

Only one, which was never enacted, S. 1268 in the 52d Cong., 1st Sess. (1892), introduced by Senator Peffer, sought to prohibit "every wilful act . . . which shall have the effect to in anyway interfere with the freedom of transit of articles in interstate commerce, ..."

When the antitrust bill (S. 1, 51st Cong., 1st Sess.), came before Congress for debate, the debates point to a similar purpose. Senator Sherman asserted the bill prevented only "business combinations" "made with a view to prevent competition," 21 Cong. Rec. 2457, 2562; see also *ibid*. at 2459, 2461.

Senator Allison spoke of combinations which "control prices," *ibid*. 2471; Senator Pugh of combinations "to limit production" for "the purpose of destroying competition," *ibid*. 2558; Senator Morgan of combinations "that affect the price of commodities," *ibid*. 2609; Senator Platt, a critic of the bill, said this bill proceeds on the assumption that "competition is beneficent to the country," *ibid*. 2729; Senator George denounced trusts which crush out competition "and that is the great evil at which all this legislation ought to be directed," *ibid*. 3147.

In the House, Representative Culberson, who was in charge of the bill, interpreted the bill to prohibit various arrangements which tend to drive out competition, *ibid*. 4089; Representative Wilson spoke in favor of the bill against combinations among "competing producers to control the supply of their product, in order that they may dictate ⊥ the terms on which they shall sell in the market, and may secure release from the stress of competition among themselves," *ibid*. 4090.

The unanimity with which foes and supporters of the bill spoke of its aims as the protection of free competition, permit use of the debates in interpreting the purpose of the act. See White, C. J., in *Standard Oil Co.* v. *United States*, 221 U. S. 1, 50; *United States* v. *San Francisco, ante*, p. 16.

See also Report of Committee on Interstate Commerce on Control of Corporations Engaged in Interstate Commerce, S. Rept. 1326, 62d Cong., 3d Sess. (1913), pp. 2, 4; Report of Federal Trade Commission, S. Doc. 226, 70th Cong., 2d Sess. (1929), pp. 343-345.

A second significant circumstance is that this Court has never applied the Sherman Act in any case, whether or not involving labor organizations or activities, unless the Court was of opinion that there was some form of restraint upon commercial competition in the marketing of goods or services and finally this Court has refused to apply the Sherman Act in cases like the present in which local strikes conducted by illegal means in a production industry prevented interstate shipment of substantial amounts of the product but in which it was not shown that the restrictions on shipments had operated to restrain commercial competition in some substantial way. *First Coronado* case, *supra*; *Leather Workers* case, *supra*. *Levering & Garrigues Co. v. Morrin*, 289 U. S. 103.

The common law doctrines relating to contracts and combinations in restraint of trade were well understood long before the enactment of the Sherman law.[17] They were contracts for the restriction or suppression of competition in the market, agreements to fix prices, divide marketing territories, apportion customers, restrict production and the like practices, which tend to raise prices or otherwise take from buyers or consumers the advantages which accrue to them from free competition in the market. Such contracts were deemed illegal and were unenforcible at common law. But the resulting restraints of trade were not penalized and gave rise to no actionable wrong. Certain classes of restraints were not outlawed when deemed reasonable, usually because they served to preserve or protect legitimate interests, previously existing, of one or more parties to the contract.

In seeking more effective protection of the public from the growing evils of restraints on the competitive system effected by the concentrated commercial power of "trusts" and "combinations" at the close of the nineteenth century, the legislators found ready at their hand the common law concept of illegal restraints of trade or commerce. In enacting the Sherman law they took over that concept by condemning such restraints wherever they occur in or affect commerce between the states. They extended the condemnation of the statute to restraints effected by any combination in the form of trust or otherwise, or conspiracy, as well as by contract or agreement, having those effects on the competitive system and on purchasers and consumers of goods or services which were characteristic of restraints deemed illegal at common law, and they gave both private and public remedies for the injuries flowing from such restraints.

That such is the scope and effect of the Sherman Act was first judicially recognized and expounded in the classic opinion in *United States v. Addyston Pipe & Steel Co.*, 85 F. 271, affirmed 175 U. S. 211, written by Judge, later Chief Justice, Taft, and concurred in by Justice Harlan and Judge, later Justice, Lurton, of this Court. This Court has since repeatedly recognized that the restraints at which the Sherman law is aimed, and which are described by its terms, are only those which are comparable to restraints deemed illegal at common law, although accomplished by means other than contract and which, for constitutional reasons, are confined to transactions in or which affect interstate commerce.

In *Standard Oil Co. v. United States*, 221 U. S. 1, 54, 55, 58, decided in 1911, this Court, speaking through Chief Justice White, pointed out that the restraint of trade contemplated by § 1 of the Act took its origin from the common law, and that the Sherman Act was adapted to the prevention, in modern conditions, of conduct or dealing effecting the wrong, at which the common law doctrine was aimed. This, it was said is "the dread of enhancement of prices and of other wrongs which it was thought would flow from the undue limitation on competitive conditions caused by contracts or other acts of individuals or corporations, . . ." The Court declared, page 59, that "the statute was drawn in the light of the existing practical conception of the law of restraint of trade," and drew the conclusion that the restraints which were condemned by the statute are those which, following the common law analogy, are "unreasonable or undue." This view was followed and more explicitly stated in *United States v. American Tobacco Co.*, 221 U. S. 106, 179, where it was said: ". . . it was held in the *Standard Oil* case that as the words 'restraint of trade' at common law and in the

---

[17] In his explanation of the bill Senator Sherman referred to several common law cases on restraint of trade. 21 Cong. Rec. 2457–2460.

law of this country at the time of the adoption of the Anti-trust Act only embraced acts or contracts or agreements or combinations which operated to the prejudice of the public interests by unduly restricting competition or unduly obstructing the due course of trade or which, either because of their inherent nature or effect or because of the evident purpose of the acts, etc., injuriously restrained trade, that the words as used in the statute were designed to have and did have but a like significance." In thus grounding the "rule of reason" upon the analogy of the common law doctrines applicable to illegal restraints of trade the Court gave a content and meaning to the statute in harmony with its history and plainly indicated by its legislative purpose. Labor cases apart, which will presently be discussed, this Court has not departed from the conception of the Sherman Act as affording a remedy, public and private, for the public wrongs which flow from restraints of trade in the common law sense of restriction or suppression of commercial competition. In the cases considered by this Court since the *Standard Oil* case in 1911 some form of restraint of commercial competition has been the *sine qua non* to the condemnation of contracts, combinations or conspiracies under the Sherman Act, and in general restraints upon competition have been condemned only when their purpose or effect was to raise or fix the market price. It is in this sense that it is said that the restraints, actual or intended, prohibited by the Sherman Act are only those which are so substantial as to affect market prices. Restraints on competition or on the course of trade in the merchandising of articles moving in interstate commerce is not enough, unless the restraint is shown to have or is intended to have an effect upon prices in the market or otherwise to deprive purchasers or consumers of the advantages which they derive from free competition. . . .

The question remains whether the effect of the combination or conspiracy among respondents was a restraint of trade within the meaning of the Sherman Act. This is not a case of a labor organization being used by combinations of those engaged in an industry as the means or instrument for suppressing competition or fixing prices. See *United States* v. *Brims*, 272 U. S. 549; *Local 167* v. *United States*, 291 U. S. 293. Here it is plain that the combination or conspiracy did not have as its purpose restraint upon competition in the market for petitioner's product. Its object was to compel petitioner to accede to the union demands and an effect of it, in consequence of the strikers' tortious acts, was the prevention of the removal of petitioner's product for interstate shipment. So far as appears the delay of these shipments was not intended to have and had no effect on prices of hosiery in the market, and so was in that respect no more a restraint forbidden by the Sherman Act than the restriction upon competition and the course of trade held lawful in *Appalachian Coals* v. *United States, supra,* because notwithstanding its effect upon the marketing of the coal it nevertheless was not intended to and did not affect market price.

A combination of employees necessarily restrains competition among themselves in the sale of their services to the employer; yet such a combination was not considered an illegal restraint of trade at common law when the Sherman Act was adopted, either because it was not thought to be unreasonable or because it was not deemed a "restraint of trade." Since the enactment of the declaration in § 6 of the Clayton Act that "the labor of a human being is not a commodity or article of commerce . . . nor shall such [labor] organizations, or the members thereof, be held or construed to be illegal combinations or conspiracies in the restraint of trade under the antitrust laws," it would seem plain that restraints on the sale of the employee's services to the employer, however much they curtail the competition among employees, are not in themselves combinations or conspiracies in restraint of trade or commerce under the Sherman Act.

Strikes or agreements not to work, entered into by laborers to compel employers to yield to their demands, may restrict to some extent the power of employers who are parties to the dispute to compete in the market with those not subject to such demands. But under the doctrine applied to non-labor cases, the mere fact of such restrictions on competition does not in itself bring the parties to the agreement within the condemnation of the Sherman Act. *Appalachian Coals* v. *United States, supra,* 360. Furthermore, successful union activity, as for example consummation of a wage agreement with employers, may have some influence on price competition by

⊥504　eliminating that part of such competition which is based on differences in labor standards. Since, in order to render a labor combination effective it must eliminate the competition from non-union made goods, . . . an elimination of price competition based on differences in labor standards is the objective of any national labor organization. But this effect on competition has not been ⊥ considered to be the kind of curtailment of price competition prohibited by the Sherman Act. . . . And in any case, the restraint here is, as we have seen, of a different kind and has not been shown to have any actual or intended effect on price or price competition.

⊥505　⊥ This Court first applied the Sherman Act to a labor organization in *Loewe* v. *Lawlor,* 208 U. S. 274, in 1908. . . . The combination or conspiracy charged was that of a nation-wide labor organization to force all manufacturers of fur hats in the United States to organize their workers by maintaining a boycott against the purchase of the product of non-union manufacturers shipped in interstate commerce. The restraint alleged was not a strike or refusal to work in the complainants' plant, but a secondary boycott by which, through threats to the manufacturer's wholesale customers and their customers, the Union sought to compel or induce them not to deal in the product of the complainants, and to purchase the competing products of other unionized manufacturers. This Court pointed out that the restraint was precisely like that in *Eastern States Retail Lumber Dealers Co.* v. *United States,* 234 U. S. 600, 610, 614, in which a conspiracy to circulate a "black list," intended to persuade retailers not to deal with specified wholesalers, was held to violate the Act because of its restraint upon competition with unlisted wholesalers. The Court in the *Loewe* case held that the boycott operated as a restraint of trade or commerce within the meaning of the Sherman Act, and that the language of the Act, "every combination, etc." was broad enough to include a labor union imposing such a restraint. . . .

⊥506　⊥ It will be observed that in each of these cases[1.464] where the Act was held applicable to labor unions, the activities affecting interstate commerce were directed at control of the market and were so widespread as substantially to affect it. There was thus a suppression of competition in the market by methods which were deemed analogous to those found to be violations in the non-labor cases. . . . That the objective of the restraint in the boycott cases was the strengthening of the bargaining position of the union and not the elimination of business competition—which was the end in the non-labor cases—was ⊥ thought to be immaterial because the Court viewed the restraint itself, in contrast to the interference with shipments caused by a local factory strike, to be of a kind regarded as offensive at common law because of its effect in curtailing a free market and it was held to offend against the Sherman Act because it effected and was aimed at suppression of competition with union made goods in the interstate market. . . .

⊥507

⊥512　⊥ These cases[1.465] show that activities of labor organizations not immunized by the Clayton Act are not necessarily violations of the Sherman Act. Underlying and implicit in all of them is recognition that the Sherman Act was not enacted to police interstate transportation, or to afford a remedy for wrongs, which are actionable under state law, and result from combinations and conspiracies which fall short, both in their purpose and effect, of any form of market control of a commodity, such as to "monopolize the supply, control its price, or discriminate between its would-be purchasers." These elements of restraint of trade, found to be present in the *Second Coronado* case[1.466] and alone to distinguish it from the *First Coronado* case[1.467] and the *Leather Workers* case[1.468] are wholly lacking here. We do not hold that conspiracies to obstruct or prevent transportation in interstate commerce can in no circumstances be violations of the Sherman Act. Apart from the Clayton Act it makes no distinction between labor and non-labor cases. We only hold now, as we have previously held both

---

[1.464] The Court's discussion of other similar cases has been omitted.

[1.465] The Court's discussion of its previous decisions involving organized labor activities, drawing upon the distinction between "direct" and "indirect" effects upon interstate commerce, which did not imply an intention to obstruct interstate commerce, has been omitted.

[1.466] Coronado Coal Co. v. United Mine Workers, 268 U.S. 295 (1925).

[1.467] United Mine Workers v. Coronado Coal Co., 259 U.S. 344 (1922).

[1.468] United Leather Workers' International Union v. Herkert & Meisel Trunk Co., 265 U.S. 457 (1924).

in labor and non-labor cases, that such restraints are not within the Sherman Act unless they are intended to have, or in fact have, the effects on the market on which the Court relied to establish violation in the *Second Coronado* case. Unless the principle of these cases is now to be discarded, an impartial application of the Sherman Act to the activities of industry and labor alike would seem to require that the Act be held inapplicable to the activities of respondents which had an even less substantial effect on the competitive conditions in the industry than the combination of producers upheld in the *Appalachian Coals* case and in others on which it relied.

If, without such effects on the market, we were to hold that a local factory strike, stopping production and shipment of its product interstate, violates the Sherman law, practically every strike in modern industry would be brought within the jurisdiction of the federal courts, under the Sherman Act, to remedy local law violations. The Act was plainly not intended to reach such a result, its language does not require it, and the course of our decisions precludes it. The maintenance in our federal system of a proper distribution between state and national governments of police authority and of remedies private and public for public wrongs is of far-reaching importance. An intention to disturb the balance is not lightly to be imputed to Congress. The Sherman Act is concerned with the character of the prohibited restraints and with their effect on interstate commerce. It draws no distinction between the restraints effected by violence and those achieved by peaceful but oftentimes quite as effective means. Restraints not within the Act, when achieved by peaceful means, are not brought within its sweep merely because, without other differences, they are attended by violence.

Affirmed.

[ED. NOTE: The dissenting opinion of Mr. Chief Justice Hughes, which was joined in by Mr. Justice McReynolds and Mr. Justice Roberts, has been omitted.]

PARKER v. BROWN

317 U.S. 341, 63 S. Ct. 307, 87 L. Ed. 315 (1943)

MR. CHIEF JUSTICE STONE delivered the opinion of the Court.

The questions for our consideration are whether the marketing program adopted for the 1940 raisin crop under the California Agricultural Prorate Act[1] is rendered invalid (1) by the Sherman Act. . . .

Appellee, a producer and packer of raisins in California, brought this suit in the district court to enjoin appellants—the State Director of Agriculture, Raisin Proration Zone No. 1, the members of the State Agricultural Prorate Advisory Commission and of the Program Committee for Zone No. 1, and others charged by the statute with the administration of the Prorate Act—from enforcing, as to appellee, a program for marketing the 1940 crop of raisins produced in "Raisin Proration Zone No. 1." After a trial upon oral testimony, a stipulation of facts and certain exhibits, the district court held that the 1940 raisin marketing program was an illegal interference with and undue burden upon interstate commerce and gave judgement for appellee granting the injunction prayed for. 39 F. Supp. 895. The case was tried by a district court of three judges and comes here on appeal under §§ 266 and 238 of the Judicial Code as amended, 28 U. S. C. §§ 380, 345.

As appears from the evidence and from the findings of the district court, almost all

---

[1] Act of June 5, 1933, ch. 754, Statutes of California of 1933, as amended by chs. 471 and 743, Statutes of 1935; ch. 6, Extra Session, 1938; chs. 363, 548 and 894, Statutes of 1939; and chs. 603, 1150 and 1186, Statutes of 1941. Its constitutionality under both Federal and State Constitutions was sustained by the California Supreme Court in *Agricultural Prorate Commission* v. *Superior Court*, 5 Cal. 2d 550, 55 P. 2d 495.

the raisins consumed in the United States, and nearly one-half of the world crop, are produced in Raisin Proration Zone No. 1. Between 90 and 95 per cent of the raisins grown in California are ultimately shipped in interstate or foreign commerce. . . .

The California Agricultural Prorate Act authorizes the establishment, through action of state officials, of programs for the marketing of agricultural commodities produced in the state, so as to restrict competition among the growers and maintain prices in the distribution of their commodities to packers. The declared purpose of the Act is to "conserve the agricultural wealth of the State" and to "prevent economic waste in the marketing of agricultural products" of the state. It authorizes (§ 3) the creation of an Agricultural Prorate Advisory Commission of nine members, of which a state official, the Director of Agriculture, is ex-officio a member. The other eight members are appointed for terms of four years by the Governor and confirmed by the Senate, and are required to take an oath of office. § 4.

Upon the petition of ten producers for the establishment of a prorate marketing plan for any commodity within a defined production zone (§ 8), and after a public hearing (§ 9), and after making prescribed economic findings (§ 10) showing that the institution of a program for the proposed zone will prevent agricultural waste and conserve agricultural wealth of the state without permitting unreasonable profits to producers, the Commission is authorized to grant the petition. The Director, with the approval of the Commission, is then required to select a program committee from among nominees chosen by the qualified producers within the zone, to which he may add not more than two handlers or packers who receive the regulated commodity from producers for marketing. §§ 11, 14, 15.

The program committee is required (§ 15) to formulate a proration marketing program for the commodity produced in the zone, which the Commission is authorized to approve after a public hearing and a "finding that the program is reasonably calculated to carry out the objectives of the Act." The Commission may, if so advised, modify the program and approve it as modified. If the proposed program, as approved by the Commission, is consented to by 65 per cent in number of producers in the zone owning 51 per cent of the acreage devoted to production of the regulated crop, the Director is required to declare the program instituted. § 16.

Authority to administer the program, subject to the approval of the Director of Agriculture, is conferred on the program committee. §§ 6, 18, 22. Section 22.5 declares that it shall be a misdemeanor, which is punishable by fine and imprisonment (Penal Code § 19), for any producer to sell or any handler to receive or possess without proper authority any commodity for which a proration program has been instituted. Like penalty is imposed upon any person who aids or abets in the commission of any of the acts specified in the section, and it is declared that each "infraction shall constitute a separate and distinct offense." Section 25 imposes a civil liability of $500 "for each and every violation" of any provision of a proration program. . . .[1.469]

Appellee's bill of complaint challenges the validity of the proration program as in violation of the Commerce Clause and the Sherman Act; in support of the decree of the district court he also urges that it conflicts with and is superseded by the Federal Agricultural Marketing Agreement Act of 1937. . . .

Validity of the Prorate Program under the Sherman Act.

Section 1 of the Sherman Act, 15 U. S. C. § 1, makes unlawful "every contract, combination . . . or conspiracy, in restraint of trade or commerce among the several States." And § 2, 15 U. S. C. § 2, makes it unlawful to "monopolize, or attempt to monopolize, or combine or conspire with any other person or persons, to monopolize any part of the trade or commerce among the several States." We may assume for present purposes that the California prorate program would violate the Sherman Act if it were organized and made effective solely by virtue of a contract, combination or conspiracy of private persons, individual or corporate. We may assume also, without deciding, that Congress could, in the exercise of its commerce power, prohibit a state from maintaining a stabilization program like the present because of its effect on

---

[1.469] The Court's description of the program, and its controls on the sale of raisins and the establishment of prices, has been omitted.

interstate commerce. Occupation of a legislative "field" by Congress in the exercise of a granted power is a familiar example of its constitutional power to suspend state laws. See *Adams Express Co.* v. *Croninger*, 226 U. S. 491, 505; *Napier* v. *Atlantic Coast Line*, 272 U. S. 605, 607; *Missouri Pacific R. Co.* v. *Porter*, 273 U. S. 341; *Illinois Gas Co.* v. *Public Service Co.*, 314 U. S. 498, 510.

But it is plain that the prorate program here was never intended to operate by force of individual agreement or combination. It derived its authority and its efficacy from the legislative command of the state and was not intended to operate or become effective without that command. We find nothing in the language of the Sherman Act or in its history which suggests that its purpose was to restrain a state or its officers or agents from activities directed by its ⊥ legislature. In a dual system of government in ⊥351 which, under the Constitution, the states are sovereign, save only as Congress may constitutionally subtract from their authority, an unexpressed purpose to nullify a state's control over its officers and agents is not lightly to be attributed to Congress.

The Sherman Act makes no mention of the state as such, and gives no hint that it was intended to restrain state action or official action directed by a state. The Act is applicable to "persons" including corporations (§ 7), and it authorizes suits under it by persons and corporations (§ 15). A state may maintain a suit for damages under it, *Georgia* v. *Evans*, 316 U. S. 159, but the United States may not, *United States* v. *Cooper Corp.*, 312 U. S. 600—conclusions derived not from the literal meaning of the words "person" and "corporation" but from the purpose, the subject matter, the context and the legislative history of the statute.

There is no suggestion of a purpose to restrain state action in the Act's legislative history. The sponsor of the bill which was ultimately enacted as the Sherman Act declared that it prevented only "business combinations." 21 Cong. Rec. 2562, 2457; see also 2459, 2461. That its purpose was to suppress combinations to restrain competition and attempts to monopolize by individuals and corporations, abundantly appears from its legislative history. See *Apex Hosiery Co.* v. *Leader*, 310 U. S. 469, 492–93 and n. 15; *United States* v. *Addyston Pipe & Steel Co.*, 85 F. 271, affirmed 175 U. S. 211; *Standard Oil Co.* v. *United States*, 221 U. S. 1, 54–58.

True, a state does not give immunity to those who violate the Sherman Act by authorizing them to violate it, or by declaring that their action is lawful, *Northern Securities Co.* v. *United States*, 193 U. S. 197, 332, 344–47; and we have no question of the state or its municipality becoming a participant in a private agreement or combina⊥tion by others for restraint of trade, cf. *Union Pacific R. Co.* v. *United States*, ⊥352 313 U. S. 450. Here the state command to the Commission and to the program committee of the California Prorate Act is not rendered unlawful by the Sherman Act since, in view of the latter's words and history, it must be taken to be a prohibition of individual and not state action. It is the state which has created the machinery for establishing the prorate program. Although the organization of a prorate zone is proposed by producers, and a prorate program approved by the Commission, must also be approved by referendum of producers, it is the state, acting through the Commission, which adopts the program and which enforces it with penal sanctions, in the execution of a governmental policy. The prerequisite approval of the program upon referendum by a prescribed number of producers is not the imposition by them of their will upon the minority by force of agreement or combination which the Sherman Act prohibits. The state itself exercises its legislative authority in making the regulation and in prescribing the conditions of its application. The required vote on the referendum is one of these conditions. Compare *Currin* v. *Wallace*, 306 U. S. 1, 16; *Hampton & Co.* v. *United States*, 276 U. S. 394, 407; *Wickard* v. *Filburn*, ante, p. 111.

The state in adopting and enforcing the prorate program made no contract or agreement and entered into no conspiracy in restraint of trade or to establish monopoly but, as sovereign, imposed the restraint as an act of government which the Sherman Act did not undertake to prohibit. *Olsen* v. *Smith*, 195 U. S. 332, 344–45; cf. *Lowenstein* v. *Evans*, 69 F. 908, 910. . . .[1.470]

⊥ *Reversed.* ⊥368

[1.470] The Court also held the program not to be in conflict with the Agricultural Marketing Agreement Act of 1937 nor in violation of the commerce clause of the Constitution.

UNITED STATES v. SOUTH-EASTERN UNDERWRITERS ASSOCIATION

322 U.S. 533, 64 S. Ct. 1162, 88 L. Ed. 1440 (1944)

[ED. NOTE: Although the McCarran-Furguson Act, 15 U.S.C. §§ 1011-15, 59 Stat. 33 (1945), later provided a limited exemption to insurance companies from operation of the antitrust laws, the holding of the Supreme Court in this decision—that insurance is a part of interstate commerce—was not overruled by that statute. Selected portions of this decision are set forth for their interpretation of congressional intent in regulating interstate commerce by enactment of the Sherman Act. Some original Court footnotes have been omitted.]

⊥ MR. JUSTICE BLACK delivered the opinion of the Court.

For seventy-five years this Court has held, whenever the question has been presented, that the Commerce Clause of the Constitution does not deprive the individual states of power to regulate and tax specific activities of foreign insurance companies which sell policies within their territories. Each state has been held to have this power even though negotiation and execution of the companies' policy contracts involved communications of information and movements of persons, moneys, and papers across state lines. Not one of all these cases, however, has involved an Act of Congress which required the Court to decide the issue of whether the Commerce Clause grants to Congress the power to regulate insurance transactions stretching across state lines. Today for the first time in the history of the Court that issue is squarely presented and must be decided.

Appellees—the South-Eastern Underwriters Association (S. E. U. A.), and its membership of nearly 200 private stock fire insurance companies, and 27 individuals—were indicted in the District Court for alleged violations of the Sherman Anti-Trust Act. The indictment alleges two conspiracies. The first, in violation of § 1 of the Act, was to restrain interstate trade and commerce by fixing and maintaining arbitrary and non-competitive premium rates on fire and specified "allied lines"[1] of insurance in ⊥ Alabama, Florida, Georgia, North Carolina, South Carolina, and Virginia; the second, in violation of § 2, was to monopolize trade and commerce in the same lines of insurance in and among the same states. . . .

⊥ The kind of interference with the free play of competitive forces with which the appellees are charged is exactly the type of conduct which the Sherman Act has outlawed for American "trade or commerce" among the states. Appellees have not argued otherwise. Their defense, set forth in a demurrer, has been that they are not required to conform to the standards of business conduct established by the Sherman Act because "the business of fire insurance is not commerce." Sustaining the demurrer, the District Court held that "the business of insurance is not commerce, either intrastate or interstate"; it "is not interstate commerce or interstate trade, though it might be considered a trade subject to local laws, either State or Federal, where the commerce clause is not the authority relied upon." 51 F. Supp. 712, 713, 714.

The District Court's opinion does not contain the slightest intimation that the indictment was held defective on a theory that it charged the appellees with restraining and monopolizing nothing but the making of local contracts. ⊥ There was not even a demurrer on that ground. The District Court treated the indictment as charging illegal restraints of trade in the total "activities complained of as constituting the business of insurance." 51 F. Supp. 712, 713. . . . Looking at all the transactions charged, [the District Court] felt compelled by previous decisions of this Court to hold that despite the interstate character of many of [the defendants' activities] "the business of insurance

---

[1] The "allied lines" of insurance handled by appellees are described in the indictment as "inland navigation and transportation, inland marine, sprinkler leakage, explosion, windstorm and tornado, extended coverage, use and occupancy, and riot and civil commotion insurance."

is not commerce," and that as a consequence this "business," contracts and all, could not be "interstate commerce" or "interstate trade." In other words, the District Court held the indictment bad for the sole reason that the entire "business of insurance" (not merely the part of the business in which contracts are physically executed) can never under any possible circumstances be "commerce," and that therefore, even though an insurance company conducts a substantial part of its business transactions across state lines, it is not engaged in "commerce among the States" within the meaning of either the Commerce Clause or the Sherman Anti-Trust Act. . . .

The record, then, presents two questions and no others: (1) Was the Sherman Act intended to prohibit conduct of fire insurance companies which restrains or monopolizes the interstate fire insurance trade? (2) If so, do fire insurance transactions which stretch across state lines constitute "Commerce among the several States" so as to make them subject to regulation by Congress under the Commerce Clause? Since it is our conclusion that the Sherman Act was intended to apply to the fire insurance business we shall, for convenience of discussion, first consider the latter question.

I.

Ordinarily courts do not construe words used in the Constitution so as to give them a meaning more narrow than one which they had in the common parlance of the times in which the Constitution was written. To hold that the word "commerce" as used in the Commerce Clause does not include a business such as insurance would do just that. Whatever other meanings "commerce" may have included in 1787, the dictionaries, encyclopedias, and other books of the period show that it included trade: business in which persons bought and sold, bargained and contracted. And this meaning has persisted to modern times. Surely, therefore, a heavy burden is on him who asserts that the plenary power which the Commerce Clause grants to Congress to regulate "Commerce among the several States" does not include the power to regulate trading in insurance to the same extent that it includes power to regulate other trades or businesses conducted across state lines.[9]

The modern insurance business holds a commanding position in the trade and commerce of our Nation. Built upon the sale of contracts of indemnity, it has become one of the largest and most important branches of commerce. . . . Perhaps no modern commercial enterprise directly affects so many persons in all walks of life as does the insurance business. Insurance touches the home, the family, and the occupation or the business of almost every person in the United States.

This business is not separated into 48 distinct territorial compartments which function in isolation from each other. Interrelationship, interdependence, and integration of activities in all the states in which they operate are practical aspects of the insurance companies' methods of doing business. A large share of the insurance business is concentrated in a comparatively few companies located, for the most part, in the financial centers of the East. Premiums collected from policyholders in every part of the United States flow into these companies for investment. As policies become payable, checks and drafts flow back to the many states where the policyholders reside. The result is a continuous and indivisible stream of intercourse among the states composed of collections of premiums, payments of policy obligations, and the countless documents and communications which are essential to the negotiation and execution of policy contracts. Individual policyholders living in many different states who own policies in a single company have their separate interests blended in one assembled fund of assets upon which all are equally dependent for payment of their policies. The decisions which that company makes at its home office—the risks it insures, the premiums it charges, the investments it makes, the losses it pays—concern not just the people of the

---

[9] Alexander Hamilton, in 1791, stating his opinion on the constitutionality of the Bank of the United States, declared that it would "admit of little if any question" that the federal power to regulate foreign commerce included "the regulation of policies of insurance." 3 Works of Alexander Hamilton (Fed. Ed., N. Y. 1904) pp. 445, 469-470. Speaking of the need of a federal power to regulate "commerce," Hamilton had earlier said, "It is, indeed, evident, on the most superficial view, that there is no object, either as it respects the interests of trade or finance, that more strongly demands a federal superintendence." Federalist No. XXII, The Federalist (Rev. Ed., N. Y. 1901) 110.

state where the home office happens to be located. They concern people living far beyond the boundaries of that state.

That the fire insurance transactions alleged to have been restrained and monopolized by appellees fit the above described pattern of the national insurance trade is shown by the indictment before us. Of the nearly 200 combining companies, chartered in various states and foreign countries, only 18 maintained their home offices in one of the six states in which the S. E. U. A. operated; and 127 had headquarters in either New York, Pennsylvania, or Connecticut. During the period 1931-1941 a total of $488,000,000 in premiums was collected by local agents in the six states, most of which was transmitted to home offices in other states; while during the same period $215,000,000 in losses was paid by checks or drafts sent from the home offices to the companies' local agents for delivery to the policyholders. Local agents solicited prospects, utilized policy forms sent from home offices, and made regular reports to their companies by mail, telephone or telegraph. Special travelling agents supervised local operations. The insurance sold by members of S. E. U. A. covered not only all kinds of fixed local properties, but also such properties as steamboats, tugs, ferries, shipyards, warehouses, terminals, trucks, busses, railroad equipment and rolling stock, and movable goods of all types carried in interstate and foreign commerce by every media of transportation.

Despite all of this, despite the fact that most persons, speaking from common knowledge, would instantly say that of course such a business is engaged in trade and commerce, the District Court felt compelled by decisions of this Court to conclude that the insurance business can never be trade or commerce within the meaning of the Commerce Clause. We must therefore consider these decisions.

In 1869 this Court held, in sustaining a statute of Virginia which regulated foreign insurance companies, that the statute did not offend the Commerce Clause because "issuing a policy of insurance is not a transaction of commerce." *Paul* v. *Virginia*, [75 U.S.] 8 Wall. 168, 183. Since then, in similar cases, this statement has been repeated, and has been broadened. . . .

In all cases in which the Court has relied upon the proposition that "the business of insurance is not commerce," its attention was focused on the validity of state statutes—the extent to which the Commerce Clause automatically deprived states of the power to regulate the insurance business. Since Congress had at no time attempted to control the insurance business, invalidation of the state statutes would practically have been equivalent to granting insurance companies engaged in interstate activities a blanket license to operate without legal restraint. As early as 1866 the insurance trade, though still in its infancy, was subject to widespread abuses. To meet the imperative need for correction of these abuses the various state legislatures, including that of Virginia, passed regulatory legislation. *Paul* v. *Virginia* upheld one of Virginia's statutes. To uphold insurance laws of other states, including tax laws, *Paul* v. *Virginia's* generalization and reasoning have been consistently adhered to.

Today, however, we are asked to apply this reasoning, not to uphold another state law, but to strike down an Act of Congress which was intended to regulate certain aspects of the methods by which interstate insurance companies do business; and, in so doing, to narrow the scope of the federal power to regulate the activities of a great business carried on back and forth across state lines. But past decisions of this Court emphasize that legal formulae devised to uphold state power cannot uncritically be accepted as trustworthy guides to determine Congressional power under the Commerce Clause. Furthermore, the reasons given in support of the generalization that "the business of insurance is not commerce" and can never be conducted so as to constitute "Commerce among the States" are inconsistent with many decisions of this Court which have upheld federal statutes regulating interstate commerce under the Commerce Clause. . . .

. . . It is settled that, for Constitutional purposes, certain activities of a business may be intrastate and therefore subject to state control, while other activities of the same business may be interstate and therefore subject to federal regulation. And there is a wide range of business and other activities which, though subject to federal regulation, are so intimately related to local welfare that, in the absence of Congressional action, they may be regulated or taxed by the states. In marking out these activities the primary test applied by the Court is not the mechanical one of whether the particular activity affected by the state regulation is part of interstate commerce, but rather whether, in each case, the competing demands of the state and national interests involved can be accommodated. And the fact that particular phases of an interstate business or activity have long been regulated or taxed by states has been recognized as a strong reason why, in the continued absence of conflicting Congressional action, the state regulatory and tax laws should be declared valid.

The real answer to the question before us is to be found in the Commerce Clause itself and in some of the great cases which interpret it. Many decisions make vivid the broad and true meaning of that clause. . . . Not only, then, may transactions be commerce though non-commercial; they may be commerce though illegal and sporadic, and though they do not utilize common carriers or concern the flow of anything more tangible than electrons and information. These activities having already been held to constitute interstate commerce, and persons engaged in them therefore having been held subject to federal regulation, it would indeed be difficult now to hold that no activities of any insurance company can ever constitute interstate commerce so as to make it subject to such regulation;—activities which, as part of the conduct of a legitimate and useful commercial enterprise, may embrace integrated operations in many states and involve the transmission of great quantities of money, documents, and communications across dozens of state lines.

The precise boundary between national and state power over commerce has never yet been, and doubtless never can be, delineated by a single abstract definition. The most widely accepted general description of that part of commerce which is subject to the federal power is that given in 1824 by Chief Justice Marshall in *Gibbons* v. *Ogden*, 9 Wheat. 1, 189-190: "Commerce, undoubtedly, is traffic, but it is something more: it is intercourse. It describes the commercial intercourse between nations, and parts of nations, in all its branches. . . ." Commerce is interstate, he said, when it "concerns more States than one." *Id.*, 194. No decision of this Court has ever questioned this as too comprehensive a description of the subject matter of the Commerce Clause. To accept a description less comprehensive, the Court has recognized, would deprive the Congress of that full power necessary to enable it to discharge its Constitutional duty to govern commerce among the states.

The power confined to Congress by the Commerce Clause is declared in The Federalist to be for the purpose of securing the "maintenance of harmony and proper intercourse among the States." But its purpose is not confined to empowering Congress with the negative authority to legislate against state regulations of commerce deemed inimical to the national interest. The power granted Congress is a positive power. It is the power to legislate concerning transactions which, reaching across state boundaries, affect the people of more states than one;—to govern affairs which the individual states, with their limited territorial jurisdictions, are not fully capable of governing. This federal power to determine the rules of intercourse across state lines was essential to weld a loose confederacy into a single, indivisible Nation; its continued existence is equally essential to the welfare of that Nation.

Our basic responsibility in interpreting the Commerce Clause is to make certain that the power to govern intercourse among the states remains where the Constitution placed it. That power, as held by this Court from the beginning, is vested in the Congress, available to be exercised for the national welfare as Congress shall deem necessary. No commercial enterprise of any kind which conducts its activities across state lines has been held to be wholly beyond the regulatory power of Congress under the Commerce Clause. We cannot make an exception of the business of insurance.

II.

We come then to the contention, earnestly pressed upon us by appellees, that Congress did not intend in the Sherman Act to exercise its power over the interstate insurance trade.

Certainly the Act's language affords no basis for this contention. Declared illegal in § 1 is "every contract, combination in the form of trust or otherwise, or conspiracy, in restraint of trade or commerce among the several States . . ."; and "every person" who shall make such a contract or engage in such a combination or conspiracy is deemed guilty of a misdemeanor. Section 2 is not less sweeping. "Every person" who monopolizes, or attempts to monopolize, or conspires with "any other person" to monopolize, "any part of the trade or commerce among the several States" is, likewise, deemed guilty of a misdemeanor. Language more comprehensive is difficult to conceive. On its face it shows a carefully studied attempt to bring within the Act every person engaged in business whose activities might restrain or monopolize commercial intercourse among the states.

A general application of the Act to all combinations of business and capital organized to suppress commercial competition is in harmony with the spirit and impulses of the times which gave it birth. "Trusts" and "monopolies" were the terror of the period. Their power to fix ⊥ prices, to restrict production, to crush small independent traders, and to concentrate large power in the few to the detriment of the many, were but some of numerous evils ascribed to them.[40] The organized opponents of trusts aimed at the complete destruction of all business combinations which possessed potential power, or had the intent, to destroy competition in whatever the people needed or ⊥ wanted.[41] So great was the strength of the anti-trust forces that the issue of trusts and monopolies became non-partisan. The question was not whether they should be abolished, but how this purpose could best be accomplished.[42]

Combinations of insurance companies were not exempt from public hostility against the trusts. Between 1885 and 1912 twenty-three states enacted laws forbidding insurance combinations. When, in 1911, one of these state ⊥ statutes was unsuccessfully challenged in this Court, the Court had this to say: "We can well understand that fire insurance companies, acting together, may have owners of property practically at their mercy in the matter of rates, and may have it in their power to deprive the public generally of the advantages flowing from competition between rival organizations engaged in the business of fire insurance. In order to meet the evils of such combinations or associations, the State is competent to adopt appropriate regulations that will tend to substitute competition in the place of combination or monopoly." *German Alliance Ins. Co. v. Hale,* 219 U. S. 307, 316.

Appellees argue that the Congress knew, as doubtless some of its members did, that this Court had prior to 1890 said that insurance was not commerce and was subject to state regulation, and that therefore we should read the Act as though it expressly exempted that business. But neither by reports nor by statements of the bill's sponsors or others was any purpose to exempt insurance companies revealed. And we fail to find in the legislative history of the Act an expression of a clear and unequivocal desire of Congress to legislate only within that area previously ⊥ declared by this

---

[40] . . .

Nor was the opposition to trusts limited to the monopolization of "goods and services." At the instance of Senator Ingalls of Kansas an amendment was added to the Sherman bill designed to tax out of existence the business of dealing in futures contracts. 21 Cong. Rec. 2613. The Ingalls amendment was adopted by the Senate without a record vote. *Id.* Subsequently the Sherman bill, as amended, was redrafted by the Senate Judiciary Committee which used substantially the same broad and sweeping language which Sections 1 and 2 of the Act contain today. With that language the Sherman bill had the support of Senator Ingalls and other proponents of the Ingalls amendment. 21 Cong. Rec. 3145, 3153. . . .

[41] Representative of anti-trust platforms, resolutions, etc., of contemporary agrarian-political movements are the following: "We demand . . . the passage of a law prohibiting the formation of trusts and combinations by speculators to secure control of the necessaries of life for the purpose of forcing up prices on consumers, imposing heavy penalties" (Texas Farmers' State Alliance, Report of Committee on Industrial Depression (1888)); "The objects of the National Alliance are . . . to oppose all forms of monopoly as being detrimental to the best interests of the public" (National Farmers' Alliance, Constitution (1887)); "We hold to the principle that all monopolies are dangerous . . ., tending to enslave a free people . . ." (National Farmers' Alliance and Industrial Union, Constitution (1889)); "We oppose the tyranny of monopolies" (National Grange, Declaration of Purposes (1874)).

[42] The platforms of both the Republican and the Democratic parties in 1888 stated unqualified opposition to monopolies and trusts. Brandon, Platforms of the Two Great Political Parties 1856–1928. The recorded vote in the House on the final conference report on the Sherman Act shows 242 ayes, no nays, and 85 not voting. 21 Cong. Rec. 6314.

Court to be within the federal power.⁴⁵ Cf. *Helvering* v. *Griffiths*, 318 U. S. 371; *Parker* v. *Motor Boat Sales*, 314 U. S. 244. We have been shown not one piece of reliable evidence that the Congress of 1890 intended to freeze the proscription of the Sherman Act within the mold of then current judicial decisions defining the commerce power. On the contrary, all the acceptable evidence points the other way. That Congress wanted to go to the utmost extent of its Constitutional power in restraining trust and monopoly agreements such as the indictment here charges admits of little, if any, doubt.⁴⁶ The purpose was to use that power to make of ours, so far as Congress could under our dual system, a competitive business economy.⁴⁷ Nor is it sufficient to justify our reading into the Act an exemption for insurance that the Congress of 1890 may have known that states already were regulating the insurance business. The Congress of 1890 also knew that railroads were subject to regulation not only by states but by the federal government itself, but this fact has been held insufficient to bring to the railroad companies the interpretative exemption from the Sherman Act they have sought. *United States* v. *Trans-Missouri Freight Assn.*, 166 U. S. 290, 314-315, 320-325.

Appellees further argue that, quite apart from what the Sherman Act meant in

---

⁴⁵ We have been pointed to only one reference made to the business of insurance in the Congressional discussions preceding passage of the Sherman Act, and that is a statement of Senator Turpie which flatly challenged the reasoning of this Court in holding that insurance was not commerce, and further predicted that in the future the Commerce Clause would not be given such a limited construction:

"The Senator from Missouri [Mr. Vest] spoke the other day about the difficulty of defining the word 'commerce,' especially as contained in the phrase 'interstate commerce.' I recollect one judicial decision upon this subject very definitely. The Supreme Court has decided that insurance is not commerce, and I suppose by following the circle of negations long enough and excluding all the things not commerce we should come at last to the residuum, which must be commerce or interstate commerce, because it can be nothing else. *A fortiori*, judging from this principle, I should myself have decided that transportation is not commerce nor interstate commerce either. . . .

"I feel inclined to make the prediction, as one of the things to come in this vast domain, scarcely touched, of cases arising under the Constitution and laws of Congress, that the whole mass of merchantable paper known as negotiable by the law merchant, made at one place, negotiable at another, payable at another, transcending in its negotiation State lines, will be remitted to Congressional action, and with respect to its creation, its formation, its negotiation, with respect to all the rights and liabilities which may arise under it, the people, stunned with the eternal dissonance of conflicting decisions and judgments of forty-eight or fifty tribunals of last resort in the States upon the subject of interstate negotiable paper, will require Congress to act therein, and that, unconstitutional as I now deem it or think it, it will as a matter of necessity be done, and in any such legislation with respect to that paper, the whole bulk of it, the personal and peculiar conditions of litigants will not be inquired about, but simply whether the one party or the other is entitled to relief or liable to recovery against him by reason of being a party to interstate commercial paper, negotiable and payable and suable under the action of Congress which may finally take place upon that subject. . . .

"Nor do I think with the Senator from New York that we are discharged from duty or released from our obligation to legislate upon the subject of trusts because the States have a right to do so." 21 Cong. Rec. 2556-2557. . . .

⁴⁶ Senator George, a member of the Senate Judiciary Committee which redrafted the Sherman Act before its final passage, stated on the floor of the Senate that, "The bill has been very ingeniously and properly drawn to cover every case which comes within what is called the commercial power of Congress. . . . It is well known that the great evil of these combinations, these conspiracies, as they are called, these monopolies, as they are denominated by the bill, consists in the fact that by combination, by association, there have been gathered together the money and the means of large numbers of persons, and under these combinations, or conspiracies, or trusts, this great aggregated capital is wielded by a single hand and guided by a single brain, or at least by hands and brains acting in complete harmony and co-operation, and that in this way, by this association, by this direction of this immense amount of capital, by one organized will, to a very large extent, these wrongs have been perpetrated upon the American people." 21 Cong. Rec. 3147.

Earlier, Senator Sherman had explained, "I do not wish to single out any particular trust or combination. It is not a particular trust, but the system I aim at." 21 Cong. Rec. 2457. And in the House, Representative Stewart, delivering the last speech preceding the unanimous adoption of the present Act, stated ". . . The provisions of this trust bill are just as broad, sweeping, and explicit as the English language can make them to express the power of Congress over this subject under the Constitution of the United States. . . ." 21 Cong. Rec. 6314.

⁴⁷ Senator Sherman, explaining his bill to the Senate, stated, "It is to arm the Federal courts within the limits of their constitutional power that they may co-operate with the State courts in checking, curbing, and controlling the most dangerous combinations that now threaten the business, property, and trade of the people of the United States." 21 Cong. Rec. 2457.

1890, the succeeding Congresses have accepted and approved the decisions of this Court that the business of insurance is not commerce. . . .

The most that can be said of all this evidence considered together is that it is inconclusive as to any point here relevant. By no means does it show that the Congress of 1890 specifically intended to exempt insurance companies from the all-inclusive scope of the Sherman Act. Nor can we attach significance to the omission of Congress to include in its amendments to the Act an express statement that the Act covered insurance. From the beginning Congress has used language broad enough to include all businesses, and never has amended the Act to define these businesses with particularity. And the fact that several Congresses since 1890 have failed to enact proposed legislation providing for more or less comprehensive federal regulation of insurance does not even remotely suggest that any Congress has held the view that insurance alone, of all businesses, should be permitted to enter into combinations for the purpose of destroying competition by coercive and intimidatory practices.

Finally it is argued at great length that virtually all the states regulate the insurance business on the theory that competition in the field of insurance is detrimental both to the insurers and the insured, and that if the Sherman Act be held applicable to insurance much of this state regulation will be destroyed. The first part of this argument is buttressed by opinions expressed by various persons that unrestricted competition in insurance results in financial chaos and public injury. Whether competition is a good thing for the insurance business is not for us to consider. Having power to enact the Sherman Act, Congress did so; if exceptions are to be written into the Act, they must come from the Congress, not this Court. . . .

. . . The argument that the Sherman Act necessarily invalidates many state laws regulating insurance we regard as exaggerated. Few states go so far as to permit private insurance companies, without state supervision, to agree upon and fix uniform insurance rates. Cf. *Parker* v. *Brown*, 317 U. S. 341, 350–352. No states authorize combinations of insurance companies to coerce, intimidate, and boycott competitors and consumers in the manner here alleged, and it cannot be that any companies have acquired a vested right to engage in such destructive business practices.

Reversed.

Mr. Justice Roberts and Mr. Justice Reed took no part in the consideration or decision of this case.

Mr. Chief Justice Stone, dissenting:

This Court has never doubted, and I do not doubt, that transactions across state lines which often attend and are incidental to the formation and performance of an insurance contract, such as the use of facilities for interstate communication and transportation, are acts of interstate commerce subject to regulation by the federal government under the commerce clause. Nor do I doubt that the business of insurance as presently conducted has in many aspects such interstate manifestations and such effects on interstate commerce as may subject it to the appropriate exercise of federal power. See *Polish Alliance* v. *Labor Board, post*, p. 643.

But such are not the questions now before us. We are not concerned here with the power of Congress to do what it has not attempted to do, but with the question whether Congress in enacting the Sherman Act has asserted its power over the business of insurance.

The questions which the Government has raised, advisedly it would seem . . . , by the indictment in this case, as it has been interpreted by the District Court below, are quite different from the question, discussed in the Court's opinion, whether the incidental use of the facilities of interstate commerce and transportation in the conduct of the fire insurance business renders the business itself "commerce" within the meaning of the Sherman Act and the commerce clause. The questions here are whether the business of entering into contracts in one state, insuring against the risk of loss by fire of property in others, is itself interstate commerce; and whether an agreement or conspiracy to fix the premium rates of such contracts and in other ways to restrict competition in effecting policies of fire insurance, violates the Sherman Act. The court below has answered "no" to both of these questions. I think that its answer is right and its judgment should be affirmed, both on principle and in view of the permanency which should be given to the construction of the commerce clause and the Sherman Act in this respect, which has until now been consistently adhered to by all branches of the Government. . . .

. . . [T]he only questions open for decision here are whether the District Court's constructions of the commerce clause and of the Sherman Act, on which it rested its decision, are the correct ones. . . .

The District Court pointed out that the offenses charged by the indictment are a conspiracy to fix arbitrary and non-competitive premium rates on fire insurance sold in several named states, and by means of that conspiracy to restrain and to monopolize trade and commerce in fire insurance in those states. The court went on to say:

"To constitute a violation of the Sherman Act, the restraint and monopoly denounced must be that of interstate trade or commerce, and, unless the restraint and monopoly charged in the indictment be restraint or monopoly in interstate trade or commerce, the indictment must fall.

"It is not a question here of whether the defendants participated in some incidental way in interstate commerce or used in some instances the facilities of interstate commerce, but is rather whether the activities complained of as constituting the business of insurance would themselves constitute interstate trade or commerce, and whether defendants' method of conducting same amounted to restraint or monopoly of same. It is not a question as to whether or not Congress had power to regulate the insurance companies or some phases of their activities, but rather whether Congress did so by the Sherman Act. . . ."

In short the District Court construed the indictment as charging restraints not in the incidental use of the mails or other instrumentalities of interstate commerce, nor in the insurance of goods moving in interstate commerce, but in the "business of insurance." And by the "business of insurance" it necessarily meant the business of writing contracts of insurance, for the indictment charges only restraints in entering into such contracts, not in their performance, and the Court deemed it irrelevant that in the negotiation and performance of the contracts appellees "may use the mails and instrumentalities of interstate commerce." It held that that business is not in itself interstate commerce, and that the alleged conspiracies to restrain and to monopolize that business were not, without more, in restraint of interstate commerce and consequently were not violations of the Sherman Act. . . .

The numerous and unvarying decisions of this Court that "insurance is not commerce" have never denied that acts of interstate commerce may be incidental to the business of writing and performing contracts of insurance, or that those incidental acts are subject to the commerce power. Our decisions on this subject have uniformly rested on the ground that the formation of an insurance contract, even though it insures against risk of loss to property located in other states or moving in interstate commerce, is not interstate commerce, and that although the incidents of interstate communication and transportation which often attend the formation and performance of an insurance contract are interstate commerce, they do not serve to render the business of insurance itself interstate commerce. . . .

. . . But the power of the Congress to regulate [acts of interstate commerce] is derived, not from its authority to regulate the business of insurance, but from its power to regulate interstate communication and transportation. And such incidental use of the facilities of interstate commerce does not render the insurance business itself interstate commerce. Nor is the nature of a single insurance transaction or a few such transactions not involving interstate commerce altered in that regard merely because their number is multiplied. The power of Congress to regulate interstate communication and transportation incidental to the insurance business is not any more or any less because the number of insurance transactions is great or small. The Congressional power to regulate does not extend to the formation and performance of insurance contracts save only as the latter may affect communication and transportation which are interstate commerce or may otherwise be found by Congress to affect transactions of interstate commerce. And even then, such effects on the commerce as do not involve restraints in competition in the marketing of goods and services are not within the reach of the Sherman Act. That such are the controlling principles has been fully recognized by this Court in the numerous cases which have held that the business of insurance is not commerce or as such subject to the commerce power. . . .

These principles are not peculiar to insurance contracts. They are equally applicable to other types of contracts which relate to things or events in other states than that of their execution, but which do not contain any obligation to engage in any form of interstate commerce. The ⊥ parties to them are not engaged in interstate commerce, for such commerce is not necessarily involved in or prerequisite to the formation of such contracts and they do not in their performance necessarily involve the doing of interstate business. . . . That the principle underlying that conclusion is the same as that underlying the decisions of this Court that the business of insurance is not interstate commerce, has been repeatedly recognized and affirmed. *Paul* v. *Virginia*, 8 Wall. 168, 183; *Hooper* v. *California*, 155 U. S. 648, 654. . . .

⊥ Undoubtedly contracts so entered into for the sale of commodities which move in interstate commerce may become the implements for restraints in marketing those commodities, and when so used may for that reason be within the Sherman Act. . . . But it is quite another matter to say that the contracts are themselves interstate commerce or that restraints in competition as to their terms or conditions are within the Sherman Act, in the absence of a showing that the purpose or effect is to restrain competition in the marketing of the goods or services to which the contracts relate. . . .

In this respect insurance contracts do not in point of law stand on any different footing as regards the Sherman Act. If contracts of insurance are in fact made the instruments of restraint in the marketing of goods and services in or affecting interstate commerce, they are not beyond the reach of the Sherman Act more than contracts ⊥ for the sale of commodities,—contracts which, not in themselves interstate commerce, may nevertheless be used as the means of its restraint. But since trade in articles of commerce is not the subject matter of contracts of insurance, it is evident that not only is the writing of insurance policies not interstate commerce but there is little scope for their use in restraining competition in the marketing of goods and services in or affecting the commerce. . . .

The conclusion seems inescapable that the formation of insurance contracts, like many others, and the business of so doing, is not, without more, commerce within the protection of the commerce clause of the Constitution and thereby, in large measure, excluded from state control and regulation. . . . This conclusion seems, upon analysis, not only correct on ⊥ principle and in complete harmony with the uniform rulings by which this Court has held that the formation of all types of contract which do not stipulate for the performance of acts of interstate commerce, are likewise not interstate commerce, but it has the support of an unbroken line of decisions of this Court beginning with *Paul* v. *Virginia*, seventy-five years ago, and extending down to the present time. . . .

⊥ It would be strange, indeed, if Congress, in adopting the Sherman Act in 1890, more than twenty years after this Court had supposedly settled the question, had considered that the business of insurance was interstate com⊥merce or had contemplated that the Sherman Act was to apply to it. Nothing in its legislative history suggests that it was intended to apply to the business of insurance.[3] The legislative materials indicate that Congress was primarily concerned with restraints of competition in the marketing of goods sold in interstate commerce, which were clearly within the

---

[3] The decisions of this Court that the negotiation of a contract between citizens of different states is not interstate commerce were known to and accepted by Congress. In the course of the debates in the Senate on the original bill introduced by Senator Sherman, Senator Turpie, discussing the extent of the federal commerce power, stated, "I recollect one judicial decision upon this subject very definitely. The Supreme Court has decided that insurance is not commerce. . . ." 21 Cong. Rec. 2556. During subsequent debates on that bill Senator Hoar, who later took charge of the revised bill reported by the Judiciary Committee and ultimately enacted, 21 Cong. Rec. 3145 *et seq.*, denied the existence of federal substantive power, under the commerce clause or Article III, § 2, over contracts between citizens of different states, asserting that Senator Sherman's bill could be supported only as a regulation of the "importation, transportation, or sale of articles. . . ." 21 Cong. Rec. 2567. See also the statements of Senator Eustis at 21 Cong. Rec. 2646, 2651-2.

federal commerce power.⁴ And while the Act is not limited to restraints of commerce in physical goods, see *e. g., Atlantic Cleaners & Dyers* v. *United States,* 286 U. S. 427, there is no reason to suppose that Congress intended the Act to apply to matters in which, under prevailing decisions of this Court, commerce was not involved. On the contrary the House committee, in reporting the bill which was adopted without change, declared: "No attempt is made to invade the legislative authority of the several States or even to occupy doubtful grounds. No system of laws can be devised by Congress alone which would effectually protect the people of the United States against the evils and oppression of trusts and monopolies. Congress has no authority to deal, generally, with the subject within the States, and the States have no authority to legislate in respect of commerce between the several States or with foreign nations."⁵

In 1904 and again in 1905 President Roosevelt urged "that the Congress carefully consider whether the power of the Bureau of Corporations cannot constitutionally be extended to cover interstate transactions in insurance." The American Bar Association, executives of leading insurance companies, and others joined in the request. Numerous bills providing for federal regulation of various aspects of the insurance business were introduced between 1902 and 1906 but the judiciary committees of both House and Senate concluded that the regulation of the business of marine, fire and life insurance was beyond Congressional power. Sen. Rep. No. 4406, 59th Cong., 1st Sess.; H. R. Rep. No. 2491, 59th Cong., 1st Sess., 12–25. The House committee stated that "the question as to whether or not insurance is commerce has passed beyond the realm of argument, because the Supreme Court of the United States has said many times for a great number of years that insurance is not commerce." (p. 13.)

And when in 1914, one year after the decision in *New York Life Ins. Co.* v. *Deer Lodge County,*[1.471] Congress by the Clayton Act, 38 Stat. 730, amended the Sherman Act and defined the term "commerce" as used in that Act, it gave no indication that it questioned or desired this Court to overrule the decision of the *Deer Lodge* case and those preceding it. On the contrary Mr. Webb, who was in charge of the bill in the House of Representatives, stated that "insurance companies are not reached as the Supreme Court has held that their contracts or policies are not interstate commerce." 51 Cong. Rec. 9390.

This Court, throughout the seventy-five years since the decision of *Paul* v. *Virginia*, has adhered to the view that the business of insurance is not interstate commerce.¹¹ Such has ever since been the practical construction by the other branches

---

⁴ See Senator Sherman's original bill, S. 3445, 50th Cong., S. 1, 51st Cong., and his statement at 21 Cong. Rec. 2562. Texts of the bill throughout its various amendments are set out in Bills and Debates Relating to Trusts, Sen. Doc. No. 147, 57th Cong., 2d Sess. (1903).

⁵ H. R. Rep. No. 1707, 51st Cong., 1st Sess., p. 1. See also the statement on the floor of the House by Mr. Culberson, in charge of the bill, "There is no attempt to exercise any doubtful authority on this subject, but the bill is confined strictly and alone to subjects over which, confessedly, there is no question about the legislative power of Congress . . ." 21 Cong. Rec. 4089. And see the statement of Senator Edmunds, chairman of the Senate Judiciary Committee which reported out the bill in the form in which it passed, that in drafting that bill the committee thought that "we would frame a bill that should be clearly within our constitutional power, that we should make its definition out of terms that were well known to the law already, and would leave it to the courts in the first instance to say how far they could carry it or its definitions as applicable to each particular case as it might arise." 21 Cong. Rec. 3148. Similarly Senator Hoar, a member of that committee who with Senator Edmunds was in charge of the bill, stated "Now we are dealing with an offense against interstate or international commerce, which the State can not regulate by penal enactment, and we find the United States without any common law. The great thing that this bill does, except affording a remedy, is to extend the common-law principles, which protected fair competition in trade in old times in England, to international and interstate commerce in the United States." 21 Cong. Rec. 3152.

¹¹ For cases arising under the Anti-Trust laws in which this Court has so stated see *Hopkins* v. *United States,* 171 U. S. 578, 602; *Blumenstock Bros.* v. *Curtis Publishing Co.,* 252 U. S. 436, 443; *Federal Club* v. *National League,* 259 U. S. 200, 209; *Standard Oil Co.* v. *United States,* 283 U. S. 163, 168–9; and see *Northern Securities Co.* v. *United States,* 193 U. S. 197, 372, 377 (dissenting opinion). See also *United Mine Workers* v. *Coronado Coal Co.,* 259 U. S. 344, 410; *United Leather Workers* v. *Herkert & Meisel Co.,* 265 U. S. 457, 470–71, relying on *Ware & Leland* v. *Mobile County,* 209 U. S. 405, a case applying the insurance rule to cotton futures contracts not calling for interstate shipment or delivery.

[1.471] 231 U.S. 495 (1913).

of the Government of the application to insurance of the commerce clause and the Sherman Act. Long continued practical construction of the Constitution or a statute is of persuasive force in determining its meaning and proper application. *Pocket Veto Case*, 279 U. S. 655, 688-90; *Federal Trade Commission* v. *Bunte Bros.*, 312 U. S. 349, 351-2; *United States* v. *Cooper Corp.*, 312 U. S. 600, 613-14. It is significant that in the fifty years since the enactment of the Sherman Act the Government has not until now sought to apply it to the business of insurance, and that Congress has continued to regard insurance as not constituting interstate commerce. Although often asked to do so it has repeatedly declined to pass legislation regulating the insurance business and to sponsor constitutional amendments subjecting it to Congressional control.

The decision now rendered repudiates this long-continued and consistent construction of the commerce clause and the Sherman Act. . . .

From what has been said it seems plain that our decisions that the business of insurance is not commerce are not unsound in principle, and involve no inconsistency or lack of harmony with accepted doctrine. They place no field of activity beyond the control of both the national and state governments. . . . On the contrary the ruling that insurance is not commerce, and is therefore unaffected by the restrictions which the commerce clause imposes on state legislation, removed the most serious obstacle to regulation of that business by the states. Through their plenary power over domestic and foreign corporations which are not engaged in interstate commerce, the states have developed extensive and effective systems of regulation of the insurance business, often solving regulatory problems of a local character with which it would be impractical or difficult for Congress to deal through the exercise of the commerce power. And in view of the broad powers of the federal government to regulate matters which, though not themselves commerce, nevertheless affect interstate commerce, *Wickard* v. *Filburn*, 317 U. S. 111; *Polish Alliance* v. *Labor Board, supra*, there can be no doubt of the power of Congress if it so desires to regulate many aspects of the insurance business mentioned in this indictment.

But the immediate and only practical effect of the decision now rendered is to withdraw from the states, in large measure, the regulation of insurance and to confer it on the national government, which has adopted no legislative policy and evolved no scheme of regulation with respect to the business of insurance. Congress having taken no action, the present decision substitutes, for the varied and detailed state regulation developed over a period of years, the limited aim and indefinite command of the Sherman Act for the suppression of restraints on competition in the marketing of goods and services in or affecting interstate commerce, to be applied by the courts to the insurance business as best they may. . . .

Congress made the choice against so drastic a change when in 1906 it rejected the proposals to assume national control over the insurance business. The report of the House Committee on the Judiciary pointed out that "all of the evils and wrongs complained of are subject to the exclusive regulation of State legislative power" and added: "assuming that Congress declares that insurance is commerce and the Supreme Court holds the legislation constitutional, how much could Congress regulate, and what effect would such legislation have? It would disturb the very substructure of government by precipitating a violent conflict between the police power of the States and the power of Congress to regulate interstate commerce. To uphold the Federal power would be to extinguish the police power of the State by the legislation of Congress. In other words, Congress would admit corporations into the respective States and have the entire regulating power." H. R. Rep. No. 2491, 59th Cong., 1st Sess., 13, 15-16. See *id.* 18.

Had Congress chosen to legislate for such parts of the insurance business as could be found to affect interstate commerce, whether by making the Sherman Act applicable to them or by regulation in some other form, it could have resolved many of these questions of conflict between federal and state regulation. But this Court can decide only the questions before it in particular cases. Its action in now overturning the precedents of seventy-five years governing a business of such volume and of such wide ramifications, cannot fail to be the occasion for loosing a flood of litigation and of legislation, state and national, in order to establish a new boundary between state and national power, raising questions which cannot be answered for years to come, during which a great business and the regulatory officers of every state must be harassed by all the doubts and difficulties inseparable from a realignment of the distribution of power in our federal system. These considerations might well stay a reversal of long-established doctrine which promises so little of advantage and so much of harm. For me these considerations are controlling.

The judgement should be affirmed.

MR. JUSTICE FRANKFURTER:

I join in the opinion of the CHIEF JUSTICE.

The relations of the insurance business to national commerce and finance, I have no doubt, afford constitutional authority for appropriate regulation by Congress of the business of insurance, certainly not to a less extent than Congressional regulation touching agriculture. . . . But the opinion of the CHIEF JUSTICE leaves me equally without doubt that by the enactment of the Sherman Act in 1890, Congress did not mean to disregard the then accepted conception of the constitutional basis for the regulation of the insurance business. And the evidence is overwhelming that the inapplicability of the Sherman Act, in its contemporaneous setting, to insurance transactions such as those charged by this indictment has been confirmed and not modified by Congressional attitude and action in the intervening fifty years. There is no Congressional warrant therefore for bringing about the far-reaching dislocations which the opinions of the CHIEF JUSTICE and MR. JUSTICE JACKSON adumbrate.

[ED. NOTE: Mr. Justice Jackson's opinion, dissenting in part, has been omitted.]

UNITED STATES v. E. I. DU PONT DE NEMOURS & CO.

351 U.S. 377, 76 S. Ct. 994, 100 L. Ed. 1264 (1956)

[ED. NOTE: Selected original Court footnotes have been omitted.]

MR. JUSTICE REED delivered the opinion of the Court.

The United States brought this civil action under § 4 of the Sherman Act against E. I. du Pont de Nemours and Company. The complaint, filed December 13, 1947, in the United States District Court for the District of Columbia, charged du Pont with monopolizing, attempting to monopolize and conspiracy to monopolize interstate commerce in cellophane and cellulosic caps and bands in violation of § 2 of the Sherman Act. Relief by injunction was sought against defendant and its officers, forbidding monopolizing or attempting to monopolize interstate trade in cellophane. The prayer also sought action to dissipate the effect of the monopolization by divestiture or other steps. . . . After a lengthy trial, judgment was entered for du Pont on all issues.[1]

The Government's direct appeal here does not contest the findings that relate to caps and bands, nor does it raise any issue concerning the alleged attempt to monopolize or conspiracy to monopolize interstate commerce in cellophane. The appeal, as specifically stated by the Government, "attacks only the ruling that du Pont has not monopolized trade in cellophane." At issue for determination is only this alleged violation by du Pont of § 2 of the Sherman Act.

---

[1] *United States v. E. I. du Pont de Nemours & Co.*, 118 F. Supp. 41. . . .

During the period that is relevant to this action, du Pont produced almost 75% of the cellophane sold in the United States, and cellophane constituted less than 20% of all "flexible packaging material" sales. This was the designation accepted at the trial for the materials listed in Finding 280, Appendix A, this opinion, *post*, p. 405.[1.472]

⊥ The Government contends that, by so dominating cellophane production, du Pont monopolized a "part of the trade or commerce" in violation of § 2. Respondent agrees that cellophane is a product which constitutes "a 'part' of commerce within the meaning of Section 2." Du Pont brief, pp. 16, 79. But it contends that the prohibition of § 2 against monopolization is not violated because it does not have the power to control the price of cellophane or to exclude competitors from the market in which cellophane is sold. The court below found that the "relevant market for determining the extent of du Pont's market control is the market for flexible packaging materials," and that competition from those other materials prevented du Pont from possessing monopoly powers in its sales of cellophane. Finding 37.

The Government asserts that cellophane and other wrapping materials are neither substantially fungible nor like priced. For these reasons, it argues that the market for other wrappings is distinct from the market for cellophane and that the competition afforded cellophane by other wrappings is not strong enough to be considered in determining whether du Pont has monopoly powers. Market delimitation is necessary under du Pont's theory to determine whether an alleged monopolist violates § 2. The ultimate consideration in such a determination is whether the defendants control the price and competition in the market for such part of trade or commerce as they are charged with monopolizing. Every manufacturer is the sole producer of the particular commodity it makes but its control in the above sense of the relevant market depends upon the availability of alternative commodities for buyers: *i. e.*, whether there is a cross-elasticity of demand between cellophane and the other wrappings. This interchangeability is largely gauged by the purchase of competing products for similar uses considering the price, characteristics and adaptability of the ⊥ competing commodities. The court below found that the flexible wrappings afforded such alternatives. This Court must determine whether the trial court erred in its estimate of the competition afforded cellophane by other materials. . . .

Two additional questions were raised in the record and decided by the court below. That court found that, even if du Pont did possess monopoly power over sales of cellophane, it was not subject to Sherman Act prosecution, because (1) the acquisition of that power was protected by patents, and (2) that power was acquired solely through du Pont's business expertness. It was thrust upon du Pont. 118 F. Supp., at 213–218.

Since the Government specifically excludes attempts and conspiracies to monopolize from consideration, a conclusion that du Pont has no monopoly power would obviate examination of these last two issues.

I. *Factual Background.*—For consideration of the issue as to monopolization, a general summary of the development of cellophane is useful.

⊥ In the early 1900's, Jacques Brandenberger, a Swiss chemist, attempted to make tablecloths impervious to dirt by spraying them with liquid viscose (a cellulose solution available in quantity from wood pulp, Finding 361) and by coagulating this coating. His idea failed, but he noted that the coating peeled off in a transparent film. This first "cellophane" was thick, hard, and not perfectly transparent, but Brandenberger apparently foresaw commercial possibilities in his discovery. By 1908 he developed the first machine for the manufacture of transparent sheets of regenerated cellulose. The 1908 product was not satisfactory, but by 1912 Brandenberger was making a saleable thin flexible film used in gas masks. He obtained patents to cover the machinery and the essential ideas of his process.

It seems to be agreed, however, that the disclosures of these early patents were not sufficient to make possible the manufacture of commercial cellophane. The inadequacy of the patents is partially attributed to the fact that the essential machine (the Hopper) was improved after it was patented. But more significant was the failure of these

---

[1.472] The Court's Appendices have been omitted, and most of the references to them in the opinion have been deleted.

patents to disclose the actual technique of the process. This technique included the operational data acquired by experimentation.

In 1917 Brandenberger assigned his patents to La Cellophane Societe Anonyme and joined that organization. Thereafter developments in the production of cellophane somewhat paralleled those taking place in artificial textiles. Chemical science furnished the knowledge for perfecting the new products. The success of the artificial products has been enormous. Du Pont was an American leader in the field of synthetics and learned of cellophane's successes through an associate, Comptoir des Textiles Artificiel.

In 1923 du Pont organized with La Cellophane an American company for the manufacture of plain cellophane. The undisputed findings are that:

> "On December 26, 1923, an agreement was executed between duPont Cellophane Company and La Cellophane by which La Cellophane licensed duPont Cellophane Company exclusively under its United States cellophane patents, and granted duPont Cellophane Company the exclusive right to make and sell in North and Central America under La Cellophane's secret processes for cellophane manufacture. DuPont Cellophane Company granted to La Cellophane exclusive rights for the rest of the world under any cellophane patents or processes duPont Cellophane Company might develop." Finding 24.

Subsequently du Pont and La Cellophane licensed several foreign companies, allowing them to manufacture and vend cellophane in limited areas. Finding 601. Technical exchange agreements with these companies were entered into at the same time. However, in 1940, du Pont notified these foreign companies that sales might be made in any country, and by 1948 all the technical exchange agreements were canceled.

Sylvania, an American affiliate of a Belgian producer of cellophane not covered by the license agreements above referred to, began the manufacture of cellophane in the United States in 1930. Litigation between the French and Belgian companies resulted in a settlement whereby La Cellophane came to have a stock interest in Sylvania, contrary to the La Cellophane-du Pont agreement. This resulted in adjustments as compensation for the intrusion into United States of La Cellophane that extended du Pont's limited territory. The details do not here seem important. Since 1934 Sylvania has produced about 25% of United States cellophane.

An important factor in the growth of cellophane production and sales was the perfection of moistureproof cellophane, a superior product of du Pont research and patented by that company through a 1927 application. Plain cellophane has little resistance to the passage of moisture vapor. Moistureproof cellophane has a composition added which keeps moisture in and out of the packed commodity. This patented type of cellophane has had a demand with much more rapid growth than the plain.

In 1931 Sylvania began the manufacture of moistureproof cellophane under its own patents. After negotiations over patent rights, du Pont in 1933 licensed Sylvania to manufacture and sell moistureproof cellophane produced under the du Pont patents at a royalty of 2% of sales. These licenses, with the plain cellophane licenses from the Belgian company, made Sylvania a full cellophane competitor, limited on moistureproof sales by the terms of the licenses to 20% of the combined sales of the two companies of that type by the payment of a prohibitive royalty on the excess. Finding 552. There was never an excess production. The limiting clause was dropped on January 1, 1945, and Sylvania was acquired in 1946 by the American Viscose Corporation with assets of over two hundred million dollars.

Between 1928 and 1950, du Pont's sales of plain cellophane increased from $3,131,608 to $9,330,776. Moistureproof sales increased from $603,222 to $89,850,416, although prices were continuously reduced. Finding 337. It could not be said that this immense increase in use was solely or even largely attributable to the superior quality of cellophane or to the technique or business acumen of du Pont, though doubtless those factors were important. The growth was a part of the expansion of the commodity-packaging habits of business, a by-product of general efficient competitive merchandising to meet modern demands. The profits, which were large, apparently arose from this trend in marketing, the development of the industrial use of chemical research and production of synthetics, rather than from elimination of other producers from the relevant market. . . .

II. *The Sherman Act and the Courts.*—The Sherman Act has received long and careful application by this Court to achieve for the Nation the freedom of enterprise from monopoly or restraint envisaged by the Congress that passed the Act in 1890. Because the Act is couched in broad terms, it is adaptable to the changing types of commercial production and distribution that have evolved since its passage. Chief Justice Hughes wrote for the Court that "As a charter of freedom, the Act has a generality and adaptability comparable to that found to be desirable in constitutional provisions." *Appalachian Coals, Inc.* v. *United States*, 288 U. S. 344, 359-360. Compare on remedy, Judge Wyzanski in *United States* v. *United Shoe Machinery Corp.*, 110 F. Supp. 295, 348. It was said in *Standard Oil Co.* v. *United States*, 221 U. S. 1, 50, that fear of the power of rapid accumulations of individual and corporate wealth from the trade and industry of a developing national economy caused its passage. Units of traders and producers snowballed by combining into so-called "trusts." Competition was threatened. Control of prices was feared. Individual initiative was dampened. While the economic picture has changed, large aggregations of private capital, with power attributes, continue. Mergers go forward. Industries such as steel, automobiles, tires, chemicals, have only a few production organizations. A considerable size is often essential for efficient operation in research, manufacture and distribution.

Judicial construction of antitrust legislation has generally been left unchanged by Congress. This is true of the Rule of Reason. While it is fair to say that the Rule is imprecise, its application in Sherman Act litigation, as directed against enhancement of price or throttling of competition, has given a workable content to antitrust legislation. . . . It was judicially declared a proper interpretation of the Sherman Act in 1911, with a strong, clear-cut dissent challenging its soundness on the ground that the specific words of the Act covered every contract that tended to restrain or monopolize. This Court has not receded from its position on the Rule. There is not, we think, any inconsistency between it and the development of the judicial theory that agreements as to maintenance of prices or division of territory are in themselves a violation of the Sherman Act. It is logical that some agreements and practices are invalid *per se*, while others are illegal only as applied to particular situations.

Difficulties of interpretation have arisen in the application of the Sherman Act in view of the technical changes in production of commodities and the new distribution practices. They have called forth reappraisal of the effect of the Act by business and government. That reappraisal has so far left the problems with which we are here concerned to the courts rather than to administrative agencies. Cf. Federal Trade Commission Act, 38 Stat. 721. It is true that Congress has made exceptions to the generality of monopoly prohibitions, exceptions that spring from the necessities or conveniences of certain industries or business organizations, or from the characteristics of the members of certain groups of citizens. But those exceptions express legislative determination of the national economy's need of reasonable limitations on cutthroat competition or prohibition of monopoly. "[W]here exceptions are made, Congress should make them." *United States* v. *Line Material Co.*, 333 U. S. 287, 310. They modify the reach of the Sherman Act but do not change its prohibition of other monopolies. We therefore turn to § 2 (note 2, *supra*) to determine whether du Pont has violated that section by its dominance in the manufacture of cellophane in the before-stated circumstances.

III. *The Sherman Act, § 2—Monopolization.*—The only statutory language of § 2 pertinent on this review is: "Every person who shall monopolize . . . shall be deemed guilty . . . ." This Court has pointed out that monopoly at common law was a grant by the sovereign to any person for the sole making or handling of anything so that others were restrained or hindered in their lawful trade. *Standard Oil Co.* v. *United States*, 221 U. S. 1, 51. However, as in England, it came to be recognized here that acts bringing the evils of authorized monopoly—unduly diminishing competition and enhancing prices—were undesirable (*id.*, at 56, 57, 58) and were declared illegal by § 2. *Id.*, at 60-62. Our cases determine that a party has monopoly power if it has, over "any part of the trade or commerce among the several States," a power of controlling prices or unreasonably restricting competition. *Id.*, at 58.

Senator Hoar, in discussing § 2, pointed out that monopoly involved something more than extraordinary commercial success, "that it involved something like the use of means which made it impossible for other persons to engage in fair competition."[15] This exception to the Sherman Act prohibitions of monopoly power is perhaps the monopoly "thrust upon" one of *United States* v. *Aluminum Co. of America*, 148 F. 2d 416, 429, left as an undecided possibility by *American Tobacco Co.* v. *United States*, 328 U. S. 781. Compare *United States* v. *United Shoe Machinery Corp.*, 110 F. Supp. 295, 342.

If cellophane is the "market" that du Pont is found to dominate, it may be assumed it does have monopoly power over that "market." Monopoly power is the power to control prices or exclude competition. It seems apparent that du Pont's power to set the price of cellophane has been limited only by the competition afforded by other flexible packaging materials. Moreover, it may be practically impossible for anyone to commence manufacturing cellophane without full access to du Pont's technique. However, du Pont has no power to prevent competition from other wrapping materials. The trial court consequently had to determine whether competition from the other wrappings prevented du Pont from possessing monopoly power in violation of § 2. Price and competition are so intimately entwined that any discussion of theory must treat them as one. It is inconceivable that price could be controlled without power over competition or vice versa. This approach to the determination of monopoly power is strengthened by this Court's conclusion in prior cases that, when an alleged monopolist has power over price and competition, an intention to monopolize in a proper case may be assumed.

If a large number of buyers and sellers deal freely in a standardized product, such as salt or wheat, we have complete or pure competition. Patents, on the other hand, furnish the most familiar type of classic monopoly. As the producers of a standardized product bring about significant differentiations of quality, design, or packaging in the product that permit differences of use, competition becomes to a greater or less degree

---

[15] 21 Cong. Rec. 3151:

"Mr. KENNA. Mr. President, I have no disposition to delay a vote on the bill, but I would like to ask, with his permission, the Senator from Vermont a question touching the second section:

"'Every person who shall monopolize, or attempt to monopolize, or combine or conspire with any other person or persons, to monopolize any part of the trade, etc.'

"Is it intended by the committee, as the section seems to indicate, that if an individual engaged in trade between States or between States and Territories, or between States or Territories and the District of Columbia, or between a State and a foreign country, by his own skill and energy, by the propriety of his conduct generally, shall pursue his calling in such a way as to monopolize a trade, his action shall be a crime under this proposed act? To make myself understood, if I am not clear—

"Mr. EDMUNDS. I think I understand the Senator.

"Mr. KENNA. Suppose a citizen of Kentucky is dealing in shorthorn cattle and by virtue of his superior skill in that particular product it turns out that he is the only one in the United States to whom an order comes from Mexico for cattle of that stock for a considerable period, so that he is conceded to have a monopoly of that trade with Mexico; is it intended by the committee that the bill shall make that man a culprit?

"Mr. EDMUNDS. It is not intended by it and the bill does not do it. Anybody who knows the meaning of the word 'monopoly,' as the courts apply it, would not apply it to such a person at all; and I am sure my friend must understand that."

Id., at 3152:

"Mr. HOAR. I put in the committee, if I may be permitted to say so (I suppose there is no impropriety in it), the precise question which has been put by the Senator from West Virginia, and I had that precise difficulty in the first place with this bill, but I was answered, and I think all the other members of the committee agreed in the answer, that 'monopoly' is a technical term known to the common law, and that it signifies—I do not mean to say that they stated what the signification was, but I became satisfied that they were right and that the word 'monopoly' is a merely technical term which has a clear and legal signification, and it is this: It is the sole engrossing to a man's self by means which prevent other men from engaging in fair competition with him.

"Of course a monopoly granted by the King was a direct inhibition of all other persons to engage in that business or calling or to acquire that particular article, except the man who had a monopoly granted him by the sovereign power. I suppose, therefore, that the courts of the United States would say in the case put by the Senator from West Virginia that a man who merely by superior skill and intelligence, a breeder of horses or raiser of cattle, or manufacturer or artisan of any kind, got the whole business because nobody could do it as well as he could was not a monopolist, but that it involved something like the use of means which made it impossible for other persons to engage in fair competition, like the engrossing, the buying up of all other persons engaged in the same business."

incomplete and the producer's power over price and competition greater over his article and its use, according to the differentiation he is able to create and maintain. A retail seller may have in one sense a monopoly on certain trade because of location, as an isolated country store or filling station, or because no one else makes a product of just the quality or attractiveness of his product, as for example in cigarettes. Thus one can theorize that we have monopolistic competition in every nonstandardized commodity with each manufacturer having power over the price and production of his own product. However, this power that, let us say, automobile or soft-drink manufacturers have over their trademarked products is not the power that makes an illegal monopoly. Illegal power must be appraised in terms of the competitive market for the product.

Determination of the competitive market for commodities depends on how different from one another are the offered commodities in character or use, how far buyers will go to substitute one commodity for another. For example, one can think of building materials as in commodity competition but one could hardly say that brick competed with steel or wood or cement or stone in the meaning of Sherman Act litigation; the products are too different. This is the interindustry competition emphasized by some economists. . . . On the other hand, there are certain differences in the formulae for soft drinks but one can hardly say that each one is an illegal monopoly. Whatever the market may be, we hold that control of price or competition establishes the existence of monopoly power under § 2. Section 2 requires the application of a reasonable approach in determining the existence of monopoly power just as surely as did § 1. This of course does not mean that there can be a reasonable monopoly. . . . Our next step is to determine whether du Pont has monopoly power over cellophane: that is, power over its price in relation to or competition with other commodities. The charge was monopolization of cellophane. The defense, that cellophane was merely a part of the relevant market for flexible packaging materials.

IV. *The Relevant Market.*—When a product is controlled by one interest, without substitutes available in the market, there is monopoly power. Because most products have possible substitutes, we cannot, as we said in *Times-Picayune Co.* v. *United States*, 345 U. S. 594, 612, give "that infinite range" to the definition of substitutes. Nor is it a proper interpretation of the Sherman Act to require that products be fungible to be considered in the relevant market.

The Government argues:

> "We do not here urge that in *no* circumstances may competition of substitutes negative possession of monopolistic power over trade in a product. The decisions make it clear at the least that the courts will not consider substitutes other than those which are substantially fungible with the monopolized product and sell at substantially the same price."

But where there are market alternatives that buyers may readily use for their purposes, illegal monopoly does not exist merely because the product said to be monopolized differs from others. If it were not so, only physically identical products would be a part of the market. To accept the Government's argument, we would have to conclude that the manufacturers of plain as well as moistureproof cellophane were monopolists, and so with films such as Pliofilm, foil, glassine, polyethylene, and Saran, for each of these wrapping materials is distinguishable. These were all exhibits in the case. New wrappings appear, generally similar to cellophane: is each a monopoly? What is called for is an appraisal of the "cross-elasticity" of demand in the trade. See Note, 54 Col. L. Rev. 580. The varying circumstances of each case determine the result. In considering what is the relevant market for determining the control of price and competition, no more definite rule can be declared than that commodities reasonably interchangeable by consumers for the same purposes make up that "part of the trade or commerce," monopolization of which may be illegal. As respects flexible packaging materials, the market geographically is nationwide.

Industrial activities cannot be confined to trim categories. Illegal monopolies under § 2 may well exist over limited products in narrow fields where competition is eliminated.²³ That does not settle the issue here. In determining the market under the Sherman Act, it is the use or uses to which the commodity is put that control. The selling price between commodities with similar uses and different characteristics may vary, so that the cheaper product can drive out the more expensive. Or, the superior quality of higher priced articles may make dominant the more desirable. Cellophane costs more than many competing products and less than a few. But whatever the price, there are various flexible wrapping materials that are bought by manufacturers for packaging their goods in their own plants or are sold to converters who shape and print them for use in the packaging of the commodities to be wrapped.

Cellophane differs from other flexible packaging materials. From some it differs more than from others. The basic materials from which the wrappings are made and the advantages and disadvantages of the products to the packaging industry are summarized in Findings 62 and 63. They are aluminum, cellulose acetate, chlorides, wood pulp, rubber hydrochloride, and ethylene gas. It will adequately illustrate the similarity in characteristics of the various products by noting here Finding 62 as to glassine. Its use is almost as extensive as cellophane . . . and many of its characteristics equally or more satisfactory to users.

It may be admitted that cellophane combines the desirable elements of transparency, strength and cheapness more definitely than any of the others. Comparative characteristics have been noted thus:

> "Moistureproof cellophane is highly transparent, tears readily but has high bursting strength, is highly impervious to moisture and gases, and is resistant to grease and oils. Heat sealable, printable, and adapted to use on wrapping machines, it makes an excellent packaging material for both display and protection of commodities.
>
> "Other flexible wrapping materials fall into four major categories: (1) opaque nonmoistureproof wrapping *paper* designed primarily for convenience and protection in handling packages; (2) moistureproof *films* of varying degrees of transparency designed primarily either to protect, or to display and protect, the products they encompass; (3) nonmoistureproof transparent *films* designed primarily to display and to some extent protect, but which obviously

---

²³ The Government notes that the prohibitions of § 2 of the Sherman Act have often been extended to producers of single products and to businesses of limited scope. But the cases to which the Government refers us were not concerned with the problem that is now before the Court. In *Story Parchment Co.* v. *Paterson Co.*, 282 U. S. 555, a conspiracy to monopolize trade in vegetable parchment was held to be a violation of § 2. Parchment paper is obviously no larger a part of commerce than cellophane. Recovery, however, was based on proven allegations of combination and conspiracy to monopolize, and the scope of the market was not in issue. P. 560. Similarly, *Indiana Farmer's Guide Co.* v. *Prairie Farmer Publishing Co.*, 293 U. S. 268, ruled that a combination or conspiracy for the purpose of monopolizing the farm-paper business in the north central part of the Nation would be illegal by reason of the second section of the Sherman Act. *Lorain Journal Co.* v. *United States*, 342 U. S. 143, a case not cited by the Government, was concerned with even a smaller geographical area (dissemination of news in a community and surrounding territory). But the Court held only that defendant had attempted to monopolize, not that he had in fact monopolized. Also, this Court found in *United States* v. *Columbia Steel Co.*, 334 U. S. 495, that the "relevant competitive market" for determining whether there had been an unreasonable restraint of trade (or an attempt to monopolize) was the market for "rolled steel" products in an 11-state area. Women's dresses of "original design," *Fashion Originators' Guild* v. *Federal Trade Comm'n*, 312 U. S. 457; "first run" motion pictures, *United States* v. *Paramount Pictures*, 334 U. S. 131; the news services of one news agency, *United States* v. *Associated Press*, 52 F. Supp. 362 (S. D. N. Y.), aff'd 326 U. S. 1; and newspaper advertising as distinguished from other means of news dissemination, *Times-Picayune Co.* v. *United States*, 345 U. S. 594, have all been designated as parts of commerce. All four were concerned only with the question of whether there had been an attempt to monopolize. *United States* v. *Aluminum Co. of America*, 148 F. 2d 416 (C. A. 2d Cir.), did involve the question of monopolization. Judge Hand found that the relevant market for measuring Alcoa's power was the market for "virgin" aluminum; he refused to consider the close competition offered by "secondary" (used) aluminum. The reason for the narrow definition was that Alcoa's control over virgin aluminum permitted it to regulate the supply of used aluminum even though the latter should be actually sold by a competitor. Consequently, the case is not particularly helpful in the problem of market definition now before the Court.

do a poor protecting job where exclusion or retention of moisture is important; and (4) moistureproof *materials* other than films of varying degrees of transparency (foils and paper products) designed to protect and display." . . .

But, despite cellophane's advantages, it has to meet competition from other materials in every one of its uses. Cellophane's principal uses are analyzed in Appendix A, Findings 281 and 282. Food products are the chief outlet, with cigarettes next. The Government makes no challenge to Finding 283 that cellophane furnishes less than 7% of wrappings for bakery products, 25% for candy, 32% for snacks, 35% for meats and poultry, 27% for crackers and biscuits, 47% for fresh produce, and 34% for frozen goods. Seventy-five to eighty percent of cigarettes are wrapped in cellophane. Finding 292. Thus, cellophane shares the packaging market with others. The over-all result is that cellophane accounts for 17.9% of flexible wrapping materials, measured by the wrapping surface. Finding 280, Appendix A, *post*, p. 405.

Moreover a very considerable degree of functional interchangeability exists between these products, as is shown by the tables of Appendix A and Findings 150-278. It will be noted, Appendix B, that except as to permeability to gases, cellophane has no qualities that are not possessed by a number of other materials. Meat will do as an example of interchangeability. Findings 205-220. Although du Pont's sales to the meat industry have reached 19,000,000 pounds annually, nearly 35%, this volume is attributed "to the rise of self-service retailing of fresh meat." Findings 212 and 283. In fact, since the popularity of self-service meats, du Pont has lost "a considerable proportion" of this packaging business to Pliofilm. Finding 215. Pliofilm is more expensive than cellophane, but its superior physical characteristics apparently offset cellophane's price advantage. While retailers shift continually between the two, the trial court found that Pliofilm is increasing its share of the business. Finding 216. One further example is worth noting. Before World War II, du Pont cellophane wrapped between 5 and 10% of baked and smoked meats. The peak year was 1933. Finding 209. Thereafter du Pont was unable to meet the competition of Sylvania and of greaseproof paper. Its sales declined and the 1933 volume was not reached again until 1947. Findings 209-210. It will be noted that greaseproof paper, glassine, waxed paper, foil and Pliofilm are used as well as cellophane, Finding 218. Findings 209-210 show the competition and 215-216 the advantages that have caused the more expensive Pliofilm to increase its proportion of the business.

An element for consideration as to cross-elasticity of demand between products is the responsiveness of the sales of one product to price changes of the other. If a slight decrease in the price of cellophane causes a considerable number of customers of other flexible wrappings to switch to cellophane, it would be an indication that a high cross-elasticity of demand exists between them; that the products compete in the same market. The court below held that the "[g]reat sensitivity of customers in the flexible packaging markets to price or quality changes" prevented du Pont from possessing monopoly control over price. 118 F. Supp., at 207. The record sustains these findings. See references made by the trial court in Findings 123-149.

We conclude that cellophane's interchangeability with the other materials mentioned suffices to make it a part of this flexible packaging material market.

The Government stresses the fact that the variation in price between cellophane and other materials demonstrates they are noncompetitive. As these products are all flexible wrapping materials, it seems reasonable to consider, as was done at the trial, their comparative cost to the consumer in terms of square area. . . . Findings as to price competition are set out in the margin.[29] Cellophane costs two or three times as much, surface measure, as its chief competitors for the flexible wrapping market, glassine and greaseproof papers. Other forms of cellulose wrappings and those from

---

[29] "132. The price of cellophane is today an obstacle to its sales in competition with other flexible packaging materials.

"133. Cellophane has always been higher priced than the two largest selling flexible packaging materials, wax paper and glassine, and this has represented a disadvantage to sales of cellophane.

"134. DuPont considered as a factor in the determination of its prices, the prices of waxed paper, glassine, greaseproof, vegetable parchment, and other flexible packaging materials.

other chemical or mineral substances, with the exception of aluminum foil, are more expensive. The uses of these materials, as can be observed by Finding 283 in Appendix A, are largely to wrap small packages for retail distribution. The wrapping is a relatively small proportion of the entire cost of the article. Different producers need different qualities in wrappings and their need may vary from time to time as their products undergo change. But the necessity for flexible wrappings is the central and unchanging demand. We cannot say that these differences in cost gave du Pont monopoly power over prices in view of the findings of fact on that subject.[31]

⊥ It is the variable characteristics of the different flexible wrappings and the energy and ability with which the manufacturers push their wares that determine choice. . . . ⊥ From this wide variety of evidence, the [trial] Court reached the conclusion expressed in Finding 838:

> "The record establishes plain cellophane and moistureproof cellophane are each flexible packaging materials which are functionally interchangeable with other flexible packaging materials and sold at same time to same customers for same purpose at competitive prices; there is no cellophane market distinct and separate from the market for flexible packaging materials; the market for flexible packaging materials is the relevant market for determining nature and extent of duPont's market control; and duPont has at all times competed with other cellophane producers and manufacturers of other flexible packaging materials in all aspects of its cellophane business."

The facts above considered dispose also of any contention that competitors have been excluded by du Pont from the packaging material market. That market has many producers and there is no proof du Pont ever has possessed power to exclude any of them from the rapidly expanding flexible packaging market. The Government apparently concedes as much, for it states that "lack of power to inhibit entry into this so-called market [*i. e.*, flexible packaging materials], comprising widely disparate products, is no indicium of absence of power to exclude competition in the manufacture and sale of cellophane." The record shows the multiplicity of competitors and the financial strength of some with individual assets running to the hundreds of millions. Findings 66–72. Indeed, the ⊥ trial court found that du Pont could not exclude competitors even from the manufacture of cellophane, Finding 727, an immaterial matter if the market is flexible packaging material. Nor can we say that du Pont's profits, while liberal (according to the Government 15.9% net after taxes on the 1937–1947 average), demonstrate the existence of a monopoly without proof of lack of

---

"135. DuPont, in reducing its prices, intended to narrow price differential between cellophane and packaging papers, particularly glassine and waxed paper. The objective of this effort has been to increase the use of cellophane. Each price reduction was intended to open up new uses for cellophane, and to attract new customers who had not used cellophane because of its price."

[31] "140. Some users are sensitive to the cost of flexible packaging materials; others are not. . . . ⊥ These customers are unwilling to use more cellophane because of its relatively high price, would use more if the price were reduced, and have increased their use as the price of cellophane has been reduced.

"141. The cost factor slips accounts away from cellophane. This hits at the precarious users, whose profit margins on their products are low, and has been put in motion by competitive developments in the user's trade. . . .

"142. The price of cellophane was reduced to expand the market for cellophane. DuPont did not reduce prices for cellophane with intent of monopolizing manufacture or with intent of suppressing competitors.

"143. DuPont reduced cellophane prices to enable sales to be made for new uses from which higher prices had excluded cellophane, and to expand sales. Reductions were made as sales volume and market conditions warranted. In determining price reductions, duPont considered relationship between its manufacturing costs and proposed prices, possible additional volume that might be gained by the price reduction, effect of price reduction upon the return duPont would obtain on its investment. It considered the effect its lowered price might have on the manufacture by others, but this possible result of a price reduction was never a motive for the reduction.

"144. DuPont never lowered cellophane prices below cost, and never dropped cellophane prices temporarily to gain a competitive advantage.

"145. As duPont's manufacturing costs declined, 1924 to 1935, duPont reduced prices for cellophane. When costs of raw materials increased subsequent to 1935, it postponed reductions until 1938 and 1939. Subsequent increases in cost of raw material and labor brought about price increases after 1947."

comparable profits during those years in other prosperous industries. Cellophane was a leader, over 17%, in the flexible packaging materials market. There is no showing that du Pont's rate of return was greater or less than that of other producers of flexible packaging materials. Finding 719.

The "market" which one must study to determine when a producer has monopoly power will vary with the part of commerce under consideration. The tests are constant. That market is composed of products that have reasonable interchangeability for the purposes for which they are produced—price, use and qualities considered. While the application of the tests remains uncertain, it seems to us that du Pont should not be found to monopolize cellophane when that product has the competition and interchangeability with other wrappings that this record shows.

On the findings of the District Court, its judgment is

Affirmed.

MR. JUSTICE CLARK and MR. JUSTICE HARLAN took no part in the consideration or decision of this case.

[ED. NOTE: The concurring opinion of Mr. Justice Frankfurter and the dissenting opinion of Chief Justice Warren, joined in by Mr. Justices Black and Douglas, have been omitted.]

UNITED STATES v. TOPCO ASSOCIATES, INC.

405 U.S. 596, 92 S. Ct. 1126, 31 L. Ed. 2d 515 (1972)

[ED. NOTE: Selected original Court footnotes have been omitted.]

MR. JUSTICE MARSHALL delivered the opinion of the Court.

The United States brought this action for injunctive relief against alleged violation by Topco Associates, Inc. (Topco), of § 1 of the Sherman Act, 26 Stat. 209, as amended, 15 U. S. C. § 1. Jurisdiction was grounded in § 4 of the Act, 15 U. S. C. § 4. Following a trial on the merits, the United States District Court for the Northern District of Illinois entered judgment for Topco, 319 F. Supp. 1031, and the United States appealed directly to this Court pursuant to § 2 of the Expediting Act, 32 Stat. 823, as amended, 15 U. S. C. § 29. We noted probable jurisdiction, 402 U. S. 905 (1971), and we now reverse the judgment of the District Court.

I

Topco is a cooperative association of approximately 25 small and medium-sized regional supermarket chains that operate stores in some 33 States.[1] Each of the member chains operates independently; there is no pooling of earnings, profits, capital, management, or advertising resources. No grocery business is conducted under the Topco name. Its basic function is to serve as a purchasing agent for its members.[2] In this capacity, it procures and distributes to the members more than 1,000 different food and related nonfood items, most of which are distributed under brand names owned by Topco. The association does not itself own any manufacturing, processing, or warehousing facilities, and the items that it procures for members are usually shipped directly from the packer or manufacturer to the members. Payment is made either to

---

[1] Topco, which is referred to at times in this opinion as the "association," is actually composed of 23 chains of supermarket retailers and two retailer-owned cooperative wholesalers.

[2] In addition to purchasing various items for its members, Topco performs other related functions: e. g., it insures that there is adequate quality control on the products that it purchases; it assists members in developing specifications on certain types of products (e. g., equipment and supplies); and it also aids the members in purchasing goods through other sources.

Topco or directly to the manufacturer at a cost that is virtually the same for the members as for Topco itself.

All of the stock in Topco is owned by the members, with the common stock, the only stock having voting rights, being equally distributed. The board of directors, which controls the operation of the association, is drawn from the members and is normally composed of high-ranking executive officers of member chains. It is the board that elects the association's officers and appoints committee members, and it is from the board that the principal executive officers of Topco must be drawn. Restrictions on the alienation of stock and the procedure for selecting all important officials of the association from within the ranks of its members give the members complete and unfettered control over the operations of the association.

Topco was founded in the 1940's by a group of small, local grocery chains, independently owned and operated, that desired to cooperate to obtain high quality merchandise under private labels in order to compete more effectively with larger national and regional chains.[3] With a line of canned, dairy, and other products, the association began. It added frozen foods in 1950, fresh produce in 1958, more general merchandise equipment and supplies in 1960, and a branded bacon and carcass beef selection program in 1966. By 1964, Topco's members had combined retail sales of more than $2 billion; by 1967, their sales totaled more than $2.3 billion, a figure exceeded by only three national grocery chains.

Members of the association vary in the degree of market share that they possess in their respective areas. The range is from 1.5% to 16%, with the average being approximately 6%. . . . Topco members are frequently in as strong a competitive position in their respective areas as any other chain. The strength of this competitive position is due, in some measure, to the success of Topco-brand products. Although only 10% of the total goods sold by Topco members bear the association's brand names, the profit on these goods is substantial and their very existence has improved the competitive potential of Topco members with respect to other large and powerful chains.

It is apparent that from meager beginnings approximately a quarter of a century ago, Topco has developed into a purchasing association wholly owned and operated by member chains, which possess much economic muscle, individually as well as cooperatively.

II

Section 1 of the Sherman Act provides, in relevant part:

> "Every contract, combination in the form of trust or otherwise, or conspiracy, in restraint of trade or commerce among the several States, or with foreign nations, is declared to be illegal . . . ."

The United States charged that, beginning at least as early as 1960 and continuing up to the time that the complaint was filed, Topco had combined and conspired with its members to violate § 1 in two respects. First, the Government alleged that there existed:

> "a continuing agreement, understanding and concert of action among the co-conspirator member firms acting through Topco, the substantial terms of which have been and are that each co-conspirator member firm will sell Topco-controlled brands only within the marketing territory allocated to it, and will refrain from selling Topco-controlled brands outside such marketing territory."

---

[3] The founding members of Topco were having difficulty competing with larger chains. This difficulty was attributable in some degree to the fact that the larger chains were capable of developing their own private-label programs.

Private-label products differ from other brand-name products in that they are sold at a limited number of easily ascertainable stores. . . . It is obvious that by using private-label products, a chain can achieve significant cost economies in purchasing, transportation, warehousing, promotion, and advertising. These economies may afford the chain opportunities for offering private-label products at lower prices than other brand-name products. This, in turn, provides many advantages. . . .

The division of marketing territories to which the complaint refers consists of a number of practices by the association.

Article IX, § 2, of the Topco bylaws establishes three categories of territorial licenses that members may secure from the association:

> "(a) *Exclusive*—An exclusive territory is one in which the member is licensed to sell all products bearing specified trademarks of the Association, to the exclusion of all other persons.
>
> "(b) *Non-exclusive*—A non-exclusive territory is one in which a member is licensed to sell all products bearing specified trademarks of the Association, but not to the exclusion of others who may also be licensed to sell products bearing the same trademarks of the Association in the same territory.
>
> "(c) *Coextensive*—A coextensive territory is one in which two (2) or more members are licensed to sell all products bearing specified trademarks of the Association to the exclusion of all other persons. . . ."

When applying for membership, a chain must designate the type of license that it desires. Membership must first be approved by the board of directors, and thereafter by an affirmative vote of 75% of the association's members. If, however, the member whose operations are closest to those of the applicant, or any member whose operations are located within 100 miles of the applicant, votes against approval, an affirmative vote of 85% of the members is required for approval. Bylaws, Art. I, § 5. Because, as indicated by the record, members cooperate in accommodating each other's wishes, the procedure for approval provides, in essence, that members have a veto of sorts over actual or potential competition in the territorial areas in which they are concerned.

Following approval, each new member signs an agreement with Topco designating the territory in which that member may sell Topco-brand products. No member may sell these products outside the territory in which it is licensed. Most licenses are exclusive, and even those denominated "coextensive" or "non-exclusive" prove to be *de facto* exclusive. Exclusive territorial areas are often allocated to members who do no actual business in those areas on the theory that they may wish to expand at some indefinite future time and that expansion would likely be in the direction of the allocated territory. When combined with each member's veto power over new members, provisions for exclusivity work effectively to insulate members from competition in Topco-brand goods. Should a member violate its license agreement and sell in areas other than those in which it is licensed, its membership can be terminated under Art. IV, §§ 2(a) and 2(b) of the bylaws. Once a territory is classified as exclusive, either formally or *de facto*, it is extremely unlikely that the classification will ever be changed. See Bylaws, Art. IX.

The Government maintains that this scheme of dividing markets violates the Sherman Act because it operates to prohibit competition in Topco-brand products among grocery chains engaged in retail operations. The Government also makes a subsidiary challenge to Topco's practices regarding licensing members to sell at wholesale. Under the bylaws, members are not permitted to sell any products supplied by the association at wholesale, whether trademarked or not, without first applying for and receiving special permission from the association to do so. Before permission is granted, other licensees (usually retailers), whose interests may potentially be affected by wholesale operations, are consulted as to their wishes in the matter. If permission is obtained, the member must agree to restrict the sale of Topco products to a specific geographic area and to sell under any conditions imposed by the association. Permission to wholesale has often been sought by members, only to be denied by the association. The Government contends that this amounts not only to a territorial restriction violative of the Sherman Act, but also to a restriction on customers that in itself is violative of the Act. . . .

. . . Topco essentially maintains that it needs territorial divisions to compete with larger chains; that the association could not exist if the territorial divisions were anything but exclusive; and that by restricting competition in the sale of Topco-brand goods, the association actually increases competition by enabling its members to compete successfully with larger regional and national chains.

The District Court, considering all these things relevant to its decision, agreed with Topco. It recognized that the panoply of restraints that Topco imposed on its members worked to prevent competition in Topco-brand products, but concluded that

> "[w]hatever anti-competitive effect these practices may have on competition in the sale of Topco private label brands is far outweighed by the increased ability of Topco members to compete both with the national chains and other supermarkets operating in their respective territories." 319 F. Supp. 1031, 1043 (1970).

The court held that Topco's practices were procompetitive and, therefore, consistent with the purposes of the antitrust laws. But we conclude that the District Court used an improper analysis in reaching its result.

III

On its face, § 1 of the Sherman Act appears to bar any combination of entrepreneurs so long as it is "in restraint of trade." Theoretically, all manufacturers, distributors, merchants, sellers, and buyers could be considered as potential competitors of each other. Were § 1 to be read in the narrowest possible way, any commercial contract could be deemed to violate it. *Chicago Board of Trade* v. *United States*, 246 U. S. 231, 238 (1918) (Brandeis, J.). The history underlying the formulation of the antitrust laws led this Court to conclude, however, that Congress did not intend to prohibit all contracts, nor even all contracts that might in some insignificant degree or attenuated sense restrain trade or competition. In lieu of the narrowest possible reading of § 1, the Court adopted a "rule of reason" analysis for determining whether most business combinations or contracts violate the prohibitions of the Sherman Act. *Standard Oil Co.* v. *United States*, 221 U. S. 1 (1911). An analysis of the reasonableness of particular restraints includes consideration of the facts peculiar to the business in which the restraint is applied, the nature of the restraint and its effects, and the history of the restraint and the reasons for its adoption. *Chicago Board of Trade* v. *United States, supra,* at 238.

While the Court has utilized the "rule of reason" in evaluating the legality of most restraints alleged to be violative of the Sherman Act, it has also developed the doctrine that certain business relationships are *per se* violations of the Act without regard to a consideration of their reasonableness. In *Northern Pacific R. Co.* v. *United States*, 356 U. S. 1, 5 (1958), Mr. Justice Black explained the appropriateness of, and the need for, *per se* rules:

> "[T]here are certain agreements or practices which because of their pernicious effect on competition and lack of any redeeming virtue are conclusively presumed to be unreasonable and therefore illegal without elaborate inquiry as to the precise harm they have caused or the business excuse for their use. This principle of *per se* unreasonableness not only makes the type of restraints which are proscribed by the Sherman Act more certain to the benefit of everyone concerned, but it also avoids the necessity for an incredibly complicated and prolonged economic investigation into the entire history of the industry involved, as well as related industries, in an effort to determine at large whether a particular restraint has been unreasonable—an inquiry so often wholly fruitless when undertaken."

It is only after considerable experience with certain business relationships that courts classify them as *per se* violations of the Sherman Act. . . . One of the classic examples of a *per se* violation of § 1 is an agreement between competitors at the same level of the market structure to allocate territories in order to minimize competition. Such concerted action is usually termed a "horizontal" restraint, in contradistinction to combinations of persons at different levels of the market structure, *e. g.*, manufacturers and distributors, which are termed "vertical" restraints. This Court has reiterated time and time again that "[h]orizontal territorial limitations . . . are naked restraints of trade with no purpose except stifling of competition." *White Motor Co.* v. *United States*,

372 U. S. 253, 263 (1963). Such limitations are *per se* violations of the Sherman Act. See *Addyston Pipe & Steel Co.* v. *United States*, 175 U. S. 211 (1899), aff'g 85 F. 271 (CA6 1898) (Taft, J.); *United States* v. *National Lead Co.*, 332 U. S. 319 (1947); *Timken Roller Bearing Co.* v. *United States*, 341 U. S. 593 (1951); *Northern Pacific R. Co.* v. *United States, supra; Citizen Publishing Co.* v. *United States*, 394 U. S. 131 (1969); *United States* v. *Sealy, Inc.*, 388 U. S. 350 (1967); *United States* v. *Arnold, Schwinn & Co.*, 388 U. S. 365, 390 (1967) (STEWART, J., concurring in part and dissenting in part); *Serta Associates, Inc.* v. *United States*, 393 U. S. 534 (1969), aff'g 296 F. Supp. 1121, 1128 (ND Ill. 1968).

We think that it is clear that the restraint in this case is a horizontal one, and, therefore, a *per se* violation of § 1. The District Court failed to make any determination as to whether there were *per se* horizontal territorial restraints in this case and simply applied a rule of reason in reaching its conclusions that the restraints were not illegal. . . . In so doing, the District Court erred.

United States v. *Sealy, Inc., supra*, is, in fact, on all fours with this case. Sealy licensed manufacturers of mattresses and bedding to make and sell products using the Sealy trademark. Like Topco, Sealy was a corporation owned almost entirely by its licensees, who elected the Board of Directors and controlled the business. Just as in this case, Sealy agreed with the licensees not to license other manufacturers or sellers to sell Sealy-brand products in a designated territory in exchange for the promise of the licensee who sold in that territory not to expand its sales beyond the area demarcated by Sealy. The Court held that this was a horizontal territorial restraint, which was *per se* violative of the Sherman Act.⁹

Whether or not we would decide this case the same way under the rule of reason used by the District Court is irrelevant to the issue before us. The fact is that courts are of limited utility in examining difficult economic problems.¹⁰ Our inability to weigh, in any meaningful sense, destruction of competition in one sector of the economy against promotion of competition in another sector is one important reason we have formulated *per se* rules.

In applying these rigid rules, the Court has consistently rejected the notion that naked restraints of trade are to be tolerated because they are well intended or because they are allegedly developed to increase competition. *E. g., United States* v. *General Motors Corp.*, 384 U. S. 127, 146–147 (1966); *United States* v. *Masonite Corp.*, 316 U. S. 265 (1942); *Fashion Originators' Guild* v. *FTC*, 312 U. S. 457 (1941).

Antitrust laws in general, and the Sherman Act in particular, are the Magna Carta of free enterprise. They are as important to the preservation of economic freedom and our free-enterprise system as the Bill of Rights is to the protection of our fundamental personal freedoms. And the freedom guaranteed each and every business, no matter how small, is the freedom to compete—to assert with vigor, imagination, devotion, and ingenuity whatever economic muscle it can muster. Implicit in such freedom is the notion that it cannot be foreclosed with respect to one sector of the economy because certain private citizens or groups believe that such foreclosure might promote greater competition in a more important sector of the economy. Cf. *United States* v. *Philadelphia National Bank*, 374 U. S. 321, 371 (1963).

The District Court determined that by limiting the freedom of its individual members to compete with each other, Topco was doing a greater good by fostering competition between members and other large supermarket chains. But, the fallacy in this is that Topco has no authority under the Sherman Act to determine the respective values of competition in various sectors of the economy. On the contrary, the Sherman Act gives to each Topco member and to each prospective member the

---

⁹ It is true that in *Sealy* the Court dealt with price fixing as well as territorial restrictions. To the extent that *Sealy* casts doubt on whether horizontal territorial limitations, unaccompanied by price fixing, are *per se* violations of the Sherman Act, we remove that doubt today.

¹⁰ There has been much recent commentary on the wisdom of *per se* rules. . . .

Without the *per se* rules, businessmen would be left with little to aid them in predicting in any particular case what courts will find to be legal and illegal under the Sherman Act. Should Congress ultimately determine that predictability is unimportant in this area of the law, it can, of course, make *per se* rules inapplicable in some or all cases, and leave courts free to ramble through the wilds of economic theory in order to maintain a flexible approach.

right to ascertain for itself whether or not competition with other supermarket chains is more desirable than competition in the sale of Topco-brand products. Without territorial restrictions, Topco members may indeed "[cut] each other's throats." Cf. *White Motor Co., supra*, at 278 (Clark, J., dissenting). But, we have never found this possibility sufficient to warrant condoning horizontal restraints of trade.

The Court has previously noted with respect to price fixing, another *per se* violation of the Sherman Act, that:

> "The reasonable price fixed today may through economic and business changes become the unreasonable price of tomorrow. Once established, it may be maintained unchanged because of the absence of competition secured by the agreement for a price reasonable when fixed." *United States v. Trenton Potteries Co.*, 273 U. S. 392, 397 (1927).

A similar observation can be made with regard to territorial limitations. *White Motor Co., supra*, at 265 n. 2 (BRENNAN, J., concurring).

There have been tremendous departures from the notion of a free-enterprise system as it was originally conceived in this country. These departures have been the product of congressional action and the will of the people. If a decision is to be made to sacrifice competition in one portion of the economy for greater competition in another portion, this too is a decision that must be made by Congress and not by private forces or by the courts. Private forces are too keenly aware of their own interests in making such decisions and courts are ill-equipped and ill-situated for such decisionmaking. To analyze, interpret, and evaluate the myriad of competing interests and the endless data that would surely be brought to bear on such decisions, and to make the delicate judgment on the relative values to society of competitive areas of the economy, the judgment of the elected representatives of the people is required.

Just as the territorial restrictions on retailing Topco-brand products must fall, so must the territorial restrictions on wholesaling. The considerations are the same, and the Sherman Act requires identical results.

We also strike down Topco's other restrictions on the right of its members to wholesale goods. These restrictions amount to regulation of the customers to whom members of Topco may sell Topco-brand goods. Like territorial restrictions, limitations on customers are intended to limit intra-brand competition and to promote inter-brand competition. For the reasons previously discussed, the arena in which Topco members compete must be left to their unfettered choice absent a contrary congressional determination. *United States v. General Motors Corp., supra*; cf. *United States v. Arnold, Schwinn & Co., supra*; *United States v. Masonite Corp., supra*; *United States v. Trenton Potteries, supra*. See also, *White Motor Co., supra*, at 281–283 (Clark, J., dissenting).

We reverse the judgment of the District Court and remand the case for entry of an appropriate decree.

It is so ordered.

MR. JUSTICE POWELL and MR. JUSTICE REHNQUIST took no part in the consideration or decision of this case.

MR. JUSTICE BLACKMUN, concurring in the result.

The conclusion the Court reaches has its anomalous aspects, for surely, as the District Court's findings make clear, today's decision in the Government's favor will tend to stultify Topco members' competition with the great and larger chains. The bigs, therefore, should find it easier to get bigger and, as a consequence, reality seems at odds with the public interest. The *per se* rule, however, now appears to be so firmly established by the Court that, at this late date, I could not oppose it. Relief, if any is to be forthcoming, apparently must be by way of legislation.

MR. CHIEF JUSTICE BURGER, dissenting.

This case does not involve restraints on interbrand competition or an allocation of markets by an association with monopoly or near-monopoly control of the sources of supply of one or more varieties of staple goods. Rather, we have here an agreement among several small grocery chains to join in a cooperative endeavor that, in my view, has an unquestionably lawful principal purpose; in pursuit of that purpose they have mutually agreed to certain minimal ancillary restraints that are fully reasonable in view of the principal purpose and that have never before today been held by this Court to be *per se* violations of the Sherman Act.

In joining in this cooperative endeavor, these small chains did not agree to the restraints here at issue in order to make it possible for them to exploit an already established line of products through noncompetitive pricing. There was no such thing as a Topco line of products until this cooperative was formed. The restraints to which the cooperative's members have agreed deal only with the marketing of the products in the Topco line, and the only function of those restraints is to permit each member chain to establish, within its own geographical area and through its own local advertising and marketing efforts, a local consumer awareness of the trademarked family of products as that member's "private label" line. The goal sought was the enhancement of the individual members' abilities to compete, albeit to a modest degree, with the large national chains which had been successfully marketing private-label lines for ⊥ several years. The sole reason for a cooperative endeavor was to make economically feasible such things as quality control, large quantity purchases at bulk prices, the development of attractively printed labels, and the ability to offer a number of different lines of trademarked products. All these things, of course, are feasible for the large national chains operating individually, but they are beyond the reach of the small operators proceeding alone.

After a careful review of the economic considerations bearing upon this case, the District Court determined that "the relief which the government here seeks would not increase competition in Topco private label brands"; on the contrary, such relief "would substantially diminish competition in the supermarket field." 319 F. Supp. 1031, 1043. This Court has not today determined, on the basis of an examination of the underlying economic realities, that the District Court's conclusions are incorrect. Rather, the majority holds that the District Court had no business examining Topco's practices under the "rule of reason"; it should not have sought to determine whether Topco's practices did in fact restrain trade or commerce within the meaning of § 1 of the Sherman Act; it should have found no more than that those practices involve a "horizontal division of markets" and are, by that very fact, *per se* violations of the Act.

I do not believe that our prior decisions justify the result reached by the majority. Nor do I believe that a new *per se* rule should be established in disposing of this case, for the judicial convenience and ready pre⊥dictability that are made possible by *per se* rules are not such overriding considerations in antitrust law as to justify their promulgation without careful prior consideration of the relevant economic realities in the light of the basic policy and goals of the Sherman Act.

I

I deal first with the cases upon which the majority relies in stating that "[t]his Court has reiterated time and time again that '[h]orizontal territorial limitations . . . are naked restraints of trade with no purpose except stifling of competition.' *White Motor Co.* v. *United States*, 372 U. S. 253, 263 (1963)." *White Motor*, of course, laid down no *per se* rule; nor were any horizontal territorial limitations involved in that case. Indeed, it was in *White Motor* that this Court reversed the District Court's holding that vertically imposed territorial limitations were *per se* violations, explaining that "[w]e need to know more than we do about the actual impact of these arrangements on competition to decide whether they . . . should be classified as *per se* violations of the Sherman Act." 372 U. S., at 263. The statement from the *White Motor* opinion quoted by the majority today was made without citation of authority and was apparently intended primarily to make clear that the facts then before the Court were not to be confused with horizontally imposed territorial limitations. To treat dictum in that case as controlling here would, of course, be unjustified.

Having quoted this dictum from *White Motor*, the Court then cites eight cases for the proposition that horizontal territorial limitations are *per se* violations of the Sherman Act. One of these cases, *Northern Pacific R. Co.* v. *United States*, 356 U. S. 1

(1958), dealt exclusively with a prohibited tying arrangement and is improperly cited as a case concerned with a division of markets.[2] Of the remaining seven cases, four involved an aggregation of trade restraints that included price-fixing agreements. *Timken Roller Bearing Co. v. United States*, 341 U. S. 593 (1951); *United States v. Sealy, Inc.*, 388 U. S. 350 (1967);[3] *Serta Associates, Inc. v. United States*, 393 U. S. 534 (1969), aff'g 296 F. Supp. 1121 (ND Ill. 1968). Price fixing is, of course, not a factor in the instant case.

Another of the cases relied upon by the Court, *United States v. National Lead Co.*, 332 U. S. 319 (1947), involved a world-wide arrangement for dividing territories, pooling patents, and exchanging technological information. The arrangement was found illegal by the District Court without any reliance on a *per se* rule; this Court, in affirming, was concerned almost exclusively with the remedies ordered by the District Court and made no attempt to declare a *per se* rule to govern the merits of the case.

In still another case on which the majority relies, *United States v. Arnold, Schwinn & Co.*, 388 U. S. 365 (1967), the District Court had, indeed, held that the agreements between the manufacturer and certain of its distributors, providing the latter with exclusive territories, were horizontal in nature and that they were, as such, *per se* violations of the Act. 237 F. Supp. 323, 342-343. Since no appeal was taken from this part of the District Court's order, that issue was not before this Court in its review of the case. Indeed, in dealing with the issues that were before it, this Court followed an approach markedly different from that of the District Court. First, in reviewing the case here, the Court made it clear that it was proceeding under the "rule of reason," and not by *per se* rule; second, the Court saw the issues presented as involving vertical, not horizontal, restraints. It can hardly be contended, therefore, that this Court's decision in *Schwinn* is controlling precedent for the application in the instant case of a *per se* rule that prohibits horizontal restraints without regard to their market effects.

Finally, there remains the eighth of the cases relied upon by the Court—actually, the first in its list of "authorities" for the purported *per se* rule. Circuit Judge (later Chief Justice) Taft's opinion for the court in *United States v. Addyston Pipe & Steel Co.*, 85 F. 271 (CA6 1898), aff'd, 175 U. S. 211 (1899), has generally been recognized—and properly so—as a fully authoritative exposition of antitrust law. But neither he, nor this Court in affirming, made any pretense of establishing a *per se* rule against all agreements involving horizontal territorial limitations. . . . Although the case has frequently—and quite properly—been cited as a horizontal allocation-of-markets case, the sole purpose of the secret customer allocations was to enable the members of the association to fix prices charged to the public at noncompetitive levels. Judge Taft rejected the defendants' argument that the prices actually charged were "reasonable"; he held that it was sufficient for a finding of a Sherman Act violation that the combination and agreement of the defendants gave them such monopoly power that they, rather than market forces, fixed the prices of all cast-iron pipe in three-fourths of the Nation's territory. The case unquestionably laid important groundwork for the subsequent establishment of the *per se* rule against price fixing. It did not, however, establish that a horizontal division of markets is, without more, a *per se* violation of the Sherman Act.

II

The foregoing analysis of the cases relied upon by the majority indicates to me that the Court is not merely following prior holdings; on the contrary, it is establishing a new *per se* rule. In the face of the District Court's well supported

---

[2] There is dictum in the case to the effect that *United States v. Addyston Pipe & Steel Co.*, 85 F. 271 (CA6 1898), aff'd, 175 U. S. 211 (1899), established a "division of markets" as unlawful in and of itself. 356 U. S., at 5. As I will show, however, *Addyston Pipe* established no such thing; it was primarily a price-fixing case.

[3] I cannot agree with the Court's descripton of *Sealy* as being "on all fours with this case." *Ante*, at 609. *Sealy* does support the proposition that the restraints on the Topco licensees are horizontally imposed. Beyond that, however, *Sealy* is hardly controlling here. The territorial restrictions in *Sealy* were found by this Court to be so intimately a part of an unlawful price-fixing and policing scheme that the two arrangements fell together. . . .

findings that the effects of such a rule in this case will be adverse to the public welfare,[9] the Court lays down that rule without regard to the impact that the condemned practices may have on competition. In doing so, the Court virtually invites Congress to undertake to determine that impact. *Ante*, at 611–612. I question whether the Court is fulfilling the role assigned to it under the statute when it declines to make this determination; in any event, if the Court is unwilling on this record to assess the economic impact, it surely should not proceed to make a new rule to govern the economic activity. *White Motor Co.* v. *United States*, 372 U. S., at 263.

When one of his versions of the proposed Act was before the Senate for consideration in 1890, Senator Sherman, in a lengthy, and obviously carefully prepared, address to that body, said that the bill sought

> "only to prevent and control combinations made with a view to prevent competition, or for the restraint of trade, or to increase the profits of the producer at the cost of the consumer. It is the unlawful combination, tested by the rules of common law and human experience, that is aimed at ⊥ by this bill, and not the lawful and useful combination.
>
>   •   •   •   •   •
>
> "I admit that it is difficult to define in legal language the precise line between lawful and unlawful combinations. This must be left for the courts to determine in each particular case. All that we, as lawmakers, can do is to declare general principles, and we can be assured that the courts will apply them so as to carry out the meaning of the law . . . ." 21 Cong. Rec. 2457, 2460.

In "carry[ing] out the meaning of the law" by making its "determin[ations] in each particular case," this Court early concluded that it was Congress' intent that a "rule of reason" be applied in making such case-by-case determinations. *Standard Oil Co.* v. *United States*, 221 U. S. 1, 60 (1911). And that rule of reason was to be applied in light of the Act's policy to protect the "public interests." *United States* v. *American Tobacco Co.*, 221 U. S. 106, 179 (1911). The *per se* rules that have been developed are similarly directed to the protection of the public welfare; they are complementary to, and in no way inconsistent with, the rule of reason. The principal advantages that flow from their use are, first, that enforcement and predictability are enhanced and, second, that unnecessary judicial investigation is avoided in those cases where practices falling within the scope of such rules are found. As the Court explained in *Northern Pacific R. Co.* v. *United States, supra*, at 5,

> "[T]here are certain agreements or practices which because of their pernicious effect on competition and lack of any redeeming virtue are conclusively presumed to be unreasonable and therefore illegal without elaborate inquiry as to the precise harm they have caused or the business excuse for their use."

⊥ In formulating a new *per se* rule today, the Court does not tell us what "pernicious effect on competition" the practices here outlawed are perceived to have; nor does it attempt to show that those practices "lack . . . any redeeming virtue." Rather, it emphasizes only the importance of predictability, asserting that "courts are of limited utility in examining difficult economic problems" and have not yet been left free by Congress to "ramble through the wilds of economic theory in order to maintain a flexible approach."

---

[9] Among the facts found by the District Court are the following: private-label brand merchandising, which is beyond the reach of the small chains acting independently and which by definition depends upon local exclusivity, permits the merchandiser to offer the public "lower consumer prices on products of high quality" and "to bargain more favorably with national brand manufacturers"; such merchandising fosters "the establishment of a broader supply base of manufacturers, thereby decreasing dependence upon a relatively few large national brand manufacturers"; it also enables "[s]maller manufacturers, the most common source of private label products, who are generally unable to develop national brand name recognition for their products, [to] benefit . . . by the assurance of a substantial market for their products . . . ." 319 F. Supp., at 1035.

With all respect, I believe that there are two basic fallacies in the Court's approach here. First, while I would not characterize our role under the Sherman Act as one of "rambl[ing] through the wilds," it is indeed one that requires our "examin[ation of] difficult economic problems." We can undoubtedly ease our task, but we should not abdicate that role by formulation of *per se* rules with no justification other than the enhancement of predictability and the reduction of judicial investigation. Second, from the general proposition that *per se* rules play a necessary role in antitrust law, it does not follow that the particular *per se* rule promulgated today is an appropriate one. Although it might well be desirable in a proper case for this Court to formulate a *per se* rule dealing with horizontal territorial limitations, it would not necessarily be appropriate for such a rule to amount to a blanket prohibition against all such limitations. More specifically, it is far from clear to me why such a rule should cover those division-of-market agreements that involve no price fixing and which are concerned only with trademarked products that are not in a monopoly or near-monopoly position with respect to competing brands. The instant case presents such an agreement; I would not decide it upon the basis of a *per se* rule.[11]

The District Court specifically found that the horizontal restraints involved here tend positively to promote competition in the supermarket field and to produce lower costs for the consumer. The Court seems implicitly to accept this determination, but says that the Sherman Act does not give Topco the authority to determine for itself "whether or not competition with other supermarket chains is more desirable than competition in the sale of Topco-brand products." *Ante*, at 611. But the majority overlooks a further specific determination of the District Court, namely, that the invalidation of the restraints here at issue "would not increase competition in Topco private label brands." 319 F. Supp., at 1043. Indeed, the District Court seemed to believe that it would, on the contrary, lead to the likely demise of those brands in time. And the evidence before the District Court would appear to justify that conclusion.

There is no national demand for Topco brands, nor has there ever been any national advertising of those brands. It would be impracticable for Topco, with its limited financial resources, to convert itself into a national brand distributor in competition with distributors of existing national brands. Furthermore, without the right to grant exclusive licenses, it could not attract and hold new members as replacements for those of its present members who, following the pattern of the past, eventually grow sufficiently in size to be able to leave the cooperative organization and develop their own individual private-label brands. Moreover, Topco's present members, once today's decision has had its full impact over the course of time, will have no more reason to promote Topco products through local advertising and merchandising efforts than they will have such reason to promote any other generally available brands.

The issues presented by the antitrust cases reaching this Court are rarely simple to resolve under the rule of reason; they do indeed frequently require us to make difficult economic determinations. We should not for that reason alone, however, be overly zealous in formulating new *per se* rules, for an excess of zeal in that regard is both contrary to the policy of the Sherman Act and detrimental to the welfare of consumers generally. Indeed, the economic effect of the new rule laid down by the Court today seems clear: unless Congress intervenes, grocery staples marketed under private-label brands with their lower consumer prices will soon be available only to those who patronize the large national chains.

---

[11] The national chains market their own private-label products, and these products are available nowhere else than in the stores of those chains. The stores of any one chain, of course, do not engage in price competition with each other with respect to their chain's private-label brands, and no serious suggestion could be made that the Sherman Act requires otherwise. I fail to see any difference whatsoever in the economic effect of the Topco arrangement for the marketing of Topco-brand products and the methods used by the national chains in marketing their private-label brands. True, the Topco arrangement involves a "combination," while each of the national chains is a single integrated corporation. The controlling consideration, however, should be that in neither case is the policy of the Sherman Act offended, for the practices in both cases work to the benefit, and not to the detriment, of the consuming public.

B THE FAIR TRADE AMENDMENTS

Chapters
2   **Miller-Tydings Resale Price Maintenance Act of 1937**
3   **McGuire Resale Price Maintenance Act Amendment of 1952**
4   **Consumer Goods Pricing Act of 1975 (Fair Trade Repealer)**

2 MILLER-TYDINGS RESALE PRICE MAINTENANCE ACT OF 1937

(REPEALED EFFECTIVE 1976; SEE CHAPTER 4)

461   Introduction
465   Chronological Synopsis
469   Table of Reprinted Documents

ORIGINAL VERSION

471   Miller-Tydings Resale Price Maintenance Act
         August 17, 1937

The Origins

472   Old Dearborn Distributing Co. v. Seagram-Distillers Corp., 299 U.S. 183 (1936)

478   Message from President Franklin D. Roosevelt to the Senate transmitting a report by the Chairman of the FTC on S. 100
         April 24, 1937

House Consideration (H. R. 1611)

480   Report of the House Committee on the Judiciary (with Additional Views)
         H.R. Rep. No. 382, 75th Cong., 1st Sess.
         [to accompany H.R. 1611]
         March 11, 1937

498   Remarks of Rep. John E. Miller, 75th Cong., 1st Sess.
         April 19, 1937

504   Resolution providing for consideration of H.R. 1611
         April 23, 1937

505   Remarks of Rep. Clare E. Hoffman, 75th Cong., 1st Sess.
         April 27, 1937

506   Remarks of Rep. William R. Poage and Rep. Earl C. Michener
         75th Cong., 1st Sess.
         May 4, 1937

Senate Consideration (S. 100; H.R. 7472)

507   Report of the Senate Committee on the Judiciary
         S. Rep. No. 257, 75th Cong., 1st Sess.
         [to accompany S. 100]
         March 29, 1937

509   S. 100 as reported by the Senate Committee on the Judiciary
March 29, 1937

Senate Debate, 75th Cong., 1st Sess.
510   May 3, 1937
510   July 23, 1937

Conference Consideration (H.R. 7472)

527   House Debate, 75th Cong., 1st Sess.
July 26, 1937

527   Report of the Conference Committee
H.R. Rep. No. 1413, 75th Cong., 1st Sess.
[to accompany H.R. 7472]
August 2, 1937

528   House Debate, 75th Cong., 1st Sess.
August 3, 1937

Presidential Comment

538   Statement by President Franklin D. Roosevelt upon signing H.R. 7472
August 18, 1937

THE DECISION

539   Commentary

541   Schwegmann Brothers v. Calvert Distillers Corp., 341 U.S. 384 (1951)

Introduction

MILLER-TYDINGS RESALE PRICE MAINTENANCE ACT OF 1937

In 1937, Congress passed the Miller-Tydings Act,[2.1] granting state fair-trade statutes an exemption from the federal antitrust laws. Although this enabling legislation amended section 1 of the Sherman Act,[2.2] it was enacted as a rider to the District of Columbia Revenue Act of 1937. An examination of the legislative history of the companion bills[2.3] introduced in the 75th Congress by Representative John E. Miller (D., Ark.) and Senator Millard E. Tydings (D., Md.) reveals the reason for this action: the leadership of Congress, acting on instructions from the White House, refused to allow the bills to come to debate.[2.4]

President Roosevelt's opposition to the bills stemmed largely from the concern about rising retail prices in the post-Depression period. Indeed, the report of the Chairman of the Federal Trade Commission to the President on the proposed bills pointed out that under the legislation "[t]here is great probability that manufacturers and dealers may abuse the power to arbitrarily fix resale prices by unduly increasing prices, resulting in bitter resentment on the part of the consuming public, especially in this period of rising prices."[2.5]

[2.1] Act of Aug. 17, 1937, ch. 690, tit. VIII, 50 Stat. 693, *amending* Sherman Act § 1 (15 U.S.C. § 1). These provisions were repealed by the Consumer Goods Pricing Act of 1975, Pub. L. No. 94-145, § 2, 89 Stat. 801, the legislative history of which appears *infra* at chapter 4.

[2.2] Act of July 2, 1890, ch. 647, § 1, 26 Stat. 209, *as amended*, 15 U.S.C. § 1 (Supp. V, 1975), the legislative history of which appears *supra* at chapter 1.

[2.3] H.R. 1611, 75th Cong., 1st Sess. (introduced by Representative Miller on January 5, 1937); S. 100, 75th Cong., 1st Sess. (introduced by Senator Tydings on January 6, 1937).

Senator Tydings had sponsored a similar measure in the previous Congress. S. 3822, 74th Cong., 2d Sess. (1936). Earlier fair-trade legislation included two predecessor Capper-Kelley bills. S. 240, H.R. 11, 71st Cong., 1st Sess. (1929); S. 97, H.R. 11, 72d Cong., 1st Sess. (1931).

[2.4] *See, e.g.*, 81 CONG. REC. 3869 (1937) (remarks of Representative Hoffman), *infra* at 505; *id.* at 4180 (remarks of Representative Michener), *infra* at 506; *id.* at 4083 (remarks of Senator King), *infra* at 510.

[2.5] Letter from W.A. Ayres to President Franklin D. Roosevelt, April 14, 1937, S. DOC. NO. 58, 75th Cong., 1st Sess. 3 (1937), *infra* at 479.

Yet, ironically, it was the disastrous consequences of the Depression, particularly on small businesses, that had led to the enactment of so-called fair-trade acts by many states, which acts in turn were the raison d'être of the Miller-Tydings Act. These state fair-trade acts, passed largely to protect small business concerns from loss-leader tactics often employed by their larger competitors, generally sanctioned agreements between manufacturers of trademarked commodities and distributors or retailers which set forth the minimum or stipulated resale prices of such commodities, provided that such commodities were in "free and open competition" with commodites of the same general class produced by others.

By 1937, some 37 states had fair-trade laws on their books, and bills were pending in an additional half-dozen. Only one state, Vermont, definitely had rejected this type of legislation. Even more important, however, was the fact that on December 7, 1936, the Supreme Court had stamped its constitutional imprimatur on state fair-trade acts, holding that the Illinois fair-trade law, which was applicable to both signers and nonsigners of fair-trade contracts, was valid under the fifth and fourteenth amendments to the Constitution. In that case, *Old Dearborn Distributing Co. v. Seagram-Distillers Corp.*,[2.6] the Court ruled that the establishment by a manufacturer or distributor of stipulated resale prices on trademarked products was a legitimate means of protecting the goodwill associated with such products. Moreover, the Court held that since the retailer was not forced to purchase the products and could in any event resell them at any price if the identifying marks were removed, laws permitting such stipulated prices did not contravene the fifth amendment's proscription against the deprivation of property without due process of law. The "essence of the statutory violation," the Court held, is "in a forbidden use of the trade-mark, brand or name" in disposing of the commodity, "not in the bare distribution of the commodity" itself.[2.7] Similarly, the Court ruled that the fact that state fair-trade laws conferred a privilege on manufacturers of trademarked products to establish stipulated resale prices for such products, which privilege was not available to producers of nonidentified goods, was not an unreasonable legislative classification and hence was not violative of the equal protection clause of the fourteenth amendment.[2.8]

With the state laws thus having passed constitutional muster, proponents of fair-trade legislation had only one remaining objective; namely, to ensure that those laws could be applied in the context of interstate transactions. Simply stated, while the state fair-trade laws afforded ample protection to transactions which were wholly *intrastate* in character, such was not the case where the commodities sought to be fair-traded were produced in one state and transported to another for resale, since the Sherman Act proscribed contracts, combinations, and conspiracies in restraint of trade. Indeed, as early as 1911, in the landmark case of *Dr. Miles Medical Co. v. John D. Park & Sons Co.*,[2.9] the Supreme Court held that contracts by which a manufacturer sought to control the resale prices of his products were invalid restraints of trade under the Sherman Act insofar as they affected interstate commerce. Thus, the stage was set for the proponents of fair trade, led by the National Association of Retail Druggists, to secure from Congress legislation amending the Sherman Act so as to enable the state fair-trade laws to be applicable to goods sold within a fair-trade state but which, prior to their sale, may have been within the flow of interstate commerce.

Extensive hearings on the Miller and Tydings bills were held within the Judiciary Committees of both Houses of Congress in January and March 1937.[2.10] During the hearings, the supporters of the bills stressed the underlying reason for the passage of the various state fair-trade laws, *i.e.*, loss-leader tactics by large stores which had resulted in many small business failures. They emphasized that congressional action was

---

[2.6] 299 U.S. 183, 57 S. Ct. 139, 81 L. Ed. 109 (1936), *infra* at 472.

[2.7] 299 U.S. at 193.

[2.8] *Id.* at 197–98.

[2.9] 220 U.S. 373, 31 S. Ct. 376, 55 L. Ed. 502 (1911).

[2.10] *Hearing on S. 100 Before a Subcomm. of the Senate Comm. on the Judiciary*, 75th Cong., 1st Sess. (1937); *Hearing on H.R. 1611 Before Subcomm. No. 3 of the House Comm. on the Judiciary*, 75th Cong., 1st Sess. (1937).

INTRODUCTION

needed solely for the purpose of enabling state fair-trade laws to be fully effective, which could result only if such laws were permitted to be applicable to all trademarked commodities in free and open competition, regardless of where they may have been produced. In effect, the proponents' position was one of states' rights; namely, that Congress should not frustrate by inaction measures that all but a handful of states had declared to be necessary to protect the citizens within their boundaries.

The response from the opponents of fair trade was swift and emphatic. Led largely by consumer groups, the Mail Order Association of America, and large department stores, the opposition argued that the enactment of this type of enabling legislation would validate under federal law vertical price fixing, long outlawed under the Sherman Act, and would tend to foster vertical monopolies. Moreover, they contended, congressional approval would wholly eliminate competition in the sale of fair-traded products, with the inevitable result that the consumer would be forced to pay higher prices than would normally prevail in a free marketplace. Finally, the opponents stressed that while they did not object to so-called loss-leader legislation, which would prohibit sales below net invoice cost, they were strenuously opposed to laws granting a manufacturer or distributor the right to establish minimum or stipulated resale prices.

In March 1937, the bills were favorably reported out by their respective Judiciary Committees,[2.11] and a resolution providing for the consideration of the Miller bill (H.R. 1611) was reported by the House Rules Committee on April 23.[2.12] The following day, however, President Roosevelt sent a message to the Senate transmitting an adverse report on the measures by the Chairman of the FTC[2.13] and put an end to floor consideration of both bills.[2.14]

Two months later, though, on July 23, 1937, the provisions of the Tydings bill (S. 100) were read on the Senate floor[2.15] in the form of a committee amendment to an appropriations bill for the District of Columbia (H.R. 7472).[2.16] As Senator Tydings explained during the subsequent brief debate: "Because of my inability to get the bill up sooner and the fact that this is the second session of the Congress in which it has appeared on the calendar, I took the liberty of offering it in the committee."[2.17] Despite the opposition of Senator William H. King (D., Utah) to the rider,[2.18] it was adopted, and the entire bill as amended was passed without a record vote.[2.19] Immediately upon passing the bill, the Senate agreed to insist upon its amendments and to ask for a conference, and conferees were appointed.[2.20] The House agreed to the conference request and appointed its conferees three days later.[2.21]

[2.11] H.R. REP. NO. 382, 75th Cong., 1st Sess. (1937), *infra* at 480-98. S. REP. NO. 257, 75th Cong., 1st Sess. (1937), *infra* at 507-08. The Senate report did little more than quote the committee report on the first Tydings bill, S. REP. NO. 2053, 74th Cong., 2d Sess. (1936), *accompanying* S. 3822, 74th Cong., 2d Sess. (1936). *See also* S. 100 as reported by the Senate Committee on the Judiciary, 75th Cong., 1st Sess. (1937), *infra* at 509-10.

[2.12] 81 CONG. REC. 3775 (1937), *infra* at 504.

[2.13] S. DOC. NO. 58, 75th Cong., 1st Sess. (1937), *infra* at 478-79.

[2.14] *See* the remarks of Representative Clare E. Hoffman, 81 CONG. REC. 3869 (April 27, 1937), *infra* at 505; remarks of Representative Earl C. Michener, *id*. at 4180 (May 4, 1937), *infra* at 506; and remarks of Senator William H. King, *id*. at 4083 (May 3, 1937), *infra* at 510.

[2.15] *Id*. at 7486-87, *infra* at 510-11. At the conclusion of the reading, Senator Tydings offered a floor amendment to the committee amendment, inserting a second proviso. *Id*. at 7487, *infra* at 511. Tydings stated that the proviso had "been worked out by certain administration leaders" and himself. *Id*. It was agreed to without a record vote. *Id*. at 7497, *infra* at 525.

[2.16] The committee amendment adding "Title VIII—Amendment to the Antitrust Laws" to H.R. 7472 had been offered by Senator Tydings in the Senate Committee on the District of Columbia and agreed to by a vote of 11 to 1 (negative vote cast by Senator King). *See id*. at 7493, *infra* at 518-19. H.R. 7472 was accompanied by S. REP. NO. 879, 75th Cong., 1st Sess. (1937).

[2.17] 81 CONG. REC. 7495, (1937), *infra* at 522.

[2.18] *Id*. at 7488-94, *infra* at 511-22.

[2.19] *Id*. at 7497, *infra* at 525. The rider became Senate Amendment No. 33.

[2.20] *Id*., *infra* at 526.

[2.21] *Id*. at 7599, *infra* at 527.

Conference consideration was swift, the sentiment in favor of fair trade being overwhelming. Although one of the conferees noted that "there was considerable outspoken talk" about the practice of attaching totally ungermane riders to House bills,[2.22] the conference report itself contained only a few descriptive lines on the rider, along with the recommendation that it be adopted.[2.23] On August 3, the House considered the conference report;[2.24] the Tydings rider generated little comment and apparently no opposition. Following a speech by Congressman Charles F. McLaughlin (D., Neb.) in which he reviewed the House Judiciary Committee's deliberations on the Miller bill,[2.25] the conference report was agreed to.[2.26] The Senate approved the report without debate on August 4.[2.27]

The District of Columbia Revenue Act, title VIII of which contained the Miller-Tydings Act, was sent to the White House on August 6. On August 17, 1937, President Roosevelt signed the measure into law. In so doing, however, he vehemently attacked Congress for attaching to an important piece of tax and revenue legislation a wholly unrelated rider, the provisions of which he was on record as opposing.[2.28]

[2.22] *Id.* at 8138 (remarks of Representative Dirksen), *infra* at 528.

[2.23] H.R. REP. NO. 1413, 75th Cong., 1st Sess. 10 (1937), *infra* at 527-28.

[2.24] 81 CONG. REC. 8134, 8138-43 (1937), *infra* at 528-37.

[2.25] *Id.* at 8140-43, *infra* at 531-37.

[2.26] *Id.* at 8143, *infra* at 537.

[2.27] *Id.* at 8166-68.

[2.28] *Infra* at 538.

Chronological Synopsis

MILLER-TYDINGS RESALE PRICE MAINTENANCE ACT OF 1937

74th Congress, 2d Session

January 27, 1936

S. 3822 was introduced by Sen. Tydings and referred to the Senate Judiciary Committee [80 Cong. Rec. 1007].

May 20, 1936

Senate Judiciary Committee favorably reported S. 3822.
   [Senate Report No. 2053, reprinted in Senate Report No. 257, at 1-2] 507

June 1, 1936

S. 3822 was passed by the Senate [80 Cong. Rec. 8433].

June 3, 1936

S. 3822 referred to the House Judiciary Committee.

December 7, 1936

Supreme Court decided *Old Dearborn Distributing Co. v. Seagram-Distillers Corp.*, 299 U.S. 183 472

75th Congress, 1st Session

January 5, 1937

H. R. 1611 was introduced by Rep. Miller and referred to the House Judiciary Committee [81 Cong. Rec. 34.]
   [Comparative print in House Report No. 382, at 4] 482

January 6, 1937

S. 100 was introduced by Sen. Tydings and referred to the Senate Judiciary Committee [81 Cong. Rec. 66].

January 27, 29, 1937

Hearings on H.R. 1611 before Subcommittee No. 3 of the House Judiciary Committee.

March 4, 1937

Hearings on S. 100 before a subcommittee of the Senate Judiciary Committee.

March 11, 1937

H R. 1611 was reported favorably, with an amendment in the nature of a substitute, by the House Judiciary Committee.
   [House Report No. 382] 480

March 29, 1937

S. 100 was reported favorably, with amendments, by the Senate Judiciary Committee.
[Senate Report No. 257] 507

April 7, 12, 1937

S. 100 passed over in the Senate [81 Cong. Rec. 3221, 3370].

April 19, 1937

Remarks of Rep. Miller on the New Deal and fair trade legislation [81 Cong. Rec. A873-76] 498

April 22, 1937

S. 100 passed over in the Senate [81 Cong. Rec. 3717].

April 23, 1937

H.R. Res. 191, providing for the consideration of H.R. 1611, was reported (H.R. Rep. No. 683) by the House Rules Committee [81 Cong. Rec. 3775] 504

April 24, 1937

Message from President Roosevelt to the Senate opposing enactment of fair trade legislation and transmitting an unfavorable report by the Chairman of the FTC on S. 100.
[Senate Document No. 58] 478

April 27, 1937

S. 100 passed over in the Senate [81 Cong. Rec. 3850].

Remarks of Rep. Hoffman protesting President Roosevelt's intervention to block House consideration of H.R. 1611 [81 Cong. Rec. 3869] 505

May 3, 1937

S. 100 passed over in the Senate; remarks of Sen. King [81 Cong. Rec. 4083-84] 510

May 4, 1937

Remarks of Rep. Poage and Rep. Michener in support of fair trade legislation [81 Cong. Rec. 4180] 506

May 6, 10, 17, 24; June 1, 14, 28, 1937

S. 100 passed over in the Senate [81 Cong. Rec. 4232, 4273, 4625, 4956, 5133, 5648, 6350].

July 7, 1937

Tydings bill was reported (S. Rep. No. 879) by the Senate Committee on the District of Columbia in the form of a rider to H.R. 7472 (District of Columbia revenue bill).

July 8, 1937

Minority report of Sen. King on H.R. 7472, opposing the fair trade rider.

July 23, 1937

Fair trade rider considered by the Senate [81 Cong. Rec. 7486-97] 510

    Committee amendment adding a new title (fair trade rider) to H.R. 7472 read for debate [81 Cong. Rec. 7486-87] 510

        Amendment to the rider, to insert a second proviso maintaining the unlawfulness of horizontal arrangements to maintain minimum resale prices, was offered by Sen. Tydings [81 Cong. Rec. 7487] and agreed to [81 Cong. Rec. 7497] 511

        Fair trade rider as amended was adopted [81 Cong. Rec. 7497] 525

Senate passed H.R. 7472, insisted upon its amendments, requested a conference with the House, and appointed conferees [81 Cong. Rec. 7497] 525

July 26, 1937

House disagreed to the Senate amendment to H.R. 7472, agreed to a conference, and appointed conferees [81 Cong. Rec. 7599] 527

August 2, 1937

Conference report on H.R. 7472, recommending that the House agree to the fair trade rider (Senate amendment No. 33), was submitted in the House.
    [House Report No. 1413] 527

August 3, 1937

House agreed to the conference report on H.R. 7472 after debating the fair trade rider [81 Cong. Rec. 8134, 8138-43] 528

August 4, 1937

Senate agreed to the conference report on H.R. 7472 without debate [81 Cong. Rec. 8166-68].

August 6, 1937

Consideration of S. 100 postponed indefinitely in the Senate [81 Cong. Rec. 8374].

August 17, 1937

H.R. 7472, containing the Miller-Tydings Resale Price Maintenance Act (title VIII), was signed into law by President Roosevelt.
    [*Statutes at Large* print] 471
    [Statement by the President, issued Aug. 18] 538

Table of Reprinted Documents

MILLER-TYDINGS RESALE PRICE MAINTENANCE ACT OF 1937

Statutory Material

Miller-Tydings Resale Price Maintenance Act, ch. 690, tit. VIII, 50 Stat. 693 (Aug. 17, 1937) 471

Legislative Materials

Bill

S. 100 as reported by Senate Judiciary Committee, 75th Cong., 1st Sess. (March 29, 1937) 509

Reports and Document

H.R. Rep. No. 382, 75th Cong., 1st Sess. (March 11, 1937) 480

S. Rep. No. 257, 75th Cong., 1st Sess. (March 29, 1937) 507

S. Doc. No. 58, 75th Cong., 1st Sess. (April 24, 1937) 478

H. R. Rep. No. 1413, 75th Cong., 1st Sess. (Aug. 2, 1937) 527

Congressional Record

Volume 81 – 75th Congress, 1st Session

Date	Pages	
April 19, 1937	A873-76	498
April 23, 1937	3775	504
April 27, 1937	3869	505
May 3, 1937	4083	510
May 4, 1937	4180	506
July 23, 1937	7486-97	510
July 26, 1937	7599	527
Aug. 3, 1937	8134, 8138-43	528

Presidential Documents

President's message to the Senate transmitting FTC report on S. 100 (Franklin D. Roosevelt), S. Doc. No. 58, 75th Cong., 1st Sess. (April 24, 1937) 478

Statement by President Franklin D. Roosevelt upon signing H.R. 7472 (Aug. 18, 1937) 538

Case Reports

Old Dearborn Disributing Co. v. Seagram-Distillers Corp., 299 U.S. 183, 57 S. Ct. 139, 81 L. Ed. 109 (1936) 472

Schwegmann Brothers v. Calvert Distillers Corp., 341 U.S. 384, 71 S. Ct. 745, 95 L. Ed. 1035 (1951) 541

Original Version

MILLER-TYDINGS RESALE PRICE MAINTENANCE ACT
August 17, 1937

Ch. 690, Tit. VIII, 50 Stat. 693

[ED. NOTE: This statute was repealed by the Consumer Goods Pricing Act of 1975, the legislative history of which appears *infra* at chapter 4.]

An Act To provide additional revenue for the District of Columbia, and for other purposes.

Be it enacted by the Senate and House of Representatives of the United States of America in Congress assembled, . . .

TITLE VIII—AMENDMENT TO THE ANTITRUST LAWS

Section 1 of the act entitled "An act to protect trade and commerce against unlawful restraints and monopolies", approved July 2, 1890, is amended to read as follows:

"SECTION 1. Every contract, combination in the form of trust or otherwise, or conspiracy, in restraint of trade or commerce among the several States, or with foreign nations, is hereby declared to be illegal: *Provided*, That nothing herein contained shall render illegal, contracts or agreements prescribing minimum prices for the resale of a commodity which bears, or the label or container of which bears, the trade mark, brand, or name of the producer or distributor of such commodity and which is in free and open competition with commodities of the same general class produced or distributed by others, when contracts or agreements of that description are lawful as applied to intrastate transactions, under any statute, law, or public policy now or hereafter in effect in any State, Territory, or the District of Columbia in which such resale is to be made, or to which the commodity is to be transported for such resale, and the making of such contracts or agreements shall not be an unfair method of competition under section 5, as amended and supplemented, of the act entitled 'An act to create a Federal Trade Commission, to define its powers and duties, and for other purposes', approved September 26, 1914: *Provided further*, That the preceding proviso shall not make lawful any contract or agreement, providing for the establishment or maintenance of minimum resale prices on any commodity herein involved, between manufacturers, or between producers, or between wholesalers, or between brokers, or between factors, or between retailers, or between persons, firms, or corporations in competition with each other. Every person who shall make any contract or engage in any combination or conspiracy hereby declared to be illegal shall be deemed guilty of a misdemeanor, and, on conviction thereof, shall be punished by fine not exceeding $5,000, or by imprisonment not exceeding one year, or by both said punishments, in the discretion of the court."

THE ORIGINS

OLD DEARBORN DISTRIBUTING CO.
v.
SEAGRAM-DISTILLERS CORP.

299 U.S. 183, 57 S. Ct. 139, 81 L. Ed. 109 (1936)

⊥ MR. JUSTICE SUTHERLAND delivered the opinion of the Court.

These appeals bring here for decision the question of the constitutional validity of §§ 1 and 2 of the Fair Trade Act of Illinois (Smith-Hurd Rev. Stat., 1935, c. 121-1/2, § 188 *et seq.*; Illinois State Bar Stat., 1935, c. 140, § 8 *et seq.*), providing as follows:

"Section 1. No contract relating to the sale or resale of a commodity which bears, or the label or content of which bears, the trade mark, brand or name of the producer or owner of such commodity and which is in fair and open competition with commodities of the same general class produced by others shall be deemed in violation of any law of the State of Illinois by reason of any of the following provisions which may be contained in such contract:

"(1) That the buyer will not resell such commodity except at the price stipulated by the vendor.

"(2) That the producer or vendee of a commodity require upon the sale of such commodity to another, that such purchaser agree that he will not, in turn, resell except at the price stipulated by such producer or vendee.

⊥ "Such provisions in any contract shall be deemed to contain or imply conditions that such commodity may be resold without reference to such agreement in the following cases:

"(1) In closing out the owner's stock for the purpose of discontinuing delivery of any such commodity: provided, however, that such stock is first offered to the manufacturer of such stock at the original invoice price, at least ten (10) days before such stock shall be offered for sale to the public.

"(2) When the goods are damaged or deteriorated in quality, and notice is given to the public thereof.

"(3) By any officer acting under the orders of any court.

"Section 2. Wilfully and knowingly advertising, offering for sale or selling any commodity at less than the price stipulated in any contract entered into pursuant to the provisions of section 1 of this Act, whether the person so advertising, offering for sale or selling is or is not a party to such contract, is unfair competition and is actionable at the suit of any person damaged thereby."

Section 3 of the act provides that it shall not apply to contracts or agreements between producers or between wholesalers or between retailers as to sale or resale prices.

No. 226 is a suit brought by appellee against appellant to enjoin the latter from wilfully and knowingly advertising, offering for sale or selling, certain brands of whisky at less than prices stipulated by appellee in accordance with contracts, made in pursuance of the Fair Trade Act, between appellee and distributors or retailers of such whisky. The facts set forth by the court below follow.

Appellee is a dealer in alcoholic beverages at wholesale. It buys the products here in question from the producers. The whiskies bear labels and trade-marks, and are in fair and open competition with commodities of the same general class produced by others. Appellant is a corporation operating four retail liquor stores in Chicago, and selling at both wholesale and retail. Appellee's sales in Chicago are made to wholesale distributors. It has not sold any of the whiskies in controversy to appellant, but has sold other liquors. Contracts in pursuance of the Fair Trade Act have been executed between appellee and certain distributors, and numerous Illinois retailers. Appellee does not sell directly to any retailer. Appellant sold the products in question at cut prices—that is to say, at prices below those stipulated—and continued to do so after appellee's demand that it cease such practice. The result of such price cutting was a diminution of sales during the price-cutting period suffered by appellee and retailers other than appellant. Some dealers ceased to display the products, and notified appellee that they could not compete with appellant and would discontinue handling the products unless the price cutting was stopped. Appellant was also a party to breaches of other fair-trade contracts between appellee and certain distributors, and continued the price cutting throughout the trial of the case in the Illinois state court of first instance.

The record shows that one of the retailer's contracts drawn in pursuance of the act was signed by appellant's secretary and treasurer prior to the commission of the acts complained of. This contract, among other things provided that the product in question should not be sold, advertised or offered for sale in Illinois below the prices to be stipulated by appellee. The contract was assailed by appellant below as ineffective, and for present purposes we accept that view. It is plain enough, however, that appellant had knowledge of the original contractual restrictions and that they constituted conditions upon which sales thereafter were to be made.

No. 372 is a suit of the same character as No. 226, seeking the same relief by injunction. The facts set forth in the complaint were admitted by a motion to dismiss. These facts, fully stated in the opinion of the court below, *infra*, we find it unnecessary to repeat. It is enough to say that while they differ in detail from those appearing in No. 226, they are sufficiently the same in substance as to be controlled by the same principles of law.

Both appellants attack the validity of the act upon the ground that it denies due process of law and the equal protection of the laws in violation of the Fourteenth Amendment in the particulars which hereafter appear. The state courts of first instance in which the suits were brought sustained the validity of the act and entered decrees as prayed for in the bills of complaint. These decrees were affirmed upon appeal by the court below. 363 Ill. 559, 2 N. E. (2d) 929; 363 Ill. 611, 2 N. E. (2d) 940.

The Illinois statute constitutes a legislative recognition of a rule which had been accepted by many of the state courts as valid at common law. This rule was based upon the distinction found to exist between articles of trade put out by the manufacturer or producer under, and identified by, patent, copyright, trade-mark, brand, or similar device, and articles of like character put out by others and not so identified. The same rule was followed for a time by some of the lower federal courts; but their decisions were upset by this court in a series of cases, of which *Dr. Miles Medical Co.* v. *Park & Sons Co.*, 220 U. S. 373 is an example. In that case this court held that a system of contracts between manufacturers and wholesale and retail merchants which sought to control the prices for sales by all such dealers by fixing the amount which the consumer should pay, amounted to an unlawful restraint of trade, invalid at common law and, so far as interstate commerce was affected, invalid under the Sherman Anti-trust Act of July 2, 1890; and it was held that the rule applied to such agreements notwithstanding the fact that they related to proprietary medicines made under a secret process and identified by distinctive packages, labels and trade-marks. The argument that since the manufacturer might make and sell or not as he chose, he could lawfully condition the price at which subsequent sales could be made by the purchaser, was rejected.

"If there be an advantage to a manufacturer in the maintenance of fixed retail prices," this court said at pages 407–409, "the question remains whether it is one which he is entitled to secure by agreements restricting the freedom of trade on the part of dealers who own what they sell. As to this, the complainant can fare no better with its plan of identical contracts than could the dealers themselves if they formed a combination and endeavored to establish the same restrictions, and thus to achieve the same result, by agreement with each other. If the immediate advantage they would thus obtain would not be sufficient to sustain such a direct agreement, the asserted ulterior benefit to the complainant cannot be regarded as sufficient to support its system. . . . The complainant's plan falls within the principle which condemns contracts of this class. It, in effect, creates a combination for the prohibited purposes. No distinction can properly be made by reason of the particular character of the commodity in question. It is not entitled to special privilege or immunity. It is an article of commerce and the rules concerning the freedom of trade must be held to apply to it. . . . The complainant having sold its product at prices satisfactory to itself, the public is entitled to whatever advantage may be derived from competition in the subsequent traffic."

It is unnecessary to review the contrary state decisions. It is enough, for present purposes, to say that, generally speaking, they sustained contracts standardizing the price at which "identified" commodities subsequently might be sold, where the price standardization is primarily effected to protect the good will created or enlarged by the identifying mark or brand. Where a manufacturer puts out an article of general production identified by a special trade-mark or brand, the result of an agreement fixing the subsequent sales price affects competition between the identified articles alone, leaving competition between articles so identified by a given manufacturer and all other articles of like kind to have full play. In other words, such restraint upon competition as there may be is strictly limited to that portion of the entire product put out and plainly identified by a particular manufacturer or producer.

The ground upon which the opposing view of this court proceeds is that such an agreement, nevertheless, constitutes an unlawful restraint of trade at common law and, in respect of interstate commerce, a violation of the Sherman Anti-trust Act. A careful reading of the decisions discloses no other ground.

Following these decisions, bills were introduced in Congress from time to time authorizing standardization-of-price agreements in respect of identified goods, upon which extensive hearings were held by the appropriate Congressional committees. These bills are in all essential respects like the Illinois act. The hearings disclose exhaustive legal briefs, and testimony and arguments for and against the economic value of the proposed laws. See, for example, Hearings before the Committee on Interstate and Foreign Commerce of the House of Representatives, on H. R. 13305 (63d Cong., 2d and 3d Sess.); H. R. 13568 (64th Cong., 1st and 2d Sess.); compare Report of the Federal Trade Commission on Resale Price Maintenance, 70th Cong., 2d Sess., H. Doc. No. 546.

It is not without significance that while the proposed legislation was vigorously assailed in other respects, we do not find that any constitutional objection was urged. And the decisions of this court, far from suggesting any constitutional infirmity in such proposed legislation, contain implications to the contrary. In the *Dr. Miles Medical Co.* case (p. 405), the court said, "Nor can the manufacturer by rule and notice, *in the absence of contract or statutory* right, even though the restriction be known to purchasers, fix prices for future sales." (Italics supplied.) In *Boston Store* v. *American Graphophone Co.*, 246 U. S. 8, where this court struck down a stipulation that patented articles should not be resold at prices other than those fixed presently and from time to time by the patent owner, it was suggested (p. 26) that if this view resulted in damage to the holders of patent rights or the law afforded insufficient protection to the inventor, the remedy lay within the scope of legislative (that is to say, Congressional) action. And in a concurring opinion (p. 28), it was said, "If the rule so declared is believed to be harmful in its operation, the remedy may be found, as it has been sought, through application to the Congress . . ." The words "as it has been sought" quite evidently referred to the bills of which we have just spoken, since they had theretofore been introduced and made the subject of the hearings. See, also *Bauer & Cie* v. *O'Donnell*, 229 U. S. 1, 12. While these observations of the court cannot, of course, be regarded as decisive of the question, they plainly imply that the court at the time foresaw no valid constitutional objection to such legislation, for it cannot be supposed that the court would suggest a legislative remedy the validity of which might seem open to doubt.

In the light of the foregoing brief résumé of the question with respect to the standardization of selling prices of identified goods in the absence of statutory authority, we proceed to a consideration of the specific objections to the constitutionality of the act here under review.

First. In respect of the due process of law clause, it is contended that the statute is a price-fixing law, which has the effect of denying to the owner of property the right to determine for himself the price at which he will sell. Appellants invoke the well-settled general principle that the right of the owner of property to fix the price at which he will sell it is an inherent attribute of the property itself, and as such is within the protection of the Fifth and Fourteenth Amendments. *Tyson & Brother* v. *Banton,* 273 U. S. 418, 429; *Wolff Co.* v. *Industrial Court,* 262 U. S. 522, 537; *Ribnik* v. *McBride,* 227 U. S. 350; *Williams* v. *Standard Oil Co.,* 278 U. S. 235; *New State Ice Co.* v. *Liebmann,* 285 U. S. 262. These cases hold that, with certain exceptions, which need not now be set forth, this right of the owner cannot be denied by legislative enactment fixing prices and compelling such owner to adhere to them. But the decisions referred to deal only with legislative price fixing. They constitute no authority for holding that prices in respect of "identified" goods may not be fixed under legislative leave by contract between the parties. The Illinois Fair Trade Act does not infringe the doctrine of these cases.

Section 1 affirms the validity of contracts of sale or resale of commodities identified by the trade-mark, brand or name of the producer or owner, which are in fair and open competition with commodities of the same general class produced by others, notwithstanding that such contracts stipulate (1) that the buyer will not resell except at the price stipulated by the vendor; and (2) that the producer or vendee of such a commodity shall require, upon the sale to another, that he agree in turn not to resell except at the price stipulated by such producer or vendee. It is clear that this section does not attempt to fix prices, nor does it delegate such power to private persons. It *permits* the designated private persons to contract with respect thereto. It contains no element of compulsion but simply legalizes their acts, leaving them free to enter into the authorized contract or not as they may see fit. Thus far, the act plainly is not open to objection; and none seems to be made.

The challenge is directed against § 2, which provides that wilfully and knowingly advertising, offering for sale or selling any commodity at less than the price stipulated in any contract made under § 1, whether the person doing so is or is not a party to the contract, shall constitute unfair competition, giving rise to a right of action in favor of anyone damaged thereby.

It is first to be observed that § 2 reaches not the *mere* advertising, offering for sale or selling at less than the stipulated price, but the doing of any of these things *wilfully* and *knowingly.* We are not called upon to determine the case of one who has made his purchase in ignorance of the contractual restriction upon the selling price, but of a purchaser who has had definite information respecting such contractual restriction and who, with such knowledge, nevertheless proceeds wilfully to resell in disregard of it.

In the second place, § 2 does not deal with the restriction upon the sale of the commodity *qua* commodity, but with that restriction because the commodity is identified by the trade-mark, brand or name of the producer or owner. The essence of the statutory violation then consists not in the bare disposition of the commodity, but in a forbidden use of the trade-mark, brand or name in accomplishing such disposition. The primary aim of the law is to protect the property—namely, the good will—of the producer, which he still owns. The price restriction is adopted as an appropriate means to that perfectly legitimate end, and not as an end in itself.

Appellants here acquired the commodity in question with full knowledge of the then-existing restriction in respect of price which the producer and wholesale dealer had imposed, and, of course, with presumptive if not actual knowledge of the law which authorized the restriction. Appellants were not obliged to buy; and their voluntary acquisition of the property with such knowledge carried with it, upon every principle of fair dealing, assent to the protective restriction, with consequent liability under § 2 of the law by which such acquisition was conditioned. Cf. *Provident Institution* v. *Jersey City,* 113 U. S. 506, 514–515; *Vreeland* v. *O'Neil,* 36 N. J. Eq. 399, 402; same case on appeal, 37 N. J. Eq. 574, 577.

We find nothing in this situation to justify the contention that there is an unlawful delegation of power to private persons to control the disposition of the property of others, such as was condemned in *Eubank* v. *Richmond,* 226 U. S. 137, 143; *Seattle Trust Co.* v. *Roberge,* 278 U. S. 116, 121–122; and *Carter* v. *Carter Coal Co.,* 298 U. S. 238, 311. In those cases the property affected had been acquired without any preëxisting restriction in respect of its use or disposition. The imposition of the restriction *in invitum* was authorized after complete and unrestricted ownership had vested in the persons affected. Here, the restriction, already imposed with the knowledge of appellants, ran with the acquisition and conditioned it.

Nor is § 2 so arbitrary, unfair or wanting in reason as to result in a denial of due process. We are here dealing not with a commodity alone, but with a commodity plus the brand or trade-mark which it bears as evidence of its origin and of the quality of the commodity for which the brand or trade-mark stands. Appellants own the commodity; they do not own the mark or the good will that the mark symbolizes. And good will is property in a very real sense, injury to which, like injury to any other species of property, is a proper subject for legislation. Good will is a valuable contributing aid to business—sometimes the most valuable contributing asset of the producer or distributor of commodities. And distinctive trade-marks, labels and brands, are legitimate aids to the creation or enlargement of such good will. It is well settled that the proprietor of the good will "is entitled to protection as against one who attempts to deprive him ⊥ of the benefits resulting from the same, by using his labels and trade-mark without his consent and authority." *McLean* v. *Fleming,* 96 U. S. 245, 252. "Courts afford redress or relief upon the ground that a party has a valuable interest in the good-will of his trade or business, and in the trade-marks adopted to maintain and extend it." *Hanover Milling Co.* v. *Metcalf,* 240 U. S. 403, 412. The ownership of the good will, we repeat, remains unchanged, notwithstanding the commodity has been parted with. Section 2 of the act does not prevent a purchaser of the commodity bearing the mark from selling the commodity alone at any price he pleases. It interferes only when he sells with the aid of the good will of the vendor; and it interferes then only to protect that good will against injury. It proceeds upon the theory that the sale of identified goods at less than the price fixed by the owner of the mark or brand is an assault upon the good will, and constitutes what the statute denominates "unfair competition." See *Liberty Warehouse Co.* v. *Burley Tobacco Growers' Assn.,* 276 U. S. 71, 91–92, 96–97. There is nothing in the act to preclude the purchaser from removing the mark or brand from the commodity—thus separating the physical property, which he owns, from the good will, which is the property of another—and then selling the commodity at his own price, provided he can do so without utilizing the good will of the latter as an aid to that end.

There is a great body of fact and opinion tending to show that price cutting by retail dealers is not only injurious to the good will and business of the producer and distributor of identified goods, but injurious to the general public as well. The evidence to that effect is voluminous; but it would serve no useful purpose to review the evidence or to enlarge further upon the subject. True, there is evidence, opinion and argument to the contrary; but it does not concern us to determine where the ⊥ weight lies. We need say no more than that the question may be regarded as fairly open to differences of opinion. The legislation here in question proceeds upon the former and not the latter view; and the legislative determination in that respect, in the circumstances here disclosed, is conclusive so far as this court is concerned. Where the question of what the facts establish is a fairly-debatable one, we accept and carry into effect the opinion of the legislature. *Radice* v. *New York,* 264 U. S. 292, 294; *Zahn* v. *Board of Public Works,* 274 U. S. 325, 328, and cases cited.

Certain terms contained in the act are said to be fatally vague and indefinite, and therefore to deny due process of law under our decisions in *Connally* v. *General Construction Co.,* 269 U. S. 385, 390 *et seq.*, and other cases. The contention is directed in the main against the phrase in § 1 of the act, "fair and open competition," and "any commodity" and "any contract entered into pursuant to the provisions of section 1" contained in § 2. The point is shown to be lacking in substance by the reasoning in the *Connally* case at pp. 391–392 and the cases there cited. See particularly *Hygrade Provision Co.* v. *Sherman,* 266 U. S. 497, 501–503; *United States* v. *Cohen Grocery Co.,* 255 U. S. 81, 92, where it is said "that, for reasons found to result either from the text of the statutes involved or the subjects with which they dealt, a standard of some sort was afforded." Certainly, the phrase "fair and open competition" is as definite as the phrase contained in § 5 of the Federal Trade Commission Act, "unfair *methods* of competition," which this court has never regarded as being fatally uncertain. *Federal Trade Comm'n* v. *Gratz,* 253 U. S. 421, 427; *Federal Trade Comm'n* v. *Beech-Nut Co.,* 257 U. S. 441, 453; *Federal Trade Comm'n* v. *Raladam Co.,* 283 U. S. 643, 648. We think the phrases complained of are sufficiently definite, considering the whole statute; and that no one need be misled as to their meaning, or need suffer by reason of any supposed uncertainty. Cf. *Miller* v. *Schoene,* 276 U. S. 272, 281; *Standard Oil Co.* v. *United States,* 221 U. S. 1, 69.

Second. The contention that § 2 of the act denies the equal protection of the laws in violation of the Fourteenth Amendment proceeds upon the view that it confers a privilege upon the producers and owners of goods identified by trade-mark, brand or name, which it denies in the case of unidentified goods. As this court many times has said, the equal-protection clause does not preclude the states from resorting to classification for the purposes of legislation. It only requires that the classification "must be reasonable, not arbitrary, and must rest upon some ground of difference having a fair and substantial relation to the object of the legislation, so that all persons similarly circumstanced shall be treated alike." *Colgate* v. *Harvey,* 296 U. S. 404, 422, 423, and cases cited.

Clearly, the challenged section of the Illinois act satisfies this test. Enough appears already in this opinion to show the essential difference between trade-marked goods and others not so identified. The entire struggle to bring about legislation such as the Illinois act embodies has been based upon this essential difference. In *Radice* v. *New York,* 264 U. S. 292, 296–297, we sustained a statute prohibiting night employment of women in restaurants in large cities, against the claim that it denied equal protection of the laws in that it did not apply to small cities, or to women employed as singers and performers, or to attendants in ladies' cloak rooms and parlors, or employees in hotel dining rooms and kitchens or in lunch rooms and restaurants conducted by employers for the benefit of their employees. Former decisions of the court were cited sustaining classifications based upon differences between fire insurance and other kinds of insurance; between railroads and other corporations; between barber-shop employment and other kinds of labor; between "immigrant agents" engaged in hiring laborers to be employed beyond the limits of a state and persons engaged in the business of hiring for labor within the state; between sugar refiners who produce the sugar and those who purchase it. Other illustrations of a similar character might be cited.

But it is unnecessary to pursue the subject further; for, since the sole purpose of the present law is to afford a legitimate remedy for an injury to the good will which results from the use of trade-marks, brands or names, it is obvious that its provisions would be wholly inapplicable to goods which are unmarked.

Decrees affirmed.

MR. JUSTICE STONE took no part in the consideration or decision of these cases.

MESSAGE FROM PRESIDENT FRANKLIN D. ROOSEVELT TO THE SENATE TRANSMITTING A REPORT BY THE CHAIRMAN OF THE FTC ON S. 100
April 24, 1937

S. Doc. No. 58, 75th Cong., 1st Sess. 1 (1937)

The White House,
Washington, April 24, 1937.

The PRESIDENT OF THE SENATE.

SIR: My attention was called to S. 100, which would render legal certain contracts for the maintenance of resale prices now illegal under Federal law. I requested the Chairman of the Federal Trade Commission to give me a recommendation on this bill, and I attach his reply on behalf of the Commission.

The present hazard of undue advances in prices, with a resultant rise in the cost of living, makes it most untimely to legalize any competitive or marketing practice calculated to facilitate increases in the cost of numerous and important articles which American householders, and consumers generally, buy. You will note that the Federal Trade Commission has made no study of the effect of resale price maintenance on consumers since 1929, but the Commission does mention a reputable body of informed opinion to the effect that such control of resale prices would be harmful to the consuming public. Indeed, the Commission says: "There is great probability that manufacturers and dealers may abuse the power to arbitrarily fix resale prices by unduly increasing prices, resulting in bitter resentment on ⊥ the part of the consuming public, especially in this period of rising prices."

Since we seem to be in a period of rising retail prices, this bill should not, in my judgment, receive the consideration of the Congress until the whole matter can be more fully explored. Conceivably, the Congress might approve having the Commission bring down to date the study which it made eight years ago by examining the economic effects of resale price maintenance under the novel and rapidly changing conditions now attending business in this country.

Faithfully yours,

Franklin D. Roosevelt.

Federal Trade Commission,
April 14, 1937.

The President,
The White House, Washington, D. C.

DEAR MR. PRESIDENT: Receipt is hereby acknowledged of your memorandum of April 7, 1937, transmitting Secretary Morgenthau's letter of April 6, 1937, and requesting a recommendation on the Tydings-Miller bill. The Commission has not heretofore expressed an opinion as to the merits of this bill for the reason that it deemed it to be a matter of legislative policy for determination by yourself and the Congress.

The Tydings-Miller bill would amend the antitrust laws so as to legalize contracts and agreements fixing minimum resale prices for goods sold in interstate commerce and resold within the jurisdiction of any State where such contracts or agreements as to intrastate commerce have been legalized. A number of States now have such statutes.

Many of these State laws and the Tydings-Miller bill are directly and irreconcilably in conflict with the present Federal law on resale price maintenance. Public policy since the passage of the Sherman Antitrust Act in 1890 has been opposed to resale price maintenance. Numerous court decrees have been entered under the Sherman Act and numerous orders to cease and desist have been issued by this

Commission and affirmed by the courts in conformity with the public policy expressed in the Sherman Act and in the Federal Trade Commission Act. Enactment of the Tydings-Miller bill would in its practical effect void such decrees and orders and constitute a reversal of what has been public policy for many years.

Since State laws, legalizing resale price maintenance, differ in the various States, and since, under the proposed Federal legislation, Federal exemption from the antitrust laws would be conditioned upon the legality of similar contracts in intrastate transactions, the Tydings-Miller bill would modify the antitrust laws in differing degrees in different States. Thus, not only would it leave the Federal antitrust laws in full force and effect as to those States which do not legalize resale price maintenance, but there would be divergent policies as to those States which legalize resale price maintenance, because of the differing terms of the different statutes in the respective States. Thus, the Federal Government would be under the necessity of attempting to enforce divergent regulatory policies toward shipments made by the same manufacturer to dealers located in different States, because of the differences in the respective State statutes.

A peculiar feature of many of the State laws which would, under a recent decision of the Supreme Court, speaking through Mr. Justice Sutherland (57 S. Ct. 147), thus be made binding upon interstate commerce is that they require wholesalers and retailers to conform to the provisions of private resale price maintenance contracts to which they are not parties. Thus, a private contract, the provisions of which are determined without public hearing and apart from any public supervision as to reasonableness, is made binding upon all dealers and the consuming public.

With respect to the economic phase of this matter, the Commission has not made a recent study of resale price maintenance. However, in 1929, the Commission did undertake such a study, reporting to the Congress thereon in 1931 (H. R. 546, 70th Cong., 2d sess.). In that report the Commission said:

"The position taken by both proponents and opponents of resale price maintenance are [sic] based on the belief that such maintenance of prices will limit retail competition. * * * The real crux of the question, therefore, is whether injury done to the consumers' interests through the elimination of dealer competition with respect to price-maintained articles would be greater than the damage now alleged to be done to the interests of manufacturers and distributors of trade-marked, nationally advertised brands when they are used as leaders. Neither injury is capable of exact measurement, but, in the opinion of the Commission, the potential damage to consumers through price fixing would be much greater than any existing damage to producers through this form of price cutting."

The general opposition of economists and consumers to this type of legislation is noteworthy. A questionnaire sent to members of the American Economic Association some years ago, by Carroll W. Doten, professor at the Massachusetts Institute of Technology resulted in a vote of 401 to 87 that the manufacturer should not have the legal right to control the retail prices of his products.

There is great probability that manufacturers and dealers may abuse the power to arbitrarily fix resale prices by unduly increasing prices, resulting in bitter resentment on the part of the consuming public, especially in this period of rising prices.

Replying to your inquiry as to the five complaints issued against certain distillers by this Commission, referred to by Secretary Morgenthau, there are enclosed herewith, for your information, copies of those complaints.* In substance, these dealers are charged with maintaining uniform minimum resale prices in interstate commerce and with enforcing agreements with respect thereto by unlawful methods, such as the use of blacklists, boycott, threats of boycott, and other coercive methods incidental to the enforcement of their resale price policies.

With great respect, I am,
    Very truly yours,

W. A. Ayres, Chairman.

---

* Not reprinted herein.

HOUSE CONSIDERATION (H.R. 1611)

REPORT OF THE HOUSE COMMITTEE ON THE JUDICIARY (WITH ADDITIONAL VIEWS)
H.R. Rep. No. 382
75th Cong., 1st Sess.
March 11, 1937

Mr. MILLER, from the Committee on the Judiciary, submitted the following

REPORT

[To accompany H. R. 1611]

The Committee on the Judiciary, to whom was referred the bill (H. R. 1611) to amend the act entitled "An act to protect trade and commerce against unlawful restraints and monopolies", approved July 2, 1890, after consideration, report the same favorably to the House with an amendment with the recommendation that as amended the bill do pass.

The committee amendment is as follows: Strike out all after the enacting clause and insert in lieu thereof the following:

That section 1 of the Act entitled "An Act to protect trade and commerce against unlawful restraints and monopolies", approved July 2, 1890 (U. S. Code, title 15, sec. 1), be amended to read as follows:

"SECTION 1. Every contract, combination in the form of trust or otherwise, or conspiracy in restraint of trade or commerce among the several States, or with foreign nations, is hereby declared to be illegal. Every person who shall make any such contract or engage in any such combination or conspiracy, shall be deemed guilty of a misdemeanor, and, on conviction thereof, shall be punished by fine not exceeding $5,000, or by imprisonment not exceeding one year, or by both said punishments, in the discretion of the court. Nothing herein contained shall render illegal, contracts or agreements prescribing minimum prices or other conditions for the resale of a commodity which bears, or the label or container of which bears, the trade mark, brand, or name of the producer or distributor of such commodity and which is in free and open competition with commodities of the same general class produced or distributed by others, when such contracts or agreements are lawful as applied to intrastate transactions, under any statute, law, or public policy now or hereafter in effect in any State, Territory, or the District of Columbia in which such resale is made, or to which the commodity is to be transported for such resale, and the making of such contracts or agreements shall not be an unfair method of competition under section 5, as amended and supplemented, of the Act entitled 'An Act to create a Federal Trade Commission, to define its powers and duties, and for other purposes', approved September 26, 1914 (U. S. Code, title 15, sec. 45)."

GENERAL STATEMENT

The sole objective of this proposed legislation is to permit the public policy of States having "fair trade acts" to operate with respect to interstate contracts for the resale of goods within those States. The fair-trade acts referred to legalize the maintenance, by contract, of resale prices of branded or trade-marked goods which are in free competition with other goods of the same general class.

To accomplish this end, the reported bill amends section 1 of the Sherman Antitrust Act which declares every contract in restraint of trade illegal. The amendment adds a sentence to the section, in the nature of a limitation, to the effect, in substance, that nothing therein contained shall render illegal contracts prescribing minimum prices or other conditions for resale of branded or trade-marked goods when such contracts are lawful as to intrastate transactions under the State law of the State in which the resale is to be made; and that the making of such contracts shall not be an unfair method of competition under section 5 of the Federal Trade Commission Act.

In view of the decision of the Supreme Court in *Dr. Miles Medical Co.* v. *Park & Sons Co.* (220 U. S. 373),[2.29] and other cases, it is doubtful, at least, that such contracts are now valid in interstate commerce.

STATE FAIR TRADE ACTS

State fair trade acts typically provide, first, that contracts may lawfully be made which provide for maintenance by contract of resale prices of branded or trade-marked competitive goods. Second, that third parties with notice are bound by the terms of such a contract regardless of whether they are parties to it.

The pertinent provisions of the Illinois act, recently held constitutional by the Supreme Court in the case of *Old Dearborn Distributing Co.* v. *Seagram-Distillers Corporation* (decided Dec. 7, 1936) read as follows:

SECTION 1. No contract relating to the sale or resale of a commodity which bears, or the label or content of which bears, the trade mark, brand, or name of the producer or owner of such commodity and which is in fair and open competition with commodities of the same general class produced by others shall be deemed in violation of any law of the State of Illinois by reason of any of the following provisions which may be contained in such contract:

(1) That the buyer will not resell such commodity except at the price stipulated by the vendor.

(2) That the producer or vendee of a commodity require upon the sale of such commodity to another that such purchaser agree that he will not, in turn, resell except at the price stipulated by such producer or vendee.

Such provisions in any contract shall be deemed to contain or imply conditions that such commodity may be resold without reference to such agreement in the following cases:

(1) In closing out the owner's stock for the purpose of discontinuing delivery of any such commodity: *Provided, however,* That such stock is first offered to the manufacturer of such stock at the original invoice price, at least ten (10) days before such stock shall be offered for sale to the public.

(2) When the goods are damaged or deteriorated in quality, and notice is given to the public thereof.

(3) By any officer acting under the orders of any court.

SEC. 2. Wilfully and knowingly advertising, offering for sale, or selling any commodity at less than the price stipulated in any contract entered into pursuant to the provisions of section 1 of this Act, whether the person so advertising, offering for sale, or selling is or is not a party to such contract, is unfair competition and is actionable at the suit of any person damaged thereby.

The following States, the committee is advised, have adopted fair trade acts: California, Washington, Oregon, Montana, Wyoming, Arizona, New Mexico, Utah, North Dakota, South Dakota, Kansas, Louisiana, Arkansas, Iowa, Wisconsin, Illinois, Kentucky, Tennessee, Indiana, Ohio, Georgia, Virginia, West Virginia, Pennsylvania, Maryland, New York, New Jersey, and Rhode Island.

The committee is advised that in addition one house of each of the following States have passed a fair trade bill: South Carolina, North Carolina, Idaho, Colorado, and Oklahoma.

The committee is further advised that bills are pending in the Legislatures of Nevada, Michigan, Minnesota, Texas, Mississippi, Delaware, Missouri, Connecticut, Massachusetts, New Hampshire, and Maine; and that only one State, Vermont, has definitely rejected legislation of this character.

ECONOMIC ASPECTS

The anticipated economic effects of the legislation here proposed were presented both by proponents and opponents of the bill in the hearings held by the subcommittee

---

[2.29] 220 U.S. 373, 31 S. Ct. 376, 55 L. Ed. 502 (1911).

of the Committee on the Judiciary in charge of the bill. On the one hand it is urged that predatory price cutting is a weapon of monopolistic large distributors to crush small businessmen. On the other hand, it is contended that price-maintenance legislation tends unduly to enhance the price of goods to the consumer. To this argument it is answered that the free play of competition between products of different manufacturers of the same general class will prevent such a result.

However, in the opinion of the committee, those arguments are more properly addressed to the State legislatures considering the enactment of fair trade acts. It is the legislature's responsibility to fix the public policy of the State. This legislation merely seeks to help effectuate a public policy so fixed in a State. It has no application to any State which does not see fit to enact a fair trade act.

In this connection the committee invites attention to the following paragraph of the opinion of the Supreme Court, heretofore referred to, upholding the constitutionality of the Illinois act, the Court speaking through Mr. Justice Sutherland: [2.30]

There is a great body of fact and opinion tending to show that price cutting by retail dealers is not only injurious to the goodwill and business of the producer and distributor of identified goods, but injurious to the general public as well. The evidence to that effect is voluminous; but it would serve no useful purpose to review the evidence or to enlarge further upon the subject. True, there is evidence, opinion, and argument to the contrary; but it does not concern us to determine where the weight lies. We need say no more than that the question may be regarded as fairly open to differences of opinion. The legislation here in question proceeds upon the former and not the latter view; and the legislative determination in that respect, in the circumstances here disclosed, is conclusive so far as this court is concerned. Where the question of what the facts establish is a fairly debatable one we accept and carry into effect the opinion of the legislature. *Radice* v. *New York* (264 U. S. 292, 294);[2.31] *Zahn* v. *Board of Public Works* (274 U. S. 325, 328, and cases cited).[2.32]

EFFECTUATION OF STATE PUBLIC POLICY

Your committee respectfully submit that sound public policy on the part of the Federal Government lies in the direction of lending assistance to the States to effectuate their own public policy with regard to ⊥ their internal affairs. It is submitted that this is especially true where such assistance, as in this instance, consists of removing a handicap resulting from the surrender of the power over interstate commerce by the States to the Federal Government.

In compliance with clause 2a of rule XIII, existing law is printed below in roman, with new matter proposed to be added printed in italics:

1. Bill as introduced:

SECTION 1. Every contract, combination in the form of trust or otherwise, or conspiracy in restraint of trade or commerce among the several States, or with foreign nations is hereby declared to be illegal: *Provided, That nothing herein contained shall render illegal contracts or agreements prescribing minimum prices or other conditions for the resale of a commodity which bears, or the label or container of which bears, the trade mark, brand, or name of the producer or distributor of such commodity and which is in free and open competition with commodities of the same general class produced or distributed by others, when contracts or agreements of that description are lawful as applied to intrastate transactions, under any statute, law, or public policy now or hereafter in effect in any State, Territory, or the District of Columbia in which such resale is made, or to which the commodity is to be transported for such resale and the making of such contracts or agreements shall not be an unfair method of competition under section 5, as amended and supplemented, of the Act entitled "An Act to create a Federal Trade Commission, to define its powers and duties, and for other purposes*["], *approved September 26, 1914.* Every person who shall make any such contract or engage in any such combination or conspiracy shall be deemed guilty of a misdemeanor, and, on conviction thereof, shall be punished by fine not exceeding $5,000, or by imprisonment not exceeding one year, or by both said punishments, in the discretion of the court.

[2.30] 299 U.S. at 195–96.
[2.31] 264 U.S. 292, 294, 44 S. Ct. 325, 326, 68 L. Ed. 690, 694 (1924).
[2.32] 274 U.S. 325, 328, 47 S. Ct. 594, 595, 71 L. Ed. 1074, 1076 (1927).

II. Bill as amended and reported by committee:

SECTION 1. Every contract, combination in the form of trust or otherwise, or conspiracy in restraint of trade or commerce among the several States, or with foreign nations, is hereby declared to be illegal. Every person who shall make any such contract or engage in any such combination or conspiracy shall be deemed guilty of a misdemeanor, and, on conviction thereof, shall be punished by fine not exceeding $5,000, or by imprisonment not exceeding one year, or by both said punishments, in the discretion of the court.

Nothing herein contained shall render illegal, contracts or agreements prescribing minimum prices or other conditions for the resale of a commodity which bears, or the label or container of which bears, the trade mark, brand, or name of the producer or distributor of such commodity and which is in free and open competition with commodities of the same general class produced or distributed by others, when such contracts or agreements are lawful as applied to intrastate transactions, under any statute, law, or public policy now or hereafter in effect in any State, Territory, or the District of Columbia in which such resale is made, or to which the commodity is to be transported for such resale, and the making of such contracts or agreements shall not be an unfair method of competition under section 5, as amended and supplemented, of the act entitled "An act to create a Federal Trade Commission, to define its powers and duties, and for other purposes", approved September 26, 1914 (U. S. Code, title 15, sec. 45).

ADDITIONAL VIEWS SUBMITTED BY MR. CELLER

I shall vote for this bill—but remember—

A GOOD MEDICINE MAY BE POISON INCORRECTLY USED

This is not a statement in opposition to H. R. 1611 if it is actually legislation against "loss-leader" selling, for the reasons given below. Its purposes are instead both to make of record the views of the minority in anticipation of the verdict of the future in respect to this legislation, and to place on warning, until that verdict is rendered, those who may hope for too much from a good medicine which is also poison when incorrectly used.

It is not in opposition to H. R. 1611 on the score of "loss leaders" because the curbing of "loss-leader" selling—the use of financial strength to sell unnaturally low for the purposes of ruining weaker competitors or enticing consumers to buy high-profit goods—is applauded by all who think constructively. I have for many years advocated that this practice so harmful to the small merchant be curbed. I have not weakened in that advocacy. For years I supported the Capper-Kelly "loss-leader" bill. I shall vote for this bill, if finally I am given no alternative. In the meantime, I shall continue to attempt to amend it in the interest of the consumer.

Since trade-marked goods, particularly low-unit priced trade-marked goods, have for obvious reasons been for years favorite "loss leaders", and since H. R. 1611 would make it easier for manufacturers of trade-marked goods to prevent "loss leader" selling of their products under State laws such as those recently sustained by the Supreme Court, H. R. 1611 has a claim upon those who oppose "loss leaders" to withhold their opposition. Some evidently feel it has a claim for active support on this score.

THE CONSUMER WILL SUFFER

If H. R. 1611 was forthright legislation banning sales of trade-marked goods—or any goods, for that matter—below cost, even plus a percentage that protected the efficient distributor and his workers, it would indeed have such a claim for active support from those who are really soundly friendly to the small merchant and his customer, the consumer. For only through more efficient service to the consumer will the merchant achieve any lasting benefit, while, on the other hand, only by protecting the efficient merchant from predatory trade practices—and malicious "loss leader" selling is a predatory trade practice—will the consumer obtain any lasting benefit. The real friends of the small merchant will be shown, when the verdict of the future is rendered, to be those who emphasized this merchandising truth, and not those who encouraged exploitation of the consumer for the sake of temporary gains under guise of curbing predatory trade practices.

⊥ Moreover, H. R. 1611 purports to apply to trade marks and trade names solely, but it applies as well to mere individual and company names.

It purports to be for the sole purpose of helping manufacturers, but actually gives every owner of commodities, every distributor of them, the same tremendous grant of power that it supposedly extends to manufacturers of trade-marked goods only. With a trick phrase it sets aside the antitrust law, and the Federal Trade Commission Act as well, in the case of any condition any vendor may elect to attach to a sale, so long merely as it cannot be shown that a monopoly results, thus opening the road to sales contracts tying together two different products, while legislation is pending before Congress to outlaw that very practice.

WHY H. R. 1611 JUSTIFIES NO MORE THAN FORBEARANCE

But the basic reason that H. R. 1611 does not, at the most, have a claim to more than forbearance from those opposed to predatory "loss leader" selling is obvious. Instead of forbidding the practice in terms affording fair protection to consumer and merchant, it makes it possible for the merchants—indeed tempts the short-sighted merchants and their paid advisers—to, by "ganging up" on the manufacturer, force a maintenance of prices beyond the levels necessary fairly to protect consumers and themselves.

The only answer to this obviously accurate statement is: "Don't be afraid, the manufacturers won't put the prices that high!"

They certainly won't want to—but the real question is: "Can they be forced?" For that the attempt will be made to force them is obvious. For example, the officially avowed purpose of organized retailers in the drug field is to obtain 50 percent (on cost) profit on every sale, no matter what the size of purchase, no matter how small the cost of handling and stocking a nationally advertised, trade-marked line; no matter how rapidly the small required stock of a product turns over.

For instance, if a toothpaste, the manufacturer of which takes the responsibility of bringing customers into stores to buy it, costs 15 cents a tube in dozen lots at wholesale, and the $1.80 worth of stock sells out every 2 days, the gross profit on that $1.80 must be $165.80 a year in order to satisfy the minimum requirements of the organized retailers in the line involved, according to the statement of their president and the printed 1937 "platform" in their official journal. And the organized wholesalers in the same field will desire the manufacturer to assure them at least 15 percent on their cost before they make it possible for the retailer to thus buy in dozen lots on short notice. In my locality the drug retailers, finding that manufacturers in many instances wanted to fix the retail margin at 19 percent instead of the 50 percent demanded, are announcing they will make themselves substitutes for the manufacturers' advertised and trade-marked goods.

WHAT THE MANUFACTURER WILL BE UP AGAINST

Such organized groups of distributors in at least the retail drug trade buy the great majority of the manufacturers' goods in the lines in which "loss leader" selling is most prevalent. They can—and he knows it—make or break his most elaborate sales efforts.

⊥ So far he has resisted—the better word is "avoided"—their power by pointing out that no law existed authorizing him to fix prices. Even when State price maintenance laws were obtained in many States as a result of pressure by organized mercantile groups, the Congress consistently declining to pass a Federal law, the manufacturers raised the points that they were still subject to the Federal antitrust laws and that setting up in a number of States to qualify under their laws placed heavy operative burdens on them.

THREE FACTS THAT PROVE THE POINT

H. R. 1611 was, indeed, advanced by the organized mercantile groups to "kill off" those two points. With it passed, the manufacturers will have, supposedly, nothing left to resort to for "points", and will "get the works." Of course "manufacturers" as here used is not all-inclusive, some manufacturers feel they can risk wide distributive margins, many were willing to "play along" when only a few States were involved.

But that manufacturers, by and large, fear being forced to dangerously high prices is established by two simple facts. First, they could, if they wished, maintain prices without specific enabling legislation, and very few have done so. The Journal of the New York State Pharmaceutical Association in its current issue, I notice, describes a manufacturer's success in securing 85 percent price stabilization even though his products had been among those most notoriously used for "loss leader" selling.

Second, how many manufacturers have appeared at the hearings on H. R. 1611 supporting it? If it is needed to help them protect the rights the Supreme Court has found they have at stake, why aren't they out in force in favor of H. R. 1611? It is true that after those opposing H. R. 1611 stressed the point, an official of one of the drug manufacturers' associations appeared for it. Incidentally, I wonder if his appearance under the circumstances is not a demonstration of the power of the organized retailers over manufacturers in that field?

And some sent telegrams and letters "for the record", evidently in response to requests for them from retailers' organizations. Also an attorney from the staff of a large general manufacturers' association appeared at a hearing, evidently attracted by the "possibilities" latent in the trick phrase extending immunity from the antitrust law and the Federal Trade Commission Act to "conditions for the resale." That the fact remains that not a single manufacturer has appeared to speak a single word in the flesh and blood for this legislation which purports to be required for the protection of manufacturers using trade marks.

In this connection it is interesting to notice how few widely known manufacturers are listed in the current drug trade retail paper for my locality, which actually lists as "A" grade manufacturers those "playing ball" satisfactorily—to the retailers—price-wise. The list reads as follows and you can pick out the big national manufacturers without running out of fingers: American Druggists' Syndicate; Harriet, Hubbard Ayer; Bayer Co.; Cooper & Cooper, Inc.; Coty, Inc.; Ex-Lax, Inc.; Health Products Corporation; International Cellucotton Products, Miles Laboratories, Inc.; My-Pet Medicines, Inc.; Northam Warren Sales Co., Inc.; Pepsodent Sales, Inc.; Poloris Co., Inc.; Seeck & Kade, Inc.; Sterilek Co., Inc.; Upjohn Co.; Yardley & Co., Ltd.; and the Youngs Rubber Corporation.

No; the manufacturers in these lines so dependent on distributor friendliness do not dare oppose; of course—all they can do is to hope they won't be put on the spot. But H. R. 1611 puts them right on the spot. And that this is realized by those wanting them "on the spot" is obvious to any casual reader of the trade press. I noticed the other day these significant sentences in a trade paper published in my neighborhood:

One enthusiastic price maintenance advocate from my home city minces no words:

I would suggest that when manufacturers raise their minimum resale prices under contract terms they abolish the idea of the minimum price as it is a well-known fact that the minimum price soon becomes the maximum price. The theory that prices may be raised gradually is impracticable and may involve firms in litigation.

Another observes:

It (The Supreme Court decision upholding the State laws which would underlie H. R. 1611) will also give the retail druggists an opportunity to see which manufacturers, distributors and wholesalers are sincere in their efforts to control prices.

There is space for only a third:

From now on there will be no alibi for sincere manufacturers not to have a price-stabilization program and to put same into 100-percent operation. As for those manufacturers who do not embrace this opportunity to play fair with their retail distributors, in my opinion, it is going to be just too bad.

The last quotation is probably not far from the facts—it is going to be "just too bad" with the manufacturers who do not "come through" with the desired degree of price-upping once H. R. 1611 is enacted. And that desired degree is not—let this be emphasized again—price maintenance sufficient to protect the efficient merchant, but price maintenance sufficient to cover average costs—for the efficient and the inefficient, for slow turning and fast moving lines—at an outside, over-all national level.

It is all very well to point out that any such margins will in the end ruin those seeking them, either by attracting more into the business or opening the road to competing lines moving at lower margins. But when that happens the small merchant will have been harmed, not benefited. It is this possibility, even probability, which leads those sincerely opposed to predatory "loss leaders", and sincerely interested in the sound welfare of the small merchant, to call "stop, look, and listen" in connection with H. R. 1611.

DANGEROUS MEDICINE

In other words, permitting the fixing of prices at any level is dangerous medicine—medicine good for an obvious cancer that should be eradicated, namely, predatory price cutting—but also medicine poisonous to the lifeblood of both the consumer and the small merchants serving him if used to the extent of forcing manufacturers to fix prices at levels covering inefficiency. H. R. 1611 gives the power to use the good medicine until it poisons. And the danger is that misguided pressure, as above indicated, will be exerted to use it until it poisons while curing. A cured corpse is hardly satisfactory.

⊥ That there is ample reason for a "stop, look, and listen" warning rests not only on the individual evidences already cited indicating that the good medicine H. R. 1611 makes available will be used in poisonous doses, but as well on the fact that the Nation-wide pressure group back of this legislation is committed officially to a 50 percent profit margin, as mentioned above. All that N. R. A. could be brought to authorize was a 10-percent margin of protection, and that was given only when obligations respecting wages and hours of employees had been undertaken. Since labor costs and other direct charges of the most efficient exceed in most retail instances the 10 percent, perhaps protection should start higher, but N. R. A. after prolonged study was not prepared to risk it. But 50 percent is certainly at the other extreme. And the "autopsy" on N. R. A. just announced brands any price fixing as an error.

The following account of the thorough national organization of this pressure groop [sic] avowedly seeking that 50 percent through H. R. 1611 is certainly undisputable evidence of the pressure manufacturers will be put under once the bill is enacted. I quote from the organization's official journal:

As this is written (first week in January) only four States remain which have not set up the N. A. R. D. congressional contact committees on a county basis. In other words, 44 States of the Union are now organized as never before in history for the purpose of furthering legislation.

The final step in this organization is now being made. We have the proper contact man in nearly every county in this country. They now number over 2,000. We are now asking that each of these 2,000 men form a committee of their own in their own local community consisting of 10 other local independent businessmen who will work and move as a unit when called upon by the N. A. R. D. Washington office.

The power of this organization will be enormous and it will be irresistible * * *.

Can anyone doubt either the strength or the effectiveness of the pressure such an organization can—and will, undoubtedly—turn on the manufacturers of trade-marked articles immediately it has obtained enactment of H. R. 1611?

As an example of the sort of "ride" on which organized trade pressure, such as has avowed openly that the Tydings-Miller bill must aid in "delivering" prices maintained to assure 50-percent margins, can take even the largest of manufacturers, let me cite this remarkable instance as reported from California by Ewald T. Grether, associate professor of economics at the University of California:

The —— case was publicized nationally and had repercussions throughout the entire country. It is peculiarly well-adapted to reflect the state of mind of retail druggists throughout the Nation as well as in California. In the January 1, 1935 issue of the Northern California Drug News there is an editorial lauding a well-known national dentifrice and antiseptic manufacturer for finally issuing fair-trade contracts after months of request, including a formal petition, on the part of retailers. The company was praised particularly because it guaranteed minimum margins of 18.4 percent, 26.5 percent, and 34.2 percent, depending upon the quantity purchased. However, on July 13, 1935, dealers in California received letters from this firm advising them that it was necessary to withdraw from operation under the Fair Trade Act since they were making shipments directly from Chicago and hence were involved in interstate commerce. Immediately, a storm broke loose in California which swept into other States before it had spent itself. On July 17, the northern association passed a resolution condemning the company and urging and advising its members to "discontinue the sale of the products of any and all companies which cancel fair-trade contracts." Similar action was taken in the southern association. The response of the trade was amazing; an almost universal boycott was raised against the firm. For a ⊥ period it was possible to obtain the products of the firm only from a few cut-rate outlets. An interesting aspect was that a number of large wholesale houses also cooperated by refusing to deliver the items of the company. It appears that the company had a startling decline in sales in California. Worse still, the antagonism spread into other States and affected sales and attitudes nationally. The outcome was that the company capitulated completely, again issuing contracts in California, and likewise, so it is stated, giving a check of $25,000 to the National Association of Retail Druggists to be used in its fight for price-maintenance legislation.

In truth and in fact, this company was coerced into violation of our antitrust laws, since it sought to maintain prices in interstate commerce before passage of the Tydings-Miller bill.

THE REAL ISSUE

It is all very well to point out that the manufacturer does not have to maintain prices unless he elects to do so. The real issues are, however:

First. Can he resist against pressure of the type indicated above?

Second. If he does "elect" to fix resale prices, can he withstand fixing them so as to assure the 50-percent retail profit for which this same pressure officially stands?

Third. If he finally "elects" 100 percent and fixes prices to assure the retail margins demanded by the pressure put on him, will not the "cure" become a poison by both exploiting the consumer and finally undermining the small merchant misled into believing that there is some magic profit umbrella?

Those who care to take the trouble will find typical examples of manufacturers who are already responding to the pressure for a retail margin of 50 percent or better in almost any issue of the organization journals in the trade most energetically pushing for enactment of H. R. 1611. For example, in the current issue of the official journal of the largest national organization in that trade there are these two offers on nationally advertised trade-marked lines of the type the retailers wish manufacturers to see similarly price-maintained under H. R. 1611:

Four dollars and eighty cents investment in face creams and powders to sell to the consumer for $7.60. That amounts to a gross of 58 percent. There are 20 pieces of merchandise in this $4.80 model stock, and 20 samples, a display card and a folder of selling suggestions are thrown in. On a weekly turn-over of this $4.80 stock the retailer alone would do a $395.20 volume at a gross profit of $145.60—58 percent on the cost of the goods sold, 3,033 percent on the $4.80 tied up in the stock. These figures make no allowance for the profits of the wholesalers through whom this manufacturer offers these stocks—probably between $40–$50 in the volume assumed for the sake of illustration. In other words, for what the manufacturer would receive around $200 in the course of the transactions assumed, consumers would have expended nearly $400, and the actual investment need actually never have exceeded $5 in retail stock for the assumed trade, or probably $60 in the wholesale supplies necessary to supply that specific trade.

Two dollars and eight-five [sic] cents investment in cough drops to sell to consumers for $5.52. This amounts to a gross of 91 percent. There are 120 packages of merchandise in this $2.85 model stock, and 8 display containers and 1 display basket are thrown in. A little cost figuring will show you the profit possible on a rapid turn-over of this $2.85 stock, although allowance must be made for the seasonable character of this particular merchandise. And any way it is figured it is 91 percent on the cost of the goods.

⊥ TAKE A LEAF FROM PATMAN ACT EXPERIENCES

There is no occasion to draw on the many similar instances now being prominently advertised in the trade press—the profit margins on these fast-turning lines being from 21 to 200 percent. Since the Patman Act was passed many manufacturers are evidently tumbling over one another in an effort to make "quantity" sales of purchases of a few dollars and to "suggest" resale prices for these purchases which will gross 50 percent or more on cost for merely handling the goods over counters. Everybody seems to be taking a Roman holiday at the consumers' expense under cover of the Patman Act coupled with "suggested" resale prices—and no one seems ready to admit that such hilarious holidays are always followed sooner or later by headaches. Of course the object in pushing H. R. 1611 is to eliminate the necessity for this "suggesting" of resale prices by manufacturers. With H. R. 1611 a law they will be able to go as high—or as much higher as they are "persuaded" to—without any "suggesting." Who will dare claim it will be lower than they are now going with no right to do more than to suggest? Who will dare say that the purpose in the lines mentioned in asking for enactment of H. R. 1611 is not only the applauded one of outlawing "loss leader" selling but the purely commercial one of making it possible to "persuade" manufacturers to fix resale prices on their trade-marked articles at levels assuring 50 percent on cost? If the purpose is only to stop "loss leader" selling, why not limit it to outlawing sales at a loss?

Here is an analysis I have noticed of some advertised resale prices and margins of the sort I have mentioned as just "suggested" by manufacturers in advertisements—anyone can decide what resale prices and margins will be fixed when H. R. 1611 makes that possible:

A Squibb ad establishing a dozen bottles of cod liver oil as rating "the best quantity prices" and offering the dozen on a basis assuring 42-percent gross profit to retailers as the lowest "suggested" consumer prices—"dealers like the big profit—54 cents" this advertisement naively exclaims. Another advertiser picks three stores from its customer lists and proclaims they averaged 55-percent profit over a test period. And still another nationally known manufacturer announces in bold type: "* * * higher minimum prices (that is, higher prices to consumers) in all but 12 States." And another offers dealers, in a double-page two-color advertisement, 43-percent profit on a purchase of but half a dozen 35-cent brushes. The dealer's "quantity order" in this case comes to $1.40, the consumer pays $2.45, the dealer takes $1.05. Finally, another well-known manufacturer offers a case as a "quantity" purchase (for $4.50) on a 100-percent profit basis, while one even more widely known advertises 400-percent gross profit on each 10-cent sale of his product. And the president of the association, the official journal of which carried the advertising cited, had told its members: "I believe that the association should firmly reiterate its stand for margins of at least 33 1/3 percent (33 1/3 percent on retail prices means 50 percent on the merchant's cost price) on protected minimum resale selling prices, regardless of the quantity purchased." Since then the association journal has featured the 50-percent margin objective as "official."

If the Patman Act can bring about results as startling to consumers as the above—results, by the way, all were warned would follow enactment of that law—who can say what will happen when enactment of H. R. 1611 makes it possible for those interested to challenge manufacturers with an ominous: "Now you do not have to any longer depend on merely attempting to proceed by 'suggesting'—you can fix prices without fear of the Federal antitrust laws or without even having to domesticate in States with price maintenance laws"?

RIDICULOUS IN SOME CASES—SINISTER IN ALL CASES

Some results—not a few of them would be ridicuous [sic] if they were not so sinister—of this spreading idea that profits can somehow be created by trade ukase or governmental statute, which idea is the sinister something lurking behind the good intentions carefully draped around the Patman Act and the Tydings-Miller bill, are already beginning to appear out in the open. Often they take the shape of ridiculous refusals to sell outside certain trade channels except in large quantities under the excuse the Patman Act prohibits doing so, when, of course, it does no such thing. The real reason is to force selling in a certain way and through certain channels, which was one evil the original Patman bill actually proposed, but, being out in the open, it was possible to eliminate.

For example, I heard the other day of a woman who does bookbinding being refused less than 100 pounds of glue "because the Patman Act" prohibited it. She wanted 25 pounds; the quantity in which she bought last, and was willing to pay a fair 25-pound lot price. But she had to buy 100 pounds—or thought she did—and, incidentally, paid the price she had formerly paid for 25 pounds. Now she says she has enough glue for 15 years. Another woman I know, who had been buying an item in quantities much larger than the average druggist buys it in from his wholesaler—she had been getting a usual discount off list, of course—was recently informed she could no longer be sold as the Patman Act prohibited it. Both the instances I mention are examples of ridiculous extremes in using legislation to put an umbrella over trade.

Another amusing development is that this profit-by-law idea is spreading beyond the trades so far most energetic in using it and that some of the new followers of this easy-profit mirage are turning it against the pioneers. For example, while the retail druggists are busy trying to put their 50-percent-on-every-order-regardless-of-quantity plan on ice, the restaurant boys have crept up on them and are pushing for laws restricting prepared food sales to rooms exclusively devoted to that business. Imagine what such laws will do to the druggists. While they are endeavoring to get a few hundred dollars legislated into their cash drawers via the Patman Act and the Tydings-Miller bill, they may find thousands of dollars of their fountain luncheon business legislated over into restaurants. Of course the restaurant men say: "Why should the druggists sell everything from soup to books, and besides want 50 percent by law on the books and the fast selling trade-marked goods, and as much as they can get on everything else, with exclusive rights on drug items? If we sold 'Gone With the Wind', a lawn mower, an electric lamp, and a bottle of paregoric with our table d'hotes they would first swear out a warrant for our arrest for infringing on the pharmacy law and be yelling about unfair trade practices for a year after we had been tried and fined for dispensing the paregoric—so we think they should stop selling soup along with those items."

And so it goes—maybe getting funnier and funnier, but if so it is for everybody but the consumer. The poor old consumer will make [sic] up sooner or later, you can depend on that, just as he did in 1912 and 1920, with the result that chains came into the picture, and when he does, you can predict with a remarkable degree of assurance that something or some way to take care of his demands will appear. Maybe it will be cooperatives, if prices are pushed high enough to give them a chance.

A POINT NOT ALWAYS UNDERSTOOD

It must be remembered that by and large trade-marked articles of the low-unit-price type primarily involved in "loss leader" selling turn over very rapidly and can be stocked in very small amounts. The real object of the sponsors of the Patman Act, as this Congress was warned, is to use it to make "quantity" purchases of these small amounts. The instances cited above show how well they have already succeeded—purchases of under $5 are styled "quantity" purchases!

When the Patman Act was before Congress it was stated the result of making quantity purchases of small purchases [sic] would result in savings to the consumer. It was an assertion backed by neither probability nor fact, but it evidently sounded convincing, for the act passed—it is to be feared because it was somehow felt to be a constructive step toward controlling abuses of large purchasing power. The above examples will show where the consumer got off.

Now, H. R. 1611 is urged on the grounds it will cure predatory "loss leader" selling. But it is obvious from the facts already cited that it will also be used to "persuade" manufacturers to up prices sufficiently to assure at least a 50 percent gross on the cost of many of the items frequently used for "loss leaders."

The Members of the Congress can decide for themselves what the picture will be with H. R. 1611 and the Patman Act working together. The facts already pointed out make it easy to do so. Will a most righteous "cure" lead to a most dangerous raid on the consumer purchasing power?

But to complete all the high lights in that picture it is necessary, as stated, to bear in mind that the low-unit trade-marked items most frequently used for "loss leader" selling turn rapidly and need be stocked only in small quantities. Therefore they use a minimum of space and call for a minimum of all overhead charges.

STARTLING TRUTH

The Department of Commerce has published figures to show [(]Domestic Commerce Series No. 90, tables 37–43) that the most rapid-turning items actually move at from 24 to 36 percent of their cost. These percentages were based on actual checks in various types of drug stores.

Now, if a $100 stock of one of these fast-moving items can be turned but 12 times a year at the 50-percent margin "announced as desired" under H. R. 1611, it is plain, if the actual cost of handling is the top figure mentioned above (36 percent), that a net profit of 14 percent will be shown on the cost of the year's sales volume of $1,800 in the item, and 168 percent on the $100 tied up in stock. And in the instances cited above $5 is frequently mentioned as a quantity purchase of stock—as a matter of fact, wholesalers sell but an insignificant amount of the fast-moving trade-marked items in case lots, and retailers consider an order of a dozen of these pieces of merchandise as perfectly normal—wholesalers, indeed, are thankful for the order for a dozen pieces not being "assorted"! Figure out for yourself what ⊥ the profits become on such small stock investments in trade-marked, low-unit items such as have been favorite "loss leaders" if resale prices are fixed to assure 50 percent on the cost, and you have some idea of the merchandising "dynamite" in H. R. 1611, totally aside from its commendable power to kill off predatory "loss leader" selling. And the pity of it is that it is "dynamite" as dangerous to the retailer tempted to use it on the consumer as it is on the consumer "dynamited." It is true, of course, that persisting in "dynamiting" will finally drive away the hardiest of consumers, but then it is usually too late to save the business of the retailer misled into the "dynamiting"—some other enterprise normally has the trade by that time.

ANOTHER PROBLEM

Furthermore, if pressure groups are to secure enactment of State legislation which is then merely "sanctioned" by Federal statutes, is not a precedent of dangerous import established, in that dangerous lack of uniformity between the States will result? If Federal legislation is called for, certainly it, and not legislation State by State, is most effective. Some States may never enact legislation to which H. R. 1611 will apply—as a result, on one side of a river, for instance, prices may be maintained at a 50-percent retail profit level, while on the other side of the river a merchant able to sell at half that and still make a profit, may reap a harvest at the expense of those on the price-maintained side of the stream.

This is not, perhaps, a determining factor. On the other hand, it does point to the very important issue that forthright legislation is preferable. If "loss leader" selling is to be outlawed—and it should be—let the legislation outlaw it specifically and nationally.

SOMETHING THE HEARINGS INDICATE

The hearings before the subcommittee on H. R. 1611 themselves put us on warning. Those that appeared in opposition do not by and large oppose a curb on predatory "loss leader" selling. They oppose a "cure" which becomes a poison if used to certain extents.

The record of the hearings demonstrate [sic] that it is a case of the good 5-cent cigar. There is no opposition to a good 5-cent cigar. But there is opposition to making it possible to enforce a 10-cent or a 15-cent price for the good 5-cent cigar.

THE NUB OF THE ISSUE

Admittedly, what I now quote is the nub of the issue—again I select a reference to my own locality:

There is a pronounced tendency toward combination and concentration of trade in the retail field. Newspaper readers have noted within the past few days that apparently to all intents and purposes the United Cigar Stores and the Riker-Hegeman stores have consolidated. Within the memory of all here a great change has come over the drug business and cigar business of this city. In mentioning these companies and others, it is with no thought of attacking them, for they haven't done more than to make the most of the opportunities with which the people have provided them and probably are neither better nor worse than the general run of businessmen. To see how rapidly the drug business has become centralized here, we need only think back a few years, when there were four or five Bolton drug stores in Brooklyn. They were ably and aggressively managed. The opportunity came and they purchased the old Riker drug store at Twenty-third Street ⊥ and Sixth Avenue. Soon all of the Bolton stores became Riker stores, and in the Metropolitan district new Riker stores were opened rapidly. Thus spurred on, the old Hegeman Corporation of 200 Broadway undertook a similar extension of a system of stores, and then these two strong contenders of the market found it desirable to combine 2 or 3 years ago. * * *

Whatever the facts may be, the casual observer knows that the drug business and cigar business has become largely congested into these two chain-store systems, and the United Cigar Stores have spread from coast to coast and number now nearly 1,000. * * *

The smaller merchants of America are in distress, and their difficulties are increasing as their newly developed competitors increase. These merchants are made the scape-goat for the high cost of living by some; they are pointed out as the modern Shylock; they are pictured as incompetent, inadequate, and a burden upon the backs of the people. * * *

Abusive price cutting cannot be successfully applied to unknown goods. Most men know that a Dunlap hat has a market value of $5. Any store which could go to an agent of Dunlap's hats and get a quantity and put them on sale at a price of $2, regardless of what they cost, could fill the store by the simple announcement of this bargain. They could advertise Bunkom's $5 hats at $2 indefinitely and no one would pay attention, because no one knows anything about Bunkom's hats; they may be worth $5 or $1.50, but it is the magic of the name in which the public has confidence, which makes price cutting attractive to merchants who have other merchandise to unload; it does not apply to the great mass of bulk merchandise which goes without a name, like nails or potatoes or lumber, or any of the things where the identity of the producer is not known.

But what I have quoted is from a speech made in 1913—nearly a quarter of a century ago.

SOMETHING TO THINK ABOUT

This striking example that the run of time and events is at best difficult to foretell is offered as a warning that what may be expected of legislation in 1937 may be far different when the record is cast up 23 years later. What would the speaker quoted have said, when he spoke back in 1913, to an accurate forecast that 16 years later there would be 1,506 drug stores in Brooklyn, only 5 percent of which were chain stores; that the 2 chains he holds up as warnings would be so hard pressed they would go through financial reorganization proceedings and their representatives appear before a subcommittee of the House Judiciary Committee in January of 1937 favoring legislation giving manufacturers of trade-marked articles the right to fix prices throughout the States authorizing price maintenance, which would then be 16 in number with similar legislation pending in at least 20 others?

Does it follow that 16 years from 1937 the record will show that such a right has benefited the small merchants desiring it, or the manufacturers offered it, or the consumers subjected to it? Even if that right to place prices as high as mistaken—although well-intentioned—pressure during the 16 years may dictate, is given to prevent selling trade-marked goods at a loss in order that small merchants may be quite rightly protected from the obvious injustices of predatory "loss leader" selling?

Those two questions point out the quandry [sic] in which H. R. 1611 places all sincere well-wishers of the small merchant. They wish to protect him from predatory "loss leader" selling. For his own good they wish to protect him also from price maintenance which denies the consumer the fruits of legitimate efficiency, for they know if he falls into that trap that his trade will suffer in the end. Since H. R. 1611 makes it possible for mistaken pressure drives for higher prices ⊥ that disregard efficiency to succeed, they fear it may finally harm those who seek its enactment.

Therefore they favor it as a cure for predatory loss leader selling of trade-marked goods, but fear it may become poison to those rightly entitled to the cure, by being used to fix prices at levels which only incidentally eliminate loss leader selling, but principally seek to assure by law arbitrary profit margins based not on efficiency, but average or typical over-all costs of doing business.

THE REAL DANGER IN H. R. 1611

Such average, over-all costs do not rest on the costs of the most efficient and effective, but average all the various favorable and unfavorable factors of location, number of outlets, volume of sales, rapidity of turn-over by lines and individual storekeeping ability. They are not indexes of what is the most effective way to serve the consumer, but an average of what it costs, over-all, for a trade to pay expenses and make a profit. If enforced by law, they levy on the consumer what amounts to a tax equal to the average cost of operating a retail outlet in the line involved, regardless of what an outlet could be operated for by the most efficient merchant in a normal location with a normal number of consumers to serve. And the consumer will not pay any such tax—he never has and never will. He will rebel finally, but first he will get what he wants some other way—and as he shifts his trade, those who hoped to control him will find the lifeblood (volume) of their businesses drying up.

There lies the danger in H. R. 1611—the poison. We have, moreover, seen that the pressure to up prices to average, over-all margins is ready to be unleashed the moment H. R. 1611 becomes a law.

And it is that danger those who are both interested in the sound prosperity of the small merchant and the passage of legislation that will check predatory "loss leader" selling see in H. R. 1611. They can oppose it—but do not wish to do so because they believe in outlawing predatory price selling. They can wish that its proponents, realizing that soundness over the long pull outweighs temporary profit-margin umbrellas, would of their own volition limit it to outlawing "loss leader" selling, instead of using that worthy objective to get it for use as a dangerous weapon to fix prices at 50 percent over cost. But that is a wish they readily admit is vain so long as the temptation of legislating a 50-percent over cost gross margin exists.

A FRIENDLY BUT UNWELCOME WARNING

So about all they can do is to cry "stop, look, listen," knowing full well that doing so will be both unwelcome and discredited at the moment, but being confident that the future will demonstrate it a sound warning and hoping that perhaps running up the danger signal will result in some of the rocks underlying legislating up set profit margins being avoided before it is too late.

Certainly the present tendency to deride efficiency, and good operative direction and sound management and keen merchandising and storekeeping ability, as price fixers, and to turn the laws for profit assurance, challenges all to warn who see [sic] the inevitable catastrophe down that road which looks so easy but ends up so rough. Laws can and should make competition fair—on that score H. R. 1611 deserves ⊥ support—but laws cannot make profits without reducing real purchasing power, and therefore finally increasing the disadvantages of the unfortunate one-third our President calls upon us to help; since H. R. 1611 can be used as a weapon for profit-margin fixing—indeed, undoubtedly will be so used, as we have seen—on that score it is dangerous. Let these who accept such a dangerous weapon, on the understanding of Congress that they are only to use it to cut out the cancer of "loss leader" selling, be on warning when they use it to slash out of the consumers' purchasing power—as their intimate trade proceedings already cited show they intend to do—a fixed gross profit margin of 50 percent over the cost of goods to them. Since it is a friendly, constructive warning, it deserves being welcomed instead of the disparagement and derision it will undoubtedly receive from all but the consumer—and those who even in 1937 realize that our basic prosperity really depends on protecting the consumer's purchasing power.

STATEMENTS THAT PRICE MAINTENANCE DOES NOT INCREASE PRICES ARE MISLEADING

It is my understanding that members of the subcommittee holding hearings on H. R. 1611 have been assured by representatives of the very trade association I find pledging a 50-percent profit to its members in its meetings and official journals, that price maintenance does not increase prices to consumers. Since members of the committee last session accepted at face value similarly unsound statements in connection with the Patman Act, I fear these obviously undependable assurances regarding H. R. 1611 may also be credited.

The Patman Act, we were assured, would reduce prices to the consumer. I have sought in vain for even any indication of a lowering of prices to consumers, unassociated with fluctuating natural products, that can be even remotely attributed to the Patman Act. I do not believe any of its sponsors would today have the temerity to suggest that it has had any such effect in respect to small unit sales in trade-marked drug goods, the very goods in which they are interested and the very goods with which H. R. 1611 is most directly concerned.

What, then, I ask, may we find the facts to be in respect to H. R. 1611, 8 months after it is enacted into law, if it, like the Patman Act, is passed on the strength of such pleasant, but misleading, assurances?

It is not a happy prospect to look forward to the final accounting with the consumer in respect to legislation of this type, if after a mistake is demonstrated to have been made, unsound assurances from a trade with a fixed-profit objective at stake must be pointed to in justification. By that time the consumer's pocketbook will have been filched.

WHAT IS REALLY MEANT

When proponents of H. R. 1611 rush forward with assurances that its enactment will result in lower prices to the consumer they must really mean that outlawing "loss leader" selling may not result in higher prices to consumers. Such assurances would probably be sound, for losses on actual "leaders", really sold at a loss, must naturally be made up on other items.

But what is actually behind the pressure for enactment of H. R. 1611, as I have shown, is a stated intention to force prices to a fixed-profit level. That is an entirely different matter than eliminating "loss leaders", which, as their very name shows, are items either sold at no profit or at a loss.

No one can assure the committee with facts which can be substantiated that price maintenance at a profit level of 50, or 40, or 35 percent, results in lower prices to the consumer. I believe anyone giving the matter a moment's unbiased thought will agree that probably no one ever will be able to both offer such facts and to substantiate them.

As a matter of fact, ample evidence is available indicative of the increased prices consumers are paying already as a result of price increases which fall short of the 50 percent which proponents of H. R. 1611 avowedly have as their objective. For example, the following are one set of such facts from Chicago: "Decision refers to the recent Supreme Court decision upholding State price maintenance in Illinois."

	Price since decision	Price before decision	Occasional cut prices
Shampoo	$0.59	$0.44	$0.36
Hair tonic	.89	.79	.69
Razor blades	.29	.23	.19
Tooth brushes	.43	.39	.23
Dental cream	.33	.29	.21
Shaving cream	.37	.34	.23
Cough preparations	.49	.49	.33
Foot preparations	.33	.29	.24
Drug items	.66	.64	.59
Face powder	1.10	.89	.63
Salve	1.19	1.19	.84
Eye preparations	.89	.89	.67

THE CALIFORNIA EXPERIENCE

I have no doubt that data based on California legislation have been used in an effort to substantiate assurances that enactment of H. R. 1611 will not increase prices to the consumer. If that is the case, I point to such use as another indication that a studied effort is being made to confuse the committee between "loss leader" selling and price fixing at a fixed 50-percent profit level. Certainly the committee should be put on its guard by such efforts, or it may be placed in the position of having enacted legislation to achieve the praiseworthy end of eliminating "loss leaders", while, in fact, the real end sought was exploitation of the consumer through fixing 50-percent profit margins to the satisfaction of the proponents alleging their only interest is a ban on loss leaders.

California retailers in the line most active in sponsoring H. R. 1611 have for a matter of years openly avowed they want a 50-percent margin on the type of goods they handle with which H. R. 1611 is concerned. They have tried all avenues open to them to achieve that end, even to the extent of setting up a private price-control bureau. The State legislature has by now enacted practically every law that they have requested, short of a perfectly frank one stating consumers must pay these merchants at least a 50-percent margin on all the trade-marked items sold in that trade. The California Fair Trade Practice Act comes as near to stating that as is possible without stating it openly. Similar laws have been secured by the same trade in other States and are being pushed in almost all the remaining States.

California retailers in this trade originated the type of so-called fair-trade State law which H. R. 1611 has been created to make it more difficult for manufacturers to refrain from using.

But despite their pioneer efforts to secure their objective of a 50-percent margin, the California retailers have so far been unable to hog-tie for themselves quite that margin. That is what they hope enactment of H. R. 1611 will accomplish for them. And those in other States hope it will make it possible to get California prices.

But the California pioneers have done a good job in eliminating "loss leader" selling, and have even gotten 168 manufacturers to fix prices at levels all of which go further and guarantee them high profits, in certain instances as high as the 50 percent they desire.

Now, if elimination of "loss leaders" is the real objective, why are these California retailers pushing for H. R. 1611, since they have controlled "loss leaders" for several years, even gone further and entered the dangerous field of margin fixing? Is it not obvious they want in their cases H. R. 1611 only because of their desire to hog-tie their 50-percent margin objective? And why would not the reaction be the same in other States, if the outlawing of "loss leaders" is accompanied with a power to fix margins as high as they might "persuade" manufacturers to fix them?

ANOTHER IMPORTANT FACT

And is it not obvious from the above facts, that California price data become misleading in connection with a 50-percent profit margin situation, which is what I have shown the situation surrounding H. R. 1611 to be? These data, of course, only apply to California actualities, and these actualities are somewhat different from both the actualities the proponents of H. R. 1611 avow to their supporters they wish to create, and quite different from the actualities they tell the Congress they wish to create. Would they have dared to reveal to the Congress that their objective is what they have officially bound themselves to their supporters to achieve? That is, 50 percent at least on every purchase?

Moreover, California figures are, like all similar figures from all sections of the country, based on the elementary fact that "loss leaders" of nationally advertised drug trade-marked items are prevalent in the downtown urban communities, while prices for such items carry surprisingly generous margins outside these urban sections and in neighborhood and suburban stores. Therefore a price-control program such as has been set up in California results in no appreciable price advances—except in the downtown urban centers and to the customers of the most efficient stores in those centers. And the average results may hide this fact and be quite deceptive, of course.

THE FACTS ABOUT CALIFORNIA

But even the results obtained in California have been disastrous to consumers of the type of articles involved in H. R. 1611. For instance, the report made by a University of California professor, which ⊥ is unfortunately sometimes cited in a manner that is a bit misleading, shows very large increases in prices and margins of and on drug and cosmetic items in the most efficient downtown urban popular-priced stores. Naturally, the high-price stores not obtaining the large volumes, either because of management or location, show small price increases, or even decreases unless and until manufacturers are "persuaded" to fix prices assuring a 50 percent retail gross, or some percentage even higher. But the consumer can only make his savings at the stores with volume, or management, superiority, or location advantages, sufficient to permit passing on savings to him, and when such popular-priced outlets are forced to raise prices heavily, even if all the other outlets do not raise prices, the net result is simply that he catches it coming and going. For he has to pay high prices at all outlets, and far more than previously at the outlets benefiting him most.

However, the results already obtained in 1936 in California are alarming enough to indicate the danger ahead to the consumer if duplicated in all States and if passage of H. R. 1611 makes it possible to enforce a full 50-percent-margin level. The professor mentioned actually finds nearly a 45-percent margin already established in 1936 for

1,216 items under that State's law of the type to which H. R. 1611 is desired as a sort of Federal benediction. The professor is as a result forced to observe, in connection with this legislation to which the Congress is asked to give its blessing, that "it is rather surprising that so high an average (margin) should appear with a plan but recently introduced, for some manufacturers were loath to raise prices sufficiently from the cut-rate levels to allow wide margins." Notice the professor is now referring to recent results, not to the 1933 results when manufacturers had evidently not been "persuaded" not to "loath."

And he further observes that this legislation to which the Congress is asked to give a national standing "is not merely a loss limitation device, but allows the guaranteeing of margins to dealers." Notice that a "loss limitation device" is professorial language for what is needed to outlaw "loss leader" selling.

And the professor cannot miss noticing the consumers' plight, for he states:

Without doubt those consumers who wish to buy standard drug products with a minimum of professional attention and merchandising services, are harmed by resale-price maintenance except insofar as they are able to obtain equivalent quality under private label.

Why, one might well ask, should consumers require professional attention in buying packaged trade-marked articles, which are what the professor means by "standard drug products"? Or merchandising services, even to the extent of wrapping paper? And, if H. R. 1611 is supposedly in tune with recent court decisions stressing the importance of protecting manufacturers' trade marks, how does it come that manufacturers have been "loath", as the professor suggests, in any respect under this prioneer [sic] underlying law? And, for the same reason, how is it that that same law brings substitutes for those manufacturers' products, or private label goods, to the consumer's mind?

And the professor assuredly cannot be correctly cited as approving of the California law which is the pioneer among those to which the ⊥ Tydings-Miller bill refers, for he comes to this final condemnation of it: ⊥21

* * * The procedure of the Fair Trade Act cannot be defended as a generalized scheme (for remedying unfair trade practice) for (1) it is not applicable to the majority of goods; (2) when it is, it allows the establishing of an undue uniformity and rigidity in the price structure.

Of course "undue uniformity and rigidity in the price structure" is a technical way of saying: "Let the consumer look out—they are out after his scalp."

THE NET OF THE CALIFORNIA EXPERIENCE

But so many embarrassing questions arise once the real issues underlying H. R. 1611 are closely inspected that it is little short of pitiless to press them. For these issues are price-fixing issues, and the price-fixing issues do not fit in neatly with really meritorious motives to curb "loss leader" selling.

Incidentally, a warning against using "cut rate" in a degradatory manner, if it does not refer to actual "loss leader" selling, should be sounded. In one of the quotations above it will be noticed the professor uses the expression "cut rate."

In the sense he uses it he evidently means selling below the price established by the manufacturer. Proponents of H. R. 1611 would therefore feel any sales under a 50-percent margin a "cut rate" sale. To them such a sale may seem full of sin, but it does not follow consumers would agree with them. And if the prescribed margin is 50 percent, and a dealer is so located, and so manages his store, and is blessed with such a volume, that he can make a handsome profit on his investment and sell at a 36-percent margin, is he doing anything subject to criticism by cutting below the 50-percent margin which would give a profit to stores less favorably situated or not as efficiently operated? And certainly no "loss leader" selling would be involved.

The net of the California experience under the pioneer law of the type H. R. 1611 is intended to facilitate is simply that popular-price stores with the volume, location, and management required to sell at the most efficient prices have had to raise prices tremendously, while stores already getting very wide margins have reduced them in some cases slightly because so far the 50-percent margin desired has not yet gotten completely into force in all instances and prices based on somewhat lower margins have as a result been advertised by manufacturers in some cases. However, over 1,200 items, as noted, have been gotten up to a 45-percent level. The consumer has had his most favorable outlets hamstrung, to the tune of up to 25 percent and more, and the program to completely hog-tie them is proceeding apace. That is surely enough to indicate what the consumer is in for. Naturally, he has not rebelled yet—he can still buy from outlets which have not yet been hog-tied by either the Patman Act, the bill just introduced by the gentleman from Texas, Mr. Patman, several other bills pending—and H. R. 1611 is not yet enacted. The pity is that if he ever does have to rebel the first to suffer will be the small merchants misled into believing that price fixing spells easy profits. It is interesting to note in this connection that a number of State laws were enacted without hearings being held. It is evident that the consumers of the country know nothing about the underlying legislation.

⊥ Those contending that the Tydings-Miller bill if enacted will not lead to higher prices to the consumer, while openly avowing their objective is at least a 50-percent margin on the nationally advertised, well-known, trade-marked items they sell, go so far as actually to cite to the committee, in substantiation of their remarkable claims, a set of figures collected by one of their associations. These figures can undoubtedly be dismissed on the score that those preparing them have a fixed minimum margin of 50 percent as their real objective, but moreover, they are quite obviously but hand-picked, nonrepresentative data. They represent only 114 stores—there are 3,206 drug stores in California, and 114 is but 3.5 percent of 3,206—and their hand-picked nature is self-evident, because the entire 114 stores are in 62 different cities. Moreover these figures are not published, although it is stated in the hearings that they are published. They are, evidently, merely in the files of proponents of the bill. In other words, not over 52 competitors can be involved out of the entire State of California. Naturally, it wouldn't be difficult to select among 62 cities 114 stores which, being exceedingly high-margin stores, showed slight variations (6.7 percent upward in these hand-picked figures) from the minimum contractual prices first offered by manufacturers—and, remember, before any 50-percent minimum is achieved. Of course 114 popular-priced, low-margin stores would show absolutely opposite figures—and large price increases—and if and when the 50 percent avowed objective is attained, again the figures will be different—and reflect still larger price increases.

Therefore, those who infer to the committee, first, that the report of the California college professor mentioned indicates what the scattered instances, hand-picked by one of their associations, represents, and second that the professor approves of price fixing at least at average cost of doing business levels (which is what the 50-percent minimum margin the proponents of H. R. 1611 seek is), are in fact doing the committee a disservice, if not actually misleading it. For the college professor states very clearly: "In the metropolitan centers retail prices on advertised items were immediately raised on the average about one-third over 1933 prices * * *." Certainly the difference between a minus 6.7 percent and a positive 33 1/3 percent must still be 40 percent, and it is exactly by that tremendous percentage that such inferences might, if unchallenged, mislead. Further, the continuing of all-pervading disception [sic] running through all such contentions must be remembered, namely, that the figures cited do not reflect prices that would result from the avowed objective of those advancing them, which is a 50-percent minimum, said to represent the cost of doing business, averaged, for their line.

Regarding the second point, the California professor is very clear and definite—he does not believe it sound to fix prices at or above average costs of doing business for trades. He says:

It would be revolutionary, to say the least, as well as uneconomical and inefficient, to set up uniform average marking rates on all items in a given assembly * * *. The use of an average figure * * * would lend legal sanction to the factors making for diseconomy.

Thus out of the mouth of the very man they cite to the committee the sponsors of the Tydings-Miller bill are shown to be planning to put it to uneconomical, revolutionary, and inefficient uses, and to accomplish "diseconomy" with it while protesting they wish it only for the sound, safe, efficient, and praiseworthy objective of eliminating "loss leaders."

⊥ This incident alone of coupling the California college professor's report with the figures from the 114 stores selected in a search through 62 cities by an officer of one of the sponsor's associations, and merely part of files, and not published as represented to the committee, should put the committee on warning. It recalls to me, if it does not to others on the committee, the scandalous misrepresentation of certain leading college professors' views which were somehow foisted off on the majority report on the Patman Act.

A WARNING

Certainly that all constitutes a warning to "stop, look, and listen" before aiding and abetting a similar program in every State under the guise of quite soundly checking "loss leader" selling. And certainly it all has nothing in the world to do with checking "loss leader" selling, except that naturally "loss leader" selling does incidentally go out the window, once you embark on a program of fixing margins at anything over cost, let alone at 50 percent over cost.

A CASE IN POINT

My own experience since preparing this report is a case in point. After I announced my intention of submitting it, statements by both proponents and opponents of H. R. 1611 quickly appeared which, curiously enough, served to confirm my suspicions that a desire to check "loss leader" selling was being used as a cloak for a sinister price-fixing scheme. Proponents in my locality avowed, for example, that they are after 50 percent only in certain items, and only about 40 percent on others. This was a dead give away, surely. Opponents were provoked at me because I even assumed the bill is what it has been represented to be—a measure to check "loss leader" selling.

As a result, I am confident that the committee is being asked to act on "loss leader" selling in order to assist a Nation-wide price-fixing program, in which both the Patman Act and H. R. 1611 are two steps, and State price-control legislation a third step. There may be other steps involved in this vast scheme of consumer exploitation. Certainly curbing "loss leader" selling is no more the real motive in the case of H. R. 1611 than curbing alleged monopoly was the real motive in the case of the Patman Act. The real motive is to legalize price fixing, pure, simple, and unadulterated.

The Federal Trade Commission should investigate fully and report. The Commission should ascertain whether or not there is evidence that any of the proponents of H. R. 1611 have actually avowed a fixed profit margin as their objective. It should report the actual effects of State price-control laws on the resale prices of articles such as those with which H. R. 1611 is concerned. It should discover, if any trades have used such laws, or the Commission's own Federal Trade Practice Conferences, to raise prices or eliminate or restrict competition. It should report what the N. R. A. experience has to offer in respect to price control at levels above the cost of the goods involved. It should suggest at what levels, if any, overcost measures to check "loss leader" selling should begin to work if the consumer is to be properly protected.

Surely these are subjects in connection with which the Commission can best assemble the necessary facts the committee should have before acting. Certainly the committee cannot safely recommend legislation to the Congress which it has been shown to be directly connected with ⊥ price-fixing campaigns until it has had the advantage of a full and complete investigation. The chairman and chief counsel of the Commission appeared before the committee but they had not conducted the investigation as aforesaid.

ANOTHER ALTERNATIVE

An alternative would be to amend H. R. 1611 so that it only grants immunities so long as the prices fixed do no more than prevent "loss leader" selling. In other words, while the Congress unfortunately cannot, probably, outlaw "loss leader" selling directly, because of the intrastate nature of the transactions, it perhaps could within its constitutional rights, qualify its grant of immunity in H. R. 1611, and even specify that the use of the grant to ends in excess of controlling "loss leader" selling does not have the approval of the Congress. The Wisconsin fair trade practices law has such a consumer safety valve. Certainly such an amendment would test the sincerity of those sponsoring H. R. 1611 on the ground that controlling "loss leader" selling is their only interest.

It must be kept in mind that the Supreme Court in upholding two State laws of the type H. R. 1611 is intended to facilitate, did not sustain price-fixing as an end. The Supreme Court merely upheld price-fixing contracts, involving trade-marked articles in open competition, as binding on all (on notice as to their existence), as a means to the end of protecting intangible rights in the trade marks from destructive selling. Most States, as a matter of fact, have statutes or provisions in their constitutions running against price fixing.

Therefore the responsibility of foreseeing any use of legislation like H. R. 1611 to price-fixing ends rests heavily in the committee and the Congress. The Supreme Court, in other words, has not by any means sanctioned such uses. It has merely sanctioned a method for protecting trade marks from certain damaging practices, among which would most assuredly be included "loss leader" selling, but among which would not, also most assuredly, be included a coercive plan on the part of distributors to force price-fixing upon manufacturers at levels to assure certain up-set wholesale and retail margins. Certainly if the proponents of H. R. 1611 feel that "loss leader" selling means selling that does not gross a 50 percent profit margin—which I fear is the case—they themselves have put the committee on warning.

The committee I fear now faces the grave task, as the result of the passage of the Patman Act, the spread of State price-control laws, and the offering of H. R. 1611 of drawing a line between trade-practice regulation for the benefit of the small man and legislation permitting the small man to bring about levies on the consumer for arbitrary profit margins, levies which will sooner or later "back-kick" on the small man.

That is certainly a task tremendously important. It deserves not only the entire committee's gravest consideration, in my opinion, but the assistance of the most thorough investigation the Federal Trade Commission can make. Delay in a matter so vital is certainly inconsequential in view of the vast issues involved. I venture to recommend the steps I do only because I am confident the importance of the matter amply justifies them.

Emanuel Celler.
Robert L. Ramsay.

REMARKS OF REP. JOHN E. MILLER
75th Cong., 1st Sess.
April 19, 1937

81 Cong. Rec. A873

Mr. [JOHN E.] MILLER [D., Ark.]. Mr. Speaker, much is heard these days of the New Deal. It is the subject of bitter controversy in every nook and corner of the land. In exclusive clubs, on the street, in the country store, and on the farm it is defended and damned with equal fervor. There are some who profess to believe that the new teachings are subversive of our institutions and go so far as to undermine the foundation of the Republic. There are others, however, who see the New Deal as a belated effort to work humanity a bit closer to the top and to give all an opportunity to enjoy life, liberty, and the pursuit of happiness.

There are some who regard the new political concepts as directly contrary to the principles and purposes of our system of government. To them the new teachings are alien teachings having no place in a country devoted to democratic ideals. There are some who regard the President as an agent of destruction, bent upon tearing down the temple built by the fathers. There are others who view him as an apostle of a new political philosophy which places a greater value upon mankind and which seeks to give all a greater share of the comforts and enjoyments of life. To these the more "abundant life" is not a term of derision. These have no difficulty in catching the idealism which places human rights above property rights.

The storm of controversy will continue to beat itself against the new order. The controversy will become more bitter as the days wear on. Prejudice will vie with prejudice in adding to the general confusion. Be this as it may, I give it as my deliberate opinion that the laurel wreath of immortality will crown that doctrine which places the man above the machine which he operates. The happiness of people, the material progress of families, the well-being of millions of individuals have come to stand out as one of the major objectives of government.

The time is here when we must regard industry as a means to an end, and not the end itself. We must view labor and toil in terms of people, living people, who make it possible for the wheels of industry to hum, and we must realize that the producer is vastly more important than the goods which he produces. We are approaching the day when we shall understand that ultimately all problems are social problems, and that government, industry, economics, and philosophy must all bend themselves to the task of bringing about a fuller and more equitable existence for mankind as a whole. Man was not made for the Sabbath, but the Sabbath was made for man. Ultimately, everything shall be judged in the light of what it has contributed to human happiness and human betterment. You may call it a New Deal or anything you please, but I want to take my stand alongside of the man with the hoe, rather than with the hoe itself.

America has had many New Deals. There has always been a certain unrest in the hearts of our people that has pushed them further and further ahead. The ringing of the Liberty Bell announced the beginning of the greatest political experiment in the history of the world. Even today we can hear the clang-clang of the old Bell as it announced the glad tidings that America had cast off the old to face into the new. Each clang of the bell may be likened to the hammering of the anvil as there was beaten and forged the basic pattern of an America devoted to religious and political liberty, and which dared to proclaim that all men are created equal. Even now we can visualize the courage and devotion of our forefathers as they plunged headlong into a fight from which was to emerge a land consecrated to the principle of a square deal, and a free and open road for all. The new deal, then and now, was simply another word for opportunity.

Our present difficulties in America spring from no defect or break-down in those early doctrines. The principles born at Bunker Hill, nourished through the horrors of Valley Forge, and nailed down for posterity at Yorktown, are as immortal today as they were when first baptized with the blood of men who placed liberty and freedom above life itself. Those doctrines flourished in the early days of the Republic. They were given life and form by Jefferson, glorified under Lincoln, championed by the first Roosevelt, and consecrated anew under Woodrow Wilson, and are being brought to full fruition under the second Roosevelt.

The principles of liberty, freedom, opportunity, confront us today as the noblest expression of all that America was meant to be. The present constitutes a challenge to our right to the past. The New Deal, as I see it, is nothing but another step in giving immortality to the principles inherent in America herself. America must again become the land of liberty, liberty of opportunity, liberty of thought, liberty of action, and freedom from the heel of the despot, whether that despot be a foreign foe or a domestic foe, wrapped in the cloak of monopoly or wearing the garb of special privilege.

The difficulty is not with the basic pattern of America, but with those forces which would twist the pattern to serve their own selfish ends. For years there have been powers at work which would sacrifice our institutions if only they themselves might prosper. New forces, strange forces, forces alien to the true American way of doing things, forces bent upon having their own way, irrespective of what ruin they may bring to others, have long been at work chiseling away the foundation upon which the country rests.

Quietly, cautiously, insidiously, and cunningly, these forces have bored their way in until today they sit at the controls. They now have the power to destroy all that stands in their way. These smart lads have been building fences, pulling strings, fixing this and fixing that, until the economic scheme has become pretty much what they want it to be. They crack the whip and put the rest of us through the jumps. In a very real sense, they control the destiny of millions of people, and their imprint is now to be seen in the social status that prevails.

Vast changes have come about in our social and economic set-up, and because of these vast changes, America finds herself facing the terrifying problems of today. Wealth and power have become vested in a few to such an extent that the very existence of our ideals lies in the balance. We have sat by while the forces of monopoly have juggled the industrial and economic systems to their heart's content. The business life of every city and hamlet in the country ⊥ has become vastly disturbed by the invasion of absentee ownership and outside control. A country which was built upon the ideal of opportunity for all, has come to mean opportunity for but a few.

This is nowhere better illustrated than in the field of retail distribution. Here the destruction may be seen piled high along the roadside. Here may be seen the stark tragedy which stalks alongside the present trend of things. Here may be seen the play and interplay of the forces which would make America the mere footstool of monopoly. Here may be seen the change and interchange of the forces which have woven their own strange economic pattern for the American people. Here may be seen the course and intercourse of the powers which seek to bend our political institutions to serve the interests of the few at the expense of many. Here may be seen the charge and discharge of the forces which have distorted and disfigured American principles to the extent that the door of opportunity swings to admit only a few. Retail distribution has become so intense, so colored with the curse of special privilege, so completely under the heel of despotic powers, that it stands a challenge to all the finer things America was meant to be.

I have observed the economic trends in the retail field. First of all, retail distribution is by far our largest industry. In 1929, for instance, there were nearly a half a million stores selling food at retail, with a total sales nearly $11,000,000,000. The combined sales for all retail stores amounted to the almost legendary total of $53,000,000,000. There are about 1,500,000 retail stores in this country, employing millions of people, and affording the one service which brings the products of the farm and factory to your door. Retailing constitutes the bedrock of our national prosperity. It is the one means which permits America to carry on.

There is every reason why we should keep the channels of retail distribution clear of all obstructions. There is every reason why we should see to it that no one is permitted to gain control and to direct it to selfish ends. There is every reason why we should not permit a few to monopolize it, and to use their power for the destruction of independent business enterprises.

Yet, strange as it may seem, we are doing just these very things. In spite of its great importance, economists, political leaders, and legislators have, on the whole, shown scant interest in the problems confronting the neighborhood store. During the past decade or so many fields of retail distribution have fallen into the hands of centralized power. These fields were once in the hands of individual businessmen, each serving his place in the economic scheme and each doing his share toward building up American industry and American communities. It was the independent businessman, proud of his position in the community, who put America on her feet.

The grocer, the hardware dealer, the jeweler, the pharmacist were to be found shoulder to shoulder with the doctor, the lawyer, the clergyman in their efforts to upbuild and uplift. These men constituted the woof and fabric of our national life. It was their prowess that built an empire in the wilderness. These men built our cities, railroads, factories, churches, colleges, universities, and hospitals. These men trudged through the horrors of war that freedom might come to have a meaning far beyond the power of words to express. These were the men who met in legislative halls, who sat on the bench, and who were entrusted with executive authority to give force and life to the principles of opportunity for all and special privileges to none.

Thoughtful men, men really concerned with the economic and social future of America, have been greatly alarmed by the changes which have come about in retail distribution. These men see in the present situation forces at work which spell the doom of all that our country was meant to be. They see a break-down in the orderly processes of distribution, and a consequent break-down in the forces of production. They see, too, the beginning of a break-down in the social status of those once engaged in conducting their own independent businesses. They see the footsteps of a new feudal system with a few in complete control of the destiny of millions.

They see the present unemployment problems as the logical outcome of the centralization of distribution in the hands of a few. They ask themselves just how can unemployment be cut down by continuing a system which pushes greater and greater numbers out of work? How can there be a pick-up in business activity by continuing to squeeze a greater and greater number of stores out of business? What is there to be gained by crippling the system which heretofore at least has provided for the free and open distribution of the products of American industry? How can prosperity be restored by hammering harder and harder against the great army of independent businessmen upon whom the burden of distribution rests? How sound is that economic system which has nailed the doors and closed the shutters of hundreds of thousands of independent stores throughout the length and breadth of America?

These men have been casting about for some effective means of retaining a place for the independent merchant. They seek to retain his code of business morals; they seek to conserve his fair-minded point of view; they seek to preserve his influence in community life; they seek to maintain, in its original force and power, the doctrine of opportunity for all and a free and open road for all; they seek to engender in the great bulk of our people a sense of responsibility and awaken them to the perils which lie ahead.

Some years ago there was conceived a legislative plan which has become known as fair-trade legislation. This legislation followed closely upon the plan before Congress for many years. The first State to enact fair-trade legislation was California. This legislation has since been adopted in Oregon, Arizona, Wyoming, Iowa, Louisiana, Illinois, Kentucky, West Virginia, Maryland, New York, Rhode Island, New Mexico, Utah, Idaho, Washington, Montana, South Dakota, Kansas, Arkansas, Wisconsin, Ohio, Tennessee, Virginia, Pennsylvania, New Jersey, North Dakota, Georgia, Colorado, Indiana, Nevada, North Carolina, Minnesota, Delaware, Oklahoma, Nebraska, and South Carolina. These States comprise more than three-fourths of our entire population and include the great industrial sections of the country. Combined, these States have nearly three-fourths of the membership in the National Congress.

The purpose of this legislation is to equalize, to some extent at least, the difference between large and small business, and to strike down the unfair advantages which the big operator enjoys. This legislation is aimed at giving plain everyday honesty a place in retail distribution, and to bringing back common decency to the market place. It is intended to call a halt upon the plundering hordes which have marched roughshod over independent enterprise. It is designed to bring back peace and order to retail distribution, and to cure the madness of current commercial warfare.

In a practical sense, fair-trade legislation recognizes the naked dishonesty and gross deception of the modern predatory price cutter. Surveys without number, conducted by the Government as well as by private concerns, have shown that predatory prices are a snare and a delusion whereby the purchaser is led as a lamb to the slaughter. Once inside, the wily retailer proceeds to fleece the purchaser. Congressional investigations have shown that while a few cents are knocked off the price of standard articles to create a false impression upon the public, profits well above 2,000 percent are gouged from the pockets of the buying public by the predatory operator.

The costs of doing business must be met by the deep cut-price artist no less than by the retailer who feels that he should deal honestly and fairly with those who come to him. There is no magic in the matter of operating expense. One way to pull operating costs down is to steal wages from employees, and congressional investigations again have shown just how low the wage scale is in those stores claiming to always undersell. Millions upon millions have been gouged from the buying public and the unfortunate employees by those concerns who always sell for less. The whole predatory system is a rank deception, a hollow delusion, and a stench in the nostrils of those who know just how contemptible the game has become.

The fair-trade movement has engendered a much greater interest upon the part of our lawmaking bodies in the problems of distribution. The feeling is growing that the buying public has been sandbagged and gypped long enough. The feeling is growing, too, that the public is safer in the hands of honest independent business. The predatory cut-rater is being seen as one who must play under cover, and who cannot stand honest competition. His code is a code of destruction, he can rise only upon the ruin which he himself brings about. Predatory business is crooked business. It depends upon the blackjack, and it strikes below the belt.

Certainly such business principles are alien to American ideals, and must be crushed if the America of the past is to be the America of the future. We cannot maintain true American ideals unless the benefits and advantages of American ideals are free and open to all.

WHAT IS THE ORIGIN OF THE FAIR-TRADE MOVEMENT?

The fair-trade movement grew out of attempts to maintain free and open competition in retail trade by eliminating those business practices which tend to monopoly. Chief among these is predatory price cutting, commonly known as "loss leader" selling. Loss leader selling consists in offering standard merchandise at less than cost. Such merchandise is known as "bait" merchandise, and is offered for the purpose of creating the false impression that everything in the store is sold at correspondingly low prices. Customers are thus lured into the store and every artful device is then used to switch them from the articles offered at cut prices, upon which the dealer sustains an actual loss, to other similar articles of unknown quality, upon which the dealer makes an exorbitant profit. Prolonged selling at such predatory levels results in freezing out small dealer competition, and once such competition is destroyed, monopoly is created. Because of its pernicious, destructive, and antisocial nature, loss leader selling has been declared an unfair trade practice by the Federal Trade Commission.

One of the greatest Justices of the United States Supreme Court once referred to loss leaders in the following terms:

> When a trade-marked article is advertised to be sold at less than the standard price it is generally done to attract persons to a particular store by the offer of an obviously extraordinary bargain. It is a bait, called by the dealers a "leader." But the cut-price article would more appropriately be termed a "misleader", because the very purpose of the cut price is to create a false impression.

The only way for the customer to beat the game is to buy the bargain and nothing else, but the price cutter knows that the customer will not do this, just as a professional gambler knows that the sucker can be induced to remain in the game by permitting him to win occasionally.

The fact that cut-rate stores exist is proof that they make money, not on loss leaders, but their profit comes from the sale of merchandise of unknown quality, for which they get a higher price than is possible on standard goods of known value.

WHAT IS A FAIR-TRADE LAW?

It is an act of a State legislature aimed at the elimination of certain evils, and particularly at the elimination of the evils of loss-leader selling. Generally speaking, these acts of the State legislatures provide that contracts relating to the sale or resale of commodities which bear, or the label or content of which bears, the trade mark, brand, or name of the producer or owner of such commodities, and which are in free and open competition with commodities of the same general class produced by others, are valid, and that such contracts may provide that the buyer will not sell such commodity except at the price stipulated by the vendor. As heretofore stated, fair-trade acts have been enacted in 37 States. They are practically uniform and make provision for the closing out of the owner's stock of merchandise or for the sale of damaged or deteriorated goods or sales held under orders of any court.

ARE THESE STATE FAIR-TRADE ACTS PRICE-FIXING ACTS?

They are not price-fixing acts in any sense. It is doubtful whether any legislative body has the right to enact a price-fixing statute. Such an enactment would be contrary to the inherent attributes of property itself, and such an act would probably violate the fifth and fourteenth amendments, which in effect guarantee the owner of property the right to determine for himself the price at which he will sell. The State fair-trade acts only grant legislative authority to the interested parties to enter into a contract for the disposition of identified goods.

The Supreme Court of the United States, in the case of *Old Dearborn Co.* v. *Seagram Corporation* (299 U. S. 178), decided December 7, 1936, held that the Fair Trade Act of Illinois is constitutional; and, since all of the fair-trade acts enacted by the various States are similar, it cannot successfully be argued that such acts of the State legislatures are not valid.

DO THE FAIR-TRADE ACTS COVER ALL MERCHANDISE?

The fair-trade acts of the States are limited in their scope. By express language they apply only to commodities and merchandise which bears, or the label or content of which bears, the trade mark, brand, or name of the producer and which are in free and open competition with other merchandise of the same general class.

IS EVERY PRODUCER REQUIRED TO ENTER INTO A CONTRACT?

The contracts are purely voluntary. A manufacturer or producer may or may not desire to have his products sold in accordance with and under such contracts as are authorized by the acts. It is a matter entirely within the discretion of the owners. The legislation merely makes such contracts legal and enforceable, once the parties enter into them.

WHAT IS TO PREVENT MANUFACTURERS AND OTHER PRODUCERS FROM AGREEING AMONG THEMSELVES REGARDING RESALE PRICES?

The acts of all the States provide that they shall not apply to contracts or agreements between producers or between wholesalers or between retailers as to sale or resale prices. The acts of the State legislatures will and do prevent monopolistic combinations and agreements among the producers and manufacturers, as well as to prevent retailers themselves from entering into contracts with each other to govern the prices at which the goods will be sold to the consumer.

WHAT ASSURANCE HAS THE CONSUMER THAT MANUFACTURERS WILL NOT SET UNREASONABLY HIGH RETAIL PRICES FOR THEIR PRODUCTS?

Under the State acts the contracts are limited to the particular kinds of merchandise hereinbefore stated. Practically all identified merchandise is highly competitive. The natural effect of free competition is to lower prices. For illustration, there are probably one hundred or more trade-mark brands of tooth paste. Under the law the manufacturers or producers of tooth paste, or any other merchandise, cannot enter into agreements among themselves as to the price of their products and, therefore, not being able to enter into such unlawful combinations, the manufacturers and producers must continue to strive for as large a share of the business as he can possibly obtain. Thus he is compelled to keep his retail prices low enough to secure customer acceptance.

ARE RETAIL PRICES HIGHER IN STATES HAVING THESE FAIR-TRADE ACTS?

Retail prices on the whole have declined in the States having fair-trade acts. Carefully conducted surveys show a general leveling of retail prices. By eliminating loss-leader selling there is no need for exacting exorbitant profits on other goods and this has had a tendency to pull all prices down to a level which permits the merchant to actually give to the customer a lower price, and at the same time permits the merchant to make a reasonable return on his invested capital.

WHY IS IT NECESSARY TO ENACT H. R. 1611?

The constitutionality of fair-trade acts has been sustained, but unless section 1 of the act of July 2, 1890, is amended it is reasonably certain that the rule announced by the Supreme Court of the United States in *Miles Medical Co.* v. *Parke* [sic] *& Sons Co.* (220 U. S. 373), decided April 3, 1911, will apply, and that it will be unlawful to ship merchandise in interstate commerce into States for sale under such contracts. It is certain that the State legislation will not fully function unless H. R. 1611 is enacted, because the producers and manufacturers will be fearful of criminal prosecution if such goods are shipped in interstate commerce for sale under such contracts. Many manufacturers not domiciled in the State where the goods are to be sold are unwilling to take the risk of violating a Federal law, and the effectiveness of the State fair-trade acts is seriously impaired. H. R. 1611 does no more than to remove Federal obstacles to the enforcement of contracts which the States themselves have declared lawful. The bill does not commit the Congress to a national policy on the subject matter of the State laws and is not price-fixing legislation in any sense.

Sound public policy lies in the direction of lending assistance to the States to effectuate their own public policy with regard to their internal affairs. The States have no right to regulate interstate commerce, but they are entitled to every assistance possible from the Federal Government to regulate commerce within their own boundaries, and unless H. R. 1611 is enacted this right will be denied to the States.

It should be borne in mind that H. R. 1611 will not apply to those States that have not enacted fair-trade acts, and if the States, after giving a fair trial to the fair-trade acts, should repeal such legislation, then section 1 of the present act, approved July 2, 1890, will remain in full force and effect.

Thirty-seven States have said by these legislative enactments that they desire to regulate these matters themselves. It seems that the Congress should accept this decision of these States and render every assistance possible to carry into effect the opinion of the lawmaking bodies in the several States, not only upon this question, but on all other matters where it is possible for the States to act.

RESOLUTION PROVIDING FOR CONSIDERATION OF H.R. 1611
75th Cong., 1st Sess.
April 23, 1937

81 Cong. Rec. 3775

RESTRAINTS AND MONOPOLIES ON TRADE AND COMMERCE

Mr. [JOHN] O'CONNOR [D., N.Y.], from the Committee on Rules, reported the following resolution (H. Res. 191), providing for the consideration of the bill (H. R. 1611) to amend the act entitled "An act to protect trade and commerce against unlawful restraints and monopolies", approved July 2, 1890 (Rept. No. 683), which was referred to the House Calendar and ordered printed:

House Resolution 191

Resolved, That upon the adoption of this resolution it shall be in order to move that the House resolve itself into the Committee of the Whole House on the state of the Union for the consideration of H. R. 1611, a bill to amend the act entitled "An act to protect trade and commerce against unlawful restraints and monopolies", approved July 2, 1890. That after general debate, which shall be confined to the bill and continue not to exceed 3 hours, to be equally divided and controlled by the chairman and ranking minority member of the Committee on the Judiciary, the bill shall be read for amendment under the 5-minute rule. At the conclusion of the reading of the bill for amendment, the Committee shall rise and report the same to the House with such amendments as may have been adopted, and the previous question shall be considered as ordered on the bill and amendments thereto to final passage without intervening motion except one motion to recommit, with or without instructions.

[ED. NOTE: H.R. 1611 was never called up for consideration, however. See the communication from President Roosevelt to the Senate reprinted *supra* and the remarks reprinted immediately *infra.*]

REMARKS OF REP. CLARE E. HOFFMAN
75th Cong., 1st Sess.
April 27, 1937

81 CONG. REC. 3869

Mr. [CLARE E.] HOFFMAN [R., Mich.]. Mr. Speaker, I ask consent to proceed for 5 minutes and to revise and extend my remarks.

The SPEAKER. Is there objection to the request of the gentleman from Michigan? There was no objection.

A TRAFFIC COP IN CONGRESS

Mr. HOFFMAN. Mr. Speaker, President Roosevelt's directing thumb, regardless of congressional stop and go signals manipulated by leaders, indicates to subservient Congressmen not only what they shall pass but when they shall move.

A most striking illustration of this was given today, when Presidential action called a halt on the consideration of the Miller-Tydings bill, which would have permitted the States to regulate price fixing by contract.

In the House consideration of legislative matters is supposed to be determined by the leadership, Speaker BANKHEAD and SAM RAYBURN, and the powerful Rules Committee, and this organization, with the approval of the President, set today, Tuesday, for consideration of the Miller-Tydings bill.

Yesterday, without warning, the President decided that the enactment of this bill might acknowledge too great a power to the States. So today House membership is advised that it may consider something else.

In the meantime, the President will undoubtedly group the legislation which he desires and which relates to price fixing, wages, hours, and child labor all in one bill and then present it, at some time which suits his convenience, to the Congress and have it passed.

Beyond question, the President has in mind a bill reenacting many provisions of the N. R. A., which will give to the Federal Government absolute control over the business of the citizen. In short, and to put it bluntly, giving his administration the powers of a dictator over economic affairs.

With the help of John L. Lewis, the Civil Liberties Committee, his Labor Department, and the National Labor Relations Board, the beginning of complete domination of all industrial life is not so far away.

Congress was told today that all other legislation must await the determination of the court issue.

Like the Stuart kings of old England, the President not only desires a Supreme Court which he may manipulate, but a law which will enable him to send his "flying squadrons" of Federal circuit judges into any particular circuit in the country, somewhat as Lewis sends his "flying squadrons" of United Mine Workers into industrial communities when workers are slow in joining the C. I. O. or oppose him.

Thus again is the President's purpose to grasp the powers of an absolute dictator revealed to the people and thus again will Members of Congress be forced into a position where they must either vote for a bill embodying many objectives, complicated in its nature, and granting to the Executive increased and arbitrary power, or be, by him, branded as unfair in their consideration of human rights.

The situation is one calculated to break the heart of any conscientious, patriotic American.

REMARKS OF REP. WILLIAM R. POAGE AND REP. EARL C. MICHENER
75th Cong., 1st Sess.
May 4, 1937

81 Cong. Rec. 4180

Mr. [WILLIAM R.] POAGE [D., Tex.]. Mr. Speaker and fellow Members of the House, in our solicitude for the welfare and security of the Federal Government, we, as Members of Congress, are prone to forget that there are 48 other governments serving the same people who are served by the Federal Government, and that these 48 State governments must levy taxes on the same people who support the Federal Government. We do not always seem to realize that every time we offer the States a so-called Federal-aid project that we are imposing a double burden on the people of the country. Not only must the people of the several States pay the taxes to provide for the Federal contribution, but in addition they must, as taxpayers of their own States, pay the taxes to provide their State's contribution. No matter how meritorious the cause, the ultimate cost must and does fall on the taxpayer.

In my State, as in many of your States, we have levied excise taxes on certain usable goods of general consumption, such as cigarettes. This tax is collected from those of our own citizens who use these goods. We have had a long, hard fight to develop a system of tax collection which would be reasonably effective. We feel that we now have such a system except for the evasions that are allowed and encouraged by the application of the rules of the Federal Government in regard to the movement of interstate commerce. In Texas, as in many other States, it is a violation of the law to transport or possess an unstamped package of cigarettes. Millions of dollars' worth of unstamped cigarettes are brought into our State and into other States each year in interstate commerce, and the Federal Government protects these violators of State laws. These violations not only deprive the States of the means of collecting needed revenue from their own citizens in the manner deemed wise by the States themselves; they go further and work a serious injury to the honest dealer within the State by subjecting him to the unfair competition of a product on which no tax is paid. Instead of hampering the States in the exercise of their taxing power, the Federal Government should aid them. Instead of enabling a group of law violators to profit by unfair competition with honest local dealers, this Federal Government should help the States protect these reputable dealers. To this end I recently appeared before the Judiciary Committee of this House to urge upon its members the importance of giving consideration to this situation. I hope that appropriate provisions to accomplish this will be included in the Smith bill, H. R. 4746, and that this measure will receive your favorable consideration when it comes on the floor.

Mr. [EARL C.] MICHENER [R., Mich.]. Mr. Speaker, will the gentleman yield?

Mr. POAGE. Yes.

Mr. MICHENER. We have the Miller-Tydings bill, in which the gentleman is interested, the purpose of which is to prevent the thing that he is talking about. It is on the calendar. The committee reported it, I think, unanimously, and the leadership gave it a place. It was to be considered, but, as I understand—and I know the gentleman will correct me if I am wrong—the White House sent word that we were not to consider those things in the House; that we should consider those things in a different way, and that we might hear of some solution from the White House. Does not the gentleman think we ought to exercise our own judgment here and act on these matters ourselves?

Mr. POAGE. I am going to do that very thing. That is the very purpose of this speech. I expect to call attention to the fact that it is my belief that the Smith bill does the thing that I am suggesting and that probably the Miller-Tydings bill does not cover that whole field, although it may have meritorious spots in it. I hope we will have the Smith bill for a solution of it.

SENATE CONSIDERATION (S. 100; H.R. 7472)

REPORT OF THE SENATE COMMITTEE ON THE JUDICIARY
S. Rep. No. 257
75th Cong., 1st Sess.
March 29, 1937

Mr. HATCH, from the Committee on the Judiciary, submitted the following

REPORT

[To accompany S. 100]

The Committee on the Judiciary, having had under consideration the bill (S. 100) to amend the act entitled "An act to protect trade and commerce against unlawful restraints and monopolies", approved July 2, 1890, report the same back to the Senate with the recommendation that it do pass with the following amendments:

Amendment no. 1: In the third line of the title, after the figures "1890", strike out the period and insert the following:

: and to modify the provisions of "An act to create a Federal Trade Commission, to define its powers and duties, and for other purposes", approved September 26, 1914.

Amendment no. 2: In line 7 of section 1, on page 1, strike out the comma after the word "conspiracy".

Amendment no. 3: In line 5 of section 1, on page 2, insert a comma after the word "bears".

Amendment no. 4: In line 12 of section 1, on page 2, between the word "is" and the word "made" insert the words "to be".

Amendment no. 5: In line 19 of section 1, on page 2, strike out the word "such" between the word "any" and the word "contract".

Amendment no. 6: In line 19 of section 1, on page 2, strike out the word "such" between the word "any" and of the letters "combi-".

Amendment no. 7: In line 20 of section 1, on page 2, after the word "conspiracy" and before the word "shall" insert the words "hereby declared to be illegal".

Amendment no. 8: In line 22 of section 1, on page 2, after the symbol and figures "$5,000" insert a comma.

During the Seventy-fourth Congress, second session a similar bill (S. 3822) was reported favorably from the Committee on the Judiciary and placed on Senate Calendar No. 2155. As the language of that report is applicable to the present legislation under consideration, the report on S. 3822[2.33] is quoted at length, as follows:

> The Committee on the Judiciary, having had under consideration the bill (S. 3822) to amend the act entitled "An act to protect trade and commerce against unlawful restraints and monopolies", approved July 2, 1890, report the same back with the recommendation that the bill do pass.

[2.33] S. 3822, 74th Cong., 2d Sess. (1936), was the first fair-trade bill introduced by Senator Tydings. The report on the bill, quoted here, was S. REP. No. 2053, 74th Cong., 2d Sess. (1936).

In 1933 a law was enacted by the State of California authorizing a manufacturer or producer of a commodity which bears his trade mark, brand, or name, and which is sold in free and open competition with commodities of the same general class produced by others to make a contract that the purchaser will not resell such commodity except at the price stipulated by the manufacturer or producer.

The purpose of the California act, as expressed in its title, was to protect trade-mark owners, distributors, and the general public against injurious and uneconomic practices in the distribution of articles of standard quality under a trade mark, brand, or name, and the particular practice against which it was directed was the so-called loss-leader selling.

Since the passage of the California act similar legislation has been enacted in 12 other States, namely, New York, Illinois, Pennsylvania, New Jersey, Oregon, Washington, Wisconsin, Iowa, Maryland, Ohio, Virginia, and Rhode Island (the last 3 since the introduction of the proposed bill).

In still other States contracts stipulating minimum resale prices are valid at common law.

In the States where such contracts are lawful, it has been found that loss-leader selling of identified merchandise sold under competitive conditions operates as a fraud on the consumer, destroys the producer's goodwill in his trade mark, and is used by the large merchant to eliminate his small independent competitor.

In recommending the passage of S. 3822 the committee, while fully recognizing the evils of loss-leader selling, is not required to determine the effectiveness of the device adopted by the States to eliminate the same.

It is sufficient that this type of selling unquestionably has had a disastrous effect upon the small independent retailer, thereby tending to create monopoly, and that a large number of States have found that its evil effects can be mitigated if not eliminated, by legalizing contracts stipulating minimum resale prices.

The Congress is not called upon to pass upon the effectiveness of the remedy but it should not put obstacles in the way of efforts of the individual States to make the remedy effective.

Though there is no specific adjudication on the subject, it is believed that contracts stipulating minimum resale prices, even when they are made or are to be performed in a State where such contracts are lawful, may violate the Sherman Act whenever the goods sold under the contract move in interstate commerce.

Consequently, many manufacturers not domiciled in the state of the vendee are unwilling to run the risk of violating the Federal law, and the effectiveness of the State fair-trade laws is thereby seriously impaired.

S. 100 removes the doubt as to the applicability of the Sherman Act by expressly legalizing such contracts where legal under the laws of the State where made or where they are to be performed.

Moreover, the proposed bill declares such contracts shall not be an unfair method of competition under the Federal Trade Commission law.

The language of the bill, in describing the class of commodities to which it is applicable, follows closely the language of the State acts, and the scope of the bill is therefore carefully limited to commodities "in free and open competition with commodities of the same general class produced by others."

The State acts are in no sense general price-fixing acts. They merely authorize a manufacturer or producer to enter into contracts for the maintenance of his price, but they do not compel him to do so. In other words, they are merely permissive.

They do not authorize horizontal contracts, that is to say, contracts or agreements between manufacturers, between producers, or between wholesalers, or between retailers as to the sale or resale price of any commodity.

They apply only to commodities which are in free and open competition with commodities of the same general class produced by others, and they therefore do not in any sense restrain trade or competition. In fact, they legalize a device which is intended to increase competition and prevent monopoly.

But most important, from the standpoint of the Congress, the proposed bill merely permits the individual States to function, without Federal restraint, within their proper sphere, and does not commit the Congress to a national policy on the subject matter of the State laws.

In other words, the bill does no more than to remove Federal obstacles to the enforcement of contracts which the States themselves have declared lawful.

S. 100 AS REPORTED BY THE SENATE COMMITTEE ON THE JUDICIARY
75th Cong., 1st Sess.
March 29, 1937

⊥ Reported by Mr. HATCH, with amendments

[Omit the part struck through and insert the part printed in italic]

A BILL

To amend the Act entitled "An Act to protect trade and commerce against unlawful restraints and monopolies", approved July 2, 1890.

1 *Be it enacted by the Senate and House of Representa-*
2 *tives of the United States of America in Congress assembled,*
3 That section 1 of the Act entitled "An Act to protect trade
4 and commerce against unlawful restraints and monopolies",
5 approved July 2, 1890, be amended to read as follows:
6 SECTION 1. Every contract, combination in the form
7 of trust or otherwise, or ~~conspiracy,~~ *conspiracy* in restraint
8 of trade or commerce among the several States, or with
9 foreign nations, is hereby declared to be illegal: *Provided,*
10 That nothing herein contained shall render illegal, contracts
11 or agreements prescribing minimum prices or other condi-
12 tions for the resale of a commodity which bears, or the
13 label or container of which ~~bears~~ *bears,* the trade mark,
14 brand, or name of the producer or distributor of such com-
15 modity and which is in free and open competition with
16 commodities of the same general class produced or dis-
17 tributed by others, when contracts or agreements of that
18 description are lawful as applied to intrastate transactions,
19 under any statute, law, or public policy now or hereafter
20 in effect in any State, Territory or the District of Columbia
21 in which such resale is *to be* made, or to which the com-
22 modity is to be transported for such resale, and the making
23 of such contracts or agreements shall not be an unfair method
14 of competition under section 5, as amended and supple-
15 mented, of the Act entitled "An Act to create a Federal
16 Trade Commission, to define its powers and duties, and for
17 other purposes", approved September 26, 1914. Every
18 person who shall make any such contract or engage in
19 any ~~such~~ combination or conspiracy *hereby declared to be*
20 *illegal,* shall be deemed guilty of a misdemeanor, and, on
21 conviction thereof, shall be punished by fine not exceeding
22 ~~$5,000~~ *$5,000,* or by imprisonment not exceeding one year,
23 or by both said punishments, in the discretion of the court.

Amend the title so as to read: "A bill to amend the Act entitled 'An Act to protect trade and commerce against unlawful restraints and monopolies', approved July 2, 1890;

and to modify the provisions of the Act entitled 'An Act to create a Federal Trade Commission, to define its powers and duties, and for other purposes', approved September 26, 1914."

SENATE DEBATE
75th Cong., 1st Sess.
May 3, 1937

81 Cong. Rec. 4083

The bill (S. 100) to amend the act entitled "An act to protect trade and commerce against unlawful restraints and monopolies", approved July 2, 1890, was announced as next in order.

Mr. [KENNETH] McKELLAR [D., Tenn.]. Mr. President, may we have an explanation of the bill?

⊥ Mr. [WILLIAM H.] KING [D., Utah]. Mr. President, I read in the newspapers a few days ago what purported to be a letter addressed to the Vice President, expressing in effect opposition to the so-called Tydings-Miller bill. The communication indicated that it came from a high authority in the executive branch of the Government. I am wondering if this purported message will prove an obstacle to the consideration of the bill.

As Senators know, the bill had received strong support, and there seemed to be no possible means of preventing its passage. Now it appears that the passage of the bill is to be delayed, perhaps indefinitely.

I might add that I have indicated opposition to the bill because I believe it tends to monopoly. I am therefore quite reconciled to a course that will not call for its consideration. I think the bill should go over.

The PRESIDENT pro tempore. The bill will be passed over.

[ED. NOTE: S. 100 received no further consideration by the Senate. However, the provisions of the bill were later attached as a rider to a District of Columbia appropriations bill (H.R. 7472) by the Senate Committee on the District of Columbia and reported to the Senate floor in the form of a committee amendment adding title VIII. The debate that follows is on the pertinent portion of the District of Columbia Revenue Act.]

SENATE DEBATE
75th Cong., 1st Sess.
July 23, 1937

81 Cong. Rec. 7486

The next amendment was, at the top of page 79, to insert:

TITLE VIII—AMENDMENT TO THE ANTITRUST LAWS

Section 1 of the act entitled "An act to protect trade and commerce against unlawful restraints and monopolies", approved July 2, 1890, is amended to read as follows:

"SECTION 1. Every contract, combination in the form of trust or otherwise, or conspiracy in restraint of trade or commerce among ⊥ the several States, or with foreign nations, is hereby declared to be illegal: *Provided,* That nothing herein contained shall render illegal contracts or agreements prescribing minimum prices for the resale of a commodity which bears, or the label or container of which bears, the trade mark, brand, or name of the producer or distributor of such commodity and which is in free and open competition with commodities of the same general class produced or distributed by others, when contracts or agreements of that description are lawful as applied to intrastate transactions, under any statute, law, or public policy now or hereafter in effect in any State, Territory, or the District of Columbia in which such resale is to be made, or to which the commodity is to be transported for such resale, and the making of such contracts or agreements shall not be an unfair method of competition under section 5, as amended and supplemented, of the act entitled 'An act to create a Federal Trade Commission, to define its powers and duties, and for other purposes', approved September 26, 1914. Every person who shall make any contract or engage in any combination or conspiracy hereby declared to be illegal shall be deemed guilty of a misdemeanor, and, on conviction thereof, shall be punished by fine not exceeding $5,000, or by imprisonment not exceeding 1 year, or by both said punishments, in the discretion of the court."

Mr. [MILLARD E.] TYDINGS [D., Md.]. Mr. President, I offer an amendment to the committee amendment, which I ask to have stated.

The PRESIDING OFFICER. The amendment to the amendment will be stated.

The CHIEF CLERK. On page 80, line 1, after "1914", it is proposed to insert a colon and the following:

Provided further, That the preceding proviso shall not make lawful any contract or agreement, providing for the establishment or maintenance of minimum resale prices on any commodity herein involved, between manufacturers or between producers or between wholesalers or between brokers or between factors or between retailers or between persons, firms, or corporations in competition with each other.

The PRESIDING OFFICER. The question is on agreeing to the amendment offered by the Senator from Maryland [Mr. TYDINGS] to the amendment reported by the committee.

Mr. TYDINGS. Mr. President, I am not going to make a speech now; but I should like to say that the amendment which I have just offered has been worked out by certain administration leaders and myself and is entirely satisfactory to me; and I think I am authorized to say that with that amendment the administration is not now opposed to this title of the bill.

Mr. KING. Mr. President, may I inquire of the Senator from Maryland for whom he speaks when he says "the administration"?

Mr. TYDINGS. The Attorney General's Department.

Mr. KING. Will the Senator explain the purpose of the amendment and its significance?

Mr. TYDINGS. In my judgment, Mr. President, the amendment is unnecessary because the provision as now found in the bill allows none of the things which the amendment specifically eliminates; but, in order that there may be no misunderstanding and that the element of competition may be kept forward throughout the process projected in this measure, the amendment has been offered. I took up the matter with the Attorney General and we worked out this amendment; and so far as I know and believe, it is an accurate statement that forces which were formerly opposed to this title of the bill have no particular objection to it at the present time. . . .

⊥ Mr. KING. Mr. President, I am opposed to the amendment offered by the ⊥7488 Senator from Maryland [Mr. TYDINGS]. Even if it possessed merit, it would have no place in the measure now under consideration. It is a rider upon a District of Columbia revenue bill, and it deals with a subject of great importance, affecting the entire Nation. It is a measure which seeks to nullify in many important respects the antitrust laws and to aid in the creation and maintenance of monopolies. I repeat that it is a rider, and riders are universally condemned. Unfortunately, efforts are not infrequently made to attach to measures of importance—measures which are absolutely necessary for the public welfare—riders, so-called, which have no relation whatever to pending legislation, or to the measures to which they are sought to be attached. Advantage is taken of a situation, which it is believed will secure legislative approval of propositions which, standing alone, would not obtain the approval of Congress. Occasionally important and necessary legislation is marred and disfigured by including therein propositions entirely foreign and alien, and which, as I have indicated, if compelled to rest solely upon their own merits, would fall.

I repeat that riders are universally condemned. They have been employed to obtain approval of unjust, unsound, and often obnoxious legislation. In some legislative bodies, amendments in the form of riders to measures under consideration, are not permitted. To be considered they must ⊥ be germane, and logically connected with the bill to which they are offered as amendments. In other words, they must be legitimately connected with the subject under consideration. I need not further elaborate the point that riders are deformities which cannot be defended. They often defeat sound and wise measures, and introduce foreign and extraneous matters into the legislative arena.

We have before us a bill dealing exclusively with District of Columbia affairs. It relates solely to taxation, and its purpose is to obtain revenue to meet the expenses of the Capital of the Nation.

The Committee on the District of Columbia, after due deliberation, agreed upon a bill exclusively dealing with revenue matters. However, as an amendment to the bill the Senator from Maryland [Mr. TYDINGS] offered the rider which has just been read, and which everyone conceded was a rider and had no place upon the bill, and which could not be defended upon the ground that it was proper legislation. I opposed the rider, but it was adopted. I filed a minority report which dealt only with the rider, and in that report I stated that the amendment—

* * * is wholly irrelevant and improper. It is not intended to provide revenue for the District of Columbia, or to meet the tax situation or to aid the District in meeting its deficits. It is an indefensible provision which has no place upon H. R. 7472, and should be stricken from the bill.

I further stated:

There can be no justification in my opinion for attaching riders to revenue measures, and for that matter to any form of legislation. * * * Apparently it is thought that by attaching this rider to the bill, which must be passed within a short time to meet the imperative demands of the District of Columbia, there is a chance to secure its passage. Certainly the measure, if it has merit, can be brought before the Senate upon motion and there stand or fall according to its merits; but it is improper to take advantage of the desperate condition of the District of Columbia, which will be without funds within a few days, and employ this proposed tax bill as a vehicle to secure the passage of a measure which seeks to repeal the Sherman antitrust law and to permit price fixing in many States and thus to affect business and economic conditions throughout the United States.

The amendment seeks to repeal the antitrust laws and so, in my opinion, by legalizing price fixing, will result in monopolistic practices.

Under the misleading titles of a "fair-trade practice" bill, or an "enabling act" to enable the States to enact so-called State fair-trade-practice acts, but always under the representation that it is merely a measure to prevent loss-leading selling, we are now confronted with a demand that the Sherman Antitrust Act be rendered innocuous, if not repealed in part, and that certain types of trade, based upon price-fixing, be legalized in interstate commerce.

In my report I further stated that for a number of years an aggressive campaign had been waged to secure congressional legislation which would permit price fixing and material changes in the antitrust laws. I further added that these efforts had failed, but that during the past few years demand had been made by some organizations to attain the objectives which had been heretofore prevented by Congress.

I further pointed out the fact that a bill was pending before the Senate, known as S. 100, and that it had been offered as a rider to the revenue bill under consideration. In the minority report I pointed to the fact that the Sherman antitrust law declared illegal every contract, combination in the form of trust, or otherwise, or conspiracy in restraint of trade or commerce among the several States, or with foreign nations; and that this rider seeks to amend such law by providing that contracts or agreements prescribing minimum prices for the resale of certain commodities shall not be illegal.

The purpose of S. 100, as I indicated in the minority report, and the rider which is attached to the bill under consideration, was to permit price fixing in connection with the sale of various commodities. I stated that the Federal Trade Commission, and other Federal agencies, national consumers' organizations, farm and labor organizations, and economists of note understand the basic unsoundness of the rider and of the hidden attack on consumers, and have indicated their disapproval of the measure.

A number of States have enacted laws under the terms of which, as I interpret them, contracts may be made which will permit monopolies and the fixing of prices.

As stated by the Federal Trade Commission, many of these State laws are directly and irreconcilably in conflict with the present Federal laws in respect of resale-price maintenance. In other words, S. 100 and the Tydings rider permit resale-price maintenance and, as stated, the fixing of prices. If the antitrust laws are repealed, then it is believed by some manufacturers and many retailers that the way will be clear for resale-price maintenance, which, I may add, would inevitably mean that monopolistic practices would become numerous.

I am repeating when I state that the Senator from Maryland offered some time ago a measure (S. 100) which is now upon the calendar, the purpose of which was to repeal all antitrust laws insofar as they apply to price-fixing agreements in those States in which State legislation permits such agreements. That bill has not been acted upon by the Senate and it is now offered in the form of an amendment as a rider to the tax bill relating solely to the District of Columbia.

Mr. McKELLAR. Mr. President, will the Senator yield?

Mr. KING. I yield.

Mr. McKELLAR. Does not the amendment provide that the Sherman antitrust law and Clayton Act shall be applicable to all the rest of the country except the District of Columbia?

Mr. KING. No, Mr. President.

Mr. McKELLAR. Does not the amendment make an exception? The amendment offered by the Senator from Maryland provides—

> That the preceding proviso shall not make lawful any contract or agreement, providing for the establishment or maintenance of minimum resale prices on any commodity herein involved, between manufacturers or between producers or between wholesalers or between brokers or between factors or between retailers or between persons, firms, or corporations in competition with each other.

That does away with the Sherman antitrust law and the Clayton Act here in the District of Columbia.

Mr. [ALBEN W.] BARKLEY [D., Ky.]. Mr. President, will the Senator yield?

Mr. KING. I yield.

Mr. BARKLEY. Title VIII applies not merely to the District of Columbia. The provision with respect to the Sherman antitrust law applies to the whole country. The amendment offered by the Senator from Maryland, if it shall be adopted, will apply to the whole country, and not alone to the District of Columbia.

Mr. KING. Mr. President, the Senator from Tennessee's [Mr. MCKELLAR] position, if I understand it correctly, is not correct. I think the Senator from Kentucky [Mr. BARKLEY] has correctly stated that the amendment attached to the pending measure by the Senator from Maryland [Mr. TYDINGS] would in effect repeal the antitrust laws in all States in which legislation had been enacted permitting agreements authorizing the fixing of prices of commodities insofar as the antitrust laws related to such agreements. In other words, in a number of States, laws have been enacted which permit contracts and agreements prescribing minimum prices for the resale of commodities. As a result of these enactments, contracts are made and prices fixed without being subject to the antitrust laws unless such contracts are entered into between corporations or individuals in different States. There has been a powerful movement, largely promoted by the National Association of Retail Druggists, to repeal the antitrust laws to the extent that price fixing might be permitted in those States which enacted laws legalizing combinations and agreements fixing minimum prices and providing for price maintenance.

As I was saying when interrupted by the Senator from Tennessee [Mr. MCKELLAR], the Senator from Maryland [Mr. TYDINGS] introduced S. 100—which is in effect the amendment now under consideration—and a similar bill was introduced in the House. The Senate bill has not been acted upon by the Senate, though it has been on the calendar for some time.

⊥ Mr. President, I do not agree with the Senator from Maryland [Mr. TYDINGS] in ⊥7490 the statement which he made a few moments ago that forces which were formerly opposed to the provisions of the amendment—being S. 100—have no particular objection to it now. As a matter of fact, I know there are strong, indeed, violent objections to this measure by consumers' organizations, agricultural and labor organizations, and many groups of our citizenship. The Senator states that the subject was taken up with the Attorney General and "we worked out the amendment which has been offered."

Mr. President, my information is not in harmony with the statements of the Senator. Even if the Attorney General had assented to the amendment I would question his right to do so; and certainly I would not feel that the Senate, or any Member of the Senate, was bound thereby. I deny the right of the Department of Justice to consent to the repeal of antitrust laws, or to adopt any course that would permit monopolistic practices. The evils of monopoly have been experienced by the American people, and years ago they determined to enact legislation to protect trade and commerce against unlawful restraints and monopolies. The Sherman law was supplemented by the Clayton Act, and upon a number of occasions Congress has declared its purpose to prevent monopolies or monopolistic practices. I cannot believe that the Government, or any responsible officer of the Government, will approve of any measure that weakens or impairs the Federal antitrust laws. Indeed, I believe the sentiment in the executive departments, as well as throughout the country, is to strengthen such laws, to the end that there may be free competition and full opportunity for private persons and private interests to engage in trade and commerce, without apprehension that the heavy hand of monopoly will be laid upon them.

Mr. President, as I have stated, S. 100 is in substance the rider attached to this bill. With respect to S. 100 the President of the United States has expressed his disapproval of the same. On the 24th of April of this year the President sent a communication to the Vice President expressly dealing with S. 100, the so-called Tydings bill. . . .

The President in his letter correctly appraises the purposes and the effect of this amendment, which, as I have stated, is the Tydings-Miller bill. He states that it would render legal certain contracts for the maintenance of resale prices now illegal under Federal law.

As I have indicated, the Sherman antitrust law was to protect trade and commerce against unlawful restraints and monopolies; but it is now designed by this amendment to permit contracts and agreements which are in restraint of trade and which permit the maintenance of resale prices. Retail druggists' organizations and certain other organizations have maintained an active lobby for a number of years to secure the repeal of the antitrust laws in order that they might with impunity fix and maintain prices within their respective States. They were successful, as I have indicated, in a number of States in obtaining legislation legalizing contracts and agreements to fix prices and create monopolies. These State statutes have been effective in promoting price-fixing and monopolistic practices, so long as they were intrastate; but there was hanging over the transactions the Federal antitrust laws, which afforded some protection to the consumers in such States. It was believed by the organizations just referred to that if they could secure the enactment of a Federal statute that would lift the antitrust laws from those States in which price fixing and monopolies were legalized they would be able to carry out their purposes and fix prices and entrench themselves behind monopolistic bulwarks. If the rider is adopted and becomes law, it will permit manufacturers and distributors in New York, for instance, to enter into contracts with retailers in California, and to fix and maintain retail prices, though monopolies in the commodities referred to might result. And I might add that in California and other States it has been held that if the retail vendee gives notice to the public of his price-fixing contract with the distributor or manufacturer in New York no other person in the State may sell the commodity at a price below that fixed in such contract.

I might add, in passing, that the Federal antitrust laws would not have the same meaning in all States. In those States where laws are passed permitting resale price fixing the efficacy of the Federal statutes would be impaired, but in those States which have not legalized price fixing the antitrust laws would be effective. In the communication of the Chairman of the Federal Trade Commission it is clearly indicated that the enactment of the rider would modify the antitrust laws in differing degrees in different States. It would leave such laws in full force and effect in those States which did not legalize resale-price maintenance; but there would be divergent policies in those States which legalize resale-price maintenance; and the result would be that the Federal Government would be under the necessity of attempting to enforce divergent regulatory policies toward shipments made by the same manufacturer to dealers located in different States.

Mr. President, I affirm in all seriousness that the provisions of the rider, if enacted into law, will legalize price fixing and further monopolistic practices, the consumers of the country will be penalized, and inordinate profits reaped by manufacturers and retailers.

I refer again to the communication of Commissioner Ayres to the President, in which he states that the enactment of S. 100 would, in its practical operation, modify, if not render inoperative, existing court consent decrees and orders of the Commission against price fixers, and thus practically terminate present Federal Trade Commission proceedings against a number of distillers. It would seem, Mr. President, wholly unjustifiable to repeal or modify the antitrust laws; to legalize price fixing; to make possible, indeed certain, the increase of commodity prices; to nullify court decrees entered for the protection of consumers against monopolies; and, in my view, it is more reprehensible to bring about such results without due consideration and by a rider attached to a revenue measure dealing solely with the District of Columbia.

If the antitrust laws are to be repealed or modified, if monopolies are to be validated and legalized, then there should be a searching investigation made and all available information weighed and considered in order to determine the advantages and disadvantages that would follow such legislation.

I repeat when I say that it is not fair to the residents of the District of Columbia to have their tax bill made the vehicle of general legislation which will affect the economic and industrial life of the entire country.

May I again refer to the letter of the President to the Vice President wherein he states that—

The present hazard of undue advances in prices, with a resultant rise in the cost of living, makes it most untimely to legalize any competitive or marketing practice calculated to facilitate increases in the cost of numerous and important articles American householders and consumers generally buy.

The President further refers to the statement of the Commissioner of the Federal Trade Commission, which in substance states that the effect of resale-price maintenance would be harmful to the consuming public; and he quotes from the Federal Trade Commission report, which states that—

There is great probability that manufacturers and dealers may abuse the power to arbitrarily fix resale prices by unduly increasing prices, resulting in bitter resentment on the part of the consuming public, especially in this period of rising prices.

Mr. President, a number of Senators who were detained from the Senate by committees have returned to the Senate Chamber, and I may, therefore, be pardoned for briefly covering a few points already discussed.

There is, as I have indicated, upon the calendar S. 100. This measure has not been acted upon, though it has been on the calendar for some time. That bill seeks to legalize price maintenance and to permit contracts and agreements which I believe to be in restraint of trade. A number of States have enacted laws under which these price-fixing agreements and contracts which are in restraint of trade are legalized, as a result of which those entering into such contracts and agreements are free from prosecution under any State laws dealing with monopolies and price-fixing agreements. I have indicated that there are groups of manufacturers and retailers who are determined to have the Federal antitrust laws repealed or modified in order that they may engage in monopolistic practices and enter into contracts which in effect constitute restraint of trade. I should state, however, that many manufacturers are opposed to the so-called Tydings bill and the amendments under consideration. They do not favor monopolistic practices or price fixing. They believe in fair and legitimate competition and look with disfavor upon State laws which legalize monopolistic practices, and, as I have stated, upon the movement to nullify Federal antitrust laws. They appreciate the fact, as indicated in the communication of the President to the Vice President, that there would be an undue advance in prices, with a resultant rise in the cost of living, if the Federal antitrust laws should be repealed or devitalized in the manner permitted by this rider.

Mr. [LYNN J.] FRAZIER [R., N.D.]. It seems to me hardly fair that the manufacturers of products should say to retailers to whom they sell their products how much the consumer must pay for the products.

Mr. KING. The Senator's view is I think generally approved by the American people, but it is the purpose of the Tydings amendment to permit that to be done. To illustrate, if a Michigan manufacturer contracts at the present time to sell his commodities in the State of North Dakota, or any other State in which price-fixing laws have been enacted, the antitrust laws would be applicable; but if the Tydings amendment is enacted into law, then the antitrust laws would not be operative to prohibit price-fixing and other monopolistic practices in such States. In that event in those States prices could be fixed so high as to be oppressive, and monopolistic practices encouraged and developed.

Mr. FRAZIER. Mr. President, will the Senator yield?

Mr. KING. I yield.

Mr. FRAZIER. I should like to ask the Senator from Utah if he understands that this amendment—title VIII—would allow manufacturers to fix the prices at which retailers must sell their products to consumers.

Mr. KING. In reply may I say that if this amendment shall be enacted into law, it would seriously weaken the antitrust laws in all States which have enacted laws permitting the fixing of minimum prices for the resale of commodities. ⊥ In fact, the enactment of the amendment would permit manufacturers and distributors to fix prices at which retailers must sell their products to consumers in those States which have enacted laws permitting minimum prices for the resale of commodities.

Mr. [ARTHUR H.] VANDENBERG [R., Mich.]. Mr. President—

Mr. KING. I yield to the Senator from Michigan.

Mr. VANDENBERG. I suggest that the Senator might offer an even more fundamental complaint. Regardless of the merits of this amendment, it is perfectly obvious that not 5 percent of the membership of the Senate will know anything whatever about the amendment when the Senate votes upon it. It is perfectly obvious that the Senate has reached the point of exhaustion in respect of the consideration of legislation; and if the Senate has any prudent consideration whatever for the country, instead of trying to do some of these intricate things it will quit and go home.

Mr. KING. Mr. President, I think the Senator is substantially correct. The tax bill before the Senate has many important and complex features and complicated provisions, and the amendment now before the Senate is pregnant with difficulties and dangers which I fear are not comprehended by some Senators. Certainly any measure that modifies or repeals or changes the antitrust laws should receive most serious consideration at the hands of committees of the Senate, as well as the Senate itself. Too little consideration is being given to this amendment and its implications and the consequences, I again affirm, are not fully realized by many Members of this body.

Mr. [PAT] McCARRAN [D., Nev.]. Mr. President, will the Senator yield?

Mr. KING. I yield to the Senator from Nevada.

Mr. McCARRAN. Would the Senator consent to a unanimous-consent request at this time that the pending business be laid aside, and that Senate bill 69 be taken up by the Senate at this time?

Mr. KING. What is Senate bill 69?

Mr. McCARRAN. It is the car-limit bill with regard to interstate commerce. Would the Senator consent to that if a unanimous-consent agreement to that effect were asked for?

Mr. KING. Mr. President, does the Senator in charge of the bill, the Senator from Nevada, think it would be fair to the District and to the country to put aside the pending bill?

Mr. McCARRAN. I desire to say to the Senator what I really believe. I may be mistaken in my belief, but I really believe that the consideration of Senate bill 69 will not take more than a few hours.

Mr. KING. Since the Senator from Nevada has charge of the bill, I do not know whether I could properly interpose an objection, although I call his attention to the fact that it is imperative that this tax bill be enacted into law at the earliest possible moment.

Mr. TYDINGS. I call for the regular order.

Mr. KING. I have the floor, Mr. President.

The PRESIDING OFFICER (Mr. HATCH in the chair). The regular order is called for. The Senator from Utah has the floor.

Mr. McCARRAN. Mr. President, while the Senator from Utah has the floor, out of courtesy to me I ask the privilege of saying that when this bill shall have been disposed of I shall move for the consideration by the Senate of Senate bill 69.

Mr. KING. Mr. President, I think it would be a mistake to lay aside the pending bill, and certainly if this were done, and intervening measures occupied the time of the Senate for several weeks, the District of Columbia would be in a most unfortunate situation. It is known that there is a large deficit and that within a few days its funds will be exhausted and current obligations will remain unpaid.

I am repeating when I protest against the amendment which is under consideration, believing as I do that it will interfere with the enactment of needed tax legislation. I again protest against it because of the impropriety and unfairness of attaching riders to appropriation bills.

Mr. McCARRAN. Will the Senator yield?

Mr. KING. I yield.

Mr. McCARRAN. In view of all the concessions that have been made here this afternoon, I desire to say with reference to this amendment that I am not in accord, and I have not been in accord, with this bill from beginning to end. I only hope we may work out a bill that will be worth while. It is unfortunate to have to work it out in a conference committee. I do not believe that is the function of a conference committee, but it looks as though we shall be forced to do it in this instance.

In order to have this matter concluded, so as to go to conference, while I do not disagree with the Senator from Utah, I believe this tax matter should be worked out for the District, and the conference committee can cut off this amendment just as well as any other. It seems to me that if we destroy this amendment now we may destroy the whole bill. Let us go to conference with the whole bill and then take out that which is objectionable.

Mr. KING. Mr. President, with all due respect to my friend, I cannot follow his conclusion.

Mr. [WILLIAM E.] BORAH [R., Idaho]. Mr. President, does the Senator yield?

Mr. KING. I yield to the Senator from Idaho.

Mr. BORAH. Mr. President, I should like to ask whether it would be possible to reach an agreement to fix a definite time to dispose of the bill on the calendar. The trouble is that the Senator from Maryland has not had an opportunity to be heard. If there could be an understanding or agreement that the bill would be taken up at a certain time and disposed of, I myself would feel that that was the best way to dispose of it.

Mr. BARKLEY. Mr. President, in that connection I wish to state that it is impossible at this time to enter into any agreement as to when the bill might be taken up. Of course, we all understand that it cannot be disposed of on a call of the calendar. This sort of bill cannot be disposed of with the limited debate that is permitted when the calendar is being called. I am certain that it would be possible within the near future for the Senator from Maryland to move to proceed to the consideration of the bill, and while I am not for the bill—not that I am opposed to it, but I have never been enthusiastic about the type of legislation which it embodies—I shall be glad to cooperate with the Senator in an effort to arrange for a definite time in the near future when he may move to proceed to the consideration of the bill on the calendar, if that is any satisfaction or consolation to the Senator.

Mr. TYDINGS. Mr. President, will the Senator from Utah yield to me while I answer?

Mr. KING. I yield.

Mr. TYDINGS. That would not be satisfactory to me, because the proposal is purely nebulous. For 5 or 6 months this measure has been on the calendar, and every time it has been reached the clarion voice of the Senator from Utah has said "Over." So I have been unable to secure consideration of the bill, and it is a matter of poetic justice that finally it finds itself on a bill in charge of a Senator who happens to be the Senator from Utah.

Every Member of this body knows where he stands on this bill, and if the Senator from Utah will cease filibustering and give me an opportunity to make a few remarks about the bill, I shall be glad to have a vote, and there will be no delay.

Mr. KING. Mr. President, if the Senator were more accurate, his position would be more tenable. The fact is that this amendment has never been on the calendar. It is true that although the Tydings bill has been upon the calendar for some time, no motion has ever been made by the Senator to have the bill considered. He could have moved at any time to take the bill up for consideration; but he did not do so. Many measures which were placed upon the calendar subsequent to the Tydings bill being reported have been, by motion, taken from the calendar, considered, and passed by the Senate. But, as stated, the Senator has not availed himself of the opportunity to move for consideration of his measure. He has been content to remain silent. Perhaps ⊥ the President's communication, dated April 24 of this year, to the President of the Senate, has deterred the Senator from making a motion to take the bill up for consideration. As I have shown, the President's letter is a powerful argument against the bill; and the report of the Federal Trade Commission constitutes an almost invincible argument against its being enacted into law. It is true that upon two or three occasions during the morning hour, and under the 5-minute rule, the Tydings bill, as well as many other bills, were reached; but as Senators know, it is an almost universal rule that important measures—measures which call for discussion and consideration—are passed over when called during the morning hour. Senators frequently object to the consideration of measures which they have introduced, and which are reached upon a call of the calendar during the morning hour, because they believe due consideration during the limited period available is not possible. Upon two or three occasions during the morning hour when the Tydings bill was reached I asked that it be passed; but, as stated, no motion was made to take the bill up for consideration, notwithstanding the request made. May I say that I will join with the Senator in requesting that the so-called Tydings bill now on the calendar be taken up for consideration at an early date. While I am opposed to the bill, I shall not object to its being brought before the Senate at a time when it can be fully and adequately considered. I am objecting, however, to its being considered as an amendment to a revenue bill vital to the District of Columbia, and which must be passed within the next few days if the officials of the District of Columbia shall have funds with which to meet current obligations.

Mr. BARKLEY and Mr. TYDINGS addressed the Chair.

The PRESIDING OFFICER. Does the Senator from Utah yield; and if so, to whom?

Mr. KING. I yield first to the Senator from Kentucky.

Mr. BARKLEY. Time and time again the argument is made that it is unwise to attach substantive legislation such as the bill of the Senator from Maryland to a tax bill or some other bill. I am not out of harmony with the Senator from Utah on this question. But the bill is here, it is a part of the measure now before us, and we have to vote on it before the tax bill can be disposed of, because I take it that it will be impossible to eliminate it by unanimous consent, or by any other method except by a vote. That being true, and the proposal in title 8 being well understood, I express the hope that we may arrive at a vote on it without unnecessary delay, so that Senators may express their feelings about it. If it is stricken out on a vote, that will eliminate it and simplify the bill, and if it is left in the bill by a vote, it will then go to conference, where it can be disposed of.

Mr. TYDINGS. Mr. President, I have no objection to the conferees taking such action as the conferees may deem wise but if I may make an observation—

Mr. KING. I yield to the Senator.

Mr. TYDINGS. The Senator from Utah in the committee made the same objections to the bill being attached as an amendment that he is now making on the floor of the Senate. The vote was 11 to 1 in favor of putting it on the bill. The only vote against it in the committee was that of the Senator from Utah, who was present either in person or by proxy. With that overwhelming majority in the committee the Senator from Maryland thinks he is well within his rights in insisting that the Senate vote the amendment up or down. If the Senator from Utah had not objected so many times when the bill was reached on the calendar, it would not now be here in the shape against which he complains.

Mr. KING. Mr. President, I regret that the Senator is not accurate in the statement just made. I say again that I objected two or three times only and then during the morning hour, as we all object to bills, even our own measures, when we know it is impossible to consider proposed legislation of great importance during the morning hour. I suggest now that I shall be glad to join with the Senator in having the bill taken up at as early a day as possible, to be fixed by the leader and by the Senator.

My protest is first against the bill itself. I think the President was right in pointing out its evils, and the Federal Trade Commission was right in its objections, as stated in the letter to the President. Farm organizations of the country and many of the consumers' leagues are right in protesting against it, because they perceive its effects in increasing prices because of the virtual repeal of antitrust laws and the fixing of prices by manufacturers and retailers.

Legislation of this kind, to my mind, is inherently wrong. But the Senator from Maryland, or any other Senator, has the right, of course, to have the bill considered on its merits, under proper auspices and at a proper time, when debate upon it may reveal its virtues and disclose its vices.

Mr. President, I have evidence to show unjustifiable increase in prices which have taken place in those States which have by their laws made inoperative the antitrust laws. I desire, however, to call attention to the report made by Professor Grether, who made a careful study of the effect of the minimum-price law enacted in California. Professor Grether is connected with one of the universities of California. His report, made after extensive research and study, may be found in the California Law Review for December 1936. In his report he refers to a survey made by him showing the prices of 134 advertised drug items. I may say in passing that the protagonists of the Tydings amendment are some of the drug manufacturers and retail druggists. For a number of years they have carried on an aggressive campaign for the modification of the antitrust laws and the legalization of contracts made between manufacturers and distributors and retailers specifying prices at which their products must be sold. Professor Grether states in the Law Review referred to that the—

* * * 1934 contractual prices were approximately one-third above the average of advertised prices for the first 6 months of 1933.

The data compiled by Dr. Grether showed price variations ranging from increases of 50 percent on hospital supplies, salts, and soaps; 33 1/3 percent on cosmetics, cod-liver oils, deodorants, food tonics, laxatives, liniments, pills, and tablets to slightly smaller increases on many other articles.

While the California fair-trade laws were more or less suspended during the N. R. A. regime, the National Association of Retail Druggists endeavored to establish minimum prices under the codes which would prevent sales below cost plus heavy mark-ups. However, after careful investigation, the N. R. A. officials refused to accede to this demand, finally only a minimum resale price which was set at the delivered wholesale price of dozen lots, or practically invoice cost. Further discussing the effects of the California law, Professor Grether says:

There can be no doubt that resale-price maintenance under the California Fair Trade Act has made for higher prices on advertised products sold through cut-rate and chain-store institutions. The evidence presented above, in the discussion of price conditions in 1933 in comparison with 1934 and 1935 contractual prices, is conclusive on this point.

The data presented by Dr. Grether show clearly the effect of the California Fair Trade Act on prices in that State. The data show that the independent drug stores, which for years had been on a high-price level, did not materially increase their prices. The same situation exists in other States where there are similar so-called fair-trade-practice acts. But they also show that the chain stores and other popular-price stores were compelled to raise their prices to the higher levels fixed by resale-price contracts with manufacturers. In other words, the manufacturers fixed resale prices at about the same figure as the relatively inefficient independent dealer, or credit-and-delivery service dealer had always charged, but such prices were in many cases far above the prices at which the efficient store and the popular-price stores theretofore found profitable. It is clear that the California plan deprives consumers of cosmetics and drugs of the opportunity to buy these commodities at lower costs.

If these popular-price stores are forced to sell at approximately the same price as the full-service, high-cost neighborhood drug stores, they will lose volume to the small stores and the consumer will be permanently deprived of the opportunity to buy at lower prices through an efficiently operated distribution system. Commenting on this phase of the situation, Professor Grether states—page 697:

> Without doubt those consumers who wish to buy standard drug products with a minimum of professional attention and merchandising services, are harmed by resale-price maintenance, except insofar as they are able to obtain equivalent quality under private brands.

The Federal Trade Commission reached the same conclusion. It reported in part II, page 160, of its report on resale-price maintenance that—

> The fact is that consumers live on different economic levels and have varying standards of living. To the housewife purchasing on the basis of $10,000 family income, fine store fixtures, roomy aisles, beautiful displays, couteous [sic] salespeople, credit, and frequent and expensive delivery services may be worth the additional cost. To ask the wife of the day laborer to pay the price necessary to cover the additional cost on any goods that both families use may be asking her to pay for service which she cannot afford and which, therefore, she does not desire, because every cent saved in buying may mean ability to satisfy, to some extent, wants that otherwise would remain ungratified.

In California, at least, manufacturers have attempted to benefit by reason of this situation by demanding larger profits. Professor Grether says, in speaking of the California laws:

> * * * it is not merely a loss limitation device, but allows the guaranteeing of margins to dealers.

He shows a table on page 681 which indicates minimum retail margins on over 1,000 drug items on which he was able to obtain wholesale quotations on the July 1934 list of contractual items. This list shows an arithmetical average minimum margin of 31.02 percent—of contractual price—which hits fairly close to the 33 1/3-percent margin on the selling price—equivalent to a 50-percent mark-up on the cost—which the National Association of Retail Druggists has set as its immediate objective. And this 31.02-percent margin was in 1934. Margins have widened since that time. Professor Grether says—page 682:

> It is rather surprising that so high an average [margin] should appear with a plan but recently introduced, for some manufacturers were loathe to raise prices sufficiently from the cut-rate levels to allow wide margins.

Mr. President, New York has enacted a so-called fair-trade practice statute, and it has resulted in an unwarranted increase in prices to the injury of consumers. Under this act, known as the Feld-Crawford Act, there has been a mark-up on costs of cosmetics of 65 percent; drugs, 57 percent; liquors, 56 percent; books, 70 percent; and miscellaneous articles, 60 percent.

In other words, the efficient distributor, who does not need any such margin on these items to make a satisfactory profit on a satisfactory volume of sales, is required by law to take this additional profit. Naturally the increased price to the consumer may result in a reduced volume of sales and no more than his present total of profit for the year's business. But the consumer must pay the increased price, and particularly the consumer who thinks it worth while to make his purchases at the popular-price chain stores throughout New York City and the downtown popular-price department stores.

I invite attention to a statement made by Professor Grether in connection with his investigation which shows the intimidation and coercion which were resorted to in order to accomplish certain results favorable to those who favored the price-fixing plan. He states:

* * * through meetings, called usually at night after store hours so all might attend, personal discussions and informal contacts, the druggists often developed a collective attitude of cooperation with friendly manufacturers as well as the negative one of opposition to those who did not meet the demands of the dealers. There can be little doubt that the plan was an effective element in the whole movement for resale-price control. * * *

The amount of strength that was demonstrated by retail druggists through the organized devices discussed in the preceding pages may best be illustrated by two very famous cases. First, early in August 1934 a well-known aspirin manufacturer was requested by a petition of signatures 20 feet in length to operate under the act.

He did not want to engage in price fixing and take advantage of the State law.

When the petition did not seem to receive the reception that the dealers expected, the published statements in the Northern California Drug News became increasingly antagonistic in tone. It was made clear in these statements that the dealers had the power of substitution even in this case. The slogan was "No Fair Trade Act—No Orders."

That is, unless you accept the Fair Trade Act you get no orders.

The most terse statement of attitude was the following:

"This aspirin is a sort of Napoleon in the patent-medicine army, but then, even the great Frenchman met his Waterloo when the rest of Europe got together, decided that they had enough of him, and cooperated against him."

The outcome of the controversy was that the company issued fair-trade contracts early in 1935.

The company was compelled to issue fair-trade contracts because the opposition was so great and the combination so powerful. If it had not capitulated it would have lost its entire trade in California. Professor [sic] Grether continues:

The second case was publicized nationally and had repercussions throughout the entire country. It is peculiarly well adapted to reflect the state of mind of retail druggists throughout the Nation as well as in California.

In the January 1, 1935, issue of the Northern California Drug News there is an editorial lauding a well-known national dentifrice and antiseptic manufacturer for finally issuing fair-trade contracts after months of request, including a formal petition, on the part of retailers. The company was praised particularly because it guaranteed minimum margins of 18.4 percent, 26.5 percent, and 34.2 percent—depending upon the quantity purchased. However, on July 13, 1935, dealers in California received letters from this firm advising them that it was necessary to withdraw from operation under the Fair Trade Act, since they were making shipments directly from Chicago and hence were involved in interstate commerce.

Immediately [sic] a storm broke loose in California which swept into other States before it had spent itself. On July 17 the northern association passed a resolution condemning the company and urging and advising its members to "discontinue the sale of the products of any and all companies which cancel fair-trade contracts." Similar action was taken in the southern association. The response of the trade was amazing; an almost universal boycott was raised against the firm. For a period it was possible to obtain the products of the firm only from a few cut-rate outlets. An interesting aspect was that a number of large wholesale houses also cooperated by refusing to deliver the items of the company.

It appears that the company had a startling decline in sales in California. Worse still, the antagonism spread into other States and affected sales and attitudes nationally. The outcome was that the company capitulated completely, again issuing contracts in California, and likewise, so it is stated, giving a check of $25,000 to the National Association of Retail Druggists to be used in its fight for price-maintenance legislation.

Mr. President, pressure was brought by various retailers who were availing themselves of the provisions of price-fixing State laws to compel not only retailers but manufacturers and distributors to accept contracts that were issued pursuant to the so-called fair-trade laws. If this amendment is enacted into law, then, in every State in which the so-called fair-trade measures are enacted, the antitrust laws will be superseded, contracts will be forced upon retailers who may not desire to avail themselves of opportunities to increase and fix prices, and also upon manufacturers and distributors who likewise are opposed to such price-fixing measures.

In my opinion, the evidence is conclusive that already in those States which have enacted the so-called fair-trade acts prices have been materially increased and the consumers have been penalized. I predict that there will be a revolt among consumers against measures and policies which create monopolies and which bear oppressively upon the consuming public.

Mr. President, in conclusion, I renew my protest against this amendment. I am advised that there are sufficient votes to secure its passage. I cannot help but believe its evils and dangers are not fully understood by Senators, but I am persuaded that sooner or later there will be an aroused public sentiment against State or Federal laws which encourage or permit monopolies and monopolistic practices and increase prices until they bear oppressively upon the consuming public. . . .

⊥ 7495   ⊥ Mr. TYDINGS. Mr. President, I wish to make a very brief statement in explanation of the pending amendment.

There is on the calendar Senate bill 100, sometimes called the Miller-Tydings bill, the text of which now appears on the District of Columbia tax bill as an amendment. The bill was first introduced in the House and later in the Senate. Long and extensive hearings by the Judiciary Committee of each branch were held. Many witnesses appeared pro and con on the measure, and finally it was reported favorably both by the Judiciary Committee of the Senate and by the Judiciary Committee of the House.

Because of my inability to get the bill up sooner and the fact that this is the second session of the Congress in which it has appeared on the calendar, I took the liberty of offering it in the committee as an amendment to the District of Columbia tax bill. It is a very short bill.

Forty-two States of the Union have already adopted the provisions of the amendment which I hold in my hand, and it is a law in those States. Only six States in the Union have not enacted such a fair-trade act. Forty-two States already have it. The action upon it is almost unanimous, and will be unanimous, in my judgment, as soon as the remaining six legislatures meet.

This is not an effort to tear down the antitrust law. It is an effort to strengthen the antitrust law, to make it apply so that the small businessman shall enjoy the same privileges which larger businessmen have enjoyed under the Sherman antitrust law through all the years. The bill is against monopoly. It is in behalf of the small and independent business. Those who ask for it are the small businessmen, the Independent Retail Grocers' Association, the independent druggists of America, the book sellers of America. Why do they ask for it? It is because the practices of monopoly have tended more and more to drive the small concerns out of business. Let me give one illustration and for the purpose I will take books.

A book such as Gone With the Wind is published. It sells for a particular price. All the big department stores buy it, and all the independent book stores buy it. The independent book stores sell nothing but books. The large department stores sell a variety of articles, and Gone With the Wind can be bought in those particular stores for less than the stores paid for it from the publisher. The result is that practically all the sales of the book are made at less than cost, and are not made by the book stores of America but by the stores dealing in other commodities. As a consequence the book store soon finds it has lost its biggest opportunity to do a good business at a reasonable profit, while the other stores obviously could not stay in business and sell things at less than the price paid for them but make up the loss on the book by the sale of other articles. So in the end the public pays the full price of the book in that fashion.

There is not a line in the amendment which would permit manufacturers to combine with other manufacturers, wholesalers with other wholesalers, or retailers with other retailers.

Mr. BARKLEY. Mr. President, will the Senator yield?

The PRESIDING OFFICER. Does the Senator from Maryland yield to the Senator from Kentucky?

Mr. TYDINGS. I prefer to finish my statement, and then I shall be glad to yield. I shall only speak a moment or two longer.

Mr. BARKLEY. I merely desired a little information.

Mr. TYDINGS. What does the amendment do? It permits a man who manufactures an article to state the minimum resale price of the article in a contract with the man who buys it for ultimate resale to the public, provided—and this "provided" is mountain-high—that the article about which the contract is written is in free and open competition with other articles. If it is not in free and open competition with other articles, no such contract may be written.

For example, to show that the adoption of the amendment would not result in price increases, let us take the case of a tube of tooth paste. There are on the market 25 or 30 varieties of tooth paste. Under the amendment, manufacturers may not combine with each other for the purpose of price maintenance; but if a manufacturer wishes to say that his particular kind of tooth paste may not be sold by a retailer at less than a certain minimum price, and that minimum price is high, other tooth-paste manufacturers will come in and take his business. The very language of the amendment says that such contracts shall be legal only as to articles which are in open and direct competition with other articles. The element of competition is never absent in a single line of this measure. This is a measure for the small businessman; and the persons who appeared before the Judiciary Committee in opposition to the proposed legislation were not little-business men. They were big-business men. Those who appeared for the proposed legislation were small-business men or their representatives.

Mr. BARKLEY rose.

Mr. TYDINGS. I yield to the Senator from Kentucky.

Mr. BARKLEY. Mr. President, I am asking purely for information. I find here that after stating that every contract, combination in the form of trust or otherwise, and so forth, is illegal, the proviso goes on to say:

> That nothing herein contained shall render illegal, contracts or agreements prescribing minimum prices for the resale of a commodity which bears, or the label or container of which bears, the trade mark, brand, or name of the producer or distributor of such commodity and which is in free and open competition with commodities of the same general class produced or distributed by others, when contracts or agreements of that description are lawful as applied to intrastate transactions.

I desire to ask the Senator if that is to be interpreted to mean that the contracts which are permitted under this proviso are permitted so long as the articles are in free and open competition, and so long as the State in which they are sold permits that sort of contract to be entered into and enforced.

Mr. TYDINGS. That is correct.

Mr. BARKLEY. What would be the effect of a law of this kind in a State where there was no such authority to enter into contracts of this kind?

Mr. TYDINGS. The State law would prevail.

Mr. BARKLEY. So the proposed legislation would not in any way infringe upon State laws that might prohibit that sort of contract?

Mr. TYDINGS. Not in the slightest degree.

Mr. BARKLEY. I will say to the Senator that of course that is quite different from the provisions which have been contained in similar legislation which has been pending in Congress ever since I have been here.

Mr. TYDINGS. That is true.

Mr. BARKLEY. And, in my judgment, the change very much improves the proposed legislation.

Mr. TYDINGS. What we have attempted to do is what 42 States have already written on their statute books. It is simply to back up those acts, that is all; to have a code of fair trade practices written not by a national board such as the N. R. A. but by each State, so that the people may go to the State legislature and correct immediately any abuses that may develop. We are trying to decentralize fair trade practices rather than to have the matter dealt with as it was dealt with under the old N. R. A., which tried to put one blanket over the whole country, and which, in my judgment, allowed manufacturers to combine with other manufacturers, wholesalers with wholesalers, and retailers with retailers. Under the pending amendment it is illegal for manufacturers to combine, for wholesalers to combine, or for retailers to combine. The transaction is purely a vertical one from the manufacturer to the retailer.

I could talk longer on the subject. I think, however, every Senator is familiar with it. I believe every Senator has had opportunity to examine into it, because I feel that in every State of the Union many, many of the constituents of Senators have written to them about it, either pro or con. I have never voted for a price-fixing bill in my life so far as I can recall.

Mr. [LEWIS B.] SCHWELLENBACH [D., Wash.]. Mr. President, will the Senator yield?

Mr. TYDINGS. Yes.

Mr. SCHWELLENBACH. As I understand, the Senator has an amendment on the desk.

Mr. TYDINGS. That is true.

Mr. SCHWELLENBACH. Will the Senator explain just what the amendment does as compared to what is printed in the bill?

Mr. TYDINGS. Originally, as the Senator from Washington will recall, there was a message from the administration in opposition to this measure. I may say that I have been in consultation with the Attorney General's office, and the amendment I have offered was suggested by me and accepted by the Attorney General as curing the objections of the administration; and before I explain it briefly, I think I am now in a position to say that the original objections have been eliminated.

The amendment provides that nothing in this particular provision shall permit manufacturers to combine with manufacturers, wholesalers with wholesalers, factors with factors, or retailers with retailers. That is made absolutely certain. I do not think it was necessary, but I was glad to put it in to place the matter beyond the peradventure of a doubt.

As this is the small-business man's measure, as it is not a price-fixing measure, as the element of competition is always present, and as 42 States have already enacted similar legislation, I ask, on the further ground of State rights and decentralized government, that the action of these 42 States be supported.

Mr. [WARREN R.] AUSTIN [R., Vt.]. Mr. President, I am in favor of this measure. I sat in the subcommittee which considered it in conjunction with the Robinson-Patman bill and other similar bills, and which took much testimony, at a former session of Congress. Afterward, I acted with the present presiding officer [Mr. HATCH in the chair] and another Senator whose name I do not recall as a subcommittee, to consider the Miller-Tydings bill; and the committee reported it unanimously. It was afterward favorably reported to the Senate; but, for reasons which are well known, it never has had an opportunity to be considered.

I am for this measure for two particular reasons. One of them is the broad reason that it is in the right direction with respect to fundamental government. That is to say, it is exactly the reverse of centralization of authority in Washington to fix prices.

This Congress has passed the Guffey-Vinson Act, enabling the central Government to fix prices of coal. This Congress has passed the amendment to the Agricultural Adjustment Act giving the sanction of the Department of Agriculture and of the Federal Government to licenses and contracts for the sale of milk which fixes a minimum price to producers of milk. In effect, the Robinson-Patman law now in force is a price-fixing law which finds its authority here in Washington. My primary objection to all those bills was that they ran counter to our theory of a dual system of government in which the control of production, manufacture, and mining was expressly reserved to the several States, and that they reached over State boundaries and undertook to regulate intrastate commerce.

This proposed legislation is in just the opposite direction. Here is a measure which recognizes our form of government. Here is a measure which says, "We will not go into the State of Vermont with a regulation of prices from any other State in the Union, or from Washington, unless the State of Vermont is willing to have it done." It is that freedom which is left by this measure and expressly sanctioned by it—that freedom of every State in the Union to declare its own policy with respect to its own domestic affairs which appeals to me most strongly.

I have already seen the effect of it. That independence has already been exercised by States of the Union in anticipation of the passage of this or some similar legislation. As has been pointed out, 42 States have enacted similar statutes declaring what they call fair-trade practices with respect to prices, and preventing price cutting, which is unfair and which tends to drive little men out of business. On the other hand, my own

State, the State of Vermont, has exercised its independence and its right as a sovereign State to say, "We do not want price fixing in this State." Therefore, the State of Vermont can declare its own policy and have it effective with the cooperation of the Federal Government if this measure is enacted, because, if that is done, no manufacturer doing business in another State and transporting his goods into the State of Vermont can say there that the resale price of his product shall be so much and no less. Whether or not that is wise I am not undertaking to argue. The point is that it is more important to the people of the United States of America to save fundamental institutions than it is to declare themselves upon a mere matter of economic policy. I am more in favor of preserving the independence of the several States, and their right to manage their own affairs than of fixing prices or not fixing prices.

The other reason why I am in favor of this measure is that I think its effect would be to remove a vice in our economic system. It would remove protection to the price cutter. Notwithstanding the marvelous wisdom of the United States Congress, of course, we cannot expect that their laws will operate wisely in all cases and upon all people. That is true of the Sherman antitrust law, and that is true of the Federal Trade Commission Act, that is true of the Clayton Act, that is true of the Guffey-Vinson law, that is true of the amendment of the A.A.A., that is true of the Robinson-Patman law. Any law passed by the Federal Congress attempting to apply one uniform, horizontal rule all over the ⊥ great continent and upon all the different States, with their different types of resources, is bound to have inequities and inequalities and hardships in its operation.

Mr. President, I intend to detain the Senate for only a few more moments. I am for the measure because it restores fair competition, and because it removes protection to the price cutter.

On this question I call attention to the fact that high authority has commented upon price cutting as not a virtue but a vice which is harmful to the consumer. I read an extract from an opinion of Mr. Justice Holmes in a case decided in 1911, as follows:

> I cannot believe that in the long run the public will profit by this Court permitting knaves to cut reasonable prices for some ulterior purpose of their own, and thus to impair, if not destroy, the production and sale of articles which it is assumed to be desirable that the public should be able to get.[2.34]

I quote from another Justice, Mr. Justice Brandeis, this being from an opinion rendered before he was elevated to his present dignified position:

> The evil results of price cutting are far-reaching. * * * The process of exterminating the small independent retailer, already hard pressed by capitalistic combinations, would be greatly accelerated by such a movement (meaning permissive price cutting) * * *. Shall we, under the guise of protecting competition, further foster monopoly by creating immunity for the price cutters? Americans should be under no illusions as to the value or effect of price cutting. It has been the most potent weapon of monopoly—a means of killing the small rival to which the great trusts have resorted most frequently. It is so simple, so effective. Far-reaching organized capital secures by this means the cooperation of the short-sighted unorganized consumer to his own undoing.

Mr. President, I refrain from further comment upon the measure. I am for it. I think it is a grand step in the right direction.

The PRESIDING OFFICER. The question is on agreeing to the amendment offered by the Senator from Maryland [Mr. TYDINGS] to the amendment of the committee.

The amendment to the amendment was agreed to.

The amendment as amended was agreed to.

The PRESIDING OFFICER. The question now is on the engrossment of the amendments and the third reading of the bill.

The amendments were ordered to be engrossed and the bill to be read a third time.

The bill was read the third time, and passed.

[2.34] Dr. Miles Medical Co. v. John D. Park & Sons Co., 220 U.S. 373, 412 (1911) (dissenting opinion).

Mr. KING. Mr. President, I ask unanimous consent that the bill as passed be printed in the usual form, with the amendments adopted by the Senate numbered.

The PRESIDING OFFICER. Is there objection? The Chair hears none, and it is so ordered.

Mr. KING. I move that the Senate insist upon its amendments, ask for a conference with the House thereon, and that the Chair appoint the conferees on the part of the Senate.

The motion was agreed to; and the Presiding Officer appointed Mr. KING, Mr. MCCARRAN, Mr. TYDINGS, Mr. CAPPER, and Mr. AUSTIN conferees on the part of the Senate.

CONFERENCE CONSIDERATION (H.R. 7472)

HOUSE DEBATE
75th Cong., 1st Sess.
July 26, 1937

81 CONG. REC. 7599

Mr. [VINCENT L.] PALMISANO [D., Md.]. Mr. Speaker, I ask unanimous consent to take from the Speaker's table the bill (H. R. 7472) to provide additional revenue for the District of Columbia, and for other purposes, with a Senate amendment, disagree to the Senate amendment, and agree to the conference asked by the Senate.

The SPEAKER. Is there objection to the request of the gentleman from Maryland? [After a pause.] The Chair hears none, and appoints the following conferees: Messrs. PALMISANO, KENNEDY of Maryland, NICHOLS, DIRKSEN, and SHORT.

REPORT OF THE CONFERENCE COMMITTEE
H.R. Rep. No. 1413
75th Cong., 1st Sess.
August 2, 1937

Mr. PALMISANO, from the committee of conference, submitted the following

CONFERENCE REPORT

[To accompany H. R. 7472]

The committee of conference on the disagreeing votes of the two Houses on the amendments of the Senate to the bill (H. R. 7472) to provide additional revenue for the District of Columbia, and for other purposes, having met, after full and free conference, have agreed to recommend and do recommend to their respective Houses as follows:

That the Senate recede from its amendments numbered 11, 12, 29, 30, 31, and 32.

That the House recede from its disagreement to the amendments of the Senate numbered 1, 2, 3, 4, 5, 6, 7, 8, 13, 14, 15, 16, 17, 18, 19, 20, 21, 22, 23, 24, 25, 26, and 33; and agree to the same. . . .

STATEMENT OF THE MANAGERS ON THE PART OF THE HOUSE

* * * *

Amendment no. 33: This amendment provides for an amendment to the antitrust laws under which contracts and agreements stipulating minimum resale prices of certain commodities, and which are similar to contracts and agreements which are lawful as applied to intrastate commerce, are not to be regarded as being illegal under the antitrust laws. The House recedes.

> Vincent L. Palmisano,
> Ambrose J. Kennedy,
> Jack Nichols,
> Everett M. Dirksen,
> Dewey Short,
> *Managers on the part of the House.*

HOUSE DEBATE
75th Cong., 1st Sess.
August 3, 1937

81 Cong. Rec. 8134

Mr. PALMISANO. Mr. Speaker, I call up the conference report upon the bill (H. R. 7472) to provide additional revenue for the District of Columbia and for other purposes, and ask unanimous consent that the statement be read in lieu of the report.

The SPEAKER. The gentleman from Maryland calls up the conference report upon the District tax bill, H. R. 7472, and asks unanimous consent that the statement be read in lieu of the report. Is there objection?

There was no objection. . . .

⊥ 8138 ⊥ Mr. [EVERETT M.] DIRKSEN [R., Ill.]. . . .

Finally, the Senate added a new title which contained the substance of the Miller-Tydings bill. There was considerable outspoken talk about the procedure whereby a wholly ungermane rider is attached to a House bill and some insistence that the House conferees stand adamant in demanding its removal from the bill. Conferees can, of course, be adamant, but it must not be forgotten that the technique of the conference committee is to give and take, to compromise and harmonize in order to effect a bill in agreeable form. The difficulty lies not in the derelictions of conferees but in the rule which permits the attaching of ungermane items to House bills in the form of riders. This practice has prevailed for a long time and probably will prevail for a much longer time unless there be an alteration of the rules which make such legislative technique possible.

I do not condone this practice, but I might say that I did favor and do favor the enactment of the Miller-Tydings bill. It resulted from an Illinois case that went to the Supreme Court. The Illinois Legislature had enacted a law prior to 1936 making it possible for the manufacturer of merchandise to set the price at which it must be resold. In other words, it empowered the manufacturer to tell the retailer what he must get as a retail price and if he refused to do so, the manufacturer could refuse to sell him further and also had an action at law. It so happened that the Seagram's Distillers Corporation, located in Indiana, sold some of its products to the Old Dearborn Distributing Co. in Chicago. Evidently, the distiller indicated the price at which the liquors must be sold and when the distributer [*sic*] refused to abide by such a price, there was a violation and court action. Thus the case found its way to the Supreme Court on a question of constitutionality of the statute. The Court ruled that this was a matter of policy for the States to determine, and thereby upheld the Fair Trade Act of Illinois.

A question then arose as to whether or not the maintenance of such resale prices under a State fair trade act might not be in violation of the Sherman Anti-Trust Act of 1890 insofar as these transactions sprang from a contract in interstate commerce. This question was presented to the House Judiciary Committee and there determined by the reporting of the Miller bill. It was essentially nothing more than an enabling act which placed the stamp of approval upon price maintenance transactions under State acts, notwithstanding the Sherman Act of 1890. The bill was reported to the House and was ready for action but for some unknown reason it was withdrawn and began to gather dust. Then came the District revenue bill and this Tydings-Miller bill was attached as a rider. It was slightly modified from its original text by a proviso which I am informed was acceptable to the Attorney General and acceptable to the authors. I, for one, trust that it will be approved by the Senate and by the President because it will be of immense importance to the retailers, the wholesalers, and the manufacturers of the country.

Thus, while the conferees were perfecting a revenue measure for the Nation's capital, they were also, by a quirk in the rules, enacting one of the most important pieces of general legislation that has come before this session of Congress. Such are the vagaries of human and legislative destiny. . . .

⊥ Mr. [FRANCIS D.] CULKIN [R., N.Y.]. I am interested in amendment no. 33, ⊥ 8139 which has to do with the Miller-Tydings bill. Can the gentleman tell me whether that amendment, in its general scope, contains the provisions of the Miller-Tydings bill?

Mr. PALMISANO. I understand so.

Mr. CULKIN. The action of the conferees is satisfactory to the gentleman from Arkansas, the author of the bill in the House?

Mr. PALMISANO. I understand it is.

Mr. MILLER. Yes.

Mr. CULKIN. I think the bill is sound legislation and should be on the books.

Mr. Speaker, this legislation carries into effect one of the principles of the Kelly-Capper Act. It does it through the medium of fair-trade acts passed by the State legislatures. It is perhaps sounder in principle than the Kelly-Capper Act, in that it applies the basic principle of that legislation through the medium of home rule. Having supported the Kelly-Capper Act and urged its passage, I am even more vigorously for this measure. I wish to congratulate the learned proponent of the bill, our distinguished colleague from Arkansas [Mr. MILLER], upon bringing this bill to the floor.

This bill will aid the independent merchant, the efficient independent retailer, and protect them from predatory price cutting by chain outfits. But the independent must not be lulled into the belief that legislative enactment alone will save him, for his case depends even more largely upon his own initiative, industry, and energy. His present precarious situation is due to the tremendous economic waste in distribution. This is aggravated to a more serious extent by his failure to so organize his group that he is able to participate in mass buying and mass distribution the way the chain organizations do. Former President Hoover is quoted as saying that no less than $8,000,000,000 is lost annually through inefficient marketing. A large portion of this loss is due to the present procedure in retail business circles. In my judgment, the time is now ripe for the independent retailer and wholesaler to mass their buying powers through cooperative procedure and successfully meet the chain store by bringing about reduced prices.

It is stated that about 4,000,000 men are engaged in the retailing business in America and that 3,000,000 of these are independents. The force of numbers and buying power is therefore still in the hands of the independents, and they can hold the fort by the application of mass buying and mass distribution. Such procedure would eliminate the tremendous waste that now handicaps the local retailer and would put him economically on all fours with the chain. The independent retailer, furnishing as he does a delivery and credit system which appeals to many groups, provided he sets up in addition the machinery of cooperative buying, has nothing to fear.

THE AMERICAN RETAILER

Here in America the retail merchant was a potent influence in the political field during the Revolutionary period. The first retailers were the traders who pioneered the woods before the settlements came. In the development of America, past and present, the independent retailer has had a tremendous social and political part. In community life everywhere they are the backbone of church and other local organizations. The retail merchant largely supports the local hospitals, the fraternal organizations, service and social clubs, and all other charitable activities. The solicitor for such various and worth-while activities as the Boy Scouts, Red Cross, Young Men's Christian Association, and the other activities that stand for community betterment makes the store of the retail merchant his first port of call. Incidentally, a worthy cause is never rejected by the community-minded retailer. But let the selfsame solicitor visit the chain store. Its managing clerk tells him that he has no authority in the premises and he will have to communicate with the headquarters of the chain 1,000 or 2,000 miles away. The local merchant educates his children in the professions, arts, and sciences, and from this blood we recruit much of our leadership today. He is an outstanding influence not only for civic but for political betterment. He is invariably a useful and constructive citizen. He is frequently called into the public service and acts on the school board or in other municipal activities without pay.

Nor is this the only service of the merchant to community life. There are also certain of the humanities in the picture. Take the case of John Smith, who is taken ill. He has a wife and five small children depending on him for support. The family income stops and he desires credit from the retailer pending his return to health and employment. Based on his record of honesty and payment the merchant extends the credit and John Smith is tided over his adverse days. Financial help is frequently extended by the local retailer to his customers who are in temporary monetary distress. Chain stores are impersonal and no such accommodation is possible there. In many other ways does the local retailer, in direct and indirect matters, serve the community. The local retailer is perhaps a director in the local bank or building association and gives freely of his time in the upbuilding of the community. His profits are invested locally or on deposit in the local bank.

CHAINS WILL DESTROY COMMUNITY LIFE

On the other hand, the receipts of the chain store remains [sic] in the town overnight and then are sent on to some distant city. This procedure is draining the communities dry by the withdrawal of profits from circulation. This is one of the most pernicious results of the outside chain. In a recent article on Efforts [sic] of Chain Operations on Community Welfare, Lt. Gov. Henry A. Huber, of the State of Wisconsin, states:

> Community life is being robbed of its profits and its industries. Chain stores, chain oil stations, chain drug stores, chain insurance companies, and mail-order houses are taking the profits of the storekeeper and the farmer and the businessman of Wisconsin and distributing outside of the State.
>
> Blind, indeed, is he who cannot decipher these fundamental economic facts. A mere reading of them should convince any person that it is time Wisconsin awoke and protected its own people, its own industries, its own businessmen, and its own profits. It is time that the links of the chain shackle were broken.

EFFECTS ON LABOR

The chain store is equally disastrous in its effect on industrial wages. The chain-store buyer goes to the manufacturer of a standard article and makes him a proposition to take a large portion of his output at a low figure. This is the basis upon which the chain store works; namely, to purchase in mass and distribute in mass. He drives a hard bargain with the manufacturer, and the manufacturer like all mortals thinks of himself first and passes on the decrease in the price to his workmen. This is not a psychological proposition, but an actual fact. As I have heretofore stated, copyrighted and standardized articles which the chain or department stores frequently use as bait, mirror in their low prices a reduced wage to the industrial worker. As the buying power of the chains increases they will more and more vigorously dictate prices to the manufacturer. Failing this, they will build a plant alongside of him and engage in manufacturing the particular articles themselves. In either case it will result in a reduced wage to the industrial group and a consequent reduction in comforts and clothes and food and education for his children. Of what avail will the nominal saving which the industrial worker now makes in the chain stores be to him under such circumstances?

This measure complements existing State law and will make legal what was condemned by the Supreme Court in 1910 [sic] in the case of *Dr. Miles Medicine Co.* v.

Parks [sic] *& Sons Co.* (220 U. S. Rep. 373). The report of the proponent of the bill, Mr. MILLER, calls attention to the opinion of Judge Sutherland, upholding the constitutionality of the Illinois Price Fixing Act. The House will be interested to know that such price-fixing acts supplemented by this legislation will write into law the minority opinion of Mr. Justice Holmes, filed in the Miles case. Mr. Justice Holmes' language in this dissenting opinion was vigorous and incisive, and the principle laid down in his dissenting opinion is the genesis of this pending measure. Mr. Justice Holmes stated:

> I cannot believe that in the long run the public will profit by this Court permitting knaves to cut reasonable prices for some ulterior purpose of their own and thus to impair, if not to destroy, the production and sale of articles which it is assumed to be desirable that the public should be able to get.[2.35]

We lately hear a good deal about the minority opinion becoming the majority opinion of the Court. This has been the history of our jurisprudence in matters involving social progress and broader definitions of human rights. It has been especially true of the remarkable forensic foresight which has characterized the notable dissents of the late Justice Holmes. In the pending measure is an evidence that these historic dissents amount almost to prophecy of what is certain to finally become the law. In saying this I voice no disrespect or criticism of the majority of the Court but desire to emphasize the psychic ability of this extraordinary man, now passed away, to peer into the future and forecast the social and economic needs of the Nation. At the time the Kelly-Capper bill was pending in 1930, I had the temerity to write to Judge Holmes and send him a copy of my speech. You can imagine my delight when, a few days later, I received an autographic [sic] letter from him, which I ask permission to read to the House:

Beverly Farms, Mass.,
June 17, 1930.

Hon. Francis D. Culkin,
House of Representatives,
Washington, D.C.

MY DEAR SIR: Please accept my thanks for your kind letter and very interesting speech. Of course I am gratified by the generous expressions concerning myself. I do not feel competent to express an opinion upon what if any legislation is desirable, although I see no reason to change that expressed in the Dr. Miles Medicine Co. case.

Very truly yours,

O. W. Holmes.

My opinion in 1930 was that the principle of this legislation was sound and meritorious. My opinion was that the legislation was in the interest of the manufacturer and laborer working in industry. My opinion was that this legislation would be an aid to the efficient independent retailer who was playing an important part in community life in America. I stated then that this legislation in nowise would foster monopoly. I have not changed my mind on any of these conclusions. I am vigorously for this legislation and trust the House and Senate will write it into law. . . .

Mr. [CHARLES F.] MCLAUGHLIN [D., Neb.]. The adoption of the conference report now before the House will result in the enactment of the Miller-Tydings bill. That bill, H. R. 1611, has been acted on favorably by the Committee on the Judiciary and by the Rules Committee.

In these remarks I shall refer to the Miller-Tydings amendment, which is included in the conference report, as H. R. 1611.

House bill 1611 is known as the Fair Trade Enabling Act because it is an act which enables fair-trade legislation passed by individual State legislatures to become effective and to be fully operative within the respective States. It is not legislation which puts into effect a new national policy originating in Congress. Rather it is legislation which helps the States to put into effect a policy originating within the States themselves. It constitutes a method through which States are enabled to enforce their laws through the cooperation of the Federal Government. It lends to the States the

---

[2.35] 220 U.S. at 412.

assistance of national legislation making effective fair-trade practice acts passed in the State legislatures.

Lengthy and exhaustive hearings on this proposed law were conducted before subcommittee no. III of the Committee on the Judiciary, of which subcommittee, Mr. MILLER, the introducer of the bill is chairman and upon which subcommittee I have the honor to serve. Many witnesses for and against the bill were heard. Briefs and printed statements in support of the bill and in opposition to it were filed and made a part of the printed record of the hearings. Oral arguments were made upon the bill pro and con. The subcommittee considered the testimony. After long study and discussion I was commissioned to report the bill favorably to the full Committee on the Judiciary, and it was so reported. The full committee held executive sessions on the bill and the Chairman and General Counsel of the Federal Trade Commission accepted the committee's invitation to attend one of these meetings and to discuss the bill with the committee. Finally the Judiciary Committee voted unanimously to report the bill to the House with approval. Objections to parts of the bill were made by one member of the committee. These objections will be answered later in these remarks. A hearing was had on the bill before the Rules Committee and the committee passed a resolution for a rule. The bill has passed through the conventional course of procedure and the standing committee who have thoroughly considered it recommend to the House that it be enacted into law, in order that the fair-trade practice acts passed by so many of the States of the Union may become vital laws, fully operative and capable of performing the great service which they are designed to perform.

The State laws cannot function completely and satisfactorily without the enactment by Congress of a fair-trade enabling act.

Forty-two States of the Union have enacted fair-trade legislation. These States are California, Arizona, Wyoming, Iowa, Louisiana, Illinois, Kentucky, West Virginia, Maryland, New York, North Carolina, Oregon, Maine, Connecticut, Rhode Island, New Mexico, Utah, Idaho, Washington, Montana, South Dakota, Kansas, Arkansas, Wisconsin, Minnesota, South Carolina, Michigan, Florida, Oklahoma, Ohio, Tennessee, Virginia, Pennsylvania, New Jersey, North Dakota, Georgia, Colorado, Indiana, Nevada, Nebraska, Massachussetts, and New Hampshire.

The State acts are substantially identical. They were enacted by the individual State legislatures and represent the wishes of the people of the respective States. The wisdom and soundness of the legislation has been passed upon by 42 State legislative bodies. H. R. 1611 will in effect confirm and ratify the judgment of the State legislatures which have passed State fair-trade practice acts.

What is a State fair-trade practice act and what is its purpose? A State fair-trade practice act is a legislative act which provides that contracts for the resale of a commodity which bears, or the label or container of which bears, the trade-mark, brand, or name of the producer or distributor of such commodity and which is in free and open competition with commodities of the same general class produced or distributed by others, are valid contracts where the parties thereto agree therein that the buyer will not sell the article below the minimum price stated in the contract. The act applies only to articles or commodities which are in free and open competition with other articles or commodities of the same general class.

In other words, a State fair-trade practice act is an act which allows a seller of a trade-marked or identified commodity and the purchaser of such commodity to agree that the purchaser of that commodity shall not sell the commodity at less than the price agreed upon between the buyer and the seller where the commodity is one which is in open competition with commodities of similar character. The State fair-trade practice acts in the respective States practically uniformly provide that any retailer selling a trade-marked commodity which comes within the provisions of the act, ⊥ knowing that the owner of the commodity has provided by contract that the article shall not be sold at less than a certain price, is bound by that contract although he may not be a party to it, and is liable for the penalties set up in the act against those who sell the trade-marked article at a price less than the price named as the selling price by the owner. So much for the definition and description of a State fair-trade practice act. Now, as to the purpose and effect.

The purpose of the State fair-trade practice acts is to eliminate an evil which has resulted in untold hardship to the small merchant and the independent merchant seeking to conduct a business in a fair, honorable, and reasonable way. The evil to which I refer is the evil of price cutting and this evil normally manifests itself in the practice known as the loss leader. The loss-leader practice is the practice of the advertising and selling of well-known, reputable, trade-marked articles of merchandise for which a demand has been created, at a price less than the cost price of the article to the retailer. It is obvious that the sale of an article by a merchant at less than its cost to him is an unprofitable sale in itself. It has all the earmarks of the Greek bearing gifts. Its purpose is not to give the customer something for nothing but on the contrary is intended to get something from the customer by creating in the customer's mind the belief that he is getting something for less than its real and actual cost. Wherever the loss-leader practice is made use of the loss on the individual article sold below cost is made up by the increased price of other articles. Thus the customer is lured into the store of the loss-leader retailer by the belief that he will be able to buy goods cheap, only to find that the goods, other than the loss leaders, are purchased at a price sufficiently high to make up for the loss taken by the merchant in the sale of the loss leader. The loss-leader practice is a form of unfair competition which was exposed by witnesses before the committee and which has been condemned by legitimate trade associations as an outstanding evil in the retail merchandising.

The effects of the State acts may be judged by the experience in California, and this experience is being duplicated, so far as can be determined at this time, in the States which have since enacted fair-trade laws except that the full operation of the laws is handicapped by the provisions of the existing Federal statutes which H. R. 1611 is designed to correct.

The experiences under the California and other State fair-trade acts show that the level of prices for the products coming under their provisions has not advanced and the indications are that they will be reduced as floor levels are established. The cost of living has not increased following the enactment of these laws, and, so far, there has been no consumer resistance, as is shown by the fact that the legislatures of about 25 States have adopted the laws since January 1 of this year and after public hearings on the merits of the legislation.

Having examined the State fair-trade practice acts, let us consider the bill before Congress.

What is the fair-trade practice enabling act now pending before us, and how does it operate?

H. R. 1611, known as the Miller-Tydings Fair Trade Practice Enabling Act, is simple in its mechanics. It is a recognition of the sovereign rights of the individual States, respectively, to govern themselves in matters of commerce within their respective State borders. The act merely amends the existing Federal law—the Sherman Act—so as to provide that goods shipped from one State to another may be subject to the fair-trade practice act of the State into which the goods are shipped and that the contracts covering the resale of such goods in accordance with that State law are valid contracts.

H. R. 1611 is in no sense a price-fixing statute. No prices are fixed by the act. It is entirely a permissive act. It merely allows the seller and buyer of trade-marked or identified goods, sold in free open competition with similar goods, to contract for resale of goods according to the State law, if they want to do so. It does not compel the buyer and seller to enter into the contract but only authorizes them to do so if they so desire. It removes the existing barrier which now prevents the free execution of such contracts.

It is to be particularly noted that the act makes valid, as to goods flowing in interstate commerce, only those contracts in which the goods included therein are sold in open competition with other goods of similar character. Thus the act is in no sense a measure which will sanction contracts creating monopolies or combinations in restraint of trade. The provisions of the Sherman Act specifically prohibiting such contracts are not changed by this act but continue to remain in force. The act does not legalize contracts to maintain prices between manufacturers or sellers of different trade-marked articles of the same class or character. It only authorizes or permits contracts between the seller and the buyer, regarding resale price, as to a particular article, and then only provided that article is in free and open competition with articles of a similar character produced or distributed by others, and further provided only that the contract is authorized under the laws of the State in which it is to be carried out. The act, as amended in the Senate, and as now before the House in the conference report, specifically provides that the act shall not make lawful any contract or agreement providing for establishment or maintenance of minimum resale prices on any commodity covered by the act, between manufacturers, or between producers, or between wholesalers, or between brokers, or between factors, or between retailers, or between persons, firms, or corporations in competition with each other. As an example, the act would not allow two manufacturers of similar trade-marked articles, as, for instance, articles of food or drugs or clothing or soap or fountain pens, or any other competing articles of similar kind, to agree between themselves as to the price at which their respective articles shall be sold. The act does not alter the provisions nor the effect of the Sherman Act as to such contracts. In other words, it simply authorizes contracts, permitted by the States, between the seller and buyer of one article—contracts known as vertical contracts. It does not permit contracts between seller and seller of different articles—contracts known as horizontal contracts. The latter contracts, if violative of the Sherman Act now, will still be violative of that act if H. R. 1611 becomes a law.

State fair-trade practice acts have been declared constitutional and valid by a number of the courts of last resort of the States. Notable among these cases is the case of Old Dearborn against Seagram, in the State of Illinois, later upheld by the Supreme Court of the United States, to which case I shall presently refer more particularly, and the recent case of Doubleday, Doran Co. against R. H. Macy & Co. [sic], in the State of New York—Two hundred and Seventy-third New York Reports, page 167.[2.36]

The Supreme Court of the United States, in the case of *Old Dearborn Distributing Co. v. Seagram Distillers Corporation* (299 U. S. 178), decided on December 7, 1936, held that the State Fair Trade Practice Act of the State of Illinois was constitutional and valid. The United States Supreme Court, in its decision of that case, made a statement with reference to the wisdom of the State acts which is pertinent to the discussion of this bill in Congress today. The Supreme Court of the United States examined the constitutionality of the State statute and declared that the statute was constitutional. It was argued before the Court that the legislature of the State should not have enacted the law because it was an unwise law. The Supreme Court of the United States in handing down its opinion said:

> There is a great body of fact and opinion tending to show that price cutting by retail dealers is not only injurious to the good-will and business of the producer and distributor of identified goods but injurious to the general public as well. The evidence to that effect is voluminous, but it would serve no useful purpose to review the evidence or to enlarge further upon this subject. True, there is evidence, opinion, and argument to the contrary; but it does not concern us to determine where the weight lies. ⊥ We need say no more than that the question may be regarded as fairly open to differences of opinion. The legislation here in question proceeds upon the former and not the latter view; and the legislative determination in that respect, in the circumstances here disclosed, is conclusive so far as this Court is concerned. Where the question of what the facts establish is a fairly debatable one, we accept and carry into effect the opinion of the legislature (*Radice* v. *New York*, 264 U. S. 292, 294; *Zahn* v. *Board of Public Works*, 274 U. S. 325, 328; and cases cited).[2.37]

The same situation exists here today. The legislatures of 42 States of this Union have solemnly declared that in the exercise of their wisdom and judgment they desire that certain contracts be made valid within their State borders. We are today discussing a law which, if enacted, will enable those States to carry out the wishes of their respective people as expressed by their legislative act. The wisdom of the respective State acts has been passed upon by 42 individual legislatures.

The unicameral Legislature of my own State of Nebraska enacted a State fair-trade

---

[2.36] 273 N.Y. 167, 7 N.E.2d 30 (1937) is the citation to Bourjois Sales Corp. v. Dorfman. In *Dorfman*, the New York Court of Appeals, in following the Supreme Court's holding in *Old Dearborn*, overruled Doubleday, Doran & Co. v. Macy & Co., 269 N.Y. 272, 199 N.E. 409 (1936).

[2.37] 299 U.S. at 195-96.

CONFERENCE CONSIDERATION (H.R. 7472) 535

practice act by an almost unanimous vote. In voting for H. R. 1611 we are voting to permit these States to enforce their own fair-trade laws—to carry out their express desire. If we vote against it, we vote to prevent the State laws from operating effectively. Although 42 States have passed fair-trade acts governing contracts for the sale of trade-marked or identified goods within their respective State borders, these State statutes cannot function fully and freely and satisfactorily unless we pass this act. There exists grave doubt whether goods transported from an outside State into a State having a fair-trade act can be legally made the subject of the type of contract permitted by the State act. The enactment of this bill (H.R. 1611) would so amend the existing Federal law—the Sherman Act—as to allow these goods shipped in interstate commerce legally to become the subject of a State fair-trade contract. The enactment of this bill into law will remove the only existing barrier to the complete functioning of the State fair-trade acts in those States which have passed such acts.

Are we going to deny these States their rights? Surely not. Are we going to say to 42 of our sovereign States which have passed a fair trade practice act—and every one of the 48 States will eventually pass the act—are we going to say to the States, "You want an effective fair-trade act, but we will not let you have it?" That is what we will say in effect if we do not enact this legislation. Rather, shall we say to the States, "A barrier exists which prevents you from receiving the full benefit of your own fair-trade law within your own State borders. It lies in our power to remove that barrier. We will remove it. We recognize your right to govern yourself. We will cooperate with you to that legitimate end." H. R. 1611, which we have under discussion today, would remove that barrier and thus enable the States to have the benefit of the legislation which they have enacted for their own welfare.

In the hearings before the committee and in the debates upon the bill in the committee itself, it was suggested that there are two points which may be considered in the nature of objections to the bill. The committee discussed these points and considered that they did not constitute valid objections. However, in order to present the matter fully to the House, these objections should be referred to. These objections are:

First. That H. R. 1611, if enacted, would impose a penalty upon a seller of merchandise for selling such merchandise below the minimum price agreed upon in a contract to which he is not a party.

Second. Objection is made that no allowance is made in the contract of resale authorized by the respective State laws for difference in cost of doing business between different individual businesses, and that a resale price which might be fair to one concern might not be fair resale price to another concern because of the difference in the overhead or the cost of doing business existing between the two firms.

The objections were overruled by the committee after a consideration of the testimony bearing upon them and after full discussion of the objections.

The first objection, namely, that H. R. 1611, if enacted, will permit resale contracts to be binding upon parties other than the parties to the contract itself, is fully answered by the statement that the respective State laws make provision that the contract shall be binding upon all those who sell the trade-marked article which is the subject of the resale contract whenever the person selling the article below the contract resale price does so willfully and knowingly. This argument is well answered by the controlling opinion of the Supreme Court of the United States in the case of Old Dearborn against Seagram, supra, upholding the validity and constitutionality of the Illinois State Fair Trade Practice Act, where the Court says:

> A challenge is directed against section 2, which provides that willfully and knowingly advertising, offering for sale or selling any commodity at less than the price stipulated in any contract made under section 1, whether the person doing so is or is not a party to the contract, shall constitute unfair competition, giving rise to a right of action in favor of anyone damaged thereby.
>
> It is first to be observed that paragraph [sic] 2 reaches not the mere advertising, offering for sale or selling at less than the stipulated price, but the doing of any of these things willfully and knowingly. We are not called upon to determine the case of one who has made his purchase in ignorance of the contractual restriction upon the selling price, but of a purchaser

who has had definite information respecting such contractual restriction and who, with such knowledge, nevertheless proceeds willfully to resell in disregard of it.[2.38]

Appellants here acquired the commodity in question with full knowledge of the then-existing restriction in respect of price which the producer and wholesale dealer had imposed, and, of course, with presumptive if not actual knowledge of the law which authorized the restriction. Appellants were not obliged to buy; and their voluntary acquisition of the property with such knowledge carried with it, upon every principle of fair dealing, assent to the protective restriction, with consequent liability under paragraph [sic] 2 of the law by which such acquisition was contained.[2.39]

Further complete answer to this objection is that the respective States in the exercise of their wisdom and judgment imposed the penalties provided in the respective State acts. The bill before us today, if enacted, merely makes effective the law which has been enacted by the respective State legislatures to govern transactions within their own borders.

The second objection that no allowance has been made for difference in cost of doing business between different firms engaged in sale of trade-marked articles which are subject to price resale contracts, is again answered by the statement that no such allowance is set forth in the State acts and that the bill which we have before us for consideration merely makes effective the State acts and does not attempt to legislate substantively on the subject of resale price maintenance. However, this question was considered so seriously by the committee that members of the Federal Trade Commission were called into the conference by the committee in executive session and after a full discussion and consideration of the question the committee accepted the conclusions expressed by the representative of the Federal Trade Commission. They pointed out that the plan of attempting through the Federal Trade Commission, or through any other body, of fixing a specific resale price for each merchant for each commodity upon which resale contracts have been entered into, would be a task so gigantic and stupendous as to be an utter impossibility. The opponents of this bill urge as their strongest objection the claim that this is a price-fixing bill. This claim is untrue. However, the very ones who oppose this bill as a price-fixing measure bring forth a suggestion that the bill be so amended as to require price fixing of commodities in every case in which a State authorized price resale contract is entered into. The full and complete answer to this, as in the case of the first objection, is that the State acts authorize the price resale contracts in which it is agreed between the manufacturer, the producer, and the seller that the commodity shall be sold at a price agreed upon between the parties to the contract. H. R. 1611 merely makes possible the full and complete operation of these State acts.

In conclusion, I repeat that the purpose of H. R. 1611 is merely to allow the people of the respective States to carry out a public policy which they have determined for themselves. It removes an existing Federal barrier which prevents the operation of State laws within the borders of the ⊥ States which have enacted these laws. It merely validates contracts operative within the respective States as to goods transported into those States in interstate commerce. The States have enacted their fair-trade practice laws for the benefit of the producer, the distributor, and the consumer, and for the protection and continuance in business of the independent merchant.

The States in which the acts have operated are satisfied with them. The other States which have recently enacted them based their enactment upon the beneficial results shown in the States where they have been in operation. However, State fair-trade practice acts have never had an opportunity to function fully, and they never will operate with complete effectiveness, nor produce the full benefit which they are capable of producing until the removal of the existing Federal barrier by the passage of the Miller-Tydings Fair Trade Practice Act, H. R. 1611. That act is now before us as an amendment to the conference report under consideration.

Forty-two States of the Union today look to the House of Representatives to pass

---

[2.38] At this juncture Representative McLaughlin, in reading this excerpt from *Old Dearborn* into the *Record*, omitted a paragraph.

[2.39] 299 U.S. at 193–94.

this law which will remove the barrier now standing in the way of the full and complete operation of the respective State fair-trade practice acts.

Mr. PALMISANO. Mr. Speaker, I move the adoption of the conference report.

The conference report was agreed to.

A motion to reconsider was laid on the table.

[ED. NOTE: The Senate approved the conference report on H.R. 7472 without debate on August 4, 1937. 81 CONG. REC. 8166-68 (1937).]

PRESIDENTIAL COMMENT

STATEMENT BY PRESIDENT FRANKLIN D. ROOSEVELT UPON SIGNING H.R. 7472
August 18, 1937

There has been before me for ten days an important and lengthy bill to provide additional revenue for the District of Columbia. To this bill, during its discussion in the Senate, was attached a wholly unrelated amendment pertaining to existing anti-trust laws, insofar as they affect retail sales.

This is the first instance during my term of office that this vicious practice of attaching unrelated riders to tax or appropriation bills has occurred.

The country will recognize the unfairness of placing any President in the position of having to disapprove a major bill just because an extraneous rider has been attached to it. In the present case, I have no hesitation in approving the tax legislation for the District of Columbia, but I have distinct hesitation in approving the rider which weakens the anti-trust laws.

Several of the Departments of the Government have pointed out, in reports they have given me, extremely objectionable features in this rider and recommended my veto of the whole bill on this account. There is, on the other hand, some estimable opinion that the effects of this rider will not be as serious as it is feared by the Departments that favor a veto.

I have decided to sign the bill in the hope that it will not be as harmful as most people predict, and I call attention to the fact that one of the principal objections to the rider is that the Departments opposing it believe it will seriously raise the cost of many articles to the consuming public.

But in signing it, I express again the objection to this unusual method of passing laws, and I sincerely trust that future sessions of the Congress of the United States will forego the practice of attaching unrelated riders to important and specific bills.

The Decision

Commentary

The Miller-Tydings Act was signed into law in August 1937; by the end of the year, 42 states had enacted fair-trade laws. Each of these, following the early lead of the 1933 California Act, by their own terms were applicable both to actual signers of fair-trade agreements and to so-called nonsigners—those who had notice of the existence of a fair-trade agreement in their state and who "willfully and knowingly" advertised, offered for sale, or sold any fair-traded commodity at less than the price stipulated in such agreement.

Since some 37 states already had fair-trade statutes covering nonsigners on their books at the time the Miller-Tydings Act became law, since the Supreme Court had upheld the constitutionality of such statutes in its decision in the *Old Dearborn* case,[2.40] and since the purpose of the Miller-Tydings Act was to give full effect to those state statutes with respect to goods that had moved in interstate commerce prior to their resale, it was assumed virtually without question that the Miller-Tydings Act exemption from Sherman Act liability for resale price maintenance agreements encompassed both actual signers to such agreements and those persons having notice of such agreements who willfully and knowingly violated their provisions. For almost 14 years following the enactment of the Miller-Tydings Act, the assumption of its applicability to nonsigners was manifested in the enforcement of fair-trade agreements against nonsigners. But on May 21, 1951, the Supreme Court handed down its decision in *Schwegmann Brothers v. Calvert Distillers Corp.*,[2.41] and in so doing sent out a shock wave that jolted the proponents of fair trade.

The *Schwegmann* case involved the attempted enforcement by Calvert of its minimum retail price schedule against a nonsigning Louisiana retailer who had refused to comply with Calvert's fixed retail prices. The district court entered an order enjoining Schwegmann from further violations of the Louisiana fair-trade law (which was specifically applicable to nonsigners) and the Fifth Circuit Court of Appeals affirmed. The issue in the Supreme Court was a simple one: Did the Miller-Tydings Act permit enforcement of fair-trade agreements as to products previously in interstate commerce against nonsigners who had notice of such agreements? The answer of the Supreme Court, in a six-to-three decision written by Mr. Justice Douglas, was a resounding "no."

The majority opinion first reviewed the history of events leading up to the enactment of the Miller-Tydings Act in 1937, pointing out that resale price maintenance on products within the flow of interstate commerce had been held unlawful under section 1 of the Sherman Act by the Court's 1911 decision in the *Dr. Miles* case.[2.42] It then tackled the core question of whether the immunity from Sherman Act liability contained in the Miller-Tydings Act was applicable to nonsigners. The Court held that the Act's immunity was a limited one, since it did not contain a

---

[2.40] Old Dearborn Distrib. Co. v. Seagrams-Distillers Corp., 299 U.S. 183, 57 S. Ct. 139, 81 L. Ed. 109 (1936), *supra* at 472.

[2.41] 341 U.S. 384, 71 S. Ct. 745, 95 L. Ed. 1035 (1951), *infra* at 541.

[2.42] Dr. Miles Medical Co. v. John D. Park & Sons Co., 220 U.S. 373, 31 S. Ct. 376, 55 L. Ed. 502 (1911).

nonsigner provision and, by its terms, sanctioned only "contracts or agreements."[2.43] The Court then stated that what Calvert sought in this case was "not price fixing by contract or agreement" but rather "price fixing by compulsion."[2.44] This, the Court ruled, was clearly not permitted on the face of the statute itself.

Moreover, the Court held that state fair-trade laws which force nonconsenting retailers to follow a "parallel price policy" violate the proviso contained in the Miller-Tydings Act which forbids horizontal price fixing. "A real sanction can be given the prohibitions of the proviso," according to the Court, "only if price maintenance power granted a distributor is limited to *voluntary* engagements. Otherwise, the exception swallows the proviso and destroys its practical effectiveness."[2.45]

Finally, the majority found that the legislative history of the Miller-Tydings statute supported its conclusions. Neither that Act, nor its predecessor Capper-Kelly fair trade bills (first introduced in 1929 but never passed), contained nonsigner provisions, a fact which the Court found to be persuasive as to legislative intent. Moreover, while conceding that there were some statements in the legislative history, particularly in the House report on the Miller bill,[2.46] supportive of Calvert's position, the Court decided "not [to] take these remarks at face value" because the thrust of the legislative history made clear "that the voluntary contract is the core of the argument" for the legislation.[2.47] In support of this finding, the Court cited a floor speech by Senator Tydings in which no suggestion was made that the bill affected anyone other than actual signers[2.48] and stated that it was unable to find any indication "that coercive as well as voluntary schemes or arrangements are permissible" under the Act.[2.49]

In a separate concurring opinion, Mr. Justice Jackson, joined by Mr. Justice Minton, stated he saw no reason to go back into the legislative history of the Miller-Tydings Act because, in his view, "[r]esort to legislative history is only justified where the face of the Act is inescapably ambiguous."[2.50] Justice Jackson further added that he could "think of no better example of legislative history that is unedifying and unilluminating than that of the [Miller-Tydings Act]."[2.51]

In dissent, Mr. Justice Frankfurter, joined by Justices Black and Burton, cited references in the House report on the Miller bill, remarks on the floor by Senator Tydings and by then Representative Dirksen, and interpretations given the bills by the Federal Trade Commission, by the Department of Justice, and by other opponents, to demonstrate that the legislative history clearly supports the position that the Act was intended to be applicable to nonsigners as well as to signers of fair-trade agreements. Justice Frankfurter concluded his dissent by stating that "[t]he 'fair trade' laws may well be unsound as a matter of economics. . . . [However], [t]hese are matters beyond the Court's concern. Where both the words of a statute and its legislative history clearly indicate the purpose of Congress, it should be respected. We should not substitute our own notion of what Congress should have done."[2.52]

Although clearly a significant setback to fair traders, the Supreme Court's decision in *Schwegmann* was not the deathknell of fair trade in the United States. Within days of the Court's ruling, the proponents of fair trade were back in Congress, this time pressing for additional legislation to validate nonsigner provisions in the context of interstate transactions. The result of their efforts was the enactment of the McGuire Act, the history of which is contained in the next chapter.

[2.43] 341 U.S. at 388.

[2.44] *Id.*

[2.45] *Id.* at 389 (emphasis in original).

[2.46] H.R. REP. No. 382, 75th Cong., 1st Sess. 2 (1937), *supra* at 480–81.

[2.47] 341 U.S. at 393.

[2.48] *Id.* at 394.

[2.49] *Id.*

[2.50] *Id.* at 395 (Jackson, J., concurring).

[2.51] *Id.* at 397.

[2.52] *Id.* at 402 (Frankfurter, J., dissenting).

SCHWEGMANN BROTHERS v. CALVERT DISTILLERS CORP.

341 U.S. 384, 71 S. Ct. 745, 95 L. Ed. 1035 (1951)

MR. JUSTICE DOUGLAS delivered the opinion of the Court.

Respondents, Maryland and Delaware corporations, are distributors of gin and whiskey. They sell their products to wholesalers in Louisiana, who in turn sell to retailers. Respondents have a price-fixing scheme whereby they try to maintain uniform retail prices for their products. They endeavor to make retailers sign price-fixing contracts under which the buyers promise to sell at not less than the prices stated in respondents' schedules. They have indeed succeeded in getting over one hundred Louisiana retailers to sign these agreements. Petitioner, a retailer in New Orleans, refused to agree to the price-fixing scheme and sold respondents' products at a cut-rate price. Respondents thereupon brought this suit in the District Court by reason of diversity of citizenship to enjoin petitioner from selling the products at less than the minimum prices fixed by their schedules.

It is clear from our decisions under the Sherman Act (26 Stat. 209) that this interstate marketing arrangement would be illegal, that it would be enjoined, that it would draw civil and criminal penalties, and that no court would enforce it. Fixing minimum prices, like other types of price fixing, is illegal *per se*. *United States* v. *Socony-Vacuum Oil Co.*, 310 U. S. 150; *Kiefer-Stewart Co.* v. *Seagram & Sons*, 340 U. S. 211. Resale price maintenance was indeed struck down in *Dr. Miles Medical Co.* v. *Park & Sons Co.*, 220 U. S. 373. The fact that a state authorizes the price fixing does not, of course, give immunity to the scheme, absent approval by Congress.

Respondents, however, seek to find legality for this marketing arrangement in the Miller-Tydings Act enacted in 1937 as an amendment to § 1 of the Sherman Act. 50 Stat. 693, 15 U. S. C. § 1. That amendment provides in material part that "nothing herein contained shall render illegal, *contracts or agreements* prescribing minimum prices for the resale" of specified commodities when "*contracts or agreements of that description* are lawful as applied to intrastate transactions" under local law.[1] (Italics added.)

Louisiana has such a law. La. Gen. Stat., §§ 9809.1 *et seq.* It permits a "contract" for the sale or resale of a commodity to provide that the buyer will not resell "except at the price stipulated by the vendor." The Louisiana statute goes further. It not only allows a distributor and retailer to make a "contract" fixing the resale price; but once there is a price-fixing "contract," known to a seller, with any retailer in the state, it also condemns as unfair competition a sale at less than the price stipulated even though the seller is not a party to the "contract."[2] In other words, the Louisiana statute enforces price fixing not only against parties to a "contract" but also against nonsigners. So far as Louisiana law is concerned, price fixing can be enforced against all retailers once any single retailer agrees with a distributor on the resale price. And the argument is that the Miller-Tydings Act permits the same range of price fixing.

The argument is phrased as follows: the present action is outlawed by the Sherman Act—the Miller-Tydings Act apart—only if it is a contract, combination, or conspiracy

---

[1] Resale price maintenance is allowed only as respects commodities which bear, or the label or container of which bear, the trade mark, brand, or name of the producer or distributor and which are in free and open competition with commodities of the same general class produced or distributed by others. Excluded are agreements between manufacturers, between producers, between wholesalers, between brokers, between factors, between retailers or between persons, firms or corporations in competition with each other.

[2] The nonsigner clause in the Louisiana Act reads as follows: "Wilfully and knowingly advertising, offering for sale or selling any commodity at less than the price stipulated in any contract entered into pursuant to the provision of section 1 [§ 9809.1] of this act, *whether the person so advertising, offering for sale or selling is or is not a party to such contract*, is unfair competition and is actionable at the suit of any person damaged thereby."

in restraint of trade. But if a contract or agreement is the vice, then by the terms of the Miller-Tydings Act that contract or agreement is immunized, provided it is immunized by state law. The same is true if the vice is a conspiracy, since a conspiracy presupposes an agreement. That was in essence the view of the Court of Appeals, which affirmed by a divided vote a judgment of a district court enjoining petitioner from price cutting. 184 F. 2d 11.

The argument at first blush has appeal. But we think it offends the statutory scheme.

We note to begin with that there are critical differences between Louisiana's law and the Miller-Tydings Act. The latter exempts only "contracts or agreements prescribing minimum prices for the resale." On the other hand, the Louisiana law sanctions the fixing of maximum as well as minimum prices, for it exempts any provision that the buyer will not resell "except at the price stipulated by the vendor." We start then with a federal act which does not, as respondents suggest, turn over to the states the handling of the whole problem of resale price maintenance on this type of commodity. What is granted is a limited immunity—a limitation that is further emphasized by the inclusion in the state law and the exclusion from the federal law of the nonsigner provision. The omission of the nonsigner provision from the federal law is fatal to respondents' position unless we are to perform a distinct legislative function by reading into the Act a provision that was meticulously omitted from it.

A refusal to read the nonsigner provision into the Miller-Tydings Act makes sense if we are to take the words of the statute in their normal and customary meaning. The Act sanctions only "contracts or agreements." If a distributor and one or more retailers want to agree, combine, or conspire to fix a minimum price, they can do so if state law permits. Their contract, combination, or conspiracy—hitherto illegal—is made lawful. They can fix minimum prices pursuant to their contract or agreement with impunity. When they seek, however, to impose price fixing on persons who have not contracted or agreed to the scheme, the situation is vastly different. That is not price fixing by contract or agreement; that is price fixing by compulsion. That is not following the path of consensual agreement; that is resort to coercion.

Much argument is made to import into the contracts which respondents make with retailers a provision that the parties may force nonsigners into line. It is said that state law attaches that condition to every such contract and that therefore the Miller-Tydings Act exempts it from the Sherman Act. Such a condition, if implied, creates an agreement respecting not sales made under the contract but other sales. Yet all that are exempted by the Miller-Tydings Act are "contracts or agreements prescribing minimum prices for the resale" of the articles purchased, not "contracts or agreements" respecting the practices of noncontracting competitors of the contracting retailers.

It should be noted in this connection that the Miller-Tydings Act expressly continues the prohibitions of the Sherman Act against "horizontal" price fixing by those in competition with each other at the same functional level.[3] Therefore, when a state compels retailers to follow a parallel price policy, it demands private conduct which the Sherman Act forbids. See *Parker* v. *Brown*, 317 U. S. 341, 350. Elimination of price competition at the retail level may, of course, lawfully result if a distributor successfully negotiates individual "vertical" agreements with all his retailers. But when retailers are *forced* to abandon price competition, they are driven into a compact in violation of the spirit of the proviso which forbids "horizontal" price fixing. A real sanction can be given the prohibitions of the proviso only if the price maintenance power granted a distributor is limited to *voluntary* engagements. Otherwise, the exception swallows the proviso and destroys its practical effectiveness.

The contrary conclusion would have a vast and devastating effect on Sherman Act policies. If it were adopted, once a distributor executed a contract with a single retailer setting the minimum resale price for a commodity in the state, all other

---

[3] "*Provided further,* That the preceding proviso shall not make lawful any contract or agreement, providing for the establishment or maintenance of minimum resale prices on any commodity herein involved, between manufacturers, or between producers, or between wholesalers, . . . or between retailers, or between persons, firms, or corporations in competition with each other." 15 U. S. C. § 1.

retailers could be forced into line. Had Congress desired to eliminate the consensual element from the arrangement and to permit blanketing a state with resale price fixing if only one retailer wanted it, we feel that different measures would have been adopted—either a nonsigner provision would have been included or resale price fixing would have been authorized without more. Certainly the words used connote a voluntary scheme. Contracts or agreements convey the idea of a cooperative arrangement, not a program whereby recalcitrants are dragged in by the heels and compelled to submit to price fixing.

The history of the Act supports this construction. The efforts to override the rule of *Dr. Miles Medical Co.* v. *Park & Sons Co., supra,* were long and persistent. Many bills had been introduced on this subject before Senator Tydings introduced his. Thus in 1929, in the Seventy-First Congress, the Capper-Kelly fair trade bill was offered.[4] It had no nonsigner provision. It merely permitted resale price maintenance as respects specified classes of commodities by declaring that no such "contract relating to the sale or resale" shall be unlawful. As stated in the House Report, that bill merely legalized an agreement "that the vendee will not resell the commodity specified in the contract except at a stipulated price."[5] That bill became the model for the California act passed in 1931—the first state act permitting resale price maintenance.[6] The California act contained no nonsigner clause. Neither did the Capper-Kelly bill that ⊥ was introduced in the Seventy-Second Congress.[7] So far as material here it was identical with its predecessor.

The Capper-Kelly bill did not pass. And by the time the next bill was introduced—three years later—the California act had been changed by the addition of the nonsigner provision.[8] That was in 1933. Yet when in 1936 Senator Tydings introduced his first bill in the Seventy-Fourth Congress[9] he followed substantially the Capper-Kelly bills and wrote no nonsigner provision into it. His bill merely legalized "contracts or agreements prescribing minimum prices or other conditions for the resale" of a commodity. By this date several additional states had resale price maintenance laws with nonsigner provisions.[10] Even though the state laws were the models for the federal bills, the nonsigner provision was never added. That was true of the bill introduced in the Seventy-Fifth Congress as well as the subsequent one. They all followed in this respect the pattern of the Capper-Kelly bill as it appeared before the first nonsigner provision was written into state law. The "contract" concept utilized by Capper-Kelly before there was a nonsigner provision in state law was thus continued even after the nonsigner provision appeared. The inference, therefore, is strong that there was continuity between the first Tydings bill and the preceding Capper-Kelly bills. The Tydings bills built on the same foundation; they were no more concerned with nonsigner provisions than were their predecessors. In view of this history we can only conclude that, if the ⊥ draftsman intended that the nonsigning retailer was to be coerced, it was strange indeed that he omitted the one clear provision that would have accomplished that result.

An argument is made from the reports and debates to the effect that "contracts or agreements" nevertheless includes the nonsigner provisions of state law. The Senate Report on the first Tydings bill, after stating that the California law authorized a distributor "to make a contract that the purchaser will not resell" except at the stipulated price, said that the proposed federal law "does no more than to remove

---

[4] S. 240, 71st Cong., 1st Sess.; H. R. 11, 71st Cong., 1st Sess. See H. R. Rep. No. 536, 71st Cong., 2d Sess.

[5] H. R. Rep. No. 536, 71st Cong., 2d Sess. 2.

[6] Cal. Stat., 1931, c. 278. The California Act was sometimes known as "the Junior Capper-Kelly." See Grether, Price Control Under Fair Trade Legislation (1939), p. 54.

[7] S. 97, 72d Cong., 1st Sess.; H. R. 11, 72d Cong., 1st Sess.

[8] Cal. Stat., 1933, c. 260: The California law is now found in Business & Professions Code, Pt. 2, c. 3, § 16904.

[9] S. 3822, 74th Cong., 2d Sess., 80 Cong. Rec. 1007.

[10] See Ill. Laws 1935, p. 1436; Iowa Laws 1935, c. 106; Md. Laws 1935, c. 212, § 2; N. J. Laws 1935, c. 58, § 2; N. Y. Laws 1935, c. 976, § 2; Ore. Laws 1935, c. 295, § 2; Pa. Laws 1935, No. 115, § 2; Wash. Laws 1935, c. 177, § 4; Wis. Laws 1935, c. 52.

Federal obstacles to the enforcement of contracts which the States themselves have declared lawful."[11] The Senate Report on the second Tydings bill, which was introduced in the Seventy-fifth Congress, did little more than reprint the earlier report.[12] The House Report, heavily relied on here, gave a more extended analysis.[13]

The House Report referred to the state fair trade acts as authorizing the maintenance of resale prices by contract and as providing that "third parties with notice are bound by the terms of such a contract regardless of whether they are parties to it"; and the Report also stated that the objective of the Act was to permit the public policy of the states having such acts to operate with respect to interstate contracts for the sale of goods.[14] This Report is the strongest statement for respondents' position which is found in the legislative history. The bill which that Report endorsed, however, did not pass. The bill which became the law was attached by the Senate Committee on the District of Columbia as a rider to the District of Columbia revenue bill. In that form it was debated and passed.

⊥ It is true that the House Report quoted above[15] was referred to when the Senate amendment to the revenue measure was before the House.[16] And one Congressman in the debate said that the nonsigner provision of state laws was validated by the federal law.

But we do not take these remarks at face value. In the first place, the House Report, while referring to the nonsigner provision when describing a typical state fair trade act, is so drafted that the voluntary contract is the core of the argument for the bill. Hence, the General Statement in the Report states that the sole objective of the Act was "to permit the public policy of States having 'fair trade acts' to operate with respect to interstate *contracts* for the resale of goods"; and the fair trade acts are referred to as legalizing "the maintenance, *by contract*, of resale prices of branded or trade-marked goods."[17] (Italics added.)

In the second place, the remarks relied on were not only about a bill on which no vote was taken; they were about a bill which sanctioned "contracts or agreements" prescribing not only "minimum prices" but "other conditions" as well. The words "other conditions" were dropped from the amendment that was made to the revenue bill. Why they were deleted does not appear. It is said that they have no relevance to the present problem, since we are dealing here with "minimum prices" not with "other conditions." But that answer does not quite hold. The question is the amount of state law embraced in the words "contracts or agreements." It might well be argued that one of the "conditions" attaching to a contract fixing a minimum price would be the liability of a nonsigner. ⊥ We do no more than stir the doubt, for the doubt alone is enough to make us skeptical of the full implications of the old report as applied to a new and different bill.

We look for more definite clues; and we find the following statement made on the floor by Senator Tydings: "What does the amendment do? It permits a man who manufactures an article to state the minimum resale price of the article in a contract with the man who buys it for ultimate resale to the public. . . ."[18] Not once did Senator Tydings refer to the nonsigner provisions of state law. Not once did he suggest that the amendment would affect anyone but the retailer who signs the contract. We search the words of the sponsors for a clear indication that coercive as well as voluntary schemes or arrangements are permissible. We find none.[19] What we do find is

---

[11] S. Rep. No. 2053, 74th Cong., 2d Sess. 2.
[12] S. Rep. No. 257, 75th Cong., 1st Sess.
[13] H. R. Rep. No. 382, 75th Cong., 1st Sess.
[14] *Id.*, p. 2.
[15] *Id.*
[16] See, *e. g.*, the statement of Rep. Dirksen, a House conferee, in 81 Cong. Rec. 8138.
[17] H. R. Rep. No. 382, 75th Cong., 1st Sess. 2.
[18] 81 Cong. Rec. 7495.
[19] H. R. Rep. No. 1413, 75th Cong., 1st Sess. 10 (the Conference Report of the House) merely stated: "This amendment provides for an amendment to the antitrust laws under which contracts and agreements stipulating minimum resale prices of certain commodities, and which are similar to contracts and agreements which are lawful as applied to intrastate commerce, are not to be regarded as being illegal under the antitrust laws."

the expression of fear in the minority report of the Senate Committee that the nonsigner provisions of the state laws would be made effective if the law passed.[20] These fears were presented in the Senate debate by Senator King in opposition to the amendment.[21] But the Senate Report emphasizes the "permissive" nature of the state laws,[22] not once pointing to their coercive features.

The fears and doubts of the opposition are no authoritative guide to the construction of legislation. It is the sponsors that we look to when the meaning of the statutory words is in doubt. And when we read what the sponsors wrote and said about the amendment, we cannot find that the distributors were to have the right to use not only a *contract* to fix retail prices but a *club* as well. The words they used—"contracts or agreements"—suggest just the contrary.

It should be remembered that it was the state laws that the federal law was designed to accommodate. Federal regulation was to give way to state regulation. When state regulation provided for resale price maintenance by both those who contracted and those who did not, and the federal regulation was relaxed only as respects "contracts or agreements," the inference is strong that Congress left the noncontracting group to be governed by preexisting law. In other words, since Congress was writing a law to meet the specifications of state law, it would seem that if the nonsigner provision as well as the "contract" provision of state law were to be written into federal law, the pattern of the legislation would have been different.

We could conclude that Congress carved out the vast exception from the Sherman Act now claimed only if we were willing to assume that it took a devious route and yet failed to make its purpose plain.

Reversed.

MR. JUSTICE JACKSON, whom MR. JUSTICE MINTON joins, concurring.

I agree with the Court's judgment and with its opinion insofar as it rests upon the language of the Miller-Tydings Act. But it does not appear that there is either necessity or propriety in going back of it into legislative history.

Resort to legislative history is only justified where the face of the Act is inescapably ambiguous, and then I think we should not go beyond Committee reports, which presumably are well considered and carefully prepared. I cannot deny that I have sometimes offended against that rule. But to select casual statements from floor debates, not always distinguished for candor or accuracy, as a basis for making up our minds what law Congress intended to enact is to substitute ourselves for the Congress in one of its important functions. The Rules of the House and Senate, with the sanction of the Constitution, require three readings of an Act in each House before final enactment. That is intended, I take it, to make sure that each House knows what it is passing and passes what it wants, and that what is enacted was formally reduced to writing. It is the business of Congress to sum up its own debates in its legislation. Moreover, it is only the words of the bill that have presidential approval, where that approval is given. It is not to be supposed that, in signing a bill, the President endorses the whole Congressional Record. For us to undertake to reconstruct an enactment from legislative history is merely to involve the Court in political controversies which are quite proper in the enactment of a bill but should have no place in its interpretation.

Moreover, there are practical reasons why we should accept whenever possible the meaning which an enactment reveals on its face. Laws are intended for all of our people to live by; and the people go to law offices to learn what their rights under those laws are. Here is a controversy which affects every little merchant in many States. Aside from a few offices in the larger cities, the materials of legislative history are not available to the lawyer who can afford neither the cost of acquisition, the cost of housing, or the cost of repeatedly examining the whole congressional history. Moreover, if he could, he would not know any way of anticipating what would impress enough members of the Court to be controlling. To accept legislative debates to modify

---

[20] S. Rep. No. 879, 75th Cong., 1st Sess.

[21] 81 Cong. Rec. 7491. And see S. Rep. No. 879, Part 2, 75th Cong., 1st Sess.

[22] S. Rep. No. 879, 75th Cong., 1st Sess. 6.

statutory provisions is to make the law inaccessible to a large part of the country.

By and large, I think our function was well stated by Mr. Justice Holmes: "We do not inquire what the legislature meant; we ask only what the statute means." Holmes, Collected Legal Papers, 207. See also *Soon Hing* v. *Crowley,* 113 U. S. 703, 710–711. And I can think of no better example of legislative history that is unedifying and unilluminating than that of the Act before us.

MR. JUSTICE FRANKFURTER, whom MR. JUSTICE BLACK and MR. JUSTICE BURTON join, dissenting.

In 1890, Congress passed the Sherman Law, which declared illegal "[e]very contract, combination in the form of trust or otherwise, or conspiracy, in restraint of trade or commerce among the several States, or with foreign nations." Act of July 2, 1890, § 1, 26 Stat. 209, 15 U. S. C. § 1. In 1937, Congress passed the Miller-Tydings Amendment. This excepted from the Sherman Law "contracts or agreements" prescribing minimum prices for the resale of trade-marked commodities where such contracts or agreements were valid under State statute or policy. Act of Aug. 17, 1937, Title VIII, 50 Stat. 673, 693, 15 U. S. C. § 1. It would appear that, insofar as the Sherman Law made maintenance of minimum resale prices illegal, the Miller-Tydings Amendment made it legal to the extent that State law legalized it. "Contracts or agreements" immunized by the Miller-Tydings Amendment surely cannot have a narrower scope than "contract, combination . . . or conspiracy" in the Sherman Law. The Miller-Tydings Amendment is an amendment to § 1 of the Sherman Law. The category of contract cannot be given different content in the very same section of the same act, and every combination or conspiracy implies an agreement.

The setting of the Miller-Tydings Amendment and its legislative history remove any lingering doubts. The depression following 1929 gave impetus to the movement for legislation which would allow the fixing of minimum resale prices. In 1931, California passed a statute allowing a manufacturer to establish resale prices binding only upon retailers who voluntarily entered into a contract with him. This proved completely ineffective, and in 1933 California amended her statute to provide that such a contract established a minimum price binding upon any person who had notice of the contract. Grether, Experience in California with Fair Trade Legislation Restricting Price Cutting, 24 Calif. L. Rev. 640, 644 (1936). This amendment was the so-called "non-signer" clause which, in effect, allowed a manufacturer or wholesaler to fix a minimum resale price for his product. Every "fair trade" law thereafter passed by any State contained this "non-signer" clause. By the close of 1936, 14 States had passed such laws. In 1937, 28 more States passed them. Today, 45 out of 48 States have "fair trade" laws. See Report of the Federal Trade Commission on Resale Price Maintenance XXVII (Dec. 13, 1945).

A substantial obstacle remained in the path of the "fair trade" movement. In 1911, we had decided *Dr. Miles Medical Co.* v. *Park & Sons Co.,* 220 U. S. 373. There, in a suit brought against a "non-signer," we held that an agreement to maintain resale prices was a "contract . . . in restraint of trade" which was contrary to the Sherman Law. To remove this block, the Miller-Tydings Amendment was enacted. It is said, however, that thereby Congress meant only to remove the bar of the Sherman Law from agreements between the manufacturer and retailer, that Congress did not mean to make valid the "non-signer" clause which formed an integral part of each of the 42 State statutes in effect when the Amendment was passed.

The Miller-Tydings Amendment was passed as a rider to a Revenue Bill for the District of Columbia. The Senate Committee which attached the rider referred the Senate to S. Rep. No. 2053, 74th Cong., 2d Sess.[1] The House Conference Report (H. R. Rep. No. 1413, 75th Cong., 1st Sess.), contains only five lines concerning the rider. But the rider was not a new measure. It came as no surprise to the House, which already

---

[1] The Senate Report on the District of Columbia Revenue Bill, S. Rep. No. 879, 75th Cong., 1st Sess., quoted S. Rep. No. 2053, 74th Cong., 2d Sess. See S. Rep. No. 257, 75th Cong., 1st Sess., which also quotes the text of the earlier report.

had before it practically the same language in the Miller Bill, reported favorably by the Committee on the Judiciary. H. R. Rep. No. 382, 75th Cong., 1st Sess. Both the House and Senate, therefore, had before them reports dealing with the substance of the Miller-Tydings Amendment. These reports speak for themselves, and I attach them as appendices to this opinion, *post*, p. 402. Every State act referred to in these reports contained a "non-signer" provision. I cannot see how, in view of these reports, we can conclude that Congress meant the "non-signer" provisions to be invalid under the Sherman Law—unless, that is, we are to depart from the respect we have accorded authoritative legislative history in scores of cases during the last decade. See cases collected in *Commissioner* v. *Estate of Church*, 335 U. S. 632, 687, Appendix A. In many of these cases the purpose of Congress was far less clearly revealed than here.[2] It has never been questioned in this Court that committee reports, as well as statements by those in charge of a bill or of a report, are authoritative elucidations of the scope of a measure.

It is suggested that we go to the words of the sponsors of the Miller-Tydings Amendment. We have done so. Their words confirm the plain meaning of the words of the statute and of the congressional reports. Senator Tydings made the following statement: "What we have attempted to do is what 42 States have already written on their statute books. It is simply to back up those acts, that is all; to have a code of fair trade practices written not by a national board such as the N. R. A. but by each State, so that the people may go to the State legislature and correct immediately any abuses that may develop." 81 Cong. Rec. 7496.

Representative Dirksen made a statement to the House as a member of its Conference Committee. He referred to the case of *Old Dearborn Co.* v. *Seagram Corp.*, 299 U. S. 183, in which this Court had held that the "Non-signer" provision of the Illinois "fair trade" statute did not violate the Due Process Clause. Mr. Dirksen continued: "A question then arose as to whether or not the maintenance of such resale prices under a State fair trade act might not be in violation of the Sherman Anti-Trust Law of 1890 insofar as these transactions sprang from a contract in interstate commerce. This question was presented to the House Judiciary Committee and there determined by the reporting of the Miller bill. It was essentially nothing more than an enabling act which placed the stamp of approval upon price maintenance transactions under State acts, notwithstanding the Sherman Act of 1890." 81 Cong. Rec. 8138.

Every one of the 42 State acts which the Miller-Tydings Amendment was to "back up"—the acts on which the Miller-Tydings Amendment was to place a "stamp of approval"—contained a "non-signer" provision. As demonstrated by experience in California, the State acts would have been futile without the "non-signer" clause. The Court now holds that the Miller-Tydings Amendment does not cover these "non-signer" provisions. Not only is the view of the Court contrary to the words of the statute and to the legislative history. It is also in conflict with the interpretation given

---

[2] The intricate verbal arguments used to support the Court's decision do not affect the clarity of the statute and its legislative history. (1) It is said that the proviso to the Miller-Tydings Amendment makes it inapplicable to "non-signer" clauses in State acts. But the proviso only made explicit that the Amendment applied only to vertical agreements and did not make legal horizontal agreements, for example, those between retailers or between manufacturers. See statements of Senator Tydings, 81 Cong. Rec. 7487, 7496. The wording of the proviso, in fact, follows closely a statement of what the Senate Committee thought was implicit in the State acts. See S. Rep. No. 2053, 74th Cong., 2d Sess. 2. (2) The fact that the 1931 California statute used wording similar to the Miller-Tydings Amendment and was later amended to refer to nonsigners is beside the mark. The words of the 1933 amendment to the California statute make clear that it was not, like the Miller-Tydings Amendment, designed to remove the bar of an antitrust act. It was enacted to give an affirmative right to recover from nonsigners, something the Miller-Tydings Amendment does not purport to do. In such a statute specific language referring to nonsigners would of course have to be used. (3) It is said that H. R. Rep. No. 382, 75th Cong., 1st Sess., refers to a bill containing the phrase "other conditions." The words "other conditions," when used in conjunction with a phrase referring to minimum prices, could scarcely mean anything except "conditions other than minimum prices." We are here concerned with minimum prices. (4) "Permissive" was used in the Senate Report not to refer to retailers but to manufacturers. "[The State acts] merely authorize a manufacturer or producer to enter into contracts for the maintenance of his price, but they do not compel him to do so. In other words, they are merely permissive." S. Rep. No. 2053, 74th Cong., 2d Sess. 2.

the Miller-Tydings Amendment by the Federal Trade Commission,[3] by the Department of Justice,[4] and by practically all persons adversely affected by the "fair trade" laws.[5] The "fair trade" laws may well be unsound as a matter of economics. Perhaps Congress should not pass an important measure dealing with an extraneous subject as a rider to a revenue bill, with the coercive influence it exerts in avoiding a veto; perhaps it should restrict legislation to a single relevant subject, as required by the constitutions of three-fourths of the States. These are matters beyond the Court's concern. Where both the words of a statute and its legislative history clearly indicate the purpose of Congress, it should be respected. We should not substitute our own notion of what Congress should have done.

---

[3] See letter addressed to the President by the Chairman of the Federal Trade Commission, S. Doc. No. 58, 75th Cong., 1st Sess., pp. 2–3. See also Report of the Federal Trade Commission on Resale Price Maintenance LXII (Dec. 13, 1945).

[4] The Department of Justice appears to have instituted no prosecutions because of enforcement of "fair trade" acts against nonsigners. The Assistant Attorney General who played an important part in enforcement of the antitrust laws called for repeal of the Miller-Tydings Amendment because it made legal the nonsigner provisions of the State "fair trade" acts. Statement of Mr. Thurman Arnold, T.N.E.C. Hearings, pp. 18162–18165.

[5] The contention that the "non-signer" provisions are not within the Miller-Tydings Amendment appears to have been made in only two reported cases since the Amendment was passed in 1937. *Calamia v. Goldsmith Bros., Inc.*, 299 N. Y. 636 and 795, 87 N. E. 2d 50 and 687; *Pepsodent Co. v. Krauss Co.*, 56 F. Supp. 922. In both, the argument was rejected.

3 McGUIRE RESALE PRICE MAINTENANCE ACT AMENDMENT OF 1952

(REPEALED EFFECTIVE 1976; SEE CHAPTER 4)

551	Introduction
555	Chronological Synopsis
559	Table of Reprinted Documents

ORIGINAL VERSION

560	McGuire Resale Price Maintenance Act Amendment July 14, 1952

The Origins

562	Remarks of Rep. John A. McGuire introducing H.R. 5767 82d Cong., 1st Sess. October 17, 1951

House Consideration (H.R. 5767; H.R. 6925)

565	H.R. 5767, 82d Cong., 1st Sess. October 17, 1951
566	Remarks of Rep. Louis B. Heller, 82d Cong., 2d Sess. January 15, 1952
567	Report of the House Committee on Interstate and Foreign Commerce H.R. Rep. No. 1437, 82d Cong., 2d Sess. [to accompany H.R. 5767] February 26, 1952
577	H.R. 5767 as reported by the House Committee on Interstate and Foreign Commerce February 27, 1952
579	Report of the House Committee on the Judiciary (with Minority Views) H.R. Rep. No. 1516, 82d Cong., 2d Sess. [to accompany H.R. 6925] March 13, 1952
632	H.R. 6925 as reported by the House Committee on the Judiciary March 13, 1952
634	Remarks of Rep. Charles A. Wolverton, 82d Cong., 2d Sess. May 6, 1952

	House Debate, 82d Cong., 2d Sess.
639	May 7, 1952
701	May 8, 1952

Senate Consideration (H.R. 5767)

751	Senate Debate, 82d Cong., 2d Sess. May 9, 1952
752	Report of the Senate Committee on Interstate and Foreign Commerce S. Rep. No. 1741, 82d Cong., 2d Sess. [to accompany H.R. 5767] June 12 (legislative day, June 10), 1952
	Senate Debate, 82d Cong., 2d Sess.
764	July 1, 1952
824	July 2, 1952

Presidential Comment

925	Statement by President Harry S. Truman upon signing the "Fair-Trade Laws" bill (H.R. 5767) July 14, 1952

THE DECISION

927	Commentary
929	United States v. McKesson & Robbins, Inc., 351 U.S. 305 (1956)

Introduction

McGUIRE RESALE PRICE MAINTENANCE ACT AMENDMENT OF 1952

Shaken by the Supreme Court's decision in *Schwegmann Brothers v. Calvert Distillers Corp.*[3.1] holding that the Miller-Tydings Act[3.2] did not exempt from liability under section 1 of the Sherman Act nonsigner provisions in state fair-trade laws insofar as they affected goods which had moved in interstate commerce prior to their resale, the proponents of fair trade had but one avenue of relief: additional legislation in Congress to circumvent the *Schwegmann* holding.

Led again by the National Association of Retail Druggists,[3.3] the proponents wasted no time in securing congressional action. On October 17, 1951, less than five months after the *Schwegmann* decision, Representative John A. McGuire (D., Conn.) introduced the bill that was later enacted into law bearing his name.[3.4] The McGuire bill, offered as an amendment to section 5(a) of the Federal Trade Commission Act, specifically validated under federal law the nonsigner provisions in the various state fair-trade acts.

The McGuire bill was favorably reported out of the House Committee on Interstate and Foreign Commerce on February 27, 1952.[3.5] Some two weeks later a similar measure,[3.6] this one introduced by Representative Eugene J. Keogh (D., N.Y.) as an amendment to the Sherman Act, was reported out of the House Judiciary Committee.[3.7] Although the Keogh bill also permitted state fair-trade contracts to be applied to

---

[3.1] 341 U.S. 384, 71 S. Ct. 745, 95 L. Ed. 1035 (1951), *supra* at chapter 2.

[3.2] Act of Aug. 17, 1937, ch. 690, tit. VIII, 50 Stat. 693, the legislative history of which appears *supra* at chapter 2.

[3.3] The association had also played a significant role in the passage of the Miller-Tydings Act of 1937. See chapter 2, *Introduction*, *supra*.

[3.4] H.R. 5767, 82d Cong., 1st Sess. (1951), *infra* at 565–66.

[3.5] H.R. 5767 as reported by the House Committee on Interstate and Foreign Commerce, 82d Cong., 2d Sess. (1952), *infra* at 577–78, *accompanied by* H.R. REP. NO. 1437, 82d Cong., 2d Sess. (1952), *infra* at 567–76.

[3.6] H.R. 6925, 82d Cong., 2d Sess. (introduced March 6, 1952) (a clean bill superseding H.R. 6367).

[3.7] H.R. 6925 as reported by the House Committee on the Judiciary, 82d Cong., 2d Sess. (1952), *infra* at 632–34, *accompanied by* H.R. REP. NO. 1516, 82d Cong., 2d Sess. (1952), *infra* at 577–631. Three

nonsigners, it differed from the McGuire bill in that it would have specifically made the failure of the fair trader to fully enforce its stipulated or minimum resale prices a defense to a fair-trade enforcement action. More important, the Keogh bill would have created a federal cause of action for unfair competition under the Federal Trade Commission Act for advertising, offering for sale, selling, transporting for sale or resale, or delivering pursuant to a sale, in interstate commerce, a product for which the resale price had been set at less than the price set in a state having a fair-trade statute.

In the subsequent debate on the floor of the House (on May 7–8, 1952), the McGuire and Keogh bills were jointly considered. The debate consisted mainly of tributes by the proponents of fair trade to the salutary effects of the Miller-Tydings Act and state fair-trade legislation; little was said in opposition to the demand for legislation covering nonsigners. In the end, the House opted for the McGuire bill, largely because the Keogh bill would have injected the federal government one step further into the enforcement of fair trade by creating a federal cause of action for violations and possibly by requiring the Federal Trade Commission to take affirmative enforcement action. On May 8, 1952, the House voted in favor of the McGuire bill as reported by an overwhelming margin of 196 to 10.[3.8]

On the Senate side, the McGuire bill's road to passage was somewhat rockier. To begin with, the report of the Senate Committee on Interstate and Foreign Commerce on H.R. 5767 contained no recommendation; it merely excerpted the statements of the various proponents and opponents who had appeared before the committee and testified with respect to the proposed legislation.[3.9] Moreover, when the bill was finally brought to the Senate floor on July 1, 1952, no Senator chose to rise in support of it. This prompted the following exchange between Senators Paul H. Douglas (D., Ill.) and Wayne L. Morse (R., Ore.):

Mr. DOUGLAS. Mr. President, are we going to pass this bill without its sponsors saying a word in its behalf? Is this child to be born without any statement as to the nature of the child?
SEVERAL SENATORS. Vote! Vote! . . .
Mr. DOUGLAS. . . .
This is really an extraordinary situation. No Senator has risen on the floor of the Senate to expound the bill. I may point out that the bill has come from the committee without recommendation. The hearings have not been printed. No sponsor has risen to explain the bill or give the reasons why he favors it. It is extraordinary that no Senator is willing to assume that burden. . . .
Mr. MORSE. Does the Senator think there might be some possibility that the reason no Senator has seen fit to father the child is that there may be some question as to its paternity?
Mr. DOUGLAS. I was trying to imply that, but I did not wish to be invidious in my references. I think perhaps there might be some doubt about the quality of the child itself.[3.10]

Whatever else the above exchange may have accomplished, it triggered a fierce debate on the floor of the Senate on the entire question of fair-trade legislation. The debate lasted two full days and at times seemed headed for a full-blown filibuster by the opponents, led by Senator Morse. Only the voting strength of the proponents prevented this. Although silent at first in the hope of securing passage of the bill without extended debate, the proponents were not to be denied their say. Led primarily by Senator Hubert H. Humphrey (D., Minn.), a former druggist and avid supporter of fair trade, they argued passionately and at length in support of the McGuire bill and fair-trade legislation generally.

Ironically, the Senate debate on the McGuire bill (on July 1–2, 1952) was far more extensive than that on the Miller-Tydings Act some 15 years earlier. As with the Miller-Tydings Act, however, the sentiment of the Senate was overwhelmingly in favor of congressional approval of fair-trade enabling legislation. On July 2, 1952, the Senate

---

other bills relating to resale price maintenance had been introduced in the first session of the 82d Congress and referred to the Judiciary Committee: H.R. 4365 (Curtis bill), H.R. 4592 (Poulson bill), and H.R. 4662 (Morano bill).

[3.8] 98 CONG. REC. 4956 (1952), *infra* at 749.

[3.9] S. REP. NO. 1741, 82d Cong., 2d Sess. (1952), *infra* at 752–64.

[3.10] 98 CONG. REC. 8716–17 (1952), *infra* at 764–65.

voted 64 to 16 in favor of the McGuire bill.[3.11] Nevertheless, as a concession to the opponents and in an effort to mollify the White House, Senator Humphrey submitted a concurrent resolution[3.12] to authorize the establishment of a Joint Committee on Fair Trade Practices to study further the effects of the McGuire Act and a resolution[3.13] to have the Senate Select Committee on Small Business make further and continuing studies in the same field. These resolutions were cited with approval by President Truman in his statement on signing the McGuire Act into law on July 14, 1952.[3.14]

[3.11] *Id.* at 8891-92, *infra* at 923.

[3.12] S. Con. Res. 87, 82d Cong., 2d Sess., 98 CONG. REC. 8892 (1952), *infra* at 923. This resolution was referred to the Senate Committee on Interstate and Foreign Commerce, but no further action was taken.

[3.13] S. Res. 348, 82d Cong., 2d Sess., 98 CONG. REC. 8892 (1952), *infra* at 924. This resolution was referred to the Senate Committee on Interstate and Foreign Commerce, but no further action was taken.

[3.14] 1952-1953 PUBLIC PAPERS OF THE PRESIDENTS, HARRY S. TRUMAN 477-78 (1953), *infra* at 925-26.

Chronological Synopsis

McGUIRE RESALE PRICE MAINTENANCE ACT AMENDMENT OF 1952

81st Congress, 1st Session

December 8, 1950

Sunbeam Corp. v. Wentling, 185 F.2d 903 (3d Cir.), decided.

82d Congress, 1st Session

May 12, 1951

Schwegmann Brothers v. Calvert Distillers Corp., 341 U.S. 384, decided .... reprinted in chap. 2

June 4, 1951

Rehearing denied in *Schwegmann Brothers,* 341 U.S. 956.

June 7, 1951

H.R. 4365 (to repeal Miller-Tydings Act) was introduced by Rep. Curtis and referred to the House Judiciary Committee.

June 25, 1951

H.R. 4592 (to amend Sherman Act § 1) was introduced by Rep. Poulson and referred to the House Judiciary Committee.

June 29, 1951

H.R. 4662 (to amend Sherman Act § 1) was introduced by Rep. Morano and referred to the House Judiciary Committee.

October 17, 1951

H.R. 5767 (to amend FTC Act § 5(a)) was introduced by Rep. McGuire and referred to the House Interstate and Foreign Commerce Committee [Remarks upon introduction, 97 Cong. Rec. 13404-05]... 562
 [Bill print] 565

82d Congress, 2d Session

January 15, 1952

Remarks of Rep. Heller on H.R. 5767 [98 Cong. Rec. A321] 566

February 2, 1952

FTC submitted comments to the House Interstate and Foreign Commerce Committee opposing enactment of H.R. 5767.
  [Printed in House Report No. 1437, at 10-12] 574

February 4-20, 1952

Hearings on H.R. 5767 before a subcommittee of the House Interstate and Foreign Commerce Committee (minimum resale price maintenance hearings).

February 8, 1952

FTC submitted comments to the House Judiciary Committee recommending enactment of H.R. 4365 (Curtis bill) and opposing enactment of H.R. 4592 (Poulson bill) and H.R. 4662 (Morano bill).
  [Printed in House Report No. 1516, at 53-59] 622

February 13-27, 1952

Hearings before the Antitrust Subcommittee of the House Judiciary Committee on bills related to resale price maintenance (H.R. 4365, H.R. 4592, H.R. 4662, H.R. 6367).

February 27, 1952

H.R. 5767 (McGuire bill) was reported favorably, with an amendment in the nature of a substitute, by the House Interstate and Foreign Commerce Committee.
  [House Report No. 1437] 567
  [Bill print] 577

February 28, 1952

Bureau of the Budget submitted a statement to the House Judiciary Committee that passage of H.R. 4592, H.R. 4662, or H.R. 6367 would not be in accord with the President's program.
  [Printed in House Report No. 1516, at 61] 630

March 6, 1952

H.R. 6925 (clean bill superseding H.R. 6367) was introduced by Rep. Keogh and referred to the House Judiciary Committee.

March 11, 1952

H.R. 6986 was introduced by Rep. Celler and referred to the House Judiciary Committee.

March 13, 1952

H.R. 6925 (Keogh bill) was reported favorably, with a minor amendment, by the House Judiciary Committee.
  [House Report No. 1516] 579
  [Bill print] 632

April 4, 1952

FTC report on H.R. 5767 and H.R. 6925 [98 Cong. Rec. 4946] 728

May 6, 1952

Remarks of Rep. Wolverton upon inserting a comparative analysis of H.R. 5767, H.R. 6925, and H.R. 6986 in the *Record* [98 Cong. Rec. A2742-43, A2752-53] 634

May 7, 1952

House adopted H.R. Res. 586, a rule providing for the consideration of both the McGuire and Keogh bills and making the committee amendment to the McGuire bill in order as an original bill [98 Cong. Rec. 4896-900] 639

CHRONOLOGICAL SYNOPSIS 557

General debate on H.R. 5767 in Committee of the Whole [98 Cong. Rec. 4900-26] 647
    Committee substitute for H.R. 5767 read [98 Cong. Rec. 4926] 700

May 8, 1952

House debate in Committee of the Whole [98 Cong. Rec. 4933-56] 701

    H.R. 6925 was offered as a substitute by Rep. Reed [98 Cong. Rec. 4934-35] and rejected by a vote of 12-111 [98 Cong. Rec. 4948] 704

    Celler amendment, providing a cause of action for persons injured by loss-leader practices, was offered and rejected [98 Cong. Rec. 4948-51] 733

    Javits amendment, providing that the exemption be applicable only to commodities in free and open competition with non-fair-traded commodities, was proposed and rejected [98 Cong. Rec. 4951-52] 739

    Cole amendment, providing a federal cause of action for persons injured by interstate sales of goods to buyers in fair-trade states at a price less than that specified by the applicable resale price maintenance contract in the buyer's state, was proposed and rejected [98 Cong. Rec. 4952-54] 740

    Crawford amendment, providing that the manufacturer's failure to make reasonable efforts to ensure compliance with resale price maintenance would be a complete defense to an action brought by that manufacturer, was proposed and rejected [98 Cong. Rec. 4954-55] 745

    Committee substitute for H.R. 5767 was adopted and the bill as thus amended reported to the House from the Committee of the Whole [98 Cong. Rec. 4956] 749

House agreed to the substitute for H.R. 5767 adopted in the Committee of the Whole and passed H.R. 5767 without further amendment by a vote of 196-10 [98 Cong. Rec. 4956] 749

May 9, 1952

H.R. 5767 referred to the Senate Interstate and Foreign Commerce Committee [98 Cong. Rec 5002] 751

May 21, 1952

FTC submitted comments to the Senate Interstate and Foreign Commerce Committee opposing enactment of H.R. 5767.
    [Printed in Senate Report No. 1741, at 1-4] 752

June 12, 1952

H.R. 5767 was reported, without amendment and without recommendation, by the Senate Interstate and Foreign Commerce Committee.
    [Senate Report No. 1741] 752

July 1, 1952

Senate began debate on H.R. 5767 [98 Cong. Rec. 8716-47] 764

    Motion made by Sen. Douglas to table H.R. 5767 was rejected by a vote of 7-64 [98 Cong. Rec. 8716] 765

    Douglas amendment to substitute a modified version of H.R. 6986 (Celler bill) for H.R. 5767 was proposed [98 Cong. Rec. 8731-34] 791

    Sen. Long submitted two amendments. The first required a state agency determination that the prescribed minimum resale price was reasonable for the antitrust exemption to become applicable. The second, in the nature of a substitute, replaced the language of the bill with a provision making it illegal under certain circumstances for sellers to discriminate among commodities of different manufacturers by selling one's product at below cost [98 Cong. Rec. 8748] 824

July 2, 1952

Senate debate on H.R. 5767 [98 Cong. Rec. 8819-26, 8833-58, 8865-73, 8881-91] 824

July 2, 1952 — *Cont.*

Sen. Morse introduced two amendments. The first added language requiring a state agency to determine that the prescribed price was fair and reasonable in order for the resale price maintenance contract to be exempt from the antitrust laws. The second made the antitrust exemption inapplicable to resale price maintenance contracts prescribing stipulated, rather than minimum, prices [98 Cong. Rec. 8856-57] 881

Douglas amendment (proposed July 1) was considered and rejected by a vote of 12-69 [98 Cong. Rec. 8887-88] 916

First Morse amendment was considered and rejected [98 Cong. Rec. 8889] 919

Long amendment in the nature of a substitute (introduced July 1) was called up, considered, and rejected [98 Cong. Rec. 8889-90] 919

Second Morse amendment was considered and rejected [98 Cong. Rec. 8891] 922

H.R. 5767 was passed by the Senate, without amendment, by a vote of 64-16 [98 Cong. Rec. 8892] 923

S. Con. Res. 87, to authorize the establishment of a Joint Committee on Fair Trade Practices, and S. Res. 348, directing the Senate Small Business Committee to make further and continuing studies in the same field, were submitted by Sen. Humphrey, received, and referred to the Senate Interstate and Foreign Commerce Committee [98 Cong. Rec. 8892] 923

July 14, 1952

H.R. 5767 was signed into law by President Truman.
[*Statutes at Large* print] 560
[Statement by the President] 925

Table of Reprinted Documents

McGUIRE RESALE PRICE MAINTENANCE ACT AMENDMENT OF 1952

Statutory Material

McGuire Resale Price Maintenance Act Amendment, ch. 745, 66 Stat. 631 (July 14, 1952) 560

Legislative Materials

Bills

H.R. 5767, 82 Cong., 1st Sess. (Oct. 17, 1951) 565

H.R. 5767 as reported by House Interstate and Foreign Commerce Committee, 82d Cong., 2d Sess. (Feb. 27, 1952) 577

H.R. 6925 as reported by House Judiciary Committee, 82d Cong., 2d Sess. (March 13, 1952) 632

Reports

H.R. Rep. No. 1437, 82d Cong., 2d Sess. (Feb. 26, 1952) 567

H.R. Rep. No. 1516, 82d Cong., 2d Sess. (March 13, 1952) 579

S. Rep. No. 1741, 82d Cong., 2d Sess. (June 12 [legislative day, June 10], 1952) 752

Congressional Record

Volume 97 – 82d Congress, 1st Session

Date	Pages	
Oct. 17, 1951	13404-05	562

Volume 98 – 82d Congress, 2d Session

Dates	Pages	
Jan. 15, 1952	A321	566
May 6, 1952	A2742-43, A2752-53	634
May 7, 1952	4896-926	639
May 8, 1952	4933-56	701
May 9, 1952	5002	751
July 1, 1952	8716-48	764
July 2, 1952	8819-26, 8833-58, 8865-73, 8881-926	824

Presidential Document

Statement by President Harry S. Truman upon signing H.R. 5767, 1952-1953 Pub. Papers 477 (July 14, 1952) 925

Case Report

United States v. McKesson & Robbins, Inc., 351 U.S. 305, 76 S. Ct. 937, 100 L. Ed. 1209 (1956) 929

Original Version

McGUIRE RESALE PRICE MAINTENANCE ACT AMENDMENT
July 14, 1952

Ch. 745, 66 Stat. 631

[ED. NOTE: This statute was repealed by the Consumer Goods Pricing Act of 1975, the legislative history of which appears *infra* at chapter 4.]

An Act To amend the Federal Trade Commission Act with respect to certain contracts and agreements which establish minimum or stipulated resale prices and which are extended by State law to persons who are not parties to such contracts and agreements, and for certain other purposes.

Be it enacted by the Senate and House of Representatives of the United States of America in Congress assembled, That it is the purpose ⊥ of this Act to protect the rights of States under the United States Constitution to regulate their internal affairs and more particularly to enact statutes and laws, and to adopt policies, which authorize contracts and agreements prescribing minimum or stipulated prices for the resale of commodities and to extend the minimum or stipulated prices prescribed by such contracts and agreements to persons who are not parties thereto. It is the further purpose of this Act to permit such statutes, laws, and public policies to apply to commodities, contracts, agreements, and activities in or affecting interstate or foreign commerce.

SEC. 2. Section 5 (a) of the Federal Trade Commission Act, as amended, is hereby amended to read as follows:

"SEC. 5. (a) (1) Unfair methods of competition in commerce, and unfair or deceptive acts or practices in commerce, are hereby declared unlawful.

"(2) Nothing contained in this Act or in any of the Antitrust Acts shall render unlawful any contracts or agreements prescribing minimum or stipulated prices, or requiring a vendee to enter into contracts or agreements prescribing minimum or stipulated prices, for the resale of a commodity which bears, or the label or container of which bears, the trade-mark, brand, or name of the producer or distributor of such commodity and which is in free and open competition with commodities of the same general class produced or distributed by others, when contracts or agreements of that description are lawful as applied to intrastate transactions under any statute, law, or public policy now or hereafter in effect in any State, Territory, or the District of Columbia in which such resale is to be made, or to which the commodity is to be transported for such resale.

"(3) Nothing contained in this Act or in any of the Antitrust Acts shall render unlawful the exercise or the enforcement of any right or right of action created by any statute, law, or public policy now or hereafter in effect in any State, Territory, or the District of Columbia, which in substance provides that willfully and knowingly advertising, offering for sale, or selling any commodity at less than the price or prices prescribed in such contracts or agreements whether the person so advertising, offering for sale, or selling is or is not a party to such a contract or agreement, is unfair competition and is actionable at the suit of any person damaged thereby.

"(4) Neither the making of contracts or agreements as described in paragraph (2) of this subsection, nor the exercise or enforcement of any right or right of action as described in paragraph (3) of this subsection shall constitute an unlawful burden or restraint upon, or interference with, commerce.

"(5) Nothing contained in paragraph (2) of this subsection shall make lawful contracts or agreements providing for the establishment or maintenance of minimum or stipulated resale prices on any commodity referred to in paragraph (2) of this subsection, between manufacturers, or between producers, or between wholesalers, or between brokers, or between factors, or between retailers, or between persons, firms, or corporations in competition with each other.

"(6) The Commission is hereby empowered and directed to prevent persons, partnerships, or corporations, except banks, common carriers subject to the Acts to regulate commerce, air carriers and foreign air carriers subject to the Civil Aeronautics Act of 1938, and persons, partnerships, or corporations subject to the Packers and Stockyards Act, 1921, except as provided in section 406 (b) of said Act from using unfair methods of competition in commerce and unfair or deceptive acts or practices in commerce."

THE ORIGINS

REMARKS OF REP. JOHN A. McGUIRE
INTRODUCING H.R. 5767
82d Cong., 1st Sess.
October 17, 1951

97 CONG. REC. 13404

Mr. McGUIRE [D., Conn.]. Mr. Speaker, I am this day introducing a bill (H.R. 5767) to amend the Federal Trade Commission and other acts regulating trade practices. The purpose of this measure is to clarify the status of certain State laws, to affirm within specific limits the right of each State to determine its own policy with respect to the regulation of its internal affairs, and to enable each State to protect its domestic trade from unfair trade practices.

THE NEED FOR AMENDING THE MILLER-TYDINGS ACT

Specifically, the bill is designed to restore the Miller-Tydings Act to the status it occupied prior to the Court decision last May in Schwegmann Bros. against Calvert Distillers Corp.[3.15] This decision deprived the Miller-Tydings Act of much of its effectiveness and struck a heavy blow at State fair-trade laws.

The Miller-Tydings Act was enacted in 1937 as an amendment to the Federal Trade Commission and Sherman Acts. Its purpose was to make it possible for the several States—if they so desired—to legislate on matters theretofore considered to be wholly within the orbit of Federal authority. Under this amendment the States could enact fair-trade laws affirming the right of a manufacturer of a proprietary article to exercise a measure of control over the price at which the product can be resold. It declared that the Federal Trade Commission and Sherman Acts did not render illegal a contract between a producer of a trade-marked article and his dealers prescribing minimum prices for the resale of the commodity when such contracts are lawful under State law. The act stipulated that the article must be in free and open competition with commodities of the same general class, and also specifically forbade horizontal price-fixing agreements between manufacturers or between dealers.

A total of 42 States had enacted fair-trade legislation prior to the passage of the Miller-Tydings Act. Since then three additional States have acted. Nearly all of this legislation has been placed in jeopardy by the Schwegmann decision. If Congress intended to make it possible for States to exercise control over this matter as I believe it did and if Congress is still of the opinion that the States should have this right as I believe they should, then additional legislation is necessary.

THE SCHWEGMANN CASE

The issue confronting the courts in the Schwegmann case was whether the Miller-Tydings Act permits the States to enact laws which require dealers who are not parties to specific written contracts, the so-called nonsigners, to observe the prices stipulated by the manufacturer. In spite of the fact that every State law in existence at the time the

---

[3.15] 341 U.S. 384, 71 S. Ct. 745, 95 L. Ed. 1035, *rehearing denied,* 341 U.S. 956 (1951), *supra* at chapter 2.

Miller-Tydings Act was passed, as well as every law which has been enacted since, contains these nonsigner clauses, the Court said "No." The Miller-Tydings Act, according to the Court, grants only a limited immunity and does not authorize a State to permit a seller to enforce his prices on those who are not parties to specific contracts.

I am convinced that in 1937 Congress intended that the Miller-Tydings Act should exempt noncontractive price maintenance as well as contractive. Otherwise, the law made little sense. There would have been no reason to enact it. Doubtless the Court had good reasons for deciding otherwise. But that is not the point. The point is that now we must indicate to the Court in unmistakable language that Congress does intend to support existing State laws on this subject. The present bill does this.

PROVISIONS OF THIS AMENDMENT

The bill declares that it is the intention of Congress to reaffirm the inherent right of each State to regulate its internal affairs and specifically to enact legislation authorizing contracts prescribing minimum prices for the resale of commodities and to extend these prices to persons not parties to the contract. Section 5 (a) of the Federal Trade Commission Act is to be amended by inserting a statement that the section does not apply to "contracts or agreements prescribing minimum prices for the resale of a commodity which bears the trade-mark, brand, or name of the producer or distributor of such commodity and which is in free and open competition with the commodities of the same general class produced or distributed by others," when such contracts "are lawful as applied to intrastate transactions." The bill further provides that all rights of action created by State laws may be exercised against nonsigners. The making of such contracts and their enforcement are not to be illegal under the Sherman Act. The bill specifically forbids agreements between manufacturers, or between wholesalers, or between retailers, or between "persons, firms or corporations in competition with each other."

PROTECTION AGAINST MONOPOLY

This bill is merely an enabling measure. It merely turns a specified and very limited area of trade regulation back to the States. It is not coercive. The States are not forced to do anything. All we are doing is to make it possible for States which believe in the principles of price maintenance to enact appropriate legislation. And I call your attention to the fact that the great bulk of the American people do believe in price maintenance. Otherwise we would not have these laws in 45 of our States.

If a State does not believe in price maintenance, it is not forced to tolerate the practice. In the absence of State legislation authorizing price maintenance, the Federal law remains unchanged. No State need fear any encroachment on its internal affairs by neighboring States pursuing a different policy.

The bill represents no change in our antitrust policy. It contains more than adequate protection against undesirable restraints of trade. The commodity whose price is under control must be "in free and open competition with commodities of the same general class produced or distributed by others." It will not be possible for a manufacturer to use price maintenance as an adjunct of monopoly because the law does not apply to any product which is not sold in a competitive market.

Nor need one fear that consumers will be charged higher prices under resale price maintenance. Stabilized prices do not mean high prices. The penalties for charging excessive prices are exactly the same as in any competitive economy, namely, loss of sales and reduced profits. Remember that monopoly involves horizontal control of the market. Resale price maintenance is vertical control.

NEED FOR FAIR TRADE LAWS

We believe the principles underlying fair trade legislation to be entirely sound for two basic reasons. First, price cutting is the favorite device of the mass distributor to force the independent out of business and to obtain a monopolistic position. Unfair pricing practices are a potent weapon in the hands of the monopolist and would-be monopolist. The preservation of our thousands of independent retailers is a basic necessity if the competitive system is to survive. The manufacturer who stabilizes his prices is merely placing the small retailer on an equal competitive footing with the massive chain store. Price maintenance is necessary to preserve competition at the retail level.

Secondly, the right to control resale prices is inherent in the very concept of a proprietary article. We believe that a manufacturer who develops a product, attaches his name to it, and spends huge sums in convincing the consuming public of its virtues should have a continuing interest in that product. He must be able to protect his investment against the depredations of the price cutter who uses the good will of the real owner for his own personal gain.

HOUSE CONSIDERATION (H.R. 5767; H.R. 6925)

H.R. 5767
82d Cong., 1st Sess.
October 17, 1951

Mr. McGuire introduced the following bill; which was referred to the Committee on Interstate and Foreign Commerce

A BILL

To amend the Federal Trade Commission Act with respect to certain contracts and agreements which establish minimum resale prices and which are extended by State law to nonsigners.

1 *Be it enacted by the Senate and House of Representa-*
2 *tives of the United States of America in Congress assembled,*
3 That it is the purpose of this Act to protect the right of
4 States under the United States Constitution to regulate its
5 internal affairs and more particularly to enact statutes and
6 laws, and to adopt policies which authorize contracts and
7 agreements prescribing minimum prices for the resale of
8 commodities and to extend the minimum prices prescribed by
9 such contracts and agreements to persons within the State
10 even though such persons are not parties thereto. It is the
11 further purpose of this Act to make certain of such statutes,
12 laws, and public policies applicable to commodities, shipped
13 in interstate or foreign commerce.
14 SEC. 2. Section 5 (a) of the Federal Trade Commission
15 Act, as amended, is hereby amended by inserting after the
16 first sentence thereof, the following new matter: "Nothing
17 herein contained shall render unfair or unlawful contracts
18 or agreements prescribing minimum prices for the resale of a
19 commodity which bears, or the label or container of which
20 bears, the trade-mark, brand, or name of the producer or
21 distributor of such commodity and which is in free and open
22 competition with commodities of the same general class
23 produced or distributed by others, when contracts or agree-
24 ments of that description are lawful as applied to intrastate
25 transaction [sic], under any statute, law, or public policy now or
26 hereafter in effect in any State, Territory, or the District of
27 Columbia in which such resale is to be made, or to which
28 the commodity is to be transported for such resale, or render
29 unfair or unlawful the enforcement of any right of action
30 created by any statute, law, or public policy now or hereafter

22 in effect in any State, Territory, or the District of Columbia,
23 which declares that willfully and knowingly advertising,
24 offering for sale, or selling any commodity at less than
25 the price stipulated in such contracts or agreements, whether
1   the person so advertising, offering for sale, or selling is or
2   is not a party to such contract or agreement, is unfair
3   competition and is actionable at the suit of any person
4   damaged thereby; and the making of such contracts or
5   agreements, or such enforcement thereof against a contracting
6   or noncontracting person, shall not be illegal under section
7   1 of the Act entitled 'An Act to protect trade and commerce
8   against unlawful restraints and monopolies', approved July
9   2, 1890, as amended; nor shall the making of such contracts
10 or agreements, or the enforcement thereof against a con-
11 tracting or noncontracting person constitute a burden, re-
12 straint, or interference with interstate commerce. The pre-
13 ceding sentence shall not make lawful any contract or agree-
14 ment, providing for the establishment or maintenance of
15 minimum resale prices on any commodity herein involved,
16 between manufacturers, or between producers, or between
17 wholesalers, or between brokers, or between factors, or
18 between retailers, or between persons, firms, or corporations
19 in competition with each other. Every person who shall
20 make any contract or agreement hereby declared to be unfair
21 or unlawful shall be deemed guilty of a misdemeanor, and, on
22 conviction thereof, shall be punished by fine not exceeding
23 $5,000 or by imprisonment not exceeding one year, or by
24 both said punishments, in the discretion of the court."

REMARKS OF REP. LOUIS B. HELLER
82d Cong., 2d Sess.
January 15, 1952

98 CONG. REC. A321

Mr. [LOUIS B.] HELLER [D., N.Y.]. Mr. Speaker, on October 17, 1951, our distinguished colleague, Representative JOHN A. MCGUIRE, introduced a bill, H. R. 5767, legalizing the nonsigners provisions of the State fair trade laws as they apply to interstate and intrastate commerce. This bill was referred to the House Committee on Interstate and Foreign Commerce, which is headed by the Honorable ROBERT CROSSER, of Ohio, and of which I have the honor to be a member.

By a 6-to-3 decision handed down on May 21, 1951, the Supreme Court nullified the interstate application of the nonsigner provisions in the State fair trade laws and thereby reopened the question of these laws.[3.16] Since then widespread interest has been aroused regarding the possible need for new congressional action in support of the 45 separate State resale price maintenance laws.

Congressman MCGUIRE'S bill rightfully seeks to amend the Federal Trade Commission Act by correcting it through legislation in the public interest so that it would work effectively for consumers, manufacturers, and retailers, as was the situation

---

[3.16] Schwegmann Bros. v. Calvert Distillers Corp., 341 U.S. 384 (1951).

before the Supreme Court upset the fair-trade laws. His bill applies the nonsigner provisions of the State acts to goods in interstate commerce.

It is clear that a bill of this nature which deals with problems of interstate commerce logically and properly belongs in the House Interstate and Foreign Commerce Committee. According to the Legislative Reorganization Act of 1946, known as Public Law 601, Seventy-ninth Congress, this committee was vested with the legislative jurisdiction over interstate and foreign commerce generally.

I understand that efforts are being made to take this bill out of our committee and refer it to the House Judiciary Committee. I am unalterably opposed to any such move because of the nature of the bill, as indicated above, and because I regard such move as an infraction of the rules under the Reorganization Act of 1946. H. R. 5767 belongs in the House Interstate and Foreign Commerce Committee and nowhere else. It is for that committee to consider it and to suggest the necessary action.

REPORT OF THE HOUSE COMMITTEE ON INTERSTATE AND FOREIGN COMMERCE
H.R. Rep. No. 1437
82d Cong., 2d Sess.
February 26, 1952

Mr. PRIEST, from the Committee on Interstate and Foreign Commerce, submitted the following

REPORT

[To accompany H. R. 5767]

The Committee on Interstate and Foreign Commerce, to whom was referred the bill (H. R. 5767) to amend the Federal Trade Commission Act with respect to certain contracts and agreements which establish minimum resale prices and which are extended by State law to nonsigners, having considered the same, report favorably thereon with amendments and recommend that the bill, as amended, do pass.

The amendments are as follows:

The amendment to the text of the bill strikes out all after the enacting clause and inserts a substitute which appears in the reported bill in italic type.

The other amendment modifies the title of the bill.

GENERAL STATEMENT

The primary purpose of the bill is to reaffirm the very same proposition which, in the committee's opinion, the Congress intended to enact into law when it passed the Miller-Tydings Act (act of August 17, 1937, title VIII, 50 Stat. 673, 15 U. S. C. sec. 1), to the effect that the application and enforcement of State fair-trade laws—including the nonsigner provisions[1] of such laws—with regard to interstate transactions shall not constitute a violation of the Federal Trade Commission Act or the Sherman Antitrust Act. This reaffirmation is made necessary because of the decision of a divided Supreme Court in *Schwegmann* v. *Calvert Distillers Corporation* (341 U. S. 384, May 21, 1951). In that case, six members of the Court held that the Miller-Tydings Act did not exempt from these Federal laws enforcement of State fair trade laws with respect to

---

[1] The nonsigner provisions permit enforcement of minimum or stipulated prices against any person who willfully and knowingly advertises, offers for sale, or sells any fair-traded commodity at less than the price stipulated in a resale price maintenance contract, whether or not such person is or is not a party to such contract.

nonsigners. Three members of the Court held that the Miller-Tydings Act did so apply.

The end result of the Supreme Court decision has been seriously to undermine the effectiveness of the Miller-Tydings Act and, in turn, of the fair-trade laws enacted by 45 States. H. R. 5767, as amended, is designed to restore the effectiveness of these acts by making it abundantly clear that Congress means to let State fair-trade laws apply in their totality; that is, with respect to nonsigners as well as signers.

The bill further provides that the application of these State laws to interstate transactions shall not constitute a burden upon interstate commerce. The purpose of this provision is to remove any obstacle, as far as Federal law is concerned, which might stand in the way of a broader interpretation of State fair-trade laws so as to make them applicable to retail transactions and retail advertising which cross State lines. The possible existence of such an obstacle was suggested by the United States Circuit Court of Appeals for the Third Circuit in its recent decision in *Sunbeam Corporation* v. *Wentling* (185 F. 2d 903, December 8, 1950).[3.17] In that case the court held that the Pennsylvania law should not be construed to apply to sales by Pennsylvania retailers to consumers in other States, or to advertisements in publications published in other States, because, so construed, the Pennsylvania statute might be considered a burden upon interstate commerce and might, therefore, be declared unconstitutional.

The committee, through its Subcommittee on Fair Trade Legislation, held extensive hearings on H. R. 5767, in the course of which proponents and opponents of fair trade were heard. The bill has the support of a great number of trade associations and organizations which represent a large segment of American wholesalers and retailers, including druggists, jewelers, hardware merchants, sporting-goods distributors, photographic-equipment stores, and so forth. It also has the support of several prominent manufacturers who volunteered to testify before the committee.

The hearings before the Committee on Interstate and Foreign Commerce were as complete as they could be made. The committee not only heard all of the witnesses who offered to testify, but it invited to testify all the known opponents of fair trade, several of whom, unfortunately, failed to appear.

In the course of the hearing, the bill was endorsed by the House Select Committee on Small Business, whose chairman, Hon. Wright Patman, of Texas, appeared as the first witness and presented an extensive report of the Select Committee on Small Business entitled "Fair Trade: The Problem and the Issues" (H. Rept. 1292). That report contains the following conclusions and recommendations:

> The Select Committee on Small Business has studied carefully the arguments presented both by the advocates of fair trade and the opponents. It is impressed by the complexity of the problem and by the weight of evidence on both sides of the issue. The committee is convinced that deceitful and misleading price cutting is not in the public interest and that small-business enterprises in particular need protection against loss-leader and similar unfair business practices. It believes the States should retain jurisdiction over retail trade practices and that Congress should make it possible to enforce fair trade contracts in interstate commerce.

The report of the House Select Committee on Small Business is comprehensive in its discussion of the nature and development of the fair-trade problem, the legal basis of fair trade, and the issues with respect to fair trade both for fair trade and against fair trade.[2]

---

[2] The Senate Select Committee on Small Business, in its annual report filed January 21, 1952 (S. Rept. No. 1068), likewise gives careful attention to the effects of the Schwegmann decision upon fair trade. The report takes cognizance of the introduction of H. R. 5767 and states in its conclusions as follows: "Your committee intends to keep a close watch on fair trade during the coming months. It will scrutinize closely the efforts of the business community to police itself. It will also be vitally interested in the progress of pending legislation on fair trade. The advantages of fair trade are evident, and your committee will be awake to any opportunities in the legislative field that would renew the stability and security of small business. The Nation's economic well-being depends to a large extent on the vitality of America's small businesses. Threats of price wars must be eliminated if that vitality is to endure."

[3.17] The judgment of the court of appeals in the *Wentling* case was vacated and the case remanded by the Supreme Court for reconsideration in light of the *Schwegmann* case. 341 U.S. 944 (1951). The opinion of the court of appeals on remand can be found at 192 F.2d 7 (3d Cir. 1951).

The testimony with respect to fair trade reflects considerable differences of opinions with respect to the economic merits or faults of vertical resale price maintenance. Some witnesses expressed opposition to H. R. 5767 because, in their opinion, vertical resale price maintenance tends to produce economic rigidities which would thwart the orderly evolution of our economy and stand in the way of the development of new and efficient channels of mass distribution. Proponents of fair trade, on the other hand, pointed out that the fair-trade laws are not the only legal basis for vertical resale price maintenance. Consignment selling and exclusive franchises, for example they contend, offer other legal bases for the practice of vertical resale price maintenance. Even if all State fair-trade laws and the Miller-Tydings Act were to be repealed tomorrow, so the proponents argue, manufacturers in many industries will be able to continue the practice of vertical resale price maintenance by adjusting their operations in accordance with one or another of the legal means available. Many smaller manufacturers, on the other hand, it is contended, would find it impracticable to use consignment selling or exclusive franchises, and they, therefore, together with numerous small distributors handling their merchandise, would not be able to enjoy the advantages of vertical resale price maintenance.

Proponents of fair trade further emphasize that the existence during the past 20 years of fair-trade laws apparently has not hindered the remarkable developments in production and distribution that have taken place during this period.

The record of testimony contains divergent observations concerning the effect of fair trade on prices. Opinions were expressed by some witnesses that fair trade means higher prices to the consumer because many merchants can sell items for less than fair-trade prices if permitted under the law to do so. Proponents of fair trade, on the other hand, point out that merchants who sell one item or another for less at some time or other than the regular mark-up must make up the losses incurred by reason of such "bargains" by charging higher prices for other items. This system, the proponents of fair trade argue, constitutes "price juggling" rather than "price cutting" which would be in the interest of the consumer.

Proponents of fair trade also contend that prices on fair-traded merchandise have risen less than other prices and far less than the cost of living, since 1939. Opponents of fair trade contend that if this was so, the reason for the lesser rise in prices must be found in the high level of fair-traded prices prevailing prior to 1939.

Proponents of fair trade argue that the consumer actually determines the price at which competing fair-traded articles are sold because the consumer has complete freedom of choice not only among fair-traded articles but also may turn from fair-traded articles to ⊥ private brands promoted by department stores, chains, and mail- ⊥ 4 order houses. Opponents of fair trade point to the very same factor as an argument against fair trade because, so they argue, the growth of private brands is proof of excessive prices charged for fair-traded nationally advertised merchandise.

Opponents of fair trade charge that the margin of profits permitted by vertical resale price maintenance is high enough to enable the most inefficient retailer to earn a profit from the sale of fair-traded merchandise. Proponents of fair trade, on the other hand, argue that fair-traded prices reflect average rather than low efficiency, and that many retailers have found it necessary to revise downward the prices for fair-traded merchandise carried on their shelves.

Opponents of fair trade charge that fair trade legislation has blunted individual initiative and has slowed down the dynamism of the market place. Proponents of fair trade point to the fact that the greatest evolution in retailing methods experienced in this country has taken place during the past two decades and that merchants who are outstanding opponents of fair trade have themselves enjoyed their greatest growth during the past 20 years.

Proponents of fair trade contend that price juggling and similar predatory pricing practices threaten the very foundation of small business. Opponents of fair trade minimize the magnitude of these admittedly unfair trade practices and point to the fact that the extreme price wars following the Schwegmann decision lasted only for brief periods and affected only limited areas in the United States.

Proponents of fair trade argued that resale price maintenance constitutes the only effective weapon against such predatory price practices. Opponents, on the other hand, argue that the fair trade laws are not the proper remedy and point to other laws like the Robinson-Patman Act, for example, and anti-loss-leader laws as the proper weapons against predatory price cutting.

The committee has studied diligently the economic arguments for and against fair trade given at the committee hearings. The committee has, likewise, studied the arguments pro and con contained in the report of the Select Committee on Small Business. The committee is aware of the honest differences of opinion which prevail as regards the economic merits of fair trade legislation. However, the committee is ever mindful of the effects on our economic and political institutions that would result from the wholesale destruction of small business concerns.

In this connection, the committee was greatly interested in the testimony of the Federal Trade Commission. The Commission opposed the bill H. R. 5767 on economic and legal grounds. The representative of the Federal Trade Commission stated that the Commission had on several occasions, on these grounds, recommended in favor of the outright repeal of the Miller-Tydings Act. The Commission witness, however, was frank enough to state that there were grounds other than economic and legal grounds which might be considered as furnishing valid arguments in favor of Federal validation of State fair trade legislation.

First, the Commission witness stated, the maintenance of a strong, healthy small-business community is the best bulwark that we have against the growth of collectivism either in the form of fascism or communism. Secondly, the witness' own studies showed that in those ⊥ communities in which there exists a healthy small-business group, the level of civic welfare and the interest taken by small-business leaders in health, recreation, and education tend to be higher than in those communities in which business consists principally of a few large concerns owned and operated by distant managers and distant corporations. Finally, the third argument is to the effect that small independent community drug stores or other specialty stores, on which people depend for special services, cannot make a living solely on the basis of selling those services (like, for example, the filling of prescriptions). They cannot stay in business unless they can get protection, through fair trade laws, with respect to the sale of nationally advertised products which are sold over the counter by such specialty stores.

Under all these circumstances, the committee feels amply justified in recommending enactment of H. R. 5767, as amended, which would permit the several States to experiment further with fair-trade legislation.

If price rigidities do later result from fair-trade laws that are determined to be evils greater than the benefits derived from such laws, the States may want to modify these laws and policies appropriately. However, for the time being, as far as the Federal Government is concerned, the committee feels the States should be left free to protect their trade in the best manner known to them from predatory price practices.

SECTION-BY-SECTION ANALYSIS OF THE BILL AS AMENDED

First section. Declaration of purposes

The first section provides that it is the purpose of the act to protect the rights of States to regulate their internal affairs, and more particularly to enact laws and adopt policies which authorize contracts prescribing minimum or stipulated prices for the resale of commodities and to extend the prices prescribed by such contracts to persons who are not parties thereto. The section also provides that it is the purpose of the act to permit such laws and policies to apply to transactions in or affecting interstate commerce.

Section 2. Amendment of Federal Trade Commission Act

Section 2 rewrites section 5 (a) of the Federal Trade Commission Act; as amended by the bill, section 5 (a) consists of six paragraphs as follows:

Paragraph (1).—This paragraph, which is the same as the first sentence of the existing section 5 (a), provides that unfair methods of competition in interstate or foreign commerce, and unfair or deceptive practices in interstate or foreign commerce, are unlawful.

Paragraph (2).—With the two exceptions referred to below, this paragraph contains substantially the same provisions as those contained in the first proviso of the Miller-

Tydings Act. In substance, this paragraph provides that neither the Federal Trade Commission Act nor any of the antitrust acts[3] shall make unlawful a contract prescribing minimum or stipulated prices for the resale of a trade-marked commodity in open competition with other commodities when such a contract is lawful under applicable State law. This paragraph differs from the Miller-Tydings Act in two respects. First, it includes a provision expressly covering contracts which prescribe "stipulated" prices; such contracts are not expressly covered by the Miller-Tydings Act. Second, it includes a provision expressly covering a contract which requires a vendee to enter into another contract prescribing a minimum or stipulated price; such a contract is not expressly covered by the Miller-Tydings Act.

Paragraph (3).—This is a new paragraph, covering the situation presented in the *Schwegmann* case referred to above. It provides that neither the Federal Trade Commission Act nor the antitrust acts shall render unlawful the exercise or the enforcement of any right or right of action created by any law or public policy of any State, Territory, or the District of Columbia which provides that willfully and knowingly advertising, offering for sale, or selling any commodity at less than the prices prescribed in such contracts, whether the person so advertising, offering for sale, or selling is or is not a party to the contract, is unfair competition and is actionable at the suit of any person damaged thereby.

Paragraph (4).—This is a new paragraph, included because of the *Wentling* case referred to above. It provides that neither the making of a contract as described in paragraph (2) nor the exercise or enforcement of any right or right of action as described in paragraph (3) shall constitute an unlawful burden or restraint upon, or interference with, interstate or foreign commerce.

Paragraph (5).—This paragraph contains substantially the same provisions as those inserted in the Sherman Act by the second proviso of the Miller-Tydings Act. It provides that nothing contained in paragraph (2) shall make lawful any contract providing for the establishment or maintenance of minimum or stipulated resale prices on any commodity, between manufacturers, or between producers, or between wholesalers, or between brokers, or between factors, or between retailers, or between producers, firms, or corporations in competition with each other.

Paragraph (6).—This paragraph is the same as the second sentence of the existing section 5 (a).

CHANGES IN EXISTING LAW

In compliance with paragraph 2a of rule XIII of the Rules of the House of Representatives, changes in existing law made by the bill, as introduced, are shown as follows (new matter is printed in italics, existing law in which no change is proposed is shown in roman):

SECTION 5 (a) OF THE FEDERAL TRADE COMMISSION ACT

SEC. 5. (a) Unfair methods of competition in commerce, and unfair or deceptive acts or practices in commerce, are hereby declared unlawful. *Nothing herein contained shall render unfair or unlawful contracts or agreements prescribing minimum prices for the resale of a commodity which bears, or the label or container of which bears, the trade-mark, brand, or name of the producer or distributor of such commodity and which is in free and open competition with commodities of the same general class produced or distributed by others, when contracts or agreements of that description are lawful as applied to intrastate transaction [sic], under any statute, law, or public policy now or hereafter in effect in any State, Territory, or the District of Columbia in which such resale is to be made, or to which the commodity is to be transported for such resale, or render unfair or unlawful the enforcement of any right of action created by any statute, law, or public policy now or hereafter in effect in any State, Territory, or the District of Columbia, which declares that willfully and knowingly advertising, offering for sale, or selling any commodity at less than the price stipulated in such contracts or agreements, whether the person so advertising, offering for sale, or selling is or is not a party to such contract or agreement, is unfair competition and is actionable at the suit of any person damaged thereby; and the making of such contracts or agreements, or such enforcement thereof against a*

---

[3] By definition in the Federal Trade Commission Act the term "Antitrust Acts" means the Sherman Antitrust Act and certain other laws prohibiting unlawful restraints and monopolies.

contracting or noncontracting person, shall not be illegal under section 1 of the Act entitled "An Act to protect trade and commerce against unlawful restraints and monopolies", approved July 2, 1890, as amended; nor shall the making of such contracts or agreements, or the enforcement thereof against a contracting or noncontracting person constitute a burden, restraint, or interference with interstate commerce. The preceding sentence shall not make lawful any contract or agreement, providing for the establishment or maintenance of minimum resale prices on any commodity herein involved, between manufacturers, or between producers, or between wholesalers, or between brokers, or between factors, or between retailers, or between persons, firms, or corporations in competition with each other. Every person who shall make any contract or agreement hereby declared to be unfair or unlawful shall be deemed guilty of a misdemeanor, and, on conviction thereof, shall be punished by fine not exceeding $5,000 or by imprisonment not exceeding one year, or by both said punishments, in the discretion of the court.

The Commission is hereby empowered and directed to prevent persons, partnerships, or corporations, except banks, common carriers subject to the Acts to regulate commerce, air carriers, and foreign air carriers subject to the Civil Aeronautics Act of 1938, and persons, partnerships, or corporations subject to the Packers and Stockyards Act, 1921, except as provided in section 406 (b) of said Act, from using unfair methods of competition in commerce and unfair or deceptive acts or practices in commerce.

APPENDIX

Reports of Department of Commerce and Federal Trade Commission on H. R. 5767

Department of Commerce,
Washington, February 27, 1952

Hon. Robert Crosser,
Chairman, Committee on Interstate and Foreign Commerce,
House of Representatives, Washington, D. C.

  Dear Mr. Chairman: Enclosed herewith is a statement on the legislation relating to resale price maintenance in reply to your letter of October 19, 1951.

  This statement presents my views and those of the Department of Commerce. I am most grateful for the opportunity you have afforded me to present my views on this subject to your committee.

  Due to the urgency of this matter, we have been unable to secure the views of the Bureau of the Budget.

Sincerely yours,

Charles Sawyer,
Secretary of Commerce.

Views of the Department of Commerce Concerning Legislation Providing for Minimum Resale Price Maintenance

  Title 8 of the act of August 17, 1937 (ch. 690, 50 Stat. 693) (popularly known as the Miller-Tydings amendment), amended the Sherman Antitrust Act to provide that nothing contained in that act shall make illegal contracts or agreements to fix minimum prices for resale of a commodity which bears, or the label or container of which bears, a trade-mark, brand, or name of the producer or distributor thereof and which is in free and open competition with commodities of the same general class produced or distributed by others if such contracts or agreements are lawful as applied to intrastate transactions under any statute, law or public policy in any State, Territory, or the District of Columbia in which such resale is to be made or to which the commodity is to be transported for such resale. Title 8 also provided that such contracts or agreements would not be an unfair method of competition under section 5 of the Federal Trade Commission Act. It also included a specific statement that horizontal price agreements were not authorized or made legal. Shortly after the enactment of this legislation many States passed laws making lawful resale price-maintenance contracts or agreements with respect to intrastate transactions. Most, if not all, of those laws contained the so-called nonsigners clause which provided that such contracts or agreements made with one distributor within the State applied to every other distributor of the commodity within the State who was provided with notice of the terms of the contract or agreement. The clause allowed such contracts or agreements to be enforced against both signers and nonsigners of the contract or agreement.

  In 1951 the Supreme Court of the United States in the case of *Schwegmann Brothers et al*

v. *Calvert Distillers Corp.* (341 U. S. 384) held that contracts establishing minimum prices for resale of commodities in commerce could not be enforced against distributors not parties to such a contract. Recognizing that the practical effect of the Schwegmann case was to nullify the Miller-Tydings amendment and therefore the minimum resale price laws of the States, several Members of the Congress have introduced bills providing that such contracts may be enforced against nonsigners if the State law contains a "nonsigners clause," without constituting a violation of the Federal Trade Commission Act or the antitrust acts. Legislation to repeal the Miller-Tydings amendment has also been introduced.

The position of the Department of Commerce, in commenting on this legislation, is influenced by the organic responsibilities of the Department in encouraging higher standards of business ethics and operations and also by the responsibility of the Department in protecting the interests of small business.

Without the Miller-Tydings Act, State fair-trade laws would be largely inoperative since, without this enabling act applying to interstate trade, it would undoubtedly be necessary for a manufacturer to be incorporated in each State in which he wished to issue fair-trade contracts. This procedure would add materially to the cost of distribution, a policy to which the Department is justifiably opposed; and it is manifest that a large number of manufacturers now working under fair-trade contracts would drop such contracts under those conditions and that the State fair-trade laws thereupon would become a matter of only academic interest. Since a repeal of the Miller-Tydings amendment would nullify State fair-trade laws, the Department's attitude regarding this amendment reasonably might be based on its view of the fair-trade laws themselves. And with reference to these State laws, since 45 States have enacted them, there seems to be a clear-cut matter of public policy, affecting 45 States, involved in support or opposition to the Miller-Tydings amendment.

The same reasoning applies to the "nonsigner" clause typical to a State fair-trade law. In considering the wisdom of this clause, however, we must recognize that without the clause, fair-trade contracts in any State would be meaningless, because the firms who precipitate price wars are the very ones who would not sign the fair-trade contract. If all competitor retailers were not treated alike in this respect, the stage would be set for wide-open price wars in any State. In considering the "nonsigner" clause, therefore, we must conclude that without such a clause, fair-trade laws would be meaningless.

Since either of the above two features spells life or death for State fair-trade laws themselves, a decision for or against the Miller-Tydings amendment, or the nonsigner clause, must be made with due consideration of the values attached to this type of resale price maintenance law, and upon the basis of public policy with reference to fair-trade laws.

In contemplating policy regarding fair-trade laws, the following aspects are worthy of consideration:

These laws protect the capital investment of small retailers in inventories which have been purchased at prevailing market prices, in that the retailer is protected against killing price wars. Faced by predatory price cutting by powerful retail organizations, the small retailer must either sell his goods at a loss, or lose his trade to these competitors on the "loss leader" items and also lose the store traffic thus diverted to the price-cutting stores for the purchase of such items. This result we believe is destructive of small-business enterprise and constitutes a deception of the consuming public.

Price wars disappeared with a few exceptions, with the widespread acceptance of fair-trade contract procedures, and the businesses of many small retailers were thus saved.

Studies have been made from time to time of the results of fair-trade laws on consumer prices. Those studies have been unconvincing in demonstrating the effect of these laws on prices. Some studies have shown tendencies toward higher prices. Other studies have shown that average prices are lower under fair-trade laws. It is known that in a great many neighborhood and other independent retail stores, prices on fair-trade products have been reduced as standard practice, because the fair-trade minimum price became a standard price in the trade and this price was lower than the price printed on labels which was the price formerly charged by these stores. Fair-trade prices are, in general, fair to the consumer and to the dealer, allowing the latter only a reasonable mark-up in order to cover his operating costs and a nominal profit on his business investment.

Opponents of fair-trade laws claim that monopolistic practices are thereby promoted. We know of no evidence which supports such a belief, and are of the opinion that opposition on this ground is based wholly on theory. It is our opinion, and we believe that opinion to be substantiated by the Report of the Federal Trade Commission on Resale Price Maintenance (submitted to the Congress, December 13, 1945), that ardent support for minimum resale prices is found in the ranks of small business, independent proprietors of corner drug stores and similar retail establishments. These persons are the least likely to favor legislation encouraging the growth of monopolies in their field. Among others, those groups identified with monopolistic practices and tendencies, such as loss-leader selling to the deception of the public and to the benefit of their own competitive position in the market at the expense of small business, usually were opposed to fair-trade legislation.

⊥ The opposition to fair-trade laws comes from two principal sources: (1) Large distributing groups including chains and large department stores which have historically used price cutting to drive weaker competition out of the way, thus, in restraint of trade, attempting to create a monopoly in the field of retailing; (2) lawyers and economists, both in the Government and in private practice, who cite a violation of the economic principle of a free price based on supply and demand and the theoretical harm resulting from such violations. Equally eminent practitioners, in Government and private practice take a contrary view, citing favorable price and other economic results flowing from these laws. We believe that theory and practice must be separated when considering the merits of this type of legislation.

Price control is a practical, not theoretical, problem. Price ceilings are at times necessary, and at other times, during buyers' markets price floors are needed to prevent business chaos.

To condemn price control under the fair-trade laws is to close one's eyes to other types of price control sponsored by manufacturers and producers without regard to fair-trade contracts. In a very substantial segment of business, represented by sales of automobiles, major appliances, home furnishings and some lines of men's clothing, resale prices are maintained by fear that the manufacturer will refuse to sell to the dealer in the event he violates the manufacturer's price policy.

There are other types of price maintenance in operation in this country without regard to fair-trade contracts. In one type merchandise is distributed through the retailer on a consignment basis. In this type of merchandising the manufacturer owns the retail stock and the retailer does not pay for it until it has been sold to the ultimate consumer. Obviously, under this system, the dealer has nothing to say about prices. He is merely an agent executing the orders of his principal.

CONCLUSION

There is reason to conclude that the case against fair trade is more theoretical than real; that fair trade is beneficial to small business; that facts regarding its causing higher prices in total are unconvincing; that monopoly does not result from fair-trade laws; and that fair-trade laws have a stabilizing influence on the economy. For these reasons we recommend against repeal of the Miller-Tydings amendment, and, further, recommend that the amendment be strengthened by the adoption of H. R. 4592, H. R. 5767 or similar legislation.

Due to the urgency of this legislation we have been unable to obtain the views of the Bureau of the Budget with respect to the transmission of this report.

Federal Trade Commission,
February 2, 1952.

Hon. Robert Crosser,
Chairman, Committee on Interstate and Foreign Commerce,
House of Representatives, Washington, D. C.

MY DEAR MR. CHAIRMAN: In response to the request made in your letter of October 19, 1951, for a report, together with such comment as the Commission may desire to make, upon H. R. 5767, Eighty-second Congress, first session, introduced October 17, 1951, in the House of Representatives by Congressman John A. McGuire of Connecticut, the following is submitted.

The principal purpose of the proposed legislation is to overcome the effect of the recent decision of the Supreme Court in the Schwegmann case *(Schwegmann Bros. v. Calvert Distillers Corporation,* 341 U. S. 384, decided May 21, 1951). In that case the Supreme Court held that the Miller-Tydings Act does not make binding upon nonsigners resale prices fixed in contracts under State resale price-maintenance laws, insofar, of course, as interstate commerce is concerned. The bill proposes to reenact as an amendment to the Federal Trade Commission Act (and to limit the application of the Sherman Antitrust Act accordingly) [*sic*]. The presently existing Miller-Tydings amendment to the Sherman Act but with the addition of the nonsigner clause, and with a provision that resale price maintenance contracts and the enforcement thereof against a signer or nonsigner shall not constitute a burden upon interstate commerce.

Prior to the Miller-Tydings Act, decisions in a number of cases under the Sherman and Federal Trade Commission Acts had made it clear that the failure of a retailer to observe the resale prices marked on trade-marked or branded goods did not create a cause of action in favor of the manufacturer either under the ⊥ common law or under the patent or copyright laws. Moreover, the courts held that where a manufacturer maintained the resale prices of his identified goods by a system of contracts or equivalent cooperative methods, those contracts were void and such methods illegal under both the Sherman and the Federal Trade Commission Acts.

The Miller-Tydings Act amended the Sherman Act by legalizing minimum resale price agreements or contracts respecting trade-marked or otherwise identified goods sold in interstate commerce provided that the commodities affected were resold in any State that had legalized this type of contract, or agreement with respect to resales made within its boundaries. The act also amended the Federal Trade Commission Act by providing that the making of such contracts should not constitute an unfair method of competition under section 5 of the Federal Trade Commission Act.

Resale price-maintenance laws—that is, laws declaring as not in violation of the law of the particular State certain kinds of price-maintenance contracts and providing that nonsigners of such contracts with knowledge thereof should be bound by the price stipulations therein—were on the statute books of 45 States as of May 1, 1941. Most of these States adopted price-maintenance laws in 1937 soon after the decision of the Supreme Court in *Old Dearborn Distributing Company* v. *Seagram Distillers Corporation* (299 U. S. 183 (decided December 7, 1936)),[3.18] declaring as constitutional the principal provisions, including the nonsigner clause, of the Illinois price-maintenance law.

The legal principle involved in the proposed legislation and in the State laws concerning resale price maintenance is not a mere authorization of contracts for the fixing of resale prices. That authorization now exists under the Miller-Tydings amendment as interpreted by the Supreme Court in the Schwegmann case. The new principle introduced by this bill is that the Congress shall specifically approve the so-called nonsigner clause. Thus, if this bill is enacted, a private contract, the provisions of which would be determined without public hearing and apart from any public supervision as to reasonableness, would be made binding upon all dealers and the consuming public.

In an effort to prescribe the freedom of business enterprise, the courts have been circumspect in recognizing even the authority of governments to fix the prices that businessmen shall charge. Such price fixing is invalid unless it is undertaken for a public purpose and by reasonable means. In the State resale price-maintenance laws and in the present bill, however, the power to fix prices would be entrusted not to a government, but to private persons: the purpose to be served by the price fixing would be whatever purposes such private persons might have, presumably that of serving their own pecuniary interests rather than that of the public interest; and the prices fixed would not be tested for reasonableness by any instrumentality, public or private; nevertheless, a person who is not a party to this private contract is to be deemed guilty of unfair competition and subject to a suit for damages if he fails to observe the prices, regardless of whether or not they are arbitrary or extortionate.

In granting to such private persons the power to fix prices, the proposed legislation goes much further than Congress saw fit to grant to the Government itself in the National Industrial Recovery Act (act of June 16, 1933). In that act, consideration was given labor and to the consuming public and there was always a representative of both who participated in the fixing of prices, while in the present bill no consideration whatsoever is given to the interests of labor or the consuming public.

The effect of adding the nonsigner clause to resale price maintenance is the de facto nullification of our Federal antitrust laws prohibiting horizontal conspiracy to fix prices. Nothing is more clearly established in Federal policy than the principle that horizontal price fixing shall not be tolerated. The proposed legislation pays lip service to that principle: yet its effect would be that a minimum price fixed by contract with one retail distributor would become the minimum price for all other retail distributors who were placed upon notice of the existence of the contract. The rigidity and uniformity of the price would be exactly that of the most rigid horizontal price-fixing conspiracy; the level of the price would be likely to be at least as high as in a horizontal conspiracy; and the public control of the reasonableness of the arrangement would be as nonexistent as in the case of a horizontal conspiracy. Thenceforward, any group of distributors desiring to fix prices horizontally would be foolish to take the direct road to that end. Instead some one of their number would make a vertical contract with a supplier and then place the other members of the group on notice of the existence of the contract. Through this means, the group could not only negate the objections of the Government, but could actually use the courts as devices to enforce the arrangement.

In considering this problem, under the provisions of the Miller-Tydings Act in the Schwegmann case, the Supreme Court stated:

"It should be noted in this connection that the Miller-Tydings Act expressly continues the

---

[3.18] 299 U.S. 183, 57 S. Ct. 139, 81 L. Ed. 109 (1936), *supra* at chapter 2.

prohibitions of the Sherman Act against 'horizontal' price fixing by those in competition with each other at the same functional level. Therefore, when a State compels retailers to follow a parallel price policy, it demands private conduct which the Sherman Act forbids. (See *Parker* v. *Brown*, 317 U. S. 341, 350.)[3.19] Elimination of price competition at the retail level may, of course, lawfully result if a distributor successfully negotiates individual 'vertical' agreements with all his retailers. But when retailers are forced to abandon price competition, they are driven into a compact in violation of the spirit of the proviso which forbids 'horizontal' price fixing."[3.20]

One of the stated purposes of the proposed legislation is "to make certain of such [State] statutes, laws, and public policies applicable to commodities, shipped in interstate or foreign commerce." The Miller-Tydings Act exempted from the application of the Sherman and Federal Trade Commission Acts, contracts prescribing minimum prices for the resale of an identified commodity where such contracts are lawful "as applied to intrastate transactions, under any statute, law, or public policy now or hereafter in effect in any State, Territory, or the District of Columbia, in which such resale is to be made, or to which the commodity is to be transported for such resale." Thus, it appears to be a purpose of the present bill to make State laws and public policy applicable to commodities transported in interstate and foreign commerce which would extend both the purpose and provisions of the Miller-Tydings Act. If this extension is made by the enactment of this bill, an area of interstate commerce would be made subject to regulations in accordance with the provisions of State law. In other words, the present bill proposes that Congress exempt from the application of Federal antitrust law an area of interstate commerce and to give consent to State regulation thereof.

It is noted that the bill provides for punishment to the extent of a fine not exceeding $5,000 or by imprisonment not exceeding 1 year, or by both said punishments, in the discretion of the court. It is stated that such punishments are for the making of a contract or agreement "hereby declared to be unfair or unlawful." The bill does not make clear what "contract or agreement" is thereby involved. A similar provision appearing at the end of section 1 of the Sherman Antitrust Act, following the Miller-Tydings amendment, clearly applies to contracts, agreements, combinations, and conspiracies there made unlawful. The penal provisions in the present bill appear to have application to contracts and agreements in restraint of trade violative of section 5 of the Federal Trade Commission Act because they constitute unfair methods of competition. Thus, it appears that the entering into contracts or agreements which violate section 5 of the Federal Trade Commission Act would, by the terms of this bill, be made subject to a penalty of $5,000 or by imprisonment not exceeding 1 year, or by both said punishments, in the discretion of the court.

In our opinion economic conditions are not the same at the present time as existed in 1937 which prompted the enactment of the Miller-Tydings Act. At present there is no necessity for Federal resale price maintenance legislation with respect to interstate commerce. Furthermore, the Congress has already pointed the way toward elimination of the evils, which sponsors of the Miller-Tydings Act sought to remedy, through legislation prohibiting price discrimination and other unfair methods of competition. It is the elimination of these evils rather than legislation legalizing price fixing which will minimize the inequities between the smaller businessman and his more powerful competitor.

During previous years, the Commission has expressed its opposition to resale price maintenance in two reports to the Congress, the first of which was presented in 1931 (70th Cong., 2d sess., H. Doc. No. 546), and the second entitled "Report on Resale Price Maintenance," which was submitted on December 13, 1945.

Consistent with the foregoing observations, the Commission is opposed to H. R. 5767 (the McGuire bill).

By direction of the Commission.

Jas. M. Mead, Chairman.

February 4, 1952.

N.B.—In view of your request that we expedite the matter, this report has not been cleared with the Bureau of the Budget.

Jas. M. Mead, Chairman.

[3.19] 317 U.S. 341, 63 S. Ct. 307, 87 L. Ed. 315 (1943), *supra* at chapter 1.
[3.20] 341 U.S. at 389.

H.R. 5767 AS REPORTED BY THE HOUSE COMMITTEE ON INTERSTATE AND FOREIGN COMMERCE
82d Cong., 2d Sess.
February 27, 1952

Reported with amendments, referred to the House Calendar, and ordered to be printed

[Strike out all after the enacting clause and insert the part printed in italic]

A BILL

To amend the Federal Trade Commission Act with respect to certain contracts and agreements which establish minimum resale prices and which are extended by State law to nonsigners.

Be it enacted by the Senate and House of Representatives of the United States of America in Congress assembled, . . . [3.21] That it is the purpose of this Act to protect the rights of States under the United States Constitution to regulate their internal affairs and more particularly to enact statutes and laws, and to adopt policies, which authorize contracts and agreements prescribing minimum or stipulated prices for the resale of commodities and to extend the minimum or stipulated prices prescribed by such contracts and agreements to persons who are not parties thereto. It is the further purpose of this Act to permit such statutes, laws, and public policies to apply to commodities, contracts, agreements, and activities in or affecting interstate or foreign commerce.

SEC. 2. Section 5(a) of the Federal Trade Commission Act, as amended, is hereby amended to read as follows:

"SEC. 5 (a) (1) Unfair methods of competition in commerce, and unfair or deceptive acts or practices in commerce, are hereby declared unlawful.

"(2) Nothing contained in this Act or in any of the Antitrust Acts shall render unlawful any contracts or agreements prescribing minimum or stipulated prices, or requiring a vendee to enter into contracts or agreements prescribing minimum or stipulated prices, for the resale of a commodity which bears, or the label or container of which bears, the trademark, brand, or name of the producer or distributor of such commodity and which is in free and open competition with commodities of the same general class produced or distributed by others, when contracts or agreements of that description are lawful as applied in intrastate transactions under any statute, law, or public policy now or hereafter in effect in any State, Territory, or the District of Columbia in which

---

[3.21] H.R. 5767 as introduced is reprinted *supra* at 565–66.

such resale is to be made, or to which the commodity is to be transported for such resale.

"(3) Nothing contained in this Act or in any of the Antitrust Acts shall render unlawful the exercise or the enforcement of any right or right of action created by any statute, law, or public policy now or hereafter in effect in any State, Territory, or the District of Columbia, which in substance provides that willfully and knowingly advertising, offering for sale, or selling any commodity at less than the price or prices prescribed in such contracts or agreements whether the person so advertising, offering for sale, or selling is or is not a party to such a contract or agreement, is unfair competition and is actionable at the suit of any person damaged thereby.

"(4) Neither the making of contracts or agreements as described in paragraph (2) of this subsection, nor the exercise or enforcement of any right or right of action as described in paragraph (3) of this subsection shall constitute an unlawful burden or restraint upon, or interference with, commerce.

"(5) Nothing contained in paragraph (2) of this subsection shall make lawful contracts or agreements providing for the establishment or maintenance of minimum or stipulated resale prices on any commodity referred to in paragraph (2) of this subsection, between manufacturers, or between producers, or between wholesalers, or between brokers, or between factors, or between retailers, or between persons, firms, or corporations in competition with each other.

"(6) The Commission is hereby empowered and directed to prevent persons, partnerships, or corporations, except banks, common carriers subject to the Acts to regulate commerce, air carriers and foreign air carriers subject to the Civil Aeronautics Act of 1938, and persons, partnerships, or corporations subject to the Packers and Stockyards Act, 1921, except as provided in section 406 (b) of said Act, from using unfair methods of competition in commerce and unfair or deceptive acts or practices in commerce."

Amend the title so as to read: "A bill to amend the Federal Trade Commission Act with respect to certain contracts and agreements which establish minimum or stipulated resale prices and which are extended by State law to persons who are not parties to such contracts and agreements, and for certain other purposes."

REPORT OF THE HOUSE COMMITTEE ON THE JUDICIARY (WITH MINORITY VIEWS)
H.R. Rep. No. 1516
82d Cong., 2d Sess.
March 13, 1952

Mr. ROGERS of Colorado, from the Committee on the Judiciary, submitted the following

REPORT

[To accompany H. R. 6925]

The Committee on the Judiciary, to whom was referred the bill (H. R. 6925) to amend the act entitled "An act to protect trade and commerce against unlawful restraints and monopolies," approved July 2, 1890, and for other purposes, having considered the same, report favorably thereon with an amendment and recommend that the bill do pass.

The amendment is as follows:

Page 2, line 21, insert a comma after "trade-mark", delete "or" before the word "brand", insert a comma after the word "brand" and insert the words "or name" immediately thereafter.

I. INTRODUCTION

The committee, after exhaustive hearings on the subject, recognizes that restoration of the law permitting resale price maintenance to operate effectively is necessary to achieve some measure of protection to small and independent retailers and to manufacturers of trade-marked products. Such legislation is therefore recommended for the consideration of the Congress. This recommendation, however, is not unanimous because of the plethora of close, complex, and weighty arguments advanced by those who oppose, in practice and theory, resale price maintenance.

It may be stated that the committee is cognizant of these arguments and their validity but feels, after weighing all of the equities, that such legislation is necessary at this time. Moreover, in reporting H. R. 6925, the committee believes that it has done nothing more than seek to do what the proponents of the law claim was done by the Miller-Tydings amendment to the Sherman Act.[1] In addition, it is felt that H. R. 6925 will ameliorate the effects of the recent court decisions which have made virtually inoperative the resale price maintenance statutes of the several States.

The Miller-Tydings amendment to the Sherman Act was enacted into law in 1937. Prior to that, and in almost every session of Congress since 1914, numerous bills were introduced to permit manufacturers to set a minimum price on products which bear unique and distinctive trade-marks and styles.[2] In all of these bills the same philosophy appears, namely that the manufacturer's trade-mark, name, and good will must be protected from diminution in value by virtue of the use of such a brand-name product as a loss leader or in a cut-rate sale.

It was principally on this argument that all the bills were defeated. In the 1930's, however, a more persuasive argument was advanced as the result of and supported by the economic chaos extant during the depths of the depression years. Existing in those years and coupled with the great incidence of retail failures and bankruptcies was the unprecedented collapse of the price structure generally. Valiant efforts to ease the plight of manufacturers and small, independent, as well as large, retailers and to bolster the

---

[1] 26 Stat. 209 (1890), as amended by 50 Stat. 693, as amended.
[2] Beginning with H. R. 13305, 63d Cong., 2d sess.

shattered price structures were then the order of the day. The National Industrial Recovery Act, the Agricultural Adjustment Act, and similar drastic measures became the means of stabilizing the economy and were the watchwords of recovery. Thus in many States, legislatures sought legal methods to stabilize and fix prices in order that retailers and others, with huge capital reserves, could effectively be prevented from driving their competitors out of business by means of slashed prices and loss-leader selling. Additional means of preventing ruinous competition, such as sales-below-cost statutes, were drafted.

The State of California, in 1931, enacted what is conceded to be the first of all resale price maintenance statutes. The 1931 act merely legalized voluntary agreements to maintain resale prices and, as in the post-Schwegmann era, was found to be ineffectual. In 1933, therefore, the statute was amended to include a nonsigners provision, making the resale price binding on all vendors having notice of the price set by the manufacturer. In the ensuing years up to and including 1949, 45 State legislatures enacted the same or similar laws as fundamental portions of the public policy of the several States.

State resale price-maintenance laws

State fair-trade laws are basically the same and contain two principal features in common. The first of these features is that the laws permit vertical contracts between producers, distributors, and retailers setting a resale price on the commodity. The second is that the statutes create a cause of action against persons who willfully and knowingly sell below the price set.

Generally, it may be stated that the laws are permissive in the sense that no one is compelled to enter into a contract; but, upon notice, it is enforcible as against all dealers whether they be parties to the contract or not. Only in extraordinary cases, such as in bankruptcy or discontinuance of a line may the price be cut by a merchant so that he may liquidate his inventory of price-fixed goods. Under all of these laws the manufacturer was permitted to set a minimum (or in some cases a stipulated price) below which a retailer could not sell thereby virtually eliminating the impairment of the manufacturer's good will and the ruinous competition then so rampant.

Under these laws the manufacturer was permitted to set a price by contract with his retailer below which the latter was not to sell under penalty of injunction and/or damages in a civil suit for breach of contract. The Miller-Tydings amendment when enacted merely extended this theory and provided an exemption of such contracts from the effects of the Sherman Act, under the terms of which such contracts or agreements would otherwise be illegal. In any event, contracts for minimum resale price maintenance could only be made by setting a minimum resale price on products in interstate commerce where such contract was made in a State having a fair-trade law.

In addition, the numerous State statutes contained what is colloquially called the nonsigners' clause. By this device, the States created a cause of action on the part of the manufacturer permitting a suit to be maintained on the theory of "unfair competition" where a person, not a party to the fair-trade contract, willfully and knowingly sold below the minimum or stipulated price established by the manufacturer.

It was in this context that such State statutes and the Miller-Tydings amendment of the Sherman Act have been declared not to be unconstitutional.[3] And it was not until the recent case of *Schwegmann Brothers* v. *Calvert Distillers Corp.*[4] that the exemption granted by the Miller-Tydings Act was judicially defined. In effect the decision rendered unenforceable the cause of action provided for by the "nonsigners' clause" in the State statutes as it relates to the intrastate sale of fair-traded goods in interstate commerce.

---

[3] In 1936 the Supreme Court of the United States held that the Illinois and California laws were not unconstitutional in the Old Dearborn and Pep Boys cases respectively. These cases were decided at about the same time and gave judicial sanction to the laws of the States which protected a manufacturer's valuable trade-mark and good will. The principal attack made upon these statutes was that the nonsigners clause violated the due process and equal-protection clauses of the fourteenth amendment of the Federal Constitution *(Old Dearborn Distributing Co.* v. *Seagram-Distillers Corp.,* 299 U. S. 183, and *The Pep Boys, Manny, Moe & Jack of California, Inc.* v. *Pyroil Sales Co., Inc.,* 299 U. S. 198 [57 S. Ct. 147, 81 L. Ed. 122]).

[4] 341 U. S. 384.

B. LEGAL ASPECTS

Throughout the years since 1937, it was believed that the Federal obstacles to successful operation of resale price maintenance had been eliminated by the Miller-Tydings amendment to the Sherman Act. The Supreme Court of the United States, however, in the Schwegmann case seriously impaired the effectiveness of the State laws. And although there can be no doubt that the Schwegmann decision effectively emasculated fair trade, the coup de grâce was administered in the case of *Sunbeam Corporation* v. *Wentling*.[5]

The committee has studied the development of the laws relating to resale price maintenance and has concluded that where public policy has given protection to many aspects of commerce, it may be a matter of legislative intent to extend such protections to include trade-marks, brand-named articles and manufacturer's good will from unrestricted and ruinous competition. As Mr. Rivers Peterson of the National Retail Hardware Association stated, on February 27, 1952:

> I think it worthy of consideration by your committee that fair-trade legislation has been enacted by the legislatures of 45 of the 48 States of this Nation. Surely, if it was the evil thing its opponents would have you believe, all of these 45 State legislatures would not have been hoodwinked and misled into enacting such legislation.

Development of the law

Prior to the Sherman Act, the basic law regarding resale-price maintenance was found to exist in the statutes of the several States relating to monopoly and trade practices. The strict common-law rule that any restraint of trade, such as price fixing, however slight, was unlawful, was ameliorated by a series of decisions beginning with the English case of *Mitchie* v. *Reynolds*.[6] From these decisions came the modern common-law rule that the reasonableness of the restraint was to be considered in adjudicating the legality of the restraint. And this was the common law at the time of the American Revolution, consequently becoming the law of the several States. Thus a limited or partial restraint of trade even under the Sherman Act, if reasonable, would not be considered unlawful.[7]

From this basic principle and its enunciation by stare decisis, there have been decisions which relate directly to the problem of resale price maintenance. The right of producers to set prices on patented or copyrighted products, or to control their product by way of consignment sales have been recognized in many cases. Thus a patentee may fix the resale price of an article made under his patent by a licensee.[8] And a patentee may place restrictions on the price at which his licensee sells an article which the latter makes and only can make legally under the license.[9] Although some modification of these rules of law is attributed to later cases,[10] it is clear that these modifications only apply where the result would be to permit horizontal conspiracies in the restraint of trade as between licensees, patentee and others. Under the modified rule enunciated above, it would appear that the state of the law now permits certain resale price maintenance arrangements to exist legally so long as the restraints caused thereby were reasonable and connected with a vested right of the producer. Moreover, it will be noted that courts have, from time to time indicated that price fixing contracts might apply legally to other commodities not patented.

In the famous Dr. Miles case, for example, it was claimed that a manufacturer had the right to fix a resale price on a product manufactured under a "secret process."[11] And while the Supreme Court did not permit such a deviation from existing law, it is interesting to note that the Court observed, at page 405:

---

[5] 185 F. 2d 903 and 192 F. 2d 7.

[6] 1 P. Wms. 181 (1711).

[7] *Eastern States Retail Lumber Dealers* v. *U. S.*, 234 U. S. 600, [34 S. Ct. 951, 58 L. Ed. 1490] 1914.

[8] *Edison Phonograph Co.* v. *Kaufman*, 105 Fed. Rep. 960, 1901.

[9] *U. S.* v. *General Electric*, 272 U. S. 476, [47 S. Ct. 192, 71 L. Ed. 362] 1926.

[10] *U. S.* v. *U. S. Gypsum Co.*, 333 U. S. 364, [68 S. Ct. 525, 92 L. Ed. 746] 1948; and *U. S.* v. *Line Material Co.*, 333 U. S. 287, [68 S. Ct. 550, 92 L. Ed. 701] 1948.

[11] *Dr. Miles Medical Co.* v. *Park and Sons, Inc.*, 220 U. S. 373, [31 S. Ct. 376, 55 L. Ed. 502] 1911.

Nor can the manufacturer, by rule and notice, in absence of contract or *statutory right,* even though the restriction be known to purchasers, fix prices for future sales. [Emphasis added.]

The inference is clear, from the decision, that patent medicines may differ from other patented products and in that regard may not be eligible for the consideration given those products but that, nevertheless, there could be a situation in which manufacturers could set a resale price where there is a statutory right so to do.

Mr. Justice Holmes, in the dissent in the Dr. Miles case, recognized that price cutting not only injures the manufacturer but the public as well when he stated, at page 412:

I cannot believe that in the long run the public will profit by this Court permitting knaves to cut reasonable prices for some ulterior purpose of their own and thus to impair, if not to destroy, the production and sale of articles which it is assumed to be desirable that the public should be able to get.

The broad language by which the Court, in the Dr. Miles case, indicated that a statutory right could be afforded to permit manufacturers, under statute and by contract, to set minimum resale prices and prevent ruinous competition and destruction of good will gave rise to the fair-trade movement. The public policy of the several States resulted in the passage of many State fair-trade laws and culminated, in 1937, in the enactment of the Miller-Tydings Act. Thus the statutory right envisioned by the Court in the Dr. Miles case was realized by the States and the bar of the Sherman Act was lifted by enabling legislation to sanction the full operation of the State laws as they affect goods in interstate commerce. The exemption to the Sherman Act was limited, it is admitted, to those contracts and agreements made under the laws of the several States which had declared resale price maintenance as a cornerstone of their economic public policy.

The major test of the validity of fair trade laws came in 1936 when the Illinois Fair Trade Act was attacked as being unconstitutional in the case of *Old Dearborn Distributing Company* v. *Seagram Distillers Corp.*[12] It was claimed in that case that such a law, which included a nonsigners clause, denied to the contracting retailer due process of law. It was also contended that the statute was contrary to public policy. The court held, however, that such a method of resale price maintenance was not unconstitutional and that the Illinois Legislature not only considered price cutting by retailers injurious to manufacturers but injurious to the public welfare as well. And, the Supreme Court stated, at pages 195–196, when that is the case, in spite of opinion and evidence to the contrary, "Where the question of what the facts establish is a fairly debatable one, we accept and carry into effect the opinion of the legislature."

Until the decision in the Schwegmann case, therefore, it was commonly accepted that the fair-trade laws were effective as to signers and nonsigners both under the State laws and the Miller-Tydings amendment to the Sherman Act. In the Schwegmann case Calvert sought to restrain Schwegmann, an independent supermarket owner, by injunction from selling its products below the price fixed in fair-trade contracts with other retailers. Schwegmann was a nonsigner. The Circuit Court of Appeals, Fifth Circuit, affirmed the district court decree which provided for injunctive relief and said—

* * * what that amendment (Miller-Tydings) did was to remove all Sherman Act restrictions on agreements restraining trade in States, where, by State law, these agreements had been validated as to intrastate commerce.[13]

But in the Supreme Court it was held that the Miller-Tydings amendment exempts only "contracts and agreements prescribing minimum prices for resale" and that unless the Supreme Court was to read language into the amendment, the omission of the nonsigner provision in the Miller-Tydings amendment is "fatal to the respondent's (Calvert's) position."[3.22]

---

[12] 299 U. S. 183.

[13] 184 F. 2d 11 et seq.

[3.22] 341 U.S. at 388.

Three Justices of the Court, Frankfurter, Black, and Burton, strongly dissented from the above majority opinion. They stated that all fair-trade statutes in the States have, as parts thereof, nonsigners provisions and that the legislative history of the Miller-Tydings amendment, if not severally limited, shows that congressional intent was to legalize the existing types of fair-trade acts extant in the States. It was stated in the dissent that a study of the legislative history of Miller-Tydings removes doubt as to the intent of Congress in this regard. A strong position was taken by the minority of the Court to the effect that the Miller-Tydings exemption to the Sherman Act was merely an "enabling act" designed to place the "stamp of approval" upon transactions maintaining a resale price under State laws when such transactions entered the flow of interstate commerce. It is apparent, therefore, that Congress must clarify, by way of legislation, the exact status of the 45 laws of the several States providing for resale price maintenance.

It may be stated without equivocation that the Schwegmann case did not question the constitutionality of the Miller-Tydings amendment and that the amendment was not declared invalid as unconstitutional. The Schwegmann case merely made inapplicable the nonsigners clause as it relates to the intrastate resale of fair-traded articles in interstate commerce. Furthermore the Court indicated in its majority opinion that—

> Had Congress desired to eliminate the consensual element * * *, we feel that different measures would have been adopted—either a nonsigner provision would have been included or resale price fixing would have been authorized without more.[3.23]

As was stated by Mr. Herbert Levy, counsel for Maryland Pharmaceutical Association, Inc., and Baltimore Retail Druggists Association, Inc., before the Antitrust Subcommittee:

> What the legislation now before the Congress seeks to do is just what the Congress thought it was doing in 1937, when it enacted the Miller-Tydings Act—no more and no less—and what everyone else thought the Congress had done until the unfortunate and (as I see it) unsound Schwegmann and Wentling decisions were rendered.
>
> This was a great shock to proponents of fair trade, and most of us still feel that the reasoning of the dissenting opinion in the Schwegmann case should have prevailed.
>
> As a coauthor, with Mr. Edward S. Rogers, of the Miller-Tydings Act, I can say that the omission of any reference to the nonsigner was not an oversight. It was deliberate, because as legislation designed to make the State acts effective, it was thought, as the minority of the Supreme Court decided, that every provision of the State acts tending to implement fair trade would be given full effect.[14]

The importance of the decision in the case of *Sunbeam Corp.* v. *Wentling*[15] cannot be underestimated in considering the effects of H. R. 6925 on State resale price maintenance statutes. In the Wentling and Schwegmann cases, the Court held, in effect, that not only did the State fair trade act not apply to nonsigners in interstate commerce but also did not apply to nonsigners in intrastate commerce; the former holding conformed to the Supreme Court's decision in the Schwegmann case which was decided in the interim between the remand of the first Wentling case and the decision in the second.

The legal effect of the Miller-Tydings amendment at this time

The Miller-Tydings amendment, according to the Schwegmann decision, exempts only those types of vertical price maintenance schemes which are created under State law by contract or agreement. Both the Miller-Tydings amendment and all the State laws expressly forbid horizontal pricing agreements between manufacturers, distributors, retailers and others who are thereby specifically enjoined and prevented from eliminating price competition by combination or conspiracy.

The Schwegmann case, by narrowing the exemption claimed under the Miller-Tydings amendment, illustrates the necessity for this legislation should the Congress

---

[14] Hearings, February 15, 1952.
[15] 185 F. 2d 903 and 192 F. 2d 7.

[3.23] *Id.* at 390.

decide, as a matter of national policy, that ⊥ vertical price fixing should be permitted in limited cases. Since the Miller-Tydings amendment was held not to cover nonsigners, any agreement between a producer and a nonsigner as to resale prices would render the former, if his product be in interstate commerce, liable to a Sherman Act criminal prosecution, or to either a civil suit by the Government or a private treble-damage suit by any one claimed to be injured. The question of the constitutionality of the Miller-Tydings amendment was not raised and so the problem of extending the exemption to include nonsigners must, perforce, await judicial determination. As a consequence, the state of the law now rests squarely, as to constitutionality, on the Old Dearborn and Pep Boys cases. All State laws, in addition, remain in force except insofar as the nonsigners clause relates to goods in interstate commerce.

The committee has had testimony to the effect that manufacturers have attempted to remedy this situation by signing as many contracts with distributors and retailers of their products as possible. But this has led to a task that is all but impossible of accomplishment since, numerically, dealers of popular trade-marked items number into the thousands. Where one retailer does not cooperate, however, all of the efforts made to protect his trade-mark and good will can be of no avail to the manufacturer. Other manufacturers, the committee understands have attempted to set up, for domiciliary purposes, warehouses or sales offices in each State in which they do business. These attempts to impart an intrastate aspect to such transactions can likewise be burdensome on the production and distribution of goods, which, heretofore free, have provided this country with the highest standard of living civilization has ever known.

C. THE SHERMAN ACT AND H. R. 6925

The Sherman Act is the "charter of freedom" of the American free-enterprise system. It, together with other auxiliary legislation, has been declared by the Congress to be the basis for political as well as economic freedom, for, it is said, economic freedom can coexist with political freedom only in an atmosphere free from monopolistic restraints. In spite of the fact that proponents of resale price maintenance claim that H. R. 6925 does not declare Federal economic policy, it is evident that the measure reported is more than an enabling act. It is positive law by way of an exemption to the basic antitrust statutes of the Nation. Other exemptions to the antitrust laws may largely be classified into two separate categories. The exemptions granted to industries whose operations are intricately interwoven with the public necessity and convenience in interstate commerce, such as railroads and shipping companies are one category. Of this classification, the Interstate Commerce Act (including the Reed-Bulwinkle Act), the Civil Aeronautics Act of 1938, and the Shipping Act of 1916 are prime examples.[16]

The other category of exemptions from the basic policies set forth in the Sherman Act are those which protect small business from the activities of larger, more powerful and concentrated competitors. It is in this classification that the Miller-Tydings amendment falls and it is in this context that the committee deals with H. R. 6925. As a practical matter the committee realizes that the legislation proposed in H. R. 6925 goes even beyond the typical limited exemptions given business in the Capper-Volstead Act,[17] Public Law 464, Seventy-third Congress,[18] and other acts in one important respect. The supervision of the exemptions in the last-named legislation has been entrusted to departments or agencies of the Federal Government.

H. R. 6925 is a departure from this principle and practice. Enforcement of the rights granted under the Miller-Tydings amendment as amended by H. R. 6925 will be left to private individuals or corporations. It is the hope of this committee that the enforcement of such rights will not be abused nor will any activity arising therefrom necessitate future legislative action to eliminate such abuses.

---

[16] As amended, 54 Stat. 905 (1940); 62 Stat. 472 (1948); 52 Stat. 973 (1938); 39 Stat. 733 (1916), as amended by 41 Stat. 996 (1920); with limited repeal 54 Stat. 950 (1940), respectively.

[17] **42 Stat. 388 (1922).**

[18] **48 Stat. 1213 (1934).**

II. The Importance of Fair Trade to Manufacturers and Retailers
A. Protection of Trade-Marks, Brand Names, and Good Will

"Fair trade," one species of resale price maintenance, operates in and provides protection for two main areas or levels in our economy. The two areas, production and distribution, are, however, intricately woven together so that they must be viewed as a whole rather than separately. Viewed from the production level, fair trade is a type of resale control, a method by which a manufacturer may vertically control the pricing of his commodity as it flows through the channels of distribution. Viewed from the level of distribution, fair trade has the effect of stabilizing prices and preventing ruinous competition on the part of retailers who may often reduce an uncontrolled price to force competitors out of business.

The primary aim of fair trade from the manufacturer's point of view is to protect his trade name or mark, while curbing the loss-leader practice so abhorred by retailers. The term "loss leader" implies that an unscrupulous retailer or distributor may exploit the good will of the manufacturer of a known and respected article by lowering the price on the product for the purpose of advertising and selling all of his other wares to the public. In this manner, the retailer hopes to satisfy many other needs of the consumer attracted by the extremely low price promoted by this device. It is natural that loss leaders, without exception, are products of known value produced by manufacturers who spend much time and energy in "preselling" their product by large expenditures for advertising. The great increase in national advertising given products by means of radio, television, newspapers, and magazines has materially enhanced the attractiveness of these items for use as loss leaders by retailers. Such uses are not only promotional devices and advertisements for the retailer, but constitute a serious diminution in value of the product of the manufacturer. Testimony adduced by the subcommittee indicates the evils involved and how fair trade prevents the diminution complained of. Lacking such protection, both the manufacturer and consumer suffer. Thus Mr. John W. Anderson, President of the American Fair Trade Council, states:

> Often from 80 to 90 percent or more of a manufacturer's total sales come from the straightforward smaller retailer who understandably discontinues the active sale of the favored product—and puts a competitive product out in front—when the favored product is advertised in the area as a store-traffic lure. Thus, the manufacturer's total sales go down and production costs go up as overhead expense must be piled up on lowered volume. Thus the "cut-price spiral" produces the "quality squeeze." [9]
>
> Predatory cut prices tend to spiral downwardly so long as there remains, within the community affected, sufficient good will for the trade-mark under attack to make it useful for lurist purposes of retail trade diversion. Cut-price wars sometimes spiral the retail price of a popular product down to a mere fraction of its actual cost of manufacture.
>
> The cut-price spiral produces diminishing retailer good will, and diminishing consumer sales, to create what has come to be known as the quality squeeze.
>
> The quality squeeze results from compulsions upon the manufacturer to reduce his costs, so as to meet the demands of retail monopolists for still further reductions in their costs of acquisition, to support continuing downward spiraling of retail prices.
>
> The quality squeeze created by the cut-price spiral of loss-leader competition reduces the "mileage" a consumer receives per unit of retail price. In that process the public suffers from what is, in effect, an inverted form of concealed inflation. Unit prices may remain at low levels and may gravitate even lower, but values per unit of price go down much faster, under such conditions, than do prices. This is because it is the plus percentages of added prime costs of producing the item that yield to the public its greatest values per unit of sales price. Often by increasing the prime factory cost of an item by as much as 5 or 10 percent the value of the product to the consumer may be increased by 200 or 300 percent—or more. By the same token, an arbitrary reduction of as much as 5 or 10 percent in the prime factory cost of a product may readily reduce the value of that product to the consumer by half or more, without noticeably altering its appearance.
>
> Omitting the hardening operation on the wearing parts of the lowly can opener, for example, might reduce slightly its factory cost to meet relentless pressures of predatory competition, but would most certainly reduce its usefulness as a can opener to almost zero, without making any change in its appearance.

As the quality squeeze continues, the consumer's good will for the manufacturer's product is destroyed, and the once-honored product may disappear from the marketing area affected. The lurist retailer who uses loss-leader principles to bait a bear trap for the consumer hurts everyone else, from manufacturer to consumer.[19]

The necessity and desirability of protecting the manufacturer's property right in trade-marks and brand names from diminution in value is, to that segment of our economy, the most important argument for the restoration of resale price maintenance. Mr. Anderson, president of the American Fair Trade Council, forcefully and succinctly stated that proposition when he said:

Laws prohibiting larceny protect the manufacturer against the theft of his physical property. Fair-trade laws protect the manufacturer against the theft of perhaps his most valuable asset—though intangible—his good will.

The necessity for restoring to full stature the fair-trade laws of the several States has been dramatically demonstrated by the wave of violent price wars touched off by the Schwegmann decision. The effects of price cutting, selling below cost and damage to good will of the manufacturers has not yet been estimated from the point of view of financial loss. It is apparent, however, that the system which has operated successfully for many years can no longer continue to protect those who most need the application of the law. As Mr. S. Ralph Lazarus [sic], chairman of the board, Benrus Watch Co. said to the committee:

I am before you today because I believe that the repeal of the Miller-Tydings amendment, and the automatic nullifying of sound fair-trade laws in 45 States have now brought both the retail and manufacturing industries of the United States to the most critical and dangerous test of our system of distribution that we have faced for more than two decades. This action has brought fear, mistrust, and panic into the market, and raised the specter of mass bankruptcy to help disorganize the systems of production and distribution which are the cornerstones of the American way of life.[20]

B. PROTECTION AGAINST MONOPOLY OF DISTRIBUTION

Justification for resale price maintenance can also be found in the value attributed the device by the other of its principal exponents; the small retailer. The small retailer and business man declare that resale price maintenance prevents an eventual monopoly in distribution of goods by compelling all retailers to sell fair-traded products at or above the minimum price set by the manufacturer of the product. Mr. George J. Burger, vice president in charge of legislative activities, National Federation of Independent Business, succinctly stated this protection of small business by means of fair trade when he said to the committee:

The bald fact is that for successful operation, for continued incentive to remain in private enterprise, small, independent firms need the protection afforded by an effective fair-trade law.

He continued:

Essentially they need it for protection against unchained monopolistic strength of some giant firms who do from 5 to 10 percent of their volume on branded, nationally advertised items, on which they may have equal or slightly larger margins than their smaller, independent competitors, while doing from 90 to 95 percent of their volume on private or unbranded goods, on which their margins run at times one hundred fold the margins on their branded products. Small, independent businessmen by and large do not have access to this private or unbranded low-cost merchandise. They cannot, as their giant rivals have in the past and may in the future, juggle prices on nationally advertised goods, and offer phony bargains, to lure trade to purchase vast amounts of lucrative private or nonbranded goods. In a few words, when the giants begin to juggle, the small firms cannot compete.[21]

Likewise larger distributors or retailers who desire quick profits on seasonal sales can be held in check and prevented from selling such items as drugs, electrical

---

[19] Hearings, February 22, 1952.
[20] **Hearings, February 20, 1952.**
[21] Hearings, February 13, 1952.

appliances, watches, and other branded articles at noncompetitive prices. Mr. Rivers Peterson, managing director, National Retail Hardware Association objected, in his testimony of February 27, 1952, to the use of a relatively small number of items as seasonal loss leaders by stores who do not traditionally, the year round, carry such items when he stated:

> Why do these price cutters insist on giving consumers the benefit of these especially low prices on a relatively small number of nationally advertised brands and why do they consistently select items that are not a part of the lines in which the establishment deals primarily but are the bread and butter merchandise for retailers in other lines?

The protection afforded that important segment of our economy represented by small business must be strengthened lest it be eliminated as the result of the ability of the larger retailer to hold and take a loss while driving the little merchant from his stand.

In addition to the small-business men who desire protection from retail monopoly, manufacturers also condemn, with much vigor, the growth of monopoly in channels of distribution for they, like the small retailer, would be completely at the mercy of retail outlets of enormous size, if the small independent merchant were forced out of business. When store traffic is built up by means of loss leaders and the small merchant becomes extinct the retail monopolist has both the manufacturer and consumer at his mercy. He, the user of loss leaders, may then set any price he wishes upon an article and force the manufacturer to sell to him after all other avenues of distribution have withered away. As Louis D. Brandeis, late an Associate Justice of the Supreme Court of the United States, wrote, with respect to the monopolistic aspects of price cutting:

> Americans should be under no illusions as to the value or effect of price cutting.
> It has been the most potent weapon of monopoly—a means of killing the small rival to which the great trusts have resorted most frequently. It is so simple, so effective. Farseeing organized capital secures by this means the cooperation of the short-sighted unorganized consumer to his own undoing. Thoughtless or weak, he yields to the temptation of trifling immediate gain, and, selling his birthright for a mess of pottage, becomes himself an instrument of monopoly.[22]

The manufacturers further realize the dangers inherent in a distributive monopoly and this is evidenced by the statement of Mr. Anderson in this regard when he said:

> The Miller-Tydings Act retards monopoly of distribution by preventing the use of honored trade-marked products with well-known standards of value (quality and price) as loss leaders to build store traffic and destroy the competition afforded by the small merchants.
> There is but one goal of predatory price cutting—to gain a monopoly of distribution in the area affected. The retail monopoly erects itself between the consumer and the sources of the things he must have for good living. Once entrenched, the retail monopolist price-fixes, to suit his own notions of what profit he wants, every item the consumer must buy in his store, the only exception having been fair-traded products. The would-be monopolist, of course, desires the repeal of fair-trade laws so that the popularity of honored brand-name products may be used, through noisily cut prices, to lure customers away from his smaller competitors.
> The Schwegmann decision loosened the reins on would-be monopolists. Six justices of the United States Supreme Court set in motion a devastating price war that has turned the eyes of small business and fair-trading manufacturers throughout the country to this committee and Congress for corrective and remedial legislation. This price war, as devastating as it was, may have been only child's play compared to that to come unless Congress acts.

And further he states:

> The growing threat of monopoly of distribution is evidenced by the following:
> 1. Approximately 90.4 percent of the 1,770,000 retail outlets employ five persons or less. These stores did only 45.8 percent of the total retail business. The stores employing six or more persons represented approximately only 9.6 percent of the total number of retail stores, yet did approximately 54.2 percent of the total annual retail trade.[23]
> 2. Exactly 20 giant retailers will turn in, during 1951, a combined volume of some $18 billions. In the merchandise categories in which these 20 giants did at least $15 billions, total retail volume in 1951 will probably be about $75 billions. Thus, very roughly, these 20 huge

---

[22] Cutthroat Competition—The Competition That Kills, Harper's Weekly, November 15, 1913.
[23] 71 United States statistical abstract, 1950, table 1046, p. 893.

retailers took into their tills $1 out of every $5 spent by the public for these merchandise categories.[24]

3. The director of merchandising of Grey Advertising Agency, Inc., New York City, E. B. Weiss, points out in his recent book, Mass Marketing to the "400" Mass Retailers, that some 400 giant retailers do over half the Nation's retail business in such major merchandise classifications as drug, food, variety, dry goods, and apparel.

The vicious use of the loss-leader formula to build monopoly of distribution is spelled out in detail in recent suits filed by fair-trading manufacturers.

To check the growing threat of monopoly of distribution, restoration of fair trade to its former effectiveness as a public servant is urgently needed. Fair trade is one of the few weapons the consumer possesses to combat this ruthless form of monopoly.

III. THE NECESSITY FOR RESTORATION

Arguments have been advanced by the proponents of resale price maintenance which point up the practical economic feasibility and desirability of the amendatory legislation reported by the committee.

A. TO THE MANUFACTURER AND RETAILER

Fair trade prevents disastrous, ruinous and totally destructive competition on the distributive level of our economy. A product which is in demand by the general consuming public should be sold at a price that allows to the wholesaler and retailer a proper margin of profit and at the same time prevents the damage and injury which price cutting causes to the good-will and reputation of the manufacturers of that product. By means of setting a minimum price for the resale of the product, the manufacturer assures the reputation of his product while permitting the retailer to have sufficient mark-up to enable him to compete with other stores. If this right were not legally protected by legislation of the type here reported, retailers could, without scruples, reduce the price on a popular branded item. Resale price maintenance prevents this.

At the outset, the general public would question the regular price for which the article was sold in the first instance. He would have the right to say "Why can I now buy this same product for X dollars when before it was priced at X plus Y dollars." The tendency for the product to lose its popular appeal is apparent and the damage is suffered both by the manufacturer and the retailer. Resale price maintenance prevents this.

The customer would also have the right to question whether the manufacturer, in good faith, has not already been marketing an overpriced item or that this particular product has been found to be so inferior as to require drastic price reduction in order to sell it. Resale price maintenance prevents this.

The retailer on the other hand must explain why his larger competitor can sell the product at such low prices, which undoubtedly has a bad effect on his customer relations. In addition, and most important, the retailer either has to reduce the price of the article to the consumer to meet in good faith the lower price competition or discontinue the handling of the item. In either of these alternatives he is forced to engage in an uneconomic practice. Carried to the extreme this would lead to the virtual elimination of the small retailer who does not have the economic staying power of his larger competitor. Resale price maintenance prevents this.

The damage to the manufacturer is not as obvious although it must be conceded that his good will and future sales potential will be impaired. After the temporary exploitation of the product has been achieved by lowering the price, even those who engage in that practice lose interest in handling the product. For then they find it uneconomical to continue to operate on low margins or at a loss. Again the manufacturer suffers and the retailer who has set aside the goods, not selling them at reduced prices, has on his hand [sic] the proverbial white elephant which he cannot move except at a loss. Resale price maintenance prevents this. Thus there is need for some device, such as the resale price maintenance scheme, to protect both the small retailer and bona fide manufacturer from ruinous competition.

---

[24] Grey Matter, a publication of Grey Advertising Agency, Inc., January 15, 1952.

B. TO THE CONSUMER

Proponents of fair trade have also presented and documented a case for resale price maintenance to the effect that the consumer receives ⊥ the protection that is his ⊥ 13 due when he buys a reputable product at a fixed price no matter where he may be. Under the theory of uniformity in quantity and quality of nationally known and advertised branded goods, there can be no form of deception practiced either by the retailer or the manufacturer in offering such goods for sale. Thus a consumer knows that there is a standard price that he may pay for an article and if he does not want that protection he may, of his own free choice, buy another item the quality and reputation of which has not been established. In addition, and equally important, is the fact that the exceptional bargain that the consumer receives when he buys a branded article at less than the set price is often offset by the promotional attempts of the retailer who uses such practices either to "switch" the customer from the true path of his intent, that is to buy that particular product, and offer to the customer another less well-known item. The common practice of advertising and holding sales on such loss-leaders often results in the rapid sale of the article, the quantities of which are quickly exhausted. Or, on the other hand, the promotional user of the loss-leader often shifts the purchaser's attention to another item or to items on which there is a higher mark-up to recoup that which the retailer has lost on the loss-leader promotion. All of these things do not benefit the consumer and often, in fact, operate to his detriment.

C. TO THE ENHANCEMENT OF COMPETITION AND THE DEVELOPMENT OF FAIR PRICES

Price setting by the manufacturer leads to the development of fair prices and enhances competition on all levels of the economy.

When a manufacturer, A, sets a price on his product, he will not consciously price it out of the market; and that is common good business judgment on his part. Similarly other manufacturers of goods in free and open competition with goods of like and similar nature will price their products competitively with A. Thus you will find adequate competition on the manufacturing level as to price. Any horizontal arrangement between manufacturers to maintain the same price in combination or conspiracy is still illegal under the Sherman Act and is so stated expressly, by way of reaffirmation, in H. R. 6925. It has been said that competition will not work in a field where one manufacturer does not wish to fair-trade his product which is similar to or in competition with other fair-traded products. This in essence means that one manufacturer may price his product at a set resale level leaving others free to undersell him. But that in itself makes for a truly competitive economy. The former must either lower his price to meet that form of competition or depend on his own trade name and reputation to keep control of his segment of that particular market. This again shows how resale price maintenance encourages competitive pricing policies among manufacturers.

Likewise on the retail or distribution level, the retailer or wholesaler has the free choice to buy and stock non-fair-traded articles as well as fair-traded brands. Thus, the corner store may compete with his neighbor for the consumer's market. Fair trade does not prevent competition on the distributive level even if both carry a product on which the manufacturer has set a resale price. And this is so because fair-trade contracts generally set a minimum price below which the ⊥ product may not be sold. Since the ⊥ 14 average retailing establishment is considered to be as efficient as its supermarket or chain-store brethren, it can keep its overhead down to the point where its mark-up may vary to such an extent as to permit the existence of several different prices on the same fair-traded article, even within a given area. In determining the mark-up to cover all items of expense and a normal profit there is much room for varying prices and for various modes and methods of doing business. The retailer who provides credit for his customers, special services, deliveries, plush carpets, and elaborate displays must expect to have greater overhead as items to be considered in his mark-up. Another merchant, doing business on a less grand scale, can compete by offering the fair-traded product at lower price than his "full service" competitor and thus the forces of competition remain intact.

The placing of a minimum resale price on an article, as is recognized by the statutes of 45 States of the Union merely protects the retailer from ruinous competition and does not, in many respects, guarantee a margin of profit to him. By placing a minimum price on a brand-name article, the manufacturer does not necessarily limit or freeze the retail margin. And this is so, first, because he does not want to and will not intentionally price himself out of the market; secondly, because he does not control the actual maximum price charged by the retailer; and, thirdly, because he cannot, in all practicality, regulate the activities of the large number of retailers with whom he must deal in order to have, himself, an efficient operation.

D. TO THE PUBLIC POLICY OF THE SEVERAL STATES

The nonsigners' clause is the keystone of resale price maintenance

Conceding that fair trade is part of the economic public policy of the many States which have adopted such laws, and that the Miller-Tydings amendment, ambiguous though the Court may interpret it, was designed to effectuate such State policy, the committee is of the opinion that the nonsigners clause is the keystone of such legislation and must therefore be sanctioned.

This is so even though the committee realizes that the nonsigners' clause has been the subject of much litigation and criticism throughout the years. Without such clause, fair-trade contracts or agreements alone cannot provide for resale price maintenance, as experience has plainly shown in the Schwegmann and Wentling cases. The merchant who does not wish to sign a fair-trade contract can easily demoralize and shatter the whole structure of resale price maintenance with the consequence of rendering any number of products subject to price cutting. The retailer who does not adhere to a trade policy as expressed in the declaration of public policy in State laws must effectively be bound lest all other merchants lose the protection afforded by such laws. It has been said that the nonsigners clause creates a new form of contractual obligation unknown in the history of the common or statutory law.

The absence of the consensual element imposed by the nonsigners' clause is claimed by the opponents of fair trade as a violation of the basic tenets of contract law; namely, that a person, not a party to a contract, should, nevertheless by the nonsigners' clause be bound by its provisions. It has been said, and there is much merit in the argument that price cutting and destruction of a manufacturer's good will is no less offensive whether free of the effects of contractual obligation or under contractual obligations for the economic and social effects are the same in any case. The nonsigners' provision effectuates State as well as National policy and only provides a remedy rather that [sic] a new right of action. The many acts that are in effect in the several States as well as H. R. 6925 require that such improper and immoral economic practices, if "willfully and knowingly" made by persons not party to a fair-trade contract, leaves any nonsigning party in this situation. First, he may choose to sign a contract in which case the ordinary remedies under contract law would apply in case of a breach thereof. Second, he need not carry the product which has been fair traded. But, thirdly, if he, as a nonsigner, does choose to carry the article, he may not sell it at less than the minimum price set or in the alternative, be held liable if he is on notice that such a resale price restriction is in force.

The declaration that it is an act of unfair competition willfully and knowingly to sell below the fair-trade price is a matter not only of direct and immediate interest to retailers and manufacturers but it sets forth a principle of public economic policy not inconsistent with established policy in the Robinson-Patman Act[25] and the Federal Trade Commission Act[26] as well as other Federal laws relating to trade and commerce.

In the dissent in the case of *Dr. Miles Medical Co.* v. *Park and Sons Co.*,[27] Mr. Justice Holmes said:

> The Dr. Miles Medical Co. knows better than we do what will enable it to do the best business. We must assume its retail price to be reasonable, for it is so alleged and the case is

---

[25] 49 Stat. 1526 (1936).

[26] 38 Stat. 717 (1914).

[27] Op. cit.

here on demurrer; so I see nothing to warrant my assuming that the public will not be served best by the company being allowed to carry out its plan.[3.24]

Opponents of fair trade assert that such price fixing destroys competition on the distributive level and even more so when a nonsigner's [sic] clause applies. But Mr. Justice Holmes states, in general terms that:

> I think we greatly exaggerate the value and importance to the public of competition in the production or distribution of an article (here it is only distribution), as fixing a fair price. What really fixes that is the competition of conflicting desires. We, none of us, can have as much as we want of all the things that we want. Therefore, we have to choose. As soon as the price of something we want goes above the point at which we are willing to give up other things to have that, we cease to buy it and buy something else. Of course, I am speaking of things that we can get along without. There may be necessaries that sooner or later must be dealt with like short rations in a shipwreck, but they are not Dr. Miles' medicines. With regard to things like the latter it seems to me that the point of most profitable returns marks the equilibrium of social desires and determines the fair price in the only sense in which I can find meaning in those words.[3.25]

Thus in the case of all fair-traded products, like Dr. Miles' medicines, competitive forces and prices are supported by consumer-demand preference and not destroyed by the fixing of a price under a fair-trade contract or by means of the nonsigners' clause.

SECTION-BY-SECTION ANALYSIS OF H. R. 6925, AS AMENDED

Section 1 of the act entitled "An act to protect trade and commerce against unlawful restraints and monopolies," approved July 2, 1890, as amended, is amended in the following respects:

Subsections (a) and (b) reenact the Miller-Tydings amendment to the Sherman Act insofar as that amendment exempts from the Sherman Act "contracts and agreements" prescribing minimum prices for the resale of commodities bearing the trade-mark, brand, or name of the producer when such contracts and agreements are lawful under State law.

The committee intends that the phrase "minimum prices" contained in line 8, page 2,[3.26] shall be the only subject matter of the contract or agreement exempt from the operation of the antitrust laws. In the contemplation of the committee, provisions or conditions in the contract other than price provisions shall not be included in the exemption granted by the bill considered herein.

The phrase "minimum prices" follows exactly the language of the original Miller-Tydings amendment.

The committee does not intend that the words "minimum prices" are to mean "stipulated" prices or price even though language to that effect may be found in some State statutes. This is so because, in the committee's opinion, stipulated prices set not only a minimum but also a maximum price which leads to rigidity in the price structure, and limited margins which may adversely affect small retailers.

The word "prices" is used to connote more than one price because of the fact that a producer of trade-marked goods may wish to set more than one price on the same product. Such language is designed to meet the situation where the producer desires to set a price for sales at wholesale and set a price for sales at retail. By the use of the word "prices" the committee does not intend to indicate that the manufacturer may set different prices at the same level of distribution within the same general area. The committee realizes that differences in prices may be caused by differences in cost in applying the rule enunciated in the Robinson-Patman Act, that prices may vary making due allowance for different costs of manufacture, sale, or delivery resulting from the differing methods or quantities in which such commodities are to such purchasers sold or delivered.

[3.24] 220 U.S. at 412.

[3.25] *Id.*

[3.26] Reference is to H.R. 6925 as introduced by Representative Keogh on March 6, 1952.

The Miller-Tydings amendment has been modified, by deletion of the word "distributor," so that only products bearing the name, trade-mark, or brand of the producer may be covered (line 11). The purpose of this deletion is to give the protection deemed necessary to the person who owns the valuable trade-mark. The use of the words "producer or distributor" may give rise to a horizontal price-fixing contract which would be in violation of the Sherman Act if a trade-mark owner is both the producer of his own brand and the distributor of a similar product in competition with his own brand.

A new sentence has been added beginning with line 18, page 2, which limits the words "contract or agreement" to those instruments to which the party prescribing the price is the owner of the trade-mark, name, or brand for it is his valuable property right, good will, which is sought to be protected by this legislation.

Subsection (c) exempts from the effects of the Sherman Act the exercise or enforcement of the right or rights of action created under State law against a person not signatory to a resale price maintenance contract where that person "willfully and knowingly" sells at less than the price prescribed in such contracts. This is a nonsigners' clause designed to ameliorate the decision of the Supreme Court in the Schwegmann case. Thus the section extends the enforcement of the unfair competition sections of State laws in interstate commerce and amplifies the Miller-Tydings amendment.

The proviso contained in section 1 (c) starting on line 9, page 3, declares that in the exercise of the rights or right of action as may be exempted from the antitrust laws the owner of the trade-mark, brand, or name must diligently supervise and maintain compliance with his set price in all cases legally possible. Such supervision and prosecution of violators is a condition precedent to the enforcement of his right of action as well as a condition precedent to the right of any other party aggrieved to maintain a suit. Thus the failure to protect retailers and to supervise and prosecute violators of resale price maintenance then in force will be a complete defense barring the enforcement of the rights or right of action exempted from the Sherman Act.

Subsection (d) provides a Federal cause of action for a signer or nonsigner to willfully and knowingly, in interstate commerce, (1) advertise for sale, offer for sale, or sell or (2) have transported for sale or resale or (3) deliver pursuant to a sale, or otherwise deliver, commodities upon which a resale price has been set at less than the price set in a State having a resale price maintenance law.

Subsection (d) is designed specifically to remedy the situation exemplified by the Wentling decision and attempts to provide a remedy for the injuries arising from the type of conduct enumerated above in those States having resale price maintenance laws. Thus the advertising, offering, selling, transporting, or delivery of such goods from fair-trade States into non-fair-trade States at prices lower than the resale price would not be actionable; nor would the commerce from non-fair-trade States, such as Texas, Vermont, and Missouri, and the District of Columbia, into fair-trade States be subject to the resale price maintenance laws of the fair-trade States. By the proviso on line 24, page 4, the committee intends not to encroach upon the sovereignty of the States not having fair-trade laws. Thus the Federal cause of action created under this section shall not apply to advertisements for sale, offers for sale or sales originating from or directed into Texas, Vermont, or Missouri, together with the District of Columbia.

The committee intends that the right of action created under subsection (d) shall be limited only to those having a proprietary interest in the commodity and the words "any person, firm, or corporation," appearing at line 6, page 4, shall be limited to persons actually engaged in commerce and not trade associations or groups engaged in "educational, eleemosynary, charitable, or social" purposes. The subsection also provides for remedies by way of injunctive relief for such violations. The proviso on line 4, page 5, declares, as in subsection (c), that the owner of the trade-mark, brand, or name must diligently maintain compliance of his set price in all cases lest his failure so to do be a complete defense to his action to enforce his rights against some but not all of the violators of the resale price set by him.

Subsection (e) reenacts the Miller-Tydings amendment in declaring that neither the making of resale price maintenance contracts nor the establishment or enforcement of the rights of action prescribed in sections (c) and (d) of this act shall constitute an unfair method of competition under section 5 of the Federal Trade Commission Act.

Subsection (f) specifically prevents contracts and agreements between competitors, so-called "horizontal" agreements between producers or distributors on the same level of commerce.

This concludes the majority report on H. R. 6925. The changes in existing law, in compliance with paragraph 2a of rule XIII of the Rules of the House of Representatives, are shown on page 62 of the appendix to this report and thereafter.

Mr. Celler submitted the following minority views on H. R. 6925 on behalf of himself, Mr. Jonas, and Mr. Bakewell:

MINORITY VIEWS IN OPPOSITION TO RESALE PRICE MAINTENANCE

We oppose this legislation exempting resale price maintenance agreements from the antitrust laws and making violations of State resale price maintenance laws actionable in the Federal courts on all interstate transactions. Because of the serious consequences to our competitive economy resulting from resale price maintenance legislation and the impact of such laws upon the consumer, we have delineated the reasons underlying our opposition to this proposed legislation in the succeeding pages at considerable length. The substance of our objections, which finds documentation in the main text, is contained in the following summary:

Summary

Resale price maintenance is a system whereby large manufacturers of branded or trade-marked items are permitted, by means of resale price maintenance contracts with retail outlets, to determine the selling price of their products charged by the retailer to the consumer. Under resale price maintenance as now proposed, retailers are bound to adhere to the prices determined by the manufacturer under penalty of fine and injunction. The minimum prices established by the producer in his contracts are binding upon all retailers throughout a State regardless of whether the retailer has signed such resale pricing agreements or not.

Resale price maintenance has been advanced as a solution to the competitive problems besetting the independent retail merchant in vying for trade with the modern giants of retail distribution—the chain store, the department store, and the mail-order house. It is also claimed that resale price maintenance affords the manufacturer legitimate protection for his trade-marked article. While both of these objectives are laudable, we do not believe that resale price maintenance is the appropriate method to achieve either.

Insofar as the small retailer is concerned, retail price maintenance as a long-term measure injures his competitive standing. High margins on articles sold under fair trade contracts already have enticed the supermarket and other large distributive outlets into the retail market place formerly occupied by the small merchant. This trend has been particularly noticeable in the drug field where studies reveal that 85 percent of the large grocery outlets now dispense dentifrices, certain pharmaceuticals, and health and beauty aids formerly sold primarily in drug stores. The magnitude of profits guaranteed by fair-trade contracts covering drug items have made up for lower mark-ups demanded by competition on food products and have converted some of the large supermarkets into ardent advocates of fair trade. This legislation only hastens the day when numerous small drug stores will fall victim to the competition of large supermarkets and chain stores.

Conversely, when resale price maintenance contracts fail to provide for adequate profits on the retail level, the small retailer is unable to extricate himself from the fair trade price squeeze. In periods of rising costs or inflationary cycles, the laments of the individual merchant may well go unheeded by the manufacturer and, as has recently occurred in certain instances, bankruptcy may threaten hundreds of small storekeepers throughout the country. Retailers have been able to meet this problem in the past only by acting collectively in open violation of the antitrust laws to impress upon large manufacturers their need for adequate mark-ups.

Even when prices established by the manufacturer under resale price maintenance agreements do not result in either of these dire consequences, the very fact that his prices have been rigidly established at the retail level prevent the small merchant from meeting the price competition offered by his powerful competitors—the chains, department stores, and mail-order houses. Again fair trade serves only to fetter the small and independent retailer.

With these consequences clearly in mind, it is obvious that resale price maintenance results in transforming independent businessmen into mere conduits for the large manufacturers of fair-traded merchandise. Thus, concentration of economic power, loss of economic freedom, and restriction of competition is the inevitable aftermath of resale price maintenance legislation.

Already, concentration of economic power in principal fair-trade industries such as drugs and pharmaceuticals, small arms, silverware, pens and pencils, and electrical appliances is high according to figures contained in the latest Census of Manufactures. In many of these sectors of the economy, concentration has been on the increase within recent years and reliable testimony indicates that fair-trade legislation has been of substantial assistance to this growth. When it is remembered that of the 100 largest advertisers in the United States through various media, more than half fair-trade some or all of their products, it becomes evident how fair-trade legislation succors big business rather than small, promotes the growth of monopoly power, and relegates the independent merchant to a humble and subservient position in our economy.

Besides promoting the concentration of economic power, resale price maintenance agreements serve as incentive for boycotts, intimidation, discrimination, and other collective measures prohibited by the antitrust laws. Since passage of the Miller-Tydings amendment the Department of Justice has brought numerous proceedings in which it was charged that resale price maintenance agreements had served as a guise for illegal activities in restraint of trade. Included were indictments against the Colorado Wholesale Wine and Liquor Dealers Association, the National Association of Retail Druggists, the National Wholesale Druggists Association, the New York Pharmaceutical Association, and the Record Dealers Association. Resale price maintenance has also been an important factor in many cases instituted by the Federal Trade Commission.

The list of manufacturers who have been the subject of coercion under fair trade is long. The Pepsodent Co. was the victim of a campaign by retailers to put its toothpaste under the counter when it temporarily abandoned resale price maintenance agreements. In more recent times, the editorial policies of the Luce publications, which have been deemed inimical to fair trade, have resulted in an important trade association notifying retailers and manufacturers that "Luce magazine your enemies" and urging them to refrain from selling or placing advertisements in Time or Fortune. Currently, a cartoon portraying fair trade in an unfriendly light has resulted in an organized program of retaliation among groups of retailers to cut prices of the St. Louis Post-Dispatch.

On the retail level, organized pressure has been placed upon independent sellers who have not cooperated in resale price maintenance programs. Price-cutting outlets have been "persuaded" to revise their policies; wholesalers have been exhorted in trade publications to boycott retailers who refuse to conform.

These and other illegal activities in restraint of trade are the inevitable results of resale price maintenance agreements no matter how carefully Congress may surround this legislation with protective safeguards. The Department of Justice avers that the overwhelming majority of fair trade contracts, if examined closely, would be found to contain violations of the antitrust laws either in their content, their execution, or their enforcement. The frankest proponents of fair trade themselves admit that resale price maintenance programs cannot work effectively unless accompanied by collective action among retailers and between retailers and manufacturers.

While resale price maintenance injures competition and promotes the concentration of economic power, its most immediate impact is felt by the consumer. Any comparison shopping tour will readily disclose the large savings which can be had on purchases made in the District of Columbia, as against those made across the District line in the fair trade jurisdictions of Virginia or Maryland. Numerous studies have been made which bear these conclusions out. The consumer will no doubt be surprised to discover that Congress intends to prohibit efficient retail establishments from reducing prices on his wares. It will also certainly appear anomalous to the voters of the United States for Congress, during a severe inflationary period, which has necessitated rigid governmental controls to prevent prices from going up, seriously to consider legislation which, under the penalties of Federal law, prohibits the prices of many important commodities from coming down.

Numerous consumer organizations have testified against this bill, among them, notably the CIO on behalf of labor, the American Farm Bureau Federation and the National Grange on behalf of farmers, and the General Federation of Women's Clubs for the American consuming public.

There has been no showing whatever of the existence of an economic situation necessitating resort to such a drastic remedy as fair-trade legislation. In retail sales and in number of retail outlets, non-fair-trade States such as Missouri and Texas have prospered equally as well as—if not in many instances better than—their fair trading sisters. Retail sales in fair trading outlets such as drug stores and jewelry stores have in many cases, shown substantial increases in the months subsequent to the Schwegmann decision as compared to the same periods of the year before when fair trade was safely ensconced. Despite the Schwegmann decision, which declared that the Miller-Tydings exemption of resale price maintenance agreements from the antitrust laws did not permit the binding of nonsigners, 1951 has ⊥ been a banner year for sales of many fair-traded commodities and much optimism exists among industry spokesmen for a repetition of these favorable conditions in 1952. Manufacturers of fair-traded commodities have testified frankly that they were unable to say that they would suffer through lack of fair trade.

True enough, competitive evils have been shown to exist, both in fair-trade and non-fair-trade jurisdictions, but remedy for these lies not in exempting resale price maintenance agreements from the antitrust laws. At the appropriate time, we shall advance what we consider to be appropriate legislation designed to prevent such unfair trade practices as "loss leader" selling which advocates of fair trade claim is the evil they seek to extinguish. We don't believe it proper to behead our economy in order to cure the headache of loss leaders.

Regardless of the merits of resale price maintenance, we feel that this legislation as it is written leaves much to be desired. Extending the provisions of resale price maintenance agreements made pursuant to State law so as to bind retailers who are in nowise parties thereto lends congressional sanction to economic servitude. As the Supreme Court recently declared in the Schwegmann decision:

> When they seek, however, to impose price fixing on persons who have not contracted or agreed to the scheme, the situation is vastly different. That is not price fixing by contract or agreement; that is price fixing by compulsion. That is not following the path of consensual agreement; that is resort to coercion.[1]

When Congress thereafter makes it a Federal offense (as it does in sec. (d) of H. R. 6925) for signers and nonsigners of resale price maintenance agreements alike to violate State resale price maintenance laws in interstate transactions, it is treading on highly dangerous constitutional grounds. Lending Federal sanction to the enforcement of retail prices fixed by manufacturers may well raise the question of unconstitutional delegation of legislative powers. To afford no procedural safeguards, such as appeals, hearings, and submissions, to those affected adversely by resale price maintenance agreements appears to violate our fundamental due process procedures applicable to all administrative determinations. That no adequate standards are established for assuring a fair return to the retailer whose selling prices are fixed without his consent under resale price maintenance contracts could legitimately be said to deprive him of property without due process of law. The confusion in this statute as to which State law is

---

[1] *Schwegmann Bros.* v. *Calvert Corp.*, 341 U. S. 384, 388 (1951).

applicable to interstate transactions may well render the statute unconstitutionally void for vagueness.

While it is no doubt true that Congress may constitutionally encumber interstate commerce at its pleasure, we may also seriously question the wisdom of Congress in damming the channels of interstate commerce with exactly those obstructions which the States themselves are constitutionally prohibited from erecting. We can see resulting from this type of legislation only a morass of chaos and confusion.

I. RESALE PRICE MAINTENANCE PROMOTES THE CONCENTRATION OF ECONOMIC POWER

Principal arguments which have been advanced in favor of fair-trade legislation are two: First, that it protects the small retailer from the unremitting competition of large marketing outlets; and second, that it affords a legitimate safeguard to the manufacturer of trade-marked articles in protecting the proprietary interest said to vest in his mark.

At first blush, there is much to be said for each of these two propositions. One can indeed lend a sympathetic ear to the plea of the House Small Business Committee in its recent report that—

> deceitful and misleading price cutting is not in the public interest and that small business enterprises in particular need protection against loss-leader and similar unfair business practices.[1a]

The desire of the producer to maintain the value of his commodity in the eyes of the consumer is equally understandable.

It is submitted, however, that none of the proponents of the above arguments has examined with care the economic ramifications inherent in the advancement of fair trade as a solution to these problems. Earnest and vigilant protectors of the small business community in our economy have supported resale price maintenance legislation as an antimonopoly measure. It is not their sincerity but their vision that we question. Legitimate concern over the growing aggrandizement of power on the part of chain stores, mail-order houses, and department stores and perhaps undue alarm over the actions of a few "discount" houses and "cut rate" dealers, has led to the insistence upon resale price maintenance as a panacea for the competitive evils besetting the small merchantman. The failure to comprehend the consequences resulting from the abdication of pricing freedom by the independent retailer must be attributed either to preoccupation or to oversight.

Who are the manufacturers in whose favor the independent seller is now forced, by this legislation, to abrogate one of the few of his remaining privileges, that of freely and independently pricing his merchandise? A recent study conducted by the American Fair Trade Council showed that among those companies which fair trade all or part of their products were 51 of the 100 largest national advertisers using newspapers, periodicals, and/or radio. These are many of the concerns among the giants of American industry and include such well-known companies as: Sterling Drug, Inc., Firestone Tire & Rubber Co., Westinghouse Electric Corp., E. I. du Pont de Nemours & Co., General Electric Co., Eastman Kodak Co., Colgate-Palmolive-Peet Co., International Silver Co., General Motors Corp., Procter & Gamble Co., and Lever Bros. Co. Included in the membership of the American Fair Trade Council which drafted, authored, and sponsored the Keogh bill (H. R. 6925) were a subsidiary of the Aluminum Corp. of America, Miles Laboratories, Inc., Minnesota Mining & Manufacturing Co., Olin Industries, Inc., Stewart Warner Corp., and the Goodyear Tire & Rubber Co.

Do proponents of this legislation seriously believe that it is in the interest of small business to permit large manufacturers such as those listed above to determine the retail level of their prices throughout each of the 45 States in the Union having resale price maintenance laws, and to allow such companies to dictate prices to every independent outlet in these areas? The retail outlet of today has already gone far on the road

---

[1a] H. Rept. 1292, 82d Cong., 2d sess. (1952), p. 1.

toward becoming a mere outlet for the distribution of the manufacturers' wares to the consumer. Nothing can sooner hasten the day when the "independence" of the small retailer will exist in name only than to place one of the principal competitive weapons at his disposal, his pricing policies, in the hands of his large supplier.

The present-day attitude of large fair-trading manufacturers toward retailers was candidly revealed when Mr. S. Ralph Lazrus, chairman of the board of directors of the Benrus Watch Co., explained in answer to the chairman's query that the independent retailer was, for all intents and purposes, a mere channel for the dispersal of the manufacturer's products:

> The CHAIRMAN. All the retailer would be would be a mere channel for the wholesaler.
> Mr. LAZRUS. In a true sense, within my judgment and in the opinion of people I come in contact with, we do consider a retailer nothing else but that for all merchandise because after all he is the man who meets the consumer. However, the competition does exist very keenly on the manufacturers' level.[2]

Mr. Lazrus still believed however, that there existed for the small retailer a measure of freedom. As he expressed it, "The independent retailer has a great deal of independence because he can see fit to buy my product or not as he sees fit."

It is clear that in the present economy, the small merchant is caught between Scylla and Charybdis. On the one hand, he is confronted with the hard bargaining of the spawning department store, the chain, and the mail-order house. On the other he is faced by the powerful manufacturer whose only concept of the retailer's independence is that "he can see fit to buy my product or not as he sees fit." To say, however, as do those who now advocate this legislation, that the solution to this dilemma lies in turning the vast number of small retail outlets of the country into mere adjuncts of the large producer by allowing the latter to determine even the selling price of his product in every corner store throughout 45 States of the Union, is to make the word "independent business" a fancy rather than a reality.

It is argued by those in favor of fair-trade legislation that competition among retail outlets can be easily dispensed with inasmuch as such competition still exists on the manufacturing level. If it is the desire of Congress to eliminate competition throughout the Nation among retail outlets, it could not deliver a more fitting eulogy to the demise of the independent merchant than that contained in this legislation. A brief examination of the structure of some of those industries where resale-price maintenance has been prevalent, will soon dispel the notion that the retailer, the wholesaler, and the consumer alike will be benefited or protected by extant competition at the manufacturing level.

In the jewelry field, where resale-price maintenance is effective on something less than 50 percent of the merchandise sold,[3] principal items under fair-trade contracts are watches, pens and pencils, silverware, clocks, china, glass, electrical appliances, lighters, and compacts. As shown in the following table, concentration of economic power in the largest companies manufacturing these products in many cases is already extremely high:

TABLE 1.—Concentration of output in largest manufacturing companies in the jewelry industry (1947)

Industry	Number of companies	Value of shipments	1947 concentration ratios	
			First 4 companies	First 8 companies
Watches and clocks	183	$341,199,000	40.7	59.4
Electrical appliances	310	466,009,000	35.8	46.9
Pens and mechanical pencils	180	147,368,000	57.6	68.4
Pressed and blown glassware	107	234,795,000	50.6	64.8
Silverware and plated ware	221	219,131,000	61.2	72.2

Source: Department of Commerce, Census of Manufactures (1947).

---

[2] Hearings, February 20, 1952.
[3] Henebry, hearings, February 15, 1952.

A similar situation prevails in the hardware field where retail hardware stores currently dispose of such assorted items as insecticides, electrical appliances, glue, vacuum cleaners, abrasives, and animal traps under resale price maintenance contracts. As shown in the following chart, concentration of economic power among the manufacturers of these products in numerous instances is likewise high.

TABLE 2. — Concentration of output in manufacturing of representative fair-trade merchandise sold in hardware stores

	Number of companies	Value of shipments	1947 concentration ratios		1935 ratios	
			First 4 companies	First 8 companies	First 4 companies	First 8 companies
Electrical appliances	310	$466,009,000	35.8	46.9	—	—
Watches and clocks	183	341,199,000	40.7	59.4	37.7	59.1
Small arms	32	57,067,000	64.0	87.1	81.9	92.4
Silverware and plated ware	221	219,131,000	61.2	72.2	56.6	68.0
Abrasive products	236	223,386,000	49.4	56.4	67.4	74.3
Glue and gelatin	60	99,262,000	44.5	66.1	37.3	58.4
Files	34	24,943,000	91.6	95.8	85.8	94.9
Vacuum cleaners	34	160,184,000	61.0	86.7	—	—
Scales and balances	73	54,542,000	53.9	71.1	54.8	72.9
Cutlery	192	142,571,000	41.0	54.1	—	—
Insecticides and fungicides	146	73,068,000	37.4	54.2	—	—
Paints and varnishes	1,154	1,248,841,000	27.3	35.7	—	—

Source: Department of Commerce, Census of Manufactures (1947).

Turning to the drug industry, where demands for resale price maintenance legislation are particularly evident, we again find economic power concentrated in the hands of a relatively few large concerns. A Federal Trade Commission report in 1949 indicated that over 40 percent of the capital assets of manufacturers in the drugs and medicine industry were owned by the six largest concerns.[4] While this was not as great a degree of concentration as the Commission has found to exist in other industries, figures did not include the assets of McKesson & Robbins, one of the largest corporations in the drug business because that company was classified as a wholesaler. Figures revealed by the Department of Commerce in its Census of Manufactures, 1947, provide perhaps a more accurate indicia of the concentration now existing among manufacturers in the drug industry.

TABLE 3. — Concentration of output in drugs and medicines

Product	Number of companies	Value of shipments	1947 concentration ratios	
			First 4 companies	First 8 companies
Medicinal chemicals	88	$201,761,000	68.5	83.1
Botanical products	13	16,395,000	92.1	98.8
Pharmaceutical preparations	1,123	941,713,000	28.0	44.0
Biological products	79	38,752,000	37.9	50.9

Source: Department of Commerce, 1947 (Census of Manufactures).

In a number of fair-trading industries, concentration of economic power among the top few concerns has increased within the last several years. Thus, in silverware and plated ware, the top four companies controlled only 56.6 percent of the industry in the

---

[4] Federal Trade Commission, The Concentration of Productive Facilities, 1947, (1949) p. 51.

pre-Miller-Tydings year of 1935, while by 1947, 61.2 percent of the output in the industry was accounted for by four leading concerns. In 1935, four companies manufacturing watches and clocks accounted for 37.7 percent of the industry's output, but by 1947, the control resting in the dominant four concerns in the industry had increased to more than 40 percent.

That legislation authorizing resale price maintenance has contributed substantially to this increase in concentration was attested to by responsible sources at the Judiciary Committee's hearings on pending resale price maintenance legislation. Leon J. Engle, representing the National Wholesale Jewelers Association, responded as follows to questioning as to the effect of resale price maintenance on the increasing concentration of power in the silverware industry.

> Mr. GOLDSTEIN. Do you think fair trade had anything to do with it?
> Mr. ENGEL. I definitely do; yes, sir.
>   *   *   *   *   *   *   *
> The CHAIRMAN. So, as you indicated, the fair-trade laws did help further that concentration?
> Mr. ENGEL. I think they were definitely helpful.[5]

What has been said heretofore goes far toward answering the question of whether the manufacturer needs minimum resale price-maintenance laws to preserve the proprietary interests in his trade-mark. We think that large companies which can afford to spend millions of dollars in advertising need little assistance from Congress in fending for themselves in the competitive arena. Permitting the owner of a trade-marked article to determine the retail price for every retail outlet would far exceed even the permitted authority granted to owners of patents under the present laws. As a United States circuit court observed in a recent case:

> A patentee is given a monopoly by legal grant. But even a patentee, who can exclude everyone else from making his patented article, cannot control the price at which others may sell his articles to consumers. The protection given to the owner of a trade-mark certainly should not be greater than that given to the holder of a legal monopoly, the patentee.[6]

Where concentration of output is already highly centralized among a small coterie of producers, it is highly imperative that all efforts be made to encourage the free flow of competitive forces. How to deal with competitive conditions in these "oligopolistic" industries under existing antitrust laws has been one of the central problems under investigation by a subcommittee of the House Committee on the Judiciary for almost 3 years. Characterized by such phenomenon as price leadership, price uniformity, pricing systems, and other indicia of competition's absence, certainly the economic magnitude of the problems posed by these industries can only be increased if dominant manufacturers are allowed by this legislation to fix retail prices throughout the length and breadth of the market place. To grant to such producers an exemption from the Sherman Act for price-fixing practices which have long been considered illegal would go far toward vitiating the potency of our antitrust statutes and increasing the growth of monopoly power.

II. RESALE PRICE MAINTENANCE INJURES THE COMPETITIVE STATUS OF INDEPENDENT RETAILERS

As has already been pointed out, advocates of resale price maintenance legislation claim it affords the small retailing merchant protection from inroads into his trade made by large chains, department stores, mail order houses, and other large retail outlets. In practice, throughout many important segments of the economy where fair trade prevails, the reverse has actually proven to be true. Resale price maintenance in

---

[5] Hearings, February 20, 1952.
[6] *Sunbeam Corp.* v. *Wentling,* 192 F. (2d) 7, 9 (1951).

many instances has substantially injured the independent merchant to the advantage of his larger retail competitors.

Let us take the retail drug trade as an example. Here, resale price maintenance has enhanced the power of the chain drug stores at the expense of independent retail competitors. As Dr. Corwin Edwards, former economic consultant to the Department of Justice, described the benefits derived by the chain drug stores from resale price maintenance in a memorandum to the Assistant Attorney General in charge of the Antitrust Division of the Department of Justice on February 10, 1941:

> Resale price maintenance has served the chains in two ways: First, it has relieved them from the competition of the pineboard independent and thus protected them from the newest and most effective channel through which fast-moving packaged drugs can reach the consumer at low prices. Second, it has enabled the chains to organize a low-price raid against any independent drug store without fear of retaliation. This second effect is due to the recognition which chains have established for their own private brands. With national brands of drug products price-controlled, the chain can collect substantial margins upon such products while reducing the price of its own private brands whenever it desires to use them as leaders or to make a raid upon the national brand business enjoyed by other stores. Since these other stores are bound not to cut prices upon the national brands and do not control private brands which have acquired prestige through extensive advertising, retaliation by the victims is not possible. Thus the most obvious effect of resale price maintenance upon the relations between chain and independent is to deprive the independent of a price-cutting weapon still available to the chain. The complacency with which chains have accepted the operation of the state laws is no doubt partially due to this fact.[7]

Despite (or perhaps because of) the protection afforded retail druggists through fair-trade legislation:

> The retail drug store has not kept pace with general business development. Although its sales volume increased 2 1/2 times between 1939 and 1949, it ended up by getting less of the consumer's dollar simply because sales through other outlets had expanded more rapidly than drug-store business. * * * The ⊥ retail druggist cannot allow himself to be fooled by today's high sales volume; the drug store has simply ridden the trend and, compared with other outlets, has not done a very good job at that.[8]

Principal beneficiary of the drug store's drop in its share of the consumer's dollar from almost 4 to less than 3 cents in the decade between 1939 and 1949 has been the grocery supermarket. The NARD Journal, on October 15, 1951, reported the extent to which grocery stores had invaded established lines handled by drug stores as follows:

> Non-food items traditionally sold by drug stores show a 59 percent penetration into grocery stores, according to a survey made by Selling Research, Inc., New York. Rating high on the list were sanitary napkins, now sold in 98 percent of grocery stores; shampoo, in 84 percent; tooth paste, 77 percent; shaving cream, 72 percent; and bandages, 70 percent. Geographically, the presence of drug items in grocery stores is most prevalent in the western portion of the country (p. 1646).

According to a recent survey conducted by the Progressive Grocer "eighty-five per cent of the nation's leading supermarkets and superettes now sell selected health and beauty aids, compared with only 37% 10 years ago."[9] By October of 1951 the last major grocery chain which had yet to promote the sale of drug items, the A. & P., had decided to enter the field by offering to it's [sic] customers tooth paste, first-aid items, shaving accessories, shampoos, and so forth. The following chart graphically shows this tremendous growth in the distribution of drug items by leading food stores during recent years:

---

[7] Cited in hearings, February 25, 1952.

[8] J. O. Peckham, vice president, A. C. Nielsen Co., Druggists Must Merchandise To Survive, NARD Journal, August 21, 1950, p. 1253.

[9] R. W. Mueller, managing editor, Food Stores Make Sensational Gains in Drug and Toiletry Sales, Progressive Grocer, February 1952, p. 50.

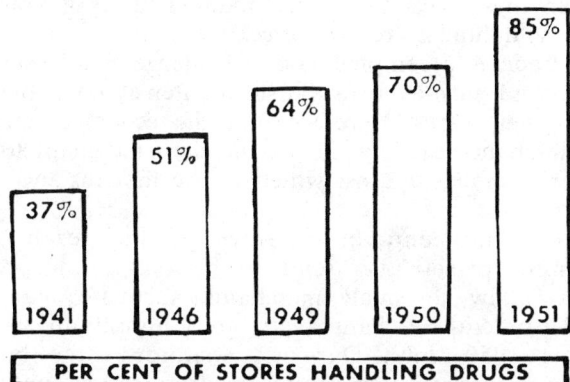

Source: Progressive Grocer, February 1952.

What has prompted this successful venture of the large supermarket into the retail trade of the retail druggist?

⊥ Main consideration—

says the NARD Journal in its August 6, 1951 editorial—

is the dynamics of competition which has forced the supermarkets to reduce margins on food items over the years and various lines with higher mark-ups were added to compensate for the lower returns from food items (p. 1154).

Lush margins on fair-trade items provide a windfall to the giant grocery mart whose profits on food items have, over the years, been reduced as a result of "the dynamics of competition." Thus, whereas a self-service drug department located in a high traffic location of a modern supermarket takes in about 2 percent of total store volume, "with 'drugs' yielding a margin of over 30% on sales, the line contributes 4% or more of store's total dollar margin."[10]

There can be little doubt that fair trade has been a boon to the supermarket in encroaching upon the retail market of his small drugstore competitor. When the Schwegmann case determined that nonsigners were no longer bound to adhere to minimum resale price schedules supermarkets showed little propensity toward reducing their large margins guaranteed by fair trade. As John W. McPherrin, former editor of the American Druggist, observed in the August 1951 issue of that periodical:

Incidentally, did you notice that very few supermarkets broke prices on drug products when fair trade was crippled. It is said that they don't want to lose the profit they are now making on drug products, and that unless they can continue to make at least 25 percent profit on drug items, they prefer to sell food items (p. 164).

Reasons prompting the large grocery chains to be ardent advocates of fair trade were succinctly stated in the February 1952 survey of drug item sales by major grocery outlets made by the Progressive Grocer. Many operators participating in the survey, Progressive Grocer noted, came out wholeheartedly in favor of fair-trade prices for these commodities, "The margins on drugs are extremely generous when compared to traditional grocery margins," it continued,

---

[10] Progressive Grocer, February 1952, p. 51.

and leading food merchants are anxious to maintain them, for they do not expect any let-up in price competition in the period ahead. To some extent drugs are compensating for the extremely low margins on many regular food products, and operators are not anxious to disturb fair-trade prices.[11]

It is evident from these facts that when manufacturers guarantee excessively high margins on articles sold under resale price maintenance arrangements, the small retailers['] stock and trade is preempted bodily by large retail establishments who find high profits on the rapid turn-over of fair-trade items more than compensating for reduced margins on other wares. Here we find the economic circumstances resulting from resale price maintenance causing the independent merchant to fall ready victim to those large and powerful outlets against which in the first instance fair-trade legislation was directed.

The paradox does not end here. Since, under resale price maintenance arrangements minimum prices also tend to be maximum prices as well, when manufacturers fail to allow to small merchants adequate mark-ups on price-fixed merchandise, the independent merchant again finds himself in sad competitive straits. Thus, on October 16, 1950, John Dargavel, writing in the NARD Journal about inadequate margins on certain items sold in drug stores, indicated the dangerous financial plight in which many small retailers currently found themselves:

The point I wish to make—

emphasized Dargavel—

is that the problem of margins is critical to the degree that it must be solved before thousands of independent druggists are pushed over the brink of bankruptcy (p. 1612).

Such was the distressed condition of the retail druggists over inadequate margins on some items during the year 1950 that one of the 1951 objectives of the National Association of Retail Druggists was—

To bring to the attention of the manufacturers that many mark-ups are inadequate for the reason they fail due to present economic conditions, to cover the costs of overhead and a reasonable profit.[12]

Margins on tobacco products during this period were characterized by certain druggists as "ridiculous," while one proprietor expressed the candid opinion that "the gross margins of the tobacco concerns are pins in the flesh of the retailers."[13] With regard to other drug store commodities, Aaron Lauter, a retail druggist in Delaware County, Pa., pointed out in August of 1950 that "many manufacturers have rigged their list prices so that when one sells at the stipulated minimum there is no profit."[14]

In view of this prevailing situation it is little wonder that the bewildered retailers began to suspect that fair trade had returned to plague them. A leading editorial in the NARD Journal of March 21, 1949, charged in bold-face headlines that manufacturers who had failed to raise margins for retail druggists were acting "like a pack of wolves."[15] The NARD subsequently bemoaned the many examples of inadequate mark-ups which could be cited to show "that the druggists have been made the goats of a cock-eyed situation which has been coupled to fair trade."[16]

The price squeeze imposed upon independent retailers by resale price maintenance agreements is not a phenomenon peculiar only to the retail drug trade. In the jewelry field, for example, the situation with regard to inadequate margins on silverware recently became so critical that it was necessary at the annual convention of the

---

[11] Id., pp. 55–56.
[12] NARD Journal, December 18, 1950, p. 1981.
[13] NARD Journal, June 20, 1949, p. 874.
[14] NARD Journal, August 7, 1950, p. 1162.
[15] NARD Journal, March 21, 1949, p. 413.
[16] NARD Journal, January 16, 1950, p. 82.

American National Retail Jewelers' Association in August of 1951 to adopt the following resolution:

> Whereas it has long been the practice for members of the Sterling Silversmiths' Guild and others to bill their sterling products at suggested retail prices with which practice the American National Retail Jewelers' Association agrees in principle, and
>
> * * * * * * *
>
> Whereas the retailers' net profits are now seriously menaced by ever-rising costs of operation, and
> Whereas the current margin is now insufficient to produce adequate net return on the sale of sterling silverware; now therefore be it
> *Resolved,* That we urge all sterling silver manufacturers to revise both the manufacturing and retail profit picture in the light of retail jewelers' current pressing needs . . . .[17]

Leo F. Henebry, president of the American National Retail Jewelers' Association, complained to the committee during the recent hearings on fair-trade legislation that "in most cases the fair-trade mark-up is inadequate rather than being more than adequate" referring, by way of illustration, to the fact that two of his three retail jewelry stores lost money in 1951 because of inadequate volume and "inadequate margin of profit on the volume we did do."[18] In the retail hardware trade, Rivers Peterson, managing director of the National Retail Hardware Association, confessed to the committee that, "We have lines in the hardware business that dealers have complained about for years, that their margin is too low."[19]

Indeed, we may well pity the poor retailer caught in the toils of fair trade. When the manufacturer fixes retail prices at levels permitting him choice margins, his principal competitors, the large supermarkets, stock well of his goods and make sharp inroads into his consumer traffic. When the manufacturer establishes low retail levels for fair-trade items or if margins fail to keep pace with rising costs and inflationary cycles, he becomes the unwitting victim of the fair-trade price squeeze. Should the manufacturer fortuitously choose the optimum price to alleviate both of the aforesaid conditions, price rigidity prohibits the retailer from meeting the price competition of private brands sold by large department stores and mail order outlets. In view of these facts, even the most ardent proponent of fair trade must confess that resale price maintenance legislation has not been altogether an unmixed blessing.

III. Resale Price Maintenance Fosters Violations of the Antitrust Laws

While section (f) of H. R. 6925 purports to prohibit horizontal agreements among retailers, among wholesalers, or among manufacturers under the act, this language is at best a piece of wishful thinking. By making resale price maintenance agreements applicable to nonsigners, there is no meaning whatever to this bit of legislative double talk. The Federal Trade Commission pointed out very clearly to the committee the effect which resale price maintenance would have upon the time-honored principle of antitrust policy condemning horizontal price-fixing agreements among competitors. Said the Commission:

> Moreover, when the nonsigner clause is added to resale price maintenance, the effect is the de facto nullification of our Federal laws against horizontal conspiracy, notwithstanding the fact that the proposed legislation expressly prohibits horizontal price fixing. Nothing is more clearly established in Federal policy than the principle that horizontal price fixing shall not be tolerated. The proposed legislation pays lip service to that principle, yet its effect would be that a minimum price fixed by contract with one retail distributor would become the minimum price for all other retail distributors of the manufacturer's product who were placed upon notice of the existence of the contract. The rigidity and uniformity of the price would be exactly that of the most rigid horizontal price fixing conspiracy; the level of the price would be likely to be at

---

[17] The Manufacturing Jeweler, September 6, 1951, p. 12.
[18] Hearings, February 15, 1952.
[19] Hearings, February 27, 1952.

least as high as in a horizontal conspiracy: and the public control over the reasonableness of the arrangement would be as nonexistent as in the case of a horizontal conspiracy.[20]

It is clear that insofar as economic effect is concerned, there exists no difference between a horizontal price-fixing arrangement among ⊥ competing retailers on the one hand, and a price agreement between one manufacturer and one retailer which is in turn binding on all competing retailers on the other. As a practical matter, expediency would dictate that conspiring retailers should hereafter achieve their illegal objectives through the now legalized device of having a manufacturer enter into a resale price maintenance agreement with a single retailer which would henceforth apply to the sales of all competitors. In this context, the prohibition against horizontal price conspiracy now becomes meaningless.

That this law will encourage violations of the antitrust laws on a wholesale basis is not just idle speculation on our part. Past experience under the Miller-Tydings law yields abundant evidence of resale price maintenance legislation serving as a cloak to conceal price fixing and other undesirable activities in restraint of trade.[3.27]

In 1942, the Colorado Wholesale Wine and Liquor Dealers Association[3.28] was indicted by the Department of Justice under section 1 of the Sherman Act for engaging in a conspiracy to fix retail prices of liquor sold in the State of Colorado. Retail prices, it was charged, were agreed upon, out of State producers were persuaded to enter into fair-trade contracts embodying agreed upon prices, and wholesalers and producers refusing to comply were boycotted. Pleas of nolo contendere were filed by the defendants and fines were imposed.

Similarly, the National Associaton of Retail Druggists,[3.29] today the loudest advocate of fair-trade legislation, was fined in 1947 on a plea of nolo contendere to an indictment charging them with having engaged in a conspiracy to fix the retail and wholesale prices of drug items, to eliminate price competition among retail druggists, and to restrain competition. This conspiracy was perpetrated despite the existence of a consent decree filed in 1907 perpetually enjoining the association from engaging in such activities as boycotts, etc. Methods employed by the NARD to achieve its illegal objectives were summarized for the committee by the Assistant Attorney General in charge of the Antitrust Division, Department of Justice, as follows:

> They threatened to refuse to handle, or to boycott, or to urge their customers and prescribing physicians to accept substitutes for drug-store items, where margins of profits had not been approved, and refused to carry in stock, boycotted, and urged their customers to accept substitutes for such drug-store items; agreed to sell drug-store items whose retail prices had been established by producers at prices not below those so established and sold said drug-store items at prices not below those so established; persuaded, induced, and compelled producers of drug-store items to establish wholesale prices in relation to the retail prices demanded by defendants; threatened producers with lack of cooperation in the sale of drug-store items on which the wholesale prices were not established at levels bearing the relation to retail prices demanded by defendants and refused to cooperate in the sale of such drug-store items.[21]

---

[20] Hearings, February 14, 1952.
[21] Hearings, February 13, 1952.

[3.27] Most of the data in the following eight footnotes (notes 3.28–.35) was obtained from the CCH Antitrust "Blue Book." *See* CCH, THE FEDERAL ANTITRUST LAWS, WITH SUMMARY OF CASES INSTITUTED BY THE UNITED STATES 1890–1951 (1952).

[3.28] United States v. Colorado Wholesale Wine & Liquor Dealers Ass'n, Crim. No. 9514 (D. Colo., indictment returned March 12, 1942). Pleas of nolo contendere were accepted and fines were imposed. *See also* United States v. Colorado Wholesale Wine & Liquor Dealers Ass'n, 47 F. Supp. 160 (D. Colo. 1942), *rev'd sub nom.* Frankfort Distilleries, Inc. v. United States, 144 F.2d 824 (10th Cir. 1944) (*en banc*), *rev'd,* 324 U.S. 293 (1945) (affirming district court's denial of defendants' motions to quash the indictment).

[3.29] United States v. National Ass'n of Retail Druggists, Crim. No. 683-C (D.N.J., indictment returned March 26, 1942). Pleas of nolo contendere were accepted and fines were imposed on January 29, 1947.

The National Wholesale Druggists' Association[3.30] was also indicted under the Sherman Act for conspiring to raise, fix, and stabilize wholesale selling prices of drug items. Alleged devices utilized to further the objectives of the conspiracy included lack of cooperation with recalcitrant manufacturers, boycotts, and refusals to sell from or carry in stock. Again, nolo contendere pleas were filed and fines levied.

In the *United States* v. *New York State Pharmaceutical Association*,[3.31] the National Association of Retail Druggists was again indicted, this time in conjunction with the New York State Pharmaceutical Association and others, for fixing, stabilizing, and maintaining the retail and wholesale prices of drug-store items through the adoption of uniform prices and methods of sale, interchange of information, boycotts, and blacklists. Pleas of nolo contendere and fines also ended this litigation.

Proceedings involving the abuse of resale price maintenance legislation are extensive. The Department of Justice has brought cases of a similar nature against the Tri-State Record Dealers Association,[3.32] the Record Dealers Association,[3.33] and has currently pending cases against the Allegheny County Retail Druggists' Association[3.34] and the Sunbeam Corp.[3.35] Proceedings instituted by the Federal Trade Commission where resale price maintenance was an important factor include:

Docket No. 4526: Law Book Publishers Co.[3.36]
Docket No. 4900: Refractories case[3.37]
Docket No. 5448: Rubber manufacturers group[3.38]
Docket No. 5734 [*sic*]: Mid-Atlantic Distributors Corp. (which just recently has been appealed to the United States Court of Appeals for the District of Columbia Circuit)[3.39]
Docket No. 5635: Cycle jobbers[3.40]
Docket No. 5636: American Dental Association[3.41]
Docket No. 4093: Wholesale Liquor Distributors Association of Northern California et al.[3.42]
Docket No. 4132: Western Confectioners Association[3.43]

[3.30] United States v. National Wholesale Druggists' Ass'n, Crim. No. 618-C (D.N.J., indictment returned Feb. 6, 1942). Pleas of nolo contendere were accepted and fines were imposed on January 4, 1946. *See also* United States v. National Wholesale Druggists' Ass'n, 61 F. Supp. 590 (D.N.J. 1945) (denying defendant McKesson & Robbins' motion to quash indictment and to inspect grand jury minutes).

[3.31] United States v. New York State Pharmaceutical Ass'n, Crim. No. 114-75 (S.D.N.Y., indictment returned March 4, 1943). Pleas of nolo contendere were accepted and fines were imposed on January 28, 1947.

[3.32] United States v. Tri-State Retail Record Dealers Ass'n, Crim. No. 13008 (W.D. Pa., indictment returned Nov. 11, 1949). Pleas of nolo contendere were accepted and fines were imposed on January 18, 1950.

[3.33] United States v. Record Dealers Ass'n, Crim. No. 15755 (E.D. Pa., indictment returned June 2, 1950). Pleas of nolo contendere were accepted and fines were imposed on March 19 and June 21, 1951.

[3.34] United States v. Allegheny County Retail Druggists' Ass'n, Crim. No. 13470 (W.D. Pa., indictment returned Oct. 22, 1951). Pleas of nolo contendere were accepted and fines were imposed on October 8, 1953. *See also* United States v. Allegheny County Retail Druggists' Ass'n, 12 F.R.D. 249 (W.D. Pa. 1952) (granting defendants' motion for a bill of particulars).

[3.35] United States v. Sunbeam Corp., Civil No. 52-C-479 (N.D. Ill., complaint filed Feb. 28, 1952). On December 11, 1953, the complaint was dismissed without prejudice by stipulation of the parties. *See* note 3.58 *infra* and accompanying text.

[3.36] American Ass'n of Law Book Publishers, 39 F.T.C. 101 (1944), *modified sub nom.* Callaghan & Co. v. FTC, 163 F.2d 359 (2d Cir. 1947).

[3.37] American Refractories Institute, 44 F.T.C. 773 (1948).

[3.38] Rubber Mfrs. Ass'n, 44 F.T.C. 453 (1948).

[3.39] Middle Atlantic Distribs., Inc., 48 F.T.C. 511 (1951), *petition for review dismissed,* (D.C. Cir. May 2, 1952). The correct docket number in this case is 5634.

[3.40] Cycle Jobbers Ass'n of America, 47 F.T.C. 930 (1951).

[3.41] American Dental Trade Ass'n, 46 F.T.C. 482 (1950).

[3.42] Wholesale Liquor Distribs. Ass'n, 31 F.T.C. 1453 (1940), *petition for review dismissed,* 121 F.2d 455 (9th Cir. 1941).

[3.43] Western Confectioners Ass'n, 34 F.T.C. 1431 (1942).

Docket No. 4168: National Retail Liquor Package Stores Association[3.44]

The success of the antitrust agencies in the above litigation belies the serious competitive problems raised by the exemption of resale price maintenance programs from the antitrust laws. The Department of Justice was quoted in 1945 as having said that—

> if its Antitrust Division had sufficient men and money to examine every resale price maintenance contract written under State and Federal legislation, and to proceed in every case in which the arrangement goes beyond the authorization of the Tydings-Miller amendment, there would be practically no resale price maintenance contracts * * *.[22]

The Assistant Attorney General in charge of the Antitrust Division, Mr. Morison, confirmed this view as of the present by averring that from the experience of the Antitrust Division the vast majority of resale price maintenance contracts, if examined fully, would be found in violation of the antitrust laws.[23] A study of how resale price maintenance has operated in practice goes far to reinforce Mr. Morison's conclusion.

To begin with, many manufacturers who fair trade their products have done so with extreme reluctance and only upon the persistent and heated insistence of retailers. As the NARD Journal quoted a prominent observer in commenting upon the attitude of manufacturers toward fair trade:

> There are two classes of manufacturers with products under fair trade. One believes in the system and the other plays along with it in a way that gives only lip service to fair trade.[24]

How manufacturers unwilling to fair trade their products have been convinced of the desirability of entering into resale price maintenance contracts is well illustrated by the case of Pepsodent. The method by which the manufacturer of this product was persuaded to return to the folds of fair trade was eloquently described by the executive secretary of the Northern California Retail Druggists Association at the thirty-seventh annual convention of the National Association of Retail Druggists in September 1935 as follows:

> Mr. Chairman, fellow druggists, the Pepsodent Co. was operating in the State of California under the California Fair Trade Act. In all the time that they were operating under the Fair Trade Act they made no attempt to enforce their contract and like a bolt of lightning from the blue sky, they informed us that the California fair-trade contract was canceled, and the general sales manager, Mr. Kermott, came out to California, called upon me in the California office to make excuses and he had with him one of the California salesmen. I expressed my heartfelt sympathy to the two young men who were in my office because I told them they would have the toughest time any salesmen had had in any territory. We passed a resolution at our meeting and we published that resolution in our journal, and we sent that resolution to every member in California in which we urged and advised them to discontinue the sale of any product that had canceled their fair-trade contract. Brothers, it was a slap in the face of our Fair Trade Act. It makes no difference what firm it was. It was unwarranted. It was the first cancellation. And to my great delight and the great delight of our executive committee all the druggists in California refused to sell Pepsodent toothpaste or Pepsodent products. They put them in the basement. Some were enthusiastic enough to throw them into the ashcan. I wouldn't bring this out except that I want you to really understand how the sales of Pepsodent products in all of California dropped off.[25]

The lesson taught by the druggists to the Pepsodent Co. were [sic] readily employed to convince other producers that adoption of resale price maintenance agreements with retailers would be to their decided advantage. Said one manufacturer with regard to the compelling reasons prompting him to adopt said resale price maintenance on his products:

---

[22] Federal Trade Commission, Report on Resale Price Maintenance (1945), p. LXI.

[23] Hearings, February 13, 1952.

[24] NARD Journal, July 2, 1951, p. 1046.

[25] Cited in Federal Trade Commission Report on Resale Price Maintenance (1945), p. 143.

[3.44] National Retail Liquor Package Stores Ass'n, 43 F.T.C. 379 (1947).

The retail outlets, particularly the independent retail druggists, through their State associations and many of them individually, pressed us to establish minimum retail prices for our products from the time the respective States enacted so-called fair-trade laws. Pressure similarly was put on us by drug wholesalers and their associations."[26]

Reported another maker of articles sold through retail drug outlets:

The retail price maintenance contracts we have made were made and any wholesale "price maintenance contracts, agreements, or arrangements," if any, which we may make in the future will be to enable us to get wholesalers' and retailers' cooperation and to cause wholesalers and retailers to discontinue discriminating against us in favor of our competitors who have either voluntarily or at the insistence of wholesalers and retailers, already entered into resale price maintenance contracts, agreements, or arrangements.[27]

John Dargavel, executive secretary of the NARD, writing to the sales company of a manufacturer of toilet preparations on February 10, 1936, in an effort to influence its selling policies, referred in a veiled manner—

to the Pepsodent Co. and some others in regard to what concerted action by the druggists of this country did to their volume—

and threatened that—

if we start a campaign through our journal, carrying it through the officers of each State and local association in this country, you are going to find that it will cause you more trouble and take away more business from you than you had ever realized.[28]

Dr. Corwin Edwards, then economic consultant to the Department of Justice, summed up many of the boycotting activities which had at that time occurred under resale price maintenance legislation in a special memorandum written to the Assistant Attorney General in charge of the Antitrust Division on February 10, 1941.[29] Stated Edwards:

Meanwhile, every effort was made to throttle public discussion and to intimidate business opposition. In California an aspirin manufacturer was forced by boycott to issue resale price contracts against his will. The druggists' intention to coerce was indicated in the following language: "This aspirin is a sort of Napoleon in the patent-medicine army, but then even the great Frenchman met his Waterloo when the rest of Europe got together, decided that they had enough of him, and cooperated against him." In the same State the manufacturers of Pepsodent toothpaste, who had experimented with resale price contracts under the California law, decided to withdraw these contracts, apparently under advice of counsel who believed that the contracts violated the antitrust laws. Thereupon the druggists organized a campaign to put Pepsodent under the counter and to switch customers to other brands. This campaign was so effective that the offending company made public apology at a subsequent convention of the National Association of Retail Druggists and, as a token of its contrition, subscribed $25,000 to a fund to lobby for resale price maintenance in other States. On one occasion an expression of opposition to resale price maintenance by the New York Times and the New York World-Telegram led to an effort by organized druggists to demoralize the dealers who distributed these papers, by selling them at less than 3 cents. On another occasion Harper's magazine carried an article against resale price maintenance and thereupon received a letter from a druggists' association in a mid-western city, demanding information as to whether Harper's endorsed the views expressed in the article and indicating that if these views were not repudiated they intended to sell Harper's at a substantial discount, presumably in an effort to create trouble among its distributors. Within the last 2 months the newspaper PM in New York has carried a series of articles against resale price maintenance, and the same tactics of intimidation have been attempted by the sale of PM at less than its customary price. The editors, having more sense of humor than some of the other victims of this policy, ran a photograph of a cut-rate advertisement in a store and gave it the caption "the best bargain in the city."[30]

---

[26] Id., p. 167.

[27] Ibid.

[28] Id., p. 166.

[29] TNEC, Final Report and Recommendations, 77th Cong., 1st sess. (1941), exhibit No. 2793, p. 233.

[30] Cf. Business Week, March 3, 1952: "Fair trade war * * * Has Been Declared by Druggists on St. Louis Post-Dispatch. Paper's Anti-Fair-Trade Cartoon Started It. Fair-trading druggists in St. Louis are

In referring to these examples of organized boycotts on the part of retailers in an effort to coerce manufacturers into adopting resale price maintenance programs, we are by no means rattling ancient skeletons. As recently as April 17, 1950, the NARD Journal printed a letter to Seeman Bros., Inc., from a wholesaler under the headline: "Airwick Goes Off Fair Trade; Wholesaler Criticizes Move." In a prior issue, the NARD had observed in an editorial that a prominent manufacturer—without mentioning names—had dropped a popular product from fair trade and warned ominously that "The manufacturer knows the outcome of the action it took * * *."[31] In any event, by 1951, Airwick, according to the Drug Topics Red Book (1951-52 edition) was again being fair traded at 59 cents for the 5 1/2-ounce bottle and $1.29 for the 15-ounce bottle. Inquiries by the committee addressed to Seeman Bros., Inc., as to reasons prompting return of Airwick to fair-trade contracts evinced absolutely no response.

The case of the Luce magazines is even more flagrant. Claiming that Time and Fortune had proven, through their editorial policies, to be enemies of fair trade, the NARD Journal, in a recent message from its executive secretary, proclaimed in banner headlines: "Luce ⊥ magazines your enemies!" Thereupon denouncing these publications for various activities, the NARD sounded the following clarion call for manufacturers and retailers to boycott:

> How long do you druggists intend to continue to serve as peddlers of periodicals you know to be subversive to your individual and collective welfare and also to the consumers? How long will it be before manufacturers in the drug field cease to go along with magazines out to bring destruction to fair trade?[32]

Boycotting activities have by no means been confined to the National Association of Retail Druggists. The following invitation to boycott recently appeared in a leaflet published by a prominent wholesaler of drug products and distributed to retailers under the heading: "What Should Believers in Fair-Trade Laws Do Now?"

> Retailers should refuse to patronize wholesalers or other suppliers who are not in sympathy with the fair-trade laws. (An example would be a wholesaler who refused to sign a manufacturer's wholesale fair-trade contract and then offers you a cut price or greater discount than allowed under the fair-trade contract.) If you patronized such a wholesaler you would be an enemy of fair trade.

Whereas boycotts are freely employed against those who do not follow the fair-trade line, cooperation is openly extended by retailers to manufacturers who yield to their demands. Thus Cosmopolitan magazine, which has published in its pages glowing articles in favor of fair trade, received an enviable reception in the N. A. R. D. Journal compared to that accorded the much-maligned Luce publications. Urged the NARD Journal of its subscribers in the December 3, 1951, issue:

> Many of you druggists continue to overlook the valuable services of Cosmopolitan magazine to the drug stores of America. Hence you fail to give the magazine the sales push it is entitled to receive (p. 1906).

In the January 3, 1949, issue of the NARD Journal, retail druggists were encouraged to acknowledge in some tangible manner the cooperative attitude which certain manufacturers had shown druggists on numerous occasions. The Journal stated:

> The third of the facts is that it is important for you to recognize your friends among the manufacturers. You know you can count on many of them through thick and thin. They have proved it to you on numerous occasions. You called for larger discounts to cover increases of

---

cutting prices—on the Post-Dispatch, a leading anti-trade newspaper * * *. Suddenly, placards appeared in drugstore windows all over St. Louis, announcing that the Post could be had for 4 cents daily and 13 cents on Sunday (it normally sells for 5 cents daily, 15 cents on Sunday)."

[31] NARD Journal, March 20, 1950, p. 426.

[32] NARD Journal, February 7, 1949, p. 177.

overhead costs that inflation brought, and a large number of your friends among the manufacturers gave them to you with the spirit of cooperation. You always find the policies they adopt are favorable to you. They are regular advertisers in your magazine—the NARD Journal—and they are also otherwise stanch supporters of the National Association of Retail Druggists (p. 17).

Retailers in the jewelry field adopted a resolution at the annual convention of the American National Retail Jewelers Association in August of 1951 stating their determination to cooperate with manufacturers selling under resale price maintenance agreements. This resolution read in part:

> By all means that are legally open to us, we will continue to encourage our members to cooperate with those manufacturers who evidence a sincere desire and a firm determination to maintain their fair-traded prices.[33]

In response to questioning by counsel at the committee's recent hearings on fair-trade legislation, Mr. Henebry, president of the association, admitted that it would be natural for retail jewelers to cooperate with manufacturers who fair traded their merchandise and that this was the prevailing attitude of members prior to the Schwegmann decision as well as the probable situation that would exist if pending fair-trade legislation were enacted. Mr. Henebry denied, however, that this cooperation would take the form of concerted action.[34]

Manufacturers have not been the only victims of collective action on the part of retailers in seeking to obtain fair trade by coercion. Drug Topics, a trade publication in the drug field, pointed out in an editorial in its July 30, 1951, issue how boycotting of recalcitrant retailers would be "helpful action" in preserving fair-trade prices. Said this journal:

> If all wholesalers, acting in their individual capacities, would refuse to sell outlets which did not maintain fair-trade prices, the outlook would become much more promising. * * *
>
> Once a price violator is denied goods, or is cut off for his refusal to comply with the invoice notice, he is likely to reshape his selling operations so as to comply with fair-trade principles (p. 38).

How secretaries of state and local associations of druggists could assist in maintaining prices by "persuading" retailers to refrain from cutting prices on fair-traded articles was described in the NARD Journal of July 2, 1951:

> The secretaries of state and also the local associations of druggists can do much to help prevent extension of price wars—

it advised.

> Many owners of drug stores have been persuaded to refrain from copycat slashes of fair-trade minimums a la Macy's Department Store in New York City. One of them was induced to be sensible after he had made a kick-off through the newspapers of the community (p. 1032).

As Mr. Morison, Assistant Attorney General in charge of the Antitrust Division of the Department of Justice, explained to the committee when his attention was called to this action, "It indicates the beginning of a violation of the Sherman Act."[35]

Efforts to restrain the pricing policies of competing retail outlets received the personal endorsement of John Dargavel, executive secretary of the NARD, in his message printed in the NARD Journal of April 18, 1949. Describing a fringe of druggists who were cutting prices as "wreckers of fair trade," Dargavel informed readers that "Violations stimulate agitation against the system of stabilized prices and out of it may come a Nation-wide movement of consumers to bring about the end of fair trade." Worried lest this disaster occur, he proclaimed openly that "The chiselers and cheaters among the druggists must be made to see the light" (p. 589).

---

[33] Cited in hearings, February 15, 1952.
[34] Hearings, February 15, 1952.
[35] Hearings, February 13, 1952.

As we have indicated before,[36] resale price maintenance frequently puts the independent retailer in competitive jeopardy because of inadequate margins established by manufacturers. Unable to cope independently with this problem vis-à-vis the powerful producer, the small merchant often finds himself acting in collusion with his competitors in an effort to obtain an adequate profit on fair-traded items. Thus in October of 1950, it became necessary for the executive committee of the National Association of Retail Druggists to take under consideration the narrow margins allowed by certain companies because of the major slash in profits suffered by independent druggists during the prior year. It was the consensus of the executive committee that "the desperate situation must have immediate correction to eliminate the economic injustice of the lopsided discounts."[37]

In the January 17, 1949, issue of the NARD Journal, John Dargavel, executive secretary of the National Association of Retail Druggists, deplored the fact that minimum resale prices on many items had been too low:

> I don't like to use bad language in my editorials—

apologized Dargavel—

> but there is only one name for prices of that kind—the word starts with "b" and ends with "d" (you know what illegitimate children are called)—and that is the kind of pricing that some of the manufacturers in the drug field are trying to put across (p. 101).

In a subsequent issue of the journal, Dargavel warned manufacturers that it was ridiculous to believe that the products they produced were immune from negative sales activities in the drug store and issued the following caveat:

> Loaded quantity discounts create resentment . . . and retaliation . . . to make them hazardous . . . unwise . . . stupid . . . and justification for them is nil . . . zero.[38]

Because of the serious problems posed for the druggists by inadequate margins, the association's activities were not limited solely to exhortations in the journal. John Dargavel confessed that:

> On numerous occasions in the past 5 years, I called on the manufacturers to increase markups to enable the druggists to cope with the spiral of overhead costs, and the arguments I submitted were based on the obvious situation. Quite a number of the companies responded with revised gross margins. Many more replied with arrogant silence or they insisted it was unwise to increase prices for the reason that it would antagonize the consumers.[39]

Herbert Levy, one time counsel for the NARD and coauthor with the late chairman of the board of the Sterling Drug Co., of the original Miller-Tydings amendment, pointed out to the committee the seriousness of the activities outlined by Mr. Dargavel above. Advised Levy:

> If he made that statement, it was an improper statement, and if he did what he said he did, I think he is subject to another prosecution under the Sherman Act, because the Miller-Tydings Act very clearly provides that horizontal agreements are in violation of the law.[40]

We have in this section taken considerable pains in describing in detail how resale-price maintenance operates in actual practice. Boycotts, threats, and coercion on either the manufacturing, retail, or wholesale level are frequent occurrences. Favoritism, discrimination, and collusion, common vices. These practices will persist no matter how carefully the legislation passed by Congress may be couched in terms of safeguards and protections. Unless we are prepared to grant huge appropriations to the Antitrust Division of the Department of Justice and place every resale-price-maintenance agreement made in the United States under constant surveillance, resale-price-maintenance legislation will provide a hotbed for recurring violations of our antitrust laws.

---

[36] Supra, p. 29, ff.
[37] NARD Journal, October 16, 1950, p. 1579.
[38] NARD Journal, October 16, 1950, p. 1613.
[39] NARD Journal, February 19, 1951, p. 292.
[40] Hearings, February 15, 1952.

⊥ By its very nature, resale-price maintenance cannot function effectively without collective action among competitors. In this opinion we are joined not only by the antitrust enforcing agencies but also by those whose views are sympathetically directed toward fair trade. A survey article appearing in a recent trade journal succinctly summarized this general opinion of fair-trade proponents as follows:

> even dealers most vigorous in their defense of fair trade are agreed that it will not accomplish anything unless there is *wide and steadfast cooperation between retailers and between retailers and manufacturers.* [Italics added.][41]

IV. Fair Trade Unfair to the Consumer

While there is no evidence showing that fair trade has assisted small retailers to a greater extent than it has injured them, one fact does remain crystal clear: Under resale price maintenance, it is the consumer who ultimately suffers.

Many studies have been published by advocates of resale price maintenance in an effort to rebut this conclusion, the most recent of these being a survey by the drug firm of McKesson & Robbins, Inc., purporting to show that fair-trade prices in drug items had risen only slightly between January 1, 1947, and December 1, 1950, compared to the rise in the cost of living reflected by the prices of other articles. "There would be no need whatsoever for Government price controls of any kind in the United States in the immediate future," smugly concluded the Bureau of Education on Fair Trade after the results of this study had been announced, "if the price behavior of all items in our economy since 1947 had been comparable to the price behavior of fair-traded products, and particularly fair-traded drug products."

The defects in this eloquent statistical defense are many, the principal one being that it compares wholesale price levels in fair traded drug products with the general retail price index reflecting the over-all cost of living.

It should be noted that the starting point for the McKesson & Robbins survey was January 1947 when the wholesale drug index had reached its highest point in more than 20 years, 181.7. At the same time the wholesale index of other commodities lagged far behind at 141.5.

Since by December of 1950 the wholesale drug index was practically equivalent to the index for all other commodities (175.1 to 175.3), it is obvious that statistics for the interim period only reflect the adjustment of other commodities in keeping pace with the previous sharp rise in the wholesale drug index. The only conclusion that may be legitimately drawn from these figures is that in the long run period, the wholesale prices of drug products have increased to exactly the same extent as have the wholesale prices for other commodities.

That manufacturers of fair-traded drug products have done exceptionally well insofar as net profits are concerned during the period of fair trade would lead one to conclude that no matter how retail prices of fair-traded drug commodities have increased or decreased compared to those of different products, resale prices have been fixed ⊥ so high in the first instance as to insure a remarkably profitable rate of return. According to the National Association of Retail Druggists:

> The manufacturers in the drug field made much more money in the last 5 years than they ever had before, and the reports show that in 1949 the profits they took were about 13 percent over 1948 or better than 15 percent over and above the average for 565 corporations . . . the profits of the manufacturers in 1948 were the highest in the history of the country . . . 70 percent over the peak of 1946.[42]

As shown in the table below profits of Abbott Laboratories increased more than fivefold between 1939 and 1950; profits of American Home Products increased more than two and a half times between 1939 and 1950; profits of Merck & Co. increased almost six times between 1939 and 1951; profits of Parke, Davis & Co. more than doubled between 1939 and 1951; while prices of other large concerns have increased proportionately.

---

[41] The Sporting Goods Dealer, November 1949, p. 49.
[42] NARD Journal, October 16, 1950, p. 1612.

Net income, actual and as percent of net worth, of 7 large drug-manufacturing companies, 1939–51

[Years ending Dec. 31]

Year	Abbott Laboratories Actual	As percent of net worth	American Home Products Corp. Actual	As percent of net worth	Merck & Co., Inc. Actual	As percent of net worth	Parke, Davis & Co. Actual	As percent of net worth
1939	$2,048,094	14.1	$4,205,611	50.7	[1] $2,356,830	25.1	$9,254,202	24.2
1946	10,820,623	28.3	8,897,921	15.9	[2] 6,169,791	17.7	13,336,582	33.8
1948	11,120,983	23.6	9,107,168	16.8	[3] 8,520,250	19.9	9,704,467	19.4
1949	10,010,500	19.8	10,673,161	18.3	6,921,927	13.1	12,411,570	22.3
1950	10,880,301	20.0	11,844,030	18.9	[4] 11,276,604	19.2	17,864,830	27.7
1951	([5])	([5])	11,565,373	([5])	[4] 12,508,774	13.9	19,053,742	([5])

Years	Sharp & Dohme, Inc. Actual	As percent of net worth	E. R. Squibb & Sons[6] Actual	As percent of net worth	Sterling Drug, Inc. Actual	As percent of net worth
1939	$902,271	8.9	[7] $2,060,978	12.5	$9,140,026	23.4
1946	3,048,186	21.0	[8] 5,063,994	15.2	13,939,073	21.1
1948	3,910,872	19.9	[8] 3,691,778	8.3	12,721,610	17.6
1949	4,759,641	17.5	[8] 6,883,927	13.6	13,006,961	18.1
1950	5,275,858	17.4	[8] 8,057,980	13.9	13,481,870	18.5
1951	4,556,854	([5])	[8] 9,704,801	12.2	([5])	([5])

[1] Before provision for contingencies of $500,000.
[2] Before provision for contingencies of $123,583.
[3] Before provision for contingencies of $30,904.
[4] Includes domestic subsidiaries only.
[5] Not available.
[6] Years ending June 30, except for 1939 which ends Dec. 31.
[7] Excludes European subsidiaries.
[8] Excludes Argentina's subsidiary.

Source: Moody's Industrial Securities, Moody's Investors Service; Standard Corporation Records. Standard & Poor's Corp. prepared by Hamilton D. Gewehr, analyst in industrial organization and corporation finance, Economics Section, Legislative Reference Service, Library of Congress, Mar. 7, 1952.

So profitable have been drug field items for manufacturers that in 1949 drug field profits rose 0.7 percent over the year before despite a 2.5 percent drop in sales figures, according to Drug Trade News' annual analysis of year-end financial statements of 111 manufacturing firms and drug store chains.[43] By 1950—

Earnings after taxes were 22.0 percent greater * * * than in 1949 for 114 companies in the drug and allied industries covered by Drug Trade News' * * * annual analysis of year-end financial statements.[44]

Resale price maintenance has often guaranteed equally high returns for wholesalers and retailers. On insulin, for example, "The price set by Eli Lilly & Co. * * * guarantees the retailer a 50 percent gross profit on cost and 25 percent profit on cost to the wholesaler," Samuel Rosenthal, owner of retail drug outlets in the District of Columbia, told the committee.[45] A hasty glance at the advertisements appearing in any random issue of a trade publication such as the American Druggist reveals retail profits on fair-trade items such as the following:[46]

Dolcin, 44.3 percent profit.
Argyrol, up to 57 1/2 percent profit.
Kessling fever thermometers, 45-percent profit.
Wyanoids, up to 50-percent profit.

[43] Drug Trade News, June 12, 1950, p. 2.
[44] Drug Trade News, June 11, 1951, p. 2.
[45] Hearings, February 25, 1952.
[46] All profits as claimed by manufacturers in American Druggist, January 1, 1951.

Ampho-Jel, up to 53.4-percent profit.
Dichloricide moth crystals, up to 42-percent profit.
Breck, 40-percent profit.
McKesson & Robbins: "You get an average of 50-percent profit."

How high fair-trade profit margins adversely affect the consumer is illustrated by a study of 208 major items in which selling prices in the 45 fair-trade States is compared to prices at which such commodities can be purchased in the non-fair-trading areas of Texas, Missouri, Vermont, and the District of Columbia.[47] The composite selling price for all of these products in fair-trade States totaled $945.10 compared to only $740.86 in the non-fair-trade jurisdictions. Profits for the retailer in fair-trade States was 38.5 percent while in non-fair-trade areas it was only 21.5 percent, a saving to the consumer in non-fair-trade locations of 17 percent.

A survey appearing in the St. Louis Star-Times on April 19, 1951, also discloses how consumers pay more for liquor products which are sold under resale price maintenance agreements in the State of Illinois than they do across the border in non-fair-trade Missouri. Prices for 35 different fifths of nationally advertised liquors cost only $139.67 in St. Louis while consumers paid $22.25 more, or $161.92, in Illinois, a difference of 15.9 percent.

Similarly, the subsequent table comparing prices of important products sold on a fair trade basis in drug stores in 45 States with prices for the same items presently prevailing in the District of Columbia is another graphic illustration of why the consumer is heavily penalized by resale price maintenance legislation.

	Fair trade price	District of Columbia price		Fair trade price	District of Columbia price
Aspirin:			Liquid shampoo — Con.		
100 Bayer	$0.59	$0.46	Kreml	$0.59	$0.47
100 Squibb	.54	.47	Laco	.43	.39
100 St. Joseph	.49	.43	Conte Castille	.49	.33
100 APC Co.	.39	—	Packers	.48	.43
Toothpaste:			Watkins Coconut	.48	.39
Colgate	.47	.33	Richard Hudnut	1.00	.79
Ipana	.47	.33	Wildroot	.48	.44
Pepsodent	.47	.39	Woodbury's	.43	.29
Phillips	.39	.27	Halo	.57	.43
Squibb	.47	.39	Fitch	.59	.47
Lyons	.47	.33	Deodorants:		
Ammident	.53	.47	Veto	.59	.53
Clordent	.69	.53	Arrid	.63	.47
Afco	.47	.39	Fresh	.59	.43
Pebammo	.49	.39	Sanite	.39	.38
Shaving cream:			Chad	.43	.39
Colgate	.53	.47	Coty	1.00	—
Barbasol	.39	.33	Hush	.49	.43
Palmolive	.53	.41	Mum	.59	.39
Burmashave	.40	.33	Odorono	.48	.37
Mollé	.43	.37	Barz	.39	.33
Noxzema	.59	.47	Five-day pads	.59	.47
Mennen	.53	.43	Ydoro	.59	.43
Gillette	.43	.37	Zipp	.50	.47
Williams	.47	.37	Stoppette	.60	.47
Hair tonics:			Dyrad	.49	.37
Wildroot	.48	.43	Mennens	.59	.41
Kreml	.57	.43	Amolin	.59	.47
Vitalis	.49	.33	Heed	.59	.47
Vaseline	.47	.39	Hand lotions:		
Jeris	.49	.39	Hinds	.49	.39
Lucky Tiger	.48	.39	Italian Balm	.45	.37
Liquid shampoo:			Cashmere Bouquet	.43	.37
Admiration	.49	.43	Frostilla	.47	.43
Breck	.60	.53	Jergens Lotion	.49	.31
Wonder	.48	—	Trushay	.49	.33
Drene	.57	.47	Pacquin	.49	.39

Source: Standard Drug Co., Washington, D. C.

---

[47] See hearings.

With the benefits resulting to the consumer in such non-fair-trade areas as the District of Columbia being so obvious, one can well sympathize with the reluctance of the American Fair Trade Council, sponsors of the Keogh bill, to urge a national Fair Trade Act. Such a bill, which would impose fair trade upon all non-fair-trade areas throughout the Nation "would perhaps be opposed by many who, in the District of Columbia, enjoy cheap liquor and other special privileges," warned John W. Anderson, president of the council in a release to members on December 7, 1951.[48]

Resale price maintenance also injures the consumer by prohibiting retailers from passing on savings achieved by virtue of economies, efficiency, location, services, etc., to the purchaser through lower prices. To illustrate this statement with a concrete example, the committee was informed that Solari, New Orleans' finest store, offers central location in the high-rent district, telephone service, fast delivery, air conditioning, extended credit, experienced personnel, and frequent advertising, while Schwegmann's supermarket, located 8 miles from the center of New Orleans in the low-rent district, does not furnish to its customers telephone service, delivery, credit, or air conditioning. At the same time, Schwegmann, under resale price maintenance, is forced to maintain mark-ups more appropriate for the luxury mart. As Gus Blancand, Louisiana wholesaler and importer of fine wines indicated to the committee in adverting to these very facts:

> Under the principles of fair trade, Solari can offer all the service inducements without penalty.
>
> Yet the consumer who chooses to drive 8 miles to get his goods, waits on himself, pays cash, delivers the goods and inspects them. He, the consumer, is denied the privileges of obtaining any of the economies which Schwegmann has made. Because two people whom he doesn't know made a price contract, both of these stores must charge the same price or be subjected to lawsuit with penalties.[49]

Julius Westheimer, president of Julius Gutman & Co., a Baltimore retail store with "no fancy frills, no thick carpets, no maze of offices or battery of secretaries, no luxurious extras or extravagant service," also told how fair trade legislation prohibited him from passing on legitimate price savings to the consumer. Said Westheimer:

> We sell the 63-cent tube of Colgate toothpaste for 51 cents, 49-cent can of Johnson baby powder for 44 cents, 28-cent box of Kleenex for 23 cents, $77.50 Community silver-plate set for $49.50, $39.95 GE electric mixer for $29.95, $1.65 Belle Sharmeer nylons for $1.39, $100 Benrus Elegance watch for $75, $29.95 Dulane Fryryte for $19.95, $3.75 Curity diapers for $2.99.[50]

These savings to the consumer, he proceeded to explain, would have to be eliminated, if Congress passed pending resale price maintenance legislation despite the fact that the question of loss leader selling was in no way involved and that—

> our profit margin on many of these items, at the low prices referred to above, is greater than on many of our non-price-fixed merchandise.[51]

V. NECESSITY FOR RESALE PRICE MAINTENANCE NOT DEMONSTRATED

While certain competitive pricing practices, occuring in both fair-trade and non-fair-trade areas, have occasioned considerable concern—and these we shall advert to at length at a later time—there has been no showing whatever that resale price maintenance is necessary to protect the independent retail outlets of the United States. In fact, the converse has proven true—retailing has thrived and prospered in areas not covered by fair trade.

In the retail drug field, for example, the Federal Business Census in 1948 showed that only 10 States in the Union had more than 1,000 drug stores with fountains serving their populace. Among these were Texas, a non-fair-trade State, which ranked

---

[48] Hearings, appendix.
[49] Hearings, February 21, 1952.
[50] Ibid.
[51] Ibid.

fourth with 1,926 retail drug stores containing fountains, and Missouri, another non-fair-trade area, which ranked ninth, with 1,191 stores. According to the same census, there were only nine States of the Union with total drug store sales amounting to more than $100,000,000. Among these States, Texas, without fair trade, ranked fifth with $162,404,000 in sales volume, and Missouri, also without fair trade, ranked ninth with a sales volume of $103,757,000. Insofar as drug stores without fountains are concerned, the non-fair-trade States of Texas and Missouri, according to 1948 Business Census figures, ranked seventh and ninth, respectively.

In total number of drug and proprietary stores together, Texas, without benefit of fair trade, was fourth in the United States, according to 1948 Business Census figures, while Missouri ranked eighth. Texas led all States in the total number of proprietary stores while the State of Missouri, in fair trade's absence, had more drug and proprietary stores in 1948 than did the fair-trading States of Montana, Idaho, Wyoming, Colorado, New Mexico, Arizona, Utah and Nevada, combined.

The sales volume of the average retail drug store in the United States during 1948 was $78,340. Leading all States of the Union in that year was the District of Columbia, a non-fair-trade area, where the average retail drug store's sales volume totaled $171,769.

A similar favorable picture for non-fair-trade areas is depicted by statistics in the retail jewelry trade. According to a release accompanying the 1948 Business Census figures, "In 1948, the five leading States in terms of sales volume of jewelry stores were New York, California, Pennsylvania, Illinois, and Texas. This ranking is the same as that for 1939 except that Texas rose from seventh to fifth place."[52] Texas is a non-fair-trade State.

With regard to the number of retail jewelry outlets, the 1948 Business Census shows Texas ranking sixth with 960 stores and Missouri tenth with 571 stores. Insofar as the volume of wholesale jewelry sales is concerned, the Manufacturing Jeweler recently reported that "States recording the largest dollar volume for the trade during 1948 included New York, Illinois, California, Pennsylvania, Ohio, Massachusetts, and Missouri in the order named. Together these States contributed 80 percent to the national total."[53] The high standing of the non-fair-trade State of Missouri in this instance should be observed.

Nor does it appear that the sales of retail outlets have, on an over-all basis, suffered since the Schwegmann decision invalidating the application of fair trade contracts to nonsigners. The sales of retail drug stores have increased substantially in the post-Schwegmann period over corresponding months of the immediately prior year. In June of 1951, retail drug sales were up 7 percent over June of 1950; in July, up 8 percent; in August, up 7 percent; in September, up 2 percent; in October, up 7 percent; in November, up 7 percent; in December, up 3 percent; and in January of 1952, up 9 percent over January of 1951. Total drug store sales shattered all records in 1951 by climbing to a grand total of $3,905,000,000, according to estimates of Drug Trade News.[54] The average gain in sales volume for all retail drug stores for 1951 was 7.3 percent above the pre-Schwegmann year of 1950.[55]

Corresponding figures may be cited for the retail jewelry trade. According to the Manufacturing Jeweler, "A year of record prosperity for the jewelry business—aided by heavy holiday-season sales—was forecast by trade leaders" at the forty-sixth annual convention of the American National Retail Jewelers' Association held in August of 1951.[56] This optimism would appear confirmed by latest statistical data available. According to National Jeweler, excise tax collections in the retail jewelry business during 1951 were 9 percent above 1950 collections. The months of July, August, October, and December saw excise tax collections exceed the equivalent periods of the

---

[52] Cited in hearings, February 20, 1952.
[53] The Manufacturing Jeweler, February 1, 1951, p. 17.
[54] Drug Trade News, January 21, 1952, p. 1.
[55] Drug Topics, January 28, 1952, p. 1.
[56] The Manufacturing Jeweler, September 6, 1951, p. 4.

year before. "These figures," claimed National Jeweler, "tend to confirm NJ's contention that 1951 was a bigger 'jewelry year' than 1950."[57]

It is highly probable that this growth in jewelry sales which has occured subsequent to the Schwegmann decision will continue in 1952. According to Dr. A. O. Dahlberg, president of the United States Economic Corp., "An increase of 2 percent over 1951 can be expected for retail jewelry sales in the first 6 months of the year."[58] At the same time Dahlberg also forecast that sales for July of 1952 would exceed sales for the month of July 1951 by 15 percent.

A comparison of bankruptcies in retail drug stores occurring in non-fair-trade States with those resulting in surrounding fair trade areas also shows that absence of fair trade has not resulted in the destruction of independent business. The American Druggist in a recent issue observed that "In 1948, failure per 1,000 drug stores in fair-trade States were almost exactly the same as for those in non-fair-trade States."[59] The following table, taken from a study made for the Federal Trade Commission in 1947 by the firm of Dun & Bradstreet, reveals that non-fair-trade jurisdictions have frequently fared much better in this regard than their fair-trading counterparts.

Failures of retail drug stores in selected States, 1939, 1940, 1946, and 1947

States Without Fair-Trade Laws				Adjacent States With Fair-Trade Laws			
1939				1939			
	Number	Liabilities	Rate per 1,000 concerns		Number	Liabilities	Rate per 1,000 concerns
Vermont	—	—	—	New Hampshire	2	$8,000	8.9
Washington, D. C.	1	$4,000	3.0	Maine	4	30,000	10.1
Texas	16	132,000	4.8	Maryland	3	7,000	4.1
Missouri	9	77,000	4.1	Oklahoma	17	119,000	15.0
				Illinois	52	217,000	14.1
				Kansas	8	72,000	7.4
1940				1940			
	Number	Liabilities			Number	Liabilities	
Vermont	—	—		New Hampshire	2	$11,000	
Washington, D. C.	3	$29,000		Maine	4	24,000	
Texas	19	108,000		Maryland	3	154,000	
Missouri	11	49,000		Oklahoma	11	48,000	
				Illinois	45	224,000	
				Kansas	7	25,000	
1946				1946			
Vermont	—	—		New Hampshire	1	$2,000	
Washington, D. C.	—	—		Maine	—	—	
Texas	—	—		Maryland	—	—	
Missouri	—	—		Oklahoma	—	—	
				Illinois	—	—	
				Kansas	—	—	
January-October 1947				January-October 1947			
Vermont	—	—		New Hampshire	—	—	
Washington, D. C.	—	—		Maine	—	—	
Texas	1	$13,000		Maryland	—	—	
Missouri	1	2,000		Oklahoma	—	—	
				Illinois	1	$50,000	
				Kansas	1	7,000	

[57] National Jeweler, February 1952, p. 178.
[58] Retail Jewelers' Bulletin, February 1952, p. 2.
[59] American Druggist, August 1951, p. 164.

From the figures cited previously it certainly does not appear that any substantial injury to retail trade as a whole has accrued by virtue of the decision of the Supreme Court in the Schwegmann case. While a number of merchants may have suffered temporarily from the brief flurry of price cutting which followed immediately upon the Schwegmann case, this type of competition was severely limited both as to area and duration. According to Henry Abt, president of Brand Names Foundation:

> The so-called price war began with one store—and one store only (Macy's). All kinds of careless observation has since tended to confuse the issue. As far as the participation of other New York firms is concerned, their action has been purely defensive.[60]

By July of 1951, a scant month and a half after the Supreme Court had handed down the Schwegmann opinion, Maurice Mermey of the Bureau of Education of Fair Trade observed that—

> The expected tidal wave of price slashes has failed to materialize since the United States Supreme Court, on May 21, nullified interstate application of the nonsigner provision of the fair trade laws. It is only in a few cities that retailers have initiated cutthroat competition.[61]

A careful study undertaken by Dun & Bradstreet at the behest of the Senate Small Business Committee and the Joint Committee on the Economic Report confirmed the ephemeral nature of the much-heralded price wars. Said the respective chairman of these two august committees in transmitting the Dun & Bradstreet report:

> The results of the study speak for themselves, but it is fair to say that in general the price cutting took place in a rather narrow area, both geographically and by way of commodities. The managers of the Dun & Bradstreet offices which cooperated in the study have indicated that the price-cutting campaign has waned.[62]

The fact that independent druggists had not been injured competitively by the practical elimination of the nonsigner provision by the Schwegmann decision was cause for serious alarm on the part of those interested in restoring fair trade. The executive secretary of the NARD noted that one of the obstacles to overcome in the drive to have Congress enact a nonsigner provision to the Miller-Tydings Act was the complacent attitude of retail druggists. Reporting on a conference of fair trade leaders, he stated:

> The representatives of the organizations at the conference made it plain that the big job is to eliminate extensive attitudes of complacency. "The druggists must be hurt more than they have to date to take more than a casual interest in plans of action to restore the potency of the nonsigner provision" was in substance the opinion of perhaps the majority of the spokesmen at the conference.[63]

By November of 1951, independent druggists had as yet felt little if any injury from the Schwegmann case. Complained the NARD of the difficulties encountered in interesting its members in the fair-trade cause:

> The hardest task will be to arouse enough druggists to join in the fight for fair trade. The executive committee will discuss the situation in an effort to develop an effective plan to overcome complacency among the drug store owners as to the system of stabilized prices. The expected wave of cutthroat competition failed to materialize and it is difficult to stimulate the concern that generates the needed united action to save fair trade.[64]

All these facts tend to confirm the conclusion that no showing has been made of economic injury compelling resort to such drastic measures as resale-price maintenance. We agree wholeheartedly with the following excerpt from an editorial appearing in the June 1951 issue of the American Druggist immediately after the Schwegmann decision

---

[60] Quoted in NARD Journal, July 2, 1951, p. 1058.
[61] NARD Journal, July 16, 1951, p. 1098.
[62] Prevalence of Price Cutting of Merchandise Marketed under Price Maintenance Agreements, committee print. 82d Cong., 1st sess[.] (1951), p. V.
[63] NARD Journal, August 6, 1951, p. 1171.
[64] NARD Journal, November 5, 1951, p. 1757.

and earnestly commend it to the attention of all retail establishments who mistakenly feel that their salvation lies in further extension of resale-price maintenance regulation.

Before any fair dealing retailer assumes that he is washed up, let him be aware that although fair trade created a more stable market for well-known products, there is no evidence that it kept any druggist in business who would otherwise have failed. Loss of fair trade will not drive any druggist out of business if he serves the public better than his competitors, not by meeting crazy prices, but by better display of goods and more friendly personal attention to every customer.

We have heard it said that this court opinion means the end of drug stores. That is poppycock! This Nation likes its drug stores—especially those that still look like drug stores. Before any fair trade laws were enacted, there were just as many drug stores as there are today. And they suffered some of the worst price wars that ever happened.

To succeed without fair trade is a little harder, but it is not impossible. Now is the time to stand up and fight for business—as the druggists of Vermont, Missouri, Texas, and the District of Columbia have always had to do.[65]

VI. SPECIFIC OBJECTIONS TO H. R. 6925

A. H. R. 6925 DOES NOT PROVIDE APPROPRIATE REMEDY FOR ABUSES

According to proponents of resale price maintenance, the evil sought to be remedied by this legislation is so-called loss leader selling; i. e., sales below cost of brand-name merchandise. Thus, Representative Allan Oakley Hunter told the Committee on the Judiciary:

> Wild price cutting is an example of one of the evils resulting from the lack of adequate fair trade laws. I do not, of course, refer to normal competitive pricing, but to the practice of cutting prices on nationally advertised items to a figure below cost. This "loss leader" will fool customers, while prices of unfamiliar products are raised. * * * Prolonged selling at below-cost prices will force a little dealer out of business, while the large retailer can absorb the loss, or make it up through other branches of his store. Fair trade laws prevent this.[66]

Similarly, Representative Morano, author of one of the fair trade bills considered by the Judiciary Committee, in response to the questioning of Congressman Rogers of the committee, described his conception of the objective of this legislation:

> Mr. MORANO. * * * I am in favor of punishing a chain store if they exercise cutthroat competition to knock out a small retailer across the street and then come back and sell that same article for more than what the little fellow was selling it across the street.
> Mr. ROGERS. You feel that your bill would accomplish that thing?
> Mr. MORANO. Exactly.
> Mr. ROGERS. And that is the objective of this legislation so far as you are concerned, and nothing else?
> Mr. MORANO. Exactly.[67]

The Honorable Fritz Lanham, former distinguished colleague in the House of Representatives, told the committee on behalf of the American Fair Trade Council:

> I think it is axiomatic that there could have been but one outstanding and predominant purpose of such legislation and that was to make properly effective the fair trade laws of the various States. It was to prevent the operation of self-serving schemes of uncreative commercial pirates by resort to loss-leader lures of well-known fair-traded commodities * * *.[68]

While the alleged purpose of those advocating this legislation is to prevent loss-leader selling and sales below costs, the content of this bill goes much further. By making it mandatory upon signers and nonsigners of resale price maintenance agreements alike to adhere to minimum resale prices despite differences in costs, rents, location, and efficiency, this legislation prevents all types of price cutting of fair trade merchandise whether done legitimately in an effort to pass on savings to the

---

[65] Editorial, American Druggist, June 1951, p. 53.
[66] Hearings, February 27, 1952.
[67] Hearings, February 13, 1952.
[68] Hearings, February 18, 1952.

consumer or whether done in a predatory manner by intentionally selling below cost. It fails to separate the sheep from the goats and rigidifies the price structure in the hope that by so doing the evil will be entrapped with the good. Thus, Julius M. Westheimer, president of Julius Gutman & Co., Inc., a retail store in Baltimore, Md., explained in the following colloquy with Mr. Rogers of the committee how resale price maintenance would prohibit him from making legitimate price reductions:

Mr. ROGERS. You testified on page 3 that this was price fixed by the manufacturer at 49 cents a can, and that you were now selling it at 44.
Mr. WESTHEIMER. Yes, sir.
Mr. ROGERS. Prior to the Supreme Court decision were you offering that merchandise at 44 cents rather than 49 cents?
Mr. WESTHEIMER. No, sir; we were not allowed to.[69]

If loss-leader selling is what is desired to be condemned, it would seem only logical that legislation aimed directly at this evil should have been introduced. The chairman has introduced a bill, H. R. 6986,[3.45] designed to meet squarely the loss leader problem by prohibiting loss leader sales affecting commerce which involve any commodity, and which by utilization of the State resale price maintenance laws, prohibits intrastate loss leader sales of commodities which bear a trade-mark or brand or the name of a producer. Persons sincerely interested in the well-being of small business and the preservation of competition may well lend their support to this measure rather than to resale price maintenance legislation with all the concomitant difficulties we have attempted to point out. In this regard, we agree with the following statement made by Ewald T. Grether, Flood professor of economics, and Dean, School of Business Administration, University of California, in his statement submitted to the Committee on the Judiciary:

I do not believe, however, that resale price maintenance under fair-trade legislation is the appropriate way to deal with abuses and conflicts in the channels of marketing. Resale price fixing by manufacturers of branded goods represents a highly unselective approach to a solution rather than a general solution. In addition, this approach, especially when implemented, as it has been, by the so-called nonsigner's clause, introduces difficulties and problems of its own. Widespread resale price maintenance over a period of years could produce effects which would be more damaging to our price system and to healthy competition than the evils at which it is allegedly directed.[70]

B. H. R. 6925 PERMITS STATE FAIR-TRADE CONTRACTS TO BE APPLIED TO NONSIGNERS

If it is found desirable to permit resale price-maintenance agreements between manufacturers and retailers, it does not therefore follow that it is equally as desirable to make such contracts applicable to all retailers who are not immediate parties thereto. Such extension of the doctrine of liberty of contract is certainly novel, to say the least, in the annals of Anglo-American jurisprudence. Where, in this instance, are all the customary constituents of a contract as found in the traditional common law? Where is there any element of consent? of consideration? of mutuality? Where are our notions of justice in permitting State legislatures to bind those who do not even participate in agreements made between others?

It should be carefully noted that many retailers object strongly to fair-trade agreements and feel that it works substantial injury upon them. A recent fair-trade survey conducted by the Sporting Goods Dealer among retail outlets concluded that there is "by no means anything resembling agreement on the subject." This was by far the most startling fact uncovered by the survey, because, observed the Dealer, "it has

---

[69] Hearings, February 21, 1952.
[70] Hearings, appendix.

[3.45] H.R. 6986, 82d Cong., 2d Sess. (introduced by Representative Emanuel Celler on March 11, 1952). A comparative analysis of H.R. 5767, H.R. 6925, and H.R. 6986 was inserted in the *Record* by Representative Charles A. Wolverton, 98 CONG. REC. A2743 (1952), *infra* at 635–36.

been generally accepted that dealers were almost unanimously in favor of fair trade."[71] Despite this assumption, 31 percent of retail sporting goods stores covered were either opposed to fair trade or presented serious objections or misgivings.

In a poll of the National Federation of Independent Business conducted by George Burger in which members were questioned: "Are you for or against immediate congressional action to restore the fair-trade laws?" Twenty-eight percent of those responding indicated outright opposition to such legislation and another 4 percent expressed no positive opinion on the subject.

Among many manufacturers, there exists strong sentiment against fair trade. Of 715 manufacturers selling through hardware channels responding to questionnaires dispatched recently by Hardware Age, only 131 manufacturers reported sales of their products under fair-trade contracts. "As might be expected," summed up Hardware Age, "because there are less manufacturers who fair trade than those who don't, there are even more reasons offered against the fair-trade principle."[72]

On December 15, 1941, Modern Industry asked in its pages, "Does resale price maintenance benefit the consumer and industry?" Vote of its readers on this subject was as follows:

[Percent]

	Yes	No
New England	34.1	65.9
Mid-Atlantic	30.8	69.2
North Central	35.7	64.3
South	37.5	62.5
West	42.2	57.8
Pacific coast	19.1	80.9

We believe it would be shocking for Congress to authorize the States to coerce small-business men under contracts to which they were never a party when there exists, as shown above, such substantial opposition to resale price maintenance.

C. H. R. 6925 SUBJECT TO SERIOUS CONSTITUTIONAL OBJECTIONS

We think that there are many fundamental objections to H. R. 6925 of a constitutional nature, particularly section (d) thereof which makes it a Federal civil wrong for both signers and nonsigners of resale price maintenance agreements to offer, sell, advertise, deliver, or have transported for sale in interstate commerce fair traded commodities at prices less than those established in resale price maintenance agreements in those States where such contracts are lawful. We feel that this legislation, if enacted, may be legitimately challenged upon a number of constitutional grounds, including the following:

(1) Unconstitutional delegation of legislative powers

Section (d) of this bill makes a person selling beneath the price established by a manufacturer in a resale price maintenance contract subject to suit in the Federal courts whether party to the agreement or not. In effect, Congress intends to sanction punishment of those who sell beneath prices established by private individuals.

It is now beyond doubt that Congress itself has the power to regulate the prices of retail products as an emergency measure,[73] and it is equally well settled that the States themselves may prescribe minimum retail prices of commodities when it is deemed necessary for the welfare of their populace.[74] But in this instance, neither Congress nor the States themselves have prescribed the prices below which retail commodities may not be sold. Instead, this has been left for determination to private individuals.

---

[71] The Sporting Goods Dealer, November 1949, p. 48.

[72] Hardware Age, September 8, 1949.

[73] *Yakus* v. *United States,* 321 U.S. 414 [64 S. Ct. 660, 88 L. Ed. 834] (1944).

[74] *Nebia* [sic] v. *New York,* 291 U.S. 502 [54 S. Ct. 505, 78 L. Ed. 940] (1934).

The factual situation in this instance is comparable to that confronting the Supreme Court when it considered the constitutionality of the National Industrial Recovery Act. Under the NRA, legislative power had been delegated—

not to a public official responsible to Congress or the Executive, but to private individuals in the industries to be regulated.[75]

The Court held, Mr. Chief Justice Hughes speaking, that—

Such a delegation of legislative power is unknown to our law, and is utterly inconsistent with the constitutional prerogatives and duties of Congress.[76]

(2) Deprivation of property without due process of law

Whenever Congress has promulgated statutes regulating industrial behavior, it has generally provided procedural safeguards to protect the individual from arbitrary power exercised by officials. Thus the Interstate Commerce Commission in regulating railroad rates and other matters must act upon notice, hearing, and its orders must be supported by facts sustained by the evidence.[77] In the Defense Production Act of 1950, Congress has provided that any rule, regulation, or order issued under authority of the act—

shall be accompanied by a statement that in the formulation thereof there has been consultation with industry representatives, including trade association representatives * * *.

and has authorized appeals by persons aggrieved by administrative rulings.[78] In the Administrative Procedure Act, elaborate procedural standards for Federal administrative agencies have been delineated at length.[79]

In this instance, however, no protection has been accorded to retailers bound by contracts which may be negotiated between a manufacturer and a single seller. No hearing is provided to determine the reasonableness of the minimum price established under resale price maintenance agreements; no appeal is allowed those substantially injured by prices established in such agreements; no standards exist for insuring prices of a reasonable nature. Congress, if it enacts this bill into law will be granting to private individuals more arbitrary authority than it has ever deemed it proper to bestow upon Government agencies, while at the same time it proffers no legislative safeguards to those who may be adversely affected thereby.

It is clear that a fair hearing is one of the essential elements in the constitutional regulation of the activities of private persons. As Mr. Justice Hughes expressed it in *Railroad Commission of California* v. *Pacific Gas & Electric Co.*:[80]

The right to a fair and open hearing is one of the rudiments of fair play * * *. There must be due notice and an opportunity to be heard, the procedure must be consistent with the essentials of a fair trial, and the Commission must act upon evidence and not arbitrarily (p. 393).

Mr. Justice Hughes spoke again for the Court in the case of *Morgan* v. *United States*, where the constitutional issue of a fair hearing was involved and declared that such a hearing was—

essential alike to the legal validity of the administrative regulation and to the maintenance of public confidence in the value and soundness of this important governmental process.[81]

---

[75] *Yakus* v. *United States,* 321 U.S. 414, 424 (1944).

[76] *United States* v. *Schechter Poultry Corp.,* 295 U.S. 495, 537 [55 S. Ct. 837, 846, 79 L. Ed. 1570, 1584] (1935).

[77] *Interstate Commerce Commission* v. *Louisville & Nashville Railroad Co.,* 227 U.S. 88 [33 S. Ct. 185, 57 L. Ed. 431] (1913).

[78] Secs. 709, 408, Public Law 774, 81st Cong., 2d sess. (1950).

[79] Public Law 404, 79th Cong., 2d sess. (1946).

[80] 302 U. S. 388 [58 S. Ct. 334, 82 L. Ed. 319] (1938).

[81] 304 U. S. 1, 15 [58 S. Ct. 773, 775, 82 L. Ed. 1129, 1130-31] (1938).

(3) Void for vagueness

In *Small Co.* v. *American Sugar Refining Co.*,[82] the Court determined that section 4 of the Lever Act providing that it was unlawful for—

any person willfully * * * to make any unjust or unreasonable * * * charge in * * * dealing in or with any necessaries—

was void for vagueness. It declared that even in a civil action, penalties of the act constituted—

the exaction of obedience to a rule or standard which was so vague and indefinite as really to be no rule or standard at all (p. 239).

This bill raises the same problem. Which State resale price maintenance law is to apply in any given interstate transaction falling under the prohibitions of section (d)? How is the seller to determine which of two or more minimum prices he must adhere to in interstate sales? What portion of his business may be said to be in interstate commerce demanding adherence to resale price maintenance agreements under penalty of Federal law? What commodities are in "free and open competition" so as to be amenable to fair trade contracts? All these questions remained unanswered by H. R. 6925.

Emanuel Celler, Chairman.
Edgar A. Jonas.
Claude I. Bakewell.

APPENDIX

THE BILLS INTRODUCED AND REFERRED TO THE COMMITTEE ON THE JUDICIARY RELATING TO RESALE PRICE MAINTENANCE

Originally the committee had referred to it four bills relating to resale-price maintenance. They were H. R. 4365, H. R. 4592, H. R. 4662, and H. R. 6367. The first of these bills repealed the Miller-Tydings amendment to the Sherman Act. H. R. 4592 and H. R. 4662 amended the Miller-Tydings amendment to take care of the Schwegmann case. The last bill introduced (H. R. 6367) was designed to ameliorate the effects of the decisions in both the Schwegmann and Wentling cases. H. R. 6925 is a clean bill version of H. R. 6367. It was prepared after the Antitrust Subcommittee of the Committee on the Judiciary completed its hearings and executive sessions on H. R. 6367.

As is the committee's custom when bills of this nature are referred to it, copies are sent to the agencies believed to be most vitally interested for their comment and opinion. The replies are contained herein. It will be noted that the Federal Trade Commission bill reports are directed only to the first three bills introduced and do not cover H. R. 6367. The Department of Justice gave its views at the hearing of February 13, 1952. Both the Federal Trade Commission and the Department of Justice were opposed to resale-price maintenance. On the other hand, there is contained herein the views of the Department of Commerce in favor of resale-price maintenance.

The Bureau of the Budget, which customarily is charged with the responsibility of ascertaining whether or not a department's position taken on any bill referred to it is in accord with the President's policy, declared, in a letter dated February 28, 1951, and made a part hereof, that the positions taken by the Department of Justice and the Federal Trade Commission were in accord with the program of the President and that the views of the Department of Commerce were not.

February 8, 1952.

Hon. Emanuel Celler,
Chairman, Committee on the Judiciary,
United States House of Representatives, Washington, D. C.

MY DEAR MR. CHAIRMAN: In response to the request made in your letter of January 14, 1952, for an expression of the Commission's views on H. R. 4365, Eighty-second Congress, first

---

[82] 267 U. S. 233 [45 S. Ct. 295, 69 L. Ed. 589] (1925).

session, introduced June 7, 1951, by Congressman Thomas B. Curtis, of Missouri, the following is submitted:

The purpose of the proposed legislation is to repeal the Miller-Tydings Act and to eliminate its provisions from section 1 of the Sherman Antitrust Act (act of July 2, 1890).

Prior to the Miller-Tydings Act, decisions in a number of cases under the Sherman and Federal Trade Commission Acts had made it clear that the failure of a retailer to observe the resale prices marked on trade-marked or branded goods did not create a cause of action in favor of the manufacturer either under the common law or under the patent or copyright laws. Moreover, the courts held that where a manufacturer maintained the resale prices of his identified goods by a system of ⊥ contracts or equivalent cooperative methods, those contracts were void and such methods illegal under both the Sherman and the Federal Trade Commission Acts.

⊥ 54

The Miller-Tydings Act amended the Sherman Act by legalizing minimum resale price agreements or contracts respecting trade-marked or otherwise identified goods sold in interstate commerce provided that the commodities affected were resold in any State that had legalized this type of contract, or agreement with respect to resales made within its boundaries. The act also amended the Federal Trade Commission Act by providing that the making of such contracts should not constitute an unfair method of competition under section 5 of the Federal Trade Commission Act.

Resale-price-maintenance laws—that is, laws declaring as not in violation of the law of the particular State certain kinds of price-maintenance contracts and providing that nonsigners of such contracts with knowledge thereof should be bound by the price stipulations therein—were on the statute books of 45 States as of May 1, 1941. Most of these States adopted price-maintenance laws in 1937 soon after the decision of the Supreme Court in *Old Dearborn Distributing Company* v. *Seagram Distillers Corporation* (299 U. S. 183; decided December 7, 1936), declaring as constitutional the principal provisions, including the nonsigner clause, of the Illinois price-maintenance law.

Resale-price maintenance, as practiced prior to the decision of the Supreme Court in the Schwegmann case (*Schwegmann Bros.* v. *Calvert Distillers Corporation*) (341 U. S. 384; decided May 21, 1951), is a system of pricing trade-marked, branded, or otherwise identified products for resale in which, pursuant to laws legalizing such arrangements, the manufacturer, producer, or brand owner, his authorized agent, factor, or wholesale distributor, prescribes by contract the minimum price or the resale price at which such products may be sold at wholesale, and the producer or manufacturer and his factors or wholesalers prescribe the minimum price or the resale price at which a product may be sold at retail in a specified State, or in a specified portion thereof, with the effect of legally binding all other distributors in the specified area to conform to such practice. This was done by entering into contracts with at least one such distributor of such product and serving notice upon all other distributors, who were thereupon obligated to maintain the minimum price or the resale price named in the contract. In some cases wholesale distributors, acting without the authorization of the manufacturer or brand owner, have entered into contracts with retailers for the maintenance of retail prices.

In the Schwegmann case the Supreme Court held that the Miller-Tydings Act does not make binding upon nonsigners resale prices fixed in contracts under State resale price maintenance laws insofar, of course, as interstate commerce is concerned.

Notwithstanding the Schwegmann decision, the Miller-Tydings Act and the State laws concerning resale-price maintenance would continue to authorize the making of contracts for the fixing of resale prices. And notwithstanding the fact that the Miller-Tydings Act expressly continues the prohibition of the Sherman Act against "horizontal" price fixing by those in competition with each other at the same functional level, elimination of price competition at the retail level may lawfully result if a distributor successfully negotiates individual "vertical" agreements with all of his retailers. Thus, under the Miller-Tydings Act and the State laws concerning resale-price maintenance, private contracts, the provisions of which would be determined without public hearing and apart from any public supervision as to reasonableness, would be made binding upon all dealers executing such contracts, and the consuming public.

In an effort to prescribe the freedom of business enterprise, the courts have been circumspect in recognizing even the authority of governments to fix the prices that businessmen shall charge. Such price fixing is invalid unless it is undertaken for a public purpose and by reasonable means. Under the provisions of the Miller-Tydings Act and the State resale-price-maintenance laws, however, the power to fix prices would be entrusted not to Government but to private persons; the purpose to be served by the price fixing would be whatever purpose such private persons might have, presumably that of serving their own pecuniary purpose rather than that of the public interest; and the prices fixed would not be tested for reasonableness by any instrumentality, public or private. In granting to such private persons the power to fix prices, the Miller-Tydings Act and the State resale-price maintenance laws grant to such persons much greater authority than Congress saw fit to grant to the Government itself in the National

Industrial Recovery Act (act of June 16, 1933). In that act consideration was given labor and to the consuming public and there was always a representative of both who participated in the fixing of price, while in the Miller-Tydings Act and the State resale-price-maintenance laws, no consideration whatsoever is given to the interests of labor or the consuming public.

Nothing is more clearly established in Federal policy than the principle that "horizontal" price fixing shall not be tolerated. Where a distributor has negotiated individual "vertical" agreements with all of his retailers, elimination of "horizontal" price competition at the retail level will result. The rigidity and uniformity of the price will be exactly that of the most rigid "horizontal" price-fixing conspiracy; the level of the price would be likely to be at least as high as in a "horizontal" conspiracy; and the public control over the reasonableness of the arrangement would be as nonexistent as in the case of a "horizontal" conspiracy. Thus, under the Miller-Tydings Act and the State resale-price maintenance laws any group of distributors desiring to fix prices horizontally would be foolish to take the direct road to that end. Instead, such distributors should make "vertical" contracts with the producer and through this means "horizontal" price competition between such distributors will be eliminated, the objections of the Government would be negated, and the courts could be used to enforce the arrangement.

In our opinion economic conditions are not the same at the present time as existed in 1937 which prompted the enactment of the Miller-Tydings Act. At present there is no necessity for resale-price maintenance legislation with respect to interstate commerce. Furthermore, the Congress has already pointed the way to elimination of the evils which sponsors of the Miller-Tydings Act sought to remedy, through legislation prohibiting price discrimination and other unfair methods of competition. It is the elimination of these evils rather than legislation legalizing price fixing which will minimize the inequities between the smaller businessman and his more powerful competitor.

During previous years, the Commission has expressed its opposition to resale-price maintenance in two reports to the Congress, the first of which was presented in 1931 (70th Cong., 2d sess., H. Doc. No. 546), and the second entitled "Report on Resale Price Maintenance," which was submitted on December 13, 1945.

Consistent with the foregoing observations, the Commission is in favor of the enactment of H. R. 4365 (the Curtis bill).

By direction of the Commission.

Jas. M. Mead, Chairman.

Commissioner Mason does not concur in the above report.

N. B.—In view of request that we expedite the matter, this report has not been cleared with the Bureau of the Budget.

Jas. M. Mead, Chairman.

February 8, 1952.

Hon. Emanuel Celler,
Chairman, Committee on the Judiciary,
United States House of Representatives, Washington, D. C.

MY DEAR MR. CHAIRMAN: In response to the request made in your letter of January 14, 1952, for an expression of the Commission's views on H. R. 4592, Eighty-second Congress, first session, introduced June 25, 1951, by Congressman Norris Poulson, of California, the following is submitted.

The principle purpose of the proposed legislation is to overcome the effect of the recent decision of the Supreme Court in the Schwegmann case (*Schwegmann Bros. v. Calvert Distillers Corporation* (341 U. S. 384; decided May 21, 1951)). In that case the Supreme Court held that the Miller-Tydings Act does not make binding upon nonsigners resale prices fixed in contracts under State resale-price-maintenance laws insofar, of course, as interstate commerce is concerned. The bill proposes to amend the first proviso of section 1 of the Sherman Antitrust Act (the Miller-Tydings amendment) so as to include therein the nonsigner clause.

Prior to the Miller-Tydings Act, decisions in a number of cases under the Sherman and Federal Trade Commission Acts had made it clear that the failure of a retailer to observe the resale prices marked on trade-marked or branded goods did not create a cause of action in favor of the manufacturer either under the common law or under the patent or copyright laws. Moreover, the courts held that where a manufacturer maintained the resale prices of his identified goods by a system of contracts or equivalent cooperative methods, those contracts were void and such methods illegal under both the Sherman and the Federal Trade Commission Acts.

The Miller-Tydings Act amended the Sherman Act by legalizing minimum-resale-price agreements or contracts respecting trade-marked or otherwise identified goods sold in interstate commerce provided that the commodities affected were resold in any State that had legalized this type of contract, or agreement with respect to resales made within its boundaries. The act also amended the Federal Trade Commission Act by providing that the making of such contracts should not constitute an unfair method of competition under section 5 of the Federal Trade Commission Act.

Resale-price-maintenance laws—that is, laws declaring as not in violation of the law of the particular State certain kinds of price-maintenance contracts and providing that nonsigners of such contracts with knowledge thereof should be bound by the price stipulations therein—were on the statute books of 45 States as of May 1, 1941. Most of these States adopted price-maintenance laws in 1937 soon after the decision of the Supreme Court in *Old Dearborn Distributing Company* v. *Seagram Distillers Corporation* (299 U. S. 183; decided December 7, 1936), declaring as constitutional the principal provisions, including the nonsigner clause, of the Illinois price-maintenance law.

The legal principle involved in the proposed legislation and in the State laws concerning resale-price maintenance is not a mere authorization of contracts for the fixing of resale prices. That authorization now exists under the Miller-Tydings amendment as interpreted by the Supreme Court in the Schwegmann case. The new principle introduced by this bill is that the Congress shall specifically approve the so-called nonsigner clause. Thus, if this bill is enacted, a private contract, the provisions of which would be determined without public hearing and apart from any public supervision as to reasonableness, would be made binding upon all dealers and the consuming public.

In an effort to prescribe the freedom of business enterprise, the courts have been circumspect in recognizing even the authority of governments to fix the prices that businessmen shall charge. Such price fixing is invalid unless it is undertaken for a public purpose and by reasonable means. In the State resale-price-maintenance laws and in the present bill, however, the power to fix prices would be entrusted not to a government, but to private persons; the purpose to be served by the price fixing would be whatever purpose such private persons might have, presumably that of serving their own pecuniary interests rather than that of the public interest; and the prices fixed would not be tested for reasonableness by any instrumentality public or private; nevertheless, a person who is not a party to this private contract is to be deemed guilty of unfair competition and subject to a suit for damages if he fails to observe the prices, regardless of whether or not they are arbitrary or extortionate.

In granting to such private persons the power to fix prices, the proposed legislation goes much further than Congress saw fit to grant to the Government itself in the National Industrial Recovery Act (act of June 16, 1933). In that act consideration was given to labor and the consuming public and there was always a representative of both who participated in the fixing of prices, while in the present bill no consideration whatsoever is given to the interests of labor or the consuming public.

The effect of adding the nonsigner clause to resale-price maintenance is the de facto nullification of our Federal antitrust laws prohibiting horizontal conspiracy to fix prices. Nothing is more clearly established in Federal policy than the principle that horizontal price fixing shall not be tolerated. The proposed legislation pays lip service to that principle; yet its effect would be that a minimum price fixed by contract with one retail distributor would become the minimum price for all other retail distributors who were placed upon notice of the existence of the contract. The rigidity and uniformity of the price would be exactly that of the most rigid horizontal price-fixing conspiracy; the level of the price would be likely to be at least as high as in a horizontal conspiracy; and the public control of the reasonableness of the arrangement would be as nonexistent as in the case of a horizontal conspiracy. Thenceforward, any group of distributors desiring to fix prices horizontally would be foolish to take the direct road to that end. Instead some one of their number would make a vertical contract with a supplier and then place the other members of the group on notice of the existence of the contract. Through this means, the group could not only negate the objections of the Government, but could actually use the courts as devices to enforce the arrangement.

In considering this problem, under the provisions of the Miller-Tydings Act in the Schwegmann case, the Supreme Court stated:

"It should be noted in this connection that the Miller-Tydings Act expressly continues the prohibitions of the Sherman Act against 'horizontal' price fixing ⊥ by those in competition with each other at the same functional level. Therefore, when a State compels retailers to follow a parallel price policy, it demands private conduct which the Sherman Act forbids. See *Parker* v. *Brown* (317 U. S. 341, 350). Elimination of price competition at the retail level may, of course, lawfully result if a distributor successfully negotiates individual 'vertical' agreements with all his retailers. But when retailers are forced to abandon price competition they are driven into a compact in violation of the spirit of the proviso which forbids 'horizontal' price fixing."

⊥ 57

In our opinion economic conditions are not the same at the present time as existed in 1937, which prompted the enactment of the Miller-Tydings Act. At present there is no necessity for Federal resale-price-maintenance legislation with respect to interstate commerce. Furthermore, the Congress has already pointed the way toward elimination of the evils, which sponsors of the Miller-Tydings Act sought to remedy, through legislation prohibiting price discrimination and other unfair methods of competition. It is the elimination of these evils rather than legislation legalizing price fixing which will minimize the inequities between the smaller-business man and his more powerful competitor.

During previous years, the Commission has expressed its opposition to resale-price maintenance in two reports to the Congress, the first of which was presented in 1931 (70th Cong., 2d sess., H. Doc. 546), and the second entitled "Report on Resale Price Maintenance," which was submitted on December 13, 1945.

Consistent with the foregoing observations, the Commission is opposed to H. R. 4592 (the Poulson bill).

By direction of the Commission.

Jas. M. Mead, Chairman.

N. B.—In view of your request that we expedite the matter, this report has not been cleared with the Bureau of the Budget.

Jas. M. Mead, Chairman.

February 8, 1952.

Hon. Emanuel Celler,
Chairman, Committee on the Judiciary,
United States House of Representatives, Washington, D. C.

MY DEAR MR. CHAIRMAN: In response to the request made in your letter of January 14, 1952, for an expression of the Commission's views on H. R. 4662, Eighty-second Congress, first session, introduced June 29, 1951, by Congressman Albert P. Morano, of Connecticut, the following is submitted:

The principle purpose of the proposed legislation is to overcome the effect of the recent decision of the Supreme Court in the Schwegmann case (*Schwegmann Bros.* v. *Calvert Distillers Corporation* (341 U. S. 384) decided May 21, 1951). In that case the Supreme Court held that the Miller-Tydings Act does not make binding upon nonsigners resale prices fixed in contracts under State resale-price-maintenance laws insofar, of course, as interstate commerce is concerned. The bill proposes to amend the first proviso of section 1 of the Sherman Antitrust Act (the Miller-Tydings amendment) so as to include therein the nonsigner clause.

Prior to the Miller-Tydings Act, decisions in a number of cases under the Sherman and Federal Trade Commission Acts had made it clear that the failure of a retailer to observe the resale prices marked on trade-marked or branded goods did not create a cause of action in favor of the manufacturer either under the common law or under the patent or copyright laws. Moreover, the courts held that where a manufacturer maintained the resale prices of his identified goods by a system of contracts or equivalent cooperative methods, those contracts were void and such methods illegal under both the Sherman and the Federal Trade Commission Acts.

The Miller-Tydings Act amended the Sherman Act by legalizing minimum-resale-price agreements or contracts respecting trade-marked or otherwise identified goods sold in interstate commerce provided that the commodities affected were resold in any State that had legalized this type of contract, or agreement with respect to resales made within its boundaries. The act also amended the Federal Trade Commission Act by providing that the making of such contracts should not constitute an unfair method of competition under section 5 of the Federal Trade Commission Act.

Resale-price-maintenance laws—that is, laws declaring as not in violation of the law of the particular State certain kinds of price-maintenance contracts and providing that nonsigners of such contracts with knowledge thereof should be bound by the price stipulation therein—were on the statute books of 45 States as of May 1, 1941. Most of these States adopted price-maintenance laws in 1937 soon ⊥ after the decision of the Supreme Court in *Old Dearborn Distributing Company* v. *Seagram Distillers Corporation* (299 U. S. 183: decided December 7, 1936), declaring as constitutional the principal provisions, including the nonsigner clause, of the Illinois price-maintenance law.

The legal principle involved in the proposed legislation and in the State laws concerning resale-price maintenance is not a mere authorization of contracts for the fixing of resale prices. That authorization now exists under the Miller-Tydings amendment as interpreted by the Supreme Court in the Schwegmann case. The new principle introduced by this bill is that the Congress shall specifically approve the so-called nonsigner clause. Thus, if this bill is enacted, a private contract the provisions of which would be determined without public hearing and apart from any public supervision as to reasonableness, would be made binding upon all dealers and the consuming public.

In an effort to prescribe the freedom of business enterprise, the courts have been circumspect in recognizing even the authority of governments to fix the prices that businessmen shall charge. Such price fixing is invalid unless it is undertaken for a public purpose and by reasonable means. In the State resale-price-maintenance laws and in the present bill, however, the power to fix prices would be entrusted not to a government, but to private persons: the purpose to be served by the price fixing would be whatever purpose such private persons might have, presumably that of serving their own pecuniary interests rather than that of the public interest; and the prices fixed would not be tested for reasonableness by any instrumentality public or private; nevertheless, a person who is not a party to this private contract is to be deemed guilty of unfair competition and subject to a suit for damages if he fails to observe the prices, regardless of whether or not they are arbitrary or extortionate.

In granting to such private persons the power to fix prices, the proposed legislation goes much further than Congress saw fit to grant to the Government itself in the National Industrial Recovery Act (act of June 16, 1933). In that act consideration was given labor and to the consuming public and there was always a representative of both who participated in the fixing of prices, while in the present bill no consideration whatsoever is given to the interests of labor or the consuming public.

The effect of adding the nonsigner clause to resale-price maintenance is the de facto nullification of our Federal antitrust laws prohibiting horizontal conspiracy to fix prices. Nothing is more clearly established in Federal policy than the principle that horizontal price fixing shall not be tolerated. The proposed legislation pays lip service to that principle; yet its effect would be that a minimum price fixed by contract with one retail distributor would become the minimum price for all other retail distributors who were placed upon notice of the existence of the contract. The rigidity and uniformity of the price would be exactly that of the most rigid horizontal price-fixing conspiracy; the level of the price would be likely to be at least as high as in a horizontal conspiracy; and the public control of the reasonableness of the arrangement would be as nonexistent as in the case of a horizontal conspiracy. Thenceforward any group of distributors desiring to fix prices horizontally would be foolish to take the direct road to that end. Instead some one of their number would make a vertical contract with a supplier and then place the other members of the group on notice of the existence of the contract. Through this means, the group could not only negate the objections of the Government, but could actually use the courts as devices to enforce the arrangement.

In considering this problem, under the provisions of the Miller-Tydings Act in the Schwegmann case, the Supreme Court stated:

"It should be noted in this connection that the Miller-Tydings Act expressly continues the prohibitions of the Sherman Act against 'horizontal' price fixing by those in competition with each other at the same functional level. Therefore, when a State compels retailers to follow a parallel price policy, it demands private conduct which the Sherman Act forbids. See *Parker* v. *Brown* (317 U. S. 341, 350). Elimination of price competition at the retail level may, of course, lawfully result if a distributor successfully negotiates individual 'vertical' agreements with all his retailers. But when retailers are forced to abandon price competition, they are driven into a compact in violation of the spirit of the proviso which forbids 'horizontal' price fixing."

In our opinion economic conditions are not the same at the present time as existed in 1937, which prompted the enactment of the Miller-Tydings Act. At present there is no necessity for Federal resale-price-maintenance legislation with respect to interstate commerce. Furthermore, the Congress has already pointed ⊥ the way toward elimination of the evils, which sponsors of the Miller-Tydings Act sought to remedy, through legislation prohibiting price discrimination and other unfair methods of competition. It is the elimination of these evils rather than legislation legalizing price fixing which will minimize the inequities between the smaller businessman and his more powerful competitor.

During previous years, the Commission has expressed its opposition to resale-price maintenance in two reports to the Congress, the first of which was presented in 1931 (70th Cong., 2d sess., H. Doc. No. 546), and the second entitled "Report on Resale Price Maintenance," which was submitted on December 13, 1945.

Consistent with the foregoing observations, the Commission is opposed to H. R. 4662 (the Morano bill).

By direction of the Commission.

Jas. M. Mead, Chairman.

N. B.—In view of your request that we expedite the matter, this report has not been cleared with the Bureau of the Budget.

Jas. M. Mead, Chairman.

⊥ 59

Department of Commerce,
Washington 25, February 27, 1952.

The Honorable EMANUEL CELLER,
Chairman, Committee on the Judiciary,
House of Representatives, Washington, D. C.

DEAR MR. CHAIRMAN: Enclosed herewith is a statement on the legislation relating to resale-price maintenance in reply to your letter of February 25, 1952.

This statement presents my views and those of the Department of Commerce. I am most grateful for the opportunity you have afforded me to present my views on this subject to your committee.

Due to the urgency of this matter, we have been unable to secure the views of the Bureau of the Budget.

Sincerely yours,

Charles Sawyer,
Secretary of Commerce.

VIEWS OF THE DEPARTMENT OF COMMERCE CONCERNING LEGISLATION PROVIDING FOR MINIMUM-RESALE-PRICE MAINTENANCE

Title 8 of the act of August 17, 1937 (ch. 690. 50 Stat. 693) (popularly known as the Miller-Tydings amendment), amended the Sherman Antitrust Act to provide that nothing contained in that act shall make illegal contracts or agreements to fix minimum prices for resale of a commodity which bears, or the label or container of which bears, a trade-mark, brand, or name of the producer or distributor thereof and which is in free and open competition with commodities of the same general class produced or distributed by others if such contracts or agreements are lawful as applied to intrastate transactions under any statute, law, or public policy in any State, Territory, or the District of Columbia in which such resale is to be made or to which the commodity is to be transported for such resale. Title 8 also provided that such contracts or agreements would not be an unfair method of competition under section 5 of the Federal Trade Commission Act. It also included a specific statement that horizontal price agreements were not authorized or made legal. Shortly after the enactment of this legislation many States passed laws making lawful resale-price-maintenance contracts or agreements with respect to intrastate transactions. Most, if not all, of those laws contained the so-called "nonsigners clause," which provided that such contracts or agreements made with one distributor within the State applied to every other distributor of that commodity within the State who was provided with notice of the terms of the contract or agreement. The clause allowed such contracts or agreements to be enforced against both signers and nonsigners of the contract or agreement.

In 1951, the Supreme Court of the United States in the case of *Schwegmann Brothers et al v. Calvert Distillers Corp.* (341 U. S. 384) held that contracts establishing minimum prices for resale of commodities in commerce could not be enforced against distributors not parties to such a contract. Recognizing that the practical effect of the Schwegmann case was to nullify the Miller-Tydings amendment and therefore the minimum-resale-price laws of the States, several Members of the Congress have introduced bills providing that such contracts may be enforced against nonsigners if the State law contains a "nonsigners clause," without constituting a violation of the Federal Trade Commission Act or the antitrust acts. Legislation to repeal the Miller-Tydings amendment has also been introduced.

The position of the Department of Commerce, in commenting on this legislation, is influenced by the organic responsibilities of the Department in encouraging higher standards of business ethics and operations and also by the responsibility of the Department in protecting the interests of small business.

Without the Miller-Tydings Act, State fair-trade laws would be largely inoperative since, without this enabling act applying to interstate trade, it would undoubtedly be necessary for a manufacturer to be incorporated in each State in which he wished to issue fair-trade contracts. This procedure would add materially to the cost of distribution, a policy to which the Department is justifiably opposed; and it is manifest that a large number of manufacturers now working under fair-trade contracts would drop such contracts under those conditions and that the State fair-trade laws thereupon would become a matter of only academic interest. Since a repeal of the Miller-Tydings amendment would nullify State fair-trade laws, the Department's attitude regarding this amendment reasonably might be based on its view of the fair-trade laws themselves. And with reference to these State laws, since 45 States have enacted them, there seems to be a clear-cut matter of public policy, affecting 45 States, involved in support or opposition to the Miller-Tydings amendment.

The same reasoning applies to the nonsigner clause typical to a State fair-trade law. In considering the wisdom of this clause, however, we must recognize that without the clause fair-trade contracts in any State would be meaningless, because the firms who precipitate price wars are the very ones who would not sign the fair-trade contract. If all competitor retailers were not treated alike in this respect the stage would be set for wide open price wars in any State. In considering the nonsigner clause, therefore, we must conclude that without such a clause, fair-trade laws would be meaningless.

Since either of the above two features spells life or death for State fair-trade laws themselves, a decision for or against the Miller-Tydings amendment, or the nonsigner clause, must be made with due consideration of the values attached to this type of resale-price-maintenance law, and upon the basis of public policy with reference to fair-trade laws.

In contemplating policy regarding fair-trade laws, the following aspects are worthy of consideration:

These laws protect the capital investment of small retailers in inventories which have been purchased at prevailing market prices, in that the retailer is protected against killing price wars. Faced by predatory price cutting by powerful retail organizations, the small retailer must either sell his goods at a loss, or lose his trade to these competitors on the "loss leader" items and also lose the store traffic thus diverted to the price-cutting stores for the purchase of such items. This result we believe is destructive of small-business enterprise and constitutes a deception of the consuming public.

Price wars disappeared, with a few exceptions, with the widespread acceptance of fair-trade-contract procedures, and the businesses of many small retailers were thus saved.

Studies have been made from time to time of the results of fair-trade laws on consumer prices. Those studies have been unconvincing in demonstrating the effect of these laws on prices. Some studies have shown tendencies toward higher prices. Other studies have shown that average prices are lower under fair-trade laws. It is known that in a great many neighborhood and other independent retail stores, prices on fair-trade products have been reduced as standard practice, because the fair-trade minimum price became a standard price in the trade and this price was lower than the price printed on labels which was the price formerly charged by these stores. Fair-trade prices are, in general, fair to the consumer and to the dealer, allowing the latter only a reasonable mark-up in order to cover his operating costs and a nominal profit on his business investment.

Opponents of fair-trade laws claim that monopolistic practices are thereby promoted. We know of no evidence which supports such a belief, and are of the opinion that opposition on this ground is based wholly on theory. It is our opinion, and we believe that opinion to be substantiated by the Report of the Federal Trade Commission on Resale Price Maintenance (submitted to the Congress, December 13, 1945), that ardent support for minimum resale prices is found in the ranks of small business, independent proprietors of corner drug stores, and similar retail establishments. These persons are the least likely to favor legislation encouraging the growth of monopolies in their field. Among others, those groups identified with monopolistic practices and tendencies, such as loss-leader selling to the deception of the public and to the benefit of their own competitive ⊥ position in the market at the expense of small business, usually were opposed to fair-trade legislation.

The opposition to fair-trade laws comes from two principal sources: (1) Large distributing groups, including chains and large department stores, which have historically used price cutting to drive weaker competition out of the way, thus, in restraint of trade, attempting to create a monopoly in the field of retailing; (2) lawyers and economists, both in the Government and in private practice, who cite a violation of the economic principle of a free price based on supply and demand and the theoretical harm resulting from such violations. Equally eminent practitioners, in Government and private practice, take a contrary view citing favorable price and other economic results flowing from these laws. We believe that theory and practice must be separated when considering the merits of this type of legislation.

Price control is a practical, not theoretical, problem. Price ceilings are at times necessary, and at other times during buyers markets price floors are needed to prevent business chaos.

To condemn price control under the fair-trade laws is to close one's eyes to other types of price control sponsored by manufacturers and producers without regard to fair-trade contracts. In a very substantial segment of business, represented by sales of automobiles, major appliances, home furnishings, and some lines of men's clothing, resale prices are maintained by fear that the manufacturer will refuse to sell to the dealer in the event he violates the manufacturer's price policy.

There are other types of price maintenance in operation in this country without regard to fair-trade contracts. In one type merchandise is distributed through the retailer on a consignment basis. In this type of merchandising the manufacturer owns the retail stock and the retailer does not pay for it until it has been sold to the ultimate consumer. Obviously, under this system, the dealer has nothing to say about prices. He is merely an agent executing the orders of his principal.

CONCLUSION

There is reason to conclude that the case against fair trade is more theoretical than real; that fair trade is beneficial to small business; that facts regarding its causing higher prices in total are unconvincing; that monopoly does not result from fair-trade laws; and that fair-trade laws have a stabilizing influence on the economy. For these reasons we recommend against repeal of the Miller-Tydings amendment, and, further, recommend that the amendment be strengthened by the adoption of H. R. 4592, H. R. 5767 or similar legislation.

Due to the urgency of this legislation we have been unable to obtain the views of the Bureau of the Budget with respect to the transmission of this report.

Executive Office of the President,
Bureau of the Budget,
Washington 25, D. C., February 28, 1952.

Hon. Emanuel Celler,
Chairman, Committee on the Judiciary,
House of Representatives, Washington 25, D. C.

MY DEAR MR. CELLER: This is in response to your inquiry about the Bureau's action on agency reports on H. R. 4592, H. R. 4662, and H. R. 6367, now pending before your committee.

All these bills would amend the Miller-Tydings Act for the purpose of modifying the recent ruling of the Supreme Court in the case of *Schwegmann Brothers et al.* v. *Calvert Distillers Corp.* (341 U. S. 384).

As you indicated, because of the urgency of your committee's time schedule, the adverse report of the Federal Trade Commission and the favorable report of the Department of Commerce on these bills were sent directly to the committee without awaiting the usual action by this office under Budget Circular A–19.

Copies of these reports and the adverse testimony of Assistant Attorney General Morison have now been reviewed and we are advising the agencies that, in light of the considerations advanced by the Commission and Mr. Morison, we believe that enactment of the legislation would not be in accord with the program of the President.

Sincerely yours,

F. J. Lawton, *Director.*

CHANGES IN EXISTING LAW

In compliance with paragraph 2a of rule XIII of the Rules of the House of Representatives, changes in existing law made by the bill, as introduced, are shown as follows (existing law proposed to be omitted is enclosed in black brackets, new matter is printed in italics, existing law in which no change is proposed is shown in roman):

ACT OF JULY 2, 1890, AS AMENDED (SHERMAN ANTITRUST LAW)

SECTION 1. *(a)* Every contract, combination in the form of trust or otherwise, or conspiracy, in restraint of trade or commerce among the several States, or with foreign nations, is hereby declared to be illegal[: *Provided,* That nothing herein contained shall render illegal, contracts or agreements prescribing minimum prices for the resale of a commodity which bears, or the label or container of which bears, the trade mark, brand, or name of the producer or distributor of such commodity and which is in free and open competition with commodities of the same general class produced or distributed by others, when contracts or agreements of that description are lawful as applied to intrastate transactions, under any statute, law, or public policy now or hereafter in effect in any State, Territory, or the District of Columbia in which such resale is to be made, or to which the commodity is to be transported for such resale, and the making of such contracts or agreements shall not be an unfair method of competition under section 5, as amended and supplemented, of the Act entitled "An Act to create a Federal Trade Commission, to define its powers and duties, and for other purposes", approved September 26, 1914: *Provided further,* That the preceding proviso shall not make lawful any contract or agreement, providing for the establishment or maintenance of minimum resale prices on any commodity herein involved, between manufacturers, or between producers, or between wholesalers, or between brokers, or between factors, or between retailers. or between persons, firms, or corporations in competition with each other]. Every person who shall make any contract or engage in any combination or conspiracy hereby declared to be illegal shall be deemed guilty of a misdemeanor, and, on conviction thereof, shall be punished by fine not exceeding $5,000, or by imprisonment not exceeding one year, or by both said punishments, in the discretion of the court.

(b) Nothing contained herein or in any of the antitrust laws of the United States shall render illegal any contract or agreement prescribing minimum prices for the resale of a commodity which bears, or the label or container of which bears, the trade-mark, brand, or name of the producer of such commodity and which is in free and open competition with commodities of the same general class produced or distributed by others, when contracts or agreements of that description are lawful under any statute, law, or public policy now or hereafter in effect in any State, Territory, or the District of Columbia in which such resale is to be made, or to which the commodity is to be transported for such resale. For the purposes of this Act the words "contract or agreement" shall mean a contract or agreement in which the party prescribing the minimum prices shall be the owner of the trade-mark or brand of the commodity or commodities to which this Act is applicable.

(c) Nothing contained herein or in any of the antitrust laws of the United States shall render illegal the exercise or enforcement of any right or right of action created by any law, now or hereafter in effect in any State, Territory, or the District of Columbia, which provides in substance that willfully and knowingly advertising, offering for sale, or selling any commodity at less than the minimum prices prescribed in any such contract or agreement whether the person so advertising, offering for sale, or selling is or is not a party to such contract or agreement, is unfair competition and is actionable at the suit of any person damaged thereby: Provided, however, That in the exercise or enforcement of any right or right of action as is exempted from the antitrust laws by this subsection, it shall be a complete defense to a charge of unfair competition for the defendant to show that the party prescribing the minimum prices has failed to make reasonable efforts to insure compliance by those in competition with the defendant, with such prescribed minimum prices.

(d) Whenever by contract or agreement described in subsection (b) minimum resale prices may be established for a commodity in any State, Territory, or the District of Columbia, where such a contract or agreement is lawful, it shall be an act of unfair competition, actionable at the suit of any person damaged thereby, to willfully and knowingly, in interstate commerce, (1) advertise for sale, offer for sale, or sell or (2) have transported for sale or resale or (3) deliver pursuant to a sale, or otherwise deliver, such commodity in any such State, Territory, or the District of Columbia, where such a contract or agreement is lawful, at less than the prices so established in such contract or agreement, whether the person so advertising for sale, offering for sale, or selling is or is not a party to any such contract or agreement; any person, firm or corporation, injured in his or its business or property because of the violation of this subsection (d) may sue for and recover the damages by him or it sustained and shall be entitled to sue for and have injunctive relief against threatened loss or damage by a violation of this subsection (d) when and under the same conditions and principles as injunctive relief against threatened conduct that will cause loss or damage is granted by courts of equity, under the rules governing such proceedings, and upon the execution of proper bond against damages for an injunction improvidently granted and a showing that the danger of irreparable loss or damage is immediate, a preliminary injunction may issue; action to recover such damages or for such an injunction may be maintained in any court of competent jurisdiction of the several States, or of the United States, having jurisdiction over the parties; in suits within the provisions of this subsection (d) the provisions of section 7 of this Act providing for threefold damages shall not apply: Provided, That nothing contained herein shall apply to advertisements for sale, offers for sale, or sales which originate from or are directed to or are completed within any State, Territory, or the District of Columbia, where such contracts or agreements as are described herein are not lawful by statute: And provided further, That in any proceeding involving alleged violation of this subsection it shall be a complete defense to a charge of unfair competition for the defendant to show that the party prescribing the minimum prices has failed to make reasonable efforts to insure compliance, by those in competition with the defendant, with such prescribed minimum prices.

(e) Neither the making of such contracts or agreements as described in subsection (b) nor the exercise or enforcement of any right or right of action as described in subsections (c) and (d) shall be an unfair method of competition under section 5, as amended and supplemented, of the Act entitled "An Act to create a Federal Trade Commission, to define its powers and duties, and for other purposes", approved September 26, 1914.

(f) Nothing in this Act contained shall make lawful any contract or agreement, providing for the establishment or maintenance of minimum resale prices on any commodity herein involved, between manufacturers, or between producers, or between wholesalers, or between brokers, or between factors, or between retailers, or between persons, firms, or corporations in competition with each other.

H.R. 6925 AS REPORTED BY THE HOUSE COMMITTEE ON THE JUDICIARY
82d Cong., 2d Sess.
March 13, 1952

⊥ 1   ⊥ Reported with an amendment, referred to the House Calendar, and ordered to be printed

[Omit the part struck through and insert the part printed in italic]

A BILL

To amend the Act entitled "An Act to protect trade and commerce against unlawful restraints and monopolies", approved July 2, 1890, and for other purposes.

1   *Be it enacted by the Senate and House of Representa-*
2   *tives of the United States of America in Congress assembled,*
3   That section 1 of the Act entitled "An Act to protect trade
4   and commerce against unlawful restraints and monopolies",
5   approved July 2, 1890, be amended to read as follows:
6   "SECTION 1. (a) Every contract, combination in the
7   form of trust or otherwise, or conspiracy, in restraint of trade
8   or commerce among the several States, or with foreign na-
9   tions, is hereby declared to be illegal. Every person who
10   shall make any contract or engage in any combination or

⊥ 2   ⊥1   conspiracy hereby declared to be illegal shall be deemed
2   guilty of a misdemeanor, and, on conviction thereof, shall
3   be punished by fine not exceeding $5,000, or by imprison-
4   ment not exceeding one year, or by both said punishments,
5   in the discretion of the court.
6   "(b) Nothing contained herein or in any of the anti-
7   trust laws of the United States shall render illegal any
8   contract or agreement prescribing minimum prices for the
9   resale of a commodity which bears, or the label or con-
10   tainer of which bears, the trade-mark, brand, or name of
11   the producer of such commodity and which is in free and
12   open competition with commodities of the same general class
13   produced or distributed by others, when contracts or agree-
14   ments of that description are lawful under any statute, law,
15   or public policy now or hereafter in effect in any State,
16   Territory, or the District of Columbia in which such resale
17   is to be made, or to which the commodity is to be trans-
18   ported for such resale. For the purposes of this Act the
19   words 'contract or agreement' shall mean a contract or
20   agreement in which the party prescribing the minimum
21   prices shall be the owner of the ~~trade-mark or~~ *trade-*
22   *mark, brand, or name* of the commodity or commodities to
23   which this Act is applicable.
24   "(c) Nothing contained herein or in any of the anti-
25   trust laws of the United States shall render illegal the exer-

cise or enforcement of any right or right of action created by any law, now or hereafter in effect in any State, Territory, or the District of Columbia, which provides in substance that willfully and knowingly advertising, offering for sale, or selling any commodity at less than the minimum prices prescribed in any such contract or agreement whether the person so advertising, offering for sale, or selling is or is not a party to such contract or agreement, is unfair competition and is actionable at the suit of any person damaged thereby: *Provided, however*, That in the exercise or enforcement of any right or right of action as is exempted from the antitrust laws by this subsection, it shall be a complete defense to a charge of unfair competition for the defendant to show that the party prescribing the minimum prices has failed to make reasonable efforts to insure compliance, by those in competition with the defendant, with such prescribed minimum prices.

"(d) Whenever by contract or agreement described in subsection (b) minimum resale prices may be established for a commodity in any State, Territory, or the District of Columbia, where such a contract or agreement is lawful, it shall be an act of unfair competition, actionable at the suit of any person damaged thereby, to willfully and knowingly, in interstate commerce, (1) advertise for sale, offer for sale, or sell or (2) have transported for sale or resale or (3) deliver pursuant to a sale, or otherwise deliver, such commodity in any such State, Territory, or the District of Columbia, where such a contract or agreement is lawful, at less than the prices so established in such contract or agreement, whether the person so advertising for sale, offering for sale, or selling is or is not a party to any such contract or agreement; any person, firm or corporation, injured in his or its business or property because of the violation of this subsection (d) may sue for and recover the damages by him or it sustained and shall be entitled to sue for and have injunctive relief against threatened loss or damage by a violation of this subsection (d) when and under the same conditions and principles as injunctive relief against threatened conduct that will cause loss or damage is granted by courts of equity, under the rules governing such proceedings, and upon the execution of proper bond against damages for an injunction improvidently granted and a showing that the danger of irreparable loss or damage is immediate, a preliminary injunction may issue; action to recover such damages or for such an injunction may be maintained in any court of competent jurisdiction of the several States, or of the United States, having jurisdiction over the parties; in suits within the provisions of this subsection (d) the provisions of section 7 of this Act providing for threefold damages shall not apply: *Provided*, That nothing contained herein shall apply to advertisements for sale, offers for sale, or sales which originate from or are directed to or are completed within any State, Territory, or the District of Columbia, where such contracts or agreements as are described herein

8   are not lawful by statute: *And provided further,* That in
9   any proceeding involving alleged violation of this subsection
10 it shall be a complete defense to a charge of unfair competi-
11 tion for the defendant to show that the party prescribing the
12 minimum prices has failed to make reasonable efforts to
13 insure compliance, by those in competition with the defend-
14 ant, with such prescribed minimum prices.
15   "(e) Neither the making of such contracts or agree-
16 ments as described in subsection (b) nor the exercise or
17 enforcement of any right or right of action as described in
18 subsections (c) and (d) shall be an unfair method of compe-
19 tition under section 5, as amended and supplemented, of the
20 Act entitled 'An Act to create a Federal Trade Commis-
21 sion, to define its powers and duties, and for other purposes',
22 approved September 26, 1914.
1   "(f) Nothing in this Act contained shall make lawful
2   any contract or agreement, providing for the establishment
3   or maintenance of minimum resale prices on any commodity
4   herein involved, between manufacturers, or between pro-
5   ducers, or between wholesalers, or between brokers, or be-
6   tween factors, or between retailers, or between persons, firms,
7   or corporations in competition with each other."

REMARKS OF REP. CHARLES A. WOLVERTON
82d Cong., 2d Sess.
May 6, 1952

98 Cong. Rec. A2742

Mr. [CHARLES A.] WOLVERTON [R., N.J.]. Mr. Speaker, a very careful and worth-while study has been prepared by American Enterprise Association, Washington, D. C., in the form of a comparative analysis of H. R. 5767, introduced by Representative MCGUIRE, of Connecticut, and reported favorably by the House Committee on Interstate and Foreign Commerce; H. R. 6925, introduced by Representative KEOGH, of New York, and reported favorably by the House Committee on the Judiciary; and H. R. 6986, introduced by Representative CELLER, of New York. The comparative analysis to which reference is made is as follows:

HISTORICAL BACKGROUND

Fair trade laws have been enacted in all the States except Missouri, Texas, Vermont, and the District of Columbia. The major objective of such laws is to prevent price cutting below a minimum which may be prescribed in a contract between a manufacturer or wholesaler and a retailer. Under the provisions of the State laws, if such a contract is entered into between any manufacturer or wholesaler and retailer, such contract is binding upon all other retailers who have notice of the agreement irrespective of whether they have entered into a contract.

Before the passage in 1937 of the Miller-Tydings amendment to section 1 of the Sherman Antitrust Act, the laws and contracts thereunder applied only to intrastate transactions. The purpose of this amendment was to remove from the application of the antitrust laws those interstate transactions affected by the State fair trade laws. The amendment provided, in effect, that agreements prescribing minimum prices for commodities when lawful within a State would also be legal as to commodities shipped in interstate commerce for resale within a fair trade State.

The protection afforded to the maintenance of minimum resale prices in interstate transactions was limited in 1951 by the Supreme Court decision in *Schwegmann Bros.* v. *Calvert Distillers Corp.* (341 U. S. 384 (1951)) to situations where a contract had been entered into between a manufacturer and a retailer. The case held that the Miller-Tydings amendment did not cover State fair-trade laws when applied to nonsigners, and that enforcement would place an undue burden on interstate commerce.

As a result of this decision several bills have been introduced in the Eighty-second Congress.

H. R. 5767, introduced October 17, 1951, by Representative MCGUIRE, would amend the Federal Trade Commission Act by using the language of the Miller-Tydings amendment and extending it to apply to nonsigners as well as signers under resale price maintenance contracts. Also it would extend the provisions in reference to minimum prices to include contracts for "stipulated" prices, and contracts requiring vendors to enter into another contract. In addition, it would clarify the present law as modified by *Sunbeam Corporation* v. *Wentling* (185 F. 2d 903 (1950)) to permit a broader interpretation of State fair-trade laws in connection with retail sales across State lines.

H. R. 6925, introduced March 6, 1952, by Representative KEOGH, would amend the Sherman Antitrust Act, as amended. It too would abrogate the effect of the decision in the Schwegmann case by validating enforcement of State fair-trade laws applicable to nonsigners, but would limit its application to contracts for minimum resale price maintenance. It would clarify the decision in the Wentling case, but would not validate transactions originating within or consummated in non-fair-trade States. Also it would provide as a complete defense to an action a showing that the party prescribing minimum prices had failed to make reasonable efforts to insure compliance by others in competition with defendant.

H. R. 6986, introduced March 11, 1952, by Representative CELLER, would amend the Clayton Act and the Sherman Antitrust Act, as amended, and would make the provisions of the Miller-Tydings amendment applicable to nonsigners. However, it would make the law applicable only to loss leader sales and provides a number of exceptions to meet certain business requirements.

Another bill, H. R. 4365, introduced by Representative CURTIS, would repeal the Miller-Tydings amendment.

H. R. 5767 was reported with amendments by the House Committee on Interstate and Foreign Commerce on February 27, 1952. H. R. 6925 was reported with amendments by the House Committee on the Judiciary on March 13, 1952. H. R. 6986 has not yet been reported by the House Committee on the Judiciary.

The House Rules Committee cleared H. R. 5767 for floor debate and voted a special rule permitting H. R. 6925 to be offered as a substitute.

COMPARATIVE ANALYSIS

H. R. 5767	H. R. 6925	H. R. 6986
Acts amended by the proposed legislation		
Would amend section 5 (a) of the Federal Trade Commission Act with respect to certain contracts and agreements which establish minimum or stipulated resale prices and which are extended by State law to persons who are not parties to such contracts and agreements.	Would amend the Sherman Antitrust Act by reenacting and extending the provisions of the Miller-Tydings amendment, but would limit application to minimum prices and would extend act to nonsigners.	Would amend the Clayton Act and the Sherman Antitrust Act for the purpose of prohibiting loss-leader sales.
General objectives of the proposed legislation		
The bill would make the provisions of the Miller-Tydings amendment apply to nonsigners in fair trade law States and to sales by a retailer in one State to buyers in another. In effect it would provide that with regard to interstate transactions, State price maintenance laws shall not constitute a violation of the Federal Trade Commission Act or the Sherman Antitrust Act.	Same as H. R. 5767.	The bill would prohibit loss-leader sales, but would not restore State resale price maintenance.

	Specific provisions	
1. Unfair methods of competition are prohibited by reenacting existing law contained in first sentence of section 5 (a) of the Federal Trade Commission Act.	1. Existing law which prohibits unfair methods of competition under section 5 of the Federal Trade Commission Act is incorporated by reference in subparagraph (e) of section 1 of the Sherman Antitrust Act as it would be amended by this legislation.	1. While no reference is made in this bill to section 5 (a) of the Federal Trade Commission Act, that act would remain unchanged by this legislation.
2. The language of the Miller-Tydings amendment to the Sherman Antitrust Act is included in this bill and extends the provisions to cover "stipulated" prices, which also appears in some State statutes. The bill would also extend to cover contracts requiring a vendee to enter into a contract prescribing minimum or stipulated prices for resale of a commodity bearing the trademark, brand or name of a manufacturer or distributor.	2. The Miller-Tydings amendment is reenacted to cover contracts and agreements prescribing minimum prices, but does not cover "stipulated" prices nor does it apply to contracts by a distributor.	2. The language of the Miller-Tydings amendment is reenacted with the following substantial changes: (a) nonsigners would be bound, (b) contract must not prescribe minimum prices higher than "delivered cost" to the seller, however, sales would be permitted at lower than "delivered cost," when, in good faith, the items are discontinued; damaged; sold by order of the court; sold to certain charitable institutions; are perishable; sold in inventory liquidation to avoid bankruptcy; or are sold in seasonal clearance sales.
3. The effects of the Schwegmann decision are invalidated by providing that nonsigners may be bound by contracts to which they are not parties when so provided by State law.	3. Same as H. R. 5767.	3. Same as H. R. 5767, but specifically renders unenforceable those rights under contracts which prescribe a price higher than delivered cost.
4. Obstacles suggested by the Wentling decision are removed by providing that the making of contracts or the enforcement of rights under the proposed legislation would not constitute an unlawful burden or restraint upon or an interference with interstate commerce.	4. The Federal cause of action created by this bill would not apply to transactions originating from, directed to, or completed within any non-fair-trade State. (Subparagraph (d) of sec. 1 of the Sherman Antitrust Act as it would be amended by this legislation.)	4. The application of the Miller-Tydings amendment to loss leader sales, as provided for in this bill, would cover goods transported, sold, or resold to vendees in a fair-trade State.
5. The so-called horizontal agreements between manufacturers or between producers or between wholesalers or between brokers, or between factors, retailers, firms, or corporations in competition with each other remain outlawed under this proposed legislation.	5. Same as H. R. 5767.	5. Reenacts section 1 of the Sherman Antitrust Act outlawing agreements in restraint of trade, but omits that part of the language of the Miller-Tydings amendment which refers specifically to agreements between manufacturers or between producers, etc., who are competitors. (The original provisions of the Sherman Antitrust Act and sec. 5 (a) of the Federal Trade Commission Act which have been held to outlaw horizontal price agreements remain unchanged by this bill.)

Enforcement of the proposed legislation

Damage suits are authorized in the State courts by any person damaged by price cutting. (The provision for criminal penalties as contained in the original bill was dropped by committee action.)	Section 7 of the Sherman Antitrust Act, as amended, which provides for threefold damages would not be applicable. However, where a person or corporation has been damaged, suit in damages or injunctive relief is authorized. A price-cutting retailer would be afforded a complete defense to an action where he could show that the party prescribing minimum prices has failed to make reasonable efforts to insure compliance by defendant's competitors.	The bill would permit persons damaged by loss-leader selling to file suit for treble damages or to seek injunctive relief. It specifically provides that section 15 of the Clayton Act (providing for suits by United States district attorneys to restrain violations under the act) shall not apply to loss-leader practice.

• • • •

Mr. Speaker, some doubt or confusion has been expressed with reference to the purpose and effect of the McGuire fair-trade bill, H. R. 5767, reported favorably by the House Committee on Interstate and Foreign Commerce, and the Keogh bill, H. R. 6925, relating to the same subject. In an effort to bring some clarity to the subject, I herewith submit the following subject matter in question-and-answer form:

Question 1. What is the purpose of the McGuire bill?

Answer. The purpose of the McGuire bill is to permit the application and enforcement of State fair-trade laws in their entirety with respect to interstate transactions. In so doing, the bill seeks to remove several actual and potential obstacles to such complete application and enforcement:

I. With respect to the nonsigner clauses of the State fair-trade laws, the McGuire bill seeks to remove the obstacle raised by the Supreme Court in the Schwegmann case to the effect that enforcement of State fair-trade laws in interstate commerce with respect to nonsigners constitutes a violation of the Federal antitrust laws.

II. With respect to retail transactions which cross State lines, the McGuire bill seeks to remove the obstacle raised by a court of appeals in the Wentling case through its holding that the Pennsylvania State Fair Trade Act should be construed narrowly so that it will not apply to retail transactions by a nonsigner which cross Pennsylvania borders (the court's reasoning seems to apply equally to fair-trade laws of other States).

III. With respect to "stipulated" prices (as distinct from "minimum" prices), the McGuire bill seeks to remove a possible obstacle (which has not as yet been raised by any court) that the Miller-Tydings Act might not exempt contracts prescribing "stipulated" prices.

IV. With respect to agreements requiring a vendee to enter into resale price maintenance contracts, the McGuire bill seeks to remove the possible obstacle (not as yet raised by any Federal court) that the Miller-Tydings Act does not exempt such agreements.

Question 2. How do the State fair-trade laws affect nonsigners?

Answer. They provide that willfully and knowingly advertising, offering for sale, or selling any fair-trade commodity at less than the price prescribed in a fair-trade contract is unfair competition, and subjects the advertiser, offerer, or seller (even though he is not a party to the fair-trade contract) to suit by any person damaged by the advertisement, offer, or sale. This means a manufacturer who has signed a fair-trade contract with one retailer can, by giving other retailers notice of the contract, prevent them from selling below the fair-trade price.

Question 3. What is the Miller-Tydings Act?

Answer. The Miller-Tydings Act is an amendment to section 1 of the Sherman Antitrust law. The amendment exempts interstate vertical price maintenance agreements from the Sherman Antitrust Act and the Federal Trade Commission Act in those States which have enacted Fair Trade laws.

The Miller-Tydings Act was enacted on August 17, 1937. Congress passed the Miller-Tydings Act as an amendment to a District of Columbia Appropriation bill. Bills containing substantially the same provisions, however, had previously been reported favorably by the Judiciary Committee of both the Senate and the House.

4. The Schwegmann case (*Schwegmann Bros.* v. *Calvert Corp.* (341 U. S. 384, May 21, 1951)).

Question 4 (a). What is the problem raised by the Schwegmann case?

Answer. In the Schwegmann case, Calvert, having entered into resale price maintenance contracts with a number of Louisiana retailers, sued to enjoin Schwegmann, who had not signed such a contract, from selling Calvert products at retail in Louisiana at less than the price stipulated in the contracts. The Court (3 justices dissenting) found that this was an interstate price-fixing scheme which violated the Sherman Act. Although resale price maintenance contracts are lawful in Louisiana and although the Louisiana Fair Trade law has a nonsigner clause, the Court held that the Miller-Tydings Act applied only with respect to contracts authorized by State law, and did not permit the nonsigner clause of the State law to apply in this situation.

Question 4 (b). What does the McGuire bill do about this problem?

Answer. The bill provides that nothing in any of the Federal antitrust acts shall prevent the exercise or enforcement of any right or right of action created by the nonsigner provision of any State law.

Question 4 (c). Can this be done under the Constitution?

Answer. Yes. The Supreme Court in an earlier case (*Old Dearborn Co.* v. *Seagram Corp.,* 299 U. S. 183) held that the nonsigner provisions contained in fair-trade statutes are constitutional. Furthermore, the Court in the Schwegmann case did not say that Congress could not permit the nonsigner provisions of State fair-trade laws to apply to interstate transactions; it merely said that Congress did not intend to do so in passing the Miller-Tydings Act. The majority opinion apparently assumes Congress has power to accomplish this result if it wishes to do so.

5. The Wentling case (*Sunbeam Corp* v. *Wentling* (185 F. (2d) 903, Dec. 8, 1950)).

Question 5 (a). What is the problem raised by the Wentling case?

Answer. In the Wentling case the Court held that the Pennsylvania State Fair Trade Act should not be construed to apply to sales by a Pennsylvania retailer (who was a nonsigner) to consumers in other States or to advertisements in publications published in other States, because, so construed, the Pennsylvania statute might be considered a burden upon interstate commerce and might, therefore, have to be declared unconstitutional.

Question 5 (b). What does the McGuire bill do about this problem?

Answer. The McGuire bill provides that the application of State fair-trade laws shall not constitute a burden upon interstate commerce.

Question 5 (c). Does this provision in the McGuire bill assure that State fair-trade laws will apply to all interstate retail transactions?

Answer. No; it does not. Congress cannot amend State laws. However, in the light of the congressional declaration contained in the McGuire bill, the courts may be willing to give a broader interpretation to State fair-trade laws. In the Wentling case, only fear of burdening interstate commerce appears to have kept that court from making the Pennsylvania law applicable to retail transactions which cross the Pennsylvania State lines. Congress could enact a Federal fair-trade act but for reasons set forth below under question 6, the McGuire bill purposely refrains from so doing.

6. Enactment of Federal policy (as opposed to enabling legislation).

Question 6 (a). Does the McGuire bill contain a Federal prohibition against selling below fair-trade prices?

Answer. No; it does not. It merely permits the States (and 45 States have fair-trade acts) to apply and enforce their fair-trade laws. Many, if not most, retail transactions are intrastate transactions, and the States should be permitted if they so desire, to apply their fair-trade policy to such transactions.

Question 6 (b). Could Congress enact a Federal fair-trade act to prohibit sales below fair-trade prices in interstate commerce?

Answer. Yes; Congress could do so. As a matter of fact, such legislation was introduced and considered during the Sixty-ninth Congress. The Keogh bill, while still permitting application and enforcement of State fair-trade laws, would create Federal causes of action and defenses in case of sales below fair-trade prices in interstate commerce. (For details, see below, the comparison between the Keogh and McGuire bills.)

Question 6 (c). Are there Federal laws which are directed toward loss-leader selling and other methods of predatory price cutting?

Answer. Yes; the Federal antitrust laws make predatory price cutting illegal in interstate commerce where such price cutting is engaged in for the purpose of eliminating competition or establishing a monopoly. If no such purpose can be shown, or if it is done in intrastate commerce, predatory price cutting is not illegal as a matter of Federal law. However, H. R. 6986 (Mr. CELLER) would prohibit loss-leader selling per se in interstate commerce.

⊥ Question 7. What are the principal differences between the McGuire bill and the Keogh bill?

Answer. (1) The Keogh bill creates a Federal cause of action against retailers (regardless of whether they are signers or nonsigners) who sell below fair-trade prices across State lines from a State which has a fair-trade law to a State which likewise has a fair-trade law. No cause of action would exist in cases where the sale originates from a State which does not have a fair-trade law or is directed to or completed in such a State. The McGuire bill does not create a Federal cause of action but merely states that the application of State fair-trade acts to retail transactions which cross State lines shall not constitute a burden on interstate commerce.

(2) The Keogh bill also creates a Federal defense in actions to maintain fair-trade prices. It would be a complete defense in any such action (under a State fair-trade law or in any action aimed at prosecuting the new cause of action created by the Keogh bill) to show that the owner of the trade mark, brand, or name failed to make reasonable efforts to insure compliance by those in competition with the defendant in such action.

(3) The McGuire bill, like the Miller-Tydings Act and most State fair-trade laws, permits resale price maintenance for commodities bearing the trademark, brand, or name of the producer or distributor. The Keogh bill permits resale price maintenance only for commodities bearing the trademark, brand, or name of the producer.

(4) Most State fair-trade laws authorize agreements which require the buyer to enter into resale price maintenance contracts with persons to whom he resells. The Miller-Tydings Act does not specifically exempt such agreements from the Federal antitrust laws, although it may do so by implication. The McGuire bill removes any doubt on this question by specifically exempting such agreements from the antitrust laws. The Keogh bill apparently reaches the opposite result:

It seems to exempt from the antitrust laws only contracts to which the owner of the trademark, brand, or name is a party. This provision, combined with the provision referred to in paragraph (3), apparently means that only contracts to which the producer is a party are exempt.

(5) The McGuire bill specifically permits application of State fair-trade acts which authorize contracts prescribing stipulated prices. (Several State fair-trade acts use the term stipulated price.) The Keogh bill does not exempt contracts prescribing stipulated prices from the Federal antitrust laws.

HOUSE DEBATE
82d Cong., 2d Sess.
May 7, 1952

98 Cong. Rec. 4896

Mr. [RAY J.] MADDEN [D., Ind.]. Mr. Speaker, by direction of the Committee on Rules, I call up House Resolution 586 and ask for its immediate consideration.

The Clerk read the resolution, as follows:

Resolved, That upon the adoption of this resolution it shall be in order to move that the House resolve itself into the Committee of the Whole House on the State of the Union for the consideration of the bill (H. R. 5767) to amend the Federal Trade Commission Act with respect to certain contracts and agreements which establish minimum resale prices and which are extended by State law to nonsigners, and all points of order against said bill are hereby waived. That after general debate, which shall be confined to the bill and continue not to exceed 4 hours, to be equally divided and controlled by the chairman and ranking minority member of the Committee on Interstate and Foreign Commerce, the bill shall be read for amendment under the 5-minute rule. It shall be in order to consider without the intervention of any point of order the substitute committee amendment recommended by the Committee on Interstate and Foreign Commerce now in the bill, and such substitute for the purpose of amendment shall be considered under the 5-minute rule as an original bill. It shall also be in order to consider without the intervention of any point of order the text of the bill (H. R. 6925) as a substitute for the committee amendment to the bill H. R. 5767. At the conclusion of such consideration, the Committee shall rise and report the bill to the House with such amendments as may have been adopted, and any Member may demand a separate vote in the House on any of the amendments adopted in the Committee of the Whole to the bill or committee substitute. The previous question shall be considered as ordered on the bill and amendments thereto to final passage without intervening motion except one motion to recommit.

Mr. MADDEN. Mr. Speaker, I yield 30 minutes to the gentleman from Ohio [Mr. BROWN], and I yield myself such time as I may desire.

Mr. Speaker, this legislation, H. R. 5767, would permit States to authorize minimum-price contracts for the resale of commodities and make such minimum prices applicable to the sellers even though they are not parties to the contract. It would provide that such contracts when lawful under State law would not be prohibited under the Federal Trade Commission Act, nor would such act prevent the enforcement of the contracts in accordance with the State law.

The bill specifies that the making and enforcement of such minimum resale-price contracts would not be illegal under section 1 of the Sherman Antitrust Act, as amended, nor would the making or enforcement of such contracts constitute a burden, restraint, or interference with interstate commerce. However, the bill would not make legal such contracts between manufacturers, producers, and certain other specified persons in competition with each other, and the bill would provide a penalty involving $5,000 fine and imprisonment for violations.

I might say that if passed this bill would amend the Federal Trade Commission Act and would permit fair-trade agreements to be enforced against nonsigning retailers under the State fair-trade law.

The bill would apply only to products that are labeled, branded, or trade-marked with the name of the producer and distributor thereon, and in open competition with similar products of other manufacturers. This would not authorize horizontal agreements between producers and retailers. The Clayton Act prohibits any person from discriminating in prices between different purchasers of commodities where the fact of such discrimination may be to substantially lessen competition and tend to create a monopoly in the line of commerce.

The rule provides for 4 hours of general debate. Our law early recognized the illegality and the impropriety of price cutting on a certain product in order to freeze out small independent retailers. Our courts, under the antitrust laws, have enjoined sales at less than fair and reasonable prices, and at less than a fair and reasonable profit, or at less than cost with the purpose and intent of injuring or destroying the business of competitors. This legislation, if enacted into a law, will be of great aid in protecting the independent and small retailer in all lines of business. When a dealer cuts the price of his goods, he never does so with the intent of injuring his own trade or business, nor is he a benefactor of mankind. He hopes and expects by cutting prices, particularly on well known and popular products, he will draw patronage from his competitors and that he will thus be able to dominate the field, and then if his competitors fail, he can sell at higher prices and can gouge the public to his own desires. It is important to note, I believe, that this legislation has the approval of a great number of retailers, including druggists, grocers, hardware dealers, jewelers, and automobile accessories, retailers of photo equipment and supplies, radio and electric businesses, and so on.

Mr. [EMANUEL] CELLER [D., N.Y.]. Mr. Speaker, will the gentleman yield?

Mr. MADDEN. I yield.

Mr. CELLER. Can the gentleman point to one consumer organization that favors the bill—just one?

Mr. MADDEN. There are a great number of people who are familiar with the bill who are consumers and who favor it for the reason that eventually it will militate to the benefit of the consumer.

Mr. CELLER. I might say to the gentleman that such consumer organizations as the CIO, the National Grange, the American Farmers Union, the Farm Bureau Federation, are all opposed to the bill, and they are consumers who are very much concerned by the high markups which result from so-called fair-trade laws.

Mr. MADDEN. From the standpoint of the eventual effect of the legislation, it will eventually benefit the consumers because it will aid the independent retailers who are the real backbone of the home community throughout America.

Mr. CELLER. Even if it means—

Mr. MADDEN. Mr. Speaker, I refuse to yield further.

The resulting confusion brought about by the serious situation that developed up in New York, in the gentleman's home city, by one of New York City's largest retailers, brought about a price war which was detrimental to the retailing business, and eventually it was detrimental to the consumers also.

Mr. Speaker, I reserve the balance of my time.

Mr. [CLARENCE J.] BROWN [R., Ohio]. Mr. Speaker, I yield myself such time as I may consume.

Mr. Speaker, as the gentleman from Indiana has so well explained, the House Resolution 586 makes in order, under 4 hours of debate, the consideration of H. R. 5767, the McGuire bill. This rule is rather peculiar inasmuch as it also makes in order the consideration of the bill, H. R. 6925 as a substitute.

I shall repeat, in case anyone should be interested in this rule: It provides that H. R. 6925, the so-called Keogh bill shall be in order as a substitute for the McGuire bill. This rule has been written in that way purposely to give to the House the opportunity to pass upon which piece of legislation or bill it may favor.

There has been, as most of you know, a conflict as to jurisdiction between two important committees on this question. By the adoption of this rule the House will have an opportunity to debate this fair-trade question fully and pass judgment upon the two different measures which have been reported from the two different committees.

This is a very important issue that we have before us, the question of maintenance of fair trade and its consideration by the House has been made necessary, as a result of certain recent court decisions. I am not going to discuss the details of either bill because there are many Members who are much more conversant with the pending legislation and problem than I.

The McGuire bill, as I understand it, would place the control of fair-trade practices with the States—or return that power to the States, which in the past have exercised control of fair-trade practices.

The Keogh bill would place the responsibility for enforcement and supervision of fair-trade rules and practices in the Federal Government. Of course there are a few other differences between the bills. Personally, I favor the McGuire bill, because I believe fair trade is a matter which the States can handle far more fairly and more expeditiously than can the Federal Government. I think we have reached the place where we have already placed in the hands of the Central Government here in Washington about all the power it should have.

Mr. CELLER. Mr. Speaker, will the gentleman yield?

Mr. BROWN of Ohio. I yield to the gentleman from New York.

Mr. CELLER. I think the gentleman said the Keogh bill would place responsibility up to the Government. I do not understand just what the gentleman meant.

Mr. BROWN of Ohio. The supervision would come under the Federal Government.

Mr. CELLER. The Keogh bill would provide that? I do not think the gentleman is correct.

Mr. BROWN of Ohio. Perhaps I misunderstood the testimony that members of your committee gave before the Rules Committee. In other words, it is a question between Federal Government supervision on the one hand and State supervision on the other. If I am incorrect, the gentleman can correct me in his own remarks.

However, there is another issue involved in this legislation I do want to discuss for a few minutes, because I have been interested in this particular matter for a long, long time. I served on a special committee of this House, the Boren committee, during the war, when this whole question was discussed rather thoroughly. That is to whether trade names and labels are worth anything; whether they mean anything; and whether advertising in support of trade names or labels given to goods to set them apart from goods made by other manufacturers really means anything; whether advertising does add to the cost of goods purchased by the consumer or whether or not it actually brings lower prices to the consuming public, because advertised goods are sold widely.

Opponents of legislation to restore the State fair-trade laws to their full strength have contended in hearings before committees of this House that fair trade maintains high prices and high profit margins on nationally advertised products which, these opponents allege, are overpriced. They further imply that these products are overpriced largely because they are nationally advertised.

This whole approach seems to stem from the familiar misconception that advertising makes the cost of distribution too high. It is implied that the consumer is both hypnotized and victimized by national advertising into paying more than she should for a product. By contrast, private brands are alleged to be consistently lower priced, apparently just because they are not nationally advertised.

There is, of course, nothing sacred about nationally advertised brands, as such, or private brands. They must both compete with each other for the consumer's dollar in terms of the value and price they have to offer. Indeed, with the revolutionary growth of giant retailing that has taken place in the past 20 years, the distinction between the national brand and the private brand is fast disappearing, so far as advertising is concerned. Business statistics show, for instance, that the A. & P. in 1951 spent $30,000,000 in newspaper advertising alone for its private brands, and the sales volume of its private brands totaled approximately $300,000,000. The same statistics show that Sears, Roebuck last year spent $50,000,000 in advertising its private brands in newspapers and direct mail catalogs and this company's sales of its private brands amount to $2,200,000,000.

Such advertising expenditures for private brands are many times larger than the advertising budgets for most national brands. So any insistence that private brands are not advertised and are, therefore, somehow cheaper fails to recognize the actual facts of retail merchandising today.

But what about this notion that advertising, and especially national advertising, is a superfluous factor that simply makes the consumer pay through the nose? What is the function of advertising, anyway? Is it not to make the consumer aware that a particular product is available to serve a particular need of his? Advertising, in short, creates a consumer demand for goods, and national advertising creates a mass market built on this demand. In a larger but very real sense, advertising creates a higher standard of living. It stimulates people to brush their teeth every day, to buy cars, radios, television sets, refrigerators—all the things that go to make life more healthful, convenient, and pleasant.

In building a mass market for goods of all kinds, advertising is indispensable to out [sic] free-enterprise economy based on massed production. If goods could not roll off the assembly lines in a continuous flow to the consumer via the great network of outlets in our huge Nation-wide market, these assembly lines would stop. They did stop back in the depression. So did the income of labor, of the farmer, and of millions of other people. So did a great deal of advertising. We had rock-bottom prices for everything in those days, but few people had any money with which to buy even 15-cent pork chops.

Our economy is a highly interdependent one and the role of advertising in it is by no means fully recognized. Our newspapers, our national magazines, our radio and television programs are paid for to a very large extent by advertising. If this were not so, we would have no nickel newspapers, no 15-cent magazines, no free radio and television programs. We would pay much higher prices for these things, and in many cases we would not be able to get them at all. We would also pay much higher prices for goods of all kinds if mass production, mass distribution and mass advertising did not work together to turn out an abundance of goods at ever lower prices. What would we have to pay for a washing machine or a television set today if it were made by hand? As for the great life-saving drugs—penicillin, the sulfas, antibiotics—their whole history has been one of continual price reductions, thanks to mass production, mass distribution, and national advertising.

Many manufacturers of national brands have pioneered in building a market for new products. They take a tremendous financial risk in producing and advertising such products. They invest heavily in research to improve quality and performance, to develop other new products. Private brands can move into this market, thus created, without any such risk or investment and take advantage of the customer demand built up by the national brand manufacturer. This is all to the good. It makes for more and more intense competition, to the ultimate benefit of the consumer.

Under conditions of competition, as the late Justice Brandeis noted, every manufacturer sets his price at his peril. If the allegation were true that nationally advertised brands are overpriced, the consumer has every opportunity to buy competing private brands if she chooses. To imply that the consumer, under the alleged spell of national advertising will buy products at prices she considers too high, not just once but over and over, when alternatives do exist, is to indict the good sense and intelligence of the American public.

Because nationally advertised brands are identified by the manufacturer's trade-mark or brand name, they can be sold on his reputation to millions of consumers. The national brand, therefore, is the stock in trade, the bread and butter of the smaller retailers who does [sic] not have the capital resources for promotion to sell private brands extensively, as giant retailers do. But the very fact that nationally-advertised brands are widely known and in demand makes them ideal customer bait from the price-juggler's viewpoint. But when the reputation of a national brand is appropriated for trick pricing devices by a merchant who does not own the trade-mark symbolizing that reputation, a three-fold damage is done—to the manufacturer who spent many years and dollars building up that reputation; to other retailers whose business centers around the sales of such national brands; and to the consumer who may or may not be taken in by the price-juggler, but who certainly has her confidence shaken in the quality and value of the product.

In this latter connection, it is worth noting that the consumer today cannot be an expert on the intrinsic quality of the many goods she needs, as the housewife once tended to be a century or more ago when the home was in effect the factory for everything from clothing to candles. The consumer must now rely on the integrity of the standard brand which, when coupled with an established price, as under fair trade, gives the consumer a yardstick of value for her money.

Price juggling and the price wars it leads to, however, destroy the consumer's yardstick of value. When prices on well-known national brands are being driven down, day after day, to bankruptcy levels, a consumer is going to feel cheated, no matter what price she pays. She will always feel that if she had waited until tomorrow she could have got the product for less. She will assume too that the national brand was too high priced to begin with and that the price juggler's bargain price represents the real value of the trade-marked product; in short, that it is a cheap product of inferior quality.

Effective fair trade helps to prevent such a train of developments which are a genuine disservice to the consumer and a threat to the welfare of our interdependent economy in which national advertising builds a mass market to sustain mass production.

So I feel that any argument, any contention which may be made, that unnecessary advertising will be protected by the adoption or the passage of this legislation, and that it will lead to higher prices, is based upon a false premise. Instead, most of us from experience know that brand names and advertised goods are usually quality goods which can be trusted and are usually sold at prices which represent their true value.

Mr. [CLARE E.] HOFFMAN [R., Mich.]. Mr. Speaker, will the gentleman yield?

Mr. BROWN of Ohio. I yield to the gentleman from Michigan.

Mr. HOFFMAN of Michigan. Why are the farm organizations against it?

Mr. BROWN of Ohio. I do not know that the farm organizations are against it.

Mr. HOFFMAN of Michigan. Well, some of them are.

Mr. BROWN of Ohio. I know many farm organization [sic] which brand their own products, their own goods, and send them to market under trade names because they established and required certain qualities therein. I know that they also advertise these brands and also fix the prices at which such products shall be sold to the consuming public. These prices have always been a fair reflection of the true value of the food products so labeled and advertised by the farmer owned and controlled organizations.

Mr. MADDEN. Mr. Speaker, I yield 5 minutes to the gentleman from New York [Mr. CELLER].

Mr. CELLER. Mr. Speaker, it is well for the membership to know that there are many, many organizations, particularly consumer organizations that are uninhibitedly opposed to this price-fixing legislation. Among them are the General Federation of Women's Clubs, the CIO, representing labor, and, I will say to the membership with a great deal of emphasis, the Farm Bureau Federation and the National Grange, representing the farmers. Representatives from both those groups testified unalterably against this bill. The American Bar Association has gone on record as opposing it; the Housewives United oppose it; the Federation of Citizens Clubs of the District of Columbia as well, and practically every important newspaper in the country opposes it, among them the Des Moines Register, the Christian Science Monitor, the Washington Post, all Scripps-Howard papers, the New York Times, the New York Herald Tribune, the St. Louis Post-Dispatch, the Richmond News-Leader, the Denver Post, and the Louisville Courier-Journal.

The difficulty stems, as I see it, from the fact that the consumer is not organized. The consumer throughout has not been represented. We are supposed to represent the consumer. But, the National Association of Retail Druggists has drummed up a tremendous propaganda campaign in favor of these bills; have [sic] ballooned the bills far out of proportion, and this is the same organization that twice was indicted by the Antitrust Division and fined by the courts of this country for violation of the antitrust laws, based upon their boycott, upon their undue interference with those who refuse to knuckle down to their decrees to boost mark-ups. The same holds true for a number of pharmaceutical associations. They are organized. The consumer is treated as a stepchild. He makes no noise, no outcry. We should, indeed, help the consumer. We are derelict in that regard. The consumer cannot fight back. He is unorganized.

It is like the story I told this morning in committee. In the old slave days the master said to a powerful slave weighing 210 pounds and all muscle, "I want you to go out in the field and harness that wild bull." The slave, with his tremendous, giant strength, grabbed the horns of the bull and he tamed and harnessed the bull. "Now," said the master, "I want you to bridle that wild horse." And he went out and using his mass of strength, he subdued and bridled the horse. Then the master said to the slave, "You see that hornet's nest up there in the tree? I want you to go up that tree and pull it down.["] The slave said, "No; I cannot do that." "Why can you not do it? Look what you did with the bull; look what you did with the horse." "I still cannot do it, boss." "Why not?" "Well, dem hornets are organized."

Well, that is the answer. The druggists are organized. They frighten this membership. Many of the Members have come to me and indicated their opposition to these bills. I said, "What are you going to do about it?" "Well, I am worrying about the National Association of Retail Druggists." What are we, mice or men?

I have felt the ire of the National Association of Retail Druggists for years. I opposed the Miller-Tydings Act when it was first proposed. I was told by the National Association of Retail Druggists that if I would continue my opposition to these bills I would feel their venom and sting. I nonetheless opposed them, and they sought to defeat me. Every time I ran they sought to organize against me. But the voters of my district, the consumers of my district, knew better, and they elected me every time with greater pluralities. So I tell you, do not be afraid of the druggists or any of these organizations that have been whipped in line.

It is outrageous that this great body, supposed to represent the great people of the United States, are going to hearken unto the orders, the demarches, of dictators, and you are going willy-nilly to accept what the National Association of Retail Druggists give you. I cannot, will not follow their orders. That is why I am opposed to these bills and opposed to the rule.

Mr. BROWN of Ohio. Mr. Speaker, I yield 6 minutes to the gentleman from Illinois [Mr. REED].

Mr. [CHAUNCEY W.] REED [R., Ill.]. Mr. Speaker, it is quite apparent that among the Members of the House there are three schools of thought on this legislation. Some favor the McGuire bill, some the Keogh bill, and some do not favor any kind of fair-trade legislation whatsoever.

I might say that I was a member of the Committee on the Judiciary in 1937 when the Miller-Tydings act was first considered. Its object was to protect small business from unfair competition brought about by systematic price-cutting, loss-leader practices and other similar unethical conduct indulged in largely by chain stores and which had an alarming tendency toward ruining the small independent merchants. The Miller-Tydings act became a law, and, after it had been in operation a short time, it, too, generated abuses that have continued to this very day. Vertical price-fixing authorized by that law, as a legal exception to the Sherman Antitrust Act, have [sic] in many cases resulted in unfair, unreasonable and exorbitant prices to the consuming public. The legislation before us today, whether we choose the McGuire bill or the Keogh bill, will not cure those abuses. It will require an entirely new approach than that taken by the Miller-Tydings Act and followed by the proposed McGuire and Keogh bills to remove the present inequities and at the same time protect independent merchants from the unfair practices to which they were subject before the advent of so-called fair-trade laws. There is not sufficient time in this Congress to formulate and pass such desirable legislation. Hence we are today faced with the alternative of either scrapping the present proposals or passing one of them as a stopgap which will make effective present State fair-trade laws until such time as Congress can study the matter and bring forth a more desirable remedy.

I am, therefore, in favor of some fair-trade legislation, now. I desire the most effective, fair and equitable bill we can get at the present time. The Keogh bill, in my judgment, is the better bill. I am however, not so wedded to it as to preclude me from supporting what in the sound judgment of the Committee of the Whole House, is most desirable and more sure of ultimate enactment.

However, as I have before mentioned, the remedy we are trying to administer today will be only temporary. In the near future we must formulate new legislation, that will discard the abuses that have grown up under fair trade.

I might say that we had a sort of jurisdictional dispute between the Committee on

Interstate and Foreign Commerce and the Committee on the Judiciary. The former came to the Committee on Rules sponsoring H. R. 5767 (the McGuire bill) and the latter appeared sponsoring H. R. 6925 [(]the Keogh bill). Both bills sought to accomplish the same end. The McGuire bill would amend the Federal Trades [sic] Commission Act whereas the Keogh bill would amend the Sherman Anti-Trust Act. The latter, in my judgment, was based upon a more solid foundation. Its approach is direct and if enacted it would take its place in the Federal Code with existing antitrust statutes. The former is indirect. If enacted it would be tucked away as an amendment to the Trade Commission Act when in reality it would actually amend the Sherman Act. So far as orderliness and legislation consistency are concerned, the Keogh bill is the more preferable. It amends the right law in the right place.

The Committee on Rules did not see fit to pass on the jurisdictional claims but granted a rule on the McGuire bill making in order the consideration of the Keogh bill as a substitute.

Mr. [EDGAR A.] JONAS [R., Ill.]. Mr. Speaker, will the gentleman yield?

Mr. REED of Illinois. I yield.

Mr. JONAS. Probably the gentleman from Illinois can explain a question about which I am in a quandary. Have I a right to assume that the McGuire bill merely attempts to supply what was taken out of existing law, which was passed because of a decision in the Supreme Court in the Sunbeam Corporation against Wentling case? Is that all the McGuire bill proposes to do, to supply what was taken out of existing law?

Mr. REED of Illinois. The McGuire bill affects only one of the two recent decisions of the Supreme Court affecting the Miller-Tydings Act.

Mr. JONAS. Would you say what the Keogh bill proposes to do that you cannot get out of the McGuire bill?

Mr. REED of Illinois. The Keogh bill will supply the remedy which is deemed necessary on account of both of the decisions of the Supreme Court, whereas the McGuire bill only takes care of one decision.

Mr. JONAS. But both bills are directed at establishing a universal fair-trade law; are they not?

Mr. REED of Illinois. That is right.

Mr. JONAS. Subject to State rule in one instance, and to Federal regulation in the other?

Mr. REED of Illinois. The gentleman from Ohio [Mr. BROWN] was in error in his address a few minutes ago, when he said that the McGuire bill left enforcement to the States and the Keogh bill to the Federal Government. Both bills are designed to augment and implement the State laws which now exist.

Mr. [OREN] HARRIS [D., Ark.]. Mr. Speaker, will the gentleman yield?

Mr. REED of Illinois. I yield.

Mr. HARRIS. Is it not true that the McGuire bill is purely enabling legislation?

Mr. REED of Illinois. Both bills are.

Mr. HARRIS. And is it not also true under the McGuire bill, the State may take any further action they [sic] desire in order to meet the Wentling decision that the gentleman referred to?

Mr. REED of Illinois. I think the gentleman is right, and that, too, applies to both of the bills.

Mr. CELLER. Mr. Speaker, will the gentleman yield?

Mr. REED of Illinois. I yield.

Mr. CELLER. I think the gentleman will find on close scrutiny that other differences exist between the Keogh bill and the McGuire bill. For example, the McGuire bill permits not only a minimum price, that is, a price below which an article cannot be sold, but it also goes further and provides for a stipulated price; that is, it provides for a ceiling—a floor and a ceiling. And the Keogh bill provides only for a minimum price. The McGuire bill allows not only the manufacturer to fix the price, but also the distributor. The Keogh bill does not permit the wholesaler or the distributor to fix the price. So that under the Keogh bill you cannot have a number of different prices in a given State, whereas under the McGuire bill you could have. In addition to that, another important item is that the McGuire bill amends the Federal Trade Commission

Act, which was done for reasons best known to the author and those behind the bill, namely, to circumvent the Committee on the Judiciary. The Keogh bill provides for the amendment to the Sherman Act. The McGuire bill, strangely enough, affects foreign commerce. The Keogh bill has no such provision concerning foreign commerce. The Keogh bill protects the independent retailer against fair-trading manufacturers who pay lip service to fair trade; the McGuire bill has no such provision.

The wholesaler, under the McGuire bill, has the right to price fix competitive articles—thus horizontal price fixing under the guise of vertical price fixing. The Keogh bill does not permit this.

Mr. BROWN of Ohio. Mr. Speaker, I yield 1 minute to the gentleman from New York [Mr. JAVITS].

Mr. [JACOB K.] JAVITS [R., N.Y.]. Mr. Speaker, I wish to call to the attention of the House that I intend to introduce a solution to represent this middle ground, about which my colleague the gentleman from Illinois [Mr. REED] spoke. I shall offer an amendment, which will provide that a fair-trade pricing scheme under either bill—McGuire or Keogh—cannot be put into effect unless there is competition between items sought to be fair-trade priced under these bills and similar items which are not fair-trade priced whether or not they carry a brand name.

My amendment would completely open up the field of competition, therefore, so that the consumer who does not want to pay say 50 cents for a certain brand of tooth paste which is under the fair-trade law, can buy another tooth paste which is not subject to fair-trade pricing, otherwise the first tooth paste cannot be priced under the fair-trade law. It seems to me that protects the consumer and takes care of the difficulties of the independent retailers; they claim fair-trade laws are necessary in order to maintain their over-all business position which is their fundamental reason for these bills.

The responsibility will be on the manufacturer who wants to set up his branded product on a fair-trade-price basis to be sure that there is competition from similar non-fair-traded items, otherwise the exemption from the antitrust laws contained in these bills does not apply to him. That is not an onerous burden because he is doing all his business subject to the antitrust laws right now.

The text of my amendment follows:

To H. R. 5767 (Mr. MCGUIRE): Page 4, line 24, after the word "others", insert "and not subject to contracts or agreements prescribing minimum or stipulated prices as aforesaid."

To H. R. 6925 (Mr. KEOGH): Page 2, line 13, after the word "others", insert "and not subject to any contract or agreement prescribing minimum prices as aforesaid."

Mr. BROWN of Ohio. Mr. Speaker, I yield the remainder of the time to the gentleman from Iowa [Mr. DOLLIVER].

Mr. [JAMES I.] DOLLIVER [R., Iowa]. Mr. Speaker, as has already been revealed by the discussion of this legislation, unhappily a conflict of jurisdiction has arisen in the House between the committee of which I am a member, the Committee on Interstate and Foreign Commerce, and the Committee on the Judiciary. I am not able to explain, nor do I understand why or how that difficulty has arisen, but I feel sure that is in the background of some of the discussion we have heard here today.

I can readily understand, being a member of the Committee on Interstate and Foreign Commerce, why the members of my committee are, many of them, very strongly prejudiced in favor of the McGuire bill, because that was the result of our labors in the committee and came out of the hearings. Likewise, I think I can understand why some members of the Judiciary Committee are considerably enthused about the Keogh bill, which in like manner was the result of their efforts.

But that conflict of jurisdiction emphasizes one point which I sincerely trust will be developed during the course of the general debate and the reading of this legislation. I hope the membership of the House not belonging to either of these great committees will look at this situation from its four corners and then decide which is the better legislation. That is the way to get good legislation in the Congress.

This body is to deliberate over these matters and decide what is best for the country.

Some allusion was made to the fact that there is no representative here of the consumers. Of course, I most respectfully disagree with that viewpoint, because actually all of us are consumers, whether we belong to the Congress or whether we belong to one trade organization or another. We are actually all consumers.

⊥ Indeed, one of the prerogatives and one of the necessities of this body is to protect the interest of the consumer. Surely that part of this debate has already long since been disposed of when you realize what we are going to consider, both in the McGuire bill and in the Keogh substitute. Back in 1938 this fair-trade legislation was originated in the Miller-Tydings law, which in effect was an exception, where the States wanted it, to vertical price fixing, an exception from the antitrust laws. ⊥ 4900

During the period from 1938 to the present time, 45 of the 48 States have decided that they wanted fair-trade legislation in their States. Only three States do not have fair-trade legislation, and they are Texas, Missouri, and Vermont. The legislatures of those States have decided they want none of this program for the maintenance of retail prices. That is perfectly all right.

But the point I am making now is that the question of consumer protection was taken care of back 14 years ago when the Miller-Tydings bill was first adopted, and it has been taken care of since in the 45 States that have adopted this kind of legislation.

What is the purpose of these particular bills? The particular purpose that we have for consideration is to decide whether or not we are going to let the States make fair-trade laws effective within the various jurisdictions, because about a year ago the courts decided, by a divided opinion, as has already been pointed out, that fair-trade legislation would not be effective insofar as the so-called nonsigners of fair-trade agreements are concerned.

The whole purpose of these bills that are now before us, or at least the main purpose, is to correct those decisions that were made by the courts, so that the States in question if they decide so to do may sustain and have in their respective jurisdictions vertical retail price fixing.

Mr. MADDEN. Mr. Speaker, there are no further requests for time. I therefore move the previous question.

The previous question was ordered.

The resolution was agreed to.

Mr. HARRIS. Mr. Speaker, I move that the House resolve itself into the Committee of the Whole House on the State of the Union for the consideration of the bill (H. R. 5767) to amend the Federal Trade Commission Act with respect to certain contracts and agreements which establish minimum resale prices and which are extended by State law to nonsigners.

Pending that motion I ask unanimous consent that the time be equally divided between myself in the absence of the gentleman from Tennessee [Mr. PRIEST] for our side, and the gentleman from Iowa [Mr. DOLLIVER] for the other side.

Mr. CELLER. Mr. Speaker, will the gentleman yield?

Mr. HARRIS. I yield.

Mr. CELLER. What disposition will be made of the time with reference to allotment to members of the Judiciary Committee who may be for or against these bills?

Mr. HARRIS. I may say, Mr. Speaker, insofar as this side is concerned we will be very generous with the committee.

The SPEAKER. The rule fixes the matter of who shall control the time. The rule states that it shall be equally divided and controlled by the chairman and ranking minority member of the committee.

The question is on the motion.

The motion was agreed to.

Accordingly the House resolved itself into the Committee of the Whole House on the State of the Union for the consideration of the bill H. R. 5767, with Mr. MILLS in the chair.

The Clerk read the title of the bill.

By unanimous consent the first reading of the bill was dispensed with.

The CHAIRMAN. Under the rule, the time is equally divided between the chairman of the committee—and in the absence of the chairman of the committee the

Chair will recognize the gentleman from Arkansas [Mr. HARRIS]—and the ranking minority member of the committee, the gentleman from Iowa [Mr. DOLLIVER], who is present on the floor.

The gentleman from Arkansas is recognized.

Mr. HARRIS. Mr. Speaker, I yield 10 minutes to the gentleman from Connecticut [Mr. MCGUIRE], the author of the bill.

Mr. MCGUIRE. Mr. Chairman, as enabling legislation to restore the effectiveness of the State fair-trade laws, the McGuire bill, H. R. 5767 amends section 5 (a) of the Federal Trade Commission Act. Section 5 (a) (1) of the Federal Trade Commission Act says:

Unfair methods of competition in commerce, and unfair or deceptive acts or practices in commerce, are hereby declared unlawful.

The McGuire bill, in its entirety, amends this section of the Federal Trade Commission Act. The provisions of the McGuire bill specifically referring to the Federal Trade Commission Act are as follows:

(2) Nothing contained in this act or in any of the antitrust acts shall render unlawful any contracts or agreements prescribing minimum or stipulated prices, or requiring a vendee to enter into contracts or agreements prescribing minimum or stipulated prices, for the resale of a commodity which bears, or the label or container of which bears, the trade-mark, brand, or name of the producer or distributor of such commodity and which is in free and open competition with commodities of the same general class produced or distributed by others, when contracts or agreements of that description are lawful as applied to intrastate transactions under any statute, law or public policy now or hereafter in effect in any State, Territory, or the District of Columbia, in which such resale is to be made, or to which the commodity is to be transported for such resale.

(3) Nothing contained in this act or in any of the antitrust acts shall render unlawful the exercise of the enforcement of any right or right of action created by any statute, law, or public policy now or hereafter in effect in any State, Territory, or the District of Columbia, which in substance provides that willfully and knowingly advertising, offering for sale, or selling any commodity at less than the price or prices prescribed in such contracts or agreements whether the person so advertising, offering for sale, or selling is or is not a party to such a contract or agreement, is unfair competition and is actionable at the suit of any person damaged thereby.

The question has been raised as to whether the McGuire bill, H. R. 5767, directs or authorizes any action by the Federal Trade Commission with respect to the enforcement of State fair-trade laws where interstate commerce is involved.

The McGuire bill does not have this effect, in the judgment of the Chairman of the Federal Trade Commission. In a letter of April 4 on this point, written to Representative J. PERCY PRIEST, chairman of the House Interstate and Foreign Commerce Subcommittee, which considered and reported out the McGuire bill, the Chairman of the Federal Trade Commission says:

DEAR MR. PRIEST: Reference is made to your letter of March 21, 1952, regarding H. R. 5767 and H. R. 6925, as reported by the Committees on Interstate and Foreign Commerce and on the Judiciary, respectively, and the request in your letter for a statement of the views of this Commission as to whether or not these bills, or either of them, might be construed to empower the Commission to proceed against persons who offer for sale or sell merchandise in interstate commerce below the price fixed in a resale price maintenance contract, and your request for any suggested amendments which would prevent such a construction.

Neither of these bills contains any language which either directs or specifically authorizes any action by this Commission. This still leaves open, however, a substantial question. Briefly stated, this question is whether or not, if the Congress establishes a policy which in effect declares that the selling of merchandise in interstate commerce at prices lower than those fixed in resale price maintenance contracts is an act of unfair competition, such acts are then an unfair method of competition or unfair * * * acts or practices within the meaning of those terms as contained in section 5 (a) of the Federal Trade Commission Act.

In the case of H. R. 5767, the policy it would establish appears to be negative rather than affirmative. That is, the bill provides exceptions to the provisions of laws which would otherwise apply. The bill does not make the offering for sale or selling of merchandise at prices less than those fixed by resale price maintenance contracts an act of unfair competition under Federal law. In this setting the Commission believes that any argument that this bill would empower it to proceed against persons who sell merchandise in interstate commerce below the price fixed in a resale price maintenance contract would be quite tenuous. While it would be preferable in further minimizing such an argument, if the provisions concerning resale price maintenance were inserted at the end of the present section 5 (a) of the Commission act instead of between the first and second sentence of that section, as is now the case, the possibility of such an argument prevailing seems so remote as not to warrant suggesting any amendment.

Thus, the Chairman of the Federal Trade Commission clearly indicates that, in his judgment, the McGuire bill does not direct, authorize, or empower the Commission to proceed against those who violate State fair-trade laws where interstate commerce is involved. The McGuire bill adds no new powers to the Federal Trade Commission Act. It ⊥ merely exempts from the Federal Trade Commission Act and the Antitrust Acts so far as interstate commerce is concerned that type of resale price maintenance contract which is permitted by the fair-trade acts of 45 States.

⊥ 4901

In so doing, the McGuire bill does not inject any agency of the Federal Government into a new area of business supervision. It does not add one penny to any Federal budget. The McGuire bill is merely permissive. It says to the States, in effect, that the Congress recognizes the rights of the States to enact and make effective policies respecting unfair competition. That is all the McGuire bill does and that is all it is intended to do. But in doing this, it will help, in a very tangible way, to safeguard our small-business economy.

The Commission in the same letter points out, however, that where a provision, as in H. R. 6925, declares it, by an act of Congress, to be an "act of unfair competition," it will "permit a persuasive argument that the act of unfair competition thus defined also constitutes a violation of section 5 (a) of the Commission act." Under these circumstances, the Commission would be required to proceed against those who violate fair-trade laws where interstate commerce is involved.

Mr. DOLLIVER. Mr. Chairman, I yield myself 25 minutes.

Mr. Chairman, this is a continuation of the remarks that I have made in the House when the rule was being discussed. When my time expired I was discussing the effect of fair trade legislation on the consumer. Of course, as was pointed out, I believe by the gentleman from New York [Mr. CELLER] in his discussion during debate on the rule, there were no consumer organizations represented, and the consumer did not have representation in connection with this legislation.

Now there have been some interesting surveys and statistics brought out on this subject which I think are worth talking about. We all know that there has been a very great increase in the cost of living since, let us say, 1939. That has been the result of a great war, perhaps two great wars, and also, some of us think, on account of some exceedingly improvident fiscal policies that have been followed. Whatever the cause may be, the fact is that the cost of living has increased very, very greatly, to the extent of 85 percent, according to the statistical information which appears on page 53 of the hearings.

Now what about the increase in the cost of fair-traded articles? I am now quoting from a statement appearing on page 53 of the hearings:

Prices have only risen 10 percent on fair-traded merchandise since 1939.

Of course, I do not know where those statistics came from: I am not a statistician, but I do know that the testimony throughout, as is revealed in the printed hearings, indicates that there had been far less of a percentagewise increase in the retail price of fair-traded articles than the general price increase on articles that were not fair traded.

Now let us turn for a moment to another very important aspect of this legislation which has been alluded to already by several of the speakers. To me this is really the touchstone of all this bill. This is a permissive statute. This is not a statute which requires any coercion or compulsion on any of the citizens of the States, or of the United States. We merely say by this legislation that the separate 48 Commonwealths of the United States can do something about retail prices if they want to. But we do not say to anybody, anywhere, that you must do something.

Mr. [GEORGE A.] DONDERO [R., Mich.]. Mr. Chairman, will the gentleman yield?

Mr. DOLLIVER. I yield to the gentleman from Michigan.

Mr. DONDERO. When the gentleman refers to the statute, does he mean the statute on the books, the McGuire bill, or does he mean the Keogh bill?

Mr. DOLLIVER. I mean all three of them. I must make a reservation as far as the Keogh bill is concerned, however, and I will go into that a little later if time permits.

Mr. [PAUL] CUNNINGHAM [R., Iowa]. Mr. Chairman, will the gentleman yield?

Mr. DOLLIVER. I yield to the gentleman from Iowa.

Mr. CUNNINGHAM. This bill, if enacted, would permit the States to take the necessary steps to protect small business without in any way endangering the stability of big business; is that not correct?

Mr. DOLLIVER. The gentleman is absolutely correct. This legislation, the McGuire bill, if enacted, in my judgment would protect the small-business man from the price-cutting tactics and the loss-leader tactics of the great and powerful and wealthy chain-merchandising organizations of this country.

Mr. CUNNINGHAM. In addition, all it does is restore to the several States of the Union the right to pass legislation to protect small business that these States had prior to the recent decision of the United States Supreme Court.

Mr. DOLLIVER. That is entirely correct. It restores to the States the rights they thought they were exercising up to the time of this court decision about 12 months ago.

Again, I emphasize that this is permissive legislation. It is not sumptuary legislation, it is not coercive, and it will not cost one penny of Federal funds for enforcement. Not one man will be hired by anybody to see to the enforcement of this on a Federal level. It is no burden on the Federal taxpayers of this country. So I want to bear down on that particular point as hard as I can. This recognizes the rights of the States to control their businesses and the business enterprises in their States as they see fit. It is merely permissive.

Mr. CUNNINGHAM. In addition to being a fair-trade bill, the bill if enacted would enable the States to pass legislation or take appropriate steps not only to promote fair trade but to prevent unfair trade and prevent certain monopolistic companies from freezing out the small-business man, who is the backbone of America.

Mr. DOLLIVER. That is one of the objectives of this legislation, to protect the small-business man who, as the gentleman says, is the backbone of American business.

Mr. DONDERO. Mr. Chairman, if the gentleman will yield further, this example has been presented to me. You go into a chain drug store and they will sell you a tube of Pepsodent tooth paste, say for 50 cents, and give you an extra one for 1 cent. The little-business man, the drug-store dealer, cannot do that. Will this legislation affect that kind of situation?

Mr. DOLLIVER. If that particular item or brand is fair-traded, it will protect the little-business man.

Mr. DONDERO. I want to comment and simply say that that kind of advertising is simply what is known in business as a loss leader, in order to get the people to come in to buy that particular, special arrangement. They buy other things to make up whatever loss the dealer sustains by reason of that advertising sale. But the little man on the corner cannot do that. Will this control that kind of situation?

Mr. DOLLIVER. As I said a moment ago, one of the objectives of this bill is to protect the small retailer in the merchandising of fair-traded articles.

Mr. [FRED L.] CRAWFORD [R., Mich.]. Mr. Chairman, will the gentleman yield?

Mr. DOLLIVER. I yield to the gentleman from Michigan.

Mr. CRAWFORD. I believe every Member of this House knows that the Rexall drug stores of this country are owned and operated by small-business men. In those stores you find the 1-cent sale. There is no question about that. We might just as well keep this record straight. I can take you out here and show you the Rexall stores in your district and my district. Those little fellows have the 1-cent sales to maintain their volume. I have checked it with them within the last 15 days.

Mr. [NOAH M.] MASON [R., Ill.]. Mr. Chairman, will the gentleman yield?

Mr. DOLLIVER. I yield to the gentleman from Illinois.

Mr. MASON. We have a Rexall store in my home town. They do have a 1-cent sale, but they have not been selling this fair-trade in the 1-cent sale because the laws of the State of Illinois prevent it.

HOUSE CONSIDERATION (H.R. 5767; H.R. 6925)   651

Mr. DOLLIVER. I can only offer this oblique rejoinder to what has been said. The laws which ultimately control fair trade are made not by this Congress but by the separate States. These various problems, which have been presented in these questions which have been offered here, ultimately will have their answer in the laws passed by the State of Illinois, the State of Michigan, or the State of Iowa, or wherever it may be.

Mr. CRAWFORD. Mr Chairman, will the gentleman yield?

Mr. DOLLIVER. I yield.

Mr. CRAWFORD. In other words, if the State law provides that a selling agreement may be arranged between the manufacturer and the wholesaler and retailer and the broker, or whoever the middleman is, to fix those prices, if the ⊥ State law ⊥ 4902 provides that, this enabling legislation, [sic] will back up that State law?

Mr. DOLLIVER. That is right.

Mr. CRAWFORD. That is a fact; is it not?

Mr. DOLLIVER. That is correct.

Mr. CRAWFORD. We are not legislating any prices whatsoever in this. Here is the thing that bothers me about this proposition. I certainly believe in the free-enterprise system. I sincerely believe with all my soul that the only protection there is for the consumer in the private-enterprise system is in the free play of the forces of competition. Here we are, we who claim to be in favor of free enterprise in a way—and I will have to answer to my people for making this statement—in a way supporting those who claim that Government can do the job better, and that Government can protect the enterpriser and that competition should be eliminated and that there will be less damage done by laws fixing prices than there will be if competition is allowed to flow freely.

Mr. DOLLIVER. If the gentleman will permit me to proceed, I think I will have something to say about the proposition of competition and the fixing of prices a little later in my statement.

Mr. MASON. Mr. Chairman, will the gentleman yield?

Mr. DOLLIVER. I yield.

Mr. MASON. As I see it, the Government is just becoming an umpire to see that fair dealing exists between the little-business man and the big-business man. And that is the business of Government, to see that the big-business man does not squeeze the little one, because in the long run that is better for the consumer.

Mr. CUNNINGHAM. Mr. Chairman, will the gentleman yield?

Mr. DOLLIVER. I yield.

Mr. CUNNINGHAM. Will the gentleman in his splendid presentation at some point in his remarks explain what he means by an article that is fair-traded?

Mr. DOLLIVER. I will endeavor to do so.

Mr. CELLER. Mr. Chairman, will the gentleman yield?

Mr. DOLLIVER. I yield.

Mr. CELLER. I understand the position of the gentleman, and of others, is that these bills are antichain store bills.

Mr. DOLLIVER. I do not concede that to be my position. I will define that for myself and not depend on the gentleman from New York to define my position.

Mr. CELLER. It might interest the gentleman, and the members of the committee generally, to know that one of the reports, while under the lobbying act, indicated that the association of chain drug stores contributed in one quarter $10,000 to the Bureau of Education on Fair Trade, which is an offshoot of the National Retail Druggists Association for the passage of these bills. How can these bills be against chain stores, when the chain stores themselves contributed funds to further the passage of this legislation?

Mr. DOLLIVER. Mr. Chairman, I cannot obviously answer that question. I do not know anything about the accuracy of the statement made by the gentleman.

Mr. HARRIS. Mr. Chairman, will the gentleman yield?

Mr. DOLLIVER, I yield.

Mr. HARRIS. In reply to the statement made by the distinguished chairman of the Committee on the Judiciary, is it not a fact that the McGuire bill is legislation which is directed to anyone who endeavors to take advantage of unfair competition whether it is a chain store or anyone else?

Mr. DOLLIVER. My answer to that question is in the affirmative.

The second point I want to emphasize at this point in this debate is this. The legislation which we are considering today is to correct some court decisions which were made. Of course, nobody could anticipate the views or the slant that the Federal or the State courts will take upon a particular question. For 13 years it was thought by anybody who had anything to do with this fair-trade legislation in the States that it bound not only the signers of the agreements as to fair trade, but also the nonsigners.

About a year ago, the courts came up with a couple of decisions which held that the nonsigners of these fair-trade agreements were not bound, and that they could sell the fair-traded merchandise at any price they chose. You all remember a year ago there were some large department stores in one or more of the metropolitan centers that began to slash prices on some fair-traded articles.

There is still some litigation pending about these very drastic price slashes. As [has] been pointed out in the debate, those price slashes were on loss leaders, for the purpose of getting customers into those large retail centers. This legislation that we are considering today has for its purpose to correct that situation, created by the decision of the court.

Mr. DONDERO. Mr. Chairman, will the gentleman yield?

Mr. DOLLIVER. I yield to the gentleman from Michigan.

Mr. DONDERO. Take this subject of gasoline. I recall a gasoline war where one competitor reduced the price below cost in order to drive another competitor out of business. Is there anything in this legislation which would correct or lay down a policy that no competitor can sell at less than cost?

Mr. DOLLIVER. No. There is nothing of that kind here. Of course, the example which you have given is clearly inapplicable to this legislation, because I know of no gasoline that is fair-traded. I do not think it could be fair-traded under this legislation.

A theory is advanced that vertical resale price maintenance has the same effect as horizontal price fixing which is prohibited by law the argument goes, vertical resale price maintenance forces retailers to abandon price competition. For some curious reason, this argument has been advanced only in respect of vertical resale price maintenance through fair trade, which accounts for from $6 to $10 billions of sales at retail per year. It has not been advanced in connection with vertical resale price maintenance achieved through other legal means, which accounts for some $30 billions of sales at retail per year. The argument seems a bit inconsistent.

The history of marketing of the past 20 years has demonstrated that vertical resale price maintenance, as it is permitted under the fair-trade laws of 45 States, has enhanced competition, not restricted it. According to the Department of Commerce, the number of retailers in the United States has increased by 300,000 in the 20 years since the inception of fair trade. This growth in the number of retailers, which means a growth in competitors, has taken place in the face of an unprecedented development in giant retailing.

As to price competition at the retail level, the very nature of the market in which fair-traded products must compete for customers both with other fair-traded products and with non-fair-traded products insures price competition. The manufacturers of fair-traded national brands compete with each other, pricewise. This competition is reflected at the retail level. It is keen competition, as an examination of the number of products and prices available in any retail store will prove.

In terms of its practical effects, vertical resale price maintenance through the State fair-trade laws has had a salutary effect upon the economy. This is the exact opposite of the destructive consequences of horizontal price-fixing. Indeed, the antitrust prohibition against horizontal price fixing, as a means of fostering monopolies and thereby restricting full and open competition, is specifically continued by every State fair-trade act, by the Miller-Tydings Act and by the McGuire bill, H. R. 5767. The latter measure, now before this House, contains in this connection the following provision:

(5) Nothing contained in paragraph (2) of this subsection shall make lawful contracts or agreements providing for the establishment or maintenance of minimum or stipulated resale prices on any commodity referred to in paragraph (2) of this subsection, between

manufacturers, or between producers, or between wholesalers, or between brokers, or between factors, or between retailers, or between persons, firms or corporations in competition with each other.

Horizontal price fixing by agreements between competitors is prohibited because it stifles and restricts free and open competition and invariably results in the creation and growth of monopolies. However, vertical resale price maintenance under the State fair-trade laws, prevents the juggling of resale prices which eliminates competitors by stifling and restricting fair and open competition.

It is important to note that in order to foster an economy based upon full and open competition, it must follow that there be competitors. Only full and fair competition will and can maintain free competitive policies.

There is abundant evidence and opinion from such distinguished Supreme Court Justices as Mr. Holmes, Mr. Brandeis, Mr. Roberts, and Sutherland, from former Chairmen of the Federal Trade Commission itself, from a broad representation of businessmen, small and large, and from recent committee reports ⊥ of this Congress to ⊥ 4903 the following effect: Predatory pricing practices on trade-marked products tend to eliminate competition and are, therefore, unfair and destructive competition.

The House Select Committee on Small Business, in its report, Fair Trade: The Problem and the Issues, issued on February 4, 1952, says in part:

> The Select Committee on Small Business has studied carefully the arguments presented both by the advocates of fair trade and the opponents. The committee is convinced that deceitful and misleading price cutting is not in the public interest and that small-business enterprises in particular need protection against loss-leader and similar unfair business practices. It believes the States should retain jurisdiction over retail trade practices and that Congress should make it possible to enforce fair-trade contracts in interstate commerce.

In connection with this whole question of legislative policy, State or Federal, with respect to the problem of unfair competition, Mr. Justice Roberts, of the Supreme Court, in the case of Nebbia against New York had this to say:

> The lawmaking bodies in the past endeavored to promote free competition by laws aimed at trusts and monopolies. The consequent interference with private property and freedom of contract has not availed with the courts to set these enactments aside as denying due process. Where the public interest was deemed to require the fixing of minimum prices, that expedient has been sustained. If the lawmaking body within its sphere of government concludes that the conditions or practices in an industry make unrestricted competition an inadequate safeguard of the consumer's interests, produce waste harmful to the public, threaten ultimately to cut off the supply of a commodity needed by the public, or portend the destruction of the industry itself, appropriate statutes passed in an honest effort to correct the threatened consequences may not be set aside because the regulation adopted fixes prices reasonably deemed by the legislature to be fair to those engaged in the industry and to the consuming public.[3.46]

The broad purpose of the antitrust laws is to prevent the growth of monopoly power and the evils it produces. Accordingly, as means toward this end, the antitrust laws prohibit horizontal price fixing. The broad purpose of the State fair-trade laws is likewise to prevent the growth of monopoly power and the evils it produces. Accordingly, as a means toward this same end, the State fair-trade laws permit vertical resale price maintenance under conditions of full and fair competition.

Mr. HARRIS. Mr. Chairman, I yield 3 minutes to the gentleman from Colorado [Mr. ASPINALL].

Mr. [WAYNE N.] ASPINALL [D., Colo.]. Mr. Chairman, I wish to thank the gentleman from Arkansas in charge of the time on our side for giving to me an opportunity to voice my wholehearted support of the legislation now before the House in the form of the McGuire bill. I support the McGuire bill, not after an all-inclusive and thorough study of the legal questions that are involved, but primarily because of the successful operation of the Fair Trades Act of Colorado which was passed in 1937, when I had the privilege of serving as Speaker of the House. It has proved a great

---

[3.46] 291 U.S. 502, 538 (1934).

success among the people of Colorado. At that time a minority member of the rules committee helped to pass the legislation. He is now the representative of the small-business men in Colorado. He has sent to me a letter which I received this morning which letter I believe explains in great detail the position of the consumer as well as the small-business man in my State on this legislation. We are not so much concerned in the fight between large business and small business in Colorado, because we have very little there of what might be denominated large business. I have already secured permission to make his letter a part of my present remarks. I am sure you will find it well worth your careful reading.

Mr. Chairman, resale price maintenance is the guiding principle of fair trade. Fair trade is called price fixing by its opponents who nevertheless do not call other forms of resale price maintenance price fixing.

The fact is that fair trade is one—and only one—legal framework for resale price maintenance. At least $30,000,000,000 worth of goods are sold every year in this country, without recourse to fair trade, through methods of distribution under which producers are legally permitted to establish the retail prices for their trade-marked products.

All newspaper and magazine publishers can and do require all news dealers to sell their publications at the price established by the publisher. The legal framework used by publishers and by other producers of trade-marked items is consignment selling. Another method of resale price maintenance is exclusive dealerships used by manufacturers of automobiles and many other products.

Under the fair-trade laws, passed by the legislatures of 45 States, manufacturers of trade-marked products—national brands—may establish minimum resale prices, if they choose, for their products through contracts with their distributors. However, no product may be fair-traded unless it is in free and open competition with similar products produced by others. This safeguard against monopoly is not always found in other forms of legal resale price maintenance.

All forms of resale price maintenance are used to guard a trade-mark's reputation and to protect a manufacturer's channels for mass distribution—all the dealers who handle his products—from the havoc of competitive indecency as exemplified in price wars.

Newspaper and magazine publishing and the automobile industry would not have developed and contributed to our economy, as they have, if they had not long ago adopted the forms of resale price maintenance they now use to insure the orderly distribution of their products.

The State fair-trade laws have the same purpose and operate in the same way. Fair trade is needed by many manufacturers, particularly the smaller ones, who, in the interest of keeping prices down for the consumer, find it more economical to sell through wholesalers and thousands of independent retailers.

These independent dealers who form the vast majority of the country's 1,770,000 retailers—and many thousands of wholesalers, together comprise the backbone of small business in America. They also need effective fair trade if they are to have even the chance to compete, in terms of efficiency and skill, in this age of giant retailing.

Accordingly, whether or not the fair-trade laws are restored to their former effectiveness, there will be plenty of legally accepted resale price maintenance in this country. If fair trade is to be destroyed because it is resale price maintenance, then by the same logic all vertical resale price maintenance in this country should be prohibited.

The fact that the use of resale price maintenance is so widespread through various legal frameworks is graphic evidence that manufacturers need fair trade and employ it voluntarily, just as they do other forms of resale price maintenance. They are not forced into it by their distributors, as some opponents of fair trade have alleged. They need fair trade to guard the years of hard work and the large investments which have gone into building up the reputation of their trade-mark. This reputation can be destroyed when that trade-mark is exploited by a price juggler to further his own merchandising tricks.

What happens when a consumer sees a well-known brand advertised for much less than its regular price? She thinks that it was too high priced in the first place or that it has deteriorated in quality. During last spring's price wars, when Bayer aspirin was being sold for 4 cents—less than the cost of its container—the company making Bayer aspirin received a number of calls from customers asking whether this 4-cent Bayer aspirin was a second, a batch that was damaged in some way? The seeds of doubt about that product's quality had already been implanted in the minds of these customers. Price wars nourish this doubt to a point where a trade-marked product cannot be sold any longer at its regular price.

In the analysis of fair trade in the 1951 annual report of the Senate Select Committee on Small Business, the case history of the Ingersoll dollar watch is presented. The price of this watch was driven down to 57 cents. Customers would no longer pay a dollar for it. Retailers would not handle it at 57 cents. They could not afford to take the losses involved. The Senate committee report says:

> The result was that the manufacturer lost his market and was forced out of business. * * * The consuming public also lost because they were no longer able to buy a serviceable watch for a dollar.

Many manufacturers support the State fair-trade laws, then, and use them voluntarily because they know how price wars can start the process of consumer doubt, of the deterioration of the reputation of their trade-marked products. They also know how such free-for-all competition can destroy the very channels through which their products reach the market. This is why some manufacturers need and support the State fair-trade laws. This is why many other manufacturers use other legal forms of resale price maintenance.

The scope and the need for fair trade on the part of the manufacturer can be measured by the efforts a number of manufacturers are making today to work out some method of operating, even with weakened fair trade. Some are trying to have all their dealers sign fair-trade contracts. When you have thousands of dealers, this becomes a large and expensive undertaking. It adds to the cost of distribution. Others who can afford to do so are shifting to methods of consignment selling or exclusive dealerships. But what does this do to the wholesalers and the independent retailers? It will put many of them right out of business eventually. For distribution through consignment selling and exclusive dealerships tends to eliminate the wholesalers and many dealers in smaller communities. It has to, in order to be economical and competitive.

The Schick Electric Razor Co., for example, shifted in February to direct selling through its own salesmen. The company did this to stop the price-juggling in the New York area which had driven down the price of its electric razors from $27.50 to $6.99, less than half the wholesale cost. This was brought out by a witness at the hearings on the McGuire bill before the subcommittee of the House Interstate and Foreign Commerce Committee. The witness, Herman C. Nolen, vice president of McKesson & Robbins, Inc., said that his wholesale house and others would no longer be able to distribute this product, and that many small retailers would no longer get Schick razors to sell. The shift to direct selling forced the company to contract its distribution, to concentrate on larger dealers.

The weakening of fair trade has already upset an intricate network of marketing centering around small business in this country. The larger manufacturers will and are finding other legal forms of resale price maintenance because they have to, in order to guard their market. But these more expensive forms will raise consumer prices. The smaller manufacturers, the wholesalers, and many small retailers have no workable substitute for fair trade. Their livelihood and that of their families and employees, adding up to millions of people, will be progressively endangered unless Congress restores effective fair trade to the States by passing the McGuire bill, H. R. 5767. In doing so, Congress will be merely making available to these manufacturers and distributors one needed form of legal resale price maintenance which, as a basic method of distribution, is and will continue to be widely used in other legal ways by many other producers in this country. How can we justify the prohibition of fair trade because it is resale-price maintenance and permit other forms of resale-price maintenance to flourish?

Civic Association of America,
Denver, Colo., May 5, 1952.

Hon. Wayne N. Aspinall,
House Office Building, Washington, D. C.

DEAR WAYNE: In response to your telephone call this morning, I am enclosing a copy of Colorado's fair-trade act passed by our general assembly and approved by the Governor March 15, 1937. As you know, this law is similar to the other 44 State laws enacted along about the same time.

Since the enactment of our fair-trade law there have been attempts to repeal it made by interests and factions who would like to repeal the Ten Commandments if they felt they interfered with their free-swinging tactics to build up a monopoly from which they alone would benefit, and would eventually allow them to exact the pound of flesh from the heart of orderly, competitive enterprise in this State. They have always failed.

A great deal of misinformation has been promulgated in the press and otherwise that the McGuire bill is only desired and being strongly advocated by the retail drug business through their National Association of Retail Druggists. This certainly is not true in Colorado and other Rocky Mountain States. The Civic Association of America is representative of all lines of retail and wholesale independent business, of which the retail and wholesale drug people are a relatively small percent. All of hundreds of members are strong advocates of the McGuire bill.

We are of the sincere opinion that the McGuire bill, without any amendment taken from the Keogh bill, will do the job of restoring fair trade and orderly and fair marketing in this country. In matters of this kind pertaining to law and legislation, the businessmen must rely upon the judgment and advice of those whom we consider reliable and competent attorneys. We did not rely upon 1 attorney's opinion and advice but 22 whom we feel are outstanding in their experience and study of legislation and constitutional law in this country.

A great deal of emphasis seems to have been put upon the Wentling case decision by the American Fair Trade Council, Inc., in their endeavor to push the Keogh bill, or, failing in that, to have a section out of the Keogh bill inserted by amendment to the McGuire bill. We are informed that the Judiciary Committee of the House refused to accept section D of the Keogh bill and voted out a bill that was entirely different in language and provisions. Yet the AFTC now is attempting to insert section D in the McGuire bill. It is difficult for us to understand how the House would even consider an amendment that had been refused and the section eliminated by one of its committees.

We believe it would be a pertinent question to ask the proponents of the section D amendment to the McGuire bill to name the attorneys whose judgment they claim to rely upon that section D is sound and constitutional and will get the job done which they propose it will. I am sure that John Dargavel or Mr. Frates will submit the names of the attorneys upon whose advice we have relied. We want a bill passed that we sincerely believe will stand up constitutionally before the Supreme Court.

It is the consensus of businessmen in Colorado that the Members of Congress will not be misled by a number of statements made by those whom we feel want to kill the revival of fair trade in this country.

Your district, like all of Colorado, is made up, from a business standpoint, of small, independent merchants. It has been since statehood was accorded us. You know a great many of them by their first names. You know they are honorable, upright citizens. A large number of them started small when our State was young and have grown along with our natural progress. These businessmen are not asking for a law that would benefit them and hurt the position of their customers. Their customers are their friends of long standing, and without them a businessman could not continue. He has made these friends by years and years of fair, honest merchandising and dealings. He has extended credit in times when the faith he has in his customers caused him embarrassment in meeting his own obligations. His mark-up percentages have always been fair and just; otherwise he could not have continued. His competition under fair trade had the same opportunity he had. It is simply the honest, fair, American way of doing business that has made this country the greatest in the world.

It isn't the consumers that are fighting fair trade as a whole, but those who purport to represent the consumers. Businessmen are consumers themselves, and they certainly would not advocate something they felt would damage themselves. Unrestrained price wars, such as occurred last year, threaten all small business and the health of our whole economy.

I would like to have you refer to the minimum resale price hearing before the subcommittee of the Committee on Interstate and Foreign Commerce, on H. R. 5767 of February 4–20, 1952, page 9, "a dozen reasons why your Congressman should vote for fair trade." Mr. Dargavel has set forth 12 reasons in support of fair trade, upon which I do not have the ability to improve.

Your long experience as a legislator, both in the House and Senate of our own State and in Congress, has undoubtedly demonstrated to you that businessmen are willing and anxious to work for the benefit of all others. They are fair-minded people and are always found ready to help consumers, farmers, labor, in fact all segments of our life and economy. Fair trade is one of the rules of the game of business. When predatory interests attempt to prevent fair and equitable rules of the game, they can have no other motive except elimination of small business in America. It was small business that made this country. Some have grown to the extent that they no longer wish to be restrained by a fair and just law. They want the law of the jungle to prevail so that the strong can eliminate the small and weak.

In Colorado where they have, in addition to the enclosed fair-trade law, a law known as the Unfair Practices Act, which was passed subsequent to the fair-trade law.

These two are separate and distinct laws. Many adversaries of fair trade in Colorado have endeavored to confuse the public into believing the two laws are one and the same. The Unfair Practices Act deals with loss-leader selling while the fair-trade law pertains only to fair-traded articles and permits fair trade in Colorado.

At our visit in Denver during the Christmas recess, I remember your stating Congressman JOHN A. MCGUIRE was a close personal friend of yours. I am sure you have great faith and confidence in his integrity and judgment. JOHN MCGUIRE, like yourself, is a true friend of small business, yet would do nothing that would benefit small business alone to the detriment of your and his many other friends, neighbors, or constituents. I know there are people in Colorado who do not favor fair trade, but without doubt they are not small-business men, but businesses, who are large enough, strong enough to feel that it is to their best advantage to allow them unrestrained, unbridled opportunity to crush out competition. If they have their way, opportunity to make a decent living through a small business will be eliminated and chaos will prevail, and our economy will move into the area of advantage to the few to the detriment of the many.

Thank you sincerely, Wayne, for calling me and asking for our views, as representing thousands of small businesses on the fair-trade fight. We have full and complete confidence in you and your ability to fight to the last ditch for us.

Sincerely your friend,

Civic Association of America,
Marion E. Strain, President.

⊥ Mr. WOLVERTON. Mr. Chairman, I yield myself 15 minutes. ⊥ 4905

Mr. Chairman, it is my intention, in speaking on this bill, to refer in general terms to the objectives sought by the bill.

First, however, I wish to commend the gentleman from Ohio [Mr. BROWN] who spoke in favor of this bill when the rule was under consideration before the House. He made one of the finest, plainest, clearest, most logical and forceful statements I have ever heard in connection with the legislation. His remarks are entitled to great consideration in determining the meritorius [sic] character of this legislation.

Mr. Chairman, there has been much doubt or misconception as to the purpose and effect of the different bills that have been offered to the Congress to give Federal sanction and strength to the fair-trade laws that have been passed in 45 of our 48 States.

As a member of the Committee on Interstate and Foreign Commerce, I favor the McGuire bill, H. R. 5767, as favorably reported by the committee.

The primary purpose of this bill is to reestablish what I believe was the intention of Congress when it passed the Miller-Tydings Act in 1937. I was a Member of the Congress when that bill was passed and became law. It was not until May 21, 1951, when because of a decision of a divided Supreme Court in the case of *Schwegmann* v. *Calvert Distillers Corporation* (314 U. S. 384), that any doubt was cast upon the original intent and purpose of Congress. Until that decision, nearly 14 years after the act was passed, it had been generally recognized by all parties that the act as passed by Congress provided that the application and enforcement of State fair-trade laws, including the nonsigner provisions of such laws, with regard to interstate transactions, did not constitute a violation of the Federal Trade Commission Act or the Sherman Antitrust Act. Thus, for approximately 14 years this principle had been recognized as the law of the land. It was not shown in our long and very complete hearings that during this 14 years had the rights of the consumer nor anyone else suffered as a result of the law that Congress had passed in 1937. It is not often that there is such a long period of trial without discovery of any harm done to any citizen. The fact that such a long period did exist before any court found it to be technically unconstitutional bears witness to its lack of substantial wrong. The primary purpose of the McGuire bill, now before the House, is merely to reaffirm, clarify, and make certain the very same proposition which, in the committee's opinion, the Congress intended to enact into law when it passed the original law in 1937. In other words, the McGuire bill reenacts provisions of the Miller-Tydings Act in language that leaves no doubt as to the original or present intent of Congress.

Many specious arguments will be made during the consideration of the bill to the effect that it is harmful to the best interests of consumers. It is the studied opinion of the committee that all such are without foundation. While these arguments may sound plausible at times, yet, when examined in the light of practical experience, it will be found that they are neither sound or real. In this connection it should be borne in mind that 45 out of 48 of our States have adopted the fair-trade laws. Surely, this preponderance of judgment upon the part of our legislatures in 45 of our 48 States must indicate that there is substantial reason for the adoption of fair-trade laws. It is inconceivable that the 45 legislatures could all be wrong. All that the pending law provides is recognition of these State laws in interstate transactions between each other. Certainly there is nothing unreasonable or wrong on the part of Congress in doing this. I think we would be remiss in our duty if we did not do it.

It is also significant that the bill was endorsed as to its objectives by the House Select Committee on Small Business, whose chairman appeared during our hearings and presented an extensive report of the Select Committee on Small Business entitled "Fair Trade: The Problem and the Issues"—House Report No. 1292. After a fair and impartial statement of all the arguments for and against this type of legislation, the report contains the following conclusions and recommendations:

> The Select Committee on Small Business has studied carefully the arguments presented both by the advocates of fair trade and the opponents. It is impressed by the complexity of the problem and by the weight of evidence on both sides of the issue. The committee is convinced that deceitful and misleading price cutting is not in the public interest and that small-business enterprises in particular need protection against loss-leader and similar unfair business practices. It believes the States should retain jurisdiction over retail trade practices and that Congress should make it possible to enforce fair-trade contract [sic] in interstate commerce.

The attention of the Members of the House is directed to the record of hearings held by your Committee on Interstate and Foreign Commerce on this bill. You will be impressed with the thoroughness with which the committee has examined into this important subject. You will find in a reading of the hearing that every conceivable question either for or against the proposed bill has been given consideration before the favorable report of the committee was submitted to this House. But, in my opinion one of the most impressive arguments, in favor of this bill, that will appear from a reading of the testimony and statements submitted to the committee during its hearings, is the unanimity with which small-business men give their support to the bill, together with the great number of trade associations and organizations which represent a large segment of American wholesalers and retailers, including druggists, jewelers, hardware merchants, dealers in electrical appliances, wearing apparel, sporting-goods distributors, photographic-equipment stores, and a multitude of others. The bill also has the support of great numbers of manufacturers, both large and small.

Time does not permit me to answer or explain all the unfair and untrue arguments that have been made by opponents of this type of legislation. But there is one to which I will make reference. Frequently the charge is made that price competition is destroyed under fair trade. This is not true. The fact is that there is a wide range of price competition that does exist under fair trade. However, the charge against fair trade is made that it puts a dead hand on all price competition and makes for price uniformity, thus robbing the consumer of the opportunity to shop around and take advantage of price differentials among products. But when the facts of fair trade in the actual market place are examined, this charge falls flat.

In the first place, all the 45 State fair-trade laws require that a product, in order to be fair-traded, be sold in free and open competition with articles of a similar kind. This is not just an empty legalism. Even the most casual shopper can testify that fair-traded products compete with non-fair-traded national brands and with the strong private brands of the big retailers. They all are found side by side on the shelves of the stores. Whether the purchaser buys a fair-traded or non-fair-traded brand, and which one, is entirely up to the individual purchaser. They each have full freedom of choice among a variety of brands.

The purchaser is also the boss when it comes to the price they are willing to pay for any product, fair-traded or not. The purchaser is the price boss because he or she alone determines whether the price is right. They can buy or refuse to buy a particular product at a particular price. If we examine what is available in the stores, be it face powders or fountain pens, typewriters or toasters, we discover that the consumer is confronted with a host of brands showing a wide range of prices. As evidence of this observation, let us look for a moment at some data taken from Consumer Reports Buying Guides, introduced in testimony at the hearings before the committee last February 4. It gives a valuable insight into the extent of the consumer's opportunity to choose any price under fair trade.

These data list some, but not all, of the brands and prices found among 25 different categories of products. The fewest number of brands found in any category was eight, among exposure meters, with a price range from $14.95 to $32.50. The greatest number of brands found was 81, among cold creams, with a price range from 4 cents to 75 cents per ounce.

To give an idea of the number of brands and prices in some typical product categories, we can glance at a sampling of them:

Silverware: 67 brands—price range $21.50 to $69.75.
Face powder: 56 brands—price range 9 cents per ounce to $1.20 per ounce.
Laundry soaps, flakes: 51 brands—price range 28.3 cents to 69.3 cents per pound of dry soap content.
Household ammonia: 48 brands—price range 4.5 cents per ounce to 46 cents.
Inks: 27 brands—price range 4 cents per fluid ounce to 25 cents.
Fountain pens: 16 brands—price range 69 cents to $12.50.
Portable typewriters: 9 brands—price range $76.85 to $119.67.
Carbon paper: 45 brands—price range 56 cents to $4.25 for 100 sheets.
Washing machines: 31 brands—price range $92.95 to $399.95.
Talcum and dusting powders: 57 brands—price range 19 cents an ounce to $1.08 an ounce.

There are many others that could be enumerated.

This broad range of brands and prices under fair trade aptly illustrates the axiom that any manufacturer sets a fair-trade price on his product at his own peril. If this price does not meet the competition offered by rival products, then the product must eventually fail and go off the market. This is as it should be under our competitive system. The ultimate beneficiary of this strenuous competition among products and prices is the consumer. Under fair trade, price competition is full, it is free, and it is fair.

In conclusion, I think it is appropriate and well to make reference to the views of the Department of Commerce concerning this legislation. In recommending the adoption of H. R. 5767 or similar legislation it was said:

Opponents of fair-trade laws claim that monopolistic practices are thereby promoted. We know of no evidence which supports such a belief, and are of the opinion that opposition on this ground is based wholly on theory. It is our opinion, and we believe that opinion to be substantiated by the report of the Federal Trade Commission on resale price maintenance (submitted to the Congress, December 13, 1945), that ardent support for minimum resale prices is found in the ranks of small business, independent proprietors of corner drug stores, and similar retail establishments. These persons are the least likely to favor legislation encouraging the growth of monopolies in their field. Among others, those groups identified with monopolistic practices and tendencies, such as loss-leader selling to the deception of the public and to the benefit of their own competitive position in the market at the expense of small business, usually were opposed to fair-trade legislation.

The opposition to fair-trade laws comes frequently from large distributing groups including chains and large department stores which have historically used price cutting to drive weaker competition out of the way, thus, in restraint of trade, attempting to create a monopoly in the field of retailing.

To condemn price control under the fair-trade laws is to close one's eyes to other types of price control sponsored by manufacturers and producers without regard to fair trade contracts.

In a very substantial segment of business, represented by sales of automobiles, major appliances, home furnishings, and some lines of men's clothing, resale prices are maintained by fear that the manufacturer will refuse to sell to the dealer in the event he violates the manufacturer's price policy.

There are other types of price maintenance in operation in this country without regard to fair-trade contracts. In one type merchandise is distributed through the retailer on a consignment basis. In this type of merchandising the manufacturer owns the retail stock and the retailer does not pay for it until it has been sold to the ultimate consumer. Obviously, under this system, the dealer has nothing to say about prices. He is merely an agent executing the orders of his principal.

There is reason to conclude that the case against fair trade is more theoretical than real; that fair trade is beneficial to small business; that facts regarding its causing higher prices in total are unconvincing; that monopoly does not result from fair-trade laws, and that fair-trade laws have a stabilizing influence on the economy.

It is my opinion that the legislation contained in H. R. 5767, is meritorious and entitled to the support of the Members of this House. I trust it will receive your support.

Mr. [J. PERCY] PRIEST [D., Tenn.]. Mr. Chairman, I yield 5 minutes to the gentleman from Florida [Mr. ROGERS].

Mr. [DWIGHT L.] ROGERS [D., Fla.]. Mr. Chairman, this is a very important bill. I wish every one of you had had the time to read the hearings. This is a simple bill, and it merely does this: It is the enabling act, which enables the State to do business across State lines. Remember that. In its simplicity, it just permits a State to do business with an adjoining State if they have similar laws. In other words, if New York and Pennsylvania have similar laws concerning fair trade, this bill permits business to extend across the State line and permits the contracts made in compliance with the laws of those two States to be enforced in interstate commerce. That is all it does.

In order to get to the merits of any legislation, we have to know the present conditions. We have to know the relief that we want to bring about to correct the evil that exists. In 1931, the State of California passed the first fair-trade act. Since that time, 45 States have passed fair-trade acts. This is even more binding than a constitutional amendment. I would like to ask each Member of the House this question. Suppose you had a constitutional amendment which was consented to and approved by 36 States, which is all that is necessary to adopt an amendment to the Constitution? Do you not think you would be bound by it? That is the way we amend the Constitution. Now, here are 45 States that have passed fair-trade laws. The laws are on the statute books of these 45 States. Only three States, Missouri, Texas, Vermont, and the District of Columbia, do not have such laws. All of the 45 States have fair-trade laws. You think it is fair, do you think it is honest, do you think it is equitable for the Congress to say to these 45 States that they cannot have fair-trade laws, to say "We are not going to let you have fair-trade laws although you are entitled to govern your internal affairs so far as fair-trade laws and acts are concerned, but that we, the Congress, who have the authority to pass the laws in interstate commerce, are going to say that you cannot have that"?

Are we going to say that we are going to take that right away from them, and put them in a position where these cut-throat prices can exist and disturb the economy of this Nation? This bill is intended to avoid that. I, as a Member of this Congress, think that I ought to give some consideration to what these States want. I am one of the Members of Congress who believes in States rights. I think the States ought to have something to do with legislation that is passed by these States.

I do not think in a case like this, this Congress should come in and say to the States that "Although your legislature passed such law, we are going to cut you down. We are going to take the right away from the 45 States."

Is that fair? Do you think that is your duty? I think the Fair Trade Act is meritorious. We ought to look into whether the States have the right. Let us see what the history of this is and why this legislation is necessary.

In 1937 the Miller-Tydings Act was passed. All the States have [sic] been operating under the Miller-Tydings Act until 1951.

The CHAIRMAN. The time of the gentleman from Florida has expired.

Mr. PRIEST. Mr. Chairman, I yield the gentleman five additional minutes.

Mr. ROGERS of Florida. In 1936 the United States Supreme Court in a unanimous decision upheld the constitutionality of each of these State fair trade acts.[3.47] That is constitutional. The following year the Miller-Tydings Act was passed by this Congress to give full effect to the State fair-trade laws by permitting the operation of fair trade in interstate commerce. As I say, we continued to operate very peacefully until 1951 from 1937. Everything was done by the States which this act today will enable them to continue to do.

In 1951 the Supreme Court weakened the fair-trade structure, so laboriously built up by the States, by holding that the retailer who did not sign a fair-trade contract could not be required to respect fair-trade prices where interstate commerce was involved.[3.48]

As I say, this is a simple bill, and I see no reason why the 45 States of this Union desiring to proceed under a Fair Trade Act, why this Congress should come in and try to take that right away from them.

The McGuire bill merely places Congress on record that Congress means to have State fair-trade laws apply in their entirety. That means the so-called nonsigner clauses, as well as the rest of the State fair-trade laws, could be enforced with respect to interstate commerce.

Now, what is a so-called nonsigner clause? A nonsigner clause is a provision in a State fair-trade law which provides that any merchant who had knowledge of the fact that the resale price of a certain toothpaste, for example, is fixed at 39 cents, may not sell such toothpaste at less than 39 cents, even if such merchant failed to sign any agreement to that effect with the manufacturer of the toothpaste. If the merchant feels that under these circumstances he prefers not to carry this particular brand of toothpaste, he is free to carry other brands which are not fair traded. That is up to him.

The constitutionality of these so-called nonsigner clauses has been specifically upheld by the Supreme Court. Therefore, there is no question of the constitutionality of the bill in legalizing the application of nonsigner clauses with respect to interstate transactions.

The hearings before our committee showed that there is considerable controversy with respect to the economic merits of permitting the application of ⊥ the nonsigner ⊥ 4907 clauses to interstate commerce. A great number of trade associations representing a large segment of American retailers and wholesalers favored the enactment of the McGuire bill. Likewise, several prominent manufacturers have supported this measure before the committee.

The committee felt, after long hearings—and I wish every Member of this House could read them—the committee felt that the 45 States which have seen fit to enact these laws have a right to insist that their laws may be applied and enforced, regardless of the fact that some of the merchandise covered by these laws may have crossed State lines. That is all this means. That is the only thing it is applicable to.

Mr. [CHESTER B.] McMULLEN [D., Fla.]. Mr. Chairman, will the gentleman yield?

Mr. ROGERS of Florida. I yield to my distinguished colleague.

Mr. McMULLEN. I want to congratulate the gentleman, my colleague, on his statements about States' rights. I am wondering if my colleague has given any consideration to the rights of the consuming public and whether or not it is his opinion that the consumers and buyers of the Nation will pay more or less under this bill which is labeled a fair-trade law.

Mr. ROGERS of Florida. Answering the gentleman, may I say that I always want to give consideration to the consumer but I want to say that first and foremost we

---

[3.47] Old Dearborn Distrib. Co. v. Seagram-Distillers Corp., 299 U.S. 183, 57 S. Ct. 139, 81 L. Ed. 109 (1936), *supra* at chapter 2.

[3.48] Schwegmann Bros. v. Calvert Distillers Corp., 341 U.S. 384, 71 S. Ct. 745, 95 L. Ed. 1035 (1951), *supra* at chapter 2.

should give consideration to the laws passed by the States. If representatives of the various legislatures pass bills of this type for their States and fortify it [sic], then a small minority of the people should not come down here and want to repeal such legislation.

Mr. McMULLEN. I will ask the gentleman to answer the question whether he believes under this legislation the consuming public will pay more or less for the products they buy.

Mr. ROGERS of Florida. On the general average about the same. But going back to the fair treatment of distributors of the products of America, thousands and thousands of little independent merchants and druggists will be taken care of, under the provisions of the fair-trade laws.

Mr. WOLVERTON. Mr. Chairman, I yield 12 minutes to the distinguished gentleman from Colorado [Mr. HILL].

Mr. [WILLIAM S.] HILL [R., Colo.]. Mr. Chairman, for several years as a member of the Select Committee on Small Business I have had the opportunity to observe first hand the difficulties arising in our complex economic system surrounding the operators of small-business units. Our committee has held field hearings in many parts of our country. All these hearings indicated the precarious situation surrounding our small-business operators.

BY PASSING THE M'GUIRE BILL WE CAN ASSIST SMALL-BUSINESS FIRMS, BOTH RETAIL AND MANUFACTURING UNITS, TO REMAIN IN BUSINESS

Many important reasons have been offered as to why we need a good, workable, fair-trade law. To me the most important reason is that we must do all in our power to protect and maintain the small-business firms. The small-business man is truly the typical American. He is the backbone of our towns and villages. He is the church member, the scoutmaster, school-board member, the luncheon-club member, and civic leader.

The 1948 census of business shows that there were 1,769,540 retail units in the United States and that they did a total dollar volume of $130,500,000,000 during the year.

Of these retail units, 669,317—over one-third—were family operated; they hired no employees, using only family help; 289,000 establishments hired 1 employee; 217,597 employed 2 persons; 149,109 employed 3 persons; and 170,213 employed 4 to 5 outsiders. Only 3,674 retail units employed 100 or more persons. Thus 84 percent of the total retail units in the United States were operated with fewer than 6 employees in 1948, while two-tenths of 1 percent of the units employed 100 persons or more.

The 84 percent of the retail units employing fewer than 6 persons did 40 percent of the total dollar volume, but the two-tenths of 1 percent of the units employing 100 or more persons did 11 percent of the total retail dollar volume.

On these bases I favor the enactment of the McGuire bill which will insure the protection of the small-business man and provide State control and enforcement of such legislation.

Now I would like to speak on the question of who may initiate a fair-trade contract, and discuss both the McGuire and Keogh bills in this regard.

WHO MAY INITIATE A FAIR-TRADE CONTRACT?—PROVISIONS DEALING WITH THIS QUESTION IN THE M'GUIRE BILL, H. R. 5767 AND THE KEOGH BILL, H. R. 6925

As simple enabling legislation to permit the fair-trade laws of 45 States to be carried out effectively, the McGuire bill, H. R. 5767, does not designate who shall have the right to initiate a fair-trade contract. Like its other provisions, the McGuire bill, as reported out favorably by the House Interstate and Foreign Commerce Committee, leaves this point up to the States to determine.

This approach is particularly required by the fact that 24 out of the 45 State fair-trade acts specifically provide that the owner of the trade-mark, or his duly authorized distributor may initiate a fair-trade contract. The fair-trade acts of 21 other States simply provide that the producer may initiate the fair-trade contract.

The Keogh bill, H. R. 6925, however, on line 11, page 2, omits the words "or distributor" after the word, "producer." It thereby limits the initiation of fair-trade contracts to the producer alone. This limitation expressly nullifies the acts of the 24 States which permit that a person other than the producer or owner of the trade-marked product, when authorized, may initiate a fair-trade contract. There is also a legal question as to the constitutionality of this limitation, since it seeks by a congressional act to enlarge in some respects and to restrict in other respects the application of a State law.

The provisions in the 24 State fair-trade acts permitting the initiation of a fair-trade contract by an authorized distributor are designed to take account of those situations in the market place where distributors of trade-marked products have their products produced for them by others. Limiting the initiation of a fair-trade contract to the producer alone, as the Keogh bill does, is therefore an unreasonable and impractical restriction on the purpose of the State fair-trade acts. Also, this limitation reflects a failure to recognize the realities of marketing conditions in a number of industries concerned with fair trade.

As for the charge that wholesalers, in their capacity of distributing the trade-marked products of others, may initiate fair-trade contracts under the McGuire bill, the fact is that there have been no fair-trade contracts initiated by wholesalers since the inception of fair trade, 20 years ago. The reason for this is simple: Such a procedure would be impractical.

In the drug industry, for example, there may be 10 or 12 wholesalers serving the retail druggists in a single trading area. If any one of the wholesalers in such a trading area decided to initiate a fair-trade contract establishing the minimum resale price of a given trade-marked product, another wholesaler in the same area, in competition with the first wholesaler, could also initiate a fair-trade contract establishing a lower resale price on the very same product. A third wholesaler in the area could do likewise. Such a situation would be difficult and impractical. For this reason, it has never arisen. And if it ever did develop, no manufacturer, in his own defense as the owner of a trade-marked product, could permit such a situation to exist.

As for the possibility of wholesalers agreeing to establish a uniform price in their respective contracts, both the Federal antitrust laws and the State fair-trade acts specifically prohibit any such agreement. Such agreements would constitute collusion of a horizontal nature among competitors and are barred both by the Federal and State statutes involved.

The provision in the Keogh bill limiting the initiation of fair-trade contracts to the producer alone, as provided by the express language in the bill commencing after the period on line 18 and ending with the period on line 22 of page 2, will nullify, if strictly construed, the following uniformly provided clause in every State fair-trade act:

Actionable at the suit of any person damaged thereby.

Such nullification would violate the gist of the self-enforcement provisions of the State fair-trade acts.

In this connection, serious dangers are also posed by the criminal provisions of the Keogh bill, starting in line 6, page 1 and ending with line 5, page 2. This portion of the Keogh bill provides that—

Every person who shall make any contract * * * hereby declared to be illegal, shall be—

And so forth. The above provision could be construed as exempting or rendering legal only fair-trade contracts meeting the specified requirements of the Keogh bill with respect to the initiation ⊥ of contracts by producers only and with respect to the establishment of minimum prices only. In short, every fair-trade contract entered into by others than the producer, as authorized by the fair-trade acts of 24 States, could be held illegal and the initiators of such contracts could be subject to prosecution for violation of these provisions—of the Keogh bill—along with the criminal penalties provided.

In addition, any fair-trade contract which had only the words "stipulated price" instead of "minimum price," as authorized by the fair-trade acts of 17 States, could also be held illegal and the parties to the contracts subject to prosecution and criminal penalties under the provisions of the Keogh bill.

It is hardly conceivable that the Congress would enact Federal legislation like the

Keogh bill which could have the effect of subjecting many businessmen who have made fair-trade contracts in accordance with the laws of their own States, to criminal prosecution for making such contracts. The only alternative, under the Keogh bill, would be to make it necessary for all States, whose fair-trade acts do not specifically conform to the provisions of this bill, to pass new legislation which did conform. This would indeed mark a new invasion by the Federal Government of the rights of States "under the United States Constitution to regulate their internal affairs." The McGuire bill, H. R. 5767, specifically recognizes this right in its first section. And every provision in the McGuire bill is designed to enable the States with fair-trade laws— namely, 45 out of the 48 States—to carry out their respective policies on resale price maintenance without Federal restriction or interference.

Mr. [CHET] HOLIFIELD [D., Cal.]. Mr. Chairman, will the gentleman yield?

Mr. HILL. I yield to the gentleman from California.

Mr. HOLIFIELD. I just want to say that the gentleman has made a wonderful statement on this matter. His background as a merchandiser puts him in a position where he can speak with authority on the problems of the small-business man, and I want to concur in the statement he has made.

Mr. HILL. I thank the gentleman from California.

Let me read at this time a special message from George J. Burger, vice president, National Federation of Independent Business:

> On basis of our Nation-wide membership vote and in line with our testimony before both House Committee on Interstate and Foreign Commerce and House Judiciary Committee, we urge you to vote for the strongest fair-trade law possible.
>
> Such a law must permit manufacturers to enter into fair-trade contracts with their retailers, and enforce these contracts against both signers and nonsigners, across State lines in fair-trade States. It must permit the establishment of a fixed minimum price, but must prohibit establishment of a fixed maximum price. It must permit disposal of goods at close-out or bankruptcies, with option of fair-trading manufacturer to pick up his goods to preserve his price, but it must clearly prohibit distribution to fair-trade States from warehouses located in States without fair-trade laws, where intent or effect is to cut below established minimum prices. The law must also prohibit any and all effort toward collusion between dealers of competit[ive] manufacturers (note p. 920, Study of Monopoly Power, hearings before the Antitrust Subcommittee of the Committee on the Judiciary, House of Representatives, February 13 to 27, 1952, inclusive). It must also provide no loopholes for evasion on technicalities by price jugglers.

Next I want to read a special release to all Members of Congress, emanating from that same source:

> Since 1931, 45 States enacted fair-trade laws. In 1936 the United States Supreme Court, in a unanimous decision, upheld their constitutionality. The Congress passed the Miller-Tydings Act which permitted the operation of fair trade in interstate commerce. In a recent decision, the United States Supreme Court held that a retailer who did not sign a fair-trade contract (which obviously a certain class of price jugglers refuse to do), was not amenable to the law "where interstate commerce was involved." The McGuire bill seeks to remedy this. It recognizes that the States have a right under the Federal Constitution to pass laws to restrain unfair competition. The passage of legislation to enable the interstate seller of trade-marked goods (when it is in free and open competition with other items of similar character) is essential to the well-being of 1,500,000 merchants. We, therefore, respectfully urge your active support of fair-trade enabling legislation as sponsored by Representative MCGUIRE (H. R. 5767) which, we understand, will come before you this week.
>
> *Ed Wimmer,*
> *Forward America Publishing Guild.*
> *Cincinnati Retail Grocers & Meat Dealers' Association,*
> *August Meyer, Jr., Secretary.*
> *Northern Kentucky Independent Food Dealers' Association,*
> *Arthur Menne, Secretary.*
> *Dayton & Montgomery County Grocers' Association,*
> *Howard Heisterman, Secretary.*

Mr. WOLVERTON. Mr. Chairman, I yield such time as he may desire, to the gentleman from Pennsylvania [Mr. HUGH D. SCOTT, JR.].

Mr. HUGH D. SCOTT, JR. [R., Pa.]. Mr. Chairman, I support H. R. 5767. My support is based upon many things: One, the fact that I have discovered over the years the gradual disappearance of the corner drug store and the corner grocer in proportion to the large and expanding operations of the chain stores. I have felt that it is up to the States to protect the small-business man as well as the large. I felt that wherever the States can suitably control the flow of commerce in the interest of the consumer, that they should do so, and that the Federal Government's interference should be restricted to an absolute minimum.

Therefore, I agree with the committee's report, in which the statement is made that as far as the Federal Government is concerned the committee feels the States should be left free to protect their trade in the best manner known to them from predatory price practices. I also agree that resale price maintenance constitutes the only effective weapon against such predatory price practices.

I hope the bill will pass without restrictive or crippling amendments.

Mr. WOLVERTON. Mr. Chairman, I yield such time as he may desire to the gentleman from California [Mr. HUNTER].

Mr. [ALLAN OAKLEY] HUNTER [R., Cal.]. Mr. Chairman, I favor the bill introduced by the distinguished gentleman from Connecticut. I, too, hope that it passes without any crippling amendments.

Of the 48 States, 45 have enacted laws legalizing fair-trade practices. These laws allow a manufacturer and a retailer to enter into minimum-price contracts, and in addition, after one contract is signed, the manufacturer may establish his price by notification and announcements, enforcing it on other retailers in the State, even though they have not signed contracts. This is the nonsigner provision.

State fair-trade laws normally apply only to trade within that State, but under the Miller-Tydings Act of 1937, State law was extended to interstate sales taking place within each State and minimum prices were enforced. In 1951, however, the Supreme Court ruled that the act does not require the maintenance of prices against retailers who are not parties to actual contracts.

The issue now confronting Congress is whether existing laws should be amended so as to legitimatize the nonsigner provisions of State fair trade laws.

I believe that nonsigner provisions should be so legitimatized. Growth of the use of trade-marks, brands, and producer names has come about through a feeling of responsibility on the part of the manufacturer to produce a consistently good article at a fair price. If better manufacturing methods, increased sales, and better distribution have produced a fine article at a competitive price, I feel that the manufacturer should have the right to protect his product with fair-trade provisions which apply even to nonsigners.

Wild price cutting is an example of one of the evils resulting from the lack of adequate fair trade laws. I do not, of course, refer to normal competitive pricing, but to the practice of cutting prices on nationally advertised items to a figure below cost. This loss leader will fool customers, while prices of unfamiliar products are raised. This policy of juggling prices is unfair to the customer, and should be prevented by fair trade laws.

Freezing out independent merchants is made possible through such wild price cutting as just described. Prolonged selling at below-cost prices will force a little dealer out of business, while the large retailer can absorb the loss or make it up through other branches of his store. Fair trade laws prevent this.

Equalized competitive strength made possible by established minimum prices is the weapon with which the neighborhood store can fight off the big monopoly. It keeps competition alive, and competition is the whip which brings cheaper prices to the consumer and better products.

Competition, under fair trade laws, is stimulated between manufacturers who have the power to react with better products and lower prices, while competition between dealers who have no constructive effect over the product, is eliminated.

Fair trade pricing is permissive, for no manufacturer is compelled to put his trade-marked article on fair trade, though he may do so if he wishes. Fair-traded items compete with non-fair-traded items, and with each other. Neither does fair trade force consumers to pay higher prices, nor has it had that effect according to studies made.

A standard of quality is established under fair trade, by which consumers may judge the value of an article. Price cutting means a lack of standardization, while a standard price, like a brand name, gives the buyer a yardstick of value.

And lastly, loss-leader selling results in a financial loss which must be borne by the consumer. The public cannot get something for nothing, even though they seem eternally intent on trying.

In conclusion, I want to say that I am convinced that the practice of fooling the consumer by misleading price cutting is detrimental to the public interest, and that further, small business houses need protection against monopolistic tendencies, loss leader, freeze out, and other similar unfair practices of big business. In view of these facts I urge that the States retain their jurisdiction over retail trade practices and that Congress enact legislation making it possible to enforce fair trade contracts in interstate commerce. The McGuire bill will do this. I am, therefore, supporting it.

Mr. PRIEST. Mr. Chairman, I yield 20 minutes to the distinguished chairman of the House Committee on the Judiciary, the gentleman from New York [Mr. CELLER].

Mr. CELLER. Mr. Chairman, I am going to read from remarks I have made which were the basis of a minority report on fair trade submitted by certain members of the Committee on the Judiciary. I am going to read in part from that minority report:

While resale price maintenance injures competition and promotes the concentration of economic power, its most immediate impact is felt by the consumer. Any comparison shopping tour will readily disclose the large savings which can be had on purchases made in the District of Columbia, as against those made across the District line in the fair trade jurisdictions of Virginia or Maryland. Numerous studies have been made which bear these conclusions out. The consumer will no doubt be surprised to discover that Congress intends to prohibit efficient retail establishments from reducing prices on his wares. It will also certainly appear anomalous to the voters of the United States for Congress, during a severe inflationary period, which has necessitated rigid governmental controls to prevent prices from going up, seriously to consider legislation which, under the penalties of Federal law, prohibits the prices of many important commodities from coming down.

I went on one of those shopping tours referred to, and I want to give you the results, in terms of the prices of certain ordinary articles that are purchased at a drugstore, and indicate to you how the public is getting a rooking from so-called fair trade.

I purchased 10 cubic centimeters of u. 40 protamine zinc Lilly insulin, used by diabetics. The price in the District of Columbia was 98 cents. The price in Maryland was $1.29. The Maryland price was 32 percent above the District price. In Virginia, in Richmond, for example, the same article, Lilly's insulin, was sold at $1.48. If you can tell me that the public is protected by fair trade, I would like to know why those differences in prices.

I purchased a BD Yale 26 gage, one-half inch hyponeedle, used to inject insulin into a sick person's body. In the District of Columbia the price was 15 cents. In Virginia the price was 20 cents—33 percent higher in Virginia. In Maryland the price was 23 cents—53 percent more in Maryland.

I purchased 100 Bayer aspirin tablets in Virginia, Maryland, and the District of Columbia. In the District of Columbia, the price is 46 cents. What was the price in Virginia? The price was 59 cents. I paid 28 percent more for the same article in Virginia. What was the price in Maryland? Fifty-nine cents. Again, I paid 28 percent more for the same article in Maryland.

I purchased some 12-ounce bottles of Phillips milk of magnesia. Here are the bottles. In the District of Columbia, the price was 34 cents. In Virginia, it was 14 percent higher, or 39 cents. Similarly in Maryland, it was 14 percent higher, or 39 cents.

I purchased some large tubes of Ipana tooth paste. See the difference in these purchases. I paid 27 percent more for the Ipana tooth paste in Virginia than I did in the District of Columbia. In the District of Columbia, the price was 37 cents. In Virginia, the price was 47 cents; and likewise in Maryland, it was 47 cents.

I purchased packages of 20 Gillette Blueblades. In the District of Columbia, the price was 87 cents, whereas in Virginia I paid 11 percent more, or 98 cents, and also 11 percent more in Maryland, namely, 98 cents.

I purchased 50 cubic centimeters of Mead's Oleum Percomorphum. These are baby vitamins which are very essential to the health of infants and growing children. It is a very, very important product. I paid in the District of Columbia $2.63. When I went to Virginia I had to pay not $2.63 but $3.29, or 25 percent more. In Maryland I had to pay 32 percent more, or $3.49.

Take a laxative like Ex-Lax. In Virginia the price was 25 cents, and in the District of Columbia the price was 19 cents. In Maryland, the price was 28 cents. To take a laxative costs you 47 percent more in the State of Maryland than it does in the District of Columbia. And it costs you 32 percent more in the State of Virginia.

Here are some Dr. West tooth brushes. They were the same price in all three States, an indication that I am not guilty of any particular selectivity to indicate deliberately that the prices are more in one place than in another. When it came to Dr. West's tooth brushes, the price in all three locations was 59 cents.

Now, take the large-size Mennen baby powder. Here they are. In the District of Columbia, the price was 47 cents. In Virginia it was 49 cents, and in Maryland 49 cents.

Mr. Chairman, these are 10 ordinary articles that are everyday needs for housewives, diabetics, and others. The total price in Virginia is $8.23. The total price in the District of Columbia is $7.05; and the total price in Maryland is $8.80. On these 10 articles in Maryland, I paid 25 percent more than I did for the 10 articles when purchased in the District of Columbia. When I went into Virginia I paid 17 percent more for these very same articles that I had purchased in the District of Columbia.

Here is a recapitulation:

Item	Virginia price	Virginia percent increase over District of Columbia price	District of Columbia price	Maryland price	Maryland percent increase over District of Columbia price
10 cubic centimeters U. 40 protamine zinc Lilly insulin	{ $0.98 {[1] 1.48	0 51	$0.98 —	$1.29 —	32 —
BD Yale 26-gage, ½-inch hypo needle	.20	33	.15	.23	53
100 Bayer aspirin	.59	28	.46	.59	28
12 ounces Phillips milk of magnesia	.39	14	.34	.39	14
Large Ipana toothpaste	.47	27	.37	.47	27
20 Gillette Blueblades	.98	11	.87	.98	11
50 cubic centimeters Meads oleum percomorphum (baby vitamins)	3.29	25	2.63	3.49	32
18 Ex-Lax	.25	32	.19	.28	47
Dr. West toothbrush	.59	0	.59	.59	0
Large size Mennen baby powder	.49	4	.47	.49	4
Total	8.23	17	7.05	8.80	25

[1] Richmond, Va.

Now I hesitate to place in the well of the House two whisky bottles that I purchased, but I did purchase the whisky, and I have the bottles in this basket.

Mr. [H. R.] GROSS [R., Iowa]. Mr. Chairman, will the gentleman yield?

Mr. CELLER. I yield to the gentleman from Iowa.

Mr. GROSS. On the items you have just mentioned, did that include tax, or was that the price without the tax?

Mr. CELLER. That, I understand, is without tax.

Mr. [ARTHUR G.] KLEIN [D., N.Y.]. Mr. Chairman, will the gentleman yield?

Mr. CELLER. I yield to the gentleman from New York.

Mr. KLEIN. Did the gentleman ever hear of the expression "loss leaders"? I might call the gentleman's attention to the fact that it is the practice in many, many stores, not only in the District of Columbia but throughout the country, in order to induce people to come in and purchase in that store, to have articles on which they obviously lose money. I would like to call the gentleman's attention to the fact that on many other articles in the same store the purchaser pays a great deal more.

⊥ Mr. CELLER. I am going to offer a substitute which gets at the evil of loss leaders, but let us not burn down the house to roast a pig. Let us not indulge in price-fixing, which in [sic] contrary to the very concept of our antitrust and anti-monopoly laws, just to get at loss leaders. In these bills you have a cure worse than the disease. To get at loss leaders you usher in all the evils of price-fixing, an evil for [sic] worse than loss leaders. In other words, make a direct attack on loss-leaders. Do not seek to protect those who want to garner in these huge profits by virtue of vertical as well as horizontal price-fixing. Horizontal price-fixing is permitted indirectly under the provisions of this bill.

Mr. HARRIS. Mr. Chairman, will the gentleman yield?

Mr. CELLER. I yield to the gentleman from Arkansas.

Mr. HARRIS. I do not want to interrupt the gentleman, but on that particular point the gentleman has for the first time just advised the House that he proposes to offer a substitute in which he will get at loss leaders. Now, the gentleman is chairman of the Judiciary Committee. Has he at any time proposed any such bill to get at loss leaders?

Mr. CELLER. Of course. The bill has been in the hopper for a long, long time. Certainly I have offered it, and it has been considered. The bill is H. R. 6986, and was introduced on March 11, 1952, some 2 months ago.

As to the whisky, I will not exhibit it. The bottles may disappear too rapidly. But, in any event I purchased a fifth of Black Label Schenley whisky in the District of Columbia at $3.23. What did I pay in Maryland, just across the border, for the same identical bottle? I paid $4.32, a difference of $1.09. So that where fair trade prevails for that particular article, the public has to pay $1.09 more. If you can tell me there is anything fair in that kind of practice, I fail to see it. If you can call that fair trade, then I do not know what the meaning of fair trade is nor does anyone else.

Mr. PRIEST. Mr. Chairman, will the gentleman yield?

Mr. CELLER. I yield to the gentleman from Tennessee.

Mr. PRIEST. Does the gentleman have any information indicating whether a part of that difference was due to the State tax in the State of Maryland?

Mr. CELLER. No. That has nothing to do with the tax. This was on a straight retail. I am not saying there is no license tax. Naturally, you cannot buy without paying the Federal tax. The Federal taxes are uniform. The Federal and State taxes are involved, but the State tax in those States is of no consequence. Actually the tax in the District of Columbia is 15 cents a fifth, in Maryland the tax is 19 cents a fifth—just 4 cents difference—the total retail price difference due to fair trade is $1.09.

Mr. PRIEST. But the gentleman knows there is a difference in the State taxes.

Mr. CELLER. A very trifling difference, only 4 cents a fifth.

Mr. CRAWFORD. Mr. Chairman, will the gentleman yield?

Mr. CELLER. I yield to the gentleman from Michigan.

Mr. CRAWFORD. Would the gentleman mind yielding to let the gentleman from Arkansas tell what the difference is?

Mr. CELLER. I am agreeable to having him tell it.

Mr. HARRIS. I will get that and give it to the gentleman.

Mr. CELLER. I will put the information in the RECORD, namely, that the Maryland tax is only 4 cents higher.

I do not care what the tax is; the difference is so inconsequential as to nullify any argument that we are helping the general public by this kind of legislation.

Mr. CRAWFORD. Mr. Chairman, will the gentleman yield for a question?

Mr. CELLER. I yield.

Mr. CRAWFORD. And it is a further indication that each day it becomes more and more impossible for the poor man to drink liquor if he wants to; it is a rich man's drink. Why not fix it so the poor man can take a drink, too?

Mr. CELLER. What does the National Grange say in this regard? The National Grange—patrons of husbandry—is a very reputable organization and their word should mean a great deal to this body. It says:

> The truth is, it is not a fair-trade bill at all but a plan to extort over a billion dollars a year in excess margins from the American people; it is legalized price fixing.

What has happened during the period we have had these so-called fair-trade laws? I will read you a statement that appears in the hearings, which comes from the Journal of the National Association of Retail Druggists of August 1950, showing that despite, or perhaps because of, the protection afforded retail druggists through fair-trade legislation, they are suffering from the competition of large retailers. This association journal goes on to say the following:

> The retail drug store has not kept pace with the general business development. Although its sales volume increased 2 1/2 times between 1939 and 1940, it ended up by getting less of the consumer's dollar simply because sales through other outlets have expanded more rapidly than drug-store business. The retail druggist cannot allow himself to be fooled by today's high sales volume; the drug store has simply ridden the trend and, compared with other outlets, has not done a very good job at that.

All this, mind you, in the face of these fair-trade acts which have been on the statute books in the various States for a number of years.

The principle beneficiary of the drug store's declining share of the consumer's dollar from almost 4 to less than 3 cents in the decade between 1939 and 1949 has been the grocery supermarket and similar outlets. This same Journal of the National Association of Retail Druggists in the issue of October 15, 1951, reported the extent to which grocery stores had invaded the established lines handled by drug stores as follows:

> Nonfood items traditionally sold by drug stores show a 59-percent penetration into grocery stores, according to a survey made by Selling Research, Inc., New York. Rating high on the list were sanitary napkins, now sold in 98 percent of grocery stores; shampoo, 84 percent; tooth paste, 77 percent; shaving cream, 72 percent; and bandages, 70 percent. Geographically, the presence of drug items in grocery stores is most prevalent in the western portion of the country (p. 1646).

According to a recent survey conducted by the Progressive Grocer, "85 percent of the Nation's leading supermarkets and superettes now sell selected health and beauty aids, compared with only 37 percent 10 years ago." By October of 1951 the last major grocery chain which had yet to promote the sale of drug items, the A. & P., had decided to enter the field by offering to its customers tooth paste, first-aid items, shaving accessories, shampoos, and so forth. The following chart graphically shows this tremendous growth in the distribution of drug items by leading food stores during recent years:

Growth of drug distribution in leading food stores
PERCENT OF STORES HANDLING DRUGS

	Percent
1941	37
1946	51
1949	64
1950	70
1951	85

Source: Progressive Grocer, February 1952.

What has prompted this successful venture of the large supermarket into the retail trade of the retail druggist? Why did so many people retail these same articles, formerly promoted by druggists, in the supermarkets, in the grocery chains, in the automatic vending machines, gasoline stations, and stationery stores, and cigar stores? Do you know why? Because of the constant pressure brought by the Retail Druggists Association in the various States on the manufacturers of the trade-marked articles to push up the prices, to increase the mark-ups. The druggists have been hoist by their own petard. The profits have been so lush on many of these items that these other channels of distribution have gone into the business of cosmetics, beauty aids, infant foods, pharmaceuticals, soaps, and perfumery—articles they never handled before—to the detriment of the independent druggists.

Lush margins on fair-trade items provide a windfall to the giant grocery mart whose profits on food items have, over the years, been reduced as a result of the dynamics of competition. Thus, whereas a self-service drug department located in a high traffic location of a modern supermarket takes in about 2 percent of total store volume, "with 'drugs' yielding a margin of over 30 percent on sales, the line contributes 4 percent or more of store's total dollar margin."

Accordingly, we now find the economic circumstances resulting from resale price maintenance causing the independent merchant to fall ready victim to those ⊥ large and powerful outlets against which in the first instance fair-trade legislation was directed.

There is a tremendous amount of evidence in the record to show that there is a constant drive on the part of the druggists illegally, and I will show that in a moment, as well as legally to push up the mark-up. Not all druggists; most are law abiding. But a militant group are guilty. The result is that they have created more and more competition for themselves from big chain stores and supermarkets with the result that the druggist today is getting less and less of the consumer's dollar. That is what always happens when you seek to interfere unduly with the ordinary forces of competition and the law of supply and demand.

When you apply these unofficial restraints and crutches, as it were, especially to some inefficient retail druggists—and there are some of them—you have the result I have indicated.

The same NARD Journal in the October 16, 1950, issue deplored inadequate mark-ups on certain items. It said—then Mr. Dargavel speaking:

> The point I wish to make is that the problem of margins is critical to the degree that it must be solved before thousands of independent druggists are pushed over the brink of bankruptcy.

Such was the distressed condition of the retail druggists over inadequate margins on some items during the year 1950 that one of the 1951 objectives of the National Association of Retail Druggists was "to bring to the attention of the manufacturers that many mark-ups are inadequate for the reason they fail to present [sic] economic conditions, to cover the costs of overhead and a reasonable profit."

Margins on tobacco products during this period were characterized by certain druggists as "ridiculous," while one proprietor expressed the candid opinion that the gross margins of the tobacco concerns are pins in the flesh of the retailers. With regard to other drug-store commodities, Aaron Lauter, a retail druggist in Delaware County, Pa., pointed out in August of 1950 that many manufacturers have rigged their list prices so that when one sells at the stipulated minimum there is no profit.

In view of this prevailing situation it is little wonder that the bewildered retailers began to suspect that fair trade had returned to plague them. A leading editorial in the NARD Journal of March 21, 1949, charged in bold-faced headlines that manufacturers who had failed to raise margins for retail druggists were acting like a pack of wolves. The NARD subsequently bemoaned the many examples of inadequate mark-ups which could be cited to show that the druggists have been made the goats of a cockeyed situation which has been coupled to fair trade.

Mr. ROGERS of Florida. Mr. Chairman, will the gentleman yield?

Mr. CELLER. I yield to the gentleman from Florida.

Mr. ROGERS of Florida. I would like to ask the gentleman if he does not think the proper forum to correct this inequality, the inequity he has described, is in the State legislatures? Does not the gentleman think the consumers should get hold of the members of the legislatures of the various States to repeal the fair-trade laws?

Mr. CELLER. The National Association of Retail Druggists can bring and exert much pressure in this body with the result which we will see this afternoon or tomorrow. How much easier is it for the National Association of Retail Druggists to exert pressure on the local legislatures? When the original State Fair Trade Acts were passed they were passed so rapidly that the acts, in many instances, contained the same stenographic errors; the same typographical errors appeared in any number of the State legislature enactments, which shows you they went through the State legislatures willy-nilly, without consideration, without forethought, without deliberation, without hearings, only as the result of this constant drive and pressure on the part of these organizations that are primarily benefited, these same organizations which have been time out of mind guilty of offenses against the antitrust laws.

The CHAIRMAN. The time of the gentleman from New York has expired.

Mr. [LOUIS E.] GRAHAM [R., Pa.]. Mr. Chairman, I yield the gentleman three additional minutes.

Mr. PRIEST. Mr. Chairman, I yield the gentleman five additional minutes.

Mr. CELLER. Mr. Chairman, past experience under the Miller-Tydings law yields abundant evidence of resale price maintenance legislation serving as a cloak to conceal price fixing and other undesirable activities in restraint of trade.[3.49]

In 1942, the Colorado Wholesale Wine and Liquor Dealers Association was indicted by the Department of Justice under section 1 of the Sherman Act for engaging, under the guise of fair trade, in a conspiracy to fix retail prices of liquor sold in the State of Colorado. Retail prices, it was charged, were agreed upon; out-of-State producers were persuaded to enter into fair-trade contracts embodying agreed-upon prices; and wholesalers and producers refusing to comply were boycotted. Pleas of nolo contendere were filed by the defendants and fines were imposed.

Similarly the National Association of Retail Druggists, today the loudest advocate of fair-trade legislation, was fined in 1947 on a plea of nolo contendere to an indictment charging them with having engaged in a conspiracy to fix the retail and wholesale prices of drug items, to eliminate price competition among retail druggists, and to restrain competition. This conspiracy was perpetrated under the guise of fair trade despite the existence of a consent decree filed in 1907 perpetually enjoining the association from engaging in such activities as boycotts, and so forth.

The National Wholesale Druggists Association was also indicted under the Sherman Act for conspiring to raise, fix, and stabilize wholesale selling prices of drug items by means of fair-trade agreements.

Again nolo contendere pleas were filed and fines levied.

In United States against New York State Pharmaceutical Association, the National Association of Retail Druggists was again indicted, this time in conjunction with the New York State Pharmaceutical Association and others, for fixing, stabilizing, and maintaining the retail and wholesale prices of drug store items through the adoption of uniform prices and methods of sale, interchange of information, boycotts, and black lists. Pleas of nolo contendere and fines also ended this litigation.

The Department of Justice has brought cases of a similar nature involving fair trade against the Tri-State Record Dealers Association, the Record Dealers Association, and has currently pending cases against the Allegheny County Retail Druggists' Association and the Sunbeam Corp. Proceedings instituted by the Federal Trade Commission where resale price maintenance was an important factor include:[3.50]

Docket No. 4526: Law Book Publishers Co.

Docket No. 4900: Refractories case.

Docket No. 5448: Rubber manufacturers group.

Docket No. 5734: Mid-Atlantic Distributors Corp., which just recently has been appealed to the United States Court of Appeals for the District of Columbia Circuit.

Docket No. 5635: Cycle jobbers.

Docket No. 5636: American Dental Association.

Docket No. 4093: Wholesale Liquor Distributors Association of Northern California, et al.

Docket No. 4132: Western Confectioners Association.

Docket No. 4168: National Retail Liquor Package Stores Association.

Let me tell you something else about the National Association of Retail Druggists.

[3.49] *See* notes 3.28–.35 *supra.*

[3.50] *See* notes 3.36–.44 *supra.*

This organization, under the McGuire bill, is given the right to bring an action against anybody that it is alleged has violated the so-called fair-trade laws. That is something new in our jurisprudence. An association can bring an action. That is in the McGuire bill. You are buying a pig in a poke, I tell you. Here is the NARD, guilty so often of violations, able to bring actions in its own name. It will harass and annoy any number of innocent dealers. Such a right of suit will make it even more powerful.

A State counterpart and constituent organization of the National Association of Retail Druggists boycotted the Pepsodent company because the Pepsodent company refused to fair trade Pepsodent products in California. As a result of the boycott, as a result of undue interference and unlawful conduct on the part of this California druggist association, the pressure was successful. Pepsodent then wanted to resume fair trade on their articles and in order to show their contrition, they were required to pay $25,000 to the fair-trade lobbying fund of the druggists' association. That was an unlawful tribute—blood money—a penalty imposed by a private group.

Now, those are the tactics upon which you put the imprimatur of your approval, if you pass this kind of legislation. Those are the tactics that you countenance if you pass this legislation. The Department of Justice, through the head of the antitrust division, testified in confirmation of this view to the effect that the experience of the antitrust division was that a vast majority of resale price maintenance contracts, if examined fully, would be found in violation of the antitrust laws. That is what we are going to sanction if we pass this bill.

Furthermore, I am unalterably opposed to this legislation because of the undemocratic coercion involved therein. I am not so much against fair trade if it is limited to those who sign a fair-trade contract that involves a contractural, a consensual relationship. But, this goes further and says, "even if you do not sign, you are bound." That means if a manufacturer goes into any State and he signs one contract with one retailer, all the other retailers in the same State are ipso facto bound by that single contract.

In the Schwegmann case the Supreme Court said that that was unfair, and to get around the Schwegmann case they now provide that all the nonsigners shall be bound by the contract made with as few as one retailer throughout the length and breadth of the State. This is how the Supreme Court, in its majority opinion, characterized the binding of a nonsigner:

> When they seek, however, to impose price fixing on persons who have not contracted or agreed to the scheme, the situation is vastly different. That is not price fixing by contract or agreement; that is price fixing by compulsion. That is not following the path of consensual agreement; that is resort to coercion.[3.51]

Further, the Court said:

> Contracts or agreements convey the idea of a cooperative arrangement, not a program whereby recalcitrants are dragged in by the heels and compelled to submit to price fixing.[3.52]

Mr. PRIEST. Mr. Chairman, will the gentleman yield?

Mr. CELLER. I yield to the gentleman from Tennessee.

Mr. PRIEST. I am sure, in line with what the gentleman has just said about the nonsigner or nonsigner provision, that he will want it to be clear to the House that under the Miller-Tydings Act from May 1937 to May 1951 the nonsigner provision was in effect at that time.

Mr. CELLER. No, the Supreme Court has indicated that that was unfair and improper. It takes a long time for a case to reach the Supreme Court, but in the interval see the great damage that was done. Many thought that the nonsigner would be bound. I did not. I gave an opinion sometime ago that I felt a nonsigner would not be bound, but it was the practice to bind nonsigners, with the unhappy results that I have indicated.

Profit margins have been higher, particularly in the drug industry, that is the main beneficiary of all this, whereas in the grocery line prices and mark-ups have

---

[3.51] 341 U.S. at 388.
[3.52] *Id.* at 390.

deliberately dropped due to free competition throughout that period. Throughout the last two decades, all during the period of resale price maintenance, the comparative price of groceries and the mark-ups on groceries have dropped. Why? Because grocery articles have not so far been fair traded. Druggist articles are fair traded. Margins are high on drug items; prices come down on grocery items. So I say to the gentleman from Tennessee that just because people did not know what the law was should not freeze that practice into law.

It was not the law and never was the law, because the Supreme Court said it was not the law.

It does not take much imagination to discover for whose benefit these fair-trade bills will ultimately inure. A look at those manufacturers who employ fair-trade contracts readily discloses who will be primarily rewarded by the bills which are now offered under the guise of a friendly congressional hand to small and independent business. A recent study conducted by the American Fair Trade Council—sponsors of the Keogh bill—disclosed that 51 out of the leading 100 largest national advertisers, using newspapers, periodicals, and/or radio, were manufacturers who fair-trade part or all of their products. Included were such small businesses as the following: Procter & Gamble Co., General Foods Corp., General Motors Corp., General Mills Corp., American Tobacco Co., General Electric Co., American Home Products Corp., and Goodyear Tire & Rubber Co.

Who supports fair trade in the drug field? Well, large manufacturers contributed handsomely to the Bureau of Education on Fair Trade which is a lobbying organization registered with the Clerk of the House under the provisions of law, and which is behind much of the efforts to enact the McGuire bill. An examination of the steering committee of the Bureau of Education on Fair Trade shows that its composition includes the following typical representatives of small business: Charles S. Beardsley, chairman of the board, Miles Laboratories; Henry Bristol, chairman of the board, Bristol-Myers Co.; Philip Cortney, president of Coty, Inc.; W. Rutherford James, president, Towns & James, Inc.; Harry W. Meyer, vice president, International Cellucotton Products Co.; William J. Murray, Jr., chairman of the board, McKesson & Robbins, Inc.; E. Allen Newcomb, executive secretary, National Wholesale Druggists' Association; Carl H. Willingham, secretary, National Association of Chain Drug Stores; and Earl S. Ritter, vice president, Eli Lilly & Co.

While representatives of some of these big companies shed many a crocodile tear for the welfare of the poor independent druggists when they appeared before the Interstate and Foreign Commerce Committee in support of the McGuire bill, I am sure you will not be beguiled by their solicitous demeanor. It is no secret why these large companies want fair trade—it appears in black and white right on their balance sheets. Here is how the small druggists described the munificent profits which these concerns reaped from fair trade during the postwar period—and I quote from the annual report of the executive secretary of the National Association of Retail Druggists in 1950:

> The manufacturers in the drug field made much more money in the last 5 years than they ever had before, and the reports show that in 1949 the profits they took were about 13 percent over 1948 or better than 15 percent over and above the average for 656 corporations. * * * The profits of the manufacturers in 1948 were the highest in the history of the country.

It is no wonder these large drug manufacturers are now urging Congress to enact fair-trade legislation. Under fair trade, the profits of Abbott Laboratories increased more than five times during the fair-trade years of 1939 through 1950; American Home Products Corp. and Parke, Davis & Co. more than doubled their profits in the same period. Profits of Merck & Co. increased almost six times. In 1939, under fair trade, the profits of American Home Products Corp., was 50.7 percent of its net worth—in other words, a rate of return which within a period of 2 years, would equal its entire capital investment. In 1950, Parke, Davis & Co., selling under fair trade, was able to earn a net income of 27.7 percent on its net worth—the equivalent of a profit rate returning its total capital expenditures within a period of less than 4 years.

Such are the great profits assured these large producers who fair-trade their products that they can afford to spend extravagant sums for advertising and still net the handsome returns I have just referred to. Let me cite a few advertising expenditures for some of the important fair-trading companies during the year 1950 to show you where the consumer's dollar spent on fair-trade articles goes:

Procter & Gamble Co.	$27,023,122
Lever Bros.	13,464,077
Colgate-Palmolive-Peet	12,026,080
Sterling Drug	10,692,019
Miles Laboratories	8,731,493

It is no wonder that these large concerns are ardent advocates of fair trade. Some of them perhaps share a portion of their fair-trade profits with the small retailer to assure his support of the program. But in so doing the independent businessman is converted into a mere outlet for the sale of goods. In exchange for the mark-up supposedly guaranteed by fair trade, the small-business man puts his pricing policies, his right to make a profit, and his net total income at the absolute mercy of large manufacturers. There is no longer meaning for the independent merchant in this state of subjugation. The control of these large entities which can afford to spend millions of dollars on advertising over the entire economy is strengthened, while the retail field becomes filled with hundreds of economic vassals bound by the feudal bonds of the fair-trade contract to perform fealty to big business.

It is for the reasons that I have set forth that I believe that the sincere advocates of small business in this House who have suggested fair trade as the panacea for the independent retailers' woes have failed to see the forest for the trees. I have no doubt of their sincerity which their past record here on the floor of the House has proven. They have been splendid and stalwart supporters of small business. I can understand, too, why they have been sympathetic to the demands of numerous small merchants for the enactment of these bills. But I want to remind you that there are hundreds and thousands of small merchants throughout the United States who have not written you who are opposed to fair trade and who do not want to be coerced by you without counsel, without hearing, or without appeal into contracts to which they were never a party.

The eyes of these thousands of small merchants are watching you today, just as are those of the giant manufacturers who are eagerly waiting to reap the rich profits of fair trade. Watching also are the millions of consumers throughout this country, the much harried house-wives and their heavily taxed spouses, the farmers throughout the Nation, and the laboring man. They want to know if you are going to guarantee fat profits to the big fair-trading corporations of America at the expense of their independence, their freedom, and their pocketbook.

Mr. PRIEST. Mr. Chairman, I yield 10 minutes to the gentleman from Arkansas [Mr. HARRIS].

Mr. [PAUL] BROWN [D., Ga.]. Mr. Chairman, will the gentleman yield?

Mr. HARRIS. I yield.

Mr. BROWN of Georgia. The gentleman from New York just stated that the laws passed by the respective States were passed without much consideration and in great haste. I wish to state that none of the 45 States has repealed the act, and they have had sufficient time, every one of them, to repeal it.

Mr. HARRIS. I thank the gentleman for his comment.

Mr. Chairman, in trying to reply to some of the statements that have been made here I shall undertake to clear up some of the confusion that evidently some would like to see prevail here in the House.

The gentleman from New York, the distinguished chairman of the Committee on the Judiciary, has just given you his own viewpoint with reference to fair-trade laws. The gentleman has maintained the same position and the same attitude since the first time this issue was presented to the Nation. The gentleman has given you the argument on which he bases his own best judgment as to the advisability or inadvisability of a national or Federal fair-trade law. His viewpoint has nothing whatsoever to do with the question with which we are faced here today, so let us not be confused as to the problem that is up for consideration. Let us see for a moment just what it is.

I think you would be interested in a little background. In 1890 the Sherman Act was passed, which declared illegal contracts and agreements in restraint of trade throughout the Nation. Most everyone in the country is aware and advised of just what the full import of that act of Congress was. It is still the law today.

In 1931 the State of California enacted a fair-trade law. It did not include a nonsigner clause. In 1933, the State of California saw that this law was not a workable or a practical solution to the problem and amended it to include a nonsigner provision.

In 1937, to a District of Columbia appropriation bill, there was attached an amendment. It became known as the Miller-Tydings amendment. It amended the Sherman Act to provide that State legislation on fair trade, if applied to merchandise which moved in interstate commerce, does not violate the Federal antitrust laws.

Prior to 1937, when that amendment was adopted, the majority of the 48 States in the union had adopted fair trade laws. The gentleman talks about the haste of these States. Why, since that time, there are a number of States that have adopted fair-trade laws, and as late as 1950, the State of Louisiana amended its own fair-trade act. Within recent months, the State of Florida has reenacted, I believe, its own fair-trade law. So the gentleman's argument about the States rushing in with haste—that haste has lasted from 1931, insofar as the record shows until this recent time.

What brought this question here today? For 13 years—after 45 of the States of this Union had adopted fair-trade laws—for 13 years fair-trade laws were effective. They were not questioned. Then in 1950, the Schwegmann case in the State of Louisiana was presented to the district court. The District Court upheld the State law, including the nonsigner provision.[3.53] It was appealed to the court of appeals on its way to the Supreme Court, and that court agreed with the District Court.[3.54] The Supreme Court of the United States, however, held—and that is what we are here to correct today—that the Miller-Tydings Act applied only to those who were parties to the contract. The majority of the court held that in nonsigner cases, the Miller-Tydings Act did not apply.

About the same time, another problem arose with reference to articles which cross State lines in the course of a retail sale. That case came from Pennsylvania—the Wentling case. The court of appeals said that the fair-trade law of the State of Pennsylvania could not apply to articles which were sent across Pennsylvania State boundaries into other States.

As a consequence of these decisions we bring the McGuire bill to you today. It is purely and simply enabling legislation. It says to the States of Arkansas, California, Tennessee and the other 45 [sic] States, "You are permitted, under your own State procedure, to provide legislation to effect fair trade within your own boundaries." That is all it does. That is what we are here for. So the philosophy involved here today, the issue which we must pass on, is a fundamental issue. That is, are you going to permit the State of Mississippi to enact through its legislature legislation on this subject as a State under the Constitution is authorized to act, or are you going to say that such legislation is a burden on interstate commerce and the Federal Government is going to step in and say, "You cannot do that, even though the Constitution gives you that right"?

I recognize there was a problem that developed between our Committee, the Committee on Interstate and Foreign Commerce, and the Committee on the Judiciary. Certainly I did not feel too good about it. Neither did anyone else.

The CHAIRMAN. The time of the gentleman from Arkansas has expired.

Mr. HARRIS. Mr. Chairman, I yield myself five additional minutes.

We endeavored to avoid that situation as did all other Members. However, there was urgent need to bring this matter to the attention of this House so that it could correct it. The Miller-Tydings Act, as it was originally written, should be made effective, and without bringing the Federal Government into it and saying that the Federal Government is going to set up a bureau or a commission or an authority over commerce and industry and business throughout this Nation.

The Committee on the Judiciary did report its bill. I was certainly not in favor of that bill because it would have set up a fair-trade policy of the Federal Government. We are saying in the McGuire bill—and understand this is all it does—that the Federal

---

[3.53] Apparently the district court opinion was never reported.

[3.54] Schwegmann Bros. v. Calvert Distillers Corp., 184 F.2d 11 (5th Cir. 1950).

Government recognizes the action of the States. If you set up a Federal fair-trade policy you establish a Federal cause of action in the courts. You might even bring Government agencies into it, and consequently you may have a Government bureau down in my State and in your State jumping on this little business or that little business, and of course you know what will be the result there. So, consequently, we bring to you the problem, not trying to establish Federal policy, as the gentleman from New York would try to bring in here to confuse the issue.

He referred to the certain articles which allegedly cost more in fair-trade States than in non-fair-trade States. Certainly we could take some articles and say that in fair-trade States they will cost more than in non-fair-trade States. By the same token, however, we can go down here and get certain articles in the District of Columbia, which is a non-fair-trade territory, that will cost you more than the same articles in the State of Virginia, which is a fair-trade State. But you have to get the general picture. The testimony before our committee was to the effect that the percentage increase in the price of 24 nationally known articles was greater in the non-fair-trade areas than it was in the fair-trade States. We could argue the question of economics and prices in the various areas and territories, and establish proof that certain articles in one area are higher than articles in another area. That condition prevailed a long time before there were any fair-trade laws whatsoever. But the point I want to try to impress on your minds is the fundamental issue which you are going to have to determine, and that is: Do you believe in the philosophy of permitting the States to enact legislation that will be effective in the field in which they are authorized to act? Regardless of all of these other technical issues brought in from the outside, you are finally going to have to determine this basic question of whether or not you are to permit conditions to exist such as happened in New York about a year ago. Incidentally, that was immediately after the decision of the Supreme Court in the Schwegmann case. It was one of the most damaging experiences insofar as business is concerned which has occurred in recent years. You are all familiar with it.

Loss leaders were used to the extreme. Somebody sells aspirin or this product, or that product way below cost. But what does he do it for? The record shows that time after time it was done for the purpose of getting the consumers to come in, in order that they can sell other products the price of which is way above normal. That is what we are trying to protect against and that is what we wish to do here.

Mr. [ARTHUR] WINSTEAD [D., Miss.]. Mr. Chairman, will the gentleman yield?

Mr. HARRIS. I yield.

Mr. WINSTEAD. Then do I understand the gentleman to say that all this bill does is to permit each business in the respective States to operate under the State law without Federal interference?

Mr. HARRIS. That is all it does; that is the purpose of the legislation.

Mr. KLEIN. Mr. Chairman, will the gentleman yield?

Mr. HARRIS. I yield.

Mr. KLEIN. The gentleman referred to the price war in New York City immediately after the Supreme Court decision. I would like to call to his attention the fact that one of our large department stores which was guilty of price cutting was enjoined by the court in the State of New York, mind you, after the Supreme Court decision. So that the decision had nothing to do with the right of the stores to cut prices to that extent. I just wanted to point that out.

Mr. HARRIS. That is true; and it is a very important point to make.

Mr. [HAROLD C.] OSTERTAG [R., N.Y.]. Mr. Chairman, will the gentleman yield?

Mr. HARRIS. I yield.

Mr. OSTERTAG. Will the gentleman explain why the States cannot enact their own fair-trade laws without an enactment of the so-called McGuire bill?

Mr. HARRIS. That is what I endeavored to explain a moment ago. The Supreme Court in the Schwegmann case, which involved the Miller-Tydings Act, brought out several points. The Court held that the Miller-Tydings Act permitted the States to enact fair-trade laws so far as parties to the contract were concerned. However, they could not affect nonsigners. Consequently, if the State laws applied only to signers, you can very readily understand why there are some people who are looking for a loophole—people who want cut-throat competition whether through loss leaders or through something else. They would engage in predatory practices to the detriment of the signers of agreements.

The State of California, as I mentioned a moment ago, had the experience which proved to them the necessity of adjusting their own law.

Mr. KLEIN. Mr. Chairman, will the gentleman yield?

Mr. HARRIS. I yield.

Mr. KLEIN. I think the gentleman from Arkansas might point out to the gentleman from New York that the very State laws in all of these 45 States which do have fair-trade laws at the present time apply to nonsigners as well as signers. The Miller-Tydings Act was held not to apply to nonsigners. What we are trying to do in the McGuire bill presently under discussion is, as far as we can, to permit the laws of the States to apply to nonsigners.

Mr. GRAHAM. Mr. Chairman, the Committee on Interstate and Foreign Commerce has very generously tendered time to the Committee on the Judiciary. I now yield 10 minutes of that time to the gentleman from Michigan [Mr. CRAWFORD].

Mr. CRAWFORD. Mr. Chairman, I think the debate thus far demonstrates that we have had a tough problem on our hands here.

The element of compulsion which is written into this bill is exceedingly distasteful to me. I can understand what retailers are up against and what manufacturers are up against, what wholesalers are up against. I have had a little experience in some of those fields myself.

Mr. DOLLIVER. Mr. Chairman, will the gentleman yield?

Mr. CRAWFORD. For a question?

Mr. DOLLIVER. Yes.

Mr. CRAWFORD. I yield.

Mr. DOLLIVER. Mr. Chairman, will the gentleman yield?

Mr. CRAWFORD. I yield to the gentleman from Iowa.

Mr. DOLLIVER. Will the gentleman state whether he is referring to compulsion in the McGuire bill, in which there is no compulsion?

Mr. CRAWFORD. I refer to the language, and I will yield to any member of the committee to correct me if I am in error, which makes it possible to impose these restrictions on a person who does not sign one of these agreements.

Mr. DOLLIVER. My answer to that is that such laws are within the province of the State legislatures. They are not implicit in this law.

Mr. CRAWFORD. I am talking about the bills now before us. As I read H. R. 5767, and as I understand it, this language is enforceable against a merchant who does not sign an agreement; is that correct?

Mr. HARRIS. Mr. Chairman, will the gentleman yield?

Mr. CRAWFORD. I yield to the gentleman from Arkansas.

Mr. HARRIS. Just what particular language does the gentleman refer to?

Mr. CRAWFORD. The gentleman is an expert on this bill and he is a member of the committee. I am asking if this bill, together with the State laws, will impose enforcement on people who do not sign the agreements?

Mr. HARRIS. If the gentleman will permit me to answer, I will be glad to do so.

Mr. CRAWFORD. Proceed to answer.

Mr. HARRIS. I assume the gentleman was referring to the language on page 5, which is subsection (3) of section 5 (a). I should like to say to him that is a paragraph which specifically authorizes the nonsigner provisions. It does exactly what the gentleman says. This is enabling legislation. It permits the States to provide for the nonsigner clause, and, therefore, it would be effective on business that was not a party to the agreement.

Mr. CRAWFORD. I think the gentleman has answered my question and has corroborated what I said, is that correct?

Mr. HARRIS. I endeavored to answer the gentleman's question.

Mr. PRIEST. Mr. Chairman, will the gentleman yield?

Mr. CRAWFORD. I yield to the gentleman from Tennessee.

Mr. PRIEST. I understand the gentleman in framing his question to use the word "imposed," whether or not this imposed something on the States. The gentleman from

Arkansas [Mr. HARRIS] I think very clearly answered that. It does not impose anything. It permits whatever provision is in the State laws to be operative, to be effective, but it does not impose that on the States.

Mr. CRAWFORD. Then if a State law reads to the effect that signers and nonsigners must abide by this agreement, we are authorizing the State laws to make that enforcement. That is plain understandable layman's language. There are no technicalities involved in it. That is exactly what this language does. I have retailed enough to understand that.

Now, I have had letters from all of my druggists like you folks have. Why should we impose such a burden on a person, or be the means of imposing such a burden on a person, who does not sign the contract? That is something new. I may have to eat this crow, and take the consequences.

Here is another proposition. I am familiar with the arguments that are made that the private enterprise system eats itself up through competition. I am familiar with the argument that the controllist promotes all the time the philosophy that private enterprise is not capable of managing its affairs in such a way that it can survive, therefore, it is argued by the controllist that the States and the bureaus should take over and control the people and write the rules and regulations so that there will not be any warfare between competitors. In other words, it is argued that the State always knows what is best to be done, that the individual is never capable of taking care of himself, that he permits competitive forces to come about and destroy the operator. I can understand that language, too. Now, if I may speak very bluntly to my friends on the left, may I say that we are about to endorse a proposition, as Republicans we are about to endorse a proposition, which says to our people: You are not capable of surviving in the cockpit of retail merchandise; the States must look after you.

We are coming along here and are about to sanctify the theory that the State knows best. Of course, the Members of the legislative body are elected by the people. I understand that, too. ⊥ But I also understand the strength of great organized minorities, and if we do not understand that we should learn some lessons about it. So that is the proposition we have to deal with here. Take a fellow, for instance, who has a great excess of inventory. He is having to either unload that inventory in order to survive to pay off his creditors, or he can go back and not unload the inventory. What is he going to do in a proposition like this? Will the gentleman answer that?

Mr. HARRIS. The various State laws have provisions that permit just what the gentleman has said; that the man can unload his stock if such a condition exists.

Mr. CRAWFORD. Under what conditions? Will the gentleman tell us some of those conditions?

Mr. HARRIS. If it is necessary for him to unload it because of his financial condition, or if he was going bankrupt, or if he was going out of business, or if he was disposing of a stock that he did not want to handle any more; various conditions that permit it.

Mr. CRAWFORD. Who is going to determine the necessity of unloading the inventory to meet the creditor's demand? Who determines that?

Mr. HARRIS. That is your State jurisdiction. It is determined within your own State.

Mr. CRAWFORD. In other words, the State agency does it; the State machinery?

Mr. HARRIS. The businessman does it within the State. If he is in accord with the provisions of the State law, then it is permitted.

Mr. CRAWFORD. He may not be in accord with the provisions of the State law.

Mr. HARRIS. Then the jurisdiction is within the State.

Mr. CRAWFORD. He may entirely have refused to sign an agreement, and the State law provides that he is covered in the agreement, so he is compelled to go along, and he must liquidate his inventory on the basis of what the State law or the State bureau or the State regulating agency says he must do; is that correct or not?

Mr. HARRIS. No; that is not correct at all, if the gentleman will permit me.

Mr. CRAWFORD. Does the man have the liberty to run his own affairs and liquidate when he gets ready and to discount his bills; to meet his obligations?

Mr. HARRIS. Absolutely, under State provision.

Mr. CRAWFORD. Who makes the State provision?

Mr. HARRIS. The State legislature makes the provision.

Mr. CRAWFORD. And the State legislature creates the State enforcement agency.

Mr. HARRIS. No, except the courts.

Mr. CRAWFORD. You mean he has to go to court and deal with this thing of running his own business affairs?

Mr. HARRIS. Not at all, but if he violates the State law he goes into the State court.

Mr. CRAWFORD. Who says he violates the State law? What enforcement agency says he violates the State law?

Mr. HARRIS. Well, I suppose it would be like any other violation. If some competitor did not like what the man was doing and claimed he was violating the law, he would report it.

Mr. CRAWFORD. Say a man exercises his own individual business judgment, that he gets behind with his accounts payable and he wants to liquidate, and he proceeds, his competitor brings suit against him, and he is thrown into court.

Mr. KLEIN. Mr. Chairman, will the gentleman yield?

Mr. CRAWFORD. I yield to the gentleman from New York.

Mr. KLEIN. Let me explain the procedure as if it happened in the State of New York. Let us take the druggist trade. We are talking about druggists now.

Mr. CRAWFORD. No; I am talking about retailers, generally.

Mr. KLEIN. All right. If a retailer is violating the act which is called the Feld-Crawford Act in the State of New York, a complaint is usually made to the manufacturer or the distributor of that particular article. He then notifies this person who is allegedly underselling the regular price, and he says,"I want to remind you that under the laws of the State of New York you are violating the law in that you are selling this particular product, whatever it may be, at less than the fair-trade price." Now the man usually accedes to that, and either he says he did it unknowingly or for some other reason, and he raises his price. If he does not, the manufacturer then, or his agent, goes into court for an injunction to prevent this man from violating the law in that he is under-selling this particular article, and the court then decides whether he has the stock, and at that time it becomes pertinent whether he is underselling the goods, whatever it may be.

Mr. CRAWFORD. In other words, it comes down to the proposition where the retailer may or may not be thrown into court to answer as to how and why he is running his business according to his own judgment. Now that is exactly the way I see the situation.

Mr. PRIEST. Mr. Chairman, will the gentleman yield?

Mr. CRAWFORD. I yield to the gentleman from Tennessee.

Mr. PRIEST. Is that not true of the violation of any State law? Is it not the same procedure, whether it be the State bankruptcy laws or whatever it may be; the same procedure is followed?

Mr. CRAWFORD. All that I am talking about here is freedom of enterprise, free enterprise. Let the competitive forces operate. Protect the consumer. Take your gains and your losses, enjoy them or regret them, but stay in the cockpit if you can. If you cannot, get out. Play the game according to the rules or else forget free enterprise.

Mr. HARRIS. Does the gentleman believe in what are generally referred to as cutthroat practices, then?

Mr. CRAWFORD. I believe in competition. The only defense you can put up for the free-enterprise system is that it permits competition. If there is no competition you cannot justify free enterprise.

Mr. HARRIS. The gentleman believes in fair competition, I am sure; does he not?

The gentleman from Michigan [Mr. CRAWFORD], who preceded me, indicated he felt this may be an encroachment on free enterprise. I do not so view it. How can free trade and fair trade stifle free enterprise? Our Government was founded upon the theory of free trade, but that also meant equality in trade and when one segment of our economy is able by unfair trade practices to harm another segment of our economy then it is the duty of Government to prevent such an injustice. This bill makes it possible for the several States to do just that.

Last December at the Savery Hotel, in Des Moines, Iowa, there was a splendid meeting held under the auspices of the Iowa Pharmaceutical Society. It was presided over by the secretary, Mr. D. L. Bruner. There were four [sic] principal speakers, one representing the manufacturers, one the wholesalers, one the jobbers, one the retailers, and one the consumers. Each stressed the importance of fair-trade. Each recognized that fair-trade practices are essential not only for the consumer and the retailer but for the jobber, the wholesaler and the manufacturer. Each endorsed the principle of the McGuire bill. I trust it will pass the House by a large majority.

The CHAIRMAN. The time of the gentleman from Michigan has expired.

The Chair understands some agreement was made with the Committee on the Judiciary for an allocation of time. Did either the gentleman from Tennessee or the gentleman from Iowa propound a unanimous-consent request for such a division of the time?

Mr. DOLLIVER. Mr. Chairman, I ask unanimous consent that 45 minutes of the time allotted to this side be allocated to the ranking minority member of the Committee on the Judiciary.

The CHAIRMAN. Is there objection to the request of the gentleman from Iowa?

There was no objection.

Mr. DOLLIVER. Mr. Chairman, I yield such time as he may desire to the gentleman from Iowa [Mr. CUNNINGHAM].

Mr. CUNNINGHAM. Mr. Chairman, this legislation is needed for the fair treatment of the small-business man. I commend and congratulate the Committee on Interstate and Foreign Commerce and, especially my colleague, the gentleman from Iowa [Mr. DOLLIVER], a member of the committee, for its work and statesman-like approach to the problem as evidenced by H. R. 5767. I favor the passage of this measure. It is not an encroachment on free enterprise but rather a recognition of the right of the States to see that fair-trade practices are employed by those who do business within the States, whether engaged in interstate commerce or not. It restores to the several States the rights they enjoyed previous to recent decisions of the United States Supreme Court. It ⊥ will benefit and protect the manufacturer, wholesaler, jobber, retailer, and consumer. Last December a meeting was held at the Savery Hotel in Des Moines, Iowa, under the auspices of the Iowa Pharmaceutical Society. It was presided over by the society's secretary, D. L. Bruner. There were five principal speakers; one represented the manufacturer, one the wholesaler, one the jobber, one the retailer, and one the consumer. Each one favored this piece of legislation as necessary for the future of all five. They recognized that what is harmful to one segment of our economy will eventually harm all and may destroy all. America was founded upon the principle of free and fair trade. The States should have the right to see that it is fair to all and that competitive, unfair practices are not indulged in by any. This bill does just that. I hope the House passes it overwhelmingly.

Mr. PRIEST. Mr. Chairman, I yield 5 minutes to the gentleman from New York [Mr. KLEIN].

Mr. [WILLIAM M.] McCULLOCH [R., Ohio]. Mr Chairman, will the gentleman yield for a question?

Mr. KLEIN. I yield to the gentleman from Ohio.

Mr. McCULLOCH. Did I correctly understand the gentleman from New York to say that there was a violation of law involved if an item of merchandise was sold below the fair-trade price?

Mr. KLEIN. That was an unfortunate use of the term. The State law provides that there can be fair trading of articles, which applies both to nonsigners and to signers of the agreement. When I use the term "violation" I do not necessarily mean a criminal violation. I do not want the gentleman to get that idea. It is a civil action.

Mr. McCULLOCH. Yes; I understood that.

Mr. KLEIN. A man goes into a court because he claims he is being damaged by reason of the fact that he has entered into agreements throughout the country, and particularly in that State, that a particular item should be sold at not less than a specified price. The State law stipulates that such agreement shall affect and be binding on, not only those who sign the agreement, or contract, but those who do not, as well, after the nonsigner has received notice. Mind you, it must be a willful violation in order for the courts to step in and enjoin him, and there also must be notice to the nonsigner that there is such a law in effect, and that he is in violation by reason of the fact he is not living up to those agreements, although he himself has not signed.

Mr. McCULLOCH. Will the gentleman yield further for a brief question? I make the request so that we may not confuse the issue. I think I understand the method of procedure under fair-trade legislation. I do not wish to have any confusion left in the House. There is no violation of any criminal law involved in the breach of a contract by selling an item below the fair-trade price?

Mr. KLEIN. Of course not.

Mr. McCULLOCH. The violation is only a violation of contract, which results in a civil action and not in a criminal action of any kind whatsoever.

Mr. KLEIN. That is correct. I thank the gentleman for clearing up that point.

Mr. [JAMES G.] DONOVAN [D., N.Y.]. Mr. Chairman, will the gentleman yield?

Mr. KLEIN. I yield to the gentleman from New York.

Mr. DONOVAN. Will the gentleman tell the House whether or not any of these so-called fair-trade laws enacted by the 45 States have been tested constitutionally?

Mr. KLEIN. I believe the gentleman from Arkansas [Mr. HARRIS] in tracing the history of this legislation from the date of initial enactment, I believe 1913, up to 1950, made this statement, and if I am incorrect I trust the gentleman from Arkansas will correct me, that the Supreme Court never held that any of these State acts were unconstitutional. Whether they had ever gone up or were upheld, I really cannot say. Can the gentleman clear up that particular point, as to whether the fair-trade laws of the States have been tested in the Supreme Court?

Mr. HARRIS. I think there have been a number of fair-trade laws before the Supreme Court. I do not think any of them have ever been held unconstitutional.

Mr. DONOVAN. I have asked the question as to whether the constitutionality of these acts have [sic] ever been questioned in the Supreme Court.

Mr. KLEIN. The gentleman's answer was that they had been.

Mr. HARRIS. The Supreme Court by inference in the Schwegmann case upheld the constitutionality of the act, but it held that the language of the Tydings Act was not effective as to nonsigners.

Mr. DONOVAN. I am sure the gentleman will not mind if my opinion is just to the contrary, having just recently read the Schwegmann case.

Mr. HARRIS. In the case of *Old Dearborn Company* v. *Seagram* (299 U. S. 183), a case which the Supreme Court decided in 1939, the Supreme Court specifically upheld the constitutionality of the fair-trade law.

Mr. KLEIN. I thank the gentleman.

Mr. OSTERTAG. Mr. Chairman, will the gentleman yield?

Mr. KLEIN. I am happy to yield, to my colleague from New York.

Mr. OSTERTAG. There are many of us who feel—at least I feel it is rather dim in my mind—as to why the Congress of the United States has to enact any law to give the States the right to do something, which you are arguing they have that right in the first instance. I cannot get it through my head, and I would like to have it cleared up.

Mr. KLEIN. I am glad the gentleman brought that up. May I say, of course, that any time we legislate here, we can only legislate with regard to some facility or phase of interstate commerce where we have jurisdiction. Clearly the gentleman is correct, where an article is manufactured in the State and sold in that same State, we of course have no jurisdiction, and we could not go in and tell the State what to do with regard to enforcement of its own laws. Our problem arises in the case of an article manufactured in one State, and then shipped over the State line to another State and sold in that State.

The CHAIRMAN. The time of the gentleman from New York has expired.

Mr. KLEIN. Mr. Chairman, may I have five additional minutes? I hate to impose upon the gentleman, but I have not yet had an opportunity to present my own argument.

Mr. PRIEST. Mr. Chairman, I yield five additional minutes to the gentleman.

Mr. OSTERTAG. Following that point, let me ask the gentleman, assuming that a State enacts a law, a fair-trade law, then the formula or the standard that goes with that law will apply to any article shipped anywhere within the United States?

Mr. KLEIN. Providing the Federal law permits it. That was the purpose of the

Miller-Tydings Act, which was passed here, but unfortunately the Supreme Court held in this case, and it was by a divided opinion, that the Congress had never intended that act to apply to nonsigners of the agreement, and that is why we are here today, to correct that.

Mr. OSTERTAG. This will clear that up so that it will be legal when it is interstate commerce.

Mr. KLEIN. That is the only purpose of this legislation. It is clearly permissive.

Mr. HARRIS. Mr. Chairman, will the gentleman yield?

Mr. KLEIN. I yield.

Mr. HARRIS. To further clear up the question, which the gentleman just brought up, as an example, Texas is not a fair-trade State. An article manufactured in Pennsylvania, or some other fair-trade State, going into the State of Texas, of course, would not come under the fair-trade laws.

Mr. KLEIN. If I may be permitted to try to get at the argument I intended to make in the first place, the gentleman from New York [Mr. CELLER] made a very dramatic appeal here, a very dramatic appearance in which he brought all these different items that he had purchased, and showed the difference in prices here in the District of Columbia where there is no fair-trade act and Virginia and Maryland, where there are fair-trade acts. As happens very often in a dramatic production, in a theatrical production, the facts are not as important as the dramatic effect, and without impugning the motives of my friend, the gentleman from New York [Mr. CELLER] and I admire him very much—I rarely, if at all, oppose him on any question—I must say was not entirely factual. The reason is this. The gentleman for one thing did not say where he purchased these articles in the District of Columbia, at prices so much less than in the fair-trade States. They obviously were purchased at stores which make a practice of resorting to loss-leaders.

There is no question that the store in the District of Columbia which sold him these articles lost money on those articles, or at least, made no profit on them, and it is obvious, of course, that retailers are not in business to lose money. The answer to that I believe is equally obvious. They use this under-priced article to bring people into the store, and, in fact, quite often you cannot even get the product at the low price at which it is advertised, but if you do get it, once you are in that store you usually buy other articles on which the store will make a large profit, thus making up for the lack of profit on the loss-leader articles. So, where a person goes into a store and buys only the article on which they are losing money, they are defeating their own purpose. They do not want customers like that. As to him they have lost money. But that is not usually the case. As a general rule, he buys other articles to which he may be attracted, once he is in the store.

I might point out that a survey was made by the A. C. Nielson [sic] Co., a statistical agency which is well known throughout the Nation, as to whether in fair-trade States on the one hand and non-fair-trade States on the other hand the price to the consumer is less—and that is the thing we all want to do; we want to help the consumer—and these are very interesting figures. In the year 1949 the general price in fair-trade States was lower by one-tenth of 1 percent than it was in non-fair-trade States. In 1951 the saving was even greater. It was 1.75 percent less in the fair-trade States than in the non-fair-trade States. So that the argument that where you fair-trade an article it results in higher prices, is fallacious.

I want to make another point. With regard to those who feel that the small-business man ought to be protected, if the small retailer is selling an article at less than his competitors, it does not necessarily follow that the consumer is benefited. He might save money on that particular article, or even on a list of articles, but that does not mean he is going to continue to do so. In a suit by the Government against the Atlantic & Pacific Tea Co., the A. & P. was found guilty of an antitrust violation and fined $175,000.[3.55] I want to call your attention to what they did. They were accused of cutting prices, and by that method putting a number of small businesses in the community out of business. Small grocery dealers, small meat stores, and such. Any

---

[3.55] United States v. New York Great A & P Tea Co., 67 F. Supp. 626 (E.D. Ill. 1946), *aff'd*, 173 F.2d 79 (7th Cir. 1949).

meat dealer will tell you that often the A. & P. will sell meat at less than what it cost them wholesale to buy it. The court found in this particular case that their motive was not so much to pass on savings to the consumer but to stifle competition, put these small people out of business, and then they could put their prices up again.

So do not think for a moment that by cutting prices you are helping the consumer, because, in the long run, you are not.

Mr. [E. L.] FORRESTER [D., Ga.]. Mr. Chairman, will the gentleman yield?

Mr. KLEIN. I yield to the gentleman from Georgia.

Mr. FORRESTER. I want to compliment the gentleman on his observation concerning the articles bought by the gentleman from New York [Mr. CELLER]. It nowhere appeared that in Virginia or in Maryland he bought those articles at the lowest price he could have got them.

Mr. KLEIN. That is correct.

The CHAIRMAN. The time of the gentleman from New York has expired.

Mr. DOLLIVER. Mr. Chairman, I yield 5 minutes to the gentleman from Indiana [Mr. BEAMER].

Mr. [JOHN V.] BEAMER [R., Ind.]. Mr. Chairman, my approach to a consideration of this bill H. R. 5767, known as the McGuire bill, is not from the legal point of view.

The Interstate and Foreign Commerce Committee conducted studies and held hearings on H. R. 5767. As a member of this subcommittee I sat through all of these hearings and I would like to condense, if I may, my own personal impressions that I secured from the facts and the arguments that were presented to our committee.

I am not a lawyer, but as one who has been in business all of my life I feel that there are certain moral and economic considerations that are important. In the first place, I join with my friend from Florida who so emphatically stated that he was opposed to further extension of Federal control and most especially when there were adequate and fair-trade laws in respective States, particularly in these 45 States.

I do not feel that we establish a Federal policy of fair-trade practices. That is probably the most important consideration in this bill. You can talk about all the prices of products that you can secure from half a dozen different stores, there still will be different prices. But let us get down to the State level.

H. R. 5767, the McGuire bill, very specifically places the authority for the promulgation and execution of these so-called fair-trade laws back to the State level where they belong.

All the proponents of H. R. 5767 propose is to enable the fair-trade laws of these 45 States to function in interstate commerce according to the expressed policies of the respective States, and to accomplish only that, without in any way affecting or interfering with any sales of any products within any State not having a fair-trade act. At the present time, Missouri, Texas, Vermont, and District of Columbia.

During the hearings it was pointed out that there are some 1,770,000 retailers, and thousands of small wholesalers who form the backbone of the merchandising segment of our economic society. It is estimated that some 10,000,000 people—15 percent of our working population—earn their living in retailing and wholesaling. Therefore, I submit that they are the consumers and are entitled to consideration. In the words of some of their spokesmen and as expressed in their letters and statements not only here but to the committee, they merely asked for the same protection and the right that has been given labor in the minimum wage law, that has been given agriculture with a floor for the prices of their products, and that is given to millions of other citizens in social security and other guaranties.

Fair-trade laws have been in existence, as has been pointed out, for more than 20 years; in fact, one set of facts and conditions that impressed the committee and impressed me especially were the undisputed resale prices of large lists of common household products that actually had—and I call this particularly to the attention of the chairman of the Judiciary Committee—actually had a lower average selling price in the 45 fair-trade States than was the case in the other three States and the District of Columbia that do not have fair-trade laws.

Also, it was pointed out in our committee that in spite of rising costs and inflated conditions consumers paid 1 percent less for these products under fair trade, on the average, than they paid in the pre-fair-trade, depression days. Let us take a few examples. In the 15-year period from 1937 to 1952 non-fair-traded goods increased in price as follows:

Food—very few food items are fair-traded. Food has increased in price 127 percent in that 15-year period.

Steel, a non-fair-traded product, increased 72 percent.

Clothing increased 104 percent.

Opposed to that, fair-traded goods increased in the same period of time as follows:

Prescriptions and drugs, only 28 percent.

Toilet goods, 59.4 percent.

Electrical appliances, 43 percent.

Briefly, the proponents of this legislation state that they are asking only for the privilege of standard pricing which helps sell goods and broadens distribution. At the same time, the manufacturers of trade-mark products can secure the protection which the patent laws of the United States intended them to have. These people ask the privilege of continuing their interest in their own products even after they have passed title to a wholesaler, to a dealer, and finally to the consumer.

To repeat, I have attempted to give briefly only the arguments that were presented to our subcommittee. Of the hundreds of letters pertaining to fair trades that have come to my office during the recent weeks only a very small number opposed H. R. 5767 and all of the other statements coming from a large variety of interests supported it.

I hope that this Congress can and will resolve these proposals into legislation that will be fair and equitable for all—to the small retailer as well as to the consumers.

Mr. PRIEST. Mr. Chairman, I yield 1 minute to the gentleman from New York [Mr. CELLER].

Mr. CELLER. Mr. Chairman, unfortunately I was absent when the distinguished gentleman from New York [Mr. KLEIN] made some statements concerning my remarks and indicated that I did not state where I had purchased the articles which were exhibited by me this afternoon.

Those articles were purchased in the Peoples Drug Store, store No. 102, in the District of Columbia. I purchased the same articles for higher prices (because they were fair trade) in a store of the same drug chain in Virginia, the store located in Kann's shopping center. In Maryland I purchased the articles in the Cottage City Pharmacy.

Undoubtedly, in the District of Columbia, some of the articles could have been bought cheaper. Here the articles are subject to competition. My survey would be of no value unless I bought the articles from the same type of stores; therefore I bought them from the Peoples Drug Store in Washington where there was no fair trade and from the Peoples Drug Store in Virginia where there was fair trade and from a third store in a State where there was fair trade. These exhibits conclusively show that "fair trade" enhances prices.

Not one of these items were loss leaders. They are all regular day-to-day prices.

Mr. PRIEST. Mr. Chairman, I yield 10 minutes to the gentleman from California [Mr. HOLIFIELD].

MC GUIRE FAIR-TRADE BILL WILL PRESERVE FREE ENTERPRISE BY INSURING SMALL-BUSINESS COMPETITION

Mr. HOLIFIELD. Mr. Chairman, I rise to speak in favor of the McGuire fair-trade bill, H. R. 5767, because I believe that it will help to maintain our free enterprise system. I speak not as a theoretician but from a background of over 30 years' experience as a small-business man, a merchandiser serving the people of my community.

During that 30 years I have seen a drastic change occur in the business methods in my home town and the other home towns throughout America. Thirty years ago every business in my home town was owned by an independent merchant. Gradually that scene has changed. Many of the drug stores, grocery stores, filling stations, banks, et cetera are now operated by managers and owned by absentee capital. Maybe this is progress; maybe it is justified on an economic basis; but there is serious doubt in my mind as to the social impact on the community in the elimination of locally owned and operated small business. There is a serious doubt in my mind if free enterprise can continue to thrive by continuing to organize each classification of retail merchandising into larger, more closely knit and powerful units.

There are still a few individually owned small businesses and it is important to realize their method of operation and their main reasons for survival in the competitive struggle against their powerful competitors. Many of them survive because of neighborhood convenience, longer hours of service and the personality of their owners. In my opinion, however, the most important factor is that they can offer to their neighbors standard quality merchandise under well advertised and widely known brand names at fair-trade prices.

The small merchant's greatest protection is in being able to fill the demand of his customers for highly advertised brands of food, clothing, medicine and other types of merchandise—at the same fair price as his large competitor.

The consumer has confidence in brand merchandise; he has the desire to purchase brand merchandise, and if he can have confidence in a uniform price, he will trade in many instances with the small-business man.

If the customer wants variety, he has the choice between many brands representing a great variety of prices and qualities in each classification. If he desires to buy unbranded merchandise, he also has this field to explore, but he does so on his own judgment and at his own risk. He may also experiment with new brands belonging to new companies competing for the consumer's dollars, in addition to the competition already existing between well-established brands.

Let no one tell you that competition is eliminated by fair-trade practices. Competition today is very, very keen among the big and little businessman, and the way to keep that competition keen is to insure the quantity of competitors. Always keep the small-business opportunity alive. This will be done as long as fair competition is insured. It will cease when the unfair competition of the chiseler is allowed to thrive.

Small business will live as long as the large business establishment is prevented from bringing the deadly price chiseling deceptive, cut-rate "loss-leader" type of competition against it.

Nationally branded merchandise in each classification must compete with other nationally branded merchandise. I can assure you from personal experience that the consumer who buys an Arrow, Manhattan, or Van Heusen shirt pays the same percentage of retailer's profit in either case. The competition is in the quality of styling of the product in each particular price range. The same is true in the hat line or shoe line or automobile field. The prices of competing brands may be very close within the quality range, but the competitive factor remains.

The theoretician may ask, Why should not we have unrestrained price competition within a specific brand or quality range? In other words, why should not an Arrow-brand shirt with a fair-trade price of $3.50 be offered to the public at any price the retailer decides to put on it? There are many reasons. First, that price is not an accident. It is the culmination of a series of economic facts. I will mention a few:

Cost of the cotton, which had what amounts to a fair-trade price because it was supported by a parity formula; price of transportation to the mill because it was another controlled-price factor, including labor and rates; then the cloth-weaving process with its controlled labor and material costs; then the manufacturer who deals with almost rigid cost factors of labor, utilities, patented machinery, cost of distribution, and so forth. Finally, the shirt gets to the retailer, who also deals with almost rigid retailing costs—organized labor; regulated utility and transportation costs; recognized rental percentages of his gross sales; controlled advertising costs. In all of these steps from raw product to retailer there is competition, which regulates the profit yield at every point. It actually cost the average United States department store or haberdasher from 32 to 35 cents of each dollar to run its business in 1950. The average gross profit on nationally branded lines of men's wear is 40 cents of each dollar.

Deducting the cost of operation leaves a theoretical net profit before income taxes of 5 to 8 cents. The whole structure of American manufacturing and merchandising rests on that net profit of 5 to 8 cents on each dollar. That is why ruinous price cutting of retail prices on branded merchandise is deadly to the small-business man who has found it necessary to sell the merchandise that the people ask for when they buy in his store. A 10-percent cut on branded merchandise by a powerful competitor with cash-operating reserves or with mixed lines of nonbranded merchandise with long profit margins can put him out of business, for when the legitimate retailer's profit margin is squeezed he must stop handling the brand. This in turn forces the manufacturer to either cut the quality of the product or go out of business.

In conclusion, 45 States out of the 48 have seen fit to enact State fair-trade laws in the public interest.

Customers are protected against exorbitant prices by the competition between similar brand-named articles. Customers are protected by guaranteed standards of uniform quality which must exist behind a popularly accepted brand name.

The retailer is protected against selfish, chiseling competitors who practice deceptive price cutting on popular-brand articles which they use as bait to lure the customer into their stores to buy their inferior articles which carry long profit margins.

The principles I have traced are valid in practically all fields of merchandising, although the gross profit margins vary from smaller percentages on some staples to higher percentages in the luxury field, but each field has its own problems of merchandising and costs.

An important point to remember is that fair-trade prices apply only to products which are identified by advertised brand names, products which are competing in the full sense of the word with other products branded and unbranded in the same classification. Fair-trade regulation seeks only relief from vicious chiseling practices within each brand classification, practices which tend in the last analysis to destroy confidence in first, the price; second, the quality of the product; and last, but not least, the wages of labor from the raw product producer through every step to the consumers' purchase of the finished product. By this chain of protection of the legitimate wages and profits, the whole system of legitimate, high-standard, American free and fair enterprise is maintained.

I am confident that my colleagues in the House will vote favorably on the McGuire bill, H. R. 5767.

Mr. Chairman, the one thing in this fair-trade bill that bothered me was the nonsigner clause. I have gone into that matter very thoroughly, and have done a great deal of research on it, and I am including in my remarks an analysis of the nonsigner clause, which I believe is the thing that is most in the minds of the Members of the House. Because I do not have the time to read that now, I hope the Members will avail themselves of the opportunity to read it in the RECORD tomorrow.

⊥ Again I say I am giving you this from the standpoint of 30 years of merchandising in a small-business man field. I believe it is more valid than some of the theoretical arguments of men who have never stood behind a counter, who have never had to meet competition from big business, and who never have had to pay high wages to their employees and meet rigid cost conditions. The small-business men of whom I speak cannot possibly meet those conditions unless they get a fair and reasonable margin of profit on national-branded type of merchandise.

Mr. PRIEST. Mr. Chairman, will the gentleman yield?

Mr. HOLIFIELD. I yield to the gentleman from Tennessee.

Mr. PRIEST. The gentleman has stated that he will place in the RECORD his analysis of the nonsigner clause. May I ask the gentleman, who has had 30 years of business experience, if, on the basis of that experience and his knowledge of the conditions, he believes the nonsigner clause should remain applicable in the fair-trade laws?

Mr. HOLIFIELD. Unless the nonsigner clause is made applicable, there is no such thing as fair trade. The basic reason for that is that the manufacturer cannot control the merchandise once it leaves the point of the primary purchaser. When it goes to the secondary or third purchaser or retailer or distributor of that merchandise, and the manufacturer tries to control it, he becomes guilty of conspiracy under the antitrust law. For that reason, the nonsigner clause must be put in the bill. It is a recognition of the principle of fairness between the manufacturer of an article and the retailer. Other handlers, whether on the wholesaler, jobber, or retail level of business, must respect that basic principle of fairness.

Mr. Chairman, the statement to which I have referred about the nonsigner clause is as follows:

That we are here today debating the merits of the McGuire bill, H. R. 5767, is dramatic evidence of the crucial importance of the so-called nonsigner clause to the fair-trade structures of 45 States.

What does the so-called nonsigner clause, uniformly contained in all the 45 State fair-trade laws provide? Briefly it states:

> Willfully and knowingly advertising, offering for sale or selling any commodity at less than the price stipulated in any contract entered into pursuant to the provision of section 1 of this act, whether the person so advertising, offering for sale, or selling is or is not a party to such contract, is unfair competition and is actionable at the suit of any person damaged thereby.

The nonsigner clause came into being in 1933. It will be recalled that California enacted the first State fair-trade law in 1931. It contained no nonsigner clause. The act proved completely ineffective in restraining the unfair competition at which it was aimed because the very persons most likely to engage in predatory pricing practices were, and are, precisely the persons who would not sign a fair-trade contract. After 2 years of frustrating experience, the California Legislature amended its fair-trade act by adding the famous nonsigner section which I have quoted.

You will note that the nonsigner clause establishes and enunciates a policy of unfair competition, insofar as the State is concerned. That policy is made applicable to all, rather than to a selected group. It applies to signers of fair-trade contracts, obviously, because these persons have full knowledge of the existence of such contract and of its terms as regards minimum resale price. It applies to nonsigners only when they have similar knowledge because the clause specifically states "willfully and knowingly advertising, offering for sale or selling" and so forth. In short we are dealing here with a system of fair competition on a State-wide basis as elaborated in a State fair-trade act. The fair-trade contract is not the system; rather, it is the means by which the system is put into operation. In this respect, the fair-trade contract is not unlike the electric light switch which is, obviously, not the electrical system but merely the means for starting the system.

Legally this provision has been adjudicated and held valid in 16 State supreme courts, as well as the Supreme Court of the United States. The gist of all these decisions is to the effect that the so-called nonsigner clause is an appropriate and constitutional means to that perfectly legitimate end, namely, a means of avoiding the spread of unfair methods of competition in the market place. Even in the Schwegmann decision in 1951, the United States Supreme Court did not invalidate the so-called nonsigner clause in the State fair-trade laws. It mainly held that the Miller-Tydings Act did not by express language embrace the nonsigner clause as an exemption from the Sherman Act, when transactions with respect thereto involve interstate commerce.

The nonsigner clause is the heart of the State fair-trade laws. Without it, fair trade is a weak instrument—as the experience since last May amply shows. Without it, fair trade cannot operate effectively within the 45 States which have enacted fair-trade laws.

It has been asked whether fair trade can operate in interstate commerce without the nonsigner clause. The fact that we are here today shows that, with a few exceptions, it cannot. In certain cases it can and it does. The manufacturer who sells direct to retailers can refuse to sell to any retailer who refuses to sign a fair-trade contract of the manufacturer. In such cases, retailers known for predatory pricing practices have signed fair-trade contracts since the Schwegmann decision in order to be able to stock and sell the manufacturer's trade-marked merchandise.

Most manufacturers, however, sell through wholesalers as well as direct. These manufacturers may refuse to sell retailers who refuse to sign fair-trade contracts but they may not, under penalty of law, require wholesalers to refuse to sell retailers who will not sign fair-trade contracts. Such requirement on the part of manufacturers would be regarded as being in violation of the Federal antitrust laws because it involves conspiracy. Accordingly, any retailer who refuses to sign a fair-trade contract can obtain the merchandise of any manufacturer who distributes through wholesalers; and he can sell such merchandise as much below the minimum fair-trade price as he chooses, provided only that interstate commerce is involved.

Conceivably, one method by which manufacturers could continue to sell through wholesalers would be to sell on a consignment basis. Thus the wholesaler would become the manufacturer's agent and would legally be in a position to respond to the manufacturer's requirement that sales be made only to those retailers who would sign a fair-trade contract. Another suggested method would be for the manufacturer to domicile in every fair-trade State and thereafter contend in court that all sales made by him within that State were intrastate sales. But for the vast majority of manufacturers these suggestions are impractical and uneconomic and represent no realistic alternatives at all.

The testimony before the Interstate and Foreign Commerce Committee discloses that manufacturers are seeking to find a way out of this situation. They are still trying to protect the good name of their products against the ravaging damages of unfair competition. The case of Schick razors was cited in the testimony as an illustration of how the predatory pricing retailer could be brought to respect fair-trade prices. It is a case of tragic irony for small business. Schick razors, priced at $27.50, were sold in the New York area for as little as $6.99. Small retailers could no longer afford to take the losses which such sales prices involved; they put Schick razors under the counter. Schick was hurt. It did something about it. Schick decided to sell direct to retailers in the New York area. It notified wholesalers that it would no longer distribute through them in that area. And Schick decided that it would sell only to those retailers who would sign a fair-trade contract. Unfortunately for small business, Schick had neither the sales organization nor the distribution facilities to cover all its distributors in the New York area; so it concentrated only on the larger distributors, including the very distributors, the big, predatory-pricing retailers who had put Schick in a mess in the first place. So you see, these big retailers got more and more volume which it sold at fair-trade prices, while the poor, little retailers—the storekeepers who had respected Schick's fair-trade prices—got frozen out entirely. No fault of Schick's, mind you. They could not do anything else in the circumstances.

What is true of Schick is true of other manufacturers. Those who have sold through wholesalers—and they are in the great majority—have done so because it was more economical for them, their retailers and the ultimate consumers to operate in this manner. Wholesaling obviously serves a most useful and important function in the logistics of the American economy, else it could not have grown to its present stature. To eliminate it entirely for whatever reason would be a national economic calamity. To eliminate it piece by piece so that manufacturers can be in a position to refuse to sell retailers whose pricing practices would damage the good will of their products, is likewise folly and calamity.

No, the nonsigner clause does not dragoon the unwilling into a fair-trade system. No fair-trade law requires a retailer to stock anybody's merchandise, nor does any fair-trade law require a consumer to buy anybody's merchandise. But the nonsigner clause does make every retailer who stocks fair-traded merchandise responsive and responsible to the State's policy of unfair competition. And it avoids the necessity of doing a merchandising ring-around-the-rosie, with the disastrous consequences that must ensue.

The McGuire bill, H. R. 5767, enables the State fair-trade acts to become effective again in respect of their nonsigner clause. For the McGuire bill explicity validates the nonsigner clause in interstate commerce through the following provision:

(3) Nothing contained in this act (the Federal Trade Commission Act) or in any of the antitrust acts shall render unlawful the exercise or the enforcement of any right or action created by any statute, law, or public policy now or hereafter in effect in any State, Territory or the District of Columbia, which in substance provides that willfully and knowingly advertising, offering for sale, or selling any commodity at less than the price or prices prescribed in such contracts or agreements, whether the person so advertising, offering for sale, or selling is or is not a party to such contract or agreement, is unfair competition and is actionable at the suit of any person damaged thereby.

Please note that this provision does not in any way establish a Federal fair-trade policy. It only enables the State acts to function by validating the nonsigner clause in respect of interstate commerce.

It is contended by some that the concept of the nonsigner clause is not needed by those producers who really desire to maintain resale prices for their products, that all they need to do is to adopt the permitted plan of refusing to sell to those who disregard an established resale price-maintenance policy. I am advised, however, that legally as well as practically such a plan is ineffective, that while in accord with the Supreme Court decision in the Colgate Co. Case,[3.56] one may refuse to sell his products to anyone for any reason or no reason at all. However, to make effective such refusal to sell, the Supreme Court in a later case, the Beech-Nut Co. case,[3.57] held that while one may adopt a refusal-to-sell policy he cannot pursue such policy after the goods have been sold without running afoul of the Sherman antitrust law.

The fallacious contention that the refusal-to-sell plan, may adequately take the place of the nonsigner clause, uniformly provided in all the 45 State fair-trade laws, in order to enable one to maintain his resale price-maintenance policy is vividly demonstrated by the recent Department of Justice suit against the Sunbeam Corp.[3.58] In that case the Department of Justice charges the Sunbeam Corp. with violation of the antitrust laws because of the refusal to sell to those who were not willing to sign resale-price agreements in the States permitted by law, and for pursuing a policy of policing the shipment of their merchandise to distributors who have not signed such contracts.

While the complaint by the Department of Justice, a copy of which I have before me, consists of some nine differently stated charges, the gist of the charges nevertheless is that Sunbeam Corp. illegally pursued a policy of enforcing its resale-price maintenance for refusing to sell, and asked those that it did sell, to refrain from selling to those distributors who have not signed a legal resale price-maintenance contract as permitted by the State fair-trade laws.

When I view the problem in the light of actual experience in the market place, I cannot, as I once could, subscribe to the contention that the refusal-to-sell plan, can take the place of the seemingly harsh concept of the nonsigner provision contained in all of the State fair-trade laws. In my own mind I can now justify the assertion made by the proponents of fair trade that whenever the nonsigner provision was challenged in the State supreme courts, as well as in the Supreme Court of the United States, in each instance the clause was held constitutional and an appropriate means to accomplish the end; namely, to curb unfair and deceptive methods of competition in the sale of nationally advertised, trade-marked products.

Accordingly, I urge favorable consideration of H. R. 5767, the McGuire bill, which does no more than enable the States to effectively carry out their adopted policy in an effort to restrain unfair methods of competition in the market place.

Mr. DOLLIVER. Mr. Chairman, I yield 5 minutes to the gentleman from Pennsylvania [Mr. DENNY].

THE SUPPORT OF SMALL BUSINESS FOR THE M'GUIRE BILL

Mr. [HARMAR D.] DENNY [JR.] [R., Pa.]. Mr. Chairman, the support which the McGuire bill has from small business is known to every Member of Congress because of the mail which each of us has had from our constituents, especially from large numbers of independent retailers, and I have hundreds of them in my district. Yet an advertisement in this morning's Washington Post seeks to have you believe that only the retail chains and big manufacturers and wholesalers are in favor of the McGuire bill. The advertisement lists contributions from these businesses and businessmen as evidence in support of the argument. Let me show you how a little information can be twisted and distorted to lead to a wholly unwarranted conclusion, this question having been raised here today.

The contributions referred to in the advertisement were made to the Bureau of Education on Fair Trade, a nonprofit organization which collects and disseminates information on fair trade. The Bureau is supported entirely by contributions from the drug industry—although many other industries, I am told, were willing to add their contributions as well. The Bureau has an annual budget of $120,000. Of this sum, $40,000 is contributed by retailers, with like amounts coming from wholesalers and

---

[3.56] United States v. Colgate & Co., 250 U.S. 300, 39 S. Ct. 465, 63 L. Ed. 992 (1919).

[3.57] FTC v. Beech-Nut Packing Co., 257 U.S. 441, 42 S. Ct. 150, 66 L. Ed. 307 (1922).

[3.58] *See* note 3.35 *supra*.

manufacturers. Of the $40,000 contributed by retailers, $30,000 per year comes from independent retailers, and $10,000 from retail chains. The independent retailers choose to contribute as individuals, and more than 8,000 independent retail druggists contribute $5 to $25 per year. The chains chose to contribute as a group so that their contribution of $10,000 is made from the treasury of the National Association of Chain Drug Stores. As to manufacturers and wholesalers, their contributions are made to reflect their proportion of sales volume in their respective fields. It is just as simple as that. Virtually all of the wholesalers in the drug industry and most of the fair-trading manufacturers have contributed to the Bureau's support, I am told. Incidentally, all contributions have been purely voluntary.

The distortion respecting small business' interest in fair trade is no greater or less than the distortion concerning other aspects of fair trade which the author of the advertisement—a multi-million-dollar retail operator in Florida—indulges in.

This gentleman tries to tell us that fair trade is costing the American people $2,000,000,000 a year. He has not a single fact on which to base the statement. He dare not place his supposed evidence on this subject before any group of marketing experts because they would laugh him right out of court.

The gentleman tries to tell you that he could sell such and such a product at such and such a price which is lower than the fair-trade price. Sure he can, now. He can sell it for less, but the cost to the American people in the loss of its small business through such unfair competition would be very great. This is the same gentleman who sold $1 bills for 95 cents. What miracles of efficiency did he achieve in being able to sell good American dollar bills for less than $1? None, of course. He used the dollar bill as customer bait to sell the customers other merchandise with hidden high profits. It is an old, old game. Incidentally, this gentleman, in two advertisements now, has studiously refrained from telling the people what his highest profit margins are, as well as his lowest; nor has he cared to take the people into his confidence as to his over-all gross profit margin; not he. He wants you to do his bidding so he can go on fooling the public, eliminating competing retailers by unfair competition, and debasing the good names of honored products.

Forty-five States, including that in which the gentleman does business, have enacted fair-trade laws to protect all the people—not just the multi-million-dollar retailer. I hope the Congress will enable the States to realize the full effectiveness of their fair-trade laws and equitable policy.

I earnestly urge the merits of the McGuire bill.

Mr. GRAHAM. Mr. Chairman, I yield 13 minutes to the gentleman from Kansas [Mr. COLE].

Mr. [ALBERT M.] COLE [R., Kan.]. Mr. Chairman, following the startling Schwegmann decision of last year, a number of bills have been introduced to repair the damage done to fair trade by that decision. Considerable discussion has ensued as to the adequacy of one of those bills, the McGuire bill, to restrain mail-order and other long-distance types of retailers from selling across State lines into fair-trade States at prices lower than provided in contracts in effect in such States under their fair-trade laws.

To restore fair trade to its former potency for public service remedial legislation is needed not only to cure the much-publicized Schwegmann decision but also the equally dangerous Wentling decision.

In the Schwegmann case the United States Supreme Court ruled that fair-trade contracts could not be enforced in interstate commerce against noncontracting resellers. Mere statutory construction was at issue. There was no question of constitutionality of the Miller-Tydings Act, the same Court having held years ago that State fair trade acts, including the nonsigner clause, were valid.

In the Wentling decision the United States Circuit Court of Appeals for the Third Circuit held that the application of a State fair-trade act was limited to transactions within the enacting State.

Therefore, if legislation is enacted here to correct only the Schwegmann decision, this anomaly will exist. A noncontracting reseller in a fair-trade State selling a product involved in interstate commerce to consumers within his own State will be bound to adhere to the fair-trade minimum price. However, if that same, or any other noncontracting reseller makes a sale across State lines to a consumer in a fair-trade State, he is not bound to adhere to the fair-trade minimum price effective in either State unless legislation enacted here also cures the Wentling decision. Thus the vital need for the amendment here proposed. Without the amendment I shall propose many predict that fair trade would be full of embalming fluid before another session of Congress could arrive with the needed penicillin.

The only provision in the McGuire bill—H. R. 5767—that could provide any restraint on such destructive activities is its subsection (4) which, as it is now up for discussion reads as follows:

(4) Neither the making of contracts or agreements as described in paragraph (2) of this subsection, nor the exercise or enforcement of any right or right of action as described in paragraph (3) of this subsection shall constitute an unlawful burden or restraint upon, or interference with, commerce.

It is understood that eminent counsel, experienced in constitutional and fair-trade problems, have advised major segments of industry interested in fair trade that, in their opinion, the above quoted subsection (4) of the McGuire bill offers very doubtful and remote prospects of restraining such disruptive attacks upon the fair trade economy of the 45 States now having fair-trade laws. It is understood that those same lawyers, at the request of those segments of fair-trading industry, suggested, in two sentences, wording to be added to such subsection (4), without suggesting any other change in the present text of the McGuire bill. That wording sets up a provision which they stated would, in their opinion, provide the desired assurance of restraint now lacking in said section (4) of the McGuire bill. The wording they suggested has come to be known as the Keogh amendment—perhaps from the fact that it follows almost verbatim text carrying the substance of subsection (d) of the original Keogh bill. That text, with minor clarifications, altering in no way its sense, I shall later submit, for the consideration of the House, as an amendment to be added to subsection (4) of the McGuire bill (H. R. 5767), in words as follows:

Whenever by contract or agreement described in subsection (2) a stipulated or minimum resale price may be established for a commodity in any State, Territory, or the District of Columbia, where such a contract or agreement is lawful, it shall be an act of unfair competition, actionable at the suit of any person damaged thereby, to willfully and knowingly, in interstate commerce (1) sell or (2) have transported for sale or resale or (3) deliver pursuant to a sale, or otherwise deliver, such commodity in any such State, Territory, or the District of Columbia, where such a contract or agreement is lawful, at less than the price or prices so established in such contract or agreement. Any person, firm or corporation injured in his or its business or property because of the violation of this subsection (4) shall be entitled to sue for and have injunctive relief against threatened loss or damage by a violation of this subsection (4).

Mr. HARRIS. Mr. Chairman, will the gentleman yield?

Mr. COLE of Kansas. Briefly.

Mr. HARRIS. As I understand, the gentleman is advising the Members of the House that he will propose what is referred to as the Keogh amendment as an amendment to the McGuire amendment.

Mr. COLE of Kansas. That is right.

Mr. HARRIS. Should the gentleman's amendment prevail, would it not establish a Federal fair-trade policy?

Mr. COLE of Kansas. No; I think not; it leaves in the States the same authority they now have. Let me give you an illustration of what I mean. You may recall that a few years ago Kansas was known as a dry State, a State in which they did not permit the sale of intoxicating liquor. That was a State law not approved of by the Federal Government. However, the Federal Government did have a law which prohibited the distribution of intoxicating liquor into the State. Why? Not because it was a Federal law, but because it was a State law. The Federal Government attempted to and did protect the State in the enactment of laws within the powers of the State.

Mr. HARRIS. Is it not true that when the Federal Government provided legislation that would protect the State of Kansas, it at the same time provided that anyone who violated that would be subject to Federal law?

Mr. COLE of Kansas. Oh, yes; that is true.

Mr. HARRIS. And is it not true that it would be taken in Federal court?

Mr. COLE of Kansas. Yes.

Mr. HARRIS. And is it not true that a defendant would have the right of a Federal defense?

Mr. COLE of Kansas. Oh, yes.

Mr. HARRIS. Then would not that by itself be a Federal policy?

Mr. COLE of Kansas. We are balancing words on the point of a needle, may I say to the gentleman. Wait just a minute. The fact that it may or may not be a Federal policy is not important. What I am saying is that it is not an interference in any shape, manner, or form by the Federal Government of States' rights in this amendment. Why? Because this amendment provides for no action on the part of the Federal Government; it merely provides that the Federal Government shall recognize the right of the State to enact such laws and shall help protect that State; it does not give anybody in the Federal Government, anybody in Washington, anybody connected with the Federal Government any right to prosecute, to bring any suit or anything of the sort; it merely protects the State in its right.

Mr. HARRIS. Mr. Chairman, will the gentleman yield?

Mr. COLE of Kansas. I do not have too much time. I wish the gentleman would let me proceed, for I want to discuss the Keogh amendment.

It perhaps should be said at this point, in explanation of the deletion from the original text of the proposed amendment, of the words "advertise for sale, offer for sale, or," has been recommended as a means of making more clear that it never has been the intent to interfere in any way with the incidental distribution across State lines of newspapers—or radio or TV broadcasts—carrying advertisements offering prices on fair-trade products below those effective in a neighboring fair-trade State, as could not be avoided as to such advertisements originating within non-fair-trade States.

Reactions of the press to that deletion from this proposed amendment have been highly favorable.

Of several prevailing misunderstandings with relation to the true significance of the amendment here proposed is the erroneous notion, which at times has seemed to be self-propelled, that the proposed amendment would impinge upon States' rights by setting up a Federal fair-trade law which would take away from the States their sovereign right to determine for themselves what constitutes unfair competition within their borders. Nothing could be further from the truth. In fact, the intent and effect of the amendment is exactly contrary to that misunderstanding. The fact that the amendment has no effect as a Federal fair-trade act becomes apparent when you consider that the amendment would be a dead law if all States repealed their fair-trade acts.

With the Keogh amendment the McGuire bill will remain purely an enabling act and nothing else. By it the Federal Government merely enables a fair-trade State to choose for itself the terms and conditions upon which trade-marked products may be fair-traded within its borders. Without the Keogh amendment the fair-trade economy of each of the fair-trade States would be, most assuredly, completely disabled, with the resultant entrapment of innocent consumers and demoralization of practically every distributive structure now serving individual communities from the main streets of America.

What this can mean to your constituents may be made abundantly apparent in a telegram to various Members of the House sent May 5 from the Kansas Pharmaceutical Association. That telegram reads as follows:

In the light of the recent New Jersey and California court decisions sustaining the Wentling case damage to fair trade, we beg of you to strengthen the McGuire bill with the Keogh amendment or a similarly strong-language amendment in order to protect States like Kansas that are now unquestionably without protection from the mail-order business onslaught from over the borderline from non-fair-trade States. If this is not done, we will be forced to request repeal of our fair-trade act in order to give our retailers a fighting chance for survival in the old dog-eat-dog non-fair-trade market.

Kansas Pharmaceutical Association.
Clara Miller, Secretary.

I have chosen to offer the amendment here discussed, in part because perhaps no State of the Nation is more dangerously exposed to persistent uneconomic price raids across its borders than is my own State of Kansas. Kansas joins Missouri, which has no fair-trade act. Under the present status of the law, all States are exposed to all sorts of mail order rackets, from the fly-by-night cut price operator perhaps palming off obsolete or damaged merchandise, to the strongly financed cut-rate store striving constantly to eliminate its smaller competitors. Those pirates will continue to keep Kansas, and your State, under increasing bombardment from out-of-State predatory price cutters who pay no taxes within the State and contribute nothing to the civic growth and health of our communities. The McGuire bill needs the Keogh amendment to restrain such pirates.

Far from inviting interference by the Federal Government in the internal affairs of any State having a fair-trade act or having no fair-trade act, the suggested amendment says clearly to residents of each State that they must not outrage the fair-trade structure under which any other State has chosen, by its own legislation, to live.

Therefore, representations that the Keogh amendment puts the Federal Government into the fair-trade business are wholly without foundation. Federal courts have always been open in fair-trade controversies where there has been a diversity of citizenship of the parties. In the Keogh amendment the Federal Government does only what it has done often before—such as in forbidding the shipment of prison-made goods from one State into another [(]*Kentucky Whip and Collar Co.* v. *Illinois Central Railroad Co.* (299 U.S. 334 (1936)).[3.59] The proposed amendment simply makes it a matter of unfair competition for residents of one State to raid the economy of another State, as established under that other State's own laws. The Keogh amendment has no effect whatsoever upon sales—either intrastate or interstate—made in or into any State, or the District of Columbia, having no fair-trade act. Any vendor—either inside or outside a non-fair-trade area—could sell in or into that area, under the Keogh amendment, at any price desired.

Thus the Keogh amendment simply, and only, achieves, clearly and directly, what no doubt sincere drug-trade sponsors of the original McGuire bill have insisted its present subsection (4), with its vague and doubtful text, would accomplish. So what could be the value of any opposition to the Keogh amendment?

That the text of the present subsection (4) of the McGuire bill is vague and doubtful, the counsel for the Interstate and Foreign Commerce Committee of the House makes clear on page 4 of its official analysis of fair-trade bills as then pending. Counsel disposes of the entire question in the following words:

> Question: "Does this provision (subsec. 4) in the McGuire bill assure that State fair-trade laws will apply to all interstate retail transactions?"
> Answer: "No; it does not. Congress cannot amend State laws."

It is indeed unfortunate that some Members of this House have accepted, as indicated by their recent comment, the fallacious representation that the suggested amendment impinges upon States' rights and for that reason its adoption would impel all Members of this House who believe in States' rights to vote against the McGuire bill if it carries the amendment. It is hard to understand how the Federal Government could offer to the various States any more positive and definite protection of States' rights than it would through your enactment of the proposed amendment. It is true that this amendment is a declaration of a Federal policy making it unfair competition to invade any fair-trade State from outside its borders with sales and deliveries of trademarked products at prices less than those established by fair-trade contracts within the State. It should be clear that this is an act in support of States' rights, not otherwise, as claimed. Under the proposed amendment such competition is declared unfair by the Federal Government, and could be enjoined by any injured party, in any appropriate State or Federal court.

It has been chanted erroneously that, to serve the interests of retail druggists, who we all agree provide a most vital service to our people, the McGuire bill must be

---

[3.59] 299 U.S. 334, 57 S. Ct. 277, 81 L. Ed. 270 (1937).

passed without amendment and without substitution. Admittedly drugs ordinarily do not lend themselves well to interstate sale at cut prices. However, while most drugstores do sell drugs, most druggists rely, for sales necessary to keep them in business, upon sales of a wide range of nondrug products, from fountain pens to household appliances. Thus any druggist who pauses to study this problem from the standpoint of his own self-interest, it seems, would welcome your support of the Keogh amendment, or, the Keogh amendment failing, might soon be looking, perhaps too late, for someone upon whom to fix the blame for his miseries.

In each of your districts unless it is a rare exception, there are more than 10 retailers of diversified fair-trade products to every 1 drug store. For example, gas stations, jewelry, tobacco, hardware, book, furniture, clothing, sporting goods, camera and photofinishing, electric appliance, and many other types of nondrug stores rely greatly upon their sales of fair-traded products. These 10 times more numerous nondrug retailers know what they want. They want those products, their business, and their customers to have protection that the McGuire bill without the Keogh amendment does not provide.

Subsection (4) of the McGuire bill is regarded by outstanding legal authorities as an invitation to widespread and hopeless litigation which few fair-trading manufacturers could hope to finance. Why not give, in every fair-trading industry, the hundreds of thousands of little fellows, the very fountainheads of our economy, a chance to keep on building strength into our thousands of marketing areas?

It is felt that they are entitled to the greater certainty of protection from the McGuire bill with the Keogh amendment. So are the consumers of this Nation.

What rivalries could possibly transcend in importance the need for rendering to our constituents an objective service in this important legislation? . . .

⊥ Mr. PRIEST. Mr. Chairman, I yield such time as he may desire to the gentleman from South Carolina [Mr. BRYSON].

Mr. [JOSEPH R.] BRYSON [D., S.C.]. Mr. Chairman, when the House Committee on Interstate and Foreign Commerce held hearings on the pending bill, H. R. 5767, I was privileged to testify before the subcommittee, presided over by our colleague, the gentleman from Tennessee, Congressman PRIEST. I stated then, and here reiterate, that in my opinion the provisions of the McGuire bill meant the fair-trade problem, which arose by reason of the decisions of the United States Supreme Court.

In recent weeks it has been my privilege to confer with the druggists of my congressional district, all of whom favor the passage of the pending bill. As you gentlemen know, this is a very technical subject. Ordinarily, those of us who are not familiar with the difficulties involved, must of necessity depend largely upon those who have dealt in a practical way with the subject.

It is urgent that proper legislation be passed at this session of Congress. I have supported, and expect to support, the McGuire bill as is, without amendments or substitutes.

Mr. PRIEST. Mr. Chairman, I yield 10 minutes to the gentleman from North Carolina [Mr. DURHAM].

Mr. [CARL T.] DURHAM [D., N.C.]. Mr. Chairman, I do not think I ever listened to a finer explanation than the gentleman from Arkansas [Mr. HARRIS] gave us on this measure. In the declaration of the purposes of the bill, it states:

> That it is the purpose of this act to protect the rights of States under the United States Constitution to regulate their internal affairs and more particularly to enact statutes and laws, and to adopt policies, which authorize contracts and agreements prescribing minimum or stipulated prices for the resale of commodities and to extend the minimum or stipulated prices prescribed by such contracts and agreements to persons who are not parties thereto. It is the further purpose of this act to permit such statutes, laws, and public policies to apply to commodities, contracts, agreements, and activities in or affecting interstate or foreign commerce.

Mr. Chairman, I have spent about 30 years of my life in a small retail business. This was during the period of war, inflation, and depression. I believe I am pretty well qualified to pass an opinion on this measure which is before us, not only from the standpoint of the owner of the small retail business but also from the standpoint of the consumer.

I do not think that any American would ever want to see an economy in which small retail business did not play a part, and a vital part at that. An economy in which all the channels of distribution were in the hands of a few giant monopolies would run counter to all our conceptions of a healthy society. One of the best means we have for insuring that small business remains a part of our economy and flourishes in the years ahead is to restore the State fair-trade acts to full effectiveness by enacting the McGuire bill, H. R. 5767, now before us.

Not that small business is asking for any special favors in its behalf. I personally believe that the public desires to preserve it, just as it desires to keep a sound economy for agriculture and all other parts of our economy. But fair trade is not a subsidy, in the form of higher prices or in any other form.

Fair trade is merely competitive decency in the market place that enables small business, if it is efficient and capable enough to compete on equal terms with the biggest and most powerful retailing giants in the country. Fair trade curbs predatory commercial behavior and price wars, a pernicious type of unfair competition which wreaks great damage on small business. Competition by means of loss leaders is based on the ganging up of dollar power, on the huge resources needed to sell goods at a loss and still stay in business. Its final outcome is the destruction of the small by the big. Only the mastodons of the market place have the resources for such jungle warfare.

Many small retailers still remember, out of their own grim experience, how in the pre-fair-trade, depression days, bitter price wars forced thousands of small stores to close their doors. Since the weakening of fair trade by the Schwegmann decision almost a year ago, we have learned again just how devastating price wars can be. In the New York price wars of last spring, it is reported that 10 weeks of price-footballing Sunbeam Mixmasters by the big department stores caused 5,000 small retailers to lose their Mixmaster business permanently. The United States Senate's Select Committee on Small Business, in its annual report for 1951, estimate that if the price war had lasted 6 months, 20,000 stores would have gone out of business.

Had the price wars continued—

The report said—

they might have done incalculable harm to countless small businesses. * * * The Nation's economic well-being depends to a large extent on the vitality of America's small business. Threats of price wars must be eliminated if that vitality is to endure.

Unfortunately, these threats are very much with us. A recent Associated Press report tells us that price wars are going on right now around the country. They are undercover, unofficial price wars which kill small retailers more slowly, but just as surely as the all-out spectacular price battles that get on the front pages. When and if business should recede, this cold war will become a hot war as the giant retailers fight for the consumer's dollar, with no holds barred, regardless of the effects on the economy as a whole.

The age of giant retailers with huge stakes in the market is here, and to stay. A comparative handful of great retailers—some 400 out of the almost 2,000,000 retail establishments in the country—now account for more than half the total national sales volume in many of the lines of merchandise they handle.

These 400 mammoth retailing organizations directly or indirectly control about 100,000 store units. In 1948, they had a sale volume of some $31,000,000,000, or slightly over half of the total $60,000,000,000-volume in the retail fields in which they operate. In other words, the big ones are now big, on a scale never before imagined. They are big enough to create their own private brands, some of which are as national in sales and reputation as national brands. Through heavy expenditures on advertising and merchandising, they compete intensively with well-known national brands. Such growth and competition are most certainly in the consumer's interest. For they intensify, among other things, the price competition between fair-traded national brands and other brands.

Fair trade takes nothing away from these big retailers. It does not hamper their growth nor penalize their bigness. In point of historical fact, the two decades which witnessed the rise of giant retailing has been the very period in which fair trade has existed in this country. Fair trade, in the spirit of the antitrust laws, merely restrains the few from misusing their power to snuff out the many.

Fair trade gives the little fellows a chance to compete successfully too. In the same period that the giants became bigger, the number of retail stores increased by 300,000. Fair trade has thus enabled small, independent stores to exist and to compete side by side with the giants. Fair trade has helped to preserve a mixed economy of small and big business, an economy which is typical of a free-enterprise system.

If our nearly 2,000,000 small retailers disappeared from the scene to be entirely replaced by huge centralized organizations, we Americans would lose a great part of our freedom to shop and buy where we pleased. Our present system of mass production of national brands, which depends on a distribution network of hundreds of thousands of small outlets, would be upset. It is facts such as these that point up urgently the importance of preserving small business. The restoration of State fair-trade laws, as provided in the McGuire bill, is a necessary step in that preservation.

As a druggist, I am for the McGuire bill to restore fair trade because like every druggist in America and like a lot of other independent retailers I know what fair trade has meant to me in the past. And I have a pretty good idea of what the future is going to be like for all independent retailers unless fair trade is restored.

Right now, the small businesses, the stores in all the neighborhoods across the land are scared. Why? Let me tell you why.

Have you ever felt as though something big, something you could not fight with was pushing you under, taking away all you had worked for, all your plans and dreams? That is the way I felt back before fair trade when some of the big operators in town started price wars on drug-store products. I was working 12, 16 hours a day every day. It was no snap, but I liked being my own boss. You can call it independence or stubbornness or maybe even the thing that drove our pioneer forefathers out to settle the wilderness.

But the price wars hit our stock in trade—the national brands of toothpaste, aspirin, shaving cream, razors—the things that a lot of our customers came in to buy. One day we would be able to sell these things at the regular price which gave us back what we had paid out for the merchandise plus enough to help us stay in business. The next day the price jugglers would be selling these brands below cost and plugging their bargains with big promotions. Our customers would come and expect to get the same below-cost prices from us. It put us behind the eight-ball any way you looked at it. If we met these below-cost prices, we were actually giving our merchandise away. You cannot keep a business going very long that way. But if we tried to charge the regular price, our customers would just walk out and most of them did not come back. You cannot keep a business going very long that way, either.

What made us just plain mad was the fact that we were losing our business in a fast shuffle that made the rich price juggler richer, but certainly did not give the public a break. You see, it was a kind of "the hand is quicker than the eye" game. Sure, they slashed prices to the bone on hand-picked popular brands so everybody would come running for the bargains. But what did they do to the prices on all the other stuff they sold at the same time? They marked them up, of course, so they could make money on the whole deal. Otherwise, why would they have a price war? Customers cannot tell when they are getting rooked in a set-up like this. And believe me, they get rooked.

The best example I know of how this price-war thing works is the big Florida operator who sold Uncle Sam's dollar bills for 98 cents. He lost 2 cents on every sale, no matter how many sales he made. Figure it out for yourself. What was he charging for the other stuff he sold to the crowds that poured in? Was he a miracle man, was he deliberately trying to go broke or was he a smart man who made his customers think he was wonderful and then took them for all the traffic would bear?

My State of North Carolina adopted a fair-trade act. It was supposed to help small-business men like ours by stopping price wars. And it did. It made it possible for manufacturers of national brands to say to price jugglers: "You can't kick my trademark around and make it look like junk in the public's eyes by selling it below cost. And you can't put the small retailers who sell most of my products out of business with price wars. If you want to handle my brands, you've got to charge a minimum fair-trade price for them."

Of course, this was not a new idea. The public had been paying a regular standard price on newspapers and magazines and new cars and lots of other things for years and nobody questioned it. The fair-trade laws simply made it possible to do the same thing with national brands and at the same time help to keep small-business men from being stepped on and crushed.

Well, fair trade has worked better than anyone dreamed it would. We managed to keep our business going and we have kept it going under fair trade ever since. We still have to work just as hard. We are still in competition with the big stores and all the other little ones. But we do our best to serve our customers well, to give them their money's worth, to come through in an emergency when someone is sick and needs a prescription at midnight. Thanks to fair trade and hard work, we have been able to pay our taxes and meet our community responsibilities.

But hard work, without fair trade, would not have saved our business, nor the business of all the other independent stores threatened by price wars. That is why they are scared. They have been scared ever since last spring when the Supreme Court knocked the props out from under the fair-trade laws. They have reason to be scared. The price wars broke out again. Some national brands were sold for less than the cost of their containers. And unless this Congress acts to restore the fair-trade laws, a lot of these little fellows may be looking for a job this time next year. This is a grim prospect for men who have devoted years to building up their own small business.

There are a lot of operators who are trying to kill fair trade for good. They say everything would be just wonderful and prices would go way down without it. Funny thing is, prices have not gone down since fair trade was weakened. The figures put out by the Government show the cost of living has kept on going up.

I know from my own experience as a retailer that the prices of fair-traded drug store products have not gone up much at all, compared with other merchandise or the cost of food or clothing or rent. I have seen research figures showing that fair-traded national brands in drug stores sell for less in States with fair-trade laws than these very same brands do in the States without fair trade. I am not surprised. You see, many retailers now tend to sell such brands close to the fair trade minimum price—the bottom price—which is less than the price appearing on the product. They do this to meet the competition. But it is fair competition. It is not forcing you to sell something for less than you paid for it—but it gives the customer a break at the same time.

I just hope that the American People and the Congress will not be fooled by the attacks on fair trade. It reminds me of all the noise and confusion stirred up to keep the antitrust laws from being passed. "The country will go to the dogs and free enterprise will be ruined." the opponents screamed. Well, the country has not gone to the dogs and free enterprise is doing better than ever, judging by this year's figures on production, employment and profits. Free enterprise has done mighty well under fair trade, too, in the past 20 years. Big business has broken all records but small business has grown too. And that is the kind of country we want, with plenty of room and opportunity for the big and the little.

Some people have attacked fair trade because it does not fit in with their theories of economics. But theories can be way off the beam when it comes to how things actually work out for human beings. The Secretary of Commerce understands this and that is why he has come out for fair trade. He recognizes that fair trade is a matter of human beings and not ciphers on an adding machine.

That is the most important thing about any law, is it not—what it does for human beings? Fair trade has helped a lot of druggists, like me and a lot of other small retailers, to keep their businesses going, to raise families, to work and hope for the future, and to be their own bosses. In a way, that is what America adds up to. It would not be very good for the kind of America we want to have, just a few big companies, with millions of people working for them. That is what monopoly means to me and I do not want it. I do not believe the American people want it.

Fair trade helps to keep monopoly away from America's door. That is why I am for the McGuire bill, H. R. 5767, which will restore the fair-trade laws to their full strength.

The average hourly wage in the last quarter of 1951 selected from major industries shows that retail trade is listed third from last at a wage of $1.26. This affects

1,700,000 retailers and a total of 6,000,000 people, which includes their employees.

I would like to mention the wage scale of major industries for the last quarter of 1951:

Mining, bituminous	$2.23
Contract construction	2.21
Petroleum refining	2.09
Tires and inner tubes	2.01
Automobiles	1.96
Railroad equipment	1.89
Blast furnaces, steel works, rolling mills	1.83
Shipbuilding	1.83
Aircraft and parts	1.81
Machinery (except electrical)	1.80
Railway wages	1.77
Electrical machinery	1.65
Wholesale trade	1.60
Stone, clay, glass products	1.58
Local railways and bus lines	1.58
Paper and allied products	1.54
Food and food products	1.49
Lumber and wood products (except furniture)	1.49
Furniture and fixtures	1.43
Textiles	1.33
Road building, common labor	1.33
Retail trade	1.26
Tobacco manufacturers	1.16
Laundries	.92

Mr HARRIS. Mr. Chairman, will the gentleman yield?

Mr. DURHAM. I yield to the gentleman from Arkansas.

Mr. HARRIS. At this point I think it would be well to point out that the gentleman has been very helpful to the Committee on Interstate and Foreign Commerce and the House, as well as the Congress, on matters wherein the druggists are concerned. I recall specifically ⊥ the very fine assistance that he gave to us in getting a bill that he sponsored through this Congress known as the Durham bill. So I join with other Members of the House in expressing appreciation for what he is doing in behalf of the drug industry and in helping us with these problems that the drug people are concerned with.

Mr. DURHAM. I thank the gentleman very much. That is very nice of him.

Mr. DOLLIVER. Mr. Chairman, I yield such time as he may desire to the gentleman from Colorado [Mr. CHENOWETH].

Mr. [J. EDGAR] CHENOWETH [R., Colo.]. Mr. Chairman, I intend to vote for the McGuire bill just as it was reported by our committee, and without amendments. I feel that this legislation is necessary in view of conditions prevailing in our retail markets today.

As has been explained by previous speakers, this bill does not establish a Federal fair-trade policy, and it does not impose upon the Federal Government any responsibility to police or enforce the fair-trade laws of the different States. The sole purpose of this legislation is to enable the States to enforce their own laws as they may see fit.

I would be opposed to any movement to have the Federal Government adopt fair-trade laws, which would supplement or supersede the State fair-trade laws. I feel very strongly that this is a field belonging exclusively to the States.

The fact that 45 States now have fair-trade laws on their statute books would indicate that the overwhelming sentiment in this country is for some type of fair-trade protection. Some of these State laws have been on the books for more than 20 years and seem to have met with general approval. So all that we are doing today by passing this legislation is to approve what has already been established as a merchandising policy of this Nation.

In supporting this bill I certainly have not the slightest intention of injuring the consumer. I want to see the public purchase merchandise at the lowest possible figure. Neither do I want to injure any merchant, large or small, as I realize he must make a profit on his merchandise in order to remain in business.

The argument is being made against this bill that fair-trade laws compel the consumer to pay higher prices for articles in certain fields. I have seen various estimates of the amount this legislation will cost the American consumer. There is a wide difference of opinion on this matter. Proponents of fair trade contend that in the long run fair-trade laws result in lower prices to the consumer. As on every issue, there are two sides to the question. However, I would not vote for this bill if I thought it would penalize the consumer.

Friends of mine who are in the retail merchandise business have indicated to me that they must have the protection of fair-trade laws in order to remain in business. I fully realize that present-day competition is indeed severe, and that much merchandise is handled on a small margin of profit. The little merchant on the corner must compete with the larger stores and I believe both are essential in our economy. It would be most unfortunate and tragic if the man on the corner is forced out of business. It is obvious that this legislation is more in the interest of the small retailer than the large operator. However, I do not believe it will be detrimental to the larger stores.

It is my opinion that the fair-trade laws of the different States have had a stabilizing effect on our economy. If the time should come when these laws should be used to promote monopolies, or to gouge the public, then I will be among the first to advocate their repeal. It is my observation that up to this time these fair-trade laws have worked fairly well. If there have been abuses they have been negligible as compared with the over-all benefits attained.

Mr. DOLLIVER. Mr. Chairman, I have no further requests for time.

Mr. PRIEST. Mr. Chairman, I yield 5 minutes to the gentleman from Minnesota [Mr. McCarthy].

Mr. [EUGENE J.] McCARTHY [D., Minn.]. Mr. Chairman, the report on the bill, as well as the evidence presented in the hearings, and in the debate today indicates quite clearly the divergence of opinion with regard to the specific economic effects of this bill. I suppose we could go on forever hearing contradictory testimony. I do not believe that in the long run the effect upon costs or prices to the consumer will be very substantial. Undoubtedly in a program as comprehensive as this there will be some abuse. I do not believe that the economic argument is really the principal one involved here. We should take particular notice of the statement attributed in the report to the spokesman for the Federal Trade Commission, who said that the Commission was opposed to the bill on economic and legal grounds, and only on those grounds.

He then went on to say that the Commission wanted it recognized that fair-trade legislation might be desirable for these reasons: First, that the maintenance of a strong and healthy small-business community is the best bulwark we have against the growth of collectivism.

Second, that the witnesses' own study showed that in those communities in which there exists a healthy small-business group, the general level of civic welfare, and the interest taken by small-business leaders in health, recreation, and education, tend to be higher than in those communities in which business consists principally of a few large concerns owned and operated by outside managers and distant corporations.

Third, that the small independent drug store and other specialty stores on which the people depend for special services cannot make a living solely on the basis of selling those specialized services, such as prescription filling.

Our considerations here should not be solely economic. In any legislation touching upon the economy of this country we should be concerned about other factors and other values, namely, the social benefits and the cultural benefits or values that may result from it. We in the United States have never accepted that man should be considered purely to be an economic functionary. When we have been properly concerned about increasing our standards of living or increasing the productivity of our economy it has generally been with the purpose in mind of not only improving the material welfare of our citizens but also of establishing a system or of providing means which will foster intellectual and spiritual growth as well. We all know that that kind of growth cannot be accomplished in a vacuum, and it cannot be accomplished in a society in which the only consideration is the materialistic one of increased productivity or greater economic efficiency.

A few years ago a study was made of two areas of California, one in which the large-scale commercial farm predominated, and the other in which the small privately owned family farm was much more common. The results of that study showed that in the area where private ownership and where small farms predominated the civic life, the social life, the educational life, and the religious life was much more vital and much more wholesome. We should give most weight to the social and cultural implications of this legislation. Recognizing the value of competition and of free trade, we should avoid making these the only criteria and only standards by which we judge legislative proposals which come before us in this Congress.

I think it important, too, for us to keep in mind that actually the small-business group is the principal economic group in this country which has not been given some protection. In the case of the farmer we have provided a price-support program and a credit system which has blunted the sharp edge of competition and given some stability and security to the farmer, although he still takes many risks. In the case of labor, too, we have provided a minimum-wage law which, although inadequate in many respects, nevertheless does establish a minimum standard. Certainly this does not eliminate all risks for the working-man. In the case of the small-business man, however, who, like the farmer and laborer, is providing essential economic service to the people of the country, and who is making a great contribution to the social, civic, and the general cultural life of America, little or no protection has been given.

What is proposed in this bill will not give him any kind of complete security. It will not insure his income, but simply eliminate one slight element of risk and uncertainty from his business activities. In my opinion, the House should not hesitate to take the action which is called for in the McGuire bill.

Mr. PRIEST. Mr. Chairman, I yield myself 1 minute.

Mr. Chairman, the debate today on this bill, in my opinion, has developed very completely the issues that are at stake. As I told the Rules Committee when we asked for a rule on the bill, it is a simple matter. There may be some complexities in the economic situation that the bill seeks to solve. I hope to have a few more remarks on some particular points to make under the 5-minute rule.

⊥ Mr. Chairman, I have no further requests for time on this side.

The CHAIRMAN. Under the rule the amendment is considered as an original bill. The Clerk will read the amendment.

The Clerk read as follows:

Be it enacted, etc., That it is the purpose of this act to protect the rights of States under the United States Constitution to regulate their internal affairs and more particularly to enact statutes and laws, and to adopt policies, which authorize contracts and agreements prescribing minimum or stipulated prices for the resale of commodities and to extend the minimum or stipulated prices prescribed by such contracts and agreements to persons who are not parties thereto. It is the further purpose of this act to permit such statutes, laws, and public policies to apply to commodities, contracts, agreements, and activities in or affecting interstate or foreign commerce.

SEC. 2. Section 5 (a) of the Federal Trade Commission Act, as amended, is hereby amended to read as follows:

"SEC. 5. (a) (1) Unfair methods of competition in commerce, and unfair or deceptive acts or practices in commerce, are hereby declared unlawful.

"(2) Nothing contained in this act or in any of the antitrust acts shall render unlawful any contracts or agreements prescribing minimum or stipulated prices, or requiring a vendee to enter into contracts or agreements prescribing minimum or stipulated prices for the resale of a commodity which bears, or the label or container of which bears, the trade-mark, brand, or name of the producer or distributor of such commodity and which is in free and open competition with commodities of the same general class produced or distributed by others, when contracts or agreements of that description are lawful as applied to intrastate transactions under any statute, law, or public policy now or hereafter in effect in any State, Territory, or the District of Columbia in which such resale is to be made, or to which the commodity is to be transported for such resale.

"(3) Nothing contained in this act or in any of the antitrust acts shall render unlawful the exercise or the enforcement of any right or right of action created by any statute, law, or public policy now or hereafter in effect in any State, Territory, or the District of Columbia, which in substance provides that willfully and knowingly advertising, offering for sale, or selling any commodity at less than the price or prices prescribed in such contracts or agreements whether the person so advertising, offering for sale, or selling is or is not a party to such a contract or agreement, is unfair competition and is actionable at the suit of any person damaged thereby.

"(4) Neither the making of contracts or agreements as described in paragraph (2) of this subsection, nor the exercise or enforcement of any right or right of action as described in paragraph (3) of this subsection shall constitute an unlawful burden or restraint upon, or interference with, commerce.

"(5) Nothing contained in paragraph (2) of this subsection shall make lawful contracts or agreements providing for the establishment or maintenance of minimum or stipulated resale prices on any commodity referred to in paragraph (2) of this subsection, between manufacturers, or between producers, or between wholesalers, or between brokers, or between factors, or between retailers, or between persons, firms, or corporations in competition with each other.

"(6) The Commission is hereby empowered and directed to prevent persons, partnerships, or corporations, except banks, common carriers subject to the acts to regulate commerce, air carriers and foreign air carriers subject to the Civil Aeronautics Act of 1938, and persons, partnerships, or corporations subjects to the Packers and Stockyards Act, 1921, except as provided in section 406 (b) of said act, from using unfair methods of competiton in commerce and unfair or deceptive acts or practices in commerce."

Mr. PRIEST (interrupting reading of the amendment). Mr. Chairman, I ask unanimous consent that the committee amendment be considered as read, that it be printed in the RECORD, and that it be open to amendment at any point.

Mr. CHAIRMAN. Is there objection to the request of the gentleman from Tennessee?

There was no objection.

Mr. PRIEST. Mr. Chairman, I move that the Committee do now rise.

The motion was agreed to.

Accordingly the Committee rose; and the Speaker having resumed the chair, Mr. MILLS, Chairman of the Committee of the Whole House on the State of the Union, reported that that Committee, having had under consideration the bill (H. R. 5767) to amend the Federal Trade Commission Act with respect to certain contracts and agreements which establish minimum resale prices and which are extended by State law to nonsigners, had come to no resolution thereon.

HOUSE DEBATE
82d Cong., 2d Sess.
May 8, 1952

98 CONG. REC. 4933

Mr. PRIEST. Mr. Speaker, I move that the House resolve itself into the Committee of the Whole House on the State of the Union for the further consideration of the bill (H. R. 5767) to amend the Federal Trade Commission Act with respect to certain contracts and agreements which establish minimum resale prices and which are extended by State law to nonsigners.

The motion was agreed to.

Accordingly the House resolved itself into the Committee of the Whole House on the State of the Union for the further consideration of the bill H. R. 5767, with Mr. COOPER in the chair.

The Clerk read the title of the bill.

The CHAIRMAN. When the Committee rose on yesterday it was agreed that the committee amendment in the nature of a substitute, now in the bill, be considered as read and open to amendment at any point.

Are there any amendments to the committee amendment?

Mr. McGUIRE. Mr. Chairman, I move to strike out the last word.

Mr. MCGUIRE [*sic*]. Mr. Chairman, the chairman of the Judiciary Committee yesterday tried to convince you that retailers are in business for their health, rather than for profit. He purchased a number of drug items in Peoples, the drug chain, here in Washington and compared the prices of these items with prices of the same items under fair trade and came to the ringing, but vastly erroneous, conclusion that fair trade costs consumers money.

What the gentleman from New York [Mr. CELLER] did prove was that highly popular national-branded items are used as customer bait, to bring customers into the store by offering merchandise at low profit, at no profit, or even at a loss. Retailers who engage in these practices know from experience that whatever losses they incur on the bait items are more than made up because the customers will buy other merchandise on which the retailer makes high profits.

I think the Members of the House will be interested in knowing the true facts about Peoples. I am told on unimpeachable authority that the over-all gross profit margin of Peoples stores in Washington is precisely the same as that of Peoples stores outside of Washington. In other words, customers who shop at Peoples in Washington pay, on the whole, no less and no more for the merchandise they buy than do customers who shop in Peoples stores outside Washington. I am further informed that Peoples in Washington do not engage in the practice of price-juggling, whereby retailers overprice many items in order to make up for the losses on their customer-bait items. What Peoples does is to advertise certain customer-bait items at certain times—generally on days when Government employees are paid—whereas during the rest of the month Peoples prices reflect the margin that Peoples must have to make a profit. What is most interesting about the customer-bait prices is that total sales over the year in these loss leaders is so small that they do not affect the total gross-profit margin of the store by as much as half a percentage point. For this reason, Peoples over-all margin in Washington is not lower than in its stores outside Washington.

It can be argued, I suppose, that Mrs. Smith may be smart enough and determined enough to buy only the customer-bait items. If she does, she will get a bargain; but Mrs. Jones and Mrs. Brown and all the other customers will surely pay for Mrs. Smith's bargains. If all customers were smart enough and determined enough to see through the price-juggling tricks of retailers who prefer to compete unfairly, you can be sure that loss leaders would no longer be profitable and would, therefore, immediately disappear from the market place. Any time a retailer comes to you and tries to convince you that he is in love with dispensing charity to his customers during business hours, recognize him for what he is—an individual who has little respect either for the truth or for your intelligence, or for both.

Fair trade is usually discussed in economic terms. The economic benefits it brings to consumers, to retailers, and to manufacturers have been often pointed out—lower prices, fair competition in the market place, the protection of valuable trade-marks. But, important as are the economic advantages of fair trade, they do not tell the whole story of how fair trade affects the American people. For fair trade affects their lives, as well as their livelihoods.

In the first place, fair trade plays a vital role in keeping our society what we might call an open society rather than a closed one. By that I mean a society in which the doors of opportunity are kept open to everyone, a society in which everyone has the chance to move upward or to become his own boss, if he has the initiative and the ability. This freedom of opportunity, available to everyone, is one of our proudest traditions. Fair trade guards freedom of opportunity in our land because it helps small business to survive and thrive even in an age of huge retail organizations with vast aggregates of capital. By restraining the unfair competition of price-juggling—a powerful weapon by which the giants of retailing can destroy and eliminate their small rivals—fair trade ensures the continuing existence of small business. Unless small business is kept in the running by fair trade, all those Americans who have that unquenchable urge to work for themselves rather than for others, will find the door of opportunity slammed tight against them. The good old American dream ⊥ of the right of the little fellow to achieve independence will become empty and mocking delusion.

Let us put the issue this way: Do we want a nation of 150,000,000 proletarian workers employed by a handful of bosses? The answer is obvious.

It is not exaggerating to say that fair trade can affect the future of democracy in this country. As a witness from the Federal Trade Commission testified before the House Interstate and Foreign Commerce Committee hearings, the maintenance of a strong, healthy small business community is the best bulwark that we have against the growth of collectivism either in the form of fascism or communism. This is undeniably true.

When we examine the history of the rise of totalitarianism, we find that people turn to it when their lives are without hope, when a bleak future of poverty and economic subjection stretches endlessly before them, out of which they see no opportunity of rising. That is when they throw themselves into the arms of an all-powerful dictator or an all-powerful state that promises them bread in return for freedom. But when millions of citizens own their businesses, own property, work their own land—and when those who do not are guaranteed the chance to rise into these economic groups—they are then secure against the blandishments of the false messiahs of collectivism.

The Federal Trade Commission witness advanced another argument which eloquently supports measures, such as fair trade, which preserve small business in our society. Democracy is most alive when it flourishes at the grass roots. This requires a strong sense of civic and community responsibility in citizens who take an active part in community affairs. We all know from our own experience that in those communities in which there exists a healthy small-business group the level of civic welfare and the interest taken by small-business leaders in health, recreation, and education tend to be higher than in those communities in which business consists mainly of a few large concerns owned and operated by distant managers and distant corporations.

Most Americans live in small towns and villages. The manner in which the citizens of each community manage their own local affairs, when multiplied many thousandfold, determines the character of our democracy as a whole. Small-business men have a very personal stake in making their communities better places in which to live and work. Absolute ownership of the community's business enterprises deprives the community of much of the leadership and initiative needed to make community life strong and active. When local leadership is replaced by absentee control and direction, the citizens become apathetic and passive about their own affairs. Democracy then withers at the roots, and it is not long before the creeping malady of civic indifference spreads to the trunk and branches.

It should be clear that whether or not small business remains intact is more than a matter of economic preferences. It involves some of our most cherished political and social institutions.

Small business is essential to our social and political democracy. Fair trade is essential to the continued existence of small business. There can, in my opinion, be no stronger statement of the case for restoring to effectiveness the fair-trade laws of the 45 States, as provided by the McGuire bill, H. R. 5767, now before the House.

Mr. [EDMUND P.] RADWAN [R., N.Y.]. Mr. Chairman, I ask unanimous consent to extend my remarks at this point in the RECORD.

The CHAIRMAN. Is there objection to the request of the gentleman from New York?

There was no objection.

Mr. RADWAN. Mr. Chairman, the McGuire bill, H. R. 5767, has had my attention ever since its introduction. I have given consideration to both sides of the question before us, and I have come to the conclusion that the McGuire bill is good legislation and in the people's best interest.

A study of the history of fair-trade laws will reveal that the public has never hesitated to curb competition which it regards as unfair and monopolistic. The antitrust laws, the Securities and Exchange Act, as well as the Robinson-Patman Act, together with many other measures, curb unfair competition in order to promote fair competition. Fair competition is just as essential to the well-being of our economy as is free competition. Free enterprise in America was never meant to permit illegal and unfair acts any more than our freedom in America permits any individual to commit illegal or immoral acts.

Fair-trade laws such as the McGuire bill before us, curbs ruthless, commercial behavior which would destroy competition by using superior dollar power to eliminate small competitors. The fair-trade laws restrain the unfair competition of retailers who use price tricks and price juggling to bewitch the consumer without benefit to her pocketbook.

Of course, such retailers do not want to be fenced in. Like the many who bitterly opposed the antitrust laws and similar measures, they want to do as they please, even when what they please to do harms society.

This legislation, Mr. Chairman, is for the protection of small-business men as well as the public. There is a great feeling in this country against bigness in government, big business, and labor. This fair-trade legislation protects the small-business man against the bigness of would-be general monopolies. In the long run, it protects the public because it insures fair and moral dealing. It is morally and legally sound, and I trust it will be adopted and enacted into law.

Mr. REED of Illinois. Mr. Chairman, as provided for in the rule I offer the bill H. R. 6925 as a substitute for the bill H. R. 5767.

The Clerk read as follows:

Amendment offered by Mr. REED of Illinois as a substitute for the committee amendment.

"*Be it enacted, etc.,* That section 1 of the act entitled 'An act to protect trade and commerce against unlawful restraints and monopolies,' approved July 2, 1890, be amended to read as follows:

" 'SECTION 1. (a) Every contract, combination in the form of trust or otherwise, or conspiracy, in restraint of trade or commerce among the several States, or with foreign nations, is hereby declared to be illegal. Every person who shall make any contract or engage in any combination or conspiracy hereby declared to be illegal shall be deemed guilty of a misdemeanor, and, on conviction thereof, shall be punished by fine not exceeding $5,000, or by imprisonment not exceeding 1 year, or by both said punishments, in the discretion of the court.

" '(b) Nothing contained herein or in any of the antitrust laws of the United States shall render illegal any contract or agreement prescribing minimum prices for the resale of a commodity which bears, or the label or container of which bears, the trade-mark, brand, or name of the producer of such commodity and which is in free and open competition with commodities of the same general class produced or distributed by others, when contracts or agreements of that description are lawful under any statute, law, or public policy now or hereafter in effect in any State, Territory, or the District of Columbia in which such resale is to be made, or to which the commodity is to be transported for such resale. For the purposes of this act the words "contract or agreement" shall mean a contract or agreement in which the party prescribing the minimum prices shall be the owner of the trade-mark, brand, or name of the commodity or commodities to which this act is applicable.

" '(c) Nothing contained herein or in any of the antitrust laws of the United States shall render illegal the exercise or enforcement of any right or right of action created by any law, now or hereafter in effect in any State, Territory, or the District of Columbia, which provides in substance that willfully and knowingly advertising, offering for sale, or selling any commodity at less than the minimum prices prescribed in any such contract or agreement whether the person so advertising, offering for sale, or selling is or is not a party to such contract or agreement, is unfair competition and is actionable at the suit of any person damaged thereby: *Provided, however,* That in the exercise or enforcement of any right or right of action as is exempted from the antitrust laws by this subsection, it shall be a complete defense to a charge of unfair competition for the defendant to show that the party prescribing the minimum prices has failed to make reasonable efforts to insure compliance, by those in competition with the defendant, with such prescribed minimum prices.

" '(d) Whenever by contract or agreement described in subsection (b) minimum resale prices may be established for a commodity in any State, Territory, or the District of Columbia, where such a contract or agreement is lawful, it shall be an act of unfair competition, actionable at the suit of any person damaged thereby, to willfully and knowingly, in interstate commerce, (1) advertise for sale, offer for sale, or sell or (2) have transported for sale or resale or (3) deliver pursuant to a sale, or otherwise deliver, such commodity in any such State, Territory, or the District of Columbia, where such a contract or agreement is lawful, at less than the prices so established in such contract or agreement, whether the person so advertising for sale, offering for sale, or selling is or is not a party to any such contract or agreement; any person, firm, or corporation, injured in his or its business or property because of the violation of this subsection (d) may sue for and recover the damages by him or it sustained and shall be entitled to sue for and have injunctive relief against threatened loss or damage by a violation of this subsection (d) when and ⊥ under the same conditions and principles as injunctive relief against threatened conduct that will cause loss or damage is granted by courts of equity, under the rules governing such proceedings, and upon the execution of proper bond against damages for an injunction improvidently granted and a showing that the danger of irreparable loss or damage is immediate, a preliminary injunction may issue; action to recover such damages or for such an injunction may be maintained in any court of competent jurisdiction of the several States, or of the United States, having jurisdiction over the parties; in suits within the provisions of this subsection (d) the provisions of section 7 of this act providing for threefold damages shall not apply: *Provided,* That nothing contained herein shall apply to advertisements for sale, offers for sale, or sales which originate from or are directed to or are completed within any State, Territory, or the District of Columbia, where such contracts or agreements as are described herein are not lawful by statute: *And provided further,* That in any proceeding involving alleged violation of this subsection it shall be a complete defense to a charge of unfair competition for the defendant to show that the party describing the minimum prices has failed to make reasonable efforts to insure compliance, by those in competition with the defendant, with such prescribed minimum prices.

⊥ 4935

" '(e) Neither the making of such contracts or agreements as described in subsection (b) nor the exercise or enforcement of any right or right of action as described in subsections (c) and (d) shall be an unfair method of competition under section 5, as amended and supplemented, of the act entitled "An act to create a Federal Trade Commission, to define its powers and duties, and for other purposes," approved September 26, 1914.

" '(f) Nothing in this act contained shall make lawful any contract or agreement, providing for the establishment or maintenance of minimum resale prices on any commodity herein involved, between manufacturers, or between producers, or between wholesalers, or between brokers, or between factors, or between retailers, or between persons, firms, or corporations in competition with each other.' "

Mr. REED of Illinois (interrupting the reading of the amendment). Mr. Chairman, I ask unanimous consent that further reading of the amendment be dispensed with, the amendment to be printed in full.

The CHAIRMAN. Is there objection to the request of the gentleman from Illinois?

There was no objection.

Mr. REED of Illinois. Mr. Chairman, I am sure that it is the earnest desire of those who wish to enact fair-trade legislation to provide for the best possible bill. I think there are three major criteria which must be applied in determining whether or not the legislation meets the situation presented by both the Schwegmann and Wentling cases last year. The first of these is that the legislation must clearly rectify the effects of the Supreme Court decision in the Schwegmann case which related to intrastate retail sales and the circuit court opinion in the Wentling case which held that nonsigners were not bound in cases involving interstate mail-order transaction. The second test is whether the legislation is aimed primarily for the benefit of the independent retailer as distinguished from legislation more beneficial to manufacturers, wholesalers, or trade associations. The third gage of this type of legislation is whether or not complete recognition is given to the sovereignty of both the fair-trade and non-fair-trade States.

I submit that H. R. 6925 on all of these counts is better legislation. First of all, both bills, the McGuire bill and H. R. 6925, do provide for the rectification of the Schwegmann decision. However, the language in subsection 4 of the McGuire bill is so indefinite as to be almost meaningless with regard to the Wentling decision regarding mail-order sales. However, subsection (d) of the Keogh bill clearly takes care of the Wentling situation and with reference to my third test also protects the sovereignty and the public policy of both the fair-trade and non-fair-trade States.

The most important of these tests is the one regarding the independent retailers. It has been said that this provision for a stipulated price, namely ceiling prices in the McGuire bill, is designed to protect the present State legislation. However, much of this legislation was enacted subsequent to the Miller-Tydings Act in 1937. The Miller-Tydings Act, under which fair trade operated successfully until May 1951, speaks only of minimum prices and not of stipulated prices. Stipulated prices are a danger to the independent retailer for he may often be squeezed by inadequate profit margins.

Moreover, if we are realistic we recognize that there are some manufacturers who may pay lip service to fair trade that sets up fair-trade prices on one hand and on the other hand dispense surplus inventory to known price cutters. The independent retailer must be protected against this abuse of fair trade to his disadvantage. Therefore, H. R. 6925 gives the independent retailer a defense against this type of activity. Time does not permit a further exposition of the comparison of both of the two bills. I do have available a mimeographed analysis of the two measures which is available to the Members and I earnestly suggest that you read this analysis so that you may more fully understand that the Keogh bill, H. R. 6925, is more clearly designed to protect the independent retailer and is not a special interest bill for any group of manufacturers, wholesalers, or trade associations.

Mr. PRIEST. Mr. Chairman, will the gentleman yield?

Mr. REED of Illinois. I yield to the gentleman from Tennessee.

Mr. PRIEST. I notice that the bill the gentleman has offered as a substitute has stricken-out language. The gentleman is offering that language which I presume to be a committee amendment in italics in the bill rather than the original bill?[3.60]

Mr. REED of Illinois. That is correct.

Mr. PRIEST. I thank the gentleman.

The CHAIRMAN. The time of the gentleman from Illinois has expired.

Mr. HARRIS. Mr. Chairman, I ask unanimous consent that the gentleman be permitted to proceed for 5 additional minutes, because this is a most important phase of this whole legislation, and I think the gentleman should be permitted to explain his viewpoint.

The CHAIRMAN. Is there objection to the request of the gentleman from Arkansas?

There was no objection.

Mr. CRAWFORD. Mr. Chairman, will the gentleman yield?

Mr. REED of Illinois. I yield to the gentleman from Michigan.

Mr. CRAWFORD. Where in H. R. 6925 is the protection for the small retailer against the manufacturer giving surplus inventory products to the fellow who sells at the cut rate?

Mr. REED of Illinois. I think it is in the latter part of section (b).

Mr. [EDWIN E.] WILLIS [D., La.]. Mr. Chairman, will the gentleman yield?

Mr. REED of Illinois. I yield to the gentleman from Louisiana.

Mr. WILLIS. I want to associate myself with the views expressed by the gentleman from Illinois, to the point that both of us want the best possible bill in the interest of fair trade. I regard the Keogh bill as being the better bill, but certainly the McGuire bill should at least be amended as will be proposed by the gentleman from Kansas [Mr. COLE]. If the gentleman's substitute does not prevail I will support the McGuire bill. May I ask the gentleman this question? Is it not correct that under the McGuire bill, if a reseller by mail, say a mail-order house from the gentleman's State of Illinois, should ship goods to the neighboring State of Pennsylvania under the bill, such reseller may violate the laws both of Illinois and Pennsylvania, fair-trade States, under the Wentling decision? Is that not correct?

Mr. REED of Illinois. I am so informed.

Mr. WILLIS. And is it not correct that in such a situation where goods are shipped from Pennsylvania to the gentleman's State of Illinois both fair-trade States, with the mail-order house from Pennsylvania thus violating the laws of both States, under the Wentling decision, that the people of Illinois could not protect themselves by meeting these undercutting prices, because that practice is permitted by the Wentling decision, and is it not correct that the Keogh bill meets that situation, meets not only the Schwegmann decision, but the Wentling decision, and that the McGuire bill does not?

Mr. REED of Illinois. The gentleman is correct, and that is stated in this analysis which we have prepared and which I hope every Member of the House will take the opportunity to examine.

[3.60] Reference is to H.R. 6925 as reported by the House Judiciary Committee on March 13, 1952, which appears *supra* at 632–34.

Mr. HARRIS. Mr. Chairman, will the gentleman yield?

Mr. REED of Illinois. I yield to the gentleman from Arkansas.

Mr. HARRIS. I should like to ask the gentleman then, in view of the question that has been asked by the distinguished gentleman from Louisiana, is it not a fact that in the substitute bill a sale from a non-fair-trade State may be made into a fair-trade State below the price established for the product in the fair-trade State?

Mr. REED of Illinois. I am not so informed.

Mr. HARRIS. I would like to remind the gentleman that it is a fact, under his own bill, so consequently at the same time then you try to make a Federal fair-trade policy out of it you leave the loophole in your Federal fair-trade policy insofar as those non-fair-trade States are concerned?

The CHAIRMAN. The time of the gentleman from Illinois has expired.

(On request of Mr. CELLER, and by unanimous consent, Mr. REED of Illinois was allowed to proceed for five additional minutes.)

Mr. CELLER. Mr. Chairman, will the gentleman yield?

Mr. REED of Illinois. I yield to the gentleman from New York.

Mr. CELLER. Is it not true that there is no protection whatsoever in the McGuire bill with reference to the sales between States, whether the States are fair-traded or non-fair-traded? The only language we have with reference to that in the McGuire bill is on page 5, subsection (4), lines 18 to 23, and I shall read them:

Neither the making of contracts or agreements as described in paragraph (2) of this subsection—

Those are the price-maintenance contracts—

nor the exercise or enforcement of any right of action as described in paragraph (3) of this subsection shall constitute an unlawful burden or restraint upon, or interference with, commerce.

Those words are very vague. One might say they are weasel words. They look in both directions. Certainly in a bill as important as this the words should be clear, definite, and distinct, so that he who runs may read. This would make a field day for lawyers. It is a little difficult to know what was in the mind of the author when he penned these words. It probably was put in for ambiguity's sake, so that there would be the widest divergence of opinion, so that the authors of the McGuire bill, or rather, the National Retail Druggists' Association, which wrote the bill, could satisfy critics on both sides of the line.

Mr. COLE of Kansas. Mr. Chairman, will the gentleman yield?

Mr. REED of Illinois. I yield.

Mr. COLE of Kansas. May I apprise the gentleman of the fact, as he did not know it, that I plan to offer an amendment to the McGuire bill which I think will cure the situation the gentleman from New York was mentioning a moment ago.

Mr. HARRIS. Mr. Chairman, will the gentleman yield?

Mr. REED of Illinois. I yield to the gentleman from Arkansas.

Mr. HARRIS. May I ask the gentleman from Kansas, is it not a fact that the substitute bill which is proposed by the gentleman from Illinois includes the amendment of which the gentleman speaks?

Mr. COLE of Kansas. Yes, I think it does include that amendment. However, it approaches the entire problem from a different point of view than the McGuire bill.

Mr. REED of Illinois. Mr. Chairman, as I stated at the beginning of my remarks, I offer this bill, H. R. 6925, as a substitute for the pending measure because I believe it is the better of the two bills. I do so because H. R. 6925 was the subject of exhaustive hearings by a subcommittee of the Committee on the Judiciary and is believed by the majority of the members of that committee to be a more practical and workable bill, and one which is more likely to survive legal assaults thereon. I believe the House should have the opportunity to choose which of these two bills it prefers. I trust H. R. 6925 will be the one so selected. If not, however, I shall cheerfully support H. R. 5767, the McGuire bill, because of the present need for fair-trade legislation necessitated by the two Federal court decisions which have been mentioned.

Mr. PRIEST. Mr. Chairman, I rise in opposition to the amendment.

Mr. Chairman, we debated this subject yesterday afternoon, and I think the debate was very helpful. I appreciated the fact that the debate was kept on a very high plane, that it discussed the issues involved.

As I told the Rules Committee when I appeared on behalf of the Committee on Interstate and Foreign Commerce to ask for a rule on the McGuire bill, the bill itself is a very simple matter. The economic problems it seeks to solve are not simple, they are very complex, because they affect the whole economy of this country. However, the bill itself, I repeat is a simple bill.

The McGuire bill came out of the Committee on Interstate and Foreign Commerce after rather extended hearings. I was appointed by the chairman of that committee, as chairman of a subcommittee, to conduct these hearings. We called witnesses of every varying viewpoint on the subject. We heard every witness, as far as I know, that asked to be heard on the subject, and we invited many others to appear, in order that the committee itself could get the widest possible testimony on a rather complicated economic and legal question.

May I say to the committee today that at the very beginning of these hearings I was personally somewhat doubtful about the approach taken by the McGuire bill, but during the hearings, as we listened to witness after witness, and then as we went into executive session and studied the bill with our own legal counsel, I came more and more to the conclusion, and it is now a very firm conviction, that the best possible approach legislatively insofar as the Congress is concerned, is the approach made by the McGuire bill.

I have regretted that there has developed in the consideration of this legislation somewhat of a jurisdictional battle between two committees of the House.

I will at all times do everything possible to avoid such jurisdictional controversies. As a matter of fact, it is inevitable in the consideration of this bill, and I say that because the Committee on Interstate and Foreign Commerce without any question has complete jurisdiction over the Federal Trade Commission Act. There is no question there. The Committee on the Judiciary has complete jurisdiction over the Sherman Act and other acts of that nature.

So we have a proposition here, which results in a head-on collision between two committees of the House. The Committee on Interstate and Foreign Commerce reported the McGuire bill. I believe it is a better bill to do the job. I believe that for this reason. It does not create a cause for Federal action. It simply says, as was brought out time after time in the debate of yesterday, that State fair-trade laws may operate and be effective without constituting a burden on interstate commerce. That is what the bill says.

Mr. CELLER. Mr. Chairman, will the gentleman yield?

Mr. PRIEST. I yield to the chairman of the Committee on the Judiciary.

Mr. CELLER. I wholly subscribe to what the gentleman has said. He will agree both he and I and the leading members of both committees tried to resolve this difficulty as best we could. None of us like this jurisdictional fight. But will the gentleman, shall I say, pledge himself to support me and others who are like minded with us, that this situation will never happen again and that the gentleman's committee will abide by its jurisdiction, which covers the Federal Trade Commission Act, and that he will allow us, the members of the Committee on the Judiciary, to abide by our jurisdiction which concerns the Sherman law, the Robinson-Patman Act, and the Clayton Act?

Mr. PRIEST. Of course, I appreciate the spirit in which the question is asked, but I am sure the distinguished gentleman from New York knows that the gentleman from Tennessee cannot make a pledge here, which would commit a great committee of the House. The gentleman from Tennessee will always, to the very best of his ability, attempt to abide by the jurisdiction of his own committee.

Mr. Chairman, to get back to the question of the differences between the two bills, as I stated in the beginning, I was a little doubtful at first as to what approach should be taken. I am fully convinced that some legislation is needed in this field. I believe most of the members of both committees are convinced that legislation is needed in this field.

The CHAIRMAN. The time of the gentleman from Tennessee has expired.

(Mr. PRIEST asked and was given permission to proceed for three additional minutes.)

Mr. PRIEST. Mr. Chairman, granting that legislation is needed to clarify a situation which developed after the Supreme Court decision in the Schwegmann case, then the question confronting our committee was what type of legislation is best to meet that situation.

We concluded in the Committee on Interstate and Foreign Commerce that the best approach was to pass legislation permitting, mind you, permitting the State fair-trade laws that have been enacted and adopted by the States to be operative and to be effective without constituting a burden on interstate commerce. The bill does not create any Federal cause for action. The Keogh bill does create a cause for Federal action.

⊥ Mr. [BYRON G.] ROGERS [D., Colo.]. Mr. Chairman, will the gentleman yield? ⊥ 4937

Mr. PRIEST. I yield.

Mr. ROGERS of Colorado. Under the McGuire bill, do you not visualize in interstate commerce that anyone can go into a Federal court under the present procedure?

Mr. PRIEST. Certainly, I agree with the gentleman. I do not want to becloud the issue. Of course, they can go into a Federal court on that issue, if it involves interstate commerce. But the bill itself does not create such a cause for Federal action.

Mr. [WILLIAM J.] GREEN [JR.] [D., Pa.]. Mr. Chairman, will the gentleman yield?

Mr. PRIEST. I yield.

Mr. GREEN. Mr. Chairman, I compliment the gentleman on his fine presentation and just make the observation that the interesting thing about this is that jurisdictional disputes are not just confined to labor. Are they?

Mr. PRIEST. No; they are not; that is quite true. They happen in many other fields of endeavor and activity quite frequently, I might say to the gentleman.

Mr. Chairman, the Keogh bill, as I see it—and if I am wrong in my interpretation, I hope someone will get me clear on that point—the Keogh bill creates a Federal defense in an action to maintain fair prices. It would be a complete defense, as I see it, in any such action under State fair-trade law, or in any action aimed at prosecuting the new cause of action created by the Keogh bill to show that the owner of the trademark, brand, or name failed to make reasonable efforts to insure compliance by those in competition with the defendant in such action.

As I see it, that is the one great difference between the Keogh bill and the McGuire bill. I notice my good friend, who is a very fine lawyer, nods in concurrence with that idea. I yield to the gentleman from Louisiana.

Mr. WILLIS. I compliment the gentleman on his stand. He and I agreed to support fair-trade legislation.

In respect to the last point that the gentleman made, that the Keogh bill creates a cause of action, may I suggest two thoughts: The gentleman from Ohio in general debate said that the Keogh bill placed the Federal Government in fair-trade business. The gentleman does not agree with that statement, does he? Is this not the situation: The only thing the Keogh bill does is to grant a cause of action. It does not any more place the Federal Government in fair-trade business than it places the Federal Government in the insurance business because the Federal court has jurisdiction over an insurance policy between two persons living in different States.

Mr. PRIEST. I think I agree with the gentleman from Louisiana, that the statement that it placed the Federal Government in fair-trade business perhaps goes a little far, but I would say further in reply to the gentleman—we have worked together on this matter in an honest effort, he and I, to get a bill in which there was no dispute, because we both believed legislation was necessary. I believe it does go one or two steps nearer putting the Federal Government into fair-trade business than the McGuire bill.

Mr. WILLIS. The gentleman stated that under the Keogh bill it would be a defense, when a manufacturer brings a cause of action against a retailer for violating a fair-trade contract, for the retailer to retort and to say, "Well, perhaps I may not carry on my contract with you, but you are not attempting to enforce your contracts with other people who are in competition with me." The point I ask the gentleman is this: Is it not within the jurisprudence of the States right now? Under the State Law—and the only thing we are doing is to implement the State law—we are not creating any new law—under the State law right now, if a manufacturer in the gentleman's State of Tennessee, a fair-trade State, sues a druggist for violating the fair-trade contract, that druggist right now can plead as defense that that manufacturer is not honestly enforcing his fair-trade contracts against other druggists in Tennessee. That is the gentleman's jurisprudence in Tennessee, and the only thing in the Keogh bill is to carry that jurisprudence into Federal law.

The CHAIRMAN. The time of the gentleman from Tennessee has expired.

Mr. BROWN of Ohio. Mr. Chairman, I ask unanimous consent that the gentleman may proceed for two additional minutes.

The CHAIRMAN. Is there objection to the request of the gentleman from Ohio?

There was no objection.

Mr. BROWN of Ohio. I have asked for this time so that I might ask the gentleman to yield.

Mr. PRIEST. I yield.

Mr. BROWN of Ohio. The statement has just been made on the floor that the gentleman from Ohio said that the Keogh bill would put the Government in the fair-trade business. The gentleman from Ohio made no such statement. Somebody is trying to give the gentleman from Ohio the business instead of the Federal Government. What the gentleman from Ohio did say is in the CONGRESSIONAL RECORD. If you will refer to the remarks of the gentleman from Ohio, you will find that I made this statement:

> The McGuire bill, as I understand it, would place the control of fair-trade practices with the States, or return that power to the States which in the past have exercised supervision and control of fair-trade practices.

The Keogh bill would place the responsibility for enforcement and supervision of fair-trade rules and practices with the Federal Government; and that is exactly what you do under this Keogh bill when you give the Federal courts jurisdiction over its enforcement and you go in there to bring your suit. So the gentleman was misquoted on the floor, and I hope the gentleman from Louisiana will correct the RECORD.

Mr. WILLIS. Mr. Chairman, will the gentleman yield?

Mr. PRIEST. I yield to the gentleman from Louisiana.

Mr. WILLIS. I certainly did not intend to place words in the gentleman's mouth, and I accept his word for it.

Mr. BROWN of Ohio. The CONGRESSIONAL RECORD speaks for itself, sir.

Mr. WILLIS. I say I accept not only the CONGRESSIONAL RECORD but the gentleman's version of what he said. I am sorry I misunderstood the gentleman.

Mr. CELLER. Mr. Chairman, will the gentleman yield?

Mr. PRIEST. I yield.

Mr. CELLER. I may say to the gentleman from Ohio that even presently, under present conditions, the Federal courts have jurisdiction. The Wentling case arose in the Federal court; the Schwegmann case arose in the Federal court

Mr. BROWN of Ohio. But the Keogh bill would pin point it, just as I say.

The CHAIRMAN. The time of the gentleman from Tennessee has again expired.

(On request of Mr. HARRIS, and by unanimous consent, Mr. PRIEST was allowed to proceed for one additional minute.)

Mr. HARRIS. I asked for this additional minute for the purpose of replying to the statement made by the distinguished chairman of the Judiciary Committee. The reason those cases were in the Federal court was because of diversity of citizenship, was it not?

Mr. PRIEST. That is my understanding.

Mr. CELLER. Mr. Chairman, will the gentleman yield further? The Keogh bill grants jurisdiction to both State courts and Federal courts.

Mr. PRIEST. Let me say in this last 30 seconds of this last minute that I have, that I hope the Committee of the Whole will vote down the substitute and approve the McGuire bill.

Mr. DOLLIVER. Mr. Chairman, I rise in opposition to the substitute.

Mr. Chairman, as I said in my statement yesterday during general debate, unhappily a conflict of committee jurisdiction has arisen. Perhaps it was inevitable because of the nature of this legislation. The McGuire bill, to get a little technical, is an amendment to the regulations and the laws of the Federal Trade Commission; and the Keogh bill allegedly is an amendment to the antitrust law. That is a pretty tenuous difference, I may say, but perhaps that is the fundamental basis for this dispute of jurisdiction.

I am opposed vigorously to the Keogh substitute, and what I shall say in opposition I presume will in some regard also be a repetition of what has already been said. It has been pointed out that the Keogh bill puts the Federal Government right into the middle of this whole enforcement proposition. If you do not believe that read the first section of H. R. 6925 which provides a $5,000 penalty or imprisonment for not exceeding 1 year.

Mr. CELLER. Mr. Chairman, will the gentleman yield?

Mr. DOLLIVER. I have but 5 minutes; the gentleman can get time in his own right.

Mr. CELLER. That is the law now.

Mr. DOLLIVER. Why repeat it then? It is in the Keogh bill; it is the first paragraph of the bill. If it is in the old act why did it have to be repeated? It is not in the McGuire bill at all; there is no such sumptuary enforcement provision in the McGuire bill. It is hard for me not to believe there is some reason for this criminal provision in the Keogh substitute.

What we want to do in this legislation is to solve a problem that came about by reason of some court decisions. That is what the McGuire bill does.

Another phase in which the McGuire bill is superior is this: The McGuire bill permits what was going on prior to these court decisions of a year ago. It allows the distributor, as well as the wholesaler, as well as the manufacturer, to set up fair trade practices.

Why is that? As I understand the Keogh bill—and if I am wrong in this, I hope I will be corrected—it permits only a manufacturer to establish retail minimum prices. Why is the McGuire bill framed otherwise? The testimony before our committee showed that of necessity in some lines all of their business is carried on not directly from the manufacturer to the retailer but through an intermediary. Sometimes there are two steps, the wholesaler and the distributor.

The McGuire bill, I think properly, permits the wholesaler or distributor to set up a fair price schedule. It does not limit it solely to the manufacturer, as does the Keogh substitute. That is a very important thing from a practical standpoint if you are going to make this kind of legislation work.

The third thing, which has already been alluded to in this discussion, in my judgment, as I have studied these two bills, the Keogh bill puts the Federal Government right in the middle of the enforcement picture so far as fair-trade legislation is concerned. Because it undertakes to deal with a problem with which perhaps the McGuire bill does not effectively deal. That is the problem of interstate violations of fair-trade practices. Maybe the time will come when this omission will have to be dealt with. But it may transpire that the three States not having fair-trade laws may soon pass them. That will solve the problem.

However, I would call your attention to the fact that the McGuire bill merely reestablishes what was the situation prior to May 1951. Small business did not have a great deal of difficulty in most places concerning this particular part of the situation.

I hope the Keogh substitute will be rejected.

M'GUIRE BILL OR KEOGH BILL

Mr. [WRIGHT] PATMAN [D., Tex.]. Mr. Chairman, I move to strike out the requisite number of words.

IN FAVOR OF H. R. 5767

Mr. Chairman, I rise to urge the adoption of H. R. 5767, the McGuire bill for one fundamental reason, even if there were no other reason. To me this reason is completely compelling and would itself justify the adoption of the measure by this committee. This reason is that the bill will return to the States the right to regulate fair-trade practices if they so desire. I base my argument for H. R. 5767 not on the intrinsic merits of fair trade but on the rights of the States to regulate what are essentially purely local transactions.

This is the real issue before us: Whether the several States shall have the right to formulate for themselves their policy in respect to fair-trade practices. Today 45 of the 48 States have enacted statutes supporting fair trade. Every one of these laws makes it possible for a manufacturer to enforce fair-trade practices against all dealers who elect to handle his products regardless of whether the dealer has or has not signed a specific fair-trade contract. Public support for this legislation is overwhelming. The American people have rarely expressed themselves on any matter of public policy as wholeheartedly as they have on fair trade. Are we, the duly elected representatives of the people, to say no to this expression of the public will? I am sure that no Member of this House will want to be in the position of admitting that he has deliberately thwarted public policy in this fashion.

No substantive policy of Congress is being changed. It is these State laws that are in jeopardy if we do not act. The proposed bill is nothing but an enabling act which permits two or more States to exercise the same kind of control over trade practices across their boundaries that each State may exercise over its local trade. This is all that the Miller-Tydings Act does. It merely gives to the States the opportunity to decide for themselves what fair-trade policy they believe suitable to their respective needs. The only purpose of the Miller-Tydings Act, as it is of the present bill, was to support the laws enacted by the States. All of us are well aware that fair-trade legislation can never offer effective protection to the small retailer unless all businessmen in a community are bound by the same rules. The Miller-Tydings Act provided a partial grant of authority whereby the States could establish those rules if they chose to do so. The McGuire bill completes the grant.

When the Miller-Tydings Act was enacted, only 17 States had fair-trade laws. Today with 45 States having such laws, how much more cogent is the argument for supporting State legislation than it was in 1937.

I am afraid that some of us have not understood just how narrow the issue now before us is. We are merely trying—as you have been told—to restore the law to its status prior to the decision in the Schwegmann case. That decision held merely that the immunity granted by the Miller-Tydings Act does not extend to the provisions of State laws which make fair-trade contracts enforceable against nonsigners. The decision was thus very limited. It had nothing to do with the merits of fair trade in general, nor with the validity of State laws when applied to purely intrastate trade, nor even with the right of the States to control certain aspects of interstate trade. We thus have the following anomalous and confusing situation:

First. A manufacturer may contract to maintain prices with retailers in intrastate trade.

Second. He may even reach across State lines and contract with retailers in other States if the latter have fair-trade laws. These contracts are enforceable against the parties even though interstate trade is involved.

Third. He may also enforce his contracts against nonsigners in his own State.

Fourth. But if interstate trade is involved, the manufacturer cannot enforce fair-trade contracts against nonsigning retailers even though the latter reside in States which have laws specifically authorizing such enforcement.

I feel certain that each of us stands for the strengthening of the fast-ebbing power of the States when this can be done without interfering with national policy. All of us believe that the States should be left in control of their own affairs wherever possible. Certainly, then, we cannot justify a failure to provide this enabling legislation in view of the great declaration of the American people—indicated by the action of 45 States—in favor of resale-price maintenance including the nonsigner provision.

We are not foisting fair-trade practices upon the people of those few States which have not enacted such legislation. On the contrary, they are left free to deal with the whole matter as they see fit. States which do not believe in fair-trade practices are fully protected. The limitations imposed in the Miller-Tydings Act are more than adequate to conserve the public interest. No State is forced to enact fair-trade legislation. If a State disapproves of the nonsigner feature, it has full right not to enact such a clause. Only those commodities which carry a trade-mark or the brand name of the producer or dealer are subject to price maintenance. Under State law, no manufacturer is forced to distribute his products under fair-trade arrangements. Both Miller-Tydings and State laws declare that to be subject to fair trade, a commodity must be in free and open competition. Monopolistic practices are forbidden.

I do not believe there is any sound justification for opposition to this bill. If we fail to act positively in this matter, we are, in effect, willfully nullifying the fair-trade laws of 45 States. In today's vast and complex distribution systems, no single State can commercially isolate itself sufficiently to exercise the measure of control it may desire over commerce within its boundaries. State policy inevitably affects interstate commerce. But here is one area that can safely be left to State action.

The policy of the States is clear. There is no doubt as to their wishes. Congress must now recognize its responsibility to the States; not to censor, but to provide the legal mechanism that will allow the States to exercise the control over commerce they have deemed necessary to their welfare.

Mr. Chairman, the question at this time seems to be whether or not we should favor the McGuire bill or the Keogh bill. Personally, I favor the McGuire bill and I expect to state some ⊥ reasons why I am opposed to the Keogh bill.   ⊥ 4939

No. 1: The reasons for this legislation. Prior to May of 1951 there was no need for this legislation; however, the Supreme Court of the United States in a decision that you are familiar with made a ruling that upset State laws. The decision of the Court was that certain conditions and requirements of the laws of the different States were illegal and could not be enforced. The object of this bill is to put the independent merchants back in the same position they were in before that Supreme Court decision. That is the McGuire bill.

The Keogh bill goes much further than that, according to my view. The reason for this bill, in addition to the Supreme Court decision, is to do justice to a large group of independent retailers, including manufacturers and producers in this country, whose products have been abused by being used as loss leaders in deceitful, misleading, and untruthful advertising—an unfair business practice.

No one is in favor of practices that have been engaged in, and laws of this type will prevent that. There is a difference between vertical price fixing and horizontal price fixing. I have always opposed and do now oppose horizontal price fixing. I oppose manufacturers getting together and fixing prices. That is horizontal. I oppose wholesalers getting together and fixing prices. That is horizontal. One of these days the farmers, through their farm cooperatives selling their branded merchandise, will be the ones screaming for this type of legislation more than any other one group, because it will give them protection. It will protect them from the producer right on down to where the goods are delivered over the counter to the customer. That is the object of this legislation. Now as long as you can fix a price from the producer or manufacturer, whether it is a farmer or manufacturer of any type, on down to where it is delivered to the customer, that is entirely different to different groups getting together and fixing prices, as long as they are in free and open competition with other commodities of similar and like grade, quality, and kind. That is exactly the fair-trade law. It does not ordinarily apply to a commodity unless that commodity, where the price is fixed vertically, is in competition with other commodities of like grade and kind, so you have competition. Vertical price fixing in this respect is not repugnant or obnoxious to our antitrust laws, and I think it is in the public interest.

(By unanimous consent, Mr. PATMAN was allowed to proceed for five additional minutes.)

Mr. PATMAN. The State laws in 45 States provide for these fair-trade prices. This particular bill, the McGuire bill, does not go into the merits of fair trade at all; it does not go into the merits of fair trade; it does not say that your law in your State is a fair law or unfair law; it does not touch a law. It merely says what the Constitution says is the duty of Congress to regulate commerce among the States, and if two States have similar laws it is the duty of Congress to allow the people in those two States to cross State lines with their transactions in interstate commerce where it is legal in the two States. That is exactly what we are doing here, except 45 States are involved instead of two States. It is the duty of Congress in a case like that, the way I conceive it to be my duty, at least, to enact laws to allow the States to do business among themselves across State lines where it is not immoral or otherwise obnoxious and contrary to the traditions of our country and the laws and Constitution of our country. So this is just an enabling act, just to enable those 45 States to do business across State lines. I do not see anything objectionable to it. I know a good group of independent merchants of this country have sponsored this bill. I know that other groups have recently joined—Johnny Come-Lately's. They are in here now when the druggists have been carrying this ball for 25 or 30 years.

The druggists that I know that have been appealing to me to get relief through this bill are the small, independent retail druggists. They are not the large, national chains, they are the small, independent, corner drug stores. The National Association of Retail Druggists is composed of between 30,000 and 40,000 of that type of druggists, with not one chain among them, not one chain. They are every one, small, independent merchants, every one of them. All they ask is equality of opportunity in business, just a fair and square deal. That is all they ask for.

Mr. PRIEST. Mr. Chairman, will the gentleman yield?

Mr. PATMAN. I yield to the gentleman from Tennessee.

Mr. PRIEST. I asked the gentleman to yield simply to state that I doubt if any other Member of the House has studied small business more than the gentleman from Texas, as the chairman of the House Small Business Committee. Recently that committee has, under his direction, made a study of this question. The gentleman appeared before our committee to give testimony in support of the bill. The Committee on Interstate and Foreign Commerce appreciated very much having the benefit of the information given by the gentleman in his own study of this particular question.

Mr. PATMAN. I thank the gentleman very kindly.

Our committee went to the trouble of getting up the arguments for and against this type of legislation, for and against. We secured the services of people who were partisan in favor of it. We received the services of people who were prejudiced against it. We have the arguments for and against this type of legislation in a booklet of about 50 pages, made available to every Member of this House.

Our committee of 11 members, after considering the arguments in favor and against this legislation, our 11 members of this Small Business Committee of the House, your agents, unanimously agreed to recommend this bill, the McGuire bill, as being the type of bill that should be passed. We are unanimously for it. We have studied it for years. We are not for monopoly, we are against monopoly.

Mr. [CHARLES A.] HALLECK [R., Ind.]. Mr. Chairman, will the gentleman yield?

Mr. PATMAN. I yield to the gentleman from Indiana, who is a ranking member of the House Small Business Committee on the Republican side, the minority side of our committee, and has been for many years. He is one of the more constructive and valuable Members of Congress and the small independent merchants have a real friend in him.

Mr. HALLECK. I just wonder if the gentleman would not include in his remarks the rather brief statement that the House Small Business Committee got out on the matter of the necessity for fair trade legislation.

Mr. PATMAN. I shall be glad to do that, and I thank the gentleman for calling it to my attention.

I am inserting herewith a part of my testimony before the Committee on Interstate and Foreign Commerce of the House which includes the statement referred to:

Mr. HARRIS. Mr. Chairman, I believe it will be appropriate if my colleagues will permit me at this time to say that Mr. PATMAN has been in the Congress a good many years, coming from Texarkana, Tex. As chairman of the Small Business Committee, a special committee of the House of Representatives for many years, he has had occasion to study this problem quite a lot over the years. I believe that is true, is it not, Mr. PATMAN?

Mr. PATMAN. Yes, sir. We have given lots of consideration to it.

Mr. CROSSER. I think we all realize that.

Mr. PATMAN. It is my understanding that you have before you for consideration H. R. 5767, the McGuire bill, being a bill to amend the Federal Trade Commission Act with respect to certain contracts and agreements which establish minimum resale prices and which are extended by State law to nonsigners.

That bill was introduced by Mr. McGuire some time ago.

Now, if you have before you the confidential committee print entitled "Fair Trade: The Problem and the Issues," that booklet was gotten up by the Committee on Small Business. We have been working on this problem for many months.

The views expressed are partisan views, partisan on each side. It presents the arguments pro and con. Every argument that can be built up in favor of the bill is contained in this booklet. Every argument that can be presented in opposition to this bill is contained in this booklet.

And, the committee, after giving, our Committee on Small Business, after giving fair consideration to the views expressed in this booklet and other information came to the following conclusion and made the following recommendations:

"CONCLUSIONS AND RECOMMENDATIONS

"The Select Committee on Small Business has studied carefully the arguments presented both by the advocates of fair trade and the opponents. It is impressed by the complexity of the problem and by the weight of evidence on both sides of the issue. The committee is convinced that deceitful and misleading price cutting is not in the public interest and that small-business enterprises in particular need protection against loss-leader and similar unfair business practices. It believes the States should retain jurisdiction over retail trade practices and that Congress should make it possible to enforce fair-trade contracts in interstate commerce."

⊥ Under the Constitution it is the duty of Congress and the sole and exclusive duty of ⊥ 4940 Congress to regulate commerce among the several States. No other legislative body has the power. The President does not have that power. The judiciary does not have the power. It is a legislative function that only the Congress can exercise and only the Congress has sole and exclusive jurisdiction.

The way I construe this bill is that it is an enabling act, enabling States to do business across State lines where the State laws are similar. In other words, if Maryland and Pennsylvania have similar laws concerning fair trade, this bill permits business to extend across the State line and the contracts made in compliance with the laws of these two States to be enforced in interstate commerce.

It occurs to me it is a very simple question. I do not see why anyone should oppose the Congress permitting two States to do business across the State line where they have similar laws unless, of course, it is something immoral or on questions like that which should be raised, which is not raised in this particular issue.

Small business is not a partisan question. On the questions relating to small business, there is no division of opinion at the aisle, with the Republicans on this side and the Democrats on that side. There are ardent supporters in this Congress of the small, independent merchant on both sides of the aisle. This has been a nonpartisan measure. We have worked on it together. There has never been partisanship in the consideration of bills for the small-business man, the independent-business man. We are strong for this. We believe it is necessary.

I will tell you why I am opposed to the Keogh bill. It sets up Federal action, in the aggressive and also in the defensive. It would provide that the Federal Trade Commission enforce it, because the law makes it an unfair method of competition, and under section 5 of the Federal Trade Commission Act they would be right up here asking you for a million or half a million dollars to enforce it. That should not be necessary. So when you vote for the Keogh bill, you vote for a half million or a million dollars to enforce it, because you will have to have money to enforce it.

The CHAIRMAN. The time of the gentleman from Texas has expired.

(By unanimous consent, Mr. PATMAN was allowed to proceed for five additional minutes.)

Mr. CELLER. Mr. Chairman, will the gentleman yield?

Mr. PATMAN. I yield to the gentleman from New York.

Mr. CELLER. I call the gentleman's attention to the report to which he adverted, the Fair Trade Report of the Select Committee on Small Business of the House of Representatives. I read in the conclusions and recommendations the following:

It believes the States should retain jurisdiction over retail-trade practices and that Congress should make it possible to enforce fair-trade practices in interstate commerce.

There is no question whatsoever as to the binding of nonsigners.

Mr. PATMAN. I will discuss that later. I do not have time to do it now.

Mr. CELLER. Why was that left out of the report, as to nonsigners being bound?

Mr. PATMAN. The nonsigner business does not mean anything. These State laws could have provided that a manufacturer could file his contract, or his desire to fix prices vertically with the Secretary of State in each State, and made it just as binding. Instead of doing that, it was said, "We will just have one person to sign it, and when one person signs it, everybody will be bound by it." There has been a great deal said about that, but it does not mean anything. It does not go to the merits of it. That is just a matter of procedure, making it possible for the manufacturer or producer to bring his particular commodity under the fair-trade law of that State, just as a matter of procedure.

Mr. CELLER. Mr. Chairman, will the gentleman yield?

Mr. PATMAN. I cannot yield. I know the gentleman took a great deal of time here yesterday, but he ought not want to take my time too. The gentleman is honest and conscientious in his views. He does not like a law like this. Of course, he is entitled to his opinion, just as I am entitled to have my opinions.

SURGEON WHO WIELDS KNIFE

In this case, I think we want to hear from people who are sympathetic to this proposal. In other words, the surgeon who wields the knife should want the patient to live. Now Surgeon CELLER, as nice a man as he is, as good a Congressman as he is, and as fine a statesman as he is, in this case is the surgeon and he does not want this patient, the McGuire bill, to live. I am not willing to accept his words of advice, and his cautions and his suggestions in a case of this kind because he does not want the patient to live.

Mr. [WINGATE H.] LUCAS [D., Tex.]. Mr. Chairman will the gentleman yield?

Mr. PATMAN. I yield.

Mr. LUCAS. I hope the gentleman from Texas [Mr. PATMAN] will explain the effect of the McGuire bill and the Keogh bill in the States where no fair-trade laws are on the statute books.

Mr. PATMAN. In Texas we do not have any and the McGuire bill will not affect Texas. Under the Keogh bill, which I have just read hurriedly, seems to make it unlawful to advertise for sale in a fair-trade State a commodity that is lower than the fair-trade law. In other words, our publishers in Texas, on the radio and in the newspapers, if that interpretation is correct, will have to stop everything at the State line, under the Keogh bill. Otherwise, they would be criminals, they would be violating a law. That just shows that they have not thought this thing through, because the surgeon who is wielding the knife did not want the patient to live. They have not thought it through. There are many serious and fatal defects in the Keogh bill, and it shows that it has not been carefully gone into.

Mr. JAVITS. Mr. Chairman, will the gentleman yield?

Mr. PATMAN. I yield.

Mr. JAVITS. I would like to ask the gentleman when he spoke of competition, it is a fact, is it not, that under this bill and under the Miller-Tydings Act, competition is adequate under the bill, if it is with other fair-trade priced items. It does not have to be with non-fair-trade priced items?

Mr. PATMAN. Under the McGuire bill, that is correct. I am not impugning the motives of anyone on this question about which Members can differ, and honestly differ. I know they honestly do differ. I am not impugning their motives. I am not questioning their judgment. I do not know. I just believe the McGuire bill is the best bill.

Mr. McCULLOCH. Mr. Chairman, will the gentleman yield for a question concerning a statement which was made before?

Mr. PATMAN. If it was made about me, or if I made it, I will yield.

Mr. McCULLOCH. I understood the gentleman from Texas to say that it would be illegal to advertise the sale of an item at below a fair-trade price in the State of Texas.

Mr. PATMAN. No; I meant for our people to advertise it to go over into a fair-trade State. If you will read page 3, at the bottom, it says advertise for sale or offer for sale. You cannot stop the reading of newspapers at the State line. You cannot stop television or radio at the State line. You cannot possibly do it. Yet, you are placing an impossible burden upon them, if I have correctly read the bill, which shows that the bill has not been carefully gone into. I will show you another illustration here. It says here in the Keogh bill that if one is charged with violating the law his defense could be that the person charged, or the person who fixed the prices, the manufacturer or producer, has failed to make a reasonable effort to insure compliance.

The CHAIRMAN. The time of the gentleman from Texas has expired.

Mr. PATMAN. Mr. Chairman, I ask unanimous consent to address the House for two additional minutes.

The CHAIRMAN. Is there objection to the request of the gentleman from Texas?
There was no objection.

Mr. PATMAN. Let me analyze that for just a minute. Suppose you are out here on the highway, where the speed limit is 50 miles an hour, and you are going 60 miles an hour, and the cop stops you. If you have the same law as they have proposed here in the Keogh bill you would say, "Mr. Cop, you cannot convict me unless you show that those fellows who have passed me—there they go up the road—unless you show that the law is enforced against them, too. You cannot enforce the law against me unless you make a reasonable effort to enforce the law against them. So turn me loose and go after these fellows who have passed me." That is the kind of defense they want. If you catch them red-handed violating the law they can say for a defense that there are other people violating the law, and you have not made a reasonable effort to stop them, and therefore you cannot convict them under this Keogh bill, unless you can show that you have made a reasonable effort to catch the other people who are also violating the law. It is almost on the ridiculous side. I am surprised that the great Committee on the Judiciary, great as it is, composed of fine Members of this House, some of the finest and most able Members of the House, would let that slip by. I know it slipped by, because it would never be deliberately put in in that way. But it is absolutely in here.

⊥ 4941

Now, another thing: Stop the newspapers at the State line. Stop the voice at the State line. It is a violation of the Federal law if you do not. So I ask you, if you are in favor of a fair-trade bill, one that will do a good job, one that the independent merchants of this country want, vote for the McGuire bill and vote down all of these amendments.

The CHAIRMAN. The time of the gentleman from Texas has again expired.

Mr. CRAWFORD. Mr. Chairman, I move to strike out the last word.

Mr. Chairman, I want to refer to the language on page 3 of the bill, H. R. 6925, lines 10 to 17. Let us see how ridiculous that language is. I think that is what the gentleman from Texas [Mr. PATMAN] just referred to.

Provided, however, That in the exercise or enforcement of any right or right of action as is exempted from the antitrust laws by this subsection, it shall be a complete defense to a charge of unfair competition for the defendant to show that the party prescribing the minimum prices has failed to make reasonable efforts to insure compliance, by those in competition with the defendant, with such prescribed minimum prices.

That is not referring to one retail competitor as related to another retail competitor. It is referring to the manufacturer or distributor who sets the minimum price. Let us see if it is so ridiculous.

My friend sits in front of me. He is a distributor. He sets a retail price under this bill for me to sell on. Then he goes to my competitor down the street or across town and he makes an agreement with him, and he gives him an extra case of goods as an inducement to pick up a new customer. He does not give me an extra case of goods. I am on a noncompetitive basis with my competitor who received the extra case of goods. Then the distributor comes to me and he wants to bring me into court and cause me trouble because I am not complying. Now, is it ridiculous to have language in this bill that protects me against that type of distributor? I do not think so. And if the gentleman from Texas [Mr. PATMAN] wants to answer that question, I will yield to him.

Mr. PATMAN. I am sorry. I did not hear the gentleman. I apologize.

Mr. CRAWFORD. I dislike to take the additional time to go into it, but I will let somebody else answer it later. I can show you sales records where some of these slick dudes pick up as high as $180 a car secret rebates. That is a fortune in big volume basic commodities. Twenty dollars a car is a fortune. But when you can pick up 30 or 40 cents or 10 cents per unit, with 600 units in a carload at 10 cents per unit, you will pick up $60 premium. At 20 cents you pick up $120 premium. If we want to protect the little retailers of this country, let us get some of these practices removed from the trade.

I think this language on page 3 should be included in whichever bill is adopted, whether it is the McGuire bill or the Keogh bill. Unless we put it in there we are not protecting the little retail merchant.

Now, going to the other phase of this. As I understand H. R. 5767, it is an amendment to the Federal Trade Commission Act. I want to ask the gentlemen who are supporting H. R. 5767, members of the committee, this question: Does H. R. 5767 remove from the statutes now on the books the $5,000 penalty and the 1-year prison sentence which is in the law?

Mr. HARRIS. Mr. Chairman, will the gentleman yield?

Mr. CRAWFORD. I yield.

Mr. HARRIS. It does not.

Mr. CRAWFORD. All right, then; why make a defense of the McGuire bill to the effect that it does not contain the $5,000 or 1-year penalty although the Keogh bill does contain it?

The Keogh bill is simply an amendment to the 1890 Sherman antitrust law, and it simply leaves what is now in the law with respect to the $5,000 fine and 1-year imprisonment penalties; so we are not changing that part of the law when we adopt either one of the bills. Is not that correct?

Mr. HARRIS. The gentleman is correct; we are not changing the law; neither does the penalty provision, and I respectfully disagree with the interpretation of the gentleman from Iowa; neither does the penalty provision provided in the Keogh bill or the McGuire bill.

Mr. CRAWFORD. I thank the gentleman. May I ask the gentleman another question? Going back to H. R. 5767, an amendment to the Federal Trade Commission Act, on page 4, legalizes the agreements made in the State and permits the producer or distributor to set the prices. That is correct, is it not?

Mr. HARRIS. That is right; yes.

The CHAIRMAN. The time of the gentleman from Michigan has expired.

(On request of Mr. HARRIS, and by unanimous consent, Mr. CRAWFORD was allowed to proceed for three additional minutes.)

Mr. CRAWFORD. Then, on page 5 of the bill, subparagraph (4), it is provided that the nonsigners of the contract must comply. That is correct, is it not?

Mr. HARRIS. That is true, but I would like to remind the gentleman that the Keogh bill has the same proviso.

Mr. CRAWFORD. I understand; I am not criticizing that now; I am just getting the thing clear.

Then in subparagraph (4) to which the gentleman from New York [Mr. CELLER] referred a while ago there is this interesting proviso. I do not know how far it goes; my study has not gone that far as yet.

(4) Neither the making of contracts or agreements as described in paragraph (2) of this subsection, nor the exercise or enforcement of any right or right of action as described in paragraph (3) of this subsection shall constitute an unlawful burden or restraint upon, or interference with, commerce.

We are amending the Federal Trade Act, and that language is thrown in there so as to say to us in substance that these States in regard to State agreements, that the performance shall not constitute an unlawful burden or restraint upon or interfere with interstate commerce. I think that is fairly well stated there.

Now, paragraph (5) reads:

Nothing contained in paragraph (2) of this subsection shall make lawful contracts or agreements providing for the establishment or maintenance of minimum or stipulated resale prices on any commodity referred to in paragraph (2) of this subsection, between manufacturers, or between producers, or between wholesalers, or between brokers, or between factors, or between retailers, or between persons, firms, or corporations in competition with each other.

That is to prevent combination in restraint of trade, as I understand.

Mr. HARRIS. Mr. Chairman, will the gentleman yield?

Mr. CRAWFORD. I yield to the gentleman; yes.

Mr. HARRIS. That is the second proviso under the Miller-Tydings Act; that is a restatement of present law.

Mr. CRAWFORD. And I think is very properly in the bill. Then, going back to the Keogh bill which is offered as a substitute, this bill amends the Sherman antitrust law as I understand; it O.K.'s the State statutes, limits the setting of these prices to owners, does not permit distributors to set the prices; while the Keogh bill does permit distributors to set prices, and the Keogh bill also provides for compliance on the part of nonsigners, and I think that is about the set-up that we face here.

Mr. CELLER. Mr. Chairman, I move to strike the usual number of words, and ask unanimous consent to proceed for five additional minutes.

The CHAIRMAN. Is there objection to the request of the gentleman from New York?

There was no objection.

Mr. CELLER. Mr. Chairman, I ask the members to turn to page 4 of the McGuire bill and read lines 7 to 10; most unusual provisions are contained therein.

That clause reads as follows:

It is the further purpose of this act to permit such statutes, laws, and public policies to apply to commodities, contracts, agreements, and activities in or affecting interstate or foreign commerce.

That provision was deliberately omitted from the Keogh bill. The Judiciary Committee refused to consider it.

Mr. PRIEST. Mr. Chairman, will the gentleman yield?

Mr. CELLER. I yield to the gentleman from Tennessee.

Mr. PRIEST. May I state to the gentleman that that language is the same language that is in the Federal Trade Act now. In that act commerce is defined as interstate and foreign. That is identically the same language.

Mr. CELLER. But its position here indicates an abdication of the power of Congress to regulate foreign commerce—vis-a-vis state resale price arrangements. If we pass this McGuire bill with the language as stated we hereby say to a State: You can empower in turn manufacturers to set prices for resale even where foreign commerce is involved. And that can be, for example, in contradiction to a treaty, it can be in violation of the reciprocity acts. So that in a way we abdicate our powers to the States over foreign commerce. If you want to approve such a barbarous provision as that, then pass the McGuire bill.

Mr. McCULLOCH. Mr. Chairman, will the gentleman yield?

Mr. CELLER. I yield to the gentleman from Ohio.

Mr. McCULLOCH. Is it a fact that the McGuire bill departs from the old Miller-Tydings Act to include foreign commerce, as indicated by the gentleman who is now speaking?

Mr. CELLER. Yes, that is correct. The Miller-Tydings Act had no relation to foreign commerce as in the case of the instant bill before us.

Mr. McCULLOCH. Therefore, if this provision be enacted into law, it will give the States more authority than they had under the Miller-Tydings Act?

Mr. CELLER. Beyond question that is so.

Mr. HARRIS. Mr. Chairman, will the gentleman yield?

Mr. CELLER. I yield to the gentleman from Arkansas.

Mr. HARRIS. As I understood the gentleman who propounded the question a moment ago, he said the McGuire bill amended the present law to include foreign commerce. I should like to call the gentleman's attention to the Sherman Act. The Miller-Tydings law, the present law, is an exception to section 1, which provides:

Every contract, combination, in the form of trust or otherwise, or conspiracy in restraint of commerce in the several States or with foreign nations.

If it is in the present law, then this makes no change whatever.

Mr. CELLER. But here you tie up signers as well as nonsigners under State laws, and thereby abrogate the power of Congress to control interstate as well as foreign commerce in that way. I cannot conceive that we would adopt such a provision.

Mr. HALLECK. Mr. Chairman, will the gentleman yield?

Mr. CELLER. I yield to the gentleman from Indiana.

Mr. HALLECK. The gentleman seems quite disturbed about the possibility that the States might gain some power at the expense of the Federal Government. I have been here for 17 years and I have observed this headlong rush of centralized authority and power until the States today are not much more than geographic boundaries. If there is something that can reestablish the authority of the States, so far as I am concerned, I am for it.

Mr. CELLER. The gentleman's statement is utterly irrelevant to the controversy involved in this legislation.

Mr. CRAWFORD. Mr. Chairman, will the gentleman yield?

Mr. CELLER. I yield to the gentleman from Michigan.

Mr. CRAWFORD. Is there anything in the Federal Constitution or in the statutes now on the books which gives the States the power to exercise control over foreign commerce?

Mr. CELLER. There is no such provision.

Mr. CRAWFORD. Will the gentleman tell us whether or not there is language in any statute at the present time similar to that which appears on page 4, lines 7 to 10, of the McGuire bill?

Mr. CELLER. I know of no such language tying it up to these retail price maintenance statutes or contracts.

Mr. CRAWFORD. In the Miller-Tydings Act or any other act.

Mr. CELLER. In addition, what is meant by "activities"? What is meant by "public policy"? Those are words which are difficult not only of comprehension but involve great difficulty in defining, and the courts would be hard put to it to unravel. It opens a pandora's box of confusion and chaos.

Furthermore, the McGuire bill gives the right—and this is most unusual—to trade associations to bring actions in the State or Federal courts for infractions of these resale price maintenance contracts. Now can you imagine what the Association of Retail Druggists would do in that regard? They have been very powerful. Their power has been manifested here right in this Chamber. There has been a tremendous lobby developed and directed against Members of the House. These organizations have been the subject of repeated indictment by the United States Government for coercion and for harassment and for undue interference and violations of our antitrust laws. Yet in a very cavalier manner we now seek to give to those organizations the right, in 45 States, to bring actions. Can you imagine the power that is inherent in granting to an organization of this sort the right to bring actions, the right to harass, the right to annoy and to trump up all manner and kinds of charges so that the retailer will be bent to the will of these powerful organizations? I defy any man to show me—and I think I am correct in this—any statute which gives similarly the right to such organizations to bring an action in the Federal or State courts. It is most unusual and dangerous.

Mr. MASON. Mr. Chairman, will the gentleman yield?

Mr. CELLER. I yield to the gentleman from Illinois.

Mr. MASON. I would like to know this: Does the McGuire bill provide for anything that the 45 States did not have, or at least, supposed they had, before the Supreme Court interfered with their rights?

Mr. CELLER. Oh, yes. The McGuire bill, for example, grants more power.

The McGuire bill does not give any more power than the State has over intrastate commerce, but you have interstate features here where the States are given considerable additional power, and I have indicated a situation where the State was given power over foreign commerce. That certainly gives them more than they have now if you pass the McGuire bill.

Furthermore, in the McGuire bill, unlike the Keogh bill, a vendee has a right to set a resale price; not only the manufacturer can set the price, but the wholesaler or distributor. The vendee can set the price. You may have more than one price set in a State, creating considerable confusion and difficulties to the retailers. You might permit, thereby, horizontal price fixing, which was inveighed against particularly by the gentleman from Texas [Mr. PATMAN]. Take the case of McKesson & Robbins;[3.61] they are a distributor in one sense but they also have their own trade-marked and branded products. As a trade-mark owner they could fix a price; as a distributor they could fix a price on a competing article, so that in a sense you would have horizontal price fixing as far as that particular distributor was concerned on several levels because he is also a packager and distributor of his own products which are in competition with similar products that he sells as a distributor for others. That is another provision that is contained in the McGuire bill and not in the Keogh bill.

The CHAIRMAN. The time of the gentleman from New York has expired.

(On request of Mr. MCMULLEN, and by unanimous consent, Mr. CELLER was allowed to proceed for three additional minutes.)

Mr. McMULLEN. Mr. Chairman, will the gentleman yield?

Mr. CELLER. I yield to the gentleman from Florida.

Mr. McMULLEN. I would like to get the benefit of the gentleman's views on lines 16, 17, and 18, page 4, of the McGuire bill which reads:

> Nothing contained in this act or in any of the antitrust acts shall render unlawful any contracts or agreements prescribing minimum or stipulated prices.

Mr. CELLER. That is another difference. I am very glad the gentleman pointed that out.

The Keogh bill does not provide for the maintenance of a stipulated price. A "stipulated" price means a ceiling. A "minimum" price means a floor. The Keogh bill is limited to minimum prices. It has nothing to do with stipulated prices. In some instances goods are sold so that the individual retailer cannot make a profit, and he wants the goods to be sold at a higher rate. That is the case, I understand, with Anacin. They set in some States a stipulated price beyond which the retailer cannot go, and he finds that the cost of his operations, merchandising, and rents is unduly high, so he wants to raise his price, but he dare not raise his price. Here again you have an additional burden superimposed upon the retailer, namely, a stipulated price in the McGuire bill as well as a minimum price, a floor as well as a ceiling. In the Keogh bill you have no such situations developed. The Miller-Tydings Act did not contain any provision for stipulated price.

There is one thing that annoys me considerably in this matter, and that is that if only one contract is made with one retailer as to retail price then, ipso facto, every single retailer who is a customer of that manufacturer is bound. That is what we call binding nonsigners. That provision, which was attempted by a distilling firm against a retailer in Louisiana, caused the Supreme Court very properly to say:

> That is not price fixing by contract or agreement; that is price fixing by compulsion. That is not following the path of consensual agreement; that is resort to coercion.[3.62]

I repeat, that type of coercion should not be contained in any kind of bill we adopt. It is contrary to the Anglo-American concept of jurisprudence. It is contrary to fair play. It is not fair trade. It is coercion pure and simple, unadulterated coercion.

It is interesting to note that the gentleman from Tennessee [Mr. PRIEST], our very beloved whip of the House, engaged in a colloquy before his committee with a man named Mr. Cawley. I will read it:

> Mr. PRIEST. Suppose that I am a retailer and I am in Tennessee and that I have a fair-trade contract with Miles Laboratories, and I am going to sell those products that I buy and I am, at least, not going below a minimum specified in this contract, and that Mr. HALE here—
>
> Another member of the committee—

[3.61] *See generally* United States v. McKesson & Robbins, Inc., 351 U.S. 305, 76 S. Ct. 937, 100 L. Ed. 1209 (1956), *infra* at 929.

[3.62] Schwegmann Bros. v. Calvert Distillers Corp., 341 U.S. 384, 388 (1951).

is a dealer who has not signed any contract, but he also has those products for sale, and he is a nonsigner. He would be forced, on a horizontal basis, at least, not to go below a certain minimum in the sale of the product.

So he has signed no contract to that effect. It seems to me that, actually, although maybe not legally, since it would come under the terms, we will say, of the Sherman Act, but, actually, it is in effect forcing on Mr. HALE a price fixing on a horizontal basis because he is horizontal from me as another retailer, although a nonsigner.

That, to me, is the most troublesome feature in this legislation, one that I thought over more and more, and I can easily see the legal explanation and yet it does not quite, to me, satisfy a sort of moral or ethical feeling that I have about it as being forced horizontal price fixing.

I share the perturbation of the gentleman from Tennessee. I think it immoral to bind an individual who has not signed, just as the gentleman from Tennessee felt that there was something immoral, or shall I say unjust, if not barbarous, about that type of coercion.

Mr. HARRIS. Mr. Chairman, will the gentleman yield?

Mr. CELLER. I yield to the gentleman from Arkansas.

Mr. HARRIS. I understood the gentleman was speaking in behalf of the Keogh bill as a substitute for the McGuire bill.

Mr. CELLER. At this point I want to say my general remarks are addressed against this type of legislation.

Mr. HARRIS. The gentleman is for the Keogh bill, then?

Mr. CELLER. When the time comes the gentleman will see my vote in that regard.

I am in general opposed to all legislation of this coercive type. I feel it brings in its train far more evils than the evils that are sought to be evaded. If I have a pain in my leg, I do not amputate the leg. This is amputation without trying to cure the pain. Let us cure the pain by getting after loss leaders only and purely and simply. Let us get after loss leaders. They are the cause of the pain. Remove the cause. Do not cut off the leg.

This is far more than enabling legislation, as the proponents of the bill claim it is. This is clearly legislation designed to repeal an important segment of our antitrust laws. This is an abrogation of power granted by the Constitution to the Federal Government, namely, the control of interstate and foreign commerce. The States have never had the power to control interstate commerce and Congress, through the enactment of the Sherman Act, has laid down what Chief Justice Hughes has called a charter of economic freedom. Today the proponents of so-called fair-trade legislation are asking this Congress to revoke in part this charter of our economic freedom so that, as the Supreme Court has said, recalcitrants can be dragged in by the heels under legislation which would legalize price fixing in interstate commerce through the device of binding nonsigners.

Who are the manufacturers in whose favor the independent seller is now forced, by this legislation, to abrogate one of the few of his remaining privileges, that of freely and independently pricing his merchandise? A recent study conducted by the American Fair Trade Council showed that among those companies which fair trade all or part of their products were 51 of the 100 largest national advertisers using newspapers, periodicals, and/or radio. These are many of the concerns among the giants of American industry and include such well-known companies as Sterling Drug, Inc., Firestone Tire & Rubber Co., Westinghouse Electric Corp., E. I. du Pont de Nemours & Co., General Electric Co., Eastman Kodak Co., Colgate-Palmolive-Peet Co., International Silver Co., General Motors Corp., Procter & Gamble Co., and Lever Bros. Co. Included in the membership of the American Fair Trade Council which drafted, authored, and sponsored the Keogh bill, H. R. 6925, were a subsidiary of the Aluminum Corp. of America, Miles Laboratories, Inc., Minnesota Mining & Manufacturing Co., Olin Industries, Inc., Stewart-Warner Corp., and the Goodyear Tire & Rubber Co.

Do proponents of this legislation seriously believe that it is in the interest of small business to permit large manufacturers such as those listed above to determine the retail level of their prices throughout each of the 45 States in the Union having resale price-maintenance laws, and to allow such companies to dictate prices to every independent outlet in these areas? The retail outlet of today has already gone far on the road toward becoming a mere outlet for the distribution of the manufacturers' wares to the consumer. Nothing can sooner hasten the day when the independence of the small retailer will exist in name only than to place one of the principal competitive weapons at his disposal, the pricing policies, in the hands of his large supplier.

If this bill were really in the interests of small business and the independent druggists and other merchants, I would really give it my earnest support. I have been one of the strongest supporters of small business in the Congress. But these small retailers are just being utilized as a front by a number of large manufacturers who are vitally concerned that the fair-trade bills be enacted in order to insure their big profits obtained at the expense of the consumer.

While it is true that many other industries fair-trade their products, the great majority of resale price-maintenance agreements occur in the drug and cosmetic industry. We have no record of the number of such price-fixing agreements in effect throughout the Nation, but in the one State where some count of the number of contracts in force is available, the State of Utah, out of 552 contracts filed with the State, 441 of them—or some 80 percent—appertained to drugs and cosmetics. It is probable that similar percentages prevail in other areas.

Now, why have these drug, pharmaceutical, and cosmetic manufacturers been so eager to adopt fair trade? Why do they lurk in the background while the small retailer is used as a convenient front to enact fair-trade legislation? Why was the chairman of the board of the Sterling Drug Co. one of the original drafters of the Miller-Tydings Act? Why was the McGuire bill drawn up by lawyers representing manufacturers in the drug field?

One look at the cost and profit figures of these large producers on fair-trade items sold under brand names will clearly reveal why these big corporations are so covetous of their fair-trade returns.

Let us take Bayers aspirin for example. This product is manufactured by the Sterling Drug Co., a corporation which has been indicted and fined under the antitrust laws for engaging in a world-wide cartel to apportion the sale of pharmaceuticals. Now, the Bureau of Labor Statistics prepared some figures which appear in TNEC—Temporary National Economic Committee—Monograph No. 1 which showed that at the wholesale level, the price of acetylsalicylic acid was 13 cents an ounce while the wholesale price of the identical substance sold under the Bayer aspirin trade-mark was 75 cents an ounce. In other words, the consumer paid 62 cents or 82.7 percent more for the identical substance because it had the name Bayer attached to it. I will let you figure for yourself the large profits which the Sterling Drug Co. has obtained because, by attaching the trade-mark Bayer to its product, it is then permitted under fair-trade to fix a price of 75 cents for the identical commodity which sells for only 13 cents without fair trade.

This same study by economists of the Bureau of Labor Statistics showed similar mark-ups because fair trade permitted trade-mark owners to fix prices far out of proportion to the costs of manufacture. For example, it showed that while the retail cost of the ingredients in Coty's rouge refill was .037, the retail price under the brand name ⊥ was .38—a difference of over 1,000 percent. The ingredients at retail for Coty's special astringent cost .071, but the consumer paid $1—an increase of 1,400 percent.

⊥ 4944

Is it any wonder, therefore, that Mr. Lewis G. Bernstein, counsel for Coty, Inc., testified before the Priest committee in favor of this bill? Why did he say Coty's wanted fair trade? Well, the reason he gave the committee was to protect the little retailer and the consumer. He said, and I quote:

> The small independent retailer, which in the main, in our industry, means the small drug stores and the consumers, are the ones most seriously hurt by lack of fair trade.

Now Coty's solicitude for the small retailer and for the consumer is indeed touching when viewed in light of what I have said before. But Coty's real reasons for preferring fair trade are reflected in the above figures and its counsel's statement before the Priest committee that—

> If it had not been for fair trade, Coty would not be the great name today that it is.

As its counsel further described the economic strength of Coty because of fair trade:

> Coty is about the largest producer and distributor of cosmetics and perfume products in the United States and Coty products throughout the world.

Now, I have nothing against Coty—in fact my wife buys its perfume and likes it very much. But I do want to make it clear to this House that fair trade is not a small-business measure but one designed to aid the large manufacturers such as this concern which admits that it is the largest producer of cosmetics in the United States.

Let us see how fair trade helps another small business—Lever Bros.—in obtaining high profits at the expense of the consumer. One of its subsidiaries produces Harriet Hubbard Ayer products. Now, the same study by the economists of the Bureau of Labor Statistics, to which I referred before, revealed that the retail cost of ingredients which comprised Harriet Hubbard Ayer face powder was 0.066 but the retail price to the consumer was 0.60 or an increase of almost 1,000 percent. Harriet Hubbard Ayer's cream rouge cost the consumer 0.55 while the retail cost of the ingredients was only 0.038—a difference of about 1,500 percent.

Mr. Chairman, I wish to say again that I have nothing against these manufacturers. But there is no doubt that they are the ones who will benefit from this legislation, which now passes under the guise of a small-business bill. This is a big-business bill; it is big business which supports it, and it is big business who will profit from it at the expense of the consumer.

Now, Mr. Chairman, just how badly is the McGuire bill needed? While certain competitive pricing practices, occurring in both fair-trade and non-fair-trade areas, have occasioned considerable concern—and these we shall advert to at length at a later time—there has been no showing whatever that resale price maintenance is necessary to protect the independent retail outlets of the United States. In fact, the converse has proven true—retailing has thrived and prospered in areas not covered by fair trade.

In the retail drug field, for example, the Federal Business Census in 1948 showed that only 10 States in the Union had more than 1,000 drug stores with fountains serving their populace. Among these were Texas, a non-fair-trade State, which ranked fourth with 1,926 retail drug stores containing fountains, and Missouri, another non-fair-trade area, which ranked ninth with 1,191 stores. According to the same census there were only nine States of the Union with total drug store sales amounting to more than $100,000,000. Among these States, Texas, without fair trade, ranked fifth with $162,404,000 in sales volume, and Missouri, also without fair trade, ranked ninth with a sales volume of $103,757,000. Insofar as drug stores without fountains are concerned, the non-fair-trade States of Texas and Missouri, according to 1948 business census figures, ranked seventh and ninth, respectively.

In total number of drug and proprietary stores together, Texas, without benefit of fair trade, was fourth in the United States, according to 1948 business census figures, while Missouri ranked eighth. Texas led all States in the total number of proprietary stores while the State of Missouri, in fair trade's absence, had more drug and proprietary stores in 1948 than did the fair-trading States of Montana, Idaho, Wyoming, Colorado, New Mexico, Arizona, Utah and Nevada combined.

The sales volume of the average retail drug store in the United States during 1948 was $78,340. Leading all States of the Union in that year was the District of Columbia, a non-fair-trade area, where the average retail drug store's sales volume totaled $171,769.

A comparison of bankruptcies in retail drug stores occurring in non-fair-trade States with those resulting in surrounding fair-trade areas also shows that absence of fair trade has not resulted in the destruction of independent business. The American Druggist in a recent issue observed that "In 1948, failure per 1,000 drug stores in fair-trade States were almost exactly the same as for those in non-fair-trade States." Studies made for the Federal Trade Commission in 1947 by the firm of Dun & Bradstreet, also reveals that non-fair-trade jurisdiction have frequently fared much better in this regard than their fair-trading counterparts [sic].

If the druggists or any other retailing group really believe this bill essential, let them hark to the excellent advice appearing in the June 1951 issue of the American Druggist. Said this prominent journal in the drug field:

> Before any fair dealing retailer assumes that he is washed up, let him be aware that although fair trade created a more stable market for well-known products, there is no evidence that it kept any druggist in business who would otherwise have failed. Loss of fair trade will not drive any druggist out of business if he serves the public better than his competitors, not by meeting crazy prices, but by better display of goods and more friendly personal attention to every customer.
>
> We have heard it said that this court opinion means the end of drug stores. That is poppycock. This Nation likes its drug stores—especially those that still look like drug stores. Before any fair-trade laws were enacted, there were just as many drug stores as there are today. And they suffered some of the worst price wars that ever happened.
>
> To succeed without fair trade is a little harder, but it is not impossible. Now, is the time to stand up and fight for business—as the druggists of Vermont, Missouri, Texas, and the District of Columbia have always had to do.

Mr. [ALBERT P.] MORANO [R., Conn.]. Mr. Chairman, I move to strike out the last word.

Mr. Chairman, I rise in opposition to the Keogh bill. I am in general agreement with the McGuire bill, and will support that bill.

Mr. Chairman, I made a national radio broadcast last week, and I ask unanimous consent to revise and extend my remarks and include a copy of that radio address.

The CHAIRMAN. Is there objection to the request of the gentleman from Connecticut?

There was no objection.

(The address referred to is as follows:)

Mr. Chairman, one morning in May 1951, the good people of New York picked up their morning papers and found emblazoned in two-page bold-faced advertisements wonderous values in name-brand products offered for sale in a New York department store.

Here were offered prices on utilities, typewriters, clothing, drugs, furniture, and other commodities, unheard of since the depression days. And to the value-wise consumer, the wonder of it all was that these products offered were all well-known brands, heretofore sold at one standard price.

The rest is history. The response was terrific. Hordes of bargain-hungry shoppers stormed the gates of the department store. Business was tremendous at this particular store. Naturally sales fell off in other stores carrying the same merchandise at the standard set prices.

The next day another large department store, not to be outdone, announced a similar policy on name-brand merchandise. Their experience was similar to that of the first department store.

In a few days the lid was off. The large New York department stores were cutting each other's prices. The price war was on, and in some instances hourly reductions were being made.

The price-war fever spread from New York to large department stores throughout the country. These stores were stampeded with purchasers. The smaller stores, maintaining the price standards on name-brand products, found more and more of their customers being lured away to take advantage of the bargains being offered in the larger stores. Thousands upon thousands foresaw bankruptcy and a dead-end to their dreams of security in their own little businesses.

The price war was brought on by the Supreme Court decision on May 21, 1951, that the immunity granted by Congress in the Miller-Tydings Act does not extend to the maintenance of prices against retailers who are not parties to specific contracts.

The large department store which drastically slashed prices on formerly standard-priced articles had never signed a fair-trade contract—therefore when the Supreme Court ruled that the Miller-Tydings Act was not binding on nonsigners, this department store ⊥ proceeded to cut into the prices of price-fixed merchandise in order to lure customers into the store.

⊥ 4945

The effect on the signers of fair-trade contracts and on stores not able to sell articles at cost—and in some cases below costs—was disastrous. The effect on the manufacturers of the articles was equally bad.

Something had to be done to bring about some semblance of sanity from this chaotic economic mess which was spreading throughout the country.

I introduced a bill which proposed to amend the Sherman Antitrust Act to permit contracts between suppliers and retailers and wholesalers to hold up in courts, and to bind nonsigners who sell similar trade-marked merchandise to conform to the price standards accepted by the contract signers.

I introduced this amendment on June 29, 1951, as a result of the economic chaos brought on by the Supreme Court decision on May 21, 1951, ruling that the immunity granted by the Congress in the Miller-Tydings Act does not extend to the maintenance of prices against retailers who are not parties to specific contracts. This decision rendered the nonsigner provisions of State laws null and void as applied to interstate commerce.

My proposed amendment would make effective the congressional policy which 15 years ago resulted in the Miller-Tydings amendment to the Sherman Antitrust Act. With no coercive power behind it, the fair-trade exemption carved out from the Sherman Act in 1937 merely removed Federal obstacles to the enforcement of contracts which the States themselves had declared lawful. The decision of the Supreme Court in the *Schwegmann Brothers* v. *Calvert Corp.* case defeated the purposes of the Miller-Tydings amendment. It is to remedy the judicial limitation imposed and to permit effectively the public policy of the State fair-trade acts to operate that my amendment was introduced.

It must be noted that all of the Federal legislation concerning fair-trade contracts rests on the fundamental premise that the merits or defects of fair-trade laws are not the primary concern of Congress. The economic evils of cut-throat competition and loss-leader selling demand a remedy, and the State legislatures, being most susceptible to the will of the people and most familiar with local and regional economic problems, are the proper forum to determine the nature of the remedy. That this was clearly recognized when the Miller-Tydings amendment was passed, is demonstrated in the words of one sponsor, Senator Tydings:

"What we have attempted to do is what 42 States have already written on their statute books. It is simply to back up those acts, that is all: to have a code of fair-trade practices written not by a national board such as the N. R. A. but by each State, so that the people may go to the State legislature and correct immediately any abuses that may develop."

Today, 45 of the 48 State legislatures have recognized the fair-trade contract as the best solution to the complex problem of balancing the best interests of consumer, distributor, and manufacturer. The congressional permission giving to these fair-trade laws the same effect over interstate commerce as the States permit over intrastate commerce has, as a result of recent decisions, become a permission in name only. Every one of the 45 States adopting fair-trade laws has recognized the complete inadequacy of enforcement against signers only. Every one of the 45 fair-trade laws contains, in some form, a nonsigner provision. As demonstrated by experience in California, the pioneer fair-trade State, an act without the nonsigner clause is futile. The very competitors whose loss-leader selling has created the necessity for fair-trade laws are immune from the operation of the law unless they sign a fair-trade contract. A fair-trade law enforceable only against those reputable merchants willing to sign fair-trade contracts is an empty gesture. Yet the Supreme Court has, through its interpretation of the Miller-Tydings amendment, excluded enforcement against nonsigners from the fair-trade exemption carved out of the antitrust laws.

The policy that 45 of the States has chosen as the best economic solution is effectively frustrated. All a merchant need do today to evade the law of his State is to attempt to cloak himself in the immunity of interstate commerce, leaving him free to flaunt the fair-trade laws and destroy a reputable commodity through use as a loss-leader. The fair-trade exemption must be clarified by Congress in order to obviate the effects of the recent judicial decisions. The nature of our Federal system demands that the 48 States should be permitted to choose for themselves whether or not to adopt fair-trade laws. Forty-five States have so chosen but the express will of the people of those States will be frustrated unless Congress gives practical effect to the verbal permission in the Miller-Tydings Act. My proposed amendment would do this and nothing more. It would not force a fair-trade law on any State but merely prevents the laws already enacted by 45 States from languishing on the statute books, incapable of enforcement in any situation involving interstate commerce.

The entire function of Federal laws concerning fair trade, serving merely as enabling legislation, makes any discussion of the merits of fair-trade laws irrelevant. Nevertheless, recognition of the necessity for action concerning the economic evils involved in cutthroat competition impels congressional action to render the State laws effective. The evil effects of cutthroat competition are clearly apparent in the case of a manufacturer and a small retailer. The manufacturer's most important property right, the value of his product, is threatened by its use as a loss-leader. The small retailer, unable to continue selling below cost as long as the big chains and department stores, faces extinction. The effect of this not only on the retailers involved, but on the national economy is apparent from the records of the Treasury Department, indicating that these small retailers paid a large percentage of the billions of dollars collected in corporation profits. The loss of this revenue, particularly when the cost of running our Government and our military program is ever increasing, will put an even greater tax burden on the consumer. For the greatest sufferer is the one who at first seems to be the sole beneficiary of a price war, the consumer. Once the ruthless and unfair methods of cutthroat competition have destroyed competition, the laws of supply and demand can no longer protect the consumer from artificially and destructively high prices. The consumer, lured into the store, purchases unneeded and unnecessary articles, initiating the very spiral of hoarding and inflation that our Government is now seeking to prevent and defeat. In the words of one of the great justices, Mr. Justice Brandeis, of the very Court which today has rendered fair-trade laws ineffective, "Far-reaching organized capital secures by this means the cooperation of the short-sighted unorganized consumer to his own undoing."

The fair-trade exemption in the Miller-Tydings Act and pending amendments making it effective permit the individual States to protect the consumer, retailer, and manufacturer from the evils of cutthroat competition, and in no way commits the Congress to a national policy. The seriousness of the economic problem has commanded action by the States. Only immediate action by Congress can prevent the complete inefficacy of State enforcement of the fair-trade laws, with the inevitable chaos of unrestrained cutthroat competition.

The fair-trade issue will shortly be brought before Congress. In hearings before the House Committee on the Judiciary, my bill and others were considered. Finally, the committee, cognizant of the fact that restoration of the law permitting resale-price maintenance to operate effectively was necessary to achieve protection for small and independent retailers and for manufacturers of trade-marked products, recommended that fair-trade legislation be considered by Congress and reported out its own bill, H. R. 6925.

Previously the Interstate and Foreign Commerce Committee had reported out H. R. 5767, a bill designed for the same purpose, but written as an amendment to the Federal Trade Commission Act.

Discussion of these bills on the House floor will add greatly to the Washington heat already beginning to envelop us.

But it is my hope that my colleagues will be mindful of the conclusions reached by the House Select Committee on Small Business, which concluded:

"The events of the past year in the field of fair trade have been of grave concern to your committee. In particular, the Schwegmann decision and the ensuing price wars were viewed as matters of tremendous import to small business. Had the price wars continued, they could have done incalculable harm to countless small businesses. The memory of the early 1930's and the great numbers of small independent concerns that were then lost to the economy directly as a result of similar price wars is still fresh. The possibility is strong that the damage to fair trade wrought by the Schwegmann decision might well precipitate similar business failures should our economy suffer a sudden reversal. * * * It is not only the small independent merchant who suffers in a price war. The manufacturer and the consumer also suffer.

"And the leaders of price-cutting campaigns should realize that injury to other segments of the retail trade cannot benefit them. Gains realized from loss-leader selling are short-lived. The practice is a vicious one and defeats itself. No merchant, no matter how large, can afford to continue loss-leader selling indefinitely. He must engage in other practices in order to recoup his losses. And such other practices of necessity require that he sell other merchandise at high profits. The consumer must sooner or later discover the fallacy of the loss-leader-selling technique, and then the retailer loses the good will of his customer and their patronage. The good sense and recognition of their responsibilities should impel the overwhelming mass of the business community to the logic and wisdom of fair trade."

Mr. JAVITS. Mr. Chairman, I rise in opposition to the pro forma amendment.

Mr. Chairman, yesterday I served notice in the discussion on the rule that I would submit an amendment which sought to hew to the middle ground between satisfying the needs of the retailers and the needs of consumers. That amendment, in a word, would take the provision to which the gentleman from Texas [Mr. PATMAN] referred—that an item which is fair-trade priced had to be in competition with similar items—and expand that not only to similar items that are fair-trade priced but to similar items which are not fair-trade priced. I think the consumer needs that protection.

I just want to inform the Committee that I think it would be a mistake and would jeopardize my amendment, which ⊥ I think is very important, to introduce it at this stage and get it into this difficulty between two bills and two committees. So I shall refrain from introducing it. I do not intend to support the substitute until the McGuire bill is up for consideration, as I believe the House can work its full will on the terms and conditions on the McGuire bill.

⊥ 4946

Mr. PRIEST. Mr. Chairman, I ask unanimous consent that all debate on the pending substitute amendment, and all amendments thereto, close in 15 minutes.

Mr. CELLER. Mr. Chairman, reserving the right to object, will that involve the substitute which I will offer in the event that the Keogh substitute is defeated?

Mr. PRIEST. The request was only to the substitute which is pending, of course.

The CHAIRMAN. Is there objection to the request of the gentleman from Tennessee?

There was no objection.

Mr. HARRIS. Mr. Chairman, as one Member who has endeavored to give a great deal of attention and study to this very technical and difficult problem, I want to express my appreciation for the manner in which this debate has been conducted in order that the issues involved here might be brought to the attention of the House. I do want to say, however, I have somewhat of an aversion to many of the things that have been said. I think we should not get away from the basic problems that we seek to reach here with this legislation. There have been many things and many contentions thrown here in the debate, which, in my opinion, have for their purpose to deliberately confuse the issue that we are trying to settle. Everyone, I believe, recognizes that both bills before us now, the McGuire bill and the so-called Keogh substitute, offered by the distinguished gentleman from the Committee on the Judiciary, the gentleman from Illinois [Mr. REED], does get to the problem brought about by the Schwegmann case.

The additional issue that we try to reach is the problem that is brought about by the Wentling case. I yield to any member of the Committee on the Judiciary if they disagree with that statement.

Now, that being true, the problem that we must decide in trying to reach this issue is whether or not we are going to stick to the basic concept of enabling legislation in recognizing the States, or whether or not we are going to adopt a Federal fair-trade policy.

Mr. ROGERS of Colorado. Mr. Chairman, will the gentleman yield?

Mr. HARRIS. I yield briefly.

Mr. ROGERS of Colorado. Do I understand you to contend that under the McGuire bill the Federal Government would not be involved in any manner whatsoever?

Mr. HARRIS. I contend that all the McGuire bill does is to recognize the action of the States to legislate on this subject.

Mr. ROGERS of Colorado. But does it amend the Federal Trade Commission Act?

Mr. HARRIS. Yes; it does.

Mr. ROGERS of Colorado. Do you not concede in the Federal Trade Commission Act—

Mr. HARRIS. I get what the gentleman is after. My time is very limited and I cannot yield further. It does not set up a Federal fair-trade policy; it does not establish a Federal defense; nor does it establish a Federal cause of action; neither does it permit the Federal Trade Commission to become involved. Now, if you have any doubt about it, this being an amendment to the Federal Trade Commission law, let us see what the Chairman of the Federal Trade Commission said in a letter addressed to the gentleman from Tennessee [Mr. PRIEST]:

April 4, 1952.

Hon. J. Percy Priest,
Chairman, Subcommittee on Federal Trade Commission,
Committee on Interstate and Foreign Commerce,
House of Representatives, Washington, D. C.

DEAR MR. PRIEST: Reference is made to your letter of March 21, 1952, regarding H. R. 5767 and H. R. 6925, as reported by the Committees on Interstate and Foreign Commerce and on the Judiciary, respectively, and the request in your letter for a statement of the views of this Commission as to whether or not these bills, or either of them, might be construed to empower the Commission to proceed against persons who offer for sale or sell merchandise in interstate commerce below the price fixed in a resale price maintenance contract, and your request for any suggested amendments which would prevent such a construction.

Neither of these bills contains any language which either directs or specifically authorizes any action by this Commission. This still leaves open, however, a substantial question. Briefly stated, this question is whether or not, if the Congress establishes a policy which in effect declares that the selling of merchandise in interstate commerce at prices lower than those fixed in resale price maintenance contracts is an act of "unfair competition," such acts are then an "unfair method of competition" or "unfair * * * acts or practices" within the meaning of these terms as contained in section 5 (a) of the Federal Trade Commission Act.

In the case of H. R. 5767, the policy it would establish appears to be negative rather than affirmative. That is, the bill provides exceptions to the provisions of laws which would otherwise apply. The bill does not make the offering for sale or selling of merchandise at prices less than those fixed by resale price maintenance contracts an act of unfair competition under Federal law. In this setting the Commission believes that any argument that this bill would empower it to proceed against persons who sell merchandise in interstate commerce below the price fixed in a resale price maintenance contract would be quite tenuous. While it would be preferable in further minimizing such an argument, if the provisions concerning resale price maintenance were inserted at the end of the present section 5 (a) of the Commission act instead of between the first and second sentence of that section, as is now the case, the possibility of such an argument prevailing seems so remote as not to warrant suggesting any amendment.

In the case of H. R. 6925, however, subsection (d) of section 1 makes it an "act of unfair competition" under Federal law to offer for sale or sell, have transported for sale or resale, or deliver merchandise at prices less than those fixed by resale price maintenance contracts. This permits a persuasive argument that the act of unfair competition thus defined also constitutes a violation of section 5 (a) of the Commission act. The possibility of such a construction prevailing is believed to be sufficient to warrant an amendment to the bill.

The first sentence of subsection (d) of section 1 of H. R. 6925 now reads in part as follows:

"(d) Whenever by contract or agreement described in subsection (b) minimum resale prices may be established for a commodity in any State, Territory, or the District of Columbia, where such a contract or agreement is lawful, it shall be an act of unfair competition, actionable at the suit of any person damaged thereby, to wilfully and knowingly, in interstate commerce. [. . .]"

It is believed that the possibility of this Commission sustaining any action under the bill would be eliminated by amending the language quoted above to read as follows:

"(d) Whenever by contract or agreement described in subsection (b) minimum resale prices may be established for a commodity in any State, Territory, or the District of Columbia, where such contract or agreement is lawful, it shall be an act of unfair competition and actionable exclusively at the suit of any person damaged thereby, to wilfully and knowingly, in interstate commerce, * * *"

As stated in reports made to your committee and to the Committee on the Judiciary upon the various bills to authorize resale price maintenance, the Commission is strongly opposed to any such legislation. The comments submitted herewith in response to your request should not be construed as indicating any change in the Commission's views respecting such legislation.

By direction of the Commission.

Sincerely yours,

Jas. M. Mead,
Chairman.

Therefore, unless you provide an amendment to the Keogh bill, the Commission would be authorized to proceed under the Keogh bill. Consequently the Keogh bill gives to a bureau in the Federal Government authority to come before you and ask for funds in order that the provisions of the Keogh bill may be carried out.

Mr. ROGERS of Colorado. Mr. Chairman, will the gentleman yield?

Mr. HARRIS. I have only a short time.

The question of stipulated prices is one that has been brought in here. It is not the maximum price, as the gentleman said a moment ago. No one who does not volunteer to enter into an agreement can be proceeded against for anything except selling at less than the established price.

The Keogh bill is based on an altogether different concept than the McGuire bill, notwithstanding what they say. What we do in the McGuire bill is to give the States authority to correct existing situations with respect to predatory price practices. I say to you, if we adopt this substitute bill, we will be taking on a Federal fair-trade policy.

The CHAIRMAN. The time of the gentleman from Arkansas has expired.

The Chair recognizes the gentleman from North Carolina [Mr. DURHAM].

Mr. DURHAM. I do not think it is necessary for me to take up much time after the explanation given by the gentleman from Arkansas. He always makes a plain explanation of measures so one can understand the bill. If you adopt this amendment which we are considering here at the present time, you are going to place 1,700,000 little small-business people under the jurisdiction of the Federal courts. The little-business man should not be subject to the Federal courts. It is expensive; he has got to pay larger lawyer fees and is much more expensive than State courts.

The other thing that is somewhat confused here is the fact that the McGuire bill does not force anybody to do one thing. Unless the manufacturer goes into the State and says "I want to put my article under fair trade"—if he does not do it he is still in the free commerce of the country and the retailer can sell it for any price.

If you adopt this Keogh amendment, you will place all business on a Federal basis where he can be told he has got to do it. That is just the main difference, as I see it.

So let us not force the little-business man to go into the Federal courts with every little thing that happens, because when a Federal inspector goes out he usually gets his man into court, for any trivial violation.

Another thing that has been somewhat confused is the fact also that the Keogh amendment nullifies the Sherman Act. I have never heard the gentleman from New York down here before advocating that we do away with laws to let monopolies run free, but that is exactly the situation he put himself in here when he argued that point.

The McGuire amendment amends the Federal Trade Act and does not amend the Sherman Act. That is another difference.

Let us not adopt this Keogh amendment. I am speaking here personally as a little-business man; I have experienced this and know what it will do to the little grocery store and the little drug store. They are already harassed with all kinds of taxes, and even the little drug store today has to take about half of the space of one side wall to tack up the permits to do business under Federal laws. For goodness sake, let us not put him in the position of having to go to the Federal courts; let this thing operate in the States. Forty-five States have adopted it; we should let them run it. Vote down the amendment and then let us adopt the McGuire bill.

The CHAIRMAN. The Chair recognizes the gentleman from Ohio [Mr. SCHENCK].

Mr. [PAUL F.] SCHENCK [R., Ohio]. Mr. Chairman, it would seem to me that we are letting ourselves become involved in some hair-splitting legalities. No other question has precipitated so much concern in my district among the small-business men, who form the very backbone of our economy. My mail has been very heavy from this group, from grocers, druggists, hardwaremen, and many other small-business men. I have sent copies of both the McGuire bill, the Keogh bill, and all pertinent information to the small-business men in my district. They have examined these things very, very carefully and have gone over them with their own attorneys. They have come to the unanimous conclusion that they want the McGuire bill as it is written now, without any amendments whatsoever.

The CHAIRMAN. The Chair recognizes the gentleman from Ohio [Mr. REAMS].

Mr. [FRAZIER] REAMS [I., Ohio]. Mr. Chairman, I rise in support of the McGuire bill and to oppose the Keogh amendment.

Mr. Chairman, when the United States Supreme Court ruled that State laws permitting the enforcement of minimum prices on brand merchandise were not binding on merchants who do not sign such an agreement, I made a public statement that I would sponsor or support a bill to enable the States to support such a regulation. Under these laws which had been adopted by 45 States all retailers selling brand merchandise were bound by an announced agreement between the manufacturer and any one of them.

The immediate effect of this Supreme Court decision was a wave of price wars with each merchant attempting to undersell the other. This did much damage to the small businessmen who could not afford "loss-leaders" as a come-on to attract customers. Only the very large firms profited by these price wars.

Believing that the merchant on the corner in our American neighborhoods is in many ways the cornerstone of our free enterprise and the community institution, I have, ever since this Supreme Court decision was announced, sought to aid in the passing of a bill to restore to the States the right to regulate fair trade on the State level.

Therefore, I am enthusiastically in support of the McGuire bill, H. R. 5767.

The Keogh bill, in my judgment, is not a substitute for the McGuire bill. It is a bill which would create Federal regulation of fair trade. It is an enabling bill calling for no appropriation but, undoubtedly, it would, if passed, be followed by an appropriation bill to implement it. I would estimate that to enforce the Keogh bill as a law $1,000,000 a year would be spent. The Keogh bill would produce a law which sets up a new enforcement body and new penalties to be policed by the Federal Government. It would forbid any person to advertise or offer for sale any fair trade article in interstate commerce.

The McGuire bill, H. R. 5767, on the other hand, gives the State the right to have a fair trade law and the responsibility of enforcing such if it is passed.

There are undoubtedly some members in each of three categories with reference to this matter. In the first group are those who do not want any regulation at all. They favor the very large stores which can afford to lose money on leading brands and nationally advertised items in order to draw customers who will make up for these losses in the purchase of other articles. The second group are those who want the Federal Government to extend itself further into private business by a fair trade law which would place the responsibility for enforcement and supervision of fair trade laws and practices on the Federal Government. The third group, and the one in which I fall, are those who favor the McGuire bill because it does protect the small-business man, the corner grocer and druggist, and because it leaves all regulation and enforcement of this fair trade law with the individual States. These States do not have to adopt such a law if they do not want to.

Texas, Missouri, Vermont, and the District of Columbia have not, as yet, adopted fair-trade laws. The other 45 States do have them and want the right to enforce them. This, in my judgment, is as it should be. I believe that we have reached the place where we should not burden the central government here in Washington with more bureaus, more power and more regulation of the individual.

I believe in and support the McGuire bill, H. R. 5767.

The CHAIRMAN. The Chair recognizes the gentleman from Tennessee [Mr. PRIEST].

Mr. PRIEST. Mr. Chairman, first of all I want to refer to the colloquy mentioned by the distinguished gentleman from New York [Mr. CELLER] which occurred during the hearings, in which I was quoted, and properly quoted.

May I say that in the beginning of this study I had some very grave doubts in my mind about the nonsigner clause; but the more I studied the question the more I came to the conclusion that if we are to provide adequate protection to the small independent businessman in this country, particularly if any sort of business recession develops, we must have the nonsigner clause to make fair trade laws effective. I was properly quoted and, as I say, I had some grave doubts about it at the time, but I became convinced as the hearings proceeded and the more we heard testimony from small dealers that had been squeezed by price wars in some of our larger cities.

Mr. Chairman, in this closing minute of debate on the substitute, I simply want again to say that, in my opinion, we need legislation of this character, we need that legislation, as I see it, without making it a Federal policy.

We need legislation that will permit the States' fair trade laws to operate as they did operate from 1937 until May 1951, when the Supreme Court ruled in the Schwegmann case. We need that law, in my opinion, as soon as possible.

I believe the bill reported by the Committee on Interstate and Foreign Commerce amending the Federal Trade Act is the best possible legislative approach to the problem and I say that with great respect for all members of the great Committee on the Judiciary. I hope very much that the Committee will vote down the substitute and proceed, then, to approve the bill known as the McGuire bill, H. R. 5767.

Mr. COLE of Kansas. Mr. Chairman, will the gentleman yield?

Mr PRIEST. I yield to the gentleman from Kansas.

Mr. COLE of Kansas. The gentleman from New York commented upon the fact that nonsigners were bound by the signature of one who was not a member ⊥ of that ⊥ 4948 contract. May I point out, and ask the gentleman whether he agrees with me, that the nonsigner is not bound because he is not required in any way to buy any of the products which are covered by the agreement?

Mr. PRIEST. That is exactly true. May I go one step further. When a manufacturer signs a contract with a retailer under a fair trade law in a State, no other dealer in that State is bound until he has received notice that such contract has been signed. Then he may dispose of his inventory if he does not desire to continue to sell that product at a fair trade price. He is not required to sell that product at all. If he sells the product after he has been notified that a contract has been signed, he is supposed to follow the agreement insofar as it affects minimum resale prices.

Mr. [OVERTON] BROOKS [D., La.]. Mr. Chairman, I ask unanimous consent to extend my remarks at this point in the RECORD.

The CHAIRMAN. Is there objection to the request of the gentleman from Louisiana?

There was no objection.

Mr. BROOKS. Mr. Chairman, H. R. 5767 is an excellent bill. It should pass and become the law. It is a State rights bill and recognizes the ability of the State legislatures and of the State governments to pass and enforce laws at a State level with wisdom and judgment.

Ordinarily, Mr. Chairman, I am not much in sympathy with laws that reach down into the ordinary level of business transactions and seek to regulate them. Our country is vexed with regulations at a national level and our people feel that there is entirely too much red tape and Federal interference. This bill, however, puts the matter on the State level and permits the several States to act as they desire and in accordance with the wishes of their own people.

I am informed that 45 of the 48 States already have laws which seek to set forth what is known as fair-trade practices. The recent ruling of the Supreme Court of the United States, however, in the case of *Schweigman* v. *Calvert Distillery Corp.* [sic] (341 U. S. 384), May 21, 1951, knocked out the State laws and made them nonenforceable. This bill will have the effect of permitting the States to work out their own destinies and to protect the small-business man against certain cut-throat competition if they so desire. I am glad to say that Louisiana is one of the States which has enacted this type of legislation.

The best bulwark in this country which we have against the growth of collectivism in the form of communism is of course the small-business man. In communities where there exists a healthy small-business group, the level of civic welfare and interest taken by the small-business leaders in health, recreation and education tends to be higher than in those communities in which the business consists principally of a few large concerns. When these concerns are owned and managed from a distance the situation is much more pronounced. The small independent businessman, having a store on the corner in a community, performs a most necessary and worth-while service. Often times he makes a hand to mouth existence by working long hours at odd times to take advantage of a few sales and eeks [sic] out a difficult existence. When larger corporations, controlling vast output, engage in unfair-trade practices, the corner drug store faces an impossible existence. In a ruthless type of competition he is often forced out of business, although as a corner store with groceries or drugs he is vitally needed to serve the nearby community.

It is argued that this measure will result in price rigidity and will not have a wholesome affect in the competitive market. There may be some truth to this contention. This is an experimental field for legislation and some States may pass unwise and unsound laws and the cure in some instances may be worse than the disease. These laws, however, are under control of the States themselves and may be changed from time to time. In a field of 48 States much good can be accomplished by letting the States attempt to work out this type of problem so long as they do not try to burden interstate commerce.

In closing what I have to say, Mr. Chairman, I make a strong appeal for assistance to small business. I have lived in both large and small communities. I have lived in cities and in rural areas. From the time I was a little boy I can remember back over the years of the services rendered by the corner drug store and grocery store. I know that they render a real worth-while service in our economy. They have made an effort to protect themselves, at times very ineffectively against the encroachment of huge combines of wealth spreading out fan-like throughout our country, usually having their origin in Wall Street. They have tried one means of protecting themselves after another but the situation of the small-business man, I have noticed, has become increasingly difficult and acute. It is, therefore, timely that we, the Congress of the United States, take some action recognizing the very valuable services rendered to our people by the small, independent businessman and passing a law which will have the effect of at least permitting him to obtain legislation on a local level which will be beneficial to him. I hope this measure is adopted by an overwhelming vote.

The CHAIRMAN. The question is on the substitute offered by the gentleman from Illinois [Mr. REED.]

The question was taken; and on a division (demanded by Mr. HARRIS) there were—ayes 12, noes 111.

So the substitute was rejected.

Mr. CELLER. Mr. Chairman, I offer a substitute amendment.

The Clerk read as follows:

Amendment offered by Mr. CELLER: Page 1, strike out everything after the enacting clause and insert the following: "That section 5 (a) of the Federal Trade Commission Act, as amended, is hereby amended to read as follows:

" 'SEC. 5. (a) For the purposes of this section—

" '(1) The term "delivered cost" shall mean invoice cost to a seller less the value of discounts received by a seller in money or the equivalent, plus the cost of transportation incident to delivery to the seller, and plus applicable excise and sales taxes to the seller.

" '(2) The term "seller" shall mean a vendee, as used in this act, who purchases for resale.

" '(3) The term "loss-leader practice" shall mean selling a commodity, or advertising or offering a commodity for sale at retail at a price below the delivered cost of the commodity to the seller except that it does not include any of the following sales, or any advertisement or offer in connection therewith:

" '(A) Any sale of a commodity for the bona fide purpose of discontinuing dealing in such commodity or of discontinuing the seller's business, when plain notice of that fact is given to the public.

" '(B) Any sale of a commodity which is substantially damaged or deteriorated in quality if plain notice of the fact is given to the public.

" '(C) Any sale by an officer acting under an order of court.

" '(D) Any sale to any association organized and operated exclusively for religious, charitable, scientific, literary, or educational purposes, or for the prevention of cruelty to children or animals, no part of the net earnings of which inures to the benefit of any private shareholder or individual.

" '(E) Any sale of a perishable commodity if further retention of the commodity by the seller could reasonably be expected to result in a loss to the seller.

" '(F) Any sale which reasonable business practices require the seller to make in order to liquidate an inventory of a commodity to avoid insolvency or bankruptcy.

" '(G) Any seasonal clearance sale made in accordance with customary business practices in order to dispose of excess inventory.

" '(b) Any loss-leader practice which affects commerce is hereby declared to be unlawful and actionable at the suit of any person damaged thereby.

" '(c) (1) Any person injured in his business or property by any loss-leader practice hereby declared to be unlawful may sue therefor in any district court of the United States, as provided in section 4 of the Clayton Act, approved October 15, 1914, or in any State court of competent jurisdiction, and recover threefold the damages by him sustained, and the costs of suit, including a reasonable attorney's fee. Any person threatened with injury by any loss-leader practice shall be entitled to injunctive relief against such threatened injury in any court of the United States, as provided in section 16 of the Clayton Act, or to sue for and have such relief in any State court of competent jurisdiction when and under the same conditions and principles as injunctive relief against threatened conduct that will cause loss or damage is granted by courts of equity in that State, under the rules governing such proceedings, and upon the execution of proper bond against damages for an injunction improvidently granted and a showing that the danger of irreparable loss or damage is immediate, a preliminary injunction may issue.

" '(2) Section 15 of the Clayton Act (providing for suits by the United States district attorneys to restrain violations of this act), shall not apply with respect to any loss-leader practice.

" '(d) (1) Nothing contained herein or in any of the antitrust acts shall render illegal any contract or agreement prohibiting a seller from reselling at a price below his delivered cost, any commodity which bears, or the label or container of which bears, the trade-mark, brand, or name of the producer or distributor of such commodity and which is in free and open competition with commodities of the same general class produced or distributed by others, when contracts or agreements prescribing minimum prices are lawful under any statute, law, or public policy now or hereafter in effect in any State, Territory, or the District of Columbia in which such resale is to be made, or to which the commodity is to be transported for such resale, or for delivery to a vendee pursuant to a sale.

" '(2) Nothing contained herein or in any of the antitrust acts shall render illegal the exercise or enforcement of any right or right of action created by any statute, law, or public policy now or hereafter in effect in any State, Territory, or the District of Columbia, which provides in substance that willfully and knowingly advertising, offering for sale, or selling any commodity at less than the minimum prices prescribed in any such contract or agreement whether the person so advertising, offering for sale, or selling is or is not a party to such contract or agreement, is unfair competition and is actionable at the suit of any person damaged thereby: *Provided, however,* That the rights or right of action created by or under such contracts and agreements shall not apply where the minimum price prescribed in such contract is higher than the delivered cost to the seller: *And provided further,* That the rights or right of action created by or under such contracts and agreements shall not apply to any of the following sales, or advertisement or offer in connection therewith:

" '(A) Any sale of a commodity for the bona fide purpose of discontinuing dealing in such commodity or of discontinuing the seller's business, when plain notice of that fact is given to the public.

" '(B) Any sale of a commodity which is substantially damaged or deteriorated in quality if plain notice of the fact is given to the public.

" '(C) Any sale by an officer acting under an order of court.

" '(D) Any sale to any association organized and operated exclusively for religious, charitable, scientific, literary, or educational purposes, or for the prevention of cruelty to children or animals, no part of the net earnings of which inures to the benefit of any private shareholder or individual.

" '(E) Any sale of a perishable commodity if further retention of the commodity by the seller could reasonably be expected to result in a loss to the seller.

" '(F) Any sale which reasonable business practices require the seller to make in order to liquidate an inventory of a commodity to avoid insolvency or bankruptcy.

" '(G) Any seasonal clearance sale made in accordance with customary business practices in order to dispose of excess inventory.

" '(e) The Commission is hereby empowered and directed to prevent persons, partnerships, or corporations, except banks, common carriers subject to the acts to regulate commerce, air carriers, and foreign air carriers subject to the Civil Aeronautics Act of 1938, and persons, partnerships, or corporations subject to the Packers and Stockyards Act, 1921, except as provided in section 406 (b) of said act, from using unfair methods of competition in commerce and unfair or deceptive acts or practices in commerce'."

Mr. CELLER (interrupting the reading of the substitute). Mr. Chairman, I ask unanimous consent that the further reading of the substitute be dispensed with and that it be printed in the RECORD at this point.

The CHAIRMAN. Is there objection to the request of the gentleman from New York?

There was no objection.

Mr. CELLER. Mr. Chairman, all that this amendment does is to provide for the abolition of so-called loss leaders. Throughout the length of this debate we have heard tell that everybody in favor of either the Keogh bill or the McGuire bill was opposed to so-called loss leaders where retailers, in order to attract patronage to the store, would deliberately undercut and sell below cost, and indulge thereby in so-called loss-leader practices. I abhor that practice; I believe it is wrong and very hurtful and therefore I have offered this substitute amendment to punish it, to bar it, and to invoke sanctions upon those who are guilty of loss-leader selling. I think it is a vicious practice and should be condemned in the strongest terms. But in prohibiting sales below cost need we at the same time prevent all other types of legitimate competition which has proven to be the backbone of our Nation? Must we go to such extremes as to grant exemptions from our time honored antitrust laws and place our approval upon price-fixing contracts? That is going too far in my opinion. That is like, as indicated before, if you had a pain in your leg, why then just amputate the leg instead of getting at the cause of the pain and removing those causes. The cause of all the difficulty stems from the loss-leader selling. Therefore, what we should get at deliberately and without hesitation is loss-leader selling. Let us not get after ordinary and legitimate sales practices indulged in by wide awake and efficient merchants. Must we at the same time insure handsome profits to large fair-trade manufacturers and to certain concerns which support fair-trade bills? I put in the RECORD yesterday information and I will put more information in the RECORD today in my extension of remarks, facts which clearly indicate that about 51 out of 100 of the largest national advertisers, the largest concerns in the country, are in favor of these bills. Why are they in favor of them? Because they then have a grip, an ironclad grip upon the Nation, and they make of the retail merchant a mere conduit for the sale of the product that is thus nationally advertised. They are in favor of these bills, these very large oligarchic companies.

I also put in the RECORD and will put additional information in the RECORD to the effect that the chain store organizations are in favor of the fair-trade bills. Why are they in favor of them? Because of the high mark-ups that have been caused and created as the result of these fair-trade bills. There are higher profits in fair-traded articles, and these supermarkets and chain aggregations covet the sale of those types of goods. They thereby make up the differences that they may lose on grocery items. But the fair-trade articles in the main are pharmaceuticals and drugs. That is why these huge chain aggregations and these huge manufacturers are behind this bill.

Why, it is ridiculous to say this bill is primarily for the little merchant. The little merchant is deprived of his only strong weapon, competition, and his growth will be stunted. It is proof positive that in the District of Columbia and in the three fair-traded States there are less bankruptcies as far as retail establishments are concerned than there are in the fair-trade States where they have these fair-trade laws.

So I ask you, get at the seat of the trouble, vote against loss-leader selling, as is embodied in my substitute amendment.

I have pointed out to you already the dangers to small business which arise from permitting large manufacturers of fair-traded commodities to fix prices throughout the Nation. It is essential to recognize the threat to competition which extending the powers of these large producers entails. In the drug industry, four companies already control 68.5 percent of the output of medicinal chemicals, 92.1 percent of botanical products, 28 percent of pharmaceutical preparations, and 37.9 percent of biological products. The control of a few giant corporations in other fair-trading fields such as electrical appliances, small arms, and silverware is equally as high. Permitting these producers to enlarge their control of the Nation's economy even further by fixing the prices to be charged for their products in every retail outlet in 45 States of the Nation can only enhance the growth of these oligopolies and the concentration of economic power in a few large concerns.

I believe that the evils which those in favor of fair trade seek to extirpate can be dealt with in a manner which will not throttle the freedom of small business and enhance the already strong grip upon the economy exercised by the big manufacturers. Just what is the main objective which is urged in behalf of this measure? It is to prevent the unfair practice of so-called loss-leader selling in which important articles are disposed of by competitors below cost in order to destroy the business of their small rivals.

The distinguished gentleman from Texas [Mr. PATMAN] testifying before the Priest committee in favor of H. R. 5767 stated as follows:

Loss-leader selling is not only deceitful and misleading which of course will be brought about if this is not enacted; but it is detrimental to the country (p. 12).

Mr. Nicholas S. Gesoalde, executive secretary of the New York State Pharmaceutical Association, in support of the McGuire bill, pointed out, and I quote:

The public is protected through fair trade by preventing the use of predatory loss leaders to build up store traffic (p. 85).

The Senate Small Business Committee, in its latest annual report, speaking of the advantages of fair trade to the manufacturer, states:

Fair trade does protect him against the evils of loss-leader selling and the possible destruction of his product and his business through price cutting (Annual Report, p. 214).

And, insofar as the retailer is concerned, the committee said:

His margin of profit is fixed to yield him a fair return, and he is protected from destructive competition from others who might be able to afford to use the item as a loss leader (id., pp. 214–15).

Maurice Mermey, executive director of the Bureau of Education on Fair Trade, which is comprised of druggists and drug manufacturers who support the McGuire bill, averred in his statement submitted to the Priest committee:

> In curbing loss-leader selling, fair trade checks a pernicious type of unfair competition which particularly harms small business (p. 27).

It is abundantly evident from these statements that the abuse which those in favor of this legislation are endeavoring to curtail is that of loss-leader selling. It is to curb this evil of loss-leader selling that I now move to strike out everything after the enacting clause and insert the provisions of my loss-leader bill, which I have previously introduced into the House as H. R. 6986.

I wish to emphasize that in endeavoring to prohibit the sale of loss leaders through the device of resale price-maintenance agreements, not only is price cutting which is detrimental to competition prohibited, but all price reductions which are the very essence of competition are banned as well. Thus under fair trade, merchants may not reduce prices even one penny to reflect competitively legitimate savings accruing by virtue of greater efficiency, better selling practices, quantity purchases, or lower rents.

I am in favor of prohibiting loss-leader sales. I think it is a vicious practice which serves to injure small business and should be condemned in the strongest terms. But in prohibiting sales below cost, need we at the same time prevent all other types of legitimate competition which has proven to be the backbone of our Nation? Must we at the same time insure fat and handsome profits to large fair-trading manufacturers and to certain stores which support the fair-trade bills? Must we also penalize consumers by exacting from their already heavily taxed budgets the added tribute imposed by fair-trade legislation? Must we coerce all independent retailers throughout the 45 States to abide by a form of price fixing to which they were never a party?

If we must do all these things to prevent loss-leader selling, we place ourselves in the anamolous position of beheading our economy to prevent the headache of loss leaders, of amputating the limb because the leg is broken. And we will find ourselves emulating that notable physician of fable whose operation was a resounding success but whose patient died.

It can be shown that fair trade promotes monopoly and economic concentration; that it injures the competitive status of independent retailers; fosters the violations of the antitrust laws; and mulcts the consumer. How and why it does this, I cannot now set forth at length but wish that you would read my views in opposition to fair trade contained in House Report 1516 of this Congress beginning on page 19 where I have delineated these conclusions, with proper documentation, at considerable length.

I thereupon urge all of those who honestly wish to eliminate loss-leader selling to support my amendment which is designed to remedy this competitive abuse without incurring the concomitant dangers which inhere in resale price-maintenance agreements. Prohibiting loss-leader selling will aid small and independent business and promote competition. Fair trade will destroy the independence of small merchants and restrict competition and free enterprise.

In conclusion, I wish to read a letter in support of the loss-leader amendment which I have received from the Honorable W. T. Kelley, General Counsel of the Federal Trade Commission. In light of what I have said and in view of this letter, I sincerely request Members to support this amendment.

March 12, 1952.

Hon. Emanuel Celler,
Chairman, Committee on the Judiciary,
House of Representatives,
Washington, D. C.

DEAR CHAIRMAN: I have your press release No. 29 announcing the introduction of a bill to prohibit loss-leader selling.

I am in favor of such a bill as I believe selling below cost for an ulterior purpose is unfair and injurious to legitimate competition. The so-called fair trade bills in part prevent unfair competition but primarily, and in large part, prevent fair and legitimate competition. In fact, they eliminate all distribution efficiency between retailers and no longer would the public be benefited by a competition based on efficiency, service and the willingness of dealers to do business at a fair return.

My own conclusion is as follows: Where a retailer sells a branded article at a price determined by him with reference to an honest estimate of his own selling costs and the margin of profit which he considers legitimate for his whole business, he is not guilty of unfair trade or unfair competition even though the price is below that prescribed by the manufacturer. But where a retailer sells below cost or at so low a figure that he is obviously making an unreasonably low profit, and where his motive is not primarily to sell those goods but to advertise other goods, this is unfair and under those circumstances such methods should be forbidden. While illegitimate competition should not be tolerated, the law, in my judgment, should not go so far as to wipe out legitimate competition.

Congratulations on your efforts to protect the public from monopolistic enhancement of prices.

Sincerely yours,

W. T. Kelley,
General Counsel.

Mr. HARRIS. Mr. Chairman, I ask unanimous consent that all debate on this amendment close in 5 minutes.

The CHAIRMAN. Is there objection to the request of the gentleman from Arkansas?

There was no objection.

The CHAIRMAN. The Chair recognizes the gentleman from California [Mr. HOLIFIELD].

Mr. HOLIFIELD. Mr. Chairman, this is in effect a substitute bill that the gentleman from New York [Mr. CELLER] has presented. I have just read it on the Clerk's desk. It is several pages long. It attempts to do what the States will do within their own jurisdictions. They will write their own State fair-trade laws. I am sure it will be voted down.

In the little remaining time I have, I would just like to say that I have had 30 years of experience as a merchandiser, and I doubt very much if the gentleman from New York has had a year's experience in the retail merchandising business. I know what the problem is. I will tell you it is not the big chain stores and the others who want to put this thing through; it is the little-business man who has been forced to handle fair-trade merchandise in order to exist. In other words, he has to handle nationally branded merchandise because through the power of advertising the people demand it, and the people have confidence in nationally branded merchandise, and nationally branded merchandise is not as exorbitantly priced and the margin of profit for the retailer is smaller than that of nonbranded merchandise. Consumer acceptance makes it necessary for the small merchant to handle it; and if you take away the fair-trade protection from him, it means that you are going to kill the little-business man in America. The people have confidence in brand merchandise and confidence in the price because it is universally sold by the big stores as well as the little stores at the same price.

Mr. Chairman, I ask that this amendment be voted down.

The CHAIRMAN. The Chair recognizes the gentleman from Texas [Mr. PATMAN].

Mr. PATMAN. I have not had time to read and understand this amendment. It is several pages long. It has not received the consideration and the approval of the committee headed by the distinguished gentleman from New York who introduced the amendment. It appears to be an attempt to deal directly with something that is entirely local. It is placing a Federal agency in charge of or supervising business activities of the smallest, independent businessman in the United States, who is doing just an intrastate business, or a very small local business—it makes no difference. It goes entirely too far. It is something that the Congress should not legislate on. It is something that might be all right for a State to legislate on, but I do not know that I would be in favor of the amendment even in a State. No one knows what it is, and certainly we should not adopt it as a substitute for a bill that has received the consideration of a fine committee, like the Committee on Interstate and Foreign Commerce for many weeks, which heard testimony of witnesses on both sides. The committee has presented a good bill to us, the McGuire bill, and I hope it is accepted without amendments.

FAIR TRADE: IN THE PATTERN OF THE ANTITRUST LAWS

Our economy is rightly called a free-enterprise economy. It is based on the theory that the fostering of full, vigorous competition is the best means of achieving the economic well-being of the American people. Nonetheless, under our economic system, free competition, like other forms of freedom, has never existed in an absolute and unlimited manner.

The whole growth of a free civilization has consisted in tempering, in the interest of society, the liberty of the individual to do as he pleases. This applies to the liberty to compete also. If by free is meant unbridled, there is no such thing as free competition in our society. The American people would not tolerate such competition. No businessman is allowed to compete entirely on his own terms. He is always limited by what the public considers fair for all.

A great landmark in the recognition of this principle was the passage by Congress of the Sherman Antitrust Act in 1890. On the face of it, the Sherman Act restrained competition regarded as harmful to the public interest. But in a deeper sense, it safeguarded and preserved competition. For it outlawed those predatory activities of a small minority of businessmen which were aimed at destroying all their rivals and thus abolishing competition altogether.

Since the Sherman Act, Congress has successively enacted other measures which curb certain kinds of antisocial competition regarded as unfair or monopolistic. Among them were the Clayton Act, the Federal Trade Commission Act, the Food and Drug Act, the Securities and Exchange Act, and the Robinson-Patman Act.

The purpose of the fair-trade laws of the 45 States is also to curb unfair competition in order to promote fair competition. They restrain ruthless, commercial behavior which destroys competition by using superior dollar power alone to eliminate small competitors. The fair-trade laws curb the ruthless competition of those retailers who do not scruple to use trick prices and price-juggling to bewitch the consumer without benefit to her pocketbook.

Such retailers do not want to be fenced in. Like their predecessors in our history who bitterly opposed the antitrust laws and similar measures, they want to do as they please even when what they please to do harms society. They cry out that the right of free competition is being invaded, when what they mean by "free competition" is competition whose final outcome is the ending of all competition.

The legislative forerunners of the fair-trade laws were similarly viewed with alarm. The Sherman Act, in the course of congressional debate, was condemned as a statute which would crush competition. The Federal Trade Commission Act was called an infringement upon our basic liberties. It was prophesied that the Securities and Exchange Act would destroy the operations of the stock market and undermine the savings of the American people. I need hardly say, of course, that these laws are now universally regarded as among the most constructive legislation on our statute books.

The broad purpose of the antitrust laws is to prevent the growth of monopoly power and the evils consequent upon it. Accordingly, as a means toward this end, the antitrust laws prohibit horizontal price fixing, that is, any getting together of competitors who agree not to compete on price.

The broad purpose of the fair-trade laws is likewise to prevent the growth of monopoly power and the evils it produces. They also prohibit horizontal price-fixing. But as a means of restraining unfair competition, the fair-trade laws permit vertical resale price maintenance under conditions of full and fair competition. Vertical resale price maintenance must not be confused with horizontal price fixing. They are entirely different, and one has nothing to do with the other.

Horizontal price fixing is essentially an agreement among those who are on the same level in the distributive process, be they manufacturers or distributors, not to compete. Vertical resale price maintenance takes place between a manufacturer and his distributors, who are not on the same level in the distributive process and thus, of course, are not competitors. Furthermore, every fair-trade law requires that any product, in order to be fair-traded, be in free and open competition with similar articles produced by others.

It would be a mistake to concern ourselves with the technicalities expressed by the geometric adjectives, horizontal and vertical, to the exclusion of the human equation. For that is what really counts here. Both the antitrust laws and the fair trade exist for the sake of human beings, not abstract principles. They are designed to help the millions of ordinary men and women who constitute small business in this country, to make their livelihoods through, honest, hard competition, free of the threat of being crushed by monopoly power.

The CHAIRMAN. The Chair recognizes the gentleman from Arkansas [Mr. HARRIS].

Mr. HARRIS. Mr. Chairman, the Committee on Interstate and Foreign Commerce unanimously reported the McGuire bill. There were two reservations, but they did not express opposition. It is my information that the great Committee on the Judiciary had three viewpoints. One viewpoint was in favor of the McGuire bill. A second viewpoint was in favor of the Keogh proposal, which the committee reported favorably; and the third viewpoint was to do nothing at all to correct this situation. That viewpoint is expressed by the distinguished chairman of that committee, who offers this proposal as a substitute. In order to reach just exactly what he has in mind, he offers this amendment which does nothing.

I ask that the amendment be voted down.

The CHAIRMAN. The question is on the substitute amendment, offered by the gentleman from New York [Mr. CELLER].

The substitute amendment was rejected.

Mr. JAVITS. Mr. Chairman, I offer an amendment.

The Clerk read as follows:

Amendment offered by Mr. JAVITS to the committee amendment: On page 4, line 25, after the word "others", insert "and not subject to contracts or agreements prescribing minimum or stipulated prices as aforesaid."

Mr. JAVITS. Mr. Chairman, this amendment is designed to quiet the fears of consumers in respect of this bill. I believe that many Members sympathetic to the McGuire bill, like myself, have been impressed with arguments made by consumer groups, and feel that they should be taken into account. This amendment represents recognition and consideration of their viewpoint, and will not impede the essential purposes of the bill.

Mr. HARRIS. Mr. Chairman, will the gentleman yield?

Mr. JAVITS. I yield to the gentleman from Arkansas.

Mr. HARRIS. Is it not a fact that the gentleman understands the purpose of the McGuire bill is enabling legislation?

Mr. JAVITS. I do, and I will explain my amendment in exactly those terms.

Mr. HARRIS. If the gentleman will yield further, is it not true that under the gentleman's restricting amendment, if it were to be adopted it would completely nullify the proposal to make this enabling legislation?

Mr. JAVITS. I do not feel that is so, and I will explain why.

Mr. HARRIS. I will be glad to hear the explanation.

Mr. JAVITS. The bill now provides that anyone who proposes to establish or stipulate a fair-trade price is to be exempted from the antitrust laws, and I quote:

If the particular item is in free and open competition with commodities of the same general class produced or distributed by others.

Otherwise, the person who seeks to establish a fair-trade price under this bill is not exempted from the Federal antitrust laws. We are, therefore, already giving limited exemption only, to wit, that the manufacturer or distributor must make up his mind that there are other items in competition with the item which he expects to submit to fair-trade law pricing. What my amendment does is add to this limitation. It says, in effect, "You shall not be exempt from the antitrust laws unless the items which are in competition with the items which you expect to price under the McGuire bill are items which are non-fair-trade priced." It was made clear a while ago that what is contemplated in this bill is that the item sought to be fair-trade priced shall be in competition with other items which are also fair-trade priced. The consumer is, therefore, in this position: His range of choice is only in buying among a group of items, all of which can be, and in most cases are, priced under the fair-trade laws. So that if he wants to buy toothpaste, if he is going to buy any standard brand, he must pay for some item which is priced under the fair-trade law. Under my amendment the manufacturer or distributor of toothpaste could fair-trade price his item only if in the toothpaste market generally there were non-fair-trade priced items in competition with his item.

Mr. PATMAN. Mr. Chairman, will the gentleman yield?

Mr. JAVITS. My time is limited. I cannot yield right now, but will do so if I can get a few minutes more time and the gentleman will then renew his request.

The specific point I would like to make is this: The only arguments that can be made against what I am here proposing are, "Let us leave this bill unamended; it is sacrosanct." We know that is not so. Or, "Let us not change anything which is contained in any State law," ⊥ and the point will be made, as the gentleman from Arkansas [Mr. HARRIS] just made it, that this bill repeats words which are in most of the State fair-trade laws. But we are not dealing with words. We are dealing with substance.

⊥ 4952

The substance is this: The State fair-trade laws generally exempt the seller in the State from the State antitrust law, if there is one. This bill is an effort to exempt sellers on an interstate basis from the Federal antitrust laws. By my amendment we place on a further limitation of our own on that already in the bill itself, upon the exercise of that option to fair-trade price his item, which gives a particular seller the exemption from the Federal antitrust laws. I say we should add to the limitation already in the bill the necessary provision which will protect consumers and quiet their fears that they will have no range of purchase in a particular item, except among commodities all of which are fair-trade priced. By introducing the competition of non-fair-trade priced items, we say to the consumer: "If you want to buy any national brand of toothpaste and you want to pay for it, that is your privilege, but you do not have to." We say to them, "There is a toothpaste you can buy which is not fair-trade priced."

I submit this amendment is very important. It goes to the heart of what consumers have been disquieted about in respect to this bill, and if adopted will give the independent retailer everything he wants, which is protection for his over-all business position, and at the same time will protect the consumers.

The CHAIRMAN. The time of the gentleman from New York has expired.

The question recurs upon the amendment offered by the gentleman from New York [Mr. JAVITS].

The question was taken; and on a division (demanded by Mr. JAVITS) there were—ayes 12, noes 93.

So the amendment was rejected.

Mr. COLE of Kansas. Mr. Chairman, I offer an amendment.

The Clerk read as follows:

Amendment offered by Mr. COLE of Kansas to the committee amendment: On page 5, line 23, after the period insert the following: "Whenever by contract or agreement described in subsection (2) a stipulated or minimum resale price may be established for a commodity in any State, Territory, or the District of Columbia, where such a contract or agreement is lawful, it shall be an act of unfair competition, actionable at the suit of any person damaged thereby, to willfully and knowingly, in interstate commerce (1) sell or (2) have transported for sale or resale or (3) deliver pursuant to a sale, or otherwise deliver, such commodity in any such State, Territory, or the District of Columbia, where such a contract or agreement is lawful, at less than the price or prices so established in such contract or agreement. Any person, firm or corporation injured in his or its business or property because of the violation of this subsection (4) shall be entitled to sue for and have injunctive relief against threatened loss or damage by a violation of this subsection (4)."

Mr. COLE of Kansas. Mr. Chairman, the McGuire bill has corrected all of the difficulties involved by reason of the decision in the Schwegmann case. However, the decision in the Wintling [sic] case has pointed out another situation with respect to fair trade which has not been corrected in the McGuire bill. The amendment which I offer today merely plugs the loopholes in the fair-trade legislation.

My amendment provides for the protection of the merchants and retailers who are doing business in a fair-trade State; it protects them from raids on the part of mail-order houses and cut-rate retailers and wholesalers in non-fair-trade States. It protects them in this way: It provides enabling legislation which permits a person who has been damaged by these raids from un-fair-trade States by shipping into the fair-trade States commodities at a lower price than could be obtained in the fair-trade States. This legislation does not create a Federal fair-trade law in any shape, manner, or form; this amendment does not permit any Federal agency to do anything; it does not permit any Federal prosecutor to take action; it does not permit anybody in Washington to take any steps to enforce the fair-trade laws of any State; it is merely enabling legislation.

Mr. HARRIS. Mr. Chairman, will the gentleman yield?

Mr. COLE of Kansas. I yield.

Mr. HARRIS. Would the gentleman explain to the committee, then, the meaning of the term in the gentleman's amendment: "It shall be an act of unfair competition"?

Mr. COLE of Kansas. The words must be read in connection with the entire amendment. They mean this: It shall be an act of unfair competition which may be corrected by a suit, and that suit may be brought by the party damaged. By that I mean it may not be brought by anybody in the Federal Government, may not be brought by any State, may not be brought by any agency of the Federal Government; it may not be brought by any Federal prosecutor. It means only that those who have been damaged by it can bring the action. It does not attempt to tell the States what sort of law they must pass.

This merely permits the States, may I say again, to pass such enabling legislation as they desire, and it will prevent other States from sending into that State commodities at a lower price than fair trade.

If you do not have this amendment, if you do not enact this amendment, you will not have a fair-trade law. Why? One of the best illustrations I can give is what occurs in my own State. We are adjacent to the State of Missouri, which is a non-fair-trade State. Merchants in Missouri attempt to send merchandise into Kansas, merchandise which in Kansas can be sold only under the fair-trade law. The merchants in Missouri attempt to send into Kansas and sell in that State, merchandise at a price lower than is permitted by law in Kansas. Thus they are circumventing the fair-trade law of Kansas. This amendment merely permits Kansas to protect itself from the unfair competition of a non-fair-trade State. Without this type of amendment you cannot have a true fair-trade State. With this amendment you can protect Kansas, a fair-trade State, from those who would attempt to circumvent its laws.

Mr. Chairman, I suggest that the membership consider this amendment very, very carefully because it violates no principle of the McGuire bill.

Mr. [ROBERT T.] ROSS [R., N.Y.]. Mr. Chairman, I ask unanimous consent to extend my remarks at this point in the RECORD.

The CHAIRMAN. Is there objection to the request of the gentleman from New York?

There was no objection.

Mr. ROSS. Mr. Chairman, the McGuire fair-trade bill, H. R. 5767, has my wholehearted support. Its passage is essential because the fair-trade practices of producers and retailers that have proved themselves so beneficial over the years are now in serious danger. Briefly, this is what has happened. During the 1930's more and more businessmen, retailers and manufacturers alike, found the practice of resale-price maintenance advantageous. Resale-price maintenance is the setting of minimum retail prices of branded products by the manufacturer of those products.

This practice was encouraged by an ever-growing number of State legislatures that passed so-called fair-trade laws. Under these laws a manufacturer and retailers of his product can enter into contracts whereby the former establishes minimum resale prices which the latter are obligated to observe. All of these laws provide further that if a manufacturer negotiates a contract with one retailer in the State and announces the terms of this contract including his minimum prices to other retailers, he may enforce these prices on the latter, even though they have not entered into any such contract themselves. This is the so-called nonsigner provision.

The Miller-Tydings Act, passed in 1937, extended the provisions of State fair-trade laws which apply directly only to intrastate trade to interstate sales taking place within each State. It specifically exempted from the Sherman and the Federal Trade Commission Acts contracts to maintain prices in interstate sales in States which have laws authorizing such contracts.

However, last May, in the Schwegmann case, the majority of the Supreme Court ruled that contracts between a manufacturer and a seller were not binding on nonsigning retailers. In other words, the nonsigner provision was declared invalid, and thereby much of the effectiveness of the fair-trade laws was lost.

The McGuire bill, introduced by Congressman JOHN A. MCGUIRE, of Connecticut, last October, is designed to overcome the defects of the Miller-Tydings Act while at the same time restoring the full effectiveness of the fair-trade laws, including the nonsigner provision. Other bills have also been introduced in the Congress since the Schwegmann case to restore fair-trade laws to full effectiveness, but no other is as comprehensive, and no other has the support of as wide a segment of the retail trade. H. R. 5767 has also received the endorsement of the Department of Commerce, the Small Business Committees of both Houses, and the House Committee on ⊥ Interstate and Foreign Commerce which favorably reported the bill.

The enactment of H. R. 5767 would remove the threat of price cutting by giant retailers and unethical operators in the 45 States having fair-trade laws for all the manufacturers and retailers who choose to carry on business in accordance with them. It provides further protection to small business in the case of fair-traded goods sold by mail order, by prohibiting setting prices to an out-of-State buyer lower than the minimum prices in the State where the mail-order operation is located.

Important as the language of McGuire bill is in the interests of clarity, constitutionality, and legislative workability, the legal and technical wording of the bill need not detain us now. The important thing to recognize is the contribution this bill would make to fair trade, and to understand how important the restoration of effective fair trade is to the country.

Why should we have fair trade? Let me outline just a few of the reasons why I believe fair trade is in the best interests of the American people. Fair trade protects the consumer from the harmful effects of misleading loss-leader and price-baiting practices. Where the consumer is lured into a store by a low price on a well-known trade-marked item, only to be induced then to buy other items that have been correspondingly overpriced; he, the customer, has been unfairly victimized. That is unfair competition and the consumer is the loser.

Fair trade protects the reputation of the manufacturer on branded and trade-marked merchandise. Below-cost price cutting often reflects adversely on the quality of the trade-marked item, marked down to serve as a loss leader. Competitors tend to stop featuring the item, and may withdraw it altogether. Price cutting in this sense can be as adverse to the producer as physical misrepresentation.

Price cutting hurts not only the manufacturer; the effect on small retailers is even worse. Price cutting by giant distributors or sharpshooters may force independents out of business. As the Bureau of Education on Fair Trade rightly says:

> Fair trade is designed to give the small-business man a chance to compete fairly and on equal terms with large distributors, and thereby to preserve for small enterprises the field in which they can function most efficiently—that of distribution.

The consumer benefits from the use of standard brands and standard prices. Together they enable the customer to determine for himself whether he is getting the proper quality at the right price.

There is every evidence that fair-trade prices are fair prices and that they are competitively arrived at. Fair-traded items and other items are always in competition with each other. Surveys have shown that prices of fair-trade items have indeed resisted inflation better than prices of other goods. Fair-trade prices are not, as too many people mistakenly believe, rigid prices. They are changed by the manufacturer in response to the forces of supply and demand.

There is no evidence that fair-trade laws increase the cost of distribution. On the contrary, there is evidence that stores in fair-trade States have no higher, and sometimes lower, operating costs than those in the non-fair-trade areas.

Fair trade is the rule in the great majority of our States—45 of them in all—all except Missouri, Texas, Vermont, and the District of Columbia. The Miller-Tydings Act was expressly intended as enabling legislation designed to support existing State fair-trade statutes. The McGuire bill likewise is enabling legislation permitting the fair-trade States to carry out the principle of resale minimum price maintenance of branded goods where they wish, without at the same time interfering with the non-fair-trade States or the national interest.

Fair trade is, as we have seen, advantageous to the manufacturer, the wholesaler, the retailer, and the consumer. I like the way in which these advantages have been set forth in a clear and simple statement by the American Fair Trade Council, consisting of manufacturers practicing fair trade—resale price maintenance—as follows:

Fair trade is fair to the manufacturer because: First, he establishes his retail prices at a level that helps him maintain and improve quality; second, he eliminates the danger of entire markets being destroyed by ruthless price cutters; and, third, his salesmen can concentrate on selling without having to defend prices and discounts.

Fair trade is fair to the wholesaler because: First, he can maintain adequate inventories at more stable prices; second, his salesmen can concentrate on selling alone; third, he can have confidence in the quality of the product he sells; fourth, he becomes more the merchandiser and less a speculator; and, fifth, he knows fair trade is a real benefit to his retailers.

Fair trade is fair to the retailer because: First, he can recommend the products because of their quality; second, predatory retailers cannot steal his business because of loss leaders, causing him heavy inventory and operating losses; and, third, larger stocks are practical because speculation is reduced.

Fair trade is fair to the consumer because: First, quality is protected with products built up to a standard—not down to a price; second, long-term average prices are low; and, third, fair-trade prices tend to combat inflation. While all prices increased 59.3 percent from 1939 to 1947—prices of 7,334 fair-traded products increased only 1.39 percent.

The McGuire bill will assure the effective continuation of fair-trade practices. It will provide equal rights and equal protection to the great and the small of the business world. It will assure the consuming public trade-marked goods of highest quality at reasonable prices. It will provide, in the truest sense of the word, fair trade.

In the interest of the consumer and strengthening our American free-enterprise system, I urge passage of the McGuire bill.

Mr. HARRIS. Mr. Chairman, I ask unanimous consent that all debate on the pending amendment and all amendments thereto close in 8 minutes.

The CHAIRMAN. Is there objection to the request of the gentleman from Arkansas?

There was no objection.

Mr. PATMAN. Mr. Chairman, I rise in opposition to the amendment offered by the gentleman from Kansas [Mr. COLE].

Mr. Chairman, in practice let us see what this amendment will do. It applies to the non-fair-trade States in particular—Texas, Missouri, Vermont, and the District of Columbia. It means in the case of a merchant in Texarkana, Tex., who advertises a certain product for sale and delivers anywhere in that territory, if some of his orders should come by telephone, mail, or otherwise from the State of Arkansas, where they have a fair-trade law, the merchant would have to stop his shipment at the State line. He could not go over into Arkansas at all. In other words, he would be prevented from selling to his Arkansas customers at the same price he sells to his Texas customers. That same example could be used for Kansas City, Mo., and Kansas City, Kans. It could be used in the case of other States and State lines.

It is going rather far in the Federal field in encroachment upon the rights of the

States. The McGuire bill is justified as an enabling act to permit the States to do what is lawful in other States. But this amendment goes beyond that. This is an attempt to place the power of the Federal Government and a Federal agency in a State where the law does not apply at all.

Texas did not pass a fair-trade law. I think the Senate passed it one time and I believe the House passed it one time but for some reason unknown to me they never did get together and the law never got on the statute books. I am not familiar with what took place in our State legislature on this proposal but I do know it is not effective in Texas.

The fact is that Texas does not have it, Missouri does not have it, Vermont does not have it, and the District of Columbia does not have it, because Congress has never legislated a fair-trade law for the District of Columbia. This is an attempt to compel fair-trade prices in States that have never adopted the law at all. It is entirely contrary to the concept we have in advocating the McGuire bill. In advocating the McGuire bill we say it is a States' rights bill. We just permit the States to carry out the contracts that the States have said that they want carried out, and because there is a State line between them, why we will permit it in interstate commerce under the McGuire bill. But here you are placing a burden upon the merchants in those States where they have no fair-trade law. You restrict his efficiency, you restrict the value of his advertising. You take in cities like Kansas City, half of the benefit of advertising goes over into Kansas, and vice versa. But here you could not deliver the goods in one of these States; you would be absolutely stopped at the State line. It would be a violation of the law to deliver the goods.

⊥ 4954 ⊥ Mr. COLE of Kansas. Mr. Chairman, will the gentleman yield?

Mr. PATMAN. I yield to the gentleman from Kansas.

Mr. COLE of Kansas. Of course, it would be a violation of the law if the gentleman please. Why? Because the sale is a Kansas transaction, is it not? It is the Kansas law. We are attempting to protect the fair-trade law in Kansas.

Mr. PATMAN. But we do not give Kansas the right to enforce interstate commerce laws. Here is a case where you are giving Kansas the power to stop interstate commerce, and I doubt that you could give Kansas that power under the Constitution if you wanted to. You do not have the power to do it. Only the Congress can exercise the power over interstate commerce.

Mr. COLE of Kansas. The Federal Government has done it on numerous occasions: One, where Kansas was protected in its prohibitory law and the other in the sale of cigarettes.

Mr. PATMAN. This is an attempt to anticipate a great injury, a bad loophole. I do not think it will ever occur. You are anticipating exceptions, and you are trying to make arrangements to take care of an exception that will probably never happen. It will probably never occur. So let us pass the bill like it is, and then if we should discover something that is badly needed, if it is needed, later on we can take care of it.

Mr. McGUIRE. Mr. Chairman, will the gentleman yield?

Mr. PATMAN. I yield to the gentleman from Connecticut.

Mr. McGUIRE. Is it not true that the State legislatures could correct the situation raised in the Wentling decision?

Mr. PATMAN. Yes. The other States will probably pass a law, and there will be no necessity for this. You are anticipating a situation that will probably never exist in the world, and in the administration of this law, if you discover evils, if you discover loopholes, if you discover things that will happen that should not happen, we will come back to the Congress with that, and if there is a bad loophole in connection with this legislation or if there is a great injury, we can correct it later on.

The CHAIRMAN. The Chair recognizes the gentleman from Arkansas [Mr. HARRIS].

Mr. HARRIS. Mr. Chairman, this is one of the provisions that was contained in the substitute offered by the gentleman from Illinois a little while ago which the Committee did not agree to. This is paragraph (d) of section 1 of that bill, and where it says "it shall be an act of unfair competition" that would be an amendment to the

Federal Trade Commission Act. It definitely does establish a Federal cause of action, and therefore I think that the Committee will take the same action, from my own viewpoint on the proposal, as it did on the Keogh proposal.

Mr. Chairman, I ask for a vote.

The CHAIRMAN. The question is on the amendment offered by the gentleman from Kansas [Mr. COLE].

The amendment was rejected.

Mr. CRAWFORD. Mr. Chairman, I offer an amendment.

The Clerk read as follows:

> Amendment by Mr. CRAWFORD to section (3) of H. R. 5767: Paragraph (3) is amended by adding at the end thereof the following proviso: "*Provided, however,* That in the exercise [or] enforcement of any right or right of action as is exempted from the antitrust laws by this subsection, it shall be a complete defense to a charge of unfair competition for the defendant to show that the party prescribing the minimum or stipulated prices has failed to make reasonable efforts to insure compliance, by those in competition with the defendant, with such prescribed or minimum prices."

Mr. CRAWFORD. Mr. Chairman, this amendment is designed specifically for the purpose of protecting retail merchants against distributors or wholesalers who desire to give competitors of a merchant, free goods as a special inducement. The language I have used is taken from page 3, lines 10 to 17, of the Keogh bill. It plainly states:

> That in the exercise or enforcement of any right or right of action as is exempted from the antitrust laws by this subsection, it shall be a complete defense to a charge of unfair competition for the defendant to show that the party prescribing the minimum prices has failed to make reasonable efforts to insure compliance, by those in competition with the defendant, with such prescribed minimum prices.

This is language which should be in the bill.

If groceryman A is selling something and sells it below the price set by the distributor or the wholesaler, and you bring charges against him and he can show that the wholesaler or the distributor gave free goods to a competitor of groceryman A, you have no right in equity or otherwise to prosecute groceryman A when you are feeding free goods to a competitor down the street somewhere. This amendment is designed specifically for that purpose. If anybody on the Committee wants to object to it, I would like him to ask me about it and give me the reasons why.

Mr. HARRIS. As I understood the gentleman's question, he would like to have the reason why we would be opposed to the amendment?

Mr. CRAWFORD. Why it should not be in the bill.

Mr. HARRIS. Because it violates the concept that we are trying to reach here, and that is enabling legislation recognizing the action of States. The gentleman's amendment would set up a Federal defense in connection with the problems that arise under State fair-trade laws.

Mr. CRAWFORD. Where does it set up any Federal defense?

Mr. HARRIS. The language the gentleman just read. It is the language of the Keogh bill, beginning in line 12 on page 3.

Mr. CRAWFORD. That is right.

Mr. HARRIS. It is an amendment to a Federal statute. The gentleman says, "It shall be a complete defense to a charge of unfair competition," and so forth. That would certainly establish a Federal defense.

Mr. CRAWFORD. It simply amends your Federal Trade Act, and that is exactly what the McGuire bill does. It amends the Federal Trade Act, and it puts the proviso in here that you cannot crucify a small groceryman or druggist by prosecuting him for not complying when the distributor or producer who set the prices on the goods are giving his competitor down the street free goods to enable the competitor to put him out of business. If there is anything unfair about that kind of an amendment, I will take the consequences. That ought to be in the bill.

Mr. PATMAN. Mr. Chairman, will the gentleman yield?

Mr. CRAWFORD. I yield to the gentleman from Texas.

Mr. PATMAN. I am in sympathy with what the gentleman says, that we should stop such unfair practices.

Mr. CRAWFORD. Surely.

Mr. PATMAN. However, I appeal to the gentleman that he is not stopping it here.

Mr. CRAWFORD. No, I am not stopping it. I am simply making it so that you cannot prosecute one man for doing a thing while you are feeding his competitor down the street to do it.

Mr. PATMAN. Is not the gentleman writing into this bill here something that has never been done in law? In other words, the gentleman says, "If you do not enforce it against other people you cannot enforce it against me." If you had all laws written that way you never could enforce any of them.

Mr. CRAWFORD. You are sanctifying a proposition here. It is not the little retailer down the street that is doing the harm, it is the distributor or the producer who fixes the prices and who feeds the free stuff to the competitor that does the harm.

Mr. PATMAN. Does not the gentleman have his argument mixed up in this? I know he is sincere in this and I know he knows a lot about it. I know all about his experience. I see the reason for his concern. But he is talking in one place about dealing with the merchant, and this law relates to the merchant dealing with the customer. There is a great difference between the manufacturer dealing with the merchant and the merchant dealing with the customer.

Mr. CRAWFORD. The McGuire bill provides that the producer or the distributor may set these minimum prices.

The CHAIRMAN. The time of the gentleman from Michigan has expired.

(On request of Mr. HARRIS, and by unanimous consent, Mr. CRAWFORD was allowed to proceed for three additional minutes.)

Mr. CRAWFORD. The McGuire bill provides the distributor and producer may set the price. That is on page 4, subparagraph 2. The bill also provides that you could prosecute this fellow, the signer or the nonsigner. On what ground, and by what line of reasoning can you justify prosecuting grocery man A for not complying when the producer or distributor who initiates the deal is feeding free goods to some competitor down the street to grocery man A.

Mr. PATMAN. Mr. Chairman, will the gentleman yield?

Mr. CRAWFORD. I yield.

Mr. PATMAN. For the same reason that you prosecute every person who violates the plain law.

Mr. CRAWFORD. That does not apply at all because you are starting out by letting the producer or distributor fix the price. They set the pattern. Why do you want to prosecute a fellow, when the fellow who fixes the price shovels free goods to a competitor down the street.

Mr. PATMAN. I respectfully suggest that the two are not related. The two are not related. One is with reference to unfair practices as between the manufacturer and the producer to the retailer, and the McGuire bill relates to the transaction between the retailer and the consumer.

Mr. CRAWFORD. They are related, but if you do not want to protect the little man, that is your affair.

Mr. CELLER. Mr. Chairman, will the gentleman yield?

Mr. CRAWFORD. I yield.

Mr. CELLER. The gentleman's amendment provides for what is commonly known in the law as the clean hands doctrine; is that not correct?

Mr. CRAWFORD. Yes.

Mr. CELLER. And it is the present law even under the present situation where a retailer who is complained of says that the manufacturer has not in good faith endeavored to maintain the price that he shall be absolved from that price. That is the present law, and your amendment simply restates the present law; is that not correct?

Mr. CRAWFORD. Exactly.

The CHAIRMAN. The question is on the amendment offered by the gentleman from Michigan [Mr. CRAWFORD].

The amendment was rejected.

AN ANSWER TO THE OPPONENTS OF FAIR TRADE

Mr. [CLINTON D.] McKINNON [D., Cal.]. Mr. Chairman, in the debate Wednesday on the McGuire bill, H. R. 5767, the opponents of fair trade made a number of charges which must not go unanswered. It is hard to understand how such a false indictment can be made by anyone who believes in the importance of strengthening the small business economy and our system of free competition.

If this country is to lead the nations of the world along the road to democracy, we must demonstrate to them that a democracy guarantees freedom of opportunity. Freedom of opportunity means, above all, that new firms can compete with established business without being driven to the wall by predatory and oppressive tactics of price cutting, unfair methods of competition, and monopoly. It is not by mere chance that we have the highest standard of living in the world. It is due, rather to a constant fight to maintain the status of small and independent business in our communities. It has been demonstrated time and time again that our future as a free and democratic nation depends upon the success and survival of small business.

California was the pioneer State in developing fair-trade legislation. As early as 1931 the people of that State decided that the independent retailer needed protection from the predatory tactics of mass distributors. We know the charges made by the opponents of fair trade are unfounded. Let me reply to these accusations, one by one.

THE CHARGE THAT FAIR TRADE DOES NOT HELP SMALL BUSINESS

The most extravagant argument of all against fair trade is the claim that it does not help even the small firms in whose interests it is adopted. Can it be that the nearly 2,000,000 independent retailers who have learned from harsh experience that unrestrained price cutting is a threat to their very existence have been wrong all these years? I just cannot believe that.

Fair trade merely helps to place the independent retailer on a par with the mass distributors. The latter rarely have any advantage in lower costs of operation. Their competitive strength lies in purely strategic weapons derived through unfair concessions in buying, ability to absorb local losses, and the sheer weight of massed capital. They have many devices at their command which do for them what fair trade does for the small-store keeper. They can distribute through agencies. Or, like the chain stores, they can control prices all the way from producer to consumer. Fair trade merely equalizes these advantages.

Small business needs fair trade so that it can compete for the customer's favor on the basis of honesty, efficiency, services, and skill. Fair trade is designed to give the small-business man a chance to compete fairly and on equal terms with large distributors and thereby to preserve for small enterprises the field in which they can function most efficiently—that of distribution.

THE CHARGE THAT FAIR TRADE IS MONOPOLISTIC IN CHARACTER

Then there is the assertion that fair trade is inherently monopolistic in character; that it means the elimination of price competition among retailers; and that it is a general denial of the principles of free competition. Actually, nothing could be further from the truth.

Do not forget that fair trade, control, such as it is, operates on a vertical basis rather than horizontal. Competition between manufacturers continues to exist. A fair-trade law merely permits the making of contracts by which an individual producer establishes minimum resale prices on his own products. These prices vary with each producer and respond fully to consumer preferences and the laws of supply and demand. National brands compete with each other and with private brands. The consumer is always protected.

Furthermore, to be on the fair-trade list, an article must be in free and open competition with similar articles produced by others. A fair-trade product is always a competitive product. Collusion between manufacturers of different brands to establish the same price and thereby to eliminate price competition with each other is specifically forbidden by the fair-trade laws as it is by the Miller-Tydings Act itself. No less an authority than the United States Supreme Court declared, in upholding the constitutionality of the Illinois Fair Trade Act, that the act does not attempt to fix prices nor does it delegate such power to private persons.

Finally, fair trade is itself a positive deterrent to monopoly. Price cutting is discriminatory in effect and a powerful tool for the suppression of competition. By preventing price cutting, fair trade is a strong barrier to price discrimination and hence monopoly. It serves to curb predatory and unfair commercial practices.

THE CHARGE THAT FAIR TRADE INJURES THE CONSUMER

In the debates on fair trade many members of the House expressed concern over the effects of fair trade on the consumer. The assumption is that the retailer can be helped only at the expense of the consumer. This concern is quite proper. Nevertheless I am convinced that fair trade is as much in the interest of the consumer as it is of the retailer.

In the first place, there is no reliable evidence that fair trade prices are high prices. It is very easy to find specific commodities which sell for less in the District of Columbia or in any other non-fair-trade area than in fair-trade States. It is just as easy to find articles which sell for more. Only a broad statistical study can really supply a satisfactory answer. Many of these have been made. Putting them all together, one must recognize that in general the consumer pays nothing for fair trade. If anything, fair-trade prices seem to be lower than non-fair-trade prices.

A recent study, for instance, indicates that since 1939 prices of fair-trade articles have resisted inflation better than prices of other goods. According to this study, the prices of 7,334 controlled drug products increased only 3.1 percent from 1939 to 1947, whereas food prices went up 93 percent and the over-all cost of living rose 59 percent. If all prices had behaved like fair-trade prices, we would not be burdened today with such a high cost of living.

The reason that fair trade does not raise prices is simple. A manufacturer establishing fair-trade prices must set them low enough so that he will not be undersold by his competitors. No manufacturer who has spent thousands, or perhaps millions, of dollars to establish his brands would take such a risk. He will put his prices as low as possible, and those prices will be in effect everywhere.

We must not overlook the fact that fair-trade pricing is merely one of many manifestations of standard pricing. Only $5,000,000,000 worth, or approximately 4 percent of total retail sales, represented national brands sold under fair trade. Standard pricing is used without recourse to fair trade and would continue to be used if all the fair-trade laws were repealed. Daily newspapers, magazines, automobiles, household appliances, gas and oil products, home furnishings, some wearing apparel, and many other products are sold at standard prices.

Furthermore, loss-leader selling is a form of advertising. The more loss leaders a store offers, the higher its operating costs go. Generally, therefore, the types of stores which depend on price cutting to attract patronage are the ones which exact the highest average margins. In the last analysis all operating costs are paid by the consumer. The public cannot get something for nothing.

There is no reason to assume that fixed prices will weaken the drive toward greater efficiency and the reduction of costs. Fair trade results in uniform prices but not in uniform profits. A given reduction in costs has as great an effect on profits under fair trade as under free trade. The drive for efficiency is no whit less now than it was prior to general fair trade. Eventually the consumer shares with the retailer in the advantage of fair trade.

THE NONSIGNER ISSUE

The real issue before us is whether the Miller-Tydings Act should be amended so as to validate the provisions in State laws which authorize sellers to enforce price maintenance against retailers who refuse to cooperate on the basis of voluntary agreements. Some who believe in fair trade on a so-called voluntary basis object to the supposed coercive character of these nonsigner clauses.

A little study will show that these objections are groundless. The basic reason for the nonsigner provision is the very practical fact that, without it, systematic price maintenance is usually not effective. The confirmed price cutter naturally will not voluntarily sign a contract that deprives him of the bait he uses in his type of selling.

Now, the number of confirmed price cutters is very small, but the presence of even a single price cutter in a market has a demoralizing effect on the entire price structure. "One bad oyster spoils the stew and one price cutter makes the whole market sour." If one retailer starts to cut prices, others must follow. There is no limit to the extent to which prices may be slashed or to the number of dealers that may become involved. The only way to avoid the flood is to stop the first trickle.

If one accepts the basic philosophy of fair trade, there is no sane reason for objecting to the nonsigner clauses. Obviously, if price cutting is unfair, the restrictions must be directed at price cutters. These are the ones who refuse to sign contracts.

Enforcement against nonsigners is necessary for the protection of contract rights. To hold that fair-trade contracts are good when voluntarily signed but that they cannot be protected against noncontract nullification "is to say that the body may live but the heart must die."

The proposed bill is fair, democratic, and the American way of doing things. It is merely the principle of majority rule applied to commercial practices. The retailer is not forced to sell articles subject to price maintenance. He can sell only free goods or can develop his own private brands. Only if a retailer elects to deal in fair-trade goods and to retain their distinguishing trade-marks is he affected by the fair-trade contract. The McGuire bill is necessary to protect small business, preserve our competitive institutions, and to maintain a sound foundation to our entire economic system.

The CHAIRMAN. The question is on the committee amendment.

The committee amendment was agreed to.

The CHAIRMAN. Under the rule, the Committee will rise.

Accordingly the Committee rose; and the Speaker having resumed the chair, Mr. MILLS, Chairman of the Committee of the Whole House on the State of the Union, reported that that Committee, having had under consideration the bill (H. R. 5767) to amend the Federal Trade Commission Act with respect to certain contracts and agreements which establish minimum resale prices and which are extended by State law to nonsigners, pursuant to House Resolution 586, he reported the bill back to the House, with an amendment adopted in the Committee of the Whole.

The SPEAKER. Under the rule, the previous question is ordered.

Mr. DOLLIVER. Mr. Speaker, I make the point of order that a quorum is not present.

The SPEAKER. The Chair will count. [After counting.] Two hundred and twenty-one Members are present; a quorum.

The question is on agreeing to the amendment.

The amendment was agreed to.

The SPEAKER. The question is on the engrossment and third reading of the bill.

The bill was ordered to be engrossed and read a third time, and was read the third time.

The SPEAKER. The question is on the passage of the bill.

The question was taken; and on a division (demanded by Mr. HARRIS) there were—ayes 196, noes 10.

Mr. CELLER. Mr. Speaker, I object to the vote on the ground that there is no quorum present.

The SPEAKER. The Chair has just counted, and there were 221 Members present; a quorum.

Mr. CELLER. Mr. Speaker, I ask for the yeas and nays.

The yeas and nays were refused.

So the bill was passed.

The title was amended so as to read: "A bill to amend the Federal Trade Commission Act with respect to certain contracts and agreements which establish minimum or stipulated resale prices and which are extended by State law to persons who are not parties to such contracts and agreements, and for certain other purposes."

A motion to reconsider was laid on the table.

Mr. PRIEST. Mr. Speaker, I ask unanimous consent that all Members have five legislative days in which to revise and extend their remarks on the bill H. R. 5767.

The SPEAKER. Is there objection to the request of the gentleman from Tennessee?

There was no objection.

[ED. NOTE: H.R. 5767 **as passed by the House was identical with the substitute version reported by the House Committee on Interstate and Foreign Commerce on February 27, 1952, reprinted** *supra*.]

SENATE CONSIDERATION (H.R. 5767)

SENATE DEBATE
82d Cong., 2d Sess.
May 9, 1952

98 CONG. REC. 5002

The VICE PRESIDENT. If Senators will suspend for a moment, the Chair has before him a message from the House of Representatives concerning House bill 5767, a bill to amend the Federal Trade Commission Act with respect to certain contracts and agreements which establish minimum or stipulated resale prices and which are extended by State law to persons who are not parties to such contracts and agreements, and for certain other purposes.

The Chair has been looking into this act, and also into the terms of the bill, itself, and the report of the Committee on Interstate and Foreign Commerce of the House upon it. The object of the bill is to amend the Federal Trade Commission Act. In one or two sections of the bill, it is provided that nothing in this act, or in the antitrust laws, shall prevent the accomplishment of the purposes of this bill. The last paragraph provides what the Federal Trade Commission may or may not do, what it is empowered and directed to do, and so forth.

The Chair thinks this bill should go to the Committee on Interstate and Foreign Commerce, because it deals with interstate commerce. It is an amendment of an act which came from the Committee on Interstate and Foreign Commerce. In the House, the bill which has come to the Senate was referred to the Committee on Interstate and Foreign Commerce. The Chair feels that it should go to the Senate Committee on Interstate and Foreign Commerce, and therefore makes the reference.

Mr. [LEVERETT] SALTONSTALL [R., Mass.]. Mr. President, will the Senator from Nevada yield so that I may address a question to the Chair?

Mr. [PAT] McCARRAN [D., Nev.]. In a moment. I should like to make an inquiry of the Chair on the same subject, if the Senator from Massachusetts will permit me to do so for a moment.

Mr. President, without attempting to take issue with the ruling of the Chair, which I understand is that the bill shall be referred to the Committee on Interstate and Foreign Commerce—

The VICE PRESIDENT. That is correct.

Mr. McCARRAN. I think, if the Chair will read the bill through, he will see that it is in reality a bill which affects antitrust laws in general, rather than interstate commerce.

The VICE PRESIDENT. The Chair has read the bill through. According to the House report, the bill is made necessary because of a decision of the Supreme Court dealing with the Miller-Tydings Act, which was a fair-trade act, and which came from the Committee on Interstate and Foreign Commerce. The Chair feels that this bill is predominantly an amendment to the Federal Trade Commission Act, dealing with resale prices in interstate commerce. The mention of the antitrust laws appears to the Chair as being more or less incidental, because it says that nothing in this act, or in the antitrust laws, shall prevent the accomplishment of the things attempted by the bill itself. The Chair feels that while the mention of the Antitrust Act might give some color to a reference to the Judiciary Committee, yet the dominant purpose is to amend the Miller-Tydings Act, in view of a decision of the Supreme Court construing that act, and the Chair therefore feels that the bill should go to that committee.

Mr. SALTONSTALL. Mr. President, I think the Senator from Nevada has raised the question I was thinking of raising. I have nothing to add to what the Senator from Nevada has said.

REPORT OF THE SENATE COMMITTEE ON INTERSTATE AND FOREIGN COMMERCE
S. Rep. No. 1741
82d Cong., 2d Sess.
June 12 (legislative day, June 10), 1952

Mr. JOHNSON of Colorado, from the Committee on Interstate and Foreign Commerce, submitted the following

REPORT

[To accompany H. R. 5767]

The Committee on Interstate and Foreign Commerce, to whom was referred the bill (H. R. 5767) to amend the Federal Trade Commission Act with respect to certain contracts and agreements which establish minimum or stipulated resale prices and which are extended by State law to persons who are not parties to such contracts and agreements, and for certain other purposes, having considered the same, report thereon without amendment and without recommendation.

United States Senate,
Committee on the Judiciary,
June 7, 1952.

Hon. Edwin C. Johnson,
Chairman, Committee on Interstate and Foreign Commerce,
United States Senate, Washington, D. C.

MY DEAR MR. CHAIRMAN: My attention has been called to H.R. 5767, to amend the Federal Trade Commission Act with respect to certain contracts and agreements which establish minimum or stipulated resale prices, which passed the House of Representatives on May 8, 1952, and on which the Committee on Interstate and Foreign Commerce held hearings beginning June 2, 1952.

Under the Legislative Reorganization Act of 1946, the Committee on the Judiciary was specifically given jurisdiction over "all proposed legislation * * * relating to * * * protection of trade and commerce against unlawful restraints and monopolies".

The bill in question (H. R. 5767) would assert and declare to be lawful certain contracts or agreements prescribing minimum or stipulated prices irrespective of the antitrust acts and the Supreme Court decision in the Schwegmann case decided May 21, 1951.

Because of the impact that the enactment of H. R. 5767 would have on the Sherman Act, I respectfully request that upon completion of consideration by the Committee on Interstate and Foreign Commerce, this bill be referred to the Committee on the Judiciary.

I solicit your cooperation to this end and will appreciate having your views on this matter.

Kindest personal regards.

Sincerely,

Pat McCarran, Chairman.

Federal Trade Commission,
Washington 25, May 21, 1952

Hon. Edwin C. Johnson,
Chairman, Committee on Interstate and Foreign Commerce,
United States Senate, Washington, D. C.

MY DEAR MR. CHAIRMAN: In response to the request made in your letter of May 12, 1952, for comment of the Commission upon H. R. 5767, Eighty-second Congress, second session, which has been referred to your committee for consideration, the following is submitted:

The principal purpose of the proposed legislation is to overcome the effect of the recent decision of the Supreme Court in the Schwegmann case (*Schwegmann Bros.* v. *Calvert Distillers Corporation*, 341 U. S. 384, decided May 21, 1951). In that case the Supreme Court held that the Miller-Tydings Act does not make binding upon nonsigners resale prices fixed in contracts under State resale price maintenance laws, insofar, of course, as interstate commerce is concerned. The bill proposes to reenact as an amendment to the Federal Trade Commission Act (and to limit the application of the Sherman Antitrust Act accordingly) the presently existing Miller-Tydings amendment to the Sherman Act but with the addition of the nonsigner clause, and with a provision that resale price maintenance contracts and the enforcement thereof against a signer or nonsigner shall not constitute a burden upon interstate commerce.

Prior to the Miller-Tydings Act, decisions in a number of cases under the Sherman and Federal Trade Commission Acts had made it clear that the failure of a retailer to observe the resale prices marked on trade-marked or branded goods did not create a cause of action in favor of the manufacturer either under the common law or under the patent or copyright laws. Moreover, the courts held that where a manufacturer maintained the resale prices of his identified goods by a system of contracts or equivalent cooperative methods, those contracts were void and such methods illegal under both the Sherman and the Federal Trade Commission Acts.

The Miller-Tydings Act amended the Sherman Act by legalizing minimum resale price agreements or contracts respecting trade-marked or otherwise identified goods sold in interstate commerce provided that the commodities affected were resold in any State that had legalized this type of contract, or agreement with respect to resales made within its boundaries. The act also amended the Federal Trade Commission Act by providing that the making of such contracts should not constitute an unfair method of competition under section 5 of the Federal Trade Commission Act.

Resale price maintenance laws—that is, laws declaring as not in violation of the law of the particular State certain kinds of price maintenance contracts and providing that nonsigners of such contracts with knowledge thereof should be bound by the price stipulations therein—were on the statute books of 45 States as of May 1, 1941. Most of these States adopted price maintenance laws in 1937 soon after the decision of the Supreme Court in *Old Dearborn Distributing Company* v. *Seagram Distillers Corporation* (299 U. S. 183, decided December 7, 1936) declaring as constitutional the principal provisions, including the nonsigner clause, of the Illinois price maintenance law.

The legal principle involved in the proposed legislation and in the State laws concerning resale price maintenance is not a mere authorization of contracts for the fixing of resale prices. That authorization now exists under the Miller-Tydings amendment as interpreted by the Supreme Court in Schwegmann case. The new principle introduced by this bill is that the Congress shall specifically approve the so-called nonsigner clause. Thus, if this bill is enacted, a private contract, the provisions of which would be determined without public hearing and apart from any public supervision as to reasonableness, would be made binding upon all dealers and the consuming public.

In an effort to prescribe the freedom of business enterprise, the courts have been circumspect in recognizing even the authority of governments to fix the prices that businessmen shall charge. Such price fixing is invalid unless it is undertaken for a public purpose and by reasonable means. In the State resale price maintenance laws and in the present bill, however, the power to fix prices would be entrusted not to a government, but to private persons; the purpose to be served by the price fixing would be whatever purposes such private persons might have, presumably that of serving their own pecuniary interests rather than that of the public interest; and the prices fixed would not be tested for reasonableness by any instrumentality public or private; nevertheless, a person who is not a party to this private contract is to be deemed guilty of unfair competition and subject to a suit for damages if he fails to observe the prices, regardless of whether or not they are arbitrary or extortionate.

In granting to such private persons the power to fix prices, the proposed legislation goes much further than Congress saw fit to grant to the Government itself in the National Industrial

Recovery Act (act of June 16, 1933). In that act, consideration was given labor and to the consuming public and there was always a representative of both who participated in the fixing of prices, while in the present bill, no consideration whatsoever is given to the interests of labor or the consuming public.

The effect of adding the nonsigner clause to resale price maintenance is the de facto nullification of our Federal antitrust laws prohibiting horizontal conspiracy to fix prices. Nothing is more clearly established in Federal policy than the principle that horizontal price fixing shall not be tolerated. The proposed legislation pays lip service to that principle; yet its effect would be that a minimum price fixed by contract with one retail distributor would become the minimum price for all other retail distributors who were placed upon notice of the existence of the contract. The rigidity and uniformity of the price would be exactly that of the most rigid horizontal price-fixing conspiracy; the level of the price would be likely to be at least as high as in a horizontal conspiracy; and the public control of the reasonableness of the arrangement would be as nonexistent as in the case of a horizontal conspiracy. Thenceforward, any group of distributors desiring to fix prices horizontally would be foolish to take the direct road to that end. Instead some one of their number would make a vertical contract with a supplier and then place the other members of the group on notice of the existence of the contract. Through this means, the group could not only negate the objections of the Government, but could actually use the courts as devices to enforce the arrangement.

In considering this problem, under the provisions of the Miller-Tydings Act in the Schwegmann case, the Supreme Court stated:

"It should be noted in this connection that the Miller-Tydings Act expressly continues the prohibitions of the Sherman Act against 'horizontal' price fixing by those in competition with each other at the same functional level. Therefore, when a State compels retailers to follow a parallel price policy, it demands private conduct which the Sherman Act forbids. See *Parker* v. *Brown* (317 U. S. 341, 350). Elimination of price competition at the retail level may, of course, lawfully result if a distributor successfully negotiates individual 'vertical' agreements with all his retailers. But when retailers are forced to abandon price competition, they are driven into a compact in violation of the spirit of the proviso which forbids 'horizontal' price fixing."

One of the stated purposes of the proposed legislation is "to permit such [State] statutes, laws and public policies to apply to commodities, contracts, agreements and activities in or affecting interstate or foreign commerce." The Miller-Tydings Act exempted from the application of the Sherman and Federal Trade Commission Acts, contracts prescribing minimum prices for the resale of an identified commodity where such contracts are lawful "as applied to intrastate transactions, under any statute, law or public policy now or hereafter in effect in any State, Territory, or the District of Columbia, in which such resale is to be made, or to which the commodity is to be transported for such resale." Thus, it appears to be a purpose of the present bill to make State laws and public policy applicable to commodities transported in interstate and foreign commerce which would extend both the purpose and provisions of the Miller-Tydings Act. If this extension is made by the enactment of this bill, an area of interstate commerce would be made subject to regulations in accordance with the provisions of State law. In other words, the present bill proposes that Congress exempt from the application of Federal antitrust law an area of interstate commerce and to give consent to State regulation thereof.

In our opinion economic conditions are not the same at the present time as existed in 1937 which prompted the enactment of the Miller-Tydings Act. At present there is no necessity for Federal resale price maintenance legislation with respect to interstate commerce. Furthermore, the Congress has already pointed the way toward elimination of the evils, which sponsors of the Miller-Tydings Act sought to remedy, through legislation prohibiting price discrimination and other unfair methods of competition. It is the elimination of these evils rather than legislation legalizing price fixing which will minimize the inequities between the smaller-business man and his more powerful competitor.

During previous years, the Commission has expressed its opposition to resale price maintenance in two reports to the Congress, the first of which was presented in 1931 (70th Cong., 2d sess., H. Doc. No. 546), and the second entitled "Report on Resale Price Maintenance," which was submitted on December 13, 1945.

Consistent with the foregoing observations, the Commission is opposed to H. R. 5767 (the McGuire bill).

It is understood that your committee will start hearings on H. R. 5767 on Monday, June 2, 1952. It will be appreciated if this Commission can be afforded an opportunity to have representatives appear at these hearings and present the views of the Commission on H. R. 5767 in more detail.

By direction of the Commission.

Sincerely yours,

Jas. M. Mead, Chairman.

N. B.—Pursuant to regulations, this report was cleared orally with the Bureau of the Budget on May 21, 1952, and on that date the Commission was advised that there would be no objection to the submission of the report to the committee.

Jas. M. Mead, Chairman.

The following is a listing of the opponents and proponents which appeared before the Committee on Interstate and Foreign Commerce, and testified on H. R. 5767:

OPPONENTS

Mr. Everette MacIntyre, Assistant Director of Bureau of Monopoly, Federal Trade Commission
Mr. John Blair, Assistant Chief Economist, Federal Trade Commission, Washington 25, D. C.
Mr. H. Graham Morison, Assistant Attorney General, Justice Department
Mr. John J. Schwegmann, Jr., with Mr. C. F. Fort, drug department manager, Schwegmann Bros. Giant Supermarket, Airline Highway, New Orleans, La.
Prof. Joseph Klamon, Washington University, professor of marketing, 7464 University Drive, University City, St. Louis 5, Mo.
Mr. Julius M. Westheimer, president, Julius Gutman & Co., Lexington Street and Park Avenue, Baltimore 1, Md.
Mr. Wendell Berge, Ring Building, Washington, D. C.
Mr. B. E. Webb, Webb City, Inc., St. Petersburg, Fla.
Mr. Angus McDonald, National Farmers Union, Washington, D. C.
Mr. Matt Triggs, assistant legislative director, American Farm Bureau Federation, 261 Constitution Avenue NW., Washington, D. C.
Mr. Lloyd C. Halvorson, economist, National Grange, 744 Jackson Place, Washington 6, D. C.
Mr. Samuel Rosenthal, Standard Drug Co., Post Office Box 1556, Richmond, Va.
Mr. Jenkins Garrett, The Texas Merchants Association, associated with Leonards Department Store, Fort Worth, Tex.
Mr. Donald Montgomery, Washington representative, United Auto Workers, CIO (Congress of Industrial Organizations), 718 Jackson Place NW., Washington 6, D. C.
Mr. Jack M. Eckerd, Eckerd Drug Stores, 1107 State Street, Erie, Pa.
Mr. Herman Luckoff, Luckoff's Mutual Stores, Inc., 257-259 East Main Street, Columbus 15, Ohio.
Mrs. Hilda Smith (Mrs. Ralph Smith), department of business administration, State University of New York, Harpur College, Endicott, N. Y.
Mr. Bert C. Abrens, executive secretary, National Association of Educational Buyers, 1461 Franklin Avenue, Garden City, Long Island, New York, N. Y.
Prof. Phillip Gamble, Consumers Union of the United States, Inc., 17 Union Square West, New York 3, N. Y.
Prof. William Heller, Jr., Northampton Consumer Club, University of Massachusetts, Amherst, Mass.
Mr. Ralph S. Brown, Jr., Yale University Law School, New Haven, Conn.
Mr. Sidney Margolis, National Association of Consumers, 265 Henry Street, New York City, N. Y.
Mrs. Frances Wright, Housewives United, 2915 Foxhall Road NW., Washington, D. C.
Mrs. Clarence D. Wright, General Federation of Women's Clubs, Washington, D. C.
Mr. P. L. Saunders, representing John Q. Public, Washington, D. C.
Mr. L. L. Lyons, New Orleans, La.

PROPONENTS

Mr. John W. Anderson, president, American Fair Trade Council, 1434 West Eleventh Avenue, Gary, Ind.
Mr. Maurice Mermey, director, Bureau of Education on Fair Trade, 205 East Forty-second Street, New York, N. Y.
Mr. Herman S. Waller, general counsel, National Association of Retail Druggists, 32 West Randolph Street, Chicago, Ill.
Mr. George J. Burger, vice president, National Federation of Independent Business, Washington, D. C.
Mr. Leo F. Henebry, president, American National Retail Jewelers, Roanoke, Va.
Mr. Leo J. Heer, vice president, National Retail Furniture Association, 1028 Connecticut Avenue NW., Suite No. 822, Washington 6, D. C.
Mr. Lloyd C. Nelson, president, Cal-Dak Co., 225 Acacia Street, Colton, Calif.
Mr. Gordon L. Uhl, jeweler, 1410 Potomac Avenue, Dormont, Pittsburgh 16, Pa.
Mr. Millard Tydings, Joseph E. Seagrams Distillers, Baltimore, Md.

Mr. Stanley Smiley, general counsel, R. H. Macy & Co., Inc., New York, N. Y.
Mr. Fritz Lanham, American Fair Trade Council, 1434 West Eleventh Avenue, Gary, Ind.
Hon. John J. Sparkman, United States Senator of Alabama.

The following excerpts taken from the testimony of the opponents and proponents on H. R. 5767 seem to be pertinent to the basic issues involved:

OPPONENTS

Justice Department

It is inconsistent with the basic philosophy of the Sherman Act. * * * It is susceptible of use as a cloak to hide general price-fixing activities; and it impairs competition at all levels of production and distribution.

Federal Trade Commission

* * * The potential damage to consumers through price fixing would be much greater than any existing damage to producers through this form of price cutting.

* * * In analyzing the testimony of the witnesses supporting the fair-trade laws, resale price maintenance laws, testimony which was given before both the House Judiciary Committee and the House Interstate and Foreign Commerce Committee, it will be found that the overwhelming bulk of the arguments and evidence presented in behalf of the legislation is to the effect that it is necessary in order to protect the small-business man against predatory and discriminatory practices waged against him by his larger and more powerful rival.

Now if there is another means and a less onerous and less injurious or, might I say, a noninjurious method of meeting that particular problem, an alternative to fair trade which would meet that particular problem, I would say the overwhelming bulk of arguments advanced in behalf of fair trade would lose whatever foundation they now have.

* * * The resale price maintenance laws are a price-fixing measure, giving manufacturers the right to fix the exact level of retail prices; * * * it ignores the question of efficiency.

Mr. Stanley Smiley, general counsel R. H. Macy & Co., Inc.

Private price fixing invariably and inevitably works against consumers. Public policy requires the protection of millions of consumers, not the self-interest of a handful of manufacturers and retailers.

Congress should not apply to interstate commerce the systems of private price fixing now permitted under the falsely labeled "fair trade" laws of 45 States. Giving legal sanction to private price fixing merely spreads an economic umbrella over a favored few while the many stand out in the downpour of higher prices.

Under the protection of these laws, before the Schwegmann case more and more manufacturers were climbing aboard the price-fixing wagon. The effect of this trend was to hog-tie competition at the retailing level. Public policy demands an end to this unhealthy trend and a return to the healthy principle of a competition that sets prices according to consumer demand, and not by fiat of manufacturers.

No matter how it may be camouflaged, private price fixing never benefits consumers by lower prices. On the contrary, price fixing always results in price raising.

Congress has wisely recognized the need for competition among producers. Congress should similarly recognize the need for competition in distribution.

Arguments that price fixing is necessary to protect small-business men are not substantiated by the facts.

Experience demonstrates conclusively that fair-trade laws are not fair. They don't work in the manner claimed any more than prohibition did. They are unenforceable because of the American consumer's continued insistence on the right to buy at the lowest price he can find.

Fair-trade laws seriously inhibit all retailers and distributors who, like Macy's make it a cardinal point of business policy to endeavor to offer more and better goods at lower prices to more people all the time.

Congress should not surrender, even if it can, its constitutional power to regulate commerce among the States by delegating that power to the legislatures of the several States.

After the United States Supreme Court decision of May 21, 1951, had rendered the fair trade nonsigner clause illegal, more than 2,000 editorials in the Nation's publications praised the decision as a great victory for the American consumer and the free competitive system.

Fair-trade legislation eliminates our constitutional rights of contract.

Dr. Joseph M. Klamon, professor of marketing, Washington University, St. Louis, Mo.

The proponents of fair trade are anxious to eliminate the remaining few States which have failed to enact fair-trade legislation, in order to remove any basis for comparison of prices in fair-trade and non-fair-trade States.

If competition among producers of an item is good for the public, why should competition among retail sellers of that item be denied?

If the public is deceived by loss-leader prices, what would prevent equal deception as to fair-trade prices which are and have always been rather exorbitant?

Fair-trade practices as heretofore in use are potentially dangerous. They invite manufacturers and distributors of competing articles to enter into understandings to maintain prices higher than would otherwise prevail.

Remove the coercive pressure of organized retailers and often not all, but many, manufacturers lose interest in fair-trade price fixing.

Fair trade is a contradiction in a free-enterprise society.

Lloyd Halvorson, the National Grange

In substance, what this means is a request to let the States invalidate the national antimonopolistic laws.

Section 8 of the Constitution gives Congress the power "To regulate commerce with foreign nations and among the several States."

Resale price fixing, which eliminates normal price competition on individual products at retail. * * *

Legalized price fixing will add greatly to the problems of Congress through its effect on other segments of our economy.

Fixed mark-up margins, above the free competitive level, will restrict the amount of goods consumers and * * * buy and * * * will soon curtail production and cause unemployment and all sorts of economic, social, and political ills and evils.

To members of the National Grange it is shockingly un-American to suggest that a contract between private parties be enforced upon others.

H. R. 5767 goes so far as to allow associations of merchants to sue noncomplying retailers if the manufacturer does not take action.

H. R. 5767 would kill normal price competition to get at "loss leaders."

We should let competition decide what is a proper mark-up on goods sold at wholesale and retail.

If the Congress thinks that "loss leaders" are a serious evil, it should legislate to curb that evil without providing the basis for destroying normal price competition as does resale price fixing.

We of the grange want to let small business be the Gibraltar of free enterprise, and not the appendage of a corporate state and a leech upon society.

Resale price fixing is a barrier to new low cost methods of selling and a barrier to the expansion of efficient firms.

Small-business men complain about "price raids" and "loss leaders." Again we say, small-business men should be told to come up with a solution to that problem without destroying normal price competition.

If "loss leaders" are an evil used by big business to put small business out of business, then again I say we should have a bill to eliminate that evil. * * *"

The proponents of H. R. 5767 would have one believe that they are very afraid of big, powerful businesses or monopolists.

Resale price fixing tends to curtail competition among manufacturers as well as among retailers.

The reason vertical price fixing tends to curtail competition among manufacturers, as well as destroy it at wholesale and retail, is that it is a way of prearranging price.

Farmers strongly resent being forced to pay high fixed prices when some retailers would prefer to charge a lower price.

John Schwegmann, Jr. (Supermarket operator)

The supermarket operation is the greatest mass retailer of goods of all time. By incorporating the economical features of the department store, the wholesalers, the chain stores, and the cooperative groups, it is possible for the supermarket to move tons of merchandise at lower retail prices—up to 20 percent on many items.

It is impossible to protect the inefficient or unnecessary retailer through legislation.

Fixed price or fair trade is a devilish scheme to eliminate competition at all levels.

If the retail price is pegged, the price chain is secure and everyone is happy except the consumer.

We supermarket operators and millions of Americans need economic freedom to escape from a manufacturers' dictatorship, which can cause inflation as dangerous as the present national defense emergency.

Fair-trade legislation, which is retail price fixing by manufacturers, eliminates competition between retailers.

Under the fair-trade legislation, commodities of the same general class are not in free and open competition.

When a leading brand manufacturer fixes his retail price, the other manufacturers automatically fall in line and peg their prices in line with the leader.

Fair-trade legislation gives arbitrary governmental authority to individuals, companies, and corporations.

Donald Montgomery, UAW-CIO

The McGuire bill is bad medicine for consumers and is a quack remedy for the economic ills it is aimed at. While forcing consumers to pay high fixed prices, it will not solve the competitive problems of small retailers.

Some of the very manufacturers who, under the McGuire bill, will freeze prices of the nationally advertised lines will put up products under private labels at lower prices for the cut-price retailers.

The fundamental problem facing small retailers is the fact that nationally advertised products already are priced too high.

* * * The trend in merchandising has just about reduced the independent retailer to the status of agents for national manufacturers.

The remedy for the infirmities which the Supreme Court found in the Miller-Tydings Act is not to patch it up, but to repeal it.

Jack M. Eckerd (drug store owner)

* * * This bill is unfair to the consumer.

For anyone to say that prices are no lower without fair trade than with is a simple untruth.

The resulting boycott (of Pepsodent) was so effective that they soon were forced back on fair trade and even felt it necessary to put up $25,000 for the California fair trade pot to whip other nonsigners into line.

I believe that any bill to rigidly fix the gross profit on the sale of an item is un-American and will fail to serve its purpose.

To druggists who feel that fair trade has caused their good business the past 10 years, I ask "What type business hasn't been good the past 10 years?"

* * * The McGuire price-fixing bill is contrary to our system of free enterprise, unfair to the consumer, and of no value in protecting the small merchant against the giant retailer.

Mr. Julius Westheimer, president, Julius Gutman & Co., Inc., Baltimore, Md.

Can you conceive of anything less fair than a law which compels a store to perform an act which it never agreed to do, either verbally or in writing—namely to force that store to sell articles of merchandise at the manufacturer's dictated price level, higher by far than the price which the store would establish for the merchandise? * * *

This toothbrush is fair-traded (price-fixed) at 29 cents and in our store we sell it for 23 cents. It costs us 16 cents showing us a mark-up of 43 percent even at the reduced price we sell it for.

All stores—big and little—occasionally advertise specially priced merchandise to stimulate business It's not a question of loss-leaders. It is merely promotional merchandising. And we draw no line of distinction between price-fixed goods and price-free goods.

* * * If a store buys and pays for its goods, the store itself should establish the retail price for that goods.

* * * If you pass H. R. 5767, the price-fixing bill with the nonsigner clause in it our hands would be tied. * * * Someone else would be telling us what to sell our aspirin for. Anything fair about a fair-trade law like that, gentlemen?

* * * It is store policy * * * to save our customers money right down the line and therefore I submit that the "loss leader" argument * * * falls flat on its face under examination.

Mr. Wendell Berge

* * * The (Supreme) Court went on to say that we cannot find that the distributors were to have the right to use not only a contract to fix retail prices but a club as well.

* * * The effect * * * is to put the whole retail industry of a given State under absolute price dictation.

The present bill * * * not only permits the manufacturer to dictate minimum prices but it also permits him to prescribe stipulated prices if such are authorized by State law.

In a free economy the conflicting interests of the consumer and the retailer find their proper level through the forces of normal competition.

The proponents of fair-trade legislation have managed to stir up a great deal of emotional sympathy by identifying themselves with the small independent retailer as against the larger so-called predatory chain stores.

* * * It is a well-known fact that the resale price maintenance of branded goods is wholly ineffective as against the larger chain operations.

Although the Miller-Tydings Act only legalizes agreements prescribing minimum prices, the McGuire bill also applies to stipulated prices; in other words, specific or maximum prices as well as minimum prices.

* * * The McGuire bill legalizes agreements relating to stipulated prices in or affecting interstate or foreign commerce.

* * * The McGuire bill is directed to the Federal Trade Commission Act and reaches the Miller-Tydings amendment to the Sherman Act only by reciting, in the language amending the Federal Trade Commission Act, that "nothing contained in this (Federal Trade Commission) act or in any of the antitrust acts shall render unlawful," etc. That is certainly a back-handed method of cutting down the Sherman Act.

* * * Practically all the newspapers of the country which have commented on this matter have opposed this and similar bills.

* * * There has been no support for this bill except from special interests who think they would benefit from the enactment of the bill.

Informed consumers everywhere are against this bill, but we are all aware that consumers as a group are not highly organized or articulate. * * *

* * * The Senate of the United States (should) not be stampeded by high pressure lobby tactics into approving a bill so obviously against the public interest.

Jenkins Garrett (speaking for various Texas owned independent stores)

By this bill its proponents are asking the legislative branch of the National Government to declare a national policy in the field of interstate commerce.

* * * In these hearings the proponents are telling you the price-fixing laws are permissive laws and should be called "voluntary trade" laws. It reminds me of the words of the little colored boy talking to a little catfish he had just caught in the creek—"Hold still little fish, I ain't going to do anything to you—but just gut you."

This thing is bigger than the drug industry and the few manufacturers outside the drug field sponsoring this bill. This legislation covers every field of retailing and all fields of manufacturing.

A large number of small druggists support the doctrine of manufacturers setting prices, because under the system it guarantees them a 50 percent or better mark-up.

There has never been a greater boom to monopoly, a greater blow to private initiative in retailing, or a greater enemy of the small progressive merchant than this unrestrained power of the manufacturer to set retail selling prices. * * *

An enterprising independent merchant can whip the socks off a national chain operator any day of the week if the small merchant is left free to set his own retail selling prices. * * *

We see that this movement is dominated by the druggist, that few manufacturers support the movement outside the drug field, and that its leading advocates are the National Association of Retail Druggists, the American Fair Trade Council and the National Association of Chain Drug Stores.

* * * This form of legislation * * * justified the exemption of manufacturers from the Antitrust Act.

If independent merchants who oppose this bill are price conscious, it may be because we have gone to the school of experience of which the national chain is headmaster.

This bill will increase the cost of merchandise to the consumer.

If this bill decreased prices and caused the retailer to sell for less, it does not seem reasonable that the hundreds of thousands of dollars being spent now in trying to get this legislation through Congress would be expended.

Failures of druggists are nonexistent in the free competition States.

We are against this legislation because it does not eliminate loss leaders—it does not reduce prices—and it is not for the little man.

This legislation * * * deprives an enterprising retailer of the right to pass on to the customer savings affected by him by varying methods of doing business.

The ultimate objective of the retail associations, such as the Drug Association, is to force all manufacturers of drug products to set and enforce the retail selling price of their products at a mark-up acceptable to the association.

This Senate has in its power to grant these proponents the instrumentality to accomplish their objective * * *. All is needed is immunity from our revered antitrust laws and the power to bind a man on a contract to which he does not consent and which he will not sign.

J. E. Webb (drug store)

If the same keen spirited competition that built America is to be continued, this unfair trade act must not pass the Senate.

The manufacturer is fully protected without fair trade. No one can take his trade names away from him and he can reserve the right by law either to sell or not to sell, whomever he pleases.

No merchant can truthfully say that he believes in free enterprise and still be for fair trade. Free trade and fair trade are * * * far apart * * *.

Angus McDonald, National Farmers Union

We are opposed to the weakening of our antitrust laws in any way, especially in regard to price fixing.

Matt Triggs, American Farm Bureau Federation

We are opposed to all forms of price fixing, but the nonsigner provision incorporated in H. R. 5767 is, in our opinion, a particularly undesirable form of price fixing.

We know of no convincing evidence to indicate that those retail trades which have generally resorted to fair-trade price practices have been more profitable than those retail trades which have not. * * *

Farm price supports are comparable to minimum wages for labor or loss-leader legislation for the distribution trade.

Samuel Rosenthal (Standard Drug Co., Richmond, Va.)

The proponents claim that this law is needed to protect the small independent retailer against predatory loss-leader selling, but the proponents have not and cannot produce any proof that such predatory selling has in the past been the cause of eliminating competition at the retail level.

* * * Most manufacturers were coerced and forced into price fixing their merchandise and that these prices were fixed by various retail groups acting through associations * * * the consumer who pays the bill has no say whatsoever.

The proponents fail to tell us that the fair trade contract prices of the other manufacturers are exactly the same as that of Eli Lilly & Co.

Canada, which had such a price-fixing law for years, recently repealed this law. The only country that has absolute price fixing on everything is Russia.

The sponsors of this bill are aiming to destroy all competition at the retail and wholesale level.

⊥ It is plainly for the benefit of producers, distributors and retailers, and the welfare of the public is not considered.

It subsidizes certain retailers at the expense of the public.

Statutes such as this give evidence of the ability of organized minorities to procure legislation * * * at the expense of the unorganized purchasing public.

It involves an unlawful delegation of legislative power in permitting private individuals to fix prices binding upon another.

Mrs. Frances Wright, a housewife

Drug Topics said in the April 7 issue: "* * * The bill must win in the House with a majority so big that it will have a salutary effect upon the Senate * * *."

The bill did win, of course—196 to 10.

"Write your Senators and Congressmen today," the editor of Drug Topics advises, "and let them know you want them to get tough in their support of fair trade. Tell them you expect them to write H. R. 5767, as recommended by the (House) Commerce Committee, into law not only to help you but to help themselves as well."

I feel sure that Senators and housewives want the same thing: a country where the weak are protected * * * a country whose laws are made by the people not by the pressure groups.

National Association of Consumers

Resale price maintenance, establishing uniform prices or setting a floor under prices for particular branded articles is contrary to our proudly proclaimed principle of a free competitive economy.

* * * A system of private price fixing unregulated by public authority.

* * * Fair trade committees set up to police these price-fixing arrangements have also to come out of the consumer's dollar.

The assertion that small-business men will be ruined unless resale price maintenance is strengthened and even extended by nonsigner clauses hardly seems to be borne out by experience in those few States and the District of Columbia which so far have been able to resist the pressures for private price agreements.

Professor Brown, Yale University

Unless competition in distribution is preserved and encouraged by law, consumers may well be deprived of most of the advantages of technological progress in production.

Resale price maintenance is incompatible with the principles of a market economy.

Prof. Phillip Gamble, Consumers Union

* * * The problem of the "loss-leader" can be handled best for all concerned by fixing invoice cost as the minimum price if any legislation of this type is deemed necessary.

* * * The Miller-Tydings Act is much like the prohibition amendment, more likely to be dishonored than honored.

* * * This proposal is against the American tradition of free enterprise and is of doubtful constitutionality as an unconstitutional delegation of legislative powers * * *.

Bert C. Ahrens, National Association of Educational Buyers

Price fixing stifles competition and subverts the welfare of the public as a whole to the welfare of a select few.

The additional cost to the public as a whole can be estimated therefore as from 1,200 to 1,800 million dollars annually.

Mrs. G. Ralph Smith, Harpur College, Endicott, N. Y.

* * * It gives private parties power to fix prices greater than that of the States granting these powers.

* * * The violation of the laws or other merchandising practices should not be adequate justification for extending this type of legislation.

Herman Luckoff (store owner)

Fair-trade law will add to the poor man's burden, protecting the large interest by insuring the cost of advertising schemes.

Fair trade is highjacking the public * * *.

* * * The retailer, big and small, is complaining about Government intervention in business, yet he runs to the Government for a license to hold up the public and perpetuate all his schemes.

PROPONENTS

Mr. Maurice Mermey, director, Bureau of Education on Fair Trade

* * * The fair-trade laws are State laws.

* * * The fair-trade laws are laws of fair competition.

* * * Consumers pay less in fair-trade States.

* * * Fair-trade prices have resisted inflation.

* * * Fair trade is beneficial to small business; that facts regarding its causing higher prices in total are unconvincing: that monopoly does not result from fair-trade laws: and that fair-trade laws have a stabilizing influence on the economy.

Mr. John W. Anderson, president, American Fair Trade Council

* * * It is of high importance that H. R. 5767 be amended to assure that it will be fully effective in support of the traditional right of each individual State to determine for itself the "ground rules" under which its competitive economy may be enhanced in its capacity for service to its communities?

Subsection 4 of H. R. 5767 is widely regarded among outstanding fair-trade lawyers as falling far short of such exacting requirements of the courts for specific language * * *. It is not proposed that subsection 4 be eliminated or altered—nor that H. R. 5767 be altered in any other way except to add the "home town" amendment to its subsection 4.

Mr. George J. Burger, vice president, National Foundation of Independent Business

We of the federation want a strengthened fair-trade law. We do not, however, want any law written so it will be used for collusion among competitors.

We believe that had the antitrust agencies carried out these duties fully over past years there might be little need for fair-trade legislation. Had the Justice Department enforced the Sherman Act fully, monopolistic practices would not be as attractive as they are and have been * * *. Federal Trade Commission has not enforced section 5 of the Federal Trade Commission Act, which prohibits sales below the sellers' cost where the effect is to promote monopoly, and had both agencies enforced Robinson-Patman Act sections dealing with price discrimination fully, the functions of a fair-trade law would be cared for, to a great extent.

We do not believe that exclusive reliance on the laws indicated above would be an adequate substitute for fair-trade legislation now.

While we want a strengthened law to back existing State statutes, we do not want a law which would permit the fixing of maximum as well as minimum prices.

I believe that the fair-trade contract should be exclusively between the manufacturer-seller and his outlets. I do not believe it is wise for the States or any other agency to enter the picture, either as originating or enforcing agencies. * * *

Our federation urges you to enact this fair-trade law, together with sections which:

1. Permit manufacturer-sellers to enforce observance of fair-trade agreements on all sellers in a State as long as some have agreed to abide by these agreements.

2. Compel observance of fair-trade prices structures within fair-traded States by sellers operating out of non-fair-traded States.

3. Provide for the fixing of minimum resale prices only.

4. Provide effective penalties against those who would use the law to engage in collusive, rigged prices among the various competitive brands and items of merchandise.

Mr. Herman S. Waller, general counsel, National Association of Retail Druggists

This measure is urgently needed by the 45 States in the Union for the adequate enforcement of their respective State fair-trade laws, in order that they may properly promote fair and constructive competition in the field of distribution.

* * * This measure in no way commits the Congress to a Federal policy concerning fair trade; nor does it make any provision which will require or burden any governmental agency with the enforcement of this measure or any of the provisions of the State fair-trade acts; nor does this measure add any burdens to the Federal courts in the enforcement of these State laws.

H. R. 5767 is no more than a Federal enabling act to accommodate the States to carry out an adopted policy which was repeatedly declared to be constitutional and to be an appropriate means in an effort to regulate fair methods of competition in the field of distribution, as far as it may concern interstate transactions.

⊥ This measure is a constitutional prerogative of the Congress to promote and encourage State rights in the regulation of their internal affairs for the advancement of their respective communities.

Mr. Millard E. Tydings, representing Joseph D. Seagram & Sons and in his individual capacity

The philosophy of this act applies only to identified products.

The philosophy of the law is vertical, not horizontal.

The operation is directly downward. It goes from the creator and owner of an article, the manufacturer, all the way down to the man who finally purchases that article.

When an owner sells a piece of real property he usually insists, if he desires, to have inserted in the deed or contract of sale certain provisions concerning the property he is selling, which bind the purchaser and all subsequent purchasers. These provisions are known in law as covenants running with the land * * *.

* * * The article that was manufactured belongs to the man who manufactures it and it seems to me that he ought to have the right, as a real estate dealer has a right, to say under which terms and conditions it can be sold, provided that those terms and conditions are not such as to destroy competition between the manufacturer of that article and some other one or a large group of manufacturers making the same article.

Mr. Leo F. Henebry for American National Retail Jewelers Association

We are in favor of the basic merchandising principles which underlie the fair-trade laws * * *.

We believe that without the "home-town amendment," H. R. 5767 will not adequately protect the small retail merchant.

Mr. Leo J. Heer, National Retail Furniture Association

It is our strong conviction that fair-trade laws are of benefit only when they are capable of proper enforcement * * *.

We recommend to your committee three primary objectives to be incorporated in fair-trade legislation:

(1) Restoring the effectiveness of the nonsigner clause in State fair-trade law.

(2) Preventing the shipment with impunity into fair-trade States of merchandise at less than fair-trade prices.

(3) Making the responsibility for fair-trade observance a mutual one on both retailer and manufacturer.

The bill before you does not attain all those objectives and should therefore be amended to eliminate loopholes.

Mr. Lloyd C. Nelson, president, the Cal-Dak Co.

By setting a fair-trade price on our two products, we are not attempting to fix the retail price of this type merchandise * * *.

Price cutting is one of the strongest forces that can be used to develop monopoly * * *.

* * * Based on our experience, we contend that those manufacturers and retailers choosing to operate under fair trade on one or more products that they sell will stimulate competition among manufacturers and make possible lower prices on quality merchandise.

Mr. Gordon L. Uhl, jewelry store owner and operator

I cannot afford to compete with these loss-leaders by matching the cut prices of the other stores. You see I do not have any other types of merchandise that are unbranded and which I could sell at a higher price than they are worth to give me a fair average.

I am sure it is not the intention of the Government to ignore this kind of deceptive loss-leader selling, which takes business away from me every day * * * make it possible for me to stay in business by restoring fair-trade protection for me and thousands of other small jewelers all over the country.

Senator John J. Sparkman

* * * I would like to have permission to put in the record that part of the Annual Report of the Select Committee on Small Business of the Senate dated January 21, 1952, that deals with fair trade laws. It will be found at page 213, continuing through page 226.

I think the above represents a fairly objective study of the problem of fair trade legislation.

⊥ Our interest in the fair trade laws was drawn into this thing at about the time the price wars took place during last year, the Macy price wars. ⊥ 13

* * * It is not the imposition of Federal legislation upon a state or a community or a people. It is a recognition by the Federal Government of statutes which legislatures of various States have already enacted into law.

I am a great believer * * * in States Rights * * * it seems to me that this is the very essence of States Rights legislation. If fair trade laws are wrong, the wrong has been committed when the Federal Government takes notice of the fact that those States have, through the action of their own legislatures, put the laws on the book.

* * * The Joint Committee on the Economic Report under the chairmanship of Chairman O'Mahoney, of which I am a member, and the Small Business Committee joined in having a staff study made of this problem of price wars.

We had the services of Dunn [*sic*] and Bradstreet in making a survey. The results of that survey are shown in the report of the committee.

CHANGES IN EXISTING LAW

In compliance with the amendment to rule XXIX of the Standing Rules of the Senate set forth in Senate Resolution 95, Eighty-first Congress, first session, changes in existing law made by the bill (S. 1907) [*sic*] as reported are shown as follows (existing law proposed to be omitted is enclosed in black brackets, new matter is printed in italics, existing law in which no change is proposed is shown in roman):

THE FEDERAL TRADE COMMISSION ACT (ACT OF SEPTEMBER 26, 1914, 38 STAT. 717, AS AMENDED; 15 U. S. C. 41)

*   *   *   *   *   *   *

SEC. 5. (a) (*1*) Unfair methods of competition in commerce, and unfair or deceptive acts or practices in commerce, are hereby declared unlawful.

(2) Nothing contained in this Act or in any of the Antitrust Acts shall render unlawful any contracts or agreements prescribing minimum or stipulated prices, or requiring a vendee to enter into contracts or agreements prescribing minimum or stipulated prices, for the resale of a commodity which bears, or the label or container of which bears, the trade-mark, brand, or name of the producer or distributor of such commodity and which is in free and open competition with commodities of the same general class produced or distributed by others, when contracts or agreements of that description are lawful as applied to intrastate transactions under any statute, law, or public policy now or hereafter in effect in any State, Territory, or the District of Columbia in which such resale is to be made, or to which the commodity is to be transported for such resale.

(3) Nothing contained in this Act or in any of the Antitrust Acts shall render unlawful the exercise or the enforcement of any right or right of action created by any statute, law, or public policy now or hereafter in effect in any State, Territory, or the District of Columbia, which in substance provides that willfully and knowingly advertising, offering for sale, or selling any commodity at less than the price or prices prescribed in such contracts or agreements whether the person so advertising, offering for sale, or selling is or is not a party to such a contract or agreement, is unfair competition and is actionable at the suit of any person damaged thereby.

(4) Neither the making of contracts or agreements as described in paragraph (2) of this subsection, nor the exercise or enforcement of any right or right of action as described in paragraph (3) of this subsection shall constitute an unlawful burden or restraint upon, or interference with, commerce.

(5) Nothing contained in paragraph (2) of this subsection shall make lawful contracts or agreements providing for the establishment or maintenance of minimum or stipulated resale prices on any commodity referred to in paragraph (2) of this subsection, between manufacturers, or between producers, or between wholesalers, or between brokers, or between factors, or between retailers, or between persons, firms, or corporations in competition with each other.

(6) The Commission is hereby empowered and directed to prevent persons, partnerships, or corporations, except banks, common carriers subject to the Acts to regulate commerce, air

carriers and foreign air carriers subject to the Civil Aeronautics Act of 1938, and persons, partnerships, or corporations subject to the ⊥ Packers and Stockyards Act, 1921, except as provided in section 406 (b) of said Act, from using unfair methods of competition in commerce and unfair or deceptive acts or practices in commerce.

⊥ 14

NOTE.—Section 4 of such act (15 U. S. C. 44) contains the following definition:

"Antitrust Acts" means the Act entitled "An Act to protect trade and commerce against unlawful restraints and monopolies," approved July 2, 1890; also sections 73 to 77, inclusive, of an Act entitled "An Act to reduce taxation, to provide revenue for the Government, and for other purposes," approved August 27, 1894; also the Act entitled "An Act to amend section 73 and 76 of the Act of August 27, 1894, entitled 'An Act to reduce taxation, to provide revenue for the Government, and for other purposes' ", approved February 12, 1913: and also the Act entitled "An Act to supplement existing laws against unlawful restraints and monopolies, and for other purposes," approved October 15, 1914.

SENATE DEBATE
82d Cong., 2d Sess.
July 1, 1952

98 CONG. REC. 8716

The VICE PRESIDENT. The Chair lays before the Senate the unfinished business. The clerk will read the title of the bill for the information of the Senate.

The CHIEF CLERK. A bill (H. R. 5767) to amend the Federal Trade Commission Act with respect to certain contracts and agreements which establish minimum or stipulated resale prices and which are extended by State law to persons who are not parties to such contracts and agreements, and for certain other purposes.

The VICE PRESIDENT. The bill is open to amendment. If there be no amendment, the question is on the third reading of the bill.

Mr. [PAUL H.] DOUGLAS [D., Ill.]. Mr. President, is there to be discussion of this bill, or is it to go through with supersonic speed?

The VICE PRESIDENT. The Senator from Illinois is recognized.

Mr. [ERNEST W.] McFARLAND [D., Ariz.]. Mr. President, will the Senator from Illinois yield?

Mr. DOUGLAS. I will yield for a question.

Mr. McFARLAND. If it goes through with that speed, we shall not have a night session.

Mr. DOUGLAS. I am reminded of the old maxim, "Marry in haste and repent at leisure."

SEVERAL SENATORS. Vote! Vote!

Mr. DOUGLAS. Mr. President, are we going to pass this bill without its sponsors saying a word in its behalf? Is this child to be born without any statement as to the nature of the child?

SEVERAL SENATORS. Vote! Vote!

The VICE PRESIDENT. The Senate will be in order.

Mr. DOUGLAS. Mr. President, if no other Senator will discuss the bill, I shall.

Mr. President, I move that the bill be laid on the table.

The VICE PRESIDENT. Does the Chair understand that the Senator from Illinois moves to lay the bill on the table?

Mr. DOUGLAS. I so move.

The VICE PRESIDENT. The motion to lay on the table is not debatable.

Mr. DOUGLAS. Mr. President, I ask for the yeas and nays.

The yeas and nays were ordered.

Mr. SALTONSTALL. Mr. President, am I correct in my understanding that the motion before the Senate is a motion to lay on the table the fair-trade bill?

The VICE PRESIDENT. That is correct. A vote of "yea" is a vote to lay the bill on the table; a vote of "nay" is a vote against laying the bill on the table. The clerk will call the roll.

The legislative clerk called the roll. . . .

The result was announced—yeas 7, nays 64. . . .

So Mr. DOUGLAS' motion to lay the bill on the table was rejected.

The VICE PRESIDENT. The bill is before the Senate and open to amendment.

Mr. DOUGLAS. Mr. President, I made a motion to table, knowing that it would fail, as an opening shot, so that Members of the Senate might pause to know what they are doing. I had no desire to stop debate on this bill or prevent its consideration.

This is really an extraordinary situation. No Senator has risen on the floor of the Senate to expound the bill. I may point out that the bill has come from the committee without recommendation[.] The hearings have not been printed. No sponsor has risen to explain the bill or give the reasons why he favors it. It is extraordinary that no Senator is willing to assume that burden. Therefore the Senator from Illinois made the motion to table in order the Senators might have more time to consider their action. It is an extremely important bill.

Mr. [WAYNE] MORSE [R., Ore.]. Mr. President, will the Senator yield?

Mr. DOUGLAS. I yield.

Mr. MORSE. Does the Senator think there might be some possibility that the reason no Senator has seen fit to father the child is that there may be some question as to its paternity?

Mr. DOUGLAS. I was trying to imply that, but I did not wish to be invidious in my references. I think perhaps there might be some doubt about the quality of the child itself.

Mr. [JOHN J.] SPARKMAN [D., Ala.]. Mr. President, will the Senator yield?

Mr. DOUGLAS. I shall be glad to yield for any Senator to explain the merits of the bill. Then I should like to rise and state the reasons why I intend to oppose it.

Mr. [MATTHEW M.] NEELY [D., W. Va.]. Mr. President, will the Senator yield?

Mr. DOUGLAS. I yield.

Mr. NEELY. The purpose of the bill is to fix prices and increase the cost of living.

Mr. DOUGLAS. It certainly is.

Mr. NEELY. It is a bill to enable certain merchants and druggists to charge 155,000,000 American people three-fourths of a billion dollars a year more than they are now paying for the necessaries of life. The bill, if enacted, will increase the distress of every poor family and every poor man, woman, and child in the land. Under its operation six cans of milk, corn, beans, peas, soup, or other food products will cost approximately as much as seven cans cost now. A hundred other similar illustrations could be given. If the people who will be forced to bear the burden of this legislation, were as well organized and as impressive in making their wishes known as the druggists and merchants have been and still are, the Senate would, in my opinion, defeat the measure before it as decisively as it would defeat a bill to legalize highway robbery.

Since I entered the Chamber I have heard two Senators say, in effect, "This bill ought not to be passed. But the pressure for it is so great that we have decided to vote for it." Mr. President, I cannot vote for it because, regardless of the good intentions of its supporters, which are unquestioned, the effect of the bill would, in my opinion, be just as injurious to the people as it would be if it had been conceived in greed and born in iniquity. Neither the good intentions nor the benign wishes of those who favor it will help those who have to pay the cost of its operation.

This is a fight between a few thousand grocers and a few thousand druggists, on the one hand, and 155,000,000 consumers on the other. Therefore, as usual, put me down on the side of the people for whom I never fail to vote.

Mr. DOUGLAS. Mr. President, I share the general convictions of the Senator from

West Virginia, although perhaps on certain points I would not castigate certain groups as vigorously as he has done. I have tried to help some of the groups favoring this particular bill by trying to prevent them from being subjected to arbitrary price discriminations not justified by cost savings.

This is a bill to legalize resale price maintenance. What it does is to permit the manufacturers of trade-marked and branded commodities, if they make an agreement with one retailer, to determine the prices which all retailers shall charge for the commodity. It would enable them to determine not only the prices charged by a retailer who was a signer of the agreement, but the prices, in 45 States, which every other retail merchant charges, whether he signs the agreement or not.

Mr. SPARKMAN. Mr. President, will the Senator yield?

Mr. DOUGLAS. No; I should like to continue and develop the argument.

The VICE PRESIDENT. The Senator from Illinois declines to yield.

Mr. DOUGLAS. This is a private price-fixing bill. What it does is to permit a manufacturer to fix prices in the retail market, even though other retailers may not wish to charge such prices. What it does is to permit the manufacturer, if he can obtain one signer in a given State, to fix the prices which all other retailers in that State may charge. All the other retailers in 45 States would be bound to charge the same price, whether they wished to do so or not.

Mr. [J. ALLEN] FREAR [JR.] [D., Del.]. Mr. President, will the Senator from Illinois yield?

Mr. DOUGLAS. I yield.

Mr. FREAR. The Senator has raised a point which I should like to have cleared up. Does he say, as I have understood him to say, if a retail grocer or a retail druggist in Dover sells a price-fixed commodity and signs a contract for price fixing, that a retail druggist in Smyrna must charge the same price for that particular commodity?

Mr. DOUGLAS. That is correct; for that commodity.

Mr. FREAR. Even though the second merchant does not sign an agreement?

Mr. DOUGLAS. Even if he does not sign an agreement.

Mr. FREAR. Does it bind all the other druggists?

Mr. DOUGLAS. It binds all the other druggists who trade in that commodity.

Mr. FREAR. Why is it true in Delaware, as the Senator from Illinois has stated?

Mr. DOUGLAS. It is true in every State in which there is a State resale price maintenance law. Forty-five States have resale price maintenance laws. The only States which do not have such a law are Vermont, Texas, and Missouri, and the District of Columbia. If a manufacturer can get one person in each of the 45 States to sign a contract it applies for very nearly the whole United States.

Mr. FREAR. Mr. President, will the Senator from Illinois yield further?

Mr. DOUGLAS. I yield.

Mr. FREAR. Suppose a manufacturer of a certain product wants his price established at the retail level in one of the 45 States to which the Senator has referred. Is it possible for him to own a drug store or a grocery store in the State, in one way or another, directly or indirectly, and make a contract for a particular product and in that way force all the other retail merchants in the State to abide by that contract on that particular item?

Mr. DOUGLAS. Yes; I should think that would be possible. Generally, however, it is not necessary for a manufacturer to own a store and make an agreement with himself. Generally he can find one out of a number of merchants who is willing to make an agreement. It is not necessary that he have a "front." But he can work through one, if he wishes.

Mr. FREAR. Mr. President, will the Senator from Illinois yield further?

Mr. DOUGLAS. I yield further.

Mr. FREAR. That is what I wish to have determined. Suppose he wants to fix prices so badly that he buys a store and makes a contract. Is it possible for him to do that under this bill, if it is passed?

Mr. DOUGLAS. I know of nothing that would prevent that.

Mr. [WARREN G.] MAGNUSON [D., Wash.]. Mr. President, will the Senator yield?

Mr. DOUGLAS. I yield.

Mr. MAGNUSON. I think the record ought to be clear on that point. I know a little bit about our State laws. We have been living under such a law in Washington for a number of years. Everyone has been happy with it. Most of the State laws—and I looked into the subject when I was a member of the legislature in Washington—provide very severe penalties for doing what was suggested by the Senator from Delaware. They provide not only fines but prison terms. Forty-five States have been living under such laws. No Senator should stand up and say that Senators are cowardly in this matter, when the States which they represent have fair-trade laws. I represent the people of my State.

Mr. DOUGLAS. I have made no such statement.

Mr. MAGNUSON. I represent the State of Washington. I know the Senator from Illinois has not made such a statement.

Mr. [SPESSARD L.] HOLLAND [D., Fla.]. Mr. President, will the Senator yield?

Mr. DOUGLAS. May I be permitted to develop my argument?

Mr. HOLLAND. Mr. President, if the Senator will yield for a moment, the Senator from Florida wishes to support the statement which was just made by the distinguished Senator from Washington. The Senator from Florida was the author in his State on two occasions of similar State fair trade acts which have well served the people of the State of Florida.

Mr. [HUBERT H.] HUMPHREY [D., Minn.]. Mr. President, will the Senator from Illinois yield?

Mr. DOUGLAS. I am very glad to yield to the Senator from Minnesota.

The VICE PRESIDENT. Under the rule a Senator may yield only for a question, not for speeches.

Mr. HUMPHREY. I thank my illustrious friend for yielding to me.

Mr. President, we can discuss the measure before us without invective and without emotion. I honestly believe that the two points of view can be legitimately presented. I have very strong feelings about the bill. They are not engendered by textbooks, catalogs, or documents. I have feelings which arise from a great deal of experience from living at a time when there were no fair-trade laws.

I should like to say, with respect to the charge of price fixing, or whatever it may be called, that it is interesting to observe, when the Senate has provided price supports for American farmers, and justly so, that there are a great many people who want cheap food and would have it even if it would drive the farmer out of business. Who would benefit? The alleged consumer, apparently. Mr. President, among the consumers is the American farmer himself. He can consume nothing without a fair price.

The same Senators who have voted for labor laws on the floor of the Senate, which would give the right of collective bargaining, the union shop, and the closed shop, and would give the workingmen and the consumer a chance to have some money with which to buy food, oppose fair-trade laws. There are a great many people who want no unions because they want cheap labor. They do not believe in minimum wage laws. They want cheap labor.

I am in favor of minimum wage laws. I am in favor of trade-unions. I am in favor of price supports. I have seen what happened when we had no unions and no price supports. I have seen what happened when we did not have minimum wage laws and no child labor laws.

Mr. President, I shall produce evidence before this debate is over which will show what will happen to thousands upon thousands of independent merchants who will be at the mercy of the monopolistic powers in America that will drive them out of the markets. I say to the lovers of the consumer that those interests have rigged prices time and again. I saw my father-in-law driven out of business by those methods. I saw my own father suffer from them. I feel very deeply about this matter.

There are two sides to this question, Mr. President, the side of monopoly and the side of the Clayton-Sherman Antitrust Acts. I want those laws enforced. I say to the Federal Trade Commission and the other Federal agencies: "Get busy and enforce those laws." But I also want to make sure that there is such a thing as fair play and equity, and a fair deal, to which some of us have been pledged.

There is such a thing as a fair price for an honest day's labor and a professional service. I think we shall be able to join the debate on these issues, Mr. President.

I wish to thank my very esteemed and wonderful friend, the Senator from Illinois, for giving me this chance to submit my views. He knows there is an honest difference of opinion between us.

I have the greatest respect for the distinguished Senator from Illinois; I do not have greater respect for any other man, either in connection with this matter or in connection with any other matter. The Senator from Illinois knows that we are good friends, and that we shall continue to be after we have fought out this issue.

Mr. DOUGLAS. Mr. President, I am glad the exchange of shots has brought forth some arguments in behalf of this measure. I think we shall develop some discussion of it before the evening is over.

Mr. [HERBERT H.] LEHMAN [D., N.Y.]. Mr. President, will the Senator from Illinois yield to me?

Mr. DOUGLAS. No; I should like to finish one sentence before I yield.

The VICE PRESIDENT. The Chair wishes to remind all Senators that we are approaching the end of the session. The Chair wishes to have the business of the Senate transacted in an orderly way. Although we are more or less lenient when we have plenty of time, Senators should understand that a Senator who has the floor cannot yield to other Senators for speeches without endangering his place on the floor.

Mr. DOUGLAS. Very well. Then, Mr. President, in the future I shall yield only for questions. I am very glad the Chair did not make the rule prior to this point, because I wanted my friend, the Senator from Minnesota, to have a chance to make his statement.

The VICE PRESIDENT. The Chair did not make the rule; the Chair merely has called attention to it. [Laughter.]

Mr. DOUGLAS. First, Mr. President, I should like to take up the point which has been made by my friend, the Senator from Minnesota, namely, that we have price fixing for agriculture, and we have collective-bargaining agreements, and now we have rulings by the Wage Stabilization Board in regard to wages and salaries, and so forth. I wish to say that certainly a society in which prices are fixed by compulsion is not an ideal society. Certainly the ideal society should be one with a competitive economy.

Mr. [GEORGE D.] AIKEN [R., Vt.]. Mr President, will the Senator from Illinois yield for a question?

Mr. DOUGLAS. I am willing to yield for a question, although I wish my good friend would permit me to finish a paragraph before I yield.

Mr. AIKEN. A moment ago I observed that the Senator from Illinois asked other Senators who requested that he yield to wait until he had finished a sentence. I wonder why at this point the Senator from Illinois asks that I wait until he finishes a paragraph.

Mr. DOUGLAS. Mr. President, I love my friend, the Senator from Vermont, so much that I yield to him at this point for a question.

Mr. AIKEN. I thank the Senator from Illinois. My question is this: Is not the pending bill comparable to a closed shop for merchandise?

Mr. DOUGLAS. I think it is much worse than a closed shop—very much worse than a closed shop, because a closed shop, after all, merely applies to those who sign the agreement. On the other hand, this measure applies not only to those who sign the agreement but also to all those who do not sign the agreement.

BILL WOULD DELEGATE CONGRESSIONAL POWERS TO PRIVATE INDIVIDUALS

This bill constitutes a surrender to the manufacturer and to a handful of retailers, to permit them to determine what shall be the price for a given brand of commodity within a given State.

Let me point out to my good friend, the Senator from Minnesota, that in the case of most of the prices for which there is universal application—in fact, for nearly all of them for which there is universal application—those prices are subject to decisions by public bodies. Congress fixes the parity formula in the case of agricultural price support. An administrative board fixes wages and salaries. Wages and salaries are fixed administratively after due notice, after public hearing, and an opportunity for all parties to be represented.

But in the case now before us, private parties get together and fix prices not only for themselves but for the entire society. So I think there is a very great difference on this point.

What this measure does is to give public power to private persons to fix prices.

This bill arises, of course, as a result of the decision of the Supreme Court of the United States in the Schwegmann Bros. case, last year. In that case the Court declared that when Congress passed the Miller-Tydings Act, Congress had not intended it to apply to retailers who had not signed contracts. It was this decision of the Court—which, in my judgment was correct, namely, that a contract could not be enforced against nonsigners—which has led to the drive for the enactment of the McGuire bill, which now is before the Senate.

LOSS LEADER IS THE REAL EVIL

Mr. President, I wish to be fair in this matter, of course. I am well aware of the forces which led to the adoption of the so-called fair-trade laws in the various States. I believe those laws are really resale price maintenance laws, and I am well aware of the reasons behind the passage by Congress of the Miller-Tydings Act in 1937.

The argument which was used in support of those measures, and which swayed tens of thousands of honest merchants, was the threat of the loss leader. I think all of us know what the loss leader is. For example, during the depression the drug-store chains would advertise a sale of well-known products, such as Colgate's toothpaste and Bayer aspirin, at prices far below wholesale costs. In this way, consumers were drawn away from independent druggists. The loss leader was profitable to the chains since, although losses were taken on the advertised products, the customers thus drawn into the store would purchase drugs and other items on which there were much larger mark-ups. The independents, not having the resources for advertising, could not compete.

An even better example is the case of the department store. If a department store offered Kodak photographic materials at less than cost, as a loss leader, it could mark up prices on other goods. The customers would buy the Kodak items on which the department store would lose money. But while in the store, customers would buy other goods, not knowing that the mark-ups had been increased. The items thus marked up were called sucker items, and proponents of retail price maintnance claimed that there was not price cutting, beneficial to the consumer, but was price juggling, whereby the consumer paid more.

Meanwhile, the neighborhood camera shop was made to look like a high-cost operation. The fact is that it may have been actually more efficient than the department store, having less advertising and general overhead, but it could not sell its only items at less than cost, and thus had to go out of business.

The same problem existed for the small bookstores, jewelry stores, clothing stores, sporting-goods stores, and others.

The problem of the loss leader was what brought popular support behind the measure now before us.

SENATE SHOULD PASS A BILL OUTLAWING LOSS LEADERS

I wish to say that I am opposed to the loss leader, and one of the amendments which I shall submit is an amendment to outlaw the loss leader. It should be done. The loss leader can serve no valid competitive purpose. One cannot be efficient by selling below cost.

It is not necessary for us to establish resale price maintenance all over the country, merely to eliminate the loss leader. A measure to prohibit the loss leader is really equivalent to the Robinson-Patman Act to prohibit discriminatory sales—or, in other words, an extension of the principle of the Robinson-Patman Act. I favor the Robinson-Patman Act.

On the other hand, the loss leader has been improperly used as the excuse to fasten private price fixing upon the country.

The solution which was sought by the small concerns—and I wish to say they have been egged on by the manufacturers of the branded products—was resale price maintenance, which would stop loss leaders.

THE BAD FEATURES OF THE SOLUTION

The solution sought by the small concerns was resale price maintenance, which would stop loss leaders. Manufacturers took up this cause, since it enabled them to fix prices at whatever level they chose. This was, perhaps, justifiable in the sense that the manufacturers wanted as many outlets as possible, in order to be able to prevent price cutting, especially price cutting which had the effect of squeezing out numerous outlets in the form of the smaller concerns or smaller stores.

However, resale price maintenance not only stopped loss leaders but it permitted—and I wish to emphasize this point—retail mark-ups to be fixed at excessively high prices, and thus permitted very large profits. As a result of high retail prices, not only did the retailer obtain a big mark-up but the manufacturer also obtained a big mark-up over cost. In many cases—in fact, I think in the majority of cases—the retailers have been used as catspaws for the manufacturers of the branded and trade-marked products.

Mr. HUMPHREY. Mr. President, will the Senator yield at this point for a question?

Mr. DOUGLAS. Certainly I yield for a question.

Mr. HUMPHREY. My question is whether the Senator from Illinois has any information or evidence which would lead him to believe that when fair-trade laws were passed by the respective States, the manufacturers really were the proponents of those laws; or were they the opponents.

Mr. DOUGLAS. Mr. President, I believe that the move for resale price maintenance was begun by manufacturers. At any rate what is the Biblical phrase? Is it "the hand may be the hand of Esau, but the voice is the voice of Jacob"? Or is it just the other way around?

Mr. President, I have consulted my good friend, the Senator from West Virginia [Mr. NEELY], and he says that I have completely reversed that Biblical quotation. Both manufacturers and some retailers now favor it.

Mr. HUMPHREY. But I take it that the quotation from the Bible, as the Senator from Illinois gave it, is somewhat apropos in this case, because it happens that those who were opposed in the beginning to what the Senator from Illinois alleges to be price-fixing laws were the manufacturers. They were opposed because they got a big market through their cut-rate stores, and they did not care a bit about to whom they sold or how the sales were made, so long as the sales were made. Is not that correct?

Mr. DOUGLAS. Of course history is a difficult thing to plumb 20 years after the date. But would my good friend from Minnesota say that the big drug companies now are opposed to this bill?

Mr. HUMPHREY. No, I may say to the Senator that the manufacturers are for this bill.

Mr. DOUGLAS. Most certainly they are for the bill.

Mr. HUMPHREY. And I would like to ask the Senator further, whether he can name important items, the prices of which were sharply increased in order to get the gap between the regular price and the fair-trade price.

Mr. DOUGLAS. Yes. We have studies by the Federal Trade Commission indicating the increase in prices which followed upon the introduction of the resale price maintenance laws, and they show very real increases in those items compared with other commodities, particularly after passage of the Miller-Tydings Act. For instance, let us take fixed-price items before and after passage of the Miller-Tydings Act in Michigan, in Knoxville, and in New York City. The increase in Knoxville after the passage of the Miller-Tydings Act was 10 1/2 percent; in Michigan, 15.7 percent, in New York City, 25.8 percent. I ask that this material, which I shall furnish for the RECORD, be printed as part of my remarks at this point.

There being no objection, the material was ordered to be printed in the RECORD, as follows:

Price increase on fixed-price items, before and after Miller-Tydings Act, in Michigan, Knoxville, and New York City

	Percentage increase
Knoxville, Tenn.	10.5
Michigan	15.7
New York City	25.8

Source: Study of Monopoly Power, hearings before House Judiciary Committee, February 13, 1952, p. 504.

Average prices in cut-rate drug stores of free-priced and fixed-price items before and after Miller-Tydings Act in Knoxville, Tenn. (196 branded items)

Free-priced items, percentage change between 1937 and 1938; 4 percent decrease.

Fixed-price items, percentage change between 1937 and 1938; 10.5 percent increase.

Source: Study of Monopoly Power, hearings before House Judiciary Committee, February 13, 1952, p. 506.

Mr. DOUGLAS. In contrast to the increases I have indicated, prices, as a whole, were falling during this period.

Mr. HUMPHREY. Mr. President, will the Senator yield?

Mr. DOUGLAS. Certainly.

Mr. HUMPHREY. Is it not true that the figures which the Senator is citing are related to cut-rate, below-cost prices which were being used as a means of inducing customers to enter the store, but that the legitimate price is an entirely different thing? I can give the Senator an example.

Mr. DOUGLAS. It is difficult to determine what is a legal price.

Mr. HUMPHREY. I can tell the Senator.

Mr. DOUGLAS. I wish the Senator would do so.

Mr. HUMPHREY. It is a price which will at least enable a merchant to get out of a commodity what he has put into it. I can give the Senator example after example of instances in which commodities were sold for 10 cents or 15 cents below the wholesale cost. It was because of the gap evidenced by the Federal Trade Commission's report.

Mr. DOUGLAS. Mr. President, I have said that I understand the motive on the part of most merchants, and their desire to check the use of loss leaders is a worthy motive. In no sense do I regard the proponents of this measure as evil men. I think they are mistaken, but I can understand the reasons for their position. I should like to point out, however, what happens when we permit this type of price fixing. The first result is that prices to the consumer go up. That is not only true historically, but there are many current illustrations of it. Fortunately, there are 3 States and the District of Columbia which do not have the resale price maintenance laws. We can compare prices in those States and in the District with prices in the States which do have resale price maintenance laws. I should like to give certain illustrations.

Mr. HUMPHREY. What are those States?

Mr. DOUGLAS. Mr. President, the States which do not have such laws are Missouri, Vermont, and Texas, and the District of Columbia.

I have in my hand the House hearings on this point. I am going to read from page 433. A man by the name of Rosenthal, whose testimony was not questioned, submitted a list of 208 items. They were priced in each of the 45 resale price maintenance States. They were also priced in Texas, Missouri, Vermont, and the District of Columbia. Let the Senate listen to this: The average total price of those 208 items in the 45 States which had price-maintenance laws was $945.10. The average total selling price of the same items, in Texas, Missouri, Vermont, and the District of Columbia was $740.86.

In other words, the price was $205 greater in the 45 resale price maintenance States than in the four jurisdictions which did not have such a law. The price was 28 percent higher in the resale price maintenance States than in the nonresale price maintenance States.

Mr. BENTON rose.

Mr. DOUGLAS. I yield to the Senator from Connecticut.

Mr. [WILLIAM] BENTON [D., Conn.]. While the Senator is checking his figures, will he yield for a question about them?

Mr. DOUGLAS. Certainly.

Mr. BENTON. As a very outstanding example, will not the Senator agree that manifestly, in line with his position, it is impossible, of course, for prices to go up 25 percent in New York City, while prices throughout the country are falling?

Mr. DOUGLAS. Does the Senator refer to the items on the list of 208 articles?

Mr. BENTON. Is it not manifestly true that the 25 percent figure, which is the figure cited in the four areas, applies only to certain items, whether 20 or 208?

Mr. DOUGLAS. They were the so-called fixed-price items. But the illustration I am giving is not a historical one; it is a current cross-section comparison of prices in the 45 States which have so-called fair trade or resale price maintenance laws, compared with the four jurisdictions which do not have such laws. . . .

Mr. HUMPHREY. The Senator from Illinois would make a good druggist.

Mr. BENTON. I suggest that the Senator has made with that list the very point I was about to make, namely, that the total impact of those items on the cost-of-living index is relatively small. Is it not true that the total annual sales of the nationally advertised drug items the names of which the Senator has been reading, or at least many of them, do not represent a volume of $2,000,000 a year? Is it not true that their total impact on the cost-of-living index is small, and is it not true that the trick of the loss leader, which the Senator has twice stated he opposes, is in the small volume items of the type he has read, and, to give to the customer the illusion that, because the price, for example, of Carter's Little Liver Pills, or whatever the item may be, is cut, all the items in the store are cheap? Such a practice gives to the customer, does it not, the illusion, that, because he can buy an item of standard price, such as Carter's Little Liver Pills, at a low cost, he also can get his bread cheaper.

Mr. DOUGLAS. What is the question of the Senator from Connecticut? I do not want to lose my right to the floor.

Mr. BENTON. Is it not true that the 208 items may be higher in price and at the same time the cost of living or the general price level may fall? Does he make the point—

Mr. DOUGLAS. Just a moment. These are commodities to which this system is applied.

The argument of the Senator from Connecticut is apparently that, because one takes only a little from the consumer's pocket on each item, even though it is taken on hundreds of items, it does not matter in the long run.

That is the argument which has been used time and time again. The druggist says, "It is only a matter of a few cents to the consumer—why should he mind it?" The money in the consumer's pocketbook, however, goes to the purchase of a wide variety of commodities, and, if he gets "soaked" on each commodity, he then loses heavily. Small individual losses make for huge collective deficits.

This same argument has been applied in the case of gas and power rates by those who would profit at the expense of the consumer.

Mr. BENTON. I may ask the Senator if he is not misinterpreting my question. Is it not true that if the customer pays a little bit more for Carter's Little Liver Pills, while at the same time he pays less for bread and potatoes, he is not going to be out money?

Mr. DOUGLAS. I may say that sickness plays no favorites, and that the prices fixed on drug items must be paid by the poor as well as by others in the community.

Mr. BENTON. But does not the Senator know that the trick of the loss leader is to take a loss of the pennies, so that the merchant can reap profits in the terms of dollars? Does he not know that the merchants all build their volume through the use of the loss-leader illusion, and make up any loss by higher charges on other items?

Mr. DOUGLAS. The loss leader is not in dispute here. I am not advocating the loss leader. I have an amendment which will outlaw the loss leader. In order to cure the evil of the loss leader, it is recommended by the unknown sponsors of this bill that we embark upon price fixing. The Senator's argument is beside the point.

Mr. HUMPHREY. How many commodities did the Senator mention?

Mr. DOUGLAS. I mentioned 208 drug items.

Mr. HUMPHREY. Is the Senator familiar with the retail study made by A. C. Nielsen?

Mr. DOUGLAS. No.

Mr. HUMPHREY. It is an independent market research agency, the world's largest independent market research agency, with an outstanding reputation for reliability.

Mr. BENTON. It is one of the best.

Mr. HUMPHREY. It analyzed 24 leading fair-trade drug-store products. The study covered the 6-months period from March through August 1951. It showed that the over-all average prices under the fair-trade items in the fair-trade stores, instead of being over, were equal to or lower than the prices paid by consumers in non-fair trade areas for 24 products.

Mr. NEELY. Mr. President, will the Senator from Illinois yield?

Mr. DOUGLAS. I yield.

Mr. NEELY. If the facts, as stated by my distinguished and beloved friend, the Senator from Minnesota, are correct, and it is true that in the stores to which he refers the prices were lower than they were in the cut-rate stores, why is this proposed law desired?

Mr. HUMPHREY. May I have a moment to reply to the Senator? I ask unanimous consent to make a brief reply to the Senator from West Virginia, without the Senator from Illinois losing the floor.

The VICE PRESIDENT. Without objection, the Senator from Minnesota may proceed.

Mr. HUMPHREY. The Senator from West Virginia has said that if my statement with reference to the Nielsen study is correct, why is it that anyone would want this law. Is that correct?

Mr. NEELY. Yes.

Mr. HUMPHREY. I will tell the Senator. It is because of a decision by the Supreme Court involving the Tydings Act. All the bill does is to enable States to take certain action of their own, and it legitimatizes action taken in 45 State legislatures.

I want to say to my friend from West Virginia that the reason why merchants are concerned—I think they may be over-apprehensive about it—is that they can see that a man can start a store across the boundary of a State and be able to evade the fair-trade laws. In other words, he can sell cigarettes cheaper because they are shipped into the next State. He can literally give away goods.

As a union man does not like a scab to take his job, so a legitimate merchant does not like to have a cutthroat artist take his business. A scab takes a union man's job at lower wages and with poor working conditions. All that a cut-rate artist does is to lower the whole standard of business enterprise and drive legitimate merchants out of business. There is real apprehension and real fear.

There is no small-town merchant in the world who can stand competition with large concerns who would drive them out of business, by the use of loss leaders or by some other means.

Mr. DOUGLAS. My amendment outlaws loss leaders. That is not the question. The question is whether retail price fixing is justified by a manufacturer entering into an agreement with one or two merchants with respect to a certain commodity which will then apply to the entire list of retail outlets for that commodity, and then whether the Government will make such agreements enforcible upon nonsigners as well as upon signers.

Mr. HUMPHREY. May I ask the Senator from Illinois, if he feels so strongly about it, why was it that in the Committee on Labor and Public Welfare, when we were objecting to the Fulbright amendment, which calls upon the Government to pay extra prices in order to get commodities—

Mr. DOUGLAS. That had to do with an action which was subject to court review, after public hearing. This is a proposal to allow a private manufacturer to reach an agreement with a single merchant without being subject to any public considerations or procedures. It then becomes enforcible, and the Government allows the full weight of the common law to be used.

I am opposed in theory to price fixing as a whole. I believe in the competitive system, but I most certainly believe that if prices are to be fixed it should be done by a public authority and not by a private one.

Mr. HUMPHREY. Does the Senator not know what is provided in section 5, paragraph (2) of the bill? That is the paragraph which is the heart of this bill.

It provides:

> Nothing contained in this act or in any of the antitrust acts shall render unlawful any contracts or agreements prescribing minimum or stipulated prices—

And so forth. In other words, if they try to do horizontal price fixing to lessen competition, they are subject to the full penalties of the law. The fact of the matter is that during World War II prices were the least on commodities which were under fair-trade laws as compared with commodities which were not.

Mr. MOODY rose.

Mr. DOUGLAS. Mr. President, the Senator from Minnesota, in one sentence—

The PRESIDING OFFICER (Mr. HOLLAND in the chair). Does the Senator from Illinois yield to the Senator from Michigan?

Mr. DOUGLAS. I want to finish a paragraph without being interrupted.

Mr. [BLAIR] MOODY [D., Mich.]. I had not even asked the Senator to yield.

Mr. DOUGLAS. Mr. President, what we do if we pass this bill is to protect vertical price fixing. We permit a manufacturer to determine the prices which shall be charged all the way through to the ultimate customer.

The Senator from Minnesota says, "Ah yes; but we are still outlawing horizontal price fixing. In other words, the chain is around our feet, but not around our hands." I say we should not have chains on either hands or feet. We should have neither horizontal price fixing nor vertical price fixing.

The Senator from Minnesota is a very sophisticated gentleman, and I have heard him argue that agreements can be reached quietly without any evidence existing that the agreements have been reached; and from the similarity of the prices which are frequently fixed for similar products by drug stores and other stores, I have the feeling that these gentlemen know each other and that there is covert horizontal price fixing as well as vertical price fixing.

The extraordinary thing about aspirin is that it tends to sell or used to sell at about the same price when it is put on the market. There are many other drug commodities, the names of which I could read into the RECORD, the prices of which tend to be relatively uniform among the various drug houses. There are many kinds of consumers' durable goods where the prices tend to be relatively uniform.

I believe it was Lincoln who said that if and when Stephen—meaning Stephen A. Douglas—and James—meaning James Buchanan—and Roger—meaning Roger Taney—all acted, in a given way, he presumed there might be some understanding between Stephen, James, and Roger. So I presume there is some understanding on horizontal levels, as well as on vertical levels.

Mr. MOODY and Mr. NEELY addressed the Chair.

The PRESIDING OFFICER. Does the Senator from Illinois yield; and if so, to whom?

Mr. DOUGLAS. I should yield first to the Senator from Michigan.

Mr. MOODY. I should like to ask the distinguished Senator from Illinois whether he considers horizontal price fixing or vertical price fixing to be more important.

Mr. DOUGLAS. I consider both of them bad. I know it will be said that if there is vertical price fixing, but not horizontal price fixing, there will then be competition between brands.

Mr. MOODY. That is just the point.

Mr. DOUGLAS. That is partially true. I do not wish to overstate my case, but I wish to make two points in reply to that suggestion. The first is that there is not as much price competition between brands as we think. The second point I wish to make is that to the low and moderate income families, retail price is very important. If prices are high, it means a definite reduction in their standard of living. The matter of price is extremely important.

Assuming, for the moment, that there is competition among competing brands, price maintenance still destroys price competition among retailers. Competition in store advertising and service works in favor of the stores with access to the greatest amounts of credit. These are not the independents. Furthermore, low-income consumers must be subjected to lower living standards by high prices. So far as living standards are concerned, decorations, store advertising, and convenience do not help the consumer to buy more. The only thing that will do this is to lower prices.

Mr. HUMPHREY. Will the Senator yield?

Mr. DOUGLAS. No. I am in the full flight of my oratory. [Laughter.]

There seems to be a design, somehow, to make people feel that it is improper of them to think of money. One of the reasons why I am against this bill, why I want to have competition, is that it would enable consumers to think of money. I do not believe it is ignoble to think of money. I believe the hard-pressed consumers of the country have a right to think of money and to get the best bargains they can obtain at competitive prices.

Mr. HUMPHREY. Mr. President, will the Senator yield?

Mr. DOUGLAS. This is an extraordinary experience, to be challenged by my dearest friends.

Mr. HUMPHREY. And we love him dearly in spite of all. [Laughter.]

Mr. MOODY and Mr. HUMPHREY addressed the Chair.

The PRESIDING OFFICER. Does the Senator from Illinois yield; if so, to whom?

Mr. DOUGLAS. I will take the Senator from Michigan first.

Mr. MOODY. I hope the Senator will not be able to take him, but I am glad the Senator will yield.

Is it not true, as the Senator said a few minutes ago, that there is an honest difference of opinion with respect to the bill, as to which form of price fixing will harm the consumer less?

Mr. DOUGLAS. There are honest differences, and there are a great many misguided people.

Mr. MOODY. It is obvious that someone is misguided. The question is, Who is misguided?

Mr. DOUGLAS. I have my own opinion about that.

Mr. MOODY. So do I.

Mr. HUMPHREY. Mr. President will the Senator yield?

Mr. DOUGLAS. I yield.

Mr. HUMPHREY. The Senator has made a great to-do about the consumer and his regard for prices and money. That is very good. I appreciate that.

Mr. DOUGLAS. Before the Senator from Minnesota interjects—well, let him go ahead.

Mr. HUMPHREY. I should like to get my statement into the RECORD. The Senator must consider something else. He must consider the fact that in many communities where the proposed law would apply to certain merchants, they are the merchants who contribute to the community chest. Has the Senator ever tried to get a contribution from a merchant for a community chest? Some ⊥ merchants have to rush to their headquarters in New York before they can open their back door.

Has the Senator ever tried to get a contribution for the municipal band, or to establish a new park? I have, and I am here to tell the Senator that by the time such a contribution is forthcoming to do the community a service, the whole program will be dead.

Mr. DOUGLAS. I wish to make a reply to my good friend, the Senator from Minnesota. I take it he is well acquainted with the operas of Gilbert and Sullivan.

Mr. HUMPHREY. Yes.

Mr. DOUGLAS. The Senator is familiar with the Mikado. One of the stanzas of a famous song begins with the words:

> The flowers that bloom in the spring, tra la, have nothing to do with the case.

The matter of getting a subscription for the village band, or of getting milk for the children on the other side of the tracks has nothing to do with the present issue. As a matter of fact, if the Senator desires to get milk of magnesia for the children on the other side of the tracks, let him help the prices come down. The idea that one should permit others to pick his pocket, if in turn they will dish it out for support of the community is a non sequitur. Post hoc ergo propter est non sequitur.

Mr. HUMPHREY. I wish to say to the Senator that with his pleasing eloquence and his flights of oratory, he should tell the consumers that they do not have to buy the advertised products. For instance, he mentioned aspirin. If he wants to get aspirin, he can step into any store in the United States and get aspirin for a tenth of what he would have to pay for a standard brand. It is not fair trade that holds up the price of aspirin. After all, there are other commodities in competition. The Senator has assumed that there is no competition, but there are more brands of milk of magnesia than there are cows.

Mr. DOUGLAS. If each manufacturer tried to raise prices and was successful through agreements, it would stand to reason that the sum total of prices would be higher than they otherwise would be, because the whole which is made up of the sum of its parts, must be greater if the parts are greater.

Mr. HUMPHREY. I may say to the Senator briefly that the trouble with his argument is that there are so many different manufacturers engaged in manufacturing, they do not dare raise their prices so high that they will go out of business.

Mr. DOUGLAS. Some minutes ago, and several pages back in the RECORD, the Senator from Connecticut implied that this was a minor matter and did not substantially affect the consumer. During the progress of the debate I have been searching for a reference which I should like to give from Fortune magazine. Fortune is not biased against resale price maintenance laws. Like other great national publications, it gets a major portion of its revenue from the manufacturers of trade-marked, branded products.

In January and April of 1949 Fortune magazine conducted a survey of prices on many items in the District of Columbia and comparable prices on identical articles in surrounding fair-trade territory, primarily Virginia and Maryland. On the basis of this and other surveys, Fortune conservatively estimated that fair-trade—and that is a euphemism, it is really resale price maintenance—was costing the American public no less than three-quarters of a billion dollars annually. Three-quarters of a billion dollars is not something to be sneezed at or laughed at on the floor of the Senate.

Another illustration I was trying to refer to before my good friends interrupted to interrogate me was a comparison in my own State of Illinois.

We have a so-called fair trade retail price maintenance law. The State of Missouri on the opposite side of the Mississippi River does not have such a law. There are twin cities—the city of St. Louis, which is in Missouri, and the city of East St. Louis, which is in Illinois. The St. Louis Star-Times made a study of the prices of drugs and liquors in both those cities. It was found that the average prices on liquor were approximately 16 percent lower in St. Louis, Mo., than in East St. Louis, Ill. The average prices on drug items were no less than 12 percent lower.

We on the Illinois side of the Mississippi were held up for higher liquor prices and higher drug prices because of the law which we had. That statement is supported by a number of surveys. More important than the efforts of the drug industry to pass this bill are the efforts of the liquor industry, and these price comparisons help to explain why.

Mr. NEELY. Mr. President, will the Senator yield?

Mr. DOUGLAS. I yield to the Senator from West Virginia.

Mr. NEELY. Mr. President, it was my intention to refer to a statement made by the distinguished Senator from Minnesota [Mr. HUMPHREY] but he has momentarily retired from the Chamber. Therefore I shall wait until he returns.

Mr. HUMPHREY. I am right here.

Mr. BENTON. Mr. President, may I ask a question in the interim?

Mr. DOUGLAS. Mr. President, the contestants have returned. I am glad to yield.

Mr. BENTON. I am only too happy to wait.

Mr. NEELY. Mr. President, I inquire of the distinguished Senator from Illinois whether he recalls that the able Senator from Minnesota attempted to show that the philosophy of the pending price-fixing, cost-of-living-boosting bill is similar to that of union labor organizations in relation to so-called scab competition, and if he does, will he not inform us why no labor organization favors the measure?

The argument of the Senator from Minnesota was, as usual, very interesting, but it should be remembered that he was the inspiration for the skeptic poet Timon's couplet:

The two-edged tongue of mighty Zeno who,
Say what one would, could argue it untrue.

Mr. DOUGLAS. I think that in this case the labor unions are considering their members and the families of their members in their capacity as consumers, and are trying to protect the interests of consumers. This, I think, is a very praiseworthy step on their part, because all too often economic groups become interested simply in their incomes, how they receive their money, and not in how they have to spend their money.

I gave the comparative figures on drugs and liquor in East St. Louis and St. Louis. Now I should like to give some figures showing a comparison between the District of Columbia and neighboring States. Representative CELLER, of New York, sent out a shopper who purchased identical items in the District of Columbia, which does not have resale price maintenance, in Maryland which has resale price maintenance, as well as across the river in Virginia, which has resale price maintenance. The comparison was made among the three communities in close geographical juxtaposition. The central community did not have price fixing. The other two had price fixing. It is very interesting to compare such prices.

I should like to read some of the comparisons.

The first item is 10 cubic centimeters of u. 40 protamine zinc Lilly insulin, used by diabetics. Insulin is extremely important in the treatment of diabetes. Poor people as well as well-to-do people have diabetes. Let us see the price comparison. The price in the District of Columbia was 98 cents. The price in Maryland was $1.29. The Maryland price was 32 percent above the District price. In Virginia the price was $1.48, or 51 percent more.

Another item purchased by the shopper was a B. D. Yale 26-gage, 1/2-inch hypo needle. In the District of Columbia the price was 15 cents. In Virginia the price was 20 cents, or 33 percent higher. In Maryland the price was 23 cents, or 53 percent more.

Let us take Bayer aspirin, which has been introduced into the debate several times. The price in the District of Columbia was 46 cents. The price in Virginia was 59 cents, or 28 percent more for the same article in Virginia. The price in Maryland was 59 cents, also 28 percent more for the same article in Maryland. It is interesting that there should be the same mark-up in Maryland as in Virginia.

The next item is a 12-ounce bottle of Phillips milk of magnesia. The District of Columbia price was 34 cents. In Virginia the price was 39 cents, or 14 percent higher. In Maryland the price was 39 cents, 14 percent higher.

The next item is a large tube of Ipana tooth paste. The shopper paid 27 percent more for the Ipana tooth paste in Virginia than in the District of Columbia. In the District of Columbia the price was ⊥ 37 cents. In Virginia the price was 47 cents; and likewise in Maryland it was 47 cents.

The next item was 20 Gillette Blue Blades. In the District of Columbia the price was 87 cents, whereas in Virginia it was 11 percent more, or 98 cents, and also 11 percent more in Maryland, namely, 98 cents.

The next item was 50 cubic centimeters of Mead's Oleum Percomorpheum. The price in the District of Columbia was $2.63. The price in Virginia was $3.29, or 25 percent more. In Maryland the price was $3.49, or 32 percent more. These are baby vitamins which are essential to the health of infants and growing children.

The next item was 18 units of Ex-Lax. The price was 19 cents in the District of Columbia. In Virginia the price was 25 cents. In Maryland the price was 28 cents. The price in Maryland was 47 percent more than in the District of Columbia and in Virginia it was 32 percent more.

The next item was a Dr. West toothbrush. This was the only article which was sold at a uniform price in all three communities. The price was 59 cents.

The next item was the large-size Mennen baby powder. In the District of Columbia the price was 47 cents. In Virginia it was 49 cents, and in Maryland 49 cents.

The total price of these commodities in the District of Columbia was $7.05. The total price of the commodities in Virginia was $8.28; and in Maryland, $8.80. The Virginia prices were 17 percent more than the prices in the District of Columbia.

Maryland prices were 25 percent higher than the prices in the District of Columbia. . . .

Let me introduce personal testimony indicating that this is not merely a drug problem. A member of my staff wanted an exhaust fan to help his family survive the recent heat. He was interested in a Westinghouse Mobilaire fan. The fixed retail price was $79.95. He decided that this was too much money. Then he found a small neighborhood appliance store willing to sell the same item for $59.95. At that price he decided to buy it. The small store had signed no price-fixing agreement. The firm which does not sign an agreement is now free to charge whatever price it wishes, at least so far as the law is concerned. It would not be if this bill becomes law. That shows two things. At the fixed price, the fan would not have been purchased; it would have priced itself out of the market. If it had been purchased at the fixed price the consumer would have had to pay $20 more for the same item.

Mr. President, I think we can produce abundant evidence to indicate that resale-price maintenance results in higher prices to the consumer than would otherwise be the case. . . .

My good friend from Minnesota, for whom we have great affection, said a few minutes ago that during the recent increase in prices the advance in the trade-marked, branded commodities under resale-price maintenance had been less than on other commodities.

Mr. HUMPHREY. During World War II, I said.

Mr. DOUGLAS. During World War II. That is probably true. There is a reason for it. The reason for it is that the mark-up on these items was so great originally that they could absorb the increase in cost without passing it on. It is characteristic of virtually all monopoly prices during the war. A very interesting article was written by Dr. Kenneth Galbraith, who was a leading official of OPA, which was published in the Quarterly Journal of Economics in 1946 or 1947. In that article he showed that one reason why they had been able to restrain the increase in prices during the Second World War was because in the industries dominated by monopoly, quasi-monopoly, or an oligopoly, or industries which are dominated by a few firms, the profit margins were large originally and cost increases had been absorbed; and they were able to control prices much better when there was an agreement between manufacturers than in the competitive market.

However, that is proof not of good health, but of ill health. It is proof of an original high-profit margin. The opposite situation would hold true if we were to have a depression. The price of the branded commodities subject to resale-price maintenance would not fall as rapidly as commodities in general. As a result, the profit margin would widen.

Mr. HUMPHREY. Mr. President, will the Senator yield?

Mr. DOUGLAS. I yield.

Mr. HUMPHREY. I fully agree with the Senator on his analysis. I think he is persuasive and he has made a telling point on that subject. I should like to say, however, that if he is looking for cheap prices, I will tell him how he can get cheap prices. He can do away with union plumbers and other union workers and go into the open market and pick up anyone he can. However, we have said that as a matter of social policy we do not want to do it. I should like to remind my good friend from Illinois that the man who gets a cheap price and buys cheap goods will wind up getting a cheap wage, because the same argument can be used again and again.

Mr. DOUGLAS. I may say to my dear friend from Minnesota that the fundamental question is whether we want competition or do not want competition. I know that competition is a very rigorous business. It means that firms and stores which can undersell other firms and stores push out of business those who sell at higher prices. No one likes to see that happen. No one likes casualties. I want to make competition fair. We should do that. But we should not eliminate it.

Mr. HUMPHREY. That is correct.

Mr. DOUGLAS. If we remove competition from life, we substitute inefficiency. The less efficient continue in business. Those who are somewhat efficient become with time somewhat less efficient, because their profit margins are guaranteed. Experience on the whole shows that, rigorous as competition is, it is on the whole a beneficent force. It stimulates men to effort, and it is largely self-regulatory.

Mr. HUMPHREY. Mr. President will the Senator yield further?

Mr. DOUGLAS. I yield.

Mr. HUMPHREY. It was Lord Keynes, I believe, who said at one time, as between the short run and the long run he came to the conclusion that in the long run we die; and that it is the short run that really counts. I would remind the Senator that we must have some modicum of protection, and that it is more than just a matter of loss leaders. Loss leaders are sold at zero, and no one can stay in business without a profit.

Mr. DOUGLAS. My loss leader amendment defines loss leaders not merely as articles that are sold at less than the wholesale price, but at less than the wholesale price plus 6 percent.

Mr. HUMPHREY. The Harvard School of Business Administration in a recent survey estimated that the cost of doing business for retail merchants was an average of 28.8. How is a merchant going to stay in business with a 6-percent mark-up?

Mr. DOUGLAS. Should we guarantee a profit to any man in business?

Mr. HUMPHREY. The leading question of the Senator from Illinois can be answered "no"; we do not guarantee a profit. Neither do we guarantee a profit on the ultimate aggregate total. Every one of the items which the Senator has mentioned suffer competition. It is not as if we considered only one item. They are all in competition with one another. That applies even to commodities like tooth paste. There is a variety of them; there are hundreds of them. Many of them are not fair-traded at all. The question is whether a manufacturer is going to establish a price on his commodity. It is the same question that is involved in a doctor fixing his fee at $5, and a lawyer fixing his fee at something else, at a certain profit. They are methods of maintaining the price structure.

I shall develop my theme when I speak in my own time. I may say that I shall be glad to yield to the Senator from Illinois very liberally when I speak in my own time.

Mr. DOUGLAS. The Senator from Minnesota is always fair, and I know that he will give me the same rights, and even yield to me more than I have yielded to him. Mr. President, there is no doubt that under resale price maintenance three things happen: Very high prices to the ultimate consumer, high mark-ups to the retailer, and high profits to the manufacturer. The relationship of the ultimate sale price to manufacturing costs tends to be like the ratio of the Washington Monument to a pygmy.

Mr. President, I should like to put into the RECORD some figures on the profits of the big drug companies. I want to say that this does not apply purely to drug companies; it applies to other companies as well.

In the Celler minority report of the Committee on the Judiciary of the House, at page 40, there was placed in the record the net income in dollars, and in percentages the net worth, of seven large drug manufacturing companies, 1939 to 1951. . . .

Mr. HUMPHREY. Will the Senator read the names?

Mr. DOUGLAS. Yes; I shall read them. Let us take one in my own State, of which we are very proud, namely, the Abbott Laboratories.

Mr. HUMPHREY. Mr. President, will the Senator yield?

Mr. DOUGLAS. I yield.

Mr. HUMPHREY. Does the Senator realize that the Abbott Laboratories manufacture pharmaceuticals and crude drugs and very few fair-trade items? They manufacture prescription drugs, which have no relationship to fair-trade items.

For example, Abbott Laboratories manufacture very few over-the-counter items.

Mr. DOUGLAS. What would the Senator from Minnesota like me to read? To which company would he like me to refer?

8726

Mr. HUMPHREY. I will ask the Senator to give me, for example, the profit structure on what we call regular fair-trade items. Does he have the figure for Colgate's toothpaste? Does his list contain the name of Colgate-Palmolive-Peet?

Mr. DOUGLAS. It is very hard to break down the profits into particular items.

Mr. HUMPHREY. I appreciate the Senator's commentary. Does the Senator have

Lilly, Merck, or Parke-Davis? Abbott Laboratories basically produce pharmaceuticals. Pharmaceuticals are prescription drugs, and they are not fair-traded. That is where the big mark-ups occur.

Mr. DOUGLAS. Are these companies opposed to price fixing?

Mr. HUMPHREY. No; they are not.

Mr. DOUGLAS. No. They favor it. If these manufacturers are not subject to these laws, and if that is their chief business, why are they so concerned about the proposed legislation?

Mr. HUMPHREY. Because they are concerned about having a number of outlets for their products through retail pharmacists spread all over the United States, so that prescription druggists will be able to fill prescriptions with Parke-Davis products.

In other words, Parke-Davis, when it sells Ortal Compound, which is a phenolbarbitol compound, is not engaging in fair trading, but it does a tremendous business.

Mr. DOUGLAS. I have put these figures in the RECORD for what they are worth. The Senator from Minnesota may tear them to pieces—if he can.

Mr. BENTON. Mr. President, will the Senator from Illinois yield to me, so that I may make a comment in regard to what he has said?

Mr. DOUGLAS. I yield.

Mr. BENTON. It would not surprise me at all if these firms favored fair-trade laws, even though they themselves sell very few private proprietaries. These companies want large numbers of retail outlets. They do not want themselves to be at the mercy of the monopoly power represented by the development of the big chains.

Mr. DOUGLAS. In a moment I shall have something to say about the big chain business. This price-fixing business encourages the big chains.

Mr. BENTON. But this would explain their interest in fair-trade legislation. They have a deep, basic interest in the health and welfare of the independent drug store. They would prefer to deal with 50,000 customers scattered all over the country, than with 500 or 50 or 20, each with hundreds or thousands of outlets. That is sufficient to explain the situation, even though they themselves are not selling private proprietary, trade-marked items.

Of course, these products sell on narrow margins, as compared with the Abbott or Eli Lilly items which go into prescriptions, on which the consumer cannot tell what the mark-up is, for he does not know what he is paying a dollar for, whereas in the case of similar trade-marked items, he might pay a dime.

Mr. DOUGLAS. I thought the Senator from Connecticut stated—and I believe he did state—that in the case of the fair-traded items, the mark-up is enormous. Did not the Senator from Connecticut say that?

Mr. BENTON. No. On the contrary, in the case of the non-fair-trade pharmaceuticals which come over the counter in the form of prescriptions which are made up from little slips of paper which the consumers cannot read, and which list the names of ingredients which the consumers cannot understand, there is a far higher margin of profit, as the Senator from Minnesota will attest, than in the case of the fair-traded items of pharmaceuticals.

Mr. HUMPHREY. Mr. President, let me say that the Senator is correct in the case of a number of items. Many of these companies have hundreds of fair-traded items.

Mr. DOUGLAS. And they play a part in building up their profits.

Mr. HUMPHREY. Yes; there is no need for us to try to stretch the point, of course.

Mr. DOUGLAS. Mr. President, I have not yet been allowed to develop even the facts in this instance, because my good friends, the Senator from Minnesota and the Senator from Connecticut, have jumped down my throat before it has been possible for me to submit these figures here on the floor.

Let me read the figures for the profits of some of these companies: In 1939, which may not have been a fair year, Abbott Laboratories made profits of $2,048,094; in 1946, $10,820,623; in 1948, $11,120,983; in 1949, $10,010,500; in 1950, $10,880,301. When stated as a percentage of net worth, those profits amount to 14.1 percent, 28.3 percent, 23.6 percent, 19.8 percent, and 20 percent, respectively.

Then I shall read the percentages of profit in the case of American Home Products

Corp. These figures are on the basis of net worth: 50.7 percent, 15.9 percent, 16.8 percent, 18.3 percent, and 18.9 percent, respectively, for those years.

For Merck & Co.: 25.1 percent, 17.7 percent, 19.9 percent, 13.1 percent, 19.2 percent, and for 1951, 13.9 percent.

For Parke, Davis & Co.: 24.2 percent, 33.8 percent, 19.4 percent, 22.3 percent, and 27.7 percent.

For Sharpe & Dohme: 8.9 percent, 21 percent, 19.9 percent, 17.5 percent, and 17.4 percent.

For E. R. Squibb & Sons: 12.5 percent, 15.2 percent, 8.3 percent, 13.6 percent, 13.9 percent, and 12.2 percent.

For Sterling Drug: 23.4 percent, 21.1 percent, 17.6 percent, 18.1 percent, and 18.5 percent.

Those are very large profits.

If we consider the proprietaries and if we could isolate them, I think we would find that not only is the retail mark-up large, but the unit profits to manufacturers on those items are large. I can give some illustrations on percentage retail mark-ups, although, of course, we cannot obtain unit profits for manufacturers.

For instance, in the case of Dolcin—and these figures come from the American Druggist for January 1, 1951—the retail profit is 44.3 percent.

Argyrol, up to 57 1/2 percent; Kessling fever thermometers, 45 percent; Wynoids, up to 50 percent; Ampho-Jel, up to 53.4 percent; Dichloricide moth crystals, up to 42 percent; Breck, 40 percent; McKesson & Robbins, an average of 50 percent profit.

Presumably these figures are based on retail prices. These are profits claimed for manufacturers, as stated in the American Druggist magazine, the January 1, 1951, issue.

Mr. President, where does all the money for advertising in the magazines and over the radio and on the television come from? It comes from the high unit prices.

I shall tell you, Mr. President, why manufacturers want these laws. They want to hold up the retail prices because they are afraid that if the retail prices start slipping, the retailers will insist that manufacturers' prices be reduced, in order to keep the retailers in business. Therefore, the manufacturers are pushing the retailers out in front, as a sort of a bumper to protect themselves against competition. The manufacturers are using the retail druggists as hostages, to maintain the large unit, total profits of the manufacturers, just as an army which seizes women and children puts those women and children out in front, between themselves [sic] and the enemy, so that the enemy will not fire.

Mr. HUMPHREY. Mr. President, will the Senator from Illinois yield at this point?

Mr. DOUGLAS. I decline to yield at this point; I wish to finish submitting these figures.

Mr. President, this is where the poor druggists have been caught in the struggle. They do have an economic stake, but behind them are the manufacturers who use them, not for the sake of the retail druggists, but for the sake of the manufacturers.

What is true in the case of drugs is also true in the case of household appliances and in the case of liquor, and that is an extremely important fact, and in the case of sporting goods and in the case of a whole series of other goods.

Now I am glad to yield for a question.

Mr. NEELY. Mr. President, will the Senator from Illinois yield to me?

Mr. DOUGLAS. Yes, indeed.

Mr. NEELY. Let me inquire of the able Senator if it is not true that an additional reason for the pushing of the local druggists and merchants out front by the manufacturers lies in the fact that the local druggists and merchants have political influence which the manufacturers do not have?

Mr. DOUGLAS. Mr. President, I have before me a statement of contributions to the so-called fair-trade or resale-price-maintenance lobby. I believe this list is correct. It has been filed under the lobby law.

I do not believe in singling out persons for castigation, nor in citing their names, because that exposes them to invidious criticism. These firms have a ⊥ perfect right to contribute; they have a perfect right to lobby. On the other hand, I think it is significant that the list of persons which I have before me indicates contributions of

⊥ 8727

$45,905 in the third quarter of 1951, or for one-fourth of last year, namely, the next to the last quarter of 1951, before Congress came into session this year. It would be interesting to see how much has been contributed during the first two quarters of 1952.

These are contributions by these large drug companies. I do not wish to read into the RECORD the specific contributions they made, lest it seem that I would be putting them in the pillory; and I do not believe in doing that. On the other hand, I have the list before me, and I believe it to be correct. It indicates contributions of virtually $46,000 in one quarter.

Mr. President, what is the purpose behind these contributions? Those firms have a perfect right to make those contributions, but the purpose is to protect the prices on their products, the prices which they charge the retailers; and they do that by protecting the retailers' prices, so that the retailers will not put pressure on them to lower prices. Ultimately this monopoly business results in high prices to the consumers.

Mr. President, it is said that retail price maintenance is necessary in order to help small business. It does protect the profit margins of the merchants, the small-business men. It may well be that, taking small business as a whole, it may help. But there are very important qualifications to be attached. The first is that when the retailer has such high mark-ups, it encourages grocery chains, such as A. & P. and Safeway, to carry price-maintenance items, thus decreasing the amount of sales by the small stores. The Progressive Grocer has conducted a survey of this matter. It finds that 85 percent of the Nation's leading supermarkets now sell health and beauty aids, as compared to only 37 percent 10 years ago. In other words, the profit margins are so great that the grocery stores are entering the drug business. They are also going into the liquor business for similar reasons.

Mr. HUMPHREY. Mr. President, will the Senator yield?

Mr. DOUGLAS. I yield.

Mr. HUMPHREY. I am sure the Senator wants to be accurate. A while ago he quoted profit percentages which have absolutely no relationship to fact.

Mr. DOUGLAS. They were correct.

Mr. HUMPHREY. They were correct as to the gross profit.

Mr. DOUGLAS. I meant percentages of net worth.

Mr. HUMPHREY. The Senator quoted items.

Mr. DOUGLAS. Yes.

Mr. HUMPHREY. But the fact of the matter is, I may say to the Senator, that the items quoted by the Senator represented the maximum price the manufacturer places on the commodity. For example, a tube of Ipana toothpaste has on the tube the price 50 cents. That is the normal price. It costs the retailer 17 cents wholesale. That is a 33-cent gross mark-up. Now, what was the fair-trade price of a tube of Ipana toothpaste prior to June 1950? What was the fair-trade price? Thirty-seven cents. Does the Senator know how much gross profit the dealer got from that? Three cents. Does the Senator know how much that is? It amounted to—8 1/2 percent. The Senator will take note that the trouble in these figures is that one gets a gross mark-up which is the market price, but the fair-trade price is a breakdown of the lowest price at which the commodity can be sold; and that is true of every single item. It is true of any product such as Carter's Little Liver Pills. What is the fair price?

The Senator gave the profit figures for the drug companies. I am not protecting them. So far as I am concerned, they contribute to a good many things that I do not like. I say their profits are tremendous. But there is some truth in what the Senator has said about their using druggists as a front. Sometimes I think the druggists ought to look into this a little bit themselves and not be so tied up all the time. But the fact of the matter is that the gross-profit figures are misleading, because the fair-trade figure is considerably less than the gross figure; and I want the Senator to know that. There are the regular retail price and the fair-trade price. The fair-trade price offers a basic minimum to the retailer; that is, at least as to the commodities with which I am familiar. I cannot say anything about the electric fan about which the Senator was talking.

Mr. FREAR. Mr. President, will the Senator from Illinois yield so that I may ask a question of the Senator from Minnesota?

Mr. DOUGLAS. It has been some time back, but certainly with respect to the figures submitted by Representative CELLER, those were actual prices. They showed that prices in resale price-maintained States were higher than in the District. I ask unanimous consent that I may now yield to the Senator from Delaware for that purpose without losing the floor.

The PRESIDING OFFICER. Without objection, it is so ordered.

Mr. FREAR. I do not think I quite understood what the Senator from Minnesota said. If a fair-trade price is paid, there should be a reasonable profit in it for the retailer.

Mr. HUMPHREY. That is correct.

Mr. FREAR. There should also be a reasonable profit for the manufacturer, and so on down the line.

Mr. HUMPHREY. That is correct.

Mr. FREAR. There may be a difference between the fair-trade price and the established retail price for a particular product.

Mr. HUMPHREY. That is correct.

Mr. FREAR. If the retail price set by the manufacturer is, let us say, to use a round figure, $1, and the fair-trade price is 89 cents, it is some kind of a—

Mr. HUMPHREY. Some kind of a cut price.

Mr. FREAR. A cut price—yes, that is correct. But in that there is still a reasonable profit for the retailer, as well as for the manufacturer.

Mr. HUMPHREY. Not a reasonable profit.

Mr. FREAR. What happens to the difference of 11 cents in the case of an article whose price is established by the manufacturer at $1, as against a retail price of 89 cents. Where does that difference of 11 cents go—to the retailer? Or to the manufacturer?

Mr. HUMPHREY. It all goes to the retailer. That is a very good question, and I should like to give a very honest and accurate answer, if the Senator will yield.

Mr. FREAR. Mr. President, will the Senator from Illinois yield for that purpose?

Mr. DOUGLAS. I yield, provided I do not lose the floor.

Mr. HUMPHREY. I shall try to make the answer very brief. The Senator has posed a problem which relates to the figures used when an article is priced in a non-fair-trade territory, such as the District of Columbia, which is a highly competitive territory. When one goes into Virginia and buys an article, Virginia being a fair-trade State, what happens? There are many little stores in Virginia, particularly in small towns, where they do not give any fair-trade prices. They cut prices, and there is, therefore, not a fair profit. It amounts to 3-cents on a 33-cent item. It is not a fair profit, and no merchant can continue in business a month on a profit of that kind. What happens? One may go to the drug store in Woodstock, Va., and buy a bottle of Sal Hepatica, for which he pays 30 cents, as the regular price. That is what should be charged. It costs the druggist from 20 to 21 cents to buy that item. He must pay all of his operating costs out of his profits. What is the fair-trade price on that article? The fair-trade price would be 25 cents, possibly 24 cents. In Woodstock the druggist may charge 30 cents, because there is no hot competition in that community. What a fair-trade price does is to put the price right down to a minimum, and to prevent the sale of an article for less than it costs. That is what it amounts to. What should be charged is a legitimate price. A merchant ought to be able to make a legitimate profit by selling at a legitimate price. But the fair-trade price frequently leaves the merchant without a fair return. It leaves him with some loss. It amounts to this—that everyone plays the same game. If one does not like a particular druggist, he may simply go across the street. One druggist may be selling an article for 18 cents, the other for 25 cents.

Mr. DOUGLAS. Let me say that the reason for the supermarkets taking the so-called fair-trade price on resale-price-maintenance items, is because the price is held up by a retail agreement. The supermarkets, with lower costs, come in to take the field. The druggist would do better with a smaller percentage of mark-up. It would make it impossible for the supermarket groceries to come into the health and beauty business.

Mr. FREAR. Mr. President, will the Senator yield? Perhaps I am monopolizing the time of the Senator from Illinois.

Mr. DOUGLAS. That is all right.

Mr. FREAR. I think it might be carried just a step further. Does the druggist in

Woodstock who is selling Sal Hepatica at 24 or 25 cents have a fair margin of profit?

Mr. HUMPHREY. He does not, at that price—any more than he could make a profit by selling cigarettes at 5 cents a pack.

Mr. FREAR. And no more than a person could make a profit selling milk at 5 cents a quart.

Mr. HUMPHREY. In the grocery business, a profit of 12 1/2 percent is considered satisfactory. The profit of the retail drugstore is usually abnormally low. The supermarket, with a fair-trade price on Jergen's lotion of 37 cents, may compete with a drug store across the street selling the same article at 50 cents.

Mr. DOUGLAS. If we had so-called fair trade, it would be unable to do that.

Mr. HUMPHREY. Yes; that is what fair trade does. We have had fair trade for 17 years. The supermarkets are able to sell a 50-cent jar of Jergen's lotion for 37 cents, as they have been doing for many years; but they cannot go further and give it away. I have known stores to have the experience of replenishing their stocks on their shelves by going across the street and buying goods from Montgomery Ward, in order to meet their competition. They bring it in at the back door and sell it to the customers who enter through the front door.

Mr. FREAR. Mr. President, the reference made to canned milk—I do not want to bring in the name of the Pet milk company, but they are very fine competitors in fluid-milk industry. I do not think there is any product which comes nearer to being properly priced than is milk. I am sure the Senator from Minnesota would agree with that statement.

Mr. DOUGLAS. Just a minute. I know the cow has many admirers here. The affection that attaches to the cow is extraordinary.

Mr. President, I should merely like to point out that the drug stores have been meeting terrific competition from food stores which have been gradually taking on drug and liquor distribution. I have some figures indicating that from 1941 to 1951 the percentage of food stores selling drug products has grown from 37 percent to 85 percent. That is because the merchants were doing so well that it tempted the big chains to go into the drug business, so that the drug stores, by putting a tent over themselves, were inviting competition to come in from these other fields.

Mr. [RUSSELL B.] LONG [D., La.]. Mr. President, will the Senator from Illinois yield?

Mr. DOUGLAS. I yield for a question.

Mr. LONG. It seems that one item we should consider is that a store doing a great volume of business can afford to give the consumer the benefit of lower prices. Other stores in more remote localities, not having so great a volume of business, might not be able to reduce their prices. Sometimes a housewife goes across town to buy something from a store which is doing a large volume of business, although, by and large, she buys groceries and various other items from a local store near her, which has somewhat higher prices.

A fair-trade law does not permit a store which is able to do a large volume of business to lower its prices on price-fixed items.

Mr. HUMPHREY. Mr. President, the Senator fails to recognize what is the regular price for a commodity. The Senator's argument is my argument. A 50-cent article should sell for 50 cents, just as a carpenter should receive $1.75 an hour instead of $1.13. The fair-trade price is an unfair price because it is below the cost of operating the business, but, at least, it provides a minimum mark-up and a uniform one across the boards.

That is what it amounts to. A 50-cent article should sell for 50 cents. The fair-trade price is 37 cents. The little merchant cannot sell the article at 37 cents. It gives him some rules; he cannot go below that price. That is what it amounts to.

Mr. LONG. If we could help the independent merchant to refrain from loss leaders, and could protect him from the destructive effect of discrimination against him so far as the pricing of commodities is concerned, we would not have any great need for a fair-trade law.

Mr. DOUGLAS. I am glad to have the support of my good friend from Louisiana. We fought shoulder to shoulder against the basing-point bill. We fought shoulder to shoulder for the Robinson-Patman Act. Now I see him entering the lists on the side of the people and my heart leaps up. A powerful champion has ridden into the arena.

Mr. LONG. Just as we pointed out in the debate on the basing-point bill, it was our feeling that if we could protect the independent merchant from the destructive effects of price discrimination which favored the large businesses over the small businesses, we would not have too much to worry about in connection with the little fellow being run out of business.

Mr. DOUGLAS. We could protect him as a buyer by outlawing discrimination and then competitition would see to it that as a seller he could deal with the consumer at lower prices and fair terms.

Mr. LONG. The Senator from Illinois made a fight on previous occasions to protect the independent merchant from discriminations in favor of large buyers against small buyers. If we had been successful in that fight, which some of us are still endeavoring to carry on, we would not have any need for a so-called fair trade law which I fear may have the effect of reducing certain elements of price competition among the retail trade.

Mr. DOUGLAS. I am very glad that the Senator from Louisiana has made his point.

Mr. [HERMAN] WELKER [R. Idaho]. Madam President, will the Senator from Illinois yield to me?

Mr. DOUGLAS. Certainly.

Mr. WELKER. I did not want to interrupt my distinguished friend from New York, but from this time on the acting minority leader will insist upon the regular order of business, remembering the admonition given to us by the Vice President earlier this afternoon. I do not want to interrupt, and I trust I shall not have to do so.

Mr. DOUGLAS. I thank the Senator from Idaho for his very clear statement. I wish to make it clear that while I shall be very glad to yield to any Senator, I shall now, according to the ruling of the Chair, be allowed to yield only for a question.

Earlier in this discussion I pointed out that resale price maintenance resulted in such high retail mark-ups that the grocery chains have gone into the drug business in order to take advantage of the high mark-ups, and that therefore the drug business and the druggists have reared up competitors for themselves because of the high margins which have been guaranteed.

I should now like to turn to the development of private brands.

Mr. SPARKMAN. Madam President, before the Senator leaves that point, will he yield to me for a question?

Mr. DOUGLAS. Provided it is a question. I am at the mercy of the Senator. It is understood that if he makes a statement I lose my right to the floor. The penalty falls not on him but on me.

Mr. SPARKMAN. Madam President, I assure the Senator that I shall certainly state it in the form of a question.

A little while ago the Senator was speaking about the impact of this system on small business.

Mr. DOUGLAS. I think the Senator from Alabama was not in the Chamber during the entire course of my speech. I have said that in my judgment it probably does give larger margins to the units which are already in business, but that this is not an unmixed blessing for them, because there are forces operating to diminish the apparent advantage which they get initially. That is my argument. I am not arguing that it is adverse to small business. I am merely arguing that it is not as beneficial as is claimed.

Mr. SPARKMAN. Let me say to the Senator that I was in the Chamber and heard him make the statement. As a matter of fact, I was in the chair at the time.

I was wondering if the Senator was familiar with the survey which was made in New York last year at the time of the cut-price war which was carried on. The estimate was made that 20,000 of the approximately 105,000 small retailers in the New York area would have been forced into bankruptcy if the price war had continued for 6 months.

Mr. DOUGLAS. The point is that the price war did not continue for 6 months.

That was an exuberance largely started by the big department stores in New York around Thirty-third Street, which went on a spree, seeking to get the better of one another. One store started to cut the throat of another store. The other store responded by trying to cut the throat of the first store. Then two or three others joined in the melee, but after a few days it was called off, and since then there has not been large-scale price cutting. In other words, freedom sometimes leads to excesses. But is this a reason why we should have perpetual slavery?

Mr. SPARKMAN. Of course I agree with what the Senator said, except that the price war lasted longer than merely a few days. It lasted for several weeks, and presented a very serious question.

Is it not true that the splurge which those big stores made was made at the expense, first, of the United States Government, because they were in the high-tax brackets, and second, at the expense of the little store down the street, which simply could not meet the cut prices?

Mr. DOUGLAS. The Senator from Alabama, like the Senator from Connecticut [Mr. BENTON], and the Senator from Minnesota [Mr. HUMPHREY], ignores the fact that I am proposing an amendment in the nature of a substitute, which would outlaw loss-leaders. Under my proposal, we would not have Gone With the Wind selling for 99 cents. Furthermore, we define a loss-leader as something which is sold for less than the wholesale price plus 6 percent—not merely less than the wholesale price, but less than the wholesale price plus 6 percent. So for heaven's sake do not try to put the brand of Cain on me and say that I am defending loss-leaders. I am opposed to them.

Mr. SPARKMAN. Madam President, will the Senator yield for one further question?

Mr. DOUGLAS. Yes, indeed.

Mr. SPARKMAN. I assure the able Senator from Illinois that I certainly would never be in the position of helping to put the brand of Cain upon the Senator from Illinois. I know that he is sincere in what he is presenting here—

Mr. DOUGLAS. Madam President, the acting minority leader has said that he will invoke the rule of the Senate if I yield for the purpose of a statement.

Mr. SPARKMAN. I do not wish to make a statement.

Mr. DOUGLAS. I do not wish to have the Senator from Alabama trespass upon the rules of the Senate in order that I may receive the penalty. If the penalty is invoked, it will not be the fault of the Senator from Idaho. I beg my friend to conform to the parliamentary rules and at least put his statements in the form of a question.

The PRESIDING OFFICER. Does the Senator from Illinois yield for a question?

Mr. SPARKMAN. I assure the Senator that I will ask a question.

Mr. DOUGLAS. I yield.

Mr. SPARKMAN. I am familiar with the rules of the Senate. I am a lawyer. I believe I know how to lay the predicate for a question. I assure the Senator that whatever I say will be for the purpose of laying the predicate for a question. Here comes the question:

Does the Senator, or does he not, agree with this statement, which was contained in what I think is a very competent business publication, namely, Business Week magazine, when it summarized the situation in its June 1951 issue as follows—

Mr. DOUGLAS. What publication is this?

Mr. SPARKMAN. Business Week. I quote:

Fair trade has always been another major prop for the small, independent merchants during the past decade. This has been particularly true in the drug and jewelry businesses. Under the fair-trade umbrella, the small merchant has been protected from price cutting and provided with a healthy mark-up.

Mr. DOUGLAS. Strike out "healthy" and substitute "large."

Mr. SPARKMAN. There are two more sentences:

The end of fair trade on a national scale now throws this disadvantage into reverse. How much it will hurt the small retailer remains to be seen, but it's sure to leave its mark.

Mr. DOUGLAS. What does the Senator from Alabama think he proves by that quotation?

Mr. SPARKMAN. I ask the Senator from Illinois if he agrees with that statement.

The article says that the system has a very serious impact on small business, and that during the past decade fair-trade laws have constituted a prop to aid small business.

Mr. DOUGLAS. The so-called fair-trade system is a system of resale price maintenance. The term "fair trade" is a euphemism, designed to cover up the smell. It is a deodorant, so to speak, applied to these practices.

With respect to the feared fate of small business, I ask unanimous consent to insert at this point a comparison of drug store failures in fair-trade and non-fair-trade States. It shows that such laws have no real force in stopping such failures.

There being no objection, the material was ordered printed as follows:

Failures of retail drug stores in selected States, 1939, 1940, 1946, and 1947

States Without Fair-Trade Laws				Adjacent States With Fair-Trade Laws			
1939				1939			
	Number	Liabilities	Rate per 1,000 concerns		Number	Liabilities	Rate per 1,000 concerns
Vermont	—	—	—	New Hampshire	2	$8,000	8.9
Washington, D. C.	1	$4,000	3.0	Maine	4	30,000	10.1
Texas	16	132,000	4.8	Maryland	3	7,000	4.1
Missouri	9	77,000	4.1	Oklahoma	17	119,000	15.0
				Illinois	52	217,000	14.1
				Kansas	8	72,000	7.4
1940				1940			
	Number	Liabilities			Number	Liabilities	
Vermont	—	—		New Hampshire	2	$11,000	
Washington, D. C.	3	$29,000		Maine	4	24,000	
Texas	19	108,000		Maryland	3	154,000	
Missouri	11	49,000		Oklahoma	11	48,000	
				Illinois	45	224,000	
				Kansas	7	25,000	
1946				1946			
Vermont	—	—		New Hampshire	1	$2,000	
Washington, D. C.	—	—		Maine	—	—	
Texas	—	—		Maryland	—	—	
Missouri	—	—		Oklahoma	—	—	
				Illinois	—	—	
				Kansas	—	—	
January-October 1947				January-October 1947			
Vermont	—	—		New Hampshire	—	—	
Washington, D. C.	—	—		Maine	—	—	
Texas	1	$13,000		Maryland	—	—	
Missouri	1	2,000		Oklahoma	—	—	
				Illinois	1	$50,000	
				Kansas	1	7,000	

Source: Minority Views, H. Rept. 1516, p. 46.

Mr. DOUGLAS. There is no doubt that the use of this system has resulted in much higher prices to the consumers than would otherwise have been the case. It has protected retailers and manufacturers from competition. The real test is whether we believe in competition or not. I suppose every one of us in this Chamber has delivered orations at one time or another declaring in favor of competition, and against price fixing. The test is whether we are really opposed to it. Generally we are for competition for someone else. Most people are for price fixing where they are concerned. The question is whether we will permit manufacturers of trade-marked and branded commodities to fix the prices at which such commodities can sell at retail, whether or not the retail merchant has made such an agreement.

As I pointed out originally, and as the Senator from New York [Mr. LEHMAN] has reemphasized, the purpose of the bill is to provide that the nonsigner shall be compelled to charge the same prices as the signer. It delegates the power of the country to enable a private concern to determine its own price and protect itself from competition, except for such lateral competition as may exist between the various products as substitutes for one another.

Madam President, I had hoped to continue with the discussion of private brands. If I may be permitted to do so, then I shall be glad to yield for questions.

Mr. HUMPHREY. Mr. President, will the Senator yield so that I may ask him a question with reference to the non⊥signer clause, since we have taken up that point now?

Mr. DOUGLAS. Certainly.

Mr. HUMPHREY. The Senator mentioned the subject of the nonsigner clause. I wonder whether he is familiar with the fact that 45 State laws have the nonsigner clause. The first State to have it was California in 1933. The New York law contains a nonsigner clause.

Mr. DOUGLAS. There is a very real difference between a State legislature operating within a State and the exercise of Federal power over interstate commerce. Congress is not a State legislature. We are the National Legislature. What we are being asked to do is to turn over the power of the Federal Government over interstate commerce to permit a private manufacturer to fix the retail price of his products. In other words, we are delegating away the commerce powers of the Federal Government. We are furthermore violating the Sherman antitrust law and the Clayton act, and all the other statutes which declare combinations in restraint of trade to be violations of the basic law.

Mr. HUMPHREY. I do not mean to interrupt the Senator, but—

Mr. DOUGLAS. No. I hope the Senator from Minnesota will not regard the vehemence of my reply as indicative of an unfriendly feeling.

Mr. HUMPHREY. No; of course not. My only other question is this. As I understand the McGuire bill, which is the bill before us, in the Whettling [sic] case, which was the second Supreme Court case under the Miller-Tydings Act, the Supreme Court said there would be no respect between the States for the laws of the respective States. In other words, a nonsigner clause in North Dakota, for example, would have no effect in Minnesota, or vice versa. Therefore a mail-order house across the line could operate in the other State without any regard to the State laws.

Mr. DOUGLAS. I want to make the case of the Senator from Minnesota for this bill being merely an enabling act as persuasive as I can. The Webb-Kenyon Act prohibited the sending of liquor into a prohibition State, and the Ashurst-Summers Act prohibited the interstate shipment of prison-made goods in competition with free labor. Have I correctly stated the situation?

Mr. HUMPHREY. The Senator from Illinois has stated the situation very well, but I am afraid that it will not hold up after the Senator is through with me.

Mr. DOUGLAS. The Senator's proposal is to put State laws, so far as interstate commerce is concerned, ahead of Federal laws. So far as interstate commerce is concerned, the Constitution establishes congressional laws superior to State laws.

Mr. [BURNET R.] MAYBANK [D., S.C.]. Mr. President, I should like to ask the Senator a question. I do not know whether he wishes to answer it. But I should like to ask it of him.

Mr. DOUGLAS. I should like to finish my answer to the Senator from Minnesota. In the case of prison-made goods and in the case of the sale of liquor, there were no previously existing Federal laws which the State laws violated. Therefore it was proper for the Federal Government to withdraw the use of interstate commerce as a means of breaking down State laws, since there were no Federal laws prior to that.

In this case there are prior Federal laws, namely, the Sherman Antitrust Act and the Clayton Act. What is now being proposed is that the Federal Government shall give away its delegated power over interstate commerce so that State fair-trade laws may be made superior to the Sherman Antitrust Act and the Clayton Act.

There was good reason why Congress never passed a resale price-maintenance law for the District of Columbia. Congress is the legislative body for the District of Columbia. It was not the intent of Congress in its legislative capacity to repeal the Sherman Antitrust Act or the Clayton Act.

Mr. MAYBANK. Mr. President, will the Senator yield?

Mr. DOUGLAS. I yield.

Mr. MAYBANK. The Senator is making a very able argument, and we are all interested in the argument which he is making. I know the situation with respect to prison-made goods, because I was governor of my State.

Mr. WELKER. Mr. President, will the Senator speak louder?

Mr. MAYBANK. I do not know whether the Senator from Illinois will wish to answer my question. If he does not I will understand. I am wondering how long the distinguished Senator from Illinois and his colleagues will debate this bill, because I have an engagement, very frankly, and I wonder whether it would be possible for me to leave for a few hours. I mean that in all sincerity, because when I have talked a long time on the floor of the Senate I have said that I would talk all night, as I did in 1948.

Mr. DOUGLAS. I have no intention of filibustering.

Mr. MAYBANK. I would never suggest that the distinguished Senator from Illinois would filibuster.

Mr. DOUGLAS. I am not going to filibuster. I was startled at the beginning of the discussion when the bill started to go through without anyone rising in support of it and when there was no discussion about it. I thought I should take the floor to show that there is real discussion needed on this measure. I have already flushed two very handsome birds out of the thicket in the persons of the Senator from Minnesota [Mr. HUMPHREY] and the Senator from Connecticut [Mr. BENTON]. They are beautiful birds with beautiful plumage.

Mr. MAYBANK. How many more birds does the Senator from Illinois expect to flush out of the thicket? Perhaps I will be able to judge the time in that way. I am in favor of the Senator flushing the birds out of the thicket.

Mr. DOUGLAS. That is conjectural.

Mr. MAYBANK. Does the Senator think it may be one or two more?

Mr. DOUGLAS. It is beyond my power to determine (a) how many Senators will rise in opposition to me or (b) how many Senators will rise in support of the position which I take. I can only say that I am not filibustering this bill. I expect to conclude, if I am permitted to continue with my remarks, within half an hour.

Thus far, if the RECORD will be examined, it will be found that for every sentence which I have spoken there have been paragraphs of interruptions.

If I had been allowed to proceed, I could have finished my speech in half an hour. The delay has not been mine. Incidentally I do not think it is bad for us to spend a few hours discussing a bill like this, which may involve $750,000,000 to $1,000,000,000 a year.

Mr. President, a long time ago I started to speak about private brands, but I was diverted by the questions which were put to me. I should like to point out that frequently the quality of private brands is as good as the nationally advertised brands. A good many brands which are not advertised and which do not have national advertising, but which are frequently sold to wholesalers who put on their own brands, are just as good in quality even though they do not have the build-up by having beautiful movie stars advertise them or have full-page displays in the weeklies. The quality is good nevertheless. By holding up the price of the branded product a field is opened up for the private brand to come in. If we hold up the prices of the branded nationally advertised products we permit unadvertised brands to come in. I used to know something about the soup business. I had friends who ran a small soup cannery, and I had some relationship to the business. My friends would produce soup which they could sell to wholesale grocers, who would put on the cans of soup their own labels, and would sell the soup in competition with nationally advertised brands. There were chiefly only two nationally advertised brands. My friends thought their product was about as good in quality as the nationally advertised brands. The high prices of the nationally advertised brands permitted my friends to furnish their soup to the wholesalers, who in turn would use it to provide competition with the nationally advertised brands.

In other words, Madam President, I am trying to say that by means of these high percentage mark-ups, although they result in higher prices to the consumers, the gain to the retailers is less than one would think, because the high mark-ups invite the nonadvertised, private brands to come into the market. Sometimes there develops the extraordinary situation that a manufacturer will produce both nationally advertised brands and private brands, and the two brands will be almost identical, but each will skim a different market.

For instance, I am told that a Sears, Roebuck Kenmore washing machine is the same as a Whirlpool washing machine, and that there is really no difference between the two. However, the Whirlpool washing machine is nationally advertised and sells at a higher price. So one machine is sold to the snob market, so to speak, and the lower-priced machine is sold to the nonsnob market.

Madam President, should not snobs be permitted to cease being snobs? Should not they be permitted to have the advantage of price competition if they want it?

At present the whole attempt by advertising by brands is to attempt to protect prices and to make consumers believe that their future is bound up in purchasing those particular brands. Out of that process, great advertising fortunes have been built in radio, in television, by advertising copy writers—all the men who live in the happy suburbia outside of New York City, running up to Hartford, Conn., and beyond, and in Westchester County, N. Y., and out on Long Island. Out of that come the big incomes of the national weeklies. From it comes a great deal of money for the television stars and radio stars. From it come huge profits and huge mark-ups. But, Madam President, who pays the bill? Poor Mrs. Housewife pays the bill.

I believe it is about time that we had a little price competition going, and that "blue sky" no longer be sold to the American public.

Mr. MOODY. Madam President, will the Senator from Illinois yield to me?

Mr. DOUGLAS. I am glad to yield.

Mr. MOODY. I have been listening with great care and great interest to my illustrious and eloquent friend, the Senator from Illinois. I am wondering whether he is not arguing that when private brands come into the market, they provide competition, and therefore that the bill as it is now written would not bar competition, because it stimulates the creation of new business and new brands. If prices go too high, new competitors will come into the market.

Mr. DOUGLAS. That is like saying that we should load down a man with chains on his feet and on his hands; and we should chain him to a rock, and that still there will be an element of freedom for him, in that he will want to move.

If we load down the economic system with restrictions, we may not kill it entirely; fortunately, there will still be some vitality and some spirit of competition.

The point really is that competition is not an easy theory to believe in. It involves losses, as well as profits; it involves exits from business, as well as growths and successes in business. It operates by elimination from industry, as well as by rewards for the efficient and successful. It is a stern process, but on the whole it is a beneficial one, for it stimulates men to greater energy and effectiveness.

We want to put certain floors under it; but those floors, to the degree that they are put under it, will be put under it by the community. Each one should not fix his own floor, or else he will favor himself.

One of the things that is disconcerting is how people will give lip service to competition, and then will assist every possible measure to stifle, cripple, restrict, and prevent competition. If we have faith in the competitive system, we must be willing to let it operate and to abide by its results—if we really believe in it.

Where shall we go if we permit private price-fixing, Madam President? I have heard eloquent speeches on the floor of this body against public price-fixing. I do not like public price-fixing; it involves too many decisions and too many complicated factors of costs. I prefer competitive prices. But at least the price-fixing we have been hitherto discussing has been price-fixing by the community, with an attempt made to protect the consumers.

But what we are now being asked to legitimatize is private price-fixing, prices fixed by the interested parties, and only by a fraction of them; and the prices they would fix would thus have the force of law, a system infinitely worse than the public system of price-fixing, which so many of my colleagues have denounced.

So, Madam President, I hope very much that this will not pass.

I think it probably is unconstitutional, because the Supreme Court, in the Schechter case,[3.63] declared unconstitutional the delegation of legislative powers, such as the delegation to private individuals of the power to set prices. The decision of the Supreme Court in that case was a unanimous one. The NRA was declared unconstitutional, even though under the NRA system, representatives of labor played a part, and there were at least nominal representatives of consumers. I myself sat on some of those boards, as a representative of the consumers. I admit we were somewhat useless, but at least we were there for window dressing.

If the NRA was declared unconstitutional, in the Schechter case, by the unanimous opinion of the Supreme Court, what shall we say to provisions by which it is proposed to surrender to a single manufacturer—not to an entire industry, but to one manufacturer—the power to fix the prices at which his goods will be sold, and to give him the power to enforce these agreements against nonsigners? I think the bill is unconstitutional. I doubt that it will hold up in the Supreme Court. Even if it did, it would be bad public policy.

Madam President, in the few years I have spent in this body, I believe I have fought hard for competition for small business, so that small business cannot be hit over the head by big business. I have tried to protect small business against unfair advantages which big business sometimes is able to obtain by means of financial power. I want a broad distribution of ownership in the United States.

But can we depend on price-fixing, which strikes at the consumers, to protect small business? We shall do well if we can just permit small business to compete without being subjected to arbitrary power through price discrimination on the goods they purchase.

We do not need to give business, in addition, the power to gouge consumers.

Madam President, in order to crystalize the discussion, I now send to the desk my amendment outlawing the loss-leader, and ask that it be read. It is an amendment in the nature of a substitute.

The PRESIDING OFFICER. The amendment of the Senator from Illinois will be stated.

The legislative clerk proceeded to read the amendment.

Mr. MAYBANK. Madam President, I wonder whether the Senator from Illinois will yield. This is new business, and very important business. I suggest the absence of a quorum. . . .

The PRESIDING OFFICER (Mr. HILL in the chair). A quorum is present.

Mr. McFARLAND. Mr. President—

The PRESIDING OFFICER. The junior Senator from Arizona is recognized.

Mr. DOUGLAS. Mr. President, a parliamentary inquiry.

The PRESIDING OFFICER. The Senator from Arizona is recognized.

Mr. McFARLAND. Mr. President, I do not yield for a parliamentary inquiry at this time.

Mr. DOUGLAS. Mr. President, does the Senator—

Mr. McFARLAND. I do not yield for anything at this time. I shall be only a few minutes, and then the Senator can propound his parliamentary inquiry.

Mr. President, we are trying to expedite the work of the Senate. In my humble opinion, there is no question but what, by and large, the majority of the Senate will favor the passage of this bill when it comes to a vote. I hope that we can come to some agreement in regard to a vote. I dislike very much that Senators, in the last days of the session of the Senate, have to work long hours, but we must drive to do the work of the Senate so that Congress can adjourn. This bill has been listed as one of the bills that should be passed. . . .

[3.63] A.L.A. Schechter Poultry Co. v. United States, 295 U.S. 495, 55 S. Ct. 837, 79 L. Ed. 1570 (1935).

I am not trying to force this bill on anyone, nor is any other Senator trying to force it. I have tried to get a unanimous-consent agreement to vote upon it at any time tomorrow, but Senators have told me they wanted to debate it for a long time. That is their privilege; if they want to debate it for a long time, they can do so. There are only a few days left, and we must work long hours. There is no question of giving full opportunity to every Senator to present his views. . . .

Mr. [DENNIS] CHAVEZ [D., N.M.]. Does not the majority leader feel that when statements on the floor have indicated that the bill might cost American consumers more than a billion dollars, the bill should at least be debated?

Mr. McFARLAND. I am perfectly willing to have the bill debated. The only question I should like to have answered is, How much time is desired to debate the bill? . . .

Mr. President, I ask unanimous consent that beginning tomorrow at 10 o'clock the debate on the pending bill be divided equally between the proponents and the opponents, the time until 12 o'clock to be controlled on the one side by the Senator from Minnesota, and on the other side by the Senator from Illinois; that thereafter debate be limited on amendments to 40 minutes to an amendment, 20 minutes to a side, the time to be controlled by the proponent of the amendment on the one side, and by the Senator from Minnesota on the other side, in the event that he is opposed to the amendment; and in the event the Senator from Minnesota is in favor of the amendment, then the time to be controlled by the distinguished minority leader, or any Senator whom he may designate; and that thereafter debate upon the bill be limited to 1 hour, 30 minutes to a side, the time to be controlled by the distinguished Senator from Illinois on the one side, and the distinguished Senator from Minnesota on the other side. . . .

Mr. DOUGLAS. Reserving the right to object, and I do not intend to object, I wish to make it clear that I do not desire to delay the vote upon this bill after it has received proper consideration. I have not engaged in a filibuster, I will not engage in a filibuster, I do not believe in filibusters. But I should like to point out certain extraordinary circumstances connected with the way in which the bill was brought to the floor and the way in which it almost passed.

If my understanding is correct the bill came to the Senate without a favorable report of the committee. The committee merely reported the bill without recommendation. The hearings have not been printed. I have before me a typewritten copy of the hearings, but I do not believe the hearings as such have been printed or are available.

The bill was about to be passed without discussion and without sponsorship, when the Senator from Illinois, fortunately, thought that he should rise and see that there was at least some discussion—and during the last 3 hours, we have had a very interesting, although disconnected, discussion upon the merits of the bill. There has been no attempt to prevent the Senate from reaching a conclusion, but there has been an attempt, and I am proud to say we shall continue it, to see that the issues are raised, so that the Senate will have a basis for reaching a conclusion.

I shall not object to the proposal, because I thoroughly agree that after Senators have read the RECORD and have had a chance to hear the arguments, there should be a vote upon the bill tomorrow. I hope the amendment which I have suggested can be read, that I may have a chance to explain it, and that it may be printed and lie on the desk. I believe the Senator from Louisiana [Mr. LONG] has an amendment which he may intend to offer, and which, if he wishes, could be printed and lie on the desk. But I desire to clear the air, lest any imputation of filibustering be thrown upon the Senator from Illinois and other Senators who have tried to have the bill discussed.

Mr. MORSE. Mr. President, reserving the right to object, the junior Senator from Oregon has no intention to filibuster the bill, but he does intend to present his views on the bill at whatever length it may take to present them. He is going to object to the unanimous-consent request. He has already made it clear to the majority leader that he will object to any proposal for a unanimous-consent request in regard to the bill. I object.

The VICE PRESIDENT. The Senator from Oregon objects.

Mr. McFARLAND. Mr. President, I regret very much that there has been objection to the unanimous-consent request. . . .

⊥ The VICE PRESIDENT. The Chair feels that it would be better to have the ⊥ 8733 amendment appear in the RECORD as a whole, without being interrupted by the proceedings. Is there objection?

There being no objection, the amendment offered by the Senator from Illinois [Mr. DOUGLAS] was ordered to be printed in the RECORD entire, as follows:

Strike out all after the enacting clause and insert:

"That the act entitled 'An act to supplement existing laws against unlawful restraints and monopolies, and for other purposes,' approved October 15, 1914, is amended by adding at the end thereof the following new section:

" 'SEC. 27. (a) For the purposes of this section—

" '(1) The term "delivered cost" shall mean invoice cost to a seller less the value of discounts received by a seller in money or the equivalent, plus the cost of transportation incident to delivery to the seller, and plus applicable excise and sales taxes to the seller.

" '(2) The term "seller" shall mean a vendee, as used in this act, who purchases for resale.

" '(3) The term "loss leader practice" shall mean selling a commodity, or advertising or offering a commodity for sale at retail at a price below the delivered cost of the commodity to the seller plus 6 percent of such cost, except that it does not include any of the following sales, or any advertisement or offer in connection therewith:

" '(A) Any sale of a commodity for the bona fide purpose of discontinuing dealing in such commodity or of discontinuing the seller's business, when plain notice of that fact is given to the public.

" '(B) Any sale of a commodity which is substantially damaged or deteriorated in quality if plain notice of the fact is given to the public.

" '(C) Any sale by an officer acting under an order of court.

" '(D) Any sale to any association organized and operated exclusively for religious, charitable, scientific, literary, or educational purposes, or for the prevention of cruelty to children or animals, no part of the net earnings of which inures to the benefit of any private shareholder or individual.

" '(E) Any sale of a perishable commodity if further retention of the commodity by the seller could reasonably be expected to result in a loss to the seller.

" '(F) Any sale which reasonable business practices require the seller to make in order to liquidate an inventory of a commodity to avoid insolvency or bankruptcy.

" '(G) Any seasonal clearance sale made in accordance with customary business practices in order to dispose of excess inventory.

" '(b) Any loss leader practice which affects commerce is hereby declared to be unlawful and actionable at the suit of any person damaged thereby.

" '(c) (1) Any person injured in his business or property by any loss leader practice hereby declared to be unlawful may sue therefor in any district court of the United States, as provided in section 4 of this act, or in any State court of competent jurisdiction, and recover threefold the damages by him sustained, and the costs of suit, including a reasonable attorney's fee. Any person threatened with injury by any loss leader practice shall be entitled to injunctive relief against such threatened injury in any court of the United States, as provided in section 16 of this act, or to sue for and have such relief in any State court of competent jurisdiction when and under the same conditions and principles as injunctive relief against threatened conduct that will cause loss or damage is granted by courts of equity in that State, under the rules governing such proceedings, and upon the execution of proper bond against damages for an injunction improvidently granted and a showing that the danger of irreparable loss or damage is immediate, a preliminary injunction may issue.

" '(2) Section 15 of this act (providing for suits by United States district attorneys to restrain violations of this act) shall not apply with respect to any loss leader practice.

" '(d) (1) Nothing contained herein or in any of the antitrust acts shall render illegal any contract or agreement prohibiting a seller from reselling at a price below his delivered cost, any commodity which bears, or the label or container of which bears, the trade-mark, brand, or name of the producer or distributor of such commodity and which is in free and open competition with commodities of the same general class produced or distributed by others, when contracts or agreements prescribing minimum prices are lawful under any statute, law, or public policy now or hereafter in effect in any State, Territory, or the District of Columbia in which such resale is to be made, or to which the commodity is to be transported for such resale, or for delivery to a vendee pursuant to a sale.

" '(2) Nothing contained herein or in any of the antitrust acts shall render illegal the exercise or enforcement of any right or right of action created by any statute, law, or public policy now or hereafter in effect in any State, Territory, or the District of Columbia, which provides in substance that willfully and knowingly advertising, offering for sale, or selling any commodity at less than the minimum prices prescribed in any such contract or agreement whether the person so advertising, offering for sale, or selling is or is not a party to such contract or agreement, is unfair competition and is actionable at the suit of any person damaged thereby: *Provided, however,* That the rights or right of action created by or under such contracts and agreements shall not apply where the minimum price prescribed in such contract is higher than the delivered cost to the seller: *And provided further,* That the rights or right of action created by or under such contracts and agreements shall not apply to any of the following sales, or advertisement or offer in connection therewith:

" '(A) Any sale of a commodity for the bona fide purpose of discontinuing dealing in such commodity or of discontinuing the seller's business, when plain notice of that fact is given to the public.

" '(B) Any sale of a commodity which is substantially damaged or deteriorated in quality if plain notice of the fact is given to the public.

" '(C) Any sale by an officer acting under an order of court.

" '(D) Any sale to any association organized and operated exclusively for religious, charitable, scientific, literary, or educational purposes, or for the prevention of cruelty to children or animals, no part of the net earnings of which inures to the benefit of any private shareholder or individual.

" '(E) Any sale of a perishable commodity if further retention of the commodity by the seller could reasonably be expected to result in a loss to the seller.

" '(F) Any sale which reasonable business practices require the seller to make in order to liquidate an inventory of a commodity to avoid insolvency or bankruptcy.

" '(G) Any seasonal clearance sale made in accordance with customary business practices in order to dispose of excess inventory.'

"SEC. 2. That section 1 of the act entitled 'An act to protect trade and commerce against unlawful restraints and monopolies' approved July 2, 1890, as amended, is amended to read as follows:

" 'SECTION 1. Every contract, combination in the form of trust or otherwise, or conspiracy, in restraint of trade or commerce among the several States, or with foreign nations, is hereby declared to be illegal. Every person who shall make any such combination or conspiracy, shall be deemed guilty of a misdemeanor, and on conviction thereof, shall be punished by fine not exceeding $5,000, or by imprisonment not exceeding 1 year, or by both said punishments, in the discretion of the court.' "

Mr. LONG. Mr. President, I wish to say only a word or two about the parliamentary situation. . . .

The Senator from Arizona speaks of filibustering. The junior Senator from Louisiana has no scruples against filibustering if he believes the situation justifies it. Nevertheless, if filibustering is an irregularity, what shall we say of the situation when a bill is brought up without a committee report, without the hearings being printed, and without a single speech being made in favor of a bill which would affect the prices which consumers all over the Nation would have to pay for certain commodities. In this instance only one Senator rose to make a speech, and before he was three-fourths of the way through his speech, some other Senator says that a filibuster is under way, before any other Senator had an opportunity to make a speech on the subject, and before a single speech had been made in favor of the bill. . . .

If Senators wish to insist on a vote on the bill, there should be plenty of votes to carry a cloture petition, if they want to shut off debate without the bill being properly debated. . . .

Mr. McFARLAND. I appreciate the position of the Senator from Louisiana. We did not displace the bill at all, because at all times notice was given that an appropriation bill would take precedence. The misunderstanding was caused by the colloquy which occurred last Saturday. The RECORD shows that I have done everything possible to expedite the consideration and passage of this bill.

It is all right with me if Senators want to say that they believe in unlimited debate. I strongly believe in it myself. I will not ask for cloture on this bill. I have tried to give Senators an opportunity to vote on the bill. If it is defeated or if it goes over so that we cannot pass it, at least the Senate will have had an opportunity to vote on it. I think the Senate is ready to vote on the bill now. The reason no one—

Mr. DOUGLAS. Will the Senator yield at this point? I have yielded to him on my time.

Mr. McFARLAND. Very well.

Mr. DOUGLAS. Does the Senator from Arizona say that Senators are ready to vote on the bill now when they have not heard one speech in favor of the bill and have not read the report on the bill and do not have before them the hearings on the bill? How can the Senator from Arizona say that we are ready to vote on the bill?

Mr. WELKER. Mr. President, will the Senator yield?

Mr. McFARLAND. I thought the Senator from Illinois was ready to vote on the bill, because he was the one who moved to lay the bill on the table.

Mr. DOUGLAS. I am ready to vote on my amendment.

Mr. McFARLAND. The Senator was the one who made the motion to table, even before the bill was discussed. I believe every Senator knows how he will vote on the bill. The Senator from Illinois konws [sic] how he will vote on the bill. The Senator from Arizona knows how he will vote on it. I think we can dispose of it. The reason why the Senator from Illinois made his motion to table, I ⊥ presume, was because he ⊥ 8735 thought the Senate was fully informed with regard to the measure. Let the small independent merchant and the small independent druggist, the men who are the balance wheel of the Nation know who is responsible for the defeat of this measure.

I merely wanted to make it absolutely clear that the Senator from Arizona is eager to bring this measure to a vote. I meant no criticism of the Senator from Minnesota, though I think he unduly chastised me. He is my friend, and I know he has a right to do it, but I thought he laid it on a little too hard; but I know how to take it.

I want the people throughout the country, especially the small druggist who is trying to eke out an existence, and who wants to be able to fight the big chain, to know who is holding up the bill. Call the roll of the Senate, Mr. President, and you will find those who are behind the small merchants and businessmen of the country.

Mr. DOUGLAS. Mr. President, I wish the Senator from Arizona would not leave the Chamber.

Mr. McFARLAND. I am not leaving the Chamber. I moved over here to speak to a friend who wanted to congratulate me. I am always willing to be congratulated.

Mr. NEELY. Mr. President, will the Senator from Illinois yield?

Mr. DOUGLAS. No; I wish to say something on my own time.

The VICE PRESIDENT. The Senator from Illinois declines to yield.

Mr. DOUGLAS. I am glad that the Senator from Arizona is staying in the Chamber. At first I thought he was going to emulate Captain Shotover, the character in Bernard Shaw's play Heartbreak House, who would ask a question and then go out the door before anyone had a chance to reply.

Mr. McFARLAND. That is an unfair comment.

Mr. DOUGLAS. I was merely citing a play by Bernard Shaw.

Mr. McFARLAND. It is all right to cite plays, but not to cast reflections.

SEVERAL SENATORS. Vote! Vote! Vote!

The VICE PRESIDENT. The Senate will be in order.

Mr. DOUGLAS. I made my early motion to table merely in order that there might be a preliminary skirmish on this bill. I must confess that I was shocked that the bill was on the point of being passed without anyone speaking in its favor and without any statement being made concerning it and without any report of the committee being before us.

Mr. [JOHN L.] McCLELLAN [D., Ark.]. Mr. President, will the Senator yield?

Mr. DOUGLAS. I decline to yield at this time.

The VICE PRESIDENT. The Senator declines to yield.

Mr. DOUGLAS. I should like to finish my statement.

Mr. McCLELLAN. The motion to table was defeated.

Mr. DOUGLAS. The motion was defeated. Mr. President, the amendment has been read. I wish to make it clear that my amendment is in the form of a substitute. It is in effect the so-called Celler bill, H. R. 6986. I have a limited number of copies of the bill and I shall ask the pages to distribute copies of it to the Senators in the Chamber. It is the same as the Celler bill, with one exception. It prohibits a sale below cost which affects commerce, and it defines cost as the delivered cost of a commodity to the retailer plus 6 percent. In other words, it is more liberal to the retailer than the Celler bill. The Celler bill merely forbade sales at below delivered price.

Mr. AIKEN. Mr. President, will the Senator yield for a question?

Mr. DOUGLAS. May I first finish the sentence? Then I shall yield.

The VICE PRESIDENT. The Senator declines to yield at this time.

Mr. DOUGLAS. The present amendment defines cost as the delivered cost of a commodity to the retailer plus 6 percent. Therefore it is more liberal than the Celler bill. It permits a suit for damages in a Federal court by anyone who is hurt by loss-leaders. It exempts sales under bankruptcy, sales to organizations organized and operated exclusively for religious, charitable, literary or scientific purposes, seasonal clearance sales, and so on. The terms of the bill were worked out by Representative CELLER and experts of the House Judiciary Committee. Now I shall be glad to yield to the Senator from Vermont for a question.

Mr. AIKEN. I merely wanted to ask the Senator from Illinois if he has any knowledge as to whether the bill is in accord with the President's program.

Mr. DOUGLAS. I am not acquainted with all the details of the President's program. Certainly all members of his party are not justified in speaking for it. I can say that if the administration really means business—and I think it does—and if it opposes monopoly and opposes private price-fixing, the pending bill would seem to me to be a violation of the President's program. But I think it would be better if this information were obtained, as the English used to say, "out of the horse's mouth."

Mr. AIKEN. Has the bill been referred to any executive agency for study and report?

Mr. DOUGLAS. To the best of my knowledge it has not been. Pardon me; when I have been speaking of "the bill," I have been referring to the McGuire bill, the price-maintenance bill, as being a violation of the antimonopoly laws.

So far as I know, my amendment has not been referred to any of these agencies. However, I believe the amendment does constitute a legitimate protection to retailers. It seems to me that the amendment really continues the principles of the Robinson-Patman Act.

Mr. AIKEN. Will the Senator from Illinois explain the meaning of the letter from the chairman of the Judiciary Committee, which appears on the first page of Report No. 1741? Has the bill been referred to the Judiciary Committee, and has that committee held hearings on the bill and subsequently reported the bill?

Mr. DOUGLAS. Is the Senator from Vermont referring to the so-called McGuire bill, House bill 5767; or is the Senator from Vermont referring to the Celler bill?

Mr. AIKEN. Does the Senator from Illinois believe this bill should be considered by the Judiciary Committee?

Mr. DOUGLAS. Does the Senator from Vermont refer to the McGuire bill, the one now under consideration by the Senate?

Mr. AIKEN. That is correct.

Mr. DOUGLAS. I am not an expert on the rules of the Senate, and I shall not pass judgment on the question of whether that bill should have been considered by the Committee on Interstate and Foreign Commerce, which reported it without recommendation, or whether the bill should have been considered by the Judiciary Committee. I have made it clear that it was not my intention to insist that the bill be referred to the Judiciary Committee. I think that is another indication that I do not seek to prevent a vote on this bill.

I am perfectly willing to have the bill debated here on the floor of the Senate, and I do not wish to have the bill killed in committee.

So I shall not make any move to have the bill referred to the Judiciary Committee, but I believe the bill should be debated on the floor of this body.

Mr. AIKEN. Mr. President, will the Senator from Illinois yield further?

Mr. DOUGLAS. Yes, I yield.

Mr. AIKEN. Does the Senator from Illinois know of any instance in which any so-called monopoly bill has not been considered by or referred to the Judiciary Committee?

Mr. DOUGLAS. As I have said, I have not had the experience in this body that the Senator from Vermont has had. I know that frequently jurisdictional disputes arise over such matters. It is not my purpose to raise such a jurisdictional issue.

Mr. AIKEN. Does the Senator from Illinois know what reply, if any, was made to the request of the chairman of the Judiciary Committee to have the bill referred to the Judiciary Committee?

Mr. DOUGLAS. The letter of the chairman of the Judiciary Committee was addressed to the eminent Senator from Colorado [Mr. JOHNSON], the chairman of the Committee on Interstate and Foreign Commerce, and I shall have to ask him to reply to that question. . . .

Mr. [EDWIN C.] JOHNSON [D., Colo.]. Mr President, as I understand the question, this is the answer: The Committee on Interstate and Foreign Commerce received a request, by letter, from the Senator from Nevada [Mr. McCARRAN], chairman of the Committee on the Judiciary, asking that the bill be referred to the Committee on the Judiciary.

The Committee on Interstate and Foreign Commerce explored the matter, and took it up with the Parliamentarian of the Senate. We were informed that inasmuch as the bill had been referred to the Committee on Interstate and Foreign Commerce, we did not have a right to refer the bill to another committee; that the only thing we could do with the bill was to handle it in our own committee or report it to the Senate.

We sent the bill to the floor of the Senate, where the Senate has complete authority and jurisdiction over the bill. The Senate can re-refer the bill if the Senate wishes to do so.

Mr. AIKEN. Would not it be more appropriate to have the bill taken up for consideration at a time when the chairman of the Judiciary Committee is present?

The VICE PRESIDENT. The Chair may be able to answer the question.

When this bill came to the Senate from the House of Representatives, the question of the committee to which the bill should be referred was a matter to be ruled on by the Chair.

The Chair read the bill, and decided that it should be referred to the Committee on Interstate and Foreign Commerce. The Chair referred the bill to that committee. In that decision the Chair had the concurrence of the Parliamentarian of the Senate.

What happened to the bill thereafter, is a matter over which the Chair has no control.

Of course, any Senator could have moved that the bill be re-referred to the Committee on the Judiciary, but no such motion was made.

The Chair referred the bill to the committee to which the Chair thought the bill was entitled to go.

Mr. AIKEN. I thank the Chair for that information. I merely thought it strange that the request to which I have referred appear on the first page of the report.

The VICE PRESIDENT. So far as the Chair knows, no request was made to refer the bill to any particular committee. The Chair acted under the rules of the Senate, and referred the bill to the Committee on Interstate and Foreign Commerce.

Mr. AIKEN. I am very glad to obtain the explanation of what happened.

Mr. DOUGLAS. Mr. President, it is not my purpose to hold the floor any longer.

I shall merely say that if we wish to stop loss-leaders, the way to do so is to prohibit them—which my amendment does. In order to stop loss-leaders, it is not necessary to give to manufacturers the power to fix retail prices—in fact, not only to fix prices to those who sign agreements, but also to fix prices to all retailers, many of whom do not sign agreements.

In other words, Mr. President, in order to deal with the proximate and immediate evil, it is not necessary to take such a heavy dose as the McGuire bill proposes.

Since the Senator from Vermont has raised the issue as to the attitude of the President or of the President's office in regard to this matter, let me say that it is my information that the Bureau of the Budget—I do not know whether it can be said to speak for the President, but at least it thinks it can—has said that the fair-trade bill, the so-called McGuire bill, is not in accord with the President's program; and the Federal Trade Commission, as a substitute for the McGuire bill, has endorsed the type of bill which I have suggested, or another type of bill which, as I understand, is to be proposed, quite possibly by the Senator from Louisiana.

However, in order to make it clear that I am not trying to filibuster, I shall now yield the floor.

The VICE PRESIDENT. The Senator from Illinois has a right to yield at any moment.

Mr. LEHMAN. Mr. President, will the Senator from Illinois yield for a question?

Mr. DOUGLAS. Mr. President, I shall yield at this time for a question, but I hope I shall be permitted to take my seat, so that no charge of filibustering can be leveled at me.

Mr. LEHMAN. Mr. President, I sympathize entirely with the Senator's attitude. However, I wish him to yield to me for a question.

Mr. DOUGLAS. Very well; I yield.

Mr. LEHMAN. I am sure the Senator from Illinois heard the distinguished majority leader refer to his deep interest in the druggist and in the grocer, and I know that the interest of the distinguished Senator from Illinois, as well as my own interest and that of all other Members of the Senate, is also in the grocer and in the druggist. On the other hand, is it not a fact that what we who are opposing this bill are trying to do is to protect the 155,000,000 consumers of the United States?

Mr. DOUGLAS. That is correct.

Mr. LEHMAN. They are the ones who need protection. They are the ones who are being charged unduly high prices in many cases, the ones who are being mulcted out of hundreds of millions of dollars, without, in my opinion, any commensurate or corresponding gain on the part of the grocer and the druggist.

Is it not a fact that that is what we are fighting for—that we are not trying to hurt anyone, but we are trying to help all the people? At the present time we are particularly concerned in opposing this bill because of our desire to protect the 155,000,000 customers in the United States.

Mr. DOUGLAS. The Senator from New York is quite correct. We are trying to protect the really forgotten men and women of the country—the consumers.

Mr. [A. S.] MONRONEY [D., Okla.]. Mr. President, will the Senator yield for two short questions?

Mr. DOUGLAS. I yield for a question. Let it be understood that I am doing this out of courtesy. It is my desire to yield the floor.

Mr. MONRONEY. The questions I wish to ask are addressed strictly to the Senator's bill, which I think he can best explain.

Mr. DOUGLAS. It is the Celler bill.

Mr. MONRONEY. But the Senator from Illinois is sponsoring it.

Mr. DOUGLAS. That is correct.

Mr. MONRONEY. Would the Senator tell the Senate whether his bill would, in fact, put every commodity or product sold at retail, and sold below 6 percent of the delivered cost plus 6-percent profit to a retailer, under the arm of the Federal law?

Mr. DOUGLAS. Yes. It is an attempt to prevent industry from getting under the arm of the private price fixer.

Mr. MONRONEY. Could the Senator tell me what percent he estimates is now under the fair-trade limitation?

Mr. DOUGLAS. That affects only branded items, and I shall be very glad to modify my amendment so that it would refer only to the national brands or trademarked items.

Mr. MONRONEY. The point I was trying to make in my questioning was that the way the Celler bill is drawn, as introduced in the Senate, it would include everything sold at retail which did not bear at least a 6-percent markup, whereas the fair-trade and trademarked items add up to about 1 percent of the merchandise that is sold, and leaves it to the States to have their own fair-price system, if they so desire.

Mr. DOUGLAS. Let the RECORD show that the Senator is perfectly willing to modify his amendment in the nature of a substitute, so that it will cover only the same type of goods referred to by the McGuire bill, namely, trade-marked or branded goods. The language will have to be formulated.

The VICE PRESIDENT. The Senator has a right to modify his amendment.

Mr. DOUGLAS. I will submit appropriate language at a later time in this debate. It will be on Senators' desks tomorrow. Again, Mr. President, unless there are other questions, I yield the floor.

The VICE PRESIDENT. Does the Senator from Illinois yield the floor?

Mr. DOUGLAS. I yield the floor.

Mr. LEHMAN. Mr. President, I am, like the rest of us, greatly interested in the welfare of druggists and grocers in my State and in other States, too. They are a highly respectable and responsible group of persons for whom I have sincere regard and in whose interest I have a deep concern. I very much wish that they be enabled to make fair and consistent profits and be prosperous.

I am not worried over the profits, as such, of the large manufacturers. I want to see general prosperity in this country, and I want to see every industry make fair and equitable profits. But I am concerned most of all at this moment, and I am worried, about the plight and the position of the consumer—the 155,000,000 consumers in this country—and I do not think there is any question that the fair-trade laws in our various States, if they are allowed to operate under the terms of the pending bill, will mean that the consumers of this country will have to pay higher prices and pay out more of their income for these protected products.

Not for a very long time, probably not since I came to the Senate, have I been more in doubt about what I should do with regard to a bill. I have thought deeply about this bill and have discussed it extensively with others, and I have finally reached a decision to oppose this fair-trade bill; I have reached that decision with reluctance and with some doubt and hesitation.

My hesitation was based in part on the fact that, as Governor of New York, I had signed one of the first fair-trade bills that was enacted in any State of the Union. I signed it in 1935. I accompanied my signature of that fair-trade law with a strong message, a message which has been quoted in the courts on a number of occasions.

I think the history of that New York bill, and the story of why I signed it in 1935, may be of interest to my colleagues in the Senate.

That bill, as I have said, was enacted in 1935, when we were working our way out of a very great depression. It was enacted at a time when it was very difficult for manufacturers to dispose of their products at fair prices in the normal manner. They had considerable inventories and the consumers had insufficient money to buy these goods. The result was that manufacturers in their efforts to sell their products and reduce their inventories were willing to sell their goods to large department stores and big distributors at any terms, at almost any price. Of course, that led to a situation in which the small druggist, the small grocer, and the small merchant, who had their own inventories and who could not compete in price with the big retailer, had no opportunity to protect themselves. The little stores were being bankrupt and driven to the wall, and going out of business. That led to very great losses on the part of small dealers, for whom, I wish to say, I have the greatest regard. I think they are one of the most important and most necessary elements in our economy. They are the backbone of our country.

There was another thing that related to that bill, which I wish to mention tonight. When I signed that bill, I thought that the manufacturer would go out and sign up all or a greater part of the distributors of his particular product. Certainly there could have been at that time no objection whatsoever to a fair-trade bill that would permit the manufacturer to invoke the protection of the law for the contracts into which he had entered with distributors and merchants. To my considerable surprise, I found that the manufacturers did not sign up the majority of the distributors, but that they used the law in such a way that if they signed up one distributor or one retailer and got him to agree to maintain a certain price, that price was enforced for every other retailer and distributor in the whole State.

I did not contemplate such a development at the time the bill was before me. I can speak only from the standpoint of New York, but I can say to Senators that such a development was not generally envisioned when the bill was passed by the Legislature of the State of New York and obtained my approval. But that situation has developed and remains until the present time, namely, that the signing up of one retailer or distributor has imposed an obligation on every other distributor or retailer in the entire State. In my opinion, that is not a sound practice, and certainly it imposes restrictions on the free enterprise and trade we all wish to see maintained.

If the pending bill is enacted, I do not think there is any doubt that it will increase the cost to the consumer, and I do not believe it will mean any real or lasting profit to the distributor or the retailer. The situation today is so different from what it was 15, 16, 17, or 20 years ago, when we were in the midst of a depression, that I believe today the distributor or retailer does not require this protection or gain by it.

I do not believe that, save in isolated cases, the little merchant's trade is seriously interfered with or that his profits are seriously interfered with, in the absence of a fair-trade law. The little pharmacist or grocer or hardware dealer has the advantage of an intimate relationship with his community and has the further advantage of knowing the people with whom he deals. I do not believe that because a large department store 2, 3, or 4 miles from where the small dealer operates, for a very short time cuts prices, is going to interfere seriously with the business of the small merchant. I think the ability and the authority given to all merchants to fix their own prices, regardless of any Federal intervention, or State intervention, if you will, at least gives the guaranty, if not of lower prices, then of stabilized, reasonable prices, which would not be the case under a fair-trade law.

Mr. MOODY. Mr. President, I yield to no Member of this body, not even the distinguished and illustrious Senator from Illinois, in my interest in the consuming public. From the day I entered the Senate, I have sponsored measures and policies which I felt to be in the interest of the consuming public of America.

I feel that this measure is not only in the interest of the small-business men, but also in the long-term interest of the consumers. Therefore, I feel that the Senate should pass this bill.

Fair trade, so-called, is a complicated issue. There are good arguments on both sides, as we have heard here tonight. Those of us who believe strongly in a really free economy, and hope for a vigorous enforcement of the antitrust laws, at first hesitated to approve of fair trade.

In the best of all possible worlds, Mr. President, a fair trade act would not be necessary to protect small business. Unfortunately, we have not yet reached that happy state. We have found that when the powerful cross-currents of economic power are permitted to run unleashed they sometimes destroy not only individuals, but can cripple the economy.

The farm economy of America went through a decade of recession in the 1920's, and helped precipitate the great depression of 1930-32, until vigorous action was taken here to protect agriculture from depression. Workingmen were paid an average of $17 a week, when they could find jobs, and were threatened, blacklisted, and stink-bombed for attempts to organize, until their right of collective bargaining was assured by law. Big business itself, when governments followed its orders as a pliant stooge, plunged during 1931-32 into a slough of red ink—$3,400,000,000 worth of it—before common sense and a new administration and a new Congress came to take the practical steps needed to restore confidence and buying power.

The real danger of price fixing in America does not spring from the little-business man—the small druggist, the modest furniture dealer, the independent petroleum dealer, the neighborhood grocer. All are essential to our way of life. Mr. President, the real danger lies not so much in vertical arrangements on advertised brands, which are in competition with each other, as in the potent horizontal price-fixing alliances between some primary producers which stifle competition in some fields entirely.

It is there the antitrust laws should be enforced, Mr. President. It is there that the consumer should be protected. The consumer is not protected, in the long run, by the evanescent advantage of being able to buy a few items at less than cost, when he inevitably must make up that loss by paying higher prices for other goods, and when the result of unfair price cutting can only be to cripple or destroy small competitive business. Small business is the heart and soul of our real competitive system, which has given America the most goods at the best value, and the highest standard of living of any nation in the history of the world. When Joe's corner grocery store and Jim's drug store leave the neighborhood, something will have gone out of American life that can never be recovered. We must not let it happen, Senators, and I am confident we will not let it happen.

Should we permit small-business men to be destroyed, Mr. President, we would be undermining the basic strength that makes our country free and great.

I should like to read briefly from the report of our Senate Small Business Committee on fair trade because, under the leadership of the distinguished Senator from Alabama [Mr. SPARKMAN], this committee has gone into this matter with great care. The conclusion reached by the committee, and as stated in the report, reads:

CONCLUSIONS

The events of the past year in the field of fair trade have been of grave concern to your committee. In particular, the Schwegmann decision and the ensuing price wars were viewed as matters of tremendous import to small business. Had the price wars continued, they could have done incalculable harm to countless small businesses. The memory of the early 1930's and the great numbers of small, independent concerns that were then lost to the economy directly as a result of similar price wars is still fresh. The possibility is strong that the damage to fair trade wrought by the Schwegmann decision might well precipitate similar business failures should our economy suffer a sudden reversal.

* * * * * * *

Your committee is hopeful that the members of the business community will recognize their responsibilities in this situation and that they will realize the dangers inherent in loss-leader selling and cut-throat competition, that they will realize that such practices can result only in damaging the whole economy. It is not only the small independent merchant who suffers in a price war. The manufacturer and the consumer also suffer. And the leaders of price-cutting campaigns should realize that injury to other segments of the retail trade cannot benefit them. Gains realized from loss-leader selling are short-lived. The practice is a vicious one and defeats itself. No merchant, no matter how large, can afford to continue loss-leader selling indefinitely. He must engage in other practices in order to recoup his losses. And such other practices of necessity require that he sell other merchandise at high profits. The consumer must sooner or later discover the fallacy of the loss-leader selling technique, and then the retailer loses the good will of his customers and their patronage. The good sense and recognition of their responsibilities should impel the overwhelming mass of the business community to the logic and wisdom of fair trade. The Nation's economic well-being depends to a large extent on the vitality of America's small businesses. Threats of price wars must be eliminated if that vitality is to endure.

Mr. President, I may say parenthetically that I should like to see the Senator from Illinois offer his amendment, if he offers it, as an addition to the bill, rather than as a substitute.

Mr. President, I believe the consumers would be better protected if this bill should pass than if it should fail to pass. The danger of monopoly would be much greater without the bill than with it, I hope the Senate will pass the bill.

Mr. HUMPHREY. Mr. President, it is not my intention tonight to speak at length on this measure, but I feel that in light of the colloquy, and the very sharp debate which has gone on, some explanation is due.

First of all, the Senator from Illinois [Mr. DOUGLAS] has made a point of the fact that when this bill was called on the calendar the proponents of the bill did not speak up. I happened to be at the telephone at the time the bill was called. I came to the floor as quickly as I could, and when I arrived I found a motion had been made to table the bill. I feel that those of us who are for this measure surely must make our case. I do not believe that any Senator should expect to vote on a measure such as this without honest debate.

Let me say, with all due credit and honor to the Senator from Illinois, that rather than that he should be chastised for what he has done, he should be honored because he has brought out some issues that need to be discussed. He has given those of us who are the proponents of the measure an opportunity to speak on the bill and to reply to his charges. Furthermore, he has been most generous with his time. He has yielded again and again to those of us who have wanted to interrogate him.

I, for one, desire to say that if the debate on this measure should take a little time, it would not be time wasted, because just as there are those who think it is bad for the consumers, there are those who believe it is good for the retailers, the manufacturers, and the general economy of the country.

I also desire to pay tribute to the Senator from Louisiana [Mr. LONG] for his defense of the customer, and particularly his comments concerning the Senator from Illinois [Mr. DOUGLAS]. The fact of the matter is that we got ourselves into a parliamentary situation which was due to no one's judgment, but was just a matter of happenstance and unfortunate circumstances.

Mr. LONG. Mr. President, will the Senator from Minnesota yield?

Mr. HUMPHREY. I am glad to yield for a question.

Mr. LONG. The Senator is most fair in the position he has taken, and I believe he is entirely right in saying that matters which are of great moment to the people should be fully discussed. The Senator has been fearless in standing and fighting when he has been in the minority, and certainly he appreciates, as all of us do, that it is unfair to expect any measure to be voted upon without giving those who are opposed to it an opportunity to state their case, so that not only the Members of the Senate but the people may judge. It is unfortunate that so many Members might have made up their minds without hearing the debate. In some cases their minds may have been made up because of pressure or political appeal rather than on the merits of the issues involved.

I am very much interested in hearing what the Senator has to say. Perhaps he will convince me that I should join his side. My mind is not closed. I think we should have an opportunity to make the case clear in the RECORD, for anyone who might want to study it in the future or read it at the present time.

Mr. HUMPHREY. I thank the Senator. I know his keen interest in the question of our price laws, antimonopoly laws, and all matters which pertain to our commerce. I shall still respect his judgment if he opposes me.

Mr. MONRONEY. Mr. President, will the Senator from Minnesota yield?

Mr. HUMPHREY. I yield.

Mr. MONRONEY. Is it not a fact that perhaps one of the reasons why some Senators have made up their minds and do not require a great deal of additional debate is that the country lived for many years under this kind of an act? The Supreme Court held a certain portion of it to be unconstitutional, on a technicality, which technicality this bill would correct. Therefore, I think many of the proponents, although welcoming an adequate debate, did not feel that it would require an exhaustive debate as it would if it were an entirely new piece of legislation with which they were unfamiliar. The dome of the Capitol has not toppled; the Washington Monument still stands, although the Nation did have this kind of a law for a great many years. I think 1 percent of the retail commodities are trade-marked items, and those trade-marked items which are under fair-trade contracts have very little bearing on the general economy or the cost of living.

They are merely items that help to preserve the integrity, the ability, and the soundness of the small businesses of America. I do not remember any cases of small businesses growing into gigantic trusts or monopolies because of a fair-trade act. I do not think the people need to worry about the small-business man becoming an ogre that will destroy them because of the interpretation this bill places on the antitrust act.

Mr. HUMPHREY. Mr. President, I thank the Senator from Oklahoma because he has made comment on a subject concerning which I hope to say a few words.

What are we attempting to do in this proposed legislation known as the McGuire bill, or, as others call it, the fair-trade bill? It is not something that is new, because we have been living with fair-trade laws ever since the Miller-Tydings Act, and many years before. This bill seeks to do just one simple thing, namely, to restore in the Federal enabling statute the meaning which I believe the Miller-Tydings Act had when it was passed in 1937. I would refer to the dissenting opinion submitted by Mr. Justice Frankfurter in which Justices Black and Burton concurred. Justice Frankfurter summarized his objections to the Court decision when he said, in May of 1951, speaking for two of his learned colleagues and for himself, a learned judge:

Every one of the 42 State acts which the Miller-Tydings amendment was to back up—the acts on which the Miller-Tydings amendment was to place a stamp of approval—contained a nonsigner provision. As demonstrated by experience in California, the State acts would have been futile without the nonsigner clause. The Court now holds that the Miller-Tydings amendment does not cover these nonsigner provisions. Not only is the view of the Court contrary to the words of the statute and to the legislative history, it is also in conflict with the interpretation given the Miller-Tydings amendment by the Federal Trade Commission, by the Department of Justice, and by practically all persons adversely affected by the fair-trade laws.

* * * Where both the words of a statute and its legislative history clearly indicate the purpose of Congress, it should be respected. We should not substitute our own notion of what Congress should have done.3.64

In other words, Justice Frankfurter says that the legislative history of the Miller-Tydings Act made it perfectly clear that the so-called nonsigner clause was a very definite part of its intendment.

So, what this bill attempts to do is to plug the loophole which the Court said it found in the Miller-Tydings Act. It is intended to set at rest the doubt which has been raised by the Supreme Court's decision. It does not alter the laws of any of the 45 States which have fair-trade laws.

Mr. SPARKMAN. Mr. President, will the Senator from Minnesota yield?

Mr. HUMPHREY. I yield.

Mr. SPARKMAN. Does it in any way impose anything upon any State or any person?

Mr. HUMPHREY. It does not, in any way whatsoever, impose anything upon anyone or any State that was not considered to be in the original Miller-Tydings Act.

May I point out that the then Attorney General, Thurman Arnold, testified before a committee of the Congress asking for the repeal of the Miller-Tydings Act. He said it included the nonsigner clause which the Court said it did not include.

What are we called upon to do? To clarify the law. In other words we are to overrule in the Congress the split decision of the Supreme Court.

Mr. SPARKMAN. Is it not true that what we are trying to do by this bill is simply to take notice of or to recognize acts which have been passed by 45 of the States?

Mr. HUMPHREY. The Senator is absolutely correct.

Mr. SPARKMAN. If there is anything wrong about this bill, the trouble can be traced to the respective State legislatures, back home among the people, which passed the various State acts. The States wanted to have those acts passed.

Mr. HUMPHREY. Again the Senator is correct.

Mr. SPARKMAN. Congress now is simply saying to the States, "We recognize your wish in this matter, so we shall pass enabling legislation in order to protect commodities which move across State lines."

Mr. HUMPHREY. The Senator is correct. The very matter of which the Court took judicial notice in 1950 and 1951, in the Wentling case and in the Schwegmann case, the nonsigners' clause, is the subject matter which in 1939 and 1940 was rejected by the Court. Again what the Senator from Alabama has said is wholly true, that the bill would require no change to be made in the laws of the States. As a matter of fact, the McGuire bill, so far as Federal fair-trade policy is concerned, would do nothing whatsoever to the fair-trade acts of 45 States. It would take nothing away from any of the State acts. It would overcome the court decisions, so that it would be truly an enabling Federal statute.

I may say to Senators who have tonight raised their voices in opposition to the Miller-Tydings Act that they have had almost 17 years in which to raise their voices. I should have said 15 years, because the act has been on the books since 1937. Many States of the Union had fair trade laws before 1937. But the Miller-Tydings Act has been on the statute books since 1937. The California statute contained a proviso known as the nonsigner's clause, of which so much has been made tonight; namely, that if a particular manufacturer signed up with one firm, all others would be in the same group, even though they did not sign. The law is clear, and has been upheld by the courts since 1933. I desire to make it perfectly clear that decision after decision in the Supreme Court, in the circuit courts, and in district courts has upheld the constitutional validity of State acts. There is not a shadow of doubt as to their legality or constitutionality.

I conclude this portion of my statement by asking why, all at once, there is a torrential outpouring of criticism of fair trade, when, in fact, we have been living under it in America; when, in fact, the rules of competition have been legalized in America;

3.64 Schwegmann Bros. v. Calvert Distillers Corp., 341 U.S. 384, 401-02 (1951).

when, in fact, the retail business of America has been improved because of fair trade laws; when, in fact, State after State has proved that the laws work well when they are subject to the closest scrutiny of consumers, manufacturers, and retailers at the State level.

I heard tonight the cry about the consumer. Where does the consumer have a better opportunity to be heard than in his own State legislature? These statutes are State laws, administered by the States, which have an obligation to the citizens and consumers of the States.

If the consumer thought he was getting a bad deal because of a fair-trade law, he would have gone to his legislature. Yet it may be noted in the RECORD that not one State legislature has repealed a fair-trade law, nor has there been any substantial request for the repeal of such a statute. In fact, additional statutes have been passed in order to protect against predatory interests in the retail field.

Mr. SPARKMAN. Mr. President, will the Senator yield?

Mr. HUMPHREY. I yield.

Mr. SPARKMAN. A few minutes ago the able Senator made reference to the fact that the Miller-Tydings law was passed in 1937, and he said something about the number of States that had passed fair-trade laws up to that time.

I call the attention of the Senator to the fact that the first fair-trade law was passed by California in 1931. By the end of 1936, 14 States had passed such laws. In 1937, the same year in which the Miller-Tydings law was passed, 20 more States had passed such laws, making a total of 42 States.

In the excerpt from the Schwegmann case, from which the Senator read a few minutes ago, Mr. Justice Frankfurter made reference to the fact that when the Miller-Tydings Act was passed, 42 States had fair-trade laws, to which the Miller-Tydings Act was applicable and that all of them contained a nonsigner provision.

Mr. HUMPHREY. I may supplement the Senator's remarks by saying that it had been clearly understood by the lower courts, and also by the Federal Trade Commission, which today opposes this bill—and it is a matter of their own official records—and it was likewise clearly understood by the Department of Justice, that the Miller-Tydings Act included, through its provisions and its legislative history, enabling authority for the nonsigner clause. That is a matter of record.

Mr. LONG. Mr. President, will the Senator yield?

Mr. HUMPHREY. I yield.

Mr. LONG. I was very much interested to hear the Senator say that the matter of fair-trade laws is left entirely up to the State legislatures.

Mr. HUMPHREY. That is correct.

Mr. LONG. The States are not compelled to accept this kind of law. If they do not desire this type of fair-trade law, they do not have to have it.

Mr. HUMPHREY. That is correct.

Mr. LONG. Would the Senator be willing to have the same principle apply to the Fair Employment Practices Commission?

Mr. HUMPHREY. I desire to thank the Senator, but the Fair Employment Practices Commission measure is not enabling legislation; it is substantive legislation. When we are considering substantive legislation, I shall expect the Senator from Louisiana to give me vigorous opposition, because I know that he always feels that the States ought to have the opportunity to regulate local affairs, and the Senator has been so persuasive and eloquent throughout the years that I have been moved closer and closer to his position. I have even altered my ideas about FEPC with respect to local and State authority. If the Senator will remain with me, I venture to say that he will join with Senators who support the McGuire bill, which provides enabling legislation for the States. Otherwise he will learn that instead of having a bill providing local responsibility and the exercise of State authority to do economic justice in respect to States, he will get a bill like the Celler bill, which is being proposed here, which would empower Government agencies to check on every commodity to determine whether or not there was a 6-percent mark-up, or whether this commodity or that commodity was to be included.

Ah, I may say to the Senator from Louisiana, we States' righters have got to stand together tonight. We have got to stand together on these questions. [Laughter.]

Mr. LONG. I am pleased to hear that the Senator has made so much progress in his belief that the States should determine so many questions for themselves. I hope his views on the FEPC will come around to the idea of leaving the decision with respect to such a matter to the States, to leave it up to the people.

Mr. HUMPHREY. I may say to the very able, eloquent, and eminent Senator from Louisiana that if 45 States of the Union are as much in favor of FEPC as they are in favor of fair trade, I think the Senator will have pulled all my teeth and whittled down all my fangs, and I shall have to give up the fight.

Mr. MONRONEY. Mr. President, will the Senator yield?

Mr. HUMPHREY. I yield.

Mr. MONRONEY. Could the Senator enlighten the Senate, and in particular the junior Senator from Oklahoma, as to the approximate percentage of items ⊥ moving at retail which come under fair-trade laws? My impression is that the figure is about 1 percent, but I know that the Senator from Minnesota has given a great deal more study to the question than I have. ⊥ 8740

Mr. HUMPHREY. I must confess that I do not have accurate statistics on that question, but I know that out of the total volume of retail trade, it is a very small proportion. I believe the total volume of fair-trade products which have been sold in the past calendar year was something like $6,000,000,000 out of a total national income of approximately $278,000,000,000. That gives a good idea of what the amount of sales of fair-trade commodities would be. I would say they would amount to from 1 to 2 percent.

Mr. MONRONEY. So all the hubbub, worry, and fear are being created by a volume of from 1 to 2 percent of the business. Unless the senior Senator from Illinois can amend his loss-leader amendment, and after reading the amendment, I do not see how that can be done, without a redrafting of the whole measure, he would compel 100 percent of everything moving in the retail trade to be under the long arm of the Federal law. That would include sugar in the grocery stores, and sugar has never borne even a 6 percent mark-up. Many other items historically have never carried a 6 percent mark-up.

But this proposed substitute would force everything except distress merchandise to be sold at cost, plus at least six percent, without having anything to do with the protection of trade-marked items whose value a manufacturer has established through national advertising costing millions of dollars, in an effort to maintain fair trade on a nationally advertised product at a nationally advertised price, when any imitator or other manufacturer can produce an equal or corresponding competitive product without being under fair trade.

Mr. HUMPHREY. I thank the Senator. I think he has pointed out the real differences between the Douglas amendment, or the Celler bill, and the McGuire bill, the bill presently under consideration. That is a distinct contribution.

Mr. LEHMAN. Mr. President, will the Senator yield?

Mr. HUMPHREY. I yield.

Mr. LEHMAN. I wonder whether the distinguished Senator from Minnesota is accurate when he states that about $253,000,000,000 worth of goods are sold at retail.

Mr. HUMPHREY. No; I did not say that. I said that the total national income was over $250,000,000,000, and that the total amount of retail sales of fair-trade goods was around $6,000,000,000.

Mr. LEHMAN. The total goods sold at retail would be considerably under $100,000,000,000.

Mr. HUMPHREY. That is correct.

Mr. LEHMAN. So the trade-marked goods would not be 1 or 2 percent, but perhaps in excess of 6 percent.

Mr. HUMPHREY. In terms of volume of sales, I think the Senator is right. In terms of items covered, the percentage might be different. I think we should look at the facts, and I shall see that we get the facts, because there is no use conjecturing.

In 1950 the Third Circuit Court of Appeals, in the Wentling decision, weakened the fair-trade structure by holding that the enforcement of a fair-trade law in any other State having a fair-trade law constitutes an unlawful burden upon and an interference with interstate commerce. Under this decision mail-order houses and other retailers who sell across State lines are permitted to disregard the fair-trade laws of every State but their own.

All they have to do is to obtain a badge of innocence from their own State, and go out and literally commit economic murder. They have a type of immunity in going from one State to another. All they have to do is to behave at home. They can raise all the dickens they want to away from home. Abe Martin once said that all men are alike when they are away from home. This is exactly what is being attempted with this bill. It is said, "So long as you behave in Kansas, you can go to Nebraska and have a good time wrecking the whole economic marketplace."

That does not make sense. I do not propose to be any kind of lawyer, but that is the rule of the jungle. It is the rule of the bully. It is the rule of the bad boy, who acts like a pious, innocent soul at home, but the minute he gets out of town he starts having himself a junket, a good, frisky time, getting both himself and everybody else into trouble.

What we are trying to do under the McGuire bill is to say, "Your conduct at home shall be the same as your conduct when you leave home. If you are an economic gentleman in Kansas, when you visit your brothers and sisters in Nebraska, be an economic gentleman there." That is all we are saying under the McGuire bill.

I thought I would like to go into the legal problems, because I think they have caused a great deal of trouble. I cannot imagine anything else that has caused as much furore. We have been waiting 15 years to hear the speech tonight by the Senator from Illinois [Mr. DOUGLAS]. We have been waiting 15 years to hear what the Senator from Louisiana [Mr. LONG] has said, and 15 years to hear others. All at once we are hearing speeches about how terrible a fair-trade law is when, so far as I have been able to find out, no petitions have been filed by any consumers with respect to fair-trade laws. At least none have been brought to my attention.

Not many legislatures have had referendums, recalls, or initiative votes on the part of the citizenry on this subject, directed to the legislature or the governor. This has been an open subject. There has been no closed book. There has been no iron curtain. Everyone has had an opportunity to be heard. What has actually happened is that the retailer has been better off, the manufacturer has been better off, and the consumer has been better off. I am going to prove tonight that the argument which has been made about this being a bad bill for the consumer is an argument which cannot be based upon statistical facts or long-range good public policy.

Let us take another look at the subject of fair-trade laws. The Congress of the United States is a policy-making body. The legislatures of the respective States make policy in their sovereign areas. The Congress of the United States has established policies on many occasions which cannot be justified on the basis of dollars and cents, or profit-and-loss ledgers. Congress has at times made policies which are surely discriminatory. For example, the Congress of the United States treats a corporation one way and treats a farm cooperative another way. I am for that. I think that is good public policy. I think we need farmers' marketing cooperatives, and I think farmers' marketing cooperatives need some protection in order to flourish and grow for the benefit of the American farmer. However, I receive letters saying, "You give them special treatment." Perhaps that is right. However, the simple fact is that that is public policy.

There are other public policies. The Reclamation Bureau has a public policy. It says that a person cannot hold more than 160 acres of irrigated land upon a reclamation project. Can anyone in this body prove to me that a 160-acre farm is more economical than a 400- or 500-acre farm? As a matter of fact, the public policy of this country favors the family-sized farm. Can anyone prove by economic statistics that the family-sized farm is more economical to operate, or a better functional unit? As a matter of fact, statistics prove that a large corporation type farm can produce commodities more cheaply. It can produce larger quantities. It is more manageable from all the technical points of view. It is possible to have a better, more efficient system. But, my colleagues, America is not interested in the corporation farm as a part of its economy. America places a social value upon the family-sized farm, and we pay a price for that social value, a price which I am willing to pay, and everyone else is willing to pay. We could have farms of 100,000 acres or 50,000 acres, with absentee ownership and management, but that does not build the kind of America we want.

Public policy has something to do with other things besides dollars and cents. I have heard the argument to the effect that the consumer may save himself a few dollars if there are no fair-trade laws. Let us accept that thesis for the purpose of argument. Let us assume that the argument is correct, although I think I can prove that it is not. But even if it were correct, that does not tell us that that is the thing to do. It does not tell us that that is the kind of policy we should have.

I suppose it could be proved that if an employer could work people 60 hours a week, with a whip in his hand, he might be able to get more production. But we are not interested solely in production. We are interested in people living the good life. So we limit the workweek to 40 hours, as a matter of public law.

We establish a rule of time-and-a-half for overtime, so that employers will be encouraged to limit employment to 40 hours a week. We have many principles and policies which are social policies, and political policies, for the purpose of what? For the purpose of building the kind of society that America wants.

We are talking about a political, economic, and social decision tonight. We are not necessarily talking about whether some penny-pinching person is going to be able to save half a cent on a loaf of bread. We are talking about the kind of America we want. Do we want an America where, on the highways and byways, all we have is catalog houses? Do we want an America where the economic market place is filled with a few Frankensteins and giants? Or do we want an America where there are thousands upon thousands of small entrepreneurs, independent businessmen, and landholders who can stand on their own feet and talk back to their Government or to anyone else, in case they feel that they are being unjustly treated.

We want an America in which private property is meaningful. We want an America which preserves its property values—at least where there is equal opportunity to preserve the value of property. I submit that the best argument for a fair trade law is not what it does in terms of prices or profits. The best argument for a fair trade law is the kind of America it helps to preserve. The reason fair trade laws came into being was the cheap, cut-rate, pineboard store, backed by large financial interests which were able to step into the marketplace and drive the little merchants out of business, one after another, breaking up town after town and village after village, wrecking the whole system of freeholders and free enterprises in this country.

If this bill costs America some dollars, it is still a good bill. If this bill costs America hundreds of thousands of dollars in increased prices, it is still a good bill. Why? Because we need free, independent business in this country.

Mr. President, there is no use talking about competition if we are not going to have things to compete with. There is no use talking about free enterprise if the enterprise system is not going to have any freedom within it. All we have to do to find out what happens is to fail to have such a law on the statute books as is here proposed and when a depression comes let the law of the jungle prevail.

The argument is made that there was a time when we needed a law such as this, but not now. Let me tell Senators that the same thing can be said about other laws. I have heard people say there was a time when the labor movement needed collective bargaining, and that there was a time when they needed the right to organize and the right to the union shop, but not now, because they are big and strong. Mr. President, how long will they remain big and strong if the labor laws are repealed? It is true of farmers, too. I have heard people say that there was a time when they needed price supports, but they are now all well off and they no longer need price supports.

Mr. President, the time when we need such laws on the books is when we do not have to use them. The very fact that we do not have to use a law indicates the fact that it has done its job.

The fair-trade law has proved itself for 15 years, and it has put order into the market place. It has protected thousands of business places in America. I remind Senators that the people who operate these business places are also consumers. They have sons and daughters and uncles and aunts and cousins and nephews and nieces who consume goods.

If America ever loses its family-size farms, if we are ever willing to pay the price of failure to keep the family-size druggist, the merchant, or the hardware dealer in business, and if we are ever willing to put dollars above sound public policies, America's freedom will be gone. Our freedom and our property and human values are preserved by such principles. They are not preserved by cheap or cut-rate catalogs. No cut-rate catalog will ever take care of America's independence.

Mr. SPARKMAN. Mr. President, will the Senator from Minnesota yield?

Mr. HUMPHREY. I yield.

Mr. SPARKMAN. The Senator has said something about the possible cost in money. I am not so certain that it will cost money. I should like to ask the Senator to comment on this statement which was included in the report of the Small Business Committee with reference to fair-trade law:

> Fair-trade items have increased in price 10 1/2 percent since 1939, while the cost of living, according to the Department of Labor, has risen more than 85 percent.

Does that indicate that fair-trade laws have cost the consumer money?

Mr. HUMPHREY. It surely does not. I want to give further emphasis to what the Senator has said. My own university, the University of Minnesota, which we believe has a very good school of business administration, has compared the prices of 50 leading drug items before fair trade and under fair trade in 1939.

Prof. H. J. Ostlund of the University of Minnesota's School of Business Administration compared the prices of 50 leading drug-store products before fair trade, namely, during the depression years, and under fair trade in 1939. He and his associates did the job State by State. They found that consumers paid 1 percent less, on the average, for these products under fair trade than they paid in the prefair-trade depression days.

Mr. MONRONEY. Mr. President, will the Senator yield?

Mr. HUMPHREY. I yield.

Mr. MONRONEY. With further reference to the expense under fair trade, we all know that there is no fair-trade law in the District of Columbia. Yet the District of Columbia, month after month, has the highest living cost in the United States, according to the labor index. If fair trade were the guilty party, the District of Columbia surely would have a lower figure. The Senator is also aware of the fact that a manufacturer who spends millions of dollars on a trade-marked resale price item is not going to sit back complacently and let the industry undersell him on that item. He has too much involved, and he will replace that item with a fast mover, because it is all based on the mass-production system.

There is plenty of competition in the retail field. Anyone who has ever gone into it has found that out. Anyone who goes into the grocery, hardware, or furniture line will find that the retail industry, of all industry, means what it says when it talks about the free competitive enterprise system, because that is where competition is at its keenest, and it is competition which will always keep prices down. Fair trade is no barrier. Even if General Electric made a fair-trade refrigerator and Frigidaire made a fair-trade refrigerator, the two could not get together and fix the profit on an electric refrigerator. The bill prohibits that kind of price fixing. However, within the Frigidaire licensed dealers and within the General Electric licensed dealers, the price is maintained on their particular product.

Mr. HUMPHREY. The Senator is correct. One of the big mistakes that is made is in confusing capital goods with consumer goods. In the retail field there are literally thousands of commodities which the small retail pharmacists must handle. He handles as many as 25,000 separate items to take care of the people who come into his store. I am talking about a small store, in a medium-sized town.

Mr. President, with respect to the charge of collusion that has been made, it would take an Einstein to figure out how any collusion could occur. With that many commodities there is all kinds of competition. Let us take a refrigerator like Kelvinator. Kelvinator makes not only the Kelvinator refrigerator, which is trade-marked, but also a brand which it makes for sale through a catalog house to persons of lesser income.

There is all kinds of competition. This bill specifically outlaws any horizontal price fixing such as that to which the Senator from Oklahoma has referred in such detail and in such plan [sic] and analytical language.

Mr. President, I can argue the statistics of this bill, and I am prepared to argue statistics for a long time. I have lived fair trade. I think I feel this subject much more deeply than any other political issue. I do not care whether the druggists are for or against it. I know that people who have supported me have told me, "Don't you be for this bill." Mr. President, I am for this bill, because I remember when we did not have such a law. I saw people literally lose their economic lives before we had a fair-trade law. I saw them driven out of business. I do not want to go back to the rule of the jungle in order to give someone a chance to buy a tube of tooth paste for 2 cents less, while destroying the whole fabric of our economic system.

Some say that we must protect the consumer. It is no way to protect the consumer by driving competitors out of ⊥ the field. Senators may remember the little produce ⊥ 8742 houses that handled butter, eggs, and chickens, which they bought from the farmers. The houses were owned independently by local people. Sometimes as many as four or five of them stretched across the country from one county seat to another. Then Armour, Swift, and Fairmount came along, put trucks out on the road, started to pick up the chickens and the eggs and the butter, and paid a better price for the produce than the local produce operator could pay. Pretty soon they drove the local operators to the wall, and they bought their businesses at 50 cents on the dollar. They drove them all out of business. Today all over the Mid-West—and I suppose it is true also in the South and in the Northeast and in the far West—instead of seeing small independent produce companies, operated by one family, which contributed to the school board and the PTA and the local lodge, the business is done by the big chain outfits, operating clear across the country. What happened to the farmer after they ran out the little fellow? They said, "We have been paying you a high price long enough, and now we will pay you a lower price."

That is exactly what will happen, once we get rid of the fair-trade laws.

Mr. [HARRY P.] CAIN [R., Wash.]. Mr. President, will the Senator from Minnesota yield?

The PRESIDING OFFICER (Mr. HILL in the chair). Does the Senator from Minnesota yield to the Senator from Washington?

Mr. HUMPHREY. I yield.

Mr. CAIN. Earlier in the evening the Senator from Illinois said, I believe, that enactment of this fair trade bill would cost American consumers several billion dollars a year. Will the distinguished Senator from Minnesota comment on what he believes the Senator from Illinois was actually talking from—what set of figures, what statistics, what supporting evidence the Senator from Illinois was offering to the Senate in support of his contention that enactment of this bill would result in costing the consumers of the country an additional several billion dollars a year?

Mr. HUMPHREY. I understand that the Senator from Illinois was speaking from statistics prepared by the Federal Trade Commission, and he was using certain analytical studies which have been made by the Federal Trade Commission.

I happen to disagree with those statistics. I thank the Senator from Washington for bringing this point to my attention, because I have spent a great deal of time working on this subject, and it is included among a few pet projects which I have. In fact, I have spent a very great deal of time in studying the fair trade laws, and I wish to submit to the Senate my facts on this subject.

Mr. CAIN. Then does the Senator from Minnesota agree with me that an argument such as the one submitted by the Senator from Illinois must be destroyed, in order to satisfy the natural concern of American consumers?

Mr. HUMPHREY. I think that is correct. In fact, we have to point out that the figures which have been submitted here cannot be fully substantiated.

Let me say here, however, that if the fair trade law should cost more in terms of consumer prices, I still say it is a good "buy," because we have to think of both today and tomorrow.

Mr. CAIN. A few minutes ago the Senator from Minnesota indicated that he thought enactment of this bill would add some hundreds of thousands of dollars to consumer costs. I can readily understand such a figure.

However, there is a fundamental and very large difference between "some hundreds of thousands of dollars" and the "several billion dollars" to which I have just made reference, as previously mentioned by the Senator from Illinois.

Mr. HUMPHREY. There certainly is. My figures were given in only general terms; I was not trying to be accurate.

But now let me give some case studies which have been made.

I have the highest regard for the figures which have been submitted; but enough figures to fill a library have been collected on this subject.

Mr. CAIN. Mr. President, let me say that the Senator from Minnesota obviously must have a very high regard for the Senator from Illinois, who has offered figures to which I have referred, but at the same time the Senator from Minnesota could have neither regard nor respect for figures which in the aggregate amount to several billion dollars a year of added cost.

Mr. DOUGLAS. Mr. President, let the RECORD show clearly that I did not speak of billions of dollars. I quoted from an article in Fortune magazine, which certainly is not a magazine that is biased against big advertisers or against those who have trademarked brands, and therefore certainly Fortune magazine is not biased against the advocates of resale price maintenance. However, the article in Fortune magazine said that the cost of the present measure would be from $750,000,000 to $1,000,000,000 a year; and, Mr. President, in colloquial language "that ain't hay."

Mr. HUMPHREY. Mr. President, I am going to point out to the Senator that "that ain't hay," and also that although I have the greatest regard for Fortune magazine, yet it is known as somewhat of an intellectual vehicle for the Luce empire.

I do not think we need be concerned about whether Fortune magazine is a magazine for the big advertisers, because Fortune magazine has a little track of its own, and lets the others run their own show.

Let us consider the figures which I have here. First of all, let us consider the Federal Trade Commission's studies which have been made. As I said earlier in the debate with the Senator from Illinois, the Federal Trade Commission takes figures at the depth of the cut-rate situation, when prices were below cost, and then compares those prices with the regular prices of the commodities, and thereby gets great margins or differences between the two. In other words, it is something like telling a person how to gain weight, after he has been for 30 days on a diet of crackers and water, and has gotten down to virtually nothing but skin and bones. If at that time someone gives him milk, water and sugar, in 2 weeks he will have gained 20 pounds or more. Then it might be said, "All one need do is live on milk, water, and sugar."

Of course everyone knows that when one has starved until he is about to collapse and is in the depths of despair, a little milk, sugar, and water will prevent complete malnutrition.

On the other hand, when we obtain the proper figures, we begin to obtain the proof; and that is what I shall submit.

Mr. MONRONEY. Mr. President, will the Senator from Minnesota yield to me, for a question?

Mr. HUMPHREY. I yield.

Mr. MONRONEY. Would not the figures prepared by the Federal Trade Commission, to which the Senator from Minnesota referred when he said those figures showed a great margin or disparity, be similar to the figures arrived at in showing an increase in the price of wheat from 30 cents a bushel to 60 cents a bushel, at which point it might be said that the price of wheat had increased 100 percent?

Mr. HUMPHREY. Yes. Of course, in such a situation it might be said that a price increase of 100 percent had been had, and that therefore everything was wonderful.

Mr. MONRONEY. Yes.

Mr. HUMPHREY. When the Senator from Illinois was out of the Chamber, I paid him a tribute—I wish to assure him of it now—which is justly deserved by him for the way he opened the debate on this bill. I apologize that we who are proponents of the bill did not do a better job in joining the issue. Certainly the Senator from Illinois was absolutely correct in the criticisms he leveled against us.

A little earlier I said that one of the best research marketing agencies in the United States has made a study of this matter. Certainly it is one of the large agencies.

The Senator from Connecticut [Mr. BENTON], who knows a great deal about these matters from his former association with the advertising business, collaborated by saying that the Nielsen agency is one of the foremost research agencies, and is known throughout the United States for its independent research and its economic studies for the benefit of business institutions.

Mr. McFARLAND. Mr. President, will the Senator from Minnesota yield to me?

Mr. HUMPHREY. I yield.

Mr. McFARLAND. A few moments ago the Senator from Minnesota spoke of farm parity prices. Does the Senator from Minnesota agree with me that if there had not been farm parity prices, there might have been a depression?

Mr. HUMPHREY. There is no doubt of that.

Mr. McFARLAND. The small-business man and the farmer must have some protection.

Mr. HUMPHREY. That is correct.

Mr. McFARLAND. The small-business man and the farmer are the ones who have helped make our Nation great.

Mr. HUMPHREY. The Senator from Arizona is correct; they have been the backbone of our economy.

Mr. McFARLAND. Mr. President, will the Senator from Minnesota yield for another question?

Mr. HUMPHREY. I yield.

Mr. McFARLAND. How long does the Senator from Minnesota intend to speak?

Mr. HUMPHREY. I shall not speak very long, let me say. I took the floor tonight only because I felt that the admonition given by the Senator from Illinois was appropriately given, namely, that those of us who are the proponents of this bill should at least submit our argument in favor of it, so that those who are the opponents can "work it over."

Mr. McFARLAND. That is correct. But the Senator from Illinois admitted that we had full advice on the matter when he made the motion to lay the bill on the table.

Mr. DOUGLAS. No, Mr. President—

Mr. HUMPHREY. No, Mr. President; I do not want the Senator from Illinois, my friend, even to have to answer that statement, because I know that when he made the motion to lay the bill on the table there was not much else he could do, other than permit the Senate to pass the bill; and so the Senator from Illinois made the motion.

Mr. McFARLAND. The Senator from Illinois could have spoken, as he did afterward, for 3 1/2 hours before he made the motion.

Mr. President, I believe all Senators have made up their minds in regard to this bill. When the Senator from Minnesota concludes his presentation, which has been a very able and constructive and very convincing one—and I do not believe there is any question that the Senate will pass the bill—I believe we should adjourn and go home for tonight, for the hour is now 25 minutes to 11.

Then we can begin the session tomorrow morning at 10 o'clock, and can continue until 3 o'clock or even 4 o'clock the following morning, or to whatever time is required in order to pass the bill.

Mr. HUMPHREY. In order to have the RECORD correct, I wish to say that the 3 hours during which the Senator from Illinois was on his feet were not consumed by him alone. I am an accomplice to that alleged crime, if it is one; I was deeply involved. In addition, a number of other Senators took a great deal of the time of the Senator from Illinois. In fact, I sympathized with him for the way we were jumping up, asking him to yield; but I was so interested in the subject that I was tempted to join in the argument.

Mr. DOUGLAS. Mr. President, will the Senator from Minnesota yield to me?

Mr. HUMPHREY. I yield.

Mr. DOUGLAS. Is not our good friend, the Senator from Arizona, whistling to keep up his courage as he goes through the woods, when he says this bill is going to be passed, anyway? Is not the Senator from Arizona giving us a good example of self-induced optimism? [Laughter.]

Mr. HUMPHREY. Mr. President, I wish to say a kind word for the Senator from Illinois.

On the other hand, I must agree with the final, judicious, and considered judgment on the part of the majority leader, for I am confident that the bill will be passed, and I am confident that it should be passed.

That is all the more reason why I believe the opposition should have a chance to have its "say." If one is so sure, I believe he should be given all the time in the world.

Mr. McFARLAND. Mr. President, will the Senator from Minnesota yield to me?

Mr. HUMPHREY. I yield.

Mr. McFARLAND. If the Senator from Illinois thinks the Senator from Arizona is whistling, let us vote now on this bill.

Mr. LONG. Mr. President, will the Senator from Minnesota yield to me?

Mr. HUMPHREY. I yield.

Mr. LONG. Those of us who have been observing the actions of the majority leader can understand why he is the majority leader, for he proceeds in accordance with the theory of "if you have the votes, vote."

But, of course, those who do not favor a measure take the position that if they do not believe the measure has sufficient merit, they should let it be debated a while, to see if its weaknesses cannot be developed.

Senators whose desks are virtually covered with telegrams from druggists and grocers no doubt would like to have the vote on this bill taken at once.

On the other hand, those of us who have become convinced of the faults of the bill think it reasonable and proper for a moderate amount of time to be used in debating the bill and in disclosing its weaknesses and faults.

We desired to hear the debate, to hear the issue developed, in order that we might be more confident in our own mind that we were doing the right thing. This measure has been under consideration for a part of 1 day. I have known of measures that were not nearly so important, which took 2 or 3 weeks. Certainly the debate on this issue will not take more than perhaps 2 days. But I do not think it reasonable, after one Senator has made a speech—and the only speech I heard has been against the bill—to suggest that all debate be closed immediately, and that the Senate proceed to vote at once, before we know what we are doing, before the bill has been debated, and before we have had a full hearing.

Mr. MORSE. Mr. President, will the Senator yield?

Mr. HUMPHREY. I yield to the Senator from Oregon.

Mr. MORSE. I desire to raise an entirely different question, because the Senator from Minnesota and the Senator from Oregon are on opposite sides of this bill, up to this moment, although I may say I find the Senator from Minnesota very convincing on certain points. I want to protect the Senator from Minnesota from another standpoint. I have asked to have the ticket tear-sheet brought in, and I believe that one of the attachés of the Senate is looking for it. But, in case it does not get here before a recess is taken—and something tells me that the Senate is soon going to recess—

Mr. HUMPHREY. The Senator has that feeling, has he?

Mr. MORSE. I have that feeling.

Mr. HUMPHREY. I have been feeling that way, myself.

Mr. MORSE. I understand from one of the employees that the ticker is carrying a story stating that the Senator from Minnesota [Mr. HUMPHREY] voted to lay this bill on the table. I thought I might give the Senator from Minnesota an opportunity to correct that, because we all know that the Senator from Minnesota voted against laying it on the table; and, if that is on the ticker—and I have been advised that it is—I think in fairness to the Senator from Minnesota I should give him an opportunity to have the statement corrected now.

Mr. HUMPHREY. I thank the Senator from Oregon. If either the Associated Press or the United Press ticker service inferred that the Senator from Minnesota voted to lay this bill on the table, it has committed an error, and I know that either of them will properly and promptly correct it. I have a high regard for those two press services. So I ask them to do so, to check the wires, to see that everything is in good shape.

Mr. McFARLAND. Mr. President, will the Senator yield?

Mr. HUMPHREY. I yield.

Mr. McFARLAND. If an error has been committed in that regard, it will not be the first error that has ever been committed. I have been made a little happy. I thought my good friend from Louisiana had his mind made up, and that he was going to oppose this bill. I am glad he has an open mind. If he is seeking enlightenment, I shall be glad to suggest that the Senate remain in session tonight as long as he desires in order that he may listen. If he listens, I am sure he will be convinced; and I earnestly hope that he has an open mind. I thought he was against the bill, but . . . I believed we had enough votes without his, and was not worried about it. Of course, I should like to have him vote right, because the druggist and the small-business people of Louisiana who are struggling, trying to make a living, would want him to be right. So I am willing to give my good friend from Louisiana plenty of opportunity, and I do not want to cut off any debate unduly. I merely thought he had his mind made up. I am happy to find that that is not the case.

Mr. HUMPHREY. I want to say to the Senator from Arizona I feel sure that the Senator from Louisiana is simply being a gentleman, as he always is, and is being courteous in listening to me, because, as the good reverend said, "There are very few souls saved after the first 15 minutes of the service" and I did not see the Senator hit the sawdust trail. ⊥ I am afraid he has simply dedicated himself to this economic evil.   ⊥ 8744

Mr. McFARLAND. I hope the Senator is wrong. I hope the Senator from Louisiana is not beyond redemption. [Laughter.]

Mr. LONG. Mr. President, will the Senator yield?

Mr. McFARLAND. I yield.

Mr. LONG. I certainly hope that my good friend from Arizona will hear what few words my friend from Minnesota may have to say. The Senator from Louisiana has always felt that if we could see to it that the small merchants acquired their goods at the same price the large concerns were paying for the same commodities, we would be able to protect the little fellows, and they would not have to have a fair-trade law to provide for the fixing of prices with which they would be required to compete.

I am afraid the Senator from Arizona did not have an opportunity to hear enough of the previous debate, because all the small-business associations, who are urging us to vote for this bill, were at that time urging us to vote against the basing-point bill, or to vote for an amendment that would protect all the independent merchants. I propose to offer some of those amendments, and I hope at that time we may be able to persuade the Senator from Arizona to go along with us.

Mr. HUMPHREY. I want to complete the point that was brought up by the Senator from Oregon, following which I am going to yield the floor. I was talking about the Nielson study, and I bring this to the attention of my colleagues.

Mr. McFARLAND. Mr. President, will the Senator yield for one more question?

Mr. HUMPHREY. I yield.

Mr. McFARLAND. Does the Senator know whether the State of Louisiana has a fair-trade law?

Mr. HUMPHREY. Surely it has—and it is a good one.

Mr. McFARLAND. Fine. That is perhaps why the Senator wants to deprive the other States of the privilege of having one.

Mr. HUMPHREY. The trouble is, there are 44 other States that have them, and I am afraid the Senator is thinking Vermont, Missouri, and Texas might apply a little heat in his State.

I referred to a study with reference to consumer prices, and I want this item to be perfectly clear for the RECORD. The Nielson study compares prices gathered from 45 fair-trade States with the prices consumers paid for the very same products, in Missouri, Vermont, Texas, and the District of Columbia. The study analyzed the prices of fair-trade drug products of various kinds, products typically used for consumer bait by price jugglers. In the non-fair-trade States, they can be sold at any price or even given away. I should like to stress the fact that the prices used at that time by Neilson [*sic*] were collected for purposes quite unrelated to fair trade. These surveys took in all the druggists in the United States, rather than a selected few. Through the agencies employed, a representative sampling was taken of 770 stores of all types. The Neilson [*sic*] study covered a 6 months' period, from March through August of 1951, rather than an hour or a day, as in the case of the Federal Trade Commission studies. The results show over-all average prices, weighted to reflect the volume of goods sold at each price. Thus the survey shows the consumers as a whole, and what the consumer's [*sic*] as a whole paid in fair-trade and non-fair-trade areas during the 6 months' period. I should like the Senator from Washington to listen to this. Specifically, consumers under fair trade in the 45 fair-trade States paid an average of 1.4 cents less per volume-product.

Mr. McFARLAND. Mr. President, will the Senator yield?

Mr. HUMPHREY. I yield.

Mr. McFARLAND. Does the Senator want to finish his speech or would he like to have the floor in the morning?

Mr. HUMPHREY. In view of the lateness of the hour, I am willing to take my seat and take my chances on being heard, if I need to be heard again.

Mr. McFARLAND. Mr. President, I am willing to make a suggestion in order that the Senator may have the floor again. I ask unanimous consent that when the Senate reconvenes the Senator from Minnesota may have the floor.

Mr. HUMPHREY. I thank the Senator.

The PRESIDING OFFICER (Mr. SPARKMAN in the chair). Is there objection? The Chair hears none, and it is so ordered.

Mr. McFARLAND. Mr. President, I am about to move that the Senate stand in recess until 10 o'clock in the morning.

The PRESIDING OFFICER. Will the Senator from Arizona withhold the motion, in order that the present occupant of the chair may make a unanimous-consent request?

Mr. McFARLAND. I am glad to withhold it.

The PRESIDING OFFICER. In his capacity as a Senator, the present occupant of the chair asks unanimous consent that pages 213 to 226 of the annual report of the Senate Small Business Committee be printed at this point in the RECORD. It deals with the fair-trade law.

There being no objection, the pages were ordered to be printed in the RECORD, as follows:

CHAPTER X. FAIR-TRADE LAWS

Fair trade may be defined as a system which allows the owner of a trade-mark or a brand name to set minimum resale prices on his product. Statutes sanctioning resale price maintenance agreements apply only to products which are in free competition with similar commodities. In addition, they apply only when the retailer employs the good will of the manufacturer, by use of the name, to help him in selling. The statutes sanction only "vertical" agreements. They exclude "horizontal" agreements between manufacturers, producers and all parties who would normally be in competition with each other.

The year 1951 was a crucial one for small business and the proponents of fair-trade laws. In May the Supreme Court handed down its decision in the now famous Schwegmann[1] case. The decision all but upset 20 years of progress in the field of fair-trade legislation. It set off a series of events that threatened for several weeks to bring back the old price wars. It appeared for a time that the decision had destroyed all the work that had been done in the preceding 20 years to protect manufacturers, retailers, and consumers alike from the evils attendant upon cut-throat competition. A survey undertaken by Dun and Bradstreet disclosed that as of the middle of June, price cutting was on the wane. During the remainder of the year there was no significant trend to extend price cutting.

But the Schwegmann decision remained the law. It cut away the heart of the Miller-Tydings Act and the price-maintenance statutes enacted by the State legislatures. The door was open to the complete destruction of fair-trade laws. At year's end, friends of fair trade were marshaling their forces. Small-business retailers were especially active in the campaign to reinforce the legislation which they felt they so urgently needed if they were to survive.

---

[1] *Schwegmann Bros. et al.* v. *Calvert Distillers Corp.* (341 U. S. 384).

It will be the purpose of this chapter to review the history of fair-trade laws and their impact on small business and to appraise the outlook for small business in the light of the Schwegmann decision.

THE CASE FOR FAIR TRADE

The first advocates of fair-trade legislation were the manufacturers of name brand articles. They found that they were becoming the victims of loss-leader selling, a system whereby a retailer would advertise a popular name brand product at a low price in order to attract customers into his store. The manufacturer found that sales of his product in other outlets would suffer because the buyers were going to the store that advertised the lower price. In many cases the name brand article was being sold below cost. A large retailer could afford to do this because the customers who came to his store to buy the bargain would also buy other merchandise which returned a high profit. The small merchant could not afford this practice because his sales of other merchandise would not compensate for the loss he would have to take on the name brand item. The result was that the small merchant would lose business to his larger competitor. The manufacturer would also lose business because the small merchant and many others like him would be forced to drop the name brand item. Another result was that the item became cheap in the eyes of the consuming public. Buyers reasoned that if one merchant could sell it at a price substantially below that previously advertised, then the merchants who sold it previously and the manufacturer must have been making an excessive profit at the expense of the consumer. Oftentimes competition among large retailers of the item would precipitate price wars which would result in further contraction of the manufacturer's number of outlets.

There was the case of the Ingersoll dollar watch, a name brand item which was extremely popular several years ago. It was a very serviceable watch. It was nationally advertised as selling for $1 and the price became part of the name. Some retailers throughout the country decided to use the Ingersoll watch as a loss-leader. They began to sell it for less than a dollar. The price went down and down as competition increased, until it was finally selling for 57 cents, far below the wholesale price. The retailers who were selling it at that price were making up their losses on sales of other merchandise in their large stores. People who came to buy the watch rationalized that there must be other similar bargains in a store that would sell an Ingersoll dollar watch for 57 cents. The proprietor thus succeeded in selling at a profit a number of other items.

Small-business retailers were forced to drop the Ingersoll dollar watch. They could not sell it if they charged more than 57 cents, and they could not afford to sell the watch at that price and take the loss involved in each sale. The result was that the manufacturer lost his market and was forced out of business. Having been forced out of business and compelled to release the workers in his plant, he realized the evils of loss-leader selling. He became a leader in the fight for fair-trade laws. The consuming public also lost because they were no longer able to buy a serviceable watch for a dollar.

It may thus be argued that fair trade yields benefits for everyone—the manufacturer, the small-business retailer, and the consumer. It assures the manufacturer a steady market for his product. It does not give him an unfair advantage or a monopoly, because, even with the protection of fair-trade legislation, he must compete successfully with other manufacturers of the same or similar products. If he does not maintain the quality of his product or if he fixes the price too high, he loses out to his competitors in spite of fair-trade laws. But fair trade does protect him against the evils of loss-leader selling and the possible destruction of his product and his business through price cutting.

Fair trade benefits the small retailer by placing him on an even footing with all other retailers of the same item, large and small. His margin of profit is fixed to yield him a fair return, and he is protected from destructive competition from others who might be able to afford to use the item as a loss-leader.

The consumer benefits in a number of ways. He knows, for example, that an item covered by fair-trade legislation may be purchased at a standard price wherever he goes to buy it. Fair trade eliminates the necessity for "shopping around." He knows, too, that the price is fair. By the very nature of fair-trade laws, a price-fixed item cannot succeed unless it competes successfully with similar items produced by other manufacturers. In the drug field fair-trade items have increased in price just 10 1/2 percent since 1939, while the cost of living, according to the Department of Labor, has risen more than 85 percent. Fair trade also assures the consumer that a qualified product will remain on the market. It will not be lost to the consumer through loss-leader selling.

The advantages of fair trade prompted support not only from manufacturers of name brand articles but also from retailers and consumers. The depression following 1929 gave impetus to the movement for legislation which would allow the fixing of minimum resale prices.

LEGISLATIVE HISTORY OF FAIR TRADE

California was the first State to enact fair-trade legislation. In 1931 the California Legislature passed a statute[2] allowing a manufacturer to establish resale prices on his product. The statute was binding, however, only on those retailers who signed an agreement with the manufacturer. This proved completely ineffective since retailers not signing such agreements were free to sell the product at any price. In 1933 California amended its statute[3] to provide that an agreement entered into by a manufacturer and a retailer was binding upon all other retailers who had notice of the agreement. This amendment was the so-called nonsigner clause which, in effect, allowed a manufacturer or wholesaler to fix a minimum resale price for his product. Every fair-trade law thereafter passed by any State contained this nonsigner clause.

By the close of 1936, 14 States had passed such laws. In 1937, 28 more States passed them. There are fair-trade laws today in 45 of the 48 States. Only Texas, Missouri, Vermont, and the District of Columbia have remained outside the fold.

The Louisiana statute[4] contains a typical nonsigner clause:

"Willfully and knowingly advertising, offering for sale, or selling any commodity at less than the price stipulated in any contract entered into pursuant to the provision of section 1 (sec. 9809.1) of this act, whether the person so advertising, offering for sale, or selling is or is not a party to such contract, is unfair competition and is actionable at the suit of any person damaged thereby."

Such statutes were valid and enforceable so long as their effect was confined to goods moving intrastate. Where products moving interstate were involved, the statutes ran afoul of Federal law. The Sherman Act,[5] passed by Congress in 1890, declared illegal "every contract, combination in the form of trust or otherwise, or conspiracy, in restraint of trade or commerce among the several States, or with foreign nations."

Under this act, price-maintenance contracts would be illegal. Any attempt on the part of a manufacturer to enforce such a contract in interstate commerce would be enjoined. The manufacturer or anyone else attempting to enforce the contract would be subject to civil and criminal penalties, and no court would enforce it. Fixing minimum prices, like other types of price fixing, was illegal per se under the Sherman Act.

In 1911, the Supreme Court considered the question of resale price maintenance agreements in the case of *Dr. Miles Medical Co.* v. *Park & Sons Co.*,[6] and held them illegal under the Sherman Act. The case involved a suit brought against a nonsigner. The Court held that an agreement to maintain resale prices was a "contract * * * in restraint of trade," which was contrary to the Sherman Act.

THE MILLER-TYDINGS ACT

Supporters of fair trade tried for several years to remove the Sherman Act obstacle from the path of the fair-trade movement. A number of bills were introduced in Congress. In 1929, the Capper-Kelly[7] fair-trade bill was offered. It permitted resale price maintenance on specified classes of commodities by declaring that no such "contract relating to the sale or resale" shall be unlawful. The bill did not contain a nonsigner clause. It merely legalized an agreement "that the vendee will not resell the commodity specified in the contract except at a stipulated price."[8] It became the model for the California law passed in 1931.

The Capper-Kelly bill was reintroduced in the Seventy-second Congress.[9] It did not pass.

In 1936, Senator Tydings introduced his first bill in the Seventy-fourth Congress. It followed substantially the Capper-Kelly bills and did not contain a nonsigner clause. It legalized "contracts or agreements prescribing minimum prices or other conditions for the resale" of a commodity. The second Tydings bill was introduced in the Seventy-fifth Congress. The House then had under consideration the Miller bill[10] which contained practically the same language as Senator Tydings' bill.

The Miller-Tydings Act[11] was enacted in 1937 as an amendment to section 1 of the Sherman Act. It provided that "nothing herein contained shall render illegal, contracts or

---

[2] Cal. Stat., 1931, ch. 278.
[3] Cal. Stat., 1933, ch. 260.
[4] La. Gen. Stat., secs. 9809.1 et seq.
[5] 26 Stat. 209.
[6] 220 U. S. 373.
[7] S. 240, 71st Cong., 1st sess.; H. R. 11, 71st Cong., 1st sess.
[8] H. Rept. 536, 71st Cong., 2d sess.
[9] S. 97, 72d Cong., 1st sess.; H. R. 11, 72d Cong., 1st sess.
[10] H. Rept. 382, 75th Cong., 1st sess.
[11] 50 Stat. 693, 15 U.S.C., sec. 1.

agreements prescribing minimum prices for the resale" of specified commodities when "contracts or agreements of that description are lawful as applied to intrastate transactions" under local law.

Despite the absence of a nonsigner clause in the Miller-Tydings Act, the Department of Justice apparently has not instituted any prosecutions under the Sherman Act since 1937 because of enforcement of fair-trade laws against nonsigners. This does not appear to have been an oversight on the part of that agency. It has been fully aware of the import of the Miller-Tydings Act. In hearings before the Temporary National Economic Committee, Assistant Attorney General Thurman Arnold called for repeal of the Miller-Tydings Act because it made legal the nonsigner provisions of the State fair-trade laws.[12]

Until the decision in the Schwegmann case, and in spite of the absence of the nonsigner clause in the Miller-Tydings Act, there did not appear to be any question but that the nonsigner provisions were within the act. The contention that they were not within the act was raised in only two reported cases after 1939. In both cases, the argument was rejected.[13]

THE SCHWEGMANN CASE

In the light of the legislative and judicial history of fair trade legislation, the Supreme Court's decision in the Schwegmann case[14] was a shock to advocates of fair trade. A brief statement of the facts in that case will serve to demonstrate the dilemma it created for the fair-trade movement.

The original suit was brought by Seagram Distillers Corp. and Calvert Distillers Corp., Delaware and Maryland corporations engaged in the distribution of gin and whisky. The respondents were Schwegmann Bros., operators of a New Orleans supermarket. Seagram and Calvert had price-fixing agreements with over a hundred Louisiana retailers whereby they tried to maintain uniform retail prices for their products. Under these agreements the retailers promised to sell the products of Seagram and Calvert at not less than the prices stated in the distributors' schedules.

Schwegmann Bros. had refused to sign one of these agreements and were selling the products of Seagram and Calvert at cut-rate prices. Under the Louisiana fair-trade law,[15] Schwegmann was bound by the agreements entered into by Seagram and Calvert with the other Louisiana retailers and was guilty of unfair competition. Seagram and Calvert sought an injunction against Schwegmann, relying on the Miller-Tydings Act. They argued that the prohibition of the Sherman Act against price-fixing agreements had been immunized by the Miller-Tydings Act so long as such agreements were valid under State law.

Seagram and Calvert won an injunction in the district court and the court of appeals affirmed.[16] The Supreme Court reversed the court of appeals, saying that nothing in the Milleyr-Tydings [sic] Act sanctioned the enforcement of price-fixing agreements against nonsigners. The Court reviewed in detail the legislative history of the statutes, both State and Federal, and concluded that the Miller-Tydings Act exempted from the Sherman Act only "contracts or agreements prescribing minimum prices for the resale," and that nonsigners were not within the scope of the act.

Mr. Justice Douglas, writing for the Court, said:

"The Miller-Tydings Act expressly continues the prohibitions of the Sherman Act against 'horizontal' price fixing by those in competition with each other at the same functional level. Therefore, when a State compels retailers to follow a parallel price policy, it demands private conduct which the Sherman Act forbids. Elimination of price competition at the retail level may, of course, lawfully result if a distributor successfully negotiates individual 'vertical' agreements with all his retailers. But when retailers are forced to abandon price competition, they are driven into a compact in violation of the spirit of the proviso which forbids 'horizontal' price fixing.

"A real sanction can be given to the prohibitions of the proviso only if the price maintenance power granted a distributor is limited to voluntary engagements. Otherwise, the exception swallows the proviso and destroys its practical effectiveness.

"The contrary conclusion would have a vast and devastating effect on Sherman Act policies. If it were adopted, once a distributor executed a contract with a single retailer setting the minimum resale price for a commodity in the State, all other retailers could be forced into line. Had Congress desired to eliminate the consensual element from the arrangement and to permit

---

[12] TNEC Hearings, pp. 18162–18165.

[13] *Calamia* v. *Goldsmith Bros., Inc.* (299 N.Y. 636 and 775; 87 N.E. 2d 50 and 687); *Pepsodent Co.* v. *Krauss Co.* (56 F. Supp. 922).

[14] See note 1, supra.

[15] See note 4, supra.

[16] 184 F. 2d 11.

blanketing a State with resale price fixing if only one retailer wanted it, we feel that different measures would have been adopted—either a nonsigner provision would have been included or resale price fixing would have been authorized without more. Certainly the words used connote a voluntary scheme. Contracts or agreements convey the idea of a cooperative arrangement, not a program whereby recalcitrants are dragged in by the heels and compelled to submit to price fixing. * * *

"We could conclude that Congress carved out the vast exception from the Sherman Act now claimed only if we were willing to assume it took a devious route and yet failed to make its purpose plain."[3.65]

A dissenting opinion was submitted by Justice Frankfurter, in which Justices Black and Burton concurred. Justice Frankfurter summarized his objections to the Court's decision when he said:

"Every one of the 42 State acts which the Miller-Tydings amendment was to back up—the acts on which the Miller-Tydings amendment was to place a stamp of approval—contained a nonsigner provision. As demonstrated by experience in California, the State acts would have been futile without the nonsigner clause. The Court now holds that the Miller-Tydings amendment does not cover these nonsigner provisions. Not only is the view of the Court contrary to the words of the statute and to the legislative history, it is also in conflict with the interpretation given the Miller-Tydings amendment by the Federal Trade Commission, by the Department of Justice, and by practically all persons adversely affected by the fair-trade laws. * * * Where both the words of a statute and its legislative history clearly indicate the purpose of Congress, it should be respected. We should not substitute our own notion of what Congress should have done."[3.66]

THE PRICE WAR

The Supreme Court's decision in the Schwegmann case was announced on May 21, 1951. On May 29, the R. H. Macy Co. of New York, the world's largest department store, announced in full-page newspaper advertisements that it was reducing its prices on 5,978 price-fixed items by 6 percent. The advertisement referred to the Supreme Court's decision in the Schwegmann case and said that the store would add other items to those being reduced in price. Macy's competitors announced that they would meet the reductions.

During the following 3 weeks sales in New York department stores increased 20 percent. The newspapers carried daily accounts of the progress of the price war. (See table I.)

TABLE I.—Trend of prices for day at 3 stores in "war"—Table indicating the original fixed prices of typical items, the prices at which they opened yesterday and the closing prices at Gimbel's, Macy's, Abraham & Straus. Where stocks were exhausted the latest price quoted is given, where obtainable, for purposes of comparison

Item	Fair trade	Gimbel's		Macy's		Abraham & Straus	
		Open	Close	Open	Close	Open	Close
Toastmaster	$23.00	[1]$14.72	[1]$14.72	[1]$14.72	[1]$14.72	[1]$14.72	[1]$14.72
Sunbeam Mixmaster	46.50	[1]26.59	[1]26.59	[1]26.59	[1]26.59	26.59	26.59
Dormeyer Mixer	46.50	30.55	28.68	46.50	30.55	(2)	(2)
RCA—45 record attachment	12.95	8.24	8.24	8.44	8.24	8.24	8.19
Lewyt vacuum cleaner	89.95	58.63	58.63	(3)	(3)	(3)	(3)
Webster three-speed player	88.24	61.09	40.37	61.09	59.99	61.09	59.99
Men's Palm Beach suits	29.95	[1]16.94	[1]16.94	(3)	(3)	[1]17.94	[1]17.94
Men's Springweave suits	49.50	[1]29.69	[1]29.69	(3)	(3)	[1]29.95	[1]29.95
Men's Sunfrost suits	39.95	[1]24.29	[1]24.29	(3)	(3)	(3)	(3)
Waterman fountain pen	3.95	[1]2.11	[1]2.11	(2)	1.98	(3)	(3)
Underwood typewriter	68.60	(3)	(3)	(3)	(3)	(2)	44.95
Novel, From Here to Eternity	4.50	1.94	1.79	1.94	1.79	1.94	1.79
Proctor steam iron	15.45	(3)	(3)	(2)	12.95	13.11	13.11
Coffeematic percolator	29.95	21.69	20.34	20.39	21.69	21.69	21.69
Regina mixer	64.50	44.39	44.39	(2)	44.39	(2)	39.95
Bayer aspirin (100'2)	.59	.18	.18	.19	.19	.17	.17
Ronson lighter	6.60	4.69	4.69	4.69	4.69	4.65	4.65

[1] Latest price reported; item out of stock.
[2] Not reported.
[3] Item out of stock.

Source: New York Times, June 5, 1951.

[3.65] 341 U.S. at 389-90, 395.

[3.66] Id. at 401-02.

Department stores added hundreds of sales clerks and comparison shoppers to meet the competition. There were reports of shoppers injured in the rush to buy bargains. Stores posted changing prices on bulletin boards.

The price cuts took place largely in household appliances, drugs, and cosmetic specialties, men's clothing, and alcoholic beverages. The Sunbeam Mixmaster, listed at the fair-trade price of $46.50, was selling for as little as $26.59, which was below the wholesale price. A best-selling novel, listed at $4.50, was sold below cost at $1.79. A well-known brand of men's suits, regularly selling at $49.50, sold for $29.69 before supplies ran out.

Manufacturers of fair-trade articles threatened to withhold their product from the stores selling them at the lower prices. The stores avoided this bottleneck in the early stages of the price-cutting campaign by buying from independent jobbers.

Small retailers complained that they were losing all of their business to the stores involved in the price war. It was reported that Macy's, which normally sold 3.3 percent of the Mixmasters in New York, sold 56.2 percent during the 10 weeks following the start of its price cutting. Abraham & Straus, a large Brooklyn department store that normally sold 2.5 percent of the Mixmasters sold in Brooklyn, reportedly sold 59.6 percent during the price war.

One druggist in Queens, N. Y., succeeded in obtaining an injunction against Macy's under the New York fair-trade law and forced Macy's to discontinue selling 10 different items at reduced prices on the ground that they moved only in intrastate commerce and therefore were not affected by the Supreme Court's decision in the Schwegmann case.

But victories for the small retailer were few and far between. Generally, in the New York area their business suffered through the concentration of sales. It was estimated that 20,000 of the approximately 105,000 small retailers in the New York area would have been forced into bankruptcy if the price war had continued for 6 months.

The price war threatened for a time to spread to other cities. Reports from cities such as Denver, Detroit, Philadelphia, Boston, Cleveland, and Houston showed a tendency on the part of some large retailers to start cutting prices themselves in order to reduce their heavy inventories.

DUN & BRADSTREET SURVEY

The effects of the New York price war on small retailers was brought forcefully to the attention of your committee. Independent merchants and storekeepers by the score came to the committee asking for assistance. They told of the effects the price war was having on them, how they were losing trade, and how the large department stores were winning a monopoly on sales of many items. They reported that, unless the price war ended, many of them would be forced out of business.

By the time the price war had made evident its effects on small-business men, however, reports coming to your committee indicated that the war was subsiding. In the 3 weeks following Macy's announcement of its intention to cut prices on fair-trade items, most of the popular items were out of stock and the manufacturers had made good their threats to withhold further deliveries to the price cutters. In addition, the initial rush to buy the bargains appeared to have let up. The original demand had been satisfied and customers no longer seemed so eager to buy.

Recognizing the continuing danger of price wars, however, and cognizant of the possibility of their spreading to other sections of the country, the chairman of your committee met with the chairman of the Joint Committee on the Economic Report in a conference with Mr. A. D. Whiteside, president of Dun & Bradstreet, Inc. As a result of the conference, Dun & Bradstreet undertook a survey of the principal trading centers of the country to determine the scope of price cutting. The main portion of the survey covered the period from May 28, the day before Macy's announced its price cuts, to June 16, when the price war appeared to have subsided. A follow-up ⊥ survey was conducted on June 25 to test the trend in price cutting.

The survey sought to determine the sections of the country where price cutting was in effect, the number of stores in each community involved, and the lines of merchandise in which reductions were being made.

The survey indicated that from May 28 to June 16, some 825 stores in 43 of 123 trading centers had set prices on one or more items of merchandise below the resale price recommended or set by the manufacturers of the merchandise. With few exceptions, only a small number of stores were reported engaged in price cutting in any one of the 43 cities. Only 8 cities reported 10 or more stores cutting prices below the manufacturers' resale prices, and 20 cities reported less than 4 stores cutting prices. (See table II.)

Light electric household appliances were found to be the items most commonly sold at the lowered prices. Next in order of frequency of sales were cosmetics and drug specialties, heavy electric household appliances, men's wear, and alcoholic beverages. (See table III.)

[TABLE II]

Number of cities reporting	Number of stores in each city pricing merchandise below manufacturers' resale price
20	Less than 4.
6	4 to 5.
9	6 to 9.
2	10.
6	More than 10.

[TABLE III]

Line of merchandise	Cities reporting price cutting
Light electric household appliances	29
Cosmetics and drug specialties	23
Heavy electric household appliances	14
Men's wear	4
Alcoholic beverages	4

It was interesting to your committee to note that although a total of 825 stores were reported to have cut prices on fair-trade items, there were approximately 77,200 stores in the survey cities which might be said to handle one or more of the lines of merchandise affected by the type of price cutting reported in the survey. Table IV shows this breakdown in the stores survey. (See table IV.)

[TABLE IV]

Kind of business:	Number of stores
Department stores	988
Variety of stores	5,723
Men's and boys' clothing	9,648
Family clothing	3,294
Furniture	9,184
Household appliances	6,381
Hardware	8,081
Drug and proprietary	20,662
Liquor	13,280
Total	77,241

Source: U. S. Census of Business, 1948: Retail Trade.

The committee was also interested to note that there was no clear geographic clustering of communities engaging in price cutting. The survey showed, for example, that several major communities in the neighborhood of New York, including Albany, Hartford, Trenton, and Philadelphia, reported no price cutting in stores in those communities between May 28 and June 16. Table V sets forth complete statistics on the results of the Dun & Bradstreet survey.

TABLE V.—Price cutting of fair-traded merchandise, May 28 to June 16, 1951

[In 123 cities of the United States and for 5 classes of merchandise]

City	Total number of stores cutting prices	Merchandise lines in which prices were reduced				
		Heavy electric household appliances	Light electric household appliances	Men's wear	Cosmetics and drug specialties	Alcoholic beverages
Akron, Ohio	8				X	
Albany, N. Y.	0					
Albuquerque, N. Mex.	7		X		X	
Allentown, Pa.	4	X	X	X	X	

TABLE V — Cont.

City	Total number of stores cutting prices	Merchandise lines in which prices were reduced				
		Heavy electric household appliances	Light electric household appliances	Men's wear	Cosmetics and drug specialties	Alcoholic beverages
Amarillo, Tex.	0	......	......	......	......	......
Asheville, N. C.	0	......	......	......	......	......
Atlanta, Ga.	0	......	......	......	......	......
Austin, Tex.	0	......	......	......	......	......
Baltimore, Md.	7	......	X	......	X	......
Bangor, Maine	0	......	......	......	......	......
Billings, Mont.	0	......	......	......	......	......
Birmingham, Ala.	0	......	......	......	......	......
Boston, Mass.	0	......	......	......	......	......
Buffalo, N.Y.	0	......	......	......	......	......
Butte, Mont.	7	......	......	......	X	......
Canton, Ohio	0	......	......	......	......	......
Cedar Rapids, Iowa	8	X	X	......	......	......
Charleston, S. C.	0	......	......	......	......	......
Charleston, W. Va.	0	......	......	......	......	......
Charlotte, N. C.	2	......	......	......	X	......
Chattanooga, Tenn.	0	......	......	......	......	......
Chicago, Ill.	0	......	......	......	......	......
Cinncinnati, Ohio	3	......	......	......	X	......
Cleveland, Ohio	0	......	......	......	......	......
Columbia, S. C.	0	......	......	......	......	......
Columbus, Ga.	0	......	......	......	......	......
Columbus, Ohio	0	......	......	......	......	......
Dallas, Tex.	0	......	......	......	......	......
Davenport, Iowa	0	......	......	......	......	......
Dayton, Ohio	0	......	......	......	......	......
Denver, Colo.	300	X	X	......	X	X
Des Moines, Iowa	0	......	......	......	......	......
Detroit, Mich.	175	X	X	......	......	......
Dubuque, Iowa	0	......	......	......	......	......
Duluth, Minn.	2	......	......	......	X	......
El Paso, Tex.	0	......	......	......	......	......
Erie, Pa.	0	......	......	......	......	......
Evansville, Ind.	0	......	......	......	......	......
Fargo, N. Dak.	0	......	......	......	......	......
Fort Wayne, Ind.	0	......	......	......	......	......
Fort Worth, Tex.	0	......	......	......	......	......
Fresno, Calif.	1	X	......	......	......	......
Grand Rapids, Mich.	0	......	......	......	......	......
Green Bay, Wis.	0	......	......	......	......	......
Greensboro, N. C.	0	......	......	......	......	......
Greenville, S. C.	4	X	X	......	......	......
Harrisburg, Pa.	4	......	X	......	X	......
Hartford, Conn.	0	......	......	......	......	......
Houston, Tex.	0	......	......	......	......	......
Huntington, W. Va.	0	......	......	......	......	......
Indianapolis, Ind.	0	......	......	......	......	......
Jackson, Miss.	0	......	......	......	......	......
Jacksonville, Fla.	0	......	......	......	......	......
Kansas City, Mo.	4	......	X	......	......	......
Knoxville, Tenn.	0	......	......	......	......	......
La Crosse, Wis.	0	......	......	......	......	......
Lincoln, Nebr.	4	......	X	......	......	......
Little Rock, Ark.	1	......	X	......	......	......
Los Angeles, Calif.	0	......	......	......	......	......
Louisville, Ky.	2	......	X	X	......	......
Macon, Ga.	0	......	......	......	......	......
Madison, Wis.	0	......	......	......	......	......
Manchester, N. H.	0	......	......	......	......	......
Memphis, Tenn.	0	......	......	......	......	......
Miami, Fla.	4	......	X	......	......	......
Milwaukee, Wis.	0	......	......	......	......	......
Minneapolis, Minn.	0	......	......	......	......	......
Mobile, Ala.	2	......	X	......	......	......
Nashville, Tenn.	0	......	......	......	......	......
Newark, N. J.	3	......	X	......	X	......
New Haven, Conn.	0	......	......	......	......	......
New Orleans, La.	21	......	......	......	X	X
New York, N. Y.	100	X	X	X	X	......
Norfolk, Va.	1	......	X	......	......	......
Oklahoma City, Okla.	30	......	X	......	X	......

TABLE V — Cont.

City	Total number of stores cutting prices	Merchandise lines in which prices were reduced				
		Heavy electric household appliances	Light electric household appliances	Men's wear	Cosmetics and drug specialties	Alcoholic beverages
Omaha, Nebr.	10	X	X	.....	X	.....
Peoria, Ill.	0	.....	.....	.....	.....	.....
Philadelphia, Pa.	0	.....	.....	.....	.....	.....
Phoenix, Ariz.	1	X	X	.....	.....	.....
Pittsburgh, Pa.	0	.....	.....	.....	.....	.....
Portland, Maine	0	.....	.....	.....	.....	.....
Portland, Oreg.	8	X	X	X	X	.....
Providence, R. I.	2	.....	X	.....	.....	.....
Raleigh, N. C.	0	.....	.....	.....	.....	.....
Richmond, Va.	0	.....	.....	.....	.....	.....
Roanoke, Va.	0	.....	.....	.....	.....	.....
Rochester, N. Y.	0	.....	.....	.....	.....	.....
Rockford, Ill.	0	.....	.....	.....	.....	.....
Sacramento, Calif.	8	.....	X	.....	X	.....
Saginaw, Mich.	0	.....	.....	.....	.....	.....
St. Louis, Mo.	0	.....	.....	.....	.....	.....
St. Pl, Mauinn. [sic]	0	.....	.....	.....	.....	.....
Salt Lake City, Utah	0	.....	.....	.....	.....	.....
San Antonio, Tex.	0	.....	.....	.....	.....	.....
San Diego, Calif.	3	.....	.....	.....	X	.....
San Francisco, Calif.	6	.....	X	.....	X	.....
Savannah, Ga.	2	X	X	.....	.....	.....
Scranton, Pa.	3	X	X	.....	.....	.....
Seattle, Wash.	0	.....	.....	.....	.....	.....
Shreveport, La.	10	.....	.....	.....	X	X
Sioux City, Iowa	1	.....	X	.....	.....	.....
Sioux Falls, S. Dak.	1	X	.....	.....	.....	.....
South Bend, Ind.	0	.....	.....	.....	.....	.....
Spokane, Wash.	9	.....	X	.....	X	.....
Springfield, Ill.	3	.....	.....	.....	X	.....
Springfield, Mass.	0	.....	.....	.....	.....	.....
Springfield, Ohio	0	.....	.....	.....	.....	.....
Syracuse, N. Y.	0	.....	.....	.....	.....	.....
Tacoma, Wash.	0	.....	.....	.....	.....	.....
Tampa, Fla.	50	.....	.....	.....	.....	X
Terre Haute, Ind.	0	.....	.....	.....	.....	.....
Toledo, Ohio	0	.....	.....	.....	.....	.....
Topeka, Kans.	0	.....	.....	.....	.....	.....
Trenton, N. J.	0	.....	.....	.....	.....	.....
Tulsa, Okla.	1	.....	X	.....	.....	.....
Waco, Tex.	0	.....	.....	.....	.....	.....
Washington, D. C.	0	.....	.....	.....	.....	.....
Wheeling, W. Va.	0	.....	.....	.....	.....	.....
Wichita, Kans.	2	.....	.....	.....	X	.....
Wilmington, Del.	0	.....	.....	.....	.....	.....
Winston-Salem, N. C.	0	.....	.....	.....	.....	.....
Worcester, Mass.	1	X	.....	.....	.....	.....
York, Pa.	0	.....	.....	.....	.....	.....
Youngstown, Ohio	0	.....	.....	.....	.....	.....
	825	14	29	4	23	4

A second survey, conducted by Dun & Bradstreet on June 25 and 26 in the same 123 cities covered in the first survey, indicated that since June 16 there had been no significant increase in the cutting of prices below resale prices set by manufacturers. Five cities in which no price cutting had been reported as of June 16, reported one or more stores engaged in such price cutting after June 16. Two additional cities reported increases in the number of stores participating in price cutting, but the total number of stores involved in each city was only two. Conversely, it was reported that price cutting, reported as of June 16, had been discontinued in three cities and, in three additional cities, the number of stores engaged in such practices had been reduced.

On the basis of the Dun & Bradstreet survey, your committee concluded that price cutting was on the wane as of the end of June. A close watch was kept on the situation throughout the balance of 1951 and no further trends toward extension of price cutting were noted. Many of the leaders in the campaign to cut prices were quoted during the latter part of May and early June as being opposed in principle to the loss-leader type of retailing but stated that the lead of others forced them into the price war. They expressed relief when the price war tapered off. Many of the large department stores which were most active in the price war, including Macy's of New York, later signed price-maintenance agreements with manufacturers and thus, in effect, admitted the efficacy of fair trade. As of year's end, prices of fair-traded items had for the most part been restored to their previous levels and the threat to small retailers had diminished, for the time being at least.

NEW FAIR-TRADE LEGISLATION

Friends of fair trade were understandably shocked by the Supreme Court's decision in the Schwegmann case and alarmed by the price wars that followed. They recognized the fact that the Schwegmann decision had practically nullified the fair-trade statutes enacted in the legislatures of 45 States in the past 20 years. They realized that unless the nonsigner clauses of the statutes could be given effect in interstate commerce, the statutes were utterly ineffective. They were not reassured by the collapse of the price-cutting epidemic. They recognized a continuing danger to the fair-trade movement and took action to plug the loophole created by the Supreme Court in the Schwegmann decision.

A large segment of the small-business community, led by the National Association of Retail Druggists, drafted a bill designed to restore fair trade to full effectiveness. Sponsored by Representative JOHN A. MCGUIRE, the bill was introduced in the House in October.[17] It proposes an amendment to the Federal Trade Commission Act which would validate the operation of minimum resale price contracts on all distributors selling trade-marked brands in interstate commerce. The McGuire bill has been referred to the Interstate and Foreign Commerce Committee of the House. Although drafted under the leadership of the NARD, the bill has the active support of a number of other groups, including the retail jewelers, book sellers, tobacconists, hardware dealers, auto accessory dealers, and appliance merchants.

The American Fair Trade Council, Inc., a group of fair-trade advocates made up largely of manufacturers of fair-trade items, has announced its intention to submit a separate bill to Congress early in 1952. Their bill is aimed at amending the Sherman Act. It would provide in part that no one outside of a fair-trade State may offer for sale, or sell, or deliver in any such State, Territory, or the District of Columbia, any product in interstate commerce at any price less than the fair-trade price lawfully established in the State.

CONCLUSIONS

The events of the past year in the field of fair trade have been of grave concern to your committee. In particular, the Schwegmann decision and the ensuing price wars were viewed as matters of tremendous import to small business. Had the price wars continued, they could have done incalculable harm to countless small businesses. The memory of the early 1930's and the great numbers of small, independent concerns that were then lost to the economy directly as a result of similar price wars is still fresh. The possibility is strong that the damage to fair trade wrought by the Schwegmann decision might well precipitate similar business failures should our economy suffer a sudden reversal.

Business Week magazine summarized the situation in an article published in its June 16, 1951, issue. Noting the progress made by small retail merchants in the past decade and the factors contributing to that progress, Business Week said:

"Fair trade has also been another major prop for the small, independent merchant during the past decade. This has been particularly true in the drug and jewelry businesses. Under the fair-trade umbrella, the small merchant has been protected from price cutting and provided with a healthy mark-up

"The end of fair trade on a national scale now throws this advantage into reverse. How much it will hurt the small retailer remains to be seen. But it's sure to leave its mark."

Your committee is hopeful that the members of the business community will recognize their responsibilities in this situation and that they will realize the dangers inherent in loss-leader selling and cutthroat competition, that they will realize that such practices can result only in damaging the whole economy. It is not only the small independent merchant who suffers in a price war. The manufacturer and the consumer also suffer. And the leaders of price-cutting campaigns should realize that injury to other segments of the retail trade cannot benefit them. Gains realized from loss-leader selling are short-lived. The practice is a vicious one and defeats itself. No merchant, no matter how large, can afford to continue loss-leader selling indefinitely. He must engage in other practices in order to recoup his losses. And such other practices of necessity require that he sell other merchandise at high profits. The consumer must sooner or later discover the fallacy of the loss-leader selling technique, and then the retailer loses the good will of his customers and their patronage. The good sense and recognition of their responsibilities should impel the overwhelming mass of the business community to the logic and wisdom of fair trade.

---

[17] H. R. 5767, 82d Cong., 1st sess.

Your committee intends to keep a close watch on fair trade during the coming months. It will scrutinize closely the efforts of the business community to police itself. It will also be vitally interested in the progress of pending legislation on fair trade. The advantages of fair trade are evident, and your committee will be awake to any opportunities in the legislative field that would renew the stability and security of small business. The Nation's economic well-being depends to a large extent on the vitality of America's small businesses. Threats of price wars must be eliminated if that vitality is to endure. . . .

Mr. LONG submitted amendments in the nature of a substitute intended to be proposed by him to the bill (H. R. 5767) to amend the Federal Trade Commission Act with respect to certain contracts and agreements which establish minimum or stipulated resale prices and which are extended by State law to persons who are not parties to such contracts and agreements, and for certain other purposes, which were ordered to lie on the table and to be printed.

SENATE DEBATE
82d Cong., 2d Sess.
July 2, 1952

98 CONG. REC. 8819

Mr. [EVERETT M.] DIRKSEN [R., Ill.]. Mr. President, will the Senator from Minnesota yield to me?

Mr. HUMPHREY. I yield.

Mr. DIRKSEN. I may have to be absent from the Senate at the time when the vote is taken on the fair-trade bill. I feel that I should announce my position on that bill. If I were present and voting, I certainly should support the bill.

I thank the Senator from Minnesota for yielding this time to me.

Mr. HUMPHREY. Mr. President, I wish to continue with the debate which was developing last evening in reference to the pending bill. For a moment I shall summarize some of the arguments I attempted to make last night, and I shall try to place the bill in its proper focus.

First of all, House bill 5767 seeks to do only one thing, namely, to restore, by means of Federal enabling statute, the meaning which I think all the evidence leads one to believe the Congress intended the Miller-Tydings Act to have when it was passed in 1937.

The McGuire bill establishes no new Federal fair-trade policy. It adds nothing whatsoever to the fair-trade acts of the 45 States. It takes nothing away from any of those State acts. It overcomes two court decisions, so that it may be truly regarded as an enabling Federal statute. If we can ever get these points understood generally, I think there will be no argument about this bill.

The pending bill changes no Federal policy. It changes no State law. It adds nothing whatsoever new to the fair-trade policy. It has only one purpose, namely, to clarify a law which the Supreme Court found, by a split decision, not to cover certain practices.

Therefore, Mr. President, the purpose of the pending bill is only to plug the loopholes in the Federal Miller-Tydings Act, which is a measure to enable the States to carry out fair-trade practices.

There is a great hue and cry as to what the bill will do to consumers; but I ask any Member of this body, either present at this time or yet to come to the ⊥ floor, to point out to me what was so wrong with the fair-trade program from 1937 to 1951. From 1937 to 1951, it was clearly understood by the Department of Justice, it was clearly understood by the Federal Trade Commission, it was clearly understood by 45 States, it was clearly understood by every agent of this Government, that the fair-trade policy included all fair-trade laws of every State and between the States. Now, all at once, I hear a blistering attack upon the program of fair-trade legislation. I hear that it has been bad for the consumer. I hear that it is a violation of the antitrust laws. Yet, Mr. President, I submit that for 17 years these laws have been in effect. I submit there has been no popular demand that these laws be repealed. In fact, I submit that at this time the State legislatures are passing more laws, rather than fewer; and I submit that during this period of 17 years the policy of Congress has been, in many areas, to make some rules establishing fair competition in the economy.

Mr. WELKER. Mr. President, while the Senator from Minnesota is on that subject, will he inform me how many State legislatures throughout the Nation have passed such fair-trade laws or adopted such fair-trade regulations?

Mr. HUMPHREY. Forty-five of the States.

Mr. WELKER. Forty-five of them?

Mr. HUMPHREY. That is correct.

Mr. WELKER. I thank the Senator from Minnesota.

Mr. HUMPHREY. The first law was passed in 1931 in California. It was clarified in 1933 as the result of a court decision. By the time the Miller-Tydings Act went on the statute books, 42 States already had passed some form of fair-trade-practice law.

Mr. WELKER. Mr. President, will the Senator from Minnesota yield further?

Mr. HUMPHREY. I yield.

Mr. WELKER. Will the Senator from Minnesota be kind enough to point out the three States which have not passed a fair-trade law?

Mr. HUMPHREY. The three States are Vermont, Texas, and Missouri, in addition to the District of Columbia, a Federal jurisdiction.

Mr. McFARLAND. Mr. President, will the Senator from Minnesota yield to me?

Mr. HUMPHREY. I yield.

Mr. McFARLAND. I do not think there has been in the Senate any better friend of the consumer than the distinguished junior Senator from Minnesota. His record will so show. He has tried to keep prices down, by means of price controls. He has supported effective price controls. He has done the things we ordinarily believe to be good for the consumers.

Mr. HUMPHREY. I have tried to do so.

Mr. McFARLAND. Does the Senator from Minnesota think that in the long run this bill will hurt or will help the consumers?

Mr. HUMPHREY. I wish to say with all the sincerity at my command that if I thought this bill in the long run would hurt consumers, I would be opposed to the bill and would fight it.

I honestly believe that this bill, even in the short run as well as in the long run, is good for the consumers in every respect—good in terms of the prices consumers will pay for the commodities they buy, and good for the economy of America in which the consumers will live.

All the Senate is being asked to do by means of this measure is to clarify the law, which seemed to be perfectly clear and was operating well for a period of 15 years. I can place in the RECORD, as I did last night, a statement of the position of the Attorney General of the United States, a statement of the position of the Federal Trade Commission, a statement of the position of lower courts, and a statement of the position of innumerable Government officials, all of whom take the position that the Miller-Tydings Act included action between the States, in the States, and the nonsigners of the so-called contracts between manufacturers and retailers. To make it even more simple, it worked and it worked well. As I look over this body of Senators who represent the various States, I dare say that when they go back to their respective States they will never have a delegation call upon them to suggest that the fair-trade law of any State should be repealed; in fact, I have no doubt that person after person will say to them that the fair-trade laws should be kept on the books.

Mr. President, I have heard about consumers. In the department stores, in the retail establishments, more than 10,000,000 gainfully employed persons are working. These are the people who are the breadwinners for their families. Mr. President, a cut-rate, blind-bird, jungle-law economics operator does not pay his clerks. That is the kind of business that keeps them under poverty wages. It is the kind of operation that calls them to work at 9 o'clock in the morning, sends them home at 10 o'clock because there is no business, and calls them back at 2.

When there is fair trade, Mr. President, there are reasonable rules of competition in the market. There is opportunity for reasonable wages and reasonably good living conditions. The simple truth of the matter is that the fair-trade law, by regularizing certain competitive practices, by restraining predatory interests, by making it possible to have some semblance of economic decency in the market place, has been the best friend that the workingman ever had, because the workers—and there are 10,000,000 of them in retail establishments—have for the first time in a long while had a chance for a secure job at reasonably good wages, and have had a chance to know they are not going to be knocked out by some predatory interest that would destroy the entire economic market area, if it could have its way.

Mr. WELKER. Mr. President, will the Senator yield for a question?

Mr. HUMPHREY. I yield to the Senator from Idaho.

Mr. WELKER. I have listened to the very learned debate of my friend from Minnesota, and I should like him to tell me, as a Senator from Idaho, what effect this bill will have upon certain giant concerns, say in New York, California, or Illinois, with tremendous buying power, who engage in the merchandizing field and who have gradually come to my State. I am thinking of the small, independent market and the small, independent drug store, which have been a part of the community since the beginning of our State. What effect will this legislation have upon those concerns coming in to compete with our small merchants? I am mindful of the fact that my distinguished friend has covered this subject before, but since this is the start of a new day in the debate, I should like to hear the observations of the Senator in understandable language, so I may send the message to my people at home.

Mr. HUMPHREY. I may say to the Senator from Idaho, in view of the recent Supreme Court decision in the Schwegmann case, and the circuit court of appeals decision in the Wentling case, that if this bill does not pass, small independent merchants of the Senator's State will be at the mercy of any large chain operation that has great financial resources, great opportunities to buy in large markets, and to distribute through many outlets. The small, independent operator will be at the mercy of loss-leader sales, of competition, and competitive practices that can drive him to the wall at any time the big operator wants to do it.

However, if this bill is passed and becomes law, fair-trade standards will give the independent operator in the Senator's State a chance to survive. It will at least give him equality of opportunity in the competitive practices of the market place. It will mean that certain named items will carry a minimum resale price, and whether it is sold in the largest department store in Idaho, or in the smallest retail outlet in Idaho, it cannot be sold below that minimum price, which is a very low price. Such a law will give them a chance to live. It does not guarantee, I may say to the Senator, that the independent operator will survive, but it means that he will not be killed off by unfair, unprincipled practices.

Mr. WELKER. Mr. President, will the Senator yield for another question?

Mr. HUMPHREY. I yield.

Mr. WELKER. Does the Senator agree with me that the action of the Idaho State Legislature, and the legislatures of other States, in adopting fair-trade laws and a minimum-profit law—6 percent in Idaho, as I understand—was solely and fundamentally for the purpose of protecting the small independent merchants who have to exist by virtue of doing business in competition with the giant concern?

Mr. HUMPHREY. There is no doubt about that.

Mr. WELKER. I thank the Senator.

Mr. HUMPHREY. There is no doubt about it, and that is what has happened in 45 States. The legislatures of those States are relatively close to the people, ⊥ and it is entirely true that the State legislatures have made a safe political and policy decision in saying, "We believe it is important for Idaho, Minnesota, Michigan, and Arizona that independent enterprise be maintained as a part of the American economic and political structure." I believe so, too. I say that the consumer will be letting himself into a fool's paradise if he allows an economic policy crowd out hundred [sic] of independent merchants, only to see the market gobbled up by one or two large outfits. We will then see who sets the prices. There will be no competition?

Mr. WELKER. Mr. President, will the Senator yield for one further question.

Mr. HUMPHREY. I yield.

Mr. WELKER. The Senator will agree with me, and, I think, all the other sponsors of this bill, that we are interested in protecting the consumer as well as everyone else.

Mr. HUMPHREY. That is correct.

Mr. WELKER. But is it not a fact that when the giant store uses the device of a loss leader, as we have observed them do time after time, it will make up the loss on the next item the consumer buys?

Mr. HUMPHREY. Mr. President, the Senator has put his finger on the fallacy of the argument advanced by the opposition last night. Perhaps for the purpose of showing the difference between fair-trade prices and non-fair-trade prices, the difference betwen fair-trade prices and cut-rate or loss-leader prices was recited. An effort was made to get the United States Senate to believe that these cut-rate prices were uniform throughout the United States, and that every small store in the United States was giving away Alka-Seltzer or mixmasters, when, in fact, every time a store gives something like that away, it recovers the loss on some other article. It can be proved statistically that when there are loss-leader items in a business establishment, the gross profit on other items is stepped up.

Mr. WELKER. Mr. President, will the Senator yield further?

Mr. HUMPHREY. I yield.

Mr. WELKER. The Senator from Minnesota does not know does he, of many small merchandising concerns that engage in the practice of giving away anything to the consumer?

Mr. HUMPHREY. I want to say to the Senator that any merchant who engages in the practice of giving away things and can still continue in business, still pays [sic] overhead, still pay his employees, and still maintain his family, is a merchant that does not exist.

Mr. WELKER. I thank the Senator.

Mr. MOODY. Mr. President, will the Senator yield?

Mr. HUMPHREY. I yield to the Senator from Michigan.

Mr. MOODY. I have been very much interested in this colloquy. The Senator from Minnesota has just answered the very question I was going to ask, as to whether, in the long run, it would be damaging to the interests of the consumer if a situation were allowed to develop in which the small businesses were driven out of the market by loss leaders and price cutting.

Mr. HUMPHREY. It would be most damaging to the consumers' interests.

Mr. MOODY. The Senator has already answered the question. I appreciate his having yielded.

Mr. HUMPHREY. I thank the Senator from Michigan.

Furthermore, Mr. President, some people try to argue about this fair-trade bill as if we were talking about articles which are not in competition, as if we were talking about capital goods or producers' goods, as if we were talking, for example, about five or six major steel plants that produce 95 percent of all the steel. Mr. President, we are talking about the producers of consumer goods—hundreds of producers, thousands of producers.

We are talking about a competitive relationship in the retail field, where, first, there are hundreds and hundreds of outlets; second, thousands and thousands of merchants seeking the business; and third, hundreds and hundreds of producers of every single commodity, and only a small portion of those hundreds are in the fair-trade field. As a matter of fact, less than 6 percent of the total dollar volume of the retail business is in fair-trade items, and less than 2 percent of the total number of consumer items is in the fair-trade field.

Until a man stands behind the counter, until he has to meet this kind of cutthroat competition and, at the same time, take care of his family, pay his bills, and maintain his business establishment, he can never appreciate what it means to be under the rule of the jungle in the market place with the cutthroat artist driving out the independent merchant.

Mr. President, as a matter of record, let me say that I recall the president of one of the largest concerns in this country telling someone in the retail business, "We can come into your town, put a store on the corner, and lose money for 20 years, if we want that corner and want to drive you out of business. We can lose money for 20 years, and we will be there and you will be out." Why was that, Mr. President? Because that concern had 400 stores in the United States where they had already performed that kind of an operation.

Mr. WELKER. Mr. President, will the Senator from Minnesota yield further?

Mr. HUMPHREY. I yield.

Mr. WELKER. I should like to ask the Senator one further question, which may lead him far afield from his present discussion. The Senator from Minnesota is mindful of the fact that there are many distinguished members of the legal profession in this body. I wonder if the Senator realizes that many of those leaders of the bar—I happen to be a member of the bar—some of them, perhaps, opponents of this measure, have seen fit in their respective jurisdictions to adopt and fully practice the minimum-fee schedule of the States in which they practice law.

I am wondering if the Senator could give to the Senate his version of the philosophy of those Senators who feel they should adopt a minimum-fee schedule in their law practice and resist such a thing in the field of merchandise?

Mr. HUMPHREY. I am happy the Senator asked that question. It is perfectly true that the bar associations, in order to legitimatize practice, have a minimum-fee schedule. I am not condemning it; it is simply a recognition of the fact that there are members of the legal profession who are willing to wreck the whole code of ethics of the profession.

Mr. WELKER. The Senator realizes that the minimum-fee schedule is adopted to protect the client, does he not?

Mr. HUMPHREY. That is correct; and to give a semblance of order, decency, and ethics to the profession. The bill which we are discussing would apply the same principle in the field of wholesaling, retailing, and manufacturing.

Mr. President, there is virtually only one argument that can be made against the bill; namely, that it will increase consumers' prices by stifling competition. I submit that the burden of proof of that argument rests on the opponents of the bill, because since fair trade has been in practice, instead of competition being diminished, it has been augmented. There are more establishments doing business today, more processors of goods and services doing business today, than there were prior to the time of fair trade. Competition has not been stifled.

I have not heard any Senator on the floor condemning the Ford Motor Co. for its agency-franchise system. I have not heard anyone condemn the General Motors Co. for its agency-franchise system. If this practice has been legitimate why should fair trade, which is merely another form of vertical price maintenance, suddenly wreck the country, especially since it has been on the books for 15 years without doing so?

Mr. President, I was reading yesterday about the fair-trade program in relation to some of the studies which have been completed. The charge has been made that the fair-trade program would cost the American consumers anywhere from a billion to two billion dollars. This has been branded as a $2,000,000,000 lie. The surveys consist of shopping around for customer-bait items, or loss leaders offered by certain stores at certain times in certain places. They have been made by shopping around for information to fit a preconceived conclusion, and are not based upon normal marketing practice. When a lady goes downtown to shop in a drug store, and she is led into that store by a loss-leader item, she usually buys more than just one item. The purpose of the loss-leader is to get her to buy something else. She is not going around like Hawkshaw, with a spyglass, looking to see whether there is a loss-leader in a certain store, and then driving 10 miles to pick up a loss leader in another store.

I say to those who, in order to prove their case, present alleged facts about how much the bill will cost the consumer, that every housewife in America does not have as much time as has an investigator from the Federal Trade Commission, to run around from one State to another to see if she can buy a roll of toilet paper in Utah for less than she has to pay for it in New Jersey. The American housewife is a busy lady. She usually has two or three children at home, and when she goes to market, she gets all her goods in the one market.

Once the merchant gets the customer into the store, he has better than a 50-50 chance to sell merchandise at high mark-ups, which cover the cost of the loss leader. There will never be any proof whatsoever that a loss-leader item is not compensated for by a high-gross-profit item in the same establishment. The simple truth of the matter is that where there is a loss leader, there is a compensatory price on other items. There are compensatory items in the same place in order to take up the gap. There has never been anyone in the world who has been able to make money by giving away services and goods.

Mr. WELKER. Mr. President, will the Senator yield?

Mr. HUMPHREY. I yield to the Senator from Idaho.

Mr. WELKER. I take it from the remarks of the distinguished Senator from Minnesota that he disagrees with the philosophy of some opponents of the bill that a large New York store now doing business in the Senator's State and in my State is actually engaged, in a great portion of its business, on a very high-grade basis from the standpoint of the consumer. Is that correct?

Mr. HUMPHREY. I surely do disagree with that philosophy.

Mr. WELKER. The Senator realizes, does he not, that it is necessary to make at least a 20-percent profit in order to break even, and that the New York merchant doing business in Idaho is not engaged in the merchandise business for love?

Mr. HUMPHREY. Even though the New York merchant might love Idaho and all its people, he is not going to love them enough to give up his surplus profits in the name of the consumers' interest.

All that is being attempted by this bill is to provide a reasonable, decent code of ethics in the market place. I have spent a good deal of time examining into many so-called flash studies, which assume that in the absence of fair trade all the retailers in the country would sell national brand merchandise at consumer-bait prices.

If, for example, the Federal Trade Commission finds one store that is selling a $1.50 hot-water bottle for 19 cents in a non-fair-trade area like Washington, D. C., do Senators know what the Federal Trade Commission assumes? It assumes that every drug store in all the non-fair-trade areas in the United States, is selling hot-water bottles at 19 cents. Then they go to a fair-trade area and see that hot-water bottles are selling for 89 cents, and they say, "There is a 70-cent difference."

Anybody who wants a hot-water bottle will say, "I will buy the 19-cent bottle." But while the merchant has you in his store, he will say, "I know that for a sore back a hot-water bottle is going to help you, but may I suggest Dr. Smith's remedy?" That remedy, which cost 20 cents, will sell for $2. Because the dealer is a good salesman, he will sell that remedy, or he is not on the job.

That is what is meant by companion sales. No one ever made a dime giving his services away. No one ever made money in business by selling items at prices below cost. Every item sold below cost has to be compensated for by selling additional items above cost, and far above cost.

Fair trade has increased the output of American producers. It has not stifled production; it has augmented production. It has not placed a burden upon the consumer by giving less variety to choose from. He has a greater variety to chose [sic] from. Some day we are all going to have to make up our minds. I hope the day is at hand.

Mr. [WILLIAM] LANGER [R., N.D.]. Mr. President, will the Senator yield?

Mr. HUMPHREY. I yield.

Mr. LANGER. I wish to ask the distinguished Senator from Minnesota if it is not true that this type of law is especially needed for the reason that there has not been any real enforcement of the antitrust statutes.

Mr. HUMPHREY. If the Department of Justice, which has been taking a dim view of fair trade, and the Federal Trade Commission, which has been opposing fair trade, would really devote their energies—their full, total energies—to the enforcement of the Sherman Antitrust Act, the Clayton Antitrust Act, and the Federal Trade Commission Act, they would not need to worry at all about fair trade.

Mr. LANGER. So far as the Senator knows, is it not true that ever since Congress passed the first antitrust statute, away back in 1890, not a single defendant has ever been sent to the penitentiary or to jail for violation of the antitrust statutes, under any administration, Republican or Democratic?

Mr. HUMPHREY. I believe the Senator is correct. I am not positive of that, but I believe he is right.

Mr. LANGER. There was one exception—the case of Eugene Debs, whom the Government put in jail some 50 or 60 years ago. Is that correct?

Mr. HUMPHREY. I think he was sent to prison because he had some ideas.

Mr. LANGER. Would not the Senator say, further, that if the antitrust laws had been vigorously enforced, it might be that the proposed statute would not be needed?

Mr. HUMPHREY. I think that had they been enforced in the very beginning, that would be true. Let me say that we are all involved in the whole free-enterprise system sometimes. People become a little avaricious and predatory. Once in a while our moral values become mixed up in the economic practices of the marketplace. The trouble with all the classical, orthodox economists is that they forget who runs the economy. The people run it.

We have great spiritual leaders telling us to cease doing the things that violate moral standards, and to put spiritual values above material values. But there are a great many material values left in the world. Unfortunately, the American economic picture and the American economy are not fully in balance. It is not a world in which everybody receives fair play, so it becomes necessary for the States and the Federal Government to try to inject fair play into the marketplace by certain rules of law. We are merely trying to recognize reality.

Mr. LANGER. The distinguished Senator comes from the northwestern section of the United States.

Mr. HUMPHREY. That is correct.

Mr. LANGER. The distinguished Senator knows what happened in the dairy industry, where, almost over night, one outfit got control of practically every dairy selling ice cream.

Mr. HUMPHREY. The Senator is correct.

Mr. LANGER. That occurred in North Dakota, South Dakota, and Minnesota.

Mr. HUMPHREY. May I interrupt the Senator for a moment?

Mr. LANGER. Certainly.

Mr. HUMPHREY. Does the Senator know that one company went around appealing to the consumers to buy, saying, "We will give you 2 quarts of ice cream for a quarter"? But when they put the small ice cream dealers out of business, they stopped selling ice cream at 2 quarts for a quarter. They sold it at large profit.

Mr. LANGER. I may say further to the distinguished Senator from Minnesota that the big outfits are not satisfied with just controlling markets in the United States, but they extend their operations farther and farther and into country after country and thus get a monopoly not only in the United States, but also in the entire world. I ask the Senator if that is not true.

Mr. HUMPHREY. We have evidence to prove that there are cartels of that kind.

Mr. LANGER. There are concerns such as Lever Bros., which does business in 64 nations.

Mr. HUMPHREY. That is correct.

Mr. LANGER. They control the market for fats and oils in 64 countries.

Mr. HUMPHREY. The Senator is correct. We have evidence indicating that since the Schwegmann case was decided, in New York City a large dress manufacturing company, which has been in the dress manufacturing business for years, has also opened retail outlets. Dress manufacturing had been their whole life history, but when the fair-trade law was outlawed in the Schwegmann case, what do Senators suppose that company began to sell? They began to sell mixmasters and other electrical devices. They started to sell in a dress shop every item a woman might want around her home. At what price did they begin to sell? They sold the items at practically below cost, as loss-leader items.

The legitimate appliance dealer, who had been working all his life to build up a business in the sale of electric fans, washing machines, electric ironers, and mixmasters, found himself in competition with a dress company down the street which was marking up the price of dresses. Once they got the ladies in among the dresses, everything was fine and dandy. They made so much from dress sales they could afford to give them three mixmasters for nothing. The ladies were induced to come inside by offering them electric fans, toasters, washing machines, ironers, and other home appliances at prices either below cost, or just a few cents above cost, which meant that any legitimate merchant in competition would be driven out of business.

Let me answer the argument which was made here last night. The question was asked, "Why is it that the price wars have stopped in New York City?" In the first place, they have not all stopped. In the second place, the Macy-Gimbel war stopped when Mr. McGuire of Connecticut introduced his bill in the House of Representatives. Macy and Gimbel are going to lie low for a little while. They are going to wait and see whether we allow the fair trade laws to be emasculated. If we do, they will go at it again.

Furthermore, in a depression period, if we ever have one—pray God we do not—or in any period of regression, without fair trade practices, the people who would practice loss-leader sales, the people who would wreck the normal practices of the market place, will be doing just that. Hundreds of young men who have made investments in small establishments will find their business liquidated. That is not good public policy.

When a young man starts in business, if he borrows money from the Government or from a bank, we demand that he pay 4 percent interest. We have fair trade for the bankers. The Government of the United States, through the Federal Reserve System, says that the interest rate will be so much, whether in good times, bad times, winter, summer, spring, or fall.

There are many thousands of retail establishments all over the United States. Are we going to pull the props out from under them? Are we going to say to a young man, "You are just getting a start. You have been out of the Army for only 3 or 4 years. Your interest rate is high. Your help is unionized, farm products have price supports, and you have all kinds of fixed charges. But Mr. Small-Business Man, do you know what we are going to do to you? We are going to let the catalog house come in. We are going to let some big outfit from somewhere else come in, with its huge capital and reserves and buying power. We are going to let it pull the rug out from under you." Not with my vote, Mr. President.

I stated that I wish to conclude with a few words on the subject of social policy. I am not at all impressed with the fact some people feel that the only way to protect the consumer is to see that he gets a cheaper price. I say to the consumer protectors, "If you want cheaper prices, the Senator from North Dakota and I know that one way to get them is to ruin the American farmer. Do not give him a chance to live. Make a peasant out of him. Let him work 20 hours a day and produce cheap food for people who want cheap prices."

Sometimes cheap prices mean cheap ideas, a cheap country, and a cheap people. What America needs is reasonable prices, with a reasonably balanced economy and a reasonably good opportunity to survive.

There are people, even on the farm, who do not want to pay good wages for workers because if they can get cheap labor and receive reasonably high farm prices, they can make huge profits. There are always people who are anxious to see that their little side is well protected. That is normal. I am not being critical. That is natural. One of the first laws of nature is self-preservation. I see nothing wrong with a man taking care of his own temple—his body, his mind, and his soul.

Let me say to my good liberal friends that they cannot ask the Government of the United States to buy only goods which have been manufactured by workers who received the prevailing wages; they cannot ask the Government of the United States to buy only goods made by union labor; they cannot ask the Government of the United States to maintain price supports for farmers and give workers the right of collective bargaining, which means that they set the price for their labor with their employers, and then say to the small retail merchant, "We do not care about you. You can go out and be gobbled up."

I hear people ask, "Don't you believe in competition?" I do, but let me add a qualifying not. I believe in fair competition. There would be no competition in the ring between any Member of the Senate and Joe Louis. That would be murder. There would be no competition between a small town high school football team and Notre Dame. Supposedly there would be 11 men on each side, but there would be no competition. That would be athletic madness. I am simply saying that we want fair rules of conduct. That is what fair trade does. It does not eliminate competition, but it says that competition shall not be between a 200-pound man with big muscles and broad shoulders, and a 6-year-old child. That is not competition.

Fair trade says, "It makes no difference whether you are big or little. It makes no difference whether you are from New York, Texas, Minnesota, or California. It makes no difference whether you have reserves of a billion dollars, or reserves of $10. If you are going to sell Kolynos toothpaste you are not going to sell it for less than a certain price. We are going to give everyone a chance to survive."

The Congress determined that the farmer needed farm cooperatives to protect himself. We cannot compare the treatment of cooperatives with the normal economic treatment which we give to the rest of business. We were for farm cooperatives because we needed farm cooperatives. We are for the family-sized farm, because America needs the family-sized farm. No one can prove, on the basis of economics, that the family-sized farm is more economical to operate than the 50,000-acre corporation farm. But we do not want corporate farming. We want family-sized farming, because family-sized farming produces good citizens, and good citizens are the only hope of freedom and democracy. So we pay a price for it. I am willing to pay that price.

We would like to have in America independent banking, so we have laws on the books to protect independent banking. We would like to have in America a fair wage for every man and woman in the market place, so we have a Fair Labor Standards Act, which provides a minimum wage of 75 cents an hour. Many people are trying to get around that law. They say, "Don't include this group of workers or that group.' The more we weaken the Fair Labor Standards Act, the more meaningless it becomes.

My argument is that a policy decision must be made. It has been made. A policy decision was made in America in 1930. It was made in many States from 1931 on. In 45 States a policy decision was made. The decision is simply that the future well-being of the American business economy and the American political economy depends on hundreds of small landowners and entrepreneurs. I do not want to see my America become an America which is ruled by a monopoly not only in the producers' lines but in the retailers' lines. Anyone who really believes in free enterprise today, anyone who really wants to protect the free-enterprise system, will do it by giving free enterprises a chance to live. I was born in the free-enterprise system. I lived for a great part of my life in it, and I hope to live out my life under that system. I know that the free-enterprise system depends on something else besides words. It depends on giving people a chance to live.

Mr. President, that is my argument. I submit that for 15 years America has made its position perfectly clear on fair trade. Forty-five States have made their position perfectly clear, and thousands of merchants and hundreds of thousands of consumers have done likewise. What more do we want, Mr. President? . . .

⊥ 8824   ⊥ Mr. MORSE. Mr. President, before I proceed with my argument in opposition to the pending bill I wish to pay my sincere compliments to the Senator from Minnesota [Mr. HUMPHREY] for the very able argument he has presented, both last night and this morning, in support of his position on the bill.

When the bill came before the Senate yesterday afternoon, and there was an immediate demand for a vote, without even one proponent of the bill extending to the Senate what I thought it clearly was entitled to, namely, an explanation of the bill, and an argument in chief in support of the main provisions of the bill, I was greatly saddened. I thought the Senate was doing itself great damage in following such a course of action. It was my opinion then, and still is, that if the Senator from Illinois [Mr. DOUGLAS] had not immediately proceeded with his discussion in opposition to the bill, even prior to any explanation of the bill by its proponents, the bill would have passed the Senate. I do not think it is good for the Senate to follow that kind of procedure. . . .

Mr. HUMPHREY. I wish the Senator from Oregon to know that, as shown on page 8738 of the CONGRESSIONAL RECORD for yesterday, I did mention the very point the Senator from Oregon has discussed, namely, the contribution the Senator from Illinois made in discussing this measure. I have strong feelings about the comments which were made last night about the Senator from Illinois, in regard to an alleged filibuster.

I wish to say now, regardless of my feelings about this bill, that both the Senator from Illinois and the Senator from Louisiana, as of last night, and today the Senator from Oregon, are doing a service for both the proponents and the opponents of this measure. We need a legislative history, no matter what happens. . . .

⊥ Mr. MORSE. . . .   ⊥ 8825

Mr. President, I appreciate what the Senator from Minnesota said a few minutes ago in regard to the charge of filibuster which was made last night on the floor of the Senate. Personally, I shall ignore the charge, because I am satisfied that it was not made by any Senator who really intended to wrong a colleague.

Of course there has not been a filibuster on this bill, and there is not going to be one. The Senator from Minnesota and I are joint authors of a resolution which previously has been submitted to the Senate, to outlaw filibusters.

Although there is a dispute as to the interpretation of the facts, Mr. President, nevertheless I repeat that I have never participated in a filibuster, and I shall not do so today. . . .

I come now to the next point I desire to make regarding the matter of procedure in the debate today. I want a vote on this measure; and I hope a vote can be taken this afternoon. I told the majority leader last night that I had no intention of preventing a vote. But I intend to make my case against the bill, and so I say that, in inserting much of what I would otherwise read into the RECORD—I probably shall insert as much as two-thirds of it without reading it—I am doing it because I think it necessary to have a legislative record—a view which is shared by the Senator from Illinois [Mr. DOUGLAS]—so that the President may have before him a complete record as to the conflicting views in the Senate of the United States when he comes to consider the question of whether the bill should be vetoed.

⊥ I have no doubt, Mr. President, that the bill will pass—I think, by a large   ⊥ 8826
majority of the Senate. I do not know whether the President will veto the bill, but I do not know of any time since President Truman has been in the White House when he has knowingly walked out on the Antitrust Division of the United States Department of Justice in the enforcement of the antitrust and antimonopoly laws. I cannot and do not speak for the President of the United States, but I can guess as to what I think he will do, being probably biased somewhat in that guess by what I think he ought to do. I guess he will veto it, because I think he ought to veto it. In view of the possibility of a veto, I think those of us who oppose the bill owe a duty to the Chief Executive to make a record upon the basis of which he might obtain some help in his analysis of the bill and the preparation of his veto message.

Mr. President, I have one other point to make on the matter of procedure, because when I objected to a unanimous-consent agreement last night I expected that some of my colleagues, and people outside the Senate as well, would misinterpret my motivation. I opposed a unanimous-consent agreement to vote on this measure, and I shall continue to oppose it. . . .

Mr. President, we do not even have before us a report of the committee that really advises us as to the merits and demerits of this bill. The committee takes no position on the merits or demerits of the bill. It has met the formality of filing a committee report, though to me, at least, it is not at all a helpful report. It raises a few questions, but it does not provide the answers. So, Mr. President, I do not intend to consent to unanimous-consent requests to vote on measures which are presented to the Senate by a committee in such an inadequate fashion. . . .

⊥ This bill is of tremendous importance to the American people—to all the   ⊥ 8833
American people, businessmen as well as consumers. I wish now for a few minutes to turn my attention to the bill itself. . . .

Mr. President, the McGuire bill is not merely enabling legislation intended to allow the various States to control their own intrastate commerce. States already have and always have had that right. When Congress interferes in purely intrastate matters as it did in the NRA, the United States Supreme Court in the Schechter case[3.67] unanimously held the NRA unconstitutional, not only because it was an illegal delegation of authority, but also because Congress was legislating on purely intrastate matters. The McGuire bill seriously weakens the Sherman Antitrust Act and all our other procompetition laws. It is proprice fixing. In the broad concurrent zone where the States and Congress may both legislate, the United States Congress should not, even if it can, abdicate its control of interstate commerce. As I have said, all of our antitrust laws are procompetition. The McGuire bill is proprice fixing. It is irreconcilably at war with all our traditional affirmative policy and legislation to preserve competitition and free enterprise. The harm to the public of fixed, rigged prices will be very great. Of the total national income of over $250,000,000,000, about $150,000,000,000 represents retail trade. No less than 10 percent, or about $15,000,000,000, is retail trade in branded merchandise which would be directly affected by this bill. The best estimates as shown at the House and Senate hearings indicate that resale-price maintenance would increase prices no less than an average of 12 percent on all branded goods. This would force the consuming public to pay between $1,800,000,000 and $2,000,000,000 a year in higher prices on branded goods if this bill should be enacted.

The press of the country is almost unanimously opposed to this price-fixing bill. The United Press, the Scripps-Howard Press, the Kansas City Star, the New York Herald Tribune, the New York Times, the St. Louis Post-Dispatch, the St. Louis Globe-Democrat, the Denver Post, the Richmond (Va.) News-Leader, the Washington (D. C.) Post, and the Washington (D. C.) Daily News, Fortune magazine, and many other periodicals, are all strongly opposed to fair-trade rigged prices as very harmful to the public generally, especially during this period of high inflation. It is [sic] conceivable that the entire press of the country is in this instance opposed to the public interest in favoring free and competitive pricing? When retailers face their suppliers, wholesalers, and manufacturers, they want to buy under conditions of competition which is natural and proper. What makes price competition good among manufacturers and wholesalers and harmful among retailers?

My good friend, the Senator from Minnesota [Mr. HUMPHREY], and my good friend, the Senator from Michigan [Mr. MOODY] yesterday recalled the depression of 1930 as a reason for favoring this bill. No one expects that kind of a recession or depression within the next 6 months, or even within the next 2 or 3 years. Why then, must we rush this bill through the Senate before the Members of the Senate have even had an opportunity to examine the Senate hearings on the bill? Is it necessary to yield to the pressure and desire for haste which is responsible for this hasty lack of consideration of a bill which may seriously impair the living standards of many of the 155,000,000 consumers? Is there any need for this great rush to push this bill through in the closing days of this session even before the printed hearings have been made available to the Members of the Senate? It is interesting to recall that the Miller-Tydings Act of 1937 was rushed through as a rider to a District of Columbia appropriation bill. President Roosevelt denounced the Miller-Tydings Act at the time although he felt he had to sign the appropriation bill.

In hearings before the Celler committee more than 40 university professors signed or submitted statements in the hearings [sic] before the House Judiciary Committee last February 1952. All of these university men in economics, marketing and law, opposed all of the bills in favor of resale price maintenance. The record of the House hearings will show that these included men from the Yale Law School, Harvard, Massachusetts Institute of Technology, the University of Chicago, Northwestern, Washington University, and all the way to California, where Dean E. T. Grether of the business school at Berkeley, Calif., also filed a statement opposing all forms of fair trade price fixing.

University faculties seem as unanimous as the press is in asking that our antitrust laws not be weakened by destroying competition on the retail level on branded

---

[3.67] A.L.A. Schechter Poultry Co. v. United States, 295 U.S. 495 (1935).

merchandise. Much has been said of cutthroat competition or the "law of the jungle" price cutting. The Celler bill outlawing below-invoice selling and the amendment offered by the Senator from Illinois [Mr. DOUGLAS] outlawing below-invoice plus 6-percent retail sales is an adequate answer to the loss-lead argument. Under the guise of abolishing the "loss lead," this bill gives us unregulated, uncontrolled, private price fixing, which has been and will be ⊥ abused to the detriment of the public. The worst provision in this bill is the so-called nonsigner clause. That is the provision by which a price-maintenance contract between a manufacturer and any one retailer becomes automatically binding on all retailers in the same State who sell the product, regardless of the fact that many are self-service and, therefore, have a lower operating cost which they desire to pass on to the retail level.

⊥ 8834

As Fortune said in the March 1952 issue:

> To coerce a retailer into a contract he has never seen, let alone sign [sic], is bad law. Giving special protection to a special group is not exactly new in United States history, but that does not alter the fact that it is bad economics.

The article goes on to say that 22 fair-trade lawyers guided the hand of Congressman MCGUIRE when this bill was drawn. This is the bill we are asked to rush through without adequate debate and without even an opportunity to examine the Senate hearings, which have not yet been published and which we do not have. Our opinion cannot be any better than our information, and we have no right to substitute mere opinion or a yielding to pressure groups when the facts can and should be had. Possibly retailers, the Fortune article suggests, should be more volume conscious and less high-protected-margin conscious. In a release dated June 2, 1952, from the office of the Senator from Colorado [Mr. JOHNSON], six simple but very important questions were asked. Before debate on this bill ends, we should have clear and complete answers to Senator JOHNSON's important questions, which I here quote in full:

> There are a few elementary questions which should be discussed in this hearing by the proponents and the opponents. They are:
> 1. Does price-fixing at the resale level in States having fair-trade laws promote or destroy competition?
> 2. Will the interest and the very existence of small retailers in fair-trade States be secured and protected from the unfair competition of the large chain stores by the passage of this legislation?
> 3. If the Senate passes H. R. 5767, the McGuire bill, what is the position of the consumer? Is he denied the opportunity of purchasing a "bargain" on any brand name or trade-mark product which otherwise he might enjoy?
> 4. Would this bill reverse the action of Congress in creating OPS by enabling the States to set a minimum instead of a Federal ceiling price on brand names or trademark products for resale?
> 5. What are the advantages or disadvantages of the loss leaders and how would it affect the sale of trade-mark or brand-name articles?
> 6. How much money will this legislation cost the unorganized consumer and how much additional money will it put into the treasury of manufacturers, wholesalers or retailers?
> There are many other questions involved which this committee hopes may be cleared up by this hearing.

It may be, Mr. President, that the committee cleared them up, but if it did the evidence was not made available to the Senate. I had hoped that we would have before us the printed hearings of the committee so that we could judge for ourselves whether the committee had cleared up the questions.

These questions should not be ignored. The Senate and the public are entitled to have them answered fully and frankly. Here are a few other simple questions that were asked in the Senate hearings and also in the Celler hearings to which we should have complete answers before we vote on this bill:

First. If a cash-and-carry super store has lower costs, should not the public be permitted to benefit—in lower prices—from all such lower-cost methods of doing business?

Second. In the situation above why should all be required to sell a so-called fair-traded item at the same retail price?

Third. If competition among producers of an item is good for the public, why should competition among retail sellers of that item be denied?

Fourth. Has any pressure group ever campaigned for price-fixing privileges except to make prices higher than they are under free competition?

Fifth. What real and specific evidence is there that truly meritorious articles have ever been driven from the market by price competition?

Sixth. If a merchant wants to locate a store outside the city limits, operate at lower costs, price accordingly, and therefore sell at lower prices because of his lower costs, what good reason is there to deny him that right and forbid the public that benefit, and would not legislation directed toward this end be held invalid by the Supreme Court as an unconstitutional deprivation of property without due process of law?

As I said, by my speech along with that of the Senator from Illinois, I intend primarily to make a record on which the President, I hope, may base a veto message.

I wish now to say a few words in terms of rebuttal, and then I shall send to the desk two amendments to the bill. Before I finish my remarks, I shall present my arguments in support of the amendments, so that I will not take the floor again after I have concluded my speech, but have the amendments called up and voted on. As I have made clear to my colleagues, I do not intend to delay a vote on the bill today.

Point 1: The Humphrey argument that just as the Government sets price supports for agriculture and passes wage and hour acts for labor, so also should it protect the small-business man.

Mr. President, because I do not accept as sound the argument of my friend, the Senator from Minnesota, I think these observations in rebuttal should be made, at least for the record.

There are several answers to this point:

(a) In the case of farm price supports and minimum wages, it is the Government which determines what is a reasonable and fair support price or minimum wage. The Government does not, as would be true under resale price maintenance, turn the matter over to the farmers, to let them determine their own support prices, and to the workers, to let them determine their own minimum wages. By having the Government set these minima in agriculture and labor the public interest is protected, and the Government is acting in the interest of the public. Congress, in setting farm price supports, considers the interests not only of the farmers themselves, but also of processors, distributors, and—above all—of consumers. In setting minimum wages, it considers not only the interests of the workers, but also the interests of the employer and, again of the consumer. But under resale price maintenance the establishment of minima is exclusively done by the parties at interest—those who would gain by high prices. There is no mechanism whereby any consideration can be given to the consumers, or to small-business men, of whom there are many, who dislike resale price maintenance.

(b) The mechanics are different in still another respect. If the resale-price maintenance principle was to be applied to agriculture—to use an extreme and a really absurd example, but to illustrate the point, Mr. President—one farmer in each wheat-growing State could enter into a contract with, let us say, General Mills; and the price in that contract would govern the price paid by General Mills to all other farmers for their wheat. General Mills might enter into such a contract with a big, mechanized wheat farm, a factory in the field, and might establish in the contract a low price for wheat—a price which would break the back of the average small farmer. Yet under the resale price maintenance principle, all farmers, large and small, would have to sell to General Mills at that established contract price. In this connection, it must be remembered that the bill before us gives the manufacturer the right to set not merely a minimum price, but a stipulated price, as well.

Mr. President, the word "stipulated" is not so little in its implications, and I shall soon direct one of my amendments to that word.

Hence, in the example I have given, General Mills could set not merely a minimum price, but a stipulated price—and it would be exactly that price which each farmer would be paid by General Mills for his wheat—if we could correctly assume the absurd situation in which that kind of procedure would be applied to agriculture. However, I cite it to illustrate my difference with the Senator from Minnesota in regard to the principle he defended last night.

POINT 2. SENATOR HUMPHREY'S ATTACK ON FTC STATISTICS (P. 8933 [sic])

Next, Mr. President, my friend, the Senator from Minnesota, was very critical of some of the Federal Trade Commission's statistics. He may be correct, but I wish to make these observations about his comments. I do not know where the statistics he criticized are to be found.

Would the Senator from Minnesota kindly indicate where the figures of the FTC are to be found? He has criticized the FTC figures as being fallacious. But he gave no citation. I have not had a ⊥ chance to check the RECORD to see whether the Senator ⊥ 8835 from Minnesota cited documentation for his criticism.

I have gone over the FTC report on resale price maintenance, and I found no misuse of proper statistical techniques, such as the Senator from Minnesota has described, and which he criticized last night.

All that the FTC did was to compare prices before resale price maintenance and immediately after resale price maintenance. I wish to say that the source of my information is the Federal Trade Commission itself, because I checked with the Commission this morning. After listening to the Commission's explanation, Mr. President, I can see no impropriety in a comparison of prices before resale price maintenance and prices immediately after resale price maintenance.

There is no impropriety in such a comparison. They did not compare the before resale-price maintenance prices with the printed or posted ones, as opposed to the resale-price maintenance prices. They compared the prices before resale-price maintenance with the resale-price maintenance prices themselves. That is what the Commission should have done. Such a comparison should not be based upon some printed bulletin, as an indication of the intent. The comparison should be based upon the actual practice.

Mr. DOUGLAS. Mr. President, will the Senator from Oregon yield for a question?

The PRESIDING OFFICER (Mr. CASE in the chair). Does the Senator from Oregon yield to the Senator from Illinois?

Mr. MORSE. I yield.

Mr. DOUGLAS. I was the one who originally introduced the comparative material which is to be found on page 8719 of the RECORD for yesterday. I turned back to sources, and quoted that material from Knoxville, Tenn.; Michigan; and New York City.

For the sake of the record, I think it should be stated that the Knoxville study was made by Charles W. Lewis, director of the bureau of business research, University of Tennessee, and was published in his monograph entitled "Price Maintenance in Knoxville, Tenn., Under the Tennessee Fair Trade Act of 1937." The prices which were used for this study were the average advertised prices during those periods in cut-rate chain drug stores. The series was composed of 122 items.

The Michigan series was compiled by Edgar H. Gault, professor of marketing, School of Business Administration, University of Michigan, and was published in his brochure entitled "Fair Trade With Special Reference to Cut-Rate Stores in Michigan." The prices used for the study were taken from newspaper advertisements during the fall of 1937 and the fall of 1938. The series was composed of 160 well-known branded items which the author described as typical during those periods.

The New York series was compiled by Duncan Holthausen, of the staff of Dun & Bradstreet.

So these statistics were arrived at by means of independent students and studies, and were gathered together and presented during the House Judiciary Committee hearings held in connection with that committee's study of monopoly power during February of this year.

Mr. MORSE. Mr. President, I thank the Senator from Illinois very much for clarifying the record on that point and for making that contribution.

POINT 3. HISTORY OF PRESSURE, (A) TO GET RESALE PRICE MAINTENANCE LAWS ORIGINALLY PASSED AND (B) TO GET THE PRESENT BILL ENACTED

I believe that at this point in my remarks I should provide some material on the history of what, for a better term, I shall call pressure to get resale price maintenance laws passed originally and to get this particular bill passed.

With respect to the original resale price maintenance laws, I have taken certain material from the Federal Trade Commission's report on Resale Price Maintenance. I believe it is of interest, and I ask unanimous consent to have it inserted at this point in the RECORD, as a part of my remarks.

There being no objection, the excerpt from the report was ordered to be printed in the RECORD, as follows:

"Early in the Commission's investigation a letter was written to the secretary of state of each of the 44 States that had enacted resale price maintenance laws, requesting a transcript of testimony at hearings on the 'fair trade' bills. In case it was impossible to furnish a transcript of testimony, they were requested to furnish the names of persons and organizations appearing to testify either for or against the legislation. Each of these officials stated in answer to the first request that, so far as they knew, no record was kept of testimony before any legislative committee. Only four of these officials were able to give any definite information as to whether or not hearings were held. The information as to these four States was as follows:

"In Nebraska the bill was introduced by seven members of the legislature. At the hearings two men favored and two opposed its passage. No information was given as to the interest represented by any one of the four.

"In Massachusetts the proponents at the hearings were representatives of the druggists, liquor dealers, tobacco distributors, and grocers. No opponents were mentioned.

"In Alabama hearings were relatively short. The bill was sponsored primarily by the Retail Druggists Association. Very little opposition developed.

"In Illinois there were no hearings on the bill."

In this connection, there is also a very interesting finding by the Commission concerning the subject of typographical errors, which sheds some light on the rapidity with which these State bills were passed by these State legislatures.

On page 68 of the Commission's report it is stated as follows:

"The California law of 1931, as amended by addition of the nonsigner clause in 1933, became the model followed by a number of other States. Later the National Association of Retail Druggists developed a model law, patterned closely after the California act, but embodying certain corrections and changes in phraseology. This model was enacted by numerous States, with little or no change in the wording of its essential provisions. In the framing of the acts of a few of the States, both the California and the National Association of Retail Druggists models appear to have been considered, with the result that laws differing in phraseology from both, yet containing essentially provisions of both, were enacted.

"How closely the California law was followed by other States is indicated by the fact that a stenographic error in the California law was copied in the laws adopted by 11 States, notwithstanding the fact that, as finally pointed out by a New Jersey court, the error in transcription made the wording of an important section of the law unintelligible."

Mr. MORSE. Mr. President, I ask unanimous consent to have printed at this point in the RECORD, as a part of my remarks, some material regarding the history of what I consider to be the pressure movement to get this particular bill passed.

There being no objection, the statement was ordered to be printed in the RECORD, as follows:

Immediately following the decision of the Supreme Court in the Schwegmann case, the National Association of Retail Druggists took active steps to draft remedial legislation. Originally planned as an amendment to the Miller-Tydings section of the Sherman Act, this legislation was drawn to amend the Federal Trade Commission Act solely for the purpose of bypassing the supposedly unfriendly House Judiciary Committee and placing it in the hands of the Interstate and Foreign Commerce Committee. To assure that the legislation would not fall into the hands of the former body, members of the association were directed to barrage Congress with letters requesting that Members vote against any move to re-refer the proposed statute (H. R. 5767) to the Committee on the Judiciary.

Once it was evident that H. R. 5767 would remain with the Interstate and Foreign Commerce Committee, another avalanche of letters from members of the National Association of Retail Druggists beseiged members of the committee to hold prompt hearings and to issue a favorable report on the bill. This was done despite the fact that the Committee on the Judiciary had long since announced that fair, thorough, and comprehensive hearings on bills pending before it would be held with dispatch.

After H. R. 5767 was favorably acted upon by the Interstate and Foreign Commerce Committee, attention was focused directly upon the Rules Committee, and again members of the association were told to flood the members of the Rules Committee with requests to issue a rule, and friends of members of the Rules Committee were urged to contact these members personally for the same purpose.

Even now, Members of Congress have been alerted for the campaign which must be waged to push the legislation through the House of Representatives and have been told to stand by for the clarion call to overwhelm the Congress with mail urging passage of H. R. 5767.

The accompanying chronological survey of events recorded in the trade press, bulletins and announcements of responsible officials, discloses with utmost candor the facts set forth above and reveals how, in this instance, legislative procedures are being determined not by the Rules of the House but by a vocal group of highly organized retailers who believe that the orderly procedures of Congress can be subverted by outside pressures.

LEGISLATIVE DRAFTING

May 21, 1951:
Decision of Supreme Court in *Schwegmann Bros.* v. *Calvert Corp.* (341 U. S. 384 (1951)).

⊥ May 25, 1951, John Dargavel: ⊥ 8836
"There is only one organization with the experience and the leadership that are needed to direct effective unified activities to amend the Miller-Tydings Act. The NARD led the fight that resulted in the Miller-Tydings Act. * * * Right now attorneys of exceptional capabilities are busy on the determination of the phraseology of the amendment. * * * The NARD is also at work on the details of the plan of action for the organized activities to bring about the enactment of the nonsigner amendment" (NARD Journal, June 4, 1951, pp. 814, 823).

June 18, 1951, NARD Journal:
"Draft legislation for introduction in Congress, amending the Miller-Tydings Act so that it will cover the nonsigner clause in interstate commerce, has been developed by Herman Waller, legal counsel to the NARD and a veteran fighter for fair trade" (p. 962)

INTRODUCTION AND REFERRAL

October 29, 1951, Drug Trade News:
"Fair-trade supporters representing many industries have stamped their official O. K. on a Congressional bill (H. R. 5767) introduced by Representative JOHN A. McGUIRE (Democrat, Connecticut) that would validate the nonsigner clauses of State fair-trade laws through an amendment of the Federal Trade Commission Act rather than the Miller-Tydings Act as had been originally planned.

"The last-minute change in policy on the bill is viewed as an attempt to insure early action on fair-trade legislation. By amending the FTC Act instead of the Miller-Tydings Act, the bill is diverted from the hostile House Judiciary Committee to the friendlier House Interstate Commerce Committee, headed by Representative ROBERT CROSSER (Democrat, Ohio), who promises early action on it when Congress reconvenes" (p. 1).

November 1951: American Druggist:
"By use of legislative strategy, the bill was kept away from the House Judiciary Committee which is regarded as being hostile to fair trade. Representative CELLER, Democrat of New York, who is chairman of the Judiciary Committee, is one of the leading opponents of fair trade on Capitol Hill, and it was anticipated that he would do everything in his power to bottle up new fair-trade legislation.

"To keep it away from the Judiciary Committee, the bill was written as an amendment to the Federal Trade Commission Act rather than the Sherman Antitrust law. The House Interstate Commerce Committee has jurisdiction over legislation dealing with the Federal Trade Commission while the Judiciary Committee handles amendments to the Antitrust act" (p. 73).

PREVENTION OF TRANSFER

January 14, 1952, Drug Topics:
"At press time, a spokesman for the Interstate Commerce Committee, told Drug Topics that Mr. CELLER and Chairman ROBERT CROSSER of Interstate Commerce plan to meet early this term to decide which committee will handle the McGuire bill.

"He said various members of the committee feel the bill is an 'encroachment' on the jurisdiction of the Judiciary Committee since it would directly amend the FTC Act, rather than the Sherman Act, as a means of setting aside the recent Supreme Court Schwegmann decision which outlawed the nonsigner clauses of State fair-trade laws in interstate commerce" (p. 24).

February 4, 1952, John Dargavel:
"I have just received a report from Washington that hearings on H. R. 5767 (the NARD fair-trade bill) have been scheduled to open on February 4. It is good news indeed. It tells us that we won the fight to prevent the transfer of the bill from the House Committee on Interstate and Foreign Commerce to the Judiciary Committee of the House and also that the

House Committee on Interstate and Foreign Commerce responded to the wishes of the druggists in particular and the retailers in general everywhere in the United States.

"You members gave us magnificient [sic] cooperation. Your responses to the appeal I sent out for action on January 9 amounted to an avalanche of letters and telegrams" (NARD Journal, p. 183).

February 4, 1952, Drug Trade News:
"Mr. CELLER has abandoned efforts to have jurisdiction over the McGuire bill transferred to his committee. He has let it be known that he is 'not interested in the McGuire bill,' which will remain with the Interstate and Foreign Commerce Committee" (p. 1).

"This decision of Mr. CELLER'S can be characterized as a victory for the National Association of Retail Druggists, since druggists from all over the Nation have been deluging Members of the House with telegrams and letters demanding their support for keeping the McGuire bill in the Interstate and Foreign Commerce Committe [sic]" (p. 33).

HEARINGS

January 7, 1952, NARD Journal:
"The next action on the bill will be to have it scheduled for a hearing before the House Committee on Interstate and Foreign Commerce, of which the members are ROBERT CROSSER, of Ohio; LINDLEY BECKWORTH, of Texas; J. PERCY PRIEST, of Tennessee; OREN HARRIS, of Arkansas; DWIGHT L. ROGERS, of Florida; ARTHUR G. KLEIN, of New York; THOMAS B. STANLEY, of Virginia; WILLIAM T. GRANAHAN, of Pennsylvania; JOHN A. McGUIRE, of Connecticut; F. ERTEL CARLYLE, of North Carolina; JOHN BELL WILLIAMS, of Mississippi; PETER F. MACK, JR., of Illinois; HOMER THORNBERRY, of Texas; LOUIS B. HELLER, of New York; KENNETH A. ROBERTS, of Alabama; MORGAN M. MOULDER, of Missouri; HARLEY O. STAGGERS, of West Virginia; CHARLES A. WOLVERTON, of New Jersey; CARL HINSHAW, of California; LEONARD W. HALL, of New York; JOSEPH P. O'HARA, of Minnesota; ROBERT HALE, of Maine; JAMES I. DOLLIVER, of Iowa; JOHN W. HESELTON, of Massachusetts; HUGH D. SCOTT, JR., of Pennsylvania; JOHN B. BENNETT, of Michigan; RICHARD W. HOFFMAN, of Illinois; J. EDGAR CHENOWETH, of Colorado; JOHN V. BEAMER, of Indiana; and HARMAR D. DENNY, JR., of Pennsylvania.

"It is urgent that the druggists in the respective districts of the above-listed members of the House Committee on Interstate and Foreign Commerce request a hearing on H. R. 5767 early in 1952" (p. 19).

February 18, 1952, Drug Trade News:
"The decision of the Interstate and Foreign Commerce Committee to hold hearings came suddenly after earlier indications that it would not hold hearings until a later date. Originally, the committee scheduled a 1-day hearing for February 4 to hear Maurice Mermey, director of the Bureau of Education on Fair Trade, but NARD built pressure, plus the insistence of Mr. McGUIRE on immediate action, resulted in the decision to continue the hearings under the Priest subcommittee.

"In persuading the committee to hold immediate hearings, fair-trade proponents felt that they had 'put one over' on Representative EMANUEL CELLER, chairman of the House Judiciary Committee, who previously (January 18, 1951) had announced public hearings on several fair-trade bills before his committee, beginning February 13" (p. 16).

FAVORABLE REPORT

February 4, 1951, John Dargavel:
"More letters on H. R. 5767 urgent.

*   *   *   *   *   *   *

"Our next move centers on the members of the House Committee on Interstate and Foreign Commerce. Accordingly, I call on you druggists to write to them that it is vital to the system of small business to issue a favorable report on H. R. 5767. The legislative procedures are such that a favorable report is essential to prevent serious obstacles to enactment of H. R. 5767.

"The members of the House Committee on Interstate and Foreign Commerce are * * *.

"You druggists located in the respective districts of the above-listed Representatives can be of particular assistance right now. You are their constituents and they will give special attention to letters they receive from you. Hence, today, write to them that you expect a favorable report on H. R. 5767. The stake is great and failure to write to them might help to sound the death knell for fair trade" (p. 183).

February 25, 1952, Drug Topics:
"One of the significant developments in the fair-trade struggle is the apparent power of the NARD in Congress. Congressmen from all over the country have been swamped with telegrams and letters demanding action on the McGuire bill" (p. 63).

March 3, 1952, Drug Trade News:

"Much of the opposition which developed in the Interstate Commerce Committee to hasty action on H. R. 5767 was brushed aside by Representative MCGUIRE in his efforts to get a fast, favorable report on his bill.

"It was reported that Representative ROBERT CROSSER, committee chairman, and Representative J. PERCY PRIEST, chairman of the seven-member subcommittee on fair trade, urged a go-slow policy to see what Representative CELLER and his monopoly subcommittee would do.

"However, Mr. MCGUIRE, assisted in large part by a flood of letters and telegrams from retail druggists to their Congressmen, was able to whip his bill through the subcommittee and force the full committee to schedule the executive meeting on February 27.

"As reported by the subcommittee H. R. 5767 would amend section 5a of the Federal Trade Commission Act" (p. 23).

RULES COMMITTEE

February 28, 1952, special NARD bulletin:

"We urge all of you in the States and districts which the members of the House Rules Committee represent to do everything possible to create a flood of telegrams and letters to these Congressmen. The Rules Committee can break or make H. R. 5767. If a rule is not granted, the bill never will come up on the floor of the House. So you can see that this is one of the most important efforts we have to make. We urge your complete and wholehearted cooperation in getting telegrams and letters in to the members of the House Rules Committee.

"Those of you who happen to know a member of the Rules Committee personally should call him long distance to urge him to do all he can to have a rule for H. R. 5767 granted at an early date. We must work fast because the Rules Committee will be asked for a rule within the next few days."

March 3, 1952, NARD Journal:

"I now call for more help from you druggists.

"(1) Time is a serious factor in the fight to bring about the enactment of H. R. 5767. The bill must be granted special consideration—a rule—from the Rules Committee or it will be buried toward the bottom of the calendar in the House—and there it will repose untouched through the months left of the life of the Eighty-second Congress. Many of you druggists are constituents of the members of the Rules Committee—they are listed on page 338 of this issue of the NARD Journal. It is vital to the cause of fair trade that you wire or write them at once to support special consideration—a rule—for H. R. 5767. You may know well or be among the intimate friends of a Congressman on the Rules Committee. Then please telephone him right away. The fate of the bill hangs in a balance. Failure to procure the necessary responses from you druggists in the States of Georgia, Illinois, Indiana, Mississippi, New York, Ohio, Oregon, Texas, Virginia, and Washington, will spell death for H. R. 5767. I am confident you will come through with a flood of telegrams and letters to the members of the Rules Committee" (p. 335).

FINAL PASSAGE

February 18, 1952, NARD Journal:

"Then in that event the next move will center on your and every Representative in Congress. You will be called on at the proper time to help flood the House with letters and telegrams in support of H. R. 5767. I know you will respond as you did in January to block the scheme to have the bill transferred to the Judiciary Committee of the House" (p. 251).

February 25, 1952, Drug Topics:

"STILLWATER, OKLA.—A 'push-button' plan of action to spur passage of the McGuire fair-trade bill has been organized in Oklahoma, Elbert R. (Pete) Weaver, secretary of the Oklahoma Pharmaceutical Association told Drug Topics.

"According to this plan, 150 druggists from over the State have been appointed to serve as members of a contact committee. Through this committee, druggists in every town in the State can be alerted within a few hours when the time comes to give Congressmen an extra nudge in order to get the fair-trade bill through.

"The plan was put into effect recently when Oklahoma druggists sent 178 telegrams over the State, opposing a motion to refer the McGuire bill to the House Judiciary Committee.

"The wires went to 178 keymen in the pharmaceutical association and secretaries of other trade associations, who followed up with a similar barrage of telegrams to their membership. * * *

"This year, we are going to pass a new fair-trade law. When the order comes for more messages to Congressmen, we are going to contact our contact men, and we know they will act quickly" (p. 40).

March 3, 1952, NARD Journal:

"Once H. R. 5767 is granted special consideration (a rule) the bill will in a short time be sent to the floor of the House. Accordingly, it is also important to contact every Congressman. It must be done with speed. They should be urged to take stand in support of H. R. 5767" (p. 335).

POINT 4. COERCION TO IMPOSE RESALE PRICE MAINTENANCE

Mr. MORSE. Mr. President, the history of resale price maintenance is, in my judgment, a history of pressure by retailers and sometimes by manufacturers to impose resale price maintenance on those who wish to sell for less. Sometimes the pressure is applied by manufacturers against retailers who do not wish to sell at resale price maintenance prices, and sometimes it is applied by retailers against manufacturers who do not wish to observe resale price maintenance in the case of their products.

The manner in which manufacturers who do not wish to engage in resale price maintenance in the case of their products have been coerced is illustrated by the case of Pepsodent. The method by which the manufacturer of that product was persuaded to return to the fold of resale price maintenance was eloquently described by the executive secretary of the Northern California Retail Druggists Association, at the Thirty-seventh Annual Convention of the National Association of Retail Druggists, in September 1935.

Mr. President, at this point I ask unanimous consent to have that statement printed at this point in the RECORD, as a part of my remarks.

There being no objection, the statement was ordered to be printed in the RECORD, as follows:

"Mr. Chairman, fellow druggists, the Pepsodent Co. was operating in the State of California under the California Fair Trade Act. In all the time that they were operating under the Fair Trade Act they made no attempt to enforce their contract and like a bolt of lightning from the blue sky, they informed us that the California fair-trade contract was canceled, and the general sales manager Mr. Kermott, came out to California, called upon me in the California office to make excuses and he had with him one of the California salesmen. I expressed my heartfelt sympathy to the two young men who were in my office because I told them they would have the toughest time any salesmen had had in any territory. We passed a resolution at our meeting and we published that resolution in our journal, and we sent that resolution to every member in California in which we urged and advised them to discontinue the sale of any product that had canceled their fair-trade contract. Brothers, it was a slap in the face of our Fair Trade Act. It makes no difference what firm it was. It was unwarranted. It was the first cancellation. And to my great delight and the great delight of our executive committee all the druggists in California refused to sell Pepsodent toothpaste or Pepsodent products. They put them in the basement. Some were enthusiastic enough to throw them into the ashcan. I wouldn't bring this out except that I want you to really understand how the sales of Pepsodent products in all of California dropped off."[1]

The lesson taught by the druggists to the Pepsodent Co. were [sic] readily employed to convince other producers that adoption of resale price maintenance agreements with retailers would be to their decided advantage. Said one manufacturer with regard to the compelling reasons prompting him to adopt said resale price maintenance on his products:

"The retail outlets, particularly the independent retail druggists, through their State associations and many of them individually, pressed us to establish minimum retail prices for our products from the time the respective States enacted so-called fair-trade laws. Pressure similarly was put on us by drug wholesalers and their associations."[2]

Reported another maker of articles sold through retail drug outlets:

"The retail price maintenance contracts we have made were made and any wholesale 'price maintenance contracts, agreements, or arrangements,' if any, which we may make in the future will be to enable us to get wholesalers' and retailers' cooperation and to cause wholesalers and retailers to discontinue discriminating against us in favor of our competitors who have either voluntarily or at the insistence of wholesalers and retailers, already entered into resale price maintenance contracts, agreements, or arrangements."[3]

John Dargavel, executive secretary of the NARD, writing to the sales company of a manufacturer of toilet preparations on Febraury 10, 1936, in an effort to influence its selling

---

[1] Cited in Federal Trade Commission Report on Resale Price Maintenance (1945), p. 143.

[2] Id., p. 167.

[3] Ibid.

policies, referred in a veiled manner "to the Pepsodent Co. and some others in regard to what concerted action by the druggists of this country did to their volume" and threatened that "if we start a campaign through our journal, carrying it through the officers of each State and local association in this country, you are going to find that it will cause you more trouble and take away more business from you than you had ever realized."[4]

Dr. Corwin Edwards, then economic consultant to the Department of Justice, summed up many of the boycotting activities which had at that time occurred under resale price maintenance legislation in a special memorandum written to the Assistant Attorney General in charge of the Antitrust Division on February 10, 1941.[5] Stated Edwards:

"Meanwhile, every effort was made to throttle public discussion and to intimidate business opposition. In California an aspirin manufacturer was forced by boycott to issue resale-price contracts against his will. The druggists' intention to coerce was indicated in the following language: 'This aspirin is a sort of Napoleon in the patent-medicine army, but then even the great Frenchman met his Waterloo when the rest of Europe got together, decided that they had had enough of him, and cooperated against him.' In the same State the manufacturers of Pepsodent toothpaste, who had experimented with resale price contracts under the California law, decided to withdraw these contracts, apparently under advice of counsel who believed that the contracts violated the antitrust laws. Thereupon the druggists organized a campaign to put Pepsodent under the counter and to switch customers to other brands. This campaign was so effective that the offending company made public apology at a subsequent convention of the National Association of Retail Druggists and, as a token of its contrition, subscribed $25,000 to a fund to lobby for resale price maintenance in other States. On one occasion an expression of opposition to resale price maintenance by the New York Times and the New York World-Telegram led to an effort by organized druggists to demoralize the dealers who distributed these papers, by selling them at less than 3 cents. On another occasion Harper's magazine carried an article against resale price maintenance and thereupon received a letter from a druggists' association in a midwestern city, demanding information as to whether Harper's endorsed the views expressed in the article and indicating that if these views were not repudiated they intended to sell Harper's at a substantial discount, presumably in an effort to create trouble among its distributors. Within the last 2 months the newspaper PM in New York has carried a series of articles against resale price maintenance, and the same tactics of intimidation have been attempted by the sale of PM at less than its customary price. The editors, having more sense of humor than some of the other victims of this policy, ran a photograph of a cut-rate advertisement in a store and gave it the caption 'The best bargain in the city'."[6]

The case of the Luce magazines is even more flagrant. Claiming that Time and Fortune had proven, through their editorial policies, to be enemies of fair trade, the NARD Journal, in a recent message from its executive secretary, proclaimed in banner headlines: "Luce magazines your enemies!" Thereupon denouncing these publications for various activities, the NARD sounded the following clarion call for manufacturers and retailers to boycott:

"How long do you druggists intend to continue to serve as peddlers of periodicals you know to be subversive to your individual and collective welfare and also to the consumers? How long will it be before manufacturers in the drug field cease to go along with magazines out to bring destruction to fair trade?"

Boycotting activities have by no means been confined to the National Association of Retail Druggists. The following invitation to boycott recently appeared in a leaflet published by a prominent wholesaler of drug products and distributed to retailers under the heading: "What should believers in fair-trade laws do now?

"Retailers should refuse to patronize wholesalers or other suppliers who are not in sympathy with the fair-trade laws. (An example would be a wholesaler who refused to sign a manufacturer's wholesale fair-trade contract and then offers you a cut price or greater discount than allowed under the fair-trade contract.) If you patronized such a wholesaler you would be an enemy of fair trade."

Manufacturers have not been the only victims of collective action on the part of retailers in seeking to obtain fair trade by coercion. Drug Topics, a trade publication in the drug field,

---

[4] Id., p. 166.

[5] TNEC, Final Report and Recommendations, 77th Cong., 1st sess. (1941), exhibit No. 2793, p. 233.

[6] Cf. Business Week, March 3, 1952: "Fair-trade war * * * has been declared by druggists on St. Louis Post-Dispatch. Paper's anti-fair-trade cartoon started it. Fair-trading druggists in St. Louis are cutting prices—on the Post-Dispatch, a leading anti-trade newspaper * * *. Suddenly, placards appeared in drugstore windows all over St. Louis, announcing that the Post could be had for 4 cents daily and 13 cents on Sunday (it normally sells for 5 cents daily, 15 cents on Sunday)."

pointed out in an editorial in its July 30, 1951, issue how boycotting of recalcitrant retailers would be "helpful action" in preserving fair-trade prices. Said this journal:

"If all wholesalers, acting in their individual capacities, would refuse to sell outlets which did not maintain fair-trade prices, the outlook would become much more promising. * * *

"Once a price violator is denied goods, or is cut off for his refusal to comply with the invoice notice, he is likely to reshape his selling operations so as to comply with fair-trade principles" (p. 38).

How secretaries of State and local associations of druggists could assist in maintaining prices by "persuading" retailers to refrain from cutting prices on fair-traded articles was described in the NARD Journal of July 2, 1951:

"The secretaries of state and also the local associations of druggists can do much to help prevent extension of price wars," it advised.

"Many owners of drug stores have been persuaded to refrain from copycat slashes of fair-trade minimums a la Macy's Department Store in New York City. One of them was induced to be sensible after he had made a kick-off through the newspapers of the community" (p. 1032).

As Mr. Morison, Assistant Attorney General in charge of the Antitrust Division of the Department of Justice, explained to the committee when his attention was called to this action, "It indicates the beginning of a violation of the Sherman Act."

Efforts to restrain the pricing policies of competing retail outlets received the personal endorsement of John Dargavel, executive secretary of the NARD in his message printed in the NARD Journal of April 18, 1949. Describing a fringe of druggists who were cutting prices as "wreckers of fair trade," Dargavel informed readers that "Violations stimulate agitation against the system of stabilized prices and out of it may come a Nation-wide movement of consumers to bring about the end of fair trade." Worried lest this disaster occur, he proclaimed openly that "The chiselers and cheaters among the druggists must be made to see the light" (p. 589).

Mr. MORSE. Mr. President, what about the effect of fair trade on prices?

Mr. DOUGLAS. Mr. President, is it not important to get the wording and our semantics correct? Instead of saying "fair trade" should we not say "resale price maintenance laws"?

Mr. MORSE. The Senator from Illinois is completely right. I have been using this misnomer, "fair trade," because it has come to have this special meaning on the floor of the Senate. The definition of the subject matter which we have under debate is exactly as the Senator from Illinois states it.

POINT 5. THE EFFECT OF RESALE PRICE MAINTENANCE LAWS ON PRICES

Numerous studies have shown that prices in States which have resale price maintenance laws are substantially higher than prices on the same items in adjoining States that do not have such laws. To the same effect studies have shown that following the imposition of resale price maintenance laws prices have risen. The evidence of this question is summarized by the Celler committee report.

I ask unanimous consent to have the summary printed in the RECORD at this point in my remarks.

There being no objection, the summary was ordered to be printed in the RECORD, as follows:

Resale price maintenance has often guaranteed equally high returns for wholesalers and retailers. On insulin, for example, "The price set by Eli Lilly & Co. * * * guarantees the retailer a 50 percent gross profit on cost and 25 percent profit on cost to the wholesaler," Samuel Rosenthal, owner of retail drug outlets in the District of Columbia, told the House committee. A hasty glance at the advertisements appearing in any random issue of a trade publication such as the American Druggist reveals retail profits on fair-trade items such as the following: "Dolcin, 44.3 percent profit; Argyrol, up to 57 1/2 percent profit; Kessling fever thermometers, 45 percent profit; Wyanoids, up to 50 percent profit; Ampho-Jel, up to 53.4 percent profit; Dichloricide moth crystals, up to 42 percent profit; Breck, 40 percent profit; McKesson & Robbins: 'You get an average of 50 percent profit.'"

How high fair-trade profit margins adversely affect the consumer is illustrated by a study of 208 major items in which selling prices in the 45 fair-trade States is compared to prices at which such commodities can be purchased in the non-fair-trading areas of Texas, Missouri, Vermont, and the District of Columbia. The composite selling price for all of these products in fair-trade States totaled $945.10 compared to only $740.86 in the non-fair-trade jurisdictions. Profits for the retailer in fair-trade States was 38.5 percent while in non-fair-trade areas it was only 21.5 percent, a saving to the consumer in non-fair-trade locations of 17 percent.

A survey appearing in the St. Louis Star-Times on April 19, 1951, also discloses how consumers pay more for liquor products which are sold under resale price maintenance agreements in the State of Illinois than they do across the border in non-fair-trade Missouri. Prices for 35 different fifths of nationally advertised liquors cost only 139.67 in St. Louis while consumers paid $22.25 more, or $161.92, in Illinois, a difference of 15.9 percent.

Mr. MORSE. A recent price comparison shopping tour for 10 items of ordinary consumption purchased in drug stores cost a total of $8.23 in Virginia and $8.80 in Maryland under resale price maintenance laws and only $7.05 in the District of Columbia without such a law, savings of 17 and 25 percent, respectively. . . .

Mr. President, the effect of resale price maintenance in fostering violations of antitrust laws is one of the major reasons for my intention to vote against the bill. As one who has at least dealt with and studied to a considerable extent the whole problem of antitrust violations in this country, and who is convinced that we are rapidly moving in the direction of monopolistic control of large segments of American economic life, I think we ought to stop, look, and listen before we, here and now, vote for a bill which, in my judgment, will weaken the antitrust laws of the country. I believe the position taken by the United States Department of Justice in testimony by their witnesses on the House side, and in public pronouncements which have been made in opposition to this bill, deserves the very careful consideration of the Members of this body. Therefore, Mr. President, I ask unanimous consent to have inserted at this point in my remarks the materials which I wish to offer in opposition to this bill—a bill which, in my opinion, will weaken the antitrust laws and the administration of the antitrust laws.

⊥ 8839

There being no objection, the materials were ordered to be printed in the RECORD, as follows:

POINT 6. RESALE PRICE MAINTENANCE FOSTERS VIOLATIONS OF THE ANTITRUST LAWS

While section (f) of H. R. 6925 purports to prohibit horizontal agreements among retailers, among wholesalers, or among manufacturers under the act, this language is at best a piece of wishful thinking. By making resale price maintenance agreements applicable to nonsigners, there is no meaning whatever to this bit of legislative double talk. The Federal Trade Commission pointed out very clearly to the committee the effect which resale price maintenance would have upon the time-honored principle of antitrust policy condemning horizontal price-fixing agreements among competitors. Said the Commission:

"Moreover, when the nonsigner clause is added to resale price maintenance, the effect is the de facto nullification of our Federal laws against horizontal conspiracy, notwithstanding the fact that the proposed legislation expressly prohibits horizontal price fixing. Nothing is more clearly established in Federal policy than the principle that horizontal price fixing shall not be tolerated. The proposed legislation pays lip service to that principle, yet its effect would be that a minimum price fixed by contract with one retail distributor would become the minimum price for all other retail distributors of the manufacturer's product who were placed upon notice of the existence of the contract. The rigidity and uniformity of the price would be exactly that of the most rigid horizontal price-fixing conspiracy; the level of the price would be likely to be at least as high as in a horizontal conspiracy; and the public control over the reasonableness of the arrangement would be as nonexistent as in the case of a horizontal conspiracy."[1]

It is clear that insofar as economic effect is concerned, there exists no difference between a horizontal price-fixing arrangement among competing retailers on the one hand, and a price agreement between one manufacturer and one retailer which is in turn binding on all competing retailers on the other. As a practical matter, expediency would dictate that conspiring retailers should hereafter achieve their illegal objectives through the now legalized device of having a manufacturer enter into a resale price maintenance agreement with a single retailer which would henceforth apply to the sales of all competitors. In this context, the prohibition against horizontal price conspiracy now becomes meaningless.

That this law will encourage violations of the antitrust laws on a wholesale basis is not just idle speculation on our part. Past experience under the Miller-Tydings law yields abundant evidence of resale price maintenance legislation serving as a cloak to conceal price fixing and other undesirable activities in restraint of trade.

In 1942, the Colorado Wholesale Wine and Liquor Dealers Association was indicted by the Department of Justice under section 1 of the Sherman Act for engaging in a conspiracy to fix retail prices of liquor sold in the State of Colorado. Retail prices, it was charged, were agreed upon, out of State producers were persuaded to enter into fair-trade contracts embodying

---

[1] Hearings, February 14, 1952.

agreed-upon prices, and wholesalers and producers refusing to comply were boycotted. Pleas of nolo contendere were filed by the defendants and fines were imposed.

Similarly, the National Association of Retail Druggists, today the loudest advocate of fair-trade legislation, was fined in 1947 on a plea of nolo contendere to an indictment charging them with having engaged in a conspiracy to fix the retail and wholesale prices of drug items, to eliminate price competition among retail druggists, and to restrain competition. This conspiracy was perpetrated despite the existence of a consent decree filed in 1907 perpetually enjoining the association from engaging in such activities as boycotts, etc. Methods employed by the NARD to achieve its illegal objectives were summarized for the committee by the Assistant Attorney General in charge of the Antitrust Division, Department of Justice, as follows:

"They threatened to refuse to handle or to boycott, or to urge their customers and prescribing physicians to accept substitutes for drug-store items, where margins of profits had not been approved, and refused to carry in stock, boycotted, and urged their customers to accept substitutes for such drug-store items; agreed to sell drug-store items whose retail prices had been established by producers at prices not below those so established and sold said drug-store items at prices not below those so established; persuaded, induced, and compelled producers of drug-store items to establish wholesale prices in relation to the retail prices demanded by defendants; threatened producers with lack of cooperation in the sale of drug-store items on which the wholesale prices were not established at levels bearing the relation to retail prices demanded by defendants and refused to cooperate in the sale of such drug-store items."[2]

The National Wholesale Druggists' Association was also indicted under the Sherman Act for conspiring to raise, fix, and stabilize wholesale selling prices of drug items. Alleged devices utilized to further the objectives of the conspiracy included lack of cooperation with recalcitrant manufacturers, boycotts, and refusals to sell from or carry in stock. Again nolo contendere pleas were filed and fines levied.

In the *United States* v. *New York State Pharmaceutical Association*, the National Association of Retail Druggists was again indicted, this time in conjunction with the New York State Pharmaceutical Association and others, for fixing, stabilizing, and maintaining the retail and wholesale prices of drug-store items through the adoption of uniform prices and methods of sale, interchange of information, boycotts, and blacklists. Pleas of nolo contendere and fines also ended this litigation.

Proceedings involving the abuse of resale price maintenance legislation are extensive. The Department of Justice has brought cases of a similar nature against the Tri-State Record Dealers Association, the Record Dealers Association, and has currently pending cases against the Allegheny County Retail Druggists' Association and the Sunbeam Corp. Proceedings instituted by the Federal Trade Commission where resale price maintenance was an important factor include docket No. 4526, Law Book Publishers Co.; docket No. 4900, refractories case; docket No. 5448, rubber manufacturers group; docket No. 5734, Mid-Atlantic Distributors Corp. (which just recently has been appealed to the United States Court of Appeals for the District of Columbia Circuit); docket No. 5635, cycle jobbers; docket No. 5636, American Dental Association; docket No. 4093, Wholesale Liquor Distributors Association of northern California, et al.; docket No. 4132, Western Confectioners Association; docket No. 4168, National Retail Liquor Package Stores Association.

The success of the antitrust agencies in the above ligitation [sic] belies the serious competitive problems raised by the exemption of resale price maintenance programs from the antitrust laws. The Department of Justice was quoted in 1945 as having said that "if its Antitrust Division had sufficient men and money to examine every resale price maintenance contract written under State and Federal legislation, and to proceed in every case in which the arrangement goes beyond the authorization of the Tydings-Miller amendment, there would be practically no resale price maintenance contracts."

The Assistant Attorney General in charge of the Antitrust Division, Mr. Morison, confirmed this view as of the present by averring that from the experience of the Antitrust Division the vast majority of resale price maintenance contracts, if examined fully, would be found in violation of the antitrust laws. A study of how resale price maintenance has operated in practice goes far to reinforce Mr. Morison's conclusion.

Mr. MORSE. Mr. President, for further material by way of rebuttal to the argument of my good friend from Minnesota [Mr. HUMPHREY], in regard to the matter of analogy between support prices and this bill, I ask unanimous consent to have printed in the RECORD at this point the statement of Matt Triggs, assistant legislative director, American Farm Bureau Federation, before the Senate Committee on Interstate and Foreign Commerce, relative to House bill 5767, on June 4, 1952.

---

[2] Hearings, February 13, 1952.

SENATE CONSIDERATION (H.R. 5767)

There being no objection, the statement was ordered to be printed in the RECORD, as follows:

The opportunity of expressing the viewpoints of the American Farm Bureau Federation relative to H. R. 5767 is appreciated.

The American Farm Bureau Federation is an organization of 1,452,210 farm families located in 47 States and Puerto Rico.

The American Farm Bureau Federation opposed the enactment of the original Miller-Tydings Act and since then has periodically reiterated its opposition to resale price maintenance legislation.

At the most recent annual meeting of the federation at Chicago in December 1951, the following resolution on this issue was developed by the house of delegates:

"So-called fair-trade pricing legislation is inconsistent with the maintenance of the principles of a free competitive economy. Flexible and freely moving prices are an important element of these principles. We oppose legislative efforts to require nonsigners of fair-trade contracts to comply with their provisions. We favor legislation to eliminate fair-trade pricing provisions of law."

⊥ Our basic objection to price-maintenance legislation is our belief that flexibility of prices achieved by the interaction of supply-and-demand factors in a free market is a fundamental feature of a free competitive enterprise system. ⊥ 8840

The distinguishing feature of American private enterprise system, as compared with other economic systems, is our belief in the principle of competition. We are one of the few nations which has established competition as an economic ideal by legislation prohibiting practices or conspiracies to interfere with competition. This is an all-important element contributing to the vitality and dynamic growth of our society. It is the heart of our capitalistic system. Legislation which would restrict competition in the field of distribution is inconsistent with the most successful operation of the competitive enterprise society.

Many other private enterprise economies do not have this concept. Much of the effort of their business and governmental leadership is in the direction of the establishment of Government-industry agreements, the development of cartel arrangements, the enactment of programs to mitigate the effects of competition, the furthering of measures to protect individuals in this category or that from competitive pressures with their supposed harmful effects. By such devices they tend in the direction of providing an umbrella for the inefficient and of reducing the pressures and the incentives for increased efficiency which is so vital a part of the American economic pattern. The intermixture of public and private endeavors to regulate competition and fix prices has in many other countries been the forerunner of planned economy or socialism.

It is a basic defense of the profit system that competition compels the passing on to the consumer of any savings which may be made by efficient distribution. The enactment of H. R. 5767 would, in some measure, destroy this fundamental defense of private enterprise and serve as an argument for similar ventures in the regulation of competition in other fields.

We are opposed to all forms of price fixing, but the nonsigner provision incorporated in H. R. 5767 is, in our opinion, a particularly undesirable form of price fixing. One distributor, by contracting with a manufacturer, may establish marketing margins with which every other distributor must comply. It is contrary to our concept of contractual relationships to require people to comply with contracts to which they are not a party and with respect to the terms of which they have had no voice.

Any retailer who is able to serve the public more efficiently than other retailers, whether due to managerial ability, volume, location, or for any other reason, should be encouraged, not prevented, to reflect such reduced costs of operations in his prices and by such means keep competition alive and active.

A consumer who is willing to shop in less exclusive stores or who is willing to accept less service (credit, delivery, or other service) than is available elsewhere should have the opportunity to participate in the savings thus made.

It appears that most of the support for fair-trade legislation comes from the belief that it is helpful to small individual retail stores. We believe this is fallacious. If margins are held unduly high on some articles by fair-trade practices, this only increases the ability of low-cost retailers to compete more aggressively in pricing other articles, or providing better service, or to be more effective in merchandising display and advertising, or to provide better trade-in valuations.

On the contrary, so-called fair trading will be harmful to many small retailers. Many small concerns are insufficiently capitalized. They must have their stores in less desirable locations. They must do with less expensive fixtures and furnishings. They are unable to provide the credit, delivery, and other services that larger stores furnish. To bring customers to their shops, they must be permitted to compete on a price basis.

Furthermore, the existence of fair-trade programs with their guaranteed margins induces many competing retailers to carry such items who would not otherwise do so. An outstanding example of this is the extent to which grocery stores have undertaken the distribution of many fair-trade articles.

We know of no convincing evidence to indicate that those retail trades which have generally resorted to fair-trade price practices have been more profitable than those retail trades which have not, nor do we know of any evidence that retail trade has been made profitable in those States having resale price maintenance legislation than in those States which do not.

Resale price maintenance provisions of law provide a framework which may be used to implement undertakings and agreements contrary to the letter and spirit of antitrust legislation, and beyond the limitations contemplated by Congress. The United States Department of Justice has concluded, as a result of its experience with "fair trade" legislation, that "the Tydings-Miller Act does not serve the purposes which were urged upon Congress as a reason for its passage in that it sanctions arrangements inconsistent with the purpose of the antitrust laws, and becomes a cloak for many conspiracies in restraint of trade, which go far beyond the limits established in the amendment." The legislation would provide a mechanism for organized retail groups to bring concerted pressure upon manufacturers and wholesalers, in many instances supplemented by economic reprisal, to force such manufacturers to undertake a "fair trade" pricing program.

It may, perhaps, be demonstrated that price cutting is a practice that is occasionally harmful to other retailers, or to manufacturers, but H. R. 5767 does not endeavor to discriminate between loss-leader types of sales and legitimate price reductions; rather, it groups all price reductions together, labels them as unlawful practices and prohibits them.

The question which is frequently asked of us is "How can farmers oppose 'fair trade' legislation when they are in favor of price-support programs?"

There are some very obvious and important differences between price support and "fair trade" legislation.

Flexible farm price support programs, as set forth in the Agricultural Act of 1949, are intended to prevent disastrously low farm prices. They are not intended to fix prices. They are intended to permit a free market above floor levels established at 75 to 90 percent of parity. They leave agricultural prices generally free to fluctuate in response to free-market conditions.

Farm price supports are comparable to minimum wages for labor or loss-leader legislation for the distribution trade.

The latest annual meeting resolution of the American Farm Bureau Federation on this point states that:

"Farm price supports are an appropriate and necessary protection against unreasonable price declines. It is not, however, the responsibility of the Government to guarantee profitable prices to any economic group * * * We do not believe that action to raise the level of price support above that now provided in the Agricultural Act of 1949 is in the long-run interest of farm people."

Pursuant to this policy, the American Farm Bureau Federation has opposed in this Congress efforts to increase the level of price support by three different bills heard a few weeks ago by the Senate Committee on Agriculture. We have opposed the Brannan farm program, which would endeavor to establish a responsibility of the Government to fix and guarantee prices for farm products at profitable levels. We will continue to oppose any efforts which may be made to increase the mandatory level of price support above that now provided in the Agricultural Act of 1949. We believe this position is entirely consistent with our opposition to so-called fair trade legislation.

The American Farm Bureau Federation, therefore, recommends your opposition to the enactment of H. R. 5767.

Mr. MORSE. Mr. President, I think Mr. Trigg's statement is a clear rebuttal of the argument of the Senator from Minnesota. We should remember that farm parity supports may decline if industrial prices decline. There is no such protection to the public in the private price fixing in the McGuire bill. It will cost the public $2,000,000,000, a year.

Mr. President, I desire to have printed in the RECORD an article from one of the great newspapers of our land, the St. Louis Post-Dispatch. Let me say that the Post-Dispatch, in my judgment, has a magnificent journalistic record in placing before the public, as it discusses the great controversial issues of American public life, information of primary importance. This great newspaper fights for the public interest and the welfare of the Nation in keeping with the best of newspaper traditions. I ask unanimous consent that there be printed in the RECORD at this point in my remarks an article entitled "The Customers Didn't Write," an article written by Edwin L. Dale, Jr., first published in the New York Herald Tribune, and later republished in the St. Louis Post-Dispatch on Saturday, May 17, 1952.

There being no objection, the article was ordered to be printed in the RECORD, as follows:

THE CUSTOMERS DIDN'T WRITE
(By Edwin L. Dale, Jr., in the New York Herald Tribune)

Events in the House of Representatives on May 8 were the climax to a perfect lesson in how an organized group of citizens who want anything from Congress should go about getting it.

The group of citizens in this case was the Nation's druggists, the manufacturers and wholesalers of drug-store products, and some other retailers and manufacturers.

What they wanted was fair trade—the system under which a manufacturer or wholesaler can set the minimum retail price of his article in a State by signing a contract with a single retailer in that State.

Though fair-trade laws are State laws, the druggists—who completely dominated the fight for fair trade—needed congressional action because a Supreme Court decision of last May largely nullified the effectiveness of the State laws.

The druggists needed from Congress a law validating the nonsigner provision—the provision which makes all retailers, including the majority who do not sign specific fair-trade contracts, abide by the fair-trade price as if applies [sic] to goods shipped across State lines.

The administration was heartily against the bill, as evidenced by vigorous testimony from the Justice Department and the Federal Trade Commission.

Most of the press (conservative and liberal) was against it, and two of the four leading Washington newspapers campaigned actively against it.

[⊥ 8841]

Though there are two points of view about its effect on consumers, it has the agreed effect of keeping prices up in some cases.

But when the House voted, 196 Members supported the bill and only 10 opposed it.

The steamroller vote was only the culmination of a story that had begun during the first session of this Congress last fall.

The drug industry lobbyists, contemplating their strategy for a bill to nullify the Supreme Court decision, were well aware (1) that the original Federal fair-trade legislation had been in the form of an amendment to the antitrust laws, (2) that all legislation regarding the antitrust laws is considered by the Judiciary Committee, and (3) that the chairman of the Judiciary Committee, Representative EMANUEL CELLER, of New York, is an inveterate foe of fair-trade legislation.

So the lobbyists got their lawyers to draw up a bill amending the Federal Trade Commission Act instead. The FTC is under the executive jurisdiction of the Interstate and Foreign Commerce Committee, headed by Representative ROBERT CROSSER, of Ohio, a friend of fair trade.

Then they got Representative JOHN A. McGUIRE, of Connecticut, to introduce their bill, and the chief hurdle was passed.

The bill went to the Commerce Committee. Hearings began soon after Congress reconvened in January, a subcommittee was promptly appointed to continue the hearings, and the McGuire bill rolled out of the committee on February 27, virtually unchanged.

Meanwhile, the Judiciary Committee, which had been bypassed, attempted a rear-guard action by promptly reporting out a bill of its own which would restore fair trade but which contained a group of four limiting provisions.

When debate in the House began, it became clear immediately that there would be no effective opposition to fair trade as such. The only fight was over which bill to approve, with some private fair-trade advocates urging the Judiciary Committee's bill as containing more protection for their interests.

But the drug people had told the constituents to tell their Congressmen that the McGuire bill was the only one that would do the job. The Congressmen were so informed. And the result was that when voting began, the substitute bill was knocked down 111 to 12.

Other amendments were offered. Sensing their strength, the bill's managers cut down debate to as little as 3 minutes on some of them. They were all turned down by voice vote or overwhelming standing votes.

The whole thing took only a little over 2 hours, and the McGuire bill was passed and sent to the Senate (where there is a chance of another committee juggling act, incidentally, because the chairmen of the two committees there are in reverse positions regarding fair trade).

MR. CELLER, almost the only fair-trade opponent who took the floor, asked plaintively if there wasn't anyone in the House trying to protect the consumers. But, as the drug spokesmen frankly pointed out, the letters from their people arrived and letters from consumers didn't.

Mr. MORSE. Mr. President, I think the RECORD ought to show the names of some of the leading authorities in our country in the fields of law, economics, and business administration who are opposed to the bill. I ask unanimous consent to have printed in the RECORD at this point in my remarks materials setting forth their names and some of their comments in regard to their opposition to the bill.

There being no objection, the material and comments were ordered to be printed in the RECORD, as follows:

STATEMENT IN OPPOSITION TO FAIR-TRADE LEGISLATION

(Submitted by M. A. Adelman, Massachusetts Institute of Technology; Ralph S. Brown, Jr., Yale University Law School; Kenneth S. Carlston, University of Illinois College of Law; J. K. Galbraith, Harvard University; Harold C. Havighurst, Northwestern University School of Law; Edward S. Mason, Harvard University; Fritz Machlup, Johns Hopkins University; W. Rupert Maclaurin, Massachusetts Institute of Technology; John Perry Miller, Yale University; Prof. Frank Kennedy, University of Iowa Law School; Prof. Carl Fulda, Rutgers University Law School; James A. Rahl, Northwestern University School of Law; Lloyd G. Reynolds, Yale University; Eugene V. Rostow, Yale University Law School; O. Glenn Saxon, Yale University; Louis B. Schwartz, University of Pennsylvania Law School; George W. Stocking, Vanderbilt University; James Tobin, Yale University; John Thompson, Yale University Law School.)

We are opposed to legislation undoing the effect of *Schwegemann Bros.* v. *Calvert Distilling Corp.* (344 U. S. C. 384 (1951)) [sic]. In fact we support the outright repeal of the Miller-Tydings Act. Resale price maintenance has no place in a society which depends on the competitive market as a major instrument for determining price and output. Whatever appeal the device may have had in a depression, there are no sound arguments in its favor under present and prospective circumstances of near-inflation and of high-level employment.

The original passage of the Miller-Tydings Act, and of the State fair-trade laws to which it gave scope, rested on an erroneous analysis of the depression. The depression was a time when prices fell. Therefore, the supporters of fair-trade laws contended, we can raise prices by law, and end the depression. This was the same case advanced for the NRA, the Smoot-Hawley tariff, and other devices of protection against the consequences of depression. The argument was incorrect. Fixing retail prices, in the face of inadequate demand, could only cut the volume sold, further intensify the depression and complicate the task of recovery.

At the present time, the economy is working under the forced draft of the rearmament program, and the price system should operate to extract every possible ounce of production from industry and agriculture to absorb and offset the volume of purchasing power left in the pockets of consumers after taxes. Even after the bulge of the rearmament program is passed, the economy will in all probability be kept at high levels of employment and economic activity by the policies of business and government. Business should be required to compete vigorously for its share of the public's purchasing power. There is no excuse in a capitalist economy for the subsidy of price fixing in the ordinary distribution of food, drugs, clothing, and other consumers goods. Existing law offers fully adequate protection against genuinely predatory and cutthroat competition.

The drive for price fixing by law comes from some groups of retailers who obtain their supplies through the older channels of wholesale distribution. They want to sell in their local markets under monopolistic conditions—that is, free of price competition. Not only do they want to eliminate competition with each other. They also typically oppose the growth of chain stores, mail-order houses, cooperatives, department stores, and other techniques of distribution which have over two generations greatly increased the degree of competition in, and reduced the costs of the distribution of consumers goods in almost every local market of the United States. Experience proves that the efficient retailer, if he gives good service, can compete with the chain store and make a reasonable profit. There is no ground of public policy for restricting the development of the newer methods of distribution which have so greatly reduced the social cost of distribution in this country.

Unless competition in distribution is preserved and encouraged by law, consumers may well be deprived of most of the advantages of technological progress in production. Retail price maintenance is characteristic of economic practice in Western Europe, and is an important factor in the relatively slow rise in the standard of living of Western European countries. It has been regarded as contrary to the policy of the antitrust laws since Justice Hughes['] celebrated opinion in the Dr. Miles Medical Co. case in 1911. In a long line of cases the Supreme Court has held that devices for retail price maintenance are illegal—and that the overriding policy of the Sherman Act in favor of competition (*Standard Oil Co.* v. *Federal Trade Commission* 71 S. Ct. 240, 249 (1951))[3.68] qualifies and limits even the exception of the Miller-Tydings

---

[3.68] 340 U.S. 231, 248-49, 71 S. Ct. 240, 249, 95 L. Ed. 239, 250 (1951).

amendment, so as to confine it to the narrowest possible ground. (*United States* v. *Bausch & Lomb Optical Co.* 321 U. S. 707 (1944);[3.69] *United States* v. *Frankfort Distilleries, Inc.* 324 U. S. 293 (1945)[3.70]).

Resale price maintenance is incompatible with the principles of a market economy. This is a good time to abolish it. The repeal of the Miller-Tydings amendment now would put the economy into a better position to meet the pressures which future changes in supply and demand relationships may call for more flexibly and more effectively.

Mr. MORSE. Mr. President, I also ask unanimous consent to have printed in the RECORD at this point in my remarks a statement, in opposition to the pending bill, by Wendell Berge, of the District of Columbia bar, former director of the Antitrust Division of the United States Department of Justice.

There being no objection, the statement was ordered to be printed in the RECORD, as follows:

STATEMENT BY WENDELL BERGE BEFORE THE SENATE INTERSTATE AND FOREIGN COMMERCE COMMITTEE ON H. R. 5767, JUNE 4, 1952

For more than 15 years I have had a deep interest in opposing all efforts to nullify the application of the Sherman Act to resale price maintenance agreements. For 10 years I was a member of the staff of the Antitrust Division and later for nearly 4 years was assistant attorney general in charge of that division. As a result of this experience I gained some appreciation of the serious impact of so-called fair-trade laws upon the basic effectiveness of Federal antitrust legislation. The purpose of my appearance today is to add to the record a brief statement of my own convictions on this subject.

I shall not undertake to outline the history of the judicial decisions outlawing resale price maintenance, or of the efforts of the States, goaded on by powerful lobbies, to neutralize these court decisions. Such matters are well known to this committee. Nor is it necessary for me to recite the history of the Miller-Tydings Act which legalized to a limited extent resale price maintenance in interstate commerce. You are fully familiar with the Miller-Tydings Act and its background.

I do want to state, at the outset, that I am opposed to H. R. 5767, which undertakes to make effective in interstate commerce the so-called nonsigner clause which was held ⊥ by the Supreme Court in *Schwegmann Bros.* v. *Calvert Corp.* (341 U. S. 384) not to be authorized by the Miller-Tydings Act.

⊥ 8842

In the early days of the Sherman Act resale price maintenance commonly meant an agreement or agreements between a producer and dealers providing that the dealers would agree to observe prices dictated by the producers. In the leading case of *Dr. Miles Medical Co.* v. *Park & Sons Co.* (220 U. S. 373), the Supreme Court held that such agreements were illegal under the Sherman Act. Later, however, the Court affirmed the right of a producer to refuse to deal with particular dealers provided there was no agreement respecting price maintenance involved. *United States* v. *Colgate & Co.* (250 U. S. 300). This, of course, left the door open to refuse to deal with price cutters in the absence of an agreement to maintain prices. But in *Federal Trade Commission* v. *Beech-Nut Packing Co.* (257 U. S. 441) the Court in effect held that any effort to police retailers to assure that they were observing suggested prices was illegal. Thus, for some years the test of legality seemed to be whether or not on the facts, an agreement to maintain prices or enforcement methods, in the absence of specific agreement, existed.

But there was strong sentiment among manufacturers, particularly those who made and marketed branded products, to seek the right legally through contracts to dictate resale prices. The so-called fair-trade movement started with the first Fair Trade Act passed in California in 1931. This act, however, merely legalized resale price maintenance agreements in intrastate commerce. The really significant fact in the growth of fair-trade legislation came with the development of the so-called nonsigner clause. This clause, as you know, provides that if prices are set by agreement between a manufacturer and a dealer, thereafter all dealers in the State are bound by the dictated price. They do not voluntarily undertake any contractual obligation but, nevertheless, they are bound. California adopted this nonsigner clause in 1933 and thereafter, I believe, all State laws that were enacted contained it. By 1941 45 States had fair-trade laws.

It is my belief that the essentially undemocratic character of the nonsigner clause escaped the attention of the American people until the Schwegmann case last year. I think that many

---

[3.69] 321 U.S. 707, 64 S. Ct. 805, 88 L. Ed. 1024 (1944).
[3.70] 324 U.S. 293, 65 S. Ct. 661, 89 L. Ed. 951 (1945).

people believed that the policy of resale price maintenance might be a debatable policy, but they thought of it in terms merely of legalizing voluntary agreements between producers and dealers. Many people felt that resale-price maintenance in any form was an inadvisable restraint because it prevented competition on the dealer level. A series of resale-price maintenance contracts could have the same effect so far as dealer competition was concerned as horizontal agreements between dealers fixing prices. And, of course, such horizontal agreements were illegal per se under numerous court decisions applying to the Sherman Act.

But it occurs to me that in most of the policy discussion the importance, and the basically undemocratic character of the nonsigner clause, was overlooked. Not only had the type of resale-price maintenance condemned in the Dr. Miles case been legalized by the State fair-trade laws, but under those laws dealers having no desire to be brought into a system of resale-price maintenance or any economic interest in participating, were legally forced to accept it at the risk of losing their product, and in some instances at the risk of criminal prosecution. Thus, by the simple act of making a contract with a single dealer in a State a producer could force every dealer in that State to accept and abide by the dictated price. No more effective way of eliminating price competition on the dealer level can be imagined.

As Alfred Friendly, a reporter for the Washington Post, stated in an article in the Post last Sunday, June 1, 1952:

"Thus, if one manufacturer of a trade-marked item agreed with one retailer of the item in Maryland that the article will be sold for $1 at retail, no other retailer in the Free State could sell it for less than $1, regardless of whether he approved the contract price or not.

"It is self-evident, of course, that such an agreement—and the law that would permit it—is exactly 180 degrees opposite the philosophy and spirit of the national antitrust policy.

"The bill is advanced ostensibly to protect small business, the heart and essence of the free enterprise system. Yet it would deny small businesses all opportunities to act freely in their main field of action, price. They would remain not independent retailers, but would become conduits for disposal of a manufacturer's product, at the price the manufacturer sets, without leeway to attract customers by lower prices, or to convert what economies and efficiencies they develop into lower prices and higher volume."

The fair-trade movement grew rapidly in the 1930's but its effectiveness was impaired by the fact that fair-trade contracts were not valid in interstate commerce. Hence the movement to amend the Sherman Act which resulted in the Miller-Tydings Act.

As Assistant Attorney General Morison has pointed out, all that the Miller-Tydings Act did was to amend section 1 of the Sherman Act to provide that vertical minimum price fixing contracts shall not be in violation of the antitrust laws or the Federal Trade Commission Act when such contracts involve: (1) Trade-marked or branded commodities, (2) which are in competition with other similar commodities, and (3) when such contracts are valid under the State law of the place of resale.

Thus, as he says, the act speaks only in terms of "contracts or agreements" and makes no reference to nonsigners. In *Schwegmann Bros. v. Calvert Corp.* (341 U. S. 384), decided May 1951, the Supreme Court held that persons not parties to agreements establishing minimum resale prices are not bound by those agreements even though the State of resale does have a law binding nonsigners. The Court pointed out that the Miller-Tydings Act sanctions contracts or agreements between a distributor and one or more retailers to fix minimum prices, if State law permits, but added:

"When they seek, however, to impose price fixing on persons who have not contracted or agreed to the scheme, the situation is vastly different. That is not price fixing by contract or agreement; that is price fixing by compulsion. That is not following the path of consensual agreement; that is resort to coercion."

The Court also stated that when a State compels retailers to follow a parallel-price policy, it demands private conduct which the Sherman Act forbids. After examining the legislative history of the Miller-Tydings Act, the Court went on to say that "we cannot find that the distributors were to have the right to use not only a contract to fix retail prices but a club as well."

I think that the Schwegmann case is absolutely sound, and it is surprising that the point was not raised until nearly 15 years after the enactment of the Miller-Tydings Act.

Let us consider the real significance of the nonsigner clause. Whether the economic reason for utilizing the clause in a particular case is pressure from the dealers or from the manufacturer, the effect, once the clause has been adopted in a single contract, is to put the whole retail industry of a given State under absolute price dictation. There is no factor in such a situation to protect the public interest. Competition does not operate to protect the public interest because competition is eliminated by the nonsigner clause. There is no public representative in the transaction to protect the public interest as in the case of Government price regulation.

We are all familiar with the tendency of American businessmen to resent price regulation—the constant lashing at the old Office of Price Administration and the present Office of Price

Stabilization. Any regulatory agency that undertakes to set prices is in for a tough time. And yet, those public regulatory agencies that have taken such a beating have been agencies of the Federal Government whose powers are subject to termination by Congress and whose every act is subject to public accountability. They operate under standards laid down by congressional authority.

But all such factors to protect the public are absent in a scheme of price regulation in which the ultimate santion is the nonsigner clause. The price may or may not be reasonable. But it is imposed on a whole retail industry by a single contract to which most of the retail industry is not a party. There is no administrative or judicial review as to the fairness of price. It is hard to imagine a more absolute form of economic dictatorship.

Although the original impetus for fair-trade legislation came from manufacturers interested in protecting their brand names, the chief interest shifted and the later pressure for fair-trade legislation has come largely from the organized retail groups who saw in this device a means of legally eliminating price competition. Thus there have been many instances where retail interests have employed their combined power to coerce manufacturers to give them fair-trade contracts. This coercion has not infrequently been accompanied by threat of boycott.

But, on the other hand, the retailers themselves may often suffer by the enforcement of prices imposed by the manufacturers which require such a low margin of profit that the retailers cannot profitably operate. With the vast power of national advertising a manufacturer can build up such good will for a particular product that a retailer must carry such product whether or not he desires to do so. There are, for example, in the drug field many products where national advertising has created a good will for a particular brand name that is not possessed by other competing products of fully equal merit. The local druggist must carry the product which has the benefit of national advertising. Under fair-trade contracts containing nonsigner clauses, the manufacturer can, in effect, force the retailer to handle these nationally advertised brands at a ridiculously small margin of profit or even at no profit at all.

The present bill, it should be noted, not only permits the manufacturer to dictate minimum prices but it also permits him to prescribe stipulated prices if such are authorized by State law. This provision could well work against the interest of the retailer. Thus, one manufacturer and one retailer could agree upon a stipulated price—that is a maximum as well as a minimum—which would apply to all retailers.

Under this provision, suppose that a manufacturer find [sic] one big cut-rate drug store willing to operate on a very small margin of profit and contracts that a certain vitamin capsule product shall sell at a stipulated price of $2.98 per bottle. That price then becomes binding upon every druggist in the State. The margin may be much too low for the small druggist to handle the capsules at a profit, but because of the nationally advertised brand name of the product, the small druggist must carry it as a service to his customers and sell it at an unprofitable price.

As Mr. Friendly has said in his article:

"Multiply (such examples) by a few hundred of the brand-name items which every druggist deals in, and the result is obvious: the little fellow goes to the wall, and the cut-rate octopus, against which the bill is supposedly directed, takes over all the business.

"For this reason, and from other evidence (chiefly the contributions of big drug manufacturers to the lobby for the McGuire bill), there is considerable reason to believe that the small druggists have been made the unwitting frontmen for the manufacturers in the lobby campaign."

In a free economy the conflicting interests of the consumer and the retailer find their proper level through the forces of normal competition. It should not be our interest to give the consumer the benefit of products sold at an uneconomically low price nor to give the retailer the benefit of uneconomically high prices. But under fair trade both injustices occur. In some instances the manufacturer uses his power to impose on an industry prices so low as to be unfair to retailers. In other instances the retailers succeed through their organized associational activity in forcing manufacturers to raise prices above a normal competitive level. I understand, for example, that the record before the House committee showed that the National Association of Retail Druggists put on an organized effort to force manufacturers to increase profit margins on certain items, and I assume similar evidence has been or will be produced here.

The proponents of fair-trade legislation have managed to stir up a great deal of emotional sympathy by identifying themselves with the small independent retailer as against the larger so-called predatory chain stores. I hold no brief for the chain stores. Indeed, I was in charge of the Antitrust Division when the action against the Great Atlantic & Pacific Tea Co. was instituted at Danville, Ill. That case was based upon a number of alleged discriminatory and monopolistic practices, and in the criminal action the Government's position was sustained. The civil action is still pending.

But because chain stores may in some instances attain monopolistic proportion in their industry does not demonstrate that our method of retailing must necessarily be frozen in the nineteenth century pattern. There are undoubtedly some economic discriminations enjoyed by certain chain operations, especially when they exceed a certain point in expansion, that must be neutralized by legislation. But it is my opinion that the independent retailers are barking up the wrong tree when they seek to impose compulsory vertical price control upon a large segment of American industry in their effort to overcome what they believe to be the unfair advantage of other forms of distribution.

For example, it is a well-known fact that the resale price maintenance of branded goods is wholly ineffective as against the larger chain operations. If a manufacturer undertakes to fix a price on a nationally advertised brand which is distasteful to a large chain operation, that chain has the facilities to introduce new brands at its own price and the power to advertise them in competition with the older established brand. The small independent druggist is often dependent, as I have previously pointed out, upon nationally advertised brands and must handle them at whatever price is dictated. But the chain store can introduce its own brand at a cheaper price and exert all its sales effort on behalf of its own brand. I am sure that plenty of economic testimony could be introduced to the effect that resale price maintenance is ineffective in neutralizing certain advantages of chain stores.

A great deal of the complaint of the proponents of the McGuire bill is against so-called loss-leader practices. They contend that the McGuire bill, or legislation similar to it, is necessary to stop loss-leader sales which they claim injure the good will of a product and also result in unfair competition on the retail level.

I am not going to question that the McGuire bill would, if enacted into law and vigorously enforced, eliminate loss-leader sales in respect to the commodities to which the bill would apply. But I contend that it goes much further than is necessary to eliminate loss-leader sales. In order to stop this practice of loss-leader sales, you do not need to throw the baby out with the bath; you do not need to eliminate all price competition at the retail level. The problem of loss-leader sales should be dealt with separately, as such. Perhaps it could be done by the Federal Trade Commission under existing law or, if necessary, by adding specific provisions to the Federal Trade Commission law dealing with the subject of loss-leader sales.

But I am also impressed with a bill introduced in the House of Representatives on March 11, 1952, by Chairman CELLER, of the House Committee on the Judiciary. I refer to H. R. 6986, a bill to amend the Clayton Act and the Sherman Act for the purpose of prohibiting loss-leader sales. I am attaching a copy of that bill as an appendix to this statement but I shall not read it. In summary, the bill would add a new section to the Clayton Act which would define the term "loss-leader practices" to mean selling a commodity, or advertising or offering a commodity for sale at retail below the delivered cost of the commodity to the seller except that it does not include any of the following sales, or any advertisement or offer in connection therewith:

(a) Any sale for the bona fide purpose of discontinuing dealing in such commodity or of discontinuing the seller's business, when plain notice of that fact is given.

(b) Any sale of commodities which are substantially damaged or deteriorated, when plain notice of that fact is given.

(c) Any sale by officers acting under order of the court.

(d) Any sale to any association organized and operated exclusively for religious, charitable, scientific, literary, or educational purposes or for prevention of cruelty to children or animals.

(e) Any sale of a perishable commodity if further retention by the seller could be expected to result in loss.

(f) Any sale which reasonable business practices require a seller to make in order to liquidate an inventory of a commodity to avoid insolvency or bankruptcy.

(g) Any seasonal clearance sale made in accordance with customary business practices in order to dispose of excess inventory.

Any loss-leader practice which affects commerce is then declared to be unlawful and actionable at the suit of any person damaged thereby. Such person is given a right to sue for treble damages in the district courts of the United States, as provided in section 4 of the Clayton Act.

The above are the principal provisions of the Celler bill, but there are subsidiary provisions which may be examined by reading the bill in full.

In addition, section 2 of the Celler bill is to my mind very important in that it repeals the Miller-Tydings Act by amending section 1 of the Sherman Act so as to restore the text of section 1 as it existed before the Miller-Tydings amendment of August 17, 1937. I think there is no need for the Miller-Tydings Act, especially if the complaints against loss-leader sales can be met.

I think that time has demonstrated that the Miller-Tydings Act was a mistake. It has tended to make price competition less effective at the retail level. If we believe in competition as the primary regulator of price, and if we believe in passing economies in distribution on to the consumer, then there is no more reason why price competition should be eliminated at the retail level than at the wholesale or manufacturing level. If, on the other hand, we believe in eliminating competition at the retail level, why should we not be consistent and permit horizontal agreements between competitors, not only eliminating price competition, but competition in other matters, such as the rendering of service.

I hope that a bill similar to the Celler bill will be introduced in the Senate and that it will be given preferred consideration. I also hope that no final action is taken on the McGuire bill until a Senate bill similar to the Celler bill is considered and disposed of. I think that if a bill similar to the Celler bill is enacted, it will eliminate any necessity for further consideration of the McGuire bill.

There are several details concerning the McGuire bill which should be briefly noted. Although the Miller-Tydings Act only legalizes agreements prescribing minimum prices, the McGuire bill also applies to stipulated prices; in other words, specific or maximum prices as well as minimum prices.

The McGuire bill does not purport to be a direct amendment of the Miller-Tydings Act (which, in turn, was an amendment to section 1 of the Sherman Antitrust Act), yet the effect of the McGuire bill is to create an immunity greater than that of the Miller-Tydings Act itself, since the McGuire bill legalizes agreements relating to stipulated prices in or affecting interstate or foreign commerce.

Indeed, if one wanted to be critical of procedural matters, this method of amending the Sherman Act indirectly through an amendment to the Federal Trade Commission Act is subject to criticism. The Schwegmann case rested on an interpretation of the meaning of the Miller-Tydings amendment to the Sherman Act: the case held that such amendment did not legalize the nonsigner clause. The McGuire bill is solely an attempt to nullify the Schwegmann decision. Why did the lobby not seek to amend the act which was involved in the Schwegmann decision—the Miller-Tydings Act? Instead, the McGuire bill is directed to the Federal Trade Commission Act and reaches the Miller-Tydings amendment to the Sherman Act only by reciting in the language amending the Federal Trade Commission Act, that "nothing contained in this [Federal Trade Commission] act or in any of the antitrust acts shall render unlawful et cetera." That is certainly a back-handed method of cutting down the Sherman Act.

In conclusion, I want to call attention to the fact that practically all the newspapers of the country which have commented on this matter have opposed this and similar bills. There has been repeated strong editorial comment from at least three of the four Washington papers. The same can be said for newspapers in many other cities. In addition, there have been many consumer organizations, authorities in law and economics from faculties of many of our leading colleges and universities, and many other experts in the field of price economics who have testified against this bill, or signed letters and public statements opposing the bill.

So far as I know, there has been no support for this bill except from special interests who think they would benefit from the enactment of the bill. I am not aware that any independent experts have testified in favor of the bill in either the House committee hearing or here.

I am sure that the committee must be in receipt of resolutions, petitions, and the like, from groups of citizens who are interested ⊥ in opposing this measure simply from the viewpoint of ⊥ 8844 the public good. Informed consumers everywhere are against this bill, but we are all aware that consumers as a group are not highly organized or articulate, certainly not in comparison with the National Association of Retail Druggists or the American Fair Trade Council.

I urge that this committee and the Senate of the United States not be stampeded by high-pressure lobby tactics into approving a bill so obviously against the public interest.

TEXT OF THE CELLER BILL, H. R. 6986, AS INTRODUCED IN THE HOUSE OF REPRESENTATIVES MARCH 11, 1952

A bill to amend the act entitled "An act to supplement existing laws against unlawful restraints and monopolies, and for other purposes," approved October 15, 1914, and to amend the act entitled "An act to protect trade and commerce against unlawful restraints and monopolies," approved July 2, 1890, for the purpose of prohibiting loss-leader sales

Be it enacted, etc., That the act entitled "An act to supplement existing laws against unlawful restraints and monopolies, and for other purposes," approved October 15, 1914, is amended by adding at the end thereof the following new section:

"SEC. 27. (a) For the purposes of this section—

"(1) The term 'delivered cost' shall mean invoice cost to a seller less the value of discounts received by a seller in money or the equivalent, plus the cost of transportation incident to delivery to the seller, and plus applicable excise and sales taxes to the seller.

"(2) The term 'seller' shall mean a vendee, as used in this act, who purchases for resale.

"(3) The term 'loss-leader practice' shall mean selling a commodity, or advertising or offering a commodity for resale at retail at a price below the delivered cost of the commodity to the seller except that it does not include any of the following sales, or any advertisement or offer in connection therewith:

"(A) Any sale of a commodity for the bona fide purpose of discontinuing dealing in such commodity or of discontinuing the seller's business, when plain notice of that fact is given to the public.

"(B) Any sale of a commodity which is substantially damaged or deteriorated in quality if plain notice of the fact is given to the public.

"(C) Any sale by an officer acting under an order of court.

"(D) Any sale to any association organized and operated exclusively for religious, charitable, scientific, literary, or educational purposes, or for the prevention of cruelty to children or animals, no part of the net earnings of which inures to the benefit of any private shareholder or individual.

"(E) Any sale of a perishable commodity if further retention of the commodity by the seller could reasonably be expected to result in a loss to the seller.

"(F) Any sale which reasonable business practices require the seller to make in order to liquidate an inventory of a commodity to avoid insolvency or bankruptcy.

"(G) Any seasonal clearance sale made in accordance with customary business practices in order to dispose of excess inventory.

"(b) Any loss-leader practice which affects commerce is hereby declared to be unlawful and actionable at the suit of any person damaged thereby.

"(c) (1) Any person injured in his business or property by any loss-leader practice hereby declared to be unlawful may sue therefor in any district court of the United States, as provided in section 4 of this act, or in any State court of competent jurisdiction, and recover threefold the damages by him sustained, and the costs of suit, including a reasonable attorney's fee. Any person threatened with injury by any loss-leader practice shall be entitled to injunctive relief against such threatened injury in any court of the United States, as provided in section 16 of this act, or to sue for and have such relief in any State court of competent jurisdiction when and under the same conditions and principles as injunctive relief against threatened conduct that will cause loss or damage is granted by courts of equity in that State, under the rules governing such proceedings, and upon the execution of proper bond against damages for an injunction improvidently granted and a showing that the danger of irreparable loss or damage is immediate, a preliminary injunction may issue.

"(2) Section 15 of this act (providing for suits by United States district attorneys to restrain violations of this act) shall not apply with respect to any loss-leader practice.

"(d) (1) Nothing contained herein or in any of the antitrust acts shall render illegal any contract or agreement prohibiting a seller from reselling at a price below his delivered cost, any commodity which bears, or the label or container of which bears, the trade-mark, brand, or name of the producer or distributor of such commodity and which is in free and open competition with commodities of the same general class produced or distributed by others, when contracts or agreements prescribing minimum prices are lawful under any statute, law, or public policy now or hereafter in effect in any State, Territory, or the District of Columbia in which such resale is to be made, or to which the commodity is to be transported for such resale, or for delivery to a vendee pursuant to a sale.

"(2) Nothing contained herein or in any of the Antitrust Acts shall render illegal the exercise or enforcement of any right or right of action created by any statute, law, or public policy now or hereafter in effect in any State, Territory, or the District of Columbia, which provides in substance that willfully and knowingly advertising, offering for sale, or selling any commodity at less than the minimum prices prescribed in any such contract or agreement whether the person so advertising, offering for sale, or selling is or is not a party to such contract or agreement, is unfair competition and is actionable at the suit of any person damaged thereby: *Provided, however,* That the rights or right of action created by or under such contracts and agreements shall not apply where the minimum price prescribed in such contract is higher than the delivered cost to the seller: *And provided further,* That the rights or right of action created by or under such contracts and agreements shall not apply to any of the following sales, or advertisement or offer in connection therewith:

"(A) Any sale of a commodity for the bona fide purpose of discontinuing dealing in such commodity or of discontinuing dealing in such commodity [sic] or of discontinuing the seller's business, when plain notice of the fact is given to the public.

"(B) Any sale of a commodity which is substantially damaged or deteriorated in quality if plain notice of the fact is given to the public.

"(C) Any sale by an officer acting under an order of court.

"(D) Any sale to any association organized and operated exclusively for religious, charitable, scientific, literary, or educational purposes, or for the prevention of cruelty to children or animals, no part of the net earnings of which inures to the benefit of any private shareholder or individual.

"(E) Any sale of a perishable commodity if further retention of the commodity by the seller could reasonably be expected to result in a loss to the seller.

"(F) Any sale which reasonable business practices require the seller to make in order to liquidate an inventory of a commodity to avoid insolvency or bankruptcy.

"(G) Any seasonal clearance sale made in accordance with customary business practices in order to dispose of excess inventory."

SEC. 2. That section 1 of the act entitled "An act to protect trade and commerce against unlawful restraints and monopolies," approved July 2, 1890, as amended, is amended to read as follows:

"SECTION 1. Every contract, combination in the form of trust or otherwise, or conspiracy, in restraint of trade or commerce among the several States, or with foreign nations, is hereby declared to be illegal. Every person who shall make any such contract or engage in any such combination or conspiracy shall be deemed guilty of a misdemeanor, and, on conviction thereof, shall be punished by fine not exceeding $5,000, or by imprisonment not exceeding 1 year, or by both said punishments, in the discretion of the court."

Mr. MORSE. Mr. President, I also ask unanimous consent to have printed in the RECORD at this point in my remarks, without my taking the time to read it, a very able memorandum by Corwin D. Edwards, economic consultant of the Department of Justice, in connection with the bill pending before the Senate.

There being no objection, the memorandum was ordered to be printed in the RECORD, as follows:

Department of Justice,
Washington, February 10, 1941.

Memorandum for Assistant Attorney General, Antitrust Division.
Re grounds for the repeal of the Miller-Tydings amendment which authorizes resale price contracts.

The passage of resale price legislation has become a classic example of the use of misrepresentation by a pressure group. Since this group has boasted of its achievements, there is no longer any doubt about what happened. The so-called "fair trade" laws which legalized resale price legislation in the States were drafted and urged by lobbyists for organized retail druggists and were enacted with practically no support from any other source. Druggists were organized under captains, district by district, to bring pressure to bear upon legislators. Care was taken, however, to describe their bill as one generally supported by entire [sic] retail trade of the State. The bill was given the ambiguous and appealing name of "fair trade" law. A systematic effort was made to prevent public hearings and to secure the enactment of the bill without public debate. This effort was successful. There was a public hearing on the bill in only 3 States out of the first 32 in which it was passed, and in one of these the hearing followed the passage. Indeed, there was so little consideration of any kind that, although the original draft of the bill contained a stenographic error which made utter nonsense out of one of the most important provisions, this error appeared without change in the statutes of 11 States before it was caught and corrected. Another stenographic error, not quite so serious, was included in the laws of 17 States. Some members of State legislatures subsequently told consumers' organizations that they did not know what they were voting on.

Meanwhile, every effort was made to throttle public discussion and to intimidate business opposition. In California an aspirin manufacturer was forced by boycott to issue resale price contracts against his will. The druggists' intention to coerce was indicated in the following language: "This aspirin is a sort of Napoleon in the patent-medicine army, but then even the great Frenchman met his Waterloo when the rest of Europe got together, decided that they had enough of ⊥ him, and cooperated against him." In the same State the manufacturer of Pepsodent toothpaste, who had experimented with resale price contracts under the California law, decided to withdraw these contracts, apparently under advice of counsel who believed the contracts violated the antitrust laws. Thereupon the druggists organized a campaign to put Pepsodent under the counter and to switch customers to other brands. This campaign was so effective that the offending company made public apology at a subsequent convention of the National Association of Retail Druggists and, as a token of its contribution, subscribed $25,000 to a fund to lobby for resale price maintenance in other States. On one occasion an expression of opposition to resale price maintenance by the New York Times and the New York World-Telegram led to an effort by organized druggists to demoralize the dealers who distributed these papers, by selling them at less than 3 cents. On another occasion Harper's magazine carried an article against resale price maintenance and thereupon received a letter from a druggists' association in a midwestern city, demanding information as to whether Harper's endorsed the views expressed in the article and indicating that if these views were not repudiated they

⊥ 8845

intended to sell Harper's at a substantial discount, presumably in an effort to create trouble among its distributors. Within the last 2 months the newspaper PM in New York has carried a series of articles against resale price maintenance, and the same tactics of intimidation have been attempted by dealers of PM at less than its customary price. The editors, having more sense of humor than some of the other victims of this policy, ran a photograph of a cut-rate advertisement in a store and gave it the caption "The best bargain in the city."

The campaign of misrepresentation became the basis of the lobbying to amend the Sherman Act. The draft amendment was urged upon Congress with argument [sic] that it did not involve any acceptance of resale-price maintenance as a Federal principle, but merely committed the Congress to the view that if States desired to authorize resale-price maintenance the Federal control over interstate commerce should not stand in the way. The State laws were described as though they consisted merely in grants of authority for manufacturer and retailer to agree upon the resale price of branded goods. Actually, there is not one of the State statutes which is limited to such a grant. A statute of that kind was tried in California, and proved to be a miserable failure because many retailers would not sign such contracts. All of the State laws now provide that when a manufacturer and retailer sign a resale-price contract all other retailers who have notice of the contract price must refrain from selling below that price. In other words, these State laws give to manufacturer and retailer the right to coerce the retailer's competitors by fixing the resale price of these competitors against their will. There is no provision for public hearing, for standards in the establishment of the price, for any process of appeal of the nonsigner, or any other safeguard such as is always included in a plan for price fixing by public authority. (The State of Wisconsin is an exception to this rule. Its law provides that the State may set aside contracts which establish unreasonable price [sic].) Thus, the price-fixing power granted to private individuals by State laws is far greater than that which any Federal public official may exercise. Moreover, many of the State laws empower the contracting parties not only to fix minimum prices but to prevent the giving of premiums, to control various other terms of sale, and to require the purchaser in his turn to fix minimum prices if he resells. It is doubtful that half the Members of Congress who voted to amend the Sherman Act were aware that State laws in question granted authority broader than the fixation of a minimum price.

The Senate and the very text of the amendment demonstrate that those who amended the Sherman Act had been misinformed about the status of nonsigners under the State laws. The amendment explicitly prohibits agreements between retailers to fix minimum resale prices. Yet in practical effect such agreements would not be as severe a restraint upon competition as a grant of power to a single retailer to make an agreement with a manufacturer which then becomes binding upon all other retailers. When persons are bound by law, they do not need to be bound by contract. It is inconceivable that Congress would have enacted the prohibition upon agreements if it had intended to sanction coercion. Indeed, the report of the Senate Committee on the Judiciary concerning this amendment, which was later incorporated in the majority report of District of Columbia [sic] upon the appropriation bill to which the amendment was attached as a rider, described the State resale-price laws merely as statutes to authorize resale-price contracts, and added:

"The States acts are in no sense general price-fixing acts. They merely authorize a manufacturer or producer to enter contracts for the maintenance of his price, but they do not compel him to do so. In other words they are merely permissive. They do not authorize horizontal contracts, that is to say, contracts or agreements between manufacturers, between producers, or between wholesalers, or between retailers as to the sale or resale price of any commodity."

If this committee had been informed that the State laws require every retailer to maintain the same price upon a commodity covered by a contract, it could not in candor have described these laws as merely permissive nor have emphasized the point that horizontal agreements among retailers were not authorized.

It is noteworthy that the advocates of the Miller-Tydings amendment were unable to pass it as a separate bill and eventually secured its enactment by attaching it as a rider to the appropriation bill for the District of Columbia. In signing the bill, the President described this method of enactment as a vicious practice, said that he hesitated to approve the rider which weakened the antitrust laws, and expressed the hope that the bill "will not be as harmful as most people predict."

The campaign of misrepresentation has continued since the amendment of the Sherman Act. Although Congress was told that it was not being asked to express a view upon the merits of resale price maintenance as such, but merely to liberate the States to follow their own policy, it has ever since been told by the same lobbyists that in amending the Sherman Act it did express approval of resale price maintenance and that therefore it is inconsistent in refusing to pass a bill establishing resale price maintenance in the District of Columbia. But a campaign of misrepresentation becomes increasingly difficult as time passes; thus far no such bill has been passed.

Resale price maintenance has failed in both of its mutually conflicting announced purposes. When the State laws were tested in the Federal courts, they were represented as statutes which allowed a manufacturer to protect the good will attaching to a brand by making contracts concerning the resale price of articles carrying the brand. Thus described, the bill is intended to defend the manufacturers' property rights. Actually this interpretation of the bill was mere pretense. In the words of the counsel for the Illinois Pharmaceutical Association, "the fair-trade movement is a retailers' show, with a manufacturers' sign or label over it." The bill originated with retailers, was backed by a retailers' lobby, was passed by retailers' pressure, and has been used by retailers to force the issuance of contracts whether the manufacturer wants them or not. Retail organizations in the drug trade and elsewhere have used white lists of manufacturers issuing contracts, and black lists of manufacturers who do not, in an endeavor to coerce those manufacturers who are reluctant. Repeatedly the officials of retail drug organizations have had to urge their own members not to be too hasty in boycotting manufacturers who announce retail prices lower than the retailer thinks satisfactory. Most manufacturers using resale price contracts would rejoice at the opportunity to get rid of the so-called protection of their property which these contracts afford. They would like to control their own sales policy rather than have it dictated to them by organized retail groups.

A different purpose for the statutes was urged upon Congress and State legislators. They were told that resale price maintenance contracts were necessary to enable the small independent retailer to survive against the competition of the large chain. The legislation was presented as a part of the effort to defend little business and to avert monopoly in retailing. Actually this announcement of purpose involved a mixture of misrepresentation and self-deception. In the first place, though the independent retailer may be threatened in some industries, he was not actually threatened in the drug trade. The number of independent retail druggists was increasing during the period when the plight of the independent was being urged on behalf of this legislation. The average life of an independent drug store is greater than that of almost any other kind of retail store. The mark-up realized upon drug products is higher than that of almost any other kind of retail store. The mark-up realized upon drug products is higher than that upon other fast-moving retail lines, so much so that organized retail druggists are now trying to prevent the handling of packaged drugs by grocery stores which are attracted by the relatively high margin upon this merchandise. The statistics of the drug trade make it clear that there never was a major problem of the survival of the small druggist. Hence it has not been surprising to discover that the whole effort to represent the resale price maintenance laws as measurers [sic] directed against chain stores was a deliberate perversion of fact. The chains themselves supported these laws, although they were very careful to keep themselves in the background. There was no campaign of chain store opposition similar to the campaign against the taxation of chain stores. Instead, the secretary of the National Association of Chain Drug Stores testified before committees of the House and Senate in favor of the Miller-Tydings amendment.

Subsequent experience has made it clear that resale price legislation is admirably designed to further the interests of the drug chains. In their early days, when they were seeking a foothold, some of these chains were fond of cutting prices upon national brands. Once they became established, however, they lost interest in this kind of price cutting. They could draw trade by the prestige of their name and the size of their stock. Desiring a reputation for low prices, they continued their price cuts upon some items and particularly upon products which were allowing an unusually large retail mark-up. But the managers of the chains were afraid of the small independent cut-rate stores, sometimes described in the trade as pineboard stores, which sold fast-moving drugs [sic] items at a very low mark-up, with a minimum expenditure for rent, store decoration, and the arts of salesmanship. We have in Washington, for example, at least on [sic] independent cut-rate store which sells packaged drugs much more cheaply than any chain. ⊥ Indeed it sells so cheaply that one of the chains which established a competing store near ⊥ 8846 this independent in an effort to drive it out of business was careful not to use its own chain name upon this competing store. Parenthetically, it is reported that to the chain's surprise and embarrassment its own cut-rate establishment, expecting to lose money while driving out the independent, has actually made money at the same low level of prices.

Resale price maintenance has served the chains in two ways: first, it has relieved them from the competition of the pineboard independent and thus protected them from the newest and most effective channel through which fast moving packaged drugs can reach the consumer at low prices. Second, it has enabled the chains to organize a low-price raid against any independent drug store without fear of retaliation. This second effect is due to the recognition which chains have established for their own private brands. With national brands of drug products price controlled, the chain can collect substantial margins [sic] upon such products while reducing the price of its own private brands whenever it desires to use them as leaders or to make a raid upon the national brand business enjoyed by other stores. Since these other stores are bound not to cut prices upon the national brands and do not control private brands which have acquired prestige through extensive advertising, retaliation by the victims is not possible. Thus the most obvious effect of resale price maintenance upon the relations between chain and independent is to deprive the independent of a price cutting weapon still available to the chain. The complacency with which chains have accepted the operation of the State laws is no doubt partially due to this fact.

The actual effects of resale price maintenance have been those which are to be expected from private price fixing conspiracies unregulated by public authority, whether or not they enjoy the sanction of law. Some of these effects were summarized by Mr. Isador Lubin, Commissioner of Labor Statistics and a member of the Temporary National Economic Committee, in a letter transmitting to the chairman of the Committee Monograph No. 1, entitled "Price Behavior and Business Policy." Mr. Lubin said:

"This report indicates that there are certain important rigidities in retail prices, which prevent them from being reduced freely, and to which this Committee may well direct its attention. I refer to the so-called fair-trade laws which have been enacted by 44 States and to the Miller-Tydings Enabling Act which legalizes resale price maintenance contracts in interstate commerce. I refer also to the Unfair Practices Acts which are on the statute books of about half the States and which, while purporting merely to prohibit sales below cost, seem to lend themselves to highly restrictive activities. Further, in some lines of trade, particularly in certain drugs, there appear to be unduly wide margins between the cost of ingredients, the sale price at wholesale, and the price to the consumer."

The report by the Bureau of Labor Statistics, like other impartial studies, indicates that resale price contracts have hurt the consumer. Pineboards, chains, and independents which were operating under the pressure of competition in the downtown areas of large cities have raised their prices very substantially. The consumer who cannot afford high mark-ups upon drug items, or who is willing to seek out the most economical source of supply, has lost his opportunity to save money. Outlying drug stores which enjoy a neighborhood monopoly have often found it worth while to cut their prices slightly in order to announce that they are not being undersold.

Druggists determine the amount of selling effort they will spend upon a product in the light of the size of the operating margin which the manufacturer is willing to establish between his wholesale price and his fixed resale price; and under this pressure, manufacturers have begun to bid for business by raising the retailer's margin. The pages of the drug journals contain advertisements by some manufacturers calling attention to the fact that their contract resale prices guarantee operating margins as high as 50 and 60 percent of the retail price. Upon most products the margins are not as great; but many margins are probably lower than those which will be eventually established, for the officials of the retail organizations have frankly recognized that the safest way to raise prices is in a series of small increases spread over a period of time.

Naturally, higher margins have increased the profits of the drug business and already the druggists have begun to worry about the handling of drug items by grocery stores and about an increase in the number of drug stores. In Massachusetts, a State law which formerly required the State to grant a drug license upon proof of proper qualifications was recently changed to make it optional with the State authorities whether they will grant such a license, and the reason for the change was said to be a desire to limit the number of druggists. Organized retailers are seeking to make it unlawful for packaged drugs to be handled except through drug stores. The alternative is plain—either outsiders will push into the business of selling drugs until, in spite of his sheltered position, the druggist loses in average volume of sales what he has gained in wider margins, or else further steps will be taken to give a limited group of retail establishments a vested right to profits. Whichever happens, druggists who are blocked from competing with each other on a basis of price will be forced to compete by carrying larger stocks, displaying goods more lavishly, and thus raising the actual cost of distribution. The consumer is sure to lose; in the long run it is doubtful that the druggist will gain.

Resale price contracts have also been used widely in the gasoline industry, the liquor industry, the tobacco industry, and in bookselling, and sporadically in the sale of household appliances, musical instruments, and jewelry. In Ohio they have been used to prevent competition by retailers in selling certain kinds of food. It is still too early to see how much of American industry such contracts may eventually cover.

The economic grounds for repeal of the Miller-Tydings amendment are clear in the foregoing discussion. They are set forth in greater detail in appendix C, which contains a part of a speech which I made in 1939 before the American Economic Association. In addition there are persuasive legal reasons for repeal. The amendment has encouraged flagrant violations of the Sherman Act which it does not actually sanction. This situation is a consequence of the misrepresentations already described. When Congress passed the Miller-Tydings Act, the great body of retailers in the drug industry supposed that they had been given congressional authority to get together to fix resale prices and to force the reluctant into line. Actually they had been given no such authority. The facts had been misrepresented to Congress, and Congress had passed a statute which granted what had been asked for but not what was actually wanted. The gap between what is lawful and what is being done under the color of law has been visible ever since. Congress forbade competitors to get together to fix resale prices, extending its sanction to vertical but not to horizontal price fixing. In practice it is nearly always impossible for one manufacturer to establish a system of vertical price fixing unless he can be sure that his competitors will do likewise; and a single price-fixed commodity is exposed to the inroads of competing commodities when these articles can be sold for less than the fixed price. Consequently, horizontal collusion in violation of the law has been an indispensable part of the movement for resale price maintenance. Wholesalers' and retailers' committees have sought to force all competing manufacturers to issue contracts and have set up systems for the review and approval of contracts issued. The effort to keep nonsigners in line has been a collective undertaking of the competitors of those nonsigners, many of whom were nonsigners themselves. Although Manufacturer Jones and Manufacturer Smith cannot agree with each other about prices without violating the Sherman Act, they have found a ready means of evasion by which each makes an identical agreement with Retailer Brown. If the Antitrust Division had the men and the money to examine every resale price contract which has been written under the cloak of State and Federal legislation, and to proceed in every case in which the arrangement goes beyond the authorizations of the Miller-Tydings amendment, there would be no resale price problem, for there would be practically no resale price contracts. In the absence of such wholesale law enforcement, the system of resale price legislation has become a breeding ground for restraints of trade such as Congress never intended to sanction and did not sanction.

Attached as appendix A is a detailed statement concerning the limitations involved in the Miller-Tydings amendment and the various devices prevalent under resale price maintenance which typically violate the Sherman Act as amended. Such devices are prevalent in the issuance and enforcement of most resale price contracts.

There is also attached as appendix B a copy of recent [sic] decision by the Court of Appeals of Ohio, throwing out one resale price case because of collusion not contemplated in the statute. This case illustrates the fact that even the State laws, which enforce an effectual collusion among retailers, do not sanction the collusion among producers or wholesalers which is actually generated by such legislation. Although this proceeding also illustrates the fact that nonsigners have a remedy at law with which to defend themselves against collusive arrangements by those who supply them, it is neither practical nor fair to depend upon the ability of a small retailer to uncover such price-fixing conspiracies and to carry the burden of legal costs necessary to deal with them.

The simplest and most effective way to restore competition in such cases is to repeal the Miller-Tydings amendment. Such action would not strengthen the chains against the independents—indeed, it might have the opposite effect. It would not threaten the existence or the prosperity of independents as a group, for these were not in jeopardy when the act was passed and are not in jeopardy now. It would restore competition in retailing, destroy the unlawful monopolies and restraints of trade which now use this amendment as a pretext for their existence, and make it once more possible for the ingenuity of American business to decrease the charge to the consumer for the distribution of goods.

Corwin D. Edwards,
Economic Consultant.

Mr. MORSE. Mr. President, certainly there is one article I wish all Members of the Senate had time to read before voting on this bill, though I know the time is not going to be available to them. Nevertheless, it ought to be in the RECORD. It is a very fine article entitled "A Chance for Really Fair Trade," which was published in the March 1952 issue of Fortune magazine. I ask unanimous consent that the article be printed in the RECORD, at this point in my remarks.

There being no objection, the article was ordered to be printed in the RECORD, as follows:

A CHANCE FOR REALLY FAIR TRADE

Hearings have begun in Washington on several bills to restore the so-called fair-trade laws, which the Supreme Court knocked out in the Schwegmann decision handed down last May. That decision, it will be recalled, touched off some spectacular price wars, mostly in New York and mostly centering around Macy's, a bitter and articulate foe of legalized price fixing. For six giddy weeks consumers had a field day and then the wars petered out.

Whether Macy's was as wise as it was smart remains to be seen, for the big spree provided the powerful fair-trade lobbyists with precisely the ammunition they needed to mobilize congressional sentiment behind new and holeproof legislation. The American Fair Trade Council (the manufacturers' group) and the National Association of Retail Druggists began pamphleteering for a new Federal law that would restore the nonsigner clause, the heart of the whole fair-trade controversy. Their strategy was to introduce a new bill in Congress just before it adjourned in October and then put the heat on the local Congressmen as soon as they set foot in their home districts. With 22 NARD lawyers guilding [*sic*] his hand, Congressman JOHN A. MCGUIRE, Connecticut Democrat, completed H. R. 5676 last October 17. Actually, Congressmen MORANO and POULSON had each introduced a fair-trade bill in June, but when these were referred to Judiciary, chairmaned by anti-fair-trader EMANUEL CELLER, no great things were expected of them. The McGuire bill was designed for introduction into the more sympathetic Interstate and Foreign Commerce Committee.

The fair traders went right back to the grass roots, or as their campaign guide for fair trade counseled them, to "where the bodies are." The homeward-bound Senators and Representatives got the full treatment. Their local offices were deluged with some of the 150,000 pieces of background literature mailed out by the Bureau of Education on Fair Trade. In hundreds of personal contacts with their old friend, the druggist, or the friends of that old friend, they were told that the fate of little businessmen everywhere depended on fair trade, that the drugstore was an American forum to be cherished as one should cherish liberty itself, and that the consumer must be protected from the depredations of the price cutter. The success of the 12-week program may be summed up in the words of one Senator not so safely back in Washington. Asked whether he would vote against fair trade, his comment was: "I don't bleed good."

THE HEART OF THE MATTER

Why is it that the fair traders have no difficulty whatever in mustering formidable political support, while the arguments against fair-trade legislation can apparently be swept aside or ignored with political impunity? Fair trade is bad economics, bad law, and bad politics. Fair-trade legislation clearly violates the spirit of the Sherman Antitrust Act, which law carries immense magic with the voters. It is legislation that runs completely counter to the pocketbook interests of the voter as consumer. It is true that the neighborhood druggist occupies a unique place in the hearts of Americans. He is a local institution to which Americans are willing to trust their children, their health, and their troubles. But there just are not enough votes in the independent druggists and other interested small retailers to account for the indisputable political pressure behind fair trade. Is there some uncorrected abuse, some deeply felt fear, that fair trade satisfies, however awkwardly?

The easy answer is, of course, that small business is being threatened, and the small-business man is a universally appealing American symbol. The small retailer, and the neighborhood druggist in particular, did take a terrible beating during the great depression. The Miller-Tydings Act, the basis for the State fair-trade acts, was essentially a depression measure to meet a depression situation. It is extremely unlikely that we will see in our lifetime anything comparable to the thirties.

A repetition of last June's fancy price cutting also seems unlikely. Manufacturers have been busy signing individual resale price agreements with retailers and even Macy's has been forced to accept them in order to get certain brands of merchandise. (Sunbeam showed how serious it was about price maintenance by filing a $6,000,000 triple-damage suit against Macy's, charging that the store had unlawfully restrained trade by using mixmasters as loss leaders.) The economics of retailing seemed as well behaved without "fair trade" as "fair traders" claimed it had been with it.

But if the driving force behind "fair trade" is a mystery, at least there is nothing obscure about what needs to be done. Opposition to "fair trade" legislation should center on one thing and one thing only. That is the provision by which a price-maintenance contract between a manufacturer and one retailer is binding on all retailers in the same State who sell the product. No one can take exception to a manufacturer's right to police his own distribution. But to appeal to the Government for assistance in policing a price structure is bad political theory. To coerce a retailer into a contract he has never seen, let alone signed, is bad law. Giving special protection to a special group is not exactly new in United States history but that does not alter the fact that it is bad economics.

WHAT'S THE ALTERNATIVE?

As matters now stand, "fair trade" seems likely to pass this spring, or perhaps it will slip through in the something-for-everybody days just before the July conventions. The Celler committee began hearings February 13 on three pro "fair trade" bills and one against it. The Celler hearings, as announced, were to be all-inclusive with testimony both for and against "fair trade" by the most competent experts. Meanwhile, however, the Interstate Committee, at the prodding of the druggists, had announced hearings on the McGuire bill 9 days earlier than those of the Celler committee.

The druggists' tactics, obviously, are to rush the McGuire bill through the Interstate Committee before the Celler committee has had a chance to complete its hearings. The affair is strongly reminiscent of a previous stratagem when they slipped the original "fair trade" statute (the Miller-Tydings Act) through Congress by attaching it as a rider to an appropriations bill.

In the event the McGuire bill is favorably reported by Interstate, and gets past the Rules Committee, the opponents of price fixing are afraid that legislative timidity will permit passage notwithstanding the logic brought to bear against it. Such an eventuality has even produced a backstage split in the ranks of the Federal Trade Commission, once of a single mind on how to combat "fair trade." Part of the staff is still in uncompromising opposition; but an equal important number, though still opposed to "fair trade" as such, are murmuring about "politics being the art of the possible." Since permanent prohibition of "fair trade" seems politically impossible to them, they hope to work out a compromise.

Briefly, their proposition is to provide small business with special protection by rewriting section 2 (b) of the Robinson-Patman Act so that loss-leader selling by producers would be illegal even though prices were cut "in good faith" to meet competition. With loss leaders thus prevented at the producer level, the policing of loss-leader selling at the distributor level could be handled by triple-damage civil suits.

Unfortunately the remedy in this instance is almost as bad as the disease. The Supreme Court, in the Standard Oil of Indiana case, has already confirmed the right of a producer to price-cut, even though injury to competition might result, if the cut is motivated in good faith by a desire to meet the price of a competitor. Prevention of this competition among producers in order to forestall a bill that would restrict competition among distributors is merely robbing Peter to pay Paul.

RECIPE FOR PRICE CUTTING

The way to handle the predatory price cutter—and there is such a species, if increasingly rare—is through enforcement of the Federal Trade Commission Act, Robinson-Patman Act, the Sherman Act, by individual non-statutory agreements, and through civil suit brought by manufacturers, not by a statutory price-fixing scheme, which rides roughshod over all dissenters. If more is needed, now is the time to investigate and establish clearly the need. But the fact that the original Miller-Tydings Act was passed as a rider, the fact that the new bill is being hurried through with unseemly speed, does not make for confidence in the validity of the legislation.

The truth is that the small retailer, particularly the druggist, would do better to channel his energies and enthusiasm away from pseudo-panaceas like fair trade and into new marketing methods. He needs to become, as Prof. Joseph Klamon of St. Louis' Washington University put it, "less margin-conscious and more volume-conscious." A fixed set of minimum prices will not, for example, neutralize the competition of the joint grocery-and-drug store. These really formidable competitors operated on the sound belief that the housewife (if given the opportunity) will buy drugs along with her daily food purchases, are increasing in number. Chain food stores are putting in drug counters and chain drugstores are opening complete food sections. The 85-store Owl Drug chain has three on the west coast and its sister subsidiary, Liggets (125 outlets), will shortly experiment with two in the East. The time seems to be approaching when everyone will sell everything. The best defense for the small druggist is keener merchandising, continued reliance on service, the extension of credit, and convenience of location.

Through all the oratory that beclouds rather than illuminates the status of the American small retailer, one fact is clear. The fair traders have never been able to prove that price competition has caused more merchant bankruptcies in non-fair-trade States than in those where prices are policed. Under the circumstances they would render a service to their colleagues, themselves, and the free-enterprise system by combatting the merchants' real antagonists—low volume, lack of mobility, inertia.

Mr. MORSE. Mr. President, if I were to be limited to but one source material in opposition to this bill, and if I were told, "That is all you are going to have time to read," in order to get the main reasons for saying that the bill should not be passed, I would select the very able statement of Dr. Joseph M. Klamon, professor of marketing, School of Business and Public Administration, Washington University, St. Louis, Mo., made before the Senate Committee on Interstate and Foreign Commerce, on June 4, 1952. He is well known throughout this country for what some call a crusade against so-called fair-trade legislation by the Federal Government. His testimony speaks for itself. In my judgment, it is the best rebuttal that can be offered to the proponents of this bill. I think it is devastating rebuttal, and, on the basis of that testimony alone, after listening to the proponents of the bill, I would still vote against the bill. I ask unanimous consent to have Professor Klamon's statement before the Senate Committee on Interstate and Foreign Commerce, printed in the RECORD at this point as part of my remarks.

There being no objection, the statement was ordered to be printed in the RECORD, as follows:

OPPOSITION TO THE MCGUIRE RESALE PRICE FIXING BILL, H. R. 5767

STATEMENT BEFORE SENATE COMMITTEE ON INTERSTATE AND FOREIGN COMMERCE, BY DR. JOSEPH M. KLAMON, PROFESSOR OF MARKETING, SCHOOL OF BUSINESS AND PUBLIC ADMINISTRATION, WASHINGTON UNIVERSITY, ST. LOUIS, MO.

My name is Joseph M. Klamon. I wish to thank the committee for permitting me to appear in opposition to the McGuire price fixing bill. I live at 7464 University Drive, University City, Mo. Since September 1929, for the past 23 years I have taught marketing and related business courses at Washington University. I am professor of marketing in the school of business and public administration in our university. Prior to returning to St. Louis I was a tutor at Yale in economics, professor of economics and chairman of the department at William and Mary, instructor in marketing and business policy in the Harvard Graduate School of Business Administration, associate professor of economics at Carnegie Institute of Technology, and visiting lecturer at the University of Pittsburgh. Although I am not, at my own request, presently speaking or serving in that capacity, since 1934 I have served as marketing consultant to the consumers group in St. Louis, which was originally set up by Prof. PAUL DOUGLAS, now Senator from Illinois. This group has continued to function after the NRA ceased to function on a local level. I received the LL. B. from Washington University and the M. A. J. D. and Ph. D from Yale University. I also held a fellowship in 1926 in the Harvard Law School. I am opposed to the price fixing bill before you for in reality it will amend to the point of destruction the Sherman Act and the rest of our antitrust laws.

The price fixing bill before you, the McGuire bill, has only one purpose and that is by legislation to reverse the Schwegmann and Wentling cases and thus to destroy by legislation the restoration of competitive pricing on branded merchandise, which occurred as a result of the Supreme Court's decisions in the above two cases. I am opposed to the enactment of this so-called fair trade bill, but which in reality is price fixing on branded merchandise because it is entirely antithetical to the Sherman Act. If enacted into law it will seriously and adversely affect the living standards of a large portion of our population. It will cost the public no less than $2,000,000,000 a year. It will reach into the pocket of every man, woman, and child and be the equivalent of a 10 percent tax, virtually a 10 percent sales tax on all branded goods purchased. We must have either price fixing or price freedom. More than 40 professors signed or submitted statements in opposition to price fixing bills in recent hearings before the House Judiciary Committee. These included faculty members who major in marketing, business, and government legislation. They included professors from Yale, Harvard, MIT, Michigan, Chicago, Illinois, the University of California, and many others. Farm groups testified in opposition to price fixing. So did the Antitrust Division of the Department of Justice and staff members of the Federal Trade Commission.

Various labor groups and civic organizations have always opposed these price-fixing bills, which seriously impair consuming buying power, particularly during a period of high inflation. It is idle to suggest that the aggressive lobbyists of the retail druggists and brand name manufacturers are conducting this very expensive pressure campaign in order to help the public get lower prices for branded goods. The price-fixing bill before you is advocated by trade groups such as the NARD and similar trade associations who are interested in legislation to benefit only their members and not the public.

I hold no brief whatever for any particular channel of distribution. I have always been opposed to any legislation in favor of price-fixing or legislation that would weaken our antitrust laws and our competitive economy. I should suggest that your committee consider the desirability of securing the views on the proposed price-fixing bills before you from economists and professors of marketing in perhaps the 200 leading universities. Those who would destroy our antitrust laws and reverse by legislation the Schwegmann and Wentling cases have never been able to secure as many as five or six, it any, economists of national repute to testify that their bills for fair-trade price-fixing are in the public interest. The Miller-Tydings Act since its enactment has cost the consuming public many billions in higher fixed prices on branded goods. Legislation of this sort that is the equivalent of a 10-percent to 12-percent sales tax collected by retailers and manufacturers of branded goods, for themselves, should not be enacted without adequate information from disinterested experts as to whether or not such legislation is truly in the public interest.

Consumers are entitled to adequate information, competitive pricing on all goods, branded or unbranded, and the widest possible choice under such conditions of competition. I have been for many years unalterably opposed to all forms of price fixing, vertical or horizontal, when practiced by individuals and trade groups. Such price fixing by and on behalf of retailers, manufacturers or trade groups is essentially featherbedding. Featherbedding appears to be a form of business racketeering. It is invariably inimical to public interest and the consuming public. Featherbedding is no less harmful whether practiced by labor, agriculture, manufacturers, retailers, or any one else. The bill before you is essentially featherbedding, price fixing in behalf of retail druggists, brand name manufacturers, and others handling branded merchandise. It is designed to lessen, not widen, consumer choice. It is further designed to condition and police coercively and by compulsion the pricing practices of lower-cost, volume merchandisers; firms who are content with a smaller margin on an immense volume rather than a maintained high margin on a lesser volume.

About 12 years ago there was a bill introduced in the House known as H. R. 1. It was the Patman chain-store bill. It never became law. It attempted to carry the Indiana and Louisiana graduated tax on multiple retail outlets, a step further by multiplying such increasingly severe taxes by the number of States in which a chain did business. This would have taxed A & P, for example, 60 percent of its gross dollar receipts when at that time its average gross margin was ony [sic] 16 percent. This, of course, was not an attempt to regulate but to destroy a competitor. I suggested at the time that this type of legislation represented simply another effort to hold back the dawn, to halt the inevitable as I believed then and believe now that the giant superstore in food and drugs is here to stay. Restrictive legislation of this variety as enacted on a State level boomeranged.

The development of the immense food and drug superstore would probably have come in any event. However, legislation of this sort simply gave the chains and the independent superstores a tremendous shove in the direction in which they were headed anyway. In 1929 A & P was the first food chain to cross a billion dollars in volume. They did this in some 16,000 stores. Now they sell about $3,000,000,000 annually in approximately 6,000 stores. The restoration of fair trade by writing the compulsory nonsigner clause into Federal law will, in my judgment, even if legal, which is very doubtful, likewise boomerang. For super food stores, attracted by the high fixed margin on drug proprietaries and sundries have been moving and are now moving into the handling of drug items with incredible speed. The Nielson Service of Chicago and the Progressive Grocer of February 1952 indicate clearly that super food stores in the last 3 years have tripled the volume of drug items, proprietaries, and sundries that they are handling. Since the NARD[,] the retail-drug lobby which boasts that it secured the enactment of the Miller-Tydings Act as well as 45 State fair-trade laws[,] has been in the forefront of fair-trade price-fixing efforts, it may be of some interest to see the effect of maintained margins upon independent retail-drug stores.

Super food stores respect the maintained margins on drug items, as they have had to do in the past. However, they have such an enormous volume of traffic through their food stores that they are thus enabled to give their customers very attractive buys on many other items and then make available drug, [sic] proprietaries, and sundries on a self-service basis at or close to recently maintained prices.

The most important trend in drug marketing in the last few years has been the increasing sale of drug products in food stores. Four percent of the sales volume of the average supermarket, doing a business of better than $250,000 a year on a self-service basis, now comes from drug proprietaries alone. There are some 15,000 such supermarkets. Practically all of these now handle drug products in varying degrees. More eye-opening is the revelation that drug sales per square foot is as much as 4 to 1 over certain grocery departments. Sales of drug products in supermarkets were three and one-half times as great in 1951 as they were in 1948. Colgate reports 55 percent of its dentifrice sales are in food-store outlets. In Springfield, Mass., three supermarkets sell more Pepsodent than the top 15 drug stores in the city. A few of the more striking developments in the field of marketing in the past few years have been the establishment of branches of department stores in neighborhood shopping centers; the rack jobber or rack operator and perhaps most significant the movement of nationally advertised drug products through grocery supermarkets. The movement of these drug products through super food stores is easily the most important development in such stores since the handling of meats and produce in grocery stores.

According to the Grey Advertising Agency, women visit supermarkets at least four times as often as they visit drug stores, and signifiLcantly, women visit drug stores more often than department stores from whose housewares and hosiery departments the supermarkets will soon be taking a bigger bite. A move which will bear watching is the drug-grocery recently opened in California and operated jointly by Mayfair Markets and the Owl Drug Co. This is still in the experimental stage, and too early to tell if it constitutes a trend or an exception. The retail drug lobby, the NARD, and the brand name manufacturers lobby, the American Fair Trade Council of Gary, Ind., have been most active in promoting price fixing fair-trade laws and destroying competition in branded merchandise by legislation on a Federal and State level. This has tended to interest and attract other merchandisers in handling such margin-protected, price-fixed drug and other name-brand items. The rack jobber or rack operator as a result has recently had a surprisingly rapid growth. The margin on drug proprietaries is 30.5 percent to 33 percent on an average. On drug sundries it may be a few percent more.

The average margin in food supers is close to 16 percent or 17 percent, in some instances a little less, rarely more. The rack operator keeps his 15 percent plus an additional 6 percent to 8 percent as he offers the food super store about 22 percent to 24 percent average on drug proprietaries, and about 30 percent to 33 percent profit on drug sundries. The rack operator, therefore, in placing and servicing nationally advertised, fast-moving drug proprietaries and sundries in food stores takes his regular jobbers' or wholesalers' margin of about 15 percent plus an additional 6 percent to 8 percent on the drug items for servicing the drug rack in food stores. Dewing & Co., a rack operator, now services over 3,000 food stores in California alone with drug products. There are some 175 or more rack operators in the country. There has been a geographical expansion from the far West to the Midwestern States, then to the Southeast, then to the Mid-Atlantic, and lastly to the New England States. Recently there has been an association formed of these rack operators composed of the leading rack jobbers in the country with a former Kroger executive who pioneered drug products in Kroger stores heading this group.

One purpose of this association appears to be to get a better margin from manufacturers of nationally advertised items in order to give them a wider margin and greater leverage. The alert chains have watched the rack jobbers closely, learned all they could from them, and are now demanding that manufacturers of nationally advertised drug items sell them directly. This the manufacturers are only too glad to do and have had to do simply because they must have their nationally advertised products available and on display on a self-service basis or otherwise wherever the traffic and volume happen to be. Wholesalers in the drug field have, of course, been alert to what the rack jobber means to them in the movement of drug items through food stores. Some wholesalers have been quick to engage in rack jobbing activities themselves, taking the normal wholesaler's margin plus the same amount that the rack jobber has taken for servicing super food stores. Naturally, the independent retail druggist has taken a dim view of the activities designed to move greater quantities of nationally advertised drug, [sic] proprietaries, sundries, and other items through food stores, and in some instances has attempted to resist the movement of such drug items through food stores, all, of course, to no avail. It will do the retail druggist no good to attempt to take a change of venue from the free market of open competition to the political arena on either the Federal or State level, as is here attempted. There is tremendous traffic in practically all food stores.

Consumers seem receptive and desire to purchase packaged drug products in food stores. Super food stores seem interested only in about 100 or more of the fastest moving nationally advertised items. The average gross on food store products as indicated is around 15 percent to 17 percent. The average profit on drug items is almost twice that on food percentages. It is apparent that the movement of drug products in food stores is here to stay and perhaps to grow. Kroger's latest estimate is that its drug business last year was about $12,000,000 with its dollar profits per square foot of floor space exceeded only by three other departments—canned goods, meat, and bread. Other giant food distributors in the field include National Tea Stores, American Stores, Food Fair, Safeway, and last to enter the field, A & P, which is now testing drug and toiletries sections in a cross section of its stores.

In general it may be said that food store sales of drug products have moved most rapidly during the last 2 to 3 years and is a trend that cannot be arrested, nor is it a distribution factor that can be overlooked. The retail druggist himself will have to fight this new-found competition based on mass traffic movement through food stores, not with price fixing or other restrictive legislation, but with better merchandising of drug products in his store. The average druggist, it seems, finds it difficult to grasp the importance of turnover, which to the food merchandiser is of major importance. Too many druggists are high margin and price fixing conscious and not sufficiently volume conscious. Too many druggists display canned goat's milk, Wample's Remedy No. 82, Father John's Medicine, and a few other so-called profitable items whose rate of inventory turnover is often one time a year or less. The retail drug lobby, the NARD, and many of its members tends [sic] to look at the percentages which cannot be put in the bank instead of the dollars resulting from volume which pay bills. This refers mostly to the NARD and many of its independent druggist members and not to the alert super store chain or independent operator who runs his business as a business and not as a college of pharmacy.

Many proprietors of drug stores today are pharmacy school graduates with unfortunately little or no training or understanding of merchandising principles and the methods of operation and the formulas that will pay profits over the long term. The real solution to the problems confronting manufacturers of brand name merchandise and the retail druggist are not to be found in amending or destroying our antitrust laws with various price-fixing devices involving the policing of the pricing policies of lower-cost and perhaps more efficient distributors, but rather in better merchandising. In the Progressive Grocer of February 1952 the lead article featured on the cover and in detail from pages 50 through 58 has a few high lights that may be of interest. Among these are the following: 85 percent of stores surveyed (food supers) $300,000 or over annual volume as well as smaller stores now handle drugs and toiletries compared with 37 percent in 1941. This department adds about 2 percent to total store sales and 4 percent to total store gross margin. They sold an estimated $340,000,000 in drugs and toiletries in 1951 and indications are that they will continue to grow in these departments.

Leading drug and toiletry brands are now readily available to food stores from many sources, including manufacturers who are naturally pleased to exploit this added channel not only because of the added volume, but because it gives manufacturers leverage in bargaining with less fear when facing the demands of the NARD. Superfood operators find it pays to give drug department preferred high-traffic location [sic]. Drug sales per square foot of floor space in food stores are double over-all store average and the dollar margin is four times the store average because margin on these items is twice the average margin on all other food items. Most food stores support fair-trade prices for drug and toiletries and the average margin on these is 30.5 percent. It increases their ability to give greater values on items not fair traded, thereby increasing traffic, volume, and over-all gross profit. Sixty-four percent of the stores in the Progressive Grocer survey report drug sales up 22 percent over the previous year, and 47 percent of the stores in this survey plan to enlarge and improve the drug department in 1952. In a free economy capital naturally tends to flow where it may be most profitably employed. The above merely proves again that a fixed and false price level tends to defeat itself by inviting competition if not immediately in price competition, then by attracting other distributors to handle the product who then will give greater values in unbranded merchandise. The idea that sharp price competition in branded merchandise will automatically cause a quality dilution harmful to the public has no basis in fact.

Fair trade price fixing is but 20 years old. We have had thousands of national brands and hundreds of nationally advertised brands long before fair trade. Indeed, price competition may well cause emphasis upon greater quality in brand names. Manufacturers will not be inclined to destroy wide consumer acceptance and good will predicated upon known quality. Then, too, minimum quality standards may be had without price control. The basic assumption on the part of the American Fair Trade Council that a manufacturer should be able to write himself a ticket granting immunity from our antitrust laws merely by branding one or more of his products would seem difficult to justify. It is frequently argued that the aggressive use of loss leaders justifies fair trade price fixing. The two are, of course, entirely separate. If loss-lead selling were an evil instead of merely one of many sales promotional devices, it could be stopped by unfair sales acts alone or so-called fair trade practices acts aimed directly against below-invoice sales. Fair traders talk no end about the evils of loss-lead selling and then ask for the unrestricted right to fix sky-high margins on all branded merchandise. Present antitrust laws and powers of the Antitrust Division, Department of Justice, and Federal Trade Commission appear to be adequate to handle predatory price cutting designed to destroy competitors. The absence of any factual basis to justify the bills before you because of loss-lead selling and severe price wars is best evidenced by two items. First, the spectacular price wars that occurred right after the Schwegmann decision of May 21, 1951, ended in less than 2 months. Indeed, they did not even extend to many parts of the country. This proves that business does not commit suicide very often. Second, there is not a single price war of any major significance at the present time in any large city in the country.

There is no evidence whatever indicating a greater mortality among small retailers in free-trade Missouri, Texas, Vermont, and the District of Columbia than in fair trade territory. The States that do not have fair trade laws have not had any greater degree of mortality among marketers who did not enjoy the price fixing that prevailed in other States.

In the effort to enact a fair trade law in the State of Missouri, one of many, which came to an abrupt end with the U. S. Supreme Court Schwegmann decision of May 21, 1951, the American Fair Trade Council sent speakers in many parts of Missouri to tell Missourians that industry was staying out of Missouri because of the absence of ⊥ fair trade and because of our excellent antitrust laws. The St. Louis Chamber of Commerce repeatedly stated that there is no basis whatever in fact for this assertion. Indeed, the St. Louis Chamber of Commerce which strongly opposed a fair trade bill on many occasions proved that St. Louis with about one-third the population of metropolitan Chicago had over $300,000,000 in new industry and expanded industry which was greater than we ever had had and greater than Chicago's dollar total for the year. At the time the AFTC suggested Missouri was going downhill industrially because manufacturers were boycotting the State for lack of fair trade, our industrial area was about to be declared a scarce labor area for housing and other purposes, so great was our industrial expansion and our labor shortage. It is significant that all of our larger newspapers in the State, the Kansas City Star, the St. Louis Post-Dispatch, the Globe-Democrat, and the Star-Times before it was purchased by the Post-Dispatch for many years all strongly opposed fair trade price fixing. Missouri is indebted to its newspapers, the St. Louis Chamber of Commerce, and to

⊥ 8850

our State law enforcement officers, Attorney General J. E. Taylor, and former Assistant Attorney General H. Jackson Daniel and their staff for enforcing our antitrust laws and preventing manufacturers and retailers from treating Missourians as if we had a fair trade law. I asked former Assistant Attorney General Daniel and our attorney general to summarize Missouri's experience with antitrust violations which they consented to do. The following is significant as indicating what those who would destroy our antitrust laws really want. I include the communication below:

February 6, 1952.

Dr. Joseph M. Klamon,
Clayton, Mo.

DEAR DR. KLAMON: As per our conversations, I am enclosing herewith a brief summary of my impressions, as a result of my experiences in the office of the attorney general of the State of Missouri, during the years 1949–51. During the principal part of my appointment as an assistant attorney general, I was either in charge of or intimately connected with the prosecution of cases arising under the antitrust law of the State of Missouri.

In the antitrust division of the attorney general's office, we had a number of skilled and trained investigators, whose function it was to inquire into and report on possible violations of the antitrust statutes. I read all of these reports, talked to witnesses and prepared informations in the nature of quo warranto, with a view toward ousting those engaged in antitrust violations from the State of Missouri. The first six or seven informations that were filed resulted in the defendants (respondents) entering into consent judgments and paying penalties which ranged from $2,500 to $50,000, depending upon the size of the offending corporation and/or the gravity of the offense. The next group of defendants, being five or six in number, have apparently determined to fight the issue through, and their cases are now pending in the Supreme Court of Missouri. The issue in those cases is whether or not vertical price fixing violates the antitrust statutes of Missouri. While it is true that that specific issue has never been directly determined by the Supreme Court of the State of Missouri, it was the unequivocal opinion of the attorney general that the statutes clearly prohibit "any corporation from fixing or regulating the price of any article whatsoever" and that the language in those cases involving horizontal price fixing was sufficiently broad to condemn vertical price fixing. Since the McGuire bill and others of the similar nature are concerned with vertical price fixing, this summary will be confined to that particular field.

Missouri does not have a fair-trade statute. Each and every one of the surrounding States, as well as a vast majority of the rest of the States of the Union, do have such statutes. It was our experience that manufacturers, wholesalers, jobbers, and retailers, by and large, treat Missouri as a fair-trade State. Whether this attitude resulted from a flagrant disregard for the antitrust laws or whether it was induced by the lack of prosecutions from 1927 to 1949 is unknown, but in any event, the feeling that Missouri could be considered a safe fair-trade State was universal among manufacturers, jobbers, etc. It was our experience the [sic] manufacturers and jobbers sent to their customers suggested price lists, and we found in a number of instances that when an occasional retailer deviated from the minimum price suggested by the manufacturer or distributor, that he would be forthwith cut off from any direct supply of that article. The only reasonable deduction from this course of conduct, of course, is that the minimum prices were not suggested but were mandatory. When a retailer, who had been cut off for lowering prices below the suggested minimum, had brought this to the attention of the Attorney General, our investigation would then uniformly reveal that the manufacturing company had been consistent in punishing any retailer who deviated from the minimum price schedule. Occasional attempts were made by certain manufacturers, who were more discreet than others, to police prices in a more unostentatious manner. During the trial of the cases now pending in the Supreme Court where witnesses could not testify that they had been directly warned about prices, they did, however, state that there was a tacit understanding in the trade that certain products could be cut and others could not. Where the manufacturer directly policed prices in a vigorous manner, the usual practice was to have salesman [sic], during the course of his periodic visits to his customers throughout his territory, observe shelf prices and report by wire to the manufacturer any apparent price cutting. Advertisement in local newspapers were [sic] closely watched and clippings indicating price cutting were forwarded to the manufacturer or distributor by salesmen and also by competitors, usually small retailers. The testimony in the cases now pending in the Supreme Court uniformly revealed that price fixing in the State of Missouri is a two-way proposition, i. e., that the manufacturer himself may not have been particularly anxious, in most case [sic], to maintain prices but that small retailers of his product were. In an effort to cooperate with the small retailers, the manufacturer, who would otherwise have been indifferent, often took upon itself the duty of policing and maintaining minimum prices. Large retailers and volume merchandisers, by and large were not interested in maintaining fair-trade prices but small retailers and others who have adopted the classical 40 percent markup were the chief proponents of fair trade within the State of Missouri.

These low-volume retailers receive considerable assistance, not only from manufacturers but from certain fair-trade councils, retail druggists' associations, etc., who flooded the State of Missouri, each time the fair trade bill came before the assembly, with pamphlets, speakers, and financial assistance. These pressure organizations had a number of approaches. One was to the inefficient high-cost, low-volume merchandiser and was an out and out appeal to his selfish interest; that is, if retail minimum prices are not maintained, you will be outmarketed and outsold by the larger-volume buyers. The second was an appeal to chambers of commerce, etc., on the apparently plausible theory that manufacturers would be less likely to locate in the State of Missouri, if they did not have the protection of a fair trade law. The first approach needs no explanation. The second, however, is open to considerable criticism. Investigation revealed that manufacturers, by and large, were not interested in maintaining fair trade prices, unless there was considerable pressure by small retailers, and that actually any plants which failed to locate within the State of Missouri, had other and more compelling reasons for so doing. The phenomenal growth of industry in Texas, which is a non-fair-trade State, lends substantial support to the view that this latter approach is fallacious and incorrect.

The activities of the attorney general, in filing these antitrust proceedings, were noteworthy in many respects, but particularly in the following: When we filed an antitrust suit against the Seagram distillery, the very next day, after the announcement of the filing of that suit appeared in the press, the price of liquor in St. Louis collapsed and spiraled downward for several days. When we filed our next antitrust suit, prices in many drug products also fell and continued to fall until they had reached a competitive level. Not only was the reaction on prices noticeable but the policing methods became more cautious and in many cases disappeared altogether. Price reduction then began to appear all along the line on many previously fair-traded items. A few months after the announcement of our first prosecution, the Star-Times made a comparative price study on a number of previously fair-traded items in St. Louis, and across the river in Illinois, and found that for the most part, prices in Illinois where fair trade was still strong, were uniformly anywhere from 10 percent to 15 percent higher, resulting in a saving to the people of Missouri of uncalculated proportions and scope. Shortly before I resigned from the office of the attorney general to resume the practice of law, our investigators were noting substantial difficulty in finding any more violations and what few violations we did find had principally occurred before the announcement of our vigorous antitrust prosecutions.

Either fair-trade practices are now completely at a standstill in Missouri among manufacturers, distributors, and retailers, or else policing and maintenance methods have become so skillful and under the table that we are unable to detect them. The torrent of propaganda and informational literature speech making [sic] continues, however, and it may be assumed that the fair-trade bill will be again presented to the assembly on an even more pronounced and desperate scale. The fair-trade bill being, of course, the very antithesis of free competition, it is believed that the assembly of the State of Missouri, an island of free competition, will again reject the cloak-and-dagger tactics of the so-called fair-trade proponents.

Respectfully,

H. Jackson Daniel,
Former Attorney General (Assistant),
State of Missouri.

The activities that resulted in successful legal action for violation of the Missouri antitrust laws would be legalized if the bills before you to reverse the Schwegmann and Wentling cases were enacted into law and if Missouri likewise modified or destroyed its antitrust laws. Fortunately, this has not occurred, and if the problem is approached from the standpoint of public interest and on the high level of statesmanship that caused Congress to enact our antitrust laws is maintained, none of the price-fixing bills will be recommended.

It is suggested by those favoring fair trade that retail prices on branded goods are not greatly increased. I find it difficult to believe, however, that brand-name manufacturers represented by the AFTC and the Drug Retail lobby and the NARD in putting over the Miller-Tydings Act and in organizing an intensive campaign which secured fair trade in 45 States and until the Schwegmann and ⊥ Wentling cases established the sanctity of price-fixing and wider retail margins—I find it difficult to believe that all of this very expensive activity was only concerned with helping the consumer and the public interest. All of this activity and all of the activity in introducing the McGuire bill and in introducing the price-fixing bills presently before you involves spending a vast amount of money and effort in the interest of sheer altruism.

It is hardly necessary to point out that it is the sworn duty of the attorney general of Missouri, Texas, and every other State to enforce the laws of that State. Because Attorney General J. E. Taylor, of Missouri, and the attorney general of Texas, took steps to end flagrant price-fixing activities in violation of State antitrust laws, the Fair Trade Council of Gary, Ind., denounced our attorney general in a letter dated October 4, 1950, for operating a "speed trap." Note the assumption that there is nothing wrong with price fixing and an absence of competition on branded merchandise, and the implication that if our attorney general has an idea that the Missouri antitrust laws should be strictly enforced both against vertical and horizontal price fixing that he is thereby persecuting violators. The great Champ Clark is reported to be the author of Missouri's excellent antitrust laws. The language in the law is crystal clear, very broad, comprehensive, and in my opinion Attorney General Taylor is entirely correct in believing that they declared illegal not only vertical but also all forms of horizontal price fixing. I asked Mr. Daniel, former assistant attorney general, if he would kindly request Attorney General Taylor to write me his recent experience in enforcing the law in Missouri against illegal price fixing. I here set forth the letter from our attorney general in Missouri:

State of Missouri,
Offices of the Attorney General,
Jefferson City, Mo., February 5, 1952,

Dr. Joseph M. Klamon,
University City, Mo.

DEAR SIR: Mr. Jack Daniel has requested us to submit to you information concerning my enforcement of the Missouri antitrust laws, particularly with respect to vertical price-fixing practices in this State.

Since December 23, 1949, this office has filed 15 suits charging violation of the Missouri antitrust laws. Four of these actions involved horizontal price-fixing arrangements. The 11 remaining involved vertical price fixing. Of those 11 cases 7 have been concluded on the basis of stipulations entered into by the respondents and the payment by the respondents of various sums into the State treasury. No evidence was taken in any of those cases. The cases and amounts paid in settlement are as follows:

Supreme Court, No. 41839—*State ex inf. J. E. Taylor, Attorney General, relator,* v. *Seagram-Distillers Corp., a corporation; All-State Distributors, Inc., a corporation; Stickney-Hoelscher Cigar Co., a corporation; and McKesson and Robbins, Inc., a corporation,* respondents. Fines: Seagram, $35,000; All-States, $2,500; Stickney-Hoelscher, $2,500; McKesson-Robbins, $2,500.

Jackson County Circuit Court—*State ex inf. J. E. Taylor, Attorney General, relator* v. *Peter Digiovanni and Joseph Digiovanni, Co-Partners, Doing Business as Mid-West Distributing Co.,* respondents. Fines: Each, $1,250; aggregate, $2,500.

Cole County Circuit Court, No. 12213—*State ex rel. J. E. Taylor, Attorney General,* v. *International Cellucotton Products Co.* Fine: $50,000.

Supreme Court, No. 42050—*State ex inf. J. E. Taylor, Attorney General, relator* v. *Faultless Starch Co.,* respondent. Fine: $7,500.

Supreme Court, No. 42177—*State ex inf. J. E. Taylor, Attorney General,* v. *Central States Distributors, Inc.* Fine: $2,500.

Cole County Circuit Court—*State ex rel. J. E. Taylor, Attorney General,* v. *Ironrite, Inc.* Fine: $6,000.

Supreme Court, No. 42186—*State ex inf. J. E. Taylor, Attorney General,* v. *Swift & Co.* Fine: $10,000.

The Digiovanni case in the Jackson County Circuit Court was a companion case to the Seagram-Distillers Corp. case filed in the Supreme Court and involved Seagram products.

The Central States Distributors case and the Ironrite case are companion cases, both involving Ironrite ironers.

The case against Swift & Co. involved only the Swift product Vigoro.

In addition to the above cases, there is one case which is still pending in the Supreme Court, *State ex inf. J. E. Taylor, Attorney General, realtor [sic],* v. *Authorized Motor Parts Corp., et al., respondents,* in which five of the nine respondents have stipulated for decree of ouster from illegal practice and the payment of $2,500 each, or $12,500 for the five respondents. This case involves price-fixing practices in the distribution of Champion spark plugs.

In the following cases evidence has been presented to a special commissioner appointed by the supreme court. No report has been made by the Commissioner in any of the cases. They are:

Supreme Court, No. 42152—*State ex inf. J. E. Taylor, Attorney General, realtor [sic],* v. *Miles Laboratories, Inc., McKesson & Robbins, Inc., The McPike Drug Co., C. D. Smith Drug Co., St. Louis Wholesale Drug Co., and Meyer Bros. Drug Co.,* respondents.

Supreme Court No. 42185—*State ex inf. J. E. Taylor, attorney general,* v. *Armour & Co.*

Supreme Court No. 42407—*State ex inf. J. E. Taylor, attorney general, relator,* v. *Authorized Motor Parts Corp., Beck & Corbitt Co., Fred Campbell Auto Supply Co., Cities Service Oil Co.,*

General Auto Parts Co., Hayes Automotive, Inc., Kansas City Automobile Supply Co., Myers Motor Equipment Co., and Phillips Petroleum Co., respondents.

The case of *State ex rel. J. E. Taylor, attorney general,* v. *Sunbeam Corp.* is pending in Jackson County Circuit Court. No hearing has been held in that case.

We are enclosing herewith copy of a statement prepared for use before the Missouri State Senate in connection with senate bill No. 42, proposing the adoption of a fair-trade act for the State of Missouri. No hearing has been held on this bill by the senate committee and I have not used the statement, but you might find it of interest.

If there is any further information that you would like to have concerning any of the above cases or the activities of this department, please let us know and we will be glad to cooperate with you.

Yours very truly,

J. E. Taylor, *Attorney General.*

The proponents of fair trade point out as the public relations man of the retail drug lobby, Mr. Mermy, did on February 4, 1952, in the hearings on the McGuire bill that while 45 States have enacted fair trade laws, not one has repealed such a law. This is supposed to be evidence that price fixing laws on branded goods are in the public interest. If the retail drug lobby and the brand name lobby were as efficient in marketing as they are in applying coercive political pressure they would not need this political crutch to protect them from inefficiency in distribution. Once they succeed, it is almost impossible to restore competitive pricing in the public interest. This is certainly no evidence that such a law promotes public welfare. The opponents of fair trade in Missouri were to be heard before a legislative committee in Jefferson City toward the end of May 1951. Like a breath of fresh air, the Supreme Court on May 21, 1951, held the nonsigner clause invalid in the Schwegmann case, and the effort to enact a fair trade bill in Missouri lost much of it [sic] organized drive. Attorney General J. E. Taylor prepared a statement in opposition to Missouri Senate bill No. 42, the proposed fair trade bill in our State. It has never before been published or used, and it is so apropos and pertinent to the bills before you seeking to legalize the nonsigner clause and reverse Schwegmann that I here set forth the statement referred to in the above letter from the attorney general:

"STATEMENT BY J. E. TAYLOR, ATTORNEY GENERAL, STATE OF MISSOURI, AGAINST THE FAIR TRADE BILL FOR MISSOURI

"Senate bill No. 42 proposes the adoption of a so-called Fair Trade Act for the State of Missouri. The essential purpose of the bill is to enable a manufacturer to require that his products be sold at retail at a price not less than a minimum which he may specify.

"Missouri has been a regular target for the advocates of fair-trade legislation since the movement received the benefit of exemption from the Federal antitrust laws upon the enactment by Congress of the Tydings-Miller amendment in 1937. That act, incidentally, was passed as a rider to a District of Columbia appropriation act after the House and Senate had failed to act on a bill directly covering the subject. President Roosevelt, on signing the bill, denounced the practice of attaching extraneous rider clauses to bills and expressed his fear that the law would lead to increased prices to consumers. Experience under the law has shown such fear to have been justified.

"Despite the regular efforts to obtain passage of a fair-trade law in this State, the people and the legislature have recognized that fair-trade legislation is inconsistent with the free enterprise economy of which we are justly proud and have refused to subvert the welfare of the people as a whole to that of a special few.

"Undaunted by their rebuffs in this State, advocates of the legislation are now engaged in a vigorous campaign for the passage of Senate bill No. 42. The campaign is being directed by the American Fair Trade Council, Inc., of Gary, Ind., and the Fair Trade Education Bureau of New York.

"The president of the American Fair Trade Council is John W. Anderson, who is also president of the Anderson Co., of Gary, Ind., a corporation which engages in the manufacture of automobile accessories. The American Fair Trade Council is an association of manufacturers, all, or practically all, of which are located outside the State of Missouri. Mr. Anderson recently solicited membership in the organization among manufacturers all over the United States by means of a deliberately misleading letter in which my action in enforcing the antitrust laws of this State was described as 'a lucrative speed-trap operation.'

"The organization last year held its annual meeting at the Waldorf Astoria Hotel in New York City. At that meeting various manufacturers pointed out the results of their operations under fair-trade laws. A representative of G. & C. Merriam Co., publishers of Webster's Dictionary, pointed out that, before fair trade, the $20 Webster's International Dictionary was sold for as little as $12.34, but that with the advent of fair trade the price was restored to the $20 figure. Just how the purchaser benefited by this increase under fair trade was not explained.

"The report also contains a statement by a representative of Ronson Art Metal Works, Inc., a manufacturer of cigarette lighters, which operates under fair trade. This statement shows how under fair trade a merchant is deprived of his right to operate his business as he sees fit. The statement is as follows:

" 'We have a lighter fuel under the trade name of "Ronsonol" which is fair-traded at 25 cents. Let's say, for example, that they take our minimum-price lighter which is $6 and sell the combination for $6.19. We immediately put a stop to that.'

"Equally enlightening is a statement made at the meeting by Mr. Ivan D. Tefft, attorney for the Parker Pen Co. Mr. Tefft stated:

" 'Now (under fair-trade laws) the terms "price cutters" and "price cutting," when applied to a merchandiser are synonymous with law violator and no one likes to be adjudged a law violator.'

"Thus, under a fair-trade law, a Missouri merchant would not only lose the right to operate his business as he saw fit, but he would be a law violator should he attempt to do so.

"The Fair Trade Council has recently written its members outside Missouri requesting that they write their customers here and suggest that the customers see, write, wire, or telephone members Senate [sic] Criminal Jurisprudence Committee, urging that Senate bill No. 42 be reported out promptly for favorable action by the Senate. Missouri retailers have been flooded with such letters received from their out-of-State suppliers. A number of them have undoubtedly written members of this committee in response to these urgings from the outside manufacturers.

"Another part of the campaign has been a series of speeches delivered throughout the State by Mr. David Molthrop. Mr. Molthrop's position is described as community relations consultant for the Anderson Co. This is the company of which Mr. John W. Anderson, president of the American Fair Trade Council, is president. Mr. Moltrop's speech, which has been delivered before numerous civic organizations throughout the State, is described as a speech on attracting industry to the community. Two of Mr. Molthrop's points, as reported in the press, are:

"(1) 'Back your chamber of commerce to the fullest and the activities of its industrial committee.'

"(2) 'Support your local inventors. Fruition of their ideas means more jobs and more payrolls for your community.'

"However, Mr. Molthrop's purpose in coming into this State has not been merely to voice such obvious recommendations. The main point in his address has been that the enactment of Senate bill No. 42 is the most important factor in the obtaining of any industries for the State of Missouri. He has attacked the enforcement of the antitrust law. He has stated that a number of industries have refused to locate in Missouri because of the absence of a fair-trade law. The press reports of these speeches, however, disclose the specific mention of only one industry which has declined to locate in Missouri because of the lack of a fair-trade law. By coincidence that industry is the Anderson Co. Mr. Molthrop stated that that company proposed to build a $600,000 plant in Missouri, but erected an addition to its Gary plant instead after learning of the situation here. Just where the Anderson plant was to have been located has never been stated.

"If any answer is needed to Mr. Molthrop's statement in this regard, one need only point out that the Ford Motor Co. is now engaged in the construction of a $40,000,000 plant in Clay County. Numerous large industrial plants are under construction in St. Louis, including a $6,000,000 plant by Groves Laboratories and a large plant by Procter & Gamble.

"Mr. Molthrop delivered his speech before the Springfield Lions Club and that organization immediately passed a resolution appointing a committee to support the enactment of Senate bill No. 42. Members of that organization, in order to see the fallacy of Mr. Molthrop's argument, need only have reminded themselves that the Lily Tulip Cup Co. now has under construction in Springfield a plant costing several million dollars. That company evidently was not deterred by Missouri's lack of a fair-trade law.

"Why is all of this pressure being put on this committee by firms and organizations located outside the State of Missouri? The answer to me appears to be an obvious one. Forty-five States have enacted fair-trade legislation. No such legislation is found in Texas, Vermont, District of Columbia, and Missouri.

"The St. Louis Star-Times recently published articles in which prices of certain items on sale in Illinois under fair trade were compared with the prices of the same items in the State of Missouri. A survey of 50 drug items showed that the Illinois fair-trade price was approximately 12 percent higher than the price in Missouri. A survey of the prices of liquor showed that prices in Illinois are nearly 16 percent higher than in St. Louis.

"The proponents of fair trade are anxious to eliminate the remaining few States which have failed to enact fair trade legislation, in order to remove any basis for comparison of prices in fair trade and non-fair-trade States, because any such comparison always shows that prices to the consumers invariably are higher under fair trade laws. Furthermore, should fair trade laws be enacted in all States, there would be no limit to the extent to which the manufacturers might increase the prices of their products. The fair trade laws always render lip service to the antitrust laws by prohibiting combinations of manufacturers, but it is much simpler for manufacturers to combine and fix the price of their products when they know that their retailers can be forced to sell their products for whatever price they might fix.

"Missouri has a strong, effective antitrust law. For more than 50 years it has operated for the best interests of the people of this State. Any weakening of it by a 'fair trade law' is contrary to the best interests of the people. Therefore, I submit that this committee should resist the pressure of selfish out-State interests, and refuse to approve Senate bill No. 42."

Those who are responsible for the current effort to destroy the Schwegmann and Sunbeam-Wentling cases, to destroy by Federal legislation the restoration of competitive pricing in interstate commerce through the de facto repeal of the Sherman Act, and our other antitrust laws, should give us clear, simple answers to a few questions relative to the bills before you, which they have sponsored and introduced:

1. If a cash and carry super store has lower costs, should not the public be permitted to benefit (in lower prices) from all such lower cost methods of doing business?

2. In the above situation, why should all be required to sell a so-called fair-traded item at the same retail price?

3. If competition among producers of an item is good for the public, why should competition among retail sellers of that item be denied?

4. Has any pressure group ever campaigned for price-fixing privileges except to make prices higher than they are under free competition?

5. What real and specific evidence is there that truly meritorious articles have ever been driven from the market by price competition?

6. Why should the retail drug lobby, the NARD, set up permanent headquarters in the District of Columbia Press Building and the brand-name manufacturers' lobby, the American Fair-Trade Council, set up headquarters in the Mayflower Hotel in Washington and spend large sums of money to lobby for the McGuire bill before the Commerce Committee and all the bills before this committee, other than the Curtis bill, to make the public pay more than they now pay for aspirin, tooth paste, liquor, appliances, drug items, and almost any other branded item?

7. How much money have these and other lobbies been supplied with and how much have they spent and do they intend to spend to enact the above bills into law and to destroy the Schwegmann and Wentling cases, and, specifically, by whom has this money been provided?

8. If a merchant wants to locate a store outside the city limits, operate at lower costs, price accordingly, and therefore sell at lower prices because of his lower costs, what good reason is there to deny him that right and forbid the public that benefit and would not legislation directed toward this end be held invalid by the Supreme Court as an unconstitutional deprivation of property without due process of law?

9. If the public is deceived by loss-leader prices, what would prevent equal deception as to fair-trade prices which are and have always been rather exorbitant?

10. If we grant monopoly price privileges to the select few responsible for most of the bills before you and also for the McGuire bill, who is going to regulate those prices to make certain that the public is not mulcted by the price fixers?

11. Is the Keogh bill, H. R. 6367,[3.71] intended to regulate or to destroy and prevent interstate commerce in branded goods, mail-order fashion, at any price below a State fair-trade minimum?

12. Is it not probable that the United States Supreme Court would hold H. R. 6367 invalid on the ground that this does not regulate but destroys interstate commerce done by a mail-order house, and that such a bill would interfere with the inherent property right one has to conduct a lower-cost operation and to price accordingly for the benefit of the public?

These are but a few of many questions that suggest themselves the moment anyone attempts to modify or to destroy the affirmative faith in competitive pricing as evidenced in our Sherman Act and other antitrust laws. The Boston conference on distribution of last year developed a number of points that are very pertinent here. The public interest would seem to require that we should repeal the Miller-Tydings Act, as the Curtis bill before you proposes for we must have the complete restoration of the right of a distributor to set his own prices on his own property when he offers it for resale. We are here concerned with basic principles of national policy that should promote the public interest and that are vital to the future of efficient marketing. For many years there has unfortunately been conspicuous failure to recognize that

---

[3.71] This version of the Keogh bill was superseded by H.R. 6925 (clean version, introduced on March 6, 1952).

competitive price making among distributors is just as vital to the public as competitive price making among producers.

A number of disinterested studies indicate clearly that about one-half of the final retail price in many fields represents distribution costs. It would seem difficult logically to maintain that factory prices should be competitively determined and that the cost of distributive services should not. If price competition among producers is good for the consuming public, then price competition among distributors serves an equal and perhaps an even more important public purpose for today the greater weight is not so much in production as it is in distribution. Does it make sense from the public standpoint to effect significant economies in manufacture and then to dissipate a great part of such lower unit cost in inefficient distribution perpetuated by an absence of competitive pricing in marketing? The Miller-Tydings amendment to the Sherman Act and the Federal Trade Commission Act is a radical and dangerous denial of the fundamental principles of competition because it makes lawful the destruction of price competition among distributors in the sale of certain branded merchandise. The Miller-Tydings Act represents affirmative governmental interference in behalf of restraint of trade and is clearly diametrically opposed to the principle in the Sherman Act and the Federal Trade Commission Act. The real issue of high price fixing has not been settled by the Schwegmann decision. It can be settled by enacting the Curtis bill into law and thus repealing the Miller-Tydings Act which was slipped through Congress as a rider to a District of Columbia appropriation bill. President Roosevelt denounced it at the time and would have vetoed it had he had the item veto.

On the production side we depend upon competition to weed out the inefficient and to reward the progressive manufacturer who finds a new way to produce the same or better article at a lower cost, and to pass on to the public a part of such saving. What is it that makes a similar operation inimical to public interest when it occurs in distribution? The public must have adequate information and competitive prices and have the unrestricted right to shop for values at all times and on all goods, branded and unbranded, particularly now when we have the greatest degree of inflation we have ever had in the history of the country and when the dollar buys less than it ever has before. Competition is a great economic and social force. To be sure, it is not wholly painless in operation. But we cannot wisely curb it on the theory that lower costs for products and services are necessarily against the public interest because some producers and sellers cannot meet them. These are some of the contentions not only of economists at the Brookings Institution, the Harvard Graduate School of Business, Dr. Q. Forrest Walker, economist of R. H. Macy & Co., but they are, of course, elementary and fundamental principles of economics that are taught everywhere.

No one can study the history and development of fair-trade laws, the various State laws imposing cost plus restraints on retail price competition, unfair sales acts, and a number of other restraints on the price making freedom of distributors, without being impressed with the dangers which now seriously threaten national progress toward lower costs and more efficient distribution. If we believe sincerely in free enterprise, it becomes readily apparent that these restrictive pricing devices are definitely not in the public interest. They occur only when higher cost distributors take a change of venue from the market place of open competition to the political arena. They are essentially political devices designed to secure the votes of a small minority of distributors and manufacturers interested in trade restraint on branded goods, at the expense of the entire consuming public. The wide-awake competent small merchant and the giant independent super store such as Schwegmann in New Orleans and Doc Webb in St. Petersburg, Fla., does not need price protection. And the incompetents in distribution cannot possibly attain economic salvation by such means. We should actively promote healthy price competition among distributors as well as producers.

Restraint of price competition has never been in the public interest and has never served any useful purpose. It tends to shrink markets, not to broaden them, just as the Keogh bill before you and all other bills before you other than the Curtis bill are intended to do. The growth of the rack jobber or rack operator is merely one of the later examples of the fact that ironclad price rigidity can never capture more than part of the market. Even if the fair traders succeed only in part, they reap a rich harvest at the expense of the public. As a matter of enduring national policy we are not interested in restricted markets and reduced production. Pricing policy and the freedom to price competitively is perhaps one of the most crucial of all future marketing problems. In facing this problem it may be well to bear in mind one crisp sentence from the majority opinion in the Dr. Miles case: "The complainant having sold his product at prices satisfactory to itself, the public is entitled to whatever advantages may be derived from competition in the subsequent traffic."[3.72] This is the best answer to the brand name manufacturers who attempt to maintain that they can give themselves immunity from the Sherman Act by merely putting on a cloak on the package, or a brand name. If that is all that is necessary to avoid our antitrust laws, there will, of course, be an endless multiplication of

---

[3.72] Dr. Miles Medical Co. v. John D. Park & Sons Co., 220 U.S. 373, 409 (1911).

brands and the manufacturer and marketer of unbranded merchandise will then want to know why he cannot operate in similar fashion.

I am in favor of the Curtis bill and favor the immediate repeal of the Miller-Tydings Act because price maintenance agreements throw a monkey wrench into free enterprise, penalizing more efficient dealers. We must have competition not only between producers and dealers of similar goods, but also between retailers of identical brands. Trade restraint, rigid prices, and margins are functional featherbedding and like all featherbedding seriously injurious to competitive free enterprise. If we do not repeal the Miller-Tydings Act and if we do approve the bills before you, we shall accomplish the de-facto repeal of all of our antitrust laws. I strongly support the position taken before you by the Federal Trade Commission spokesmen and by the Anti-Trust Division of the Department of Justice. I believe the Anti-Trust Division of the Department of Justice and the Federal Trade Commission have well earned a salute of gratitude from the consuming public for having maintained the national policy and tradition in favor of competition and opposed to all forms of price fixing.

Recently the national income has been running well in excess of $275,000,000,000 a year. The volume of all retail trade is at the rate of $150,000,000,000 annually. When fair traders attempt to minimize the damaging effect of price fixing on consumers, they deliberately dilute the percentage of dollar volume fair-traded items by including many commodities that are not price-fixed in retail trade. The percentage may vary a small amount, but perhaps the best conservative estimate of the volume of branded goods fair traded before Schwegmann was approximately 10 percent of the total volume of retail trade, or $15,000,000,000. On the basis of a number of disinterested studies (not inspired by any trade group and not self-serving, or purchased special pleading) the average increases on prices on branded goods, on price-fixed fair-traded items, is not any less than 10 percent to 12 percent. This means that on drugs, appliances, liquor, and all other fair-traded goods, the American public prior to the Schwegmann decision, paid no less than $1,500,000,000 to $1,800,000,000 extra each year. This is the virtual equivalent of a 10 percent to 12 percent Federal sales tax on such items levied not for the benefit of the Public Treasury, but the groups of retailers and manufacturers who have sponsored most of the bills before you.

In January and April of 1949, Fortune magazine conducted a survey of prices on many items in the District of Columbia and comparable prices on such identical items in surrounding fair-trade territory. On the basis of this and other surveys Fortune conservatively estimated that fair trade was costing the American public no less than $750,000,000 annually. This study was made about 3 years ago and needs to be brought down to date. The St. Louis Star-Times conducted two surveys on prices in St. Louis where we have no fair trade and nearby Illinois that has a fair-trade law. Both of these studies will be made available to your committee, and while it is true they are flash surveys, they indicate clearly that average prices on liquor in Missouri are approximately 16 percent lower than in nearby Illinois, and that average prices on many drug items are no less than 12 percent lower than in Illinois.

Shortly after the Miller-Tydings Act was passed R. H. Macy & Co. of New York surveyed over 4,000 items sold under conditions of fair trade and before fair trade. This was one of the widest surveys conducted, and although it may come from an interested source, it indicated that the price of cosmetics as a result of fair trade price fixing had been raised 8.6 percent; drugs, 15.8 percent; liquors, 11.8 percent; books, 17.5; and miscellaneous items, 16.0 percent. In all the mass markets the survey indicated fair-trade laws have raised prices and have placed an added burden on the consuming public. The Chairman of the Department of Marketing in the School of Business and Public Administration of Temple University, Mr. Myron S. Heidingsfield, in a survey and article published in Women's Wear Daily of July 5, 1951, indicated that his study in Philadelphia, Pa., showed that most fair-traded items, particularly in appliances, were priced 20 percent too high for the average consumer, and that a number of devices had been resorted to by consumers, manufacturers, and retailers to get around fair trade price fixing restrictions in Philadelphia even before Schwegmann.

It would not be overstating the case to say that the annual overcharge to the public as a result of fair trade in 45 States has been closer to $2,000,000,000 a year than any other estimate that can be made. Approximately 200 discount houses in New York City alone the year before the Schwegmann case was decided sold more than $450,000,000 in brand-name appliances in violation of the New York Fels-Crawford fair-trade law. The savings to the public cannot be measured alone by the average 15 percent lower price than the fair-trade minimum for the marketing practices and prices of the competitors of the discount houses were obviously conditioned downward by the immense volume the discount houses were doing. The public saved no less than approximately $75,000,000 a year in lower prices on branded appliances bought in discount houses alone. This gives but a fair idea of the immense public benefit resulting from competitive pricing. The fair-trade laws are still on the lawbooks of 45 States and remain valid in intrastate commerce and also in interstate commerce, but do not apply to nonsigners. Such laws would be reactivated in a manner extremely harmful to public interest if the nonsigner clause should be upheld if enacted into law. This would mean that recalcitrants could be "dragged in by the heels" and their pricing policies policed by competitors to destroy competition and harmful to the public [sic].

I do not believe the United States Supreme Court would declare legal the compulsory, coercive pricing imposed by the nonsigner clause, but would hold such action to be a possible violation of the inherent right of any businessman to operate at the lowest possible cost and to price his merchandise accordingly. The statistical data of Mr. Maurice Mermy, the public relations man for the NARD, given in support of the McGuire bill on February 4, 1952, would seem to have little, if any, value. His data was designed to show that fair trade does not result in appreciably higher prices to the public. This data is anything but convincing because the number of items in the various surveys he relies on are not given; nor do we know who conducted these surveys because for the most part he speaks of disinterested surveys but does not identify them; nor does he give ⊥ the size of the sample, nor do we know when and in what cities and on what items and on what days the surveys were made, or whether the data is derived from comparable metropolitan areas. In statistics as in economics and in law and in some other fields, as Dean Roscoe Pound once pointed out, it is not too difficult to take a train that will get you where you want to go. As indicated, I find it difficult to believe that the American Fair Trade Council and the retail drug group, the NARD, two of the major organizations presently spending vast sums to restore fair-trade price fixing, and to destroy our antitrust laws, are at all dumb or do not know what they are after. On the contrary, they are well financed, well organized, and understand perfectly what they want—and I trust that the members of your committee understand equally well what they want and whether their bills are truly in the public interest. Their activities, according to the AFTC, are solely in the public interest and are not propaganda but truly educational work designed exclusively to promote the public interest.

I sometimes wonder how far the art of rationalization and self-deception can go. The AFTC states in a letter, to all members, of October 4, 1950, that all financial contributions and membership dues to the Fair Trade Council are for purely educational activities. It advises its members in the above letter that any money paid to the Fair Trade Council is a deductible item and tax-exempt. In this letter of October 4, 1950, the Fair Trade Council also advises and suggests that the advertising agencies handling its members' accounts may be asked or invited to pay a certain percentage of the advertising agencies' 15 percent to support the Fair Trade Council. This letter contained a sharp attack by the AFTC on the attorney general of Texas and the attorney general of Missouri and offered to help its members in fighting antitrust prosecutions. The letter of October 4, 1950, from which the above is taken must have been forgotten when in a later letter to all Fair Trade Council members, dated January 7, 1952, it solicited contributions from its members not for educational purposes, but on the basis of the actual financial interest of all members in fair trade. It would appear to be such a comfort when education and self-interest can properly go hand in hand; when patriotism and increased profit synchonize [sic] so beautifully. To be sure, it may sometimes be a bit difficult to draw the line, to know just where patriotism ceases, and self-interest begins. However, that is a matter that we need not concern ourselves with at this time.

Under conditions of competition that type of production and distribution will tend to survive which performs its function most efficiently, wins wide consumer acceptance, and therefore deserves to survive. The resistance of established producers and distributors to new techniques that may lower costs and give the public better values is easy to understand. There were riots and bloodshed in Scotland when textile machinery was introduced. Toll roads resisted railroads and the rails in turn have resisted lower cost methods of transportation. The department stores providing certain marketing advantages to the public were denounced as iniquitous institutions encouraging the public to buy on credit and thus go into debt. Perhaps there is a point there that we ought not to pass over too lightly? Chain-store merchandising was likewise resisted just as the movement of food stores into meats and produce was not welcomed by competitors. Retail druggists made many efforts to resist and are still making such efforts to resist the movement of drugs, sundries, toiletries, and similar products through super food stores. I trust and believe that your committee will weigh with the utmost care not only the requests of the NARD and the AFTC, but also what I believe to be the excellent recommendations of the Federal Trade Commission and the Antitrust Division. I should think it unnecessary to urge you to look beyond those who seek to destroy competition—those who seek special privileges for their groups—and instead to keep your eyes steadily on the 150,000,000 consumers who are trying to fight inflation, buy under conditions of competition, protect their living standard, and make their 50-cent dollars go a little further. I trust and believe that your recommendations will be in the public interest and designed to protect our national policy against horizontal and vertical price fixing, and our national faith in the American free competitive economy, without which it would be very difficult for political democracy to survive.

I shall make available to your committee in a few days a number of exhibits from my file on the matters before you, showing the attitude of the press and also some data on comparative price studies. The following editorial appeared in the St. Louis Post-Dispatch December 27, 1951:

"ANOTHER FAIR TRADE SCHEME

"It is an old tactic of pressure groups, faced with an unpleasant Supreme Court ruling, to try to get Congress to legalize what the Court has already declared illegal. And that is what the American Fair Trade Council hopes to do when Congress convenes. The council has drafted a proposed law to permit fair trade which, by any other name, means price fixing. Last May the Supreme Court ruled that retailers who do not sign fair trade contracts with manufacturers do not have to observe the minimum retail prices which the manufacturers set for their goods. In short, the retailers could charge what their purses and prospects allowed them to. This, of course, applies to goods in interstate commerce. The ruling knocked the wind out of a lot of efforts to fix retail prices. Moreover, the Justice Department later warned it would prosecute if it caught manufacturers trying to gang up on small retailers to make them sign the so-called fair trade contracts. So now the fair trading lobby wants to amend the Sherman Act, and there is irony in this. The Sherman Act is intended to help protect free competition. The amendment is intended to help cripple it. For the measure would make the manufacturers' retail prices binding on all retailers, whether or not they sign contracts and whether or not the goods are even in interstate commerce. Congress will quickly discover that such a bill would defeat the intent of the antitrust laws, the Supreme Court decision, and the Justice Department. It would help those few who fear that economic competition is dangerous business."

On February 7, 1952, the Wall Street Journal carried the following editorial which put the matter on some of the bills before you in rather clear fashion. The editorial reads as follows:

"THE FAIRNESS OF FAIR TRADE

"As was to be expected, friends of the so-called fair-trade laws are working in Congress to rehabilitate them. A Federal statute declares that where State-made law enables a manufacturer to bind all retailers to a fixed resale price by making a contract with a single retailer, the Federal Government will not object. But last year the United States Supreme Court ruled that no person can be bound by a contract to which he is not a party.

"Thereupon retailers all over the country reduced their prices on a great variety of merchandise. The reductions spread to goods which had not been price-fixed through fair-trade contracts and for a time the price cutting assumed the characteristics of an irrational price warfare. In a few weeks the war burned itself out, but without quieting the clamor that the Supreme Court decision had left small retail businesses at the mercy of their more effluent [sic] and therefore more powerful competitors.

"The court decision coincided with events which would doubtless have lowered selling prices in its absence. The buying mania that followed the outbreak of war in Korea had had two unsettling results. Consumers in general were more than usually well supplied with goods of many sorts while distributors had accumulated unusually large inventories. The latter had to move their goods against rising consumer resistance and price cuts were the only effective motive power.

"Now indignant protest rises against what Chairman PATMAN of the House Small Business Committee calls 'deceitful and misleading price cutting.' This is a reference to the 'loss leader,' the offering of one or a few items at prices near or below cost as a means of luring buyers into a store. The idea is, of course, that once inside they will buy other goods not similarly marked down. They are assumed to be that dumb.

"Partisans of fair trade frankly say they are out to overturn the Supreme Court decision in practical effect. It is hard to see how they can restore the dangerous privilege of manufacturers or wholesalers to control the actions of thousands of merchandisers without their consent and even against their will. The Supreme Court has said that such a power is beyond the law and certainly it should be. But in their heyday the fair-trade laws and the contracts under them did not completely freeze prices for the goods involved. There were then many indications—and complaints, too—that this putative method of protecting small business was breaking down. Traders who were active in defeating them were called chiselers and other hard names, which didn't bother them much.

"Fair trade practices as heretofore in use are potentially dangerous. They invite manufacturers and distributors of competing articles to enter into understandings to maintain prices higher than would otherwise prevail. Carried far enough, they would defeat the efforts of lawmakers and administrators to prevent unreasonable restraints of trade, which are the hallmarks of monopolism. A congressional regard for the safety of small business is proper enough, but the stake of all consumers in a free market cannot be ignored."

Ninety percent of the membership of the St. Louis Chamber of Commerce is made up of small businesses. The large retail stores do not constitute 2 percent of its membership according to Frank E. Lawrence, secretary of the chamber of commerce. However, because the chamber strongly opposed the retail druggists' fair trade bill for Missouri, the Missouri retail drug group resigned from the St. Louis Chamber of Commerce. A two-column story announcing this action appeared in the St. Louis Post-Dispatch of September 17, 1951. On the next day the Post-Dispatch carried the following editorial:

"THE DRUGGISTS WALK OUT

"The Retail Druggists' Association of Greater St. Louis got its ideas pretty thoroughly confused in the attack on the St. Louis Chamber of Commerce with which it withdrew its membership in that organization. Herman P. Winkelmann, executive manager of the druggists' association, denounced the chamber's opposition to the so-called fair trade law, a misleading name for a price-fixing device. He said the chamber 'is strictly big business and controlled by big business, principally the large retail stores.' We do not think Mr. Winkelmann can prove that there is anything wrong about bigness in business unless the bigness is used to destroy competition. The manager of the druggists' association is, however, all in favor or destroying competition, not by bigness, ⊥ but by price fixing under the guise of fair trade. The law, the association advocates, would enable druggists and manufacturers to fix prices at which a product could be sold. The chamber of commerce deserves commendation for the sensible and courageous attitude it has taken toward fair trade legislation. Fair trade is a device to soak the consumer and the chamber believes it is poor business. Do the druggists who are members of the Retail Druggists' Association think they are improving relations with their customers by this display of organized effort to deprive their customers of competitive prices?"

Remove the coercive pressure of organized retailers and often, not all, but many manufacturers lose interest in fair-trade price fixing. Often these manufacturers have reluctantly yielded to the demand to price fix, fair-trade fashion their brands, only to find they have priced themselves out of a good part of the market, thus necessitating the sale of multiple and/or unbranded merchandise, or private retailers brands, in order to utilize idle-plant capacity. Manufacturers have not forgotten the Pepsodent experience; nor has the retail drug group forgotten it. Manufacturers have been faced with a demand for a maintained resale price and margin. Then the demand takes the form of a request for a wider margin; then efforts are made to force manufacturers, for example, not to sell drug items in food stores. Until some manufacturers begin to wonder if they or their retail outlets control the manufacturers marketing policies. Some manufacturers of drug items are happy to see more of their products move through food stores, directly, by means of rack operators, or otherwise; for in this fashion the power of such groups as organized retail druggists to force manufacturers to do their bidding, ala Pepsodent fashion, is lessened.

Moving with the organized precision of a Panzer division, groups of interested retail druggists and brand name manufacturers, such as the Fair Trade Council of Gary, Ind., have successfully used enormous political pressure in first lobbying through Congress, first, the Miller-Tydings Act, and then, with the same tactics, adequately financed, lobbied through the State legislature [sic], 45 fair trade laws, in all States except Texas, Missouri, Vermont, and the Federal District of Columbia. Shortly after the Miller-Tydings Act was passed, these groups successfully pushed through 17 State legislatures, fair-trade laws. Prof. Malcolm P. McNair, of Harvard, pointed out in the April 1938 Journal of Marketing that 10 of these State laws enacting fair-trade price fixing copied the same stenographic error into their State statute. This would seem to give some idea of the organized pressure of interested groups for such legislation.

The constitutional right of citizens to assemble and peaceably petition their legislators for redress of grievances is so fundamental and important that there is no abuse too great to bear rather than to infringe upon that right. However, in some proper way, Members of Congress and of State legislative bodies, must find means to protect themselves from such political pressure and coercion, so that they may legislate fearlessly in the public interest, without threats of political reprisal of interested lobbies. I should suggest frequent and very detailed financial reports of all regular professional lobbyists as a start in the right direction. We must not confuse these organized and heavily financed pressure campaigns of interested manufacturers and retailers with the public interest.

In an Ohio Court of Appeals case, *Serer* [sic] *Cigarette Service Co.* (74 N. E. (2d) 853),[3.73] decided toward the end of 1947, it was held that in this case the Ohio unfair "Cigarette Sales Act, prohibiting a wholesaler from selling cigarettes at less than cost to wholesaler" with intent to injure competition, was declared unconstitutional. It was held that the act divested a cash and carry wholesaler of property rights, of advantages inherent in the cash and carry method of

---

[3.73] The correct citation is Serrer v. Cigarette Service Co., 74 N.E.2d 853 (Ohio Ct. App. 1947).

doing business. I do not know what may have happened in this case if it was appealed; nor do I know if there was any attempt to meet the objections by legislation, of the court decision in this case. It does serve, however, to indicate that courts are aware of the inherent property right that an individual may have in doing business with a lower operating cost factor, and the inherent property right to price accordingly; and that efforts by legislation or otherwise to deprive an individual of such right, may be an unconstitutional deprivation of property without due process of law. The above may be of interest relative to H. R. 6367 introduced by Mr. KEOGH, as an amendment to the Sherman Act of 1890. There is no misunderstanding the intent and purpose of this bill. It is aimed directly at reversing by legislation the Sunbeam-Wentling case that arose in Palmyra, Pa.

Briefly, Wentling is no Sears or Montgomery-Ward. These giant mail-order houses have their own private brands, such as All State, Cross Country, Kenmore, Silvertone, and others. Wentling appears to be essentially a discount house operator doing business in name brand merchandise, mail-order fashion. He sold Sunbeam Shavemasters at $17.25 when the fixed fair-trade minimum price in fair-trade territory was $23.50, a saving to anyone who would order from Wentling by mail, of $6.25. In the lower United States district court, those interested in fair trade won a complete victory but on appeal a three-man United States court of appeals sitting in Philadelphia reversed the lower court. It was held that Wentling would have to respect the Pennsylvania fair-trade minimum in intrastate trade, but could sell in interstate commerce for any price that he wished. Then of course Schwegmann came along May 21, 1951, to give Wentling added freedom to price competitively in interstate commerce, since he was a nonsigner and could not be "dragged in by the heels" to price as fair-traders wanted him to. Now the Keogh bill, H. R. 6367, obligates a mail-order dealer, such as Wentling to respect fair-trade minimum prices on branded goods and prevents any mail-order house from selling in interstate commerce below any fair-traded minimum price, even though he is not party to such contract. This would permit Wentling to do business in Palmyra, Pa., but effectively destroys all of his interstate, mail-order business. This does not regulate interstate commerce; it clearly destroys it. Why would anyone in his right mind sit down and take the time and effort necessary to order by mail a branded product, even if Wentling absorbed shipping charges, when with no effort at all a buyer can get immediate delivery by going to any retail outlet and buy the branded product at the same price, have the opportunity to examine the product and take it home at once?

The full import of the Keogh bill would seem to be rather shocking. In a release from the American Fair Trade Council temporary headquarters, suite 773, Mayflower Hotel, Washington, D. C., the AFTC proudly states that the "council has participated in the long series of discussions and studies which have brought about this draft regarded by the council as legislatively leakproof and economically sound." The above AFTC bulletin goes on to say the Keogh bill "has as its primary intent and certain effect, among other objectives in which consumers have a vital interest or stake," "the restriction, in the public interest, of the growth of retail monopoly, than which there is no form of monopoly more oppressive and to the public in general." "In fact, H. R. 6367." continued Mr. Anderson (head of the AFTC), "may quite properly go down in history as the Keogh antimonopoly law." This seems to be taking in quite a lot of territory. I find it difficult to believe that this bill is quite equal to the discovery of the principle of the wheel or the discovery of fire or the invention of printing. Perhaps the lady doth protest a bit too much. It should be noted that the AFTC (as above quoted in its release of February 3, 1952) now speaks not only as the trade group speaking for 5,000 brand-name manufacturers, one of the most effective and aggressive trade groups promoting fair-trade price fixing and attempting to destroy all antitrust laws, but now also is the advocate of wage earners, consumers, and the public interest. This assumption that what brand-name manufacturers and retailers want in the way of private control of pricing policies is automatically in the interest of the public is a fallacy that the advocates of fair trade almost invariably fall into.

I do not believe that Congress after careful reflection will ever pass this bill frankly and clearly intended to destroy competitive pricing of branded goods in interstate commerce. If Congress should ever do so, I do not believe that any President, of whatever political party, would ever sign such a bill, if the device of a rider, to a bill the President cannot veto, is not used; nor do I believe the United States Supreme Court would sustain it.

Mr. John Anderson, of the AFTC, in the above release of a little over a month ago, calls the Keogh bill "legislatively leakproof and economically sound." If it is ever enacted into law, I should prefer to await the judgment of the Supreme Court relative to its constitutionality; just as I should prefer to await the judgment of disinterested professional economists as to its economic soundness. My own view is that it is neither sound law nor economics. Indeed, it seems rather shocking. I should like a detailed explanation as to how you fight monopoly by preventing a low-cost mail-order house from selling a branded appliance for several dollars below the fixed higher price of a higher-cost distributor, in interstate commerce. From the standpoint of the public interest and consumers, the Keogh bill is easily one of the worst introduced at this session of Congress, though it does have some keen competition for that honor; chiefly from the bills presently before you to validate the nonsigner clause. I should venture to suggest that if H. R. 6367 is enacted by Congress, the United States Supreme Court, at the first opportunity, would declare the law invalid, on the ground that it does not regulate but destroys the free flow of commerce between the States and also that it deprives an individual of property without due process of law, in that it prevents a mail-order operator from enjoying his inherent right to do business on a lower-cost basis and price accordingly.

The bills before you to reverse Schwegmann and validate the nonsigner clause are far worse than the NRA ever was. It was a fatal weakness of the NRA that it illegally delegated legislative authority relative to pricing policies and other practices to NRA code authorities. It was declared unconstitutional by a unanimous decision of the Supreme Court. The Court also held the retailing of chickens in New York was not interstate commerce.[3.74] A basic weakness of the NRA was the belief that the industry that is to be regulated shall be the regulator. However, other groups were represented in the NRA. It had the appearance of a public body, although practically all NRA code authorities were dominated by trade groups. Many economists asserted that 90 percent of the enthusiasm of trade groups for the NRA was primarily motivated by a desire to engage in practices involving collusive restraint of trade and price-fixing ⊥ practices that were and are illegal under our antitrust laws.

It may be of interest to point out that the St. Louis consumer group, organized under the NRA successfully fought retail coal price fixing of Retail Solid Fuel NRA Code Authority No. 32 in St. Louis, and that the successful fight of the St. Louis consumer group to destroy coal-price fixing in our market led directly to the resignation of the National Coal Code Authority as well as the local code authority. This consumer organization, of which I was a charter member, with Bishop Scarlett and Father W. F. Mullally and a number of others, appointed by Prof. PAUL DOUGLAS, then with the NRA Consumers Council, functioned as a local body since 1934. In the past 18 years it has also fought high fixed retail milk prices, and on many occasions has defended the excellent Missouri antitrust laws whenever attacked by those who tried to introduce fair-trade price fixing into Missouri. The St. Louis consumer group has grown over the years and has many allied and affiliated civic bodies. Its constituent members represent organizations with a total membership of over 145,000 in the St. Louis metropolitan area.

I have served as its marketing consultant for many years, I have declined nomination to national consumer organizations as I do not have the time to serve on such bodies. Our local group of St. Louis consumers has no world shaking program, it has never advised the State Department on how to run its business, it is not interested in Spain, and wouldn't know how to start to make the world over. However its members and its executive committee does [sic] understand the Missouri antitrust laws, the Federal antitrust laws, and what all price fixers are up to. We have been interested exclusively in adequate consumer information about quality of products, and also very much interested in preserving free competitive prices against all efforts of trade restrainers. It is not too difficult to identify such groups, for sooner or later they suggest modifying our State antitrust laws; just as the bills presently before you fail utterly to achieve their true purpose, unless you agree to an end or destroy the Sherman Act and our other antitrust laws.

I should hesitate to trust the wisest and most benevolent bureaucrat with the compulsory pricing powers and the policing of competitors['] prices. Much less would I trust such compulsory pricing powers to private interested, unregulated trade groups, without any public authority to check abuses. Even public regulatory bodies do not always succeed in safeguarding adequately public interest. What justifies the assumption that the unregulated, vast pricing powers that go much further than the NRA ever permitted, may not be abused[?] I think such fair trade price fixing powers, eliminating competitive pricing on many branded items by legalizing vertical price control, and making nonsigners conform and not compete, would inevitably and unquestionably be abused. Either we want competition or we do not. If we are to legislate in the public interest then the bills before you to validate the nonsigner clause must be defeated, and the Curtis bill, to repeal the Miller-Tydings Act should be enacted into law.

Adam Smith was a professor of philosophy and a famous Scot. His great book on The Wealth of Nations is one of the classics of all time. Adam Smith is the father of political economy. You may be interested in one of his widely used quotations. This in no way disparages many excellent activities of trade groups. It is very pertinent, however, relative to resale price maintenance activities.

Adam Smith in his Wealth of Nations said: "People of the same trade seldom meet together, even for merriment and diversion, but the conversation ends in a conspiracy against the public, or in some contrivance to raise prices. * * * Though the law cannot hinder people

---

[3.74] A.L.A. Schechter Poultry Co. v. United States, 295 U.S. 495 (1935).

of the same trade from sometime assembling together, it ought to do nothing to facilitate such assemblies, much less to render them necessary."

The late Prof. Frank Fetter of Princeton University often said, "Whenever you hear any trade group advocate fair trade, it is time for all hands to be on deck for the Republic is in danger."

In a 600-page study for the Twentieth Century Fund, Dr. George W. Stocking of Vanderbilt University and Professor Watkins have this to say relative to retail maintenance. The following quotation appears on page 330 of this book published in 1951, on Monopoly and Free Enterprise:

"Originally price maintenance was designed to prevent price-cutting dealers from exploiting the brand good will of manufacturers at the manufacturers' expense; currently it is used to prevent price-cutting dealers from upsetting the rigged market for price-maintained goods to the detriment of organized retailers with a vested interest in noncompetitive distribution. From the standpoint of the public interest in revitalizing competitive forces, resale price maintenance is objectionable whatever group sponsors it. It deprives low-cost distributors of the competitive advantage of superior efficiency, and thereby deprives consumers of their full share of the benefits from improved business organization and less costly merchandising methods. In many manufacturing industries it restricts opportunities for the launching of new enterprises, or the expansion of old ones, by fostering trivial differentiation of products, irrational choice of goods by consumers, and uneconomic allocation of resources."

Those interested in resale price maintenance often refer to the pricing practices of motorcar manufacturers as a justification for fair trade. It is evident, however, that rigid retail prices are impossible to enforce wherever there is a significant trade-in problem. In motors, in a sellers' or buyers' market, the evaluation of the used car, the purchase of accessories, and frequently outright premiums or discounts provide the necessary leverage for competitive prices and consumer shopping for values.

In the food trade, relatively few food products have been placed under minimum resale price contracts. This is due to the prevalence of giant super food stores, of which there are over 15,000, the prominent place of retailers' private brands, and the fact that not for long can any food get too far out of line competitively for which there is a fairly acceptable substitute.

Fair trade is a contradiction in a free-enterprise society. If manufacturers are to tell retailers the minimum prices at which to sell products, what incentive is there for more efficient distribution? For more efficient retailing? In no case was a fair-trade law ever enacted as the result of a request of any disinterested civic group. These laws did not come as the Sherman Act did, as a result of widespread public demand for the preservation and protection of the public against collusive pricing, horizontal and vertical. Resale-price fixing, particularly during the present high inflationary period, is extremely harmful to living standards, and invariably results in sharply higher fixed prices on many branded items—drugs, appliances, liquor, and any number of other branded goods. Had it not been for the press in Missouri, the St. Louis Chamber of Commerce, farm groups, and various civic groups, those interested in enacting a fair-trade law in Missouri would likely have succeeded in our States [sic], as they did in 45 others. Certainly the organized groups sponsoring fair-trade laws tried often enough and hard enough, and I expect they may try again. For they may suffer any number of defeats, but need succeed only once. As one put it, during a period of high prices and low-purchasing power of the dollar, it is rather difficult to force many families with Third Avenue incomes to pay Fifth Avenue prices. People do not regard themselves as lawbreakers merely because they are obliged to shop for the better values and better buys. There is no mystery that surrounds the rise of 200 discount houses in New York City that did an annual volume in branded appliances of over $450,000,000. The wonder is they did not arise sooner and grow faster. Neither should we be surprised at the sharp increase in the number of rack jobbers, moving drug items through super food stores; just as drug stores took tobacco business from tobacco stores and candy trade from confectionery stores. If the public likes one step, self-service shopping, day and night, for food, drug, meat, bakery, and other items, that is the way it most certainly will be. Lower cost dealers and manufacturers, and rational buyers will find a method of circumventing artificial road blocks to competition.

Mr. MORSE. Mr. President, in the interest of saving time, I desire to read and very briefly discuss two amendments I shall call up later this afternoon, after action shall have been taken on the Douglas amendment. I shall support the Douglas amendment, because I think it meets the major argument of the Senator from Minnesota. The Douglas amendment involves a great question of public policy—yes, I believe it sets forth the duty devolving on the Congress to protect the small-business man from the type of economic blackmail involved in loss-leader tactics. The small-business man does not need protection from fair competition. He needs protection from economic coercion, duress, and monopolistic dictation of his economic opportunities to do business. We do have a public interest, Mr. President, in the economic practices of any group which, if allowed to go unchecked and uncontrolled, would work a great injustice on businessmen, on consumers, and on any other group to the detriment of which the practice is promulgated.

I think the Senator from Illinois [Mr. DOUGLAS] has put his finger on that area of legislative duty in regard to which Congress is called upon to take action. It is the amendment of the Senator from Illinois, in my judgment, that gives the small-business man the protection from the kind of economic blackmail the Senator from Minnesota [Mr. HUMPHREY] so eloquently discussed in his very persuasive speech of last night and this morning. But, Mr. President, the answer to the great evils, the great injustices, the great wrongs, which the Senator from Minnesota deplores so eloquently, is not to turn over to the retailers and manufacturers the power, legislatively unchecked, to fix prices.

The action that should be taken by legislation, as the Senator from Illinois has proposed, is to make clear that chain-store groups and manufacturers who use the kind of economic blackmail which characterizes the loss-leader technique violate sound public policy. It should be made clear to them that the practice exceeds competitive rights; that it is not in keeping with the principles of American justice, for men must so conduct themselves in a society of self-governing people as not to wrong their neighbors. Those are sound jurisdictional and juridical bases for the principle of the Douglas amendment, but, frankly, Mr. President, I have not been able to make the jump in reasoning that my good friend from Minnesota makes when he says that because there are many instances in which great injustice is being done the small retailer by the chain-store groups, and by the loss-leader proponents, therefore, we should pass legislation which, in effect, in my opinion, would take from under the purview and the check of a sound antitrust legislative program those who would profit from the adoption of resale price maintenance legislation.

So, Mr. President, I can support enthusiastically the amendment of the Senator from Illinois, but I cannot go along with the Senator from Minnesota as he proposes in the pending bill to give too much unchecked economic power, to those who seek the advantages of the pending bill.

In the course of the afternoon, Mr. President, without further comment on the amendments other than what I now make, in the interest of saving time, I shall call up, after the Douglas amendment is disposed of, two amendments, one of which is as follows:

On page 2, line 24,[3.75] after the word "resale", insert "*Provided, however,* That such minimum or stipulated prices as are prescribed in such contracts or agreements shall, after due consultation with representatives of persons substantially affected by such contracts or agreements, have been determined to be fair and reasonable by a duly constituted board or agency of the State in which such minimum or stipulated prices are to be charged."

In support of that amendment—

The PRESIDING OFFICER. Permit the Chair to state that the Douglas amendment has been offered as a complete substitute. Should it be adopted, then, of course, the amendment which the Senator from Oregon is suggesting would not be in order.

Mr. MORSE. I understand the parliamentary situation. I shall vote for the Douglas amendment. If it is agreed to, that ends it, so far as I am concerned.

I shall talk with the Senator from Illinois as soon as I finish these remarks in regard to my amendments to see if he thinks any revision of them might be worked into his substitute. If his subsitute [*sic*] fails, I shall offer these two amendments to the bill proper.

The purpose of the first amendment is to insure an impartial determination as to the reasonableness of prices established in resale price maintenance contracts which are legalized under the bill.

Under the present bill, the manufacturer, providing only that he sign a single

---

[3.75] Reference is to the House-passed version of H.R. 5767.

retail price maintenance agreement with one outlet in a given State, is able to determine the prices for fair-traded commodities. There is no one to say whether these prices are fair either to the small merchant or to the consumer.

The record shows that in many instances retailers have been victimized because large manufacturers have failed to provide them with adequate margins under resale price maintenance contracts. Conversely, consumers have at times been injured because of the extraordinary high prices set by the manufacturer.

To permit manufacturers to set prices without consultation with either groups of retailers or groups of consumers, is to authorize the exercise of power far greater than that which the Government has lawfully employed in support of its price-control activities. Ceiling prices established by Government agencies must be prefaced by consultations with representatives of industry and with other persons affected thereby. Elaborate appeal procedures have been established for persons aggrieved by price setting thereunder.

My amendment provides that the prices set in resale price maintenance contracts shall have been determined to be reasonable by a State agency after consultation with persons affected by resale price maintenance contracts or agreements. The consultation provision I have taken practically verbatim from the Defense Production Act of 1950 whereby Congress provided procedural safeguards for those affected by Government regulations fixing prices. I think it only fair that we extend these same safeguards to those whose prices are fixed pursuant to resale price maintenance contracts.

The second amendment I shall offer, Mr. President, is as follows:

Page 1, line 7, strike out the words "or stipulated."
Page 1, line 8, strike out the words "or stipulated."
Page 2, line 12, strike out the words "or stipulated."
Page 2, line 14, strike out the words "or stipulated."
Page 3, lines 21 and 22, strike out the words "or stipulated."

In regard to this amendment, I wish to say that as I understand, the purpose of so-called fair-trade legislation is to provide a minimum or floor for the independent merchant in order to assure him at least an adequate profit on many of his important selling items. Thus the Miller-Tydings Act, which the Congress passed in 1937, legalized contracts "providing for the establishment or maintenance of minimum resale prices." As I read the McGuire bill, however, it appears that it goes one step further and legalizes contracts which provide for "stipulated" prices.

I can see where it might be highly desirable to establish minimum retail prices as we have established minimum farm prices and minimum wages. However, I seriously question the desirability of authorizing so-called stipulated prices which, in effect, sanction the fixing of maximum as well as minimum retail price levels. To permit the establishment of maximum or stipulated prices is unadulterated price fixing by private businessmen with no public control and no public check, that really take care of the interests of the consumer, whereas, when we do something analogous to it, as the Senator from Minnesota was seeking to argue last night in regard to farm-support matters, we are doing it through the Government, with a Government check, and with the Government constantly in control of the procedure and determining what the minima shall be.

Permitting manufacturers to set ceiling prices as well as minimums is certainly not in the interests of the retail merchant. Mr. Herman Nolen, vice president of McKesson & Robbins, Inc., informed Mr. PRIEST'S subcommittee that independent merchants would be driven out of business if they were required to sell at the minimums prescribed by the manufacturer and were not permitted to sell some products at higher than established retail levels. Let me quote you verbatim what the vice president of McKesson & Robbins said:

I don't think that I would be talking out of school, but I can tell you this: That if every distributor sold at fair-trade minimums and I am including ourselves, we would starve to death. We have got to sell some products at more than the fair-trade minimums, because the fair-trade minimums are not high enough. When a manufacturer sets a fair-trade minimum he is not thinking of us or the retailer, he is thinking of himself and, "Where will I sell the most products?" (hearings on H. R. 5767, p. 121).

I think that was a very frank, objective, truthful statement made by the vice president of McKesson & Robbins, but I believe it proves my point as to why it is desirable to strike out of the bill that little catchy word "stipulated"; with all of its implications for economic rape of the American consumer.

While independent merchants may need the safeguards of minimum floors on the selling of their stock, I believe it would be highly detrimental to the welfare of small business to permit the manufacturer to set price ceilings as well as price floors. Minimum prices to protect our small retailers is one thing; ceiling or stipulated prices is another. To sanction price fixing of this nature by the manufacturers would saddle retailers throughout the country with a private OPA answerable to no man or government.

Accordingly, Mr. President, I urgently ask the Senate to adopt this simple amendment which would strike out the word "stipulated" wherever appearing in the McGuire bill and thereby confine the bill to its original purposes—that of guaranteeing a minimum price to our small retailer.

Mr. President, I close by saying, as I indicated at the beginning of my remarks, that while I do not deny that there is much that can be said on the affirmative side of the bill, it is my honest judgment that when we weigh the pros and cons of the bill, the public interest, the consumer interest, yes, the interest of the businessman himself, calls for a negative vote.

I say that, Mr. President, because I am worried about some signs I think I see developing in the American economy. I believe we are moving too far down the road toward a regulated economy. We can have a regulated economy that takes a variety of forms; we can have a regulated economy by a bureaucratic government that seeks to exercise unchecked, discretionary, and arbitrary power over ⊥ the economic life of all the American people; we can have a regulated economy, too, if we yield to the growing monopolistic control over more and more segments of American business.

To the druggists and the food merchants who are so displeased with the junior Senator from Oregon because he would not agree to commit himself to vote for the McGuire bill, let me say that I shall continue to fight for their right to free competition, but it must be free competition.

As to the growing tendency toward monopolistic controls in the United States, the sad fact is that the small merchants—such as the druggists and food merchants—are not nearly so free economically as they think they are.

I think the bill is an economic wolf in sheep's clothing; and if the small merchants let in the wolf, it will devour their economic freedom.

Mr. McCARRAN obtained the floor.

Mr. McFARLAND. Mr. President, will the Senator yield?

Mr. McCARRAN. I yield to the Senator from Arizona.

Mr. McFARLAND. I know that a number of Senators are anxious to address the Senate on other than pending matters, but their remarks should more properly come after the disposition of the regular business.

I believe Senators are anxious that we proceed with the consideration of the bill, so in order that that may be done I ask unanimous consent that at the conclusion of the remarks of the distinguished Senator from Nevada [Mr. McCARRAN] the debate be limited on the bill as follows:

One hour on the bill, the time to be divided equally between the Senator from Illinois [Mr. DOUGLAS] and the Senator from Minnesota [Mr. HUMPHREY]; that there be a limitation of 40 minutes on each amendment, the time to be divided equally between the proponent of the amendment and the Senator from Minnesota, in the event he is opposed to the amendment and if he favors the amendment, then the time to be controlled by the distinguished minority leader or anyone whom he may designate; and that all amendments shall be germane.

Mr. LONG. Mr. President, will the Senator yield?

The PRESIDING OFFICER. Does the Senator from Nevada yield to the Senator from Louisiana?

Mr. McCARRAN, I yield.

Mr. LONG. I see no reason why we cannot vote on the measure today without a unanimous-consent agreement. There is an amendment I might offer, which has been debated before, but it might require a greater amount of time for debate than that proposed.

Mr. McFARLAND. How much time would the Senator require? The main purpose that would be accomplished by the agreement would be that the remarks of Senators must be germane to amendments or to the bill. Other speeches would follow. I am willing to stay as late as any Senator desires to talk, but I should like to make it possible for the Senate to conclude today at an early hour. If the Senator from Louisiana desires a longer time to discuss his amendment, I will agree to an exception in that case.

Mr. LONG. It seems to me that we should be able to vote on the measure today, but I feel that rather than debate under a limitation, we should simply debate the bill. Then when the Senate is ready to vote, we can proceed to vote. I know of no Senator who is particularly anxious to delay a vote. At this time I would object to a limitation of debate.

Mr. McFARLAND. I regret very much that the Senator objects, because I would be willing to make an exception in the case of his amendment and to give him the time he needs. The purpose of the unanimous-consent agreement is to provide that remarks made during the consideration of the bill shall be germane to the issue. Senators would then know when they might rely on having an opportunity to make other speeches. Senators have been very cooperative about the situation. Many have stayed until late in the evening in order to be able to make their speeches and not interrupt the regular procedure. I hope the Senator from Louisiana will state a time which would be satisfactory in which to debate his amendment.

Mr. LONG. So far as I am concerned, I shall be happy to vote on the measure today, and I hope the Senate can do so. I do not see any reason why we should not be able to do so. However, at this time, I would not wish to agree to a unanimous-consent agreement on limitation of debate. . . .

⊥ Mr. BENTON. Mr. President, I am very pleased to see that the Senator from Minnesota [Mr. HUMPHREY] has returned to the floor. Indeed, my preceding comments on the remarkable report filed today in the House of Representatives were made at that point in the hope that the Senator from Minnesota might be able to return to the floor before I proceeded to discuss the bill now before us. ⊥ 8865

DISCUSSION OF FAIR-TRADE BILL

I wonder how many of our colleagues know how intimately the junior Senator from Minnesota knows whereof he speaks when he talks to us about fair-trade practices as applied to retail stores. The Senator from Minnesota is the only ex-pharmacist in the United States Senate. I remember once meeting him on his way to a druggists' convention, and later discovering the pride the druggists of America take in their ex-pharmacist in the Senate, as indeed they should as he is one of its most eminent and eloquent Members. Once when I was talking with him about his own background, he said to me, "Until I was 25 years old, I practically had never set foot outside a drug store." It was at the age of 25, and this is an interesting comment upon his background, that he left his father's drug store in Huron, South Dakota, to depart for academic studies at the University of Minnesota. This was his great decision, of course, which made him mayor of Minneapolis, and which later caused the people of Minnesota, in gratitude for his great public record as mayor of Minneapolis, to elect him, by a margin of a quarter of a million votes, to the United States Senate, as the first Democratic Senator to be elected in Minnesota since the Civil War.

Mr. President, without being unduly discursive, I wish to observe that I think I also know something about the field of business activities which this bill affects. For several year [sic], as a young man, I spent more than 8 hours every day at a typewriter and in the field with people who worked in retail stores, developing material for writing advertisements for Drug Topics, Hardware Age, Progressive Grocer, and countless other journals of the trade press. The earliest of my 13 years in the advertising business began as a $25- and later $50- and $100-a-week copywriter, writing trade-paper advertisements; and one cannot write good trade-paper advertisements unless he spends a large part of his time in the field talking to the dealers whom he is trying to advise and persuade. This advertising experience of mine followed more than 2 years as a salesman selling cash registers and other articles, and spending all day, and frequently far into the evening, working with the retail trade, trying to learn its problems. So I feel I have a special background which qualifies me to speak on this bill. But, in addition to this background of my own, in addition to the fact I have spent a good part of my life in the business community and as a businessman, I have had a further special interest in the bill. My distinguished colleague in the other House, Representative JOHN MCGUIRE, of Wallingford, Connecticut, is the original sponsor of this fair trade bill. Indeed, it is known as the MCGUIRE bill. Representative MCGUIRE has achieved a national reputation among those interested in this subject as a result of the hard work he has done in developing his bill and bringing it to the point of being debated today in the United States Senate.

Mr. President, this bill is regarded as vital to the future of our independent retail merchants. In my opinion, however, it is not a bill to be urged upon economic grounds alone though it seems that most of the discussion about this bill thus far has fallen into the field of economics. I suggest, Mr. President, that the bill, in addition to interesting distinguished economists, should perhaps more appropriately, or with equal appropriateness, interest sociologists and political scientists, whose views have not found expression in the discussion of this bill. I might question only one aspect of the presentation of my distinguished colleague from Minnesota [Mr. HUMPHREY] last night and this morning. His eloquent words on this subject certainly moved all who heard them. However, I myself do not think—and I doubt whether the Senator from Minnesota would advance it as a prior argument—that the major justification for this is to protect the weak from the strong. The Senator from Minnesota used some very marvelous metaphors this morning. He spoke of protecting the canary from the eagles. He spoke of what Joe Louis would do to any Senator who got in the ring with him.

He referred to what would happen to a high school football team if it found itself opposing Notre Dame. Mr. President, I admit that I should be for killing the canary, annihilating the high school football team, and letting the poor Senator wish he had never gotten into the ring, and regret it on his death bed, if need be, if I thought those things were actually in the public interest. I believe this bill should be urged solely because it serves the public interest, not because it may seem to be in the interest of the certain grocers, druggists, hardware stores, or other retailers whose representatives have been before committees of the Congress, advancing their own case from the standpoint of their own problems as they see them.

Mr. HUMPHREY. Mr. President, will the Senator yield at that point?

Mr. BENTON. I am glad to yield to the Senator from Minnesota.

Mr. HUMPHREY. I desire to concur in the thought expressed by the Senator, because the substance of my argument, which preceded the statements to which the Senator has referred, was that we are making basically a social and a policy or political decision; and certainly what we must consider is the total economy, and what is good for the total general welfare, rather than for any specific individual as such.

Mr. BENTON. I am very glad to have the Senator so express himself, and that is why I must say I was somewhat surprised when he ended his argument with the canary, the high school football team, and the Senator in the prize ring, because the gist of his argument last night and the gist of his argument this morning, up to that point, was that there must be considered first the interest of all the 155,000,000 American people.

(At this point Mr. BENTON yielded to Mr. SPARKMAN to ask questions of Mr. HUMPHREY. The colloquy which ensued, was, on request of Mr. BENTON, and by unanimous consent, ordered to be printed at the conclusion of his remarks.)

Mr. BENTON. Mr. President, I feel that the major mistake which is being made by many people who are discussing the bill and by its opponents is that they talk about it too much in economic terms. I agree that it must be talked about in economic terms. There may be a price which the economy should not pay even for important social and political benefits. However, in my judgment it is very doubtful whether, if we take a long-term instead of a short-term view, there is any price involved which the American people will ever pay for the benefits which accrue to them from this bill.

Incidentally, the figures quoted last night by my friend, whom I admire so greatly, the distinguished Senator from Illinois [Mr. DOUGLAS], on the profits of pharmaceutical houses, such as Lilly and Abbott Laboratories, have nothing to do with this bill at all as people who work in the drug trade will testify.

However, over and above the economic arguments there is the overriding fact that our independent retail businesses, usually family businesses, are a vital part of the fabric of our social and political life. They play a large part in determining our economic attitudes in this, our free American society.

Yes, Mr. President, it is the millions of independent owners and proprietors of small businesses who bring support and strength to our free institutions, our social, political, and economic attitudes. ⊥ They are the ones who will fight to the death against collectivism in all its terrifying forms. They should and must be preserved.

⊥ 8866

Mr. President, in October 1944, Fortune magazine published an article which I wrote, entitled "The Economics of a Free Society." I should like to hope that the distinguished Presiding Officer [Mr. BENNETT], in writing his book 2 or 3 years ago about our free economy, may have had this article called to his attention.

Fortune magazine stated:

The 12-point statement on the opposite page and the exposition of policy that follows were prepared by Mr. BENTON at the request of the Research Committee of the Committee for Economic Development. Though Mr. BENTON assumes responsibility for these documents, they have of course been approved in principle by top leaders of the CED and its economic advisors.

Mr. President, at that time I was the founding Vice Chairman of CED's Board of Trustees. Mr. Paul Hoffman was Chairman.

I deem certain sections of the policy statement relevant to our discussion today with reference to the pending bill. CED, as many Senators know, is dedicated to higher levels of productivity and employment. Yet CED recognizes that a healthy political and social environment is essential to sound economic progress. Indeed, Mr. President, Americans seek sound economic progress in order to create a sound and healthy political and social environment. The economic aspect is the servant of the social and political aspects, rather than the other way around.

In that CED statement—as I recall, it was the first of the CED papers printed for wide publication—I stated:

In the United States there are 4,000,000 or more farm enterprises, more than 1,000,000 self-employed who work as their own bosses, more than 2,000,000 private businesses with one or more employees. These provide enormous opportunities for innovation and experimentation. After the war—

That was written in 1944—

America must create an economic climate that will develop millions more. Can any centrally controlled economy hope to maintain the dynamic drive, the ingenuity, or the diversity of creative impulse of these millions of enterprises? Their persistent search for improvement results in progress: better products and services adapted more closely to the desires of the buyers at ever lower prices. The driving energy of private incentive thus serves the economic good of the Nation as a whole.

The effect of this drive for improvement is clearly visible in the history of the last 40 years. Since 1900 new and better machines and better methods have more than tripled manufacturing output per man-hour of work. For the economy as a whole, output per man-hour in recent decades has been increasing at the rate of 2 1/2 percent per year.

Mr. President, most students of our economy agree that the welfare of the small independent businessman is essential to a healthy political and economic climate in the United States. A very high percentage of our innovations and discoveries originates in small independent business. On this count alone, independent businesses pay off and justify their existence. They do so by means of the new kinds of competition they develop against the larger, well-established firms. This develops our American standards of productivity.

A high percentage of the innovations in selling and merchandising in the retail trades in the last 25 years has come out of Texas, the Southwest, and California. Is that because in Texas, the Southwest, and California there are great concentrations of economic power in the chain stores? No, not at all, Mr. President; it is because in

Texas, the Southwest, and California there have been more initiative, greater enterprise, a larger number of independent operators, and more enterprising and independent businessmen who have been using their ingenuity in new ways, in an effort to develop their own welfare; and in that way, of course, they have developed the American economy.

Our economy is not merely one of producing at the lowest possible cost; it is not merely one of getting the goods on the shelves of retail stores at the lowest possible cost. Our economy also consists of very important techniques of selling, of promotion, of so-called merchandising. The latter techniques, which have played such a large part in developing the high standard of living in the United States, owe much of their development to the independent businessmen who seek and find new, fresh, original angles by means of which they can compete with large businesses.

Mr. President, I do not favor pampering the small-business man, and I do not wish to subsidize him. I oppose many of the proposals made to Congress by the so-called small-business organizations who advocate certain forms of pampering and subsidization of small business.

On the other hand, certainly we must not permit the small-business man to be ruthlessly put out of business by practices which develop monopolies of a type which, as our history shows, often can readily learn how to exploit the public.

Mr. President, I ask the Senate whether it wishes to accelerate the trends toward monopoly and lack of widespread competition. I am sure the Senate will answer that it does not wish to accelerate those trends. However, if we fail to pass this bill, we gravely risk accelerating them, with consequent unfortunate and unhappy effects on the American economy and on the American people as a whole.

As suggested by the Senator from Minnesota, just as the family farm is regarded as a great and integral part of our American life, and just as we prefer it because it undergirds what we like to call our American way of life, as opposed to Soviet type of [sic] collective farms, or the large farms which have been developed in certain of our Western States, even though the latter may be more efficient and may produce more food at lower cost, so also do we Americans regard as a great national asset the million or so independent, family-owned retail businesses. Indeed, they are a far greater assets [sic] than any 10, 20, 50, or 100 chain-store systems, with a comparably large annual volume of sales, could possibly be.

So it is not only because of the economic importance of small independent business, which is the subject around which most of this debate has centered, but it is also because such business is the very warp and woof of our social and political fabric, that I have been proud to serve on the Senate Small Business Committee.

I instituted the clinics which the committee has carried all over the country, to aid and assist small business in its efforts to compete with large business. More recently, I have been active in tax hearings, aimed at the special problems of small business, in Bridgeport, Newark, and Los Angeles. Shortly I, as well as other members of the Senate Small Business Committee, expect to have major recommendations growing from these hearings. There are at present major injustices and inequities in our tax laws, as they are applied to small, independent business, and most particularly as they are applied to new business. These must be corrected in the next session of the Congress.

But to get back to my CED statement in Fortune, as Fortune said:

Mr. BENTON'S drafts, completed after criticism and advice from the research committee and its leading economists, will now go out to 2,000 CED community chairmen for local discussion and distribution to the 50,000 members.

In that statement I said:

Further, a free market open to the development of new, independent enterprises will continue to provide an economic basis for political freedom. Such a market breeds the millions of rival producers and sellers who do not need to cater to private or public overlords. They help keep the balance on the side of freedom and against the arbitrary exercise of economic power. They provide the competition that minimizes the need for Government regulation and operation. They provide an element of balance that counteracts potential dangers to our democratic institutions.

Lack of competition stifles the free market. So-called monopoly practices of business, labor, and Government, which remove the necessity of trying to undersell a competitor or to match or improve on his quality, induce complacency. Such practices have no place in a free-enterprise system designed to serve the common good. They require Government action either to remove their source or, where monopoly is essential to public service, to regulate them in the public interest.

Mr. President, I believe that the Members of this body who wish to encourage "the balance on the side of freedom and against the arbitrary exercise of economic power" should support this bill. Those who wish "to minimize the need of government regulation and operation" should favor this bill. Those who wish to prevent in the United States the development of monopoly power of the kind which inevitably leads to government regulation, should favor this bill.

Representative MCGUIRE has achieved a national reputation for his leadership in this area. I congratulate him.

Mr. President, we have been discussing some of the misinformation which has been spread abroad about this fair trade bill. It is my belief that many great organizations have been led to oppose this bill when in my judgment they would be in favor of the bill if they understood better its long-range importance and its long-range effects. There is widespread misunderstanding of the economic impact of the bill, and there has been far too little discussion of the social and political significance of the bill.

⊥ 8867

As I have previously suggested, this bill does not permit a manufacturer under State law to regulate his retail prices, and it does not regulate competition among manufacturers, among wholesalers, or among retailers. Such price fixing is strictly illegal, and will continue to be a violation of the criminal statutes, for which violations men can go to jail and, indeed, should go to jail.

The figures submitted yesterday evening by the Senator from Illinois [Mr. DOUGLAS] are reflections of what I choose to think are in part short-run effects of fair trade practices. Under the impact of the new type of competition which would develop with the enactment of this bill, those figures would alter greatly and at an accelerating rate with each passing year.

Mr. President, I was active in business in the early thirties. At that time, as a young man in the advertising business, I was responsible for developing advertising for a large number of well-known national food and drug brands. As the depression deepened, many manufacturers made the mistake of trying to hold up their prices. Many thought that merely by more advertising they could obtain the volume required.

In part, because of this, the private brands developed enormously, starting with the depression in 1929, and accelerating in 1930, 1931, and 1932. The development of those private brands forced down the prices of the manufactured products. If the products on which at that time, 20 years or so ago, I was working, such as Palmolive soap and Maxwell House coffee, had not brought down their prices to meet the competition of the private brands, they would have slowly faded away. This illustration which we see as we look backward into the history of the grocery and drug trade shows what would happen under this bill if manufacturers tried to hold their retail prices at too high a level or at an exorbitant level. There is a big incentive to the manufacturer to get his retail prices down.

Mr. President, this bill, of course, specifically includes provisions which cannot be misunderstood, provisions requiring free and open competition with articles of similar class produced by others.

Before I conclude, Mr. President, I desire to comment very quickly on the substitute measure offered last night by the distinguished Senator from Illinois. To those of us who have had experience in retail merchandising, the amendment offered by him raises a great many complicated questions. A similar amendment, of course, was overwhelmingly rejected by the House, I assume, because it raised so many complicated questions. The bill offered by the Senator from Illinois as an amendment applies to all articles of commerce, not merely to the relatively small number of items, the trademarked and branded items, which would fall under the fair-trade bill.

Furthermore, its exclusions seem to me to be most ambiguous. The proposed substitute tells the retailer that he must charge his delivered cost, whatever that may mean, plus 6 percent; and it then excludes a long list of items, such as items damaged or deteriorated in quality—whatever that may mean. It excludes items sold exclusively for religious, charitable, scientific, literary, or educational purposes—which is a puzzling loophole to many retailers. It excludes perishable commodities, and also commodities if their further retention by the seller could reasonably be expected to result in a loss.

Mr. President, who is to determine what is reasonable? Who is going to determine whether the inventory of a commodity must be liquidated in order to avoid insolvency or bankruptcy?

It seems to me that the substitute bill, if placed on the statute books, would open up a veritable paradise of activity, not for the consumer to enable him to get better goods at lower prices but for the accountants and lawyers and others who add overhead to the cost of operating a retail establishment, and who by so doing keep the prices up.

A most interesting omission—and there may be many exclusions which should be written into the substitute, but have not been written into it—is a very manifest one. Suppose the price drops on what a merchant has bought. In this country we operate, or are supposed to operate, on a profit-and-loss system. I do not want to guarantee every retailer that he will get his cost plus 6 percent on every item. I do not propose to take the loss out of the profit-and-loss system. If a retailer goes to the Chicago merchandise fair and makes the mistake of buying chairs at $10 a chair, and when he gets back to his home town he finds that his competitor has been smart enough to go to Grand Rapids and buy the same chair for $5 a chair, is retailer No. 1 to be prohibited from cutting his price in order to compete with retailer No. 2? Or suppose the manufacturer from whom the first retailer bought his chair at $10 is then forced to lower the price to $5, since an identical chair can be bought for $5, must the retailer who earlier bought the chair at $10, under the proposed substitute still sell his chair for $10 plus 6 percent, even though he can replace it for $5?

Such a bill, in my judgment, Mr. President, could take the bargain basement out of every department store. It would radically change retailing methods. It would violate the whole principle of turn-over applied to retail merchandising, in which the smart, aggressive retailer, when his goods do not sell, wisely reduces them 10 percent a week, or 10 percent a day, let us say, until he moves them off his shelves.

To me the substitute bill goes further in fixing prices at the expense of the consumer and in eliminating the competition about which the Senator from Illinois spoke so eloquently last night, than anything proposed or suggested in the fair trade bill which is now pending before the Senate.

Mr. HUMPHREY. Mr. President, will the Senator yield to me at that point?

Mr. BENTON. I am glad to yield.

Mr. HUMPHREY. I am delighted that the Senator from Connecticut has made these pertinent comments on the so-called loss leader bill which the Senator from Illinois presented last night as a substitute, because surely that bill needs to be fully discussed. I must say, however, that that bill applies to all articles of commerce except those that are exempted, which are limited in number.

Mr. BENTON. And which are hard to identify.

Mr. HUMPHREY. And which are hard to identify. There really are no standards by which they could be identified.

Mr. BENTON. There are no standards.

Mr. HUMPHREY. That is, as compared to the pending fair-trade bill, which applies only to trade-marked articles and the brand-name articles, which articles may be fair-traded only when the manufacturer and the retailer wish them to be. In other words, it is not at all mandatory. There may be manufacturers who do not want to fair-trade every commodity they produce, who do not want to break their plant and machinery, in which event they are subject to all types of competition, and to all types of price fluctuation. But the Douglas proposal says that there shall be no loss leaders, that there must be 6 percent added. It appears to me that the fair-trade measure is much less inclusive and is much more exclusive than the one proposed by the Senator from Illinois.

Mr. LEHMAN. Mr. President, will the Senator yield for a question?

Mr. BENTON. Yes, if I may first make a comment. In my opinion, there can be no doubt of the correctness of the position of the Senator from Minnesota. I will go even further. There are certain to be plenty of manufacturers who will not have anything to do with this fair-trade bill. The bill applies only to a limited number of trade-marked items. The great proportion of manufacturers will not operate under this bill, and their goods will in no way be restricted on prices.

Most assuredly, all smart merchants today often sell goods under cost.

Only the stupid merchant expects to get his cost back on each and every item. The proposed substitute bill would, in my opinion, penalize the small merchant and reward the stupid; which is exactly the kind of problem we are so often facing, when we are considering legislation in the Congress, and which we must be on guard against.

I am now glad to yield to the distinguished Senator from New York.

Mr. LEHMAN. Is it not a fact that the distinguished Senator from Minnesota, against whom I hate to argue on any question, and I have not done so very often since we have both been in the Senate, makes the statement that ⊥ the fixing of prices becomes effective only when the manufacturer and the retailer want them to be effective? I think that is not accurate. I believe it to be a source of weakness in the present system of State fair-trade laws that when the manufacturer of the trade-marked or branded article enters into a price agreement with one retailer, all the other retailers or distributors of that article are thereupon bound to maintain that price. They have no option; they must maintain the price, even though they were not parties to any agreement, and even though they objected to it. They are nonetheless completely bound by the provisions of the bill.

⊥ 8868

I do not believe the extent of the provision was fully appreciated at the time fair-trade acts were passed in many States. It certainly was not fully understood by this Senator who was Governor of the State and signed the bill setting up the fair-trade practice. It was my understanding at that time that the manufacturer of the branded article could make contracts with substantially all the distributors or retailers handling the article, and it was perfectly fair to expect them to live up to the terms of the contract. I do not understand, nor do I believe it was contemplated, that the signature of one retailer would bind all the other retailers in the State.

Mr. BENTON. Does the Senator have any knowledge of how often in the State of New York it actually happens that a manufacturer will make a deal with only one retailer which would have this effect on all other retailers?

I ask that question because any manufacturer who knows what he is doing does not make an open agreement with one retailer unless he is on the way to make such an agreement with other similar retail outlets he can reach and sign up. Otherwise, if he discriminates between similar types of outlets, he can ruin his distribution system.

Mr. LEHMAN. I have no record of the exact number, but I am quite certain that in very few instances have specific contracts been entered into between the manufacturer and all the retail outlets. If it be true, as the Senator from Connecticut alleges, that such contracts are entered into with all the retailers, then, of course, there is no need of this bill, because they would constitute binding contracts which would be enforceable. If the Senator and I agree to maintain a certain price, and we both affix our signatures to the agreement, I do not think any law is necessary. There is merely a contractual relationship.

Mr. BENTON. That may be true, but to the manufacturer the problem is serious. He would like to reach all his retail outlets. If, of the 50,000 drug stores which exist in this country—17 years ago, when I left the advertising business I knew how many drug stores there were, and there were approximately 50,000—if 500 of the 50,000 did not sign up, even though 49,500 did sign up, the 500 of the type described by the Senator from Minnesota last night can completely demoralize the 49,500. Further, there is the heavy cost of reaching and persuading the 49,500 to sign up.

Mr. WELKER. Mr. President, will the Senator from Connecticut yield?

Mr. BENTON. I yield.

Mr. WELKER. Once again, Mr. President, I invite the attention of the Senate to the fact that I shall insist on the regular order of business, in the interest of saving time.

Mr. BENTON. I do not object to that. As a matter of fact, I shall conclude my remarks in another 3 or 4 minutes, unless I am interrupted further with questions.

Mr. HUMPHREY. Mr. President, will the Senator from Connecticut yield?

Mr. BENTON. I yield.

Mr. HUMPHREY. Is the Senator familiar with the fact that the nonsigner clause was understood to have been included in the Miller-Tydings Act as passed in 1937, according to the interpretation of the then Attorney General of the United States, Mr. Thurman Arnold?

Mr. BENTON. I am glad to have that pointed out. Certainly there has never been in the Department of Justice a more vigorous and rigorous proponent of enforcing the antitrust laws than Mr. Thurman Arnold, one of our great public servants.

Mr. HUMPHREY. Is the Senator aware of the fact that there were two court cases in which a so-called nonsigner clause, under the terms of the Miller-Tydings Act and the State fair-trade acts were contested, and that in each of the two cases the court held they were legal and were in no way contrary to the Sherman Antitrust Act?

Mr. BENTON. I am glad to have that information placed in the RECORD.

Mr. HUMPHREY. Is the Senator aware of the fact that in the annual report of the Federal Trade Commission those two cases are fully discussed?

Mr. BENTON. Yes.

I wish I had, but I do not have, the figures to show the percentage of American manufacturers whose goods go into the hands of the ultimate consumer through direct sale or authorized dealers, and who are able to control their prices without any special legislation or fair-trade laws either at the State or Federal level, but the percentage must be large. All companies selling direct to the consumer control their prices and they are usually identical in every hamlet and city of the Nation.

The Encyclopaedia Britannica sells for exactly the same price everywhere because the company completely controls its distribution. Automobile companies control the distribution of automobiles through authorized dealers. All companies that own their own retail outlets or that deal with a small number of outlets or regularly franchised dealers, with which they can enter into the kind of contracts suggested by the Senator from New York, have found that it pays to have a fixed price that is identical; and no charge, to my knowledge, has been leveled against any such business that it is in any way harmful to the competitive factors we are seeking to encourage in American life.

If a lady customer does not like what the direct salesman of the Real Silk Co. charges for stockings, she can go to Macy's and buy her stockings. If she does not like Ford's prices, she can go to Plymouth.

All we are now trying to do apply [sic] that same principle, at the option of the manufacturer, to those relatively few lines of branded merchandise which have been found by practice to be subject to grave abuses which are not in the public interest.

Mr. HUMPHREY. Mr. President, will the Senator from Connecticut yield?

Mr. BENTON. I yield.

Mr. HUMPHREY. Is the Senator familiar with the fact that in 1936 the Supreme Court, in a unanimous decision, declared that fair-trade laws, including nonsigner clauses, were within the purview of the act?[3.76]

Mr. BENTON. I know the Senator from Minnesota is a distinguished pharmacist, and I am beginning to welcome him as distinguished legal counsel.

The Senator from Minnesota has compiled an article on fair trade, containing arguments pro and con, in three very interesting pages which have come to me and which I presume were sent to other Members of the Senate.

Important as are the pro arguments, I do not regard them as being so important as are some of the arguments for the bill which the Senator and I have advanced in this floor debate and which I choose to call social and political arguments. In the Senator from Minnesota's statement, he lists 14 points which show the strong economic arguments for the bill from the standpoint of the public interest.

I ask unanimous consent to have this interesting statement printed in the RECORD at the conclusion of my remarks.

The PRESIDING OFFICER. Is there objection? The Chair hears none, and it is so ordered.

(See exhibit A.)

Mr. BENTON. Mr. President, based upon my own business background, as well as upon my many years as a student of the American economy, as vice chairman of the

---

[3.76] Old Dearborn Distrib. Co. v. Seagram-Distillers Corp., 299 U.S. 183, 57 S. Ct. 139, 81 L. Ed. 109 (1936), *supra* at chapter 2.

Committee for Economic Development and in other roles, I urge upon the Senate the passage of the bill now before us. I hope that not too much further debate will be indicated, and that passage of the bill will not be further delayed.

Exhibit A

Arguments, Pro and Con, on Fair Trade

1. The McGuire bill is said to be a blanket approval of State fair-trade laws. Any State can pass or amend a fair-trade law without the competition requirement of all present State fair-trade laws.

The McGuire bill is Federal enabling legislation only, to permit the States to realize the full effectiveness of laws which they consider necessary to their welfare. The McGuire bill specifically includes a provision requiring "free and open competition with articles of similar class produced by others." Should a State remove such a restriction from its fair-trade act, then the McGuire bill would no longer be enabling insofar as that particular State is concerned.

2. Fair-trade prices are alleged to be too high. Efficient retailers are said to be able to sell fair-traded products below fair-trade prices and make a profit.

Popular national brand goods, which are fair-traded, are sold for less, on the average, in the fair-trade States than in the non-fair-trade area of the United States. Predatory pricing retailers like to shade the price on articles whose value is as familiar to the consumer as the worth of a dollar bill. Competitors, however, cannot permit these retailers to get a reputation for underselling them. This is what starts exhausting price wars so damaging to small business.

3. Fair trade, it is said, is bad for small business because it has encouraged supermarkets to stock fair-traded drugstore items which, so the charge goes, give the supermarket an invitingly high profit margin.

Supermarkets are now stocking drugstore items not only in the fair-trade States, but also in such non-fair-trade areas as Texas, Missouri, Vermont, and the District of Columbia. Furthermore, they are stocking such items as hosiery, housewares, and apparel, most of which are not fair-traded. Obviously this trend among supermarkets to expand the variety of their merchandise offerings has nothing to do with fair trade.

4. Efficiency in distribution must not be thwarted by fair trade in the mistaken notion, runs the observation, that it will help small business.

The revolution in retailing of the past decade shows clearly that efficiency in distribution has not been thwarted. During the 21 years of fair trade, small business has flourished side by side with the great growth of chains, supermarkets, and other giant retailers. And efficiency of operation has been vastly improved. Fair trade did not prevent these developments.

5. Vertical resale price maintenance provided by fair trade is bad for the economy, say theorists.

If that be so, Congress should prohibit vertical resale price maintenance based on other legal frameworks like consignment selling and exclusive franchises. There is plenty of evidence that vertical resale price maintenance is good for the economy because it assures the existence of plenty of competitors. The automobile industry, which pioneered mass production, has from the very beginning sold its cars on the basis of vertical resale price maintenance.

6. There is no public instrumentality, say opponents, to test the reasonableness of fair-trade prices.

If by public instrumentality is meant a Government bureau, the charge is correct. Of course, the consumer is herself the public instrumentality because she determines by her daily decisions to buy or not to buy this or that product whether its price is reasonable and its quality up to the standard she expects.

7. Henry Ford has shown retailers that consumer prices are lowered through efficiency.

He certainly has. Henry Ford also demonstrated that mass production depends upon mass distribution. He got mass distribution by requiring all his dealers to sell Ford cars at his suggested prices. With this protection against predatory price cutting assured, more and more men were willing to invest their savings in Ford dealerships.

8. High-priced lobbyists, it is alleged, are putting over fair trade through pressure tactics.

Not lobbyists but small business, earnestly convinced that its survival depends upon effective fair trade, are petitioning Congress. The number and vigor of their petitions reflects the scope of support for fair trade and the intensity of small business' convictions concerning it.

9. Consumers, opponents charge, would be against fair trade if they knew what is going on.

That's a matter of opinion. Friends of fair trade believe that consumers in purchasing fair-trade products in ever-increasing volume are voting "yes" on fair trade every time they step up to a retail counter. To say that consumers have permitted themselves to be hoodwinked for two decades is to underrate their intelligence.

10. Fair-trade prices do not allow for differences in operating costs, one professor notes.

Fair-trade prices reflect the average of operating efficiency. That's how all business works.

The chain organization doesn't permit its more efficient outlet to sell the same goods for less than its outlets which are not so efficient. No retailer gives the quick-buying shopper lower prices than it gives the slow buyer, despite the lower cost of selling the speedy shopper.

11. Why worry about fair trade now that price wars have stopped, ask opponents of the McGuire bill.

Price wars haven't stopped; they break out all the time although, fortunately for small business, there has been no recurrence on the gigantic scale of the June 1951 price wars. Without effective fair trade, however, small business lives at the whim and mercy of irresponsible operators who will start price wars when it suits their purpose to do so.

12. Manufacturers, it is charged, go on fair trade not because they believe in it but because they are pressured into it by retailers.

This is untrue, as anyone who is closely identified with manufacturers who practice fair trade, can testify. Additional evidence is supplied by the fact that many manufacturers who do not use fair trade nevertheless voluntarily practice its guiding principle, resale price maintenance, through consignment selling and exclusive franchise arrangements. There was a total estimated of $158,000,000,000 in retail sales in 1951. Of these $36,000,000,000 in annual United States retail sales were made by some type of price maintenance, and fair trade accounts for but $6,000,000,000 while the remaining $30,000,000,000 is accounted for by other legal means of resale price maintenance.

13. The nonsigner clause dragoons unwilling retailers, it is said, into observing the provisions of a contract to which he is not a party.

Fair trade is a State-by-State system of fair competition. The fair-trade contract does not require any retailer to carry any manufacturer's goods. The retailer is bound by the terms of a fair-trade contract only when he buys goods in the knowledge of the fair-trade limitations upon them, as the Supreme Court noted in its 1936 unanimous decision upholding the State fair-trade acts.

14. The McGuire bill contains no sharp standards of definition of "free and open competition," it is noted.

This is true. It is also true that the plaintiff in every fair-trade case at bar must first prove to the court's satisfaction that his product is in free and open competition. The courts have traditionally defined competition, in respect of all statutes involving it, in the light of facts adduced in each specific case at bar. Insofar as fair trade is concerned, the courts have sometimes found that free and open competition did not exist and that, therefore, a specific product could not be fair traded.

The PRESIDING OFFICER. The question is on agreeing to the Douglas amendment in the nature of a substitute.

Mr. WELKER obtained the floor.

Mr. [ANDREW F.] SCHOEPPEL [R., Kan.]. Mr. President, will the Senator yield?

Mr. WELKER. I yield to the Senator from Kansas.

Mr. SCHOEPPEL. I may say to the distinguished acting minority leader that I desire to ask unanimous consent that the Senator from Idaho may yield to me for about 4 minutes, so that I may speak upon the pending measure.

Mr. WELKER. I yield to the Senator from Kansas.

Mr. SCHOEPPEL. Mr. President, at the outset I wish to say that I favor the legislation which is the order of business before the Senate at the present time. I have listened to the arguments, pro and con, and I wish to point out that the fair-trade laws of 45 States were seriously weakened not only by the Supreme Court's Schwegmann decision, but also by the Wentling decision of the Third United States Circuit Court of Appeals. This latter decision also bears the authority of the United States Supreme Court, since it was appealed to the high court and sent back to the third circuit court, with the Schwegmann decision cited as guidance.

The Wentling decision holds that the enforcement of a State fair-trade act in any other State having a fair-trade law constitutes an unlawful burden upon, and an interference with, interstate commerce. The Wentling decision's practical effect is to permit mail-order houses and other retailers who sell across State lines to disregard the fair-trade laws of 45 sovereign States.

Legally, the Wentling decision creates this anomaly: A merchant who is not permitted to commit an act of unfair competition under his own State's fair-trade law can nevertheless commit such an act in another State.

In short, he can defy another State's fair-trade law if Congress fails to remedy this anomalous and untenable situation.

Paragraph (4) of H. R. 5767 would overcome the Wentling decision in the following language:

(4) Neither the making of contracts or agreements as described in paragraph (2) of this subsection, nor the exercise or enforcement of any right or right of action as described in paragraph (3) of this subsection shall constitute an unlawful burden or restraint upon, or interference, with, commerce.

This provision does not establish a Federal fair-trade policy. Like H. R. 5767 in its entirety, paragraph (4) simply recognizes the rights of States to establish and carry out policies to restrain unfair competition as they define it, within their borders, including transactions in which goods have moved in interstate commerce. The provision reflects the intention of the Congress to make the State fair-trade laws fully effective with respect to interstate commerce.

In passing H. R. 5767 as enabling legislation designed to effectuate State policy in an area touching on interstate commerce, Congress will not be departing from precedent. Congress has already enacted a number of statutes to harmonize its power over interstate commerce with the rights of the States, under the Constitution. These statutes include the Webb-Kenyon Act, the Ashurst-Sumners Act, the United States Warehouse Act and the Miller-Tydings Act. This latter act is still constitutional and effective under the restricted ⊥ interpretation of the Supreme Court in the Schwegmann ⊥ 8870 decision.

Two decisions of the United States Supreme Court are relevant to this problem of how much Congress may harmonize its power over interstate commerce with the rights of the States. In 1945, in International Shoe against Washington, the Court said:

It is no longer debatable that Congress, in the exercise of the commerce power, may authorize the States, in specified ways, to regulate interstate commerce or impose burdens upon it.[3.77]

In 1917, in Clark Distilling Co. against Western Maryland Railway Co., the Court said:

Where the subject of commerce is one as to which the State may constitutionally restrict, prohibit, or regulate in order to prevent harmful consequences, and for the protection of property rights, Congress may, if it sees fit to put forth its power and aid, to so regulate interstate commerce, so as to prevent that commerce from being used to impede the carrying out of the State policy.[3.78]

Amendments have been proposed to H. R. 5767 which seek to meet the Wentling decision by an approach which, it is believed, would establish a Federal fair trade policy and a Federal cause of action. It is significant that the House Interstate and Foreign Commerce Committee, the House of Representatives and the Senate Interstate and Foreign Commerce Committee did not find these amendments acceptable.

Mr. President, the simplest and soundest solution to the problem posed by the Wentling decision is provided in H. R. 5767. That is one of the reasons why I shall support the proposed legislation. It occurs to the Senator from Kansas that when 45 States in our great country have passed fair-trade laws, when 45 State legislatures have passed upon them, when 45 governors have signed such measures into law, this type of proposed legislation is in harmony and keeping with the great and preponderant majority of the commonwealths within our Republic. . . .

Mr. SPARKMAN. Mr. President, I should like to ask the Senator from Minnesota one or two questions in order to be absolutely clear in my own mind, and in order that the RECORD may be absolutely clear. I propound these questions to the Senator from Minnesota, because I know of the great interest he has in this proposed legislation, the work he has done on it, and his understanding of the facts and the background. Therefore, I should like to ask his opinion on these two questions.

Mr. HUMPHREY. I shall be glad to answer the Senator's questions if I can.

[3.77] 326 U.S. 310, 315, 66 S. Ct. 154, 158, 90 L. Ed. 95, 101 (1945).

[3.78] This quotation does not appear in the *Clark Distilling Co.* case exactly as cited here. *See* James Clark Distilling Co. v. Western Maryland Ry., 242 U.S. 311, 37 S. Ct. 180, 61 L. Ed. 326 (1917).

Mr. SPARKMAN. I have always been much concerned about horizontal resale price-maintenance agreements which have been considered illegal. Do I correctly understand that this bill does not make that type of agreement lawful?

Mr. HUMPHREY. The Senator from Alabama is absolutely correct. This bill does not make lawful the type of agreement to which he refers. It is entirely clear from paragraph (5) of section 5 (a) of the Federal Trade Commission Act, as amended by this bill, that horizontal resale price-maintenance agreements such as between a wholesaler and a wholesaler, or between a retailer and a retailer, or a manufacturer and a manufacturer, are not made lawful. They are illegal and subject to prosecution. It is only vertical resale price-maintenance agreements which are exempt from the antitrust laws when they meet the requirements of paragraph (2).

Mr. SPARKMAN. It would dispel any misunderstanding concerning lawful vertical resale price-maintenance agreements and unlawful horizontal resale price-maintenance agreements if the Senator from Minnesota would explain further for the RECORD the differences between the types of agreements.

Mr. HUMPHREY. I talked with the Senator about this matter, and I want to be very accurate. I have gone into it very carefully. Under this bill, a lawful vertical price-maintenance agreement is one entered into by the producer of a trade-marked or branded commodity, and the immediate or subsequent resellers of such commodity in the chain of distribution from producer to ultimate consumer, whereby the minimum resale price at either the wholesale or retail level, or both, is prescribed. If, for example, when a producer, who sells to distributors, wholesalers, retailers, and consumers, makes a resale price-maintenance agreement relative to a commodity made by him and bearing a trade-mark or brand, with a distributor, wholesaler, or retailer who resells such commodity at either the wholesale, or retail level, there exists a vertical resale price-maintenance contract which would be lawful under the bill if the requirements of paragraph (2) are met.

On the other hand, if one wholesaler enters into a resale price-maintenance agreement with another wholesaler prescribing the price at which they both sell a trade-marked or branded commodity which they both buy from the producer, that agreement would be horizontal and would not be made lawful.

In other words, wholesalers getting together on a price are acting illegally. For a manufacturer to get together with other manufacturers to maintain prices is illegal, but for a manufacturer to say that a certain product will sell at a certain price from the manufacturer down to the retailer is legal under the limitations prescribed in paragraph (2) of section 5 (a) of the Federal Trade Commission Act.

In general, the test of whether a resale price-maintenance contract is vertical is if the contract is between a seller and buyers who resell the original seller's product; whereas, the test of whether a resale price-maintenance contract is horizontal as [sic] if it is between competing sellers between whom the relation of buyer and seller or reseller does not exist as to the product involved.

It is important to keep this distinction in mind, because many producers of trade-marked items sell them to consumers, retailers, and wholesalers alike.

Under the bill, such firms may make resale price-maintenance contracts with both wholesalers and retailers because such contracts are vertical, that is, between sellers and buyers. While in one sense firms in this position function not only as producers but also as wholesalers and retailers, they may still lawfully make contracts with other wholesalers and retailers, when in making such contracts they act as producers of a trade-marked or branded commodity, rather than as wholesalers and retailers entering into forbidden horizontal resale price-maintenance contracts with other wholesalers or other retailers.

This question has been discussed in many colloquies on the floor, and I am happy to have it formalized by interrogation. But it should be clearly noted that price fixing between producers, price fixing between wholesalers, and price fixing between retailers is unlawful and should be prosecuted.

Mr. SPARKMAN. And the bill does not propose anything which would change that illegality.

Mr. HUMPHREY. That is correct. My admonition to the Federal Trade Commission and to the Justice Department is to keep a careful weather eye open on the kind of horizontal price-maintenance agreements which are entered into, because those which are illegal should be prosecuted.

Mr. SPARKMAN. I thank the Senator for setting the record straight.

Mr. LONG. Mr. President, will the Senator from Minnesota yield?

Mr. HUMPHREY. I yield.

Mr. LONG. There is some doubt in my mind as to the parallel which has been described. When a large concern fixes a price and another concern fixes the same price, then, in pursuance of the resale price-maintenance agreement, the public has no choice in price competition between the commodities. From a table placed in the RECORD yesterday by the Senator from Illinois [Mr. DOUGLAS], I notice that as to hand lotions of well-known brands, such as Hinds', Jergen's, and others, 4 out of 7 of them were selling at 49 cents, the fair-trade price. I notice that with reference to deodorants 8 out of 18 of the better-known brands were selling at the same price.

Is there anything in the bill which would tend to outlaw or prevent producers of similar articles setting the same price in the absence of any proof that they had conspired to do so?

Mr. HUMPHREY. The burden of proof would rest with the prosecution. They would have to be able to prove that there was collusion or some type of conspiratorial activity. I would say that the items to which the Senator from Illinois referred sold for the same price before fair trade as they did after fair trade. Hinds' honey-and-almond cream sold for 50 cents before and after fair trade.

Mr. LONG. Is the Senator speaking of the situation in Washington?

Mr. HUMPHREY. I am speaking of the national price prescribed by the manufacturer.

Mr. LONG. That does not mean that the product sold for the same price at retail, does it?

Mr. HUMPHREY. No. But the retail price placed on the commodity by the manufacturer was the same prior to fair trade and after fair trade.

I think the Senator has pointed up a possible abuse, and I believe it is the job of the Federal Trade Commission and the law enforcement officials of the Government carefully to watch for any sub rosa agreements or any collusive action. I would join with the Senator from Louisiana in attempting to expose any such violation.

Mr. LONG. The Senator knows that in the basing-point debate it was developed that with reference to the delivered-price system, it was very simple for those who had been found guilty of conspiracy and of monopolistic practices to make the same price without giving the public the benefit of competition. It would be fairly easy to determine whether they were in a conspiracy.

Mr. HUMPHREY. I think the Senator is correct about that. The more national advertising there is establishing a uniform market for a commodity, the more possible it is to get a uniform price. It is definitely one problem that has to be carefully watched. I do not minimize it. As one of the proponents of the bill, I say it is the responsibility of Congress and of the agencies of Government to see to it, by careful analysis and scrutiny, that there is no horizontal price-maintenance agreement. I want none of it. I want it to be carefully investigated and checked.

Mr. MONRONEY. Mr. President, will the Senator yield for a question?

Mr. HUMPHREY. I yield.

Mr. MONRONEY. I should like to ask the Senator if it is not a fact that there is genuine major-league competition in nationally advertised products. Manufacturers are not going to gamble millions of dollars in advertising a product which is priced out of range of competitive markets. There will be more price variations in noncompetitive prices in unadvertised lines than in the major-league competition. The pending bill, as I understand—and I ask the distinguished Senator, who is an authority on the subject, if it is not true—makes it absolutely unlawful for any manufacturer to conspire or to arrange with another manufacturer to fix prices.

Mr. HUMPHREY. Absolutely.

Mr. MONRONEY. The pricing agreement affects one manufacturer's line.

Mr. HUMPHREY. That is correct.

Mr. MONRONEY. His line is in strong competition with another manufacturer's line, because there are two giant competitors in one industry, one striving to outdo the other on price, on value, and on attractiveness of package. It is the cream of the merchandising field that meets in the major-league competition.

I believe the distinguished Senator from Connecticut, who is one of the Nation's great advertising experts, will testify to the fact that no national advertiser could possibly think of advertising a product which was not competitive in price and quality.

Mr. BENTON. If I may comment on the Senator's statement, one of the points that seem to have been overlooked throughout most of the discussion, and certainly throughout most of the discussion by opponents of the bill, is the long-range certainty that competition will develop. If immediately under fair-trade laws price discrepancies seem to emerge as to certain established national brands, and they may—and in some cases they may emerge to a greater extent than we would approve—still there comes then the effect of the kind of competition between manufacturers outlined by the Senator from Oklahoma. Other products and other brands will then come into the market and will narrow the gap and narrow the margin, so that what might be true during the first year will be far less true during the second, and will be eliminated over a period of 3, 4, or 5 years.

The long-range development of new kinds of competition under the fair-trade laws was not emphasized last night by the distinguished Senator from Illinois in his very brilliant and moving presentation, and, to my knowledge, it has not been emphasized by any of the opponents of the bill. So I will agree with the comments just made by the Senator from Oklahoma.

Mr. HUMPHREY. I wish to say to the Senator from Connecticut, who has had years of experience in the advertising business and knows all the secrets of advertising, that one of its objectives is to promote competition, promote expanding markets, and to promote new enterpreneurs [sic] in the different fields. Fair trade has done just that.

One point should be made. So far as branded articles or trade-marked articles are concerned, we find that there are articles of equal quality made by the same company which are not fair-traded, not branded, but frequently are produced in some of the same factories with those which become trade-marked. So there is that kind of competition. For example, a refrigerator company may make a trade-marked refrigerator which carries the name, reputation, and background of the company. Yet it may make another refrigerator which can be sold to the lower-income market, which is a competitive article, but still provides refrigeration, good facilities, and thereby competition to the trade-marked commodity.

Mr. BENTON. If under fair trade the prices of some items go temporarily out of line, or if the margin goes out of line, a fear of which the Senator from Illinois indicated last night in his remarks, let me say, first, that new trade-marked proprietaries will develop advertising to compete at a lower price; and, secondly, private brands of a high quality will be promoted by dealers in competition with the advertised brand, and will pull prices down, or the manufacturer will lose his market.

Mr. MONRONEY. It is a fact that in today's market, in the case of most fair-trade articles I know about or have had experience with, the manufacturer puts a lower mark-up on an article or accepts a lower percentage of profit, because he must say to the retailer, "I am giving you this service to help you sell. You do not have to create a market; I have created a market for you by my national advertising. Therefore, you take a 5, 10, or 20 percent lower mark-up, because this product is easier to sell. You do not have markdowns to take."

Therefore, I believe the claim that this bill will raise the cost of living and make consumers pay more falls, because it simply is not in line with the facts with respect to fair-trade items that I know anything about.

Mr. BENTON. The Senator is profoundly right with respect to the fact that the narrowest margins are on the heavily advertised lines. This would be true even under fair trade. But as I pointed out yesterday, if one takes to a drug counter a prescription to be filled, the mysterious symbols on the prescription do not tell him anything about what is inside nor do they indicate that the mark-up might be many hundred percent—not a mere 30 or 40 percent. For something on which the ingredients may cost a penny or two, to make up as the prescription, the druggist may charge a couple of dollars. The same thing perhaps can be bought in a Vick's vapo-rub bottle for 15 cents. That is the way drug merchandising is done. When one goes into a department store, such as Macy's, one can perhaps buy Bayer aspirin for 6 percent less than the usual price. But when one goes upstairs to the furniture department, where he cannot turn over a chair and look at the trade mark on the bottom, and has no standard by which he can contrast the chair with other chairs—well, Macy's obviously has to get its profit margin. It may be 6 percent less or it may be 16 percent more. If they had not secured adequate profit margins how could they have become the largest, fastest expanding department store in the United States? Profits have to come from somewhere. If they are able to sell Bayer aspirin at a low price, their tremendous margin of profit is made elsewhere, in the furniture and jewelry departments, let us say, and on other unbranded merchandise, as to which the customers do not have a definite standard of comparison. Manifestly their efficiency in buying, selling, and operating also contribute.

Mr. LONG. Mr. President, will the Senator yield?

Mr. BENTON. I yield.

Mr. LONG. One of the issues which gives me grave concern over the measure is that it is my understanding that if retailers get together and agree that they will sell, let us say, Jergen's lotion, for perhaps 35 cents, although it was not to be sold for a price less than 49 cents, that would be conspiracy in restraint of trade, it would be against the law, and those retailers would be subject to prosecution under the Sherman Anti-Trust Act.

Mr. BENTON. That is correct. That is my understanding.

Mr. LONG. On the other hand, if any of them singly signed a contract with Jergen's, agreeing with Jergen's rather than agreeing among themselves, they could accomplish exactly the same effect which Congress saw fit to outlaw as far ⊥ back as ⊥ 8872 1890 as being against the public interest. That is a question which seriously concerns me.

Mr. BENTON. If I may comment on that briefly, it was suggested last night that when the manufacturer, the wholesaler, and the retailer become accustomed along vertical lines to fixing the price at the level fixed by the manufacturer, this will further accelerate present tendencies in our economy for horizontal deals and fixing of prices among groups of retailers, groups of wholesalers, and groups of manufacturers.

I share the concern of the Senator from Louisiana. The Congress pays lip service to competition, but will then starve the Federal Trade Commission for funds, will refuse the Antitrust Division of the Department of Justice money it ought to have with which to hire lawyers to do the needed job and to foster competition on a horizontal basis.

I am the first to admit that with the passage of the pending bill, there may develop a greater danger that certain trends, which today are all too manifest in most areas of our economy, may be accelerated. It behooves the Federal Trade Commission and the Antitrust Division to raise their voices, to seek friends on Capitol Hill who can get them larger appropriations, to get improved personnel if they can, and to move in even more aggressively to enforce the antitrust laws.

I see the Senator from North Dakota [Mr. LANGER] on the floor. I was startled by his comment yesterday that nobody had ever gone to jail for violation of the antitrust laws. If that be true, it indicates the lack of aggressiveness with which those great laws have been enforced, laws which have been so essential to the development of our economy.

Mr. LONG. Of course, the criticism the Senator is making should not be aimed at the enforcement agencies as such. It should be aimed at Congress, because Congress has been the culprit in this instance, for not providing funds to enforce those laws.

For example, Congress finally passed a law to prohibit mergers that would have the effect of creating monopolistic conditions, but appropriated no money to enforce the law. So if there is no money to enforce the law, and if we do not hire a police force, how is the law to be enforced? Violations will go on in spite of the law.

Mr. BENTON. Congress is constantly debating, and frequently passing, legislation which saps at the vitality of these laws. I shared the fear just expressed by the Senator from Louisiana when I started to study this fair-trade bill. Many an evil, under the fair, euphemistic, and alluring phrase "fair trade," has been concealed in the laws of the States. I studied the bill in detail before I satisfied myself that the benefits which would accrue to the American people from the bill would considerably outweigh any danger which may be implicit in any acceleration of habits in the business community in the direction of violations of the antitrust laws.

Mr. HUMPHREY. Mr. President, will the Senator yield?

Mr. BENTON. I yield.

Mr. HUMPHREY. I appreciate what the Senator from Connecticut has said. As he knows, both from my public statements and my private conversations with him, I recognize that the bill is not foolproof. I have said again and again that there are many apprehensions over some features of so-called fair-trade laws. However, I wish to make it crystal clear that the junior Senator from Minnesota has repeatedly voted to increase the funds and personnel of the Antitrust Division of the Department of Justice and the Federal Trade Commission, just as the Senator from Louisiana and the Senator from Connecticut and other Senators have done. I believe in the enforcement of the laws. I believe that they should be vigorously enforced. Furthermore, I wish to say to the Federal Trade Commission, which Commission opposes a fair-trade law, that it has yet to present a really positive, contructive alternative which is workable. I submit that it is its job to do so, and in the meantime to continue to keep a weather eye on the practices under fair-trade legislation. It is my intention in the next session to call upon Congress to appoint a type of watch dog joint committee to watch over the whole matter of the practices and usages under the fair-trade law, and at a later time to report back to the Congress in case there is need for any amendments. This is not to say that the pending bill would not be effective. I think it would be.

I wish to conclude my part by saying that what we are talking about is what has been on the books for 15 years. This bill proposes no change in the law which has been on the books for 15 years, up until the time of the Schwegmann case, when the Supreme Court said, in a split decision, with three great Justices—Frankfurter, Burton, and Black—dissenting, that the Court felt that the nonsigners clause in State contracts was not provided for in the Miller-Tydings Act.

Last night the Senator from New York [Mr. LEHMAN] suggested what he considered to be a weakness in the bill—and the Senator from Connecticut and the Senator from Louisiana referred to the same point—namely, that if one manufacturer signed with one retailer all the others would be bludgeoned into position.

The fact of the matter is that that is not the way the law would work. That is nothing but theory. It has no relevancy in practice. When a manufacturer signs with a retailer, he notifies every other retailer in the country. If he does not, the courts will not uphold fair-trade practices with respect to that particular commodity. That has already been prescribed by court decision. In other words, if a retailer does not have complete information presented to him by the manufacturer, he cannot be held accountable under a fair trade practice law.

Furthermore, the professional journals of all retail groups make it their business to inform every retailer as to the manufacturer's price and the resale price. There is nothing to compel the retailer to sell the commodity at all. If he does not like the price of Jergens lotion he does not have to sell it. There are other products to be sold. There is no compulsion whatsoever on him, and he is not subject to any prosecution if he cuts the price, unless he has been fully informed as to the contractual relationship between manufacturer and seller. Let that be a matter of record.

Mr. BENTON. Most certainly he does not have to put Jergens lotion in his window or on his counter.

Mr. HUMPHREY. That is correct.

Mr. BENTON. He may not sell 10 percent as much of it as he would if he put it in his window and on his counter, and instructed his clerks to push it.

Mr. LANGER. Mr. President, will the Senator yield for a question?

Mr. BENTON. I yield.

Mr. LANGER. I ask the distinguished Senator if he knows of any other way to attain justice for the American people in this matter except by passing the pending bill?

Mr. BENTON. I like the way the Senator puts the question. Instead of stating it in terms of justice to the grocer, the druggist, and the hardware merchant he speaks of it in terms of justice to the American people. I shall devote the remainder of my remarks largely to that point. I think the bill should be considered from the standpoint of the interest of all the American people, and on that basis should be passed by the Senate.

Mr. LANGER. When the Senator from North Dakota was chairman of the Committee on Post Office and Civil Service we considered the question of excess employees. As chairman of that committee I consulted the head of the Federal Trade Commission, Mr. Freer, to find out how many cases were pending before the Federal Trade Commission which had been before it for more than 3 years without any decision. Would the Senator be surprised to learn that there were more than 300 cases over 3 years old?

I learned something further, I will say to my distinguished friend from Connecticut. Take the case involving spark plugs. Twenty years ago there were 40 spark plug companies. One of them brought an action before the Federal Trade Commission, claiming that it was being discriminated against and that the antitrust law was being violated. Would the Senator be surprised to learn that that case has been pending before the Federal Trade Commission for 15 years without a decision? There has been no decision unless one has been handed down within the past few weeks.

Mr. BENTON. I am not in the least surprised. While I shall not now undertake to defend the Federal Trade Commission, because I am sure it may have been negligent in many ways—most human institutions have been—yet let me say that as a member of the Small Business Committee I have received evidence that the FTC has been starved for staff and starved for funds. The responsibility therefore rests to a large extent on the Congress. Perhaps the situation is also due in part to certain practices within the Federal Trade Commission.

Mr. LANGER. Mr. President, will the Senator further yield?

Mr. BENTON. I yield.

Mr. LANGER. I agree wholeheartedly with the Senator from Connecticut. The Federal Trade Commission has had an inadequate sum of money with which to do a big job. It has been starved for funds ever since I first came to the Senate. Time and time again, after the Bureau of the Budget had recommended more money, and after the Appropriations Committee had recommended more money, its appropriations have been cut down $1,500,000 or $2,000,000, in spite of everything we could do on the floor of the Senate.

Looking at my distinguished friend from Minnesota [Mr. HUMPHREY] I remember that 30 years ago we heard much about Frank B. Kellogg, the great trust buster from the State of Minnesota. I took occasion to look up the record, and I was astounded to find how very little had been done. As a matter of fact, 99 percent of it was newspaper notoriety. Apparently some experts had been employed to build him up. As a matter of fact, until a very short time ago the Department of Justice did not have sufficient funds to enforce the antitrust statutes. The situation was taken up with the former Attorney General, Tom Clark, now a distinguished Associate Justice of the Supreme Court. The amount of money which that agency had, up until the time he took office, was pitiful. Those who control monopoly have somehow or other gained control in the Government. The Federal Trade Commission and the Department of Justice have been hamstrung. That is why I am delighted to have this entire debate take place, and to have all the facts brought out.

Mr. BENTON. I am very glad also, and I hope that the result will be renewed vigor on the part of the Federal Trade Commission. I believe that this bill today is further warranty for more aggressive [sic] efforts on its part to move in and get the needed funds, leadership, and manpower to do the job which ought to be done.

I may say that Frank B. Kellogg was my maternal grandfather's pageboy when he was the Democratic leader of the Minnesota State Senate. I never have learned what made a Republican of Mr. Kellogg. When the Senator mentioned his name, that was the first time I had thought of him in many years.

Mr. HUMPHREY rose.

Mr. BENTON. Does the Senator from Minnesota wish to ask a further question?

Mr. HUMPHREY. I wish to ask the Senator one question along the line of the questions of the Senator from North Dakota [Mr. LANGER].

Mr. BENTON. Let me make one personal comment which occurred to me when I was listening to the Senator from North Dakota.

The first job I had after I secured a college degree was as a salesman for the National Cash Register Co., which enjoyed a world-wide monopoly, not only in the United States, but everywhere in the world.

My first day as a salesman was spent sitting in the office reading a pamphlet which every salesman had to read on his first day. The pamphlet was written about Mr. John H. Patterson, and his practices. Mr. Patterson, who developed this great company, is widely called "the father of scientific salesmanship."

The pamphlet contained the story of the antitrust suit against John H. Patterson around 1913.[3.79] It described his famous knockout department, in which he had his so-called knockout men who were hired to go forth whenever a new competitor came out with a cash register. Mr. Patterson invited the competitor to come to Dayton and look at what was called the morgue. In the morgue were cash registers of every type, all of which had been knocked out. They had been made by approximately 40 companies which had vanished over the dim horizon.

If a competitor could not be prevailed upon to go into some other line of business the knockout men would open up stores alongside of his sales offices and sell cash registers at any price, perhaps for as little as a dollar, in order to put the competitor out of business. If that did not work, the men of the knockout department would seek to hire the competitor's agents at higher salaries and commissions. If that did not work they would bribe the freight agents of the railroad companies to see to it that the competitor's shipments never went through. If that did not work there were instances in which they would train their salesmen to go into stores and drop sand into the competitor's machines. If that did not work there were cases in which they would hire thugs to take the competing salesmen down a back alley and knock them out. At any rate, they knocked out all competitors.

Mr. President, that was my first day's reading as a salesman for the National Cash Register Co., which had just employed me. The reason I had to read the pamphlet was that John H. Patterson had been sentenced to 3 years in the penitentiary. Because of his work in the Dayton flood in 1913, in which I seem to remember that he turned out rowboats at the rate of one a minute for a day or two, his sentence was suspended. But in case any of the practices were resumed he could be put forthwith into jail. In other words, if I as a salesman made the mistake of dropping sand into a Remington Rand cash register the owner of my company might be put in jail.

Seemingly his fear of jail was such that every new salesman had to read the pamphlet on his first day of employment.

Mr. President, I tell that story because although persons have not gone to jail for such practices there has been the fear of jail and there has been the threat of jail. There is no doubt that the fear and the threat have had a tremendous effect on the attitude of American business.

If that fear and that threat had more teeth and if more people had actually gone to jail, we would have an even more vital competitive system. The reason we do not have it is in part due to the fact that Congress is subjected to pressure from forces which do not want the antitrust laws enforced.

Whenever we debate an adequate appropriation for the Federal Trade Commission and other agencies, men who are afraid of jail and afraid that their practices may be investigated, move in on Congress, and work in such a way as to have the budget figures cut so that the work of the agencies may be retarded.

Does the Senator from Minnesota have a final question?

Mr. HUMPHREY. Following the colloquy between the junior Senator from Connecticut and the senior Senator from North Dakota, I should like to invite attention to the fact that the co-authors of the Robinson-Patman Act were the distinguished late Senator Robinson and our colleague in the House, Representative PATMAN. WRIGHT PATMAN is known as one of the greatest defenders of the antitrust laws and the antimonopoly laws in this country. He has led the fight in session after session of

---

[3.79] United States v. Patterson, 222 F. 599 (6th Cir.), *cert. denied*, 238 U.S. 635 (1915).

Congress and has gained for himself a reputation second to none. Yet WRIGHT PATMAN of the House of Representatives, and cosponsor of the Robinson-Patman Act, is a valiant sponsor and proponent of the bill which the Senator from Connecticut is now discussing.

When I hear Senators on the floor tell of their fear as to what the bill would do if enacted into law, by killing competition and hurting consumers, I say this: Here are men like the Senator from North Dakota [Mr. LANGER] and Representative WRIGHT PATMAN, of Texas, with a lifetime of service to consumers, workers, and independent business people—and I have put in a few years on it myself—who rally to the support of the bill on the basis of equity and fair play.

I wanted to give that information to the Senator because we are not alone in this fight. They are the men who have spent a lifetime of service in the cause.

Mr. BENTON. I am glad to join in paying tribute to Representative PATMAN, with whom I have the honor of serving with the Senator from Wyoming [Mr. O'MAHONEY] on the Joint Committee on the Economic Report.

Mr. [HOMER E.] CAPEHART [R., Ind.]. Mr. President, I wish to say one word about the pending bill. I think it is a good bill. I think it ought to be passed; and I am hopeful that the Senate will pass it during the afternoon. . . .

⊥ NEED IS TO STOP LOSS LEADERS; NOT TO PERMIT PRICE FIXING ⊥ 8881

Mr. DOUGLAS. Mr. President, my amendment is on the desks of the Members of this body, and I ask the Members in the Chamber to read it. It would meet the assigned reason which is advanced in support of the private price-fixing bill, which is now the unfinished business before this body. The one argument which the advocates of the resale-price-maintenance or private price-fixing bill have made is the need for stopping the so-called loss leaders; namely, that unless action is taken, it is possible for large druggists and chain stores to sell nationally advertised branded goods for less than wholesale prices. Loss leaders draw into the large chain stores customers who seek a bargain, and who, when they are in the store, are then charged higher prices for other goods.

In other words the argument is made that the loss leader is used as a "come on" to draw in the sucker. It is said that it is necessary to have private price-fixing on goods, or resale-price maintenance in order to check these loss leaders.

That is the one argument which is advanced in support of this extraordinary bill, whose Senate paternity is unknown, whose record is obscure, and which comes to us with doubtful credentials.

AMENDMENT AFFECTS SAME PRODUCTS AS M'GUIRE BILL

Mr. President, if that is the real reason, my amendment meets the situation, because it outlaws the loss leader. It says that it is illegal—and I call this point to the attention of the Senator from Minnesota [Mr. HUMPHREY] and the Senator from Connecticut [Mr. BENTON]—for branded goods or articles to be sold for less than the wholesale price plus 6 percent.

I invite the attention of the sponsors of the pending bill to the fact that the amendment would really prohibit loss leaders.

The amendment applies to the identical groups of goods which the private price fixers would put into effect for their commodities as well. The amendment is confined to trade-marked and branded goods. I ask my good friends in the Senate to look at page 2, lines 7 to 10 of my amendment, where the term "loss leader" is defined as being a commodity "which bears, or the label or container of which bears, the trademark, brand, or name of the producer or distributor of such commodity and which is in free and open competition with commodities of the same general class produced or distributed by others."

Mr. [FRANCIS] CASE [R., S.D.]. Mr. President, will the Senator from Illinois yield?

Mr. DOUGLAS. I should like to finish this portion of my statement.

In other words, the precise commodities covered by the pending bill of unknown Senate paternity before us are those covered by my amendment.

Now I yield for a question.

Mr. CASE. Would the Senator also ask the Senators to read the exceptions created, particularly E, F, and G on page 3?

After reading those exceptions, the value of the amendment offered by the Senator from Illinois would seem to be wholly nebulous.

Mr. DOUGLAS. The amendment exempts perishable commodities if further retention would cause loss to the seller. This is reasonable.

On this floor we recently exempted perishables from OPS regulation. I believe my good friend from South Dakota voted for the exemption on fresh fruits and vegetables. Is the Senator from South Dakota saying that his vote was wrong?

Mr. CASE. I believe the Senator provides so many loopholes in the exceptions that no effective remedy would be provided.

Mr. DOUGLAS. The amendment contains a workable definition which exempts perishables if holding them would cause a loss. It also exempts sales where inventories are liquidated to avoid insolvency or bankruptcy. In such cases, selling below cost is justifiable and not really a loss leader. It also exempts seasonal sales and clearance sales which are in accordance with normal business practices, such as selling winter clothing in the summer. In all other transactions sales may not be made for less than the wholesale price, plus 6 percent.

Mr. President, this amendment will furnish the acid test as to whether the assigned reasons behind the bill are in fact the real reasons. If the assigned reasons are the real reasons, then I hope the sponsors of the bill will vote for my amendment, because it will give them protection.

A SENATOR. Vote!

Mr. DOUGLAS. It does not provide for private price fixing. Mr. President, did I hear "vote" from the other side of the aisle? I hope we will not debate under the shadow of the guillotine.

M'GUIRE BILL AFFECTS NON-SIGNERS AS WELL AS SIGNERS

My amendment does not provide for private price fixing. That is the real purpose of the bill before us. The real purpose of the bill, which nearly passed last night, is to give to manufacturers of trade-marked and branded commodities the power to fix the prices of all goods which they sell. Those manufacturers control those prices, not merely for those who sign contracts with them but for all those who do not sign the contracts as well.

In other words if in one of the 45 resale-price-maintenance States one retail dealer of a given branded line signs a contract with a manufacturer to charge a minimum price or a stipulated price, then all the retail outlets in that State must charge that minimum or stipulated price, which may be either a floor price or a dictated price. The Senator from Oregon [Mr. MORSE] earlier today hinted at what might be meant by the term "stipulated price." All that is necessary is to get the consent of 45 retailers, 45 men handling commodities, scattered in as many States. Then the power to fix the final price of the product is turned over to the private manufacturer. Mr. President, that is an extraordinary conferring of public power. In my judgment the bill is unconstitutional because it delegates legislative powers to private individuals. It turns over to private agencies the fixing of prices. This is contrary to the Supreme Court decision in the Schechter case.

It is also a direct repeal of the Sherman Antitrust Act and the Clayton Act. Therefore the bill is much more than a mere enabling act as has been asserted.

M'GUIRE BILL CAUSES CONSUMER TO PAY HIGHER PRICES

It, of course, results in higher prices to the consumers. I ask my colleagues to read the RECORD for yesterday and to go over the figures I then placed in the RECORD. This material will be found on page 8719 and subsequent pages. Those figures show that in the field of drugs, prices in the resale-price-maintenance States are from 15 to 20 percent higher than corresponding prices in the adjoining States which are not resale-maintenance States.

There are still four jurisdictions in this country, thank the Lord, which are not resale price maintenance States or jurisdictions. They are Vermont, Missouri, Texas, and the District of Columbia.

Here in the District of Columbia, drug prices are approximately 20 percent less, on the average, than drug prices in Virginia and in Maryland, which are resale price maintenance States.

In my own State of Illinois, drug prices are at least 12 percent higher in East St. Louis than they are in St. Louis, across the Mississippi River, in a non-resale price maintenance State.

In Oklahoma, a resale price maintenance State, prices are higher than prices in Texas, which is a nonresale price maintenance State. Everywhere in the drug business the comparisons are clear.

Although most of this discussion has been phrased in terms of the drug business, let me say that the drug industry is not the only one that is involved. The liquor industry is involved in this matter, because it wants high resale prices for its products. It knows that the demand for those products at any one time is relatively inelastic. The household appliance industry and the sporting goods industry and a whole series of other industries are involved in this matter.

Fortune magazine, which is a conservative magazine, has estimated that three-quarters of a billion dollars a year is at stake in connection with this proposed procedure.

THE STAKE OF THE MANUFACTURER IN STOPPING RETAIL COMPETITION

While the retail merchants have been doing most of the talking in support of the McGuire bill, the manufacturers of the trade-marked and branded products have been putting up the real money, why do they want this bill? They want to get a high manufacturers' price and then let the retail merchants in as junior partners. They are afraid that if we get competition in prices, that the reduction in retail prices to the consumer will force lower manufacturers' prices. They are, therefore, using the merchants as buffers to protect them from competition.

SCHWEGMANN CASE GAVE HOPE

Mr. President, last year the Supreme Court gave us some hope; it declared that although contracts between signers were still effective, and although a retail merchant who agreed, in a signed contract made with the manufacturer, not to sell a commodity for less than a given price, continued to be bound by that contract, such a contract did not bind the nonsigners. In the Schwegmann case the Supreme Court gave to the consumers an opportunity for the nonsigners to give lower prices to the consumers, and then allowed the manufacturers and the nonsigners to work out their own private arrangements, under the common law.

The pending bill would close that door of hope. The pending bill would reverse the decision of the Supreme Court. The pending bill would say that contracts are binding not only on signers, but also on nonsigners—a principle which seems to me to be thoroughly wrong.

The pending bill would result in a higher cost of living, not merely in the case of drugs, but in the case of all the other commodities I have mentioned.

M'GUIRE BILL A BLOW AT THE AMERICAN FAMILY

The pending bill is a blow at the American consumer and a blow at the American family.

Mr. President, I believe that all of us more or less realize that fact.

But who are the consumers? The consumers are the 155,000,000 American people, the 45,000,000 American families. Enactment of the bill would mean an additional annual cost of $5 a year for each person—or a total of $750,000,000 or $1,000,000,000. A man who loses $5 a year—or who loses 1 1/2 cents a day—and a family that loses $20 a year, which is taken from it at the rate of 6 cents a day—do not know they are being hurt. They do not know that that money or their economic lifeblood is slowly being filched from them. But it is.

Enactment of the pending bill will mean that the consumers will have to pay higher prices for aspirin, for vitamins, and for the precious drugs which in some instances mean the difference between life or death, the difference between health or sickness. It will cause higher prices for liquor, for sporting goods, for certain types of advertised foods, for household appliances, and so on.

However, that money will be slowly taken away from the American people; and since it will be taken away in only small quantities from any one person, the consumer will not know about it, will not protest, will not be articulate, and will not be organized.

CONSUMER INTEREST UNORGANIZED; SPECIAL INTEREST IS STRONG

On the other hand, the groups who are going to make the $750,000,000 or $1,000,000,000 a year as a result of enactment of this bill are powerful and are very well organized. The telegrams have been streaming into our offices and the lobbyists have been thronging the corridors.

I do not attack them for doing that, Mr. President. The United States Government maintains the right of petition for businessmen as well as for workers; for those who sell products, as well as for those who buy them. There is nothing wrong with what they are doing. But I ask my colleagues not to mistake the pressure of the lobbyists for the interests of the American people. I ask my colleagues to remember that over the United States the 45,000,000 families of Americans will lose by the enactment of this bill, even though a few thousand or possibly a few tens of thousands may gain by the bill. I ask my colleagues to remember the still, small voice of the American people.

Mr. President, without indulging in mock heroics, let me say that I know it is an extremely hazardous thing politically for one to take the floor of the Senate and oppose this bill. In a given State, only a few consumers will know the issues involved, or will particularly care. There are no votes and no political prestige in opposing the bill or in voting for my amendment. But the special interests supporting the bill will be deeply concerned and will resent our action. We can expect to lose ground by defending the interests of the consumers.

So here is a very classic case of a diffused general interest coming into conflict with a powerful and concentrated special interest. All of us are sufficiently experienced in politics to know what generally happens when that occurs.

But, Mr. President, this body also has a sense of stewardship. We are not only politicians; we have the welfare of our Nation at heart.

AMENDMENT IS FAIR

Mr. President, we have had a chance to think over this measure and to weigh the alternatives.

My amendment would meet the legitimate case of those who are sponsoring the pending bill. My amendment would protect them from loss-leaders, as I believe they should be protected. My amendment is liberal in its definition of a loss-leader.

When this amendment was proposed in the House of Representatives, it merely provided protection against sales below wholesale prices. The pending amendment, however, provides protection against sales which affect commerce which are below wholesale prices, plus 6 percent. In other words, my amendment would permit a 6-percent mark-up for distribution costs.

In the House the amendment covered all commodities. The pending amendment is confined to branded or trade-marked commodities, or the very same group that is covered in the pending bill, and these only if they affect commerce.

AMENDMENT WOULD NOT PERMIT PRICE FIXING

The pending amendment meets the legitimate complaints of the retail merchants, but it heads off private price-fixing.

So, Mr. President, we have the choice between whether we wish to have a competitive society or whether we wish to have a monopolistic and controlled society.

The competitive society about which we speak so frequently and so eloquently has in it elements of roughness. In a competitive society the inefficient are eliminated. The efficient survive, but the very process of competition makes people more efficient than they otherwise would be. The very fact that they have to meet competition stimulates people to an added effort, and is an inducement to added ability.

So, Mr. President, on the whole, a competitive society is one in which the whole level of production and of efficiency is higher than in a protected and monopolistic society. Such is the society in which we say we believe; but we tend to believe in it for the other fellow. Competition is good for the other fellow; but most people want for themselves protection, security, high prices, price rings and combinations, which we disguise under such terms as "fair trade." We do not really believe in competition, if we favor a bill like this. What is destroying free society, is in part, this tendency for each and every special group to want protection for itself—and to get it—because they are interested in that particular piece of legislation and are willing to sacrifice the general interests of the community as a whole.

So, Mr. President, I am going to close. I think, as a result of today's and yesterday's debate, the issues are now fairly well known. The measure was not rushed through as it seemed at one time it would be. We have had a chance to consider it.

I appeal to my colleagues to remember the silent citizens, the people who have not had the money to come to Washington, to stay at the elaborate hotels, to send telegrams, or to throng the galleries and lobbies—the people who have not had the money to organize, but who will pay the piper. I ask that we consider the silent American citizens, 45,000,000 families, who will pay the price.

PRICE FIXING DOES NOT HELP SMALL MERCHANTS

I would like to point out that in the States of Vermont, Missouri, and Texas, and in the District of Columbia, no more druggists have failed proportionately than in any other State, and that my amendment would give them still more protection.

As a matter of fact, so far as druggists are concerned, their share of the consumers' dollar has shrunk from 4 cents to 3 cents during the operation of the Miller-Tydings Act, when it was thought that nonsigners must comply with prices fixed by the manufacturers involved in this bill.

Why has the druggists' proportionate share of the market declined? One of the main reasons is that high mark-ups on price-fixed drugstore items encourage the grocery chains such as A. & P. and Safeway to carry these items. Ten years ago only 10 percent of the supermarkets carried these items. Now over 85 percent carry them. The grocery chains like this price fixing. But it doesn't help the druggists.

LET US HAVE FAITH IN FREE AND FAIR COMPETITION

I would prevent private price fixing. Let us have faith in competition. We can protect small business from arbitrary financial power, as has been done under the Robinson-Patman Act. The Senator from Louisiana and I sought on the floor of this body to preserve the Robinson-Patman Act. Let us not, however, permit private price fixing which hurts the consumer. We can stop the evil, namely, loss leaders which serve no valid competitive purpose; but it is not necessary to permit price fixing in order to do it. There is no reason why we should burn the barn in order to roast the pig. There is no reason why, in order to cure a minor ailment, we should swallow a major dose of poison.

I hope my amendment in the nature of a substitute will be adopted and the bill itself will be defeated.

Mr. LEHMAN. Mr. President[,] I have spoken previously on this question, but I want to express myself again, although briefly, in the light of the very fine debate that has taken place.

We have heard within the past 24 hours as fine a discussion of the issues as I have heard on any question that has come before the Senate. There was a tendency at first to try to drive this bill through by main force. Fortunately, however, that effort was abandoned.

I would be the last to pretend that all the virtue is on one side of this argument. Indeed, as I told the Senate last night, I have never approached a question in which I was in greater doubt as to the correct course to be followed. In order to take the position which I have finally decided on, namely, to oppose the fair-trade bill, I have had to reverse an established position I took while Governor of New York when I signed into law one of the first fair-trade laws adopted by any State.

Mr. President, I see very clearly the virtues in the fair-trade law now pending before us, and I can well understand and appreciate the arguments of my friends and colleagues, the junior Senator from Minnesota, the distinguished junior Senator from Alabama, the junior Senator from Michigan, and others. They are moved by deep concern for the welfare of the small-business men of America, the druggists, the grocers, and others.

I share their concern. I, too, am moved by the plight of the small-business man. I know the difficulties he confronts in the face of ruthless competition from large chains and huge merchandising organizations. I want to do everything in my power to protect the interests of these small-business men and to defend them against unprincipled and destructive competition where such competition is palpably unfair and where it is designed to drive these small-business men to the wall and to eliminate them as a competitive factor. I can understand that ruthless price competition by large organizations with huge resources can, in the end, reduce, but not enhance, free competitive enterprise.

⊥ But, Mr. President, there are other ways of getting at the problem than by means of fair-trade legislation. Indeed, there are better ways, more effective ways. We can, for instance, give the protection of the law to small-business men against the unprincipled use of the "loss-leader." We can prohibit more effectively than we already do discriminatory selling by the manufacturer to the retailer and thus assure that every retail seller gets the same article at the same cost.

O Mr. President, there are many ways whereby we can protect the small-business man. And we should pursue those ways. As the junior Senator from Minnesota has said, the protection of the small-business man is a social obligation. I want to do everything in my power toward that end.

But, Mr. President, the way of fair-trade legislation is not the right way.

The effect of this legislation is to give big manufacturers—the manufacturers of brand-name products—the unqualified power to fix prices and to set aside the economic laws of the competitive system. These big manufacturers get the chief benefit from the fair trade laws. They are given the authority to fix with finality the price which the consumer must pay. This is an authority which, if it is to be removed from the market place at all, should be reposed only in public hands, never in private hands.

It is a well recognized economic principle that price fixing is the ultimate evil in the throttling of competition. It is one of the worst manifestations of monopoly. Our whole body of anti-trust legislation is aimed at price fixing.

The Government should get into the the [sic] price fixing field only with the greatest reluctance and only where it is absolutely necessary. But the Government must never give the protection of law to price fixing by private agreement, by the fiat of manufacturers and big business. When we do that, we are attaching, as the distinguished senior Senator from Illinois said the other day, the last chains to the body of competitive enterprise.

And, Mr. President, it is not correct to say that only big chains and big stores are interested in selling at lower prices. There are many small stores with small overheads which can and do attract customers by taking a small margin of profit. Fair-trade laws cripple these small businesses and handicap them in their efforts to survive and to grow.

I have heard fair-trade legislation compared to minimum wage legislation and to farm parity legislation. That comparison is a false one. The minimum wage law sets a floor under wages, and permits free collective bargaining, and individual bargaining above that floor.

But the fair-trade law permits a single manufacturer to sign a contract with a single dealer and thus to establish the minimum price for that article wherever it is sold in that State. The Government is not setting the minimum price. It is authorizing the manufacturer to set that price. No bargaining is involved. No public determination is involved.

The same is true, in even greater measure, in regard to parity prices for farm products.

A general law aimed at helping a particular class is always dangerous; its effects may and usually do far overlap the group at whom the law is aimed and creates effects which are by no means helpful or desirable. It is obvious that the fair-trade laws are very costly indeed to the people of the country.

When I signed the New York fair-trade law, we were trying to work our way out of the depression. Goods were plentiful and dollars were scarce. It was an emergency measure and I said at the time I signed it—and that was in 1935—that it was not a perfect bill and was very much subject to improvement. I am now convinced that other measures should be taken to protect the small-businessman and to promote his interest. Fair-trade legislation is wrong in principle and at this time will do more harm than it will do good.

I hope the Congress will think today of the interest of that forgotten man and that forgotten woman of America, the consumer. He and she are the victims of this legislation. I know that the consumers are not organized and there is no such thing as a consumer's vote. Yet we dare not forget them. There are 155 million of them in America and they, too, must have their defenders among us.

I hope the substitute offered by the Senator from Illinois [Mr. DOUGLAS] will be adopted and that the fair-trade bill, as it is now presented, may be defeated.

Mr. CASE. Mr. President, whatever its merits may be, or whatever may be said about the bill which is before the Senate, the amendment which has been offered by the Senator from Illinois as a substitute ought not to be adopted. I question very much whether Senators, if they knew all that is in the amendment, would vote for it. It is bottomed on making over-the-counter sales interstate commerce, and it contains this sentence:

> Any loss-leader practice which affects commerce is hereby declared to be unlawful and actionable at the suit of any person damaged thereby.

In other words, it is bottomed on the premise that over-the-counter sales are interstate commerce.

Mr. DOUGLAS. Mr. President, will the Senator from South Dakota yield?

Mr. CASE. I should prefer to finish my statement.

The PRESIDING OFFICER. The Senator declines to yield.

Mr. CASE. The substitute provides for triple damages and for obtaining injunctive relief either in a court of the United States or in a State court.

There are several exceptions, however, which persons sued or against whom an injunction might be sought could offer as a defense. There are exceptions listed from (A) to (G). I particularly invite attention to paragraph (E) which provides as follows:

> Any sale of a perishable commodity if further retention of the commodity by the seller could reasonably be expected to result in a loss to the seller.

When I mentioned this awhile ago in the colloquy with the Senator from Illinois [Mr. DOUGLAS], he pointed out that he had made an exception of perishable products in the Controls Act. Of course, the Controls Act rests upon the interpretation of an emergency and the effect upon the national defense of the policy of control. Whatever may be the merits or demerits of it, at least it rests upon a national-defense provision, and not at all upon the premise that over-the-counter sales are interstate commerce. Courts have generally acted on the theory that over-the-counter sales are intrastate business. If they are to become interstate business, and the concern of the Federal courts, with the exceptions as here proposed, the amendment, if adopted, would bring about a regular lawyers' field day.

Another exception is as follows:

> Any sale which reasonable business practices require the seller to make in order to liquidate an inventory of a commodity to avoid insolvency or bankruptcy.

Mr. President, the judgment of all the many retail dealers may vary as to what would be necessary as a reasonable business practice to liquidate an inventory. Certainly that would suggest to any person the possibility of extended if not endless litigation.

Another exception is as follows:

Any seasonal clearance sale made in accordance with customary business practices in order to dispose of excess inventory.

Mr. President, are we going to ask the Federal courts of the country to determine as to all the retailers in the country when it is proper and in good faith to have a sale in order to dispose of an excess inventory? Are we going to make every little-business man subject to suits in Federal courts, either for triple damages or for injunctions, when he determines that he has an excess inventory and wants to have a sale, in order to determine whether he has a valid defense against the action proposed?

Mr. President, it seems to me these illustrations point out the extreme confusion that would result, the endless litigation and the endless harassment of small business throughout the country, and the overturning of all the precedents which have held that over-the-counter sales are intrastate business rather than interstate business.

Therefore, Mr. President, I hope, whatever Senators may think about the basic bill which is before the Senate, they will not accept this substitute.

Mr. HUMPHREY. Mr. President, I should like to yield to the Senator from Wyoming.

Mr. [LESTER C.] HUNT [D., Wyo.]. Mr. President, the McGuire bill, H. R. 5767, seeks to do just one simple thing, namely, to restore in a Federal enabling statute the meaning which I believe Congress intended the Miller-Tydings Act to have when it passed that act in 1937. It is significant that prevailing interpretations and court decisions during a 13-year period following passage of the Miller-Tydings Act enabled the State fair-trade laws to be effective.

The McGuire bill establishes no Federal fair-trade policy. It adds nothing whatsoever to the fair-trade acts of 45 States. It takes nothing away from any of these State acts. It overcomes two court decisions so that it may be a truly enabling Federal statute.

In 1951 the United States Supreme Court, in the Schwegmann decision, weakened the State fair-trade structure by holding that nonsigners, so-called, could not be bound by fair-trade contracts when interstate commerce was concerned because the Miller-Tydings Act did not contain a specific nonsigner clause. The McGuire bill does contain a specific nonsigner clause.

Late in 1950 the Third Circuit Court of Appeals, in the Wentling decision, weakened the State fair-trade structure by holding that enforcement of a State fair-trade act in any other State having a fair-trade law constituted an unlawful burden upon and interference with interstate commerce. Under that decision mail-order houses and other retailers who sell across State lines are permitted to disregard the fair-trade laws of every State but their own. The McGuire bill contains a specific provision, in paragraph (4), which clearly overcomes the Wentling decision.

Much conflicting testimony has been adduced as to the merit or lack of merit of fair trade. This testimony can properly be weighed by every State legislature. We are not called upon to weigh it here, because we are here dealing not with Federal fair-trade policy, but with an enabling act which recognizes the rights of the States to regulate their own internal affairs in an area in which they are competent to do so.

Mr. HUMPHREY. Mr. President, I rise to join issue with the Senator from Illinois on his amendment. I have listened to his eloquent and persuasive argument, but I must say his argument is filled more with words of eloquence than with persuasive words of fact. Let us clear up a few points—and I do so with the best of friendship and understanding.

The Senator from Illinois has insistently asked, What about the paternity of the bill? The paternity of the bill is in the tradition of a great American-Irish name, or Irish-American name—McGUIRE—Representative McGUIRE, of Connecticut. Let there be no doubt as to its legitimacy. It is an honorable name, and the proposal is an honorable one from an honorable man.

The bill passed the House of Representatives, and the amendment which the Senator from Illinois now offers was, in substantially the same form, overwhelmingly defeated in the House of Representatives. That is point number one.

Point No. 2. I may go farther back into the paternity of this measure. The measure had as its grandfathers the late Senator Robinson, of Arkansas, and a present Representative from Texas, the Honorable WRIGHT PATMAN. Mr. PATMAN, of Texas, is known as a friend of the consumer, and is one of the most able proponents of antimonopoly and antitrust legislation in Congress.

Mr. [LYNDON B.] JOHNSON [D., Tex.]. Mr. President, will the Senator yield?

Mr. HUMPHREY. I point out—

Mr. DOUGLAS. Mr. President, will the Senator yield?

Mr. HUMPHREY. I should like to continue for a moment. Well, all right, I yield.

Mr. DOUGLAS. Mr. President, the Senator has identified the paternity of the bill in the House, but would he tell us who left it at the doorstep of the Senate?

Mr. HUMPHREY. I should be delighted to do so. I am sure the Senator from Illinois is familiar with the legislative processes. When a bill has passed the House, it comes to the Senate. It was laid before the Senate by the Vice President, who for a long time has fought for fair trade and whose first assignment as a Representative in Congress was as chairman of a subcommittee where he heard a man who then was a lawyer, but later was a great liberal Justice of the Supreme Court, Brandeis, who came to Washington and pleaded with Representative BARKLEY for fair trade legislation.

I put myself on the side of Brandeis, on the side of Oliver Wendell Holmes, on the side of WRIGHT PATMAN, on the side of the Miller-Tydings Act.

I shall document for the distinguished Senator from Illinois what this is about, because the Senator from Illinois has argued today, in this year of our Lord 1952, about a bill which has been on the statute books since 1937. From 1937 until 1951, when the Schwegmann case was decided, there was not a bit of doubt about what the Miller-Tydings Act covered.

Mr. DOUGLAS. Mr. President, will the Senator from Minnesota yield? I know he wants to be fair.

Mr. HUMPHREY. I do.

Mr. DOUGLAS. Did the Miller-Tydings Act have a single thing to say about nonsigners?

Mr. HUMPHREY. Indeed it did. I would review for the Senator the decision of the Supreme Court in the Schwegmann case.

In my review, I shall cite from the record of Justice Frankfurter, with the assent and concurrence of Justice — and Justice Burton.

Mr. DOUGLAS. Is this the minority opinion?

Mr. HUMPHREY. It is.

Mr. DOUGLAS. In other words, the Senator accepts the minority opinion when it suits his purpose—

Mr. HUMPHREY. I accept the minority opinion only as to facts, I may say to the Senator.

Mr. LONG. Mr. President, will the Senator yield?

Mr. HUMPHREY. No, not now.

In hearings before the Temporary National Economic Committee, Assistant Attorney General Thurman Arnold called for repeal of the Miller-Tydings Act because it made legal the nonsigner provisions of the State fair-trade laws.

I cite to the Senator from Illinois pages 18162–18165 of the Temporary National Economic Committee hearings.

Assistant Attorney General Thurman Arnold had no doubt at that time about the nonsigner clause of the Miller-Tydings Act.

The Federal Trade Commission in its report repeatedly said the nonsigner clause was in the Miller-Tydings Act. The Department of Justice repeatedly said the nonsigner clause was in the Miller-Tydings Act. All the court cases said so. Here is the documentation: *Calamia* v. *Goldsmith Bros., Inc.* (299 N. Y., 636, 775; 87 N. E. (2d) 50, 687);[3.80] *Pepsodent Co.* v. *Krauss Co.* (56 F. Supp. 922).[3.81]

There are two court cases, one Supreme Court case and one Federal district court

---

[3.80] The correct citation is 299 N.Y. 636, 87 N.E.2d 50, *motion to amend remittitur granted*, 299 N.Y. 795, 87 N.E.2d 687 (1949).

[3.81] 56 F. Supp. 922 (E.D. La. 1944).

case, which are clearly identified with the nonsigner clause in the Miller-Tydings Act.

Justice Frankfurter, with Justice Black and Justice Burton, concurring, had this to say—

Mr. DOUGLAS. Was that the majority opinion?

Mr. HUMPHREY. Yes; minority or majority.

Mr. DOUGLAS. But there are nine Justices on the Supreme Court. The Senator from Minnesota has identified only three. What did the other Justices say?

Mr. HUMPHREY. The other Justices said it did not. There is no doubt about that. I am simply saying that the legislative history of the Miller-Tydings Act clearly points out that it did. No one has quoted the minority on the courts any more than has my distinguished friend. He has been a great follower of Brandeis, Oliver Wendell Holmes, and minority after minority. Those are the men who have spoken up in behalf of fair trade.

Listen to Justice Frankfurter:

As demonstrated by experience in California, the State acts would have been futile without the nonsigner clause.[3.82]

That was demonstrated in the year 1931, and the act was amended in the year 1933.

In 1936, the Supreme Court, by unanimous decision, upheld the constitutionality of the nonsigner clause in the State fair-trade laws.

Continuing with the minority opinion:

The Court now holds that the Miller-Tydings amendment does not cover these nonsigner provisions.[3.83]

This is the minority, speaking of the majority of the Court.

Not only is the view of the Court contrary to the words of the statute and to the legislative history, it is also in conflict with the interpretation given the Miller-Tydings amendment by the Federal Trade Commission, by the Department of Justice, and by practically all persons adversely affected by the fair-trade laws.[3.84]

The minority of the Court continues:

Where both the words of a statute and its legislative history clearly indicate the purpose of Congress, it should be respected. We should not substitute our own notion of what Congress should have done.[3.85]

I submit that there is a considerable amount of logic in the argument of the Senator from Minnesota, supported by a considerable amount of fact. The very premise upon which the Senator from Illinois bases his case is one Supreme Court decision, a 5-to-3 split decision, after what? After 14 years of successful application of the Miller-Tydings Act and the 45 State fair-trade laws. I will rest my case upon what I consider to be valuable experience that was not at any time criticized. I have yet to hear a speech on the floor of the Senate, in the 4 years I have been here, against fair trade. In 3 of those 4 years the same supposedly vicious law which was supposedly going to wreck the consumer was on the statute books. It did not wreck the consumer.

There are other people who are interested in the consumer. We are all interested in the consumer. I submit that there is no body of factual evidence to prove that the consumer has been injured by fair-trade laws. I say that the evidence of the Federal Trade Commission in this instance is not evidence that is based upon normal trade practices, normal buying habits, normal merchandising practices, or normal purchasing habits of consumers. Why do I say that? Because the Federal Trade Commission, in its sampling, took samples at a particular hour of the day, on a particular day of the week, and in a particular store.

[3.82] Schwegmann Bros. v. Calvert Distillers Corp., 341 U.S. 384, 401 (1951).

[3.83] *Id.*

[3.84] *Id.* at 401–02.

[3.85] *Id.* at 402.

Let me give some fair samples, and let us see whether or not fair trade has increased prices.

Starting back before fair trade, the University of Minnesota School of Business Administration made a survey. I think it would have as much objectivity in this matter as most people would—surely as much as the Federal Trade Commission, surely as much as any private entrepreneur group. The University of Minnesota School of Business Administration made a survey in the matter of fair-trade practices. Prof. H. J. Ostlund, one of the most eminent men in the field of business administration, compared the prices of 50 leading drug-store products before fair trade, that is, during depression years, with prices under fair trade, in 1939, after normal prices had gone up.

He took prices in the depression years, when prices were abnormally low, before fair trade, and compared them with prices in 1939, which was the best prewar year in terms of the price structure. He and his associates did a job State by State. They found that consumers paid 1 percent less, on the average, for those products under fair trade than they paid in the prefair [sic] trade, depression days. That takes us up to 1939.

Let us see what has happened since 1939. A survey was made by A. C. Neilsen [sic] & Co. A. C. Nielsen & Co. are employed by hundreds of merchandising firms throughout the United States, to obtain nothing but factual data. Such a survey provides a method by which to check commodity sales, to see what the relationship is between price and volume of sales, and so forth. A. C. Nielsen & Co. is a reputable concern. Never has its honor or integrity been contested.

Upon request they put their 1949 and 1951 price figures back in the IBM machines in order to ascertain what consumers in the 45 fair-trade States, taken as a whole, paid for a list of the best known national brand drug products, as compared with the prices paid by consumers in the non-fair-trade States for the same products.

Over-all, in 1949 the consumer in the fair-trade States paid one-tenth of a cent less, on an average, per product than did her non-fair-trade sister. In 1951, during a 6 months' period, the fair-trade State consumer paid 1.4 cents less per product, on the average, than the non-fair-trade consumer did.

Whose figures are we to take? The Federal Trade Commission has been opposed, since the beginning of fair trade, to a fair-trade law. It was opposed when the law was enacted. It has been obtaining figures in an effort to prove that the law did not work. The Nielsen Research Agency is neither for nor against fair trade. It has a job to do, and its job is to present economic data to producers, to manufacturers, to processors, and to wholesalers, so that they can understand what is happening in the market place. This is an objective business. If the Nielsen firm should become prejudiced one way or another, it would lose its clients.

There is no basic evidence to show that the consumer would be damaged. Let me tell the Senate one thing which would damage the consumer. The consumer is damaged when hundreds of outlets for products are lost. Let me give a good example. One of the best examples is Ingersoll watches.

We used to be able to buy an Ingersoll watch for a dollar. Let no one tell me that the price went up because of inflation, because the Ingersoll Watch Co. went out of business long before that. Ingersoll watches were nationally advertised to sell for a dollar. Some of the predatory boys wanted to sell them for 57 cents, which was exactly 13 cents less than the cost; and they sold them.

Mr. DOUGLAS. Mr. President, will the Senator yield?

Mr. HUMPHREY. I yield.

Mr. DOUGLAS. Does not the Senator realize that this loss leader would be outlawed by my amendment, which is the pending business?

Mr. HUMPHREY. I am coming to that.

Mr. DOUGLAS. The Senator should realize that, rather than riding off in all directions.

Mr. HUMPHREY. I will say to the Senator from Illinois that while he is a good economist, he is a poor businessman. No businessman in the world could live on 6 percent.

Mr. DOUGLAS. Does the Senator from Minnesota want to guarantee a profit?

Mr. HUMPHREY. No; the Senator from Minnesota does not want to guarantee a profit, but he would like to see the kind of economic system under which someone could possibly make a profit.

What happened to the Ingersoll watch? Let us see how good it was for the consumer. The Ingersoll Watch Co. products were taken up by people who used them for loss leaders. The Ingersoll Watch Co. lost every little outlet it had around the country, and pretty soon it had to lay off its employees. It could not pay its bonds. It could not take care of its overhead. It had to quit producing that item entirely.

During the price wars Macy's sent out their buyers to retail establishments and bought materials from retail establishments, brought them to Macy's, and practically gave them away, in a nonsensical, idiotic price war between Gimbel's and Macy's which threatened the lives of hundreds of outlets in New York. When did the price war stop? When Mr. MCGUIRE introduced his bill. Knock this bill out, and see what will happen. Mr. MCGUIRE introduced his bill in September [sic] last year. It was then that the price war stopped. Macy's and Gimbel's will start the price war again the minute this measure is defeated, if that should unfortunately happen.

Mr. President, the Senator from Illinois says that his amendment would take care of the brand names and outlaw loss leaders. I say to the Senator from Illinois that his amendment is mandatory. According to his amendment, he is going to see to it that on every item there is a profit of at least 6 percent.

Speaking of the consumers' interest, the fair-trade bill is voluntary. There is no compulsion.

Mr. DOUGLAS. There is a compulsion on the nonsigner.

Mr. HUMPHREY. Wait a minute. I will come to that. I merely say that when a manufacturer manufactures a product he has a right to place a minimum resale price on it. If someone is to sell that product, he must sell it for that minimum resale price. There is no compulsion upon the manufacturer to establish a minimum resale price. If he thinks he can obtain better volume, make more money, and get more customers with no fair-trade price, he does not have to establish it; but he establishes it because it is good for him; it is good for the outlet; and it is good for the consumer.

Let us come to the nonsigner clause. The same argument to which we have listened was made in 45 States. The situation which I have described has been true since 1933 in California. It was true in 42 States before the Miller-Tydings Act in '37, and it has been true every day of a year up until 1951. I may say again that the New York law contains one of the best nonsigner clauses in the United States. In other words, if a manufacturer signs with one outlet at a set price, the protective clauses in the law protect a retailer who has goods in his store before the agreement is signed. If he has such goods on his shelves, he is not held to the fair-trade price with respect to those goods.

In the second place, all sellers of fair-trade items must be notified when a contract is signed. The standard-trade practice is for a producer to send out contracts to every seller.

Thirdly, Mr. President, the trade journals publicize the fact of these contracts.

Mr. President, I would say that the most conclusive argument is the one which the Senator from Connecticut provided earlier today. What kind of United States do we want? What kind of country do we want? I go right back to the 15 years of history which is on my side, rather than 15 hours of talk. I have 15 years of history on my side. I say, without fear of successful contradiction, that the trade practices since 1937 have been better than they were before. I say that since 1937 the prices on the fair trade items have gone up less than the prices on non-fair trade items. It does not do any good to say, "Oh, but they were all padded ahead of time." That is no argument at all. As a matter of fact, since 1937 there has been less increase in the prices of fair trade items than in the prices of non-fair trade items. The cost of living index has shot up 85 percent since 1939, and the price on fair trade items has gone up only 16 percent.

Mr. President, how does one justify the talk about the harmful effect which a fair trade law would have on the consumer? I say that the fair trade law is good for the consumer. The fair trade law reduces prices. The fair trade law regularizes market practices. The fair trade law promotes production. Increased production reduces prices, and reduced prices work for the benefit of the consumer.

Mr. President, those are my arguments. They may be only assertions, but they can be backed up with many more facts than the assertions which were made on the other side.

Mr. AIKEN. Mr. President, will the Senator yield?

Mr. HUMPHREY. I yield.

Mr. AIKEN. Mr. President, will the Senator tell us how the bill which he is advocating would affect consumer cooperatives, which put out their own brands of items which are virtually identical with the advertised brands, except for the label? Would the bill have any effect at all on such cooperatives?

Mr. HUMPHREY. It would have no effect at all on cooperatives.

Mr. AIKEN. Perhaps the practice on the part of the consumer cooperatives had a great deal to do with holding down the price of fair-trade items in the last 15 years.

Mr. HUMPHREY. I want to say that I am in favor of consumer cooperatives. For every brand under fair trade there are 100 other items.

Mr. AIKEN. Which are virtually identical.

Mr. HUMPHREY. That is correct. We have a choice. In other words, it is not as if there was only one car to buy, only one tooth paste to buy, or only one piece of candy to buy. The choice is almost unlimited. There are many types of face powder that can be bought, and the competitive brands are not limited to one outlet, either. I dare say that there are a great many more manufacturers of cosmetics than there are women in the country who use them. The country is loaded with cosmetic manufacturers. They come and go. There is certainly a great deal of competition in that line.

What amuses me very much is to hear people talk about stifling competition. Mr. President, there is plenty of competition. Let us not worry about competition. Rather, let us look for customers. There is plenty of competition, and one must always figure every angle to get money in the cash register.

I hear a great deal of talk about fair trade squelching competition. Anyone who makes such a statement should spend 1 month in a retail store. Let him go into a drug store, grocery store, or a hardware store, with a great Western Auto Supply store, a Montgomery Ward store, or a Sears, Roebuck store facing him immediately across the street. There his store sits, the John Smith store, practically surrounded by that kind of competition. Mr. President, that is real competition. Let us not worry about competition. A man who is in that position does not have to worry about competition. All he must worry about is survival.

I think I am stating common sense. I do not know whether it is all written out in books, but it is common sense.

Mr. President, I am here to say that we do not have to worry about competition. No one in a general merchandising store need worry about competition. What he has to worry about is whether customers will come into the store and whether the price of cream goes up, or whether the price of wheat, cotton, or hogs goes up. That is competition, Mr. President. He will have to figure all the angles to get customers into his store and to try to keep his store open. He will give real service, Mr. President. He will deliver everything in order to get customers in and out of his store. That is what I mean by competition.

The fair-trade program has given an opportunity to these merchants to serve their communities.

It is very nice to talk about competition, but in order to have competition, we must have competitors.

Mr. President, what kind of competition is it if all one has is the competition of a big monstrous chain, which has driven everyone out of business or lets someone stay in business by sufferance?

The kind of economic situation which promotes competition is when there are dozens of people in a community all trying to sell the same products to the same customers, and all trying to give better service. That is competition. It is not something to be described; it is something to be felt and to be experienced. There is plenty of competition in the retail business. There is plenty of competition in the wholesale business. There is plenty of competition in the manufacture of consumer goods. I submit that there is no evidence that can be produced to the effect that in the retail business competition has been stifled since the passage of the fair-trade laws. I submit that when we have retail outlets by the hundreds we have better competition and lower prices; and I submit, likewise, that when we have predatory business practices we lose outlets, and ultimately it means less competition and higher prices.

Mr. AIKEN. Mr. President, will the Senator yield?

Mr. HUMPHREY. I yield.

Mr. AIKEN. With respect to the competition which exists between the large mail-order houses and the local stores, would the price of the large mail-order houses be controlled, or would they be enabled to sell patented varieties of merchandise at less than that at which the local stores are required to sell? We know there is no law now, but in order to make sure of getting a supply of a certain product a local merchandiser does sell at what is called a suggested price. It pretty nearly has the force of law, even though it is not a law. In other words, a mail-order house comes along with a 2,000 page catalog, and an item which is being sold locally at the suggested price of $1.25 is listed in the catalog for 93 cents. What effect would the bill have on such a situation?

Mr. HUMPHREY. The bill will have this effect. It will require that where there are trade or branded names on which fair-trade prices have been established the mail-order house will sell them at those prices in any State, just as the local retail man is required to do. However, it is not inflexible. For example, a minimum resale price may be a little higher than the suggested retail price. The fair-trade price is a minimum retail price. There may be flexibility of 10 to 15 cents on a dollar item.

Mr. AIKEN. The fair-trade price may be less or more than the suggested price?

Mr. HUMPHREY. That is correct. Mr. President, I rest my case.

SEVERAL SENATORS. Vote! Vote!

Several Senators requested the yeas and nays.

The yeas and nays were ordered. . . .

⊥ The result was announced—yeas 12, nays 69, as follows: . . .

So Mr. DOUGLAS' amendment in the nature of a substitute was rejected.

Mr. MOODY. Mr. President, earlier today the junior Senator from Oregon introduced into the RECORD evidence in support of his contention that distinguished economists and teachers of law in our universities are opposed to fair trade.

I can hardly let the opportunity pass without having inserted in the RECORD an article on the fair-trade question published in the November 1951 issue of the Detroit Law Journal. The article is written by Dr. Walter Adams, an associate professor of economics at Michigan State College, which has one of the leading economics departments in the country. I am proud to say that Dr. Adams, who holds a doctor of philosophy degree from Yale University and who enjoys a national reputation as an expert on small business, lends vigorous support to the arguments which I presented yesterday before the Senate on behalf of fair trade and the McGuire bill.

Mr. President, if the Senators will take time to read this short article, which is an economic analysis of the Schwegmann decision of the Supreme Court, I am confident that many objections raised against fair trade will be answered. Let me emphasize again that if we lived in the best of all possible worlds, fair-trade laws would probably not be necessary. If the antitrust laws had been enforced effectively prior to 1936, the Miller-Tydings Act probably would never have been enacted.

Mr. President, the sad fact is that the antitrust laws have not been enforced in such a way as to give the small merchant the protection he needs for his survival. Until we reach a stage in our national economic development when we can prove to the small-business man that he is effectively protected against unfair practices, unfair discriminations, and monopolistic exploitation, I think we should have the safeguards for the independent druggist, the independent petroleum dealer, the independent furniture dealer, and the neighborhood grocer which are embodied in the McGuire bill.

Mr. President, I ask unanimous consent that an article entitled "The Schwegmann Case: An Economic Comment," written by Dr. Walter Adams, and published in the November issue of the Detroit Law Journal, be printed in its entirety at this point in the RECORD.

There being no objection, the article was ordered to be printed in the RECORD, as follows:

The Schwegmann Case; An Economic Comment[1]
(By Walter Adams)[2]

Despite a threatened Presidential veto, Congress—on August 17, 1937—passed the Miller-Tydings amendment to the Sherman Antitrust Act.[3] The amendment legalized resale price maintenance with respect to trade-marked or otherwise identified goods sold in interstate commerce, provided that such goods were resold in a State which had a fair-trade law. The amendment further provided that the making of a resale price maintenance agreement was not to be considered an unfair method of competition within the meaning of section 5 of the Federal Trade Commission Act. While thus sanctioning vertical price fixing, the Miller-Tydings Act nevertheless specifically prohibited horizontal agreements concerning the price of goods sold in interstate commerce.[4]

Immediately upon passage of the act, the antitrust agencies—joined by such divergent groups as Business Week and Consumers Union, Fortune, and The Nation—began to urge upon Congress the repeal of the Miller-Tydings law. Thurman Arnold, speaking for the Antitrust Division, made the following recommendation to the temporary naational [sic] economic committee (February 12, 1941):

"The Department recommends the repeal of the Miller-Tydings amendment to the Sherman Act which was passed in 1937 * * *. This amendment has been in effect a little more than 3 years. Already the record shows that it does not serve the purposes which were urged upon Congress as a reason for its passage, that it sanctions arrangements inconsistent with the purpose of the antitrust laws, and that it becomes a cloak for many conspiracies in restraint of trade which go far beyond the limits established in the amendment."

The Federal Trade Commission, after an exhaustive investigation of the problem, concurred with Mr. Arnold's recommendation on the grounds that "resale price maintenance, legalized to correct abuses of extreme price competition, is subject to use as a means of effecting enhancement of prices by secret agreements and restraint of competition by coercive action on the part of interested cooperating trade groups of manufacturers, wholesalers, and retailers in such ways and to such an extent as to make it economically unsound and undesirable in a competitive economy * * *. The Commission believes that the consumer is not only entitled to competition between rival products but to competition between dealers handling the same branded product."[5]

When it became apparent that little could be accomplished by way of pressing for legislative action, the opponents of fair trade turned to the courts and instituted a number of cases to test the legality of resale price maintenance. These efforts bore fruit when the Supreme Court, on May 21, 1951, announced its decision in the Schwegmann case. By declaring the so-called nonsigner clause to constitute a restraint of trade under the Federal antitrust law, the Court dealt a crippling blow to the Miller-Tydings Act and to the fair-trade laws of 45 States.

Speaking for the Court majority, Justice Douglas held that—

"If a distributor and one or more retailers want to agree, combine, or conspire to fix a minimum price (under the Miller-Tydings Act), they can do so if State law permits. * * * They can fix minimum prices pursuant to their contract or agreement with impunity. When they seek, however, to impose price fixing on persons who have not contracted or agreed to the scheme, the situation is vastly different. That is not price fixing by contract or agreement; that is price fixing by compulsion. That is not following the path of consensual agreement; that is resort to coercion."[6]

The Court also ruled that when retailers are forced, as they are under the nonsigner clause,

---

[1] This case is also set forth in the U. S. Supreme Court summary section. Ed.

[2] Doctor of philosophy in economics, Yale University; economic consultant to the Small-Business Committee, U. S. House of Representatives, 81st Cong., 2d sess.; economic consultant, U. S. Senate, 82d Cong., 1st sess.; associate professor of economics, Michigan State College.

[3] The veto never materialized because the Miller-Tydings Act was attached as a rider to an appropriation bill for the District of Columbia. President Roosevelt reluctantly signed the measure into law (50 U. S. Stat. 693 (1937), 15 U. S. C., sec. 1 (1948)).

[4] Vertical price fixing is accomplished through agreements between manufacturers and wholesalers, wholesalers and retailers, or manufacturers and retailers. Horizontal price fixing, by contrast, is achieved through agreements among manufacturers, among wholesalers, or among retailers. Thus, a pricing contract between General Electric and its retail outlets would be a vertical agreement, while an understanding between General Electric and Westinghouse would constitute a horizontal agreement.

[5] Report of the Federal Trade Commission on Resale Price Maintenance, 1945, p. LXIV.

[6] *Schwegmann Bros. et al.* v. *Calvert Distillers Corp., Schwegmann Bros. et al.* v. *Seagram Distillers Corp.* (341 U. S. 384, 71 Sup. Ct. 491, 95 L. Ed. 684 (1951)); (rehearing denied June 4, 1951).

to abandon price competition, they are driven into a compact which violates the injunction of both the Sherman Act and the Miller-Tydings Act against horizontal price fixing. For these reasons the Court concluded that resale price maintenance arrangements are enforceable only when based on contracts freely entered into between manufacturers and retailers or between distributors and retailers.

The decision was jubilantly received, especially since 2 weeks after its announcement a price war of major proportions was touched off in New York City's department stores. And when the "massacre of Thirty-fourth Street" spread to San Francisco, Baltimore, Memphis, Newark, Harrisburg, and other cities, it appeared as if the removal of fair-trade regulations had indeed been the primary force in reestablishing price competition on the retail level. A new freedom had apparently been won by the merchant and renewed protection accorded to the consumer. In the absence of fair trade, it was argued, lower prices—or at least more competitive prices—were in prospect for an inflation-weary buying public.

In spite of these optimistic predictions, it should be pointed out that the Schwegmann decision is of relatively minor economic significance; that resale price maintenance is not—and never has been—a primary factor in determining prices on the retail level; that, after the initial flurry of price competition is over, prices will return to their former level; and that, in retrospect, the Schwegmann opinion might turn out to be a Pyrrhic victory allowing the enemies of competition to reinstitute some of their former techniques for the lessening of competition and the elimination of smaller competitors. Briefly stated, the reasons for the above contentions are as follows:

First, it seems likely that the recent price war in New York is attributable primarily to the swollen inventories under which wholesalers and retailers had been suffering rather than to the removal of "fair-trade" regulations. While the latter might have been the immediate stimulus for releasing the super-charged inventory pressure, only a logician guilty of the post hoc ergo propter hoc fallacy could argue that the Schwegmann opinion was "cause" and the New York price war "effect." A more sober and unemotional estimate of the situation is perhaps to be found in the view of a department store official who commented:

["]As soon as the competition is sold out, we raise our prices. * * * This thing will simmer down to 300 or 400 items to be used as loss leaders."[7]

It seems reasonable to expect, therefore, that when some of the inventories accumulated during the scare buying period of last fall have been liquidated, the retail price situation will once again return to normal.

Second, it should be recognized that resale price maintenance never did affect more than 10 percent of the commodities sold at retail; that, after enactment of the Miller-Tydings law, manufacturers—as a matter of policy—tried primarily to limit price competition in leader advertising rather than to raise prices above the level at which their larger customers were selling normally; that the provisions of the Miller-Tydings Act have, by and large, been rather effectively circumvented by chains and department stores; that, therefore, the anti-social effects of resale price maintenance have been exaggerated out of all reasonable proportions.

Third, it is self-evident that if a manufacturer insists on continuing resale price maintenance on his product, he is at liberty to do so regardless of the nonsigner clause. As long as manufacturers are free to select their own customers—a right guaranteed under section 2 of the Clayton Act—they can impose "fair trade" covenants on their retail distributors. Already Goodall-Sanford, Eversharp, and Haspel Bros. have announced—in spite of the Schwegmann decision—that they will withhold goods from Macy's presumably because of the latter's uncooperativeness in enforcing the suggested minimum retail prices. Other manufacturers may follow suit in order to prevent the use of their products as loss leaders by large-scale distributors.

Fourth, it may reasonably be contended that the Miller-Tydings Act—being a depression-born measure—was aimed primarily at controlling excessive loss-leader merchandising and sales below cost by chains and department stores, a practice which threatened eventually to result in the evaporation of many independent retail outlets. The act was designed to check a practice which had all the earmarks of an unfair and deceptive trade method, especially when used by large concerns to eliminate weaker competitors; a practice which was often employed as a means of price discrimination for the express purpose of lessening competition. While it is unfortunate perhaps that competition in the retail field had to be protected by a law which does not distinguish too clearly between price competition which is in the public interest and price competition which is economically unsound and inimical to the survival of independent firms, nevertheless "fair trade" appeared as the only practicable means by which the desired goal could be accomplished. Had the Federal Trade Commission and the Antitrust Division done a better job in preventing predatory and sharpshooting practices the effect of which was to lessen

---

[7] Quoted in Business Week, June 9, 1951, p. 23.

competition, passage of the Miller-Tydings Act might never have been necessary and its retention today no longer reasonably justified.

Fifth, and most important, it may be contended that the trade restraints embodied in the fair-trade laws are petty, minor, and insignificant when compared to the influence of monopolistic organizations and monopolistic practices on other levels of industry. It may also be contended that the consumer interest can be protected more vigorously by prosecuting horizontal agreements (tacit or otherwise) on the manufacturing level than by cracking down on vertical price fixing between manufacturers and retailers. It may be suggested that the Department of Justice, the Federal Trade Commission, and all the organs of public opinion who denounce the not so fair fair-trade laws might devote greater attention to the dissipation of concentrated economic power in vital sectors of the economy instead of attacking a statute which affords the little fellow some measure of protection against price competition (of both the predatory and the socially desirable variety).

In conclusion, one may query why, in an economy where many strategic areas are infested by monopoly and oligopoly; in an economy where the concentration of economic power is no less today than it was when the first antitrust law was passed 60 years ago; in an economy where labor, agriculture, and a variety of industrial pressure groups have succeeded in insulating themselves against the rigors of competition through exemption from the antitrust laws; why, in such an economy, we attempt to reestablish competition first in an industry where the small, independent merchant is predominant. Without attempting to justify the Miller-Tydings Act, the State fair-trade laws, or any other restraint on competition; without criticizing the legal basis for the Schwegmann opinion; one may nevertheless conclude that, given an effective enforcement of the antitrust laws prior to 1937, the Miller-Tydings Act would probably not have been needed; that, once the act was passed, it exerted a relatively insignificant effect on retail prices; that the outlawing of the nonsigner clause is, therefore, not likely to bring substantial benefit to the consuming public, and finally, that, if our goal is the fostering of greater competition in the American economy, a more auspicious starting place than the retail trade might have been chosen.

Mr. MORSE. Mr. President, I have proposed two amendments. I ask to have amendment No. 1 read at this time.

The PRESIDING OFFICER. The clerk will state the amendment.

The CHIEF CLERK. On page 2, line 24, after the word "resale," it is proposed to insert: "*Provided, however,* That such minimum or stipulated prices as are prescribed in such contracts or agreements shall, after due consultation with representatives of persons substantially affected by such contracts or agreements, have been determined to be fair and reasonable by a duly constituted board or agency of the State in which such minimum or stipulated prices are to be charged."

The PRESIDING OFFICER. The question is on the amendment of the Senator from Oregon.

Mr. MORSE. Mr. President, I have only a few words to say on this amendment. I explained it this morning. In my opinion, one of the greatest weaknesses in the bill in its present form is that it permits the private manufacturer and the private retailer to do what I consider to be price-fixing, with no check whatever upon their judgment. I think that certainly a procedure should be provided which will permit of some review, to determine whether the prices they have fixed are fair and reasonable. I propose that it be done by the appropriate State agency within each State, having within its jurisdiction this whole matter of fair trade.

I shall not ask for the yeas and nays on this amendment. However, I should like the courtesy of a recorded vote on the amendment which is to follow.

The PRESIDING OFFICER. The question is on the amendment of the Senator from Oregon [Mr. MORSE].

The amendment was rejected.

Mr. LONG. Mr. President, I desire to call up my amendment in the nature of a substitute.

The PRESIDING OFFICER. Does the Senator from Louisiana desire to have the amendment read in full by the clerk?

Mr. LONG. No. I shall explain the amendment.

The PRESIDING OFFICER. Without objection, the amendment will be printed in the RECORD, without reading.

Mr. LONG'S amendment is as follows:

Strike out all after the enacting clause and insert the following:

"That section 2 of an act entitled 'An act to supplement existing laws against unlawful restraints and monopolies, and for other purposes,' approved October 15, 1914, as amended is hereby further amended to read as follows:

"'SEC. 2. (a) That it shall be unlawful for any person engaged in or affecting commerce, in or affecting the course of such commerce, either directly or indirectly, to discriminate in price between different purchasers of commodities of like grade and quality, where either or any of the purchases involved in such discrimination are in or affecting commerce, or to discriminate between or among different commodities or similar commodities of different grade and quality by reselling at retail in or affecting commerce any commodity at less than net cost of such commodity delivered to the retailer's place of business where such commodities are sold for use, consumption, or resale within the United States or any Territory thereof or the District of Columbia or any insular possession or other place under the jurisdiction of the United States, and where the effect of such discrimination may be substantially to lessen competition or tend to create a monopoly in any line of commerce, or to injure, destroy, or prevent competition with any person who either grants or knowingly receives the benefit of such discrimination, or with customers of either of them: *Provided*, That nothing herein contained shall prevent differentials which make only due allowance for differences in the cost of manufacture, sale, or delivery resulting from the differing methods or quantities in which such commodities are ⊥ to such purchasers sold or delivered: *Provided, however*, That the Federal Trade Commission may, after due investigation and hearing to all interested parties, fix and establish quantity limits, and revise the same as it finds necessary, as to particular commodities or classes of commodities, where it finds that available purchasers in greater quantities are so few as to render differentials on account thereof unjustly discriminatory or promotive of monopoly in any line of commerce; and the foregoing shall then not be construed to permit differentials based on differences in quantities greater than those so fixed and established: *Provided further*, That nothing herein contained shall prevent persons engaged in selling goods, wares, or merchandise in commerce from selecting their own customers in bona fide transactions and not in restraint of trade: *And provided further*, That nothing herein contained shall prevent price changes from time to time where in response to changing conditions affecting the market for or the marketability of the goods concerned, such as but not limited to actual or imminent deterioration of perishable goods, obsolescence of seasonal goods, distress sales under court process, or sales in good faith in discontinuance of business in the goods concerned.

"'(b) Upon proof being made, at any hearing on a complaint under this section, that there has been discrimination in price or services or facilities furnished, the burden of rebutting the prima facie case thus made by showing justification shall be upon the person charged with a violation of this section, and unless justification shall be affirmatively shown, the Commission is authorized to issue an order terminating the discrimination: *Provided, however,* That unless the effect of the discrimination or sale below cost may be substantially to lessen competition or tend to create a monopoly in any line of commerce it shall be a complete defense for a seller to show that his lower price or the furnishing of services or facilities to any purchaser or purchasers was made in good faith to meet an equally low price of a competitor, or the services or facilities furnished by a competitor.'"

Amend the title so as to read: "An act to amend an act entitled 'An act to supplement existing laws against unlawful restraints and monopolies, and for other purposes,' approved October 15, 1914 (15 U. S. C. A., sec. 13), as amended."

Mr. LONG. Mr. President, the junior Senator from Louisiana understands, he believes, the logic of the fair-trade bill, most of which is based on the theory that it is necessary to protect individuals against loss-leader items. It seems to the junior Senator from Louisiana that some protection is justified and is reasonable, and should be provided, if it can be done in a proper manner. When a merchant uses a loss leader, it amounts to a form of discrimination as against his other commodities. Some commodities he is selling at a very high price, and the loss leader is sold at a loss, in order to lure customers into the store, so that when they are there the proprietor can sell them some other article, or articles, at a high price. That merchant is discriminating as between commodities, in order to lure people into his store. We have the Robinson-Patman Act, which is designed to outlaw certain price discriminations. It outlaws price discriminations in the sale of a commodity when the result is to injure competition. The Federal Trade Commission is charged with the responsibility of enforcing that act. It is the position of the Federal Trade Commission that price discriminations in the form of loss leaders should also be outlawed, simply by outlawing discriminations between commodities.

The pending bill would change the Robinson-Patman Act by adding the additional language "or to discriminate between or among different commodities or similar commodities of different grade and quality, by reselling at retail in or affecting commerce any commodity at less than net cost of such commodity delivered to the retailer's place of business."

Of course, there would be exceptions in instances where in good faith a person is discriminating, and in which event he would, himself, have a defense. For example, if he were going into bankruptcy, or if he were proposing a seasonal inventory.

Mr. President, my amendment would do the independent retailer far more good than the McGuire bill, perhaps 50 times as much good, because trade-marked items are not the only items which can be sold as loss leaders in order to lure people into a store. Let us consider sugar, for example. If granulated sugar is being sold at, let us say, 50 percent of the retail price, it can be used quite as much as a loss leader as a trade-marked article that is well known. There are many other items of that sort, ordinary standard commodities, items not subject in any way to a fair-trade law, which can be sold as loss leaders.

Let us consider, for example, the filling-station operator. In the city of Detroit it was found that the filling-station proprietors were seeking protection because gasoline was being sold to certain chains at a price far below what the ordinary filling station was being charged. This bill would not do anything to protect the filling-station operator. It would perhaps help a few retail druggists, but it would not substantially help the filling-station operator, because gasoline is not an article susceptible of fair-trade treatment.

The amendment I am offering would have the effect of reversing the Standard Oil of Indiana Co. decision, by providing that good faith would be a complete defense, except in cases where it could be shown that the effect of the discrimination was to injure competition as distinguished from the individual competitor. An individual competitor would be able to go into court, under my amendment, to protect himself, and to sue for treble damages, if someone were injuring him through the loss-leader practice.

It would then be possible for the defendant to plead as a defense that he was meeting competition in good faith, unless it could be shown that the discrimination was injuring not only him but competition in the entire market area.

For years the Federal Trade Commission has recommended this type legislation to meet the problem of loss leaders. This amendment, if adopted, would do far more good than would the proposed fair-trade bill. The reason why I say that is because the amendment I am offering would see to it that independent merchants would acquire their goods at substantially the same prices at which the large merchants acquired their goods.

My amendment would give the little fellow the same price which the big one gets. A small merchant selling Ipana and other brands of toothpaste would go out of business with a mark-up of 5 or 10 percent, if his large competitors were selling for the same price with a mark-up of perhaps 50 percent.

Mr. President, I cannot agree with the approach this [sic] fair trade makes to the problem, because it is diametrically opposed to the theory of our antitrust laws. The Sherman Antitrust Act says that a person cannot conspire with another to reduce competition or to create a monopoly. He cannot conspire where it would be in restraint of trade. Then we come to the Miller-Tydings amendment, under which, taking Ipana toothpaste again as an illustration, if two druggists get together and agree that they will not compete in connection with Ipana toothpaste, that is against the law, but, on the other hand, under a fair-trade law if the producers of Ipana toothpaste have an agreement with either one of the two druggists, that is lawful, but it is then unlawful for other merchants to sell at a different price.

Mr. President, it is my purpose to see that we have competition in this great country, and it is also my purpose to see that the little fellow has a chance to compete with the big fellow. My amendment proposes the same thing the independent merchants were supporting 2 years ago when the junior Senator from Louisiana was fighting the basing-point bill because it would legalize price discrimination. Merchants were writing Senators in support of the position I was taking. I hope they will support the position I am now taking. I understand they have been saying, "If the Senate adopts this amendment, the bill will be tied up in conference and we will not get a bill."

Without this amendment, this bill might have the effect of completely undermining the antitrust laws. If we apply one principle to the little fellow, we should be willing to apply the same principle to the large concern. I think this measure would result in inflicting more injury on the small retailers than it would furnish help to them. On the other hand, I think my amendment would be a far better approach and would give greater protection to the independent retailers in the long run.

SEVERAL SENATORS. Vote! Vote!

The PRESIDING OFFICER. The question is on agreeing to the amendment offered by the Senator from Louisiana.

Mr. DOUGLAS. Mr. President, I ask for the yeas and nays.

The yeas and nays were not ordered.

The PRESIDING OFFICER. The question is on agreeing to the amendment offered by the Senator from Louisiana.

The amendment was rejected. . . .

⊥ 8891   ⊥ Mr. MORSE. Mr. President, I ask that my amendment No. 2 may be stated.

The PRESIDING OFFICER. The clerk will state the amendment offered by the Senator from Oregon.

The CHIEF CLERK. It is proposed, on page 1, line 7, to strike out the words "or stipulated"; page 1, line 8, to strike out the words "or stipulated"; page 2, line 12, to strike out the words "or stipulated"; page 2, line 14, to strike out the words "or stipulated"; page 3, lines 21 and 22, to strike out the words "or stipulated."

Mr. MORSE. Mr. President, in my argument this morning I endeavored to demonstrate that another serious weakness in the pending bill is the stipulated price which would permit entrepreneurs to enter into an agreement fixing prices, which I think constitutes a great evil. I made my argument against it this morning. If we really want to come somewhere near improving this bill so that it will carry out a reasonable public interest, we should eliminate the so-called stipulated prices and leave only minimum prices. I have not heard anything from any of the proponents of the bill which, in my opinion, justifies the word "stipulated" in the bill. I think they have made their case from the standpoint of their major premises, which I believe to be fallacious. I think the weakness is that the bill would permit prices to be fixed by businessmen, without any public check.

Mr. President, I ask for the yeas and nays.

The PRESIDING OFFICER. There is not a sufficient number seconding the request.

The question is on agreeing to the amendment offered by the Senator from Oregon [Mr. MORSE].

The amendment was rejected.

The PRESIDING OFFICER. The bill is open to further amendment. If there be no further amendments, the question is on the engrossment of the amendments and the third reading of the bill.

The amendments were ordered to be engrossed, and the bill to be read a third time.

The bill was read the third time.

The PRESIDING OFFICER. The question is, Shall the bill pass?

Mr. DOUGLAS. Mr. President, I suggest the absence of a quorum.

The PRESIDING OFFICER. The clerk will call the roll.

Mr. DOUGLAS. Mr. President, I withdraw my suggestion of the absence of a quorum, and ask for the yeas and nays.

The yeas and nays were ordered.

Mr. McCARRAN. Mr. President, on the pending bill I want to say only a word.

The bill should have gone to the Judiciary Committee of the Senate when it came from the House. It is an amendment to the Antitrust Act. The antitrust laws should be studied and reviewed by a committee having the proper jurisdiction. I sought at the time to have the bill referred to the Committee on the Judiciary. It was not referred to that committee.

SENATE CONSIDERATION (H.R. 5767)

The bill was reported to the Senate by the Committee on Interstate and Foreign Commerce, which had a perfect right to report the bill, since it had been referred to that committee. The bill was reported without recommendation.

If after the bill had been reported by the Committee on Interstate and Foreign Commerce, a motion had been made to refer it to the Committee on the Judiciary, time would not have been available to enable the latter committee make [sic] a proper study of the bill, and the Committee on the Judiciary would have been accused of burying the bill. For that reason, I have not made such a motion, nor has any other member of the committee.

The bill is now before the Senate for a vote. I say there should be a study made in all respects, of the antitrust laws, and it should be made by a proper committee having jurisdiction to do so. The time is not now available for a study; hence no motion has been made, and hence the vote on this amendment to the antitrust law must now be taken by the Senate.

The VICE PRESIDENT. The yeas and nays have been ordered, and the clerk will call the roll.

Mr. HUMPHREY. Mr. President, a parliamentary inquiry.

The VICE PRESIDENT. The Senator will state it.

Mr. HUMPHREY. Are we now about to vote on final passage of the bill?

The VICE PRESIDENT. On the final passage of the bill.

The Chief Clerk called the roll. . . .

The result was announced—yeas 64, nays 16, as follows:

YEAS—64

Bennett	George	Kerr	O'Conor
Benton	Hayden	Kilgore	O'Mahoney
Brewster	Hendrickson	Knowland	Pastore
Bricker	Hennings	Langer	Robertson
Bridges	Hickenlooper	Magnuson	Schoeppel
Butler, Nebr.	Hill	Martin	Smathers
Byrd	Hoey	Maybank	Smith, Maine
Cain	Holland	McCarran	Sparkman
Capehart	Humphrey	McCarthy	Stennis
Case	Hunt	McClellan	Thye
Chavez	Ives	McFarland	Underwood
Clements	Jenner	McKellar	Watkins
Cordon	Johnson, Colo.	Monroney	Welker
Dworshak	Johnson, Tex.	Moody	Wiley
Eastland	Johnston, S. C.	Mundt	Williams
Ecton	Kem	Murray	Young

NAYS—16

Aiken	Ferguson	Green	Neely
Connally	Flanders	Lehman	Saltonstall
Douglas	Frear	Long	Smith, N. J.
Ellender	Gillette	Morse	Smith, N. C.

NOT VOTING—16

Anderson	Duff	Malone	Russell
Butler, Md.	Fulbright	McMahon	Seaton
Carlson	Kefauver	Millikin	Taft
Dirksen	Lodge	Nixon	Tobey

So the bill (H. R. 5767) was passed.

Mr. HUMPHREY. Mr. President, I submit a concurrent resolution to authorize the establishment of a Joint Committee on Fair Trade Practices, for the purposes of further study of the measure just passed; and I also submit a resolution directing the Select Committee on Small Business to make further and continuing studies in the same field.

The VICE PRESIDENT. The resolutions will be received and appropriately referred.

The concurrent resolution (S. Con. Res. 87), submitted by Mr. HUMPHREY, was received and referred to the Committee on Interstate and Foreign Commerce, as follows:

Resolved by the Senate (the House of Representatives concurring), That (a) there is hereby established a Joint Committee on Fair Trade Practices to be composed of three Members of the Senate to be appointed by the President of the Senate and three Members of the House of Representatives to be appointed by the Speaker of the House of Representatives. Not more than two of the members from each House shall be members of the same political party. Vacancies in the membership of the joint committee shall not affect the power of the remaining members to execute the functions of the joint committee, and shall be filled in the same manner as in the case of the original selections. The joint committee shall select a chairman and a vice chairman from among its members.

(b) It shall be the duty of the joint committee to make continuing studies of all problems involved in fair-trade practices and matters related to fair-trade practices. The joint committee shall, from time to time, make such reports to the Senate and the House of Representatives with respect to its studies as it may deem appropriate and shall make a final report to the Senate and to the House of Representatives on June 30, 1954.

(c) The joint committee, or any duly authorized subcommittee thereof, is authorized to hold such hearings, to sit and act at such places and times, to require, by subpena or otherwise, the attendance of such witnesses and the production of such books, papers, and documents, to administer such oaths, to take such testimony, to procure such printing and binding, and to make such expenditures as it deems advisable. The cost of stenographic services to report such hearings shall not be in excess of 25 cents per hundred words.

(d) The joint committee is empowered to appoint and fix the compensation of such experts, consultants, technicians, and clerical and stenographic assistants as it deems necessary and advisable. The committee is authorized to utilize the services, information, facilities, and personnel of the departments and establishments of the Government.

(e) The joint committee shall cease to exist on June 30, 1954. The expenses of the joint committee, which shall not exceed $50,000, shall be paid one-half from the contingent fund of the Senate and one-half from the contingent fund of the House of Representatives, upon vouchers approved by the chairman of the joint committee.

The resolution (S. Res. 348), submitted by Mr. HUMPHREY, was received and referred to the Committee on Interstate and Foreign Commerce, as follows:

Resolved, That (a) the Select Committee on Small Business is authorized and directed to establish a subcommittee thereof which shall make a comprehensive study of all problems involved in fair-trade practices and matters related to fair-trade practices.

(b) The subcommittee shall make such reports to the Senate with respect to its studies as it may deem appropriate, and shall make a final report to the Senate on June 30, 1954.

Sec. 2. (a) The subcommittee is authorized to hold such hearings, to sit and act at such places and times, to require, by subpena or otherwise, the attendance of such witnesses and the production of such books, papers, and documents, to administer such oaths, to take such testimony, to procure such printing and binding, and to make such expenditures as it deems advisable. The cost of stenographic services to report such hearings shall not be in excess of 25 cents per hundred words.

(b) The subcommittee is empowered to appoint and fix the compensation of such experts, consultants, technicians, and clerical and stenographic assistants as it deems necessary and advisable. The subcommittee is authorized to utilize the services, information, facilities, and personnel of the departments and establishments of the Government.

(c) The subcommittee shall cease to exist on June 30, 1954. The expenses of the subcommittee, which shall not exceed $50,000, shall be paid from the contingent fund of the Senate, upon vouchers approved by the chairman of the subcommittee.

PRESIDENTIAL COMMENT

STATEMENT BY PRESIDENT HARRY S. TRUMAN UPON SIGNING THE "FAIR-TRADE LAWS" BILL (H.R. 5767)
July 14, 1952

1952-1953 PUBLIC PAPERS OF THE PRESIDENTS, HARRY S. TRUMAN 477 (1953)

I have today signed H.R. 5767, "To amend the Federal Trade Commission Act with respect to certain contracts and agreements which establish minimum or stipulated resale prices and which are extended by State law to persons who are not parties to such contracts and agreements, and for certain other purposes."

This act has to do with the so-called fair-trade laws of 45 States. Under these State fair-trade laws, a manufacturer of a trademark or brand name product can, if he wishes, fix the price at which his product may be sold. He does this by making resale price contracts with distributors of his products—and under the State laws, if he makes such a contract with one retailer, it applies to all others in the State whether or not they have agreed to such a contract. This means that every retailer in a given State may be required to sell "fair-traded" products at the same price, and no retailer may attempt to attract customers by reducing his prices on any such product.

Such price-fixing arrangements would, of course, be illegal under the Federal antitrust laws, insofar as they applied to interstate commerce, unless special legislative exemption were given to them. The Miller-Tydings Act of 1937 was passed to grant such exemption, but recent decisions of the Supreme Court have held, among other things, that the Miller-Tydings Act did not sanction the so-called "nonsigner" clauses of the State laws, under which retailers are bound by the resale prices set by manufacturers, even if they have not agreed to be so bound. The purpose of H.R. 5767 is to exempt these "nonsigner" clauses from the Federal antitrust laws, and to extend the exemption for State fair-trade laws in certain other ways.

The central question posed by this act, therefore, is whether the limitations on competition that are established under the State fair-trade laws should be given the sanction of Federal law.

The main reason given for enacting the State fair-trade laws is to prevent some merchants from selling branded items at very low prices (often below cost) in order to drive other merchants out of business, or in order to attract customers who are then sold other items on which high prices are charged. There is no doubt that such practices exist, and that the fair-trade laws prevent them to some extent. This is the reason that the State fair-trade laws, and H.R. 5767, have such strong support among small and independent businessmen—particularly druggists, and hardware and appliance merchants—who fear they cannot survive against such unfair competitive practices.

At the same time, there is no doubt that the fair-trade laws also have the effect of removing some competitive forces which otherwise would operate to help keep prices down. Under the fair-trade laws, retailers cannot compete with each other by reducing the price of branded products, even where such reductions may reflect greater efficiency by one retailer as compared to another. Furthermore, the operation of the fair-trade laws in the past has on occasion been used as a cloak for unlawful conspiracies among retailers, wholesalers, and manufacturers—conspiracies which have gone much further in eliminating competition than the fair-trade laws actually permit. These are the reasons why so many economists, lawyers, and consumer groups oppose fair-trade laws, on the grounds that they eliminate too much of the vigorous, effective competition among sellers which should exist in our free enterprise system.

I believe that the effects of this legislation have been somewhat exaggerated by both sides. I do not believe that the fair-trade laws are as harmful to competition as some have asserted. There are and will be strong competitive forces among manufacturers, wholesalers, and retailers even with the fair-trade laws in effect.

At the same time, it is clear that fair-trade laws are no cure-all for the problems of small retailers. While the fair-trade laws protect him against some types of cutthroat competition, the local independent merchant will continue to have to offer better and more convenient service, and to sell at reasonable prices, if he is to survive against the legitimate and keen competition of such modern advances in the retail field as the supermarket, the mail-order house, and the branch department store.

I have signed this act because it does have value in eliminating certain unfair competitive practices, and thereby will help small businessmen to stay in business—which I believe is a healthy thing for our economy and our society.

At the same time, I believe the fair-trade laws do remove some competitive forces which should be retained in our progressive free enterprise economy.

Accordingly, I believe we have not yet found the best solution for the problem this legislation is intended to solve, and I urge the Congress to make a thorough investigation of this field, including not only the fair-trade laws, but the related problems of price discrimination and antitrust policy. I note that in the course of the debate on H.R. 5767, Senator Humphrey indicated that he would propose an investigation of this field at the next session of Congress. I hope very much that such an investigation will be undertaken, so that we may have a fresh and thorough review of the means for maintaining fair and vigorous competition in our economy.

The Decision

Commentary

Although both the Miller-Tydings Act and the McGuire Act exempted from Sherman Act liability vertically imposed resale price restrictions (*i.e.*, agreements between manufacturers and distributors, manufacturers and retailers, or distributors and retailers), each specifically forbade any such agreements *between* manufacturers, or producers, or wholesalers, or brokers, or factors, or retailers, or persons, firms, or corporations in competition with each other (*i.e.*, agreements which could be classified as *horizontal* in nature). As Congress recognized in enacting both fair-trade laws, such horizontal agreements had long been held to be *per se* illegal under the Sherman Act insofar as they affected interstate commerce, and this illegality was not intended to be altered by either the Miller-Tydings Act or the McGuire Act.

The congressional policy against horizontal price-fixing agreements was reaffirmed by the Supreme Court's 1956 decision in *United States v. McKesson & Robbins, Inc.*[3.86] In *McKesson*, the Justice Department brought a civil action for injunctive relief, charging that defendant's fair-trade agreements with independent wholesalers with whom it competed constituted illegal price fixing in violation of section 1 of the Sherman Act. The facts in the case showed that McKesson sold its branded products both to retailers directly through its own wholesale divisions and to independent wholesalers for resale by them to retailers; that it fair-traded all of its branded products at the retail level; and that it had fair-trade agreements, setting the wholesale price to retailers, with 21 independent wholesalers who competed with its own wholesale divisions. Moreover, in 1951 McKesson instructed its wholesale divisions not to sell any of its branded products to any independent wholesaler who had not entered into a fair-trade contract with defendant. This resulted in 73 additional independent wholesalers, who had been dealing with McKesson's own wholesale divisions, entering into fair-trade agreements whereby they agreed to adhere to the wholesale prices set by McKesson.

McKesson conceded that the 94 independent wholesalers with whom it had entered into fair-trade agreements competed with McKesson's own wholesale divisions in selling to retailers. McKesson argued, however, that in contracting with the independent wholesalers, it was acting only as a manufacturer, not as a competing wholesaler.

The Supreme Court, in holding unlawful McKesson's fair-trade agreements with the independent wholesalers, ruled that such agreements were within both the "between wholesalers" and "between persons, firms, or corporations in competition with each other" provisos contained in the Miller-Tydings Act and the McGuire Act. The Court, through Chief Justice Warren, held that "[s]ince appellee competed 'at the same functional level' with each of the 94 wholesalers with whom it has price-fixing agreements, the proviso prevents these agreements from falling within the statutory exemption."[3.87] The proviso in both Acts, according to the Court, "excludes from the exemption from the *per se* rule of illegality resale price maintenance contracts between firms competing on the same functional level."[3.88] The Court concluded by holding that

---

[3.86] 351 U.S. 305, 76 S. Ct. 937, 100 L. Ed. 1209 (1956), *infra* at 929.
[3.87] 351 U.S. at 313.
[3.88] *Id.* at 315.

"Congress has marked the limitations beyond which price fixing cannot go. We are not only bound by those limitations, but we are bound to construe them strictly, since resale price maintenance is a privilege restrictive of a free economy."[3.89]

In dissent, Mr. Justice Harlan, joined by Justices Frankfurter and Burton, contended that the protection of goodwill, implicit in all fair-trade legislation, should not be denied to a manufacturer merely because he happens also to be a wholesaler. In support of this argument, he pointed out that a fair-trade agreement between a nonintegrated manufacturer and a wholesaler eliminates all price competition on the manufacturer's products, just as does one between an integrated manufacturer and a wholesaler.[3.90] Thus, according to the dissenters, the real intent of Congress in inserting the proviso against horizontal price fixing in both the Miller-Tydings Act and the McGuire Act was to make unlawful only those agreements that were between manufacturers of competing brands, or between wholesalers with respect to products which did not bear the name of the wholesalers and over which the wholesalers thus could not justify any need for goodwill protection.[3.91]

In conclusion, the dissent argued that an integrated manufacturer "should be deemed to be acting as a 'manufacturer' rather than as a 'wholesaler' " in selling its products under fair-trade contracts to independent wholesalers.[3.92]

[3.89] *Id.* at 316.
[3.90] *Id.* at 317–18.
[3.91] *Id.* at 319.
[3.92] *Id.* at 320.

UNITED STATES v. McKESSON & ROBBINS, INC.

351 U. S. 305, 76 S. Ct. 937, 100 L. Ed. 1209 (1956)

MR. CHIEF JUSTICE WARREN delivered the opinion of the Court.

This is a direct appeal by the Government under the Expediting Act, 32 Stat. 823, 15 U. S. C. § 29, as amended by 62 Stat. 869, from a decision of the District Court for the Southern District of New York, interpreting the scope of the exemption from the antitrust laws provided by "fair trade" legislation.

Appellee, a Maryland corporation with its home office in New York, is the largest drug wholesaler in the United States. Operating through 74 wholesale divisions located in 35 States, it sells drugstore merchandise of various brands to retailers, principally drugstores, substantially throughout the nation. For the fiscal year ended March 31, 1954, its sales of all drug products amounted to $338,000,000.

Appellee is also a manufacturer of its own line of drug products, the total sales of which amounted to $11,000,000 for the year ended March 31, 1954. Its manufacturing operation is conducted through a single manufacturing division, McKesson Laboratories, located at Bridgeport, Connecticut. This division, like each of appellee's wholesale divisions, has a separate headquarters and a separate staff of employees, but none of the 75 divisions is separately incorporated. All are component parts of the same corporation and are responsible to the corporation's president and board of directors.

Appellee distributes its own brand products to retailers through two channels: (1) directly to retailers, and (2) through independent wholesalers. The major portion of its brand products is distributed to retailers through its own wholesale divisions. Appellee also makes direct sales to important retailers through its manufacturing division. Most of appellee's sales to independent wholesalers are made by its manufacturing division, but its wholesale divisions sold approximately $200,000 of McKesson brand products to other wholesalers during the fiscal year ended June 30, 1952.

To the extent possible under state law, appellee requires all retailers of its brand products to sell them at "fair trade" retail prices fixed by appellee. These prices are set forth in published schedules of wholesale and retail prices.

Appellee also has "fair trade" agreements with 21 independent wholesalers who buy from its manufacturing division. Sixteen of these independents compete with appellee's wholesale divisions. The other 5 compete with the manufacturing division for sales to chain drugstores located in their trading areas. On June 6, 1951, in accordance with appellee's "fair trade" policy, a vice president in charge of merchandising notified appellee's wholesale divisions that—

> "None of our wholesale divisions will sell any McKesson labeled products to any wholesaler who has not entered into a fair trade contract with McKesson Laboratories."

As a result, 73 of the independent wholesalers who had been dealing with McKesson wholesale divisions entered into "fair trade" agreements with McKesson by which they bound themselves in reselling its brand products to adhere to the wholesale prices fixed by it. Each of these independent wholesalers is in direct competition with the McKesson wholesale division from which it buys.

The Government, under Section 4 of the Sherman Act,[1] brought this civil action for injunctive relief against appellee in the District Court. The complaint charged that appellee's "fair trade" agreements with independent wholesalers with whom it was in

---

[1] 26 Stat. 209.

competition constituted illegal price fixing in violation of Section 1 of the Act. Appellee admitted the contracts, but claimed that they were exempted from the Sherman Act by the Miller-Tydings Act[2] and the McGuire Act.[3]

The Government moved for summary judgment on the ground that these Acts do not immunize McKesson's agreements with other wholesalers, since they expressly exclude from their exemption from the antitrust laws contracts "between wholesalers" or "between persons, firms, or corporations in competition with each other." The district judge denied the motion.[4] He recognized that price fixing is illegal *per se* under the Sherman Act, but announced that in "fair trade" cases "No inflexible standard should be laid down to govern in advance." He was "unwilling, at this stage of case law development of legislatively sanctioned resale price fixing" to apply the *per se* rule "in fair trade situations absent a factual showing of illegality." Such a showing, he said, could not be made "simply by pointing to *some* restraint of competition." The "true test of legality" of "fair trade" agreements between a producer-wholesaler and independent wholesalers, the court held, "is whether some additional restraint destructive of competition is occasioned."[5]

The case then proceeded to trial before another district judge, who concurred in the "ruling that fair trade price fixing by a producer-wholesaler was not per se illegal under the Sherman Act," and held that the Government's evidence did not establish an "additional restraint" within the meaning of the test previously enunciated in the case.[6] He ordered the complaint dismissed, and the Government took a direct appeal under the Expediting Act. We noted probable jurisdiction.[7]

The issue presented is a narrow one of statutory interpretation. The Government does not question the so-called vertical "fair trade" agreements between McKesson and retailers of McKesson brand products. It challenges only appellee's price-fixing agreements with independent wholesalers with whom it is in competition.

Section 1 of the Sherman Act provides:

> "Every contract, combination in the form of trust or otherwise, or conspiracy, in restraint of trade or commerce among the several States, or with foreign nations, is hereby declared to be illegal. . . ."[8]

It has been held too often to require elaboration now that price fixing is contrary to the policy of competition underlying the Sherman Act and that its illegality does not depend on a showing of its unreasonableness, since it is conclusively presumed to be unreasonable.[9] It makes no difference whether the motives of the participants are good or evil; whether the price fixing is accomplished by express contract or by some more subtle means; whether the participants possess market control; whether the amount of interstate commerce affected is large or small; or whether the effect of the agreement is to raise or to decrease prices.[10]

In *United States* v. *Socony-Vacuum Oil Co.*, 310 U. S. 150, in holding price-fixing agreements to be illegal *per se*, this Court said:

---

[2] 50 Stat. 693.

[3] 66 Stat. 632.

[4] 122 F. Supp. 333.

[5] 122 F. Supp., at 337–339. The district judge provided an illustration of the kind of conduct which might satisfy his test: "If, for example, it could be established that a producer became a wholesaler, though not in competition with an independent wholesaler, and stipulated prices for his own and the independent wholesaler as a first step toward and with intent to gouge consumers, that might suffice *prima facie* as violation of the Sherman Act outside the privilege of the fair trade statutes."

[6] R. 180.

[7] 350 U. S. 922.

[8] 26 Stat. 209.

[9] *E. g., United States* v. *Trenton Potteries Co.*, 273 U. S. 392, 397; *Ethyl Gasoline Corp.* v. *United States*, 309 U. S. 436, 458. See also *Standard Oil Co.* v. *United States*, 221 U. S. 1, 65.

[10] *United States* v. *Socony-Vacuum Oil Co.*, 310 U. S. 150, 221–224.

> "Congress has not left with us the determination of whether or not particular price-fixing schemes are wise or unwise, healthy or destructive. . . . the Sherman Act, so far as price-fixing agreements are concerned, establishes one uniform rule applicable to all industries alike."[11]

And it has been said by this Court:

> "A distributor of a trade-marked article may not lawfully limit by agreement, express or implied, the price at which or the persons to whom its purchaser may resell, except as the seller moves along the route which is marked by the Miller-Tydings Act."[12]

The question before us is whether the price-fixing agreements challenged herein move along that route. If they do not, they are illegal *per se*. There is no basis for supposing that Congress, in enacting the Miller-Tydings and McGuire Acts, intended any change in the traditional *per se* doctrine. The District Court was plainly in error in attempting to create a category of agreements which are outside the exemption of those Acts but which should nevertheless be spared from application of the *per se* rule.

In the Miller-Tydings Act, passed as a rider to a District of Columbia revenue bill, Congress was careful to state that its exemption of certain resale price maintenance contracts from the prohibitions of the antitrust laws "shall not make lawful any contract or agreement, providing for the establishment or maintenance of minimum resale prices on any commodity herein involved, between manufacturers, or between producers, or *between wholesalers*, or between brokers, or between factors, or between retailers, or *between persons, firms, or corporations in competition with each other.*"[13] (Emphasis supplied.)

Fifteen years later, Congress attached an almost identical proviso to the McGuire Act.[14] We are to take the words of these statutes "in their normal and customary meaning." *Schwegmann Bros.* v. *Calvert Corp.*, 341 U. S. 384, 388.

Appellee is admittedly a wholesaler with resale price maintenance contracts with 94 other wholesalers who are in competition with it. Thus, even if we read the proviso so that the words "in competition with each other" modify "between wholesalers," the agreements in question would seem clearly to be outside the statutory exemption. Appellee concedes that the proviso does not exempt a contract between two competing independent wholesalers fixing the price of a brand product produced by neither of them.[15] Yet it urges that what would be illegal if done between competing independent wholesalers becomes legal if done between an independent wholesaler and a competing

---

[11] 310 U. S., at 221–222.

[12] *United States* v. *Bausch & Lomb Co.*, 321 U. S. 707, 721.

[13] 50 Stat. 693. This proviso qualified the proviso immediately preceding it, which amended § 1 of the Sherman Act so as to make lawful resale price maintenance contracts entered into by manufacturers of branded or trade-marked goods if such contracts are authorized by state law as to intrastate transactions and if the commodity affected is in "free and open competition with commodities of the same general class produced or distributed by others . . . ."

[14] 66 Stat. 632. The McGuire Act amended § 5 (a) of the Federal Trade Commission Act by adding, *inter alia*, § 5 (a) (2). This specifically exempts from the antitrust laws price fixing under "fair trade" agreements which bind not only retailers who are parties to the agreement but also retailers who refuse to sign the agreement. As in the Miller-Tydings Act, the statutory exemption was qualified by an important proviso. This stated:
"(5) Nothing contained in paragraph (2) of this subsection shall make lawful contracts or agreements providing for the establishment or maintenance of minimum or stipulated resale prices on any commodity referred to in paragraph (2) of this subsection, between manufacturers, or between producers, or *between wholesalers*, or between brokers, or between factors, or between retailers, or *between persons, firms, or corporations in competition with each other.*" (Emphasis supplied.)

[15] Appellee's brief, p. 6. In the District Court and in its motion to affirm filed in this Court, however, appellee claimed that the proviso applies only to agreements "between manufacturers of competing products, or between wholesalers of competing products, or retailers of such products, fixing the prices at which *two or more* competitive products are to be sold." (Appellee's emphasis.) Motion to affirm, pp. 5–6.

wholesaler who is also the manufacturer of the brand product. This is so, appellee maintains, because in contracting with independent wholesalers it acted solely as a manufacturer selling to buyers rather than as a competitor of these buyers. But the statutes provide no basis for sanctioning the fiction of McKesson, the country's largest drug wholesaler, acting only as a manufacturer when it concludes "fair trade" agreements with competing wholesalers. These were agreements "between wholesalers."

Any doubts which might otherwise be raised as to the propriety of considering a manufacturer-wholesaler as a "wholesaler" are dispelled by the last phrase of the proviso in question, which continues the proscription against price-fixing agreements "between persons, firms, or corporations in competition with each other." Congress thus made as plain as words can make it that, without regard to categories or labels, the crucial inquiry is whether the contracting parties compete with each other. If they do, the Miller-Tydings and McGuire Acts do not permit them to fix resale prices. The Court stated in *Schwegmann Bros.* v. *Calvert Corp.*, 341 U. S. 384, 389, that this proviso "expressly continues the prohibitions of the Sherman Act against 'horizontal' price fixing by those in competition with each other at the same functional level."[16] Since appellee competes "at the same functional level" with each of the 94 wholesalers with whom it has price-fixing agreements, the proviso prevents these agreements from falling within the statutory exemption.

Appellee argues that a brief colloquy on the Senate floor between a supporter of the McGuire Act and an inquiring Senator shortly before the Act was passed should dictate a meaning contrary to that revealed by the Act's plain language. But, at best, the statement was inconclusive.[17] And the Senator whose statement is relied on was not in charge of the bill, nor was he a member of any committee that had considered it. Moreover, the McGuire Act was not a Senate bill, having been passed by the House of Representatives prior to this Senate discussion. There is nothing in the proceedings of the House to indicate that the meaning for which appellee contends should be given

---

[16] Previous phrases of the proviso appear in state "fair trade" laws, upon which the proviso seems to have been modeled. FTC Report on "Resale Price Maintenance," pp. 80–81 (1945). The last phrase, however, has apparently never been included in any state statute. Thus, meticulous inclusion of this phrase in the federal acts is not without significance.

[17] 98 Cong. Rec. 8870. Senator Humphrey, in answer to an inquiry by Senator Sparkman, said:

". . . If, for example, when a producer, who sells to distributors, wholesalers, retailers, and consumers, makes a resale price-maintenance agreement relative to a commodity made by him and bearing a trade-mark or brand, with a distributor, wholesaler, or retailer who resells such commodity at either the wholesale, or retail level, there exists a vertical resale price-maintenance contract which would be lawful under the bill if the requirements of paragraph (2) are met.

"On the other hand, *if one wholesaler enters into a resale price-maintenance agreement with another wholesaler prescribing the price at which they both sell a trade-marked or branded commodity which they both buy from the producer, that agreement would be horizontal and would not be made lawful.*

"In other words, wholesalers getting together on a price are acting illegally. For a manufacturer to get together with other manufacturers to maintain prices is illegal, but for a manufacturer to say that a certain product will sell at a certain price from the manufacturer down to the retailer is legal under the limitations prescribed in paragraph (2) of section 5 (a) of the Federal Trade Commission Act.

"In general, the test of whether a resale price-maintenance contract is vertical is if the contract is between a seller and buyers who resell the original seller's product; whereas, the test of whether a resale price-maintenance contract is horizontal as [sic] if it is between competing sellers between whom the relation of buyer and seller or reseller does not exist as to the product involved.

"It is important to keep this distinction in mind, because *many producers of trade-marked items sell them to consumers, retailers, and wholesalers alike.*

"*Under the bill, such firms may make resale price-maintenance contracts with both wholesalers and retailers because such contracts are vertical, that is, between sellers and buyers.* While in one sense firms in this position function not only as producers but also as wholesalers and retailers, they may still lawfully make contracts with other wholesalers and retailers, when in making such contracts they act as producers of a trade-marked or branded commodity, rather than as wholesalers and retailers entering into forbidden horizontal resale price-maintenance contracts with other wholesalers or other retailers." (Emphasis added.)

It should be noted that these remarks appear to be confined to the "between wholesalers" and "between retailers" phrases and do not deal with the "corporations in competition" phrase. And, even as to the former, it is not at all clear that Senator Humphrey was discussing the situation where actual competition exists between the manufacturer-wholesaler and independent wholesalers. As indicated in note 15, *supra*, until we noted probable jurisdiction, appellee flatly disagreed with an important part of this statement.

to the Act. Similarly, except to show congressional concern that the prohibition against "horizontal" price fixing be continued, the Senate and House debates on the proviso in the Miller-Tydings Act are of little assistance with respect to the problem before us.

The court below did not rely on the legislative history, finding it to be "unedifying and unilluminating."[18] We agree with this appraisal, but are not troubled by it since the language of the proviso in question is unambiguous.[19] It excludes from the exemption from the *per se* rule of illegality resale price maintenance contracts between firms competing on the same functional level.

Both the Government and appellee press upon us economic arguments which could reasonably have caused Congress to support their respective positions.[20] We need not concern ourselves with such speculation. Congress has marked the limitations beyond which price fixing cannot go. We are not only bound by those limitations but we are bound to construe them strictly, since resale price maintenance is a privilege restrictive of a free economy. Cf. *United States* v. *Masonite Corp.*, 316 U. S. 265, 280.

The judgment of the District Court dismissing the complaint must, therefore, be reversed and the case remanded for further proceedings not inconsistent with this opinion.

Reversed and remanded.

MR. JUSTICE HARLAN, whom MR. JUSTICE FRANKFURTER and MR. JUSTICE BURTON join, dissenting.

Lack of sympathy with an Act of Congress does not justify giving to it a construction that cannot be rationalized in terms of any policy reasonably attributable to Congress. Rather our duty, as always, is to seek out the policy underlying the Act and, if possible, give effect to it. In this instance, I think the Court has departed from that rule by giving the Miller-Tydings and McGuire Acts an artificial construction which produces results that could hardly have been intended by Congress.

The purpose of the state fair-trade laws is to allow the manufacturer of a brand-named product to protect the goodwill his name enjoys by controlling the prices at which his branded products are resold. *Old Dearborn Distributing Co.* v. *Seagram-Distillers Corp.*, 299 U. S. 183, 193-194. The necessary result—indeed, the very object—is to permit the elimination of price competition in the branded product among those who sell it. Congress has sanctioned those laws in the Miller-Tydings and McGuire

---

[18] 122 F. Supp., at 336.

[19] Cf. *Greenwood* v. *United States*, 350 U. S. 366, 374.

[20] The Government maintains that a resale price maintenance agreement between a manufacturer-wholesaler and competing independent wholesalers, in addition to eliminating competition between the parties, enables the former, because of its leverage as a manufacturer of branded products, to dictate the latter's prices on these products. Such an agreement, the Government claims, also leaves the manufacturer-wholesaler free to undersell the independent wholesalers when dealing with large retailers directly through its manufacturing division. And if the manufacturer's own wholesale outlets are inefficient, resale price maintenance permits it to insulate those outlets from the inroads of more efficient operators by setting its "fair trade" price higher than otherwise. According to the Government, none of these effects is present where price fixing exists between independent wholesalers and a nonintegrated manufacturer.

Appellee contends that the economic effects of "fair trading" are the same whether or not the manufacturer has its own wholesale outlets, since the protection which resale price maintenance provides to the manufacturer's good will "necessarily involves elimination of price competition among different outlets for the manufacturer's own branded merchandise." In both situations, appellee claims, the manufacturer makes "at the source, as a manufacturer, . . . downstream price fixing arrangements with its outlets."

The court below indicated an awareness of the economic arguments on both sides but refused to follow "either of alternate horns . . . in the dilemma of fair trade agreements with independent wholesalers by a manufacturer who is also a wholesaler . . . ." 122 F. Supp., at 337. Instead, the district judge advocated a case-by-case examination of the economic setting in which the question arises, with the burden on the Government to show "some *additional* restraint destructive of competition." 122 F. Supp., at 339.

For discussion of these economic contentions and the conclusions which they are designed to support, see Weston, Resale Price Maintenance and Market Integration: Fair Trade or Foul Play? 22 Geo. Wash. L. Rev. 658; Note, 64 Yale L. J. 426; 54 Col. L. Rev. 282.

Acts, considering them not to be offensive to federal antitrust policy.[1] Sufficient protection to the public interest was deemed to be afforded by the competition among different brands, a safeguard made express by the provision of the Miller-Tydings and McGuire Acts denying fair-trade contracts exemption from the antitrust laws unless the fair-traded product is "in free and open competition with commodities of the same general class." In short, the very purpose of the Acts is to permit a manufacturer to set the resale price for his own products while preserving competition between brands—that is, between the fair-traded item and similar items produced by other manufacturers.

If we accept the legislative judgment implicit in the Acts that resale price maintenance is necessary and desirable to protect the goodwill attached to a brand name, there is no meaningful distinction between the fair-trade contracts of integrated and non-integrated manufacturers. Certainly the integrated manufacturer has as strong a claim to protection of his goodwill as a non-integrated manufacturer, and the economic effect of the contracts is the same. In both cases price competition in the resale of the branded product is eliminated, and in neither case does the price fixing extend beyond the manufacturer's own product. While the Government concedes the right of a non-integrated manufacturer to eliminate price competition in his products between wholesalers, it finds a vice not contemplated by the Acts when one of the "wholesalers" is also the manufacturer, for then the contracts eliminate competition between the very parties to the contracts. But, in either case, all price competition is eliminated, and I am unable to see what difference it makes between whom the eliminated competition would have existed had it not been eliminated. The other bases of distinction suggested by the Government are equally tenuous and reflect a subtlety of analysis for which there is no support in either the Acts or their history.

So unsatisfactory, indeed, are the Government's attempts to rationalize the result contended for, that the Court chooses not to rely upon them, finding the language of the provisos so clear as to make it unnecessary even to hypothesize a consistent rationale attributable to Congress that might justify the discrimination against integrated producers. Indeed, not even the fact that the only legislative history directly in point is squarely opposed to the Court's reading of the statute (see note 17 of the Court's opinion, pp. 313–315) prompts enough doubt in the Court to require an inquiry into the purpose of the Acts. The Court's reasoning is this: the provisos except from the Acts contracts "between wholesalers" or "between persons, firms, or corporations in competition with each other"; McKesson is a "wholesaler" as well as a manufacturer and is also "in competition with" independent wholesalers; its contracts with independent wholesalers are therefore forbidden contracts "between wholesalers" and between "corporations in competition with each other." This verbalistic argument can be answered by the equally verbalistic one that the fair-trade contracts, being made in connection with the sale of its own branded products, were made by McKesson in its capacity as a "manufacturer" rather than as a competing "wholesaler." Neither argument being more conclusive than the other, the answer to the problem can be found only by looking to the purpose of the provisos and its relation to the basic policy of permitting resale price maintenance of branded goods.

As noted above, the Acts necessarily contemplate the elimination of price competition in the resale of a particular branded product and rely for protection of the public interest upon competition between brands. Viewed in the light of this purpose, the provisos become readily understandable. The vice of price-fixing agreements between those in competition with each other, whether at the manufacturing, wholesaling, or retailing level, is that they can be utilized to eliminate competition *between brands*. Thus manufacturers might agree to fix the resale prices of their competing brands in relation to each other; the same result, on an even broader scale, could be achieved by agreements between wholesalers or retailers. Further, agreements initiated by anyone other than the owner of the brand name are unnecessary to the protection of goodwill, the very justification for permitting fair-trade contracts. Thus an

---

[1] The Court refers to the Miller-Tydings Act as having been "passed as a rider to a District of Columbia revenue bill." It is pertinent to note that, in passing the later McGuire Act, Congress not only reaffirmed the policy of the Miller-Tydings Act but also eliminated the restrictive effect of this Court's decision in *Schwegmann Bros.* v. *Calvert Distillers Corp.*, 341 U. S. 384, as regards "non-signers" of fair-trade contracts.

agreement between wholesalers to fix the price of a product bearing the trade name of neither would serve no purpose other than the elimination of competition. Interpreting the provisos in the light of these considerations, I conclude that an integrated manufacturer selling ⊥ its products under fair-trade contracts to independent wholesalers should be deemed to be acting as a "manufacturer" rather than as a "wholesaler." This interpretation of the provisos fits with their terms and produces, rather than an arbitrary discrimination hardly intended by Congress, a result fully in harmony with the policy of the Acts to permit manufacturers to maintain the resale prices of their branded products while preserving competition between brands.[2]

⊥ 320

For these reasons, therefore, I would hold McKesson's contracts to be within the Miller-Tydings and McGuire Acts and would affirm the judgment below.

---

[2] The Federal Trade Commission, the administrative agency specially charged with administering the McGuire Act, has reached like conclusions. See *Eastman Kodak Co.*, 3 CCH Trade Reg. Rep. (10th ed.), par. 25, 291.

4 CONSUMER GOODS PRICING ACT OF 1975

(FAIR TRADE REPEALER)

939   Introduction
943   Chronological Synopsis
945   Table of Reprinted Documents

ORIGINAL VERSION

947   Consumer Goods Pricing Act
December 12, 1975

The Origins

948   Remarks of Sen. Edward W. Brooke introducing S. 4203
93d Cong., 2d Sess.
December 3, 1974

952   Remarks of Sen. Edward W. Brooke introducing S. 408
94th Cong., 1st Sess.
January 27, 1975

953   S. 408, 94th Cong., 1st Sess.
January 27, 1975

953   White House Press Release
January 29, 1975

House Consideration

955   H.R. 6971, 94th Cong., 1st Sess.
May 14, 1975

956   Report of the House Committee on the Judiciary
H.R. Rep. No. 94-341, 94th Cong., 1st Sess.
[to accompany H.R. 6971]
July 9, 1975

961   House Debate, 94th Cong., 1st Sess.
July 21, 1975

Senate Consideration

971 Report of the Senate Committee on the Judiciary (with Additional Views)
S. Rep. No. 94-466, 94th Cong., 1st Sess.
[to accompany H.R. 6971]
November 20 (legislative day, November 18), 1975

975 Senate Debate, 94th Cong., 1st Sess.
December 2, 1975

Presidential Comment

981 Statement by President Gerald R. Ford upon signing the Consumer Goods Pricing Act of 1975
December 12, 1975

Introduction

CONSUMER GOODS PRICING ACT OF 1975

On December 12, 1975, President Gerald R. Ford signed into law the Consumer Goods Pricing Act of 1975,[4.1] which repealed the Miller-Tydings[4.2] and McGuire Acts[4.3] and thus removed from the federal antitrust laws the exemption for resale price maintenance programs established pursuant to state fair-trade laws. Fair trade repeal was prompted by the depressed economic conditions of the mid-1970's[4.4] (similar conditions, ironically, were the genesis of the fair-trade laws in the 1930's) and by a congressional "mood of procompetitive and proconsumer militancy."[4.5] Repeal was considered a virtual certainty from the start of the 94th Congress.[4.6]

During the closing days of the 93d Congress, Senator Edward W. Brooke (R., Mass.) introduced a fair trade repeal bill,[4.7] and it was substantially the same bill that was later enacted by the 94th Congress.[4.8] Justice Department officials had previously announced that they favored repeal of the fair-trade exemption and that they were preparing such legislation.[4.9] No action was taken on the Brooke bill during the few remaining days of the 93d Congress.

[4.1] Pub. L. No. 94-145, 89 Stat. 801 (1975).

[4.2] Act of Aug. 17, 1937, ch. 690, tit. VIII, 50 Stat. 693. The legislative history of the Miller-Tydings Act appears *supra* at chapter 2.

[4.3] Act of July 14, 1952, ch. 745, 66 Stat. 631. The legislative history of the McGuire Act appears *supra* at chapter 3.

[4.4] *See* 120 CONG. REC. S20361-63 (daily ed. Dec. 3, 1974); 121 CONG. REC. S888 (daily ed. Jan. 27, 1975) (statements by Senator Edward W. Brooke on introducing fair trade repeal legislation). These statements are reprinted *infra* at 948-53.

[4.5] BNA ANTITRUST & TRADE REG. REP., Jan. 14, 1975, at B-1.

[4.6] *See id.* at B-6.

[4.7] S. 4203, 93d Cong., 2d Sess. (Dec. 3, 1974), *infra* at 951.

[4.8] The only differences were technical ones pertaining to the title and the renumbering of a subsection of the FTC Act.

[4.9] *See* Address by William B. Saxbe, Attorney General of the United States, Before the Legal Committee of the Grocery Manufacturers of America, Oct. 29, 1974, at 6-7; Address by Thomas E. Kauper, Assistant Attorney General, Antitrust Division, Before the Pittsburgh Antitrust Institute, Nov. 19, 1974, at 7-8; Address by William B. Saxbe, Attorney General of the United States, Before the National Association of Manufacturers, Dec. 6, 1974, at 6.

At the beginning of the 94th Congress, Senator Brooke reintroduced his bill,[4.10] and similar bills were introduced in the House of Representatives.[4.11] President Ford quickly announced his strong support for this legislation.[4.12]

These bills were referred to subcommittees of the Senate and House Committees on the Judiciary, which held hearings during the spring of 1975.[4.13] Representatives of the Federal Trade Commission,[4.14] the Antitrust Division of the Department of Justice,[4.15] consumer groups,[4.16] and large retailers[4.17] testified at the hearings in support of the legislation. The supporters of repeal argued that fair-trading practices cost consumers between $1.5 and $3 billion annually,[4.18] that repeal would reduce inflation and increase employment,[4.19] and that the original justification for fair trade—that it would protect small retailers—had been proven false.[4.20] Supporters also cited the favorable response to fair trade repeal in Britain and Canada[4.21] and pointed out that many states had reconsidered and in many cases repealed their fair-trade laws in recent years.[4.22]

At first it appeared that there was little opposition to fair trade repeal,[4.23] but as the hearings progressed, a number of manufacturers who fair-traded their merchandise[4.24] and small retailers[4.25] testified against repeal. Others who opposed the legislation apparently chose to remain silent.[4.26] The opponents of repeal argued that fair trade guaranteed quality products and services,[4.27] that interbrand competition protected the consumer from the lack of intrabrand competition,[4.28] that it was anti-states'-rights legislation,[4.29] and that the evidence showing lower business failure rates in free-trade states was out of date.[4.30]

Two modifications of the proposed legislation were suggested but received little support during the hearings. The first of these, proposed by a number of newspaper

---

[4.10] S. 408, 94th Cong., 1st Sess. (Jan. 27, 1975), *infra* at 953.

[4.11] The repealer bills introduced in the House of Representatives were: H.R. 2384, introduced January 29, 1975, by Representative Barbara Jordan (D., Tex.); H.R. 2390, introduced January 29, 1975, by Representative Robert McClory (R., Ill.); and H.R. 3411, introduced February 20, 1975, by Representative Samuel L. Devine (R., Ohio).

[4.12] *See* White House Press Release, Jan. 29, 1975, *infra* at 953-54.

[4.13] *Hearings on S. 408 Before the Subcomm. on Antitrust and Monopoly of the Senate Comm. on the Judiciary*, 94th Cong., 1st Sess., pts. 1-2 (1975) [hereinafter cited as *1975 Senate Hearings*]; *Hearings on H.R. 2384 Before the Subcomm. on Monopolies and Commercial Law of the House Comm. on the Judiciary*, 94th Cong., 1st Sess. (1975) [hereinafter cited as *1975 House Hearings*].

[4.14] *See 1975 Senate Hearings* 9-15; *1975 House Hearings* 3-23 (testimony of Lewis A. Engman, Chairman, Federal Trade Commission).

[4.15] *See 1975 Senate Hearings* 16-21 (testimony of Thomas A. Kauper, Assistant Attorney General, Antitrust Division); *1975 House Hearings* 109-21 (testimony of Keith I. Clearwaters, Deputy Assistant Attorney General, Antitrust Division).

[4.16] *See 1975 Senate Hearings* 25-30 (testimony of Mrs. Carol T. Foreman, Executive Director, Consumer Federation of America).

[4.17] *See, e.g., id.* at 70-75 (testimony of Kurt Barnard, President, Mass Retailing Institute); *id.* at 298-99 (letter from Sears, Roebuck & Co. favoring repeal).

[4.18] *See, e.g., id.* at 2.

[4.19] *See, e.g., id.*

[4.20] *See, e.g., id.* at 4. The basis for this argument was a study by Professor Stewart Munro Lee of Geneva College showing that retailer failures were at least as prevalent in free-trade states as in fair-trade states. The study was reprinted as a part of the hearings. *See id.* at 152-56. Opponents of the repeal argued that the study was out of date. *See, e.g., 1975 House Hearings* 72.

[4.21] *See, e.g., 1975 Senate Hearings* 4.

[4.22] *See, e.g., 1975 House Hearings* 108-09.

[4.23] During the first day of Senate hearings, Senators Hart, Hruska, and Brooke stated that they had been unable to find witnesses to testify against the Brooke bill. *See 1975 Senate Hearings* 5-6. Later in the Senate hearings, one opponent suggested that small retailers just did not know the legislation was being considered, *see id.* at 61, but another opposition witness felt that there was a "squeamishness among the business community" and that they "prefer[red] not to have a high visibility on this or any other issue these days." *Id.* at 123.

[4.24] *See, e.g., id.* at 93-97.

[4.25] *See, e.g., id.* at 61-70.

[4.26] *See* note 4.23 *supra.*

[4.27] *See, e.g., 1975 Senate Hearings* 126.

[4.28] *See, e.g., id.* at 127-28.

[4.29] *See, e.g., 1975 House Hearings* 47.

[4.30] *See, e.g., id.* at 72.

INTRODUCTION

publishers, would have allowed newspapers to impose maximum resale prices on their independent distributors.[4.31] The other proposal was for a "new product" exemption to allow a manufacturer to fair-trade a new product until it achieved an entry into the market.[4.32] Neither suggestion was adopted by either the Senate or House committee.

The House Committee on the Judiciary reported out a fair trade repeal bill in July 1975[4.33] and the House enacted it without voiced opposition and with only 11 negative votes.[4.34] Four months later, the Senate Committee on the Judiciary reported the House-passed bill[4.35] rather than Senator Brooke's bill in order to expedite final passage of the legislation.[4.36] The Senate approved the House bill with minimal debate and without a record vote,[4.37] and President Ford signed fair trade repeal into law on December 12, 1975.[4.38]

The legislative history makes it clear that a manufacturer concerned about retailers supplying adequate service for his product can continue to place clauses in distributorship contracts requiring the retailer to provide service and may insist on dealing only with retailers who will do so.[4.39] The Judiciary Committees thought that this would provide adequate protection to manufacturers, while the continued application of the Robinson-Patman Act and similar state laws would protect the interests of smaller retailers.[4.40] Moreover, the long-standing lawfulness under the federal antitrust laws of the noncoercive use of suggested retail prices is also expressly noted;[4.41] however, any attempts to enforce adherence to such suggested prices or to resale price maintenance generally will no longer enjoy any federal antitrust immunity and will be subject to the same proscriptions of the antitrust laws as was the case in non-fair-trade states prior to enactment of the repealer legislation.

[4.31] *See generally 1975 Senate Hearings*, pt. 2.
[4.32] This proposal was strenuously advanced by a car wax manufacturer who asserted that he would not have been able to get his business started without fair trade. *See 1975 Senate Hearings* 75-92; *1975 House Hearings* 50-73.
[4.33] H.R. REP. No. 94-341, 94th Cong., 1st Sess. (1975), *infra* at 956-61. The reported bill (H.R. 6971) was, with the exception of a few technical changes, identical to the bills introduced earlier in the 94th Congress.
[4.34] *See* 121 CONG. REC. H7103-06, H7144 (daily ed. July 21, 1975), *infra* at 961-70.
[4.35] S. REP. No. 94-466, 94th Cong., 1st Sess. (1975), *infra* at 971-75.
[4.36] *See id.* at 1-2.
[4.37] *See* 121 CONG. REC. S20871-74 (daily ed. Dec. 2, 1975), *infra* at 975-80.
[4.38] The President's statement upon signing the bill is reprinted *infra* at 981-82.
[4.39] *See* S. REP. No. 94-466, *supra* note 4.35, at 3.
[4.40] *See, e.g., 1975 Senate Hearings* 24 (statement of Senator Hart); *1975 House Hearings* 99 (statement of Representative Railsback).
[4.41] *See* S. REP. No. 94-466, *supra* note 4.35, at 3.

Chronological Synopsis

CONSUMER GOODS PRICING ACT OF 1975

93d Congress, 2d Session

December 3, 1974

S. 4203 was introduced by Sen. Brooke and referred to the Senate Judiciary Committee [Remarks upon introduction and text of bill, 120 Cong. Rec. S20361-63 (daily ed.)] 948

94th Congress, 1st Session

January 27, 1975

S. 408 (identical with S. 4203, 93d Cong.) was introduced by Sen. Brooke and referred to the Senate Judiciary Committee [Remarks upon introduction, 121 Cong. Rec. S888 (daily ed.)] 952
   [Bill print] 953

January 29, 1975

President Ford endorsed repeal of the fair trade exemption.
   [White House press release] 953

H.R. 2384 was introduced by Rep. Jordan and referred to the House Judiciary Committee.

H.R. 2390 was introduced by Rep. McClory and referred to the House Judiciary Committee.

February 18, 19-21; April 9, 10; May 12, 1975

Hearings on S. 408 before the Subcommittee on Antitrust and Monopoly of the Senate Judiciary Committee.

February 20, 1975

H.R. 3411 was introduced by Rep. Devine and referred to the House Judiciary Committee.

March 25; April 10, 1975

Hearings on H.R. 2384, H.R. 2390, and H.R. 3411 before the Subcommittee on Monopolies and Commercial Law of the House Judiciary Committee.

May 14, 1975

H.R. 6971 (clean bill agreed upon in subcommittee) was introduced by Rep. Jordan and referred to the House Judiciary Committee.
   [Bill print] 955

July 9, 1975

H.R. 6971 was reported favorably, without amendment, by the House Judiciary Committee.
   [House Report No. 94-341] 956

July 21, 1975

House debated and passed H.R. 6971, without amendment, by a vote of 380-11 [121 Cong. Rec. H7103-06, H7144 (daily ed.)] 961

July 22, 1975

H.R. 6971 referred to the Senate Judiciary Committee.

November 20, 1975

H.R. 6971 was reported favorably, without amendment, by the Senate Judiciary Committee.
[Senate Report No. 94-466] 971

December 2, 1975

Senate debated and passed H.R. 6971, without amendment and without a record vote [121 Cong. Rec. S20871-74 (daily ed.)] 975

December 12, 1975

H.R. 6971 was signed into law by President Ford.
[*Statutes at Large* print] 947
[Statement by the President] 981

Table of Reprinted Documents

CONSUMER GOODS PRICING ACT OF 1975

Statutory Material

Consumer Goods Pricing Act, Pub. L. No. 94-145, 89 Stat. 801 (Dec. 12, 1975) 947

Legislative Materials

Bills

S. 4203, 93rd Cong., 2d Sess., 120 Cong. Rec. S20623 (daily ed. Dec. 3, 1974) 951

S. 408, 94th Cong., 1st Sess. (Jan. 27, 1975) 953

H.R. 6971, 94th Cong., 1st Sess. (May 14, 1975) 955

Reports

H.R. Rep. No. 94-341, 94th Cong., 1st Sess. (July 9, 1975) 956

S. Rep. No. 94-466, 94th Cong., 1st Sess. (Nov. 20 [legislative day, Nov. 18], 1975) 971

Congressional Record

Volume 120 – 93d Congress, 2d Session (daily ed.)

Date	Pages	
Dec. 3, 1974	S20361-63	948

Volume 121 – 94th Congress, 1st Session (daily ed.)

Dates	Pages	
Jan. 27, 1975	S888	952
July 21, 1975	H7103-06, H7144	961
Dec. 2, 1975	S20871-74	975

Presidential Documents

White House press release (Jan 29, 1975) 953

Statement by President Gerald Ford upon signing H.R. 6971, 11 Weekly Comp. of Pres. Doc. 1367 (Dec. 12, 1975) 981

Original Version

CONSUMER GOODS PRICING ACT
December 12, 1975

Pub. L. No. 94-145, 89 Stat. 801

An Act To amend the Sherman Antitrust Act to provide lower prices for consumers.

Be it enacted by the Senate and House of Representatives of the United States of America in Congress assembled, That this Act may be cited as the "Consumer Goods Pricing Act of 1975".

SEC. 2. Section 1 of the Act entitled "An Act to protect trade and commerce against unlawful restraints and monopolies", approved July 2, 1890 (15 U.S.C. 1), is amended by striking out the colon preceding the first proviso in the first sentence and all that follows down through the end of such sentence and inserting in lieu thereof a period.

SEC. 3. Paragraphs (2) through (5) of section 5(a) of the Federal Trade Commission Act (15 U.S.C. 45(a)) are repealed and paragraph (6) of such section 5(a) is redesignated as paragraph (2).

SEC. 4. The amendments made by sections 2 and 3 of this Act shall take effect upon the expiration of the ninety-day period which begins on the date of enactment of this Act.

THE ORIGINS

REMARKS OF SEN. EDWARD W. BROOKE INTRODUCING S. 4203[4.42]
93d Cong., 2d Sess.
December 3, 1974

120 CONG. REC. S20361 (daily ed.)

Mr. BROOKE [R., Mass.]. Mr. President, double digit inflation is now haunting the American consumer. In the past 6 months the Consumer Price Index has risen an average of 1 1/2 percent a month; in the past 7 years the cost of living has spiraled by almost 50 percent. Dollar wages have increased at a brisk 7 percent rate over the past 2 years, but prices have increased even more. We are experiencing the sharpest decline of consumer buying power since the removal of World War II price controls. It is now time for the Congress of the United States to seize the initiative and attack our No. 1 enemy—inflation.

President Ford has held a summit conference on inflation out of which have come many ideas for fighting inflation. In his economic address to the Congress following the conference, the President presented his legislative proposals. The Congress showed itself capable of acting with speed and incisiveness in at least one instance. On September 10, 1974, Senator CRANSTON and I introduced the Home Purchase Assistance Act of 1974 to provide needed mortgage funds for the suffering home buyer and housing industry. Just 35 days later, on October 15, the final version of the bill had been reported to the floor of both Houses, debated, differences resolved, and passed by the Congress. On October 18, President Ford signed the bill into law. Congress had perceived a need, found a solution, and acted.

Today, I am introducing another anti-inflationary measure that I hope will command the same cooperation and result in the same incisive and affirmation action. This legislation repeals resale price maintenance laws. It ends fair trade.

Fair trade laws, also known as resale price maintenance or quality stabilization laws, have been in effect since the depression. In simple terms, they allow a manufacturer to enter into an agreement with a retailer setting the minimum price at which his identifiable product may be sold. California passed the first State law in 1931 and most States followed soon after. It became apparent, however, that these State laws when applied to interstate commerce, violated Federal antitrust laws. Thus, in 1937, Congress passed the Miller-Tydings Act granting State fair trade laws an exemption from the Sherman Antitrust Act. In 1952, the McGuire Act granted State fair trade laws exemption from the Federal Trade Commission Act, thus legalizing nonsigner provisions. These provisions, which had been enacted by some States, permit a manufacturer to sign a single fair trade agreement with one retailer, and then enforce the agreement against all other retailers in the State, even though they were not parties to the contract.

At the present time, 13 States have valid nonsigner provisions—Arizona, California,

---

[4.42] S. 4203, 93d Cong., 2d Sess. (1974). This bill was reintroduced at the beginning of the 94th Congress as S. 408, 94th Cong., 1st Sess. (1975), and is reprinted *infra* at 953.

Connecticut, Delaware, Illinois, Maryland, New Hampshire, New Jersey, New York, Ohio, Tennessee, Virginia, and Wisconsin. In addition, 23 other States have fair trade laws with nonsigner provisions—Arkansas, Colorado, Florida, Georgia, Idaho, Indiana, Iowa, Kentucky, Louisiana, Maine, Massachusetts, Michigan, Minnesota, New Mexico, North Carolina, North Dakota, Oklahoma, Oregon, Pennsylvania, South Carolina, South Dakota, Washington, and West Virginia. In all, 36 States have some form of fair trade laws currently in being.

The Miller-Tydings Act and the McGuire Act are permissive statutes. They allow States to enact laws that would otherwise be in violation of Federal statutes. In effect, they permit States to regulate goods that are in interstate commerce. They provide a Federal umbrella for restrictive State laws. Today, I propose we remove that umbrella and thus nullify the State laws as they apply to interstate commerce. I propose that we get the Federal Government out of the marketplace and permit competition rather than restrictive private agreements to fix prices.

It is important to note that neither the Federal nor the State government actually enforce any fair trade agreements. Should a manufacturer discover that a valid fair trade agreement into which he has entered is being violated, he must go to court and sue for damages. The Government plays no role in this action.

Exponents of fair trade agreements base their arguments on the economic and social conditions that prevailed almost a half century ago. In the first part of the 20th century, this country underwent its gravest and most prolonged depression during which real income fell by more than 30 percent, unemployment rose from 3 to 25 percent and more than 200,000 business firms failed. The country was desperate for a remedy so when resale price maintenance was proposed as a panacea to the country's grave problems, and argued with logic that appeared to be valid, it was quickly embraced.

Resale price maintenance has long been touted as our savior from the evils of predatory price cutting as a form of competition in which a retail firm lowers its prices in order to draw business away from its competitors and eliminate them from the market. Once the predatory firm establishes control over the market and somehow prevents any new firms from entering, it then raises prices in order to gain monopolistic profits. Thus, it is argued, that while in the short run the consumer will obtain goods at low prices, in the long run prices will be higher and the number of stores selling and servicing these goods will be lower. Exponents of resale price maintenance often argue that fair trade acts as a countervailing force to the market power of chain and discount stores. These outlets are often unjustifiably accused of bait merchandising and plotting to destroy independent retail outlets. However, exponents always fail to note that there are already State and Federal laws prohibiting false and misleading advertising, including the use of "bait and switch" and other discredited ruses. It is true that chain stores give retailers a run for their money by instituting more efficient marketing techniques and offering less frills. But this should be seen as a challenge to the less efficient retailers to develop new merchandising techniques, rather than as a threat to their existence. However, the evidence, including Justice Department and other studies, amply document the fact that more business failures occur in fair trade States than in non-fair trade States—proving that fair trade does not prevent business failures.

The most persuasive study supporting this assertion was done by Prof. Stewart Munro Lee of Geneva College and reported in the spring, 1965, volume of the Journal of Retailing. Professor Lee wrote:

> Data show no perceptible effect of fair trade laws on the total number of retail stores, the number of drug stores, or on the rates of failure in retailing in general or in the drug trade. Indeed, when one examines the details of this table closely, it appears that, if anything, the fair trade laws have opposite effects on [sic] those claimed.

This system of State resale price maintenance which is permitted by Federal law reduces competition and restricts our system of free enterprise at all levels of product distribution. The U.S. Department of Justice has estimated that resale price maintenance increases prices on fair traded goods by 18 to 27 percent—many economists feel that this increases the consumer price index by nearly 20 percent. Conservatively, this costs the American consumer over $2 billion a year in higher prices. For example, a set of golf clubs that lists for $220 can be purchased in nonfair trade areas for $136; a $49 electric shaver sells for $32; a $1,360 component stereo system can be obtained for $915 and a $560 19-inch color television sells for $483. The marketing techniques that have been established by chain and discount stores reduces [sic] the markup on consumer goods to 10 or 20 percent rather than the standard 40 to 60 percent. This is, of course, important to all consumers, but particularly to the 23 million low income people in the United States.

In the January 1969, Economic Report of the President, it was estimated that fair trade then cost consumers $1.5 billion annually. When that figure is updated by the consumer index, it reveals that American consumers are now paying a hidden subsidy of $2.1 billion a year for fair trade. To remove that $2.1 billion unnecessary burden from our economy would be one of the most immediate anti-inflationary steps we could take.

Prof. Hendrik S. Houthakker of Harvard, a former member of the President's Council of Economic Advisors, wrote an article entitled, "A Positive Strategy Against Inflation" in the Wall Street Journal of July 30, 1974. Professor Houthakker wrote:

> Our economy has to be made less prone to inflation and more responsive to anti-inflationary policies. This means, in particular, that institutional barriers to price declines have to be removed. . . .

Specifically, Professor Houthakker wrote that we could curb inflation by, among other actions, abolishing resale price maintenance.

At the same time, the respected publication of the Consumers Union, "Consumer Reports" ran an article in its November issue entitled "Good-Bye to Good Buys in Audio Equipment?" Following the article was an editorial entitled "What's Fair about Fair Trade Laws?" The article observed that fair trade "confers price fixing power on private individuals without any recourse for public review of these pricing decisions. While the Governor of New York, Vice-Presidential designee Nelson Rockefeller described fair trade as 'an affront to the American system of competitive free enterprise'. Rockefeller advocates repeal of existing fair trade laws. So does CU."

Aside from its inflationary effect, one of the most persuasive arguments against resale price maintenance is that it tends to freeze the channels of distribution and retard the advancement of technology. Fair trade helps protect those retail outlets that are unwilling or unable to improve their methods of operation. By restricting competition in price, fair trade provides for competition on the basis of advertising, salesmanship, and nonessential services. A Canadian committee set up to study the problem of resale price maintenance stated that:

> The crux of the problem of resale maintenance, is whether the consumer should reap the benefits of the most efficient forms of retailing or . . . should be forced to pay more in order to make retailing . . . a more comfortable occupation. . . .

In the past, the most vocal support for fair trade legislation has been from the small business community. It is this sector of our economy, it has been argued, that would be most injured by weakening or repealing fair trade. Yet, one of the most active and highly respected small business organizations in the country, the Smaller Business Association of New England—SBANE, vigorously supports the repeal of fair trade laws. In a statement issued on November 14, 1974, Oliver O. Ward, president of SBANE, called fair trade laws anticompetitive and obsolete. I ask unanimous consent that the full text of the SBANE statement be printed in the RECORD immediately following the printing of the text of the bill.

Businessmen making transactions must have the freedom to change their prices; to increase or decrease sales as they see fit. It is the price of the goods to which suppliers and consumers react. We must permit the retailer to establish the level of service and extras that he wants to include with the product along with the right to set the selling price. To permit the manufacturer the right of price fixing places the entire chain of distribution in a straitjacket.

Resale price maintenance stifles innovation and forces production in the wrong direction. It is amply documented that resale price maintenance forces entrepreneurs to engage in inefficient promotional campaigns in order to develop volume—that is costly for both the businessman and the consumer.

⊥ The consumer, the businessman, and the country are all best served by a ⊥S20363 dynamic and competitive system of marketing. We cannot on the one hand celebrate the beauties of free competition and then squelch it the moment it benefits consumers. Competition forces retailers, wholesalers, and manufacturers to provide the consumer the most for his money. A repeal of the fair trade laws will stimulate an increase in productive efficiency. This, coupled with increased volume due to lower prices, will provide all levels of distribution with increased profits while providing the consumer more goods at lower prices.

Resale price maintenance has brought about three major distortions in our economy. They are: First, artifically high prices; second, restraint of innovation and efficiency; and third, an increased reliance on costly promotional devices that increase prices.

There has been a good deal of talk in the past few months about biting the bullet to stop inflation. The time has come to stop talking and to act. Strong opinion has developed throughout the country to decrease the role of the Federal Government in business activities so that the economy can react to normal market forces. The 1930's were a time of trauma when order in the marketplace was desired regardless of cost. The 1970's and the decades ahead are a different time with different institutions and different problems requiring different solutions. Now is the time to rid the economy of inflation-causing, competition-depressing, artificial encumbrances.

Fair trade legislation was an idea whose time had come and has now gone.

Mr. President, I ask unanimous consent that the text of the bill be printed at this point in the RECORD.

There being no objection, the bill and letter were ordered to be printed in the RECORD, as follows:

S. 4203

Be it enacted by the Senate and House of Representatives of the United States of America in Congress assembled, That the first section of the Act entitled "An Act to protect trade and commerce against unlawful restraints and monopolies", approved July 2, 1890, as amended (15 U.S.C. 1), is amended by striking out the colon preceding the first proviso in the first sentence and all that follows before the period at the end of such sentence.

SEC. 2. Paragraphs (2)–(5) of section 5(a) of the Federal Trade Commission Act, as amended (15 U.S.C. 45(a)), are repealed.

SEC. 3. The amendments made by this Act shall become effective 90 days following the date on which this Act is enacted.

Smaller Business Association of New England, Inc.,
Waltham, Mass., November 14, 1974.

STATEMENT OF OLIVER O. WARD, PRESIDENT OF SBANE

"SBANE supports legislation sponsored by Senator Edward Brooke to repeal the Fair Trade Laws because they are a strict form of price maintenance which is anti-competitive and not in the public interest. We believe that not only are the laws obsolete, but through the years, their enforcement has become almost non-existent in many states.

At a time when consumer dissatisfaction is at its highest level in 25 years, and the small business community is mounting substantial efforts to re-examine, and wherever possible, abolish over-zealous federal legislation, it would seem that the Fair Trade Laws repeal would be a good beginning.

In an October meeting that representatives of SBANE held with President Ford and other small business organizations, President Ford noted with concern an increase in the apparent alarm in the business community over regulatory agencies and promised that his Administration would come to grips with bureaucracy. Senator Brooke's legislation is most welcome.

Many large companies have traditionally favored Fair Trade Laws on the basis of their sheltering effect on the small retailer from the big discounters. We believe that small businesses in the retail field can be competitive and thrive through the flexibility and extra service available from the neighborhood small retail establishment.

Laws should not protect inefficient small businesses from the open market and the overall benefits of the repeal of the Fair Trade Laws and a return to a more competitive free enterprise system, is a legislative action to everyone's benefit."

REMARKS OF SEN. EDWARD W. BROOKE INTRODUCING S. 408
94th Cong., 1st Sess.
January 27, 1975

121 CONG. REC. S888 (daily ed.)

Mr. BROOKE. Mr. President, on December 3, 1974, I introduced S. 4203, a bill to repeal exemptions in the antitrust laws relating to fair trade laws. The bill was referred to the Judiciary Committee, but did not receive consideration due to the short time remaining in the 93d Congress.

Today, I introduce the same bill in a different environment.

In the 8 short weeks since the bill was first introduced, an alarming deterioration has occurred in our economy. Inflation, formerly public enemy No. 1, has given way to recession as our major problem. Unemployment has increased dramatically. The gross national product—GNP—has declined precipitously. Yet, inflation continues at almost the same pace. Laast [sic] year, we experienced an inflation rate of 12.2 percent, the highest since price controls were removed at the end of the Second World War.

We face an increasing dilemma. Many proposals made to reduce inflation will increase the recession. And, almost all of the ideas put forth to bring us out of the recession will do so at the cost of reheating the inflationary tendencies we have tried to check. But the legislation I propose today is straightforward and uncomplicated. By ending fair trade laws, we can reduce consumer prices by $2.1 billion annually without compounding the problems of recession. A blow can be struck at inflation without exacerbating the recession. And we can do this by lessening the role of the Federal Government in the marketplace, by freeing the forces of competition, rather than by adding another layer of redtape to an already overburdened economy.

I will not repeat the history of fair trade legislation or the rationale for ridding our system of this costly anachronism. Rather, Mr. President, I ask unanimous consent that the text of the bill and the full text of my remarks of December 3 be printed at the conclusion of these remarks.

The PRESIDING OFFICER. Without objection, it is so ordered. . . .[4.43]

Mr. BROOKE. Let me add that I have been tremendously heartened by the positive support this bill has received. Such groups as the Cooperative League of the United States, Congress Watch, the Smaller Manufacturers Council of Pittsburgh, and the Smaller Business Association of New England have endorsed it. Many individuals from across the country have written to voice their support. I have been particularly heartened by the prospect that the Antitrust and Monopoly Subcommittee of the Senate Committee on the Judiciary hopes to schedule hearings within a month.

I am encouraged to have received word this morning that the administration fully supports my bill and will work for its prompt enactment. I am grateful to the President for this forthright stand and look forward to working with the administration in this effort to reduce prices for America's consumers.

In the weeks ahead, we will hear many debates on economic policy and on the course our country should take. There will be honest differences of opinion. I hope and

---

[4.43] Senator Brooke's remarks of December 3, 1974, are reprinted *supra* at 948–52.

trust that removing the burden of fair trade—of legalized price fixing—from the American consumer is one course of action on which we can all agree and can take forthwith.

S. 408[4.44]
94th Cong., 1st Sess.
January 27, 1975

Mr. BROOKE (for himself, Mr. BAKER, Mr. BROCK, Mr. HATHAWAY, Mr. KENNEDY, Mr. LEAHY, Mr. MCINTYRE, Mr. MCGOVERN, Mr. MOSS, Mr. STAFFORD, Mr. STEVENS, and Mr. TOWER) introduced the following bill; which was read twice and referred to the Committee on the Judiciary

A BILL

To repeal exemptions in the antitrust laws relating to fair trade laws.

1 *Be it enacted by the Senate and House of Representa-*
2 *tives of the United States of America in Congress assembled,*
3 That the first section of the Act entitled "An Act to protect
4 trade and commerce against unlawful restraints and monopo-
5 lies", approved July 2, 1890, as amended (15 U.S.C. 1), is
6 amended by striking out the colon preceding the first proviso
7 in the first sentence and all that follows before the period at
8 the end of such sentence.
9   SEC. 2. Paragraphs (2) through (5) of section 5(a)
1 of the Federal Trade Commission Act, as amended (15
2 U.S.C. 45(a)), are repealed.
3   SEC. 3. The amendments made by this Act shall become
4 effective ninety days following the date on which this Act
5 is enacted.

WHITE HOUSE PRESS RELEASE
January 29, 1975

The President today announced that he strongly endorsed repeal of federal legislation which enables states to enact Fair Trade Laws and indicated support of Senator Brooke's bill[4.45] to achieve such repeal. Similar legislation will soon be introduced in the House of Representatives.

The Miller-Tydings Act, which was enacted in 1937 and the McGuire Act (1952) which modified it, permit States to establish laws allowing manufacturers to dictate the retail prices at which their merchandise can be sold. This has the effect of eliminating

---

[4.44] Similar bills were introduced in the House: H.R. 2384 by Representative Barbara Jordan (D., Tex.); H.R. 2390 by Representative Robert McClory (R., Ill.); and H.R. 3411 by Representative Samuel L. Devine (R., Ohio). H.R. 6971, the bill that was eventually enacted, is reprinted *infra* at 955.
[4.45] S. 408, 94th Cong., 1st Sess. (1975).

price competition and raising the costs to the consumer on numerous commodities such as drugs, books, hardware, clothing and shoes. It is estimated that the elimination of such laws can save consumers between $1.5 and $3 billion a year.

This legislation is one of a number of laws for which recommendations for change will be considered in the coming months as important elements of the President's economic program. The President believes that the elimination of restrictive Government practices and the reform of outdated regulations is essential if we are to combat inflation and return our economy to stable growth and prosperity.

HOUSE CONSIDERATION

H.R. 6971
94th Cong., 1st Sess.
May 14, 1975

Ms. JORDAN (for herself, Mr. RODINO, Mr. BROOKS, Mr. FLOWERS, Mr. SEIBERLING, Mr. MEZVINSKY, Mr. MAZZOLI, Mr. HUGHES, Mr. MCCLORY, Mr. RAILSBACK, and Mr. COHEN) introduced the following bill; which was referred to the Committee on the Judiciary

A BILL

To amend the Sherman Antitrust Act to provide lower prices for consumers.

Be it enacted by the Senate and House of Representatives of the United States of America in Congress assembled, That this Act may be cited as the "Consumer Goods Pricing Act of 1975".

SEC. 2. Section 1 of the Act entitled "An Act to protect trade and commerce against unlawful restraints and monopolies", approved July 2, 1890 (15 U.S.C. 1), is amended by striking out the colon preceding the first proviso in the first sentence and all that follows down through the end of such sentence and inserting in lieu thereof a period.

SEC. 3. Paragraphs (2) through (5) of section 5(a) of the Federal Trade Commission Act (15 U.S.C. 45(a)) are repealed and paragraph (6) of such section 5(a) is redesignated as paragraph (2).

SEC. 4. The amendments made by sections 2 and 3 of this Act shall take effect upon the expiration of the ninety-day period which begins on the date of enactment of this Act.

REPORT OF THE HOUSE COMMITTEE ON THE JUDICIARY
H.R. Rep. No. 94-341
94th Cong., 1st Sess.
July 9, 1975

Mr. RODINO, from the Committee on the Judicary [sic], submitted the following

REPORT

[To accompany H.R. 6971]

The Committee on the Judiciary, to whom was referred the bill (H.R. 6971) to amend the Sherman Antitrust Act to provide lower prices for consumers, having considered the same, report favorably thereon without amendment and recommend that the bill do pass.

In 1937 Congress passed the Miller-Tydings Act, which created an exemption to the Federal antitrust laws for resale price maintenance agreements where such agreements were expressly permitted by State Law. In 1952 Miller-Tydings was supplemented by the McGuire Act, which permitted States to enact statutes allowing the enforcement of minimum resale prices even against retailers who refused to sign so-called "fair trade" agreements.

For a time, these antitrust exemptions were very popular. As many as 46 States at one time had so-called "fair trade" laws.

However, only 24 States retain any form of "fair trade" laws, and this number has been diminishing rapidly. Only a limited range of goods is "fair traded" today, and numerous manufacturers have decided on their own to abandon this practice.

The Judiciary Committee, after a reexamination of the justification for these special antitrust exemptions, concluded that they could no longer be supported. So-called "fair trade" laws, in the judgment of the Committee, contribute little but artificially high prices for consumers. They also facilitate horizontal price fixing by manufacturers. At the same time, the traditional justification for these exemptions—preservation of the small "Mom and Pop" retail outlet against the price competition of the discount chains—will no longer withstand scrutiny.

Thus the Committee adopted H.R. 6971, which is a simple repealer of the Miller-Tydings and McGuire exemptions, by voice vote.

THE LEGAL CONTEXT

An agreement between a manufacturer and a retailer that the retailer will not resell the manufacturer's product below a specified price is an obvious [sic] form of price fixing. As such it is *per se* illegal under section 1 of the Sherman Act, 15 U.S.C. § 1. *United States* v. *Socony Vacuum Oil Co.*, 310 U.S. 150 (1940).[4.46]

The Supreme Court first condemned resale price maintenance agreements under the Sherman Act 64 years ago. *Dr. Miles Medical Co.* v. *John D. Park & Sons*, 220 U.S. 373 (1911).[4.47] In a line of subsequent decisions the Court has consistently held that such agreements are in direct violation of the system of free competition which the antitrust laws are designed to promote. See *FTC* v. *Beech Nut Packing Co.*, 257 U.S. 441 (1922);[4.48] *Schwegmann Bros.* v. *Calvert Distillers Corp.*, 341 U.S. 384 (1951);[4.49]

[4.46] 310 U.S. 150, 60 S. Ct. 811, 84 L. Ed. 1129 (1940).
[4.47] 220 U.S. 373, 31 S. Ct. 376, 55 L. Ed. 502 (1911).
[4.48] 257 U.S. 441, 42 S. Ct. 150, 66 L. Ed. 307 (1922).
[4.49] 341 U.S. 384, 71 S. Ct. 745, 95 L. Ed. 1035 (1951), *supra* at chapter 2.

United States v. Parke, Davis & Co., 362 U.S. 29 (1960);[4.50] *Albrecht v. Herald Co.*,[4.51] 390 U.S. 145 (1968).[1]

Thus without some explicit form of Federal legislative exemption, State laws permitting resale price maintenance agreements would have no effect. *Hudson Distributors, Inc. v. Eli Lilly & Co.*, 377 U.S. 386 (1964).[4.52] And the Supreme Court has construed the exemptions granted by Congress narrowly to preserve the Sherman Act's procompetitive policies. See *Schwegmann Bros. v. Calvert Distillers Corp., supra.*

In this context, Miller-Tydings permitted the enforcement of resale price maintenance agreements in States which had enacted legislation to that effect.

The proponents of so-called "fair trade" sought to go further, however. Many retailers refused to sign such anticompetitive agreements, leaving the manufacturer with the choice of permitting price competition in his products or losing retail outlets. Some States responded by enacting so-called "non-signer" clauses, permitting the enforcement of minimum resale prices against non-signers so long as there was at least one retailer in the State who had signed an agreement with the manufacturer. The Supreme Court held in the *Schwegmann* case that this exceeded the scope of the Miller-Tydings exemption, and Congress responded with the McGuire Act, overruling *Schwegmann* and permitting States to enact "non-signer" clauses.

The Effect of "Fair Trade" Laws

Resale price maintenance agreements undoubtedly have certain advantages for both manufacturers and retailers. They have the effect ⊥ of eliminating price competition in the manufacturer's products between retailers who otherwise would be in a position to compete with each other. This is good for the retailer, who knows that there is no danger he will be undersold by anyone else. It is good for the manufacturer, who need not worry that price competition in his products will lead to pressure from his customers to lower his prices in order that they can compete successfully against others who undersell them. It also lets the manufacturer insulate a good part of his advertising budget from competitive danger.

"Fair Trade" practices are not good for all retailers or manufacturers, however. Some retailers prefer to try to enlarge their share of the market by competing vigorously in price—precisely the sort of behavior encouraged by our antitrust laws. This competition is stifled by "fair trading." And some manufacturers prefer to sell more products by encouraging price competition at both the manufacturing and retailing levels. Such manufacturers do not engage in "fair trading." More and more manufacturers and retailers have been abandoning "fair trading" in favor of active price competition. As a result, "fair trading" today is confined to a relatively small and

---

[1] The attitude of the Supreme Court to resale price maintenance is aptly illustrated by the history of two purported "exceptions" to the *per se* illegality of such conduct.

The Court held in *United States v. Colgate & Co.*, 250 U.S. 300 [39 S. Ct. 465, 63 L. Ed. 992] (1919), that a manufacturer could announce in advance a policy to terminate all retailers who undersold his suggested retail price and could unilaterally enforce that policy by refusing to do business with those who violated his price. The Court carefully distinguished cases involving agreements between manufacturers and retailers and placed its holding exclusively upon the right of the manufacturer to choose for any reason those with whom he would deal. Subsequent cases have limited *Colgate* strictly to its own facts, finding a Sherman Act violation in the slightest hint of concerted activity. See, *e.g.*, *FTC v. Beech Nut Packing Co.*, 257 U.S. 441 (1922); *United States v. Parke, Davis & Co.*, 362 U.S. 29 (1960).

In *United States v. General Electric Co.*, 272 U.S. 476 [47 S. Ct. 192, 71 L. Ed. 362] (1926), the Court found no violation of the Sherman Act in a scheme whereby the manufacturer of patented products sent those products on "consignment" to agents for sale at specified prices. In *Simpson v. Union Oil Co.*, 377 U.S. 13 [84 S. Ct. 1051, 12 L. Ed. 2d 98] (1964), the court narrowly limited *General Electric* to cases involving patents, and cast widespread doubt on its continued validity even in that narrow area.

[4.50] 362 U.S. 29, 80 S. Ct. 503, 4 L. Ed. 2d 505 (1960).
[4.51] 390 U.S. 145, 88 S. Ct. 869, 19 L. Ed. 2d 998 (1968).
[4.52] 377 U.S. 386, 84 S. Ct. 1273, 12 L. Ed. 2d 394 (1964).

shrinking line of commodities—principally cosmetics, certain appliances, some stereo equipment, some liquor and some drugs.[2]

From the consumers' point of view, "fair trade" laws have one effect—higher prices. Precisely how much "fair trading" costs the American consumer has never been determined, but studies clearly indicate that the amount is substantial. In 1956 the Antitrust Division of the Department of Justice did a detailed comparison of the prices of 119 "fair traded" items in both "fair trade" and "free trade" jurisdictions. On 77 of the items, the average price differential was 27 percent, while on all 119 items consumers in non-"fair trade" States paid an average of 19 percent less for the products than those in "fair trade" jurisdictions. A similar Antitrust Division study in 1970 showed price differentials of up to 37.4 percent on individual items between "fair trade" and "free trade" jurisdictions. A Library of Congress study commissioned by Senator Brooke of Massachusetts this year put the annual cost of [sic] American consumers of "fair trading" conservatively in the vicinity of $3 billion. A study by Lawrence Shepard of the University of California estimated the sum at $6.5 billion per year.

Whatever the exact figure, it is beyond dispute that resale price maintenance increases the cost of products to consumers.

The practice of "fair trading" has another important anticompetitive effect which has concerned those charged with enforcement of the antitrust laws. Deputy Assistant Attorney General Keith Clearwaters of the Antitrust Division told the Monopolies and Commercial Law Subcommittee:

> Furthermore, resale price maintenance provides convenient cover for patently illegal conspiracies in restraint of trade: State "fair trade" laws give rise to agreements among competing manufacturers, among competing wholesalers, among competing retailers, and among manufacturers competing with others at different distribution levels. Additional activities, such as boycotting of retailers refusing to enter "fair trade" contracts and the enforcing of resale price maintenance in States without "fair trade" statutes, have been inseparable concomitants of the "fair trade" laws.

Mr. Clearwaters explained that "fair trade" laws permit the effective exchange of price information which would otherwise be prohibited by the Sherman Act, and that this often leads to horizontal stabilization of prices in purportedly competing products:

> Price books can be exchanged. Announcements of changes in price are made to the industry. It may not be a smoke-filled room, but certainly the signals are made clear between the manufacturers and particularly where the manufacturers are few in number, the system works very well in pegging prices across the board in an industry at an artificially high level.

THE JUSTIFICATIONS FOR "FAIR TRADE" LAWS

The principal traditional justification for "fair trade" laws has been that they protect small family-owned retail outlets—the "Mom and Pop" stores—from price-gouging by the discount chains. Proponents of this view argue that these independent retailers frequently provide ongoing service of the product and individual attention to the customer's needs, which add to their overhead and prohibit them from competing effectively in price with the chain stores.

The first difficulty with this argument is that it finds no real support in the facts. A well-known 1965 study of small-business failure rates between 1933 and 1958 did not show that such firms fared any better in "fair trade" States. To the contrary, the study by Dr. Stewart Lee of Geneva College found a higher rate of small business failures in "fair trade" States than in States without such laws. Other studies by the Department of Justice and the Library of Congress, the latter in 1972, confirm that

---

[2] Some concern was expressed in hearings before the subcommittee that the repeal of Miller-Tydings and McGuire might impinge in some fashion upon the power of States to regulate liquor traffic under the second section of the 21st amendment. No such effect is intended. The repeal would terminate the power of liquor manufacturers to set resale prices under a general "fair trade" statute, but would leave unimpaired whatever power the States have under the 21st amendment to regulate the importation of liquor from outside the State.

"fair trade" States actually show higher small business failure rates. The growth rate of small businesses between 1956 and 1972 was 32 per cent higher in non-"fair trade" States. Moreover, studies conducted in places which have abandoned resale price maintenance show no adverse effect on small businesses. Experience in Rhode Island, which repealed "fair trade" in 1964, Canada, which repealed it in 1957, and Great Britain, which stopped "fair trading" in 1965, indicates generally lower prices, more vigorous competition and no adverse effects on small businesses.

Second, to the extent that the "Mon [sic] and Pop" retailer charges a higher price because he is providing more services to his customers, consumers should have the freedom to choose between paying more for those services and buying nothing but the unadorned product at a lower price from a competitor. And testimony before the Subcommittee indicated that many consumers are in fact willing to pay a somewhat higher price for the convenience, courtesy and service which small retailers are uniquely situated to provide.

Moreover, there is some indication that "fair trade" laws can actually work to stifle market entry by new small retail businesses. The most obvious device for such businesses to use to obtain a toehold in the market is price competition. Yet "fair trade" can take away this important competitive tool from a new business and help freeze it out of the market.

Another justification for "fair trade" laws advanced by the manufacturers is that it protects their "good will" investment in their trademarks—namely, their advertising budgets. It is contended that the manufacturer's investment in promotion and advertising represents an asset—the "market image" of the product—which would be destroyed if the price premium which was part of that "image" could be eliminated by intrabrand price competition at the retail level.

Chairman Lewis Engman of the Federal Trade Commission responded to this argument in his testimony before the Subcommittee:

> This argument reveals the anticompetitive essence of the fair trade laws. Simply put, the argument assumes an identity between cost and value and thereby begs the question of the competitive marketplace by denying the consumer the right to assign his own value to the intangible asset of trademark or image.

The Committee was of the view that manufacturers should not be able to insulate their advertising budgets from the effects of intrabrand competition in this fashion, and that the marketplace should be allowed to judge the value of a "brand image" without the restraints imposed by resale price maintenance.

The Subcommittee heard from one witness who offered a third justification for "fair trade" laws—that they offer a new struggling manufacturer an effective approach to retailers who otherwise would not accept his products. The witness testified from his own personal experience in the car wax industry. Both the Chairman of the Federal Trade Commission and the Deputy Assistant Attorney General rejected his conclusion and attributed the witness' own success to other elements of his highly effective sales program, particularly to his agreement to repurchase from the retailer any unsold wax, thus completely insuring the retailer against any loss. The Subcommittee agreed that no evidence had been presented which would justify any "new product" exemption from the repeal of Miller-Tydings and McGuire.

Conclusion

After reviewing the evidence before it, the Committee concluded that a continued exemption from the Federal antitrust laws for State statutes permitting resale price maintenance could not be justified. Among the witnesses before the Committee were the Chairman of the Federal Trade Commission and the Deputy Assistant Attorney General from the Antitrust Division, both of whom vigorously urged repeal of the Miller-Tydings and McGuire Acts. The Committee agreed with Deputy Assistant Attorney General Clearwaters that " 'fair trade' laws are nothing more than legalized price fixing."

The Committee urges adoption of H.R. 6971.

Statements Under Clause 2(1) (3) of Rule XI of the Rules of the House of Representatives

A. Oversight Statement.—The Subcommittee, in considering H.R. 6971, made no oversight findings pursuant to Clause 2(B) 1 of Rule X.

B. Budget Statement.—H.R. 6971 provides no new budget authority, or any new increased tax expenditures.

In addition Clause 2(1) (3) B of Rule XI is otherwise not applicable. Section 308(a) of the Congressional Budget Act of 1974 will not be implemented this year. (See last paragraph of House Report 94-25, 94th Congress, 1st Session, 1975).

C. No estimate or comparison from the Director of the Congressional Budget Office was received.

D. No related oversight findings and recommendations have been made by the Committee on Government Operations under Clause 2(b) (2) of Rule X.

E. Inflationary Impact Statement.—Pursuant to Clause 2(1) (4) of Rule XI, the Committee concludes that there will be no inflationary impact, as a result of this bill, on prices and costs in the operation of the national economy. On the contrary, H.R. 6971 will have the effect of lowering prices for consumers.

Changes in Existing Law Made by the Bill, As Reported

In compliance with clause 3 of rule XIII of the Rules of the House of Representatives, changes in existing law made by the bill, as reported, are shown as follows (existing law proposed to be omitted is enclosed in black brackets, new matter is printed in italic, existing law in which no change is proposed is shown in roman):

Section 1 of the Act of July 2, 1890

An act to protect trade and commerce against unlawful restraints and monopolies.

Be it enacted by the Senate and House of Representatives of the United States of America in Congress assembled,

SECTION 1. Every contract, combination in the form of trust or otherwise, or conspiracy, in restraint of trade or commerce among the several States, or with foreign nations, is hereby declared to be illegal [: *Provided*, That nothing herein contained shall render illegal, contracts or agreements prescribing minimum prices for the resale of a commodity which bears, or the label or container of which bears, the trade mark, brand, or name of the producer or distributor of such commodity and which is in free and open competition with commodities of the same general class produced or distributed by others, when contracts or agreements of that description are lawful as applied to intrastate transactions, under any statute, law, or public policy now or hereafter in effect in any State, Territory, or the District of Columbia in which such resale is to be made, or to which the commodity is to be transported for such resale, and the making of such contracts or agreements shall not be an unfair method of competition under section 5, as amended and supplemented, of the Act entitled "An Act to create a Federal Trade Commission, to define its powers and duties, and for other purposes", approved September 26, 1914: *Provided further,* That the preceding proviso shall not make lawful any contract or agreement, providing for the establishment or maintenance of minimum resale prices on any commodity herein involved, between manufacturers, or between producers, or between wholesalers, or between brokers, or between factors, or between retailers, or between persons, firms, or corporations in competition with each other]. Every person who shall make any contract or engage in any combination or conspiracy hereby declared to be illegal shall be deemed guilty of a felony, and, on conviction thereof, shall be punished by fine not exceeding one million dollars if a corporation, or, if any other person, one hundred thousand dollars, or by imprisonment not exceeding three years, or by both said punishments, in the discretion of the court.

*   *   *   *   *   *   *

The Federal Trade Commission Act

* * * * * * *

SEC. 5. (a) (1) Unfair methods of competition in or affecting commerce, and unfair or deceptive acts or practices in or affecting commerce, are hereby declared unlawful.

[(2) Nothing contained in this Act or in any of the Antitrust Acts shall render unlawful any contracts or agreements prescribing minimum or stipulated prices, or requiring a vendee to enter into contracts or agreements prescribing minimum or stipulated prices, for the resale of a commodity which bears, or the label or container of which bears, the trade-mark, brand, or name of the producer or distributor of such commodity and which is in free and open competition with commodities of the same general class produced or distributed by others, when contracts or agreements of that description are lawful as applied to intrastate transactions under any statute, law, or public policy now or hereafter in effect in any State, Territory, or the District of Columbia in which such resale is to be made, or to which the commodity is to be transported for such resale.

[(3) Nothing contained in this Act or in any of the Antitrust Acts shall render unlawful the exercise or the enforcement of any right or right of action created by any statute, law, or public policy now or hereafter in effect in any State, Territory, or the District of Columbia, which in substance provides that willfully and knowingly advertising, offering for sale, or selling any commodity at less than the price or prices prescribed in such contracts or agreements whether the person so advertising, offering for sale, or selling is or is not a party to such a contract or agreement, is unfair competition and is actionable at the suit of any person damaged thereby.

[(4) Neither the making of contracts or agreements as described in paragraph (2) of this subsection, nor the exercise or enforcement of any right or right of action as described in paragraph (3) of this subsection shall constitute an unlawful burden or restraint upon, or interference with, commerce.

[(5) Nothing contained in paragraph (2) of this subsection shall make lawful contracts or agreements providing for the establishment or maintenance of minimum or stipulated resale prices on any commodity referred to in paragraph (2) of this subsection, between manufacturers, or between producers, or between wholesalers, or between brokers, or between factors, or between retailers, or between persons, firms, or corporations in competition with each other.]

[6] (2) The Commission is hereby empowered and directed to prevent persons, partnerships, or corporations, except banks, common carriers subject to the Acts to regulate commerce, air carriers and foreign air carriers subject to the Federal Aviation Act of 1958, and persons, partnerships, or corporations insofar as they are subject to the Packers and Stockyards Act, 1921, as amended, except as provided in section 406(b) of said Act, from using unfair methods of competition in or affecting commerce and unfair or deceptive acts or practices in or affecting commerce.

HOUSE DEBATE
94th Cong., 1st Sess.
July 21, 1975

121 CONG. REC. H7103 (daily ed.)

Miss [BARBARA] JORDAN [D., Tex.]. Mr. Speaker, I move to suspend the rules and pass the bill (H.R. 6971) to amend the Sherman Antitrust Act to provide lower prices for consumers.

The Clerk read as follows: . . . .[4.53]

The SPEAKER. Is a second demanded?

Mr. [ROBERT] McCLORY [R., Ill.]. Mr. Speaker, I demand a second.

The SPEAKER. Without objection, a second will be considered as ordered.

There was no objection.

The SPEAKER. The gentlewoman from Texas (Miss JORDAN) will be recognized for 20 minutes, and the gentleman from Illinois (Mr. McCLORY) will be recognized for 20 minutes.

The Chair recognizes the gentlewoman from Texas (Miss JORDAN).

Miss JORDAN. I yield such time as he may consume to the chairman of the Committee on the Judiciary, the gentleman from New Jersey (Mr. RODINO).

(Mr. RODINO asked and was given permission to revise and extend his remarks.)

Mr. [PETER W.] RODINO [JR.] [D., N.J.]. Mr. Speaker, it is my pleasure to join with the gentlelady from Texas in urging the repeal of the so-called Fair Trade Enabling Acts. The Subcommittee on Monopolies and Commercial Law and the Judiciary Committee are of one mind in believing that this simple repealer may be one of the most effective single actions this Congress can take to combat inflation. At one stroke, it eliminates vertical price fixing in large segments of our economy.

The Miller-Tydings and McGuire Acts, children of the Great Depression, have lived far beyond their useful life. They have aged to the point where they preserve classic restraints of trade, which but for the protective umbrella they provide, would be considered per se violations of the antitrust laws.

Representative JORDAN noted the remarkable unanimity for repealer. The States, the courts, the antitrust agencies, consumer groups and large segments of the business community concur that these laws are no longer necessary.

We justified these measures on the theory that they would protect small businesses. They have not done so. Our competitive system recognizes that some businesses must fail. At times there are valid reasons for preventing this. But the fair trade laws never accomplished that purpose. Economic studies clearly indicate that small business failure rates are as high or higher in fair trade States as in States allowing robust price competition.

Our hearings marshaled impressive evidence that the only certainty is that these laws represent artificial and unwarranted price stabilization for an already overburdened consumer.

We are presently plagued by a unique combination of inflation and recession, aptly termed "stagflation." In such times, it is unconscionable that we should, by means of special interest legislation which artificially alters the forces of free competition, deny the consumer the benefits of prices set by a free and open marketplace.

Similar legislation, sponsored by Senator BROOKE of Massachusetts reflects similar feeling in the Senate. As he so aptly noted when he appeared before the Subcommittee on Monopolies and Commercial Law:

> I feel that competition is our safeguard. I don't know that there is any other safeguard that we can write into legislation, but I think competition will protect us.

To accomplish this, we need only repeal legislation which has for too long burdened the American consumer. I urge rapid enactment of this repealer.

Miss JORDAN. Mr. Speaker, I yield myself such time as I may consume.

(Miss JORDAN asked and was given permission to revise and extend her remarks.)

Miss JORDAN. Mr. Speaker, it is my privilege and pleasure today to move the passage of H.R. 6971, the Consumer Goods Pricing Act of 1975. Happily, this long-overdue legislation adds no bulk to the present body of Federal law—instead, it strikes that language which has for 38 years permitted what is perhaps our most pernicious form of vertical price fixing, the so-called fair trade laws.

In response to the economic conditions of the Great Depression, Congress passed the Miller-Tydings Act as a rider to an appropriation bill for the District of Columbia.

[4.53] H.R. 6971 as reported to the House floor was identical to the bill as introduced, reprinted *supra* at 955.

That act permitted States to pass legislation which, under certain conditions, legalized vertical price fixing and eliminate the right of a businessman to set his own price for the resale of his product. Of course, the result was artificially high prices to the consumer, a condition which this country can simply no longer afford

In 1952, in response to judicial hostility to this blatant form of price fixing, Congress expanded the enforcement of certain types of vertical price fixing by permitting the States to enact so-called nonsigner provisions which bound even those not a party to a fair trade contract to adhere to resale price contraacts [sic] as fixed by the manufacturer.

Together, the Miller-Tydings and McGuire Acts constituted special interest legislation that legitimized what, without the exemption granted by those acts, would be per se violations of the antitrust laws.

Acting in response to this legislation, some 46 States had, at the zenith of "fair trade," some form of resale price maintenance legislation. It is with pride that I note that as far back as 1937 the State of Texas noted its hostility to this form of price fixing when the House Judiciary Committee, under the chairmanship of Congressman Hatton Sumners of Dallas, refused to act on fair trade legislation. Again in 1952, the Judiciary Committee refused to countenance this form of price fixing.

I note that our sister States are now following the lead that we in Texas furnished so long ago. We, together with Missouri, Alaska, Vermont, and the District of Columbia, never countenanced such activity and never enacted such legislation.

Where once fair trade was in full favor, it is now in full flight. As of July 7, 1975, only 24 States retain some form of fair trade legislation. In 1975 alone, 13 States have repealed their fair trade laws.

In response to rapidly changing economic conditions, the Subcommittee on Monopolies and Commercial Law reported favorably on H.R. 6971 without a dissenting vote after 2 days of hearings and the receipt of numerous statements for the record.

That record establishes conclusively that these laws are, and always were, severely anticompetitive, serving little purpose but to shield competitors from the natural play of market forces, and artificially inflating prices to a consumer ⊥ increasingly burdened with skyrocketing costs.

The record established by the subcommittee demonstrates clearly that so-called fair trade laws, while ostensibly permitting vertical price fixing, have as well, a broader effect wholly unintended by Congress. For while the enabling statutes sanction only vertical agreements, such agreements facilitate simple horizontal price fixing at the manufacturing level. For when manufacturers who engage in resale price maintenance publish price schedules, ostensibly competing businesses have an easy reference point for their own pricing policy, thus further eliminating competition.

The standard defense for resale price maintenance is that it protects the small retailer, the "mom and pop" store which survives only because resale price maintenance insulates these stores from the procompetitive price cutting of larger businesses.

The subcommittee looked thoroughly at this argument. It was, interestingly enough, put forward more by manufacturers than retailers. In fact, one witness who favored the retention of the fair trade enabling statutes candidly admitted that since the emergence of the discount industry, fair trade has been something that manufacturers have willingly dropped as soon as they had enough volume to employ mass marketing methods.

As Senator BROOKE, the sponsor of similar legislation in the Senate, noted when he consented to testify before our subcommittee, studies simply do not support the contention that fair trade laws either lessen the number of retail failures or increase the number of retail stores. A 1962 Justice Department study found that States with fully effective fair trade laws had nearly a 150-percent higher rate of firm failure than free trade States. If any doubt remains, a Library of Congress study confirmed these findings and determined that in 1972, fair trade States had a 55-percent higher rate of firm bankruptcies than did free trade States.

Other evidence impressively confirms this. The State of Rhode Island repealed its fair trade laws in 1970. A study by the Marketing Science Institute found that prices in four of nine product lines investigated had declined anywhere from 20 to 40 percent,

Seventy-four percent of the retailers responding to the study unequivocally indicated that the repeal of fair trade had no substantial adverse effect on them one way or the other. Only one manufacturer of nine interviewed had actually encountered a decline in sales after the repeal of State fair trade law. Similar experiences in Great Britain and Canada confirm this.

Congress should note as well that there is by no means unanimous support for the retention of fair trade laws in the business community. The Small Business Association of New England supports the repeal of the fair trade laws, and I might add as well as [sic] that Corning Glass Works ended its fair trading practice effective April 19. It found, in effect, that it "had met the enemy, and it was itself"; Corning was competing against itself with products which were fair traded as well as nonfair traded.

Of course, the Federal Trade Commission's suit against Corning for their use of interstate fair trade restrictions may have had something to do with that.[4.54] Both that agency, and the Department of Justice unequivocally support the repeal of fair trade enabling statutes. Testimony before our subcommittee by the Department of Justice estimates that consumers are overcharged something like $2 billion a year for fair traded items. This is unconscionable.

In conclusion, it is rather standard criticism these days that Congress and the administration are unable to agree on anything. Happily, President Ford has publicly stated that he is fully in favor of repealing these inflationary and outmoded statutes. Thus, as Chairman RODINO has also frequently stated, Congress is placed in the unusual position of being able to react to a surprising unanimity of view on the part of large segments of the business community, Federal agencies, the States, and the administration. Our colleagues on the Interstate and Foreign Commerce Committee, and the minority of the Judiciary Committee, led by Mr. McCLORY, support the measure. I, therefore, urge rapid enactment of this legislation.

Mr. McCLORY. Mr. Speaker, I yield such time as he may consume to the gentleman from Michigan (Mr. HUTCHINSON) the ranking member of the full Committee on the Judiciary.

(Mr. HUTCHINSON asked and was given permission to revise and extend his remarks.)

Mr. [EDWARD] HUTCHINSON [R., Mich.]. Mr. Speaker, I rise in support of this legislation.

This bill knocks the legal props from under our fair trade laws. Upon enactment of this bill it would be a violation of the Federal Antitrust Act for a manufacturer to set a minimum retail price for any item he makes; that would be price fixing.

Back in the 1930's most States enacted fair trade laws to protect manufacturers' reputations for quality products and to protect small retailers from the price-cutting strategies of large discount houses. In order to validate these State laws against antitrust attack, Congress passed the Miller-Tydings Act and the McGuire Act, exempting fair trade laws from the reach of the Sherman Act and the Clayton Act.

The bill we are now considering will repeal both the Miller-Tydings Act and the McGuire Act, leaving State fair trade laws in violation of Federal antitrust law and, consequently, no longer of any force and effect.

Many States have already repealed their fair trade laws, and today those statutes are on the books of less than half of them. Even in those States where fair trade laws still operate, only about 4 percent of retail sales are fair traded.

While the hearings produced one or two witnesses in support of fair trade concepts, it would appear that fair trade laws, restrictive as they are of competition, reflect an economic policy that has lost most of its validity in today's marketplace.

I support the suspension of the rules to pass H.R. 6971.

Mr. McCLORY. Mr. Speaker, I yield myself such time as I may consume.

(Mr. McCLORY asked and was given permission to revise and extend his remarks.)

Mr. McCLORY. Mr. Speaker, I want, first of all, to commend the gentlewoman from Texas upon her leadership in the subcommittee in connection with the

---

[4.54] *See* Corning Glass Works v. FTC, 509 F.2d 293 (7th Cir. 1975).

development of this legislation and for her sponsorship of this measure which is before us today.

Mr. Speaker, it is my privilege today to speak in behalf of the passage of H.R. 6971, the Consumer Goods Pricing Act of 1975, which would repeal exemption in the Federal antitrust laws relating to fair trade. This legislation is to my mind vital to our economy at this time if we are to promote a climate conducive to the expansion of the private enterprise system and benefit the American consumer. H.R. 6971, which our Committee on the Judiciary has unanimously reported out, should be passed by the House of Representatives in order to assure to the American consumer protection from the artificially high prices being maintained through State fair trade laws. The adverse effect on our economy inherent in fair trade legislation, as well as the anticompetitive practices permitted under such fair trade statutes, have been most detrimental to the interests of the American consumer. Fair trade laws have but one effect from the consumer's point of view—higher prices.

As one of the original sponsors of this legislation, I have been personally interested in the repeal of the exemptions to the Sherman Antitrust Act, the Miller-Tydings Act of 1937—which permits States to adopt fair trade laws if they wish—and the McGuire Act of 1952—which would allow State fair trade laws to bind retailers who were not parties to the fair trade contracts. My original bill, presented in behalf of the administration as a companion measure to S. 408, introduced by our colleague, Senator EDWARD BROOKE, of Massachusetts, is virtually identical to the bill before us today, H.R. 6971. President Ford has repeatedly indicated his desire for legislation such as this. It is his belief—and mine—that the elimination of restrictive Government practices and the reform of outdated regulations is essential if we are to combat inflation and return our economy to stable growth and prosperity. The enactment of H.R. 6971 would repeal these Federal exemptions and thus invalidate State fair trade laws and the contractual provisions supported by such State laws.

The Miller-Tydings Act, passed during the depression of the 1930's, was followed by the enactment of laws by 46 States under which contracts between wholesalers and retailers may establish fixed retail prices under threat of State-imposed penalties for underselling such fair traded merchandise.

The enactment of the McGuire Act in 1952, in effect, expanded the exemption by allowing State fair trade laws to bind retailers who were not parties to the fair trade contracts to adhere to such agreements. It should be noted here that ⊥ the State laws which resulted were in several instances found to violate their own State constitutions.

Now, regardless of the effect of the fair trade laws which were thereafter enacted, it can hardly be suggested that the consumer benefited. On the contrary, price fixing practices which resulted ostensibly from the desire to eliminate predatory competition in which the small retailers were foundering have, in fact, created hardships for both the consumer and the independent retailer. According to a Justice Department study conducted several years ago, prices on fair traded items ranged from 19 to 27 percent higher than prices on identical items sold in States which had no fair trade legislation. Furthermore, there is not a significant difference between the rates of failure of small firms in fair trade States as would be expected if it were true that these fair trade laws protected the small retailer.

Mr. Speaker, taking into account today's economy, it is my view that the greatest benefit to business and industry in our private enterprise system would be the return to freer competition and an accelerated rate of production which can bring more jobs and likewise benefit the American consumer. In short, despite the appearance of benefits which the added or established profits to retailers produce, the best interests of our economic system result from the freest competition and the smallest number of price-fixing agreements between wholesalers and retailers.

During our hearings on this legislation, we made a concerted effort to investigate all of the legal ramifications of this act. It is my belief after these hearings and this investigation that "The Consumer Goods Pricing Act of 1975" is a most useful piece of legislation. Indeed, it was our feeling after these hearings that the current program of maximum price maintenance is not included within the McGuire Act, and, therefore, no exceptions need be made in this repealer for businesses operating under such a maintenance program. Furthermore, we must bear in mind that by repealing the Miller-Tydings and McGuire Acts, we are not stripping State legislatures of all authority to establish a program of price maintenance. We are eliminating these two statutory exceptions to the Federal antitrust law.

In light of the current economic situation—double-digit inflation and rising unemployment—the elimination of price-fixing agreements between manufacturers and retailers is imperative. The American consumer has suffered long enough from these statutes. It is time to repeal these provisions.

Mr. Speaker, inflated retail prices of consumer goods resulting from a variety of causes are a major concern to the American people today. One tried and proven method of bringing these high prices into line and giving the American people the proven benefit of a truly competitive economic system is to attack—and destroy—monopolistic, noncompetitive price fixing and other anticompetitive practices wherever they exist. This measure, "The Consumer Goods Pricing Act of 1975," is a most logical step in this direction, and I sincerely urge passage of this bill.

Miss JORDAN. Mr. Speaker, I yield such time as he may consume to the gentleman from California (Mr. DANIELSON).

(Mr. DANIELSON asked and was given permission to revise and extend his remarks.)

Mr. [GEORGE E.] DANIELSON [D., Cal.]. Mr. Speaker, I thank the gentlewoman from Texas for yielding.

Mr. Speaker, I strongly support this legislation. The term "fair trade law" in itself is appealingly deceptive, a better name for the law would be "Anti-Competition Law." I submit that this law is logically inconsistent and totally unacceptable in an economy such as ours, in a country which prides itself on free enterprise and the theory that free competition brings about better quality and lower prices for all.

This bill will hurt no one, but the consumers all will benefit.

I urge a unanimous vote for this bill.

Miss JORDAN. Mr. Speaker, I yield such time as he may consume to the gentleman from California (Mr. VAN DEERLIN), the chairman of the Subcommittee on Consumer Protection and Finance of the Interstate and Foreign Commerce Committee.

(Mr. VAN DEERLIN asked and was given permission to revise and extend his remarks.)

Mr. [LIONEL] VAN DEERLIN [D., Cal.]. Mr. Speaker, I thank the gentlewoman from Texas for yielding.

Mr. Speaker, is anything fair about the surviving fair trade laws?

Not if you are a consumer. Most people do not know these laws are on the books. Yet the laws deny free and open competition. They increase the cost of living. And they require consumers in some States to pay more for the same items than people in other States do.

Accordingly, I have no hesitation in supporting H.R. 6971, the Consumer Goods Pricing Act of 1975.

This is a bill that would close once and for all the gaping "fair trade" loophole in our antitrust laws.

What a misnomer, "fair trade." No doubt it referred to the benefits to manufacturers and retailers.

State "fair trade" laws are permitted under the Miller-Tydings Act of 1937 and the McGuire Act of 1952. It is these we are proposing to abolish, and not a moment too soon.

Under these statutes manufacturers are allowed, even invited, to bind retailers to honor fixed minimum sales prices. This has meant good profits for the retailers and bad prices for consumers. Without this helping hand from Washington, such price fixing would be illegal under the antitrust laws.

As if the laws permitting the negative State actions were not bad enough, there was a move in Congress in the 1960's to enact a national fair trade law, under the deceptively bland name of Quality Stabilization Act. Fortunately, this attempt never reached the markup stage in our House Commerce Committee.

Regardless of the name, the game was the same: price fixing.

Estimates of savings resulting from passage of H.R. 6971 vary from $1.5 billion to

$6.5 billion annually. This is necessarily a wide range, and no one can say for sure what the final figure will be. But one thing we do know: Elimination of the fair trade laws can only result in lower, not higher prices.

One of the hoariest of arguments used to support the fair trade laws is that they would somehow prevent the large discount stores from running small mom and pop operations out of business.

In fact, the fair trade laws have probably hurt the small businessman. While the small stores were getting locked into fixed prices on many items, the discount houses were able to use their greater resources to develop quality private label brands which sold for less than the small stores' national brands. Thus it was the small stores, not the giants, that were denied the opportunity to compete on the basis of price on many of the items which they stocked.

There is also no evidence that the failure rates for small businessmen have been any higher in States lacking the dubious benefits of fair trade laws. To the contrary, all studies done on the subject indicate there is very little difference in failure rates between fair and nonfair trade States. Small businesses also are able to offer convenience and service that few of the chain operations can match, keeping the smaller firms competitive in areas unrelated to pricing.

A total of 46 States used to have fair trade laws, but now only 24 do, reflecting the diminishing regard for this brand of protectionism.

In closing, I would like to point out that the Consumer Protection and Finance Subcommittee, which I head, shares jurisdiction over this matter with the Monopolies and Commercial Law Subcommittee which worked on this bill. Despite the overlapping jurisdiction, my subcommittee chose not to ask for a sequential referral. We saw no way to improve on the four-paragraph bill before us this afternoon.

The general opposition to the Fair Trade laws is manifested by the fact that the full House Judiciary Committee reported out the bill without a dissenting vote.

Clearly, fair trade is an idea whose time has gone.

Mr. McCLORY. Mr. Speaker, I yield 2 minutes to the gentleman from Pennsylvania (Mr. HEINZ).

Mr. [H. JOHN] HEINZ [3d] [R., Pa.]. Mr. Speaker, I take this time to commend the Judiciary Committee, the chairman of that committee and my good friend, the gentleman from Illinois (Mr. McCLORY) and the gentleman from Michigan (Mr. HUTCHINSON) for bringing to the House floor this long-awaited proposal to repeal the so-called fair trade laws.

The fair trade laws, in existence for over 40 years, have allowed manufacturers to specify minimum retail prices for designated brand name products. Rather than insuring fair trade practices, however, the fair trade laws have stifled competition, encouraged price fixing, increased costs to the consumer, and have generally denied the public ⊥ the benefits of competition at the retail level.

In 1970, the Department of Justice conducted a nationwide survey to determine the effect of fair trade laws on the costs of consumer goods. The Department found that consumers in nonfair trade States paid between 0.2 percent and 37.4 percent less for items that are fair-traded elsewhere. And in January of this year, the President suggested that fair trade laws cost the consumer between $1.5 and $3 billion annually.

Mr. Speaker, I am delighted that through the repeal of the fair trade laws we will give businessmen and manufacturers an opportunity to compete. And I am pleased that this legislation will bring about a long-overdue savings to the consumer.

Again, I want to compliment the Judiciary Committee for bringing this important, anti-inflationary legislation to the floor, and urge my colleagues to support it.

(Mr. HEINZ asked and was given permission to revise and extend his remarks.)

Miss JORDAN. Mr. Speaker, I yield 2 minutes to the gentleman from New York (Mr. ROSENTHAL).

(Mr. ROSENTHAL asked and was given permission to revise and extend his remarks.)

Mr. [BENJAMIN S.] ROSENTHAL [D., N.Y.]. Mr. Speaker, I want to commend the Committee on the Judiciary, and particularly the gentlewoman from Texas (Miss JORDAN) for bringing to the floor of the House this very, very important bill.

We have lived with the concept of fair trade and the stifling of competition for a number of years. In the early period, it was somewhat understandable, but today in the marketplace, there is no understandable reason to support the maintenance and continuation of fair trade. The fact is that it stifles competition. It really prevents the free market system from working. It is a crutch which many retailers and manufacturers have relied upon. It has caused substantial price increases to consumers. It has prevented legitimate competition in the retail field.

This bill is an important milestone in bringing free competition to the marketplace. If we are to have free enterprise, we must continue the purposes of this bill and others like it. I know that the American consumer shall and will be enormously grateful to our colleague, the gentlewoman from Texas (Miss JORDAN) and the Members of the committee, including the gentleman from Illinois (Mr. MCCLORY) who brought this bill to the floor today.

Mr. Speaker, I urge all my colleagues to support passage of this important piece of legislation.

Mr. [EDWARD] MEZVINSKY [D., Iowa]. Mr. Speaker, I support the Consumer Goods Pricing Act of 1975. For far too long we have allowed the outdated, fair trade laws to remain on the books. Passed during the 1930's to help small businesses stay solvent, these laws have outlived their usefulness, and now serve only to allow prices to be arbitrarily set and prevent retail outlets from engaging in price competition.

In a time of rampaging inflation, it is vital that the Congress take every feasible step to help the consumer get the most value for dollars spent. Estimates are that from $3 to $6.5 billion a year will be saved by the enactment of this law repealing the fair trade laws. This is good for the public and may well help fight high prices.

I am pleased to note that this bill has broad bipartisan support and urge my colleagues to support this legislation.

Mr. [WILLIAM J.] HUGHES [D., N.J.]. Mr. Speaker, I thank the gentlewoman from Texas for yielding and offering me this opportunity to speak in support of H.R. 6971, the Consumer Goods Pricing Act.

Repeal of the fair trade laws was the first piece of legislation I cosponsored in the House, because fair trade laws are neither fair nor do they promote trade. They are at once inflationary and unfair to the consumer.

I wish to express my gratitude to Congresswoman BARBARA JORDAN for the leadership she has evidenced in moving this piece of legislation. It is just the tonic we need at a time of skyrocketing prices and decreasing competition in sectors of our economy where fair trade laws continue to exist. The legislature in my State of New Jersey has shown the wisdom to repeal such legislation which, if it ever was needed, has certainly now outlived its usefulness.

While at one time 46 States had adopted the so-called fair trade laws, that number has now decreased to 24 States. Thankfully the range of goods so traded has also dwindled.

As one member of the House Judiciary Committee who desires to see competition restored to segments of our economy where market manipulation and concentrations in restraint in trade have developed, I am proud to have been a part of this move to repeal these unfair trade laws.

Mr. [JOHN F.] SEIBERLING [D., Ohio]. Mr. Speaker, I enthusiastically support the repeal of the Federal legislation which has enabled States to enact the so-called fair trade laws. The Miller-Tydings amendment to section 1 of the Sherman Act and the McGuire amendment to section 5(a) of the Federal Trade Commission Act enabled the States to legitimize and immunize resale price maintenance which otherwise would have amounted to a per se violation of the Federal antitrust laws.

The theory behind the Miller-Tydings amendment and the McGuire amendment was to preserve small retail outlets against price-cutting by larger stores, which had driven smaller stores out of the business, since Congress believed that the public would be better served by the existence of a large number of retail outlets. There is a real question whether these laws, in fact, served that end. But the question is academic.

In the 38 years since the Miller-Tydings amendment and the 23 years since the McGuire amendment, our economy has evolved to the point that it no longer requires and no longer is served by resale price maintenance under the fair trade laws.

Moreover, the fair trade laws have been abused. They have permitted a manufacturer's contract with one retailer to bind all nonsigning retailers in the State. They have been used to keep manufacturers' profits at artificially high levels. They have not prevented the large chains from displacing the small retailers. Yet by preventing retail and wholesale price competition, these laws have had inflationary effects. As a result, the fair trade laws have clearly become anti-consumer. In an economic system built on the principle of competition, they are an anachronistic anomaly whose repeal is long overdue.

Mr. McCLORY. Mr. Speaker, I have no further requests for time and I yield back the balance of my time.

Miss JORDAN. Mr. Speaker, I have no further requests for time.

The SPEAKER. The question is on the motion offered by the gentlewoman from Texas (Miss JORDAN) that the House suspend the rules and pass the bill H.R. 6971.

The question was taken.

Miss JORDAN. Mr. Speaker, on that I demand the yeas and nays.

The yeas and nays were ordered. . . .

⊥ The SPEAKER pro tempore. The question is on the motion offered by the gentlewoman from Texas (Miss JORDAN) that the House suspend the rules and pass the bill, H.R. 6971, on which the yeas and nays are ordered. ⊥H7144

The vote was taken by electronic device, and there were—yeas 380, nays 11, not voting 43, as follows:

[Roll No. 411]

YEAS—380

Abdnor	Burke, Fla.	Dingell	Grassley
Abzug	Burke, Mass.	Dodd	Green
Adams	Burleson, Tex.	Downey, N.Y.	Gude
Addabbo	Burlison, Mo.	Downing, Va.	Guyer
Alexander	Burton, John	Drinan	Hagedorn
Ambro	Burton, Phillip	Duncan, Oreg.	Haley
Anderson, Calif.	Butler	Duncan, Tenn.	Hall
Anderson, Ill.	Byron	du Pont	Hamilton
Andrews, N. Dak.	Carney	Early	Hammerschmidt
Annunzio	Carr	Eckhardt	Hanley
Archer	Carter	Edgar	Hannaford
Armstrong	Casey	Edwards, Ala.	Hansen
Aspin	Cederberg	Edwards, Calif.	Harkin
AuCoin	Chappell	Eilberg	Harrington
Bafalis	Chisholm	Emery	Harris
Baldus	Clancy	English	Hastings
Barrett	Clausen, Don H.	Erlenborn	Hawkins
Baucus	Clawson, Del	Esch	Hayes, Ind.
Bauman	Clay	Evans, Colo.	Hebert
Beard, R.I.	Cleveland	Evans, Ind.	Hechler, W. Va.
Beard, Tenn.	Cochran	Evins, Tenn.	Heckler, Mass.
Bedell	Cohen	Fary	Hefner
Bennett	Collins, Ill.	Fascell	Heinz
Bergland	Conable	Fenwick	Helstoski
Bevill	Conte	Findley	Henderson
Biaggi	Corman	Fish	Hicks
Biester	Cornell	Fisher	Hightower
Blanchard	Cotter	Fithian	Hillis
Blouin	Coughlin	Flood	Holland
Boggs	Crane	Florio	Holt
Boland	D'Amours	Flynt	Holtzman
Bolling	Daniel, Dan	Foley	Horton
Bonker	Daniel, R. W.	Forsythe	Howard
Brademas	Daniels, N. J.	Fountain	Howe
Breaux	Danielson	Fraser	Hubbard
Brinkley	Davis	Frenzel	Hughes
Brodhead	de la Garza	Frey	Hungate
Broomfield	Delaney	Fuqua	Hutchinson
Brown, Calif.	Dellums	Gaydos	Ichord
Brown, Ohio	Derrick	Giaimo	Jacobs
Broyhill	Derwinski	Gilman	Jarman
Buchanan	Devine	Ginn	Jeffords
Burgener	Dickinson	Goodling	Jenrette
Burke, Calif.	Diggs	Gradison	Johnson, Calif.

Johnson, Pa.	Milford	Rees	Steelman
Jones, Ala.	Miller, Calif.	Regula	Steiger, Ariz.
Jones, N.C.	Mills	Reuss	Stephens
Jones, Okla.	Mineta	Richmond	Stokes
Jones, Tenn.	Minish	Riegle	Stratton
Jordan	Mitchell, Md.	Rinaldo	Stuckey
Karth	Mitchell, N.Y.	Risenhoover	Studds
Kasten	Moakley	Roberts	Symington
Kastenmeier	Moffett	Robinson	Symms
Kazen	Mollohan	Rodino	Talcott
Kelly	Montgomery	Roe	Taylor, Mo.
Kemp	Moore	Rogers	Taylor, N.C.
Ketchum	Moorhead, Pa.	Roncalio	Teague
Keys	Morgan	Rooney	Thompson
Kindness	Mosher	Rosenthal	Thone
Koch	Moss	Rostenkowski	Thornton
Krebs	Mottl	Roush	Traxler
Krueger	Murphy, Ill.	Rousselot	Treen
Landrum	Murphy, N.Y.	Roybal	Tsongas
Latta	Murtha	Runnels	Udall
Leggett	Myers, Ind.	Russo	Ullman
Lehman	Myers, Pa.	Ryan	Van Deerlin
Lent	Natcher	St Germain	Vander Jagt
Levitas	Neal	Santini	Vander Veen
Lloyd, Calif.	Nedzi	Sarasin	Vanik
Lloyd, Tenn.	Nichols	Sarbanes	Vigorito
Long, La.	Nix	Satterfield	Waggonner
Long, Md.	Nolan	Scheuer	Walsh
Lott	Nowak	Schneebeli	Wampler
Lujan	Oberstar	Schroeder	Waxman
McClory	Obey	Sebelius	Weaver
McCloskey	O'Brien	Seiberling	Whalen
McCollister	O'Hara	Sharp	White
McCormack	O'Neill	Shipley	Whitehurst
McDade	Ottinger	Shriver	Whitten
McEwen	Passman	Shuster	Wiggins
McFall	Patterson, Calif.	Sikes	Wilson, Bob
McHugh	Pattison, N.Y.	Simon	Wilson, C. H.
McKay	Perkins	Sisk	Wilson, Tex.
McKinney	Pettis	Skubitz	Winn
Madden	Pickle	Slack	Wirth
Madigan	Pike	Smith, Iowa	Wolff
Maguire	Poage	Smith, Nebr.	Wright
Mahon	Pressler	Snyder	Wydler
Martin	Preyer	Solarz	Wylie
Mathis	Price	Spellman	Yates
Meeds	Pritchard	Staggers	Yatron
Metcalfe	Quie	Stanton, J. William	Young, Alaska
Mezvinsky	Quillen	Stanton, James V.	Young, Tex.
Michel	Randall	Stark	Zablocki
Mikva	Rangel	Steed	Zeferetti

NAYS—11

Ashbrook	Dent	Melcher	Rhodes
Collins, Tex.	Harsha	Miller, Ohio	Schulze
Conlan	McDonald	Moorhead, Calif.	

NOT VOTING—43

Andrews, N.C.	Flowers	LaFalce	Pepper
Ashley	Ford, Mich.	Lagomarsino	Peyser
Badillo	Ford, Tenn.	Litton	Railsback
Bell	Fulton	Macdonald	Rose
Bingham	Gibbons	Mann	Ruppe
Bowen	Goldwater	Matsunaga	Spence
Breckinridge	Gonzalez	Mazzoli	Steiger, Wisc.
Brooks	Hays, Ohio	Meyner	Sullivan
Brown, Mich.	Hinshaw	Mink	Young, Fla.
Conyers	Hyde	Patman, Tex.	Young, Ga.
Eshleman	Johnson, Colo.	Patten, N.J.	

So (two-thirds having voted in favor thereof) the rules were suspended and the bill was passed. . . .

A motion to reconsider was laid on the table.

SENATE CONSIDERATION

REPORT OF THE SENATE COMMITTEE ON THE JUDICIARY (WITH ADDITIONAL VIEWS)
S. Rep. No. 94-466
94th Cong., 1st Sess.
November 20 (legislative day, November 18), 1975

Mr. HART, from the Committee on the Judiciary, submitted the following

REPORT

[To accompany H.R. 6971]

The Committee on the Judiciary, to which was referred the bill (H.R. 6971) to repeal exemptions in the antitrust laws permitting State fair trade laws, having considered the same, reports favorably thereon, and recommends that the bill be passed.

PURPOSE

The purpose of the proposed legislation is to repeal Federal antitrust exemptions which permit States to enact fair trade laws. Such laws allow manufacturers to require retailers to resell at a price set by the manufacturer. These laws are, in fact, legalized price-fixing. They permit competing retailers to have identical prices and thus eliminate price competition between them. Repeal of the fair trade laws should result in a lowering of consumer prices.

This proposed legislation repeals the Miller-Tydings Act which enables the States to enact fair trade laws and the McGuire Act which permits States to enact nonsigner provisions. Without these exemptions the agreements they authorize would violate the antitrust laws.

SUBSTITUTION OF H.R. 6971 FOR S. 408

A bill to repeal fair trade enabling legislation (S. 408) was introduced in the Senate in January 1975 by Edward Brooke (R-Mass.) and was passed unanimously from the Antitrust and Monopoly Subcommittee on May 5. Before this committee was able to consider S. 408, the House of Representatives passed H.R. 6971 which is identical to S. 408 except for the title of the bill. This committee voted to substitute H.R. 6971 for S. 408 in order to expedite passage of this legislation. Without the substitution S. 408 would have had to be considered by the House after the Senate passed it. The substitution permits the bill to go directly to the President for consideration after passage by the Senate.

STATEMENT

Fair trade laws permit a manufacturer to enter into an agreement with a retailer setting the minimum or stipulated price at which his product may be sold. California passed the first State law in 1931 and other States followed. It became apparent, however, that any state law which applied to interstate commerce violated Federal antitrust laws. Thus, in 1937, Congress passed the Miller-Tydings Act granting State fair trade laws an exemption from the Sherman Antitrust Act. Some manufacturers attempted to set the resale prices not only of retailers who had signed fair trade contracts but of retailers who had not done so. In 1951, the Supreme Court in *Schwegmann Bros. v. Calvert Distillers Corp.*,[4.55] 314 [sic] U.S. 384 ruled this practice illegal. Congress rectified the situation in 1952 by enacting the McGuire Act which permitted States to pass fair trade laws with nonsigner clauses. However, the fair trade contract could be enforced against a nonsigner only as long as the manufacturer procured the signature of at least one retailer to a contract.

At the time S. 408 was introduced, 13 States had fair trade laws with nonsigner provisions and 23 States had fair trade laws without nonsigner provisions. The States with nonsigner provisions were Arizona, California, Connecticut, Delaware, Illinois, Maryland, New Hampshire, New Jersey, New York, Ohio, Tennessee, Virginia, and Wisconsin. The States with fair trade laws without nonsigner provisions were Arkansas, Colorado, Florida, Georgia, Idaho, Indiana, Iowa, Kentucky, Louisiana, Maine, Massachusetts, Michigan, Minnesota, New Mexico, North Carolina, North Dakota, Oklahoma, Oregon, Pennsylvania, South Carolina, South Dakota, Washington, and West Virginia. By November, 15 of those States had repealed their fair trade laws. They are: Arkansas, California, Colorado, Connecticut, Florida, Iowa, New Hampshire, New Jersey, New Mexico, New York, North Carolina, Ohio, Oregon, Tennessee, and Washington.

The principle products fair traded are stereo components, television sets, major appliances, mattresses, toiletries, kitchenware, watches, jewelry, glassware, wallpapers, bicycles, some types of clothing, liquor, and prescription drugs.

Liquor will not be affected by the repeal of the fair trade laws in the same manner as other products because the Twenty-First Amendment to the Constitution gives the States broad powers over the sale of alcoholic beverages. Thus, while repeal of the fair trade laws generally will prohibit manufacturers from enforcing resale prices, alcohol manufacturers may do such in States which pass price fixing statutes pursuant to the Twenty-First Amendment.

Seven days of hearings were held in the Senate. Six of those days were hearings on the bill proper. The seventh concerned an amendment proposed by several newspapers to amend the bill to permit newspapers to set maximum retail prices. The amendment was not brought to a vote because of lack of support for it.

Repeal of the fair trade laws was called for by President Ford, consumer groups, the Justice Department, the Federal Trade Commission, the Council on Wage and Price Stability, discount stores and smaller business associations. Editorials in newspapers across the country unanimously favored repeal.

Opponents were primarily service-oriented manufacturers who claimed retailers would not give adequate service unless they were guaranteed a good margin of profit. However, the manufacturer could solve this problem by placing a clause in the distributorship contract requiring the retailer to maintain adequate service. Moreover, the manufacturer has the right to select distributors who are likely to emphasize service.

While small business groups did not testify, a couple submitted statements expressing fear that there would be vicious price-cutting without fair trade. No evidence was presented to indicate that there were destructive predatory practices in states which had repealed fair trade laws. Nor were there bad effects in Canada which repealed its fair trade laws in 1957 or in Great Britain which repealed such laws in 1965. A study published in 1969 reports small retailers were not driven out of business and predatory price cutting was rare in the 4 years following repeal in Great Britain. Similar experiences have been reported in Canada.

Moreover, statistics gathered by the Library of Congress indicate that the absence of fair trade has not harmed small business. Using Dun and Bradstreet data, the Library of Congress found the 1972 firm failure rate in "fair trade" states which have the nonsigner provision was 35.9 failures per 10,000 firms, in "fair trade" States without the nonsigner provision the rate was 32.2 failures per 10,000 firms, while the

---

[4.55] The correct citation is 341 U.S. 384 (1951).

failure rate in free trade States averaged 23.3 failures per 10,000 firms—in other words "fair trade" States with fully effective laws have a 55 percent higher rate of firm failures than free trade states.

Finally, the traditional argument that fair trade protects the "mom and pop" store from unfair competition is not borne out by statistics. Between 1956 and 1972 the rate of growth of small retail stores in free trade States (including states which repealed "fair trade" during this period) is 32 percent higher than the rate in "fair trade" States.

Fair trade laws are in fact legalized price-fixing. They permit competing retailers to have identical prices and thus eliminate price competition between retailers.

Studies by the Department of Justice which were cited in a 1969 Economic Report of the President, indicate that the consumer would be saved $1.2 billion a year by the elimination of the fair trade laws. Updated for inflation this figure comes to $2.1 billion. Another study of the Department of Justice estimated that fair trade laws increase prices on fair traded goods by 18–27 percent. For example, a set of golf clubs that lists for $220 can be purchased in non-fair trade areas for $136; a $49 electric shaver for $32; a $1,360 stereo system for $915 and a $560 19-inch color television for $483.

The repeal of the fair trade laws does not affect the use of suggested prices by a manufacturer. However, the use of suggested prices in such a way as to coerce adherence to them would be illegal.

Changes in Existing Law

In compliance with subsection 4 of rule XXIX of the Standing Rules of the Senate, changes in existing law made by the bill are shown as follows (existing law proposed to be omitted is enclosed in black brackets, new matter is printed in italic, existing law in which no changes are made or proposed is shown in Roman):

Sherman Act (26 Stat. 209; 15 U.S.C. 1)

SEC. 1. Every contract, combination in the form of trust or otherwise, or conspiracy, in restraint of trade or commerce among the several States, or with foreign nations, is declared to be illegal [: *Provided*, That nothing contained in sections 1 to 7 of this title shall render illegal, contracts or agreements prescribing minimum prices for the resale of a commodity which bears, or the label or container of which bears, the trademark, brand, or name of the producer or distributor of such commodity and which is in free and open competition and [sic] commodities of the same general class produced or distributed by others, when contracts or agreements of that description are lawful as applied to intrastate transactions, under any statute, law, or public policy now or hereafter in effect in any State, Territory, or the District of Columbia in which such resale is to be made, or to which the commodity is to be transported for such resale, and the making of such contracts or agreements shall not be an unfair method of competition under section 45 of this title: Provided further, That the preceding proviso shall not make lawful any contract or agreement, providing for the establishment or maintenance of minimum resale prices on any commodity herein involved, between manufacturers, or between producers, or between wholesalers, or between brokers, or between factors, or between retailers, or between persons, firms, or corporations in competition with each other.] Every person who shall make any contract or engage in any combination or conspiracy declared by sections 1 to 7 of this title to be illegal shall be deemed guilty of a misdemeanor, and, on conviction thereof, shall be punished by fine not exceeding fifty thousand dollars, or by imprisonment not exceeding one year, or by both said punishments, in the discretion of the court.

Federal Trade Commission Act (38 Stat. 717; 15 U.S.C. 45)

SEC. 45(a) (1) Unfair methods of competition in commerce, and unfair or deceptive acts or practices in commerce, are declared unlawful.

[(2) Nothing contained in this section or in any of the Antitrust Acts shall render unlawful any contracts or agreements prescribing minimum or stipulated prices, or requiring a vendee to enter into contracts or agreements prescribing minimum or stipulated prices, for the resale of a commodity which bears, or the label or container of which bears, the trade-mark, brand, or name of the producer or distributor of such commodity and which is in free and open competition with commodities of the same general class produced or distributed by others, when contracts or agreements of that description are lawful as applied to intrastate transactions under any statute, law, or public ⊥ policy now or hereafter in effect in any State, Territory, or the District of Columbia in which such resale is to be made, or to which the commodity is to be transported for such resale.

[(3) Nothing contained in this section or in any of the Antitrust Acts shall render unlawful the exercise or the enforcement of any right or right of action created by any statute, law, or public policy now or hereafter in effect in any State, Territory, or the District of Columbia, which in substance provides that willfully and knowingly advertising, offering for sale, or selling any commodity at less than the price or prices prescribed in such contracts or agreements whether the person so advertising, offering for sale, or selling is or is not a party to such a contract or agreement, is unfair competition and is actionable at the suit of any person damaged thereby.

[(4) Neither the making of contracts or agreements as described in paragraph (2) of this subsection, nor the exercise or enforcement of any right or right of action as described in paragraph (3) of this subsection shall constitute an unlawful burden or restraint upon, or interference with, commerce.

[(5) Nothing contained in paragraph (2) of this subsection shall make lawful contracts or agreements providing for the establishment or maintenance or [sic] minimum or stipulated resale prices on any commodity referred to in paragraph (2) of this subsection, between manufacturers, or between producers, or between wholesalers, or between brokers, or between factors, or between retailers, or between persons, firms, or corporations in competition with each other.]

(2) [(6)] The Commission is empowered and directed to prevent persons, partnerships, or corporations, except banks, common carriers subject to the Act to regulate commerce, air carriers and foreign air carriers subject to the Federal Aviation Act of 1958, and persons, partnerships, or corporations insofar as they are subject to the Packers and Stockyards Act, 1921, as amended, except as provided in section 406(b) of said Act, from using unfair methods of competition in commerce and unfair or deceptive acts or practices in commerce.[4.56]

⊥ ADDITIONAL VIEWS OF SENATOR STROM THURMOND (R-SC) ON H.R. 6971, A BILL TO REPEAL ENABLING LEGISLATION FOR FAIR TRADE LAWS

The question should be raised as to whether it is desirable to pass Federal legislation to repeal existing fair trade laws. Under the Miller-Tydings Act and McGuire Act, the respective States are not required to enact fair trade laws and nonsigner provisions, but are merely given the opportunity to do so if they wish. Congress has permitted the States to enact fair trade laws since 1937, almost forty years ago, and reinforced that right in 1952.

I firmly believe in the fulfillment of the spirit, as well as the letter, of the Constitution of the United States regarding the Tenth Amendment's preservation of the powers and the rights of the States and the people. Some years ago, I strongly opposed the effort on the Federal level to impose a national fair trade law upon this Country. I remain concerned that the separate States be allowed to make decisions regarding fair trade laws to the greatest extent possible.

In view of my respect for the integrity of the individual States, I have given careful thought to whether the Federal Government should supplant the judgment of the States in this area. In considering this matter, I have been aware the States have not been completely insensitive to the need to make changes in this area as shown by

---

[4.56] The report did not contain a page 6.

the fact that a number of States in recent years have moved to repeal their fair trade laws.

After careful thought and analysis, I conclude that I will not dissent from the decision of this Committee to favorably report H.R. 6971. A review of the record indicates repeal of the fair trade laws in the various States should be in the best interest of the Country. Lower prices should be available to consumers, and a substantial contribution should be made in the effort to control inflation.

On balance, it appears the positive benefits produced by this legislation should outweigh any negative effects it would have. I have concluded that it is less objectionable to enact legislation disallowing fair trade laws than it is for the Congress to continue to sanction price fixing that results from the existence of fair trade laws.

SENATE DEBATE
94th Cong., 1st Sess.
December 2, 1975

121 Cong. Rec. S20871 (daily ed.)

The Senate proceeded to consider the bill (H.R. 6971) to amend the Sherman Antitrust Act to provide lower prices for consumers.

Mr. BROOKE. Mr. President, on the 27th of January, 1975, I reintroduced legislation I originally introduced in the 93d Congress on December 3, 1974, to repeal those exemptions in the Federal antitrust statutes which are commonly known as the fair trade laws. I wish to express my appreciation to Senators PHILIP HART and ROMAN HRUSKA, the chairman and ranking minority member of the Antitrust and Monopoly Subcommittee of the Senate Judiciary Committee for the full and complete hearings they accorded S. 408 on February 18, 19, 20, and 21, on April 9 and 10, and on May 12. The two-volume hearings of the subcommittee are a tribute to the thoroughness with which the members examined the question of fair trade. At the conclusion of the hearings, the subcommittee unanimously favored adoption of the bill, and so reported to the full Judiciary Committee.

Meanwhile, identical legislation was introduced in the House by Congressman ROBERT McCLORY and Congresswoman BARBARA JORDAN. Hearings, at which I testified, were held by the House Subcommittee on Monopolies and Commercial Law of the House Judiciary Committee on March 25 and April 10. Once again, there was unanimous support by the subcommittee and by the full House Judiciary Committee. On July 21, the House passed H.R. 6971 by a vote of 380 to 11. It is important to note that one technical change was made by the House Judiciary Committee, namely, to add a sentence renumbering paragraphs of the ⊥ Federal Trade Commission Act to number those paragraphs consecutively after the deletions provided for in S. 408. Otherwise, the House bill is identical to S. 408.

I was pleased that, in favorably acting on S. 408, the Senate Judiciary Committee has substituted H.R. 6971 so that, upon passage of the bill today, it may go directly to the President for his signature.

When I first introduced this legislation late in the 93d Congress, double-digit inflation was haunting the American consumer. In the nearly 11 months that have elapsed since then, some progress has been made nationally at bringing inflation under control, or at least under the double-digit range with which we had been afflicted earlier. However, in the last weeks, a rise in the wholesale price index could well indicate that inflation is heating up once again. And unemployment, which had also increased to the double-digit range and then decreased as economic recovery began, has again this month taken an ominous rise. In my own State of Massachusetts, the latest unemployment rate is 14 percent. These bitter legacies of recession, inflation, and unemployment appear likely to remain with us much longer than we had anticipated.

This situation of double-digit economic stagnation is costing our country dearly. In economic terms alone each year we are losing more than $170 billion in production.

While most solutions offered by our economic advisers either dampen inflation by fostering recession, or enhance economic activity by stoking the fires of inflation, the repeal of the so-called fair trade laws is simultaneously anti-inflationary and antirecessionary. The repeal of these laws alone will not curb inflation, nor will it provide employment for all, but it is one positive step in both directions. As was so clearly illustrated by the automobile rebate program, the lowering of prices does stimulate consumer demand. Demand which is then translated into increased production and more jobs.

The repeal of the fair trade laws has been strongly supported by the President of the United States. President Ford considers this legislation as an important element in our economic program to combat inflation and return our country to the path of stable growth and prosperity. This measure also has support from the business community, from consumers, and from both political parties. It is interesting to note that with the favorable public and press reaction given to my repeal bill, and the general expectation that Congress would act affirmatively in this session to repeal fair trade, 15 of the 36 States which had fair trade laws prior to February of 1975 have already repealed their own State statutes this year. They are: Arkansas, California, Colorado, Connecticut, Florida, Iowa, New Hampshire, New Jersey, New Mexico, New York, North Carolina, Ohio, Oregon, Tennessee, and Washington all ended fair trade within their jurisdiction. I believe it is reasonable to conclude that many of our colleagues in the State legislatures, was as [sic] the case with our colleagues in the House of Representatives, agree that fair trade is an idea whose time has passed.

Fair trade is legalized price fixing by which the owner of a brand name or trademarked article determines the price charged by the retail merchant. Fair trade statutes are State laws which amend State antitrust statutes so as to permit intrastate price-fixing agreements. The Federal fair trade laws—specifically the Miller-Tydings Act, 1937, and the McGuire Act, 1952—permit the interstate use of fair trade by manufacturers in States which permit its intrastate use. Without these Federal statutes, these interstate price-fixing conspracies [sic] would be in violation of the most basic of our antitrust laws—the Sherman Antitrust Act and the Federal Trade Commission Act.

The roots of fair trade can be traced back to the Great Depression of the 1930's. After the stock market crash in October of 1929 and the ensuing decline in economic activity, interest revived in price fixing. Retailers, mistaking falling prices as the source of the economic depression rather than the result of the depression, lobbied vigorously for the fair trade laws. Trade associations representing independent retailers, along with the National Association of Retail Druggists, led the fight.

In 1931 California became the first State to establish fair trade laws. They exempted from the State's antitrust laws any contract between a manufacturer and a retailer wherein the seller of a branded product bound the buyer, when reselling it, to charge the price that the former specified. However, the act was found to be virtually unenforceable because those retailers who refused to sign the fair trade contract could still sell at any price they chose. Therefore, in 1933 California amended its fair trade laws so as to permit the nonsigner provision. This coercive provision has been called by some, "the enforcer of fair trade." It permits manufacturers to bind all sellers of its product within a State to the price stipulated in the fair trade contract if any one retailer agrees to sign the contract.

These actions taken by California stimulated other States to pass similar legislation and by 1941 45 of the 48 States had fair trade statutes. In their head-long rush to pass these laws, 40 of the 45 States did not even hold hearings. Those few States that did failed to keep adequate transcripts.

While State statutes permitted manufacturers and retailers to engage in intrastate fair trade, when these contracts were made across State lines, they were found to be in violation of the Federal antitrust laws. Under pressure to rectify this situation, Congress in 1937 passed the Miller-Tydings Act as a rider to an appropriations bill for the District of Columbia. This Federal enabling legislation amended section 1 of the Sherman Antitrust Act so as to permit manufacturers to engage in interstate fair trade in those areas where its intrastate use was legal.

In 1951 the Supreme Court dealt a blow to fair trade in the Calvert Distillers case.[4.57] The Court ruled that retailers not signing the fair trade contract could not be forced to abide by such contracts as signed by other retailers. This decision brought swift demands for Congress to enact overriding legislation. It did so in 1952 by amending the Federal Trade Commission Act with the McGuire Act so as to permit the use of the coercive nonsigner clause.

Regardless of the background of this unfortunate legislation, the two criteria on which we should now judge whether or not it should be repealed are: First, what effect does fair trade have on retail prices? Second, what effect would the repeal of fair trade have on retail firms and manufacturers?

Two studies by the U.S. Department of Justice, one published in June 1963, and the other published in June 1970, have determined that fair trade does significantly increase the retail price of goods. The earlier and often quoted study found that fair trade increased retail prices by 19 to 27 percent. The more recent study found that these laws increase prices by as much as 37 percent on many items. Testimony produced during the Judiciary Committee hearings on my bill produced many specific illustrations of the price differentials on particular products.

Individual fair trade costs to the consumer are easier to determine than the broad statistics. These few nationwide studies that do exist are at least a few years old. Many are older. Nevertheless, the Library of Congress, at my request, has been researching the annual cost of fair trade. On the basis of recent calculations on inexact data, they estimate that fair trade laws cost American consumers enormous sums. Their middle-range estimate being an annual cost of $3 billion or more.

In testimony before the California State Attorney General's hearings on fair trade, in January 1975, Mr. Lawrence Shepard of the University of California estimated that fair trade costs consumers even more—$6.5 billion each year. He states that this means that fair trade costs each family on the order of $120 per year and he finds that "it is hard to conceive of any monopolistic conspiracy of similar proportions." Compare this figure to this year's tax rebate of about $8 billion and the true impact of a repeal of the fair trade laws is clear.

The proponents of fair trade argue that this license to engage in price fixing is needed to protect firms and manufacturers—particularly the small and weak—by providing them with a fair profit. They base their argument on two beliefs. First, they believe that the additional revenues obtained as a result of the increased retail price are "captured" by the retail firm. Second, they believe that consumers are insensitive to the retail price and, consequently, higher prices will not mean a lower sales volume. Both the economic theory and the empirical evidence refute these propositions.

While higher retail prices and increased profit margins may provide the retail merchant with windfall profits when fair trade is first introduced, they will quickly be eroded by nonprice com⊥petition. It is axiomatic in business that if competition based on price is prevented then competition based on service will be extensive.

It has been established by a U.S. Department of Justice study prepared by Dr. Leonard Weiss in 1969, that stores in fair trade States almost universally have a significantly lower volume of retail sales than stores in free trade areas. The study notes that "these results suggest, as economic theory would predict, that sales volume per store is systematically lower under fair trade.["]

However, the crucial test of the effect of fair trade on retail and manufacturing firms is whether or not firms in fair trade States have a lower level of bankruptcies and failure than do those in free trade States.

Dr. Steward Munroe Lee of Geneva College investigated firm failures between the years of 1933 and 1958. Using census data he found that "the best data available—does—not support the contention that the enactment of fair trade laws lessens the number of retail failures or bankruptcies or increases the number of retail stores." Instead, he found that firms in fair trade States have a significantly higher rate of bankruptcy than firms in free trade States.

In an Office of Management and Budget—OMB—study of small business survival patterns data is presented which confirms Dr. Lee's study. A Federal Trade Commission

---

[4.57] Schwegmann Bros. v. Calvert Distillers Corp., 341 U.S. 384 (1951).

analysis of this data prepared by Dennis Murphy, Assistant to the Director of the Bureau of Economics of the Federal Trade Commission, on February 13, 1975, finds that "there is simply no evidence to support the contention that the survival of small business in America depends upon fair trade.["] A Library of Congress analysis of the same data found that between 1956 and 1972 the rate of growth of small retail stores was 32 percent higher in free trade States than in fair trade States.

This evidence is also supported by a 1962 Justice Department study and by other data in the 1975 Library of Congress study. In the Justice Department study it was found that States with fully effective fair trade laws had nearly a 150 percent higher rate of firm failures than free trade States. The Library of Congress analysis found that this pattern continued in 1972; in that year fair trade States had a 55 percent higher rate of firm bankruptcies than free trade States.

What, then, can we expect when we repeal the fair trade laws?

Turning first to the case of Rhode Island which repealed its fair trade laws in 1970 we find, that just as would be predicted, prices fell, but firms did not suffer. In a study by the Marketing Science Institute published in August, 1974, entitled, "The Effects of Fair Trade Repeal: The Case of Rhode Island," on the effects of the repeal, they found that among other things:

First. Four out of nine product lines investigated exhibited a decline in prices.

Second. The decline in prices for these product lines ranged from 20 percent to 40 percent.

Third. 74 percent of the retailers who responded unequivocally indicated that the repeal has not substantially adversely affected them.

Fourth. Only one manufacturer out of the nine interviewed had actually encountered a decline in its sales after the repeal.

The experiences of both Canada and Great Britain confirm these conclusions. Both of these countries used fair trade extensively and both have repealed it: Canada in 1957 and Great Britain in April, 1965. The March 29, 1969 issue of The Economist analyzes the changes in the 4 years following the repeal of fair trade in Great Britain. They found that, contrary to the arguments used by proponents of fair trade prior to repeal, small retail firms were not driven out of business and the examples of so-called predatory price cutting were rare. The major change noted by The Economist was an upgrading and modernizing of the practices and techniques of both wholesalers and retailers. Where retailers wished to compete on price, they were able to do so and it was the consumers who benefited.

The Canadian experience has produced similar results. The August 1964 issue of Economica, published by the London School of Economics, contained an analysis of the results of ending fair trade in Canada. The first conclusion was that prices did, in fact, come down. Methods of distribution became more dynamic and efficient and, as in the case of Great Britain, examples of predatory price cutting were few.

We may then conclude that the marketplace will look much the same, but that price competition will be restored in areas in which it has been absent. In addition, a new vigor will be evident on all levels of our system of distribution. It will be both the American consumer and businessman who will be the beneficiary.

It is not only goods legally fair traded that will be affected, Mr. President. Individuals from every part of the country have written to me detailing subtle costs of fair trade that are not so easily identified. For example, manufacturers whose products are not and never were legally fair traded, act as if they were. Indeed, the merchandise arrives with the manufacturer's price tags already affixed. The price list is headed, "Fair Trade Price." Retailers are told which items may be reduced for sale at the end of the season and how much the reduction may be. What we have then is a frame of mind in the marketplace that subtly labels price reductions as improper, if not illegal. We have seen developed an attitude and a practice that suggest price cutting must be avoided at all costs—that somehow reducing the price of product reduces its quality. To repeal fair trade will destroy this illusion.

I believe, just as our forefathers believed, that the only means to insure the American consumer a fair deal is to insure that competition, not conspiracy, dominates the retail market. Competition forces retailers, wholesalers, and manufacturers to provide the consumer the most for his or her money. We cannot on the one hand celebrate the beauties of free competition and then squelch it at the moment it benefits consumers.

It is for these reasons that I support the repeal of the so-called fair trade laws, and I urge my colleagues to join me in this effort.

REPEAL FAIR TRADE LAWS

Mr. [ROMAN L.] HRUSKA [R., Neb.]. Mr. President, I rise in support of the pending bill, H.R. 6971, an act to repeal enabling legislation for fair trade laws.

President Ford has urged its passage with these words:

This legislation allowing fair trade laws is one of a number of laws for which recommendations for change will be considered in the coming months as important elements of the President's economic program.

(Fair trade laws have)—the effect of eliminating price competition and raising costs to the consumer on numerous commodities.

The Council of Economic Advisers and many other economic, legal, and Government experts also have urged the enactment of this bill.

Mr. President, by repealing resale price maintenance acts, competition would be encouraged resulting in a lowering of consumer prices. Evidence submitted to the Senate Subcommittee on Antitrust and Monopoly establishes numerous instances of significant price savings—for specific products—in nonfair trade States, in comparison to the price for the same products in so-called fair trade States.

So-called fair trade laws, also known as "resale price maintenance" or "quality stabilization" laws, have been enacted by the Congress, State legislatures, and many foreign governments.

Briefly, such laws allow a manufacturer to enter into an agreement with a retailer to set minimum prices at which his identifiable product may be sold—hence legalizing price-fixing.

California passed the first State fair trade law in 1931 and many states followed that pattern. However, the question of state law on this matter conflicting with certain provisions in the U.S. Constitution precipitated the passage of the Miller-Tydings Act by the Congress in 1937. This act exempted State fair trade laws from the Federal Sherman Antitrust Act.

Again legal questions arose, necessitating the Congress to pass in 1952 the McGuire Act, exempting State fair trade laws from the Federal Trade Commission Act, hence, legalizing nonsigner provisions. These nonsigner provisions, enacted in a number of States, permit a manufacturer to sign a single resale prce [sic] maintenance agreement with one retailer, and then proceed to enforce the agreement against all of the nonsigning retailers in the State.

The bill we consider today will repeal the Miller-Tydings Act and the McGuire Act. One of the stated purposes of these fair trade laws is to protect retailers from predatory pricing, cut-throat competition, and loss-loader [sic] selling. Proponents of fair trade laws contend that these laws are necessary to save small retailers from extinction.

⊥ Mr. President, however true that may have been in 1931, when California ⊥S20874 passed its law, or in 1937 when Congress passed the Miller-Tydings Act—because of the depressed economic condition of that time—the opponents of fair trade laws point out that the seriously depressed economy of the 1930's exists no longer and the laws should now be repealed to aid the consumer, and the country's battle against inflation.

The Senator from Massachusetts (Mr. BROOKE), said on December 3, 1974, as he introduced S. 4203—the predecessor bill to S. 408—that the reasons for enacting the Miller-Tydings Act in 1937 are no longer applicable. He cited statistics and arguments from experts to show that now is the time to repeal the Federal fair trade laws. He said they have shielded similar State laws, and have prevented competition in the marketplace.

A basic reason for repealing the Miller-Tydings Act and the McGuire Act is that many of the 36 States which originally enacted the fair trade laws have reconsidered the issue and have become convinced that they are not in the best interest of their citizens. In fact, 15 have repealed fair trade laws this year. Those States are: Arkansas, California, Colorado, Connecticut, Florida, Iowa, New Hampshire, New Jersey, New York, New Mexico, North Carolina, Ohio, Oregon, Tennessee, and Washington. My home State of Nebraska has not had a fair trade law for many years.

I commend the Senator from Massachusetts and Representative MCCLORY of Illinois for sponsoring the legislation we consider today. Senator BROOKE and Congressman MCCLORY, both of whom testified before the Senate Subcommittee on Antitrust, persistently followed the progress of this bill.

Since the House was in a position to act first, the Senator from Michigan (Mr. PHILIP A. HART) and this Senator, urged the Senate Judiciary Committee to accept the substitution of H.R. 6971 for S. 408 to expedite passage of this important legislation. Without this action, S. 408 would have had to be considered by the House after Senate approval, delaying the implementation of this important legislation.

Mr. President, although I was not a cosponsor of the Senate bill, I served as chairman for 3 of the 7 days of hearings before the subcommittee at the request of the chairman, hence I am familiar with much of the testimony and arguments of the witnesses.

On the fourth day of the hearings, at the request of a witness who opposed the bill, I urged the granting of 2 additional days of hearings so that persons opposing the bill would have an opportunity to testify. Those hearings were held on April 9 and 10, 1975.

This is noted, Mr. President, so the record will show that every effort has been made to hear all sides of the issues as fairly as possible. There is no doubt that the witnesses who opposed repealing the fair trade laws made some significant points. Many small retailers wrote to the subcommittee opposing the bill and their letters were placed in the printed hearings.

After due consideration, the subcommittee and the full Judiciary Committee voted—without an objection—that the bill become law.

Mr. President, so the record on this bill will not be misunderstood, there was another issue raised late in the proceedings by certain major newspaper publishers who wished to be exempted from the bill we consider today. In my judgment such an exemption would not be wise or desirable.

When the Senate Judiciary Committee met to discuss the bill, however, no amendment pertaining to this proposed exemption was offered.

Mr. President, on balance the best interest of the public will be served if H.R. 6971 is favorably acted upon by this body.

The bill was ordered to a third reading, read the third time, and passed.

PRESIDENTIAL COMMENT

STATEMENT BY PRESIDENT GERALD R. FORD
UPON SIGNING THE
CONSUMER GOODS PRICING ACT OF 1975
December 12, 1975

11 WEEKLY COMP. PRES. DOC. 1367

The President's Remarks at the Bill Signing Ceremony.
December 12, 1975

Obviously, I am extremely pleased to have the opportunity of signing this very important piece of legislation. And I congratulate my former colleagues in the Congress on a bipartisan basis for the rapid and, I think, constructive enactment of this important legislation.

The repeal of the fair trade laws will permit consumers to get the discounts in all 50 States. And the best way to ensure that consumers are paying the most reasonable price for consumer products is to restore competition in the marketplace. This legislation will do that.

This is one of the prime examples of how I intend to work with the Congress, the House and the Senate, on a bipartisan basis to get the Government out of unnecessary, inefficient regulation in the setting of prices and return that function to the marketplace.

I look forward to working with the Congress to restore competition in other areas of our economy now under inefficient government regulation. I have submitted to the Congress proposed regulation, or the abandonment of regulation, in a number of areas, including financial institutions; transportation, including the airlines, the rails, and the trucking areas; as well as energy. And I hope that we can work together to make some substantial progress in all of these areas.

I congratulate those who have worked with the Congress in getting this legislation through to give the consumer a better break in the marketplace so that competition will be the prime factor in ensuring a fair and reasonable opportunity for the consumer to be the prime beneficiary.

I congratulate the Members of Congress. And it is a real pleasure for me on this occasion to sign this legislation.

• • • •

Statement by the President Upon Signing H.R. 6971.
December 12, 1975

I am, today, signing into law H.R. 6971, which will make it illegal for manufacturers to fix the prices of consumer products sold by retailers. This new legislation will repeal laws enacted in 1937 and 1952 which amended the Federal antitrust laws so States could authorize otherwise illegal agreements between manufacturers and retailers setting the price at which a product would be sold to consumers. Altogether, over the years, 46 States enacted such laws.

The so-called "fair trade" laws were a response to the unique economic conditions of the Depression. These State laws require all retail merchants to sell brand name merchandise at a price set by the manufacturer if the manufacturer wanted his product to be labeled a fair trade item. In essence, these laws prohibit price competition between retailers on many consumer products.

If a merchant offers consumers a discount price on a fair trade item, he is subject to criminal action in those States with fair trade laws. As a result, these laws prevent the American people from receiving the benefit of lower prices on cameras, watches, sporting goods, small appliances, auto supplies, and many other brand name products. In today's economy, these restraints on competition no longer make sense.

When this new legislation takes effect 90 days from now, retailers will again be able to set prices on a more competitive basis, thereby enabling consumers in all 50 States to shop for the best products at the lowest possible prices.

Many States already have recognized the unfairness of these laws. Since January of this year, 15 State legislatures have repealed their fair trade laws. I commend the actions of these States.

I commend the Congress as well for its bipartisan recognition that price competition is important to American consumers and for its timely consideration of this legislation. Now that H.R. 6971 is law, I hope that the Congress and the Administration will continue to work together to achieve the much needed reform of other Government laws and regulations which impose hidden and unnecessary costs on American consumers. In particular, I hope that the Congress will support my program of regulatory reform in such important areas as air transportation, trucking, and financial institutions.

As I have been saying since taking office, the best way we can protect the consumer is to identify and eliminate costly, inefficient, and obsolete laws and regulations. Thus, I take particular pleasure in signing this bill for the benefit of the American consumer.